BLACK NIGHT, WHITE SNOW:
Russia's Revolutions
1905–1917

ROMANOVS

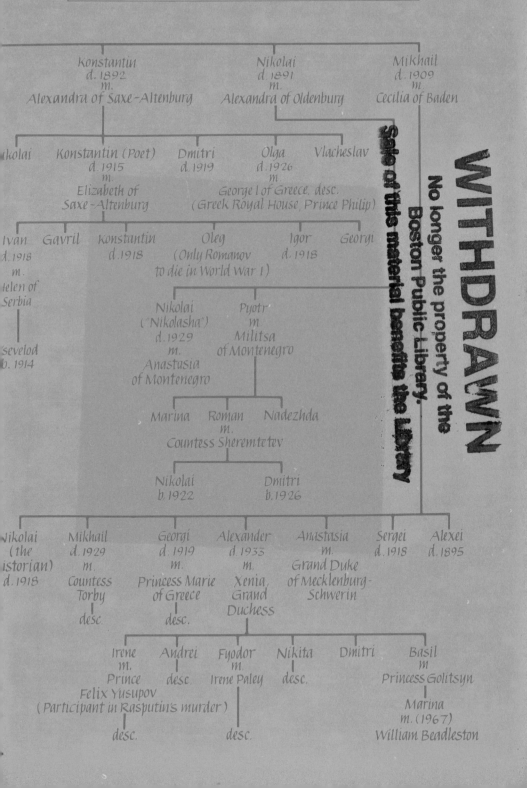

Konstantin
d. 1892
m.
Alexandra of Saxe-Altenburg

Nikolai
d. 1891
m.
Alexandra of Oldenburg

Mikhail
d. 1909
m.
Cecilia of Baden

Nikolai
Konstantin (Poet)
d. 1915
m.
Elizabeth of
Saxe-Altenburg

Dmitri
d. 1919

Olga
d. 1926
m.
George I of Greece, desc.
(Greek Royal House, Prince Philip)

Vlacheslav

Ivan
d. 1918
m.
Helen of
Serbia

Gavril

Konstantin
d. 1918

Oleg
(Only Romanov
to die in World War I)

Igor
d. 1918

Georgi

Vsevelod
b. 1914

Nikolai
("Nikolasha")
d. 1929
m.
Anastasia
of Montenegro

Pyotr
m.
Militsa
of Montenegro

Marina
Roman
m.
Countess Sheremtetev

Nadezhda

Nikolai
b. 1922

Dmitri
b. 1926

Nikolai
(the
historian)
d. 1918

Mikhail
d. 1929
m.
Countess
Torby

desc.

Georgi
d. 1919
m.
Princess Marie
of Greece

desc.

Alexander
d. 1933
m.
Xenia,
Grand
Duchess

Anastasia
m.
Grand Duke
of Mecklenburg-
Schwerin

Sergei
d. 1918

Alexei
d. 1895

Irene
m.
Prince
Felix Yusupov
(Participant in Rasputin's murder)

desc.

Andrei
desc.

Fyodor
m.
Irene Paley

desc.

Nikita
desc.

Dmitri

Basil
m
Princess Golitsyn

Marina
m. (1967)
William Beadleston

Cherny vecher.
Bely sneg.
Veter, veter!
Na nogakh ne stoit chelovek.
Veter, Veter—
Na vsem bozhem svete!

Black night.
White snow.
Wind, wind!
A man can't stand.
Wind, wind—
All over God's world!

—Alexander Blok, *The Twelve*

Harrison E. Salisbury

BLACK NIGHT, WHITE SNOW:

Russia's Revolutions
1905–1917

1978
Doubleday & Company, Inc., Garden City, New York

Library of Congress Cataloging in Publication Data

Salisbury, Harrison Evans, 1908–
  Black night, white snow.

  Bibliography: p. 611.
  Includes index.
  1. Russia—History—Revolution, 1917–1921. I. Title.
DK265.S2926 947.084′1
ISBN: 0-385-00844-9
Library of Congress Catalog Card Number 74-18830

In memory of Sir Bernard Pares,
who first urged me to study Russian history.

Contents

Principal Personages

Romanovs

Nicholas II, ruled from 1894 until 1917 (1868–1918).

Alexandra Fyodorovna (Alix of Hesse-Darmstadt), wife of Nicholas II (1872–1918).

Olga, their oldest daughter.

Tatyana, their second daughter.

Mariya, their third daughter.

Anastasia, their youngest daughter.

Alexei, their youngest child and only son, born 1904.

Ulyanovs

Ulyanov, Ilya Nikolayevich, Volga River school district inspector (1831–1886).

Ulyanova, Mariya Alexandrovna, daughter of Dr. Alexander Dmitriyevich Blank, wife of Ulyanov (1835–1916).

Ulyanova-Yelizarova, Anna Ilyinichna, their oldest daughter (1864–1935).

Ulyanov, Alexander Ilyich, their oldest son (1866–1887).

Ulyanov, Vladimir Ilyich, second son (1870–1924).

Ulyanova, Olga Ilyinichna, second daughter (1871–1891).

Ulyanov, Dmitri Ilyich, third son (1874–1943).

Ulyanova, Mariya Ilyinichna, youngest daughter (1878–1937).

Krupskaya, Nadezhda Konstaninovna, wife of Vladimir Ulyanov (1869–1939).

Yelizarov, Mark Timofeyevich, husband of Anna (1862–1919).

Veretennikov, Nikolai Ivanovich, first cousin of Ulyanov children (1871–1955).

Lozgachev-Yelizarov, Georgi, adopted son of Anna, born 1906.

Revolutionaries, Intellectuals, and Members of the Establishment

Armand, Inessa, Bolshevik, close friend and probable lover of Lenin (1874–1920).

Azef, Yevno, SR terrorist and police double agent (1869–1918).

Badmayev, Pyotr Alexandrovich, Tibetan doctor, friend of Rasputin (1851–1919).

Balmont, K. D., decadent poet and author (1867–1943).

Bely, Andrei (Boris Bugaev), mystic poet and author (1880–1934).

Blok, Alexander, great symbolist poet of the Russian Silver Age (1880–1921).

Bonch-Bruyevich, Mikhail Dmitriyevich, officer in both Czarist and Red armies (1870–1956).

Bonch-Bruyevich, Vladimir Dmitriyevich, brother of Mikhail, close associate of Lenin in 1917–18 (1873–1955).

Breshko-Breshkovskaya, Yekaterina, SR, "Little Grandmother of the Russian Revolution" (1844–1934).

Bronstein, Lev Davidovich (Leon Trotsky), revolutionary who associated himself with Lenin in spring 1917 (1879–1940).

Bryusev, Valery, decadent poet and mystic (1873–1924).

Buchanan, Sir George, English Ambassador to St. Petersburg (1854–1924).

Bunin, Ivan A., Russian novelist, opposed to Revolution, Nobel Prize winner (1870–1953).

Burenin, N. Ye., Petersburg society figure and revolutionary (1874–1962).

Burtsev, V. L., Socialist Revolutionary and famous exposer of political double agents (1862–1942).

Chernov, Viktor, leader of SR Party (1873–1952).

Dan, Fyodor, leader of SR Party (1871–1947).

Djugashvili, Iosif (Joseph Stalin), Bolshevik, member of Politburo in 1917 (1879–1953).

Figner, Vera, member of famous Narodnaya Volya Party which assassinated Czar Alexander II (1852–1942).

Fofanova, M. V., agronomist, Bolshevik, sheltered Lenin in her Petrograd apartment in late 1917 (1883–1976).

Francis, David, American Ambassador to St. Petersburg (1850–1927).

Ganetsky, Ya. S. (Furstenberg), Polish Communist, Lenin's possible liaison with Germans (1879–1937).

Gapon, Father Georgi, leader of January 9, 1905, demonstration at Winter Palace (1870–1906).

Gershuni, Grigory, SR terrorist (1870–1908).

Gilliard, Pierre, tutor to Czar's children (1880–1962).

Gippius-Merezhkovskaya, Zinaida, poet, diarist, wife of Dmitri (1867–1945).

Gorky, Maxim, Russia's major proletarian writer, early supporter of Bolsheviks, sometime critic of Lenin (1868–1936).

Ivanov, Vyacheslav, Silver Age poet, mystic, symbolist (1866–1949).

Izvolsky, Aleksandr (Alexandre Iswolsky), Foreign Minister (1856–1919).

Kerensky, Alexander Fyodorovich, Trudovik Labor Party leader, Premier of Provisional Government 1917 (1881–1970).

Kokovtsov, Count Vladimir N., Russian Premier (1853–1943).

Kollontai, Alexandra A., Bolshevik, friend of Lenin, later Soviet diplomat (1872–1952).

Kseshinskaya, Mathilde, ballerina, onetime mistress of Nicholas II, later wife of Grand Duke Andrei Vladimirovich (1872–1971).

Kuropatkin, Alexei Nikolayevich, War Minister and commander of Russian land forces in Russo-Japanese War (1848–1926).

Lepeshinsky, Panteleimon N., old Bolshevik, associate of Lenin in Switzerland (1868–1944).

Lepeshinskaya, Olga B., wife of Panteleimon (1871–1963).

Lunacharsky, Anatoly Vasilievich, old Bolshevik, intellectual, friend of Lenin (1875–1933).

Martov, Yu. O. (Tsederbaum), Menshevik Party leader (1873–1924).

Mayakovsky, Vladimir, poet, supporter of the Revolution, suicide (1893–1930).

Merezhkovsky, Dmitri, Silver Age poet, philosopher (1866–1941).

Paléologue, Maurice, French Ambassador to St. Petersburg (1859–1944)

Plehve, Vyacheslav Konstantinovich, Interior Minister (1846–1904).

Plekhanov, Georgi V., founder of Social Democracy in Russia, early disciple of Marx (1856–1918).

Protopopov, Alexander Dmitriyevich, Interior Minister 1916–17 (1866–1918).

Purishkevich, Vladimir Mitrofanovich, right-wing Duma member, member of the group which killed Rasputin (1870–1920).

Radek, Karl, Polish Communist, Lenin's agent, brilliant polemicist (1885–1939?).

Rahja, Eino Abramovich, Finnish Communist, aide and bodyguard of Lenin, 1917–18 (1886–1936).

Rasputin, Grigory Efimovich, evil genius of the reign of Nicholas II (1872–1916).

Rodzyanko, Mikhail Vladimirovich, leader of Oktobrist Party in Duma (1859–1924).

Savinkov, Boris Viktorovich, Socialist Revolutionary terrorist and author (1879–1925).

Shturmer, Boris Vladimirovich, Premier and Interior Minister 1916 (1848–1917).

Shulgin, Vasily Vitalevich, Progressive nationalist member of Duma, memoirist (1878–1975).

Simanovich, Aron, jeweler, moneylender, associate of Rasputin.

Solovyev, Vladimir, philosopher, friend of Bely and the Bloks (1853–1900).

Stasova, Yelena Dmitriyevna, early Bolshevik, secretary to Lenin (1873–1966).

Stolypin, Pyotr, Russian Premier, assassinated (1862–1911).

Sukhanov, N. L., left-wing Duma member and diarist of Revolution (1882–1940).

Sukhomlinov, Vladimir Alexandrovich, War Minister 1909–15, arrested 1916, rearrested after February Revolution (1848–1926).

Sverdlov, Ya. M., Bolshevik, close to Lenin, involved in Romanov executions (1885–1919).

Tsereteli, I. G., Menshevik, Duma leader (1881–1959).

Valentinov, N. (Nikolai Vladislavich Volsky), early Social Democrat, close to Lenin in Switzerland (1879–1964).

Voyeikov, V. N., aide-de-camp to Nicholas II.

Vyrubova, Anna (Taneyeva), confidante of Czarina Alexandra, follower of Rasputin (1884–1968).

Witte, Count Sergei Yulevich, finance specialist, Premier 1905–6 (1849–1915).

Yusupov, Prince F. F., member of the group which killed Rasputin (1887–1967).

Zenzinov, Vladimir M., Socialist Revolutionary Party leader (1880–1953).

Political Parties

Bolsheviks: Left-wing Social Democrats, led by Vladimir Lenin, believers in Socialism, Marxism, conspiratorial revolution, strict party dictatorship. Now called Communists.

Mensheviks: Right-wing Social Democrats, believers in Socialism, Marxism, democratic party organization, led by Julius Martov. Roughly equivalent to present-day European Socialists.

Socialist Revolutionaries: Populists, believers in violent revolution, terrorist acts, assassinations, all land to the peasants, headed by Viktor Chernov. Left wing, headed by Mariya Spiridonova, cooperated for a while with the Bolsheviks.

Kadets: Constitutional Democratic Party, believers in liberal democracy, parliamentarism, but considered revolutionary by Czarist government. Headed by Pavel Milyukov.

Narodnaya Volya: Small populist terrorist party responsible for assassination of Czar Alexander II in 1881 and many other terrorist acts. Extinct by the 1890s. Its tradition carried on by SRs.

Author's Note

Nearly three quarters of a century has passed since revolutionary tremors began to shake down the worm-eaten structure of the Romanov Empire.

In this time events have taken on the glaze of icons. They gleam in the histories like varnished frescoes, heroic in scope, the actors turned into gods or devils.

This is an attempt to tell the story as it happened; to uncover once again the rich reality of the stumbling, groping, conflicted men and women of Russia in the first decades of our century. In this endeavor I have gone back to the first records of those times, have talked with survivors, and have had access to many untouched and previously unknown materials, some of them in the Soviet Union.

The Lenin of whom you will read in these pages is not the one you have known before. He was no master planner. He was badly out of touch with Russia, and no one was more surprised than he when revolution came to it except, perhaps, one other man: Nicholas II, Czar of all the Russias. Yet almost singlehanded Lenin rode the tidal wave to power.

Here is the story of Russia's revolutions and of the people who made them—the dark people, as they called themselves, the *narod*, the peasants who smelled of sweat and black bread, and of the poets of Russia's Silver Age who almost alone had a premonition of the black night, the white snow, and the blood which would soak the rich Russian earth, the *chernozem*, and change it and the world irretrievably.

BLACK NIGHT, WHITE SNOW:
Russia's Revolutions
1905–1917

I

A Quiet Execution

About six o'clock on the morning of May 5, 1887, a small steamer pulled up beside the old stone wharf at Oreshok, the fortress which Peter the Great built at the point on Lake Ladoga where the Neva River starts its sixty-mile descent to the Gulf of Finland. The fortress, now called Shlisselburg, had long since lost any military significance and for one hundred years had been used as a prison for important state criminals.

On this particular morning the steamer, having ascended the Neva from St. Petersburg during the night with shrouded running lights, was moored to the Oreshok wharf for more than an hour while seven prisoners,[1] five of them in shackles and leg irons, were carefully transferred, one by one, into whitewashed cells, about ten feet long and five feet wide, with heavy iron doors, stone floors, walls more than three feet thick, and so deeply recessed in the fortress ravelins that sounds from the outside rarely penetrated. The portion of the fortress where the prisoners were quartered was called the *sarai* (barn).[2] The origin of the nickname had long since been forgotten, but the building looked like a low barn, and possibly in the distant past it had housed provisions and supplies.

Shortly after the prisoners had been placed in the cells a gang of carpenters, some of them wearing the baggy blue Dutchboy pantaloons still favored by many Russian workingmen, entered the courtyard inside the prison walls. It was a small square, surrounded by fortress buildings, squat one- and two-story structures with red-painted metal roofs and stone walls painted white. The windows were narrow and protected with double rows of massive iron bars. Working carefully and swiftly, the men began to erect a structure in a corner of the yard. The wooden sections had already been sawn and fitted together easily like the parts of a child's construction set. There was a minimum of hammering, and, indeed, so quietly did the men go about their task that, later on, it was contended that this quiet and secrecy was the product of special orders of the Czar, concerned lest his vast realm be upset or disturbed by any noise, hubbub, racket, or excitement stemming from the proceedings at Shlisselburg.

Whether or not orders had been given to act with particular discretion (and none have turned up in a meticulous search of Czarist records), the work was done with so little fuss and flourish that the workingmen would, no doubt, have been astonished to learn that the knock of their hammers would ultimately echo into the most distant reaches of the Russian land and resound decades into the future and far beyond the Czar's domain.

By the evening of May 7 the task had been completed. Three black gibbets had been put up, and at 3:30 A.M. on May 8 five of the prisoners who had been brought to Shlisselburg, the five in shackles and leg irons, were awakened in their cells and informed that, in accordance with the sentences imposed upon them at the Special Session of the State Senate April 15–19, 1887, they were now to be executed.

The news was not expected by the prisoners. Somehow they had begun to think since their transfer to Shlisselburg that the Czar had decided to commute the sentences and substitute long terms or life imprisonment for the death penalty. And, in fact, Alexander III's first impulse, on being informed of the arrest of the prisoners, was to immure them perpetually in the Shlisselburg fortress with no announcement, no trial, no public indication of their fate. He thought it desirable not to give "too great importance to these arrests" and suggested that secret imprisonment would provide "the strongest and most unpleasant punishment."[3] But later the Czar had changed his mind and put the young men on trial. Now, with what their jailers agreed was remarkable calm, they received the word that they were about to die and, having dressed, were led out about 4 A.M. into the courtyard where the three gibbets and a handful of prison officials awaited them. Because there were five men to be hanged and only three gallows, two of the prisoners had to wait until their three comrades had been hanged before they could mount the platform and surrender their lives. In a note to Czar Alexander III, written later that day, the Minister of Internal Affairs, Count Dmitri Tolstoy, apologized for the procedure, explaining that because space in the courtyard was limited it had been necessary to acquiesce in this rather awkward arrangement.

The first three prisoners to be hanged were Vasily D. Generalov, twenty years old, a member of a Don Cossack family and a student at St. Petersburg University since August 1, 1886; Pakhomi D. Andreushkin, twenty-one years old, son of a Kuban Cossack family, a student in the mathematics-physics faculty of the university; and Vasily S. Osipanov, twenty-six, son of a soldier in Tomsk, the old Siberian capital, a student in the law faculty.

The three had refused the last rites but they kissed the cross as they mounted the scaffold. Generalov and Andreushkin loudly cried:

"Long live the Narodnaya Volya!"

Osipanov tried to follow their example, but the hangman's assistant dropped the hood over his head so fast his shout was muffled. The Narodnaya Volya (People's Will) was a revolutionary party dedicated to the overthrow of the Czarist regime.

The bodies of the three young men swung free as their two comrades stood below. Then these two were led up to the gallows, one of them kissing the cross, the other pushing aside the hand of the priest. A moment later their bodies, too, hung lifeless from the yardarm, and as the sun's first thin rays slanted into the courtyard on that mild May morning, the corpses of Alexander Ulyanov, twenty years old, son of an actual state counselor and school inspector, a fourth-year student at St. Petersburg University (who had kissed the cross), and of Pyotr Y. Shevyrev, twenty-three years old, son of a well-to-do merchant at Kharkov and also a fourth-year student (who had pushed aside the priest), were removed from the gallows and placed with the other three in a common grave within the prison walls.

On the following day, May 9, the Russian press was permitted to break the silence which had been imposed since the papers had printed a brief note in early March, reporting the students' arrest. The official St. Petersburg newspaper, the *Pravitelstvenny Vestnik* (Government Herald), published on its first page an account, nearly a column long. It was sandwiched between an announcement of the departure of the Czar and the Imperial family from Novocherkassk, where they had been paying a visit on the Black Sea coast, and an announcement by the Post and Telegraph Administration of the closing of the mails for Irkutsk and Vladivostok. A notable feature of the report was its paucity of detail and sparse official tone. It did not compare with the extravagant stories which for several days had been filling the papers about the trial of a retired artillery captain named Viktor I. Normansky and his brother, Vladimir, who were charged with murdering a peasant in the Novgorod Guberniya (province).

The story did, however, present the essence of the matter. It listed the fifteen young people who had been placed on trial and said that they had been discovered to belong to a "criminal society attempting to overturn the existing state and social order by means of violent revolution." The group organized a "secret circle for terrorist activity" and plotted an attempt upon the life of His Serene Highness, Alexander III. They had been tried and convicted before a Special Session of the State Senate. The Czar had remitted several sentences but not all. The account concluded:

"The verdict of the Special Session of the State Senate of the death sentence by hanging of the defendants, Generalov, Andreushkin, Osipanov, Shevyrev and Ulyanov was carried out May 8, 1887."

The publication of additional details was forbidden. But, of course, everyone in St. Petersburg knew of the case, had talked of little else since the first announcements in March, and had followed breathlessly the rumors of the trial before the State Senate. When on May 9 newsboys ran down Nevsky Prospekt shouting: "Death of the plotters!" no one had to ask his neighbor what the headlines were about.[4]

The care with which the Government regulated the publication of details of the case and the caution which surrounded the carrying out of the executions indicated a degree of nervousness; of fear of possible repercussions in the universities and countryside; of uncertainty as to what might be expected. Nor was the uneasiness entirely without justification. The crime for which the five had been convicted was an attempt on the life of the Czar. True, it had been a ridiculously futile attempt (the bombs, experts established, could not have exploded because of defective fuses even if the young men had succeeded in throwing them), yet only blind luck had uncovered the plot at the very moment the plotters were putting it into execution. But for a careless reference in a letter; the happenstance of its being intercepted by a censor; the methodical (almost too methodical) police check to determine its sender, the young plotters would not have been detected at all. In fact, even after the arrests were made, the gendarmes had no notion they had stumbled into an attempt on the life of the Czar.[5]

When the report of the arrests was delivered to Alexander III by the police, he scrawled in the margin: "This time God saved us! But for how long? Thank goodness all the officers and agents of the police weren't dreaming and acted successfully. . . ."

II

But for How Long?

But for how long? How long would the hand of fate be stayed? How long would the great Russian Empire and its creaking, anachronistic despotism survive? When would the Czar fall?

It was a question not alone on the lips of the hard-fisted, tough-fibered Alexander III. Ever since the success of a group of young people in taking the life of Czar Alexander II on March 1, 1881, the terrible foreboding had not lifted. What had happened once could happen again. Now six years later on the same fateful first of March a new effort had been made. True, it had been thwarted. True, the times seemed less disturbed, possibly because Alexander III had taken the sternest of measures when he came to power after his father's assassination. The young terrorist group called the Narodnaya Volya, which killed Alexander II, had been smashed to bits. Or had it? How could you ever be certain that the last spark had been snuffed out?

It seemed that everything that could be done had been done. The Czar had closed the leading newspapers of St. Petersburg, the *Otechestvenniye Zapiski* and *Delo*, which he suspected of liberal and radical leanings (to the Czar liberal and radical were the same thing). He had suspended the autonomy of the universities and virtually halted the entrance of students from the lower classes. Anyone who protested the new rules was expelled. Professors suspected of liberalism were removed. Count Nikolai P. Ignatyev, as reactionary a man as the empire boasted, hobbled out of retirement to help the Emperor extinguish any smoldering dissent, and Count Dmitri Tolstoy took over as Minister of Internal Affairs. It was a time, as Lenin later was to observe, of "unbridled, unbelievably senseless, beastly reaction."

Yet despite massive repressions the terror went on. Only a year or so after the assassination of Alexander II the Odessa police officer, General Fyodor Ye. Strelnikov, notorious for his cruelty, was assassinated by the Narodnaya Volya. Two years later the Czar's remarkable security agent, Lieutenant Colonel G. P. Sudeikin, chief of Secret Police in Petersburg, a man who singlehanded was thought to have wiped out the young terrorists, was clubbed to death in his rooms by a revolutionary agent. No matter how hard the police struck, the spark still flickered. Disturbances continued in the universities—in Kazan in 1882, in Poland in 1883, in Moscow and Kiev in 1884. Kiev University was closed in 1886 after two demonstrations.

Yet, unquestionably, the situation had improved by the mid-1880s. The truth was that the Narodnaya Volya, never more than a handful of revolutionary terrorists, had been liquidated. (The police suspected but could not be certain of this.) Its fighting organization had been crushed. Most young people were turning back to their studies. They encountered no professional revolutionaries in the schools. A few read the new social economists like Karl Marx (just beginning to become known in Russia), Herbert Spencer, and John Stuart Mill, but many more read Leo Tolstoy. His *Kreutzer Sonata,* with its eloquent, melodramatic, and vaguely lewd preachment against the power of the flesh, occupied the long nights of discussion.

Some continued to be attracted to Nikolai Chernyshevsky and his famous novel *Chto Delat?* (What to Do?). This question, What to do?, had preoccupied the generation before. Indeed, it was essentially the question that had preoccupied Russia since the early nineteenth century and was to preoccupy it into the twentieth. What to do? Everyone asked the question. Even the Czar. What to do? And Alexander Herzen's question: Who is to blame? Or Tolstoy's: *Tak chto nam delat?* What are we to do? All the writers asked the question, and when the time came, so did Lenin, paraphrasing Chernyshevsky and calling his pamphlet: "What Is to Be Done?"

Questions, questions, questions. Where were the answers? Poignantly and persistently one generation of young people after another debated through the endless winter nights with the samovar bubbling and one glass of tea following another. They debated at the *vechera,* those peculiarly Russian evenings of talk, of self-examination, of moral inquiry, of self-flagellation, in which every question was asked and every possible answer was advocated and nothing was ever agreed upon. What to do? What to do with themselves; what to do with this enormous and powerful country, stumbling like a sleepwalking giant through the nineteenth century, a feudal country with a feudal government which a hundred years previously had led the world in metal production and now—after a century of lag—was rushing into the industrial revolution, doubling its industrial production, doubling its industrial workers in twenty-five years from 1865 with the expectable consequences: horrible exploitation of labor, twelve-, fourteen-, and fifteen-hour shifts, even in the iron and steel mills, more and more strikes—326 in the years 1870 to 1879 and then 446 in the first half of the 1880s[1]—workers (children of six, pregnant women of fifteen, tubercular fathers of seventeen) living in lice-ridden, heatless wooden barracks, flogged to work, shot down by the Czar's Cossacks if they ventured a complaint, brutalized, left to die on a pallet of straw or a bundle of dirty rags when all strength was drained from their bodies.

In the Ivanovo Voznesensk textile mills the workday in 1872 *averaged* 15½ hours. In St. Petersburg it ranged between 13½ and 17—at forty kopecks a day!* The governor-general of Moscow, A. A. Liven, observed in 1871 that "the labor question may, and by force of the inevitable course of events, even must take the same path in Russia that it has in the West," that is to say, strikes, economic conflict, social confrontation, mass political action.[2]

Rural teachers received less than a living wage, sometimes as little as seven or eight rubles a month. They often lived on a cot in a corner of the schoolroom. As late as 1901 the Russian press reported the scandalous death of A. M. Yeremeyeva, a teacher in the Novgorod Guberniya, who died of starvation when the authorities forgot for two months to pay her wages of 7½ rubles.[3]

What to do? Those who asked the question persistently ended, as had the five young Narodovoltsy, in Shlisselburg, in the hands of the Czar, facing the gibbet, life imprisonment (and early death) in the subterranean catacombs of Peter and Paul Fortress or exile to the mines of Nerchinsk. So it had been since the time of Alexander Radishchev, the first of the Russian *intelligents*. "My soul was wounded by the suffering of humanity," he wrote, and this sentiment caused his arrest in 1790 by the great liberal, Catherine II. He was condemned to death. The lesson was clear. Do not ask the question. The question is dangerous, the questioner more so. It was a lesson

---

* A study by P. A. Peskov of seventy-two factories in 1881 found the average working day varied between 11.55 hours and 14.25 hours with some workers on 18-to-20-hour shifts. In Vladimir and Ivanovo the pay averaged eight rubles a month in the 1880s, ten rubles in the 1890s. Often workers lost most of these wages in fines leveled by employers, (Yu. Z. Polevoi, *Zarozhdeniye Marksizma v Rossii*, p. 80, citing P. A. Peskov, *Sanitarnoye Issledoveniye Fabrik po Obrabotkye voloknistykh veshchestv v Moskve*, Moscow, 1882, p. 73.)

each generation was to learn anew, yet with the passing years a tradition grew—a tradition of violence and of repression, of irreconcilability, intransigence, maximility. On the one hand stood absolutism and the great autocrat, the Czar; on the other the most enlightened, the most idealistic, the most progressive, of his subjects. It was a struggle which waxed and waned.

In many ways and for many reasons Russia had been a laggard to European civilization. In part, perhaps, because of geography. In part (as Russians insisted), because of the heritage of 250 years of Mongol oppression. More specifically because of the schism between the Eastern and Western churches. Moscow's Orthodoxy held itself to be the true Rome. But the great schism meant that Russia experienced neither Renaissance nor Reformation. Neither Church nor Court was swept by the hurricanes of intellectual challenge which blew through western Europe. Russia knew neither Da Vinci nor Luther; neither Rousseau nor Cromwell. Peter the Great and his illustrious successor, Catherine the Great, were "enlightened" autocrats but they permitted no diminution of Imperial power. Their strong hands reinforced autocracy at a moment when it was disappearing in western Europe.

Radishchev's crime was to write a book containing an "Ode to Liberty," inspired by the American Revolution. Radishchev attacked serfdom (a form of peasant enslavement virtually indistinguishable from American slavery), called for religious freedom (Russian Orthodoxy held as tight a religious monopoly as was maintained in Spain by the Inquisition), political liberty, an end to censorship, and an end to controls over the minds of men, the establishment of a rule of law and judicial equality. (Some two hundred years later young Russian dissidents are being sent to prison for advocating virtually the same program.)

Catherine, witless with fright over the French Revolution, saw in this modest man, chief of the St. Petersburg customs house, a Robespierre or Danton. Although she eventually commuted his death sentence to ten years of exile, he was so despondent on return from banishment that he committed suicide—only the first of the intellectual sacrifices to blind Russian tyranny which has not ended to this day.

Catherine was succeeded by Paul and Paul by his "liberal" son, Alexander I (who connived at or acquiesced in Paul's murder). But Russia did not change. Alexander led the Russian armies into Paris after Napoleon's defeat. Russian officers brought back to Petersburg a whiff of enlightenment, the fresh air of Europe's new constitutional monarchies. When Alexander died mysteriously November 19, 1825, and a group of bemused young officers assembled in St. Petersburg's

Senate Square, half in revolt, half in demonstration for a constitutional monarchy under the new Czar's brother, Konstantin, the troops shouted: *"Konstantin i Konstitutsiya"*—and some said they thought Konstitutsiya was Konstantin's wife—they like Radishchev paid with their lives. The new Czar, Nicholas I, made one gesture of mercy. His Special Commission of Inquiry had decreed that the six leaders of what came to be known as the Decembrist conspiracy be drawn and quartered. Nicholas had moral objections to the shedding of blood. On his order the men were hanged, rather than chopped into hocks, like beef on the butcher's block. The remainder of the Decembrists, later joined by their wives, went into exile in eastern Siberia to become a legend that inspired generation after generation of young Russians, dedicated to bringing to their people a rule of humanity.

The Decembrists were crushed. But the spark lived. It burned in the heart of Russia's greatest poet, Alexander Pushkin. Not even Czar Nicholas I dared still Pushkin's tongue. Instead, he proposed to be Pushkin's own censor. The arrangement didn't last long. Pushkin's life was taken in a senseless duel with the coolest, most deadly gunman of the day, a duel possibly instigated by the Czar himself to rid Russia of a voice of conscience.

The 1830s gave way to the 1840s, new men, new thinkers, new writers—Alexander Herzen, Nikolai Ogarev (his question was: What do the people need?), Mikhail Bakunin, V. G. Belinsky, Nikolai Gogol, Fyodor Dostoyevsky. The 1840s yielded to the 1850s. There was no change in Russia. Nicholas I held fast—Iron Nicholas with his Third Section, the secret police . . . Iron Nicholas. Vigilant against dissent or liberalism. Herzen fled abroad, and from London his monthly, *The Bell*, tolled and tolled again—doom for the autocrat. Gogol fought the censorship—a losing battle. Pyotr Chaadayev was declared insane for writing that Russia was an egoistic nation. He was released from an asylum after two years on a promise never to write again.* Dostoyevsky was swept up in the repression of the liberal Petrashevsky group. Led out to be hanged, he was amnestied to Siberian exile as he stood on the gallows. Is it a wonder that his writing is haunted by the specter of death? Belinsky died of tuberculosis before Nicholas' agents could arrest him, and Ogarev, arrested, exiled, arrested again, was finally driven abroad. Bakunin, forced into precarious foreign existence, elaborated a philosophy of anarchistic terrorism which was to fascinate (and destroy) many brilliant members of the next two Russian generations.

---

* More than one hundred years later the Soviet Government again invoked the police insane asylum and the arbitrary verdict of insanity as a means of combating literary and political dissent.

The blood chills at the record. The Russian soil was sown with a seed so bitter that men like Bakunin turned the world upside down, proclaiming "the passion for destruction is also a creative passion."

Through the years Nicholas I vowed he would leave Russia as he found it—stern, oppressive, autocratic, orthodox. On his deathbed in 1855 he exclaimed: "My successor must do as he will; for myself I cannot change."

The new Czar, Alexander II, freed the serfs, loosened the censorship, struck fetters off universities. A new spirit seemed to be in the air. Herzen's *Bell* pealed jubilantly for the "Czar Liberator." Nikolai Nekrasov founded the great St. Petersburg monthly *Sovremennik* (Contemporary), whose influence was to dominate two decades. On its pages the thoughts of young Nikolai Chernyshevsky began to appear.

For a few years there seemed hope. Then the clouds darkened. Expectations aroused were dashed. The salt of bitterness had eaten too deep. Alongside the liberals, there appeared another breed—young men, contemptuous of life and of their own lives, convinced that only total destruction could save Russia, extremists who believed with Bakunin that to destroy was beautiful, that blood would purify their sad land, that only by bringing down the whole structure of the rotten old could the wondrous ideal of the new be built. Their names often were known to less than a handful—Pyotr Zaichnevsky, who called on his fellow Moscow students to "Get Your Axes"; Dmitri Karakozov, who fired a point-blank shot at Alexander II in April 1866; a pamphleteering student named Pyotr Tkachev whose strange friend, Sergei Nechayev, was to stamp an ultra-ist imprint on an entire revolutionary generation.

The 1850s faded into the 1860s. The men of the fifties were succeeded by those of the sixties. Those of the sixties by those of the seventies. One cannot encapsulize generations of thought, the interplay of the turgid status quo with the pull of succeeding waves of young people—university people, starving students, dignified professors with their green broadcloth suits, their garlic-and-caries breaths, their bent gold pince-nezes, and their fanatic fantasies of pure reason, ultimate triumph, and Russian universalism.

As the years passed, Czar Alexander II, never a liberal, never more than a well-meaning Conservative, drew back into the security of the Third Section, the gibbet, and sentences of exile. He was frightened to find there were no boundaries to the demands of the radicalized youth. He could not admit that reform had failed and that his regime was ingrained with terror, choking in bureaucracy, drowning in ignorance and greed. He grew more rigid, more cranky, more repressive, and now the deadly spiral spun faster and faster—more young men and women arrested; more violence against the state; more attempts at assassination; more assassinations; more arrests; more executions.

Finally came the triumph of the Narodovoltsy—the attack on the Catherine Canal March 1, 1881. Thrice the young plotters had tried and failed. They mined the railroad tracks on the Czar's route to and from the Crimea. Once, the dynamite did not explode. Once, they blew up a freight train, not the Czar's special. Then they managed to introduce a confederate into the Winter Palace, working as a carpenter. He smuggled in the dynamite stick by stick, until his bed was filled with explosive. But when the charge was hastily touched off (in fear of discovery), it merely blasted a hole in the ceiling and killed some palace servants. So came the final attempt. A tunnel was dug, foot by painful foot, under the roadway from a cheese shop at 9 Malaya Sadovaya. The dynamite sticks were placed. It was, they hoped, on the Czar's route from the Winter Palace to the Kazan Cathedral. But nothing worked right. The Czar took a different way. The revolutionaries had a fallback plan—a squad of dynamiters to attack the Czar on the street. As the Czar's entourage swept up the Catherine Canal embankment Nikolai Rysakov hurled his bomb. It dented the axle of the Emperor's carriage, killed a Cossack guard, wounded a child. The unhurt Emperor stepped out to see what had happened. An officer hurrying up said: "Where is the Emperor?" Alexander II replied: "I am safe, thank God, but . . ." He pointed to the youngster lying in agony on the pavement. Rysakov muttered (so the prosecution later was to charge): "Do not thank God yet." The Emperor walked back a few paces to where the bomb had been thrown. There another bomber Ignoty Grinevitsky, was leaning nonchalantly on the parapet of the canal. As the Emperor came up to him Grinevitsky hurled his explosive. The Emperor fell, legs shattered, his body bleeding in a hundred places. Grinevitsky fell, too, unconscious. He survived the Emperor but a few hours.

So Russia moved through the 1880s. So her course continued. So it held in the spring of 1887, the intelligentsia demoralized, the rulers traumatized. Y. A. Bunin, brother of the novelist Ivan Bunin, wrote that "chaos rules everywhere."[4]

This was the society and this was the mood which Alexander Ulyanov pictured in his last words to the court which sentenced him to be hanged until dead. He and his companions had determined to attempt the life of the Czar not because they believed this was a proper and reasoned course, but because they felt all others had been closed.

"I am confident," the young man said, speaking easily and, as his listeners conceded, with remarkable eloquence,[5] "that the natural and correct course of social action is that of propaganda by pen and word. But life showed in the most convincing way that under existing conditions such a path was impossible. . . .

"Our intelligentsia is so weak physically and so unorganized that at the present time it cannot go into open battle and only by the form of terrorism may it defend the right to its beliefs and to intellectual participation in the life of society.

"I have thought a great deal about the objection that Russian society obviously does not sympathize with terror and that, in part, it is even hostile to it. . . . Society may not be sympathetic but in so far as the demands of the struggle are the demands of the whole of Russian educated society, its urgent demands, then so long will this be the struggle of all the intelligentsia with the government. . . .

"Among the Russian people there always can be found ten persons who are so dedicated to their ideas and who so warmly feel the misfortunes of their motherland that for them it appears no sacrifice to die for their cause. . . .

"All that I have said is not with the aim of justifying my conduct from the moral point of view but to show its political value. I want to show that it is the inescapable result of the existing conditions, the existing contradictions of life. . . . That is all I want to say."

The response of Alexander III can be judged from his notations in the margin of Alexander Ulyanov's confession: "This outline is not just crazy—it is naked idiocy!" A bit further on the Czar scrawled: "Purest Communism!" He awarded bonuses of one thousand rubles and gold medals to the policemen who had stumbled upon the plot of March 1, 1887,[6] and, bundling up his household, took his family on a long and burdensome journey to the Black Sea, far from the dingy courtyard and the dark cells of Shlisselburg, where the lives of the five young university men were so quietly snuffed out.

On April 1, two weeks before delivering his final speech, Ulyanov had been permitted a meeting with his mother, Mariya Alexandrovna. The Czar gave his permission because he thought the interview would reveal to the despairing woman the "true nature" of her son. A prison official was unobtrusively present. Mother and son wept, Alexander begging his mother to forgive him for bringing her such grief. Then he talked of the dictatorial, repressive regime which held the country in thrall and of the duty, as he saw it, of every honest man to fight for the liberation of Russia.

"Yes," sighed his mother, "but with such terrible means!"

"But," replied Alexander in the classic form in which the question had been asked by so many generations of young Russians, "*Chto delat?* What is there to do, Mama, when there are no other means?"[7]

The execution of Alexander left his brother, Vladimir, just past his seventeenth birthday, the male head of the family. Years later Vladimir, now bearing the revolutionary *klichka,* or pseudonym, of Lenin, recalled the last summer of Alexander's life, his brother's hard work as a naturalist, preoccupied with his dissertation, the subject of which was the *Annelida* family of earthworms. Alexander rose early every morning to catch the best light for his microscope.

"No," Vladimir recalled thinking, "my brother will not become a revolutionary. A revolutionary cannot give so much time to annelids . . . soon I saw how mistaken I was."

III

Volga Mat'

As long as she lived, the Christmases in the old wooden house at 21 Streletskaya Street on the bluff high over the Volga at Simbirsk would sparkle in the memory of Anna Ulyanova-Yelizarova.[1] There was a solidity about life in Simbirsk, a sense of continuity and permanence which belied any thought of shaky foundations or turbulence below the placid surface. Here Russian life flowed smoothly and certainly. No sense of doom, no premonitions of apocalypse. There were six in the Ulyanov family then. Anna was the oldest. Next came Alexander. Vladimir and Olga were babies. Dmitri and Mariya had not yet been born. Their father, Ilya Nikolayevich Ulyanov, was a traveling school inspector who spent half his life on the muddy back roads of the Volga countryside. Much of the time his wife, Mariya, was left alone to cope with the household of young children.[2]

It was very much a Volga family, which is like saying that Tom Sawyer's was very much a Mississippi River family. The times were quite similar on both rivers, the endless procession of steamboats, the towns with their boatmen's taverns, the gamblers, the traders, the rowdy, raucous—often vicious—life, the broad self-contained character of the river community, its spirit, its vigor, its distance from the other Russia. These were the days of steam. But rope-drawn barges still plied the river, the chant of the Volga boatman was alive and in the air, the *burlaki,* the iron-muscled, bark-shod peasants, still drew the barges and died before they were thirty in some dirty hole, possibly the very barracks which Maxim Gorky celebrated in *The Lower*

Depths, set in his native Nizhni Novgorod, Queen City of the Volga, where the Ulyanovs lived until they moved south to Simbirsk in 1869 (and where Anna and Alexander were born). The great river with its feeling of a world apart placed a mark on all who came under its influence. It was no accident that the Russians called it Volga Mat', Volga the Mother. Years after Vladimir Ulyanov had left backwater Simbirsk and the Volga, he was seated with a group of European radicals in Brussels on the eve of World War I when the impact of it came back. He burst out to a casual acquaintance: "You've been to the Volga? You know the Volga? It is wide—unbelievably wide. When I was a child with my brother, Sasha [Alexander], we traveled on it in a boat—far, very far. . . . And we used to sing songs on the water, songs that aren't known anywhere else." The brothers used to go on what they called "around the world" trips, that is, they took long hikes or rowed along the river, venturing up one tributary and returning down another by steamboat. Sometimes, the trips took a week or more.[3]

The life of the Ulyanovs was conditioned by the great river. The father, Ilya Nikolayevich, was born at Astrakhan at the mouth of the Volga where it flows into the Caspian Sea. His school district lay along the Volga, a straggling district three hundred miles from north to south. His wife came of a different background but the Volga was in her life, too. She was of German stock. Her father, Alexander Blank, was a quite well-to-do St. Petersburg physician, a didactic, idealistic, strong-minded man who retired to a small estate on the Volga near Kazan where his daughter Mariya grew up with four sisters and a young brother under a patriarchical regime (her mother died when Mariya was three) which sternly set its face against "coddling."[4] Mariya's father believed that children should wait on themselves, sleep in heatless rooms, rise early, dress warmly, and drink hot milk in a warm kitchen to get their blood flowing. He forbade coffee or tea and was violent against the Russian samovar—a contraption suitable only for *babushkas* and *dedushkas*—grandmothers and grandfathers. His daughter was educated by her father and brought up in four languages, Russian, German, French, and English.* She was trained in music and to the end of her life played the piano often, easily, and with pleasure. She grew up a woman of beauty, moral quality, warmth, integrity, and humor, remembered by all of her children as a paramount force in shaping their characters.[5] Her father wanted her to follow in his course and study medicine—an unusual career for a

---

* Her aunt, Yekaterina Ivanovna, sister of her mother, kept house for Dr. Blank and assisted in bringing up and educating the Blank children. (Vladimir Kanivets, *Ulyanovy. Istorichesky Roman*, pp. 34–36.)

young woman of those times—but she preferred to go to Penza and prepare to be a teacher.[6]

It was Mariya Ulyanova who made Christmas the great holiday in the life of her children. Simbirsk was a dull provincial city. It boasted no factories, no trolleys, not even horsecars, and for many years there was no railroad connection. Much of the town was new. Three quarters of the buildings and houses had been consumed in the disastrous fire of 1864 which burned for nine days, destroyed twelve churches, the Spassky monastery, and more than thirty public buildings. The population was under thirty thousand.[7] The event in the life of Simbirsk was the annual fair, but even this would soon begin to fall off as the extension of railroads changed the whole life and economy of the Volga cities.[8]

In winter, life came to a halt, waiting until the ice broke on the Volga in spring and travel could resume. During Ilya Nikolayevich's long absences, the little family lived in great isolation. With the November snows Mariya Ulyanova would set the children to work with shears and paste and bright paper and scraps of ribbon to make ornaments for the Christmas tree. In the winter twilight the youngsters bustled away, fashioning tinsel stars, braiding chains of red and green paper, decorating angels of gilt, figures of the three wise men, and the animals of the crèche. It was a German—not a Russian—Christmas, and the scene of the bright-eyed children gathered around the stately figure of Mariya Ulyanova with her straight-combed hair, her gray expressive eyes, her high bosom and ruddy, handsome face could have been duplicated in ten thousand little German cottages from the Black Forest to Pomerania.[9]

The children not only made decorations for the tree. They made presents for each other and for their parents. There was no such thing as a bought present in the Ulyanov household where rubles and kopecks were never in too ample supply. The girls knitted scarves and mittens and the boys whittled letter openers, glued and decorated handkerchief boxes and tie racks.

On Christmas Eve Ilya Nikolayevich, a devout Russian Orthodox believer,[10] went to vesper services (later the older children joined him in this but not Mariya Ulyanova, who never adhered to the Orthodox belief) and then hurried home for the lighting of the candles on the tree and the festival which lay at the heart of the Ulyanovs' life. The children presented their gifts and recited verses, sometimes their own, sometimes classics chosen from Pushkin or Mikhail Lermontov. When he was eight, Alexander picked as his "present" to his parents the famous speech from K. F. Ryleyev's "Life for the Czar." "He who is Rus-

sian in his heart is brave and bold and happy to die in the right cause"
—favorite lines of his father.[11] None who heard him doubted that
Alexander was "Russian in his heart." And none, of course, knew that
the time would come when the words might be graven on his tombstone, an epitaph to his young life.

Forty years later Anna jotted down her recollection of those days
and commented: "For some reason the impression stays in my memory
very clearly of one Christmas tree when Olga was the smallest in the
family and Sasha [Alexander] was six or seven. A special feeling of
close and friendly family unity, of cosiness and cloudless childish happiness was left by this holiday."[12]

Nor did the Christmas holiday fade away when the children grew
older. It was still *the* occasion of the year, with Ilya Nikolayevich
lighting the candles on the tree as Mariya played Christmas hymns at
the piano. The occasion grew more and more jolly. The Ulyanov children invited their friends and there was dancing and games and
music. Katya Arnold, a friend of Olga's, recalled later: "Ilya Nikolayevich himself lighted the tree, danced with us and we played games—
blind man's buff and cat-and-mice. Mariya Alexandrovna played for
our dancing and I and Olga played four hands, I playing the accom-
paniment and she the melody. It was such fun I didn't want to go
home."[13] Ilya Nikolayevich was very fond of dancing. In fact, he
danced the polka and led the quadrille at a Christmas party only a
few days before his quick, sudden death January 2, 1886.[14]

Sometimes, when the small children grew bored Mariya Ulyanova
would invent games for them to play. One which they particularly
liked was troika. They moved the heavy horsehair chairs in the living
room and set them up to represent a three-horse team and sleigh.
Alexander took the coachman's place, cracking the long whip over the
horses. Mariya sat behind her oldest son with the other children and
gave a running commentary, describing to the youngsters the winter
road they were traveling, the deep fir forest, the passing coaches, the
hurrying sleighs, the plodding foot travelers whom they met on the
way.

As Anna was to recall:

"I can confidently say that no artist in my succeeding life ever
aroused in my soul such excitement or gave me such happy poetic moments as these simple games with our mother."

The warmth, the strength, the goodness, of the Ulyanov family—
their dedication to each other, to the highest of moral principles, their
concern with achievement and learning, their good humor in the face
of obstacles and hardships, the sensitivity of the relations of children

to parents, parents to children, and children to each other—all this was attested by those who knew them in those days and thereafter.

As in all traditional Russian middle-class households the Ulyanovs were blessed with a faithful *nyanya*, Varvara Grigoryevna Sarbatova, who was a member of the household for more than twenty years, sharing in every holiday, every feast, every sorrow, of their close, conventional life.[15]

They were bookish people, preoccupied with education. The father, Ilya Nikolayevich, read to his children in the evening. When Tolstoy's *War and Peace* was appearing in installments, he read each segment to them as soon as it reached Simbirsk. At four Alexander could read the newspaper, lying on the floor beside his mother. At five Anna read. Vladimir started at the same age.[16] All were taught by their mother but in spite of his long absences Ilya Nikolayevich was the authoritative head of the family. He set its tone and the tone was that of the earnest, liberal Russian educated class of the mid-century, a class which believed strongly in education; which saw Alexander II as the "Czar Liberator" and never left this view, persisting into the repressive eighties in the optimistic hopes which the reformist sixties inspired. It believed in change, redemption, improvement, enlightenment, good deeds, cold baths, fresh air, and self-discipline. When news that Czar Alexander II had been assassinated reached Simbirsk, Ilya Nikolayevich was extremely upset. He left his office immediately, came home, put on his uniform (as school inspector he had been named to a minor rank in the hereditary nobility and was a holder of the Order of Vladimir), and went to the cathedral, where a memorial service was conducted.[17] His children remarked on how shaken he was by the tragic event.[18] He was a family man, a very good family man, his children believed, and they could never recall hearing a single argument between him and his wife.

Nadezhda Krupskaya, who married Ilya Nikolayevich's second son, once said: "In order to understand to the end the character of Ilya Nikolayevich you must read *Sovremennik* [the magazine, Contemporary] under the editorship of Nekrasov and Panayev with the collaboration of Belinsky, Chernyshevsky and Dobrolyubov."[19] He was no follower of that classic of Russian family life and discipline, *Domostroi*, the medieval handbook attributed to St. Sylvester by which Russian heads of households traditionally guided their conduct, faithfully beating their wives at regular intervals, as recommended by Sylvester, for the good of both wife and husband. Ilya Nikolayevich believed in the perfectibility of man and passed on this belief strongly to his children. In later years Vladimir remembered his father talking with an-

other educator about the difficulty of getting the younger generation
to go to church. "The whip—the whip is needed," the educator said.
This was not Ilya Nikolayevich's way.[20] He took a modest interest in
science (he had taken his degree in mathematics and physics)[21] and
served as observer for the Penza weather bureau. Once he wrote a
paper on "Thunderstorms and Lightning Conductors." Another time
he designed a model of the solar system, using a lamp for the sun, a
small globe for the earth, and a silver ball for the moon.[22] He was
conscientious in his schoolwork and was proud, as were his children,
of his achievements in nearly doubling the number of pupils in his
district from 10,564 to 19,921 between 1869 and 1885.

The Ulyanov children were raised in a close-knit, intellectually
stimulating atmosphere. On the living-room table there was (as in
thousands of other middle-class Russian families) a heavily bound
gold-embossed "Album for verses," a faded wild rose pressed into the
frontispiece and the conventionally humorous and sentimental verses
contributed by the visitors ("Who loves more than me—let him write
more than me!"; "She has not died; she has passed into immortal-
ity"[23]). The Ulyanovs' bookshelves were filled with well-worn volumes of Pushkin, Gogol, Lermontov, Ivan Krylov (the Russian
Aesop), Alexei Koltsov, Sergei T. Aksakov, and Ivan Nikitin, not to
mention Jules Verne, Daniel Defoe, Sir Walter Scott (*Ivanhoe* was a
great favorite with Vladimir; Alexander didn't like the book so well),
Mayne Reid, James Fenimore Cooper, Charles Dickens, and William
Makepeace Thackeray. It was typical that a family newspaper was
published every Saturday night, called *Saturday* or *The Weekender*.
Alexander was its inspiration and editor, Anna his helper. When
Vladimir and Olga were old enough, they joined in. Vladimir's nom de
plume was "Kubyshin."[24] They loved games—chess, in particular. Also
croquet. Everyone played, all the children and their father and
mother, all but Alexander, whose nose was usually in a book. The best
player on the croquet court laid out beside the old carriage house was
Vladimir. He was merciless toward any violator of the rules but scru-
pulously fair, his brothers and sisters felt, when making decisions in
the endless wrangles that marked the game. When twilight fell, the
children lighted Japanese lanterns so that they could go on playing
deep into the long summer evenings. They made up a special vocabu-
lary, based on their father's travels about the country. They smacked
the ball "into the next county" or even farther "into the next Guberniya."[25]

The family subscribed to two children's magazines, *Rodnik*
(Spring) and *Detskoye Chteniye* (Children's Reader), which were

filled with riddles, puzzles, charades, and jokes. These they delighted in on rainy days and long evenings. For example:

> "I'm copper, I'm bone, I'm linen, I'm glass,
> I sit on the threshold bright and round
> I nestle close on guard
> And only let the owner into the house. . . ."

The answer to this one—and the Ulyanov children didn't guess it quickly—was a button.[26]

The family rented the second floor of the Zharkov house, a solid square-built house in the Russian tradition, looking out over the Old Crown—as the unpaved grassy boulevard on the top of the bluff was called—to the Volga River. Theirs was the last house on the street. Across a square stood the town jail. This was on the very outskirts of the city—a place of gardens and fruit trees and goats grazing on their tethers. On holidays it echoed with the sound of accordions and guitars. People strolled and ate sunflower seeds. Boys serenaded girls, singing *chastushki*, improvised limericks. The Old Crown was bright with kerchiefs and red shirts. At Easter time they rolled eggs and there were carousels, peddlers, and gypsies, kiosks selling fried fish, hot cakes, and vodka, and in the evening the air was filled with argument, drunken talk, and fighting. At such times Mariya Ulyanova forbade her children to go outside their yard. Over the walls of the old prison the children often heard the clank of chains, saw the haggard faces of the prisoners through the bars of the windows, heard their hoarse cries and shouts.[27] Although Anna Ulyanova in adulthood recalled the prison as a place of gloom and terror, an early glimpse into the horrors of Czardom, there is little evidence that it darkened the happy childhood of the Ulyanovs, and in any event the family moved on in 1875 to another rented house and finally in August 1878 to the house at 58 Moskovskaya Street (now Lenin Street) which they bought and where they lived until they left Simbirsk in 1887.[28]

Of the children Vladimir was the liveliest. His sisters said he was more apt to break his toys than play with them. He loved noise and jokes. Fifty years later one of his schoolboy friends still carried in his mind a picture of Vladimir in flowing blue Russian peasant blouse and wide Turkish trousers, playing tricks and teasing his sister Olga.[29] He was so noisy that more than once his mother led him into Ilya Nikolayevich's study and sat him down in a big chair covered with oilcloth—the "black chair." There he had to sit not making a sound until she released him. Once she forgot. When she came an hour later, he was peacefully sitting in the black chair, fast asleep.

The house on Moskovskaya Street had a back yard filled with apple,

plum, and cherry trees, raspberry and currant bushes, and a straw-
berry patch. The children divided the yard into the "Black Forest,"
thick with lilacs, the "Yellow Forest," overgrown with acacias, the
"Red Forest" of hawthorns, and a "Dirty Forest" where rubbish
collected. There were half a dozen kinds of apples in the orchard. The
best were anise, a prize Volga variety, and a very tasty kind called
Black Wood. Beside the back-yard gate was a well. The water was so
hard it was used only for the garden and for animals. Drinking water
was piped in from the Sviyaga, a small stream that flowed into the
Volga. There were endless games in the garden. They played soldiers
—Vladimir's favorite. He himself cut the soldiers out of heavy paper
and colored them with crayons. There were usually two armies, one
Vladimir's, the other led by his younger brother, Dmitri. The soldiers,
ten to fifteen on a side, were made to stand up on bases of folded
paper. All were the same height except for generals, who were taller.
They were set up in fighting order on facing edges of the dining-room
table and the battle began. The commanders attacked with dried peas,
snapped from their fingers. Any soldier still standing after the bombardment was awarded a medal, especially designed by Vladimir.
Once he mystified his younger brother by fastening his soldiers to the
table with light nails. Dmitri fired his peas but the soldiers merely
nodded and remained standing. Alexander's army was always Italian
with Garibaldi as its leader. Vladimir's was American. He himself
played the role of Abraham Lincoln with Generals Grant and Sher-
man leading his troops. Anna and Olga had Spanish soldiers and they
fought Napoleon (or the Americans or the Italians). The children
were partisans of Lincoln and the Northern cause. They had read and
reread Harriet Beecher Stowe's *Uncle Tom's Cabin*.[30] Vladimir was
extremely fond of military play. When he had no one else to drill, he
would command his little sister, Olga.[31]

The entertainment which stayed most vivid in the memory of Dmitri was what they called *brykaska*, or the "bucking bronco." This was
invented by Vladimir and was a kind of fright fantasy. The brykaska
was a very secret kind of ogre. As soon as their parents had left and
the house was empty, Vladimir blew out the lamps and drew the curtains. Dmitri and Olga would sit on the floor. Suddenly beyond the
door they heard an unearthly sound. A moment later a frightening,
hairy, growling thing appeared—Vladimir with a great sheepskin coat
turned wrong side out over his head. Sometimes, the brykaska was
angry and the children had to run for their lives. Sometimes, the
brykaska dragged them screaming under the divan. Or the brykaska
might be in a jolly mood. But you never knew. It came at you in the
half-shadow, all furry, on all fours. It growled and grabbed you by the

leg. Horrors! Then, suddenly, its mood changed. It let go and promised not to eat you.[32]

In summer the family took long lazy vacations at Kokushkino, the estate of Mariya's family. There they lived with the Veretennikovs, their cousins. Ivan Veretennikov had been a fellow teacher of Ilya Ulyanov at Penza. He was married to Mariya's sister and it was on a visit to the Veretennikovs in Penza that Ilya and Mariya met and were were married.[33]

"We began to dream about our move to Kokushkino and make preparations for it long in advance," Anna recalled. "We thought there was nothing better or more beautiful than Kokushkino."[34] The Veretennikov children could not wait for the arrival of their cousins. They used to set out on foot to meet them at the crossroads a couple of miles away. Sometimes they went two or three days in succession before the Ulyanovs arrived. All summer long they swam in the river. Sometimes Vladimir and his cousin, Nikolai Veretennikov, managed as many as two dozen dips before the end of the day. They played billiards in the billiard room of the estate (Vladimir was not as good a player as his cousin) and chess and checkers (at which he was better).[35] They rowed boats and took long walks in the woods, collecting birds' eggs and gathering mushrooms, the most traditional of Russian summer occupations, *podosinoviki* (under-the-aspens), *poddubniki* (under-the-oak-trees), and a dozen other succulent varieties, filling their wicker baskets and bringing the mushrooms back to be cooked with onions and dill. They sang the Volga songs and Mariya played the piano. Ilya Nikolayevich loved the student songs of his day, many of them technically forbidden by the censor. With Mariya at the piano the family often joined in Nekrasov's "Song of Yeremushka" or "Stenka Razin."[36] Years later, Vladimir passionately recalled his love for Kokushkino. "I haven't forgotten either its limetrees or its flowers. I remember with pleasure how I used to loll about in haystacks, how I used to eat strawberries and raspberries and how I used to drink fresh milk." Both Mariya Alexandrovna and her sister Anna Veretennikova loved flowers. There were mignonettes, stock, sweet peas, tobacco plant with its haunting fragrance, nasturtiums, phlox, geraniums, and hollyhocks in the flower beds. Old limes formed an arbor on the path to the pond.[37]

The Ulyanov children were excellent students—serious, well trained, devoted to their studies, and, except for Vladimir, who had a tendency to tease some of his teachers, particularly an unfortunate French instructor whose accent he mimicked, very obedient and disciplined. The boys attended the local academy or gymnasium, free of tuition because of their father's position. It was typical that when Anna asked Alexander (then eleven), "What sins are the very worst?" he immediately replied: "Lies and cowardice." It was equally typical that Anna, many years after the event, remembered that Vladimir once told a lie when visiting his aunt in Kokushkino at the age of eight. A water carafe had been broken. His aunt asked the youngsters who did it. His cousins said: "We didn't." Vladimir chimed in: "I didn't." Two or three months later Vladimir confessed his sin to his mother.[38] These attitudes did not change as the children grew older. When Alexander was fifteen or sixteen, he wrote an essay on what qualities were necessary to be a good member of society. "For useful activity," Alexander wrote, "a man needs 1, honesty; 2, love for work; 3, firmness of character; 4, intellect; 5, knowledge."

"Honesty and correct attitudes toward his obligations in relation to people around him," Alexander concluded, "should be educated in a man from early youth as from these convictions depends what branch of work he selects for himself and whether he will be guided in this choice by social usefulness or egoistic feelings of personal profit."

The essay was preserved in the family archives. It bore at its end the grade "4"—equivalent to an English "B"—and was signed "Kerensky," that is Fyodor M. Kerensky, director of the Simbirsk Gymnasium and father of Alexander Kerensky, whose Provisional Russian Government one day would be overthrown by Vladimir Ulyanov.

The conventional, idealistic view of man and his role in society expressed by Alexander in his schoolboy essay did not change. Several years later in a letter to his cousin Marusya he wrote in great detail about what he regarded as positive and negative characteristics. "In evaluating a man," he wrote, "I always use these criteria: how much he has worked for specific social ideals, ideals of another and better order of things, how basic and progressive are his convictions and how energetically and self-sacrificingly he moves toward their fulfillment." Egoism, neglect of social ills, selfish concentration on individual materialistic goals—these were the qualities he deplored. The letter was dated January 21, 1887. On May 8 he died, hanged by the neck for his part in the plot on Alexander III. He had declined to write an open plea for the Czar's mercy. It would not, he said, be honest. He had tried to kill Czar Alexander. Now it was only just that his own life be forfeit.

There were, to be true, differences in temperament between Alexander and his younger brother Vladimir. But in childhood these seemed largely superficial. Vladimir was more gay, more noisy, less serious; he liked to tease and indulge in fantasy. Alexander was quieter, more compassionate, and preferred facts. There are no moral essays like Alexander's preserved in Vladimir's archives. Both liked nature but Alexander made it his study; Vladimir (and his younger brother, Dmitri) hunted ducks and rabbits although neither was very good with a gun. A family joke on seeing a rabbit run across the field: "There is the rabbit Volodya [Vladimir] hunted all winter." Despite these differences Alexander was Vladimir's ideal. When asked his ambition as a youngster, he invariably said: "To be like Alex." "We all of us tried to emulate Sasha [Alexander]," his older sister Anna recalled. His example and influence in the family cannot be overemphasized. Another time Anna said: "He [Vladimir] loved to play just as Sasha [Alexander] played; he loved to do just what Sasha did. He loved his older brother and imitated him in everything, even the most trivial. If he was asked something—did he want to play or go for a walk or eat his porridge with milk or with meat he never answered quickly but first looked at Sasha and then said, 'The same as Sasha.'"[39] The example of his older brother, in relationship both to work and to people, was compelling to Vladimir throughout his childhood. Some critics have tried to find cruelty, single-mindedness, egocentricity, or ultraism in the record of Vladimir's early years. It does not stand up in the objective evidence of those who knew him. This was no rebel, no iconoclast, no youthful messiah. Vladimir was by all accounts as normal and pleasant a youngster as any parents could have desired.

IV

"The Best and Most Thoughtful"

The Ulyanov family, living its quiet bourgeois life in one of the sleepiest towns along the Volga, was not to be distinguished from thousands of other Russian families of the day. The mother and father dedicated themselves to bringing up their children pure of thought, clean in spirit, morally wholesome. They lived out of the mainstream of late nineteenth-century Russia where the old serf-peasant society was dying and the new landlord-sharecropper relationship was rising in the countryside, where huge and oppressive industrial establishments worked to the very point of death those peasants who straggled into the cities to find jobs; where a stubborn Imperial court sought timorously to avoid coming to grips with changing times, and reactionaries of church and bureaucracy clung with bony fingers to the ways of the past.

Duplicates of the Ulyanov family lay at every hand. The Kerensky family differed only in detail from the Ulyanov family. The elder Kerensky, an earnest, enlightened, prim, stuffy schoolmaster, brought up his children in the same out-of-tune-with-the-times liberalism, born of the brief Enlightenment which accompanied Alexander II's freeing of the serfs. Kerensky, like his colleague Ulyanov, came of poorer stock than his wife, worked hard to make something of himself, taught literature and Latin, and inculcated in his family a love for the Russian classics. Young Kerensky, like the young Ulyanovs, grew up on Pushkin, Lermontov, and Dickens. Like them he had a passion for American Indians and for *Uncle Tom's Cabin*. In his home there were great Russian—not German—celebrations of Christmas with parties and amateur theatricals that went on for days. It was a household governed by devotion to the liberal ideals of the nineteenth century, education, science, a responsible relationship of human beings to each other. This was a pattern of thought and conduct common to countless Russian families.[1]

Take, for example, the family of Viktor Chernov, later to become the leader of the great Socialist Revolutionary party. He too was a man of the Volga, born in the little town of Novouzensk in the Samara Guberniya, raised in the Volga town of Kamyshin, educated in Saratov, a city by then holding pretensions of being "the capital of the Volga." Like Ulyanov and Kerensky, Chernov's father had married a woman of greater wealth, rank, and education than himself. Like them, he by his own efforts rose into the lower nobility, winning his order of St. Vladimir and his rank of "collegiate counselor" through long and hard service in the bureaucracy. Chernov was nourished in a close, upright family, growing up on the liberal diet of the seventies, Dmitri I. Pisarev's *Russkoye Slovo*, the enlightened *Delo*, and even occasional numbers of Herzen's *Bell*. But the Chernov family was not a religious one. The elder Chernov was a freethinker, although he tended to conceal this from public view. And he held a firm and stubborn belief that sooner or later all the Russian land would go into the hands of the peasants, for, he said, they were the true children of the soil and only they genuinely loved the earth—it was a conviction which would ultimately find dramatic political expression in Chernov's own career.[2]

In the group which stood trial with Alexander for the March 1, 1887, attempt on the life of the Czar there were fifteen young people. With one or two exceptions each had the same quality of background as Alexander. They were sons or daughters of middle-class families, small merchants, minor nobility, the in-between ranks of the ecclesiastic hierarchy. In almost every case they came not from St. Petersburg or Moscow but from the provinces, particularly the Volga area, the Cossack reaches of the Don and the Kuban or the Ukraine—from what the Russians call the "periphery" as opposed to the "center."

The young people had been educated at local academies and gymnasia and then came to St. Petersburg to attend the university. They were interested in studying medicine or the law. One or two were desperately poor. But most were supported by their parents, modestly if not with luxury. Alexander received forty rubles a month from his father. He lived on thirty, saving ten which he returned to his father at the end of the university year. Of course, exceptions were plentiful to this pattern. But it was common enough to attract general attention.

For instance, Vera Figner, the sole survivor of the successful attempt on the life of Alexander II, March 1, 1881, came from the most sheltered of backgrounds, brought up on an estate in the Volga Guberniya of Kazan, far from city or town life, protected in every fashion from the harsh contrasts of Russian society. She grew up in the depths of what she called a "drowsy forest," a real bear's corner, as the Russian expression has it. Her father was a forester. The nearest neighbor was forty versts (twenty miles) away. She was educated at home in a household where her strict but devoted father laid down precise rules. She went to bed each night at a specified hour; she wore the same dark dress each day; she was taught to say good morning and good evening to her elders; to cross herself and offer thanks after every meal; not to talk while she ate; to wait her turn at table on her elders; to drink milk not tea; to eat black bread not white; not to complain about the cold; and to do her daily chores cheerfully without question. It was precisely such idealistic young people, taught to believe deeply in justice, freedom of conscience, truth, sincerity, honesty, who upon exposure to the reality of Russian life, as seen through the prism of the universities and higher educational institutions of St. Petersburg, Moscow, Kiev, or Warsaw (Poland was then an integral part of Russia), quickly, almost overnight, were transformed into extreme enemies of the Czarist system. In the case of Alexander Ulyanov the process took but a few months. Until his final year at the university, so far as can be established (and he himself testified directly on this point), he played no political role whatever.[3] He met his associates in the fateful assassination attempt in the autumn of 1886, some of them not until after New Year's, that is, less than two months before the attempt on the Czar. His violent politicization, to use the contemporary term, occurred when police brutally broke up a demonstration of university students which he had helped to organize and in which he had participated on the twenty-fifth anniversary of the death of Nikolai Dobrolyubov, the literary critic and revolutionary, November 17, 1886, at the Volkov Cemetery in St. Petersburg. It was but one quick step from the Dobrolyubov demonstration to the attempt on the Czar's life.

The ease with which young Russians of good patriotic families passed within the shortest time from being passive observers of the social, economic, and political ills of their country into the role of violent extremists, dedicated to the lethal destruction of the state and its chief figures, could not but evoke comment and astonishment both by thoughtful Russians and by state security officials charged with guarding the person of the Czar. The philosophy of these young people, to take the specific example of the group with whom Alexander was associated, was an amalgam drawn from many sources. Their emotion and passion sprang from the Narodnaya Volya which had assassinated Alexander II. They called themselves the "Terrorist Faction" of the Narodnaya Volya, but actually they had no connection with any previous or organized group other than romantic attachment. A few had peripheral exposure to Narodnaya Volya propaganda or fleeting friendships with members of the movement but nothing more. The objectives of the group were not put down on paper until the actual eve of their abortive attempt on the Czar. The reason was clear. The group had no articulated, defined program. It represented a congerie of ideals and ideas. Alexander Ulyanov wrote their manifesto in a clear neat hand for the purpose of providing the rationale for the killing of the Czar. This is not to suggest that he and his comrades had not believed in the aims which Alexander outlined. They did. They simply had never tried to put it together and on paper before. For the most part the views do not sound very radical in the context of our times. They called for free popular democratic elections "without regard to sex, religion or nationality"; local self-government and elections; recognition of the *mir*, the traditional village council, as the basic economic and administrative unit; full freedom of conscience, speech, press, assembly, and association; nationalization of land, factories, and production (it was made clear that this was an ultimate—not an immediate—objective); a popular militia to replace the standing army; and free popular education. If the Government was prepared to grant a bill of rights, popular elections, and a general amnesty for political criminals, the terror would be called off. Alexander stressed the empathy which he and his comrades felt for Russian liberals and toward the Social Democrats (Marxists) but clearly distinguished his group from both. Although enormous efforts have been made by Soviet apologists to read Marxist implications into Alexander's platform, it remains a mixture of the liberal and progressive ideas of the times. Every one of Alexander's points came from the Narodnaya Volya platform except for the point on popular education—that came from the nascent Marxist group of Dmitri N. Blagoyev.[4] Actually, one of the strongest influences on Alexander and his group was Leo Tolstoy's famous pamphlet of February 14, 1886, *Tak Chto Nam Delat?* (What Are We to Do?). Tolstoy had been inspired to write the pamphlet by the terrible glimpse into Russian life which he had gained as a volunteer census taker in 1882. He was permeated with alarm for the life of the people. "Around us," he said, "people die from back-breaking work and want." The root of the evil, he felt, was the money economy which enslaved the poor in the service of the rich. Unless men broke with the system by ceasing to benefit by this "slave labor," a workers' revolution would sweep the whole structure away.[5]

Nikolai Berdyayev, the philosopher, felt that the Russian intelligentsia had been crushed between two millstones, the autocratic monarchy above and the "dark" peasant masses below. It was propelled into extremism by the lack of middle ground, by the savagery with which the Government attacked any advocate of change or reform, no matter how reasonable. "The best, the most thoughtful and cultured people of the 19th century did not live in the present which was abhorrent to them. They lived in the future or in the past," he said.[6] He called Dobrolyubov the darling of the young people of the eighties and later, "the kind of man of whom saints are made." Dobrolyubov had a strong Orthodox upbringing, an exquisite sense of evil and of sin. He could not forgive himself if he overslept or indulged in too much jam. He loved his parents, especially his father, a stern, serious, just man. When he became aware of the nature of Russian life, he lost his faith, appalled by the evil, the inequity, the suffering, he found around him. Berdyayev saw in Andrei Zhelyabov, the leader of the 1881 attempt on the Czar's life, almost a classic example of the nihilism which turned faith inside out. To the courtroom where he was on trial for his life Zhelyabov proclaimed:

"I believe in the truth and righteousness of the [Christian] faith and I solemnly acknowledge that faith without works is dead and that each genuine Christian should fight for justice, for the rights of the oppressed and the weak and, if need be, also suffer for them; that is my faith."

One hot evening in May 1887, Dmitri Andreyev, a member of the graduating class at Simbirsk Gymnasium, finished supper at the pension where he was staying and strolled out on the Crown for a breath of fresh air before going back to his books. It was the eve of examinations but the weather was so pleasant, the sky so clear over the broad expanse of the Volga, the scent of lilac and acacia so strong, that Andreyev broke into song as he strolled along the boulevard. He passed a gazebo on the riverbank and noticed someone sitting, staring into the distance. Suddenly he heard a shout: "What's the matter— aren't you studying for exams?" It was Vladimir Ulyanov. Andreyev saw that his friend was in a gloomy, preoccupied mood, so he sat down in silence and the two looked out over the Volga. Presently Vladimir sighed deeply. "What's the matter?" Andreyev asked. Vladimir turned, started to say something, then didn't. Andreyev knew that Vladimir's father had died a year or so before and that his brother Alexander had been arrested in Petersburg. He tried to lift Vladimir's spirits. Nothing worked. Ordinarily Vladimir was gay and lively. Finally, Andreyev observed that the evening was so quiet nature itself could not help but put you into a good mood. Vladimir then spoke. He said that on May 8 his brother had been executed. The news shocked Andreyev. He fell silent, too. The boys sat a long time, neither speaking. Finally, Vladimir rose and they walked together toward the city with slow steps. Later, Andreyev felt he could almost see Vladimir mastering his emotions, taking himself under command. At last the two parted, exchanging not a word, shaking each other's hands firmly and Vladimir staring so deeply into Andreyev's eyes he could never get the look out of his mind.

Two or three weeks later Ivan M. Chebotarov, a classmate of Alexander's, returned to Simbirsk. Vladimir questioned him "quietly, even too methodically" about the circumstances of Alexander's trial, which Chebotarov had attended. Chebotarov got the impression that Vladimir was motivated by something deeper than natural curiosity. Vladimir's questions centered particularly on his brother's revolutionary mood.[7]

There are many accounts of Vladimir's reaction to the tragedy of his brother's death. His younger sister Mariya recalled (but not until February 7, 1924, after Vladimir's death) that when he heard the news he exclaimed: "We will not take that path! We must not follow that path." A possibly more reliable version of Vladimir's reaction on hearing of Alexander's execution was given by Mariya on another occasion. In the earlier version Vladimir was described as typically silent, offering no comment on the news. "The expression on his face was such that he regretted that his brother had so cheaply given his life, not using it as he might have for the good of the working class," Mariya recalled. She was only nine years old at the time of Alexander's death (Vladimir was seventeen). It seems dubious that such thoughts as these crossed her mind, but her description of Vladimir's silent stunned reaction is consistent with that of all the other witnesses of the day who picture him as shocked into inarticulateness.[8] The trauma persisted for a long time. For example, as late as 1891 when he came to St. Petersburg for law examinations, it was still present. He looked up S. F. Oldenburg, a close friend of Alexander's, and asked many questions about his brother, especially his scientific work. Oldenburg remembered Vladimir as "gloomy and silent" and said he obviously suffered deeply over his brother's death.[9] A family friend recollected that when Vladimir was first told the news of his brother's arrest, he said: "It is an affair so serious that it may finish badly for Sasha [Alexander]."

It is notable that in all the accounts no member of Vladimir's family, none of his friends, offers any other remark or expression made by Vladimir in those days in Simbirsk. Change there was. Everyone noticed that. The gay, laughing boy, full of tease and jokes and high spirits, overnight became serious, silent, thoughtful, gloomy. Of the two remarks attributed to him one is banal and meaningless; of course, anyone who attempted to take the Czar's life would be in serious trouble. The reference to "we will not take that path" has a self-serving political connotation, and the fact that it was "recalled" for the first time forty years after the event cannot help but engender skepticism. When Vladimir did enter political life, he moved on a different track than his brother. He opposed the random use of terror which cost his brother's life and substituted instead a cold policy of calculation and secret political conspiracy. But there is no evidence that this conclusion leaped full-blown into the mind of the seventeen-year-old Volga schoolboy. Had this happened, there would undoubtedly be dozens of references to it in Soviet historiography and in the many, many reminiscences about Alexander and Vladimir jotted down by the Ulyanov family and by Vladimir himself. What is clear is that the blow of Alexander's execution struck far too deep for Vladimir to verbalize it. His conduct in the gazebo with Andreyev has the hard ring of reality about it—morose, shocked, silent, unable to speak his feelings, let alone to begin to draw political conclusions.[10]

The deepest insight into what was passing through Vladimir's mind is given by his eldest sister, Anna. She had been at St. Petersburg, attending the university with Alexander, but she fell ill and came back to Simbirsk in the autumn of 1885 not long before her father died. She spent a great deal of time with Vladimir—Volodya as she always called him. She took long walks with her brother and they talked interminably. Volodya was sixteen going on seventeen. He was full of the turbulence of adolescence. He was antagonistic to the regime at the gymnasium, critical of the teaching and teachers, and had revolted against religion. In general, she said, he had a negative attitude toward authority, which was principally manifest toward school. "But there was nothing specifically political in our conversation," she emphasized. "I am confident that in the closeness of our relations Volodya never would have concealed from me such interests. At that time, in a word, he had no political beliefs."

Anna did not find this surprising, considering Volodya's youth and the "deaf alienated social life of the provinces [where] political views did not develop early."

Moreover, there was no evidence that even Alexander had begun to think politically before leaving Simbirsk for his last year at the university. He had not spoken of his opinions to Volodya or even to Anna, who was back at the university during the period when Alexander's sudden politicization was occurring.

There was another circumstance which, in Anna's view, played a role in Vladimir's reactions. Much as Vladimir admired his brother and had sought to imitate him as a little boy, the two brothers were not close in the last year or two of Alexander's life. This Anna discovered in talking with Alexander in the fall of 1886, only a few months before his death. She said to him one evening: "How do you like our Volodya?" Alexander replied: "He is undoubtedly a very talented person but we don't get on very well and we are not really close, in fact we are not close at all."

Anna asked her brother his reason for such a firm and negative opinion. He refused to answer but Anna believed she knew. "Volodya," she said, "had reached that transitional age when a youngster is especially sharp and quarrelsome. He was very brash and self-confident, and even more so after the death of father." This had disturbed Anna although probably not as much as it disturbed Alexander. She knew that Alexander could not stand Vladimir's sarcasm and rudeness and his growing superciliousness. This was particularly true when Vladimir was sharp with his mother as he began to be after the death of their father. Anna's mother told her that in that last summer when Alexander and Vladimir were both at home the two boys one day were playing chess silently. She reminded Vladimir of a chore which he had not done. He replied rudely and went on with the game. She spoke again. Again Vladimir made a sarcastic reply. Alexander then intervened. "Volodya," he said, "either you will go right now and do what Mama says or I won't play with you any more." Vladimir rose and did the chore. To Alexander, Anna felt, any kind of rudeness, sarcasm, or sharp language was completely alien whereas it was basic to Vladimir's nature—particularly after he became an adolescent.

"The different nature of the two brothers," she said, "had already made its appearance in childhood and, thus, they could never be close friends notwithstanding the boundless respect and admiration which Volodya had for Sasha in his early years. It was absolutely clear that each [of them] had his own nature and that they were entirely different individuals."[11]

Anna's reflections on her two brothers provide a clue to the processes under way within Vladimir after his brother's death. Almost certainly Vladimir suffered feelings of guilt as well as of hurt and of mystery as to what had been going on within the mind of his elder brother during their last months, months of substantial alienation. Concealed from Vladimir, his brother had developed an entire personality, a philosophy, and a way of life of which Vladimir had not even the smallest clue and which he could not have guessed in that final period, marked as it was by his sarcasm and cockiness. There was, indeed, much on which Vladimir must ponder. One thing is certain. Never again was anyone to hear of lack of politeness, concern, and sensitivity in Vladimir's relations with his family. Never again was his mother to hear him speak rudely (although rudeness, sarcasm, sharpness to the point of verbal sadism, would be imposed upon his political opponents—and not infrequently on his closest political associates). With his family, in Anna's words, his relations would always be marked by "friendliness, comradely attention and consideration."

But all of this was to become apparent later. For the moment Vladimir plunged into his gymnasium examinations with the full vigor of a brilliant, engaged mind. He graduated with honors. His score was 4 10/11 which meant that he had perfect marks of 5 in every subject but logic (in which he scored 4). In conduct, attention in class, preparation, written assignments, recitations, interest in subject matter—in all he was rated outstanding. He was the winner of the gold medal and was given by the master, Fyodor M. Kerensky, the highest recommendation for admission to Kazan University, Kerensky asserting that there had "never been a single case when Ulyanov by word or deed aroused any unpraiseworthy opinion about himself." This was not literally true—there had been some complaints about his boisterousness and sarcasm from instructors. But Kerensky was doing his best for a boy in whom he had confidence, the son of his old friend and colleague, the district school inspector who had died only a few months earlier, the son of his friend's widow who had just passed through the shock and tragedy of her oldest son's execution. He was doing what he could to get Vladimir admitted to the university knowing that questions were bound to be raised.[12]

Mariya Alexandrovna was aware of all this. She was determined not to lose her second son by the route which cost her the first. Hardly had exams finished in June 1887 than she put up most of the furnishings of the house in Simbirsk for sale and not waiting to sell the house itself, moved her family to the peace and quiet of the deep countryside, hoping there to recover her bearings and make a new start.[13]

V

Up Against the Wall

It was to Kokushkino, the estate of her father, Alexander Blank, that Mariya Ulyanova retreated with her family in the summer of 1887.[1] Here she had grown up, here the family had spent its summers, here she felt more safe and secure.* The place was quiet, isolated, stretching lazily along the reedy banks of the Ushni, an expanse of sprawling birch forests, grassy pasture, and fertile meadows, across which straggled brown and white Swiss cows, fields of barley and buckwheat, reedy thickets, marshes where ducks paused in spring on their migratory flights, and no near neighbors. It was not so isolated as the forest retreat where Vera Figner grew up, but in winter when the snows drifted five or six feet deep it might as well have been Siberia. The next two or three years of Vladimir Ulyanov's life were spent in large measure in the countryside, first at Kokushkino and later at Alakayevka. True, he had some brief interludes in Kazan, where he entered the law faculty in the autumn of 1887, but by December 1887 he was back at Kokushkino, under police observation (as was his sister Anna), expelled from the university for taking part in a demon-

---

* Kokushkino was located in the Laishsky Uyezd of the Kazan Guberniya about forty kilometers east of Kazan on the banks of the Ushni River, midway between the Kazanka and Kama rivers, tributaries of the Volga. There was a largely Tartar village called Cheremyshevo-Apokaevo about a kilometer away. By the time of the Revolution Kokushkino had ceased to exist as an independent village and the community was now called Apakaeva. The village is now called Lenino. (V. Volin, V. I. Lenin i Povolzhe, p. 54; Russiiskaya Federatsiya Evropeiskii Ugo-Vostok, p. 24; Malaya Sovetskaya Entsikolpediya, 3rd ed., p. 942.)

stration, a demonstration and arrest so routine, so expectable, so inevitable, as hardly to be worth mentioning except for a story Vladimir told long afterward. The policeman who arrested him, apparently thinking that he had fallen into trouble through the accidental influence of older comrades, said: "Why are you revolting, young man? You are up against the wall." To which Vladimir replied: "The wall is rotten—one shove and it will collapse." The response shocked the policeman into silence—or so Vladimir remembered fifteen or sixteen years later.

From the moment he arrived in Kokushkino he plunged into reading. Never before or again would he read so furiously. He devoured shelves of books of his father's which had been brought from Simbirsk —bound volumes of *Sovremennik, Otechestvenniye Zapiski*, and *Vestnik Yevropy*. He read from early morning until late at night. He was reading before his tea was hot in the morning and he was reading when the candle guttered out after midnight. He read everything that came to hand—courses for the university, the poetry of Nekrasov, philosophy, literature, and economics. He read Ivan Turgenev's *On the Eve*. He was fond of Turgenev and earlier had read his *Hours* as a textbook on "firmness of purpose" just as he had read Andrei Kolosov for dedication in life. But most of all he read Chernyshevsky. He read every article which Chernyshevsky wrote for *Sovremennik* and through him became acquainted with Belinsky, with the basic principles of the peasant question, with the political economy of Mill, with Friedrich Hegel, with materialism, with aesthetics, with the role of art and literature, with outstanding events in life abroad, with all of the preparatory groundwork he needed, as he later noted, in order to master the dialectic of Marx.[2]

He read Chernyshevsky's *Chto Delat?* five times. He read it and as soon as he finished he read it again from beginning to end. The great service of *Chto Delat?*, he was later to say, was that it proved that the *only* correct route which a thoughtful and responsible person could take was the revolutionary path and also showed how a revolutionary should conduct himself, what rules he should apply to his life, how he must work, and what methods he need employ. "To this day," he once said, "it is impossible to cite a single Russian revolutionary who with such basic penetration and force as Chernyshevsky understood and condemned the cowardly, infamous and criminal nature of every kind of liberalism."[3] From Chernyshevsky Vladimir drew the lesson: no compromise; no quarter; total dedication; intransigence in goal; flexibility in method.

Years later the first stunning impression of Chernyshevsky had not left Vladimir. He was talking in Geneva in 1904 with Nikolai Valentinov, who remarked that *Chto Delat?* was a primitive, giftless, pretentious, almost unreadable work. Vladimir burst out in anger. How could Valentinov permit himself such an extraordinarily stupid thought about the most talented figure of socialism next to Marx? Marx himself had called Chernyshevsky a great Russian writer.[4]

"He didn't say that about *Chto Delat?*," Valentinov rejoined. "This thing, Marx, doubtless, never read."

Vladimir was beside himself.

"Under its influence hundreds of people have become revolutionaries. Maybe that's because Chernyshevsky wrote without any talent and so primitively? For example, he attracted my brother and he attracted me. He shook me profoundly. When did you read *Chto Delat?* It's useless to read it if you haven't got your mother's milk off your lips. Chernyshevsky's book is too complicated, too full of thought to understand and appreciate in early youth. I myself tried to read it at about 14. It was an absolutely worthless and superficial experience. Then, after the execution of my brother, knowing that Chernyshevsky's novel had been one of his most beloved books, I sat down with it not just for a few days but for a week. Only then did I understand its depths. It is the kind of thing which gives you ammunition for your whole life."[5]

It is much easier to understand Valentinov's reaction to *Chto Delat?* than that of Vladimir. Chernyshevsky wrote the book in the Peter and Paul Fortress, where he had been imprisoned on false and forged evidence. The investigating commission found nothing wrong with the novel, and the censor, thinking it had been approved by higher authority, passed it. Thus, it was published in *Sovremennik* in 1863 but it was quickly banned and was not reprinted until after the 1905 Revolution.[6]

Chto Delat? is a utopian novel. It presents two or three simple propositions. The first and the most impressive is the concept of free love—but not in the sense of promiscuity or sensuality. Chernyshevsky preaches absolute equality and sensitivity in human relations. The heroine, Vera Pavlovna, and her husband, Lopukhov, do not make love, sleep in separate chambers, meet by appointment, see each other only when each clearly desires it, shake hands rather than kiss. It is true that eventually they indulge in an occasional kiss but never in physical love. When the husband senses that Vera has fallen in love with his best friend, he stages a false suicide to permit Vera to marry his friend. It is indicative of the novel's creakiness that the husband later returns under a painfully obvious false identity and marries again; the two couples become inseparable.

This idealistic and unworldly presentation of human relations enormously attracted the young Russian intelligentsia and violently offended the Russian reactionaries, still accustomed to the coarse brutality of the *Domostroi*, the womanizing of the upper class, and the primitive church law relative to women and divorce—the same which Tolstoy attacked with such passion in *Anna Karenina*.

There were other themes in *Chto Delat?* One was communism—but not exactly the kind which would threaten the existence of capitalism in Russia. In the novel Vera establishes a needlework co-operative which she peoples with "fallen women." The co-operative is a great success and gives rise to disquisitions by Vera Pavlovna about the new day in which exploitation of man by man, woman by man, and human beings by each other will end. The needleworkers share the profits of their enterprise. They eat co-operatively and live in communal style. It is possible to read into this a model for communization of the whole of Russia but it takes a striking reach of imagination.

Chernyshevsky preached a dedication to ideals and objectives; the hardening of will and body (his ideal revolutionary, Rakhmatov, sleeps on a bed of nails; eats raw meat; develops a physique like that of a Volga boatman; denies himself sexual relations; studies twenty-four to thirty-six hours at a time; travels widely but only to study "what is necessary" of social conditions; speaks with utmost frankness and often rudely; has no personal life, no luxuries, no caprices; reads Adam Smith, Malthus, Ricardo, and Mill; has no use for Macaulay; devours Thackeray's *Vanity Fair;* dresses badly and smokes very expensive cigars; devotes himself to the ceaseless and undeviating pursuit of revolutionary aims).[7] The students of his novel live in communes remarkably like those popular in the United States of the late 1960s and the 1970s.

Even when you read and reread the novel it is difficult to recapture the aura which it evoked in the mind of young Ulyanov. His feelings lacerated by the loss of his idealized older brother, savagely suppressing the constant welling-up of emotions, he searched for a means that would not only place his life within a rational context but justify his brother's sacrifice. That the novel did so for him there can be no doubt. Nor was he alone in attesting to the powerful impact of this unlikely work. The whole generation of young Russians to which he belonged fell under Chernyshevsky's influence. It was not only the idealistic concepts of Chernyshevsky—it was the idyllic setting, the almost Byronesque romanticism which attracted the young.

"The encyclopedic learning of Chernyshevsky, the clearness of his revolutionary views, his merciless polemic talent nourished me," Vladimir once said. He marked whole pages and read them, pencil in hand, filling notebook after notebook with jottings—unfortunately all lost. He wrote a letter to Chernyshevsky but to his regret never got a reply. Because of the censorship, of course, Chernyshevsky was not able to state his views openly. But Vladimir was convinced he could understand the underlying meaning because Chernyshevsky (and Marx, in his view) was like a musician with absolute pitch—he had "absolute revolutionary sense."[8] No one so influenced Vladimir (until he later became acquainted with Marx—and probably not even Marx) as did Chernyshevsky. His wife, Nadezhda Krupskaya, said that he never spoke of Chernyshevsky without becoming passionate. He was fond of citing Chernyshevsky as an example of revolutionary strength and often said that "a revolutionary Marxist must be ready at all times for everything"—a teaching which he drew directly from Chernyshevsky.

One more teaching Vladimir drew from Chernyshevsky—the principle of "the worse the better"; that is to say, the worse conditions become, the better it will be for the revolutionary cause. Thus, Chernyshevsky took a negative attitude toward the liberation of the serfs. And if they were to be liberated, it was better that they got no land because in that way the peasants would be more quickly driven to revolution. This terrible principle was to become one of Vladimir's. In 1891–92 crop failure brought famine to the Volga. There were no reserves of rye and wheat in the villages. All had been sold for export. Raging cholera devastated the countryside. It was one of the worst disasters to hit Russia in the late nineteenth century. Tolstoy played a leading role in organizing aid for the starving as did the author V. G. Korolenko.[9] Hundreds of progressive and liberal young Russians went to the Volga area to help out, among them, for example, the twin princes Dolgorukov, Pavel and Pyotr, then twenty-five. Both were to die eventually at the hands of the Bolsheviks, Pavel in 1927 after a romantic and pointless trip in disguise back into Soviet Russia, and Pyotr, presumably in 1945 when he was arrested in Prague where he had lived for many years. He was spirited back into Russia by the Soviet secret police. He was then seventy-nine years old.[10]

The Volga disaster was so great that it changed the whole social temper of the countryside and gave a new thrust to the cause of revolution.[11] In Samara the local burghers organized soup kitchens for the starving peasants. Vladimir scoffed at the relief efforts. He contended that the more intense the suffering of the peasant, the more violent would become his hatred for the ruling order, thus advancing the cause of revolution.[12]

Later on there were those who sought to compare Vladimir Ulyanov with Sergei Nechayev and Pyotr Tkachev, Russian preachers of pure terror and the doctrine that the end justifies any means. The comparisons are superficially apt. But no comparison is so apt as that to Chernyshevsky's ideal, Rakhmatov, resolute, completely dedicated to his task, prepared to give up everything for his goal of changing Russia but, like Vladimir, determined not to yield his life lightly, to fight with every resource at his command. It was on this pattern that Vladimir was to model himself—"an unusual man, an individual of a very rare sort," as Chernyshevsky said, "the best among the best, the mover of the movers . . . the salt of the salt of the earth."[13] The scent of elitism is heavy in Chernyshevsky's prose. It was to form an integral ingredient in Vladimir's concept of the elite revolutionary party which he conceived to be the vanguard (and surrogate) of the proletariat.

If the impression of Chernyshevsky on Vladimir was given resonance because of the emotional state in which he found himself, this was inevitably reinforced by his other reading. Second only to Chernyshevsky he studied Nikolai Dobrolyubov, particularly two articles published in Sovremennik. One dealt with Ivan Goncharov's novel Oblomov, and the other with Turgenev's novel On the Eve. Vladimir recalled that they "hit me like lightning." He saw in each profound revolutionary implications—implications which lie closer to the surface than do those of Chto Delat? Oblomov depicts a hero filled with good intentions who never managed to get up off his couch or out of his dressing gown. Dobrolyubov suggested that this had been the plague of Russia for thirty years—Oblomovitis—endless talking, endless pondering, doing nothing.

"Century after century passes," Dobrolyubov said, "and a half million stay-at-homes, sluggards and blockheads are immersed in deep slumber."

He saw Olga Ilinskaya, Goncharov's heroine, as possessing the faith of a true fighter against inertia, against Oblomovitis. The call to action which Vladimir read into the essay is there—clear and hardly concealed.

The clue to the second essay, that on Turgenev's On the Eve, is given in its title, "When Will the Real Day Come?"—the day of the real Russian revolutionary. Turgenev took for his hero a Bulgarian revolutionary, Insarov—a concession to the censor who would never have permitted a Russian revolutionary to appear as the hero of a Russian novel.

Dobrolyubov states his case bluntly: "We need a man like Insarov, but a Russian Insarov." He contends that the day of martyrs, of isolated champions of truth and virtue, has passed. Now a whole new generation, "for whom love of truth and honest strivings are no longer a novelty," has grown up. These are the "chosen people, the best people . . . the best people of our times."

"We can liberate ourselves from [the internal enemy] only by dispelling the raw, foggy atmosphere of our lives," he declared. "Is this possible? . . . Yes, it is possible. . . . Eternal banality, pettiness and apathy cannot be the lawful lot of man; . . . everywhere the unsoundness of the old order of things is understood; . . . Everybody is waiting, everybody is hoping. . . . That day will come at last! At all events, the eve is never far from the next day; only a matter of one night separates them."[14]

It is not hard to imagine Vladimir ingesting these heady words, reading them as a message directed specifically to himself. He was in the most sensitive of moods, his sister Anna recalled, "a very critical mood toward the established order and, under the impression of the execution of his beloved brother, a specially anti-government mood was created."[15] His brother's death, she said, had caused him seriously to think of that course which he should follow, and now, in the torrent of his reading and study, the lines of his future development were being established. If Chernyshevsky and Dobrolyubov confirmed Vladimir in his mission—the destruction of the hated, rotten Russian tyranny and the erection of a new order based on justice, equality, and humanity—the question remained as to what means might be employed to that end. At this point, there seems little doubt that Vladimir remained profoundly under the influence of his martyred brother's example and the example of the other young people who had laid down their lives for the cause of revolution. His sister felt that he stood at the crossroads, still attracted to the Narodnaya Volya and not yet committed to a new course.[16]

"The fate of his brother sharpened his thoughts," Nadezhda Krupskaya later observed. "He worked with extraordinary firmness, looked truth in the eye, didn't give himself a minute of attraction to phrases or illusions, worked with great honesty in his approach to all questions."[17]

Yet it was a mistake, Angelica Balabanoff always felt, to attribute Vladimir's life decisions solely to the influence of his brother's tragic death. The death of Alexander was only part of a total process. Balabanoff was a revolutionary contemporary of Ulyanov's, a woman of almost saintly convictions. She knew him intimately as she did the whole generation of whom she was an outstanding member.

"We had to uproot the deepest feelings from our heart," she recalled, "the feeling of duty, the solidarity with those whose sufferings we felt more acutely than the pain we inflicted on our parents, stifled traditions, bonds, habits."

She saw in the dilemma of her generation and that of Vladimir the image of that fateful catechism depicted by Turgenev. The dialogue ran:

"You, young woman, who are going to cross this threshold, do you know what awaits you?"

"I know."

"Cold, hunger, hostility, contempt, irony, shame, prison, disease, and death."

"I know, I am ready to endure all this."

"Even if all this were to come not only from your enemies but also from your relatives and friends?"

"Yes, even then."

"Are you even ready to commit a crime?"

"I am ready for that too."

"Have you considered that you might be subject to a delusion, that you might find you have sacrificed your young life in vain?"

"I have considered this too."

"Enter then."

"Imbecile," said someone.

"Saint!" answered the echo.[18]

VI

What Is to Be Done?

It was a moment for taking stock in Russia. As Georgi V. Plekhanov, the founder of the Russian Social Democratic party, later was to say:

"In the 1880s the intelligentsia went through a profound theoretical defeat which together with the political defeat of the Revolutionary [Narodnaya Volya] Party left it a real invalid."

These defeats were intimately aligned to the failure of the terror to shake the regime, producing instead intensified repression which crushed or smothered any kind of opposition, and to the inability of the intellectuals to discover another path which offered even faint hope of achieving their goal—the establishment in their backward and blundering country of a system of justice, equity, and integrity. Plekhanov observed in the ranks of the intellectuals "all the marks of profound demoralization, like that of a badly beaten army—the main force had departed, many fled without a backward glance, thinking only of saving themselves, others dropped their weapons and the few who preserved them bravely and who continued to struggle had neither organization nor a definite program of struggle and thought only, in the last analysis, of how to die not without glory."[1]

Industrialization was moving apace. Kazan, which Vladimir frequently visited (though theoretically confined to the Kokushkino estate), was a bustling manufacturing, trading, and administrative center. It had 133,208 residents[2] in 1888, eighty factories (most of them small), a university, a veterinary institute, a seminary, concerts, plays and even opera, an excellent library and what was more important a secret library of rare revolutionary, illegal, and unpermitted books. It had its quota of political exiles from St. Petersburg, the modest beginnings of agitational circles attempting to reach workers in the factories and a good many revolutionary-inclined youth at the university.[3] It was, of course, provincial in the extreme. It had grown rapidly in the sixties and seventies but now was losing population. There was only a small class of well-to-do and upper-rank Imperial civil servants; a goodly sprinkling of merchants, distinguished by their reddish beards, black hats, long black double-breasted coats; and many, many peasants, shuffling along the muddy streets with their typical loping gait, as though still dragging behind them great roped burdens, dressed summer and winter in greasy, worn sheepskins, feet bound with linen rags and often wearing bark shoes. The Kazan estates were neither notably profitable nor unprofitable, although there was much land speculation there and throughout the middle Volga. Tolstoy, for instance, in 1871 purchased a 6,750-acre estate in the Samara area, purely for investment. He hoped to make a fortune in horse breeding. The Russian grain trade was extremely profitable, the port figures at Odessa doubling and doubling again, under the forced draft of government policy to maximize export of grain in order to produce a favorable balance of trade. But for the most part neither estate owners nor former serfs profited. Poverty and even starvation were not uncommon at a time when a violent boom was characteristic of the Russian economy, especially in railroads, insurance companies, banks, new trading companies, and cotton textile production. Foreign capital was pouring into the country, into the oil fields of the Caucasus and the rich Donets coal and steel region of the Ukraine. Fortunes were being made by English, French, and German—but particularly English—entrepreneurs. The character of the times is clearly indicated in the investment advertisements which filled the St. Petersburg newspapers— for the Northern Insurance Society, the Southwest Railroad Society, the Don Land Bank at Taganrog, the Ivanovo Railroad, the Petersburg City Credit Society, the Azov Insurance Company, the Kursk-Kharkov-Azov Railway Company. At a time when 60 per cent of Russian peasants could not earn enough to support a minimum living standard, industry was growing more rapidly than anywhere in the world. Steel, coal, and oil production was rising faster than in western Europe or the United States. In the 1880s coal production doubled. From 1880 to 1894 oil production rose fifteen times. Mining in the 1880s grew faster than in the United States. Steel plants rose in the Donets and the Urals. Railroad construction outpaced the United

States. Moscow was typical of the industrial boom. The number of
manufacturing plants rose from 443 to 667 from 1853 to 1890, the
number of workers from 46,074 to 76,752. In St. Petersburg the working proletariat (factory population) rose from 33,458 to 73,948 from
1865 to 1890.[4]

At this time the works of Karl Marx had been known in Russia for
several years. Indeed, the censor had permitted *Das Kapital* to be
published in Russian translation in 1872 in an edition of three thousand copies in the mistaken impression that it was such a dull work of
economics that it could do no harm.[5] But there was as yet little direct
knowledge or study of Marxian views. A circle oriented toward Marx
and headed by a Bulgarian named Dmitri N. Blagoyev had existed in
St. Petersburg at the time Alexander Ulyanov was caught up in revolutionary activities there. Although Blagoyev himself was exiled from
Russia in March 1885, some tenuous connection existed between this
group and that to which Alexander was attached, and Alexander was
certainly somewhat aware of Marxist thought. But there is no evidence that Vladimir had any acquaintance with Marx's theories before
he came to Kokushkino. It then came to him secondhand, by reading
Plekhanov's *Our Disagreements* in which Plekhanov, the founder of
the Social Democratic party, outlined his disagreements with the
Narodniki (Populists), the liberals led by V. Vorontsov, and the radical Narodnaya Volya party, pronouncing anathema on the policy of
terror with the words "Bakuninism and Populism as revolutionary doctrines have outlived their time," and challenging the "Jacobin principles of conspiracy and seizure of power by a revolutionary minority."
"Never, never in my life," Vladimir later said of Plekhanov, "did I hold
for any one man such respect and honor."[6] Soon he managed to get a
copy of Volume I of *Das Kapital*, and, as his sister Anna recalled, "he
told me with great heat and enthusiasm about the basic theory of
Marx and the new horizons which it opened."[7]

By chance there lived in Kazan an excellent student of Marxism, a
man named Nikolai Fedoseyev. He was studying in the university and
was expelled at the same time as Vladimir. Vladimir actually joined a
small circle in Kazan which Fedoseyev headed but never met him because the members were carefully compartmented from each other to
minimize losses in event of police interference. It was a wise precaution. Within a few months the police swept down and took most of the
members into custody. By this time Vladimir had left Kazan. His
mother, relentless in her effort to protect her family from the fateful
consequences of revolutionary activity, had taken the proceeds of the
sale of the Simbirsk house and purchased for 7,500 rubles a small estate comprising 225 acres and a mill,[8] at Alakayevka, fifty versts

(twenty-five miles) from Samara, another Volga town, one much like Kazan but not quite so large.

Mariya Alexandrovna purchased the Alakayevka estate from a large landowner, K. M. Sibiryakov. She bought it sight unseen. The purchase was made for her by Mark T. Yelizarov, her son-in-law. It comprised an area of 83.5 desyatins (about 225 acres) of which one quarter was not arable, being gullies, ponds, and roadways.[9] The price of 123 rubles per cultivable desyatin was the highest price paid in twenty years for land in the Samara Guberniya. The estate was sold in December 1897, nine years after its purchase, for the same price that was paid for it. From 1890 through 1897 it was rented to a farmer named Krushvits, who paid rent of 500 rubles a month, out of which, however, Mariya Alexandrovna paid construction costs and an unstated share of other expenses. The purchase and the sale terms were rather unusual.[10] The Ulyanovs' neighbors in Alakayevka comprised some thirty-four families (197 souls) who together farmed only sixty-five desyatins of land—not quite two desyatins per family. Five families had no land whatever. Only 6 per cent of the male peasants and 0.7 per cent of the females were literate. In 1882 there was not a single school in the Volost.[11]

Nikolai Valentinov, the careful investigator of Ulyanov family finances, was not certain that Mariya Alexandrovna used the proceeds of the sale of the Simbirsk house to purchase Alakayevka. He pointed out that Mariya's husband, Ilya, received not long before his death an inheritance from his older brother in Astrakhan. Possibly, this was the money used to buy Alakayevka. In any event Valentinov noted that by 1897–98 Mariya Alexandrovna was putting together what he called the "Ulyanov Family Fund," comprising the proceeds of the sale of Alakayevka, the remains of her husband's inheritance, the money received for the Simbirsk house, the proceeds from the sale of Kokuskkino, plus her own inheritance from her father, who died in June 1873. This must have amounted to a comfortable sum. She herself received a pension of 100 rubles a month[12] from the time of her husband's death,[13] and although it may have been somewhat reduced in the late 1890s, it was still apparently 1,200 rubles a year at the time of her death in 1916.[14] Trotsky believed that the pension was 1,200 rubles a year from beginning to end and that the 7,500 rubles paid for Alakayevka represented Mariya's share in the Kokushkino estate and the proceeds of the Simbirsk house sale,[15] but he may be mistaken in this as he seems to be in a claim that the Alakayevka estate was increasingly mortgaged after 1891 or 1892. Valentinov's conclusion is that the "Ulyanov Family Fund," probably invested in Czarist government bonds, provided sufficient income and capital to permit not only Lenin but the whole Ulyanov family to exist comfortably with virtually no income-producing work for the rest of their lives. It paid for foreign travel by all the members of the family, modest but, of course, not lavish living, and very large purchases of books and other research resources.[16]

Samara was sometimes called the "Chicago of Russia" because it was a center of grain trade and boasted a substantial number of millionaires, crude, hearty men who had made their fortunes in wheat. It had some small food processing factories, flour mills, a tannery, a railroad shop, men's and women's gymnasia, a *real* school, a school for medical assistants, a railroad vocational school, an agricultural technical school, a seminary, no university, and 196 saloons.[17] Their new village of Alakayevka was as remote as or more remote than Kokushkino. It was Mariya Alexandrovna's hope that Vladimir would become a farmer. Instead, he interested himself in peasant economy, studied Marx and Engels, and attempted to apply his new-found knowledge of dialectical materialism to the peasant and agricultural problems. Vladimir, as he later told a friend, found no one in Samara who was interested in Marxist theory although there was a small group of Narodniki (Populists) and a fairly good, illegal library. But there was no one with whom he could carry on intelligent theoretical discussions.[18]

In Alakayevka the Ulyanovs lived in an old one-story house with a garden, long since gone to seed. There was a birch-lined walk and another bordered by limes. Vladimir sat for hours in a shady spot under the trees reading and taking notes. He worked from nine in the morning to 2 P.M. Then he sometimes walked in the nearby forest with his brothers and sisters, picking mushrooms and *malini*, wild raspberries. There was a good pond ten minutes away and twice a day in summer he went for a swim. He loved to float on his back in the water, his hands behind his head, thinking about what he had just read or letting his thoughts wander into the distance, wondering perhaps what Alexander would have done in his place and how might he expatiate his brother's martyrdom. Near the house he put up a trapeze and practiced circus stunts. There had been a trapeze in the barn when they lived on Moskovskaya Street, a rope for balancing acts, some homemade stilts on which he delighted to walk, and giant swings. He was a first-class swimmer, an indefatigable walker, and as good a skater as could be found in the countryside. If he did not have a physique to match that of Rakhmatov, he had a powerful body and he was to keep fit all his life and, as noted, to preach physical fitness eternally to his more bookish companions.[19] In the evenings he sat with an English dictionary, picking his way through David Ricardo, or poring over Gizot's *History of Civilization* in Russian translation. By this time his sister Anna had married Mark Yelizarov, his sister Olga was at the university in St. Petersburg, and Dmitri was entered at Moscow University. Because the police barred Vladimir from the higher schools, he was working to get a law degree by correspondence with St. Petersburg. In summer the family was still together. They gathered at night around the lamp in the kitchen to read and sing. Olga accompanied Vladimir in one sentimental song that was a favorite: "You have such fascinating eyes/From them I will surely die!" Vladimir clapped his hands as he sang and shouted: "Die! Die! Die!"

One evening Anna recited a poem:

> Night is still distant but all is twilight
> All around it is still.
> The night has fallen over the fields
> And the village sleeps . . .
>
> In the farmhouse only in one wing
> Burns a light
> And for the serious reading
> A circle has formed.
> All sit, poring over the book.
> All is quiet . . .[20]

It was a portrait of the family. But soon it changed. Mariya Alexandrovna's hopes for making her second son a farmer came to naught. Vladimir stayed on at Alakayevka for a year. He could not make himself into a farmer. Later he would blame this on the abnormal relationships existing between proprietors and muzhiks but actually he had neither talent nor inclination for the land. This had already become evident when suddenly Olga died of typhoid fever and Vladimir Ulyanov left Samara on August 31, 1893, for St. Petersburg. He arrived September 3, ostensibly to take up the practice of law, his degree having finally been granted. Actually, of course, he came to St. Petersburg to take up the cause of revolution.

Since 1888 his name had been entered in the secret books of the Czar's regime as one who was politically unreliable, forbidden employment in the state service, and to be watched by the police. It was a reasonable precaution and one which the police would carry out to the best of their ability so long as the Czar's regime endured.

By now Vladimir's philosophy, strategy, and tactics had been molded into a coherent whole. He had welded the extremist ideals of Chernyshevsky, the dedication of Dobrolyubov, and the economic critique of Marx into a philosophy of politics and life. Henceforth, he would change very little. He would, with Chernyshevsky, fight all liberals, all compromisers, all those prepared to settle for anything less than the ultimate goal as fiercely (sometimes, it seemed, even more fiercely) as he fought the Czar himself. He would apply relentlessly the tool of criticism which Marx with his dialectic and his dissection of the capitalist economic and social system had given him. If he had not yet fully absorbed the lessons of conspiracy, secrecy, and discipline, he was in the process of learning them. He had now broken with the hope of his brother that assassination and the example of individual heroism would bring down the system. This does not mean that he had abandoned all idea of terror. He would hold to its use all his life but only in special circumstances and not as the main revolutionary reliance.

Vladimir was still enough of an advocate of terror when he came to St. Petersburg to bother some of the young members of the Social Democratic circle in St. Petersburg to which he quickly gravitated, his way paved by the name of his martyred brother.[21] His feelings were clearly ambivalent. He had considered himself a Social Democrat (theoretically opposed to terror) in Samara before coming to St. Petersburg and later described himself as a member of the Social Democratic illegal circle in Samara for two years.[22] However, Lenin immediately began to contribute to the St. Petersburg circle papers which were radically opposed to the terrorist viewpoint. His first paper, long lost, was presented November 1893, and dealt with market problems. Early in 1894 he wrote his first major pamphlet, "Who Are the Friends of the People and How Do They Fight the Social Democrats?" His Narodnaya Volya terrorist views were materially changed in the atmosphere of St. Petersburg.

He was clearly at that stage which his wife, Nadezhda Krupskaya, later described by quoting from the concluding paragraph in his pamphlet "What Is to Be Done?" in which he said: "Many of them began their revolutionary careers as Narodovoltsy. Almost all in early youth carefully bowed before the heroes of the terror. To break with the fascinating impression of their heroic tradition cost a battle, accompanied by a breach with people who wished to remain true to the Narodnaya Volya." This, said Nadezhda Krupskaya, was a chapter from Vladimir's own biography.[23] He plunged into the work of the Social Democratic circle with enormous energy. He loved statistics and liked to discuss the great questions (largely economic) which possessed him and his Marxist-oriented companions, although at the start he seems to have been a bit shy about public confrontations.[24] Before leaving Samara he had tried his hand at some articles—a critique on a work by V.V. (V. P. Vorontsev), a review of a book by V. Ye. Postnikov called "Southern Russian Peasant Formulations" which was rejected by the magazine *Russkaya Mysl,* and a few other fugitive pieces. Obviously, he fancied himself something of a specialist on peasant questions as a result of his experience on the farm at Alakayevka. Within a few weeks he had met and become attracted to Nadezhda Krupskaya, a member of the circle even before he appeared on the scene and the woman with whom he was to spend his life. He was soon one of the leaders of the group although not quite as swiftly or as clearly as the haleographers of Moscow would now have it. He tried his hand at leading a workers' circle but had no great success and would always be a bit skeptical of this means of organization.[25] The group quickly evolved into what was called the Union of Struggle for the Emancipation of the Working Class, a union with rather more deep roots in student and university circles than in the working class. One of the principal ways it raised money was to set up booths at student balls, manned by pretty girls who sold bouquets for 25 rubles and champagne for 100 rubles; sometimes 600 or 700 rubles was raised in an evening.[26]

Ulyanov was at this time a young man of twenty-three, of medium height, strongly built with the same fresh ruddy face of his mother, a sprouting mustache, reddish beard, and reddish straggly hair. He was already growing bald, and his receding hairline gave him a very broad wide forehead. His eyes were rather small and slightly Mongolian, but they were so wide open that he seemed always intent, thoughtful, and serious. Often a light ironic smile played over his lips, and the impact he made was not always favorable. Pyotr B. Struve noted that his first impression was unpleasant and said that this remained with him all his life.[27] Because of his baldness he looked older than he was. His companions almost from the beginning called him *starik,* the Old Man. It was a nickname that never left him, unlike some of the others such as Sobakevich, Petersburzhets, Nikolai Petrovich, Comrade Tulin, or simply K.T. In all he was to use at least 151 pseudonyms, or *klichki,* in his career. But the one by which he eventually came to be known in every corner of the world was Lenin.[28]

VII

Life for the Czar

The first word which Vladimir Nemirovich-Danchenko heard of the events of May 18, 1896, came from his cook, who returned unexpectedly early from the Khodynka Fields where a people's fete celebrating the coronation in Moscow of Nicholas II and Alexandra Fyodorovna was being held.

Engaged by the journal *Niva* to write about the ceremonies, Nemirovich-Danchenko proudly sported a "Correspondent's Badge," a bronze medal with the Imperial initials "N II" and "A" in blue enamel within a wreath of crowns and lettered in gold: Moscow, May 1896. The date, in Old Slavonic, was inscribed with the broken cross of the Orthodox Church. Below appeared a pen and scroll. The medal presented to Nemirovich-Danchenko at the Kremlin in a small satin and velvet box was, he assured the readers of *Niva*, "very elegant." But this was only in keeping with the style of the coronation. Everywhere in Moscow had been erected stanchions for flags, platforms for spectators, false fronts for big buildings, pylons for patriotic displays, scaffolds for illuminations in electricity, gas, and kerosene. Everywhere the initials "N" and "A" were to be seen and the slogans "God Save the Czar" or "Glory, Glory to Our Russian Czar." Every public building and most private houses had a fresh coat of paint. Gorky thought that Moscow had gotten itself up like a widow awaiting a new bridegroom. The fireworks at the Kremlin by curious chance were in charge of the very same Kobozev whose name had been used by the plotters against Alexander II in 1881 in renting the cheese shop on the Sadovaya in St.

Petersburg. Now Kobozev was a specialist working for the foreign firm that had won the concession for the fireworks display.[1] Korday's French clothing store quickly exhausted its stocks—trains for ladies' gowns at 300 to 400 rubles and complete outfits at 2,000. Moscow was not St. Petersburg where, as Baedeker noted, every tenth person on the street wore a uniform. Nevertheless, Nemirovich-Danchenko found Kuznetsky Most, Moscow's street of fine shops, crowded with officers and so many people speaking foreign languages it made his ears buzz. The Moscow telegraph office kept open to 11 P.M. (instead of the usual 9 P.M.), and staffs were enlarged to handle the volume of messages. Some of St. Petersburg's prima ballerinas like Mariya Petipa daughter of the great choreographer, the Italian Perina Leniani, and Mathilde Kshesinskaya (the Czar's favorite and onetime mistress) had been brought in to reinforce the Bolshoi Theater Company as well as the first and second corps de ballet of the Mariinsky Theater. The interior of the Bolshoi had been refurbished at a cost of 50,000 rubles, and another 12,000 went for decorations, including electrical illuminations. The principal coronation spectacles were, inevitably, *Swan Lake* and Mikhail Glinka's *A Life for the Czar*. (The Imperial loge had been enlarged to accommodate sixty-three guests.)

Everything was planned on a scale of grandeur never seen in Russia. The Government of France appropriated 900,000 francs for the coronation, renting the Hunter's Club at 22,000 rubles. It was paying 2,000 rubles simply for the privilege of building a terrace for a grand ball, and the total cost at the club was estimated at 200,000. But France was Russia's great ally and expense did not matter. For flats and apartments (if you could find one) the going rate was 2,000 or 2,500 for the month of May. There was a good deal of gossip about the parsimony of the German ambassador who had rented the Von Derviz[2] palace at Krasnye Vorota, some distance from the center of town, for Prince Heinrich's stay. The building was beautiful, decorated with Gobelin tapestries, and it had been taken for the remarkably low price of 7,000 rubles, possibly because it was not large enough for a grand ball. Instead, the Germans were offering a musicale.

The Government had requisitioned all the Moscow hotels. The Royal Chancellery was housed at the Bolshaya Moskovskaya; foreign princes, princesses, and diplomatic representatives at the Slavyansky Bazaar[3] and the Kontinental; noblemen and officers at the new Metropol.

Rooms and flats on Tverskaya Street—the main route of Imperial processions from Petrovsky Palace on Moscow's outskirts (where the Czar and Czarina were to stay) to the Kremlin—were impossible to obtain. They rented for 200 rubles if there was a window on the street.

Just a place to crane your neck out a *fortochka* (the little Russian ventilation windows) cost 15 rubles. Carriages hired at 800 to 900 rubles for the month and coachmen at 300 rubles. The usual fee was 75. A woman sneered at Nemirovich-Danchenko when he tried to engage her carriage for Coronation Day, May 14, at 75 rubles. "How much do you want?" Nemirovich-Danchenko asked. "One hundred and seventy little rubles," she said.

"But I can buy a pair of horses for that," he retorted.

"Well, that's your business," she replied.

Places in public stands sold for 10 or 15 rubles. Balconies on the Tverskaya cost 500 rubles. The English Club (now the Museum of the Revolution) put up a fine platform for its members, each of whom was permitted to invite four lady guests. But they had to be in their places by 8 A.M. The club served a special early breakfast for which the ladies wore party dresses and the men formal morning clothes. Every building on the Czar's route was examined by the police, who paid special attention to the attics. The painters who daubed the buildings and the porters and janitors were checked out by the gendarmerie.

But for all the preparations, as Nemirovich-Danchenko noted, everyone was still at the mercy of chance and the Russian weather. No kind of modern American invention would help. The nineteenth century was on the way out and the twentieth, "from which the whole world expects miracles of beauty and comfort," was about to open but still no one could guarantee what the holiday would bring.

So it was that a little after ten on the morning of May 18, 1896 (the Czar having been formally crowned with his beautiful German Czarina at his side in the Kremlin cathedral four days earlier—police and soldiers standing shoulder-to-shoulder facing the crowds and a little boy asking his father again and again: "Why is the Czar so pale, Daddy?"[4]), Nemirovich-Danchenko was surprised to find his cook, a simple-minded country woman, already back home. She had left at 5 A.M. for the fete at the Khodynka Fields. The festival had drawn the common people from the very ends of Russia. Its site was a military training ground* on the outskirts of Moscow, just across the Petersburg chaussée from the Petrovsky Palace, the coronation residence of Nicholas and Alexandra.

Here the people of Russia were to celebrate and receive gifts from their new monarch—iron mugs enameled in red and blue with traditional Russian patterns and carrying the initials "N II" and "A" in gold

* Now the old Moscow Central Airport, formerly used for the arrival of distinguished guests.

below a double-headed Russian eagle and the date 1896. There were also silk scarves for women, *pryaniki* (a kind of Russian version of lebkuchen, German Christmas cookies) embossed with the date and occasion, *saiki* (small loaves of Russian bread), sausage, and, of course, enormous quantities of free beer.

Multitudes had been gathering at Khodynka for days—pilgrims from the countryside, from Pskov, from the deep forests of the Kama, from Siberia and the Middle Volga. Many had walked all the way from the heart of the Ukraine. All of Russia was here—that is the Russia of bast shoes, of linen foot wrappings, of shapeless blouses, blue pantaloons, *tulupy* (greasy sheepskin jackets), heavy capes, kaftans, and worn blackcloth coats. Every monastery in Moscow had been opened to feed the pilgrims. At night they gathered on the Khodynka commons, sleeping on the ground in their *burlaki* or crowding about the booths, pavilions, and tents. There were crude stages and side shows, circus performers including the most famous clown in Russia, Durov, of the classic circus dynasty, bands, gypsy entertainers, trained bears—all the traditional amusements of the Russian scene.

On the night of the seventeenth there was a gala at the Bolshoi Theater—the spectacle was *A Life for the Czar*—and a French observer said he was nearly blinded by the diamonds: the ladies in daring décolleté wore them in showers—stars, crosses, great sprays of flora and fauna.[5] Everyone was talking about the remarkable throngs assembling at Khodynka. About midnight Nemirovich-Danchenko drove out to have a look. He found the field jammed with people, possibly 100,000, maybe 300,000 or even 400,000. There was no way of guessing. They were gathered around bonfires, drinking and singing to guitars, bayans, and balalaikas. Already some tens of thousands had lined up against the wooden barriers and counters where the mugs and scarves were to be given out and the beer to be poured. This was at the south side of the rough and humpy field (it was crisscrossed with shallow trenches dug for past military maneuvers). Scattered through the vast meadow were carousels, playing merrily, and platforms where gypsy dancers would perform on the morrow. Only a handful of gendarmes was present but there was no particular disorder. Most of those who spent the night on the fields were peasants from the countryside. But the Moscow crowds had already begun to arrive. All the way back to Moscow Nemirovich-Danchenko passed people heading for Khodynka. Like everyone he was impressed by the outpouring. It seemed a good omen for the new Czar's reign. Never had such an assemblage of the common folk gathered to honor their ruler.

So it was with no little surprise that Nemirovich-Danchenko greeted the sudden reappearance of his cook.

"Did you get your mug?" he asked gaily.

"What do you mean—mug," she replied. "My God! I barely escaped with my life."

"What happened?"

"God in his heavens! You never saw so many people!" she said, hastily crossing herself. "*Slava Bogu!* God save us! I don't know how many were crushed to death. Thousands . . ."

Nemirovich-Danchenko was uncertain how literally he should take this news but he thought he had better find out. In the courtyard he met the water vendor, bringing in fresh pails of water. He too had just come back from Khodynka. There he had seen two men crushed to death before his eyes beside a beer barrel and a third whose leg was broken. On the street Nemirovich-Danchenko found his porter, hatless, wringing his hands and crying. His wife had gone to Khodynka with a friend. The friend was back but not the wife. He was sure she was dead. By this time Nemirovich-Danchenko knew that tragedy had struck. He put on his blue, white, and bronze "Correspondent's Medal" and started out Tverskaya Street, meeting a solid throng coming from Khodynka. Hundreds of thousands, he thought. He disagreed with some who later wrote that the crowd looked shaken and anguished. To the contrary he felt that the people were so enduring, so patient, so capable of long and stubbornly suppressing their real feelings, that even in this tragic moment they seemed outwardly unchanged and even indifferent. In the ability to hold within themselves their true emotions, he believed, simple Russian people were endlessly subtle and enigmatic. It was a quality which ran very deep —far beyond the comprehension of the sophisticated and cosmopolitan upper classes. In this lay the enormous strength of the *narod*, the Russian people, a tidal force when aroused.

As Nemirovich-Danchenko made his way along the Tverskaya, he met an occasional cart or wagon, laden with boxes and cases. Only much later did he realize that the wagons were bringing back corpses from Khodynka. (Others recalled seeing cart after cart bearing bodies back to the city—some bodies covered with a tarpaulin, others hastily tumbled in without ceremony.)

Moscow was famous for its "forty times forty" churches and today, their onion domes glittering with fresh gold leaf, sparkled in the sun, and from their bells came peal after peal, echoing over the silent crowds. Overhead the familiar Moscow crows wheeled and scolded.[6]

Once at the Khodynka Fields Nemirovich-Danchenko found three orchestras and a chorus of thousands of voices led by V. A. Safonov, director of the Moscow Conservatory, performing. The viewing stands were filled—men in handsome uniforms, beautiful and well-dressed women. The pavilions were decorated with flowers and gay bunting, giving the scene the aspect of a fashionable day at the races. A strong wind blew across the field, and through clouds of dust he could see small clusters of people huddled here and there. He found it hard to believe any tragedy had occurred, nor were there visible signs of disaster. At that instant came the sound of cheering. The Czar and Czarina had arrived and appeared on the balcony of the Imperial pavilion. The cheers redoubled. The band struck up the national anthem. For half an hour the handsome young Czar, just twenty-eight (and the image of his first cousin, King George of England), and his lustrous bride took the crowd's acclaim. Then they entered an open carriage and crossed to the Petrovsky Palace gates to receive deputations of citizens, according to the protocol of the coronation. How heavy, thought Nemirovich-Danchenko, is the cap of Monomakh, the Russian crown! Later on it seemed to him that the Czar was disturbed and pale. But this may have been imagination. Whether or not the Czar had been informed at this point of the Khodynka catastrophe no change was ordered in the ceremonies. The Czar and Czarina stood at the palace gates, not more than two hundred yards from Khodynka, receiving, in order, fourteen separate delegations: representatives of Uspensky cathedral; representatives of the Cathedral of Christ the Savior; Master Kolyvastsky, who presented Their Majesties with a traditional platter for bread and salt which eight men had spent nine months hewing out of rock crystal; artists of the Moscow Imperial theaters; representatives of the Moscow coachmen; representatives of the Georgiyevsky cavalry regiment; Moscow peasant-workers from seven woolen factories; the official spokesmen for the Moscow middle bourgeoisie, the *meshchanstvo;* representatives of the Moscow Old Believers, who presented the royal couple with a silver platter in which the initials of Nicholas were picked out in diamonds; the contractors who had decorated Moscow for the coronation; bakers Savostyanov and Naidenov, who had baked the *pryaniki* for Khodynka; the Moscow German colony; the Society of the Hunt; and the Moscow Racing Club.

Then the Czar and his Czarina went into the palace, where four large pavilions were set up for a feast. On one side were facilities for the nobility and on the other for the village elders.

Hurrahs rang out. First the Czar spoke to the elders: "The Empress and I heartily thank you for your expression of love and dedication. We do not doubt that these feelings are shared by your fellow villagers. Care for your welfare is as close to my heart as it is to that of our Father and Beloved Savior."

Prince Trubetskoi turned to the nobility and led the cheers for the Czar.

Two orchestras played military music as the village elders sat down to their feast—a meal they would long remember. The embossed menu, decorated with a view of the Kremlin, the cap of Monomakh, the Imperial eagle, and a rising sun, listed the courses: Poltava borsch, meat fries, cold whitefish, veal with fresh greens, roast spring chicken and duckling, fresh and pickled cucumbers, raspberry sweet, dessert, fruits, and wines.

As the elders raised their vodka glasses in toasts, *do dna* (bottoms up), to the new sovereign, Nemirovich-Danchenko returned to Khodynka. There was almost no one left in the pavilion. On the field he found the gypsy dancers and their bands performing to listless crowds. Durov was juggling a ball in the air, some men were shouldering up to the bars—possibly a few thousand persons in all. Everywhere there was paper and litter, here and there the inevitable Russian ice-cream girl with her straight blond hair, her comfortable bosom and white apron, and an occasional seller of *kisel* and *kvass*. He went from one group to another, three or four or five persons sitting or standing on the grass. They were quiet, hardly talking. Then he pushed beyond a battered row of food stands and encountered the first corpses—fifteen or more laid out, side by side. Nemirovich-Danchenko found himself unable to describe the scene—the faces, dark purple, blue-black, or violet-hued, hair drawn back, eyes closed, ribbons of blood in the corners of their mouths, clothing in shreds. On the breast of each victim a handful of coins, mostly copper, rarely of silver, left by peasants who had survived. He still could not believe the extent of the catastrophe. Then he went behind another row of stalls and another and another and everywhere it was the same—endless corpses, laid out side by side and, passing among them silent for the most part but in some cases wailing in grief, hundreds and thousands of persons searching out their dead.

Dr. Alexei Mikhailovich Ostroukhov, who lived on Leontyev Pereulok (now Stanislavsky Street), so close to the Tverskaya that he saw the masses of people fleeing from Khodynka, went to the scene to see if he could be of help. He found piles of bodies, sometimes as many as fifty in a heap, a tangle of arms, legs, and heads, the people's clothing black with dirt and often torn from their bodies. The turf on the field had been transformed to a dusty desert, as though a herd of cattle had rampaged across it. Working with crews of firemen, Dr. Ostroukhov began the dreary task of sorting through the bodies. To his surprise he found not a few persons badly hurt but still breathing. He heard of strange sights at the morgue, where some of the "corpses" suddenly started up from their slabs, having regained consciousness.[7]

It had all happened in twelve or fifteen minutes, quite early in the morning, just after six. Something, no one could ever be certain what, had set the crowd in motion. Possibly a cry that there would not be enough mugs to go around. Or that the beer was running out. Whatever it was the mass of people—the hundreds of thousands who had come in from the countryside and the new hundreds of thousands of Muscovites who assembled in the early morning hours (possibly 600,000 or 700,000 in all)—had begun suddenly to move. One stumbled. Another fell. In an instant, dozens, scores, and hundreds were down, many in the shallow unfilled trenches, and tens of thousands of others were stampeding over them. The toll? Who knows? But it was upwards of 2,000 dead and many more thousands injured. Most were buried in a "brothers' grave," a mass burial at Vagankov Cemetery at the expense of the Czar and the Czarina, who attended memorial services for the victims and provided some thousands of rubles to stricken families.[8]

There were many who raised the question of the meaning of Khodynka and not a few who saw in it an augury for the new regime. Sergei Witte, as hardheaded a statesman as Russia possessed, felt that the Czar should have canceled all festivities and particularly the French ambassador's ball. ("The saddest ball ever given," was Nemirovich-Danchenko's description. "I no longer felt shame; I was simply sick," Pierre d'Alheim wrote. But when he arrived at the fete, Witte was told by the Grand Duke Sergei Alexandrovich, governor-general of Moscow, that the "Czar did not agree with this view." The Czar, said the Grand Duke, considered Khodynka a great disaster but not one which should "darken the coronation holiday."[9] Thus, the Czar's program continued remorselessly. He and the Czarina appeared at the French party. The Czar had the first dance with Countess Montebello, wife of the ambassador, and the Czarina with the Count.* The rest of the schedule was carried out without change—the banquet at the Kremlin's Alexander Hall on the nineteenth (but the Austro-Hungarian fete was canceled due to the death of Duke Karl Ludwig); the ball of the governor-general, the Grand Duke Sergei Alexandrovich, on the twentieth; the ball of the Moscow nobility at the famous Hall of Columns with Prince Trubetskoi as host and 4,000 guests

---

* According to Grand Duke Alexander Mikhailovich, Nicholas' uncle, he and his four brothers—the Mikhailovichi as they were called in the Imperial family—violently opposed carrying on with festivities after the Khodynka disaster. They were called "revolutionaries" by the older Grand Dukes. They came to the French ball but walked out when dancing began. Grand Duke Alexei Alexandrovich remarked: "There go the four Imperial followers of Robespierre." (Grand Duke Alexander, *Once a Grand Duke*, p. 172.)

on the twenty-first; the state visit to the Troitsky-Sergeyevsky Monastery on the twenty-second; the visit to the Moscow Duma, dinner at the English ambassador O'Connor's and the palace ball in the Alexander and St. Andrew halls of the Kremlin for 3,100 guests on the twenty-third (this was the day the Czar gave 20,000 rubles to found a children's home in memory of the Khodynka victims); the musicale at the German Embassy on the twenty-fourth; the palace dinner for the ambassadors on the twenty-fifth; and, concluding it all, back to Khodynka on the twenty-sixth for the big military review. It was a hot day. Blue skies. Bright sun. A brilliant spectacle. The Imperial carriage drawn by six white horses. Some 67 generals, 1,960 officers, and 38,565 enlisted men—40,592 in all—in the march past.

Only the spiritually insensitive, thought Nemirovich-Danchenko, could fail to feel the shadow cast over the occasion by Khodynka. He had no use for those who wanted to put Khodynka out of mind and erase it from memory. (The Government "Correspondents' Bureau" officially requested correspondents "to refrain from all rhetoric in writing of the sad incident of the 18th."[10]) To what purpose? he asked. Why? Who needed it? Was it necessary in life to close one's eyes to grief and open them only to happiness? Was not the best course just the opposite? After all who could know genuine spiritual happiness who had not suffered the bitterness of woe?

In the coronation events, he thought, as in a mirror, were reflected the Russian people, their enormous strength, and the future role which they would play in determining the fate of mankind.[11]

But what was that fate to be?

VIII

The Seeds Are Planted

On the night of December 8–9, 1895, a police raid was carried out in St. Petersburg in which forty-six young men and women were arrested, twenty-nine of whom were held for investigation, including Vladimir Ulyanov. All were Social Democrats and full-fledged Marxists, who had recently been active in agitation, particularly in the St. Petersburg textile industry. A few days after the raids some of those who escaped arrest issued a proclamation in which they took the name of the Union of Struggle for the Emancipation of the Working Class—a resounding title and one which made a considerable impression on the Czar's police and, after a while, on the workers themselves. At the moment of the Khodynka disaster Ulyanov, now signing his writings with the name "Ilyin" and known to his comrades humorously as Lyapin-Tyapin, a character in Gogol's *Inspector General*,[1] was sitting in Cell No. 193 of the St. Petersburg House of Detention, composing leaflets for the Union of Struggle, corresponding with his unarrested companions, including his fiancée and fellow activist, Nadezhda Krupskaya, and his activist sister, Anna. The prison authorities wouldn't let him have ink so he was writing his messages between the lines of books invisibly in milk, using inkwells made of pinches of bread. One day, he told Krupskaya, he ate six "inkwells" to save them from discovery by the guards.

By this time Vladimir was a disciplined, dedicated revolutionary. He had been abroad the summer previous to establish contacts with the leading exiled Russian Marxists, Georgi Plekhanov and Pavel B.

Axelrod in Switzerland, heading up the Emancipation of Labor group. He made brief stops in Paris and London and came back to St. Petersburg filled with plans for establishing a new paper which would be published in collaboration with the Swiss émigrés. He was now, in a word, a mature enemy of the Czarist state, devoting himself full-time to the cause, known and respected among his associates, one of the leading members of the St. Petersburg group which included such men as Julius Martov, V. V. Starkov, A. A. Vaneyev, V. A. Shelgunov, G. M. Krzhizhanovsky, names that were to be heard in the coming years.[2]

Ulyanov had taken a hand with his comrades in agitation of the sprawling, fast-growing St. Petersburg manufacturing industry, especially in the big textile mills. He was a believer in agitation, but, contrary to legends that grew up in later years, never very active at it. His real forte was writing—writing and analysis, tactics and organization.[3]

Lodged in jail, Ulyanov was in no position to react one way or another to the Khodynka catastrophe. But events were moving in a manner which could not but deepen the shadow over the new reign of Nicholas. To mark Coronation Day the governor-general of St. Petersburg had decreed a paid holiday May 14 for all private factories and a three-day holiday for state-owned factories. (Even at this time state industry was a major factor in Russian economy.) When private workers were refused the same treatment as state workers, they walked out. By May 19 thirty thousand textile workers in Petersburg were idle—the biggest industrial disturbance the capital had ever seen. It caused a sensation. Strikes spread quickly to Moscow and then across the country. The principal demand was the 10½-hour day in place of the 13-hour day. The Union of Struggle took up the workers' cause, and although the strike failed, it gave great impetus to the Social Democratic movement of Ulyanov and his associates.[4]

As Nadezhda Krupskaya later commented:

"The year of the coronation of Nicholas II and the famous Khodynka marked the first tentative actions of the workers of the two capitals [St. Petersburg and Moscow], the first ominous tread of the workers' feet, still not political, it is true, but already marked by solidarity and mass action."[5] Or as Martov put it in more elaborate language: "The dark night of the autocratic regime is still fully enveloping our country but already one can hear the first crowing of the cocks announcing the inevitable coming of the morning."[6]

It is perhaps not too much to see in Khodynka a premonitory sign of the fate which awaited Nicholas and Alexandra, the empire which they headed, the cumbersome, outmoded autocracy, and the persistence onto the threshold of the twentieth century of a social and political system which had little or no relevance to its epoch.

The golden age of Russian industrialization, as Bertrand Wolfe called it, was in full swing.[7] Grain export was being encouraged by every device. (Odessa, the principal shipping port, was growing like Los Angeles in the 1920s.) An enormous burden of indirect taxation was sweating the peasants to build up Russia's financial reserves. Wage scales were on a par with those of Manchester in 1840 or Brockton, Massachusetts, in 1860. Russian tariffs were the highest in the world—an indirect subsidy to industrialists, paid for by the masses. Railroad building went ahead at a fantastic scale, the Trans-Siberian pushing steadily eastward through the 1890s regardless of cost. In 1891–95, 4,403 miles of railroad were built. In 1896–1900, 10,035 miles. By the end of the nineties the state (which owned almost all the railroads) had an investment in them of 4.7 billion gold rubles. Nowhere in the world except Sweden was industrial growth so rapid.

But the cost—enormously high domestic prices (the Government paid 110 to 135 kopecks per pood [thirty-six pounds] for rails which it could have imported for 85 to 87 kopecks)—came out of the hides of peasants, "the dark people," and the industrial proletariat who were driven to the edge of starvation and often over its boundary.

Such a policy would have involved dangers for the sternest, most iron-handed, most efficient dictator—a Nicholas I or a Stalin. But in Nicholas II Russia had neither a Nicholas I nor even an Alexander III. No one who knew Nicholas II casually could really dislike him. Amiability, an unwillingness to say no, a determination not to hurt the feelings of those around him, a warm personal charm coupled with ingrained indecisiveness and deep fatalism were his strongest traits. (Once in a letter to the Czarina he himself referred to "my tiny will."[8]) He was not stupid although his education left much to be desired. Witte, who came to know Nicholas II only too well, felt that he had many of the fatal weaknesses of Czar Paul Petrovich, father of Alexander I, who conspired or acquiesced in his father's murder, as well as those of Alexander himself—mysticism, cunning, guile— without Alexander's culture. Witte felt that Nicholas had about as much culture as the average "guards colonel of a good family."[*] Leon Trotsky thought much the same. In fact, the comparison of Nicholas to "an average Guards officer" was often made.[9] Trotsky, too, saw a similarity between Paul and Nicholas, "their distrust of everybody, their feeling of abnegation, their consciousness, as you might say, of

[*] Even the Grand Dukes sometimes referred to him as "the colonel." (V. Kobylin, *Imperator Nikolai II i general-adyutant M. V. Alexeyev*, p. 141.)

being crowned pariahs." He felt Nicholas was not only unstable but treacherous, a man who felt at ease only "among completely mediocre and brainless people, saintly fakirs, holy men, to whom he did not have to look up."[10] The Czar was notably pro-English—he had an English tutor, Mr. Heath, "Karl Osipovich," and he spoke English as well as Russian,[11] and he was greatly attached to his English cousins, King George V and Queen Mary, but by trying to be agreeable and polite he was often led around by the nose by his less agreeable cousin, Emperor Wilhelm II.[12] Nicholas was not, as a matter of fact, much more Russian than his German bride. From the time of Peter the Great the Romanovs had consistently intermarried with the German nobility to the point at which the French ambassador, Maurice Paléologue, calculated Nicholas to be only 1/128 Russian.[13] If the father of the German Catherine's son, Paul, was Count Saltykov rather than Peter III, as many believed, there was not a drop of Russian blood in Nicholas.[14]

Because of his indecisiveness Nicholas was forever attempting to prove his decisiveness—a trait which in the end brought him more swiftly to disaster than any other. It was endlessly played upon by the Czarina, with whom he was simply, plainly, naïvely, and hopelessly in love. The Czar was remarkably susceptible to suggestions that he lacked firmness in defending the ancient prerogatives of the throne. His most reactionary adviser, K. P. Pobedonostsev, used this approach with considerable success. It was he who persuaded the Czar to reject out-of-hand as "senseless dreams" a reasoned hope expressed by the Tver Zemstvo at the time of his accession to the throne that "the voice of the people's need" would always be heard and that "the rights of individuals and public institutions will be firmly safeguarded." "I shall maintain the principle of autocracy just as firmly and unflinchingly as it was preserved by my unforgettable dead father," the Czar insisted. It was a determination which held within itself fateful seeds of destruction,[15] and the words "senseless dreams" became an indictment repeated again and again by the Czar's critics, even the most conservative of them.

Nicholas had come to the throne a bit unexpectedly when Alexander III suddenly died in the autumn of 1894. Nicholas and his beloved Alix were betrothed in the dying Czar's bedroom.* A month after Alexander III's death Nicky and Alix, as they called each other to the end of their days when not calling each other (he or her) "Sunny,"

---

* Alix' first public appearance in St. Petersburg was in the funeral cortege which bore the body of Alexander III from the Nicholas Station to the Cathedral of St. Peter and St. Paul. Peasant women crossed themselves in the crowd murmuring: "She has come to us behind a coffin. She brings misfortune with her." (Pierre Gilliard, *Thirteen Years at the Russian Court*, p. 48.) She was thereafter known as the "funeral bride."

"Spitsbub," "Little Wife," or (she of him) "Boysy," "lovy," *"dushki"* (my soul), "my sweet one," "pussy mine," "sweety," "darling many-kins," *"Lansbub,"*[16] were married.

Alix' impression of the Czar, formed in her early days of marriage and expressed in a letter to her friend, the German Countess Rantzau, was: "I feel that all who surround my husband are insincere and no one is doing his duty for Russia. They are all serving him for their career and personal advantage and I worry myself and cry for days on end, as I feel that my husband is very young and inexperienced, of which they are taking advantage."[17]

There was much truth in her observation. And Khodynka bore this out. The fete had been managed carelessly—indeed, criminally mis-managed from the beginning. The people's *gulanye,* as such holidays were called in Russia, was a tradition of medieval origin. It was al-ways rowdy and boisterous. Deaths and injuries were not unusual. In-deed, they were expected. You could not assemble so vast a throng of peasants, fill them with beer and vodka, and expect anything else. In fact, at Alexander III's coronation gulanye thirty-two persons had died, a number of them in the rush to get the Czar's presents and free liquor.

Khodynka was planned on a scale to outdo all other gulani. It was held on the same field where the fete of Alexander III had been held. Everyone knew the commons were crisscrossed with shallow trenches. Everyone knew several hundred thousand countrymen would assem-ble. (The Czar's officials had cast no fewer than 400,000 of the enameled mugs which were the lure that brought so many to their deaths.)

It was true that the crowds proved almost twice as large as had been anticipated. But even if only 400,000 had appeared, the arrange-ments would have broken down because the responsible official, the governor-general of Moscow, the Grand Duke Sergei Alexandrovich, had carelessly failed to provide more than a handful of gendarmes to control the throngs. Once the disaster occurred the principal effort of the officials was to conceal its extent from the Czar and the public. When the Czar learned what had happened, he was appalled. He wanted to retire to a monastery and pray for the victims.[18] His inti-mates dissuaded him and the moment in which the Czar at the onset of his reign might have forged a bond of sympathy and commonality with his people vanished in intrigue and squabble over who was to blame for the catastrophe. This took a pattern which, unfortunately, was to be repeated time and again.

There were two sources of responsibility for Khodynka. One was the Minister of Court, Count I. I. Vorontsov-Dashkov, an old friend and

associate of the Dowager Empress, who lent him her support. Vorontsov-Dashkov was in general charge of the arrangements for the coronation. The other responsible official was the Grand Duke Sergei Alexandrovich, who directed the Moscow arrangements and particularly
those for security. (For several years Sergei was called "the prince of
Khodynka" behind his back.) The wrangle over blame was not clearly
resolved, but the Count submitted his resignation and Nicholas accepted it.* Because the Grand Duke was married to her sister, the
Czarina had taken up the cudgels for him. Thus, from the moment of
the young couple's coronation, the court and the Russian aristocracy,
as well as political supporters of the regime, felt that the young Empress had on personal grounds thrown her weight into a complex political question. Gossip over Alix' role in the Khodynka disaster did not
halt within the court but spread out into broad society and, thus, the
legend of the "German wife" and her remarkable influence over her
weak Emperor-husband was born. Both Nicholas and Alix returned
depressed and gloomy from Moscow, she even more silent and withdrawn than ever.[19] The pattern of the regime was set and fixed in
the tragedy. Circumstances were to change in the ensuing years, but
the aura of ineptitude, intrigue, rivalry, the Emperor's decent instincts,
quickly obliterated by indecisiveness and a willingness to be
influenced and moved from one position to another by his beloved
wife (and others), was established. The dangers which were to flow
from this syndrome could not, of course, be foreseen. But the fact that
Russia was in the most true sense of the word an absolute autocracy in
which the sovereign's word was final and total magnified and exaggerated every weakness and defect in the Czar's character and his inability to understand his role and his relationship to Russia.

Ulyanov and the other young revolutionaries had little or no knowledge of the nature of the new Czar. But this meant nothing to them.
They felt they had in Marxist dialectic the key to history—a history
which was on their side. They had turned their backs on the romantic
tradition of assassination of the Narodnaya Volya, although terror
lived on as the weapon of their rivals, the Socialist Revolutionaries, or
SRs led by Viktor Chernov. The SRs, based on the peasantry and direct inheritors of the populism of the 1860s and 1870s, employed far
more dramatic tactics than the group with which Ulyanov was associated. The SRs continued to carry out assassinations, violent attacks
on Czarist officials and institutions, and for a long time to come (even
into the days of 1917) were to be stronger in numbers, more influen-

* Witte blamed Colonel Vlasovsky, chief of Moscow police, for the disaster.
Vlasovsky resigned but soon came back to favor. (Graf S. Yu. Vitte, *Vospomonan-
iya*, Vol. I, pp. 58–64.)

tial, particularly in the countryside, and more feared by the Czarist authorities than the Marxist groups. The formal birth of the Socialist Revolutionary party was still a short time distant, but the lines of cleavage were already apparent. The Marxists in whose ranks Ulyanov was emerging as a leader based their strategy on close conspiratorial technique, intimate ties between underground revolutionary centers within Russia and exiled leaders abroad, massive distribution of pamphlets and propaganda, agitation among the rapidly growing industrial proletariat of St. Petersburg, Moscow, Kiev, Baku, and the new industrial centers of the Caucasus, and a program of economic and social goals, drawn largely from Marx and depending heavily on Plekhanov's application of these doctrines to Russia.

Thus, Lenin and his friends in the St. Petersburg House of Detention were by no means downcast or depressed by their arrest, although all of them sometimes suffered from prison blues. They looked forward to several years' exile in Siberia and had already decided that they would not seek to escape. Rather they would use their Siberian time for study, for perfecting their underground network across the vast ill-governed continent that was Russia, using the years as a period of learning and testing, of tightening their own personal bonds and flexing their revolutionary muscles. There were few government restrictions on exiles. They could read, write, and study as they pleased. Correspondence was slow but not interfered with. The local police kept them under rather slipshod observation. They were not supposed to leave their places of exile but often did move about Siberia to visit and meet with each other.

The exiles did not see the downfall of Czar Nicholas on the near horizon, but they were supremely confident that his end would not be far distant. They based this calculation on two things: the harsh economic facts of the industrial revolution in Russia and the obvious and increasing inability of the autocratic, cumbersome Czarist behemoth to adapt itself to changing conditions of life—a situation with which Vladimir Ulyanov soon was to deal in his first major work, *The Development of Capitalism in Russia*, a serious Marxist critique of the Russian system which he wrote in Siberian exile at Shushenskoye in the Krasnoyarsk region, using materials sent him by his mother and sisters and brought by Nadezhda Krupskaya. Nadezhda, too, had been condemned to exile and got permission to join Ulyanov at Shushenskoye on condition that the two promptly married. Laden with books which her fiancé had ordered (he had listed seventeen works, such as A. V. Semenov's *Historical Data on Industry and Trade* in three volumes, F. A. Shcherbina's *Economic Relations in the Region of the Vladikavkaz Railroad*, and Y. I. Ragozin's *Iron and Coal in South Russia*) and accompanied by her mother, Nadezhda Krupskaya arrived in Shushen-skoye on May 7, 1898. Ulyanov was out hunting and came back late to find the two women waiting in the rather comfortable room which he rented in a log house belonging to a man named Appolon Zyryanov.

Lenin was surprised to see the light in the window. His landlord told him his fellow exile, a Finn named Oskar Engburg, had gotten drunk and was throwing his books around. Lenin, in a state of great concern, burst in to find Nadezhda and her mother.[20] Because of Czarist red tape it was July 10 before Vladimir and Nadezhda were able to marry.[21] It was a church wedding, celebrated by the village priest with exiles from nearby places in attendance.

The details of Lenin's wedding have been suppressed by Soviet historians, apparently because it was celebrated in the traditional Orthodox fashion. Lenin wrote his mother and sister on two or three occasions inviting them to come with his brother Dmitri (if Dmitri was released from prison in time). He thought the trip would not be too hard for his mother if she came by second-class rail coach. He had hoped they could be married before the fast of St. Peter (Orthodox weddings could not be performed during the fast), but the delay of Siberian authorities in handling his papers made this impossible. Like Lenin his sister Anna had been married conventionally in the village church at Trostyanka. Vladimir was his sister's escort. The letters of Lenin to his mother describing the wedding have never been published.[22] In fact, Lenin wrote an estimated 128 letters to his family from Siberia but only 91 have been published. Letters dealing with his wedding, financial matters, etc., have been suppressed by Soviet historical censors.[23] When Lenin and Krupskaya took up residence in Switzerland in 1908, the question of their marriage certificate arose. It was needed for their registration with the police. He wrote his sister Mariya twice, February 7 and February 14, 1908, about it, first suggesting that she apply "palm oil" (a small bribe) to obtain it from the authorities at Krasnoyarsk, then suggesting that Krupskaya's mother apply to a justice of peace and obtain a court order requiring the Krasnoyarsk church authorities to issue a copy of the marriage certificate on grounds it was needed "in connection with the disposal of an inheritance."[24]

Shushenskoye was an old Siberian village of about fifteen hundred population on the Yenisei River, twenty-five miles south of Minusinsk in the Krasnoyarsk area. The peasants were poor and the "intelligentsia" was made up of two teachers, a priest, the county clerk, and the storekeeper. Their principal occupations were cards and vodka.

Ulyanov wrote his mother that he had been exiled to the "Italy" of Siberia.[25] He wrote his sister "Shu . . . shu . . . shu . . . A big village, some streets, quite dirty and dusty. Manure isn't put onto the fields but thrown on the edge of the village. To get out of town one must make his way through piles of manure."

Ulyanov became fond of his landlord, Zyryanov, and two other local inhabitants, a former clerk named Zhuravlev and a peasant nicknamed "Sosipatych." They hunted ducks and woodcock, fished, shot rabbits, gathered *kedrovy orekhi*, the tasty Siberian pine nuts. He acquired a hunting dog named Pegasus, a pair of leather breeches,[26] and bought a secondhand Berdan hunting rifle for eight rubles.* In winter he and Nadezhda skated on a rink which he and some schoolchildren made. ("With the change of weather I am skating instead of hunting. I don't think I have skated for 10 years," he wrote his mother.) Sometimes, lying on his bed and not looking at the boards, he played three chess games simultaneously.[27] He and Nadezhda worked together translating Sydney and Beatrice Webb's massive *Theory and Practise of English Trade Unionism* into Russian, for which they were paid four hundred rubles, which was a help. The Czarist Government gave political exiles an allowance of eight rubles a month so that between them Lenin and Krupskaya drew a Government ration of sixteen rubles.[28] His mother worried constantly about the cold and whether he was dressed warmly enough. He poked gentle fun at her fears. In summer they kept a small vegetable garden and raised cucumbers, carrots, beets, and potatoes. At Christmas they had a tree for the village children. The youngsters helped decorate it, then Ulyanov led them in Christmas songs. He still loved to sing and he still kept Christmas in the style his mother had set long ago in Simbirsk. Frequently there were meetings with fellow exiles, in Minusinsk or some other Siberian town. Either the authorities didn't care what the exiles did or were too lazy to interfere. He kept up a lively correspondence (the mails came twice a week) with his family and fellow revolutionaries.†

Not that exile was one long sabbatical. One of the most respected exiles, Nikolai Yevgrafovich Fedoseyev (the man who had headed a Marxist study group in Kazan at the time Ulyanov was a university student), killed himself with a revolver in despondency over false

---

* The gun was bought for him March 5, 1899, by his brother-in-law Mark Yelizarev. (*Istorichesky Arkhiv*, 1958, No. 1, p. 22, Letter of Mariya Ulyanova, Lenin's mother, to her daughter Mariya. There are according to *Istorichesky Arkhiv* a very large number of unpublished letters of Mariya Ulyanova in the archives.) The gun was later sold for Vladimir by his brother Dmitri for seventy-five rubles. (V. I. Lenin, *Collected Works*, Vol. LVII, p. 33.)

† The letters did not always deal with serious dialectic questions. Nina Struve, wife of Pyotr B. Struve, who was to become one of Lenin's political antagonists, wrote Nadezhda that her baby boy was "already holding his head up and every day we show him the portraits of Darwin and Marx and say 'Nod to Uncle Darwin,' 'Nod to Uncle Marx' and he nods in such an amusing way." (Krupskaya, *Reminiscences of Lenin*, p. 40.)

charges of being a police agent which another exile named Yukhotsky made against him. When Fedoseyev's girl friend, on her way to join him, heard of the suicide, she killed herself as well. "How terrible is this tragic history!" Ulyanov wrote. His close friend and associate, A. A. Vaneyev, had been exiled to Turukhansk, the most remote village in the Yenisei Guberniya. Vaneyev was regarded by the authorities as one of the most dangerous of exiles. Finally, despite desperate effort by Ulyanov and others to get him better treatment, Vaneyev died September 8, 1899, of a combination of pleuritis, cholera, and typhus.

Ulyanov gave the funeral oration and he and his companions ordered a cast-iron headstone from the Abakan ironworks for Vaneyev's grave. It was inscribed:

Anatoly Alexandrovich Vaneyev
Political Exile
Died 8 Sept. 1899
27 years old
Peace Be With You, Comrade

Ulyanov's principal achievement in his three years of exile was his work *The Development of Capitalism in Russia*. He finished it in autumn 1898 and sent his manuscript with its citations of more than four hundred different books and source materials back to St. Petersburg, where it was published in full legality in March 1899, under the imprint of the publishing house of M. I. Vodovozov. The only concession to the times was the nom de plume "Vladimir Ilyin," which deceived no one, especially not the police.*

By the time his exile neared its close Ulyanov was possessed with eagerness to get on with his plans for the new revolutionary paper which had been put aside by his arrest in December 1895. As his fellow exile, G. M. Krzhizhanovsky, noted:

"Our exile was coming to an end. I had received permission to work on the Trans-Siberian railroad. I well remember one of my last walks with Vladimir Ilyich on the banks of the wide Yenisei. It was a frosty moonlit night and before us sparkled the endless shroud of the Siberian snow.

---

* The police reported in this connection: "The named author is better known under his other pseudonym Tulin. Under such a pseudonym his articles have appeared in *Novoye Slovo* and in some Social Democratic collections not approved by the censor. His real name is known by few as the S.D. holds it a great secret, regarding this author as one of its leaders. In reality it is Vladimir Ilyich Ulyanov, political exile and brother of Alexander Ulyanov, executed in 1887." The report bore a notation "His Honor, the Minister, desires to acquaint himself with this edition and asks the gendarmerie to send him one example. (Done 20/IX)." (M. Moskalev, *V. I. Lenin v Sibiri*, p. 91.)

"Vladimir Ilyich told me excitedly of his plans and preparations for his return to Russia. . . . Organization of the Party press organ . . . transport of its publications from abroad . . . creation of a party for the aid of this central organ, presenting, so to say, an original framework for the building of the whole structure of the Revolutionary proletariat. This was at the center of his argument.

"To me it seemed on first sight that he over-evaluated the role of such a paper and that this arose from the long term of his being in exile and his own inevitable single-minded concentration on literary activity."[29]

It was not the first—or last—time when one of Ulyanov's comrades was to disagree with his evaluation of the revolutionary situation or the tactics to be followed.

On January 31, 1900, Ulyanov left Siberia for Russia. He caught the train from Achinsk on February 2, making a slow progress westward with frequent halts to contact his revolutionary friends. He visited Pskov, Riga, Smolensk, Podolsk, Nizhni Novgorod, Moscow, and St. Petersburg (arranging for the distribution of the underground paper he was preparing to launch) and on June 16, 1900, went abroad, there to live with only brief cat-and-mouse interludes in his homeland until the events of 1917. He was, as Trotsky was to note, thirty years old and "already fully mature." In Russia, in the student circles, the Social Democratic groups, and in exile circles, Trotsky observed, "he held first place. He could not fail to realize his power, if only because everyone he met and worked with so closely did. When he left Russia he was already in possession of a full theoretical equipment and a solid store of revolutionary experience."[30]

Lenin was an unusual man. But the path he took was well trodden.

With rare exceptions the men and women who passed through the Siberian experience went on to spend their lives working for the Czar's downfall. Many went almost directly abroad as soon as their exile was completed. In the future it would often be said that Siberian exile with its long winters, its limitless hours for thought, for study, for contemplation of Russian life in its harshest aspects, the close camaraderie which inevitably developed among the political exiles, the relative freedom which the Czarist Government permitted for correspondence, for organization, for the circulation of revolutionary materials, and even for conspiratorial meetings and assemblies, provided a remarkable forcing bed in which the seeds of the revolutionary movement took such sturdy root that flourishing growth became almost inevitable.

IX

On the Eve

Alexander Blok called the nineteenth century the "Iron Century." Now it was ending and everyone was convinced that something quite different lay ahead. The *Moskovskiye Vedomosti,* organ of the Moscow bourse, warned that the twentieth century would be "the Century of Socialism," and socialism, it explained, was "that danger which we count the most serious challenge not only at the present time but at least for the first half of the future Century."[1]

That the new century harbored critical problems for Russia and especially for the regime was apparent to all. To none was it more plain than to Witte, the Czar's Minister of Finance, a railroad builder and financier, unquestionably the most able and realistic man in the Empire—qualifications which made the Czar exceedingly uncomfortable in his company. So much so that only when Nicholas found himself in clear and present peril was he willing to give Witte a more or less free hand.

The Czar was vacationing in Yalta in October 1898, when Witte sent him a letter posing the basic question: Shall Russia go forward toward fulfillment of a magnificent destiny or will it enter into decline? To go forward, Witte emphasized, Russia must emerge from the state of semislavery which had proved to be the legacy of serfdom's abolition. It was not enough to "liberate" the serf from bondage. He must be liberated from the "slavery of production." He must be given legal status and consciousness of his rights. No longer could he be treated as a "half-person." And he must be educated. Russia was not only more illiterate than any other European land, it was more backward than some Asian countries.

"Possibly education may corrupt the people," Witte admitted. (The Czar's favorite and most reactionary minister, Pobedonostsev, was convinced of this, as were in all probability, the Czar and the Czarina.) "Nevertheless, education must advance and it must advance energetically. Our people with their Orthodox faith are churlish and dark. But a dark people cannot be improved. He who does not go forward will for that very reason go backward compared with people who are advancing forward."*

The heart of the matter, said Witte, was the peasant question—peasant instability, peasant impoverishment, peasant ignorance.

"It is the primary question in the life of Russia," he added. "It must be resolved."

How did Nicholas II react to these blunt but intelligent words? Witte had no idea. "The Czar never spoke to me on this subject," he said dryly. "Therefore the peasant question did not advance."[2]

Witte was no radical. Far from it. He was an entrepreneur par excellence, a sharp, tricky man, too tricky for his own good. He would have subscribed wholeheartedly to the Coolidge-ism "The business of business is business." But as businessman-statesman he understood only too clearly the challenges which anachronistic Russia would face in the twentieth century and devoted his every effort to creating conditions in which business and industry would grow and flourish. There was, in all honesty, little difference in Witte's analysis of Russia's dilemma and that, for example, of Lenin in his *Development of Capitalism in Russia,* although one stood at the right hand of the Czar and the other wrote in a Siberian exile cabin at Shushenskoye.

Where Witte differed from Lenin and the revolutionaries was not in diagnosis but in remedy. Witte believed he could so stimulate Russia economically that the Imperial system could survive, albeit with modifications and limitations of the Czar's powers. Lenin, the Social Democrats, the Socialist Revolutionaries, and many other radicals and

---

* Witte was remarkably echoed by Stalin at a conference of Soviet industrial managers in 1931: "To slacken the pace would mean to lag behind and those who lag behind are beaten. We do not want to be beaten. . . . The history of old Russia consisted of the fact that she was always being beaten because of her backwardness. She was beaten by the Mongol khans. She was beaten by the Turkish beys. She was beaten by the Swedish knights. She was beaten by the Polish-Lithuanian pans. She was beaten by the Anglo-French capitalists. She was beaten by the Japanese barons. She was beaten by all—for her backwardness. For military backwardness. Cultural backwardness. Political backwardness. Industrial backwardness. Agricultural backwardness. They beat her because to beat her was profitable and could be done with impunity. . . . We are 50 or 100 years behind the advanced countries. We must make good this lag in 10 years. Either we do it or they will crush us." (J. V. Stalin, *Collected Works,* Vol. XIII, p. 38.)

liberals believed change could come only with the total destruction of Czarism.*

As Witte argued in a memorandum to the Czar of March 22, 1899:

"Industry gives birth to capital; capital gives rise to enterprise and love of learning; and knowledge, enterprise and capital combined create new industries. Such is the eternal cycle of economic life and by the succession of such turns our national economy moves ahead in the process of its natural growth. In Russia this growth is yet too slow because there is yet too little industry, capital and spirit of enterprise. But we cannot be content with the continuation of such slow growth. . . .

"We have to develop mass-production industries, widely dispersed and variegated. We must give the country such industrial perfection as has been reached by the United States of America which firmly bases its prosperity on two pillars—agriculture and industry. . . ."

Point by point, he spelled out the measures which the Czar must approve to bring his backward country through the dangerous rapids of the twentieth century.

He concluded with these words:

"In submitting this program to favorable consideration by Your Imperial Highness, I respectfully ask that it may please you, my sovereign, to make certain that it may not be endangered henceforth by waverings and changes. . . ."[3]

Witte's reward was to be removed from office, largely through the intrigue of an incompetent adventurer and former cavalry officer named Alexander M. Bezobrazov (whose name, in translation, means "rude," "vulgar," or "illiterate"), who had gained enormous influence over Nicholas II—an influence almost as pernicious as would soon be exercised by the paramount adventurer Rasputin. The Czar had a fatal inclination toward hare-brained schemers and schemes,† possibly

---

* Isaac Deutscher points out the paradox that because of Russia's backwardness Russian Marxists, in contrast to their western European counterparts, often argued that capitalism must first develop in order to provide a basis on which socialism might be constructed. Thus, the arguments of some Russian Marxists could hardly be distinguished from those of the more progressive capitalists. Ultimately, a split developed between those who called themselves "legal Marxists," whose activities were not prescribed by the authorities because they did not preach revolution, and revolutionary Marxists, actively seeking to bring about the downfall of the Romanov Government. Struve, M. I. Tugan-Baranovsky, and many others became "legal Marxists" and, ultimately, the mainstays of liberal thought in Russia. M. N. Pokrovsky, the Soviet historian who fell afoul of Stalin in the 1930s, noted the irony that "in all the world the Marxists are the Party of the working class, only in Russia are they the party of big capital." (M. N. Pokrovsky, Brief History of Russia, Vol. II, 1933; Isaac Deutscher, Stalin, p. 30.)

† Nicholas was interested in building a bridge across the Bering Strait and once thought of putting an electric fence around his empire. (Alexandre Izwolsky, Mémoires, p. 291.)

inherited from his father, who once put 2 million gold rubles in the hands of a Buryat-Mongol doctor named Zhamsaryn Badmayev, who had promised to stir up a revolt of Mongols, Tibetans, and north Chinese and bring them all into the Russian camp.[4] Bezobrazov was introduced to the Czar by the Grand Duke Alexander Mikhailovich. Following the Badmayev precedent the Czar promptly gave him 2 million rubles from secret funds with which Bezobrazov promised he would manage to transfer Manchuria and Korea to Russia "without a drop of blood."[5] Witte, War Minister Alexei Kuropatkin, and Foreign Minister Vladimir Lamsdorf followed Bezobrazov's activities with open alarm. In 1903 Bezobrazov was in Manchuria setting up a detachment of six hundred in a "woodcutters' artel" (all of them former noncommissioned Russian officers) to be active on the Yalu against Korea.[*] He was in private personal correspondence with the Czar. Kuropatkin called him an "impractical dreamer and adventurer" and concluded that Russia had two policies in the Far East—"the Imperial and the Bezobrazov."[6] Nor was this the end of such plots. In January 1904, Nicholas privately received two Kalmyks named Ulyanov from the Don country—one was an officer and one a lama—and sent them off on a secret expedition to try to bring Tibet under Russian dominion.[7]

These were the kind of woolly illusions with which Nicholas filled his mind.[8] The atmosphere around the court was not healthy. As early as 1901 the aged aristocrat and historian A. A. Polovtsev, returning to St. Petersburg from taking the cure at Monte Carlo, noted in his diary that the Czar and his family were the object of gossip and scandal, centering on the society with which the Romanovs surrounded themselves.[9]

Nicholas was often stimulated by mischief-making letters from his cousin Willy, Emperor Wilhelm II of Germany, who indefatigably sought to embroil Russia in one way or another, now with Japan, now with Britain, so that she would be too weak and involved to interfere with his own grandiose plottings. The Czar was not alone in his fascination with eastern adventures. His passion for the East was shared by the Czarina, who echoed her husband's opinion (or originated it?) that the yellow race must be put in its place.[10] The Czar's distaste for Japan may have been stimulated by an attempt made on his life when he visited Japan as a young man.

In contrast to the hardheaded, tough-minded profit-and-loss concerns of Witte (and not a few other brilliant industrial empire-builders whose style was akin to the Morgan-Rockefeller-Gould-Har-

---

[*] Bezobrazov had acquired a Korean trading concession in 1902 from an Amur river merchant named Briner. The tract lay on the Yalu River. Mariya Fyodorovna, Nicholas' mother, and Mikhail, his brother, were said to have taken shares in the Yalu concession. (S. P. Melgunov, *Nikolai II*, p. 15.)

riman school in the United States) Nicholas II dreamed flamboyant dreams of Imperial grandeur and military adventure. As Minister of War Kuropatkin put it to Witte:

"Our Emperor has grandiose plans in his head: to seize Manchuria for Russia and to go on from there to unite Korea with Russia. He dreams of putting Tibet under his power. He wants to take Persia and occupy not only the Bosporus but also the Dardanelles. When we ministers hold back the Czar from achieving his dreams he feels in his disappointment all the more certain that he is right and that he understands better than we the glory and the good of Russia. That is why the Bezobrazovs, singing in unison, seem to the Czar more understanding of his purposes than we ministers."[11]*

It was no wonder that movement for change, reform, and a reorganization of the autocratic system began to appear even in what might be normally regarded as the most conservative circles of Russian society—among landowners, the wealthy bourgeoisie, and the powerful, ambitious, and newly emerging industrialists. By midsummer 1903 Count N. V. Muravyev, Minister of Justice, was telling Minister of War Kuropatkin that "all levels of society" were disaffected.[12] By November he was saying that Russia's internal situation was alarming, that provocations were everywhere; that the Government was struggling against itself and against the institutions of capital. How long this could continue he could not guess and he was himself hoping to get out.[13]

In Moscow the reform banner attracted both industrialists and patrician landowners. An informal grouping called the Symposium sprang up in 1899 under the leadership of D. N. Shipov, a well-to-do slavophile liberal. It won the participation of two of the Dolgorukov Princes, Pavel and Pyotr. New industrialists like N. I. Guchkov and M. V. Chelnokov joined in. Many of these men had been active in the Zemstvo movement, an effort to transform the ancient Russian rural assemblies into organs of participatory democracy. Naturally, it had been largely suppressed by the Czar.

Among the vigorous industrialists, men who had made huge fortunes out of textiles, steel, sugar, coal, and the new technological industries, the mood moved swiftly from palliative talk of reforms toward more and more radical proposals. By November 1904, they were demanding representative government, a State Duma (Congress), freedom of speech, freedom of assembly, city self-government, broad

---

* Witte expressed full agreement with Kuropatkin's analysis and added that it was truly awful to have to stand by watching while "these evil personalities" were dragging the Czar in one direction or another and to see such vast sums flow out of the state coffers into such stupid projects. (A. N. Kuropatkin, diary, in *Krasny Arkhiv*, 1922, Vol II, p. 32.)

powers for the Zemstvos, and free general elections. The names backing these proposals included those of Savva T. Morozov (the Morozov family was probably the richest in Moscow with huge holdings in textiles and sugar; Savva Morozov's wealth was estimated at 15 million rubles in 1899, that of his brother Vladimir at 10 million), V. P. Ryabushinsky, a great banker, N. I. and K. I. Guchkov, V. S. Bakhrushin, A. S. Vishnikov, and M. V. Chelnokov.[14]

The distance which had been swiftly traveled by these eminently respectable, wealthy, powerful members of the Russian establishment can be measured if their platform is compared with that drafted by Alexander Ulyanov for his "terrorist faction" of the Narodnaya Volya in 1886. With the single and obvious exception of nationalization of factories, land, and production there was no clause in Alexander's "manifesto" which would not have commanded the enthusiastic support of an influential segment of Russian big business and the ancient landholding aristocracy.

It was obviously true, as Leon Trotsky observed, that Russia on the threshold of the twentieth century was "a vast laboratory of social thinking."[15] The social thinking was the by-product of turmoil, of conflict, of change. The pace of events, long so slow, so glacially Russian, now took on speed and unexpectedness. In the morning a man might be a simple bystander. By nightfall he had become a revolutionist.

Nikolai Yevgenyevich Burenin, grandson of one of St. Petersburg's leading businessmen, a trader in tea and coffee, in sugar and spices, went for a stroll one winter's morning on the Nevsky. The date, as it chanced, was March 4, 1901, and Nikolai hadn't a care in the world. He was a most presentable young man, and a good many ambitious matrons dreamed of marrying off their daughters to him. His mother's father was a millionaire merchant and fur dealer. His grandmother ruled the household with an iron hand, surrounded by sycophantic priests and nuns, Metropolitans and other high dignitaries of the church. When the old lady lay dying, her relatives gathered, quarreling so sharply over the inheritance that at the moment of death no one was left with Grandma—all were drinking and arguing in an adjoining room. It was a scene out of a classic Ostrovsky play about the Moscow *kupechestvo*.

Burenin had grown up in this milieu. His father was no businessman, preferring to devote his time to horse racing. His mother was a woman of contradictory spirit, of strong aristocratic tendencies, but with an open inquiring mind. Burenin's brother was an officer in the Czar's Life Guards. His uncle was a former mayor of St. Petersburg named Glazunov, an extraordinarily wealthy man, the most rapacious of the relatives who gathered at the bedside of the dying grandmother.

Burenin had graduated from the Petersburg School of Commerce and then, having little taste for business and considerable talent as a musician and artist, went on to the Academy of Arts.

When he set out for a walk to his uncle's house, a great palace at the corner of Nevsky Prospekt and the Catherine Canal, he noticed many police and gendarmes on the street, and when he got to his uncle's house, he found it was cordoned off by soldiers. The doorman wouldn't let him in because the courtyard was filled with policemen and Cossacks.

Burenin turned away and wandered toward the Kazan Cathedral, a handsome Romanesque structure, set back on a great plaza from the Nevsky. There was a crowd of people in the square, and as Burenin started up the steps he heard shouts from all sides. At that moment police and Cossacks descended on the crowd, beating them with their scabbard-encased sabers, whipping down anyone who raised a hand. Burenin put up the fur collar of his winter overcoat just as a whip slashed across his shoulders. Jumping to the parapet beside the cathedral, he saw a woman, covered with blood, being taken off by a passing coachman to the hospital.

"Aroused to the depth of my soul by what was happening and not understanding anything," Burenin recalled, "I turned to a police officer and demanded an explanation of what this all meant."

The officer asked who he was. Burenin handed him his engraved visiting card and said that he intended to launch an investigation of this scandalous attack of the police on peaceful residents and citizens.

The officer refused the visiting card and, pointing to a group standing beside the cathedral, said: "Go and join them. They will explain it all."

Hardly had Burenin approached the crowd than police and Cossacks surrounded the group and marched them off to the Spassky police station. As he entered the station Burenin managed to toss out another visiting card on which he scrawled: "I'm all right. Held at Spassky police station."

The demonstrators were protesting the so-called temporary rules imposed on universities by the Minister of Education Nikolai P. Bogolepov; Bogolepov had been assassinated February 14, 1901, by a former student named Pyotr V. Karpovich, but his "temporary rules," which provided in some instances that students involved in demonstrations could be forcibly impressed into the Army, had not been rescinded.

When the police found out Burenin's identity (they quickly received a complaint from General Maslov, the chief prosecutor, a friend of Burenin's mother), he was released. But the events at Kazan Cathedral and his confinement with the demonstrators changed his life. A few days after his release Burenin paid a visit to the home of his friend, Dmitri Vasilyevich Stasov, a lawyer who had often defended young revolutionaries and others falling into the hands of the Czar's political police. As a result he himself had been arrested on a couple of occasions.[16] Stasov was an excellent musician and a friend of Glinka's. Together with Anton Rubinstein and Vasily A. Kologrivov, he had founded the St. Petersburg Conservatory. Stasov's brother, Vladimir, was the author of the libretto for Alexander Borodin's *Prince Igor*.[17] Burenin occasionally played concerts at the Stasov home. But now the talk was not of music.

Yelena, Stasov's dark, beautiful, intense daughter, drew Burenin aside. She was, she said, engaged in the revolutionary underground. Would Burenin like to join? He would be a particularly valuable recruit because who would suspect him with a brother and an uncle and the husband of his sister—all officers in the Czar's regiments? Without hesitation Burenin agreed. "The shooting at Kazan Cathedral had determined my relationship toward the state system," Burenin later explained. In that moment the underground organization which Lenin had established for the distribution of his émigré-produced revolutionary newspaper, *Iskra* (The Spark), gained a new recruit. Burenin had never heard of Lenin, *Iskra*, or the Social Democratic underground. It made no difference. From then onward Burenin's life became a kind of kaleidoscope, reflecting St. Petersburg existence—the conventional society of the nobility, teas, dances, balls, concerts in musical circles, all in the most fashionable surroundings—and, at the same time and often on the same day or night, bold, sometimes hairraising adventures as he and a group of well-to-do young people put the estates of their remarkably wealthy families, the villas in the suburbs, the houses in Finland, the palaces and mansions in the city, at the disposal of an expanding revolutionary underground, engaged in smuggling newspapers, pamphlets, and agitational instructions into Russia; in slipping secret agents back and forth across the frontiers; and in transporting arms and explosives from the most diverse sources (Turkey, Bulgaria, Berlin) into Russia from adjoining Finland and Poland.

The transformation of Burenin from an apolitical, artistic well-to-do young man-about-town into an imaginative and daring revolutionary agent had been accomplished within minutes by the crash of Cossack sabers and the slash of Cossack *nagaiki*. Such a transformation could occur only in an atmosphere electrically charged and close to flash point. It inevitably reminds one of the similar "radicalization" of American youth (and their middle-aged allies) in the antiwar demonstrations of the late 1960s and early 1970s.

The demonstration at Kazan Cathedral March 4, 1901, was unusual —not in the remarkable brutality of the police but in the fact that it is very well documented and that it inspired Maxim Gorky to write his "Song of the Stormy Petrel,"* which became the rallying call of a whole generation of revolutionary youth ("The Storm! Soon it will burst. Wait! Soon it will burst!") and caused Leo Tolstoy to write an appeal to the Czar in which he warned the sovereign that if simple reforms, civil rights, and electoral privileges were not quickly granted the day might come when troops and police would refuse to fire on crowds of demonstrators.[18] The Czar, to be sure, did not acknowledge Tolstoy's advice.

The Kazan demonstration had many prominent participants, among them Pyotr B. Struve, a leading Marxist who was soon to break violently with Lenin, Professor M. I. Tugan-Baranovsky, of Moscow University, whose Marxist studies are still classic sources on Russian economic development in the late nineteenth and early twentieth centuries, the writer and liberal publicist Nikolai F. Annensky, the theatrical director V. E. Meyerhold, who wrote the playwright Anton Chekhov "my blood boils,"[19] and Prince Leonid D. Vyazemsky, a member of the Council of State who tried to halt the Cossacks in their brutality, was beaten for his pains and then publicly reprimanded and banished from St. Petersburg by the Czar. When Vyazemsky sought to protest to the Ministers of Interior, Justice, and War, they refused to receive him.[20]

The presence of these prominent figures was noted by another young participant, R. V. Ivanov-Razumnik, then a student at St. Petersburg University. Ivanov-Razumnik was hauled off to jail along with fifteen hundred of his fellow students to find himself in a huge airy cell about fifteen paces long with a broad window, protected by bars, which offered a distant view of the Alexander Nevsky Lavra Gardens and the southern regions of St. Petersburg. The cell was warm, clean, well painted, provided with running water, a lavatory, comfortable folding bunks, and steam heat. Ivanov-Razumnik, who was to be imprisoned countless times in his life, first by the Czarist

---

* Petrel in Russian is *burevestnik*, literally "the harbinger of the storm." Mikhail Kalinin, a close associate of Lenin's, called the song the "call of revolution." Lenin's sister Mariya and all her friends knew it by heart and sang it endlessly. (B. Byalik, *Sudba Maxima Gorokogo*, p. 134.) The Russian censor banned its publication in an allegory which Gorky called *Spring Melodies* but inexplicably permitted its publication as a song. It was printed, reprinted, hectographed in millions of copies. (Ibid., pp. 134–35.)

police and even more often by the Bolsheviks (because he was a staunch sympathizer if not a member of the rival left-wing SRs), came to look back on the accommodations forty years later with awe and affection.

The students were permitted to move freely from cell to cell and congregate in the corridors. The only ban was on mingling with "real criminals." Nor were boys and girls permitted to share the same cell block. But the students received mountains of parcels from home. Ivanov-Razumnik got huge homemade pies which he shared with his friends. The family of Rimsky-Korsakov, the composer, sent baskets of apples, pears, oranges, and grapes. There was more food than the students could consume so they rigged up baskets and lowered the leftovers by ropes to the "real" criminals on the ground floor. A tobacco manufacturer named Shapshal whose son was in the prison sent in ten thousand cigarettes; a few days later he sent ten thousand more.

After a week or so visitors were permitted and the cell floors turned into a kind of house party. There was no surveillance. Everyone had a "fiancée" or girl friend; the warden, in despair, called in one young man and asked him to specify which of three attractive young "fiancées" was his real fiancée. (In truth none was.) The young people organized lectures and built a theater in the largest prison cell where they put on concerts and plays almost every evening. Ivanov-Razumnik gave a paper on "The Attitude of Maxim Gorky to Contemporary Culture and the Intelligentsia."

One day Ivanov-Razumnik sought and obtained an interview with the prison chief. The Moscow Art Theater was paying its first visit to St. Petersburg. Ivanov-Razumnik had a subscription ticket. Before being arrested he had seen *Uncle Vanya*, and on this night Hauptmann's *The Lonely Ones* was to be presented. He begged permission to leave jail for the evening to see the play. "I give you my word of honor as a student," he told the warden, "that I will not let you down and will be in my place in the cell again not later than midnight."

The chief of prison solemnly said that much as he respected a student's word of honor there might be dozens of others who had tickets for plays. Suppose Ivanov-Razumnik were permitted to go—what about the others? All couldn't be released. It wouldn't be fair to make an exception just for one. Ivanov-Razumnik could not but agree and returned peacefully to his cell.

After about three weeks the students were released, expelled from the university, and ordered to leave St. Petersburg. They themselves were permitted to pick their place of forced residence.

The day the doors swung open the students gave the warden an ovation. One student, in a farewell speech, said: "Although you're a jailer you're a decent fellow all the same. We hope you'll stop being a jailer and remain a human being." Then the students went straight to a photographer's studio and had a group picture taken.

"Oh, yes," Ivanov-Razumnik commented years later. "There was a prison for you indeed!"[21]

X

The Stage Is Set

It was a time of demonstrations, a time of arrests, a time of crystallization of political viewpoints. In St. Petersburg a meeting was called at the Institute of Mining to commemorate Pyotr Lavrov, the populist writer, who had died in February 1900. The principal speaker was Pavel Nikolayevich Milyukov, historian at Moscow University, a friend and associate of the most venerable of Russian historians, Professor Vasily Klyuchevsky. Already Milyukov had been exiled once. Now he was arrested, held for six months, then permitted to settle outside St. Petersburg.[1] In these years Milyukov and those like him were constantly compelled to choose between prison or exile, on the one hand, or, on the other, the suppression of their personal views and political opinions. Thus, Milyukov's philosophy took shape and hardened. He was not a radical. He was a liberal—and in due course would become Russia's leading liberal. Yet in these times he found himself as harshly repressed as the most violent revolutionary and as opposed to the Czar's regime, to V. K. Plehve, who succeeded Witte as the Czar's chief Minister, as any of the young students in the St. Petersburg Transit Prison in March 1901. Finally, he was compelled to go abroad, to teach and lecture in France, in Germany, and in the United States. But his voice was not stilled. The publication *Osvobozhdeniye*[2] (Liberation), in which he played a leading role, was founded in Stuttgart and carried to Russia the same note of challenge as did Lenin's *Iskra*, published first in London and then in Geneva.

Writing from America where he was lecturing at the University of

Chicago, Milyukov tried to explain what was happening to his country. There had, he believed, arisen two Russias.

"I should designate one as the Russia of Leo Tolstoy, the great writer [excommunicated by the Holy Synod in February 1901*] and the other as that of Plehve, the late Minister of the Interior [assassinated in July 1904.].

"The former is the Russia of our 'intellectuals' and of the people; the latter is official Russia. One is the Russia of the future, as dreamed of by members of the liberal professions; the other is an anachronism, deeply rooted in the past and defended in the present by an omnipotent bureaucracy. The one spells liberty; the other, despotism."[3]

The process of politicization was by no means confined to St. Petersburg and Moscow. It was felt with equal weight in the hinterland. One day in the spring of 1897 two eighteen-year-olds were walking down a street in Nikolayev, a sleepy provincial shipbuilding town on the Black Sea. One was Lev Bronshtein, the other Grigory Sokolovsky. They had spent the winter arguing about politics, about Russia. Neither belonged to a political party. In Bronshtein's house his father, a prosperous grain merchant and mill owner, had long forbidden any political talk, probably because as a Jew, he regarded all politics as dangerous. Yet for some months now Bronshtein and Sokolovsky had been discussing utopian socialism and other questions of the day. Bronshtein had begun as a hard-line conservative, skeptical of every socialist whisper. But now he had begun to change. He was reading John Stuart Mill, Lippert's *Primitive Culture*, Jeremy Bentham, Chernyshevsky, and Auguste Mignet's *French Revolution*. He and Sokolovsky had even made a first venture into participatory democracy by mounting a campaign against the Board of Directors of the Nikolayev Library who wanted to raise the annual subscription fee from five to six rubles. They won their campaign, electing a new Board of Directors and keeping the fee at five rubles. Then for several weeks the two collaborated in writing a play which included both populist and Marxist characters, a project which was never completed, possibly because while they were antagonistic to populism they were only weakly attracted to Marxism.

In February of 1897 a woman student named Mariya Vetrova had burned herself to death in the Peter and Paul Fortress.[4] Both young

---

* The sins for which Tolstoy was excommunicated were: (1) "He rejects the personal, living God, glorified in the Holy Trinity"; (2) "he denies Christ as the God-man risen from the dead"; (3) "he denies the Immaculate Conception and the virginity, before and after the birth, of the God-mother"; (4) "he does not recognize life after death and retribution for sins"; (5) "he rejects the benefaction of the Holy Ghost"; (6) "he rejects the benefaction of the Eucharist."

men were deeply moved by the tragedy. As they walked down the street on that spring day Bronshtein turned to Sokolovsky and said: "It's about time we started."

"Yes," said Sokolovsky, "it is about time."

"But how?"

"That's it, how?"

"We must find workers, not wait for anybody or ask anything but just find workers and set to it."

Sokolovsky said he thought he knew how to begin. He would look up a workingman he knew, a watchman who belonged to a Bible sect. He went off to find him but the man had vanished. Instead he ran into a woman who introduced him to another sectarian, Ivan Andreyevich Mukhin, who was an electrician.

The next day Sokolovsky, Bronshtein, Mukhin, and several others were sitting in a tavern. As a melodeon jangled out a tune, Mukhin began to speak. He said that he used his Gospel teaching, just as an opening gambit, in order to "explain the whole truth" to workers. Once he got a conversation going, he said, he switched the talk to navy beans.

"It's very simple," he said. "I put a bean on the table and say, 'This is the Czar.' Around it, I place more beans. 'These are ministers, bishops, generals, and over there the gentry and merchants. And in this other heap, the plain people.'"

Then, said Mukhin, "I scramble all the beans together and I say: 'Now tell me where is the Czar and the ministers?' And they answer me: 'Who can tell? You can't spot them now.'

"'Just what I say. You can't spot them now.' And so I say, 'All beans should be scrambled.'"

Bronshtein and Sokolovsky were thrilled with this introduction to the real working class, to a genuine proletarian agitator, his simplicity and wisdom. Then Mukhin added:

"Only how to scramble them, damn them. That's the problem. That's not navy beans, is it?"

Bronshtein was far from having the answer, but he set to work with enormous energy. He and his friend went to the shipyards and met more workers. The workers already had an eight-hour day and decent enough pay. But they wanted social justice, more humane treatment by the management. One was a cabinetmaker named Korotkov who wrote a proletarian march: "We are the alphas and omegas, the beginnings and endings." One was a blond giant of a young man, gloomy and mysterious, who was soon to take his life by asphyxiating himself with coal gas. They had a single tattered copy of the *Communist Manifesto*, which had been transcribed by someone in Odessa. They wrote leaflets and articles in longhand. They hadn't heard that typewriters had been invented.

Everything went swimmingly for nearly a year until the police cracked down and arrested about two hundred persons including Bronshtein. In a transit prison in Moscow in the summer of 1900 Bronshtein heard of Lenin for the first time and read his book. Then he set out for a four-year term of exile in the distant reaches of the Lena River, first at Ust-Kut and then at Verkholensk, where the winter temperature often fell to sixty below zero, there to stay, until he escaped in the summer of 1902, making his way via Zurich and Paris to London. There he knocked on the door of a Russian exile, living at 30 Holford Square under the name of Jacob Richter, very early one morning in October 1902.[5] Richter was still in bed. The door was opened by his wife, Nadezhda, who immediately led the visitor into the bedroom. Richter (the name Lenin was using at the time) exclaimed in great glee: "The Pero [the pen] has arrived!" Pero was the *klichka* Bronshtein had adopted for his revolutionary writings from Siberia. Later he was to become known as Leon Trotsky.[6]

On May 29, 1899, a notation was placed in the records of the Tiflis Theological Seminary concerning one of the students in the first division of the fifth class. It read:

"Iosif Djugashvili is dismissed from the Seminary for having missed his examinations for an unexplained reason."

In later years Djugashvili's pietistic and aged mother, who had made enormous sacrifices to place her son in the seminary, contended that he had left his studies at her insistence because a doctor feared he was coming down with tuberculosis because of overwork. Djugashvili himself liked to explain that he was expelled for political activities.

Perhaps there was some truth in each explanation. The Caucasus was no exception to the political whirlwinds swirling up in what was called the great Russian prison house of nations. While Tiflis was not as strongly affected by the industrial boom as nearby Baku and the great oil fields (largely being exploited by consortiums of British, Belgian, French, and German capital), it possessed a fervent Georgian nationalist movement and a nascent revolutionary underground.

Young Djugashvili had entered the Tiflis Seminary at the age of fifteen in 1894, matriculating from a background of grinding poverty. His father, a shoemaker, the traditional trade of drunkards, was dead (perhaps the victim of a drunken brawl), and it was only the iron determination of his mother which lifted him out of a lifetime of deprivation and poverty in the flinty mountain village of Gori.

Djugashvili was a good student and almost immediately made his mark as a poet of lyric and nationalistic emotion. His verses—"To the Moon," "To R. Eristavi" (a well-known Georgian nationalist), "Old Man Nininka"—appeared in the Georgian publications *Kvali* and *Iveria* over the signatures Soselo (Little Joe) and I. Dj-shvili. In the seminary he broadened his horizons through the "Cheap Library," a local lending institution which did a brisk business with students in works proscribed by seminary authorities. Month after month notations appeared in the seminary records: "It appears that Djugashvili has a ticket to the Cheap Library from which he borrows books. Today I confiscated Victor Hugo's *Toilers of the Sea* in which I found the said library ticket." The principal ordered him confined to a punishment cell, noting: "I have already warned him once about an unsanctioned book *Ninety-three* by Victor Hugo." In March 1897 he was sent to a punishment cell again, this time for reading Letourneau's *Literary Evolution of the Nations.* He read Gogol, Chekhov, the Russian satirist Saltykov-Shchedrin (whose *The Town of Gloops* was to be one of his favorites all his life), Hugo, Thackeray's *Vanity Fair*, Balzac, works of Darwin and, increasingly, economics and politics, possibly including the solitary copy of Marx's *Kapital* from which hand-copied transcripts circulated surreptitiously among young Tiflis radicals.

In his seminary years Djugashvili followed the inevitable path from romantic nationalist questings to more and more advanced political inquiry. He became a secret member of Messame Dassy (the Third Group), a radical Georgian political society, organized by Noah Jordaniya, N. S. Chkheidze, and I. G. Tsereteli, all names later to figure importantly on the national Russian scene.

Strikes began to sweep the Caucasus. There were risings of railroad workers in Tiflis. The expelled seminary student, now an employee of the Tiflis Observatory, helped to organize a May Day demonstration and spoke at it—his first public speech—in 1901. He helped to start an underground paper, *Brdzola* (The Struggle), and in his first contribution declared:

"Not only the working class has been groaning under the yoke of tsardom. Other social classes, too, are strangled in the grip of autocracy. Groaning is the hunger-swollen Russian peasantry . . . Groaning are the small towndwellers, petty employees . . . petty officials . . . Groaning are the oppressed nationalities and religions of Russia, among them the Poles and the Finns . . . Groaning are the unceasingly persecuted and humiliated Jews . . . Groaning are the Georgians, the Armenians and other nations . . . Groaning are the many millions of members of Russian religious sects."

Soon he moved to the oil boomtown of Batum on the Turkish frontier, assumed the underground *klichka* of "Koba," and launched an activist program. He had been under police surveillance for some time. Now the Okhrana agents put a confidential note in their files: "In Autumn, 1901, the Social Democratic Committee of Tiflis sent one of its members, Iosif Vissarionovich Djugashvili, to Batum for the purpose of carrying on propaganda among the factory workers. As a result of Djugashvili's activities . . . Social Democratic organizations began to spring up in all the factories of Batum. The results of the Social Democratic propaganda could already be seen in 1902 in the prolonged strike in the Rothschild factory and in street demonstrations."[7]

The openness and boldness of Koba's agitation stirred some concern on the part of his associates who felt (correctly, as it transpired) that it was bound to bring a police crackdown. The youthful organizer took some precautions. He moved to the Mukhmudia section of Batum, into the house of an old Moslem, Khashim Smyrba. He set up his illegal printing press there, and women, disguised in the classic long Moslem *chadra*, or black veil, smuggled the pamphlets out. But Khashim's neighbors grew suspicious. They thought he and Koba were printing counterfeit rubles and demanded a share. Koba quieted them by saying he was working to improve their lives and by tacitly agreeing to accept an offer by Khashim to provide him a beautiful wife if he became a Moslem.

These efforts did not throw off the police for long. On April 5, 1902, they moved in and arrested a prisoner whom they described as: "Height: 2 arshins 4½ vershoks [5 feet 4 inches]. Body: medium. Age: 23 [actually he was 22]. Second and third toes of the left foot fused. Appearance: ordinary. Hair: dark brown. Beard and mustache: brown. Nose straight and long. Forehead straight and low. Face long, swarthy and pockmarked." His police nickname was "Ryaboi," the pock-marked one. After considerable delay the prisoner was condemned to three years of exile in eastern Siberia. He began his journey to Novaya Uda, not far from Lake Baikal, in November 1903. Shortly after his arrival in Siberia he escaped and by February 1904 was back in Tiflis ready to take up his activity again. He was now a seasoned underground revolutionary. He regarded himself as a member of the Social Democratic party but thus far had not indicated whether his sympathies lay with the Bolshevik faction headed by Lenin or the Menshevik faction to which most of the Georgian Social Democrats inclined. In fact, he was probably little aware of these doctrinaire differences and it would be nearly ten years more before he was to adopt the party *klichka* which would distinguish him for the rest of his life and into the stream of history—Stalin.[8]

The stage was being set. The actors were taking their places— Lenin, Trotsky, Stalin, Chernov, Milyukov, Struve, the Dolgorukovs, the Morozovs, Witte, others. None yet knew their roles nor the order of scenes in which they would appear. Few had met each other. But Russia's temperature was rising. The smell of revolution was in the air. Milyukov observed in 1904 that "nearly all of the Russian young people who have passed through the schools of Dmitri Tolstoy (that eminently reactionary minister) are socialistic. All the exertions of the school authorities, with all their system of minute police supervision and their teaching of politically indifferent subjects, has availed nothing. . . . Particularly during the last few years (since 1899) the revolution is, as it were, insistent within the walls of our universities and academies."[9] Yet never had the police been so active. Never had more persons been sent into exile. The total of political exiles under police surveillance in 1880 had been a mere 2,873. In the spring of 1901 alone some 16,000 were exiled from Petersburg and in the two years of Interior Minister D. S. Sipyagin's tenure the total was estimated at 60,000.[10]

But of what avail?

A typical warning was sounded at Saratov in 1903 by a provincial lawyer named Volkenshtein who was defending a group which had participated in a mass demonstration:

"Gentlemen of the jury, you have just been told that your sentence will put an end to the demonstrations; that demonstrations disturb general tranquillity and unsettle people's well-being. Well, I assert the contrary! Apart from the demonstrations you will find no tranquillity in Russian society. The fermentation is spread everywhere. The people here accused are guilty only of having spoken aloud what is said in a thousand ways everywhere. Through the impermeable muteness of our life, through all its pores, oozes criticism of the regime. A criticism of the existing order bursts forth roaring and whistling through every crack and gap. That is what these men have seen and heard.

"And therefore they hoisted their red banner. You may convict them. But then you must realize that together with them tens, nay hundreds of thousands of Russian citizens are being judged."[11]

What, in these times, was Czar Nicholas doing? He was, as he noted in his diary, "gathering my strength." To what end? To Imperial ends. To the ends of glory, of grandeur. Bemused by the tantalizing flattery of "Cousin Willy" and by his own fantasies of empire, he was moving closer and closer to disaster in the Far East. With the dismissal of Witte he had taken Far Eastern affairs into his own hands, eagerly advised by the adventurer Bezobrazov. Tensions between Japan and Russia were growing rapidly. All during the summer and autumn of 1903 the anxieties of the Czar's more responsible Ministers, War Minister Kuropatkin and Count Lamsdorf in the Foreign Office, rose.

They could see war coming but there was almost nothing they could do to prevent it. For the fact was the Czar himself and his less than competent uncle (a natural son of Alexander II), Adm. Yevgeny I. Alexeyev, viceroy of the Far East, were itching to try their luck against the Japanese.[12] The Japanese ambassador sought in vain for meaningful discussions with Nicholas. To Ambassador Kurino's pleas for a personal audience there came the lordly response that His Imperial Majesty was otherwise occupied. At the traditional New Year's reception for diplomats, January 1, 1904, the Czar took occasion to remind one and all of Russia's great power and warned against presuming on her patience and good will. Meanwhile nothing disturbed the benign calm of his diary entries:

January 1   Got up early. Left my beloved Alix at midday and went to the city. . . .

January 2   Much snow fell and it began to thaw. . . .

January 4   Sunday. It was a clear pleasant day. . . . Read a lot. Uncle Vladimir took tea with me. . . .

January 7   Again thawing. I held a big reception. . . .

January 11   Remarkable weather and a wonderful day. The hunt was very successful; in all we took 879 birds. I shot 115, 21 partridges, 91 pheasants, a rabbit and two hare. . . .

January 14 . . . Put on my Prussian uniform and went with Alix and Misha to lunch at the German Embassy to mark Wilhelm's birthday. At 3 o'clock received two Kalmyks, Officer Ulyanov and Lama Ulyanov who are going to Tibet. . . .[13]

January 17 . . . After lunch received again Rikhter and Engineer Yugovich, designers of the Manchurian railroad. Walked in the garden. Frosty . . .

January 18   Hunted pheasants. Very successful. In all we killed 489. I shot 96, 81 pheasants and 14 partridge and a hare. . . .

January 21   Walked for only half an hour. After tea Lamsdorf came in about the Japanese agreement. The two [that is, Alix and he] of us dined together. Went to the theater. It was *Sleeping Beauty*. Outstanding. I hadn't seen it for a long time. . . .

January 23   Very successful spectacle at the Hermitage. They gave the prologue and fourth act of *Mephistopheles*. Medeya, Chaliapin and Sobinov sang. . . .

January 24 Saturday. Colder today and the temperature fell to 13 degrees. After lunch went to an exhibit of water colors. Went to the theater. They put on a very interesting *Retour de Jérusalem*. This evening received word of the end of conversations with Japan and the departure of the Japanese ambassador!

January 25 Sunday. Day was raw and snow fell. . . . Walked in the garden a whole hour. At 5 took tea at Anichkov. Nothing new from the Far East.

January 26 Monday. This morning had a meeting on the Japanese question. We decided not to start anything. . . . All day I was in an excited mood. At 8 P.M. went to the theater. Saw *Rusalka*. Very good. Returned home to receive from Adm. E. N. Alexeyev a telegram with the news that this night Japanese destroyers carried out an attack on the *Tsarevich, Retvizan* and *Pallada* standing in the open roadstead and inflicted damage. It is war without declaration. God be with us![14]

The dress rehearsal was at hand.

XI

"A Small Victorious War"

The thirtieth of January 1904 dawned cold and raw. That is, it was a
fairly ordinary winter day in St. Petersburg—skies gray and overcast,
the temperature well below freezing, a skudding wind off the frozen
Gulf of Finland, and occasional flurries of snow. It was a morning to
suit the mood of Nicholas II. This was the fourth day of war with
Japan and there had been nothing but bad news from the Far East.
Petersburg was filled with rumors that the Japanese fleet had been
sunk, but Nicholas, alas, knew that none was true. The latest dispatch
from his viceroy, Alexeyev, contained more bad news. The Russian
transport *Yenisei* had been sunk by a Japanese mine with the loss of
its commander and nearly one hundred officers and men. The Czar
had risen early with a heavy heart, and not even the sight of his beloved wife (she had now missed her second period and there was no
doubt that she was again pregnant) and children had lifted his mood.
About midmorning there was a disturbance—noise and shouting in
the square in front of the Winter Palace. It took a little time for the
Czar to realize what was going on—an enormous crowd of students
had issued from St. Petersburg University across the Neva River and,
carrying flags and banners, had paraded over the Nikolayevsky Bridge
and thronged into the square. Now, standing outside the palace, they
were singing "God Save the Czar" and "Holy Russia." The hymns
were interspersed with resounding cheers: "Hail to the Russian Army
and Fleet," "Long Live Russia," "Hail to the Czar." The vigor of the
cheers echoed back and forth from the heavy façade of the Winter

Palace to the grandiose escarpment of the General Staff Building. Gathering up the Czarina and the Imperial children, the Czar went to the Bely Zal, the White Hall, which was the state dining room and fronted on the square. The servants threw back the heavy windows and he and his family stepped out. The cheers sounded louder as they took the crowd's salute. Finally he retired and sent the palace commandant to thank the students. The crowd then swept out of the palace square and, picking up recruits, marched down Nevsky Prospekt, now filled curb to curb, to the Anichkov Palace. There beside the famous Klodt horses the throng halted and again the national hymns were sung, cheers rang out for the Czar and his armed forces. By this time it was not just students. As one observer noted: "Everyone was mixed together—generals and tramps marched side-by-side, students with banners and ladies, their arms filled with shopping. Everyone was united in one general feeling. Everyone sang."[1]

It was true. Seldom, at least in modern times, had Russia been so caught up in a single emotion. The official newspaper, *Pravitelstvenny Vestnik*, spoke of the "unity and desire for sacrifice" of the whole Russian people, of their support for "our beloved Monarch." Nor was this mere officialese. Observers agreed that "never before had the Russian people in all its raw mass shown so clearly its love for the Czar and the Fatherland." The outpouring of feeling exceeded that of any recent war—the Crimean War, the Balkan encounters, the Turkish War.[2] And what struck everyone was the manner in which the upper levels of the population, the intelligentsia, precisely those circles which had been most alienated, most influenced by revolutionary agitation, had thrown their support behind the Czar with an enthusiasm which had to be seen to be believed. It was not just the manifestation of January 30—thrilling as that was—it was the demonstrations in the days that followed, new gatherings of people who swept up to the Winter Palace to dramatize their solidarity, their love, their patriotism, and their dedication. The rallies spread over the whole country— to Moscow, Kharkov, Odessa, Kiev, Kazan, and, of course, all along the line of the Siberian Railroad. Military units were smothered with affection. The arrival and departure of commanders and regiments attracted such crowds that trains could hardly pull through the stations. There was deep emotion about the losses of Russian warships—attributed universally to the treachery of the Japanese in attacking without declaration of war, and although some cautioned that because of the distance of the theater of war from Russia's center it would take time to redress the balance, there was confidence that Russian arms would quickly triumph. In the swelling chorus of national patriotism there could be detected not a few symptoms of racial chauvinism, and the pictures and sketches of the Japanese as published in the popular press did much to feed primitive emotions. Millions of rubles were contributed to the Red Cross and defense funds. Count Orlov-Davydov gave a million rubles. The Saratov noblemen gave 250,000. The St. Petersburg merchants gave half a million.[3] The Moscow Zemstvo contributed 300,000 rubles to the fleet. A. F. Marks, publisher of *Niva*, contributed 41,236 volumes of Gogol, Chekhov, Leskov, Lermontov, Zhukovsky, Danilevsky, Bobrakin, and others for hospital libraries. Soap manufacturer O. T. Arkhipov gave 10,000 bars of soap. There were many more volunteers for service than the Army could accommodate. The new Hermitage was turned over as a collecting point for supplies for the sick and wounded troops in the Far East.[4] Even Leo Tolstoy with his deep pacifist and nonviolent convictions was moved by the national mood. On four separate days he rode horseback from his Yasnaya Polyana estate to Tula for the latest news.[5] All in all there was no doubt that the country was united—united behind the sovereign and the Russian cause in a fashion that reminded some of the way Russia had rallied against Napoleon's invasion, and in this magnificent sweep revolutionary unrest, the activities of the underground terrorists, the deep rumblings from the hard-pressed peasantry and the half-starved proletariat—all this was drowned in a flood tide of popular emotion. There had been nothing like it in the ten years of Nicholas' reign. Nor would there be anything like it in the years which lay ahead. To be sure Nicholas did not understand this. He had little comprehension of the genuine feeling of the country and, in his diary, made plain not only his deep disappointment at the disaster the fleet had suffered but his fears over the public reaction to the debacle. Some measure of his despondency was reflected in a note from his wife begging forgiveness for any hurt she might have done him and adding the hope that taking communion together "may give you strength and energy for your heavy task God has laid on you." She prayed, she said, "with heart and soul for you and our beloved [*sic!*] Country in confidence that God and our dear Friend* will help us."[6]

But if Nicholas had little inkling of the country's mood, neither did the revolutionaries, especially Lenin, far away in Geneva, so totally preoccupied with the complicated and emotionally exhausting quarrels among the factions of the Social Democratic party that he hardly noticed the start of the war. Lenin was not alone in this preoccupation with sectarian struggle. All his associates in the Social Democratic

---

* The "dear Friend" here referred to was "Doctor Philippe" of Paris, a pseudo-scientist introduced to the Czar and Czarina by the two Montenegrin Grand Duchesses, daughters of King Nicholas of Montenegro, who were married to Grand Dukes Nicholas and Peter. Later on the "dear Friend" of the Czarina's notes would be Rasputin.

ranks, both Bolsheviks and Mensheviks, were possessed by it—
Plekhanov, Martov, Axelrod, Vera Zasulich. It was a struggle which
was to determine the fate and future of both the Social Democrats
and Lenin. The principal issue concealed under endless verbiage,
debate, vitriolic polemics, was a simple one: Would the Party be organized as Lenin insisted, along highly centralized, almost military
lines with authority held at the top and strict discipline prevailing
within the ranks of a small group of men and women dedicating themselves to full-time revolutionary tasks? Or would it present itself as
Plekhanov, Martov, Axelrod, and the others advocated as a party of
more general adherence, inviting any supporter to join whether or not
he was a full-time revolutionary and preserving a relatively democratic system of debate and resolution of issues by the Party membership as a whole? Superimposed upon this issue—which had split the
Party at its London 1903 Congress into Bolshevik (majority) and
Menshevik (minority) factions—was another question not yet entirely
clear to all but already making its outline visible. This was the question of Lenin's *personal* leadership of the movement and the extraordinary determination, stubbornness, and tactical skill which he was
prepared to invest in order to create an organization of the kind he
wished and which he would head.

The struggle went on throughout the year of 1904, and so intensely
did it absorb Lenin that he showed little comprehension of the
significance of what was happening in Russia. If one examines his literary output—speeches, letters, pamphlets, editorials—for 1904, one
finds hardly a mention of the war or its dramatic effects within Russia.[7] In part this was due, as he himself conceded, to "isolation from
Russia, the engulfing atmosphere of the accursed émigré slough
[which] weighs so heavily on one."[8] In part, it was something else
—a characteristic of his personality. He threw himself into a controversy, a cause, or an endeavor with fanatical energy—what Krupskaya
called "a rage." It totally preoccupied him, drained him of physical energy, blinded him to any other aim than the one in which he was engaged. Then, when the "rage" had passed, a "psychological reaction set
in; dullness, loss of strength and fatigue."[9] He was unable to eat or
sleep, his face turned sallow, his eyes dulled. In a word, he fell into severe depression. So it was now. The quarrel with his comrades left
Lenin in a state of nervous collapse, almost of breakdown.[10] Anatoly
Lunacharsky recalled that never before nor after had he seen Lenin in
such spiritual torpor.[11] Lenin told Panteleimon N. Lepeshinsky that he
was ready to "throw everything over and go to the mountains." He
spent weeks in the late spring and summer of 1904 tramping the Swiss
alps with Krupskaya. "We chose the loneliest trails that led into the

wilds, away from any people," she recalled. "A month of this restored
Vladimir Ilyich's nerves to normal. It was as if he had bathed in a
mountain stream and washed off all the cobwebs of sordid intrigue."[12]

In these times was being fixed one of the most important of Lenin's
traits: his manic preoccupation with controversy, his insistence upon
the rightness and superiority of his own view, and an extremism of
language and tactics which already was shaking some of the older revolutionaries like Vera Zasulich. In controversy there seemed no epithet
too crude to use against his opponent, no language too bitter, too insulting. "Whether those who took part in these debates wished or not
every argument on party matters began and ended with the question
of Lenin," observed Valentinov, who was very close to him in this
time.[13] Lenin's opponents were called "cretins," "semi-idiots," or "riffraff."

Lenin's failure to concern himself with the Russo-Japanese War was
by no means something unique. Trotsky, as he later recalled, "spent
the whole year of 1904 arguing with the leading group of Mensheviks
on questions of policy and organization" and wound up abandoning all
Party affiliations for the time being.[14] Nor does Stalin, just back in the
Caucasus from Siberian exile, seem to have conducted himself in
different fashion. His published record is devoid of concern with or
perception of the implications of the war for the revolutionary cause.[15]

In the first days after the Japanese attack the Nicholas regime had
reached its apogee. Never again would it be so popular, never again
would the enthusiasm of the people be so genuine, their love for the
Czar so open and frank, never again would Russia stand as one person, united behind its ruler in a common national cause.[16] In late January 1904 and the opening of February it really seemed that war with
Japan would bring the country together and open the way to the resolution of the grave problems which divided it so. It was in these times
that Plehve, the one Minister of the Czar who had strongly supported
an aggressive policy toward Japan, said to General Kuropatkin (who
had strongly opposed this policy): "Alexei Nikolayevich, you do not
know the internal situation of Russia. In order to hold back the Revolution we need a small victorious war."[17] A small victorious war. Who
could doubt that the great Russian empire would crush the impudent
yellow upstarts of the East?

Plehve was the only cabinet Minister who had favored the war, War
Minister Kuropatkin and Foreign Minister Lamsdorf being opposed.
Some others favored it, notably Admiral Alexeyev, the Czar's Far
Eastern viceroy and commander in the Pacific, the Grand Dukes
Sergei (governor-general of Moscow) and Alexei (the Czar's cousin)

plus the congerie of dissolute adventurers like the notorious Bezobra-zov. At least one of the Czar's Ministers described Nicholas as being "hypnotized" by Bezobrazov.[18] Whether this was literally true it struck a foreboding note. The question of the "hypnosis" of the Czar was to arise in much more critical terms a few years into the future. The Czarina favored a strong hand in the Far East. She saw there a theater not only of Imperial victories for her beloved husband but a pano-ramic vision of an empire almost without limits. Then, too, Kaiser Wilhelm II for months had been writing his "beloved cousin, Nicky," trying to increase the Emperor's ardor for the Japanese adventure, plying him with tales of British perfidy and plotting. In the weeks just before the Japanese attack he had taken to addressing his cousin as "Admiral of the Pacific Ocean." He signed himself, "Admiral of the Atlantic Ocean." He dropped these designations by mid-April 1904. Such ebullience no longer seemed apropos.[19]

The mood of military adventure was hardly shared by the country. In the weeks leading up to outbreak of war, War Minister Kuropatkin spoke with the Grand Duchess Xeniya Alexandrovna (sister of the Czar) in early December. She insisted to him that "there will be no war, that her brother wanted no war, that there was no need to fight Japan and that Russia did not need Korea." Kuropatkin reminded her that the matter might not be in Russian hands, that the Czar might say "I want no war" and be told "It's too late. Now, we want war." The Grand Duchess Yelizaveta Fyodorovna, sister of the Czarina and wife of Grand Duke Sergei, told Kuropatkin that the mood of Moscow was: "We don't want war. We don't understand the aims of a war and we will not be aroused." A couple of nights later Kuropatkin was told by Alexander Petrovich, Prince of Oldenburg, that war must not be permitted, that there was growing public dissatisfaction, and that the question of war "might become a dynastic one"—a hint that the reign of Nicholas might not survive the crisis. Oldenburg described the Caucasus and Tiflis as being on the verge of rebellion and said that dissatisfaction with Prince Golitsyn, the governor-general, was so high that the Georgians and Armenians were joining hands against the Rus-sians.[20] Early in January Grand Duke Alexander lunched with the Czar and asked about the Japanese situation. "There is no question of war," the Czar said. "There will be no war with Japan nor with any-one else."

"I wish it were true," the Grand Duke recalled replying.

"It is true," the Czar insisted.[21]

There was a grand ball at the Winter Palace on January 19. Count-ess Benkendorf, wife of the Russian ambassador to London, asked the Czar at dinner: "Your Highness, will there be war with Japan? I ask not from curiosity but as a mother. My son is at Port Arthur." The Czar responded: "There will be no war. I don't want it and I'm doing all that I can to see that there is no war."[22] A few days earlier Kuropatkin had a report on conditions in Port Arthur that convinced him Russia must avoid war if possible. Admiral Alexeyev had permitted the fleet to fall into disarray, repairs were not being made, maneuvers had been canceled to avoid wear and tear, supplies were insufficient, commanders incompetent. Kuropatkin recommended on January 15, 1904, that if war was inescapable it be delayed for a minimum of sixteen months while the unfinished Trans-Siberian rail link around Lake Baikal was completed and the Chinese Eastern Railroad strengthened so as to ease the supply of the Russian Far Eastern forces. At a minimum he urged a delay of four months. Foreign Minister Lamsdorf, however, by now, was impatient with Kuropatkin, insisting that "each hour is dear."

The meeting left Kuropatkin with an uneasy impression. The fact was that Russia, partly of its ruler's volition and partly through inertia, was sliding into war. It was ten days before another general discussion was held. By this time the Japanese ambassador had announced he was quitting Moscow and breaking off talks, a certain sign that conflict must be near. Now for the first time Nicholas displayed concern over the possibility of war. Instead of his usual expression of confidence that there would be no war, he said with some irritation: "War is war and peace is peace but this uncertainty is agonizing." Lamsdorf thought war almost certain. Both he and Prince Obolensky suggested that it might well begin without a Japanese declaration. Still, nothing definite was done and the next day another meeting was held at which the possibility of an attack on Japan by the Russian fleet was discussed but rejected because of lack of confidence in the viceroy's ability to direct the armed forces.[23]

So it was that the empire slithered into war, half-willing, half-unwilling, her ruler wanting, yet not wanting, the conflict, her leaders divided, incompetent commanders in charge of key posts with no clear understanding of the nature of the enemy nor what should be the goal of national policy. It was typical that the first word of the Japanese attack came not from the Czar's viceroy but from a commercial agent in St. Petersburg.[24] First word was that the dreadnoughts *Retvizan* and *Tsarevich* and the cruiser *Pallada* had been sunk. It turned out later that they were not sunk but they might as well have been for they were so badly damaged they were effectively out of action. They had been standing at anchor without protective antitorpedo nets. The commander of the *Tsarevich* was not even aboard his ship—he was ashore attending a name day party for the admiral.[25] On the second day of war the Japanese badly damaged the *Askold,* the *Novik,* and two more Russian ships. On the following day the *Yenisei* was lost. So was the *Koreyets* and the *Varyag.* So it went. Bad and then worse. The story has a familiar ring. Thirty-seven years later the Japanese carried out an attack on Pearl Harbor which duplicated, almost measure for measure, the assault at Port Arthur. But this lay in the future. In the winter of 1904 all the Czar and his Government knew was that, regardless of the enthusiastic solidarity of the Russian people, there could not have been blacker news. When, twelve days after the start of war, War Minister Kuropatkin was named commander of land forces in the Far East, he asked Witte for advice on what to do. Witte told him:

"Admiral Alexeyev, the Commander-in-Chief, is now in Mukden. You, of course, will go straight to Mukden. Here is what I would do in your place: Arriving in Mukden I would send a detachment of officers to Alexeyev and arrest the Commander-in-Chief. In view of the prestige you have among the troops there would be no reaction to this. Then I would send Alexeyev by the train on which you arrived back to St. Petersburg under arrest and at the same time telegraph the Czar as follows: Your Highness for the successful fulfilment of that great cause which you have entrusted to me I count it necessary on arriving at the front first of all to arrest the Commander-in-Chief and send him to Petersburg since without this condition the successful prosecution of the war is unthinkable." Kuropatkin thought Witte was joking.

"I said, Alexei Nikolayevich, I am not joking," Witte recalled.[26]

It was, indeed, no joke. The viceroy was not arrested and unfortunately the dispatch of the honest but hardly brilliant Kuropatkin to the East did not change the course of events. The bad news of February was followed by the worse news of March—the sinking of the pride of the fleet, the armor-clad *Petropavlovsk,* with Admiral Makarov, hero of the Turkish War and as able a naval officer as Russia possessed, and almost all hands, including the famous battle painter Vassily V. Vereshchagin, who chanced to be aboard.[27] Nor did the news improve. In May the Japanese defeated the Russians on the Yalu and the siege of Port Arthur quickly followed. On the day the Czar got the news of the tightening of the noose around Port Arthur he noted in his diary that he had taken a walk, shot a crow, and paddled a bit in his canoe at Tsarskoye Selo. He was very fond of canoeing.[28]

XII

Not a Good Summer

A small victorious war . . . Plehve was thinking, of course, of the social and economic contradictions which wracked Russia, defying resolution and almost defying description. These were not abstractions—
they were Russian life, the reality of Russian life as experienced every
day in the cities and in the countryside.

It was not something concealed and mysterious. It was everywhere.
In August 1902 Maxim Gorky completed his play *Na Dne* (The
Lower Depths)[1] and turned it over for production by the Moscow Art
Theater. Gorky set his play in the slums of Nizhni Novgorod, in a
trushchoba, the lowest kind of den. Konstantin Stanislavsky and Nemirovich-Danchenko, eager to give the play a realistic setting, approached their friend V. A. Gilyarovsky, a writer for the Moscow
boulevard papers whose "speciality" was Khitrovka, a sprawling maze
of buildings huddled near the putrid Yauza River, a small tributary of
the Moskva in the heart of town. The Khitrovka market was notorious.
Here the most dangerous criminals gathered, here murderers plied
their craft, men traded their last shirt for a gulp of vodka, and eleven-
year-old girls were sold outright for fifty rubles or rented for half a
ruble a night. Here child beggars were hired out to work, sometimes
with dead babies wrapped in rags to whet public sympathy. Nursing
babies rented to female beggars for twenty-five kopecks a day and
three-year-olds at ten kopecks. At the age of five—if they survived—
the children went out to beg for themselves. Mothers of the infants—
usually prostitutes who were selling their bodies for the benefit of

their "cats," or pimps—sold their children at auction to professional beggars, who often were horribly mutilated men and women with pus-oozing sores and stumps of legs and arms. Ten-year-old prostitutes, graduating from street begging, were no rarity. One night Gilyarovsky watched a drunken thirteen-year-old girl with short-cut brown hair, a child's face, and red swollen eyes. She was too drunk to sit upright. Only blurred sounds issued from her small mouth. Her cat, a dandy in a fine Russian jacket, sold her for a ruble to a brawny man who picked her up and carried her out into the night on his shoulder. The women of Khitrovka were called *tyetki* (frumps). It took three to six months to turn a young girl into a *tetok*. The fate of all was the same—death in prison, in a hospital, or on the dirty floor of one of the *traktiri* (taverns). There were four principal buildings in Khitrovka—the Bunin, the Rumyantsev, the Stepanov or Yaroshenko, and the Romeiko—each named for its putative owner. The Rumyantsev housed two dens, the Peresylny (Transit) and the Sibir. The Katorga (Hard Labor) was in the Yaroshenko. Each had its own character. The Peresylny catered to the homeless, the poor, the prostitutes; the Sibir to robbers, pickpockets, horse thieves; the Katorga to highwaymen, convicts on the run, and escaped prisoners from Siberia. The police seldom entered these establishments. Never on any condition had they been known to enter a group of houses known as the Kulakovka, which ran from Khitrov Square to Svininsky Pereulok. Here were located two of the lowest dens, one called the Utyug (Flatiron) and the other the Dry Gulch. When the Katorga finally closed its doors, drinking went on for the rest of the night at the Flatiron. Tailors and seamstresses inhabited the Bunin house. Thieves brought them stolen fur coats and rich gowns. Within hours these had been cut and refashioned into hats, jackets, and muffs and put on sale in the market on the square.

Khitrovka was known as the foggiest place in Moscow. It was situated on low land, surrounded by old stone houses, paint peeling off, with peddlers and beggars huddled in rows on the pavement, cooking slumgullion in iron pots, frying sausage on charcoal fires, and boiling up messes which they called "dog's happiness." The smell of urine, manure, roasting mutton, frying onions, steaming horses, filled the air.[2] Tens of thousands of human souls lived around this square, paying five kopecks a night for a place to sprawl on a wooden shelf. Thousands of unemployed peasants and laborers gathered there each day, waiting for the labor brokers and shop bosses to pick them for manual work. If they were not hired by afternoon, they would sell a shirt or their shoes for a bite to eat and another night's lodging. At night the place rang with drunken shouts and cries for help. But no one answered.

Khitrovka was the worst slum in Moscow, possibly the worst in Russia. But it was not unusual. There were others in Moscow, particularly around two markets, the Sukharevka and the Smolenskaya. Sukharevka was called the "daughter of war" for it had sprung up after Moscow was burned in the War of 1812 and Smolenskaya the "son of cholera" for it came into being after the terrible Moscow cholera epidemic of 1771–72. Of course, the Haymarket slum of St. Petersburg (the scene of Dostoyevsky's *Crime and Punishment*) was the equal of any of these, and the "lower depths" of Nizhni Novgorod was similar except a bit smaller.

Then there was the Yama, the Pit, Moscow's famous red-light district, the two or three blocks of shabby, two-storied houses, most of them in pseudo-Russian style, with elaborate lace curtains and wood carving over windows and doors, the main streets of the Yamskaya Sloboda, once the settlement of coachmen and hostlers, of stables and taverns, now exclusively devoted to prostitution. There were two streets in the Yama, Bolshaya Yamskaya and Malaya Yamskaya. The best houses where a visitor was charged three rubles for a visit and ten rubles for the night were on Bolshaya Yamskaya. Here, too, were the second-class houses where a customer paid a ruble a visit. Malaya Yamskaya housed the dregs, the decrepit, dirty houses where a customer paid fifty kopecks or even less; where robbery was frequent and murder hardly uncommon. The number of prostitutes quartered in the Yama was estimated at five hundred. Each house was Government-licensed, each woman was Government-approved, each held the official yellow ticket, permitting her to ply her trade.[3]

Nemirovich-Danchenko wanted V. A. Simov, who was designing the sets for *The Lower Depths,* to see Khitrovka in order to reproduce as faithfully as possible every horror of Russian life. And he wanted his actors to see for themselves the real men and women who were the prototypes of Gorky's characters. For their benefit Gilyarovsky took them to the Stepanov house. The Katorga was on the lower floor. On the second floor of one wing at No. 6 was located a very large loft divided in the center by a rough wooden partition. Half of the room was occupied by beggars and the other by copyists. They copied plays at the rate of thirty-five kopecks an act. It often took all day to copy the parts for one act. The copyists usually earned no more than twenty kopecks a day, although if an act was very short they might make as much as forty. But, of course, there was not always a play to copy. Often they sat on their wooden platforms all day waiting for work that did not come. Sometimes they sat for two days or three. They dared not leave for fear work might suddenly arrive. If no work came, they sold their shirts for vodka or bread. Often Gilyarovsky found two or three copyists stark naked. Often they were too drunk to copy the plays. They had sold everything they had. How long they survived was a matter of chance.

It was to this place that Gilyarovsky led the Art Theater Group. The copyists—six of them—sat half-clothed and barefoot, waiting for work which had been promised that evening. A flickering oil lamp burned on the table. Gilyarovsky tossed down five rubles, and some bottles of Smirnov vodka, well watered by the thieving proprietor, appeared. Simov began to sketch. Suddenly Gilyarovsky noticed Vanka, the Horse, one of the thieves, moving up behind Simov, bottle in hand. There was a tense moment. Just as Vanka was about to crash the bottle on the artist's head the chief copyist, the Baron, grabbed Vanka's arm and danger was averted. But the actors quickly left before even more serious trouble erupted.[4]

This was the reality of Russia's Lower Depths. This was the foundation on which the glitter and grandeur of the empire rested. Presented on the stage of the Art Theater, Gorky's play created a sensation. There were nineteen calls for the author on opening night.[5] The Art Theater played *The Lower Depths* for fifty consecutive nights in St. Petersburg, something which had never happened before. Everyone went. The Czar quite accurately declared that the play had a "harmful state significance" and Plehve characterized Gorky "a dangerous man, leader of a party of revolutionary malcontents."[6] Accordingly, the police then banned the play in the provinces. Perhaps no one would notice.

No one would notice. If only no one would notice . . . divert public attention. That, of course, was the theory of the small victorious war. It was the theory of the pogrom, as well. One night two dragoons got into a row in the Yama. Claimed they had been shortchanged, that one of the girls had picked their pockets. The usual thing. Except that this was not. They went back to their barracks, roused some of their comrades, and returned to the Yama. Before the night was over hundreds of soldiers had pillaged the quarter, gutting the houses, beating the girls, the madams, the pimps. Fire broke out. The disorder spread through Moscow, but as it spread it took another form. Now the victims were Jews, beaten on the streets, Jewish shops, smashed and robbed. The cry *"Bei zhidov"* echoed in the city. It became a pogrom.

How did the pogroms start? There was really no mystery about them. They were carried out at the instigation and with the official but secret collaboration of the Czar's authorities. Nicholas, to be sure, was anti-Semitic. He openly expressed complete contempt for and distrust in Jews to his War Minister, Kuropatkin.[7] But this was not unusual. His father, Alexander III, had asked Witte with considerable curiosity when Witte first entered his service: "Is it true that you favor the Jews?" Witte put his reply in the form of a question. Could the Czar drown all the Jews in the Black Sea? If so, then he, Witte, would fully understand such a decision. But if he could not drown them all, then the only solution was to make it possible for the Jews to exist and to eliminate all the discriminatory laws. Jews must be given equality. Witte's view was not widely shared. The Grand Duke Sergei Alexandrovich, governor-general of Moscow, and his police chief, Gen. Dmitri F. Trepov, were among the leading anti-Semites in the empire. They carried out policies which were consistently harsh and repressive. They hated Jews on religious grounds and saw in them the chief source of revolutionary agitation. This policy, in Witte's opinion, effectively revolutionized a whole generation of young Jews who had previously been among the mildest, meekest inhabitants of the Czar's realm. "By their policies," Witte observed, "they transformed Moscow into a fully revolutionary state—Moscow, the heart of Russia, the citadel of the Russian state. The Grand Duke Sergei and Trepov, in essence, revolutionized Moscow."[8]

The policy of pogrom got its real start under Count Nikolai P. Ignatyev and was continued by Gen. Pyotr N. Durnovo, but in Witte's not unprejudiced opinion (he hated Plehve) it was carried to a peak under Plehve. Plehve himself was not anti-Semitic by conviction but knew that his policy pleased Grand Duke Sergei Alexandrovich and, more importantly, the Czar himself.[9]

This policy led to Kishinev. The very name of the city is still, three quarters of a century later, synonymous with pogrom. The horror occurred April 6, 7, 8, 1903. The cry of *"Bei zhidov"* shrilled through the ghetto. More than fifty Jews (and a few others) were killed and hundreds wounded. No fewer than thirteen hundred shops, houses, and flats were sacked. When the terror was over, the city looked as though it had been ravaged by civil war—as, indeed, it had been. The massacre of Kishinev resounded around the world. Anger and revulsion were intense in London, Berlin, Paris, and, particularly, in New York. The Government, somewhat embarrassed, sought to absolve itself of responsibility. It put the blame on local antagonisms which had gotten beyond control. But the truth was quite different. Count Musin-Pushkin, commander of the Odessa Military District, carried out a personal investigation of the slaughter. He satisfied himself that no pogrom would have occurred or could have occurred had the local authorities called upon the military garrison to intervene—as was their duty. They made no call and the troops stayed in their barracks. It was Pushkin's opinion that the pogrom had been carried out with the toleration if not the actual permission of Plehve.[10]

Plehve had a plain and simple rationale for the pogrom. Not only did it take the minds of the masses off the ills of the Government and focus attention on another target but it was directed against what he perceived as the most revolutionary element in Russian society—the Jews. The pogrom, by his definition, was an antirevolutionary counter-measure. When world opinion became more and more aroused, Plehve met with leading Jews in Paris (and also with rabbis in Russia). He told them bluntly: "If you will put a stop to the revolution I will end the pogroms." To which the Jews replied that they could not change the revolutionary mood of the young so long as the Government contin-ued its harsh measures of discrimination.

Searching as he was to produce some psychological change in the mood of the masses, Plehve backed the war with Japan and backed the pogrom against the Jews. With the first signs that the war was going badly he automatically, almost instinctively, intensified the po-groms.

A small victorious war . . . *Bei zhidov* . . . There was a third strand to the Government's policy, and as early as the summer of 1903 Witte had warned Plehve that this third strand would lead not only to catas-trophe but to Plehve's own assassination. The policy which provoked Witte's warning was a scheme set in motion by the Czar's secret police to create an organization of workers, ostensibly independent but actu-ally stage-managed by the police. The authors of this scheme were a reactionary publicist named Lev Tikhomirov and a police officer, Ser-gei V. Zubatov. The scheme was taken up by Interior Minister D. S. Sipyagin and after his assassination was carried forward by Plehve. The first organizations were set up among machine-shop workers and textile workers in Moscow, where the project was strongly supported by Grand Duke Sergei Alexandrovich and Police Chief Trepov. The police officers, analyzing the goals of the revolutionary parties, had concluded that they had three chief targets: the capitalists, the bour-geoisie, and the Government. They conceived the notion that if the workers' antagonism could be directed against the capitalists and the bourgeoisie, pressure on the Government would disappear.

The police unions rapidly acquired strength. In 1902 they brought about a large strike in Moscow which centered around a silk factory which had been established in the 1870s by a Frenchman named U. P. Goujon.[11] Goujon refused the workers' demands for more pay and to his

astonishment was confronted with pressure from Police Chief Trepov
to yield to the strikers. Goujon appealed to the Moscow Manufac-
turers Association which complained to the Finance Minister, Witte.
In the ensuing row Zubatov was removed from his post and exiled to
Vladimir.[12] The police unions suffered a setback,[13] but they played an
important role in a series of strikes in southern Russia in 1903, and
Plehve's confidence in the Zubatov movement remained unshaken. He
believed in Zubatov personally (Zubatov was credited with saving
Plehve's life three times in attempted assassinations), and the Zubatov
unions in St. Petersburg, headed by a priest named Father Georgi
Apollonovich Gapon, a student at the St. Petersburg Seminary and
later chaplain at the Kresty Prison, were not dissolved but permitted
to grow and, during 1904, rapidly acquired influence and membership
in the St. Petersburg factories.[14]

Gapon had headed the so-called Society of Russian Factory and
Plant Workers from its founding in October 1903. He was encouraged
to launch the organization by the secret police and maintained a close
connection with them, although his own early associates had no political tendencies and no links with Zubatov. In 1904 he began to display
some independence from the police. He set up "halls" in various parts
of St. Petersburg. There were monthly dues, insurance and vacation
plans, self-help projects. In some halls lending libraries were established and, in the evenings, they held occasional dances and musi-
cals to which members brought their wives. Workers who had come
under the influence of revolutionaries—the Social Democrats or Socialist Revolutionaries—were chary of Gapon's society, but, little by
little, he won the confidence of some workers and also gathered a small
group extremely devoted to him. By the end of 1904 there were,
according to one estimate, about eighty members who were so committed to Gapon they were willing to follow him "through fire and water."
As 1904 wore on there was more and more talk of society meetings
about the needs and interests of the people and there began to be discussion of political action but only a little and even that very carefully
expressed. Police were present at all meetings, usually in plain clothes,
but their presence was well known. Their attitude was ambivalent.
They did not interfere, possibly assuming mistakenly that whatever
Gapon and his followers did had been approved by higher authority.
Gapon's circles spent much time reading newspapers (30 per cent of
male workers and 70 per cent of female were illiterate).[15] Selections
were drawn not from radical or revolutionary newspapers but from
more conservative organs like *Nashi Dni* (Our Days) or *Nasha Zhizn*
(Our Life).[16] A. M. Buiko, an old worker at the great Putilov steel

plant in St. Petersburg, recalled that in the summer of 1904 in the
Narva section where many Putilov workers lived Gapon organized one
of his sections. The first meeting was opened by Gapon who declared,
"Though the Czar is far away and God is high in the heavens and although there is much which the authorities do not know we will bring
the situation of the working people to the attention not only of the
factory owners but to the powers that be."

Many older and conservative workers immediately threw their support to Gapon. They bought his portraits, put them on the wall, and
said that as the son of poor peasants in the Poltava region Gapon
knew very well the life of the people and would defend their interests.[17]

The summer of 1904 was not a good summer. It began with the assassination of the archreactionary Governor-General N. I. Bobrikov of
Finland (still a Russian Grand Duchy). He was shot June 3 by a student named Shauman, who was killed on the spot. The Czar noted the
event in his diary, adding that June 3 was a remarkably clear summer
day—for the first time that year he and his family were able to dine
outdoors on the balcony at Tsarskoye Selo. On July 15 came even
worse news—the assassination of Plehve, killed by a bomb thrown by
a Socialist Revolutionary, a member of the SR Fighting Section, Yegor
Sergeyevich Sazonov. The assassination was arranged and managed
by a man named Yevno Azef, a fat, indifferent-seeming, stone-faced
individual who looked older than his thirty-three years. Unknown to
the authorities, the terrorists had twice before attempted to kill Plehve
but the plans aborted. This time they had four bomb-throwers, each
with a sixteen-pound bomb, stationed along the route which Plehve
was traveling. Sazonov, dressed as a railroad worker and carrying his
bomb wrapped in a cotton kerchief, threw it just as Plehve's carriage
passed the Hotel Warsaw, close to the Warsaw station. Plehve was
killed instantly, Sazonov was badly wounded, but the other participants including the famous Boris Savinkov escaped.[18] Plehve was on
his way to deliver a report to the Czar in which (as Witte later heard)
"an agent of the secret police, some Jew from one of the towns of Germany," reported that an attempt was to be made on the life of the
Czar and that Witte was playing an active role in the revolutionary
plot.[19] What Witte did not then know; nor the Czar; nor, of course, the
late Interior Minister, was that Azef, the man who planned and executed Plehve's assassination, was himself an agent of the secret police
which Plehve headed. Azef was to become the most notorious of the
Russian double agents, men who carried out leading revolutionary

roles and at the same time informed on their comrades to the Russian secret police. Azef's connections with the police dated to 1892. In 1901 he had been an organizer of the SR party and in 1903 took over the direction of its "fighting organization." He betrayed almost all of his collaborators in the fighting organization and was finally exposed (after years of rumor and suspicion) by V. L. Burtsev, the famous chief of the SR's counterintelligence. He was hunted by revolutionary agents, bent on vengeance, but escaped to Germany, where he died during World War I.

No satisfactory psychological explanation of provocateurs like Azef has ever been offered. They seem to have been either split personalities or pure villains, seeking to enhance their usefulness to the police by committing ever more brutal crimes. Perhaps they were symbols of the deadly contradictions which were rending Russian society.

On the evening of July 15, having heard the news of Plehve's murder earlier in the day, the Czar and his family dined in the open on the palace balcony. The weather, he noted in his diary, was "wonderful."[20]

Not all the news was bad. Or so it seemed.

On July 30 the Czar wrote in his diary:

"An unforgettable day for us in which God clearly showed us his blessing. At 1:15 p.m. Alix gave birth to a son who with a prayer we have named Alexei. It all happened remarkably fast—for me particularly so. This morning I was at Mama's as always and then received Kokovtsov for his report and Artillery Officer Klepikov who was wounded at Wafangkow. Then I went to join Alix for lunch. She already was upstairs and within half an hour the happy event had occurred. There aren't words enough to thank God for rendering us such comfort in this year of difficult experiences. Dear Alix feels very well. Mama came at 2 and sat with me for a long time before seeing her grandson for the first time. At 5 we went to prayers with the children and all the family. I sent a mass of telegrams. Misha came from camp. He is assured that he can go into 'retirement.' [He was Mikhail Alexandrovich, the Czar's younger brother and the heir apparent.] Dined in the bedroom."

Four days later the ecstatic father wrote of the new baby: "He is a remarkably quiet infant—he almost never cries."

There was one more notable entry in Nicholas' diary before the summer ended. On September 8 the Czar noted: "Alix and I are very disturbed at the constant bleeding in little Alexei. It continued at intervals from his navel until evening.[21]

This was the first sign of hemophilia in the Czarevich.

"How difficult to live through such minutes of worry," the Czar observed. He did not know the minutes were to lengthen to hours, the hours to days, the days to weeks, the weeks to months, until finally the worry was without end.

XIII

The Night Before

St. Petersburg was more beautiful than ever on the night of January 8, 1905. There was a full moon that seemed to hover for hours, huge and red on the horizon, coloring the golden spire of the Admiralty a copperish russet and painting the dark, red Winter Palace deep purple. An enormous shadow was projected across Palace Square by the arch of the General Staff Building. On the Nevsky, along the Moika, and past the great houses of the embankment and the Millionnaya, sleighs moved swiftly with a tinkle of bells that lingered in the crisp air. The mood of the city was curious, and later, in perspective, many found it hard to define. It was as though the city were pregnant with events, the nature of which no one understood and many were afraid to guess.

There was a meeting that night at the Putilov hall of the Society of Factory and Plant Workers at 42 Peterhof Chaussée (formerly the Old Tashkent Café).[1] Father Gapon was supposed to appear, and when he did not rumors began to circulate that he had been arrested. The meeting hall was hot and close but no one left. It was late evening before Gapon arrived—worn, hoarse, distraught, a rather handsome, black-haired, black-eyed man with a thin nervous face. He spoke quietly to his supporters,[2] comparing this night to the night before the Resurrection. Tomorrow, he said, we will go to the Czar, the people will wake from the dead, a new life will dawn. But, he warned, the Czar may not receive us. "And then for us there is no Czar." The crowd solemnly chanted: "And then for us there is no Czar." One last word: "We will die together. We will swear to stand, all for one and one for all."³ Slowly the crowd dispersed. Workers thanked him, pressed his hand, and mothers held out their babies to be blessed.

Later on, those present were asked what they did when they got home. They said they slept a little and waited for the morning. Those who were religious prayed.

There were similar meetings in each of the ten other halls of Father Gapon's society. These were not the only meetings in St. Petersburg that night. In the library of the newspaper *Nashi Dni*,⁴ a group of writers and members of the intelligentsia assembled with some of the Gapon workers. They had gathered because of growing concern at what the morrow would bring. They knew that Father Gapon, in the name of the workers, had sent a letter to Interior Minister Svyatopolk-Mirsky telling of their intention to wait on the Czar, Sunday January 9, and submit to him a petition of their demands. Rumors filled St. Petersburg, and the rumor which alarmed the assemblage most was that there might be a collision between the workers and the Czar's troops.

What were the workers asking? The eight-hour day, a rule of law, freedom of speech, of press, of assembly, and freedom to strike. What, it was asked, did they propose to do in support of these demands?

"We will go to the Father and tell him how we suffer," was the answer. "We will tell him—Father, forgive us. We have come to you. Help us, your children. We know you are happy to dedicate your life for us and to live only for us but you don't know how they beat and torture us; how we starve; how they treat us like cattle; how illiterate we all are."

Suppose, they were asked, for some reason the Czar does not meet with you—do you plan more forceful action? No, was the reply. But suppose, in general, he doesn't want to talk to such a large crowd? If necessary, they said, he could receive a delegation at Tsarskoye Selo just so long as it was a real delegation selected by Father Gapon and the workers.

Then came the last question. What if the Czar would not even do that? "Then," said the workers, "then, he is not the Czar. Then, there is no Czar."

There was no doubt in the minds of those present that the workers' intentions were peaceful. Late as was the hour—it was after midnight —a delegation of nine, including Maxim Gorky, the liberal writer Nikolai F. Annensky, Academician K. K. Arsenyev, the journalist and future member of the Kadet party Iosif V. Gessen, and V. I. Semevsky, a historian and economist, was named to wait immediately upon Interior Minister Mirsky and Witte in hope of averting bloodshed. The group did not find Mirsky at home (he had gone to

Tsarskoye Selo to consult the Czar) but left word of their mission with his deputy, General K. N. Rydzevsky, who suggested that their proper course should be to talk to the workers, not the Government. Then they went to Witte's house on the Petersburg side. He received them, but said bluntly that the matter was not "in my department."

Witte later wrote that he promptly reported this meeting to Mirsky. He said he had been excluded from a cabinet meeting the evening of January 8 at which the demonstration was discussed and measures agreed upon because it was believed that he would support the workers' demands.[5] Finance Minister V. N. Kokovtsov was skeptical of Witte's version. He believed Witte was well informed as to what was going on and, perhaps, deliberately stood aside in order to benefit if things went wrong. Kokovtsov said that the cabinet meeting was calm and lacking in any sense of urgency. Most of the discussion dealt with disposition of troops to keep workers from gathering in the center of the city. Kokovtsov expressed surprise at not having been informed of the situation earlier, since, having responsibility for the Factory Inspection, it was his duty to advise employers what was going on. Mirsky told him that it had been decided on Thursday that the Czar would leave town, that he would not be in St. Petersburg on Sunday, and that the police would tell the workers of his absence in good time. Therefore, it was supposed, they would not go to the Winter Palace.[6] A day or two earlier Mirsky had asked the city police to arrest Gapon and his chief lieutenants. The authorities refused, contending this would only worsen the situation.[7] A warrant (Order No. 1827) for Gapon's arrest and for nineteen of his associates was sworn out on the evening of the eighth by General Rydzevsky,[8] but the military said they could not execute it "because he was constantly surrounded by large numbers of his supporters."[9]

Gorky and his associates returned to the meeting at *Nashi Dni* and reported their slender results. There seemed nothing more to do but wait for what the day would bring. One thing was done, however. Some members decided to scatter out to the workers' quarters and see what was going on.

Gorky went to his home, where the door was opened by his friend Savva Morozov, the radical millionaire. "I was afraid you had been arrested," Morozov said. He warned Gorky not to appear on the streets alone in the morning and to carry a revolver. Gorky said he had no gun. Morozov drew a Browning out of his pocket, shoved it ino Gorky's hand, and left him.[10]

By this time it was well after 3 A.M. on the ninth. A raw wind had sprung up and was whisking gusts of snow through the gloomy Petersburg streets. But the city was not quiet. Troops were on the march.

Guard posts were being set up at the great bridges across the Neva, at the principal intersections approaching the Winter Palace, and at the arterial streets which led from working-class areas like the Narva Gates, Kolpino, Vasilevsky Island, and the Petersburg side. Headquarters was established at Guards Staff Headquarters, 34 Millionnaya, near the Winter Palace.

There were Red Cross posts and field kitchens, and around campfires in the streets soldiers kept warm with vodka, sang camp songs, danced, told stories, and got drunk. Many of the units had been rushed in that evening from Revel and Pskov.[11] As early as January 7 there had been 3,000 troops on duty in St. Petersburg. By midnight of the eighth the number had been raised to 7,000 infantry and 3,000 cavalry—some 20 battalions of infantry, $23\frac{1}{2}$ squadrons of guards cavalry, and 8 Cossack detachments. In addition, of course, there were thousands of police, including mounted units.[12]

The Czar spent the night with his family at his beloved Tsarskoye Selo, a few miles from the city. It had been a clear frosty day, as he was careful to remark in his diary, and in spite of many preoccupations he took a good long walk. But he was disturbed by the situation in his capital. "The workers so far have been peaceful," he noted. "The number [of strikers] is estimated at 120,000. At the head of the union is a certain Socialist-Priest Gapon. Mirsky came in this evening with a report of measures he has taken."[13]

The crisis of January 8 had arisen suddenly but hardly unexpectedly. The war had gone steadily worse. Kuropatkin proved unable to hold the Japanese back at Liao Yang, thus losing all hope that the siege of Port Arthur might be lifted. The fighting for Mukden went badly. The Czar had dispatched most of his Baltic Fleet to the Far East, hoping to regain control of the seas from the Japanese. But the enterprise got off to a typically disastrous start, the Russian warships firing on and sinking some British fishing vessels off the Dogger Bank in the North Sea in the belief they were Japanese—an incident that almost led to war with England. Then, just before Christmas (January 1, new style) came the terrible news of the surrender of Port Arthur by Gen. Anatoly M. Stössel—an act which many Russians to this day regard as virtual treason. The mood within Russia steadily blackened. The assassination of Plehve not only had shocked society but served, somewhat, to revive the waning spirits of the revolutionary movements, particularly the terror-haunted SRs. (The Social Democrats were still foggy with intra-Party conflict.) The leadership of the SRs, centered around Viktor Chernov, Yekaterina Breshko-Breshkovskaya ("the Little Grandmother of the Russian Revolution"), and M. Gotz,

was strongly established in Swiss exile. Its terrorist arm, led first by
G. A. Gershuni and then (after Gershuni's arrest) by the still unex-
posed police agent, Azef, was daring and experienced. It was rapidly
beginning to occupy the same heroic role in the popular mind as had
been filled by the Narodovoltsy of the 1880s. The SRs were enhancing
their position with the peasants, based on their contention that the land
belonged to no one and that only those who labored on it were to
profit from it. All land, the SRs said, must revert from landowners,
church, and nobility and come into the hands of the nation as a whole.
It would be controlled by local peasants and they alone would reap its
benefits. This uncompromising agrarian program gave the SRs a
strength which no other revolutionary group could challenge and, as
Sir Bernard Pares observed: "The peasantry were really in the long
run all-important."[14] For the workers, the SRs offered civil rights, protective legislation, shorter hours, and taxation of wealth, a program
much like Gapon's.[15] The appeal of the SRs to the peasants can be
measured by the fact that in the forty-two years between emancipation in 1863 and 1905 peasants had acquired 52 million acres of
land but their *average* holdings were only one-half those of 1860. They
constituted 85 per cent of Russia's population but owned only 37 per
cent of the land—the state holding 34 per cent, private landowners 26,
and the church 3. Land prices had doubled, making it even more
difficult for the peasants to increase their holdings. Returns were miserable. The average yield of wheat per acre was 406 pounds compared
with 868 in Germany and 1,109 in the United States. It was the same
with rye and oats. The average peasant had an investment of 490
rubles. He paid 60 rubles a year in taxes. His other expenses totaled
160 rubles. His income was 134 rubles so that each year he wound up
86 rubles in the red. Poverty was so intense that Government relief
payments rose from an average of 12 million rubles between 1871 and
1890 to 268 million in 1901–6. The SR-sponsored Peasants Union had
almost total peasant support. To the peasants there was only one
issue: the land.[16]

    In contrast Russia was becoming more and more a boom area for
foreign investment. Between 1889 and 1894, 5.3 million rubles of foreign capital went into Russia. But from 1895 to 1899 the total rose to
370.7 million.[17] In 1900, 35.9 per cent of capital invested in Russian industry was foreign and another 43.1 per cent was raised by sale of
securities abroad, a total of 79 per cent, or 1,678 billion gold rubles. In
addition France had lent Nicholas II 9,349 billion gold francs.[18] The
historian M. Pokrovsky drew an analogy between the Russia of 1905
and Germany in the revolutionary year 1848. Russia in 1905 had a pig
iron production equal to that of Prussia in 1879—not 1848—and there

were similar figures in other industries. Within a few years—by 1909—there were more factory workers in Moscow than in Paris—130,000 compared to 108,000–112,000 in Paris.

In other words there existed in the Russia of 1905 an industrial proletariat considerably stronger than appeared at first glance. It was estimated at 3 million in 1900 and may have approached 4 million by 1905.[19]

That proletariat, that gray mass of the downtrodden, many of them former peasants from the *chernozem* (black earth), crowded into the miserable factory barracks of Vasilevsky Island, the Narva and Vyborg quarters, was now slowly but unmistakably beginning to move. These throngs, these illiterate "dark people," faithful and superstitious believers in the Orthodox creed, loyal and suffering children of the "little Father," that is, the Czar, constituted Father Gapon's flock.

There were portents enough on the horizon, and even the Czar was not entirely unaware of them. In naming Mirsky in place of the slain Plehve he had, in fact, modified Government policy slightly. Mirsky was a more moderate man than Plehve and promised a Government of "public confidence."[20] The more politically acute members of society, liberal landholders, and liberal industrialists had begun to stir. By November 1904, important meetings were being held all over the country —first the Zemstvo Congress, representing liberal countrymen, and then a series of "professional" banquets (the "banquet campaign," as it came to be called) in many cities throughout the country. Some were attended exclusively by lawyers, engineers, or doctors, others by a mixture of professional men, academics, writers, and editors. The Saratov dinner brought out 1,500 persons. The St. Petersburg banquet drew 676 guests. It was opened by Nikolai F. Annensky and among the speakers were Iosif V. Gessen and V. I. Semevsky—three of those who were to meet on the night of January 8. These assemblies, in one form or another, called on the Czar to establish constitutional government with a freely elected parliament, a rule of law, freedom of press, speech, conscience, association, and assembly. The Zemstvo called for equality of the peasant with other citizens, local self-government, and a special program to meet rural needs.[21] A number of Moscow's leading industrialists took an active part in these meetings, in particular, Savva T. Morozov, V. P. Ryabushinksy, and M. V. Chelnokov. These were the nouveaux riches, the "white city" capitalists. They were not welcome in St. Petersburg, were not consulted by the Czar or his advisers, were held in social contempt by the older nobility. They also represented the most vigorous and progressive force in Russian society with a strong sense of social conscience.

Speaking in the Moscow Duma, the city senate, these men supported, in large part, the Zemstvo demands for political liberties and establishment of a system of representative government.[22] As V. Ya. Laverychev, a contemporary Soviet historian, notes, "thus, on the very eve of the revolution of 1905–06 a number of Moscow capitalists for the first time openly entered the political arena."[23]

"Russia was the scene of activities that had never before been conceivable there," commented the historian Sidney Harcave. "It appeared that almost the entire middle and upper classes, that is the educated classes, were speaking out against the government."[24]

Many years later a member of one of these families observed that of the many mistakes made by Nicholas II probably the most fatal was the failure to bring the brilliant Moscow entrepreneurs to the side of the court—the Morozovs, the Ryabushinskys, the Guchkovs, and the rest. Instead, these vigorous capitalists, the Russian Vanderbilts, Goulds and Rockefellers were despised as upstarts.[25] They had transformed Moscow with their new mansions, clearing out blocks of dusty courtyards to build brilliant palaces in the most eclectic styles— Gothic, pseudo-Russian, Greek revival. They were not to transform Imperial Russia.[26]

The court's failure to co-opt the new capitalists sent them pell-mell into the ranks of the Czar's opponents—reform, radical, revolutionary parties—all were financed by these fantastically wealthy industrialists and bankers.

This was a certain sign of the depth of the crisis, and, indeed, it was notable and significant that the broad strata of Russia's intelligentsia— the decent, principled, well-intentioned successors to the intelligentsia of the sixties who had hailed Alexander II as the Czar Liberator— together with the masses of the St. Petersburg working class led by a religious, mystical priest who was himself largely a puppet of the police, had evolved a program of reform in which they were almost entirely in agreement on main principles and which had won the support not only of literate doctors, lawyers, and writers and illiterate factory workers but also of public-spirited entrepreneurs and landed aristocrats. The breadth of agreement on the nature of the ills of Russia and on a program to cure them was remarkable and often difficult for the participants themselves to credit.

The only elements in Russian society which were out of tune with the times were the extreme radicals, principally Lenin's Bolsheviks and their Menshevik rivals, so immersed in Talmudic strife that they had little concept of what was happening in the real world, and, of course, the Czar and his intimate circle, also caught up in Talmudism but of a very different sort.

To be sure, the Czar was aware of what he called the "revolutionary movement in Russia" (sometimes, he called it a "time of troubles" or "disturbances") and worried by it, but after long discussions with his chief advisers in mid-December, he had rejected their counsel for reform and insisted on issuing a decree in which he refused to create a popularly elected National Senate which would have been a first significant step toward constitutional rule.[27]

So December faded into January. The Czar greeted New Year's with a cri de coeur: "I pray to God that in the coming year He will give Russia a victorious end to the war, a firm peace and a quiet life without disturbances." On January 2 the Czar's children, "even our little treasure," the hemophilic Czarevich, took part in a New Year's *yolka*, a Christmas party for the palace officers. All was gaiety.[28]

XIV

Bloody Sunday

Father Gapon lived in a very small house in the workers' quarter on the Petersburg side. After the Zemstvo meetings in November he had begun to invite writers, lawyers, and other intelligentsia to his house to meet with his principal aides. The intelligentsia were suspicious of Gapon. His connection with the police and the Government was too widely known. These suspicions were not dampened when the St. Petersburg prefect, Gen. G. I. Fullon, attended the opening of a Gapon hall on the Shlisselburg Trakt in early December.[1] But suspicion or no, Gapon's movement was growing rapidly. While toward the end of December its membership was estimated at only a few thousand, the Petersburg workers as a whole were beginning to speak openly of the necessity of political action and of striking for it and they were turning to Gapon as their spokesman.[2] Gapon himself was beginning to act more and more the charismatic leader and less and less the police pawn. This was a vital and significant change, quite obvious in retrospect, but by no means entirely clear to either Gapon, his police masters, or the confused underground revolutionaries (busily fighting him) at the time.

About the middle of December a dispute broke out in the railroad car shop of the Putilov works. The shop boss, a man named A. Tetyavkin, fired four workers—Sergunin, Ivan Subbotin, Ukolev, and Fyodorov. All were members of the Gapon Society, and Vladimir Inozentsev, the Gapon leader, took up the case contending that Tetyavkin was hostile to society members.[3] It was decided to send a deputation on December 29 to Director Smirnov of the Putilov plant and also to Prefect Fullon and the State Factory Inspection.[4] Smirnov responded rudely and the delegates got no satisfaction. On January 3, 12,500 workers walked out at Putilov.[5] On January 4, 1,000 at the Franco-Russian Machine Plant struck. On the fifth 16,000 quit work at the Neva Machine and Ship Building works, 2,000 at the Neva textile factory, and 700 at the Yekaterinhof textile plant. The demands were the same at all plants—the eight-hour day, workers' rights, higher pay, removal of some hated bosses.[6] By the seventh 382 factories had been shut down. Within three days an estimated 140,000 to 150,000[7] workers were idle in St. Petersburg. Everywhere Father Gapon and his society took the lead. Efforts by the more radical parties to play a role had little or no effect. They were not ready to lead a mass movement and, indeed, were only vaguely aware of the workers' mood and of the emerging role of the Gapon Society. The Bolsheviks didn't even take note of the Putilov strike until the fifth and they carefully avoided any reference to Gapon.[8] Lenin's St. Petersburg agent, S. I. Gusev, called Gapon "a Zubatovite of the highest order." Later he suggested that he "possibly is an idealist who is being used by all and, especially I think, by the most reactionary clique."[9] All factions of the Social Democrats in St. Petersburg were weak, disrupted, and disheartened. Lenin had virtually no strength. Maxim Litvinov (the future Soviet Foreign Minister) wrote Lenin and Krupskaya December 12, 1904, from St. Petersburg: "The periphery if not everywhere against us, is almost nowhere for us. The mass of party workers up to now continue to regard us as a handful of disorganizers with no strength of our own. No kind of conference (let alone a secret one) will change this widely held view. I repeat—our situation is impossibly rickety and precarious."[10] Gusev wrote of the "terrible weakness" of the Bolshevik organization. The Mensheviks, he contended, were "incomparably better off," particularly because they had thirty to forty "young women from abroad, true and dedicated to the point of hysteria."[11] In its December meetings the Petersburg Central Committee conceded that its work was disorganized, leaflets were not being distributed, most of the workers supported the Mensheviks. The workers were saying of the Committee: "Those are the people who understand nothing—just sit there." In the Petersburg region only eight of an original thirty Bolshevik circles were still alive; in the Nevsky region only three.[12] In their official report Lenin's St. Petersburg lieutenants admitted that "the January events caught the Petersburg Committee in an extremely lamentable condition. Contacts with workers were extremely disorganized by the Mensheviks. . . . There was not a single worker on the Committee [as of the end of December]. The strike at the Putilov plant caught the Committee by surprise. Before January 9 the mood of workers toward the Committee was extremely hostile. Our agitators were beaten up, our leaflets destroyed. And the first 500 rubles we sent to the Putilov workers was received reluctantly."[13] The first Bolshevik leaflet came out only on January 8.[14]

One candid Bolshevik St. Petersburg Committee member said: "Only today can we understand the full disorganization of the Party. The St. Petersburg organization is perfectly helpless in the face of the accidental workers' protest. You only have to go out into the street and look around to see how weak we are. And what can we do? Put out a few hundred leaflets which will literally be unnoticed and send out a few speakers."[15] Gusev spoke in one report of the "chaotic condition of the organization." In the Nevsky region among an estimated 30,000 workers the Bolsheviks had six or seven circles with five or six workers in each. Projected to the whole working class of St. Petersburg this provides an estimated membership of 216.[16] The figure for January membership reported by Gusev to the Third Party Congress in London in April 1905 was 215. This included 100 students.[17]

Actually, the Mensheviks were in almost as bad a state. Both Bolsheviks and Mensheviks put out leaflets directed against Gapon. Gusev hated Gapon. He called him "that cursed Gapon" and, years later, describing him to his daughter, he used the same term. He said listening to him made him "boil with rage."[18] He used the same term, writing Lenin January 5, 1905, about the struggle against the "cursed Gapon," saying: "The exposure of Gapon and the struggle with him will be the basis of the agitation we are hurriedly organizing. We have to move all our forces into action."[19] Krupskaya was writing Gusev from Geneva the same day: "We hear from foreign papers that the Putilov plant is on strike. Do we have any connections there? Can we get some word about the strike? We need it quickly."[20]

Despite his distaste for Gapon, Gusev did make an effort to meet him, apparently for the purpose of entering into some arrangement. The appointment was set up by Pyotr Rutenberg, the SR agent who was very close to Gapon. However, Gapon didn't show up for the meeting. Rutenberg expressed enthusiasm for Gapon. Gusev remembered saying to him as he left: "The future will show which one of us is right but I strongly fear that you will suffer a severe disappointment."[21]

In St. Petersburg events moved like a praire fire. Later on, one worker was to recall that he reported to his shop January 5 at 7 A.M. There was the usual morning prayer. He lighted the lamp over his lathe and began to oil his machine. Two or three minutes later a companion came in, crying: "Get dressed, comrades, we are going with the Putilov men in search of the truth."* He thought his friend was joking but a few moments later there was a whistle and the whole shop walked out. They went to the next shop, got them to walk off, and then to a third. Another worker said he had come to his shop at 7 A.M. and found a bunch of comrades at the gates. "Why aren't you working?" he asked. "We don't want to," they replied. "Well, if you don't want to then get out of the way," he said and went in. A few minutes later he heard a window break and the shout: "Quit it. Come on out. Quit work." The shop quit and everyone donned street clothing and left.[22] D. Ya. Odintsov was a seventeen-year-old apprentice at a jewelry factory in the center of St. Petersburg. He was working as usual on January 7 when a delegate from a larger factory on the nearby Nevsky came in and persuaded everyone to join the strike. By this time Odintsov's shop was ready to close anyway because the gas supply (for lighting) had failed—cut off by striking workers. I. A. Ovsyannikov worked with his friend Izaak Petrov in Maximov's blacksmith shop on Maly Prospekt, Vasilevsky Island. Selivestrov's stables —a large establishment with more than one hundred horses—was in the courtyard. Next door was the Possel factory. Ovsyannikov and Petrov persuaded all three establishments to shut down January 7. With workers from a horseshoe factory they paraded through the streets, getting a number of droshky drivers to join them.[23]

In these days meetings were held continuously in the Gapon Society halls. The atmosphere was almost religious. Radical speakers were shouted down as "going against God and the Czar," although on several occasions students, SRs, and Social Democrats were courteously invited to speak. The crowd chanted its responses in unison. When an orator said, "To live like this—wouldn't it be better in the grave?" the crowd chanted: "In the grave . . . in the grave . . ." When an orator said: "If the Czar does not receive us . . ." the crowd roared: "Then, we have no Czar." Again and again they repeated: "No Czar . . . No Czar."[24]

The decision to draft a petition to the Czar and present it to him in a mass assemblage at the Winter Palace was made on the evening of January 6–7, and the next day Gapon sent a letter to Mirsky outlining his intentions (and enclosing a copy of the petition).

What was the word which the workers had sought to bring to their Czar? It was couched in the dark people's deeply traditional language.

---

* *Truth*, in Russian usage, has a wider, deeper meaning than in English. Here the worker is using the word in a sense almost of a religious crusade in search of the true faith.

We workers and residents of the city of St. Petersburg, of various ranks and stations, our wives, children and helpless old parents, have come to Thee, Sire, to seek justice and protection.

We have become beggars; we are oppressed and burdened by labor beyond our strength; we are humiliated; we are regarded, not as human beings, but as slaves who must endure their bitter fate in silence. . . .

Sire, there are many thousands of us here; we have the appearance of human beings but, in fact, neither we nor the rest of the Russian people enjoy a single human right—not even the right to speak, think, assemble, discuss our needs, or take steps to improve our condition. . . .

Sire! Is this in accordance with God's laws, by the grace of which Thou reignest? . . . Is it better to die—for all of us, the toiling people of all Russia, to die, allowing the capitalists (the exploiters of the working class) and the bureaucrats (who rob the government and plunder the Russian people) to live and enjoy themselves?

This is the choice we face, Sire, and this is why we have come to the walls of Thy palace.

Order these measures and take Thine oath to carry them out. Thou wilt thus make Russia both happy and famous, and Thy name will be engraved in our hearts and in those of our posterity forever. And if Thou dost not so order and dost not respond to our pleas we will die here in this square before Thy palace. We have nowhere else to go and no purpose in going.

From the moment Gapon sent his letter to Mirsky events seemed to move on their own rails. There were rumors that the authorities would not permit the January 9 assembly. But there were opposing rumors, too. Police stood by good-naturedly at the Gapon halls, sat and listened to the orators. There was no sign of hostility. On the seventh or eighth, as he later recalled, Dr. Dyakonov, a physician at the Alfuzov Hospital, noted some posters near his hospital saying: "People must not congregate in the streets or appropriate legal measures will be taken." But the posters were not put up where the workers could see them and were couched in language which they were not apt to understand.[25]

Father Gapon spent the night of January 8 in the quarters of a Putilov worker named Sinelovsky, surrounded by his "life guards," the small group of workers devoted to his security.[26] (There were rumors

of an attempt on his life.) It was midnight or later before he slept. He
was exhausted and losing his voice. A friend proposed that Father
Georgi have a bite to eat. He refused. He drank half a glass of tea and
smoked one cigarette after another. When he finally slept he slept
soundly and did not awaken until 8 A.M.[27] Already the first group was
gathering—the Kolpino workers, who had nearly ten miles to walk.
The sun had not yet risen when about one thousand began their
march at 6:30 A.M. in pitch dark. (On that early January day in St.
Petersburg the sun did not rise until 8:37.) The wind had dropped
during the night, the temperature was five degrees below freezing,
and later on the day would be clear and comparatively mild.* The
mood of the people was quiet. They were, as they said, "going to the
Czar." Other detachments did not have so far to walk but they
gathered early nonetheless. On the Shlisselburg Trakt a worker reported that a friendly gendarme had told him there would be no interference. It was first decided to organize the march with women, children, and elderly workers in the front ranks so the Czar could see that
everyone was together. Someone asked what if troops appeared. There
was a general opinion the troops would not fire. "We'll take them by
the shoulder and say: 'Brothers, what about it? You really wouldn't
fire on your own!'" In the end it was decided, nonetheless, to put able-
bodied men in the front. About 10 A.M. the Vasilevsky Island section
assembled. Some of the doormen along the Fourth Line (one of the
principal streets) said, "Well, they'll get beaten up today." A worker
made a speech: "You know why we are going. We are going to the
Czar for the Truth. Our life is beyond endurance. You remember
Minin who turned to the people in order to save Russia? From whom?
From the Poles. Now we must save Russia from the bureaucrats under
whose weight we suffer. They squeeze the sweat and blood out of us.
You know our workers' life. We live ten families to the room. Do I
speak the truth?" "True . . . true . . . ," responded the crowd. "And so
we go to the Czar. If he is our Czar, if he loves his people he must listen to us. . . . We go to him with open hearts. I am going ahead in
the first rank and if we fall the second rank will come after us. But it
cannot be that he would open fire on us." There were other speakers—
a woman, a girl, and a young man. A student wanted to speak. He was
shouted down but it was agreed students might march with the
workers if they wished because they, too, were suffering under the regime. Then, the first man spoke again: "Now, let us pray to God. Let
us say the Lord's Prayer." They crossed themselves. One old man and
many women wept.

* January 9, 1905, was one of those rare days in the year when the Czar failed
to note the weather in his diary.

Father Gapon did not speak again. Just before the march was to start, a messenger came, asking him to talk by telephone with Prefect Fullon. He refused. It was too late. "Tell the Prefect that now I and my comrades are going to the Palace," he said. Gapon joined his followers. He urged a few mothers who asked his blessing to return home because there might be trouble.

At the head of the column was placed a very large portrait of the Czar and two smaller portraits of the Czar and Czarina. There was also a large white flag on which had been spelled out in big letters: "Soldiers! Do not fire on the people." There were numbers of religious banners, large crosses, and icons. About 11 A.M. the column with Father Gapon in his priestly cassock at its head, surrounded by his bodyguard, started. The sun was bright. As they walked, they sang, "Save us, O Lord, Thy People." Police along the route took off their caps. They estimated the crowd at three thousand; the participants guessed that it totaled fifty thousand.[28]

The procession moved slowly and freely through the streets until it approached the Narva Gates when suddenly from behind the gates a cavalry squadron, of the Life Guard Grenadiers, appeared, drove straight at the crowd, breaking the first ranks, then swiftly wheeled to one side, opening the way for infantry (the 13th Irkutsk Regiment, just brought in from Pskov), stationed on and beside the small bridge to the left. The crowd was confused but joined hands and continued ahead, singing solemnly. A bugle sounded and the Pskov units opened fire. Police officer Zhultrevich shouted: "What are you doing? How can you fire on a holy pilgrimage and the portrait of the Czar?" A minute later he was struck down by a bullet.[29] The elderly workers carrying the Czar's portraits fell. So did a youngster carrying a religious torch. Cries rose from the crowd. Some, true to their oath, stood firm. Others ran. Gapon fell, struck by the body of one of those killed beside him. Rutenberg, the SR fighting squad man, lay beside Gapon. Cautiously he asked: "Are you alive, Father?" "I'm alive." "Shall we go?" "Let's go." They hurried across the street into the nearest courtyard and disappeared before anyone knew what had happened.[30] Rumors spread that Gapon had been killed.[31] Actually Rutenberg concealed Gapon in a worker's flat and shaved off his beard.[32]

The troops had been ordered to halt individual columns before they converged on the palace square. But there was no uniformity. The Kolpino group met no interference until it reached Mytninskaya, beside the Nevsky. Here an officer simply told them they could not proceed in a body but must go forward in small groups. The Nevsky group, estimated at more than five thousand, was halted on the Shlisselburg Trakt, a rather narrow street along the Neva Embankment, by a Cossack officer of the Ataman Regiment. While they argued they were fired on from the rear. They begged to be allowed to proceed. "I can't let you go ahead," the officer said, "because you are going against the Czar." "No," cried the workers. "We are going *for* the Czar. We only want to free him from the web of Capitalists and embezzlers." The Cossacks would not give way and the firing continued. An old man sank to his knees praying for mercy for the people. He was trampled by the cavalry and wounded by a saber thrust. Some of the crowd escaped over the ice of the frozen Neva and proceeded into the city.

On Vasilevsky Island the collision with the troops occurred only a few minutes after the six thousand marchers had started. When they got to the Fourth and Fifth Lines, just short of the Neva Embankment, almost at the Academy of Arts where the famous painter V. A. Serov stood watching at the window,[33] they met a detachment of the Finnish Life Guard Regiment and halted twenty-five or thirty paces away. They sent deputies forward, waving white handkerchiefs, and attempted to explain their mission but their voices were drowned out and a mounted squadron charged the crowd. Infantry appeared with raised rifles. The deputies threw off their coats and bared their breasts to the guns. Then the commander called in more cavalry and charged again. The crowd scattered in confusion, carrying off their wounded. Soon they were meeting in a nearby street, listening to fiery orations by students. Some broke into the Shaff gun shop and seized weapons, mostly sabers, swords, and knives. They began to break down telegraph poles and throw up barricades.[34]*

About 3 P.M. Colonel Skorpinsky of the 89th Belomorsky Regiment was ordered to clear the barricades. (His regiment had detrained from

---

* In contemporary Soviet literature the Bolsheviks are portrayed as organizing and leading the Vasilevsky Island action. But a report by the Petersburg Central Committee to the Third Party Congress in April 1905 makes no such claim and, in fact, only devotes a few passing words to the Vasilevsky manifestation. It is perfectly clear that the claim of Bolshevik inspiration and leadership of the most violent of the Bloody Sunday actions is an ex post facto amendation of history. (*Tretii Syezd RSDRP*, pp. 564–66.) The names of two St. Petersburg students, arrested in connection with the Vasilevsky manifestation. Leonid Davydovich Davydov and Semyon N. Rekhtsammer, have been unearthed by Bolshevik historians. Neither, however, is identified as Bolshevik. (V. I. Nevsky, *Rabocheye Dvizhniye*, p. 117; V. I. Nevsky, *Krasnaya Letopis*, 1922, No. 1, p. 51.) Gusev, the Bolshevik Committee head, spent the morning at one of the Party cells, waiting for reports of what was happening. About noon he heard that workers were being fired on. He went off toward the Alexander Garden but apparently was unable to get through the military lines. When he got back to his headquarters, he heard about the Vasilevsky Island fighting. (Yelizaveta Drabkina, *Chernye Sukari*, pp. 27–28.) A. L. Sidorov, a senior Soviet historian who edited the memoirs of D. N. Lyubimov, chief of chancellory of the Czar's Ministry of Internal Affairs, carefully corrects a reference by Lyubimov to "social democrats" as being organizers of the Vasilevsky Island barricades. The organizers, he notes, were a group of SRs. (A. L. Sidorov, *Voprosy Istorii*, 1965, No. 9.)

Revel at the Baltic Station at 5:30 A.M.[35]) He advanced on Sredny Prospekt where, as he later reported, he found a series of obstacles, hundreds of people milling about, and the red flag waving. He shouted a loud warning that if they did not disperse he would open fire. He was met, he claimed, by shouts, curses, and obscenity. Then, he told his men: Ready . . . Aim . . . Fire . . . with a pause between each command. At the third signal they fired a volley. After that, he said, all was quiet. His men advanced and demolished the barricade. They continued to clear barricades until it was dark, firing volley after volley and receiving in return an occasional revolver shot or a shower of bricks from the roofs of buildings.[36] Often they left bodies beside the demolished barricades.

The group from the Petersburg side was halted at the Troitsky Bridge. Among them was Anna Ulyanova-Yelizarova, Lenin's sister. Another was Gorky, who walked with the group as they came down Kamennoostrov Prospekt. He listened to the workers. "We can't stand any more," one said. "That's why we came." "Do you really believe he [the Czar] won't understand?" another asked. A youth appeared with a red flag and was rebuffed. "We don't need red flags," the crowd said confidently. "We are going to the Father." "He loves us," another said. The radical journalist A. N. Prokopovich said: "The main thing is —don't break any windows. Please don't break any windows."[37] When the crowd saw the line of soldiers across the Prospekt at the Troitsky Bridge, people began to murmur. "The soldiers are cold," one said. "Poor lads, they have to stand there." Another set up a cry: "Hurray for the soldiers." Even after the firing began people in the crowd kept repeating over and over: "It's a mistake. A mistake. Something went wrong." Some of the bullets flew past the balcony from which Witte was watching the crowd at his house on Kamennoostrov Prospekt.[38] In the firing forty-eight men, women, and children were killed and more than one hundred wounded, many of them in repeated charges by Cossack cavalry.

On the Nevsky at 2 P.M. there were the usual Sunday crowds—more than usual because the day was fine. Mixed among them were workers in knots and groups making their way to the Winter Palace. There were also Cossack detachments which wove through the crowd and blocked the street entirely at its lower end near the Admiralty. Alexander Kerensky was on the Nevsky that day and was among the crowd which swirled against the iron fences of the Alexander Garden on one side and across to the arch of the General Staff Building.[39]*

* Kerensky was deeply moved by the events he witnessed. That evening he went home and wrote a letter to some of his friends in the Guards officer corps, protesting the firing on the workers. (Alexander Kerensky, *Russia and History's Turning Point*, p. 50.)

Between ten and eleven in the morning Finance Minister V. N. Kokovtsov heard and saw shooting around the Police Bridge, and shots flew past the windows of his residence across the Moika. Crowds surged back and forth between the Nevsky and Volynsky Pereulok, and intermittent fighting went on until afternoon. When he went out of his house a bit later, police told him there had been only a few casualties.[40] People moved on both sides of the Admiralty Prospekt to the corner of the Nevsky. Many were strolling in the gardens and there, as usual, were idlers and children skating. The mood of the crowds was one of suppressed excitement. There was quiet conversation. Occasionally squadrons of cavalry with drawn swords moved down the Admiralty Prospekt, pushing the public close to the walls and fences. Word had begun to spread of shooting in other quarters but the workers remained confident that the Czar would appear. Some said that he was not in St. Petersburg. But few believed this. A little after two a fat red-faced officer (no one ever learned his name) appeared and began shouting, "Disperse or we'll shoot." He shouted this to the Kolpino workers standing by the General Staff Arch. Someone shouted back: "Shoot! We've come in search of the truth." The Palace Square was jammed with 2,300 troops,[41] both cavalry and infantry. Cannon had been set up around the Winter Palace. Suddenly a detachment of the Preobrazhensky Guards moved out of the square and formed two lines, opposite the Alexander Garden. The public watched perplexed. A bugle sounded. A hush fell over the crowd. The bugle sounded again. Colonel Delsal[42] shouted: "Aim." The first rank of the Preobrazhensky dropped to a kneeling position and took aim. No one moved. Faces whitened. Many crossed themselves. The salvo crashed out. Direct fire at close range on people standing beside the garden and directed into the garden, on the curious, the passers-by, the children at their games. The crowd stood frozen. No one believed these were real bullets. Then they saw. Bodies lay torn and bleeding around the square, in the gardens, against the iron railings, blood flowing out over the white snow and the frozen ice. Dark pools rapidly spreading. Nor was it ended. The soldiers wheeled about. They fired again toward the Admiralty and toward the Palace Bridge. And then toward the General Staff Arch. The army report said "more than 30" were killed and wounded.[43]* The crowds scattered in terror. H. H. Munro

---

* The number of casualties on Bloody Sunday has never been established accurately. The Government put the figure at 96 killed and 333 wounded of whom 34 later died. It was widely believed that several hundred were killed and possibly 1,500 wounded. A group of journalists compiled a list of 4,600 killed and wounded. (Sidney Harcave, *The Russian Revolution of 1905*, p. 93.) Lenin, basing himself on exaggerated Paris reports, thought the total was at least 4,600. (Walter Soblinsky, *The Road to Bloody Sunday*, p. 267.) V. I. Nevsky, a careful historian, estimated casualties at 800 to 1,000. (*Krasnaya Letopis*, 1922, No. 1, p. 56.)

(the English satirist Saki) was on the scene, covering the event for the London *Morning Post*. He narrowly escaped a volley fired by a Cossack detachment at the Hôtel de France across from St. Isaac's.[44] Yelena Stasova was walking down Bolshaya Morskaya toward the Nevsky when troops in Kirpichny Pereulok opened fire. The sweep of the panic-stricken populace literally carried her back a whole block to Gorokhovaya. Never in her life was she to forget the terror.[45]

Remarkably, the day suddenly lost its light. The writer Dmitri Merezhkovsky, who had been walking in the Summer Garden, recalled that the sun appeared to be surrounded by a great red circle and its rays were obscured.[46] Others saw two red circles as though three suns were hanging in the sky. Then, about three o'clock, a winter rainbow incredibly and briefly sparkled. In a moment the wind washed it out and snow fell heavily. It was almost as dark as night and seemed darker because the lights on the Nevsky did not go on.[47]

By chance, Andrei Bely, the symbolist poet, and his mother arrived in St. Petersburg January 9 from Moscow. In midafternoon Bely made his way to the Merezhkovsky flat on the fifth floor[48] of the Muruzi house at the corner of Panteleimon Street and Liteiny Prospekt. Zinaida Gippius Merezhkovskaya, a poetess and probably the most beautifully baroque woman in Russia, lay at full length on a divan, a white smock over her black satin dress, the flames of the fireplace playing on her golden-red hair, her lapus lazuli green eyes, her orchidaceous red lips, a lorgnette in her slender hand, a large black cross around her neck. "We picked this day for your arrival," she said languidly. The room was filled with the aesthetes of St. Petersburg— V. F. Nuvel, a close friend of Sergei Diaghilev's; the philosopher-poet N. Minsky; E. F. Lundberg, with whom Bely immediately began to talk about "chaos"; Dmitri V. Filosofov, a cousin of Diaghilev's; A. A. Smirnov, a colleague on the Merezhkovsky journal, *Novy Put*; and, of course, Merezhkovsky himself, small, thin, with cloudy eyes.

All the talk was of the events in the streets. Gapon, it was said, was dead. Hundreds had been killed. In the evening Bely and the Merezhkovskys went to the Free Economic Society. All of intellectual Petersburg was there. Zinaida Gippius sat on a chair in her black satin dress and, smiling, examined everyone through her lorgnette. Presently Gorky appeared on the balcony with a small, pale, freshly shaven man in civilian dress who began to speak in a shrill voice. The crowd stirred, a mutter ran from person to person: "It's Gapon. It's really him."[49]

And so it was. After the shooting Gapon had made his way to

He gives the first official figure as 76 killed, 233 wounded, later raised to 130 killed, 299 wounded.

Gorky's flat. Savva Morozov, who was acting as doorman and body-guard for Gorky, let him in. He was wearing a floor-length cloak and his hair and beard had been raggedly hacked away. His face was blue and his eyes wide and staring. "Give me something to drink. Wine. Everyone's dead," he cried (as Gorky recalled).

Gapon gulped down two water glasses of wine. Then Morozov attempted to trim his hair and beard a bit more carefully. Rutenberg, Gapon's SR friend and mentor, appeared and it was decided Gapon should show himself at the Free Economic Society meeting to negate the rumors of his death. Morozov then called the director of the Art Theater, Asaf Tikhomirov, who hurried over and made up Gapon's face for the occasion. After this process Gapon looked, Gorky recalled, a bit like a young barber or perhaps a shop assistant in a stylish store.[50]

Thus it was that Gapon appeared before the Free Economic Society, still on the verge of hysteria. He shouted: "Peaceful means have failed. Now we must go over to other means."[51] He read a letter to the workers ("Dear blood-welded brothers") and called down "my pastor's curse" on the soldiers who had fired on the workers and on "the traitor Czar who ordered the shedding of innocent blood." After Gapon spoke Merezhkovsky hurried to the Alexandrinsky Theater, where the performance was halted in protest against the events of the day. At the Mariinsky, as Tamara Karsavina was to recall, Olga Preobrazhenskaya's gala *Caprices de Papillon* was hastily brought to an end in fear of the mob.[52]

That night Gorky wrote an appeal: "To all Russian citizens and to the Social Opinion of the European States. We proclaim that this kind of order cannot be suffered and we invite all the citizens of Russia to immediate stubborn and united struggle with autocracy."[53] To Hearst's New York *Journal,* for which he was Russian correspondent, Gorky cabled: "The Russian Revolution has begun."[54]

Crowds roamed the streets late into evening, shouting "Brother-Murderers" at the Cossacks, who patrolled with drawn swords. Hooligans broke into stores. Rocks were hurled through windows. Finally, by midnight it was dead quiet. A heavy snow was falling. Bloody Sunday had passed into history. That night the Czar wrote in his diary: "A terrible day. Troops had to fire in many places of the city, there were many killed and wounded. God, how painful and awful. Mama came straight from the city to mass. We lunched together. Walked with Misha. Mama is staying with us for the night."

At 4 A.M. on January 10 the express train from Berlin pulled into Nicholas Station. It was twelve hours late—delayed by heavy snows. The station was deserted. Isadora Duncan, the young American dancer, descended from her compartment and, wrapped in furs against the ten-below-zero winds, entered a sleigh which whirled her down the Nevsky Prospekt to the Hotel Europa. Suddenly she saw in the half-light of the broad and empty boulevard a long procession— men, women, and children. "Black and mournful it came," she recalled. "There were men laden and bent under their loads—coffins— one after another." These were the victims of Bloody Sunday, the funeral procession, slow and mournful. The scene was etched in the artist's mind and later she recalled that it had "left its mark on all my life."[55] Two nights later she was to appear before the flower of St. Petersburg at the Salle des Nobles where it seemed to Andrei Bely and the Bloks that her dancing of Beethoven's Seventh Symphony and Chopin's Twelfth Prelude was "a symbol of the young newborn revolutionary Russia."[56]

Thus, Bloody Sunday.

"Even on the morning of January 9," wrote the contemporary historian A. Vanag, "filled with belief in the Czar these masses were not ready for revolution. But by evening with the cry: 'No longer do we have a Czar' they were ready to act. They rose against the autocrat. They began the revolution."[57]

Henceforth for the dark people there was no Czar.

XV

The Czar Sleeps

The Imperial Yacht Club, possibly the gloomiest, most grandiose building in St. Petersburg, heavy with granite, marble, pillars, enormous chandeliers, velours, and endless ballrooms, stood on the Morskaya, just around the corner from St. Isaac's, next to the new Astoria Hotel. Here Count Alexei Alexandrovich Bobrinsky, a man of noble ancestry, considerable wealth, an archaeologist by hobby, and a dabbler in education all his life, spent the evening of January 31, 1905.

It was not an evening notable for gaiety, but even so it was late by the time his troika, moving swiftly through the light snow, brought Bobrinsky, swathed in sable robes, back to his home. Late though it was he hurried to his study and, as was his habit, jotted a few lines in his diary: "Anniversary at the Yacht-Club. It is now a quarter to three and I have returned from the Club. There at dinner were the Grand Dukes Nikolai and Pyotr Nikolayevich, Nikolai and Sergei Mikhailovich. The Grand Dukes, dreadfully frightened at the approaching revolution, now are throwing off all pride and reconciling themselves to the end. . . . Among the ministers, too, there is fear and a search for a way out. . . . Things are bad in the interior. Agrarian disorders are starting. They are burning factories and plundering. The ministries fidget, the Czar fidgets, the police fidget. They all talk about the oncoming slaughter. A wicked story is being told about Pobedonostsev [the Czar's reactionary adviser]—that he had himself taken to Tsarskoye Selo in a coffin like a corpse so afraid was he of a bomb."[1]

Count Bobrinsky was a sharp-eyed and gossipy observer of considerable independence. He had long been a close friend of Dowager Empress Mariya Fyodorovna's and of late had been even closer to Czarina Alexandra, taking her side in the quarrel between the Dowager and the Czarina. He had watched the approach of the storm for years with deepening apprehension. As early as 1895 he had noted in his diary: "The Czar does nothing. He is a sphinx. He has no kind of personality. They say that more than once he has interrupted a minister's report with a request to wait a bit while he goes to consult mama." A bit later he jotted down: "The Czar continues to play hide-and-seek. No one sees him." Nine years later he wrote: "The Czar sits by himself—invisible." As the crisis of 1905 deepened he wrote (March 20, 1905): "The Czar sleeps. He sleeps on a volcano," and, a few days later: "The Czar is still without will—he sleeps. The Czar and the Czarina sit behind locked doors at Tsarskoye Selo. The Grand Dukes are absolutely terrified. . . ."[2]

Rightly or wrongly Bobrinsky felt that the Czarina had a clearer grasp of the situation than the Czar. In October and November 1904 he noted that it was being said that the Czarina favored granting a constitution and even that "she stands at the head of the Constitutional Party." He may have been expressing the Queen's own opinion because, after an audience with the Czarina January 28, he wrote: "We had a most open talk about the general situation of the country. I poured out my soul. I said all that I could. I argued the urgent necessity of summoning the representatives and warned of the advancing revolution. The Empress said that the Czar had decided to announce the coming assembly. I'm convinced there will be no delay. I pray to God this conversation will lead to some good." A few days later he put in the hands of the Empress a draft manifesto which he believed she approved. But it remained to be seen what "our weak-willed Czar" would make of it.

Bobrinsky was far from alone in his feeling of alarm. Savva T. Morozov, the wealthy Moscow industrialist and frequent angel of the Bolshevik and other radical causes ("He scurries before the Revolution like a devil before the dawn," Chekhov once said of him[3]), said to Maxim Gorky on the evening of January 9: "The Czar is a blockhead. He forgets that the people who were shot today on his order just a year and a half ago fell to their knees before his palace saying: 'God save the Czar.' If today he had come out on the balcony and said to the crowd a few pleasant words and given them two or three promises (to fulfill them is not obligatory) then these people again would have sung for him 'God save the Czar.' And even might have beaten out the brains of that priest on the Alexander Column."[4] If, said Morozov, a man like Gapon could lead thousands of people against the throne, then the cause of the Romanovs and of the monarchy was a dying cause.[5]

The shock and alienation of the intelligentsia was profound. Ivan Ye. Repin, Russia's leading artist and clearly a man of the center and not of the left, wrote in a letter to his friend V. V. Stasov on January 22: "How good that for all his base, greedy, predatory thieving nature he [the Czar] is at the same time so stupid that perhaps he will soon fall into a trap to the general happiness of all enlightened people. Ah, how tiresome."[6]

Leo Tolstoy took a somewhat different view. He attacked those who had stirred up the workers because he was convinced they could not move the Government. "The Czar is not free," he said bitterly. "He talks now to one, now to another. He listens to his uncles, his mother, Pobedonostsev. He is a pitiful, insignificant, even an unkind person."[7]

Three years earlier Tolstoy, feeling that he was near death, had tried to warn the Czar that Russia was headed for disaster. "I address you not only as a Czar but as a brother-man," he said. "I write as it were from the other world since I await death's approach." He called for democratization of the regime and urged the Czar to put himself at the head of a movement "to lead people from evil to good, from darkness to light," and thus serve both God and man. Tolstoy sent the letter privately, through Grand Duke Nikolai Mikhailovich, asking the Czar not to reveal it to his Ministers, thinking it would, thus, be more influential. The only response he got for his pains was a message from the Czar "not [to] worry for he would not show" the letter to anyone.[8]

Now, once again, the Czar was equivocal. His initial response to Bloody Sunday was to bring in the notorious General Trepov from Moscow and give him dictatorial powers to restore order. Trepov's first act was to clap Gorky and the other members of the citizens' committee which had tried to avert the catastrophe into jail. Trepov was a brave but limited cavalry officer. He could sweep the street clear with his horse guards. But he could not cure the ills of a dying social system.

What could be done? Count V. N. Kokovtsov, the Minister of Finance, wrote the Czar on January 11, the day after Trepov's appointment, an emotional letter:

> I do not believe I have the right to hold up my views until my regular reporting day because the unrest in the capital is marked by the sharpest character and each lost day makes

more and more difficult the task of the government. . . .

I do not see this ending with police measures alone. We should not expect that the use of armed force will be sufficient for this end. The police were not able to forestall the flaring up of events; they stood by without a move for long months as mere witnesses while there grew and strengthened a criminal organization approved in the beginning by the Minister of Internal Affairs himself. . . .

My conscience and an honest evaluation of the events we have just gone through leads me to conclude that only the imperial word of Your Majesty will quiet the capital and prevent the inescapable widening of disorders in other parts of your Empire—as the uprising in Moscow already shows.

But that word must be the word of authority. In a moment when the streets of the capital are red with blood the voice of a minister or even all the ministers together will not be heard by the people. This word must belong only to your Imperial Majesty and before your word all rebellious heads will bow. . . . The workers will believe your word—that it is not the hypocritical promises of their leaders but only in your mercy that they will find the source of all good and solicitude.[9]

Kokovtsov did not believe the Czar took too kindly to his views.[10] Nevertheless, a declaration designed to woo the workers back from their "false path" was issued in the Czar's name January 15.[11] Of course, it had no effect. Disorders continued to spread throughout Russia. The outbreak in Moscow was violent. So were those in the Baltic provinces and the Caucasus. Within two weeks higher education had virtually come to a standstill. Universities were closed and neither professors nor students were willing to attend under the protection of bayonets. A manifesto signed by 342 leading educators demanded complete reform of the educational system.[12] The Czar replaced the vaguely liberal Mirsky as Minister of Interior with Alexander Bulygin. A group of thirty-four carefully selected, utterly docile factory workers was taken by train to Tsarskoye Selo to be harangued by the Czar, who warned against "evil men," said that it had been necessary to sacrifice the lives of innocent victims, and bestowed God's blessing on the delegation.

"I believe in the honorable feelings of the working people," the Czar assured his listeners, "and in their unshakable devotion to me and therefore I forgive them their guilt."[13] It was the first time the Czar had ever met face to face with a worker.

After being given tea and sandwiches[14] they were instructed to go back to their factories and tell their comrades what the Czar had said. On their return some were spat upon and greeted with such hostility they had to leave.[15] "Who are these?" the workers asked. "They aren't our workers and we don't know them." Many workers refused any part of the fifty thousand rubles the Czar made available for relief of the victims of Bloody Sunday. They called it "blood money."[16] It was only too apparent that without basic, far-reaching changes the Imperial system was doomed. State Secretary A. S. Yermolov, Minister of Agriculture, a mild and rather passive liberal, deeply troubled and deeply moved, had a remarkably frank conversation with the Czar on January 17.

"Russia today," Yermolov said, "is passing through a terrible experience, the like of which has not been seen in history and the results of which it is impossible to predict.

"Even if the spilling of blood on the streets of St. Petersburg should succeed in halting the workers' movement it may not actually quiet the situation. To the contrary the opposite may occur. Rather than halting agitation it may take another form. It may be expressed in a series of attacks. . . . We know that you do not fear death and all are confident in your personal bravery but your life belongs to Russia and you must think of the consequences to the state and to the throne if an attack should succeed."

"I am not afraid of death," the Czar replied, "and I believe in God's will but I do know that I do not have the right to risk my life."

"Yes," Yermolov said. "You do not have the right to risk your life and you must think about the foundation on which the autocracy should be based. It cannot base itself solely upon armed force, solely on the troops. . . ."

"I understand that it is an impossible situation," the Czar replied.

"You can only rely on the people," Yermolov continued, "but for this it is necessary that the people believe in you and continue to see in you their defender; yet, examine what happened on January 9. Masses of workers from all ends of Petersburg sought to gather at Your Majesty's Palace not with evil intentions, not with the aim of overthrowing the throne, not even to present to you some kind of demands of a political nature. . . . They were going to their Czar in order to lay before the throne a loyal statement of their urgent needs and to pour out before you all the bitter hardships of their lot. . . .

"I think, Your Excellency, that if we had a real government it would have given you some warning. I do not know whether it would have been possible for Your Excellency to come out to this crowd but I think that its plea could have been heard and examined in timely fashion and possibly Your Majesty could have announced that you would receive a deputation from the workers, that you would examine and satisfy legitimate demands. . . .

"Among the mass of dead there was not one leader or revolutionary. It was just a crowd, among them women and children and even those who accidentally happened to be there."

Yermolov then uttered a significant warning:

"Permit me openly to tell Your Majesty that at the present time we have no government. I have the honor to sit before you and deliver a report. This is at the given moment the government but tomorrow in this place will sit another minister and there will be another government and this other minister may report to Your Majesty in an entirely different manner than his predecessor. This cannot be the foundation of a firm government.

"Some years ago the basis of the government was the nobility. . . . But now the situation is essentially changed. Not to mention the fact the nobility itself is split. . . ."[17]

A few days later, on January 31, Yermolov sent the Czar a lengthy memorandum in which he pointed out that the Moscow nobility were so badly divided that they could not even conduct elections for the chairmanship of the corps of nobles. There was no doubt, he said, that within the nobility there were individuals of the most extreme views, supporters of radical parties. The peasants were badly shaken by events which they did not understand. They no longer knew who was friend and who was foe. They never saw the Czar. Now they were listening to agitators who were stimulating their most dangerous instincts.

"Permit me, then, Your Majesty," he said, "to say that I am profoundly confident that it is necessary to act and to act swiftly while time has not yet completely run out. . . .

"We need—all Russia waits—from the heights of the throne the Czar's word, in the solemn form of a manifesto, in the form of a response to one of the loyal addresses submitted to you—your irrevocable decision to listen to the voice of the Russian people and for this purpose to create at a moment which you deem timely freely elected representatives of all levels of the Russian soil in the form of a popular duma."[18]

Again and again the same note was sounded—the plea to the Czar to act and to speak in his own voice. It was a plea that would still be echoing unanswered in the February Days of 1917.

There was, thus, within the Czar's Government and among his closest advisers a clear perception that Russia stood at the edge of total disaster. There was even an intermittent perception of the gravity of the crisis by the Czar himself. But confusion matched confusion,[19] and around the Czar there constantly sounded the "bellowing" voices of his towering uncles, the Grand Dukes, the pounding fists of Grand Duke Alexei Alexandrovich (weighing at least 250 pounds), and the top sergeant shout of the Grand Duke Nikolai Nikolayevich (Nikolasha), who stood at six feet five inches,[20] drowning out the thoughtful advice of the Kokovtsovs and the Yermolovs.[21] Nicholas II, a slender five feet seven inches beside his huge uncles, was, in the opinion of one relative, probably "the most polite man in Europe."[22] But politeness was not enough. Russia was in agony and worse lay ahead—the crushing defeat at Mukden and with it the loss of any hope of turning the tide of land war against the Japanese only to be followed by the utter disaster of Tsushima, the sinking of the fleet the Czar had sent all the way from the Baltic.* The red flare of peasant unrest was flickering across the land and soon the sky would be crimson, night after night, with the burning of estates, the destruction of barns, the firing of the crops as they stood in the fields. Ahead lay mutiny in the fleet, the famous rebellion of the sailors of the Black Sea battleship, *Potemkin,* growing anarchy in the cities. As weeks passed, observed Witte, "the psychology of all the inhabitants of Russia began to turn upside down, people became confused, at a loss to know what to do and finally, you might say, Russia simply went mad."[23]

Sergei Alexandrovich, uncle of Nicholas II, the brother of Nicholas' father, Alexander III, was a stolid, vain, ignorant man, a mediocre officer, obstinate and overbearing. In the opinion of his nephew, the Grand Duke Alexander Mikhailovich, he was disagreeable and incompetent. "Try as I will," said Alexander, "I cannot find a single redeeming feature of his character." The best thing about him was his wife, a beautiful and intelligent woman, the Grand Duchess Yelizaveta, older sister of the Czarina.[24]

Sergei served for many years as governor-general of Moscow, and he it was who was more responsible than any other for the Khodynka disaster at the Czar's coronation. He was the sponsor and close supporter of General Trepov. In the process he succeeded in alienating every level of the population from the nobility to the merchant class, from students to laboring men. He had been relieved as governor-general just before January 9 but continued to serve as Moscow commandant. On February 4 at 3 P.M. in broad daylight as Sergei drove

---

* Grand Duke Alexander reported that Nicholas received the first news of the Tsushima disaster while on a picnic with his family at Gatchina. He said the Czar went pale, lighted a cigarette, and said nothing. The Czar described the picnic on May 14, 1905, in his diary but does not mention Tsushima until the next day's entry. (Grand Duke Alexander, *Once a Grand Duke,* p. 233; Imperator Nikolas II, *Dnevnik,* p. 201.)

in his antique German coach[25] with its gray silk lining to the Nikolsky Gate of the Kremlin, the SR terrorist Ivan Kalyayev threw a bomb which instantly killed the Grand Duke and fatally wounded his coachman.[26] Kalyayev made no attempt to escape and refused to name his accomplices. When Interior Minister Bulygin said to him: "Don't you know who I am?" Kalyayev replied: "Yes, you are No. 6 [on the SR list of targets]." The Grand Duchess Yelizaveta heard the bomb explosion from her palace, where she was working with a Red Cross group, preparing clothing for the troops in Manchuria. She instantly cried: "It is Sergei!"[27] and rushed to the scene. The Grand Duke had literally been blown to bits. She collected fragments of his body with her own hands and had them taken to the chapel in her palace.[28] Later, she visited Kalyayev in prison. She said she would intercede with the Czar for his life if he would express sorrow for killing her husband. He refused, saying that his death would aid the cause of revolution more. The assassination, like that of Plehve, had been managed by the chief of the SR Fighting Section, the police agent, Azef, and his close associate, the enigmatic and legendary Boris Savinkov.

The Grand Duke Konstantin Konstantinovich, who went to Moscow for Sergei's funeral, noted in his diary for February 6: "These terrible events seem like some kind of dream. In Russia everything is getting worse; if you look back at the autumn, to September and October, you simply can't believe with what quick steps we have advanced to disaster, to unknown misfortunes."[29]

The Czar noted his uncle's death with sorrow ("A terrible crime . . . unhappy Ella, may God preserve and help her!"), attended a mass for him (but did not go to the funeral—this was regarded by the police as too dangerous; henceforth he and his family would leave Tsarskoye Selo only under exceptional circumstances), made public a statement of indignation and anger at the cruel act, and announced that he was going to call together a national assembly "of the most trustworthy men, having the confidence of the people, and elected by them," in a word, the long-awaited Duma. This, he hoped, would bring "good and calm" to Russia.[30]

The Czar's cousin Kaiser Wilhelm II offered Nicholas II the most melodramatic advice. "Il faut que l'Empereur fasse un grand acte pour affermir son pouvoir de nouveau et sauvegarder sa dynastie qui est menacée. Il faut qu'il paye de sa personne," wrote "your warmly loving cousin and friend, Willy," to his "beloved Nicky." He recommended that Nicholas assume personal command of his troops, go to Moscow, pray at St. Basil's, gather an assemblage at the Kremlin, promise no constitution or national assembly, no free speech, no free press, simply a habeas corpus act. Then, surrounded by his supporters, with the Orthodox church symbols, the crosses, the gonfalons, the banners, the holy icons, the censors, and the candles, emerge on a balcony before massed troops with naked bayonets and cannon and summon them to battle against the Japanese foe with himself at the head. Not content with writing Nicky a 4,000-word letter, Willy wrote the Czar's mother a similar, equally long letter, hoping to get the Dowager Empress Mariya Fyodorovna to back him up. "What a blow for all your House and for poor Nicky [were] the terrible Moscow events!" he wrote her. For once Nicky showed good sense. He ignored the Kaiser's Wagnerian scenario.[31]

In plain fact, as Grand Duke Konstantin Konstantinovich noted in his diary, the Czar and the Czarina were living by themselves in Tsarskoye Selo, almost as prisoners. Even as late as March 25 Konstantin Konstantinovich said in his diary that "there still can be no talk" of Their Excellencies leaving Tsarskoye Selo. In May he was so distressed by the situation that he wrote: "I'm afraid to read the papers."[32]

"Good and calm." The Czar would struggle for years trying to find the path to good and calm, and finally his reign would come to an end, the goal still as far from his grasp as it would prove to be from that of his successors.

XVI

Lenin

On the morning of January 10, a crisp winter day in Geneva, Lenin and his wife, Nadezhda Krupskaya, started out from the modest pension where they lived at 91 Rue de Carouge.[1] They were on their way to the library where Lenin was busily compiling a list of books in Russian, German, French, and English on different subjects, particularly Japan, probably in preparation for writing something on the Russo-Japanese War, a subject which he had seriously neglected. The intersection of Rue de Carouge and Quai de l'Arve was the center of the Russian emigration in Geneva.[2] There Lenin had set up offices for his new paper, *Vpered* (Forward), to which he had devoted so much of his energies in recent months; there was located at No. 93 the famous Lepeshinsky Bolshevik restaurant[3] or canteen with six long wooden tables and fifty benches (and a piano) where the hard-pressed revolutionaries were served plain but wholesome meals of borsch, *shchi*, *pirogi*, and *chorny khleb* at cheap prices,[4] and the Café Landolt where over a glass of beer or a carafe of wine the émigrés argued from ten in the morning until two at night. Here lived most of Lenin's closest collaborators abroad—Vladimir Bonch-Bruyevich, the Lyadovs (Mandelshtams), the Ilyins, and many others, including Anatoly Lunacharsky and his wife, Anna, newly arrived from Russia. And here were to be found most often M. S. Olminsky (Alexandrov), V. V. Vorovsky (Orlovsky), V. I. Krakhmal (Zagorsky), V. P. Nogin,[5] A. A. Bogdanov (Ryadovoi), and other Lenin supporters or new arrivals from the

homeland like S. I. Gusev, Lenin's chief in St. Petersburg, Maxim Litvinov, and many others.[6]

The morning of January 10 had begun for Lenin and his wife,
Krupskaya, like any other in the unending succession of mornings in
emigration. They rose early, refreshed themselves with a glass of hot
tea and a bit of bread and cheese, and then, putting their notebooks
and memoranda into worn leather portfolios, set out on foot for the
Geneva Public Library.[7]

Krupskaya, never a good-looking woman, was growing stolid and
heavy. The years of emigration had taken their strain. Her broad face
with its heavy brow now conveyed an air of perpetual tiredness, and
her slightly protruding eyes (later she was to suffer severely from
goiter) had become strained and red. Lenin had grown more and
more bald, but his glance was as piercing as ever. Both seemed ten
or fifteen years older than their chronological ages.

Lenin and Krupskaya had hardly gotten to the street when they saw
the Lunacharskys heading toward them. Anna Lunacharsky was so excited she could not talk and simply waved her muff. Lunacharsky's
pince-nez almost leaped from the narrow bridge of his nose as he
shouted out the good news of the outbreak in Petersburg. Excitement
spread through the Russian colony. All day long Lenin and his companions sat in the Lepeshinsky canteen. (Lepeshinsky had almost
swooned when, coming back from his daily trip to the butcher, he saw
the headline "La Révolution en Russie."[8]) Little was said. Everyone
was too excited. Solemnly the little group sang the revolutionary funeral march, "You Have Fallen in the Struggle." There were five editions of the *Tribune de Genève*. Each brought more details of events.
There was no immediate effort to assess the meaning of what had happened. The shock was too great, emotions too profound.[9]

Trotsky had been away from Geneva on a lecture trip and returned
only on the morning of the tenth, having sat up all night in a third-
class compartment. He picked up a paper at the railroad station but
found no mention of the workers' march (it was yesterday's paper but
he did not notice that) and decided that the demonstration had not
occurred. He called at the Iskra office a bit later and greeted Martov:
"So it didn't come off?"

"What do you mean?" Martov replied. "We've spent the whole night
in a café reading fresh cables. Haven't you heard anything?"

Martov, a night owl, had beaten Lenin to the punch by twelve
hours. Now he pushed into Trotsky's hands the reports telling of the
firing on the workers.[10] Instantly Trotsky made up his mind that he
must return to Russia. He got a new passport from a student, left for
Munich with his wife, Nataliya Sedova, within a day or two, paused in

Vienna (where he heard the news of the assassination of Grand Duke Sergei and made contact with the revolutionary adventurer Parvus), and by mid-February had arrived in Kiev with a passport in the name of a retired corporal named Arbuzov.[11]

In the general excitement the Russian émigré colony drew together. The Mensheviks proposed a common meeting with the Bolsheviks. Lenin's closest associates were enthusiastic. They went to him. "Hmmm," he said, stroking his chin. "We must fear the Greeks even when they are bearing gifts." He was adamant against a common front. His comrades were in despair. Finally, Lepeshinsky burst out: "It's a unique moment in our life. The great mass of the Social Democrats want peace. If we are obstinate this mass will pass us by." Reluctantly Lenin yielded—but insisted on strict bargaining. Russia was in flames but he was not willing to abandon any real point in his excruciating ideological warfare. The meeting was finally held but Lenin walked out halfway through it and compelled his small band of supporters to do the same.[12]

Lenin stayed on in Geneva. So did Martov. So did Axelrod. So did Plekhanov—he never did go to Russia during the '05 days. Even the fiery Rosa Luxemburg did not get back to Russian Poland until December 1905. Nor did Chernov or the other leaders of the SRs hurry home. In fact, the Little Grandmother of the Revolution, Yekaterina Breshko-Breshkovskaya, the very symbol of Socialist Revolutionary spirit, at this time was touring America with extraordinary success, raising thousands of dollars and stirring audiences from Boston's Faneuil Hall to the Pacific Coast. She did not interrupt her tour. Nor did Pavel Milyukov, the leader of the liberals, immediately cancel the course of lectures he was delivering at the University of Chicago. He returned to Russia only in April.

Why was this? Why did not men who had dedicated their lives to the overthrow of the Czar leap to the opportunity? The plain fact was that the revolutionaries, as a whole, including the underground in Russia and all of the émigré leaders (Trotsky was a very minor figure at this point, having broken with both the Bolsheviks and the Mensheviks), did not perceive that *the* revolutionary moment was at hand. Lenin's new *Vpered*, launched on the eve of January 9 (the first issue was dated December 24 and arrived in St. Petersburg just before[13] Bloody Sunday[14]), called, of course, for revolution but not in the immediate future.[15] In fact, Lenin thought that the "wave of liberal agitation," as he called it, might well quickly abate. The proletariat, he said, was "holding itself back, carefully taking its bearings." In retrospect, the words seemed appropriate to describe Lenin's own posture; but not that of the actual proletariat, now taking to the barricades. But neither Lenin nor any revolutionary figure predicted January 9. They did not realize events were moving so rapidly, and what movement they did perceive they were inclined to scorn as being either bourgeois in spirit or the product of police provocation. Revolutionary plotters though they were, they played no role in these most revolutionary events and, hence, their impulse was to doubt their relevance. Neither then nor later were they frank enough to admit their colossal error. But Lunacharsky, looking back to 1905 from the perspective of 1917–18, wrote: "I now think that the 1905–06 revolution caught us somewhat unprepared and that we lacked real political skill." And to make clear that he had Lenin specifically in mind he added, "I am bound to say that this period of Lenin's activity, in 1905 and 1906, seems to me to have been a comparatively ineffective one."[16]

Lunacharsky was close to Lenin in this period and he sought to clarify in his mind Lenin's stature as a revolutionary leader.

"I wondered," he said, "whether Lenin really was such a genuinely revolutionary leader as he had seemed to be. I began to feel that life as an émigré had somewhat reduced Lenin's stature, that for him the internal party struggle with the Mensheviks had overshadowed the much greater struggle against the monarchy and that he was more of a journalist than a real leader."[17]

Rereading the record of Lenin's activity, studying his letters and articles, it is difficult not to agree with Lunacharsky, and, in a sense, Lunacharsky's remarks applied to most of the émigré leaders—Plekhanov, Martov, and the rest. For years they had been living semisecretly in faded boardinghouses and pensions, hunted and spied upon by the police, often never knowing where the next franc was coming from, engaged in dangerous, foolhardy and futile plotting and conspiracy, arguing among themselves, becoming more and more parochial, jealous, and closed-in in their viewpoints, burning with frustration and passion which found no release. It was this, as much as the question of principles, organizational rules, centralized authority, or the dominant personality of Lenin which had produced the fateful split within the Social Democrats which in 1904 gave birth to the rival factions—Lenin's Bolsheviks and Martov's Mensheviks.

Life in emigration had changed them more than they knew. The toll on Lenin's nerves had been serious. He had passed through at least three episodes of severe melancholia. Before Iskra was moved to Geneva in 1903, Krupskaya wrote that "Vladimir Ilyich's nerves were in such a bad state that he developed a nervous disease caused by inflammation of the nerve endings of the back and chest" (shingles?).[18] At the time of the great split at the Second Party Congress in 1903 she reported that he could not sleep and virtually stopped eating.[19]. A bit later he was so preoccupied that he ran into a streetcar while cycling and nearly had his eye knocked out.[20]

In the spring and summer of 1904 Lenin was in such a state of nervous exhaustion that Krupskaya compelled him to give up all work and go hiking in the mountains for a month.[21] Nor was this something new. In Siberia the quarrels of the exiles played havoc with his nerves and on his first trip to Switzerland in 1895 he complained of "my nervous stomach."[22] A. D. Naglovsky, an Old Bolshevik, a member of the Kazan organization, met Lenin at this time in Geneva. He described Lenin as extremely nervous, fidgety, and keyed up, "obviously a neurasthenic."[23] By December 1904 Lenin's spirits were much improved (because of the impending publication of the first issue of *Vpered*), but he was too occupied by organizational problems and factional disputes to give careful attention to the evolving situation in Russia and he was far from well informed—except for ordinary newspaper reports. His chief Petersburg agent, S. I. Gusev, had been in Geneva in December 1904[24] but gave Lenin no indication of what lay immediately ahead, and the reports which Gusev and the other Bolsheviks sent back to Lenin offered little clue to the build-up of unrest among the factory workers of Petersburg. Small wonder that the contents of *Vpered* No. 1 seemed to have been written in a different era than that which opened January 9. Day after day Lenin and Krupskaya wrote their contacts in Russia imploring, begging, demanding to know what was happening. The waiting, the delay, the lack of information, played further on Lenin's nerves and gave him sleepless nights.

Lenin wrote his Central Committee in Petersburg seven days after Bloody Sunday: "We have just looked at the log of correspondence with Russia. Gusev sent 6 letters in 10 days and Bogdanov 2 in 30 days. How come? Not a whisper, not a line for *Vpered*. Not a word about business, plans, communications. This is something impossible, unbelievable, a disgrace."[25] Two weeks later he was writing: "We are putting out No. 6 of *Vpered* and from a member of the Board of Editors (Bogdanov) not a line for *Vpered*. We brag about the young forces of the Bolsheviks and after two months of work we haven't even gotten a whisper!"[26] Krupskaya wrote Gusev January 5, 1905: "Dear Friend! Why don't you write a single word? We wait your letter with impatience. You promised to write all your impressions."[27]

Some of Lenin's comrades thought that 1904 was his worst year. "For a long time he wrote nothing and even didn't speak at public meetings," M. Olminsky recalled.[28] Everything had gone wrong. On December 11, 1904, Krupskaya wrote Lenin's sister Anna Ilyinichna Yelizarova: "Correspondence goes very poorly and not by our fault.

We have no money and literally every ruble is precious." But Lenin had been stimulated by the arrival of Lunacharsky, and a public meeting at which Lunacharsky spoke had been a great success so that, she added, "Starik [the Old Man] has come to life and is young again in these last days."[29]

It was in this stifling atmosphere that many of the characteristics which were to leave a stamp not only on Lenin's leadership but upon the movement which he headed were forged. Russian political controversy had traditionally been passionate and, on the part of the radicals, it was characterized by all the extremism which marked their radical philosophy. Feelings were harsh. Rhetoric robust. Lunacharsky called Lenin a "cruel political opponent, exploiting any blunder and exaggerating every hint of opportunism. . . . He employed every weapon except dirty ones." Lunacharsky saw little difference in tactics between Lenin and his Menshevik opponents and admitted being "very much disturbed by Lenin's political ruthlessness" when it was directed against himself.[30] G. M. Krzhizhanovsky called Lenin merciless and undeviating in political struggle although "to look at he is like a well-heeled peasant from Yaroslavl, a cunning little *muzhik*, especially when he's wearing a beard."[31] Trotsky called him absolutely ruthless and said it was not without significance that "irreconcilable" and "relentless" were among his favorite words. He found Lenin's conduct unpardonable at times but later conceded that it was correct from the revolutionary point of view.[32] Vera Zasulich, comparing Plekhanov and Lenin, said that Plekhanov was like a greyhound, Lenin like a bulldog with a "deadly bite."[33] Plekhanov told Axelrod one day, speaking of Lenin: "From this dough comes Robespierres."[34] Lenin's socialist opponents spoke even more sharply. Professor Sergei Bulgakov contended that "Lenin thinks dishonestly" and added that Lenin's *Chto Delat?* (What Is to Be Done?) "reeks of a revolutionary police-station." The Marxist economist Mikhail I. Tugan-Baranovsky contended that Lenin's *Development of Capitalism in Russia* was a "weak book" "full of mistakes" and said that Lenin deliberately avoided reading works which might disturb his Marxist theories.[35]

Nikolai Valentinov (N. V. Volsky or Samsonov), a young Russian revolutionary with an indelible memory, a strong curiosity, a deep interest, and even (especially in the beginning) a genuine reverence for Lenin, spent many hours between January 5, 1904, and September 16, 1904, in discussion and argument with Lenin. Valentinov was an extraordinarily energetic and intellectually curious young man who played a considerable role in Moscow and St. Petersburg intellectual and radical life in the prerevolutionary years. Andrei Bely, who worked with him on several fleeting Social Democratic newspapers, described him as a lively companion with pale blond hair, a gift for words, a sharp wit, and very attractive.[36] Valentinov had come to Geneva as an exile after being imprisoned in Kiev. He had a keen ear for Lenin's style and quickly noted that Lenin habitually applied harsh epithets to his opponents, often drawing them from Russian literature. "Voroshilov" and "Balalaikin" or "Voroshilov-Balalaikin" were favorites. Voroshilov was a character in Turgenev's *Smoke*, Balalaikin was drawn from Saltykov-Shchedrin.[37] Sometimes, Lenin called his enemies Martynovs and Akimovs—two old party workers who Lenin believed symbolized "political cretinism, theoretical backwardness and organizational tailism."[38]

This tactic was by no means unique with Lenin. It was common among the revolutionaries and, indeed, Lenin claimed, probably quite accurately, that he had taken it from Plekhanov. Plekhanov once told him, "First, let's stick the convict's badge on him and then after that we'll examine his case."[39]

Lenin told Valentinov:

"I think that we must 'stick the convict's badge' on anyone and everyone who tries to undermine Marxism, even if we don't go on to examine his case. That's how every sound revolutionary should react. When you see a stinking heap on the road you don't have to poke around in it to see what it is. Your nose tells you it's shit and you give it a wide berth."[40]

When Valentinov reproached Lenin, saying that he had "never before seen or heard such nasty ways of settling accounts, such repulsive polemical methods and back-stabbing intrigue" as in Geneva revolutionary circles, Lenin defended this style: "You are upset, God help us, because the same tone doesn't prevail in the party as is approved in schools for daughters of the nobility." He bragged that Marx used to curse and swear and praised the skill of French politicians at "blackening an opponent's mug so well that it takes ages for him to get it clean again."[41] "Revolution is a dirty job," he once said. "You do not make it with white gloves."[42]

Lenin was deliberately coarse in his political polemics, employing rude peasant oaths and derisive street language. It was almost as though he was seeking to establish his proletarian credentials by using phrases and language that would never have been heard or permitted by his schoolmaster father or his cultured mother.[43]

Later, Lenin formulated his philosophy precisely in a speech made in his own defense before a Party court in 1906, answering charges . that he was guilty of conduct impermissible in a Party member.

He conceded that his words were "calculated to evoke in the reader hatred, aversion and contempt . . . calculated not to convince but to break up the ranks of the opponent, not to correct the mistake of the opponent but to destroy him, to wipe his organization off the face of the earth. This wording is indeed of such a nature as to evoke the worst thoughts, the worst suspicions about the opponent."

He said such conduct was not permissible within a united party but insisted that when confronted with a split (i.e., a conflict between his views and others) he would *always* act in this manner. He had, he conceded, "purposely and deliberately carried confusion into the ranks of the section of the St. Petersburg proletariat which followed the Mensheviks."

"Are there any limits to permissible struggle based on a split? There are no limits to such a struggle set by any Party standards, nor can there be such."[44]

There was nothing emotional about this tactic, in the opinion of V. S. Voitinsky, who was extremely close to Lenin in 1906–7. "He was perhaps the most unemotional man I have ever met in politics. No hate, no compassion, not even irritation against his opponents," Voitinsky said. "His ruthlessness in polemics never stemmed from a personal grudge—each word, even each slanderous innuendo in his writings was coldly calculated."[45]

This was a far cry from the fanatical standards of personal honesty with which Lenin was raised, the standards, for example, of the Ulyanov family, the standards of his elder brother, Alexander. But Alexander had broken the barrier which separates lofty goals and extreme means. He had, to the distress of his mother, been willing to kill the Czar for the sake of the revolutionary cause. (But he would not have been willing to lie; to use deceit; to call white black or honest dishonest; he refused to ask pardon for his crime.) Lenin by 1905 had also crossed a bridge. He was no longer the pleasant, attractive, fun-loving, teasing boy so passionate in his games and play in a sleepy Volga town. The passion he still had but the inner man was changed. It was a change which had begun, no doubt, as he sat in the pergola looking over the Volga in Simbirsk and pondered his brother's death. It had gone forward in the early arguments in St. Petersburg, as he put the romantic traditions of his brother and the Narodnaya Volya behind him. It had begun to harden in the long and pregnant years of Siberian exile, and now living the life of a political émigré his character had taken its final form—ruthless and merciless in political combat, fanatical in determination to attain a goal and in conviction of his own superior wisdom, but always flexible in tactics. He preserved with members of his family and a most intimate circle the old, warm, simple, honest habits of Simbirsk, the plain dicta of the truth and nothing but the truth, inculcated by his mother and his father. But in politics he was now ready to use any means to his end. Or almost any. He explained this impatiently to Angelica Balabanoff, the saintly Russian revolutionary, at about this time (probably November 23 or 24, 1904) in Zurich where she went to hear him speak.[46] She could not understand his habit of accusing honest and disinterested people of treason, dishonesty, or bribery. He told her that to seize power every means must be used.

"Even dishonest ones?" she asked.

"Everything that is done in the interest of the proletarian cause is honest," he said. He explained that when he called a dedicated socialist a traitor "I do not intend to say they are dishonest individuals; but I do want to point out that, objectively, through their attitude they become traitors."[47]

Even earlier, in Lenin's early days in St. Petersburg he had been "very flexible" on questions of tactics. V. V. Starkov said that Lenin had strongly defended the use of terror by the Social Democrats, insisting that "the principal thing was the objective." Lenin held that "each method of struggle (including terror) could be good or bad, depending on whether it aided in the given circumstance in achieving the goal." And, said Starkov, "so Vladimir Ilyich remained to the last days of his life."[48] (Starkov had been associated with Lenin in the St. Petersburg Union of Struggle for the Emancipation of the Working Class and was close to him until after 1905.) This was a characteristic of thought and tactic which would haunt Lenin's cause and throw a deep shadow far into the future.

Together with his maximalist attitude, Lenin linked belief in an elite revolutionary corps, highly disciplined, with the "conductor's baton" in his own firm hand.[49] "From the time of Iskra [that is, 1901–2] Lenin concentrated on one new organizational idea—the creation of a close-knit, solid, well-disciplined group of 'professional revolutionaries,' as outlined in his book *Chto Delat?*," M. A. Silvin believed.[50] It was, in Lenin's belief, fully matured by 1905, the only method by which the Revolution could be achieved. And this quite naturally reinforced the passion with which he sought by any means to make certain that his own views on Party organization and Party policy prevailed. It was this tendency toward extremism and total centralization which led Trotsky to make his famous (and prophetic) declaration: "The organization of the Party takes the place of the Party itself; the Central Committee takes the place of the organization: and finally the dictator takes the place of the Central Committee."[51]

Or as Gleb Krzhizhanovsky quoted the Menshevik leader Fyodor Dan as once saying:

"There was no other man who for 24 hours a day was occupied with Revolution; to whom there was no other thought except thoughts of Revolution and who even in his sleep saw only Revolution."[52]

This, then, was the Lenin who received the news of January 9 in Geneva, exuberant, impatient but by no means certain of the next move. Lenin was too shrewd not to recognize that January 9 was a quantum jump in the direction in which he hoped to move Russia. But he could not quickly determine what to do, particularly since his Bolshevik organization in Russia was so pitifully weak.

In late January Father Gapon arrived in Geneva, by way of Paris. He issued an "open letter," hoping to unite the quarreling revolutionary factions into one great movement with himself at its head. It was a naïve dream, but Lenin commented favorably in *Vpered* and, unlike some revolutionaries such as Plekhanov, eagerly met with Gapon hoping to get through his eyes a firsthand look at the situation within Russia.[53] It was typical of the isolation of Lenin and the other revolutionaries from ordinary Russian men and women that Lenin was literally to steep himself in Gapon's company. Later on, during the summer, Lenin did the same with the revolutionary sailor Matyushenko, leader in the mutiny of the battleship *Potemkin*. He used such individuals as a kind of human barometer to test the winds of Russia. The truth was that Lenin had had comparatively little contact with either workers or peasants. He had met a few peasants as a teenager on the family estate at Kokushkino, had seen a few more while living with his mother at Alakayevka, and had gotten acquainted with two or three in Siberian exile. As for workers—genuine proletarians— he saw not many more. He had met some in St. Petersburg during his textile organizing days before his exile, but once he left Russia direct personal meetings with workers became rare.

A woman SR arranged Gapon's first rendezvous with Lenin on "neutral ground" at a Geneva café. Lenin was greatly moved by Gapon but, recognizing the man's naïveté, warned: "Don't you listen to flattery, my dear man. If you don't study, that is where you'll be." And he pointed under the table.

Alas, this was to be Gapon's fate. His star flared quickly and vanished. He published his "autobiography" (a sensationalized hack writer's job), tried vainly to unify the revolutionaries in an abortive meeting of eighteen socialist parties, April 2, 1905, and finally made his way back to Russia with documents and passports provided by Lenin in connection with a plot to smuggle a shipload of arms into Russia aboard the British freighter *John Grafton*.[54] The *Grafton* affair was remarkably complex. The funds apparently were provided by a Japanese agent, Col. Motojiro Akashi, through Koni Zilliacus, a

Finnish revolutionary later to become a well-known British left parliamentarian.[55] The consignment of the ship and cargo were arranged in England by an anarchist, N. V. Chaikovsky. They were consigned to the SRs, and Gapon's role in this was very obscure.[56] However, the ship ran aground and the arms were lost. Gapon went in and out of Russia, visited Monte Carlo creating such a scandal that he lost most of his following and finally became involved in an intrigue so complex it still cannot be entirely pieced together.

Gapon had gone back to St. Petersburg, hoping to re-establish his workers' organization. Intermediaries promised him an interview with Count Witte but Witte refused to meet him, saying he thought Gapon might assassinate him. Aides to Witte and police agents promptly began to spin a web around the naïve defrocked priest. Such shadowy figures as I. F. Manasevich-Manuilov, a journalist with police connections, and the clever senior Okhrana official, Pyotr I. Rachkovsky, involved Gapon in proposals for double and triple betrayals.

At the same time Azef, chief of the SR fighting organization (and himself a double agent), ordered Pyotr Rutenberg, the SR terrorist who was still at Gapon's side, to carry out a double assassination of Gapon and Rachkovsky. This was beyond Rutenberg's ability. Finally, however, Rutenberg, finding himself more and more involved in Gapon's scandals, decided to carry out the priest's "execution."

Rutenberg lured Gapon to a cottage in the Finnish lake resort of Ozersky. He had with him four or five members of the SR fighting organization whom he told that Gapon was to be executed because of betrayal of the revolutionary cause to the police. A drumhead court-martial was held with Gapon in an adjacent room. The group "voted unanimously" (in Rutenberg's account) to hang the priest. They rushed into his room as Gapon cried: "Brothers, darlings. Stop. Give me a last word." They pinned him down, threw a rope over an iron hook on the wall, and strung him up as he cried: "Brothers. Brothers. Mercy. Forgive me in the memory of the past." The hook was so low that Rutenberg and his assistants sat on Gapon's shoulders until he choked to death.

The story leaked immediately and sensational accounts appeared in the St. Petersburg papers and abroad but the police took their time about "discovering" the body because of the involvement of so many double and triple agents. A month passed before the body was found and buried by a handful of his old supporters.[57]

While Lenin had recognized Gapon's naïveté he had found him a valued key to the mood of the Russian peasant. One day he came upon Gapon and the peasant sailor, Matyushenko, in violent argument about the Bolshevik land program. Lenin listened and quickly realized that both felt the Bolshevik program was inadequate. "All the land to the people," shouted Matyushenko. Gapon agreed and offered a slogan: "We want no Czar—let there be one master over the land—God —with all of you as his tenants." Instantly, Lenin determined that the peasants were right and he was wrong—or so Krupskaya reported. He could not win his Party to this position. (It was, of course, the basic position which Lenin's bitter enemies, the terror-oriented SRs, had taken from the beginning.) But when the time came he remembered. "All land to the peasants" was to be a cornerstone of 1917.

XVII

The Dress Rehearsal

On a fine clear morning, September 4, 1905, at 10:30, Nicholas II, his wife, the Czarina, all their children, and a small party that included Prince A. N. Obolensky, Adm. Count A. F. Geiden, Adm. Alexei A. Birilev, the Navy Minister, and a few others, including the Czarina's new lady in waiting, Anna Vyrubova, boarded the ketch *Alexandra* at Peterhof and sailed to Kronshtadt, where they transferred to the Imperial yacht, *Polar Star*. They were off for a two weeks' cruise on the Baltic with what remained of the Russian fleet after the disasters in the Far East. At last the Czar was able to relax. The worst was over.

On August 6 he had approved a new law, establishing the Duma, and even though suffrage was limited and the Duma's powers even more so, he felt confident this action would quell the political agitation which had swelled so alarmingly. On August 16 Witte had signed the Treaty of Portsmouth, ending the war with Japan on terms which were somewhat better than might have been expected. Soon seasoned troops would be on their way back to European Russia, ready to crush any disorders that might break out. It had been a hard year and the Czar frankly told Vyrubova that without the Empress "I could not have survived it."[1] The September sail was filled with long days on the blue sea and frequent halts at sandy islets for picnics, strolls, and mushroom picking. The children, including the Czarevich, were in fine fettle. The Czar even shot a woodcock and a few ducks. The Czarina and Madame Vyrubova played four hands on the piano, Beethoven and Tchaikovsky.[2] The sun shone. Nights were cold but there were fireworks for the children. Several times the Czar took his family for a row in a small dinghy. The weather held remarkably well.[3] "I'm happy as a child," the Czar wrote his mother, "with this liberty and this rest, and above all with the life on the water. Our little son is in very good spirits and I hope that he will also love the sea. The idea of getting away for some days for a change of scene has been with me for a long time. Thank God, that this dream has been realized!"[4] Toward the end of the cruise Witte joined them and was created a Count for his success at Portsmouth. The occasion overwhelmed the normally bluff statesman. According to the Czar, Witte tried three times to kiss his hand. (Witte recalled kissing it only once.[5]) As the cruise ended, the Czarina took Madame Vyrubova in her arms and said: "I thank God that He has sent me a friend."[6]

Vyrubova, a plain, deeply neurasthenic woman, was the daughter of the Czar's chief of chancery. She was superstitious, religious, and became intensely devoted to the Czar and Czarina, dedicating her entire life to the Imperial couple after the failure of an unconsummated marriage.[7]

Back at Peterhof September 19 the Czar settled into the "old routine —again begin the reports and meetings." It was tiresome but he felt refreshed and relieved that his great empire at long last was moving toward less turbulent times.

So it seemed. That night at Peterhof the Czar dined alone with his beloved Alix. Somewhere in the papers on his desk there was probably a telegram about the situation in Moscow. Nothing urgent. But on that day, September 19, the printers at the big Sytin publishing firm had gone on strike. The owners had been willing to grant a reduction in working hours but refused a wage increase.

If there was no scent of crisis at Peterhof, the same could be said for Geneva, where Lenin toiled away on the minutiae of running his underground organization. Letters, reports, articles, complaints, squabbles. His temper was bad. He was so angry with the conduct of his Central Committee in Russia that he swore: "Positively, I will bring you up on formal charges before the Fourth Congress on grounds of violating Party rules and establishing a second (rival) center. By God, I will!"[8] In July of 1905 the Bolsheviks still had only about one thousand members in St. Petersburg, mostly intelligentsia— students, *kursistki* (young female students auditing university courses), professional people, and the like. There were only about fifty members in the Narva section and still no proper organization at the Putilov works.[9] At the moment Lenin was increasingly concerned with the idea of armed insurrection. He had made a study of street fighting at the library of the Société des Lectures, he consulted the works of Marx and Engels, dipped into Karl von Clausewitz, and began to translate a book by Gen. G. P. Cluseret. Cluseret had served with Giuseppe Garibaldi, with the Union forces in the Civil War, and finally as a military leader of the Paris Commune in 1870.[10] At Lenin's insistence a Fighting Technical Group had been set up in St. Petersburg in which Nikolai Burenin, that same well-to-do young man who had been instantly revolutionized by the demonstration at Kazan Cathedral Square in 1901, was playing a leading role.[11] Its task was to smuggle arms into St. Petersburg and organize small workshops for making bombs in preparation of street fighting. On October 3 Lenin wrote to St. Petersburg, to the Fighting Committee: "I'm terrified, by God, simply terrified to watch you talking about bombs for half a year and still not a single bomb made. And you are educated people. . . . Go to the young, gentlemen! That's the one and only saving remedy. Otherwise, by God, you will be too late (I see this clearly)." He demanded that they set up fighting groups of three individuals or ten or thirty and warned that unless they created two hundred to three hundred groups within the next month or two the Fighting Committee would be dead and might as well be buried. In spite of these rousing words Lenin did not think revolution was at hand. In fact,[12] ten days later, October 13, he wrote again to St. Petersburg and expressed himself firmly against an immediate uprising, suggesting that it would be better to wait until spring and the return of the troops from Manchuria. "I'm inclined to think that, in general, it would be better to delay it," he said. "But of course, we won't be asked.[13] . . . The time of the uprising, I repeat, I would *willingly postpone* until the spring but it is difficult for me to judge from a distance."[14]

Actually at this very moment Russia was exploding.

Once again neither the revolutionaries nor the Government had sensed the flash point. Even Trotsky, who had been in Russia since spring in a maelstrom of revolutionary agitation (and far more au courant than the exiles in Geneva or the Czar at Tsarskoye Selo), was rusticating in Finland where he had taken refuge in early summer after a provocateur named Dobroskok (Nikolai of the gold spectacles) had betrayed a number of Mensheviks with whom he was in touch. By this time Trotsky was working closely with both Mensheviks and Bolsheviks. He was writing leaflets from Finland and through his close friend, Leonid Krasin, Lenin's organizing genius, was having them printed by the Bolsheviks in St. Petersburg.[15]

As Trotsky labored quietly over his pamphlets deep in the Finnish woods beside an isolated lake at an almost empty villa called Rauha (peace), Russia began to erupt.[16] The whole Moscow printing industry closed down in sympathy with the Sytin strike September 20. Other industries quickly followed. The Moscow bakeries struck. Fearing the city would be left without bread, authorities attempted to confine the workers at Fillipov's bakery, a huge six-story building in the center of town near the governor-general's palace on the Tverskaya, to their plant. A wild fight broke out. Bakers hurled cast-iron pans, cake molds, and bricks at the police. Finally two companies of the 1st Don Cossack Regiment stormed the plant.[17] Students joined the fray. Moscow University became the center of nonstop agitation. There were repeated street clashes and more than one hundred casualties. On October 2 a "Soviet," or council, was formed by striking unionists to direct activities, although by this time the Moscow movement seemed to be fading out. But almost immediately it flared up in St. Petersburg, touched off by the sudden death of the liberal Prince Sergei Trubetskoy, the new rector of Moscow University.[18] He had been a national hero since June when he gave the Czar a warning of the urgent need of achieving unity with the people. Failure, he said, would lead to a popular movement against "all who were called masters." "Do not linger, Sire," he told the Czar. "Great is your responsibility before God and Russia." To which the Czar responded: "Throw away your doubts. My will, the Czar's will, to call together representatives of the people is unchangeable."[19]

Now it was autumn. There was still no Duma, and Trubetskoy's death became the symbol and excuse for mighty demonstrations, first in St. Petersburg, then in Moscow. In St. Petersburg mourners seized red flags from passing streetcars and knelt with uncovered heads in Palace Square to honor the dead of January 9. In Moscow fifty thousand paraded with red banners, golden trumpets, wreaths of flowers. They sang the "Marseillaise."[20] Strikes spread like an epidemic. All the printers in St. Petersburg, except those of the General Staff and the Chief Government Printing Office, went on strike. So did the great shipbuilding plants, the steel factories, the naval works. By early October the railway men began to walk out. The Moscow-Kazan line was first, then Moscow-Yaroslavl, Moscow-Nizhni Novgorod, Moscow-Kursk, and quickly all other lines which radiated out of Moscow like the spokes of a wheel.[21] Service between Petersburg and Moscow tapered off. The strike spread through the country to Kharkov, the Urals, the Volga, the Ukraine, Poland, Central Asia, and Siberia. By October 12 there was not even service between Peterhof, where the Czar was in residence, and the capital, twenty miles away. The picket boats *Dozorny* and *Razvedchik* were pressed into service to carry Ministers back and forth.[22] Prices began to rise; food, especially meat, vanished from the markets. Banks halted payment on bills.[23]

Russia was experiencing—unannounced, unplanned, and initially unrecognized—a formless insurrection in which power simply flowed to the people. In St. Petersburg, following the Moscow example, a Soviet, or co-ordinating council, of workers' deputies sprang into being. The first call went out October 10 and 11 at the initiative of the Mensheviks (Lenin's Bolsheviks, once again misjudging the situation, were violently opposed to the Soviet, which they saw as a Menshevik trick, that is, a device to channel the workers into Menshevik rather than Bolshevik ranks), and it immediately leaped into life, meeting for the first time October 13.[24] Soon the Soviet was acting more like a shadow government than a strike committee. From the beginning Trotsky, back from Finland, living with his wife in the rented rooms of a stock exchange speculator under the name of Mr. and Mrs. Vikentyev, became a leading member of the Soviet under the name of Yanovsky. He had, in fact, returned from Finland with a plan in his portfolio for just such a council.[25] He was soon writing for three papers—the *Russian Gazette*, which he had taken over with the revolutionary adventurer Parvus and pushed up from 30,000 to 500,000 circulation within a month; *Nachalo*, the new Menshevik organ which towered over the Bolshevik *Novaya Zhizn* (weak and faltering with Lenin still abroad); and *Izvestiya*, a new underground paper launched as the official organ of the Soviet. The Soviet was to last for fifty days, and before those fifty days ended Trotsky had emerged as its acknowledged leader, the spirit and voice of what had become the first Russian Revolution. The 1905 Soviet was to color not only his life, his role in Russia, but the whole revolutionary experience through which Russia was to pass in coming years. In the end it would bequeath its name to the regime which emerged from the Romanov wreckage. The Soviet, coming into being almost accidentally, proved to be indispensable. As Trotsky commented: "Internal friction between two equally powerful sections of the Social Democrats, on the one hand, and the struggle of both factions with the Socialist Revolutionaries on the other, rendered the creation of a non-party organization absolutely essential."[26]

Few countries have ever seen such a general strike as developed in Russia. Doctors, bank clerks, postmen, the Mariinsky corps de ballet, droshky drivers, and stockbrokers walked out. St. Petersburg's water supply was assured only by locking in the workers. There was no electricity because the power workers had walked out. The city was as dark as it had been in the Middle Ages. It was virtually cut off from the hinterland.[27] A single searchlight was mounted atop the Admiralty building and powered by naval turbines to sweep the Nevsky Prospekt. Who could tell what might happen next?[28] The days were strange, the weather was strange, and the mood of St. Petersburg was like never before, or so it seemed to the poet Andrei Bely. It was cold and somehow noxious. The wind scampered through the city, sending clouds of dust before it. On the streets there seemed to be more and more caps and soldiers' hats and fewer and fewer gentlemen's toppers.[29]

Rail supply to Kuropatkin's troops in the Far East was cut. Even the army telegraph was affected. With newspapers closed down rumors flew. Workers by the thousand thronged into St. Petersburg University, seeking news of what was happening, seeking, too, leadership in a situation that was as confused as it was critical. Each evening thousands assembled—10,000, 15,000, 20,000, 30,000. No one could be sure how large was the crowd. The university became a hotbed of revolutionary agitation. Bolshevik, Menshevik, and SR students (many of them had only joined their factions within the past week) worked shoulder to shoulder. By October 12 St. Petersburg was paralyzed. That day the Czar gave General Trepov dictatorial powers and ordered him to crush the strike.[30] Troops began to pour into the city—using their own transport. Not a railroad wheel was turning.

On October 14 Trepov issued an order to his troops which was to resound into history: "Spare no cartridges and use no blanks." The order was plastered up in a thousand places on the St. Petersburg walls so that none would be unaware of the Government's intent.[31] Meetings at the university were banned. On October 15 Trepov warned the university he would clear it by force.[32] There were precautionary discussions—if not preparations—to remove the Czar and his family from Peterhof to a place of refuge abroad.[33] Two destroyers were ordered to stand by.[34]

At this critical moment Witte submitted to the Czar, October 9, what amounted to an ultimatum: either form a constitutional government (with himself as head) or turn the country into a military dictatorship and give the armed forces the task of putting down the rebellion by blood.

Witte's analysis was remarkable for its insight and frankness. "The basic slogan of the contemporary social movement in Russia," he wrote, "is freedom." Its roots lay not in the events of the past turbulent year but deep in history, in the ancient freedoms of Novgorod and Pskov, in the fierce independence of the Zaporozhye Cossacks, in the peasant revolts of the Volga, the rebellion in the Orthodox Church, and even in the revolt against Peter's reforms. It was the same spirit which had brought on the revolt of the Dekabristy (Decembrists), the Petrashevsky affair of the mid-nineteenth century, the end of serfdom on February 19, 1861. "Man," said Witte, "always strives for freedom, cultured man to freedom and law—to freedom, regulated by law and the security of his rights.

"The ominous signs of a terrible and stormy explosion each day make themselves felt more strongly," he wrote.[35]

Witte met with the Czar on the ninth and with the Czar and the Czarina on the tenth. The Czar consulted his closest associates, members of the royal family, Baron Frederiks, the Minister of Court (who was strongly opposed to any concessions to democracy). Each day the situation worsened, although only faint hints of crisis were reflected in the Czar's diary—as always he continued to pay more heed to the weather than to politics. On the fifteenth the Czar met with Witte, his domineering uncle Nikolasha (Grand Duke Nikolai Nikolayevich), Gen. O. V. Rikter, in whom he had great confidence, and Baron Frederiks. The basic question was whether to accept Witte's proposals for a constitutional monarchy or rely on force to put down the uprising. After four hours of talk Nikolasha and General Rikter decided in favor of Witte. Frederiks was still opposed. The Czar met with two more men, State Counselor, Ivan Goremykin and Baron Budberg. They also sided against military action and in favor of a watered-down constitution. The Czar then called in General Trepov, "the honest Trepov" as he repeatedly called him. Trepov was a bluff soldier, a cavalryman, not a politician. The Czar put before Trepov the Witte proposal for a constitution, plus a question—how long could Trepov hold St. Petersburg against the rebels without serious bloodshed? Trepov, analyzing the situation in Moscow (where the city was now in open rebellion with the Soviet holding more authority than the governor-general) and the spread of the movement in St. Petersburg (still fairly quiet although almost no enterprises, private or government, except the military were yet functioning), told the Czar that if the order was given him instantly to clear St. Petersburg of demonstrators and meetings, the cost in human life would be enormous. He opted for the Witte plan. This tipped the scales. But only by a slight margin. The Czar agreed to issue a manifesto for the Witte program. Yet at the last moment there was hesitation. Was the Czarina still trying to persuade her husband to stand firm? On the morning of October 17 the Czar summoned his uncle Nikolasha for a final conference. When Nikolasha arrived at the palace, Baron Frederiks made an emotional plea to him to abandon the Witte program. Instead, let Nikolasha become dictator with full powers to suppress the revolt by force. The Grand Duke became extraordinarily excited. He drew a revolver from his pocket. "You see this revolver?" he asked Frederiks. "I'm going now to the Czar and I will beg him to sign the manifesto

and the Witte program. Either he signs or in his presence I will put a
bullet through my head with this revolver."

Nikolasha rushed from the room and into the Czar's chamber. What
transpired there was never revealed.* But when Witte arrived at Peterhof a little later the matter had been settled.[36] That day the Czar issued his Manifesto:

> To grant the people the unshakable foundations of civil
> liberty on the basis of true inviolability of person, freedom of
> conscience, speech, assembly and association;
>
> To admit immediately to participation in the State Duma,
> without suspending the scheduled elections, and in so far as
> it is feasible in the brief time remaining before the convening
> of the Duma, those classes of the population that are now
> wholly deprived of the rights of suffrage, leaving the further
> development of the principle of universal suffrage to the new
> legislative order;
>
> And to establish as an inviolable rule that no law can come
> into force without the consent of the State Duma and that
> the representatives of the people must be guaranteed the op-
> portunity of effective participation in the supervision of the
> legality of the actions performed by Our appointed officials.

The autocratic rule of the Romanovs, which had endured almost
three hundred years, had ended. For better or for worse Russia was
embarked upon a new constitutional path.[37] It was seventeen years to
the day since the spectacular railroad accident of October 17, 1888,
when Czar Alexander III saved his own life and that of his family by
literally holding up the roof of the wrecked dining car on his
shoulders.[38] A brief memorial service was held by Father Ivan of
Kronshtadt. Then, at 5 P.M. the Czar put his signature to the document.
"After such a day one's head is heavy and thoughts begin to wander,"
he commented.[39] The Czarina remarked that these days had been like
a very difficult labor.[40]

The mood in the palace was one of menace. The Grand Dukes were
in a rage, the Duchesses in a state of hysteria, the Czarina like a caged
lioness. A visitor noticed, side by side, in the drawing room of the
Alexander Palace portraits of Marie Antoinette and the Czarina. He
did not think it a good omen.[41] The Czar, in fact, was profoundly

---

* The Czarina and most of the Imperial family always put primary blame on
Nikolasha for October 17. The report of last-minute intrigue against Witte is supported by State Secretary A. A. Polevtsev's diary. (*Krasny Arkhiv*, 1923, Vol. IV,
pp. 77–79.) Polevtsev was the father-in-law of A. A. Bobrinsky, another famous
St. Petersburg diarist. (Ibid., 1924, Vol. V, p. 128.)

shaken as he revealed in the letter he wrote his mother who was visiting her father in Denmark:

> I do not know how to begin this letter.
>
> It seems to me that a year has passed since I wrote you the last time [two weeks previously, in fact]. . . .
>
> You remember no doubt those January days which we spent together at Tsarskoye—they were miserable, were they not? But they are *nothing* compared with those of the present. . . .
>
> All kinds of meetings were permitted, in Moscow, I don't know why, by Durnovo [the governor-general].[42] . . . God knows what happened in the Universities. Every kind of person walked in, said what kind of horror he pleased and no one paid any attention. . . . It makes one sick to read the news—there's nothing but reports of strikes in the schools, the drugstores, etc., and murders of the police, Cossacks and soldiers. The Ministers instead of acting with decisiveness get together and cackle like a lot of chickens. . . .
>
> I ordered immediately that all the troops at the disposition of the Petersburg garrison be put under the orders of Trepov. . . . Here we had the only halt in the movement toward revolution because Trepov warned the populace with posters that all disorders would be put down without mercy. . . .
>
> Menacing but quiet days began—quiet because in the streets there was perfect order and everyone knew that whatever was being prepared the army was waiting for the signal and the others didn't start anything. It was like in summer before a thunderstorm. Everyone's nerves were drawn to the breaking point.
>
> During these terrible days I saw Witte constantly, our conversations began in the morning and finished in the evening towards dark. It was necessary to choose between two solutions: to find an energetic military man and crush the rebellion with every force. . . . That would cost rivers of blood and in the end we would be just where we started—that is to say, the authority of our power would have been demonstrated but the result would be the same and progressive reforms could not have been carried out.
>
> The other solution—to give to the people their civil rights, freedom of speech, of the press, of assembly and association and inviolability of person and to take on an obligation that

all laws would be approved by the Duma—that is, in a word, a constitution. Witte warmly defended this solution, realizing very well its risks but also that it is actually the only possibility. Nearly all the persons with whom I have talked agree with Witte that there is no other solution. He made it quite clear that he would accept the Presidency of the Council of Ministers only on condition his program was accepted and his actions not interfered with. . . . We discussed it for two days and in the end after a prayer I signed it. Dear mother, you cannot imagine the anguish this has cost me. I could not in a telegram explain all the circumstances which brought me to this terrible decision which nevertheless I took in full consciousness. . . . I had no one to rely upon except the honest Trepov. There was no way out but to make the sign of the cross and do what the world demanded. The only consolation is the hope that through the bounty of God this difficult decision will help Russia to emerge from the untenable chaos in which it has existed for nearly a year. . . .

We find ourselves in the midst of a revolution and the disorganization of the whole administration of the country is complete: this is the chief peril. . . .

I know that you pray for your poor Nicky. May Christ be with you. God will save and calm Russia. With all my heart.

Nicky[43]

Prince Vladimir Orlov, who had opposed the Czar's decree to the end, told of coming to see the Czar the day after the act was signed. He sat at his desk with head bowed, tears flowing from his eyes. "Don't leave me today," the Czar said. "I am too depressed. I feel that in signing this act I have lost the crown. Now all is finished."[44]

XVIII

The First Scene

"There is nothing in it for the people," was Leo Tolstoy's comment on the Manifesto. Much the same comment was made by Pavel Milyukov, now just forming his great liberal party, the Constitutional Democrats, or Kadets as they came to be called. On the evening of October 17 he had appeared at the Literaturny Kruzhok, the Literary Circle, a club on Bolshaya Dmitrovka which had been built by the sister of Margarita Kirillovna Morozova as a gathering place for Moscow's decadent poets and radical thinkers. Valery Bryusov and Andrei Bely read their verses from the platform, and in the huge hall was a gambling club filled with ordinary Moscow businessmen. Profits from the gambling paid for the literary club. On this occasion Milyukov spoke to an excited mixture of poets and gamblers, businessmen and radicals.

The Czar's Manifesto was a victory, he told them, and not a small one. Nor was it the first victory. But it was only a new link in a chain —and it was very late in coming.

"Nothing has changed," he concluded. "The war continues."[1]

Like almost everyone in Russia he believed that the Czar had acted too late and had done either too little or too much. For scarcely concealed within the instant euphoria over October 17 there was, as the savage course of events in St. Petersburg, Moscow, and throughout the empire quickly revealed, no consensus, no willingness to accept either the Czar's actions, the good faith of his chosen instrument, Witte, or, it sometimes seemed, anything else.

Ivan Shaurov was a student at the St. Petersburg Polytechnic Institute. Like all students he had for days been in the thick of agitation. He was a Bolshevik, had been one for about a year.

He did not hear of the Czar's Manifesto until October 18. Then he and a friend started to walk into town from the suburb where they lived. They made their way from the Vyborg side to Liteiny Prospekt and then to the Nevsky, where they saw some demonstrators, perhaps fifty or sixty in all, carrying five or six red flags, moving up the Nevsky very rapidly. Shaurov asked who they were and why they were moving so swiftly and was told they had been demonstrating against the Czar's Manifesto on Zagorodny Prospekt, near Five Corners, but a shot had rung out, either killing or wounding the speaker.[2] Now they were hurrying to the Kazan Cathedral Square, where there was supposed to be a big rally against the Manifesto. As they passed the Gostiny Dvor, the department store on the Nevsky, Shaurov saw another crowd moving into the street carrying the Czarist tricolor. Shaurov's group had been walking in silence. Now it began to sing the "Marseillaise." The group with the tricolor turned out to be Black Hundreds, extreme reactionaries. They also were demonstrating against the Manifesto—but in favor of complete autocracy for the Czar.[3] Shaurov's group swept ahead so rapidly that it reached Kazan Square ahead of their rivals and moved into the center, forming a line against an attack by the Black Hundreds. As the two groups approached each other a shot rang out. Shaurov could not tell from which side it came. Then another. Soon there was a brisk exchange. Shaurov himself drew a revolver and fired into the Black Hundred ranks without aiming. A moment later he saw a middle-aged man with an unbuttoned overcoat fall heavily to the ground. The man had been carrying the tricolor. The shooting lasted only a minute or so. Then a free-for-all broke out for possession of the flags. Shaurov managed to grab one tricolor. He ripped off the white and the blue segments and posted the improvised red flag in the center of the square. The Black Hundreds finally fled and the crowd milled about. Some said a naval unit had revolted and was on its way with its arms to join the demonstration. Others reported that troops with machine guns were en route to clear the square with gunfire. Shortly, however, the organizers of the Kazan demonstration appeared with real red flags. Thousands of persons gathered. There was too much noise to hear well, but the speaker, as far as Shaurov could understand, called on the crowd for vigilance, said that it was necessary to fight on, not to put away their arms, not to believe the Government, and to prepare for an armed uprising. The crowd was electrified. Shaurov managed to climb onto the staircase. He found that all traffic on the Nevsky had been halted and there was a solid human mass as far as the eye could see. The great square was filled and so was the Nevsky. There were red flags everywhere and everywhere revolutionary hymns sounded in the air. Dusk began to fall. No police or troops intervened. The speakers shouted: "Now to meetings at the University and the Academy of Arts." The crowd moved out of the square and down the Nevsky toward the Admiralty. Shaurov marched beside one of the flag bearers. "I'm tired," the bearer said. "You carry it for a while." Shaurov took up the red flag. They crossed the Moika, singing the "Marseillaise":

> "We foreswear the old world
> We shake away its dust from our feet . . ."

As they crossed the palace square Shaurov's arms grew tired. He handed the banner to another student. And the crowd marched on.[4]

Trotsky, too, was in that crowd. A student told him about the incident in which the speaker was wounded. They decided to go to the university. On the way men and women all began to rip tricolored Czarist flags from house gates, tearing off the blue and white stripes, creating dozens of improvised red flags. At the university speaker after speaker addressed the crowd from the balcony. Trotsky was the third or fourth in turn.

"Citizens!" he said. "Now that we have got the ruling clique with its back to the wall, they promise us freedom. . . . But do not be too quick to celebrate victory; victory is not yet complete. . . . If anyone among you believe in the Czar's promises, let him say so aloud. . . .

"Isn't the order to spare no bullets hanging by the side of the manifesto about our freedoms? . . . We cannot, we do not want to, we must not live at gunpoint. Citizens! Let not a single soldier remain within a radius of 25 versts from the capital. . . . Our strength is in ourselves. With sword in hand we must stand guard over our freedom."[5]

"I tore the Czar's manifesto into pieces and scattered them to the winds," Trotsky recalled.[6]* The Executive Committee of the St. Petersburg Soviet, of which Trotsky was a member, was meeting in the Women's College. The crowd called on the Soviet to lead a procession to the Kresty Prison to liberate the prisoners—on the model of the French Revolution's storming of the Bastille. The committee feared this would cause bloodshed so it named a group of three, including Trotsky, to lead the crowd off into quiet streets. Finally after a very

* The similarity of Trotsky's remarks and those attributed by Shaurov to the "unknown speaker" at Kazan Cathedral suggests that Shaurov, writing his memoirs in contemporary Soviet times, has conveniently transposed Trotsky's speech to an "unknown speaker."

long march they told the crowd to disperse and warned them against provocations.[7]

In Moscow enormous crowds gathered in the center of the city on October 18. Some were workers, some were students, some were gentry, some were sight-seers. Thousands assembled in front of Governor-General Durnovo's palace on Tverskaya,[8] demanding freedom for political prisoners in Butyrka and Taganka prisons. They carried red flags and sang the "Marseillaise." Pavel Arsky, who had escaped from Sevastopol where he had been arrested for revolutionary agitation in the fleet, was in the crowd. As red banners waved he watched the governor-general in full uniform, wearing his medals, appear on the balcony. "Take off your hat!" the crowd cried. "Amnesty!" They raised a huge white sheet on which the word "Amnesty" had been spelled out. The governor took off his hat, bowed, and slowly left the balcony. The crowd then marched to the Butyrka and Taganka prisons. One of those freed from Taganka, Zinovy Litvin-Sedoi, rushed straight from his cell to a mass meeting at the Conservatory. He was so excited he could hardly talk.[9] Columns of demonstrators moved through the streets of Moscow all day long.

One column, making its way about 2 P.M. from a meeting at the Higher Technical School to the Taganka Prison, headed down Nemetsky Street, led by Nikolai Ye. Bauman, a veterinarian and Bolshevik party man who had himself been released from Taganka Prison a few days earlier. As the column drew parallel with the Dufurmantel factory, Bauman noticed in the distance a group of workers standing outside, watching the processions. He leaped into a droshky, red flag in hand, and drove toward the factory gates, thinking to persuade the men to join the demonstration. He had hardly entered the droshky when a man rushed at him carrying an iron gas pipe. Bauman jumped from the carriage but the man knocked him to the pavement, smashed again and again at his head, wounding him fatally. The murderer was Nikolai Fedotovich Mikhalin, a peasant, a member of the Black Hundred group, the Union of the Russian People, and, quite possibly, a police provocateur.[10]

Moscow had never seen anything like Bauman's funeral. Governor-General Durnovo gave his word there would be no interference. The body lay in state in the auditorium of the Higher Technical School. On October 20 after hundreds of meetings at which tens of thousands of rubles were collected for guns and ammunition the funeral procession started. More than 200,000[11] persons joined in—workers, students, the intelligentsia, even soldiers. Konstantin Stanislavsky marched, his white hair gleaming. So did Fyodor Chaliapin, his tall figure towering over his companions. So did the painter Valentin G. Serov and the poet Valery Bryusov.[12] It took eight hours to pass through the city. The coffin was decorated with a red banner and covered with flowers and pine boughs. Surrounding it was a fifty-man armed guard, led by Zinovy Litvin-Sedoi (who had been Bauman's close comrade in Taganka Prison). They were armed with bombs, Browning revolvers, Mauser rifles, and Finnish knives. Each factory detachment had its armed group, and ahead of the procession rode skirmishers and a mounted detachment of workers. The procession started at 9 A.M. and it was dusk before the head of the column reached the cemetery. When the marchers passed the Troitsko-Sergeyevsky Barracks, someone cried out: "Soldiers! Who are you with! Tell us!" The response was: "With the People. For Freedom." At Pokrovsky Street a band of Black Hundreds waited menacingly. The funeral leaders shouted: "Comrades! It's a provocation. Your fighting units will protect you." The Black Hundreds fell back. The demonstration passed through the heart of Moscow, down Mokhovaya Street, past the thronging shops of the meat dealers, the provision merchants, past the old buildings of Moscow University, and up Bolshaya Nikitskaya past the Moscow Conservatory, where suddenly there swelled out the profound measures of the funeral march:

> "You fell in fatal combat
> With boundless love for the people . . ."

The procession halted as a Conservatory orchestra and choir saluted the revolutionary movement. Further the marchers went. Across Kudrinsky Square, up Bolshaya Presnya, and to the Vagankov Cemetery. The crowd filled the cemetery and the surrounding streets.

It was after dark when the ceremonies concluded and the demonstrators began the homeward walk. There had been no incidents. But now as throngs reached the corner of Bolshaya Nikitskaya and Mokhovaya, close to the meat and provision markets of the Okhotnaya Ryad (Hunter's Row), they encountered bands of *Okhotnoryadtsy*—as the Moscow Black Hundreds were called—men wearing the traditional old Russian kaftans and visored caps.[13] The cry went up: "Okhotnaya Ryad men!" The students rushed into the courtyard of the nearby Moscow University and started to throw up barricades. They were, Ilya Ehrenburg remembered, divided into groups of ten. He chalked a number on his student's uniform and carried stones up to the lecture halls. If the Okhotnaya Ryad men broke in, they would hurl down the stones. Campfires were lighted. The students sang all night long: "Boldly friends, boldly, never lose courage in the unequal fight."

Ehrenburg was fifteen. It was the first time he had seen blood in the snow. He would never forget it.[14]

Gorky was watching from a window of the apartment at the corner of Vozdvizhenka and Mokhovaya Street[15] which he had taken with his wife, Mariya Andreyeva. Earlier they had sent a wreath with a ribbon "To Our Comrade: Slain at his fighting post."[16] Suddenly Chaliapin, ecstatic and disheveled, burst in as the fighting raged in the street: "Ah, Alexei—do you see how fine it is? Never has there been anything so fine, do you understand? But no, you could not understand that! Think: we have freedom, equality. Ah, My God! How remarkable it is!"

At that moment bullets spattered the windowpane, and shards of glass showered about Gorky, Andreyeva, and Chaliapin.[17]

It was not until October 20 that General Kuropatkin got the news of the Manifesto at his field headquarters in eastern Siberia. On October 23 he jotted down his reflections:

"The poor Czar! What he must suffer in these days. And to think that without such advisers as [V.A.] Meshchersky, Pobedonostsev, Goremykin, Sipyagin, Plehve, Bobrikov, Bezobrazov, and most of all [Grand Duke] Sergei Alexandrovich and [Grand Duke] Nikolai Nikolayevich he might have favored freedom for his people, if he were only confident that with this freedom the people would be happier. But they convinced him that the result of freedom would be unhappiness. . . . He was convinced by that gloomy man-hater Nikolai Nikolayevich together with Sergei that he was not a mere man but a *Super-Man*, incapable of making any mistake and not responsible for any kind of fantasy that might be fatal for Russia."

Kuropatkin had no communications whatever with Russia. He was cut off by telegraph and rail. All he had to go on were wild reports coming in through Harbin. Agents of the Russian-Chinese Bank were reporting that Moscow was in flames, that a provisional government had been set up, that the Army was joining the revolution, that battles were raging in the streets of Petersburg with thirty thousand killed and wounded, that the Czar had taken refuge in Kronshtadt and the Czarina had fled to Denmark, that Witte was heading a temporary government, and that revolution had broken out in Irkutsk. But there was also some less alarming news. Kuropatkin's chief of communications assured him that the lines were open between Irkutsk and St. Petersburg, that there had been outbreaks in Irkutsk but that they had been brought under control, and that revolutionaries in Tomsk had been put under lock and key. In Odessa and Kiev, he heard, there were violent pogroms because the Jews were blamed for the revolutionary events.[18]

The most bloodthirsty pogroms Russia had ever seen now began to break out. The general strike ended but Soviets stayed in being in St. Petersburg and Moscow and, in no time, were calling out the workers again. Vicious right-wing riots struck Moscow, St. Petersburg, Kiev, and Tomsk. In Russian Poland and the Baltic capitals conditions approached anarchy. The worst anti-Semitic outrage occurred in Odessa. There was a three-day saturnalia of burning, looting, and killing of Jews. More than five hundred perished. Police and military refused to intervene, insisting the Jews had brought on the trouble themselves. In villages and across the countryside peasants, their harvests in, turned attention to the landlords' estates, burning and killing, often under the influence of violent young SR agitators who assured them that the Czar's Manifesto meant that the land was theirs. More than two thousand outbreaks occurred in the Baltic provinces alone. Within a couple of months Cousin Willy (Wilhelm II) was writing Cousin Nicky (Nicholas II) in great concern about the number of refugees from the Baltic region. He estimated there were fifty thousand in Berlin and twenty thousand in Königsberg.[19]

The failure of the Manifesto to quiet his people quickly began to convince the Czar that counsels of moderation were futile. He wrote his mother, October 27:

It is undeniable that the situation in Russia is still very difficult and serious. In the first days that followed the Manifesto the bad elements of the population raised their heads very high but very quickly strong reaction set in and the whole mass of the loyal people made itself known. The result was understandable and what one might expect here. The people are indignant at the insolence and the audacity of the revolutionaries and the socialists and since nine-tenths of them are Jews all the hatred is directed against them. Hence the pogroms against the Jews. It is astonishing with what *unity* and how *simultaneously* these occurred in all the cities of Russia and Siberia.[20] In England, naturally, they write that these disorders were organized by the police. But this is already a well-known fable. Not only have the Jews suffered —also engineers, lawyers and all other kinds of bad people. What has happened at Tomsk, Simferopol, Tver and Odessa clearly shows what can happen in a storm of fury—the houses of the revolutionaries were surrounded and set afire.

Those who were not burned to death were killed as they emerged. I have received very touching telegrams from everywhere with thanks for the gift of liberty but also with clear declarations that they wish autocracy to be preserved.[21]

Already the Czar was complaining about Witte and regretting the loss of Trepov (whom he had made commandant of the palace). Two weeks later he was complaining more strongly, pointing out (correctly) that Witte had promised that after October 17 the Government would swiftly carry out its reforms and that it would not permit disorders and violence. "The result," the Czar said dryly, "seems to be quite the contrary."[22]

Week by week the Czar wrote his mother, telling her of the growing force which he was employing to put down unrest in the country, finally giving a description of the punitive expeditions into the Baltic provinces where more than two thousand persons were to be hanged and shot with the declaration "terror must be met by terror."[23]

Sir Bernard Pares, who knew the Czar, felt that use of this quotation by the revolutionaries to depict Nicholas as a bloodthirsty tyrant was not fair.[24] But the comments made by Nicholas concerning the punitive expeditions which shot, pillaged, and burned with no pretense of legality through late 1905 and almost the whole of 1906 makes one wonder.

For instance, Gen. V. A. Bekman reported December 14, 1905, that he had refrained from razing the town of Tukkum in Latvia when the inhabitants assured him that they had driven all the rebels out and would deliver all arms and maintain peace. Short of ammunition, he accepted the proposition and called off his attack. The residents greeted the troops with the traditional bread-and-salt, turned over the bodies of an officer and a dragoon who had been killed, and surrendered sixty-two guns and forty-five revolvers. The Czar, underlining the explanation, noted in the margin of Bekman's report: "This is no reason. The city should have been destroyed." There are many, many comments of similar nature.[25] K. N. Uspensky quotes the Czar as commenting on news of the punitive expeditions, *"Cela me chatouille!"* (This tickles me!)[26]

XIX

The Last Stages

The Revolution of 1905 had reached its final stages when Lenin arrived on the scene. He did not get away from Geneva until the end of October. The October 17 Manifesto had come and gone. The murder of Bauman and the great funeral parades had occurred. The pogroms had broken out. The regime had begun to strike back with increasing force. Still Lenin lingered in Switzerland. And his journey took much longer than had been expected because the agent who was to meet him in Stockholm with documents and travel papers did not show up. Lenin waited nearly two weeks in Stockholm, out of touch with events but making a reassessment of the institution of the Soviet in which he concluded that it was the true instrument of Revolution and "ought to proclaim itself as quickly as possible the provisional revolutionary government and complete it with the representatives of all the revolutionary parties and all the revolutionary democrats." This was a 180° swing from the Bolshevik opposition to the Soviet—and, as it turned out, the paper was never published during Lenin's lifetime, probably because when he got to St. Petersburg he found his comrades violently opposed to the idea. His Stockholm views did, however, contain the germ of his attitude to the Soviet when the question again arose twelve years later.[1]

Lenin finally arrived in St. Petersburg on November 8, 1905. At the Finland Station to meet him was young Nikolai Burenin, the former man about town. Burenin was the one who had arranged for a dilatory young Finnish student named Julius Kastren to meet Lenin in Stockholm. Now Burenin engaged a droshky and took Lenin to his sister's house on Mozhaiskaya Street. Burenin's sister was the wife of a Life Guard officer, and her husband, naturally, was a strong monarchist. Unbeknownst to the sister, Lenin spent several hours in the flat, meeting with his Bolshevik comrades. Then Leonid Krasin, Lenin's most reliable man of affairs, took him to the home of another Bolshevik, P. P. Rumyantsev.[2] A few days later Krupskaya joined him. The Revolution was now entering its final paroxysm. The Czar's terrifying punitive expeditions were already ravaging the provinces of Saratov, Tambov, Penza, Voronezh, and Chernigov. But Lenin did not quickly sense the state of affairs. He was out of touch and almost pathetically eager for impressions of Russia. Krupskaya hustled about the city, talking to everyone she met—servant girls who told her the gossip, a janitor who wanted the land to be taken from the gentry, a baker who had once been in one of her Sunday school circles, and some young girls who were giving lectures to workers.[3] She brought her chitchat back to Lenin who pored over it like nuggets from a placer mine.

Party activity centered around the newspaper *Novaya Zhizn*. Its nominal publisher was Mariya Andreyevna, a beautiful actress and Gorky's wife. The editor was the "mad" poet N. M. Minsky (Vilenkin) author of a paper called "The Mystical Rose on the Breast of the Cloud",[4] and among the leading contributors were Gorky, Leonid Andreyev, Balmont, Yevgeny Chirikov, and many other non-Bolsheviks. Day by day the last remnants of censorship were being thrown off. Lenin's first article appeared November 10. He took over the editorship and in a characteristic gesture insisted in sweeping all non-Party people out of the establishment.[5] Then he took a quick trip to Moscow and gave one less-than-memorable speech at the St. Petersburg Soviet November 13 in connection with an employers' lockout.

The times were strange. One day Trotsky was invited to the home of Baroness Uexküll von Hildebrant, one of the wealthiest homes in Petersburg. A doorman took his overcoat and hung it with a long row of officers' greatcoats. The Baroness escorted him into the living room where there were sixty or seventy persons gathered, including thirty or forty officers, some of them guardsmen. Trotsky was not the only speaker. Pyotr Struve was there. So was the radical journalist S. N. Prokopovich and Fyodor Rodichev, a Constitutional Democrat. Trotsky told the assemblage that the workers were unarmed, that liberty was unarmed, and that the keys to the arsenals and guns were in the hands of the officers. At the decisive moment, he said, they must be turned over to the people.[6]

The famous SR terrorist Boris Savinkov, a price on his head, almost openly walked the streets of St. Petersburg. He was a close friend of

Serafina Pavlovna Remizova's, wife of the famous writer. He visited their flat and told of his hallucinations of Kalyayev, the man who bombed the Grand Duke Nikolai to death. He was attracted to the Merezhkovskys in his struggle with the ethical problem of terror and killing. To kill, he believed, was necessary. Yet to kill was impossible. Yet he must kill. Savinkov turned up only slightly disguised at a World of Art exhibition with Alexei Remizov. Remizov pointed him out to Bely. "There he is," Remizov said. Bely wrote some verses about him but couldn't get them printed.[7] Savinkov's followers attended meetings of the Religious-Philosophical Society. In Klara Borisovna Rozenberg's salon, members of secret revolutionary organizations gathered, arguing whether Nietzsche or Engels was right. One day a young revolutionary named Pigit dropped into the apartment Bely was sharing with L. L. Koblinsky (Ellis). Pigit had just come in from Finland with a load of Brownings for the revolutionaries. "I have some for you," he said casually.[8]

But the end was drawing near. On November 26 the Government arrested the head of the St. Petersburg Soviet, Georgi S. Khrustalev-Nosar, and Trotsky took his place. A week later Government troops surrounded the Free Economic Society building and swept into their net some 250 members of the Soviet, including Trotsky and most of the Executive Committee. Before they surrendered, the deputies, at Trotsky's word, smashed their Brownings so that the weapons would not fall into the hands of the police.[9] St. Petersburg revolutionary newspapers were closed down.

Where was Lenin at this point? Back in Finland holding a conference of his Bolshevik supporters at Tammerfors which called for an armed uprising and arranged for a coalition with the Mensheviks.[10] Nothing else of consequence occurred at Tammerfors. Lenin practiced revolver shooting in the woods between sessions. One of the Tammerfors delegates was a young man from the Caucasus, attending under the *nom de guerre* of Ivanovich. "I had hoped to see the mountain eagle of our party, a great man, great not only politically, but physically. I had painted Lenin in my imagination as a kind of giant, stately and imposing. What was my disappointment when I saw the most ordinary kind of man of middle height with absolutely nothing to distinguish him from ordinary mortals," Ivanovich recalled many years later. By this time Ivanovich was becoming known as Stalin. If Ivanovich made any particular impact on Lenin it was not recorded.[11]

And Witte, in the words of the Czar, had finally begun "vigorously to stamp out the revolution."[12] The Czar was now meeting almost daily with his military units, reviewing individual regiments and receiving their officers. His diary recorded more than twenty such meetings from late November through December.[13] By the end of the year, he was officially greeting delegations from the Union of Russian People, that is, the anti-Semitic Black Hundred organization which was the inspirer of so many vicious pogroms.[14]

The last act of 1905 opened December 7 with a general strike called by the Moscow Soviet.* It spread to St. Petersburg the next day and to other cities as well. But Moscow was its center. Almost immediately the city was paralyzed. Adm. F. V. Dubasov, a new governor-general, fresh from leading punitive expeditions in the countryside, kept police and troops largely out of sight. The Moscow Soviet seemed to be the master and energetically sought to win over the Moscow garrison. However, on the night of December 8 Dubasov surrounded the Aquarium where several thousand strikers and leaders had assembled and arrested a number—but most of the leaders escaped. The aroused revolutionaries began to throw up barricades in the city streets. Zinovy Litvin-Sedoi, a former engineering officer, was almost the only man of military experience in the workers' ranks. He was assigned to Presnya, one of the principal working-class areas. The Presnya workers had few arms; only the fighting squad of the Schmidt factory had Mausers. The Mamontov workers had hunting rifles. The rest had nothing but "bulldogs"—revolvers. There was a rumor that the Prokhorov plant had a machine gun. This was only a rumor. The first barricade went up at the junction of the Sadovaya and Tverskaya. The whole neighborhood, including men and women in elegant dress, turned out to build it.

"Many people," wrote Gorky (who was there), "believe that it was the revolutionaries who began building the barricades; this, of course, is very flattering but it is not quite correct. It was the man in the street, the non-party man who began building the barricades and therein lies the special nature of the event. The first barricades on the Tverskaya were built gaily with jokes and laughter and the widest possible variety of people took part in this cheerful labor, from the respectable gentleman wearing an expensive overcoat to the cook-general and the janitor."[15]

Overnight the Presnya area was crisscrossed with barriers that ran from the Tverskaya along the Sadovaya to Bronnaya to Kudrinsky

* Bertram Wolfe in *Three Who Made a Revolution*, p. 330, puts the "moral blame" on Lenin for the Moscow insurrectionary call, contending that it was inspired by Lenin's insistence on armed action. It was true that Lenin had repeatedly called for armed action, *whether or not* there was a real chance for success, taking the view that an armed uprising would revolutionize the proletariat and strengthen it for later struggles even if the immediate outcome was unsuccessful. Yet the dominant force in the Moscow Soviet was Menshevik and, in fact, there was close and warm collaboration at this time among all the radical factions—Mensheviks, SRs, and Bolsheviks.

Square to Novinsky Boulevard to Dorogomilovo and across the Moscow River to the Brest railroad shops and on to the Butyrka Prison. A right-wing paper estimated that ten thousand men and women were defending the Presnya barricades. The actual number was probably closer to two thousand, if that.[16] Litvin-Sedoi contended they had only 250 weapons in all. "Without a rudder and without a wind"—that was what the street urchins of Moscow were saying about the insurrectionists.

Rebel headquarters were set up in the Schmidt furniture factory on Nizhnyaya Prudovaya Street and the Prokhorov textile factory.[17] Nikolai Pavlovich Schmidt, owner of the furniture factory (regarded as the best in Russia), was a leading supporter of the revolutionary cause, and on the eve of the December uprising gave Maxim Gorky twenty thousand rubles for the purchase of arms. Earlier he had given Gorky fifteen thousand rubles to start *Novaya Zhizn*, the newspaper Lenin took over.

Dubasov, concerned over the reliability of his troops, moved very cautiously. The government had been able to hold open the St. Petersburg–Moscow railroad line, in part, at least, because the Moscow Soviet made no attempt to seize the terminal.[18] As a result when Dubasov asked for reinforcements the Czar was able to send in his crack Semyonov Regiment (about which he wrote a month earlier to his mother: "The regiment is in superb state. Min [the commander] and all the officers are in perfect spirit.")[19] to reinforce the Moscow garrison. Dubasov first cleaned up the central areas of the city. In some places troops fired into passing crowds almost at random, in others they concentrated on known strong points. On December 11 the government destroyed the Sytin printing works with cannon fire, shelled a student dormitory on the Bronnaya, and occupied several workers' strongholds.

In the midst of the fighting Fedosiya Ilyinichna Drabkina, a member of Burenin's "fighting group" in St. Petersburg, was sent to Moscow with a trunkful of so-called Macedonian bombs for the beleaguered revolutionary forces. She took along her four-year-old daughter, Lizka or Yelizaveta, to distract the suspicious. (Nadezhda Krupskaya called little Lizka the "conspiracy machine" because her baby face diverted suspicion from her mother through a whole series of risky adventures.)

Drabkina, traveling on a train filled with troops headed to put down the Moscow uprising, delivered her bombs and went straight to Gorky's apartment. There every current of the revolution flowed in and out. In the Gorky aviary—Gorky was passionately fond of birds—young revolutionaries were trained in the art of making bombs and using them. There was a table with hot food and drinks constantly replenished for the exhausted revolutionaries, and the spare rooms were used as dormitories. The samovar bubbled all night long.[20]

Gorky's charity was not to save the day. The main battle opened December 15 when the Semyonov Guards debarked from the Brest Station. That night a workers' battalion had captured A. I. Voiloshnikov, chief of the Moscow secret police, on the street and shot him in the courtyard of the Prokhorov factory.[21] Colonel Min deployed his forces skillfully. They seized the Gorbaty Bridge, the Zoological Gardens Square, and Kudrinsky Square, mounting machine guns on the Gorbaty Bridge and artillery in a circle around Presnya. Gunfire continued throughout the night of December 16–17 with heavy shells falling into the Schmidt factory. Both the Schmidt building and his home caught fire. Schmidt kept some cattle in a large fenced court. This, too, caught fire and the cattle were destroyed. The Prokhorov factory was shelled but the owner succeeded in getting the governor-general to suspend the firing. The Semyonov Guards moved in steadily, burning workers' houses and shooting anyone they saw. By Saturday morning the seventeenth the northern part of Presnya and Bolshaya Presnenskaya Street was occupied by the Guards. Hour by hour (although no one yet knew it) the 1905 Revolution was ending. All day Saturday the troops worked their way in more closely, blasting and burning as they went. By evening the revolt had been crushed. That was the evening that Lenin and his comrades, concluding their deliberations at Tammerfors, prepared to return to Russia. All day Sunday the Czar's troops mopped up Presnya, and isolated fighting went on until Monday the nineteenth. There were a thousand casualties, including one hundred troops and police and eighty-six children.[22] All of Presnya lay in ruins.[23] The Czar noted in his diary: "In Moscow, Thank God, the rebels have laid down their arms. The principal role in this was taken by the Semyonov and 16th Lettish regiment."[24]

It would be months before all the bloodletting was over but the 1905 Revolution had come to an end—a bitter, vengeful one. The Czar could hardly wait to pull the Semyonov Regiment out of Moscow and send it on new reprisals. City after city and town after town was bombarded, burned, and ravished. There were 100 to 160 executions a week.[25] Everyone blamed the other. Lenin's sister Anna told of meeting a Moscow workingwoman at the railroad station. "Thank you," said the woman bitterly, "thank you, you Petersburgers, for your support. You sent us the Semyonov Regiment."[26]

Lenin tried to rationalize and find some comfort in the situation. For a long time he was no more convinced that the Revolution had ended in failure than he had, at the beginning, been conscious of the fact that it had actually started. He showed no sense of timing, no sense of the rhythm of events, of the ripening of the revolutionary moment or the reality that, once passed, the moment had gone. He greeted the new year with an editorial: "Civil war is raging. Dubasov's guns have revolutionized new masses of the people on an unprecedented scale. . . . What now?" But he had no answer for his question. Nor had any of the other revolutionaries. The workers were crushed; the peasants, still burning estates and murdering landlords, were no match for the Cossack uhlans, the crack dragoons, the heavy infantry, and horse-drawn artillery which the Czar had set raging across the countryside, leaving gibbets and hanged men and women in hundreds of village squares.

Lenin and his Bolsheviks went back to the underground, hunted day and night by the police. Trotsky and the Soviet leaders were in Kresty Prison for a while, then transferred to the Peter and Paul Fortress. The debris of the Revolution was everywhere and it would take years to clear up.

One of those arrested in Presnya was Nikolai Pavlovich Schmidt,[27] the twenty-two-year-old student owner of the Schmidt factory. His father had died in 1902 and he came into control of the property in 1904. He was arrested at his house at 16 Novinsky Boulevard. Fortunately the police did not search the basement. It was filled with cases of Mausers and revolvers still in their shipping grease. Schmidt was subjected to prolonged interrogation, kept without sleep for eight days, refused any food, and threatened with execution. He finally signed an admission of his revolutionary activities and was taken to Butyrka Prison, where his health rapidly deteriorated in solitary confinement despite the protests of his family (his mother was the daughter of Vikula Yeliseyevich Morozov, director of the great family and a sister of Savva Morozov). On February 12, 1906, he wrote his sister that he had spent a terrible night and feared for the next one. In the morning he was found dead in his cell, two wounds in his neck, cuts on his hands, and bruises on his face. It was called suicide but suspicion has lingered that he was killed by his guards. Nikolai Valentinov, who knew Schmidt and followed the affair closely, was convinced Schmidt died by his own hand. Moscow newspapers friendly to him and to the cause of revolution so reported. They said he had cut his throat with a sliver of glass after breaking the window in his cell.[28] The editors of the Leninsky Sbornik as late as 1975 still insisted that Schmidt was "brutally killed in Butyrka prison."[29]

Schmidt had promised his fortune to the revolutionaries. But by law it passed to his brother, Alexei. The question was how to transfer the money without the authorities getting wind of what was happening.

The problem was not made simpler by a raging quarrel which arose between the Bolsheviks and the Mensheviks. Each claimed Schmidt had promised them the money.

Lenin took a leading hand in devising an elaborate plot. Alexei agreed to renounce his inheritance. It, thus, went to his sister, Yelizaveta Pavlovna. Although she was already pregnant by her revolutionary lover, Viktor Taratuta (they refused on principle to be married), she agreed to a formal (but not-to-be-consummated) marriage with a Bolshevik named Alexander Mikhailovich Ignatiyev, whose father was a general.[30] Ignatiyev's high social status, it was thought by Lenin, would throw the Czarist authorities off the scent. Ignatiyev, a member of the underground fighting squad in Petersburg, was summoned to Geneva, where Lenin told him of his assignment. He protested that he had committed himself to "fighting activity and not to marriage." Nonetheless, Lenin insisted and a formal meeting with the bride took place. The couple then went to Paris, met with the Russian consul, Prince Kugushev, and the wedding was performed October 11, 1908, in the Russian Embassy chapel. It went off without a hitch, although the priest, noting the bride's condition, observed: "I see that you have already kissed the bride. But never mind. God will bless your marriage nonetheless."[31]

Next, a Bolshevik agent in St. Petersburg, S. P. Shesternin, was given an authorization to withdraw Yelizaveta's capital and turn over her shares to the family firm of Vikula Morozov and Sons, which was headed by her uncle, Ivan. The cover story was that she and her husband wanted to invest their money in another commercial venture. Morozov accepted this story and agreed to give the money, 200,000 rubles or more, to Shesternin. He, expecting that at any moment a gendarme might appear and arrest him, went to the Morozov office on the Varvarka, got the money, took a carriage to the Lyons Credit Bank on Kuznetsky Most, ten minutes away, and handed over the money for transmission to Yelizaveta in Paris, where she received it in the form of gold francs which were promptly deposited in the Bolshevik treasury.[32]

So the Revolution of 1905 came to an end. It was, Trotsky wrote, "the dress rehearsal for the revolution of 1917," and consequently, he said, he took part in the events of 1917 "with absolute confidence and resolution," because they were merely a continuation and development of the revolutionary activity which had been interrupted by the arrest of the St. Petersburg Soviet on December 3, 1905.[33]

Whether this was really so, whether any future uprising was to be a repetition of 1905, only time would tell. No one knew what lay ahead.

Certainly not Lenin. For nearly two years he stayed in Russia and on its fringes, in the underground, frustratingly trying to get the Revolution moving again. Nothing worked. On January 7, 1908, he and Krupskaya arrived back in Geneva. The weather was frigid. Lenin had a touch of food poisoning. So did Krupskaya. To make matters worse Lenin was coming down with a bad cold. The wind blew. The lake was icy and frozen. The town seemed dead and empty. As they walked through the desolate streets, Lenin turned to Krupskaya and said: "I have a feeling that I've come here simply to be put into my coffin."[34]

The Revolution was, indeed, over. But not the story. A new act was opening, on a stage Lenin could not see. November 1, 1905, Nicholas II had jotted into his diary this entry: "We've made the acquaintance of a man of God, Grigory from the Tobolsk Guberniya." Grigory, of course, was Rasputin.

XX

From the Tower

At the turn of the century the old Potemkin Palace in St. Petersburg
was torn down and a stylish multistory apartment building, No 25
Tavricheskaya, was put up in its place. On the top floor (the sixth)
under a mansard roof was located Ivanov's Tower, the sprawling flat
of the decadent, mystic, symbolist poet Vyacheslav Ivanov, quite possibly the most urbane, cultured, and esoteric man in Europe and certainly in Russia. The walls of three flats had been demolished to create
a living space without doors, partitions, or dimensions—simply areas
divided by low bookcases or shelves. Corridors of random width connected the areas. There were no rooms, only what Ivanov called "sectors"—some square, some rhomboid. Heavy carpets muffled footsteps
and voices. Sometimes it seemed a place of whispers, but the hushed
sounds could reverberate halfway around the world. The furniture
was ornate, heavy, carved, highly polished, upholstered in rich dam-
asks and deep velours. The walls blazed with orange-red tapestries
against which marble masks and strange devices glowed like emblems
of another planet—one too ancient to be remembered or, perhaps, one
not yet born. There were candles for light and the air was heavy with
the scent of lilies.[1] Wine was always at hand as well as a multitude of
cupbearers. The tower overlooked the Tauride Palace where after
1905 the new Duma met (when the Czar permitted it) and Ivanov,
some said, poised over the parliament like a singing spider, catching
flies to feed his decadent salon.

The absence of walls in Ivanov's Tower was neither accidental nor whimsical. It was an expression of the poet's philosophy and that of a generation of Russian thinkers, philosophers, and artists of whom Ivanov was possibly the most exquisite example. Not only were there no walls in the tower. There were no clocks. Here one lost all sense of place or of country, of person, of past, of present, of future. Here was the center of the real Russian Revolution—the challenge to almost every idea, every concept, every belief, which lay at the foundation of age-old Russian autocratic, authoritarian, didactic culture and society. Here poets, philosophers, artists, ventured into dazzling flights almost beyond the bounds of human consciousness. Beside the visitors to Ivanov's Tower the political revolutionaries and their opponents, the Czar's circle and the police, seemed like grubby pygmies, mired in stale rhetoric and sad clichés.

Ivanov's famous "Wednesdays," the receptions where he presided as high priest or "Ivanov the Great," as some acolytes called him, were held not on Wednesday but only after Wednesday had passed, that is, after midnight early on Thursday morning. The Wednesdays went on and on—sometimes until six in the morning, sometimes for several days. Ordinarily Ivanov went to bed at 8 A.M. and awakened about three in the afternoon. He swigged enormous quantities of black tea as he worked in his dressing gown, lounging on the divan where he slept and where, later, he would preside over his assembly. At 7:30 P.M. shaven, fresh, rosy, fully dressed, he would breakfast. Andrei Bely (he himself had founded a "Commune of Dreamers" in Moscow) once spent five weeks in Ivanov's "camp," as Dmitri Merezhkovsky called it. This was a long time. Bely's friend Emil K. Metner fled back to Moscow after trying it for two days. Guests lived in the same kind of "dens" as did Ivanov, his wife, Zinovyeva-Annibal (and after her death, her friend Mariya M. Zamyatina, who became Ivanov's companion-housekeeper), his son, his stepdaughter, and his stepson. Somewhere beyond the demolished walls there was a small suite where the writer M. A. Kuzmin lived and where the poet Nikolai Gumilev[2] slept when he stayed overnight.

Tea was served not earlier than midnight in the orange-hung den of Ivanov. At that hour individual tête-à-têtes in the little dens came to an end, and in the orange chamber members of the Petersburg Religious-Philosophical Society and almost anyone in St. Petersburg who was interested in the fate of Russia or of man might be met.

The talk never halted and there was no more barrier to examination of ideas than there were walls to the rooms. At 5 A.M. Ivanov and Andrei Bely might begin a conversation on God, symbolism, the Dionysan mysteries, or the future of the Romanov dynasty.[3] It would continue until 7 or 8 A.M. when Ivanov would call to Mariya Zamyatina, hunched up, tired, eyes screwed open: "Can't we have some fried eggs?" Life was lived on what Bely called the principle of Einstein—no boundaries to time, all was one.[4]

What kind of thought was explored in Ivanov's Tower? What was the future as seen from this vaulting observation point? It was a vision revolutionary beyond any parameters of Marxism or anarchism. Indeed, it was one which would have united Lenin and Nicholas II in opposition had either had an opportunity to penetrate its nature. It was a panorama heavily apocalyptic, deeply tinged with the philosophy of Nietzsche, Schopenhauer, Kant, the French symbolists, Hauptmann, Hamsun, Ibsen, Maeterlinck, Verlaine, Baudelaire, Dostoyevsky, and, a bit later, that of Rudolf Steiner and the anthroposophists. Ivanov, a brilliant classical scholar, learned in Greek and Latin, dreamed of reviving the thousand-year-old cult of Dionysus. He conceived a new theater of mystery in which the Dionysan rituals—the orgiastic rites, the human sacrifices, the cannibalism—would be born anew. He dreamed of bridges between Christ and Dionysus, between Plato and the Greek cults of love, between primitive Russia and the New Jerusalem.[5] He attracted into his circle not only Bely but Bely's intimate friends, the poet Alexander Blok and Lyubov Dmitriyevna, Blok's wife, with whom Bely was hopelessly in love. Blok dreamed of creating artistic games in life. Lyubov Dmitriyevna dreamed of playing roles in the scenes which Blok created. To Bely the lines between life and fantasy had already become almost too blurred for differentiation.[6]

There were vast differences of temperament, of style, of philosophy, among those who found their way to Ivanov's Tower (and to the other exquisite salons of the day—those of the Merezhkovskys in St. Petersburg, of the Bloks, earlier and later in Moscow, of Margarita Kirillovna Morozova in Moscow, Mamontov's circle at Abramtsevo and others). But one thing each had in common—a perfect sense of the "pregnancy" of the times. Each participant knew, sensed, perceived, or dreamed of the cataclysm which was to overwhelm Russia. None doubted that the old was dying and the new was being born. None needed wait for 1905 to be convinced of this. Father Gapon appeared to them as an avenger long prophesied in the book of Daniel; the Czar as a fateful figure from the Apocrypha. The artists foretold the coming of catastrophe long before the pedantic Marxists, the romantic SRs, or the nervous Moscow millionaires began to nudge history along. The rotten scent of decaying society was pungent in poets' noses a decade before it touched the perfumed nostrils of the court. These were the men and women who in Ivanov-Razumnik's words lived "at the very edge of the edge."[7] They believed with Dmitri

Merezhkovsky that the future would be "either we—or no one."[8] Each artist, as Bely once observed, carried in his head "his" revolution and each, of course, was different from any other.[9] With the failure of 1905 they turned to the "revolution within themselves."[10] After 1905 the majority of the Russian intelligentsia, Ivanov-Razumnik thought, remained socialist, but the kind of political faith each professed frequently changed. Bely counted himself a Menshevik[11] during the days of the Moscow uprising when he fell in love with the Revolution and saw his chief mission as creating a link between Marxism and symbolism.[12] Bely's friend Sergei M. Solovyev was an SR. His friend, Ellis (the nom de plume of L. L. Kobylinsky), a Marxist; another friend, Leonid Semyonov, an anarchist. Alexander Blok was a "maximalist."[13] Valery Bryusov, heretofore an ardent monarchist and nationalist, was instantly transformed into a revolutionary and refused to have anything to do with "liberal chatter." (But he felt that the gunfire of the Cossacks and the barricades of Moscow created "very good" conditions for working on his romantic novel.)[14] The Merezhkovskys were Marxists—whatever they meant by that.

Margarita Kirillovna Morozova, pupil of Alexander Scriabin, whose mystic and erotic music attracted many women,[15] a widow of Mikhail Morozov, one of the multimillionaire Morozovs, conducted her salon in a mansion at the corner of Smolensky Boulevard and Glazovsky.[16] This was a great house in classic style with a handsome ballroom, big, rather uncomfortable, and cold[17] with a raised platform for musicians, actors, or speakers at one end. The curtains, armchairs, upholstery, colors—all had been chosen to create "an historic picture," and L. N. Pasternak, father of the famous author-to-be, and a fashionable Moscow painter, had sketched a design which was to include a grandiose picture of Madame Morozova and her guests—but for some reason this was never executed.[18] Madame Morozova, a warm, intellectually vigorous woman with flashing emerald eyes,[19] also had a beautiful drawing room, a cozy white chamber with a soft gray rug, and there might be found Pavel Milyukov, the liberal professor who talked of a constitution and soon would found the liberal Kadet party; Bely, who projected mystic visions; Vladimir Solovyev, who spoke of philosophy; Sergei N. Bulgakov, who preached romantic anarchy,[20] V. F. Ern, Filipp F. Fortunatov, Grigori A. Rachinsky, Alexander A. Kizevetter, Ye. K. Balmont, Prince G. E. Lvov, and, before his death, Prince Sergei N. Trubetskoi, whom many described as a "legal" Marxist. Their politics ranged from anarchy to autocracy.[21] Poets, philosophers, artists—all strove toward a new synthesis and many thought to marry revolutionary theory and religious mysticism. This, they believed, might create a bridge which would lead Russia through chaos into the still unknown future.

In their visions they saw with extraordinary clarity the Calvary which Russia was entering. Indeed, their own lives were testimony to the death throes of the social order. It was often difficult to mark a point at which reality ended and mystical vision began. Bely believed that he was born "under the sign of the death of the old world." Vladimir Solovyev perceived the dawn of the twentieth century as the climax of world history and the signal for the opening of the last battle, that between Christ and AntiChrist. "The approaching end of the world," he wrote a friend, "strikes me like some obvious but quite subtle scent—just as a traveller nearing the sea feels the sea breeze before he sees the sea."[22]

Bely caught the mood in a poem:

> There is nothing. And there will be nothing
> And you are dying.
> The world has vanished and God will forget it
> What are you waiting for?[23]

Bely felt that the new century had changed the psychological atmosphere of Russia. Before 1898, in his words, the wind was from the north and the heavens were gray. Balmont's verses, "Under the Northern Sky," symbolized the epoch as did Chekhov with his bemused, lost people, Nina Zarechnaya in *The Seagull* and Madame Ranevskaya in *The Cherry Orchard*. Now, new winds blew, new gods arose, especially Friedrich Nietzsche. The rubicon of 1900, Bely felt, ruptured time, fractured consciousness, introduced a new tragic epoch.[24] He and his friends saw in the volcanic eruption on Martinique in 1902 physical evidence of the new epoch—for two or three years the very atmosphere took on an unearthly rosy cast from volcanic ash suspended in the atmosphere. There were sunsets and sunrises of incredible beauty.[25]

One evening Zinaida Gippius lay full length on her divan. Clouds of perfume surrounded her as she drew from a red lacquer box a red-tipped cigarette, languidly lighted it, and exhaled a plume of smoke, heavy with her favorite scent, *tuberosa lublis*. A few days earlier she had said: "I need something—that's not on this earth." Tonight, cigarette lighted, she put to Nikolai Berdyayev, the philosopher who was just beginning his journey from Marxism to Christianity, the question: "What do you wish? That there be a God or that there not be a God?"[26] Berdyayev was agonizing, in his own words, "between the ideal of the Madonna and the ideal of Sodom," that is between purity and evil, a choice close to the Russian heart, embodying as it did the dual nature of life and a profound feeling that true redemption was to be found only through sin—a concept on which Rasputin was to play with remarkable vigor. The argument went on all night.

Ivanov's Tower was not the only place where time was turned upside down. More than once Merezhkovsky interrupted a soulful conversation between Zinaida and one of her guests[27] (often it was Bely), rapping on the wall from the bedroom where long since he had retired, saying: "Zina, for heaven's sake, let him go. It's four o'clock. You're not letting me sleep."[28]

The apocalypse was no mere figure of speech. Its tragedy drenched the lives of the generation and each life contributed to the disintegrating mosaic of Russian society. Bely's life and that of his circle piled tragedy on tragedy. Within weeks Bely lost the three persons closest and dearest to him. First, his great friend and preceptor Mikhail Solovyev died. Within hours Solovyev's wife, Olga, shot herself. Then Bely's father died. Day after day and night after night Bely walked in Novodevichi cemetery, silently pausing at the graves of the three beloved figures. Often he was accompanied by Leonid Semyonov,[29] a passionate adherent of Blok (later he became an SR terrorist, a devout follower of Tolstoy, and finally died in the Civil War). As they walked among the fragrant lilacs, the roses, the flickering icon lamps, Bely spoke Blok's verses:

> On the forgotten grave grows grass
> We have forgotten yesterday and forgotten the word
> And all around us is quietness . . .[30]

Ahead of Bely lay deeper tragedy—within months he fell in love with Nina Petrovskaya and began to act out a drama symbolic of the times. She was, in his words, "thin, not very tall, giving the impression of being all angles; although she had narrow shoulders she appeared heavy; her head was big and square, her body long and thin, her legs too short; she braided her ominous black hair in two plaits; her deep hazel, sad, surprising eyes penetrated into the soul; her face was pale yellow with deep circles under the eyes, cheeks powdered so much she seemed to wear a mask; big threatening lips painted blood red, a smile so gentle, so child-like that you forgot those lips." She was a hopelessly childish woman, living a hysterically unhappy life (she had left her husband, director of the Grif publishing house), kind, tender, suggestible, an excellent subject for hypnosis. She was one of that race of thin, pale, mysterious, dark girls who, like heroines of Maeterlinck, suddenly filled the salons of Petersburg and Moscow.[31] Daughter of an official, she had a conventional upbringing and was trained as a dentist—a past she hated. The poet V. F. Khodasevich saw in her life the epic of her age. She was attracted to symbolism but symbolism offered no direction to its adherent. He could glorify God or the devil and in this contradiction Nina Petrovskaya was soon lost. Nor was she alone. The symbolists and the decadents saw poems as real life. The poet did not write of love; he experienced love in order to write. "It was only necessary to fall in love," Khodasevich remarked, "and a man had all the necessary materials for his first lyrics—passion, despair, triumph, madness, vice, sin, hatred, etc." The symbolists did not separate the writer from the man or the literary from the personal.[32]

Thus, Nina Petrovskaya, pale face, hazel eyes, threatening lips, became the symbol of symbolism. She demanded of life fullness, excitement, tragedy, poetry—and actually, this was to be her life. First, she fell in love with the poet Balmont. Then Bely appeared and she accepted Bely as her "teacher of life." She wore a wooden rosary on a black cord and a large black cross, just like that worn by Bely. Day by day her spirits lifted. Her phobia about tuberculosis vanished, she stopped using morphine, her dreams of suicide faded. Bely saw himself as Orpheus and Nina as Eurydice. But a third poet appeared, Valery Bryusov—Bryusov, the "great magister," son of a rich Moscow merchant[33] of whom Zinaida Gippius said, "The only trouble is that if you look at his face long enough it reminds you of a chimpanzee."[34]

Nina shared with Bryusov her vision of Bely as a golden-haired prophet, possibly even an angel. It was a fateful confidence. Bryusov dabbled in black magic, spiritualism, demonology, alchemy.[35] He proposed a secret union with Nina and what seemed to her a compact with the Beast emerging from the Depths. Nina summoned Bely, and revolver in hand, poison on her cabinet, tears streaming from her eyes, told him of her descent into hell with Bryusov.

One spring day in 1905 Bely was delivering a lecture in the small hall of the Polytechnical Museum in Moscow. At the intermission Nina appeared on stage, drew a Browning (*everyone* was carrying revolvers in 1905), and fired at close range. The gun misfired and Bely grabbed it from her.* Later, she told Khodasevich: "God is with him. It is fate, but to tell the truth, I long ago killed him there in the Museum." She was speaking in the symbolist language which finds no

---

* Bely told another story of this incident. He said that it occurred in the spring of 1907; that Nina concealed the revolver in her muff, intending to shoot him, but hearing him recite his verses, her hallucination changed and she drew the gun and tried to shoot Bryusov, who was with her. Bryusov took the "dangerous toy" away, sent her home with the poet L. L. Koblinsky, then came up and coolly congratulated Bely on his reading. (Andrei Bely, *Nachalo Veka*, p. 286.)

difference between the thought and the deed. Because Nina had shot to kill Bely, he was, for her, dead, and she was his murderess.

Bryusov grew cold and Nina sought to hold him. For two days she sat on the divan, neither eating nor sleeping, her head covered with a scarf, endlessly weeping. She broke the furniture. She smashed vases. She ran away, gambling wildly at cards, drinking, and finally in 1908 returning to morphine.

On November 9, 1911, she left Moscow, knowing she would never see Bryusov again. Khodasevich went to the Alexandrovsky Station to see her off. He found her in the train compartment, sitting with Bryusov. On the floor was an open bottle of cognac, "the national drink of the Moscow symbolists." She and Bryusov finished the bottle, crying and embracing. Then the train pulled out. Bryusov and Khodasevich took a sleigh, sitting silently as the horses, bells tinkling, passed the Strastnoi Monastery and on to Bryusov's house. It was the name day of Bryusov's mother. They played cards and drank late into the night while the train carried Nina westward—to Rome, to Warsaw, to Paris. In 1913 she threw herself from the window of a hotel on the Boulevard St.-Michel. She did not die but she broke her leg and it never healed properly.

She became a Roman Catholic. Over the years she wrote Khodasevich—February 25, 1925: "It seems I can't stand any more"; April 7, 1925: "You think, I suppose, that I've died? Not yet." And September 12, 1927. "This time soon I will die." On the night of February 23, 1928, in a slum hotel in a slum section of Paris she turned on the gas in the heater and ended it. Seventeen years earlier the poet Alexander Blok (they were *all* poets and they all knew each other) had jotted in his diary November 6, 1911: "Nina Ivanovna Petrovskaya 'has died.'"[36] Why, Khodasevich asked many years later, did Blok write that Nina had died in 1911 and why did he put the quotation marks around the word? Because, of course, Nina had died long before she left Russia, in those years when the poetic legend which she was creating and living had actually ended in tragedy. Just as Bely had "died" when she pointed the pistol and pulled the trigger, so she had "died" when the last word of Bryusov's novel about her, *The Flaming Angel*, had been put to paper.[37]

Bryusov, son of a strict but politically liberal father, read at three, kept a diary at six, and at thirteen wrote three picaresque novels. He published his first work, a story about a race track totalizator, in *Russky Sport* at the age of sixteen. His first experience with a "light woman" left him profoundly disillusioned. At nineteen he had his first love affair with Yelena Maslova, whom he described as not beautiful but possessing strange eyes and a shining red face which she powdered heavily. She died a year later of typhus; Bryusov was convinced she died of love for him.[38] His most tragic affair occurred in 1912 when he and Nadezhda Grigoryevna Lvova fell in love. The poet Khodasevich described her as "intelligent, simple, spiritual." At fifteen Nadya had become an underground revolutionary, at sixteen she was arrested, at nineteen she began to write poetry, and at twenty-two she tragically exclaimed: "I'm only a poetess!"[39] She could not bear to share Bryusov (he was married) and thought of suicide. For some reason Bryusov gave her a revolver—the same which Nina Petrovskaya had fired at Bely. On the night of November 23, 1912, a Sunday, Nadezhda telephoned Bryusov. She had been translating some poems of Jules Leforgue, who wrote of the unbearable boredom of Sundays. Bryusov was busy. She called Khodasevich. He was not at home. She called V. G. Shershenevich, another poet, and suggested that they go to the movies. He couldn't. So she took Bryusov's gun and killed herself. Bryusov collapsed. A day or two later he entered a sanatorium in Riga. He began to use morphine (Nina Petrovskaya had introduced him to drugs in 1908) and came close to a nervous breakdown.[40] A Soviet commentary in a posthumous edition of Lvova's works said: "In Lvova's life no significant external events occurred."[41]

The lives of the poets and their friends overflowed with melodrama and this was the spirit of Russia. Everyone was racing away from an intolerable present into a future which only a few believed would ever exist. It was true of the Czar and his court, of the revolutionaries in their dismal Geneva cafés, and, most of all, of the Russian intellectuals. Their lives read like the scenarios of an opera by Mussorgsky. The day came when Bryusov challenged Bely to a duel. Their seconds, the poet Ellis and the poet-philosopher Sergei Solovyev, smoothed the matter over, and the next day and thereafter Bryusov and Bely went on working side by side on the magazine *Vesy*. The relations of Bely, Blok, and Blok's wife, Lyubov, marched toward disaster. Finally, Bely decided to kill her and kill himself—but didn't. He feared he was losing his mind yet amid his agony he wrote his "Fourth Symphony" (a mystical poem) in twenty days, turned out critical articles on the leading European socialists August Bebel, Karl Kautsky, and Émile Vandervelde (under the noms de plumes of Alpha, Beta, and Gamma), produced some revolutionary verse (the countryside was still ravaged by peasant uprisings and Czarist reprisals at the rate of 100 to 150 executions per week)[42]: "We wait! Hunger and cold—Prison lies ahead; Bitter strong vodka, Flames in our Breasts,"[43] and, appearing at one of Ivanov's Wednesdays in the Tower, read an essay called "Phoenix" in which he described the two forces which contended for the human spirit—the passive force of the Sphinx and the creative revolutionary force of the Phoenix—the Revelation's "word of the beast" against the "word of the eagle." The artist was the universal, eternal guardian angel. His fire melted the sphinxlike face of life; he conquered death with love; he "entered the fire, drunk with the wine of dawn and, burning, is resurrected from the dead." It was a poet's testimony to the power of love to resurrect life.[44]

There was one more episode with Lyubov. Bely met her. She told him all had ended. He decided to kill himself. The next morning they met again and agreed on a year's separation. Bely left Russia for Germany, signing his agony in a poem:

> Blood blackens like resin
> The ulcer clots
> But the old pain—
> Can it ever be forgotten?[45]

XXI

The Arts Explode

The political revolutionaries had missed their moment. Now they bitterly understood this. The Czar was slowly squelching the feeble first
life of the Duma and turning to Pyotr Stolypin to create the foundation of a new Imperial structure based on repression, an enriched middle class of peasant-farmers, and a prosperous industry. Nicholas had
long since dropped Count Witte, writing his mother, November 2,
1906: "As long as I live I will never trust that man again with the
smallest thing. I had quite enough of last year's experiment. It is still
like a nightmare to me."[1]* He was, for the moment, quite pleased with
Stolypin's vigor and style. It seemed to promise a no-nonsense regime
which would thrust into the past the horrors of the mobs and the
revolutionaries. To be sure Russia was far from quiet. But the danger
of organized overthrow seemed to be fading.

What neither the Czar nor Stolypin nor the revolutionary leaders
could grasp was that whatever might be Russia's current political
mood the earth was still shaking under their feet. Again, this was
sensed by Russia's poets and painters, a portent of the future. The political revolution might be stalled but the artistic revolution roared
forward, tearing apart lives—driving some to morphine, others to
madness. Nothing could halt it. In art, in poetry, in the theater, in philosophy, in music, the old Russia was being destroyed and a new one

* When Witte died in 1915 the Czar remarked: "Count Witte's death has been
a great relief to me. I also regard it as a sign from God." (Maurice Paléologue, *An
Ambassador's Memoirs*, Vol. I, p. 303.)

born. This had been in progress before 1905. It moved through and past 1905 without interruption. Indeed, it would surge through World War I, defying even that titanic struggle, passing through the two Revolutions of 1917 with mounting vigor only finally to founder in the early years of the new society which the poets had given their souls to create.

In these years Moscow and St. Petersburg were afire. The conflagration had been building up for a decade or more, nourished by the enthusiasm, the magnificent taste and fabulous fortunes of the millionaires—Savva Mamontov, the railroad baron whose support for painters, sculptors, composers, and dramatists even exceeded that of his rival millionaire Savva Morozov, who not only funded the Bolsheviks but financed Stanislavsky (a cousin of Mamontov's) and Nemirovich-Danchenko in founding the Moscow Art Theater.

It was the riches and taste of men like this that created the atmosphere in which flourished Nikolai Rimsky-Korsakov, Alexander Borodin, Modest Mussorgsky, the magnificent Russian ballet—Vaslav Nijinsky, Anna Pavlova, Igor Stravinsky, Mikhail Fokine—and the extraordinary flowering of Russian art: the Wanderers, Ilya Repin, Valentin Serov, Vasily Surikov, Apollinarius and Viktor Vasnetsov; the World of Art group (its credo: "a new climate and new ideas"), Alexander Benois (a "black beetle burrowing deeply in an armchair," as V. V. Rozanov called him), Mikhail Vrubel, Dmitri Filosofov ("Adonis" was Zinaida Gippius' nickname for him), the musicologist Walter Nuvel, the symbolist poets, Merezhkovsky, Blok, Bely, and Balmont, Leon Bakst ("soft Bakst with his rosy smile," in Rozanov's words), Diaghilev, Nicholas Roerich, the painter-mystic-explorer,[2] and the new Russian impressionists, Mikhail Larionov, Natasha Goncharova, and all the others whose names topple one after the other like entries in a museum catalogue: Kasimir Malevich, Vladimir Tatlin, the Burlyuks, David and Vladimir, Vassily Kandinsky, Ilya Mashkov, Pyotr Konchalovsky, Robert Falk, Lyubov Popova, Pavel Filonov, Marc Chagall, Lazar Lissitsky, Olga Rosanova, Alexander Rodchenko, Naum Gabo, Anton Pevsner.[3]

Like Ivanov's Tower the movement had no boundaries. It lived on the interchange of creative idiom—German philosophers and the French postimpressionist group, Bonnard, Gauguin, Van Gogh, Cézanne. Only in Paris was there painting as brilliant as that of the revolutionary Moscow groups—the World of Art, Blue Rose, Golden Fleece, Jack of Diamonds, Donkey's Tail, Union of Youth. The Bolsheviks, the SRs, and the Mensheviks had beaten a retreat, but the caldron of artistic change boiled over into Mussorgsky's *Boris Gudenov*, with Diaghilev as director, Chaliapin as Boris, settings and costumes by Benois and Alexander Golovin, and Borodin's *Prince Igor*, with Roerich's sets, Fokine's choreography, the dancing of Pavlova and Nijinsky. When *World of Art* died the torch was grasped by *Vesy* (its small offices were in the just-opened Hotel Metropol in Moscow, which was decorated with Golovin's dubious mosaics), by *Novy Put*, *Apollon*, *Golden Fleece*.

Boundary lines between the arts dissolved. David Burlyuk and Vladimir Mayakovsky married the word and the image. Their dress was calculated to offend, their pictures to shock, their words to arouse. Mayakovsky called his creed "a slap at public taste" and set the words of his verse against meaning, against conventional rhythm, against meter, against grammar, against spelling. Larionov carried the Revolution into form and figure, distorting the bodies of his soldiers and prostitutes, scrawling *"mat' "* (obscenities) across his paintings, violating every social convention and established artistic taste. David Burlyuk and his brother walked through Russian villages, accompanied by Mayakovsky and Vassily Kamensky, with the words "I, Burlyuk" scrawled in white grease paint across his forehead. Mayakovsky sported a yellow waistcoat. They wore earrings and placed radishes in their buttonholes, their eyes daubed green, red-and-black algebraic signs and graffiti painted on chalk-powdered cheeks. The walls of propriety were shattered as surely as the walls of Ivanov's Tower. They lived their lives in a spotlight of publicity and controversy, concocting schemes to shock the Moscow *kupechestvo* (merchants) and the stylish, symbolist-oriented salons of St. Petersburg. And, of course, they were supported by the wealthy and sometimes eccentric members of the society they had turned against. One philanthropist was a military physician, named Nikolai Ivanovich Kulbin, who financed exhibitions, bought futuristic paintings, helped out artists and poets, and himself dabbled in painting. Another was Shemshurin, a Moscow merchant who kept open house for artists—but only until 5:30 P.M. Anyone in his reception hall at 5:25 was admitted to dinner. But the doors swung shut at 5:30. He it was who invited David Burlyuk and his brother to Moscow from the Black Sea, where their father was a wealthy estate manager. Many an evening Kasimir Malevich got his first and only meal of the day at Shemshurin's table. So did Goncharova.

But Shemshurin was small-fry compared with Sergei Shchukin and his four brothers. Shchukin was taken by a friend to the Durand-Ruel gallery in Paris in 1897, where he bought Claude Monet's painting "Argenteuil Lilac." This was a tidewater date. In the next fifteen years Shchukin purchased 221 works of French impressionists and post-impressionists, more than 50 by Matisse and Picasso. He introduced the movement to Russia. Manet, Pissaro, Renoir, Degas, Cézanne, Van Gogh, Gauguin, Rousseau, and Derain. He hung the pictures on the walls of his Moscow house where they exploded in the eyes of young Russian painters and poets. The impact was as violent as the volleys which shattered Father Gapon's faithful in St. Petersburg. Shchukin became the most important collector of Matisse. Indeed, in Moscow Matisse was considered "our own Moscow artist."[4] Between 1908 and 1914 Shchukin bought more than 50 paintings by Picasso.

Ivan Morozov began collecting Matisse in 1908. His collection of 135 paintings eventually included even more Matisses than Shchukin's. There seemed to be no end to the rich Muscovites who poured their money into art—Tretyakov (whose name still adorns the principal Moscow art gallery), Ivan Ivanovich Troyanovsky, a doctor and a liberal supporter of the Blue Rose group, Bakhrushin, Ostroukhov, Rachinsky, and another doctor, Sergei Goloushev-Glagol.[5]

The revolutionary art collections, studied every day by the Russian avant-garde, affected the Russian intelligentsia deeply. Nowhere in the world did such brilliant collections exist.[6]

The alliance of wealthy capitalists and revolutionary intelligentsia bands the revolutionary years like a red cord. From 1906 through 1909 the heart and brain of the cultural revolution was *Le Toison d'Or* or *Zolotoye Runo* (the Golden Fleece), subsidized and edited by yet another great Moscow millionaire, N. P. Ryabushinsky, friend and rival of Savva Morozov, not so brilliant nor so erratic as the "Bolshevik billionaire" but a leader before and after 1905 in the movement for a new Russia. *Zolotoye Runo* became the talk of Moscow, and the Metropol Hotel Café even named a parfait after it.[7]

While the political revolutionaries drowned in frustration, while the new men of the Duma painfully tried to entice Russia onto democratic tracks, a revolutionary symbiosis of art and culture moved ahead. In the second and third Zolotoye Runo exhibitions there was no segregation of Russian and French paintings, no lines drawn between nationalities. Nor could there be. All was one; the World of Art, or Mir Iskusstva, was a society, a community of diverse but converging ideas, a journal, a sponsor of exhibitions, an inspirer of poetry and art. It envisaged the artist and poet as the priest of an order dedicated to the eternal truths. This was the turn-of-the-century mood. Within a decade emerged Larionov and his "Rayonist" movement with its challenge:

We declare: the genius of our days to be: trousers, jackets, shoes, tramways, buses, airplanes, railways, magnificent ships. . . .

We deny that individuality has any value in a work of art. . . .

Hail nationalism!—we go hand in hand with house-painters.

We demand technical mastery. We are against artistic societies which lead to stagnation. We do not demand attention from the public but ask it not to demand attention from us.[8]

And by 1915 Malevich was proclaiming:

To reproduce the hallowed objects and parts of nature is to revivify a shackled thief.

Only stupid and uncreative artists protect their art with sincerity.

In art truth is needed, not sincerity.

Things have disappeared like smoke before the new art culture. Art is moving towards its self-appointed end of creation, to the domination of the forms of nature.

Russia's atelier revolution lived and flamed while across the Russian countryside rolled the dreary ranks of the *karatelnye ekspeditsii,* the endless punitive expeditions of the Czar, shooting, burning, and hanging. Village after gray village. The hasty gibbets. The raw smell of burned thatch from the blackened huts. The screams. The obscene bodies of slaughtered cows. And from the yardarms the twisted bodies of the peasants. "Order first, reform later," as Premier Pyotr Stolypin said.

"Today, May 9," read Leo Tolstoy in his newspaper, "on the Strelbitsky field at Kherson 20 peasants were executed by hanging for a bandit attack on the estate of a landowner in the Yelizavetgrad district."

"How well we have arranged life in Russia," he remarked to his secretary. "I would have been convinced that there did not exist in Russia a man so cruel as to kill 20 people. But here it is done unnoticed: one subscribes, another reads, this wretched executioner hangs."

The year was 1908. The failed revolution lay three years in the past. But still the hangmen stalked the land. Tolstoy turned to his desk. Within two weeks he had produced the pamphlet "I Cannot Be Silent."

"It is impossible to live so!" he wrote. "I, at any rate, cannot and will not live so. That is why I write this and will circulate it by all means in my power both in Russia and abroad—that one of two things may happen; either that these inhuman deeds may be stopped or that my connection with them may be snapped and I put in prison where I may be clearly conscious that these horrors are not committed on my behalf."[9]

Leonid Andreyev put his protest into the novel *Seven Who Were Hanged*—the common thief, the mad peasant who had, he hardly knew why, killed his master, the five revolutionaries, three boys (one of whom was puttied with fear) and two calm and courageous girls. He wrote it like a stenographic transcription, blunt, raw, direct, no moralizing, no words for the Czar's censor to clutch at. They passed it for publication and the whole nation was jarred at the photographic image of relentless brutality.[10]

Day by day, week by week, month by month, the killing went on and on. On August 12, 1906, an SR suicide squad forced its way into Stolypin's country house with a charge of dynamite. They blew up the house, killing themselves and thirty more, in all, wounding Stolypin's two children and many others.[11] After that he and his family were moved into the Winter Palace for better security and he traveled to Peterhof to consult the Czar only by sea.[12] On the day after the Stolypin attack Maj. Gen. G. A. Min (the Czar had just promoted him for his suppression of the December uprising in Moscow) was shot to death with a Browning revolver by an SR terrorist, Zinaida Konoplyannikova, at the New Peterhof Station.[13] Konoplyannikova was hanged by order of a military field court,[14] but the Czar complained to Stolypin that "the ceaseless attacks and murder of government servants and the daily more bold assaults have put this country into a state of full anarchy."[15] The Dowager Empress was writing her son: "Until we exterminate all the monsters we will never have peace and quiet in Russia"[16] and the Czar was responding, "You can understand my sentiments, dear mama, at not being able to mount a horse and not going beyond the gates."[17]

A plot to kill Grand Duke Nikolai Nikolayevich as well as General Trepov and Prince Orlov in Peterhof itself was uncovered and thwarted. In December a Socialist Revolutionary assassin attacked Admiral Dubasov in Moscow. The admiral escaped with concussion of the brain and the assassin was hanged. When Kadet members of the Duma applauded the news of the attack on Dubasov, the Czar concluded that the Duma was nothing less than a "revolutionary terrorist meeting."[18] Through it all there was a curious air of unreality. The Czar and Czarina seemed to be spending most of their evenings with the "Montenegrins," as the sisters, Anastasia and Militsa, daughters of the Montenegrin Royal House and married respectively to the Grand

Dukes Nikolai Nikolayevich and Pyotr Nikolayevich, the Czar's uncles, were called. They met at Stana's in Znamensky, where they occupied themselves with spiritualism, or with Militsa in Sergeyevsky, where in a garden tower they were meeting with all kinds of "ill-assorted people."

The papers were overflowing with accounts of robberies and murders, but as observed the elderly historian A. A. Polovtsev, "In Peterhof they take no account of the situation and what is going on. They constantly vacillate, now doing one thing, then another, undecided, unconfident, holding mystic séances with those two Montenegrins, whose presence is so unfortunate for Russia."[19]

Prince G. E. Lvov visited the Czar. He expected to see him "brokenhearted, suffering for his country and his people but instead toward me came some kind of jolly sprightly little fellow in a raspberry shirt and wide pantaloons, held up by a cord." Lvov was so shocked by the Czar's conduct (the Czar was trying to get him to enter Stolypin's government) that he had a slight nervous collapse.[20]

It was a moment in which Russia seemed detached from reality, in which peasants died for the crime of being peasants, in which bombs destroyed the Czar's civil servants, in which revolutionaries lingered in the exquisite frustration of Paris and Russian ballet achieved heights of artistry never again to be approached.

The times resembled that strange moment of Valery Bryusov's "The Pale Horse," which took its inspiration from Revelation 6:8: ". . . behold a pale horse: and his name that sat on him was Death." "The street," wrote Bryusov, "was like a storm. The crowds passed by as if pursued by inevitable Fate. Cars, cabs, busses roared amid the furious endless stream of people. Signs whirled and sparkled like changing eyes high in the heavens from the terrible heights of the 30th floor. Wheels hummed proudly, newsboys screamed, whips cracked. Suddenly amid the storm—a hellish whisper. There sounds a strange dissonant footfall, a deadening shriek, a tremendous crash. And the flaming Horseman appears. The horse flies headlong. The air still trembles and the echo rolls. Time quivers and the Look is Terror. In letters of fire the Horseman's scroll spells Death. The crowd tramples madly. Terror stays no one . . . It lasts a moment. Then on the streets there is fresh movement. All is ordinary in the bright sunshine and no one notices in the noisy rush whether an apparition has passed by or simply a dream—only a woman from a whore house and an escaped madman still stretch their hands toward the vanished vision."

No poem in Russia was more popular than "The Pale Horse." No Marxist analyst, no revolutionary propagandist, captured the essence of 1905 as did this apocalyptic poet in lines written *two years* before the Revolution. The Pale Horse and his rider Death had indeed shown themselves for a moment in the streets of Petersburg. And vanished. But not for long.[21]

XXII

"What a Bad Joke Is Man!"

By 1911 the prevailing attitude of the young people of Russia (and of
many of their elders) was being described as *ogarochny,* burning the
candle at both ends. They had begun to live for the moment careless
of what the future might bring—or whether there would, indeed, be a
future. Their mood produced the cult of *tryn-trava,* an almost un-
translatable phrase which means: "What difference does it make?" or
"Who cares?" The sense of apocalypse which had possessed the intellectuals from before the turn of the century now permeated every
level of society. The contrasts and contradictions which had marked
Russia for more than fifty years had again deepened.

Economically Russia was hurtling forward. Industrial output which
in 1871 had been a little more than 500 million rubles would by 1912
reach 6 billion rubles. Pig iron production in 1884 had been 1.3 million
tons. By 1913 it would surpass 5.1 million tons. Coal extraction was expanding from 18 million tons in 1900 to 40 million in 1913. Foreign
capital poured into the country—370.7 million rubles between 1905
and 1908, and in the nine years between 1904 and 1913 Russia sold
more than 3 billion rubles of bonds abroad. By 1914, 2 billion rubles
of private foreign capital had been invested in Russia. Even agriculture, that laggard child, was making giant strides under Premier
Stolypin's simple but effective program that enabled the more successful peasants, the *kulaks,* to enrich themselves at the expense of their
poorer neighbors. There had been a series of good crop years, and
production was helped by the rapid development of peasant co-opera-

tives which by 1914 would number 33,000 with upwards of 12 million members.[1] Small wonder that Alexander Blok saw in the black coal mines and the endless stacks of the new steel mills marching across the empty steppes "the star of a new America."[2]

But even the economic boom carried a warning symptom—the growing number of strikes. In 1910 there were 226, involving 46,623 workers. Next year the figure more than doubled, and by 1912 there were 2,032, involving 725,491 workers. In 1913 the total reached 2,404, affecting 887,096 workers. More and more strikes had political as well as economic aims.[3]

The business upsurge only smeared a touch of rouge on the pale cheeks of Russian society. The press was filled with reports of the most bizarre happenings, reflecting the alienation of men and women on every level of life. Nightly a group of writers, "modernists" in the words of the boulevard press, gathered at the Vienna Café in Petersburg and drank themselves into a stupor. One evening they stole a cat from a friend's house, put it on trial, tortured it (to extract a "confession"), and, finally, hanged it from a makeshift cat's gallows. Or so the scandal-hunting press reported. It was also said that they stuck pins in the cat, drew blood and mixed it with their wine for a communion service. No one knew whether the story was true in whole or in part but everyone believed it. From that time forward the habitués of the Vienna were known as the "cat fanciers."[4]

The spiritual aspirations of the intelligentsia, their dreams of transforming Russia into a paradise on earth, the vision of a future in which men and women, as Chernyshevsky depicted, would live freely, as equals, in full respect for each other's person and personality, had almost been lost. In place of the ideals of Chernyshevsky or Tolstoy emerged the image of Sanin, hero of Mikhail Artsybashev's erotic novel—the totally amoral man who loves as he wills, who is convinced that there is no eternal life, that one must take pleasure where it is found, live for the moment, because "life is an incurable disease." Sanin believed in no "golden future." He sought salvation in the flesh —marriage, love, idealism—all was thrown over for the satisfactions of the body. Sanin looked to the day when man could freely do whatever he willed at the moment. Men (and women) should, he believed, love without barrier, without moral interdictions, and without jealousy. Artsybashev filled his novel with cold-blooded seductions, naturalistic sexual detail, the manipulation of women by men for sexual satisfaction. Almost all of his characters ended badly (particularly the women) in suicide, desertion, tragic pregnancies, or despair. In the end Sanin proclaims: "What a bad joke is man!"

In a sense Sanin was the antithesis of Chernyshevsky's moralistic

Rakhmatov, who put all bodily senses behind him in iron-minded concentration on the cause of Revolution. Small wonder that Andrei Bely felt Russia had fallen into a twilight of bawdiness in which only the candle butt of the *ogarochny* flickered dimly, in which the *koshkodavakhi* (cat writers) held their strange orgies and the mystical tower of Ivanov, that realm of intellectual voluntarism, of anarchistic ritual, was drowning in a sea of tawdry sensationalism.[5] Bely could no longer perceive distinction between the dialogue of the *koshkodavakhi* and that of Ivanov's Tower where one night in answer to the question: "What is love?" Berdyayev responded: "It is the black rose—passion!" And someone else, probably Rozanov, who divided his time between pornography, mystic criticism, and anti-Semitic pamphleteering, responded: "Love is Plato's erotic wings."[6] To Bely (and to others) there seemed a direct connection between the anarchy of the spirit born in the Tower and in the other fashionable salons of St. Petersburg and Moscow, and the new Russian age of social and political decadence. It was but a step—hardly half a step—from the lesbian novels of Zinovyeva-Annibal, Ivanov's wife, the pederastic verses of the Tower's resident poet, Mikhail Kuzmin, and the lyrics of Ivanov's "333" to the total debauchery of the *tryn-trava*, the *ogarochny*, and the Saninists. It was difficult for anyone but the participants to draw a line between Rozanov's glorification of Platonic love, by which he meant Plato's love for young men, and the homosexuality of the cheap café, and Bely raised the question as to what force had overwhelmed the symbolist movement. Did the crisis arise from a resurgence of primitive Russian sexualism, the raw physical eroticism of the *khlysti*, the ancient Russian sect of self-flagellants whose "baths" were orgies of whipping, beating, and sexual satiation, whose sadomasochism ran like a dark stain through the Orthodoxy of the deep Russian countryside, particularly in the backwaters of the Volga, the forests of the Kama, and the endless reaches of Siberia?[7]

It was a strange time. In a leading St. Petersburg whore house the portrait of one of Russia's best known writers (and most honored guests) was hung—in order to attract the trade of others. Another house catered to husbands and wives, the same courtesan often serving both husband and wife, each in their preferred manner. In another, young women of good families, having sworn an oath of secrecy, appeared naked before men and ravished them. It reminded Bely of Goethe's famous dictum—that from boundless romanticism to the whorehouse is but a single step.[8] St. Petersburg seemed to Bely like the ghost of a vampire, materializing out of the yellow fogs of the Finnish marshes. And within the city somewhere, unknown to its inhabitants, unrecognized, a bomb was ticking. Only the Bronze Horseman, that fateful symbol of Peter, the statue erected in his honor by Catherine, held the city alive by force of a mighty will.[9] Describing the city a bit later, the poetess Zinaida Gippius sensed in it something of Gogol's "fear and terror," something undefinable yet almost palpable. One day she met Alexander Blok walking the street with tragic face, and when she asked him what was the matter, he said that what he felt could not be expressed in words.[10] He dedicated to her what she thought was one of the best of his poems: "We are the children of Russia's terrible years."[11]

In this era Boris Azef, the most famous provocateur of the day, the man who directed the assassination of Grand Duke Sergei in Moscow, who played a role in the killing of Interior Minister Plehve and many others while simultaneously acting as the principal informer on the revolutionaries for the Third Section of Nicholas' police, this man, the symbol of the Janus face of Russian society, combining outward nobility with total inner evil, became a kind of folk hero, the Charles Manson of his time. To young people in St. Petersburg and Moscow, to many of those who in an earlier generation had been attracted to the heroic example of the Dekabristi and their wives (who had given themselves to Siberian exile in payment for the adolescent effort to change the Russia of Nicholas I), the figure of the ultimate rogue, the symbol of the depravity of man and the triumph of evil, was worshiped almost as an icon. Azef, traitor, provocateur, adept and culpable betrayer of everyone—police and Government, Party and revolution, his comrades, his employers, and himself—was enthroned.[12]

Scandal filled the air. One evening at the Yar, Moscow's most luxurious restaurant,[13] as the band played a tango—the city's newest, maddest passion—a young man walked up to a table where a beautiful woman sat with several older men, all in evening dress. He reproved the woman for being at the Yar in such company so late in the evening. She laughed cynically. The young man shrugged his shoulders, thrust a hand into his evening jacket, and emptied a revolver at his former wife. His trial—the Praslov case—became the sensation of Russia. The young man and woman had been bright stars in Moscow's decadent night life. They had met at the "Suicide Club" and held their wedding reception at the Villa Black Swan, a rendezvous built by a Moscow millionaire for his wildest revels. Then they had parted. After twenty-eight days of gaudy testimony and violent silence (several who were called as witnesses killed themselves rather than testify) Praslov was acquitted by a jury. The defense attorney had quoted Goethe: "I have never heard of a crime, no matter how gruesome, which I could not have committed myself."[14]

A few days later the newspapers had another sensation—two young

Petersburg students of titled families planned a champagne supper at an expensive restaurant. When their parents refused to give them money for the meal, they broke into the flat of a prominent actress, stabbed her to death, and made off with her jewelry. A newspaper columnist commented: "A real gentleman is obliged to keep his social engagements at no matter what price."[15]

The diary of Count Alexei Bobrinsky provides a mirror of the times. For a decade or more he had watched with cynical pessimism the growing decay of the Imperial system to which he, in general, had dedicated his life. He did not believe it could survive much longer. With the death of Leo Tolstoy at the railroad station at Astapovo on November 7, 1910, after his melodramatic "flight" from his estate at Yasnaya Polyana, Bobrinsky's first thought was of its political consequences. Outbreaks were certain to occur. Would they shake the throne to its foundation?[16] Since 1905 this had been his reaction, again and again, to each major political event. Nor was he alone. (Lenin had the same reaction.)

Bobrinsky's forebodings were not without basis. Tolstoy's death touched off immediate disorders—students with red flags and black flags appeared on the Nevsky to celebrate a "civil memorial service." (Tolstoy had been refused burial by the Orthodox Church because he had been excommunicated.) Police and Cossacks, sabers flashing and *nagaki* swinging, cleared the great avenue. As the demonstrations continued Bobrinsky noted: "This is the harbinger of the coming revolution." And again, on December 5, he wrote: "What is happening now is not clear. Evidently the dawn of the second revolution is at hand." A day later when students and police engaged in a gun battle in Odessa, he asked: "Is it beginning?"

Bobrinsky was wrong. The second revolution was not at hand—not yet. But his instinct was correct, and his basic conviction that society stood at the brink was supported by his other entries: a great reception at the Winter Palace, the first in a long time, so disorderly and boring that he called it "sheer anarchy." A crowning touch—he came home with someone else's hat and coat. He thought the Czar looked puffy, his eyes small and sick. He was told that the Czar was drinking heavily, staying up all night, carousing with naval officers. Whether it was true or not Bobrinsky could not say. His friend Vyazigin, talking of the coming revolution (as who wasn't?), said it would certainly succeed because the Czar in the kindness of his heart would tell the troops not to fire on the revolutionaries. The Czarina did not attend the reception. She was suffering, Bobrinsky said, from a "psychological" illness.

Bobrinsky was revising his impression of the Czarina. She was not, as he had thought earlier, a supporter of constitutional government but a very strong defender of autocracy. When the Czar said: *"Il faut consulter Stolypine,"* she would respond: *"N'es tu pas souverain? Quel besoin de demander d'autres avis?"* On the other hand, he noted, she was not as gossip portrayed her. For instance, he had been told that rumors of a lesbian relationship between the Czarina and Madame Vyrubova "are exaggerated." The Czar, he heard, was beginning to "show some signs of life" and was upset about the unpleasantness in his family and the health of the Czarina.[17]

Scandal piled on scandal. The latest centered on Kshesinskaya, the ballerina, once (before 1896) the mistress of Nicholas II, later the close friend of the Grand Duke Sergei Mikhailovich and since 1900, consort of Grand Duke Andrei Vladimirovich, the Czar's cousin. The rumor, as Bobrinsky heard it, was that the police had carried out a search of Kshesinskaya's palace.[18] In the cellar, secret artillery documents and underground revolutionary literature had been found. Kshesinskaya told the investigators that the artillery materials were given her by Grand Duke Sergei Mikhailovich (chief of Russian artillery). The Grand Duke was said to have confirmed this. Why he should have picked the ballerina's cellar as a repository for state secrets and why revolutionary pamphlets had been mixed in the packing cases no one seemed to know. One version was that Kshesinskaya had wheedled the documents out of her patron for purposes of selling them to foreign intelligence agents.

Another rumor, Bobrinsky reported, was that War Minister Vladimir A. Sukhomlinov had set up a war game simulating an attack by Germany. One side was supposed to be commanded by Grand Duke Nikolai Nikolayevich (Nikolasha). But Nikolasha refused to play the game, claiming it was a trap, designed to show up his incapability. These rumors, Bobrinsky noted, came from the Imperial Yacht Club and "therefore are not without basis."[19]

For a decade, spiritualism and séances, occultism and superstitious cults, had been growing in popularity. The royal family was not alone in its interest. The intelligentsia and ordinary citizens sought new foundations on which to rebuild their shattered faith. Everyone was reading Annie Besant, the Secret Doctrine of Agrippa Nettesgeimsky, the Cabbala, of Zohar, Merkabah, Lucius Fismicus, Ptolemy's Tetrabiblos, the *Miscellanies* of Clement Alexandria, the tracts of Hammer, the Shepherd of the People, the Cathars Canilis Supramundanus and their interpreters. Spiritualist journals sprang up like weeds— the *Spiritualist* (once a month, two rubles a year) and *From There*, a twice-a-week bulletin on the latest events in the spirit world.[20] Bely's friends had dabbled in spiritualism for years, particularly

Nina Petrovskaya, S. A. Sokolov, A. A. Lang, and Valery Bryusov. They met in regular circles with "powerful mediums."[21] Bely at first scoffed at spiritualism but by 1908 he was participating in K. P. Khristoferov's circle and, in the grip of more and more intense delusions of persecution and conspiracy, was moving toward complete immersion in theosophist spiritualism.[22] This was stimulated by his exposure to one of the strangest phenomena in St. Petersburg—Anna Rudolfovna Minstslova, a fat woman with a yellow mane of hair, half-blind blue eyes, fat stomach, short fat arms, no eyebrows, a lorgnette in her fat hand, a voice that seemed to come from an empty barrel, dressed in what looked at first glance like a black sack. This improbable creature soon put Bely (and many others) into her power. She would shake his hand, her stomach quivering, and ask him if he could not feel the power flowing from her hand to his. "You are the chosen one," she whispered. And Bely believed it. Once she whispered to him: "The Gulf calls." "Who?" he asked. "The Atlantic Ocean," she said. "I have a connection with the Ocean." Suddenly she vanished. Not a trace of her in Moscow or Petersburg. Years went by. She was never seen again. Bely and her followers were convinced that she had heard the call of the Atlantic and, following the call, had made her way to some Norwegian fiord and hurled herself into its depths.[23]

Andrei Bely broke away from Moscow for five weeks and went to the remote village of Bobrovka. There he wrote *Serebryany Golub* (The Silver Dove), a prophecy in the form of a novel which told of the tragedy of Daryalsky, a sophisticated, educated Russian *intelligent,* such a man as Bely himself, who was drawn into a secret village sect of flagellants, headed by a crafty peasant, gifted with mystical powers, a man with a face like a gnawed bone and a grasp of black magic. The peasant's pock-marked woman, Matryona, employed her shameless and earthy passion to pull Daryalsky into the sect where he abandoned his sophisticated life and plunged into the rites of the *khlysti,* the flagellants. He believed he had discovered in them the secret of Russia.

"The Russian earth knows the secret. So does the Russian forest," Bely wrote. "The Russian soul is new-born; the Russian word is strong as pitch. If you are Russian there is in your soul a 'red'* secret—to live in the fields, to die in the fields, keeping to yourself that one holy word which no one knows except those who have received it and received it in silence.

"In the West there are many books; in Russia there are many unspoken words. There is that in Russia which destroys books and smashes buildings and puts life itself to the fire; and on that day when

* The Russian word for red and for beautiful is the same.

the West comes to Russia it will be totally consumed by fire; all will burn that can be burned because only from the ashes of death does the Zhar-Ptitsa, the Firebird, fly to heaven."[24]

Within the fantasy of the Silver Dove, he captured the fateful struggle for Russia's soul and future—the forces of enlightenment against the forest-brooding Firebird; the cult of knowledge against the cult of the khlysti, their lust, their blood, their passion.

Twenty years later Bely looked back on *The Silver Dove* with wonderment, for he had, he now realized, written a symbolic novel about Rasputin before Rasputin was known on the Russian scene. He had painted Rasputin in the figure of the peasant, Mitri Kudeyarov, and he had foretold the death of Russia's intelligentsia at the hands of the primeval forces which Kudeyarov represented.

"The Silver Dove," Bely mused, "was unsuccessful in many ways but it was successful in one. It pointed a finger to a still empty place. . . ." Soon, he said, this place would be occupied by Rasputin.[25]

XXIII

The Starets

When Anna Vyrubova first met Czarina Alexandra, she was closely questioned by her new friend (or so Vyrubova recalled) about her belief in spiritualism, which Alexandra described as a "great sin." Anna evidently was able to satisfy the Empress on this count. But at the same time the Empress offered a distinction between spiritualism, by which she meant table-tipping, the evoking of spirit voices in a dark room by professional mediums, etc., and "mysticism." The Empress described herself as a profound devotee of mysticism.[1] Indeed, the House of Hesse had long been known for such devotion. Among Alexandra's ancestors was St. Elizabeth of Hungary, who had been held up to Alexandra since childhood as the figure on whom she should model her life. Alexandra's mother had maintained an intimate association with the mystical theologian David Straus. Mysticism and religion were almost synonymous in Alexandra's life, and when she cast off her Protestant faith and embraced Orthodoxy, it was not the skeptical Orthodox faith of the 1870s that she accepted but sixteenth-century Russian Orthodoxism filled with superstition, saints, and candles. There was not a single saint in the Orthodox calendar for whom Alexandra did not light a candle. Her faith resembled the dark and mystery-laden world of that most backward layer of Moscow life, the old burghers of Zamoskvorechye—the quarter south of the Moskva River where in their rambling old compounds the tight-fisted *kupechestvo* still clung to their superstitious belief in dwarfs, fools, soothsayers, and prophets.[2] The Czar's faith was very similar to that of the Empress. Both believed in the special spiritual powers of those wandering pilgrims who for centuries had been a characteristic of the Russian scene—men, often half-mad, who spent their lives ranging the Russian steppes, dependent upon the charity of the peasants or of the wealthy, performing simple miracles (easing the birth of a calf, "curing" a woman's barrenness, casting off the spell of the village witch or alternately, casting a spell on the peasant's enemy). God's slaves, as they were sometimes called. They wore ragged robes and bark shoes. Often they walked barefoot in the frozen winter. They had some knowledge of the Scriptures or the Apocrypha and their talk was of strange things—of monsters and miracles, of salvation through sin, of the wonders they had seen and which were to come to pass. They were *stranniki*, wanderers, or *bosonozhki*, barefoot pilgrims, or *startsi*, aesthetic pilgrims who often took up their abode in monasteries. These men were regarded with superstition and awe, reverence and respect, by almost all levels in Russian society.

The *starets* was a figure of special significance. Dostoyevsky in *The Brothers Karamazov* described him as "one who takes your soul and will into his soul and his will. When you select your *starets* you freely surrender your will, you give it to him in utter submission, in full renunciation. He who takes this burden upon him, who accepts this terrible school of life, does so of his own free will in hope that after a long atonement he will be able to conquer himself and become his own master. . . ."[3]

Siberia, the village, the deep forest—these were places of strange and unbelievable events. Who knew what might happen there? Who knew what secrets these men might possess, clutching their greasy brown robes, held together with a worn piece of hemp? Siberia was the home of the sectarians: the *molokani*, who drank only milk and ate no meat; the Old Believers, who sometimes huddled together within their churches, set them afire, and perished for the grace of God; the *dukhobortsi*, who submitted to no man's law (only to God's) and stripped naked in protest against the Czar's gendarmes; the *beglopopovtsi*, who regarded priests as agents of the devil; the khlysti, who beat themselves and each other with birch switches and leaded ropes; the *skoptsi*, who castrated themselves to win freedom from sexual temptation; the *dushiteli*, who offered the dying the service of choking them to death, and others. Among all these sects and aberrant peoples the tradition of the orgy, the ancient cults of lust and drunkenness, debauchery and "cleansing through sin," lived on, only slightly mantled by pseudoreligious "festivals" (*maslenitsa*, the pre-Lenten holiday *birizhovka*, May-fest, the midsummer solstice).

Despite the Czarina's brave words about spiritualism there was in the intimate circle at Tsarskoye Selo a strong belief in the supernatural. The Czar had been closely attached to his father, Alexander III, and almost certainly engaged in efforts to communicate with him in the early years after Alexander's death.[4] The great spiritual favorite of the court (and St. Petersburg) at this time was Father Ivan of Kronshtadt, whose personality was powerfully colored with mysticism. The first mystic known to have entered the intimate court circle was "Dr." Philippe—Philippe Nizier-Vachot, described by Sir Bernard Pares as "an adventurer in mysticism, a professional soul doctor." Philippe was introduced to the Czar and the Czarina during a state visit to France by the Grand Duchess Militsa, wife of Grand Duke Pyotr Nikolayevich. Militsa was one of the two Montenegrin princesses, sisters, married into the Imperial family. The other was Anastasia (Stana), wife of Nikolasha. The Montenegrins were lively, superstitious women, addicted to fashionable cults and fakirs. Regardless of whether the Czar and his wife engaged in séances (and they almost certainly did occasionally), Militsa and Stana indulged frequently. So did Stana's husband, bluff and blundering old Nikolasha.

Philippe, of course, was a charlatan. Pyotr Rachkovsky, the chief of the Russian secret police in France, presented evidence of this to the Dowager Empress, who informed the Czar.[5] Rachkovsky's reward was dismissal from service. The Dowager Empress' comment was: "*C'est un crime!*"[6] For a time Philippe had considerable influence, particularly since he claimed to be able to assist the Czarina in conceiving an heir. His influence failed somewhat when the Empress had what proved to be a false pregnancy in 1902, and in 1904 he was sent back to France—but not before giving Alexandra a bell with which to warn off advisers of the Czar whom she distrusted and an accurate prophecy that Their Majesties would one day "have another friend who will speak to them of God."[7]

Philippe was not the only wonder-worker who appeared at the court. There was a mystic named Papus and a curious figure, a simple-minded "God's Fool," a cripple named Mitya Kozelsky, or "Kolyuba," who was incapable of speech and communicated only with his hands; the barefoot *strannik* Vasya Tkachenko; the Monk Iliodor, originally from Saratov but by 1911[8] in residence at St. Petersburg. And in the background, of course, the continuing favorite, Father Ivan of Kronshtadt.

The man who came to be known as Rasputin arrived in St. Petersburg in 1903. His first name was Grigory and he had no *familiya*, or Russian family name, a common enough circumstance among peasants. His father was called Yefim, and Rasputin was known as Grigory

Yefimovich Novy, the "Novy" simply meaning "new," for he was a "new man," not native to the village of Pokrovskoye in the remote Tobolsk Guberniya of Siberia where he lived. How he acquired the name of Rasputin (which means dissolute) is arguable. Probably it stemmed from his conduct in the village. His sexual prowess was legendary and there were few young (or even older) women in the region whom he had not possessed before he emerged from young manhood. His father was a coachman, quite possibly a horse thief (as was Rasputin) and he drove widely over the Siberian backwoods. Rasputin was, it was later charged, a member of the khlysti sect but this was never proved.[9] In conduct and attitude, however, he resembled the khlysti. Fleeing his village because of the scandals, he began to wander over Russia—a *strannik*. He freely confessed that he had been a sinner but sought repentance through devotion to the works of God. He made a pilgrimage to Jerusalem (traditional for the strannik) and on December 29, 1903, appeared at the religious academy in St. Petersburg.[10] He was a strong man of medium height with sharp gray eyes which had penetrating qualities. Few people could match his gaze and many quickly fell under his hypnotic influence. He wore his hair long over his shoulders and looked like a saint or at least a monk. His chestnut hair was heavy, wiry, well combed, and greased. His beard was tangled and thick. He wore simple peasant's garb, a Russian blouse, drawn about his waist with a silk cord, wide Turkish trousers, high boots, and a loose Russian coat thrown about his shoulders. Later on he would wear silk shirts sewed for him by the Czarina herself, and in her presence he would wear gleaming Russian leather boots instead of battered peasant ones. He had no table manners. Or rather he had the manners of an animal. He ate with his fingers, plunging his hands into the platters on the table and plucking tasty heads and fillets out of his *ukha* (fish soup). He ate no meat, no sweets, no pastries. His favorite foods were potatoes and vegetables. He tore hunks of bread apart with his blackened teeth. He did not like vodka but consumed quantities of madeira and port. He was very fond of the Russian bath with its heat and steam (and heavy-breasted female attendants) and headed straight for the bath after a night of drinking and debauchery. He had a powerful body odor. The higher the society, the more coarse and vulgar his language. He rarely cursed in the presence of peasants and never in the presence of his daughters, Mariya (Matryona) and Varya. But nothing was more foul than his language and manners in the presence of fawning duchesses or importuning noblemen.[11]

In Petersburg Rasputin won the interest—and support—of several important clergymen, one of them Bishop Feophan, who was close to the court. Another champion was Germogen, Bishop of Saratov. A year or two after his first appearance Rasputin was "discovered" by the two Montenegrin duchesses who were in Kiev on a religious pilgrimage. They encountered in the courtyard of the Mikhailovsky Monastery a strannik sawing wood. The strannik gave the titled ladies an intense look and bowed low. They stopped and began to question him. He told them of his wanderings, his pilgrimage to Jerusalem, the holy places he had seen, and hinted at strange wonders. The superstitious duchesses were entranced. From the Kiev courtyard and the wood chopping it was but a simple step to Tsarskoye Selo, where he was soon the sensation of the circle centering around the Montenegrins.[12] He gave the first example of his powers by curing Nikolasha's favorite hound of the colic.[13]

This was the "man of God, Grigory from Tobolsk Guberniya," with whom the Czar and Czarina became acquainted, in the words of the Czar's diary, on November 1, 1905.[14] It is probably no coincidence that the evening before the acquaintance began Nicholas and Alexandra dined with the Montenegrin princesses (and their husbands). The party did not break up until 11 P.M. Almost certainly the next day's audience for Rasputin was arranged at that time.[15]

There is no precise record to show how rapidly the relationship between Rasputin and the Imperial couple developed. From the moment of meeting he treated them like simple peasants, greeting them with the traditional triple kiss and calling them simply "Papa" and "Mama." The Czar's diary contains two more brief allusions to Rasputin within the year. They met him at Nikolasha's July 18, 1906. And on October 13 the Czar noted that Grigory had come, bringing the holy icon of St. Simeon of Verkhoturye. "He saw the children and talked with them until 7:15," he added. Again on December 9 he wrote: "Dined with Militsa and Stana. All evening they told us stories about Grigory."[16] The key to the rapidly deepening association was, of course, the concern of the Imperial couple over the health of the Czarevich. The couple saw in Rasputin and his mysterical powers the guarantee, or so they thought, of the boy's life.

Rasputin quickly acquired enormous influence in the narrow court circle. To his principal patrons, the Montenegrin princesses and their Grand Duke husbands, he now added the royal couple and their intimates, particularly Anna Vyrubova, the closest personal friend of the Czarina. A small establishment began to grow around him. He brought his two daughters, Mariya and Varya, but not his son Mitya, a half-wit, from Siberia to live in his house. His wife Praskovya Dubrovina paid him an annual visit. To those who spoke to her of Rasputin's dissolute life she simply replied: "He can do what he wants. He has enough for all." More than once she had turned out of their house women who insisted on sleeping with her husband.[17] And he established a working relationship with a shrewd Jewish jeweler named Aron Simanovich who had already made connections with the court. (The Czarina was extremely parsimonious: Simanovich's success rested on his ability to offer her bargains in jewels which Fabergé could not match.)[18] Simanovich's good sense, prudence, and knowledge of financial matters was to prove vital to Rasputin as his affairs grew more and more complex.

Rasputin's name did not immediately arouse many echoes beyond court circles. Zinaida Gippius first heard it mentioned in the winter of 1908-9. She declined an invitation from the Baroness Uexküll to meet him at her salon. She was more interested in another starets named Shchetinin, whom she described as a "democratic" edition of Rasputin. Shchetinin dressed like Rasputin in Russian blouse and high Russian boots. Like Rasputin he was a womanizer, a carouser, a rough-mannered man. But instead of the highest levels of Russian society his followers were working-class men—and working-class women. He was finally whisked out of Petersburg by the ecclesiastic authorities after evidence had been collected of his orgies and perversions. These were the same authorities who clustered around Rasputin, currying his favor.[19]

To the cool-minded Count V. N. Kokovtsov, Rasputin seemed a "typical Siberian convict, a tramp who had shrewdly trained himself to play the fool and who carried out his role according to a tried-and-true recipe." Rasputin tried to exercise his hypnotic powers on Kokovtsov but the count dismissed him. Privately Kokovtsov commented that he was reminded of an Armenian peddler with an ace of diamonds up his sleeve.[20]

But this was not the impression Rasputin made at Tsarskoye Selo. There he swiftly emerged as the spiritual adviser of both the Czar and the Czarina, particularly after the critical illness of the Czarevich in 1906. The Imperial couple simply believed that Rasputin had saved the life of Alexei. As to how he achieved this—no questions were asked in the Imperial family. It was clear that he exercised hypnotic powers over the Czarevich. He may also have had recourse to Tibetan decoctions provided him by the Buryat-Mongol doctor, Badmayev. These were infusions of oriental herbs of uncertain composition.[21] By 1911 there was no question—Rasputin's influence was supreme. As time passed Rasputin told more and more stories of his intimacy with the throne. Once, he said, he sat with the Imperial couple, talking politics. Suddenly he banged on the table so hard the Czar trembled and the Czarevich cried out.

"Where does it beat?" Rasputin demanded, pointing his finger first to his forehead and then to his heart.

"Here," said the Czar. "Here my heart beats."

"Oh," said Rasputin. "Then, in what you do for Russia—ask not the mind but the heart. The heart is higher than the mind."

"Good," replied the Czar, kissing Rasputin. "Thank you, thank you, teacher."

On another occasion, in Rasputin's words, the Czar fell on his knees before him crying: "Grigory, Grigory! You are Christ. You are our Savior."

Sometimes, Rasputin claimed, he spent the whole day in the Czarina's bedroom. He kissed her and she put her head on his shoulder and he carried her to bed like a small child. He listened to the children's prayers and sang hymns with them.[22]

Many persons believed, undoubtedly with reason, that Rasputin, particularly when drunk, exaggerated his intimacy with the Imperial couple, but Rasputin's tales were supported by the Czarina's own letters to him. "How tedious I am without you," she wrote. "I breathe easily only when you, my teacher, sit beside me and I kiss your hand and put my head on your holy shoulder. Oh, how light I am then! I want only one thing—to sleep, to sleep an eternity on your shoulder. Oh, what happiness just to feel your presence near me. When I hear you my head bows and I feel the touch of your hand."[23] The Czarina signed her letters to Rasputin "M" (for Mama).[24] There were not a few such letters. Also schoolgirlish letters from the Imperial daughters, obviously written under their mother's persuasion and embarrassing in their gushiness ("Please write me a letter, I so love to get them from you." "I saw you in my dream." "I think of you constantly you are so good.").[25]

Rasputin once showed the Monk Iliodor a trunk in his Pokrovskoye home which he said was filled with letters from the Czarina and the Imperial daughters. That was undoubtedly an exaggeration. But there were enough to cause endless trouble. Rasputin gave Iliodor several as a "keepsake" and sooner or later they began to leak their way into the gossip of society and copies reached important political leaders like Alexander I. Guchkov and M. V. Rodzyanko. The police managed to buy up the Iliodor originals—six in all, one from the Czarina, one each from the four Imperial princesses, and one signed "A" for Alexei, the Czarevich.[26] But there were carbons, of course, and also mimeograph copies.[27]

No one close to the Czarina believed that she committed any personal improprieties with Rasputin. But this, inevitably, was the gossip of St. Petersburg, gossip which followed the Empress down through the decades. "She saw her future husband first at the glittering Russian Court when she was 14 and it is no exaggeration to say that she loved him with all the force of her sharply defined spirit, knowing no compromise and preserving that feeling inviolable to her very last breath," Kokovtsov observed.[28] This view was shared by Sir Bernard Pares, who knew the Imperial family and St. Petersburg intimately and this is the impression conveyed in pure tones by the touching memoir of Pierre Gilliard, Swiss tutor to the Czarevich. Gilliard was with the Imperial family until their last days. "She worshipped her husband as she worshipped her children and there was no limit to her devotion for those she loved," Gilliard observed. "Persuaded, as she was, that the only support for the dynasty was the nation and that Rasputin was God's elect (had she not witnessed the efficacy of his prayers during her son's illness?) she was absolutely convinced that this lowly peasant could use his supernatural powers to help him who held in his hands the fate of the empire of the Czars. . . . It was thus that in her desire to save her husband and her son whom she loved more than life itself, she forged with her own hands the instrument of their undoing."[29] As for the Czar he, too, was trapped—in part by his own superstitious belief in Rasputin's powers and in part by his dedication to his wife. Not many months before his death in 1911 Stolypin sought to persuade the Czar to send Rasputin back to Siberia, to which the Czar responded: "I know and believe, Pyotr Arkadyevich, that you are truly dedicated to me. Perhaps, all that you tell me is true. But I beg you to speak no more to me of Rasputin. There is nothing more I can do about it."[30]

On September 1, 1911, the great gilt curtain of the Kiev Opera House rose about 9 P.M. on a special performance of *The Tale of Czar Sultan* by Rimsky-Korsakov. All the senior classes of the Kiev gymnasia, both boys and girls, were assembled in the balconies under heavy security. The doors of the galleries were locked so that no one could descend to the first floor. There were police officers at every door.

In the top row of the theater sat Konstantin Paustovsky, a graduating student in the First Gymnasium, soon to be renamed Emperor Alexander I Gymnasium. It was very hot and Paustovsky could reach out and touch the ceiling of the theater with his hand.

At the second intermission he got up and went forward with his companions to crowd around the railing. As he looked down to the orchestra he thought it seemed rather misty but there was a glitter and sparkle from the diamonds in the headdresses and brilliant gowns of the ladies.

The spectacle marked a state visit of Nicholas II. By the time Paustovsky got to the front of the gallery the Czar and his daughters (the
Czarina was absent) had moved out of their box into an adjacent retiring room. The Czar's Ministers were crowded up by the orchestra
rail where the musicians in their black evening clothes sat silently.
Suddenly Paustovsky heard a sharp crack and then another. The musicians leaped to their feet. A girl cried: "Look, he sat right down on the
floor." "Who?" asked Paustovsky. "Stolypin," she said. It was true,
Paustovsky saw. The Premier, a tall man with black beard and a ribbon over his shoulder, was sitting on the floor beside the railing.

"Clear the gallery!" a policeman shouted. As the students filed out
they heard the orchestra strike up "God Save the Czar."[31]

As Nicholas II described the scene in a letter to his mother, Mariya
Fyodorovna:

"We had just left the box, as it was so hot, when we heard two
sounds, as if something had been dropped. I thought an opera glass
might have fallen on somebody's head and ran back into the box to
look. Directly in front of me in the stalls, Stolypin was standing; he
slowly turned his face towards us and with his left hand made the sign
of the cross in the air. Only then did I notice that he was very pale
and that his right hand and uniform were blood-stained. . . . Then
. . . the national anthem was sung and I left with the girls at eleven.
You can imagine with what emotions."[32]

Count Kokovtsov (who was to succeed Stolypin) had just said
good-by to the Premier as he had to return that night to Petersburg.
"If you could take me with you on the train," Stolypin said, "I would
profoundly thank you. All day long I've felt somehow harassed and
worn out."

The Count was making his way toward the lobby when he heard
two shots. They sounded to him like a firecracker.

Stolypin died four days later on the evening of September 5.
Kokovtsov had been at his bedside almost constantly but left that
night about 9 P.M. His nerves could no longer stand the terrible
screams. The Czar had not broken off his scheduled tour and did not
visit Stolypin. He arrived at the hospital only the next morning.
Stolypin's widow stood beside the bed and as the Czar entered she
said in loud and firm tones: "Your Highness, Susanin will not come
again to Rus." (Ivan Susanin was the legendary peasant savior of the
ancient Russian throne—celebrated in the Czar's favorite opera,
Glinka's A Life for the Czar.[33]

Stolypin was one more victim of the symbiotic police-terrorist relationship. He had been shot by a police stool pigeon named D. Bogrov
who had been provided with his ticket to the theater by the police,

despite the fact that he had come to them with mysterious reports of an assassination plot. Bogrov had been on the police payroll since 1907. He was paid 100 rubles a month. His father was a well-known Jewish lawyer in Kiev, a heavy gambler who on one occasion had won 100,000 rubles. Young Bogrov was also a gambler. He had dabbled in anarchism but appeared to have no firm political convictions. He was, in the opinion of those who investigated the case, obviously an unstable psychotic individual.[34]

Suspicion of police complicity in the assassination, has never died, fed by questions about the relationship of Bogrov to the police and by the conduct of the police after the assassination. The police sought to block investigation of the affair. Bogrov was summarily and secretly tried and executed shortly after midnight September 12. All records of the questioning of Bogrov and of his trial disappeared and were probably destroyed.[35] The Czar declined to act on a report which charged the security officers with slackness and misconduct; both he and the Czarina were known to have been hostile toward Stolypin at the end. The Czar did not attend the funeral and the Empress refused to pray for Stolypin's soul.[36] The Czarina told the Grand Duke Dmitri Pavlovich that "those who have offended God in the person of our friend [Rasputin] may no longer count on divine protection."[37]

Investigation disclosed that the police were at least criminally careless in the Stolypin affair. The assassin Bogrov had actually come to the Kiev police and told them that an SR plot to assassinate Stolypin was about to be carried out. He was interviewed by Gen. A. I. Spiridovich, chief of the Czar's personal security detail; Spiridovich's brother-in-law, Col. Nikolai N. Kulyabko, chief of security for Kiev; and Vice-Director of the Interior Mitrofan N. Verigin. Gen. Pavel G. Kurlov, counselor of the Interior Ministry, in general charge of security, was informed as well. Bogrov was an undercover agent employed by Kulyabko—described after the assassination as a "former agent." All of the police officers involved were reprimanded, reduced in rank, or lost their jobs, although Kurlov later became governor-general of the Baltic provinces.[38] The Czar refused to act on a report by Kokovtsov recommending more severe punishment. This was possibly the most notorious of the prerevolutionary assassinations and was extensively investigated by the Extraordinary Investigating Commission of the Provisional Government, set up in 1917.[39] An investigation by M. I. Trusevich, a member of the Duma, carried out in 1911 did not bear out widely believed rumors that Rasputin had some connection with the case.[40]

Bogrov displayed total indifference at his trial. When sentenced he said: "It's all the same to me whether I eat 2,000 more cutlets in my life or don't eat them."[41]

Some years later A. I. Guchkov said that he had never been able to rid himself of the belief that in some manner the "dark forces," the reactionary elements which were hurrying Russia down the slippery slopes of disaster played a role in the elimination of Stolypin. But the nature of that role remains a mystery.[42]

During the September days of the Czar's visit Rasputin was in Kiev, too. Several years later V. V. Shulgin, a brilliant young Conservative leader in the Duma, had a curious conversation with a Kiev official who accompanied Rasputin on the day of the Czar's ceremonial procession through the streets of Kiev. As Stolypin's carriage passed by, Rasputin cried out: "Death is following him! Death is following him!" And that evening Rasputin cried again and again: "It's terrible. It's terrible. Death is coming."[43]

Kokovtsov was named in Stolypin's place and began his service by submitting to the Czar a frank and open letter in which he warned him that those who bore the responsible burdens of government could not act with hope of success unless they enjoyed both his and the country's confidence.[44]

"Russia," commented A. I. Guchkov, "has fallen into a morass—and it is, of course, beyond the strength of V. N. Kokovtsov to pull it out."[45]

Looking back on it, Count Kokovtsov came to regard the winter of 1911–12 as *the* critical moment for the Romanov dynasty and Imperial Russia. The atmosphere in Petersburg thickened. The name of Rasputin appeared more and more often in the newspapers. His closeness to the palace was becoming apparent to all. So was his pervasive influence in policy. Stories began to circulate about his sexual activities in the Tobolsk Guberniya. References to his relations with Petersburg society women turned up in such newspapers as *Rech* and *Russkoye Slovo*. Pavel Milyukov began talking in the Duma about "dark forces" and their influence on the country—by which he meant not only Rasputin but the whole circle around the Court.[46] Every effort by police and the Czar's Ministers to quiet the scandals failed. In fact, they grew worse. Bishop Germogen and the Monk Iliodor, Rasputin's early supporters, turned against him. They confronted Rasputin on December 16, 1911. Iliodor presented his charges—that Rasputin had boasted of going to the public baths in Pokrovskoye with Anna Vyrubova, the Czarina's confidante, and other women, that he had caressed and raped the nun Vishnyakova, that he had told of his sexual conquests (while claiming that his sexual organs were "inactive"). Iliodor had collected a dossier on Rasputin's debauchery with the aid of Mitya Kozelsky, a rival "holy man." In a passion Germogen struck Rasputin on the head with his heavy bishop's cross and made him swear on a holy icon to give up women and cease his visits to the Czar's palace.[47] Rasputin was frightened but he soon recovered his courage and succeeded in having his enemies banished from Petersburg, claiming they had wanted to castrate him. At Tsarskoye Selo sympathy was on Rasputin's side. He had been, it was said there, attacked as a highwayman attacks a victim in the forest, deliberately decoyed to be attacked from the rear.

As scandal after scandal bubbled through the heated Petersburg atmosphere the Czar became more and more angry, demanding that the police and the Government put an end to newspaper comments and Duma debate. "I simply do not understand why my will cannot be carried out," he told Interior Minister Makarov. But, of course, there was little or nothing anyone could do. The scandal fed on itself. On February 13, 1912, the Dowager Empress Mariya Fyodorovna called in Count Kokovtsov and he told her frankly that the streets of Petersburg were filled with ugly and damaging gossip touching on intimate details of the life of the Emperor and Empress. The Dowager Empress was a strong-willed woman who had little love for her daughter-in-law, but she burst into tears and promised to try to speak to her son.

"My unhappy daughter-in-law does not understand that she is destroying the dynasty and herself. She truly believes in the holiness of this rogue and we are powerless to stave off misfortune," she said.[48]

Looking back on it all, A. I. Guchkov, the leader of the Octobrist party in the Duma, a staunch monarchist, declared that even before the death of Premier Stolypin he had begun to lose faith in the possibility of Russia's peaceful political evolution. Now "it became clearer to me that Russia was moving along the path of violent overthrow, a complete break with the past, and, so to say, navigating without rudder and without compass in the shoreless sea of political and social exploration."

It seemed to him that a fatal role would be played by the "irresponsible forces," that is the influence of Rasputin, Vyrubova, her father, Alexander S. Taneyev, Prince Andronikov, and others in what Guchkov called the "court camarilla." It was then that he raised the question for the first time in the Duma of the dark forces, and Rasputin.

By 1912 the question in his mind was a simple one:

Would there or would there not be a Russia?

A year later he asked himself the question: Where is the Government's policy leading? He answered: To inescapable catastrophe. He found little disagreement with his analysis among people of the most diverse social groups. All that remained to be determined was at what moment disaster would strike and what form it would take.

"But who," he asked, "could predict that?"[49]

XXIV

On the Brink

They were all leaving Russia in those years—the revolutionaries, the poets, the philosophers, the artists. They went to Rome, to Naples, to Capri, to Nice, to Geneva, to Zurich, to Brussels, to Vienna, to Berlin. But most of all to Paris. Paris . . . Everyone in Russia was there. It was almost a second capital. Zinaida Gippius was entranced. Paris in the spring! Really a pre-spring, for winter was not over although the sun was warm. At night from the balcony of their hotel on the Champs-Élysées the velvet sky sparkled with stars and the avenue flamed with lights; little bells of the fiacres danced an endless tune; on the Neva there was still ice but on the Seine it seemed that winter never came.

It was a time to be out of Russia. The Merezhkovskys were in Paris where Dmitri was plunging into his major work, *The Czar and the Revolution* ("In the house of the Romanovs . . . a mysterious curse descends from generation to generation . . . , murders and adultery, blood and mud . . . the block, the rope and poison—these are the true emblems of Russian autocracy. . . .").[1] Andrei Bely joined the Merezhkovskys. The poet Minsky, the same who had gone to prison for editing Lenin's newspaper, was there. Minsky had begun one of his poems with the words: "Workers of the world—unite!"[2] The poet Balmont arrived with one of his wives, the beautiful and luxuriant Andreyevna, from Moscow. Zinaida Gippius could not remember which wife she was, number four or number five. Balmont had dashed out of Russia after writing an inflammatory poem, "The Dagger," for which he thought he might be arrested.[3] He had called the Czar a "Bloody hangman."[4]

Here in Paris was the philosopher Dmitri V. Filosofov and the painter Alexander Benois who was working with Sergei Diaghilev. Diaghilev had brought the St. Petersburg Opera to Paris for the first time in 1908. On May 10, 1909, he presented his Russian ballet for its Paris premiere—Nijinsky, Chaliapin, Karsavina, Fokine, Pavlova. Paris would never be the same again. Neither would the Russians. In St. Petersburg Diaghilev would become known as "the Conqueror of Paris."[5]

The poets and painters were in Paris. The millionaire I. I. Shchukin —the French called him the "Russian Prince Chouquine"[6]—patron of many Russian and French artists, spent at least half his time there. So did his millionaire brother, Sergei, who created the great Moscow impressionist collection.

There were also the revolutionaries. The revolutionary center of Russia had been transferred to Paris. The Mensheviks were there— Fyodor Dan, Julius Martov, and Alexander S. Martynov—the SRs Abram Gots and Viktor Chernov. And, of course, Plekhanov. And also Boris Savinkov, co-organizer of the assassination of the Grand Duke Sergei. Savinkov was in and out of the Merezhkovskys' flat on the Rue Théophile Gautier in Auteuil constantly. So was Ivan Bunakov, another leading SR terrorist. When Savinkov was not at Merezhkovsky's he was apt to be found at the Zetlins'. Mikhail Osipovich Zetlin was a revolutionary poet who wrote under the name of Amari. But he was also one of the many revolutionary members (mostly SR sympathizers) of the family that owned the famous Vysotsky Tea Company, the biggest in Russia.[7] (Gots was a member of the same family.) One day Bely found Zinaida Gippius offering tea in a delicate china cup to a truculent revolutionary sailor from the Potemkin who roared: "We will wipe you out!" Politely she replied: "Will you have some tea? A biscuit, perhaps?"[8] Bely formed a firm friendship with the French socialist Jean Jaurès (who was to be assassinated on the eve of World War I). The Merezhkovskys were intimate with Anatole France and his constant companion, Madame de Caillavet. Vera Figner, who had been confined for twelve solitary years for her role in the assassination of Alexander II, had been released in 1905; now, she, too, was in Paris.

Years later Ilya Ehrenburg began to list the names of those you might meet on a spring evening at La Rotonde—Chagall, Soutine, Larionov, Goncharova, David Sterenberg, Fotinsky, Marevna, Vladimir Izdebsky, Archipenko, Zadkine (in over-alls with a great Dane), Meshchaninov, Savinkov, Balmont, Lunacharsky, himself—and, of course, Picasso, Juan Gris, Modigliani, Diego Rivera, Apollinaire, Cocteau, Léger, Vlaminck, and, he thought, probably a hundred others whose names did not immediately come to mind.[9]

One evening Figner and Merezhkovsky shared a platform. Figner, no longer young, her face long but somehow beautiful, awkwardly and bashfully, in a white dress, read some simple verses. Poetry, Gippius noted, was not her glory. Then they sat at table, Madame de Caillavet beside Figner. Madame de Caillavet, of course, knew that Figner had been confined "*dans une forteresse*" for twelve years. She made light conversation.

"*Vous êtes une héroïne, Madame, n'est-ce-pas? Vous êtes une héroïne?*" she said.

What was Figner to say, Gippius wondered—yes, indeed, ma'am, I am a heroine. Or no, I'm not a heroine, so please leave me alone. Figner said nothing at all and Madame de Caillavet was quite put out.[10]

Gippius helped Savinkov write the story of Grand Duke Sergei's assassination in the form of a novel. It was a poem to the cult of assassination. Savinkov wrote that he lived only to kill.[11] Gippius gave the novel the title *The Pale Horse* and sent it to Russia where it appeared in *Russkaya Mysl* under the nom de plume of V. Ropshin. Savinkov and Bunakov were trying to get the Fighting Group of the SRs going again. But it was difficult after the exposure of Azef's treachery. And Savinkov's novel didn't help matters. In 1912 Gippius sent Savinkov a birthday sonnet and he sent her one in return. She was amazed at its perfection but frightened by its message from "a soul choked in blood."[12]

Zinaida Gippius and Merezhkovsky were confident that revolution was coming to Russia—that it would be made by these very men, these SRs with whom they were so intimate.

Not all of Paris was high art or high ideals. No end of shady characters appeared—Manasevich-Manuilov, journalist and provocateur, and agent of Rachkovsky, long the director of the Czar's secret police in Paris; Baron Buksgevden, son of a Black Hundred leader believed to have carried out several notorious killings, including those of D. M. Gertsenshtein and possibly Iollos.

One night Minsky took Gippius and Bely on a tour of the Place Pigalle. He showed them the cabaret Enfer and the Bar Maurice, homosexual and lesbian haunts, and a small "local" where older women prowled for young girls. Minsky told them that in the house where he lived there were two beautiful girls, with the eyes of Madonnas. They were lesbians of seventeen and eighteen. The sophisticated Gippius and Bely were shocked. The decadence of Paris somehow seemed more

derground newspapers in Russia; bribes to be paid for the release of prisoners and to grease border crossings; large publishing projects abroad. Arms and munitions being bought. Without money the organization would wither away. And here there was a fateful crossover of moral principles. At Lenin's instigation—or at least with his approval and warm support—the technique of the "expropriation" was developed. "Expropriation" was simply a euphemism for armed robbery. The most famous of these was the holdup of a consignment of currency for the Tiflis post office in Georgia on June 26, 1907, at 10:30 A.M. The money, between 250,000 and 341,000 rubles, had been placed in sacks in a stagecoach, followed by another coach in which an armed military escort rode. It was preceded and followed by detachments of Cossack horsemen. The convoy was attacked with bombs and gunfire in the heart of the city and the treasure seized. This attack was carried out by a Bolshevik fighting detachment headed by Semyon A. Ter-Petrosyan (Kamo) which included V. K. Lominadze and K. M. Tsintsadze. It was directed by one of Lenin's chief lieutenants in the Caucasus, Iosif Djugashvili.

The Tiflis holdup caused an extraordinary uproar. All Europe knew of it, and in the following months excitement grew when one Bolshevik after another was picked up in Paris, Berlin, and Munich with 500-ruble notes bearing telltale serial numbers of the Tiflis consignment. Maxim Litvinov, eventually to be Russia's Foreign Minister, was arrested in Paris with twelve of the bills.[23] Then Kamo himself was seized in Berlin in 1908 carrying a suitcase filled with dynamite. Another "expropriation"—this one of the Mendelssohn Bank in Berlin— was being prepared.[24] He feigned mental illness and eventually was released in 1911. He promptly joined Lenin in Paris.[25] Eventually the remaining 500-ruble notes had to be burned. They were too hot to hold.[26]

The Tiflis "expropriation" set off a violent reaction within the Bolshevik movement. Expropriations had been explicitly prohibited by a 1907 London Party Conference but Lenin ordered them to go ahead regardless. The tremors recurred when Prussian police raided a Berlin warehouse, arrested a number of Bolsheviks, and seized a stock of watermarked paper used for producing counterfeit three-ruble notes. Lenin's agent, Krasin, was identified as the man who had ordered the paper.[27]

Kamo, Lominadze, Stalin, and all those involved in the Tiflis affair were expelled from the Party (later to be restored to membership through Lenin's influence) and Lenin was denounced.

The dirty money scandal was intensified by a dispute over the Schmidt inheritance. The Bolsheviks had gotten all of this money—

260,000 rubles.* But the slippery tactics which Lenin employed to obtain the inheritance (the fraudulent marriage and delivery of the money to the Bolshevik office in Paris) had become a Party scandal. For one thing, the Mensheviks contended that they were entitled to the funds. After a long wrangle Lenin agreed to turn over a substantial portion (possibly as much as 100,000 rubles—the exact sum long since has become obscure in the endless intra-Party disputes)[28] to three German socialist trustees—Karl Kautsky, Franz Mehring, and Clara Zetkin—while the matter was adjudicated by a Party court. He turned over the first of the funds in June 1911,[29] but in 1912 persuaded Kautsky to return at least part of the money—possibly 12,000 rubles, possibly much more.[30] The German comrades never did decide which of the wrangling Russian factions were entitled to it.[31]

The sordid struggles over money, the ethical quarrels as to sources and methods, tainted the whole movement. By this time Lenin professed to have no regard for what he called "bourgeois prejudices."[32] Of Viktor Taratuta, who had arranged the fictitious marriage which brought the Schmidt fortune to the Bolsheviks—a man whom all agreed had few principles and who for years was suspected of being a police spy—Lenin simply said: "A Central Committee to be effective must be made up of gifted writers, able organizers and a few intelligent scoundrels. I recommend Comrade X [Taratuta] as an intelligent scoundrel."[33] He followed his formula. "Lenin was neither blind nor indifferent to the harm personal dishonesty might do to the movement yet he used individuals who were the scum of humanity," commented Angelica Balabanoff. "The Bolsheviks used any individual as long as he proved shrewd, unscrupulous, a jack-of-all-trades, able to obtain access anywhere and a humble executor of his boss's orders."[34] V. V. Voitinsky quoted Lenin as saying: "Revolution is a dirty job. You do not make it with white gloves." He tolerated and defended the presence in the movement of scoundrels, embezzlers, and wastrels. "Ours is a big business," he said. "We can use all kinds of trash." He had, Voitinsky believed, no morals and no rules of decency in politics and "nothing but contemptuous mockery for the concept of Honor."[35]

Krzhizhanovsky recalled that in Siberia when someone would describe another as "a good man" Lenin would ask: "And what is a good man?" Krzhizhanovsky understood Lenin to mean that he was indifferent as to whether someone committed a sin in his personal conduct or violated one of the Ten Commandments. When Lenin heard of someone who had violated moral norms in his personal conduct, he

---

* Earlier estimates placed the sum at 280,000 rubles or more but the 260,000 figure seems to be established in the latest collection of Lenin documents. (*Leninsky Sbornik*, Vol. XXXVIII, p. 36.)

would say: "That doesn't mean anything to me—that's *Privatsache*" or "I close my eyes to that."[36]

This was the atmosphere of Lenin's move to Paris. He had, it was now obvious, crossed another divide. Long since he had abandoned honesty, the pure ethical reasoning, the clear distinction between good and evil which had illuminated the life of his martyred brother Alexander and which had been the rule of the plain and honest Simbirsk home in which he was reared.

Before 1905 he had moved a long way toward the view that the end justifies the means. In the decadence which characterized Russia of the interrevolutionary period he abandoned what scruples remained. Now the nature of the weapon; the nature of the technique; the nature of the tactic was no longer a test.

Perhaps this was why his mood was so somber in Geneva and why the somber mood followed him to France. He wrote his mother on the eve of his departure, November 17, 1908: "We hope the big city will put some life into us all; we are tired of staying in this provincial backwater."[37] It was not to be. In Paris, said Krupskaya twenty years later, "we spent the most trying years of our emigrant life abroad." Lenin never got used to it. "What the devil made us go to Paris!" he said again and again.[38] His reaction could not have been more unlike that of his old comrade (and now enemy) Martov who fell in love with Paris. Despite the poverty of his émigré life, Martov became such an habitué of La Rotonde, so loved sitting and talking and writing there, his friends wondered if they could ever get him back to Russia.[39] It was different with Lenin. His Bolsheviks met at a dismal café on the Avenue d'Orléans. They drank grenadine and soda, red, sticky, unpleasant.[40] From the beginning Paris to Lenin was a bore and a bother. Krupskaya had endless trouble getting them settled. She found the French bureaucracy incredible. It took three trips to town to get the gas connected. They had a fine flat at 24 Rue Beaunier, on the third floor, not far from the Avenue d'Orléans and the Parc Montsouris.[41] It was really too luxurious, "very elegant and expensive," Lenin called it. The rent was 840 francs a year plus 60 francs tax and what they paid the concierge—almost 1,000 francs, a not inconsiderable sum for those times.[42] Krupskaya was impressed by the fact that there were mirrors over all the fireplaces, the very latest Paris style, she reported. Her mother and Lenin's sister Mariya lived with them, each with her own room.

But they had left none of the quarrels behind. "Life in Paris was a hectic affair," Krupskaya remembered. "Conflict within the group was a nerve-wracking business. I remember Ilyich once coming home after having had words with the Otzovists [a Party faction]. He looked

awful and even his tongue seemed to have turned grey."[43] His old
friend and present enemy, Bogdanov, actually believed Lenin was on
the way toward leaving the revolutionary movement entirely.[44] The
tone of his letters conveyed the mood. They were filled with intra-
Party quarrels. He was publishing a book, *Materialism and Em-
piriocriticism,* in Moscow, and again and again he warned his sister
Anna, his intermediary with the publishers, "please do not tone down
anything in the places against Bogdanov, Lunacharky & Co. They
must not be toned down. You have deleted the passage about Chernov
being a 'more honest' opponent than they, which is a great pity." "I am
not suffering from nerves," he insisted to Vatslav V. Vorovsky, "but
our position is difficult."[45]

Polemics, polemics, polemics. Hardly a word about life in Paris—except complaints. Hardly a word about personal life. Hardly a question
about his family. In his letters to his mother and his sisters the tender,
intimate, loving warmth of his earlier correspondence fades into per-
functory questions, apologies for not writing, pro forma comments
about health. By May 26, 1909, he was writing his sister Anna, "Things
are bad here," and Krupskaya was adding a postscript: "I have been
in a state of utter melancholy, the time has been frittered away."[46]

Party meetings turned into physical brawls. *Never* had there been
anything like this before. Lenin sometimes walked the streets of Paris
all night long. He wrote Gorky April 11, 1910: "Living in the midst
. . . of these squabbles and scandals, this hell and ugly scum is sickening. To watch it all is sickening, too. But one must not be influenced
by one's moods. Emigrant life is now a hundred times worse than it
was before the revolution."[47]

No wonder, in this circumstance, the revolutionary movement, the
Social Democratic movement, was in disarray. "So," Lenin told Gorky,
"we have to suffer. Either—at best—we cut open the blisters, let out
the pus, and cure and rear the infant. Or, at worst—the infant dies.
Then we shall be childless for a while (that is, we shall re-establish
the Bolshevik faction) and then give birth to a more healthy infant."[48]

One day not long after Anna joined her brother in Paris she recalled
him saying on New Year's Day, 1912,[49] with as gloomy a look as she
could remember: "Do you suppose I will live to see another revolution?"[50]

Lenin was despondent over the situation in Russia. The revolutionary movement was in a state of "appalling chaos" with, as he
wrote Karl Kautsky and the other two German trustees of the Schmidt
fund in early spring, 1910, a "tremendous decline among the organizations everywhere, almost their cessation in many localities. The

XXV

Three Hundred Years

December 3, 1911, was a gloomy winter day in Paris. There was a raw wind that tore away umbrellas and an icy rain that filled the gutters. It was the day that Paris paid its last respects to Paul and Laura Lafargue, son-in-law and daughter of Karl Marx. The Lafargues had long lived at Draveil, about twenty-five kilometers outside Paris. They were too old, they felt, to work longer for the cause of revolution, and feeling their usefulness to mankind at an end they had simply killed themselves.

A few months before, Lenin and Krupskaya had called on the Lafargues, who were a kind of living icon to the revolutionaries. Lenin and Krupskaya cycled to Draveil, and while Lenin and Lafargue talked philosophy Krupskaya and Laura Lafargue walked in the garden. When the women rejoined their husbands, they found them vigorously engaged in conversation. "He will soon prove the sincerity of his philosophic convictions," Laura said of her husband, and the two exchanged a strange smile which Krupskaya did not understand until she heard the news of their death.[1]

Now the revolutionary movement met to honor these two unusual figures. The ceremonies were at the Pierre-Lachaise Cemetery, the place where the members of the Paris Commune had been executed. It was an appropriate setting. All of Europe's revolutionaries were represented at the ceremony. There was a huge crowd. The two coffins were carried under red flags. Jean Jaurès, the great French socialist leader, delivered the principal address. Kautsky spoke. So did the vet-

wholesale flight of the intelligentsia. All that are left are workers circles and isolated individuals."[51]

In August Lenin went to Stockholm and had what proved to be his
last visit with his mother. She was shocked at his appearance. "If it
hadn't been for Marusya," she wrote her daughter Anna, "I wouldn't
have known him. He is so thin and changed but he swears he feels
well."

Lenin told her that he rode his bicycle a great deal and that was
why he was so thin.[52]

In November 1910, Lenin was telling Gorky, "Things are turning
out bad. It's saddening."[53] Nor did the pattern change with the new
year, for again in January 1911 Lenin told Gorky, "I have long been
intending to reply to your letter but the intensification of the squabbling here (a hundred thousand devils take it!) had distracted me."[54]

eran French socialist Édouard Vaillant. One speaker after another took the platform. Finally it was Lenin's turn. On hearing of the suicide of the Lafargues he had told Krupskaya: "If you can't do any more work for the Party you must be able to face the truth and die like the Lafargues." He wanted to say over their graves that their work had not been in vain. There was little he could say about the movement in Russia. But China had just thrown off the Manchu mantle. The Chinese nationalist revolution of 1911 was in everyone's minds and, taking heart from this, he declared that "the Russian revolution [of 1905] ushered in an era of democratic revolutions throughout Asia and 800 million people are now joining in the democratic movement of the whole of the civilized world."[2]

It was hardly the most inspiring talk Lenin was to give. But it was the best he could do in this time of trouble, pessimism, almost unbearable personal tension, frayed nerves, and a Russian movement that was so fragmented that there were times when it seemed that you could number Lenin's supporters on the fingers of both hands. Lenin spoke in Russian. When he had finished, a slim, graceful woman, her golden hair combed into billowing waves which framed her face under a heavily ribboned hat and almost covered her small ears, a broad open brow, a large mouth, green eyes with a kind of warm sadness, went to the podium. There was a luminosity about her that contrasted with the gray and dripping day, the bitter wind, the inevitable melancholy of the graveyard. In perfect French she translated Lenin's remarks and then retired.[3]

This was Inessa Elizabeth Armand. She was thirty-seven years old. She had then known Lenin for about a year and would dedicate the rest of her life to him and to his cause. Inessa was born in Paris May 8, 1874, at 2 P.M. at the house on Rue de la Chapelle, No. 63, where her parents (her father was an opera singer, her mother an actress and music teacher) lived. But with the death of her father she was taken to Moscow and brought up there by her aunt and grandmother.

Inessa was a beauty. There is no other word for it. One has only to look at photographs (each year she was brought to have her picture taken at P. Pavlov's Photography Studio on the Myasnitskaya, in the Vyatsky House, across from the Salayev brothers' bookstore).

By the time she met Lenin, some time in 1910,[4] Inessa had already lived a full life. She was the mother of five children by Alexander Armand, son of a very wealthy Moscow manufacturer (in whose family her aunt and grandmother were tutors), one of that circle of adventurous, rich, and liberal Moscow enterpreneurs which included the Morozovs, the Prokhorovs, the Guchkovs, the Ryabushinskys, the Abrikosovs, the Khludovs, and the Katuarmamis. These were the "first families" of the "White Stone City," as the nouveaux riches of Moscow were called. The Armands were in wool textiles and they did a business estimated at 200,000 rubles a year, employing 2,000 workers in their principal works on the Yaroslavl Chaussée, twenty-eight versts from Moscow in the village of Pushkino.

Inessa had married October 2, 1893. Despite the rapidity with which she bore one child after another, she was far too spirited to settle down to the conventional life of a Moscow matron. She enlisted in good works, taking a hand in temperance campaigns, in women's education, in fighting prostitution, in the suffragette cause, and in improving conditions in the family mills at Pushkino. Like Lenin she had read Chernyshevsky's *What Is to Be Done?* and, as he had set the hero, Rakhmatov, as the model of his character so she, more and more, began to shape her life in the pattern of the idealistic heroine, Vera Pavlovna. By 1898 she was moving toward a more structured social view. She had read Pyotr Lavrov's *The Task of Understanding History* and decided, as she told her husband, that never had she found views which so corresponded with hers. Lavrov was a Narodnik, that is, a kind of agrarian populist. By 1901 she was hesitating between the SRs and the Social Democrats, apparently more inclined to the SRs. But 1903 was a fateful year for her. She went to Switzerland, gave birth to her fifth child, Andrei, and as the fictional Vera had left Lopatkin so she left her husband, Alexander, for his younger brother, Vladimir. She also read Lenin's book on the development of capitalism in Russia and this, she later said, turned her toward the Bolsheviks.[5]

Despite all this Alexander remained a close and warm friend of Inessa so long as she lived. As revolution began to absorb more and more of her interest, the children spent most of their time with Alexander. Less than a month after Bloody Sunday she found herself arrested as a member of a "terrorist group" of the SRs in Moscow. Actually, the police had hauled in a mixed bag of SRs and Bolsheviks and it took some time to sort them out. In 1907 she was sent into exile to the Arkhangelsk Guberniya but escaped late in 1908 to Switzerland, where her lover, Vladimir, in the last stages of tuberculosis, awaited her. With his death she buried herself in studies for a year in Brussels. Some time during that year she probably met Lenin for the first time. It may have been a fleeting encounter in one of the cafés where the Russian revolutionaries spent their days and argued their hearts out or possibly at the Russian library on Rue Gablein. No one knows. But in the autumn of 1910 Inessa moved to Paris, to Rue St.-Jacques, No. 241, in the students' quarter and there she lived like a student. The object of her study was Lenin. "I can see her now," Grigory Kotov recalled, "coming out of the Lenins' place. Her temperament struck me violently. She seemed to be an inexhaustible spring of life. Here was the fiery flame of revolution and the red feather in her hat was like the tongue of that flame."[6] Lyudmila N. Stal, Inessa's close friend, put it less flamboyantly. She said Inessa was "constantly attentive to her comrades and ready to share with them the last crust of bread."

Or as Krupskaya put it: "Inessa Armand arrived in Paris from Brussels in 1910 and immediately became an active member of our Paris group. . . . She was elected to the presidium of the group and started an extensive correspondence with the other groups abroad. . . . She was a passionate Bolshevik and very soon our whole Paris crowd had gathered around her." When Lenin started a school for young Bolsheviks and agitators from Russia in Longjumeau, a tannery village outside Paris, Inessa rented a house where a canteen for the school was set up and this quickly became the heart of all its activities.

As Krupskaya said of Inessa when they were together in Cracow a bit later: "All of us—our entire Cracow group—were drawn very close to Inessa. She was brimming with vitality and good spirits. . . . Things seemed cosier and more cheerful when Inessa was there. . . . There was a delightful warmth about her stories. Ilyich and I went for long walks with Inessa. . . . She loved music and persuaded us all to attend the Beethoven concerts. She was a good musician herself and played many Beethoven pieces very well. A particular favorite of Ilyich's was the Sonata Pathétique and he always asked her to play it. . . ."*

Was Inessa Lenin's lover? Did his life in those grim and dreadful Paris days become, in fact, a ménage à trois? Almost certainly. Inessa moved into the house next door to Lenin and Krupskaya, they at No. 4 and she at No. 2, Rue Marie-Rose. Lenin's comrades were well aware of his special feeling for Inessa, of the relationship which the two shared. Both Alexandra Kollontai and Angelica Balabanoff had no doubt of this.[7] There are plain hints of it in Lenin's published correspondence. None of Lenin's letters to Inessa were published before

* Lenin loved the Appassionata above all other musical works. Years later, during the civil war, he said to Maxim Gorky after hearing Issay Dobrowen perform: "I know nothing better than the Appassionata. I could listen to it every day. Wonderful, more than human music. I always think with pride, perhaps naive pride: see what miracles men can perform!" Then he added ruefully: "But I can't listen to music often. It plays on my nerves; it makes me want to say silly, tender things and stroke the heads of people who, living in a dirty hell, can yet create such beauty. But today one mustn't stroke anybody's head—he'd bite off your hand. One's got to hit men on the head, hit them mercilessly, although ideally we are against any violence toward human beings. Yes, yes—it's a hellishly difficult job." (M. Gorky, Russky Sovremennik, 1924, No. 1, p. 237.) Lidiya A. Fotiyeva, Lenin's secretary and Party associate from the time of the 1905 Revolution, recalls often playing Beethoven's Sonata Pathétique for Lenin. (L. A. Fotiyeva, V. I. Lenin—rukovoditel i tovarishch, p. 90.)

Krupskaya's death in January 1939.* But within six months in July 1939, the magazine *Bolshevik* published two Lenin letters to Inessa dealing with the question of "freedom of love."[8] Nothing more appeared until 1949, when ten more letters were published in *Bolshevik*, No. 1, for that year. These ten letters, the two which first appeared in 1939, and an additional eleven were published in Volume 35 of the fourth edition of Lenin's collected works in 1950—twenty-three letters in all, two for 1913, four for 1914, two for 1915, six for 1916, and nine for 1917 (all prior to Lenin's return to Russia). Then, when the fifth edition of Lenin's works appeared in 1964, sixty-seven more letters from Lenin to Inessa came to light—twenty-five for 1914, one for 1915, nineteen for 1916, and twenty-two for 1917.

This is the most extended correspondence Lenin ever conducted with anyone except members of his family. The most striking feature of the letters is Lenin's use of the intimate familiar pronoun *ty* in addressing Inessa instead of the ordinary *vy*, that is, the "thou" form rather than the "you" form. With perhaps two exceptions Lenin in his whole correspondence never used this form except with members of his family.[9]

The editors of Lenin's works are remarkable for their tenacity in establishing textual completeness. But Lenin's letters to Inessa are remarkable for their incompleteness. In many the superscription and closing passage are omitted without notice. In the second and larger batch of letters the editors frankly state in nine cases that the opening passages of the letters "are missing." In some cases the letter begins only on page three or five. There are other examples of an occasional missing page in the textual collection of Lenin's letters. But in no case is his correspondence so obviously mutilated. Of course, this is not necessarily the fault of the editors. Krupskaya may simply have removed more sentimental pages and passages.

Not a line from any of Inessa's letters to Lenin had been published until 1975, when two tiny impersonal extracts from her Party communications with Lenin in 1916 were quoted in an introduction to a collection of her speeches, articles, and letters to her family written by her daughter, Inna A. Armand. Lenin occasionally quoted from her letters in his own communications, showing their lively nature.

The publication in the 1975 collection of forty-nine Armand letters, principally to her children, confirmed what had been obvious for some time—that a substantial Armand archive has been preserved. Eventually, perhaps, Inessa's side of the correspondence with Lenin will see the light. Inessa's letters, incidentally, are preserved in the Central

---

* This in itself seems significant. It has been suggested that Stalin used the letters to blackmail Krupskaya.

Party Archive.[10] A critical Soviet review of the 1975 Armand collection, interestingly, expressed hope that a second edition would be published drawing more heavily on heretofore unrevealed archival materials.[11]

The touchiness of this whole subject is revealed in the official daily chronicle of Lenin's life which carefully mentions almost every letter Lenin wrote or received. It mentions each letter he wrote to Inessa but *none* of those he received.[12]

Even with all the excisions Lenin's special feelings shine through. He peppers his letters with English phrases and expressions of sentiment, often using the curious phrase "Friendly shakehands." He calls Inessa "the Holy Virgin" for her properness in argument (and then apologizes for the expression); he worries again and again that his words have offended her; he worries when she does not reply swiftly; he worries over her health; he is occasionally playful in argument (which he never permitted himself with any other correspondents); and, once in the course of trying to persuade Inessa that she was wrong to suggest in a pamphlet on "freedom of love" that "even a fleeting passion and intimacy" are "more poetic and cleaner" than "kisses without love" by a vulgar and shallow married couple, he confesses that he really doesn't want to engage in arguing with her at all and "would willingly throw aside this letter and postpone matters until we can talk about it."[13]

Alexandra Kollontai believed that Krupskaya offered to leave Lenin but that he insisted that she stay on.* Whatever the case Krupskaya's letters for this period are extremely dispirited—ordinarily she put up a good front regardless of what was going on. But she wrote Lenin's mother from Longjumeau, August 26, 1911: "Our summer has not been very fortunate, either. Mother got ill several times . . . our place here is not good; there is not the tiniest garden. . . . It is hot in the house and noisy. . . . As regards work he [Lenin] is busier at the moment although it is difficult to foresee what will happen in the autumn. . . ." On March 9, 1912, she was writing Lenin's sister Anna, "This year I have somehow fought shy of letter-writing. Life goes on so monotonously here that I don't know what to write about. This winter I have been at home, working persistently and for months on end have not left this part of town. . . . I should like to write more about Volodya [Lenin] to make the letter interesting but couldn't manage it. Another time, perhaps. . . ."[14]

Not even the pleasant and unexpected appearance of Inessa Armand in Lenin's life was capable of curing his despondency. Every-

* Balabanoff told Wolfe that Inessa bore Lenin a child but this is almost certainly mistaken. After Inessa's death the Ulyanovs are said to have taken in Inessa's oldest daughter, Inna, born long before Inessa met Lenin. (Bertram Wolfe, in *Encounter*, Feb. 1964, p. 90.)

thing seemed to go wrong. He found it difficult to work in the Bibliothèque Nationale. There was much red tape and it was a long bicycle ride from the suburbs. He arranged to leave his bicycle on the steps of a house next door, paying the concierge ten centimes a day. When the bike was stolen, the concierge shrugged her shoulders and said she wasn't being paid to watch it. Lenin liked to go out to the suburb of Juvisy and calm his nerves by watching the airplanes take off and land on a small airfield. One day he was nearly hit by a motorcar. He saved himself by leaping off but his bike was demolished.[15] The car belonged to a viscount and Lenin wrote his sister he was taking him into court to try to recover damages.[16] Whether he succeeded is not recorded.

These were grueling days for the revolutionaries. A bit later, on the eve of World War I when Lenin moved his base to Cracow on the Austria-Polish frontier with Russia, the scene brightened a bit. Contact with Russia was much easier, which was particularly important because the revolutionary movements were going over, for the most part, to open political action—participation in the Duma, legal political parties, legal newspapers (often suppressed but always revived). They kept a revolutionary underground intact, but by 1914 the revolutionaries were 95 per cent legal. The legal aboveground movement flourished as the secret underground movement never had.

Lenin's abandonment of Paris probably came just in time. In March 1912 he wrote his sister Anna, "there is more bickering and abuse of each other than there has been for a long time—there probably never has been so much before . . . in short there is so little here that is interesting or pleasant that it's not worth writing."[17]

Krupskaya put it bluntly: "Another year or two of life in this [Paris] atmosphere of squabbling and emigrant tragedy would have meant heading for a breakdown."[18]

In 1913 the Romanov dynasty celebrated its three-hundredth anniversary. There were balls—for the first time the oldest Imperial girls, Olga and Tatyana, participated—and fetes and state processionals. Madame Mathilde Kshesinskaya came out of mourning (her father had died) to dance in A Life for the Czar (sung by Chaliapin), a story of the first Romanov, Mikhail Fyodorovich.[19] Nicholas rode in a triumphal procession through the Moscow streets, on horseback, ahead of his escort, unprotected, followed by the Empress and the royal children in an open carriage. It was a daring gesture and there were audible sighs of relief when the Czar reached the Iversky Chapel at the Kremlin gates for the first of the many prayers.[20] But, of course, the Czar's act was testimony, too, to the tranquillity which now seemed to prevail. To be sure there had been an upsurge of demonstrations after the terrible shooting down of workers in the Lena gold fields in the winter of 1912. Yet now, as Leonid Andreyev put it, "the appearance of Russia is sad, her works are trifling or shoddy, and where does the gay summons to the new difficult work of revolution rise up?"[21]

Not that all was quiet. There were rumblings in Europe. A new Balkan crisis. Premier Kokovtsov was desperately worried about the state of Russian military preparedness and the incompetence of General Sukhomlinov, the War Minister. Nicholas assured him that he agreed completely with his views, but a year later, Kokovtsov grimly noted, hardly anything had been done.[22]

In the critical area of relations between Russia and Germany it seemed that all was quiet. There had been no renewal of the foreboding note struck for the first time (since it had begun in 1894) in the Nicky-Willy correspondence when Willy warned Nicky at the opening of 1909 that "between our two countries there has arisen some hostility."

"I consider it my duty before it is too late to turn your attention to the real state of affairs and the reasons for them," Willy wrote then. He wound up sending his warmest greetings to Alix and expressing pleasure that Nicholas and Alexandra had liked his Christmas present. But the note of warning—that Germany was well aware that Russia was entering into a Triple Entente with France and England—was so clear that the Czar hastened to respond, briefed extensively by his foreign policy advisers, making plain to Willy that "a similar lack of confidence has appeared on both sides."

But 1913 opened on a different note. Willy sent to Nicky his "hearty Christmas greetings and best wishes for the New Year."

"I seriously hope and believe that 1913 will flow peacefully as you telegraphed me on New Year's Day," he wrote. "I think that we can both look on the future quietly."

Willy had a good word for Nicky's War Minister, General Sukhomlinov, who had stopped by on passing through Berlin. He described him as "very nice and interesting" in his description of the campaign of 1877 in which he had participated. Nicky signed himself "your warmly loving cousin and friend."[23]

And so the three hundredth anniversary of the dynasty went off with éclat. Kokovtsov was a bit amused, a bit bitter, at one feature of the ceremonies. Nicholas decided to give the event a "family" rather than a "state character."

This, Kokovtsov thought, was due to influences in the circle of the Czar, very likely the Czarina, supporters of the "cult of the autocrat," who still thought of the throne in terms of pure absolutism. These forces were growing stronger now that Russia seemed to be more quiet. Their argument was that the Czar could lead the country on his own because all the people were with him, loved him, and were blindly devoted to him. In such a circumstance what need for the bothersome Duma and the nagging Ministers?

So, for the Romanov anniversary, the Court made no arrangements for the cabinet to accompany the Imperial family in their tour of the ancient cities linked to the founding of the dynasty—Vladimir, Suzdal, the village of Bogolyubovo, Nizhni Novgorod, Kostroma, Yaroslavl, Rostov, and Moscow. Only the Minister of Transportation was taken along. Premier Kokovtsov had to hitch a ride with him.

Everywhere the Czar and his family were greeted with outpourings of enthusiasm. He was offered the traditional *khleb-sol,* the peasant bread-and-salt, by the elders of the towns, and everywhere, very handsome in his Guards uniform, he expressed his confidence that "in the example of your glorious ancestors you will always be on guard for God, the Czar and the Fatherland." Everywhere their four beautiful daughters accompanied him, in long dresses of white voile with tight banded collars embroidered in traditional Russian designs. The Czarevich, a handsome husky-looking boy, was carried through the ceremonies in the arms of strong sailors (he was recovering from a particularly serious bout of hemophilia). The Czarina accompanied her husband, her figure imposing but her face worn, tired, and worried— little more than an echo of the slender, beautiful woman who rode at the Czar's side during coronation in 1896. The Grand Dukes made up the train—big, bulky, and beefy. Monuments to Minin and Pozharsky, the Moscow heroes, were dedicated; ancestors of the peasant Susanin, the one who "gave his life for the Czar," were discovered and decorated.

At Yaroslavl the Czar was taken to an industrial exhibition. There he was shown an enormous pine log—a tree more than three hundred years old, a mere sapling in the time when the first Romanov Mikhail Fyodorovich had taken the throne. It had been cut down in the Czar's honor. After three hundred years of vigorous growth it was to be sawed into a million planks, and soon even its memory would disappear from the Russian earth.[24]

XXVI

Last Warnings

The winter of 1914 in Petersburg was more gay than ever. True, the Imperial family, as had been the custom since 1905, kept to itself at Tsarskoye Selo, making the fewest possible appearances in the capital. But society had almost grown used to that. There was an unending procession of balls, parties, and routs. Kshesinskaya, once the Czar's favorite and now the consort of the Grand Duke Andrei, came back to St. Petersburg to give a Russian Christmas party for her son, Vova, in her grand house on the Moika (in Petersburg only the Imperial residences were called palaces). She arranged to have the famous Russian circus clown Durov appear with his animals—including an elephant. In some manner the elephant, swathed in blankets, was smuggled into the house, concealed in a cloakroom, and brought out at the climactic moment. The elephant reclined on an enormous bed and used a chamber pot to the delight of the youngsters.[1]

Of all the Petersburg parties none was more brilliant than that given by the Countess Kleinmikhel to present the three daughters of her sister-in-law to Petersburg society.[2] It was a costume ball and everyone wanted an invitation, which proved a little embarrassing to the countess, whose house could accommodate only three hundred guests. That is, as she explained, her kitchen could feed only three hundred persons and "every Russian expects to be fed at his own place at the table." She arranged an elaborate program of dances—a quadrille performed by the three Kleinmikhel girls and the beautiful young Duchess Kantakuzen, niece of Grand Duke Nikolai Nikolayevich, the elder (who had commanded Russian forces in the Turkish War); an Egyptian dance by Countess Marianna Zarnekau, daughter of Countess Paley; a Hungarian dance by Baroness Wrangel and her friend, Madame Okhotnikova, sister of the Countess Ignatyeva, a great beauty, with Count Roman Pontoni and Jacques Des Lalaig as partners; a Cossack number by Prince Konstantin Bagration; a little Russian dance by Duchess Kochubei, her brother, Victor, Count Musin-Pushkin, and Grigory Shebeko; an eastern quadrille led by the Grand Duchess Viktoriya Fyodorovna, wife of the Grand Duke Kirill Vladimirovich, and Grand Duke Boris Vladimirovich. Among those taking part in the quadrille were the Grand Duchess Olga Orlova, Countess May Kutuzova, Meriel Buchanan, daughter of the English ambassador, Mrs. Jasper Ridley, daughter of Baron Benkendorf, Russia's ambassador in Paris, the Grand Duchess Nataliya Gorchakova, and Prince Alexander Batenberg. More than a hundred persons begged for the privilege of standing on the staircase to watch the dancing. But the countess refused. "It would have spoiled the beauty of the evening," she said. Such an evening, of course, could not pass without a scandal—or threat of scandal. Pavel Rodzyanko, brother of the president of the Duma, husband of the Princess Mariya Golitsyn, wanted to attend the party with his five sons. But the countess heard from friends that he only wanted to come in order to perpetrate a public insult to Prince Bagration. When she declined to invite him, he swore he would make her weep "tears of blood." It was the last great ball before the outbreak of World War I, the diplomat Nicholas de Basily recalled. He wore to it a costume of crimson silk, modeled on that of a Venetian Renaissance portrait in his family's collection.[3]

Petersburg dances were long affairs. Dancing often started at five in the afternoon and went on until five in the morning with an interlude for supper. The interlude traditionally was marked by the playing of the march from *Lohengrin* as the guests went in to dine—a glittering affair served on plates of gold or silver, gleaming with candelabra and centerpieces of ice or pastry in the shape of the Kremlin towers or Falconet's famous statue of Peter the Great on a rearing stallion.

After supper came the cotillion which, as Princess Lidiya Vassiltchikova recalled many years later, was the "gayest and prettiest moment of the ball." Wicker carts of flowers—roses, carnations, mimosa, and violets—were trundled into the ballroom, and bright nosegays tied with ribbons of lavender, yellow, and pink were passed out to the escorts to give to their ladies. The whole room suddenly filled with the wondrous aroma of spring while outside the thermometer stood at thirty degrees below zero.[4] Then, at five in the morning the young people, swathed in ermine and mink, sparkling with diamonds, their escorts in the blazing crimson of Guards uniforms, burnished with golden epaulets, descended the marble staircases between rows of satin-breeched footmen with powdered perukes. They were handed into their troikas and sleighs to the flame of torches, then to course through the snow-piled streets of Petersburg, silver bells jangling merrily on the horses, frost-bound coachmen in their sheepskin greatcoats, cracking long whips, down the empty Neva embankment past the black and menacing façades of the hulking buildings, the broad Neva a frozen desert of ice, the gas lamps in the Champs de Mars golden halos in the murk, exhausted, excited, champagne still bubbling in their heads and hearts beating fast, back to the gloomy mansions in which they lived on the Fontanka or the Moika, tumbling into bed just as the men and women of the Narva sector and the Nevskaya Zastava began to struggle from under their thin quilts, pulling on rough clothes and felt boots, gulping down a glass of hot tea before pushing out the door and on through the polar cold to the Putilov works or the shipbuilding yards, hurrying through the frozen streets to get to their benches before the six o'clock whistle, knowing that for lateness they might be fined a half-day's pay or more, hurrying like black ants through the snow-drifted streets, heads tucked down, hands thrust in pockets, hurrying, hurrying, stomachs empty and growling, and in their heads a dull but burning resentment against the endless harshness, the endless bitterness, of their Russian life.

So the new year, 1914, slowly got under way. It seemed not unlike other years in the recent past. The magazine *Niva*, looking to the future, hoped for diplomatic success in the East and the West as 1914 moved on. And *Niva* felt the first steps had been taken toward a rise in the quality of Russian political life, "the first steps toward the liberation of it from the dying despotism of bookish doctrine, the first steps toward the working out of a path toward genuine progress for the country, based on past history and social system, the first step toward the establishment of real freedom."[5] *Niva* liked to look on the brighter side of things and an event at the Hermitage Palace theater brought hope to many in what *Niva* called "our gloomy times, filled with small and great evil, lacking in true and clear character and ideals." This was the presentation of a passion play—almost an oratorio—by K.P., the famous literary and liberal Grand Duke, Konstantin Konstantinovich. It was called *The King of the Jews*. The Grand Duke himself took the role of Joseph of Arimathaea. His brilliant son, Prince Oleg, played the role of Prefect and another son, Prince Igor, played that of Rufus. There was music by Glazunov and dances created by Fokine. *Niva* felt the production should encourage "all those wearied of our days as were Nicodemus, Rodin and Procula of theirs" and the *Times* of London felt it would mark an epoch in Christian literature.[6]

January was a long cold month and February was not well under way when a fateful event occurred—the dismissal by the Czar on February 12, 1914, of the honest, capable, energetic, plain-speaking, and intelligent Count Kokovtsov from his post of Premier and his replacement by the first in a tragic succession of declining mediocrities—Count Ivan Goremykin. Rasputin and the Czarina were responsible for Kokovtsov's fall. Rasputin had visited Kokovtsov in February 1912 and attempted to establish a working relationship with the Premier. Kokovtsov sternly dismissed him and reported his action to the Czar. From that day, Kokovtsov later concluded, "my fall was inevitable." For two years the Czar continued to be polite and kind but the Empress pointedly (and publicly) turned her back on him.[7]

The Czar did not remove from office the last able Premier who was to serve him without receiving a warning of the perils which lay ahead. Tension with Germany had been rising year by year, and with Russia's new alignment through France with England, European statesmen had become convinced that a clash between Germany and Austro-Hungary on one side and the Triple Entente of England, France, and Russia was almost inescapable. Kokovtsov had paid a visit to Berlin late in 1913 and then journeyed south to the Crimea to give the Czar a personal report. He sent ahead a written dispatch in which he said that war with Germany would be a disaster and lead to the destruction of the dynasty. He found no evidence that his words made any impression. Now he tried again. Sitting alone with the Czar in the beautiful Livadiya Palace looking out over the blue waters of the Black Sea, Kokovtsov told his sovereign that he believed war with Germany inevitable and that events were moving swiftly toward catastrophe. The Czar listened quietly, looking deep into Kokovtsov's eyes as if to judge the truth of what he was saying. Silently the Czar gazed out for a long time at the sea. Finally, he spoke: "All is in the will of God." It was Kokovtsov's last intimate conversation with the Czar.

There was a growing atmosphere of apprehension. The Czar's mother, Grand Duchess Mariya Alexandrovna, met her son in the theater on the night of Kokovtsov's dismissal and asked why he had done it. The Czar replied: "Do you think that was easy for me? Some time I will tell you about it." He never did and his mother said to Kokovtsov a few days later: "You understand me and how much I worry about the future and what gloomy thoughts possess me. My daughter-in-law doesn't love me and thinks I'm jealous of my power. She doesn't understand that I have but one desire—that my son be happy. Yet, I see that we are going by great steps toward some kind of catastrophe and that the Czar listens only to flatterers and doesn't see that under his feet is growing something that he still doesn't suspect."[8] Later Mariya Alexandrovna told Kokovtsov her son was bored with "all these forecasts and predictions which produce an impression only in Petersburg drawing rooms." No one understood, the Czar told her, the love the people bore for him.

The fall of Kokovtsov coincided with *maslenitsa*. Shrovetide, the great Russian winter holiday, the week of carnival, of feasting on the thinnest, most delicate of *blini*, or pancakes, drowned in liquid butter and smetana and heaped with gray beluga caviar, eaten to toasts of vodka, traditionally drunk *do dna*, to the bottom. St. Petersburg and Moscow turned into winter fairylands with snow slides in every park and public place, red-cheeked girls and laughing escorts sledding down the hillsides in a fury of snow and ice, sidewalk pavilions in squares vending *pirozhki*—meat pies—and apple tarts and sweetmeats; dancing bears and musicians pumping on brass trumpets and beating drums.

In former times these late January and early February days had marked the height of the St. Petersburg season—a season that opened with a grand ball for three thousand guests in the Nikolayevsky hall of the Winter Palace followed by a banquet served in the other halls. The season continued with three more balls for eight hundred guests each—one in the concert hall of the palace, another on the Thursday of maslenitsa in the Hermitage Pavilion, and a final fete held at one of the suburban palaces. This was called the *Folle-journée* (mad day) and began with dancing at four o'clock. At seven the traditional blini were served, then dancing renewed. At midnight the music stopped, a banquet was served, and the party was over.

Now all this had been given up because of the Czarina's dislike of society, and the matrons of Petersburg had one more cause for complaint against her. No longer could they present their young daughters to society against the brilliant background of the Winter Palace.

In place of these spectacles Nicholas celebrated maslenitsa with his old comrades of the guard—at a regimental dinner of the Life Guard Hussars around a long table sparkling with the regimental silver—almost three hundred pieces—trays, cups, goblets, *kovshi* (Russian drinking scoops), bowls, urns, vases, medallions, and trophies. There were no flowers. The decor was silver, gleaming under the tall silver candelabra. All was silver except for the trays and saucers, which were of gold, in accord with an old Russian folk saying that "silver must be placed on golden plates."

Trumpeters played during dinner. There were no toasts, no speeches. The celebration broke up at 4 A.M. after entertainment by singers and dancers, choruses of the regimental songs, and much storytelling. Maj. Gen. V. N. Voyeikov, long commander of the Hussars regiment and only recently named palace commandant, insisted that the Czar drank very little during this and other regimental evenings—a few glasses of his favorite port wine, a shot or two of vodka, and some champagne. Voyeikov was dedicated to Nicholas and his version may be accurate. There were many, however, who insisted that the Czar was much too fond of wine and particularly enjoyed the regimental dinners because in the company of his military friends he could indulge freely.[9]

The Czarina marked the advent of Lent with prayers and fasting.

It was at this most festive of Russian seasons that Pyotr Durnovo, Witte's Minister of Interior and since Witte's fall the leader of the right wing in the State Council, submitted to Nicholas a lengthy memorandum. Durnovo was convinced that war between England, France, and Russia on one side, and Germany, Austria, and Turkey on the other was at hand. The main burden, he believed, would fall upon Russia—a burden which Russia was not prepared to carry. She lacked military reserves, her military factories produced badly, and her network of strategic railroads was insufficient.

Durnovo felt that war would prove a disaster. Even if Russia won she would be so weakened she might not survive.

"A general European war," he warned, "is mortally dangerous for both Russia and Germany no matter who wins. It is our firm conviction based upon a long and careful study of all contemporary subversive tendencies, that there must inevitably break out in the defeated country a social revolution which, by the very nature of things, will spread to the country of the victor."

Durnovo had no fear of a revolutionary movement per se, such as might be led by Bolsheviks or Socialist Revolutionaries.

"The opponents of the Government," he said, "have no popular support. The people see no difference between a Government official and an intellectual. The Russian masses, whether workmen or peasants, are not looking for political rights which they neither want nor comprehend."

Instead, he insisted, the peasant dreamed of obtaining land (someone else's) and the workman of putting the profits of the business into his (not the owner's) pockets.

"If these slogans," he warned, "are scattered far and wide among the populace and the Government permits agitation along these lines, Russia will be flung into anarchy.

"In the event of a defeat, the possibility of which with a foe like Germany cannot be overlooked, social revolution in its most extreme form is inevitable. . . .

"The defeated army, having lost its most dependable men, and carried away by the tide of primitive peasant desire for land, will find itself too demoralized to serve as a bulwark of law and order.

"The legislative institutions and the intellectual opposition parties, lacking real authority in the eyes of the people, will be powerless to stem the popular tide aroused by themselves and Russia will be flung into anarchy, whose outcome cannot ever be foreseen."[10]

The warning of Durnovo was not unique—except for the clarity of his thinking. Kokovtsov had reached much the same conclusion, and Foreign Minister Sergei Sazonov after a review of the military situation in February with the Minister of the Navy and the Chief of the General Staff was depressed.

"I had a conviction that, although we were able to foresee events," he recalled, "it was not in our power to avert them. There was a great gulf between the determination of our aims and their attainment."[11]

What effect these sobering views had upon Nicholas II it is difficult to guess. Durnovo's memorandum was found among the Czar's papers after the Revolution. There was no indication it had been studied. Possibly it was not even read.

XXVII

Impotence Before Fate

For Russia's revolutionary parties the year 1914 offered no auspicious signs. Lenin was now quietly settled near the Russian border, in Cracow, Poland, then part of the Austro-Hungarian Empire. He had made the move quite suddenly, pulling up stakes in hated Paris June 4, 1912, and arriving June 9 in Cracow so unexpectedly that even his family had no advance warning of his plans. The move put him within a day or two's mail communication with St. Petersburg and gave him easy access to couriers and Party figures moving in and out of Russia. The convenience was obvious. Even so there is some mystery why Lenin moved from Paris to Cracow at just that moment. All his official biographies and Soviet historiography attribute the move to the fact that *Pravda*, a new legal Bolshevik daily paper, was being started in St. Petersburg. They portray Lenin as playing a major role in establishing and running the paper. The actual circumstances hardly support this theory. True, Lenin had favored the setting up of *Pravda*, but no evidence that he participated in the founding of the newspaper has turned up—no letters, no orders, no instructions, no guides as to editorial policy or anything else. Considering the care with which Lenin always dealt with such questions, his apparent disinterest in *Pravda* seems strange. His correspondence reveals only two references to *Pravda* in the weeks before its first issue, inquiries as to when it would start publishing. He wrote nothing for the first issue nor does he seem to have been asked to. His first article appeared in issues No. 13 and No. 14 for May 8 and 9, 1912.[1] Then nothing until July 12, after which his contributions gradually became more frequent, as did his quarrels with the editors whose policy was much too mild for Lenin's taste. Stalin may have had something to do with this. He had a hand in starting *Pravda* and fixed the moderate tone of its policy. All of this makes it hard to relate Lenin's Cracow move to *Pravda*. As late as May 20 Lenin was still writing his mother from Paris that "we have not yet decided on anything about summer."[2] About this time, however, he wrote Yakov Ganetsky, a Polish Social Democrat living in Cracow, about conditions there, inquiring particularly whether the Austrian police might hand him over to the Russian police. After receiving reassurances from Ganetsky (who consulted the Social Democratic representatives in the Austrian Parliament) Lenin came to Cracow on June 9 with Krupskaya and her mother. Ganetsky helped them to get established.[3]

The fact was that this was a time of growing independence of the Bolshevik movement within Russia from its long direction by Lenin. Much the same process was occurring in all of the revolutionary movements. Now, and particularly after the amnesty granted in 1913 to most of the exiled Russian political figures, the Bolshevik party and the other radical parties were taking their place in Russian society as largely legal organizations. As noted, they participated in elections, had their own representatives in the Duma, their own legal newspapers, their own publishing houses, conducted meetings, issued leaflets and pamphlets, organized insurance companies, and maintained a largely legal aboveground existence. The old underground which was Lenin's milieu was opened up. Perhaps Lenin's move to Cracow reflected a feeling that he must be closer to Russia if he was to remain a viable political leader. Cracow was not Russia but it looked like Russia, the women went barefoot and wore gay cotton dresses in summer just as in Russia, and "even the Jews are like Russians," as Lenin told his mother.[4] However, it was a dull town, no decent libraries, "no culture." (Lenin never did learn to read and speak Polish.) Yet Cracow fitted his mood. He was away from the fierce émigré quarrels that had so jangled his nerves,[5] and even the fact that *Pravda*'s editors were quite independent, frequently rejecting his articles, toning them down (they insisted that their workers audience had no interest in the narrow polemics which so absorbed Lenin), cutting his articles to more manageable proportions, and sometimes treating his requests for money and reference materials cavalierly did not seem to affect him seriously. By 1914 Lenin was forty-four years old (two years younger than the Czar). He looked his age—in fact, he looked older. His nickname "Starik" (old man) seemed entirely appropriate. He worked away at increasing his influence over *Pravda*, and the Bolshevik Duma delegation led by Lenin's favorite, Roman V. Malinovsky, and other Party figures frequently slipped over the frontier to meet with Lenin at either Cracow or Poronin in the nearby mountains where he liked to spend the summer. Money was a problem (which was why he was constantly chivying the *Pravda* editors for his hundred rubles a month contributor's fee) and so was the health of Nadezhda Krupskaya, who suffered goiter trouble and had to be taken to Switzerland for an operation by a Dr. Kocher, a specialist who, in Lenin's words to his mother, "has a huge clientele of Russians, of Jews especially."[6] It was a quiet time in a life that had seldom been quiet. For a while Inessa Armand had stayed in Cracow, had played for Lenin on the piano, had enlivened the exile colony. But it was not a long stay. Earlier Lenin had sent her to St. Petersburg to straighten out *Pravda's* affairs, an abortive mission which wound up with her arrest and her husband paying a 5,000-ruble fine for her release. Now she was off again, living in Paris for the most part, and Lenin directed an endless stream of letters to her, often on matters of strict Party business but often not and almost always flavored with the special playful affection which marked his correspondence with her and her alone. Lenin had a brief reunion with her in Paris in January 1914, when he went there to give some speeches.* That winter Lenin again went ice skating.[7] There were two groups among the exiles, the "cinemaist party" (those who liked to go to the movies) and the "anti-cinemaist" or "anti-Semitic" as they sometimes called themselves. Lenin belonged to the "anti-Semitic party."[8]

Exile life flowed smoothly. There seemed nothing on the Russian scene either particularly to encourage or discourage the professional revolutionaries. Then, the calm was shattered. At 4 P.M. on May 8, 1914, Roman Malinovsky, the leading Bolshevik deputy in the Duma, appeared in the office of Speaker Rodzyanko and, throwing onto the table a written document, dramatically exclaimed: "*Proshchaite!* Farewell!" Rodzyanko, a bull of a man, leaped to his feet crying: "What is the matter, Malinovsky? You're being very rude." "Read that," said Malinovsky as he left, "and you will see what I mean. I'm leaving the Duma."[9]

"That" turned out to be Malinovsky's resignation. He was resigning his Duma post forthwith and going abroad. When Rodzyanko announced the news, a commotion broke loose. The only Bolshevik

---

* Lenin went to Brussels from Paris and wrote Inessa on at least three successive days. The published versions of these letters as well as two he sent her just before going to Paris are unusually mutilated. In one case only a P.S. has been published. One letter begins: "I am writing you briefly on business," implying that there were others "not on business." (V. I. Lenin, *Collected Works,* Vol. XLIII, pp. 375–80.)

member present in the Duma, M. K. Muranov, could offer no clue to the riddle. Georgi Petrovsky, another Bolshevik deputy, was sent to Malinovsky to try to find out what was going on. Malinovsky, hysterical, shouted: "Judge me as you will and do what you want but I will not speak."[10]

That night he took the train for the frontier.

What had happened (although it took the Bolsheviks years to adjust to the fact) was that Malinovsky, the great champion of radical causes, the most fiery orator of the Duma, Lenin's favorite, was one more in the endless succession of police agents who had infiltrated the Party. He had been an agent before his election to the Duma and after it. Thanks to his intimate knowledge of Party affairs one leading member after another (among them Yakov Sverdlov and Stalin) had been arrested by the police. Suspicion of Malinovsky had simmered in radical circles for several years. Nikolai Bukharin and A. A. Troyanovsky had pleaded with Lenin to examine the evidence. But Lenin would not be budged.

Once Krupskaya recalled walking back from a meeting with the Zinovievs at which the rumors about Malinovsky were discussed. Lenin suddenly stopped in his traces and said in dismay: "What if they are true?" Krupskaya reassured him that they could not be true and he calmed down.[11]

Malinovsky made his way straight to Lenin when he left St. Petersburg. Lenin declined publicly to repudiate him. Instead, Lenin, Grigory Zinoviev, and Ganetsky published a statement defending "Malinovsky's political honesty." *Pravda* took the same line.[12]

The riddle of Malinovsky has still not been entirely solved. His resignation from the Duma came at the orders of the new Deputy Minister of Interior, V. F. Dzhunkovsky, who discovered to his shock on taking office that a leading member of the Duma was a police agent. He was known as "X." Dzhunkovsky ordered Malinovsky to leave the country, giving him a severance settlement of 6,000 rubles, a passport, and a train ticket.[13] Years after Malinovsky's exposure Krupskaya still wrote of him with sympathy, recalling that he "hung around Poronin, feeling utterly miserable and lonely. God knows what he must have lived through in that time."[14] When later he joined the French Army and was taken prisoner by the Germans in World War I, Lenin and Krupskaya sent him food, clothing, and revolutionary literature to distribute among his fellow prisoners.[15] After the Revolution he voluntarily returned to Russia, was tried by a revolutionary tribunal and shot. He asked a confrontation with Lenin but this was refused.

Did Malinovsky think Lenin might accept him back into the ranks?

Perhaps he had good reason. On May 26, 1917, before the Provisional Government's Extraordinary Investigating Commission Lenin gave his views on the Malinovsky affair. Lenin, usually so vitriolic about traitors and renegades, was remarkably unconcerned; indeed, he even took a *positive* view of Malinovsky's connection with the police.

"When the Okhrana achieved its aim [of placing Malinovsky in the Duma] it developed that Malinovsky was transformed into one of the links in the long and firm chain connecting our legal base with the two strongest organs of the party in influencing the masses, that is, *Pravda* and the Social Democratic faction of the Duma. The provocateur had to protect both of these organs in order to justify himself before us.

"Both of these organs were directed by us, both I and Zinoviev wrote in *Pravda* daily and the resolutions of the Party defined its line in totality. Its influence on 40 to 60 thousand workers thus was guaranteed. Also the Duma faction in which Muranov, G. I. Petrovsky and A. E. Badayev worked all the more independently of Malinovsky, widened its connections and itself influenced a wide segment of workers.

"Malinovsky could destroy and ruin a series of individuals. But the growth of party work in the sense of developing its significance and influence on the masses, on tens and hundreds of thousands [through strikes, strengthening after April 1912]—this growth he neither halted nor controlled nor 'directed'—nor could he.

"I would not be surprised if in the Okhrana the decision to sever Malinovsky from the Duma rose from the conclusion that Malinovsky had been shown to be too closely connected with the legal *Pravda* and the legal faction of deputies which was carrying the revolutionary work to the masses and that this no longer could be tolerated by 'them,' by the Okhrana."

Badayev took much the same line. He argued that Malinovsky's fiery revolutionary speeches and organizational activities damaged the Czarist Government which, by utilizing him as a provocateur, "willy-nilly poured water on the millwheel of revolution."

Badayev offered a curious comment on Lenin's evaluation of Malinovsky. Lenin, he said, did not "embellish but even more stigmatized the personality of the traitor." Perhaps. But many might come to the opposite conclusion—that even with full knowledge of Malinovsky's double role Lenin was looking for a positive explanation of his fallen comrade's conduct.[16]

The fact was that the symbiotic connection between police and revolutionaries had come full circle. Did Malinovsky know when he was speaking in the Duma whether he was raising his voice for S. P.

Beletsky, the police commissioner who maintained contact with him, or for Lenin? His speeches were often written by Lenin but edited by Beletsky. Sometimes Lenin struck something out, sometimes Beletsky did. On many matters the policy of the gendarmerie and of Lenin was identical—each, for example, was eager to split the revolutionary movement, the police in order to sow confusion, Lenin in order to increase his control over the faction which he called his party. The moral corruption of the informer system which had first struck the Socialist Revolutionaries (the double agent Azef) had gradually spread throughout all segments and parties of the radical left. Nor was it a one-way street. The police had begun to be demoralized, as well, as Beletsky pointed out. Indeed, Dzhunkovsky's determination to weed out provocateurs, double agents, and police spies (not only in political parties but in the Army and the educational system) was motivated by his feeling of moral outrage and his sense that the corrupting process was deeply harming Russian society.[17]

It was the kind of atmosphere in which even if Lenin had known the facts of Malinovsky (and he may have) he might well have concluded that Malinovsky was *his* agent, just as the police were certain that he was *theirs*. In Russian society in that pregnant spring of 1914 one could no longer be certain that black was black and white was white. Either might be the opposite. Nothing was what it seemed.

The Malinovsky case, the savage polemics which it produced, the shattering scandal, the personal tragedy, poisoned the atmosphere surrounding Lenin and his entourage during the fateful weeks leading up to July 1914. The tone of Lenin's letters turned sour and hateful once more. His thoughts and energies were once again directed into the fetid back parlor of revolutionary politics. He had not time or energy to focus on the world about him. June slipped into July and not a word about the international situation flowed from his pen. Alexei Semyonovich Kiselev, one of the Party's leading Petersburg workers, spent ten days in Poronin at the end of June, leaving on July 5. He heard nothing about the alarming European situation or impending war. He thought that Lenin was working too hard, but Krupskaya passed it off by saying (she did not know how prophetically), "Oh, he's good for another ten years."[18] Money worries overwhelmed Lenin. He agreed to do an article on Karl Marx for Granat, the big bourgeois Russian encyclopedia.[19] Then a sudden wave of strikes in St. Petersburg caught his eye. He thought a new "revolutionary situation" had arisen and hastily told the editor he would not have time to do the piece on Marx.[20] But July 8 (21 new style)—as war was about to start —*Pravda* was closed down by the Government. Only this action seems to have shaken him so that he suddenly perceived the war clouds hanging over Europe.* He reacted quickly—with a letter to Granat, saying that if they hadn't found another writer, he'd have time, after all, to do the article because "war will, it seems, interrupt a number of *urgent* political affairs with which I was burdened."[21] The italics are his. The letter was written from Cracow July 15 (28), 1914. It was Lenin's first comment on a war which, in his view, was going to take his time away from really important business.

Where were the others? Stalin could not have been more remote. After his less than successful meddling with *Pravda* he had been sent into exile again, in July 1913, and now was living on the Arctic Circle in the tiny fishing village of Kureika. He, too, seems to have been in a foul mood. He refused to give the customary lecture of the newly arrived exile on the political situation in Russia, and he expropriated for himself a small library which the other exiles were keeping for their common use. One thought Stalin acted like a Czarist general in the company of ordinary soldiers.[22] Yakov Sverdlov found him unbearable. "A comrade is with me but we know each other too well," he wrote a friend. "And saddest of all in exile or prison conditions a man bares himself and all his petty aspects are revealed. Worst of all only the trivialities of life are seen."[23]

Sverdlov and several other exiles got themselves transferred away from Kureika. Stalin tried his hand at fishing and trapping, may have lived with a peasant woman and had a son by her,[24] and rusticated. He seems not to have studied (as most exiles did); wrote virtually nothing—possibly one brief, long-lost article. He fell out of touch with revolutionary affairs, engaged in no correspondence—two or three casual letters are all that have turned up, one asking a friend to send him some picture postcards because the Arctic scenery was monotonous. No other leading Bolshevik's exile record is so bland, so empty. His collected works show a blank between February 1913 and March 1917. Always before when he had gone into exile Stalin had managed a successful escape. Not so this time. He made a few vague preparations for leaving, but after being sent to Kureika he sank into lassitude. He read little, wrote less, and was shunned because of his ill

---

* The last time Lenin had mentioned war as a possibility in Europe—and then to scoff at it—was in a letter to Gorky in January 1913, when he observed "a war between Austria and Russia would be a very useful thing for the revolution (throughout Eastern Europe) but it's not very probable that Franz-Josef and Nicky will give us this pleasure." (V. I. Lenin, *Collected Works*, Vol. XXXV, p. 75, letter to Gorky written after Jan. 25, 1913.) Lenin was not alone among the revolutionaries in not foreseeing World War I. The correspondence of other Social Democratic leaders is equally void of premonitions. (See *Sotsial-Democraticheskoye divzheniye v rossii*, 1928.)

temper and vile tongue. He had so completely vanished from the scene that Lenin could not recall his name. Twice in 1915 Lenin wrote querulously, first to Zinoviev, then to V. A. Karpinsky: "Find out the name of "Koba"—Iosif Dj—— very important."[25] No one seems to have remembered. Nor has Lenin's reason for concern come down to us.

Trotsky was living quietly in Vienna. He was supporting himself as a correspondent for the *Kievskaya Mysl*, a leading bourgeois newspaper in Kiev. He was also publishing (with some difficulty and only occasionally) his own radical newspaper, *Pravda* (he bitterly complained that the Bolsheviks had stolen his name for their paper), and watching the storm signals of the European war. He was much closer to the real world of struggle and great power policy than his radical comrades either in St. Petersburg or in Polish exile. He had served as a correspondent for *Kievskaya Mysl* during the Balkan War of 1912–13 and had experienced at firsthand the genuine horror of war. He saw the European conflagration coming, understood that it undoubtedly meant the end of the old empires—the Russian, the German, the Austro-Hungarian. But even this gave him no lift of spirits.

"A sense of the tragedy of history which words cannot suggest," he later wrote, "was taking possession of me; a feeling of impotence before fate, a burning compassion for the human locust."[26]

In Siberia, in the grim prison of Irkutsk was confined—as so often she had been in her long revolutionary life—Yekaterina Breshko-Breshkovskaya, the Socialist Revolutionary leader, the Little Grandmother of the Russian Revolution. At the age of seventy-one she had made a daring escape from exile at Kirensk, six hundred miles to the north on the Lena River. She was captured on the outskirts of Irkutsk and thrown into prison. Now in the spring of 1914 she wrote, as always, to her friends all over the world, and especially in the United States. At any moment she expected to be transported to the even more remote north. She wrote her dear friend, Alice Stone Blackwell, of Boston: "Tulips, daffodils and other spring flowers rejoice my solitude and carry my thoughts to you. In a few days the first party of convicts will start for the north. Whether I am to go with it or not they do not tell me. The summer is short here but it rejuvenates me all the same and if I can spend it in the open air, I shall be ready to meet the winter, however severe."[27]

XXVIII

"We Are Kalutsky . . ."

The date was July 11, 1914, old style; July 24, new style. On the tenth
President Raymond Poincaré of France had concluded his four-day
visit to Russia, a visit filled with diplomatic dinners, entertainments
given by the Czar, a cruise on the Imperial yacht, a grand banquet at
the Winter Palace, a review of troops, intimate and pregnant conversations on the fate of the world and on French-Russian relations. The
crisis which had been slowly building since the assassination of the
Grand Duke Ferdinand of Austria on June 15 (28) was nearly at a climax. The night of the tenth the French ambassador, Paléologue, a
stout short man with a ready wit, had been with the Czar until almost
2:30 in the morning. The Czarina retired much earlier, her nerves
strained by the formalities of the Poincaré reception. But the Czar was
in a mood to talk and he had taken Paléologue for a brief sail on the
Imperial yacht, *Alexandria*. The Czar spoke of the threat of war and
of his conviction that peace could be maintained. He was certain that
France and Russia would act together. Paléologue was not so sanguine
on the question of keeping the peace. He felt that Europe was on the
eve of war. The Czar would not believe it. "Emperor Wilhelm,"
Nicholas said, "is too cautious to launch his country on some wild adventure and the Emperor Franz Josef's only wish is to die in peace."
After making this remark the Czar looked out at the sea and the thin
line of lights, marking the Finnish shore. He was silent for a while,
then rose and paced the deck, thinking, one suspects, of the conse-

quences to Russia and the world if his assessment of Wilhelm and Franz Josef proved incorrect.[1]

On July 11 the diplomatic whirlwind continued—the notes, the threats, the ultimata. All the powers of Europe were involved. The Czar was told at about 11 A.M.[2] in a telephone call from Foreign Minister Sazonov (he hated phone calls and seldom accepted one) that Austria had delivered an ultimatum to Serbia. "That's outrageous," he exclaimed and asked to be kept informed.[3] There was horse racing in the afternoon which Nicholas attended. Later Pierre Gilliard, tutor to the Czarevich, encountered the Czar walking in the park. He found him preoccupied but not anxious.[4] In the evening the Czar went to a regimental dinner of the Horse Guards followed by the usual entertainment in the small Tsarskoye Selo theater. Kshesinskaya performed "my best Russian dance" and then waited in her dressing room, hoping that she might catch a glimpse of the Czar as she had twenty-two years before when both were young and at the height of their infatuation. This time Nicholas did not come. She was never to dance for him again, and only once more was she to be in his presence —a week later on Sunday July 20.[5]

That was the day the Czar went to St. Petersburg to announce the declaration of war. A solemn mass was held before the miraculous icon of the Virgin of Kazan which had been brought to the St. George's Gallery of the Winter Palace. A throng of five thousand attended, all of the Court in full military dress and the officers in field uniform. The Czar recited the oath which Alexander I had taken at the time of Napoleon's invasion in 1812: "I solemnly swear that I will never make peace so long as one of the enemy is on the soil of the fatherland."[6] Then he went out on the balcony of the palace facing the great square—the same square where he had taken the cheers in 1904 when war broke out with Japan and the same square into which Father Gapon had led his faithful on January 9, 1905, certain that the Czar would appear. Once again the square was filled. When the Czar emerged hundreds of thousands sank to their knees and a mighty chorus rang out: "God Save the Czar!" In this hour all Russia was united in what Sir Bernard Pares called *sobornost*, a Russian word which describes that unity which comes over a congregation of the Orthodox faithful when it gathers in the cathedral.[7] The newspaper *Kommersant* called it "a holy war." *Utro Rossii* said "war is terrible but more terrible is the nightmare of constantly expecting war." *Birzhevye Vedomosti*, the financial paper, called it "a war to end war."

But was the unity of the nation genuine unity?

True, the enormous and sudden waves of strikes which arose in

June and July (and which Lenin mistook for another revolution)
vanished as swiftly as they had appeared. Now even the Putilov
workers on whom the police had fired a fortnight earlier were throwing the rule books into the blast furnaces and working day and night
without extra pay. They were delivering in eleven days war orders
that usually required twenty-three days.[8] But this did not obscure the
fact that there had been an enormous increase in labor unrest, beginning with 1912 when the shooting down of defenseless strikers in the
Lena gold fields had shocked the world and stirred Russia's revolutionary parties to new activity. There had been 2,032 strikes affecting
725,491 workers in 1912; 2,404 involving 887,096 in 1913, and in 1914
(most of them on the very eve of the war) 3,534 involving 1,337,458.[9]
Russia entered the war with an industrial proletariat or working force
of a little more than 3,000,000.[10] This meant that nearly half of Russia's workingmen went out on strike in 1914—a total that exceeded the
unrest of 1905. In St. Petersburg alone on June 24 there had been
130,000 workers on strike and they had begun to throw up barricades
in the streets.[11] What would these workers do when and if (and most
informed persons felt the question was "when" and not "if") Russia
began to break down under the burden of war?

And what of the peasants who crowded into the mobilization points
by the million, the strong blond peasant boys with rope belts knotted
around the waists of their long gray Russian blouses, the young blood
of Russia with its blue eyes, high cheekbones, strong backs, and stolid
faces? They thronged off to war from every village followed by crying
mothers, sisters, and wives, hustled onto the freight trains or formed
up into marching columns, often still with linen-bound feet and rude
lapti. What did they think of as the bands played and the girls handed
them armloads of wild flowers picked beside the July fields of yellow-
ing grain? What of those who remained behind? Only one man from a
family went at first but everyone knew this was just the beginning.
What was the mood in the endless villages of Russia, those clusters of
thatched and whitewashed huts along a single village street, wide as a
football field, with the blue-painted shutters and the curlicue wooden
decorations? Of what did the women with their broad white skirts,
their linen shirtwaists, their bronzed arms and shoulders talk as they
gathered at dusk around the village well to work the long pole that
brought water to their wooden buckets? Viktor Chernov called them
the sphinx of Russia, and he was the leader of the Socialist Revolutionaries, a group who were closer to the peasants than any other
party. He could not help wondering whether their hearts were really
with the Czar, with this strange new war against the *nemtsi*, the
tongueless ones, the Germans.[12] Pavel Milyukov, the Kadet leader,

thought he heard an answer from the heart of Russia, the Russia of *vekovaya tishina,* eternal quiet, the Russia that lay beyond the railroads and which had not been touched even by the banal life of the drowsy little provincial towns with their dusty roads, dirty inns, and countless flies. He heard it in the response of the peasant to almost any question and particularly to the question of the war. It was a simple phrase: *my kalutsky.* The phrase told nothing. It said: We are from Kaluga. We are Kaluga-ites. But its meaning was deep. It implied a continent. We are from Kaluga, said the peasants, and the Kaiser will not come to Kaluga. In a word, it was not *their* war. It was not like the War of 1812 when Napoleon *came to them.* It was something far off and distant. And if, as many said, the peasant had boundless devotion to the Czar and boundless devotion to his motherland—this might be true—up to a point. To be sure he would fight. But he had to have arms to fight with. And if the going turned bad and he left the ranks to return to his village, his "boundless devotion" would be shown to the land and he would regard it as his land to use as he saw fit, not the land of some nobleman.[13]

The peasants' attitude toward the land was essentially mystical. They had never regarded it as *belonging* to the landlords. It belonged to God, if it belonged to anyone.[14] They had thought this was what the Czar understood in 1863 when the serfs were liberated. And they still expected that the land would be freed. But possibly now, as they were more and more beginning to think, they would have to free the land with their own hands. It was a unique understanding of this relationship between the peasant and that land which underlay the SRs' attitude toward the land problem. Chernov (although he never quite figured out how to do it) proposed that the land be made free as the air to be used on an equal basis by all of those who wished to cultivate it.[15]

But fifty years after the Czar's liberating decree the peasant was as far as ever from being master, let alone owner, of his land. There were still gigantic concentrations in possession of a handful of owners—and usually this was the best land. A census of 1905 showed that 11,000 owners held estates of 1,000 to 5,000 desyatins (one desyatin equals 2.7 acres); 1,000 held estates of 5,000 to 10,000 desyatins; 699 owned estates of larger size. Thus, the brothers Stroganov, Count Bobrinsky, and Count Musin-Pushkin owned respectively 60,000, 75,000 and 80,000 desyatins. S. Spilevsky held 100,000; the two Balashevs 385,000; a third had 600,000. Count Sheremetev owned a large cattle ranch and estates in eleven different guberniya. K. Rukavishnikov owned 850,000 desyatins; Prince Abemelek-Lazarev more than 900,000. S. M. Golitsyn owned 1,000,000 desyatins in the Perm Guberniya, 40,000 desyatins in Vyatka, more than 13,000 in Tver and Ryazan, and 5,000 in Moscow.

The concentration of landholding had dropped somewhat since 1877. There were 225 fewer holders of more than 10,000 desyatins. Much of this was under the influence of the Stolypin land reform program which was designed to create a stable class of middle-peasant farm owners. There were 113,898 owners of more than 50 desyatins in 1905 and probably no more than 100,000 in 1917. Of the 12,000 peasant families who had farmed their lands in common in the traditional Russian *obshchina* (farming commune) more than a quarter had now become private farmers, owning their own land and farming it with hired labor.

In the process peasants had flocked to the cities—59 per cent or more of St. Petersburg's population on the eve of the war was peasant, many of whom moved annually back and forth from factory to village, depending on planting and harvesting seasons. Invisible to the Government—but deeply important politically and psychologically—was this peasant majority in the capital city.[16]

It was for the peasants, the dark people of the boundless lands of Russia, that Rasputin spoke and it was in Rasputin's person that both the Czar and the Czarina saw not only a holy man (as they believed), a man of mystical vision and powers, but the incarnation of the Russian people.

"The Czar desired union with the people," Berdyayev observed. "The Czar had no intercourse with them. He was separated from them by a wall of an almighty bureaucracy. Then for the first time he met the people in the person of Rasputin. He became a symbol of the people and the people's religious life."[17]

What, then, was the attitude of this "man of the people," as the Czarina called him? Rasputin was totally opposed to the war. He was opposed to war in general and had strongly urged the Czar not to become involved in the Balkan War of 1912. Had he been in St. Petersburg or Tsarskoye Selo, he later insisted, there would have been no war in 1914. But now he was far distant in his native Siberian Pokrovskoye, where he had been lying between life and death for days from stab wounds in the stomach, inflicted by a woman named Guseva, a woman whom Rasputin had used and discarded. His life hung in balance and there was enormous concern over him on the part of the Czarina and her confidante, Madame Vyrubova. They believed the attack had been instigated by Rasputin's enemies. But evidence of that has never been found.[18] Dangerous as was his condition, Rasputin managed to send off at least one final warning to the Czar through Vyrubova: "Let Papa not plan war because war will mean the end of

Russia and yourselves and you will lose to the last man."[19] Vyrubova
put the message before the Czar but sadly conceded that he paid little
heed to it. The Czarina, terrified at the prospect of war, had sent
Rasputin a series of telegrams, begging him to "pray for us."[20]
When she learned that Russian mobilization had been ordered, she
had a violent argument with the Czar and flung herself on her bed,
crying hysterically: "All is lost. War has come and I know nothing of
it."[21]

War . . . The country was caught up in its excitement—the ordinary people, the peasants, the poets, the artists, the writers. The brilliant and perceptive Duma member V. V. Shulgin commented that the
intelligentsia, which in the course of the Japanese War adopted the slogan "the worse the better" (for achieving their objective of freedom),
had suddenly been reborn as Russian patriots. He cited the Duma session of July 26 at which speaker after speaker pledged himself to the
war.[22] And at first this seemed to be true. Mayakovsky wrote flaming
articles for the newspapers under the nom de plume of Citizen Shrapnel. He proclaimed: "The Vandal enemies have robbed Russia. . . ."
And he sent to the Moscow police chief an application in the name of
"Vladimir Vladimirovich Mayakovsky, Gentleman" in which he wrote:
"I humbly beg for the issuance of a certificate of loyalty in order to
enable me to enter active army services as a volunteer."[23]

He was, of course, refused, as "politically unreliable."[24] The application of one Boris Pasternak was also turned down. Ilya Ehrenburg was
in Paris, writing poetry. He tried to volunteer for a special Russian
unit attached to the French Army. When he was rejected, he got a job
in a freight station. Later he became a war correspondent for the
Birzhevye Vedomosti, the leading Russian financial paper. Alexander
Kuprin, famous for his sensational stories of Moscow prostitutes, now
turned his wrath on the Germans, whom he called "hydras" who must
be exterminated, and had his picture taken in uniform. The lyric poet
Fyodor Sologub hailed the cause of the holy war.[25] Maxim Gorky was
back in Russia, thanks to the amnesty of 1913, but at first he could not
decide between patriotism and pacifism. He went to Kiev to visit his
wife, Mariya Andreyeva, who was acting there. A group of tailors
asked him what he thought about the war and he said he was "tangled
up" with the question. Somewhat later, however, he came out against
it.[26*] Ivan Bunin and his brother Yuli were cruising on the Volga.
Their steamer was tied up at the wharf at Saratov when they saw

* "Poor Gorky! what a pity he has disgraced himself," Lenin wrote A. G.
Shlyapnikov, October 31, 1914, of Gorky's attitude to the war. Lenin and Gorky
had drifted far apart and never really were to come together again. V. I. Lenin,
Collected Works, Vol. XXXV, p. 171.)

newsboys running toward them crying: "Extra! Extra! Murder of the
Austrian archduke at Sarajevo!" Yuli Bunin bought a paper and, turning to Ivan, said, "It's the end of us. Russia goes to war for Serbia and
then Revolution in Russia. It is the end of our previous life." By September Bunin was writing violent denunciations of the Germans for
"their criminal conduct," their "unbelievable cruelty to the defenseless,
old people, women, prisoners and wounded."[27] Ivan Bunin was a patriot although he once told Valentin Katayev that he abandoned
Odessa for Moscow at the start of the war, fearful of an attack "by
Rumania or the Turkish Navy."[28] Vyacheslav Ivanov, of the "Tower,"
became a patriot, as did V. F. Ern, Pavel A. Florensky, Sergei N.
Bulgakov, Yevgeny N. Trubetskoi, and many other aesthetes.[29] Valen-
tin Bryusov, the necromancer, was off to the front before the month of
July was out. He became a war correspondent for the newspaper
Russkiye Vedomosti (but by 1915 he was back in Moscow translating
Oscar Wilde's "Ballad of Reading Gaol").[30]

The war came to different men in different forms. It found the
prophet of Russian apocalypse, Andrei Bely, in Dornach, Switzerland,
with his beloved Asya, her sister and her sister's husband, swinging a
five-pound hammer and building a temple to the glory of Rudolf
Steiner and his anthroposophistic faith. To Bely it seemed that out of
his own personality had sprung "hunger, disease, war, the voice of revolution."

"The catastrophe of Europe and the explosion of my personality,"
he wrote, "are the same event. You can say—I am war or I gave birth
to war." He felt himself guilty for the catastrophe. He was a bomb
threatening to blow up the earth, and the enemy—the spirit of the occult world—threatened him with destruction.[31]

Not all the other writers spoke for war. Zinaida Gippius and her
husband, Dmitri Merezhkovsky, returned to Russia from Paris on its
eve—Merezhkovsky so depressed that later Gippius wondered if he
did not have a premonition of what was coming.[32] On the day before
war started—July 19—she began a diary, her *Sinyaya Kniga* (Blue
Book). It opened on a note of despair. "What to write? Can I? There
is only one thing—WAR!" The conflict had begun, she felt, without
reason, without prelude, without slogans, without design. Everyone
had lost their heads, and she, as she wrote the words, felt that she, too,
was going out of her mind. There was nothing but trivia to put down.
What was the fatherland, after all? Was it the people or the Government or all taken together? But what if she hated the Russian Government and if the Government hated her people?

"Why is it," she wrote, "that, in general, war is evil and only this war is good? War is war and of war I say it is forever forbidden and neither now nor ever is it necessary."

The Czar ordered universal prohibition for the duration of the war (there were those who later were to say that this was a major factor in the Revolution since the poor could get no vodka, only home-brew, while the rich drank what they liked) and changed the name of St. Petersburg to Petrograd. Gippius called it "mania" and accused the Czar of trying to change Peter's city into "Nikolograd."[33] She could hardly bear to go to the streets, filled as they were with marching troops, patriotic demonstrations, crowds bearing flags, portraits of the Czar, and holy church banners.[34]

Summer had been hot, and late August brought magnificent clear blue days as the bronzed leaves began to fall, Konstantin Paustovsky remembered, on the artillery that lined the Moscow streets, waiting to be shipped to the front. But soon all this changed. The news from the front was bad. Worse than bad. Terrifying. Gen. A. V. Samsonov and his army had been lost to the Germans in the death trap of Tannenberg. There was talk of treachery, of Gen. P. K. Rennenkampf's failure to relieve Samsonov. Rennenkampf, a German name, and the suspicion and hatred of Germans ran deep. There had long been gossip of the "German Empress" (the Czarina), and violent anti-German rioting broke out in both Petrograd and Moscow, after the declaration of war. The German Embassy in St. Isaac's Square had been sacked and the bronze horses on the roof hurled into the Moika. German shops and offices were burned and pillaged. Now a pall of smoke drifted slowly over Moscow and over Petrograd as well. Rumors spread that it was the smoke of battle, that the front was coming closer, that Warsaw had fallen, that the Germans were ravaging Poland as they had Belgium. None of this was true but it was believed. Some said the forests and meadowlands around Tver were burning. Others said that half the forests of Siberia were afire as well as the peat bogs near Petrograd.[35] Autumn wore on and the smoke did not vanish. The days grew more dark and the pungent smell filled the nostrils. The peasants stood outside their thatched huts, looked at the sky, smelled the wind, and shook their heads in gloom. They did not know what it meant but they saw no good in the signs.[36]

War was taking over the country. Millions of men were moving out of the villages in an endless cloud of gray humanity, moving west toward the frontiers of Germany and Austria. There were not enough guns—only enough so that they were issued to those in the first ranks. The army marched into battle, those to the rear without arms. They got guns of their own only when those ahead had fallen. Church bells rang in the villages and the women wept. A friend of Paustovsky's watched the peasant soldiers march through Moscow. "I walked right up to the front ranks to get a look," he said. "You know they smell of bread. An amazing smell. You smell it and for some reason you believe that nobody can ever defeat the Russian people."[37] But the Germans did defeat the poorly led, badly equipped untrained peasant hordes. Four hundred thousand were lost with Samsonov's army, more than the whole number of Union deaths in the American Civil War. Victories against the Austrians took more hundreds of thousands. The snows had not yet come before the breakdowns began. The Grand Duke Nikolai Nikolayevich, the commander in chief, as the Grand Duke Andrei Vladimirovich was informed, had been opposed to the whole East Prussian strategy.[38] Why was it carried out? A gallant gesture to help Russia's French allies, battling on the River Marne to save Paris.

Toward the end of August or the first of September when M. V. Rodzyanko, president of the Duma, made his first trip to GHQ he observed the disorder in transportation. "Chaos is beginning on the railroads," he told the commander in chief when he visited him in his luxurious six-car railroad train. The Grand Duke had his offices in one car, a dining saloon in another, his bedroom in a third, which was simply fitted except for one wall completely covered with two hundred icons gleaming in golden frames before which icon lamps constantly burned. The other cars were for his staff.[39] Rodzyanko told Nikolasha that little by little the chaos would affect all transport in the immediate rear and then gradually spread into the depths of the country. The Grand Duke agreed but said he had no authority to deal with this and other nonmilitary questions. Rodzyanko took the case to Premier Goremykin, who said the Government would handle the question of the rear but that the war "ce n'est pas mon affaire."[40] The result—"unbelievable confusion" in Rodzyanko's words. The war was two months old. Already the empire was beginning to come apart.

XXIX

"A Healthy War"

The deaths began. The common man, the Ivans, the Feofans, the Mishas, the Fyodors, the Mityas, the Kostyas, died in the Masurian marshes and Carpathian passes. Death was impartial. It took a Romanov along with the others. This was Prince Oleg, a poet, the beloved and talented young son of Grand Duke Konstantin Konstantinovich, "K.P.," the poet, playwright, and scholar. Oleg went into action with the First Army in East Prussia in early August.[1] By September 29 he was dying of wounds in a Vilna hospital. The Grand Duke and his wife arrived at the bedside a few minutes before the end. K.P. gave his son his grandfather's St. George's Cross. Oleg, still conscious, held it in his hands, exclaiming: "Grandfather's cross! Grandfather's cross!" Then in a jerky voice he continued: "There was an attack . . . the horse swerved. . . . I was wounded . . . fell. . . ."

He lost consciousness, then revived and asked why everyone was standing around his bed. A moment later he died. He was the first and last Romanov to die in action in the war that was to take millions of Russian lives.[2]

The poets began to spend their nights in a Petrograd cellar called the Stray Dog. It opened at midnight. Because of wartime prohibition it served only coffee or pineapple juice in teacups. Or that is what was said. Mayakovsky read his poem "Mother and the Evening Killed by the Germans" ("Mother, what is it?" White, white, like a tombstone. "It's about him, telegram with the news, he's dead. Ah, cover, cover the eyes of the newspapers!").[3] Tamara Karsavina danced at the Stray

Dog—the walls of the staircase were decorated with paintings by Sudeikin and the cellar was lined with flowers but this did not mask the stink of urine from the ancient lavatory. Karsavina danced on a mirror. She was accompanied by a little girl dressed as cupid, and an entrance fee of twenty-five rubles was charged.[4] Anna Akhmatova, in tight black silk dress, a large oval cameo on her belt, read her famous verse:

> We are all sinners, we are all whores
> How sad we are together.[5]

And, finally, Mayakovsky, with the swift changing mood of the war, declaimed:

> For you who only love women and food
> Should I give my life for your pleasure?
> I'd rather serve pineapple juice
> To the whores at the bar.[6]

The Czar in that autumn of 1914 began to visit the front; rather, not the front but the comfortable GHQ of his uncle, Nikolasha, the commander in chief, in his private railroad cars at Baranovichi. The Czar was cheered by daily letters—sometimes more often than daily—sent to him by "Wifey" or "Sunny," as the Czarina signed herself. She was confident that "with God's help here all will go well and end gloriously" and she thought the war "has lifted up spirits, cleansed the many stagnant minds and brought unity in feeling." It was, she believed, " 'a healthy war' in the moral sense."[7] "Nicky," as he invariably signed himself, was as sentimental as "Wifey." But in one of his earliest letters, dated November 19, 1914, he captured the essence of the problem.

"The one big and serious difficulty for our army" he wrote, "is that we again haven't enough munitions. Because of this during the fighting our troops must observe care and economy and that means that all the heavy fighting falls on the infantry. Thanks to this losses quickly become colossal. Some army corps are turned into divisions, brigades into regiments and so on. . . . The replacements are good but half of them have no rifles because the troops have lost such a mass of weapons. Some pick them up on the field of battle. . . ."

Russian industry even with the most energetic efforts was not well enough developed to meet the extraordinary demands of the war, swollen by the terrible equipment losses in the early stages. Nor did

Russia's allies have much productive capacity to spare. Efforts to buy arms in America came too late to make any critical difference.

Russian official losses for the first ten months of war were 3,880,000—a figure which Sir Bernard Pares, who was asked to report it to the British Government, regarded as an understatement. Gen. Georgi N. Danilov estimated them at 300,000 a month before short-ages of munitions became acute.[8] In December 1914, Ambassador Pa-léologue was told that Russia entered the war with a supposed reserve of 5,600,000 rifles. But this was now exhausted. So was the reserve of 5,200,000 rounds of shrapnel. The armies expended 45,000 rounds a day and production was only 13,000 rounds.[9]

And so, commented the saturnine Shulgin, "We danced 'the last tango' on the rim of trenches filled with forgotten corpses."[10]

At the outbreak of war Lenin was arrested at his mountain cottage at Poronin. For the first time he genuinely feared for his life. He was taken to be a Russian spy by the local gendarmerie. Krupskaya over-heard some Polish peasant women talking (apparently for her benefit) about what they would do with a spy if the police let him go. They would put out his eyes, cut off his tongue—just as a start. Lenin was held in a little market village of Nowy Targ. Finally, Viktor Adler, the famous Austrian socialist (and bitter political enemy of Lenin's), vouched for him. "Are you sure that Lenin is an enemy of the Czarist government?" Adler was asked by the Austrian Interior Minister. "A more sworn enemy than your Excellency," said Adler.[11] The Nowy Targ authorities were ordered to release him. He and Krupskaya made their way back to Cracow, where before leaving for Switzerland Krupskaya arranged to have an inheritance of her mother's—some 4,000 rubles—transferred to a Swiss account. The Vienna broker took half the money as commission. The remainder helped support them through the war.[12]

Lenin plunged into activity—not, to be sure, related to revolution in Russia; related instead to the international socialist movement. He had little or no news of what was happening in Russia and no time to think of Russia. In his correspondence of the initial months of the war there is hardly a reference to Russia. All his attention was fixed on the socialist movement, and particularly on the split which had broken it open. Most of the socialists in each country abandoned internationalist principles and voted to support their national war effort be it German, French, or Russian. Lenin's mood was summed up in a letter he sent off to Alexandra Kollontai in Copenhagen toward the end of 1914: "The European war has brought this great benefit to international socialism, that it has exposed for all to see the utter rottenness, baseness

and meanness of opportunism, thereby giving a splendid impetus to
the cleansing of the working-class-movement from the dung ac-
cumulated during decades of peace."[13] As for revolution in Russia—
that, at best, he thought, would be a bourgeois revolution, that is, not
one led by himself and his adherents. In other countries, more advanced, like Germany, there could be talk of a socialist revolution. But
in all this he was most cautious. It could well take "a very long time,"
as he made plain in letters to his lieutenant in Stockholm, A. G.
Shlyapnikov, on whom he was dependent for such information as he
got out of Russia.[14] He also with considerable haste and no little
difficulty (since he had been compelled to abandon most of his personal library in Cracow) sent off his article on Karl Marx to the
Granat Encyclopedia. After numerous proddings on his part his sister
Mariya collected his fee of 200-odd rubles in person.[15] Lenin also
began to solicit other literary work, getting his relatives in Russia to
canvass publishing houses on the possibilities. As an old hand at exile
he was settling down for a long siege devoted almost entirely to warfare with his fellow political exiles. Once again, so far as daily activity
was concerned, revolution in Russia was on the shelf.

Russia's elder statesman, Count Witte, rejected by the Czar, long
out of office and out of favor, when war began was vacationing in
Biarritz and did not return to Petrograd until September 1914. He
came back deeply upset. "This war is madness," he told the French
ambassador. "It has been forced on the Czar's prudence by stupid and
short-sighted politicians. It can only have disastrous results. A victory
to me seems highly questionable."[16] With his usual stubbornness Witte
began to campaign for a quick exit of Russia from the war. When the
Russian armies defeated the Austrians in the Carpathians in November 1914, he urged that peace be made at once. "We have just beaten
the Austrians," he said, "and driven back the Germans. It is the utmost
we can ever do. Henceforth our military power can only wane."[17]

Witte's campaign worried the French and British—so much so that
the British ambassador, Sir George Buchanan, made an attack on him
as a "Germanophile" in a New Year's address at the English Club.[18]

But few paid Witte much heed. The only man in Russia who
seemed to hold the same views was Rasputin, a fact which Witte's political opponents were quick to mention with a smirk. On February
28, 1915, Witte died (which gave the Czar comfort) and soon Rasputin became embroiled in one of the most scandalous—if not the most
scandalous—episodes of his scandal-filled career.[19]

Rasputin had recovered with remarkable speed from his wounds.
With equal celerity he had regained his prestige with the Czar. He

had never lost it with the Czarina. The Czar met with Rasputin on several occasions during the autumn, and early in January 1915, Rasputin won his way back to full favor by rescuing Vyrubova, almost literally, from grave's edge. The Empress' confidante had been critically injured in a railroad accident January 2 in which her body was crushed by a steel girder.[20] Rasputin learned of the accident the day after it happened. He rushed to the hospital, where the Czar and Czarina were at Vyrubova's side. "Annushka!" Rasputin cried. "Look at me!" Vyrubova opened her eyes saying: "Grigory. Thank God. It's you." Rasputin staggered from the room and fell into a faint.[21] Vyrubova's recovery proceeded smoothly from that moment. On February 26 the Czar set out for GHQ after receiving Rasputin's blessing, reporting to his wife that in his heart he felt a "genuine pascal peace." It was this moment which Rasputin chose for a brief visit to Moscow, where, as he told the Czarina, he planned to pray at the tombs of the Orthodox patriarchs.

Deputy Interior Minister Vladimir F. Dzhunkovsky had assigned two details of police to watch Rasputin—an open detail for Rasputin's protection, a secret squad to observe his comings and goings from the house at 64 Gorokhova where he lived. The reports of the secret agents offered a day-by-day and hour-by-hour account of Rasputin's existence.

> *12 February. Rasputin with an unknown woman visited No. 15–17 Troitsky Street, Prince Andronikov's. At 4:30 A.M. he came home in company of six drunken men (with a guitar) who stayed until 6 in the morning singing and dancing. . . . March 10. About 1 A.M. seven or eight men and women headed by Ensign Karpotiny arrived and stayed until 3 A.M. The company shouted, sang songs, danced and the whole drunken band left with Rasputin for an unknown destination. . . . March 11. At 10:15 Rasputin met someone on Gorokhova Street and went to No. 6 Pushkin Street to visit the Prostitute Tregubova. Then he went to the baths. . . . March 13 . . . At 6:30 Rasputin went with two women to No. 76 Yekaterinsky Canal to Savelyev's where he stayed until 5 A.M. and then lay in bed ill all day.*[22]

On March 25 Rasputin left for Moscow. There, in the words of Pares, either his praying at the tombs was too much for him or he felt that he had some credit in hand.[23] In any event two days later he visited the famous Yar, the gypsy restaurant on the outskirts of Moscow which had been the downfall of so many noblemen who tossed their last gold rubles into the skirts of a gypsy singer and then walked out to put a pistol into their mouths in the cold dawn of a wintry Moscow morning.

Rasputin's conduct at the Yar was not unusual—for him—but it was public. He occupied a loge with two Moscow journalists and three young women, one of whom moved in social circles. They drank and caroused while a balalaika band played. Then the gypsy women sang and danced, provocatively shaking their loose breasts. Rasputin became more and more excited. He began loudly to proclaim his amorous prowess, naming the women he had had and describing their particular sexual attractions. He shrugged off his kaftan and pulled out his embroidered blouse. "The old woman [the Czarina] made this for me," he said, adding, "I can do what I like with her." He further exposed himself and sought to embrace the women in the loge, then the gypsy entertainers. At this point waiters and police tried to quell him. He shouted that he was behaving just as he did in the presence of the Czarina. Finally, he was arrested and hauled away "snarling and vowing vengeance" (in the words of Bruce Lockhart, the famous British agent, who saw it all).[24]*

Dzhunkovsky, the honest policeman, thought he now had enough evidence to procure Rasputin's downfall. He presented his case to the Czar, holding back nothing, arguing that this was only an extreme example of Rasputin's conduct, that the issue threatened both dynasty and state, that Rasputin was a weapon in the hands of those who wished to destroy Russia. He asked permission to continue the investigation and observation of Rasputin. The Czar replied: "I not only give you permission but I beg you to do it." The talk lasted from 10 P.M. to half after midnight.[25]

But things did not turn out as Dzhunkovsky imagined. Rasputin promptly called on the Czar in the role of a penitent, saying that like all people, he was a sinner and not a saint.[26] His words probably did not entirely convince the Czar, but the image of the sinner repentant and the weakness of the flesh is a powerful one in Russia. Soon enough Rasputin's counteroffensive was in full swing and the Czarina was writing her husband at GHQ: ". . . my enemy Dzhunkovsky. Ah dear, he is not an honest man, he has shown that vile filthy paper (against our Friend) to Dmitri. . . . Such a sin & as tho you had said to him, that you have had enough of these dirty stories and wish him

---

* Immediately on his return to Petrograd Rasputin sent off a telegram to Princess Tenisheva in Moscow: "Happy for the revelation, sorry for waiting, kiss you dearly." He sent another to Anna Dzhanulova, wife of a Moscow merchant, one of his followers: "Lovely treasure I kiss you strongly." These may have been two of his companions at the Yar. (*Krasny Arkhiv*, 1925, Vol. V, p. 273.)

[Rasputin] to be severely punished. You see how he turns your words and orders around—the slanderers were to be punished . . . ah, it's so vile—always liars, enemies—I long knew Dzhunkovsky hates Gregory. . . . Ah, my Love, when at last will you thump with your hand upon the table & scream at Dzhunkovsky and others when they act wrongly. . . . Oh my Boy, make one tremble before you—to love you is not enough, one must be affraid [sic] of hurting, displeasing you. . . ."[27]

To no one's surprise Dzhunkovsky was sacked a day or two after Rasputin had told one of the plain-clothes agents: "Your Dzhunkovsky is finished."[28] Dzhunkovsky understood why this happened. The Empress regarded him as "an enemy of the Imperial house." The Empress, he believed, was "so blind, so sick, if you could call it that, so much under the influence of Rasputin, that she was not conscious of what she did. Moreover, she had the firm belief that if it were not for Rasputin the Czarevich would die. It was her *idée fixe*. The Czar had once told Stolypin that it was better to have ten Rasputins than one hysterical Empress,[29] and Rodzyanko after long investigation was inclined to agree with Premier Goremykin that the problem of the Czarina and Rasputin was *"une question clinique."*[30]

But Gen. V. N. Dedulin, sometime commandant of the palace, took another view. He quoted the Czar as once saying of Rasputin:

"This is a brave Russian man, simple and pious. I love to talk with him during my moments of uncertainty and doubt because calm and serenity revive in my heart after I've talked with him."[31]

Pious, brave, simple, wastrel, vagabond, wonder-worker or fraud, adventurer, Rasputin was the man who within the year would grasp complete and total control of Russia.[32] He had behaved his worst to find his power over the Czarina growing stronger and stronger. Only a few weeks remained before the Czar would take a fatal step. He would put himself in supreme command of Russia's military machine. And Rasputin, through domination of the Czarina and the Czarina's domination of her husband, would be the dictator.

XXX

The Little Comb

At 7:39 P.M. August 23, 1915, Nicholas sent the following telegram from "The Czar's Stavka" (Staff headquarters) at Mogilev on the Dnieper to his wife back in Tsarskoye Selo:

"The meeting went extraordinarily well and simply. He is leaving the day after tomorrow but the change is effective today. Now all has been done. I tenderly kiss you and the children."

The Czarina replied within an hour of the delivery of the Czar's telegram:

"Thank God, my beloved for you and your brave decision. Thank God that all has gone well. We 'all' kiss you. I am writing. Sleep well and peacefully. Very touched by the first telegram in my name from the Czar's Stavka."

This event—the Czar's taking over of Supreme Command from his uncle, the Grand Duke Nikolai Nikolayevich—satisfied the most passionate longings of the Empress who felt, with some justice, that Nikolasha was a rival of her husband's for public favor. It played to the powerful ambition of Rasputin. The Grand Duke and Rasputin had long since broken relations because of Rasputin's intrigues against the Grand Duke. The Grand Duke had, in fact, warned on hearing that Rasputin wanted to visit GHQ: "Come and I'll hang [him]."[1]

Little more could be said of the Czar's action. All of the omens were bad. It had been a bad summer; indeed, a bad year. The war could hardly have gone worse. True, the Russians achieved tremendous success against the Austrians in late autumn and winter, 1914–15, occupy-

ing Galicia and the Carpathians, including the almost impregnable
fortress of Peremyshl. But this had now come apart. Rapidly the Germans and Austrians reversed the tide, rolling back the Russians in
Galicia, wiping out the salient in the Carpathians, recapturing the
mountain strongholds. At the very moment the Czar assumed command the Germans were about to take Warsaw, and soon most of
Poland would be in their hands. They were pushing along the Baltic
coast, occupying Lithuania, and there was fear that Riga would fall
which would menace Petrograd. On August 10, 1915, Minister of Education Pavel N. Ignatyev inquired about plans for removing art treasures from the capital, and the next day Gen. Nikolai V. Ruzsky, commander of the northwest front, could do no more than tell the Council
of Ministers that he hoped the autumn rains would hold up the German advance short of Petrograd.[2] Nowhere could a break be seen in
the clouds.

The Grand Duke Andrei Vladimirovich (whose consort was the
ballerina Kshesinskaya) had a discussion with Gen. F. F. Palitsin, regarding the situation at Warsaw.

"What should the High Command do?" the Grand Duke asked.

"I don't know," the general replied.

"But you have some idea?"

"I've an idea—a very good idea."

"Should the Russians attack?" the Grand Duke asked.

"Well," the general said, "that's not possible because we must husband our strength."

"Then we should hold our lines and fight where we are?"

"When we take a stand," the general said, "we should do it in a better place."

"Then we must retreat?"

"God save us!" the general exclaimed. "How can we retreat? Theory
shows that when you retreat you lose much more than when you attack."

"Then what should we do?"

"I don't know but I have a very good, an excellent plan."

The Grand Duke walked away from the general with a feeling of
horror. What kind of a nightmare was this? Or was it reality. The
words "a very good, an excellent plan" kept reverberating in his ears.[3]

It was indeed a nightmare but it was reality. Not only was Russian
military planning adrift in a fog but the shortages of men, of arms, of
material, were desperate. There was not enough oats and hay. The
ministry's answer was to cut the daily ration. Let the horses eat ten instead of twenty pounds of oats and five instead of fifteen pounds of
hay. It was the same with rations for the troops, especially meat.[4] As

for food for the workers a government survey in autumn, 1915, found that of 659 cities 500 had food shortages, 348 being short of rye flour and 334 short of wheat, and Interior Minister Alexei Khvostov warned that in all of the center and northwest of Russia and particularly in Petrograd, the situation had become "extraordinarily dangerous."[5] The peasants weren't selling supplies and what was sold was being held by speculators. What would happen? the Grand Duke Andrei asked himself. As early as May 1915, he had been informed there were only two hundred shells, on the average, available for each battery, and firing was limited to two and a half shells per gun every twenty-four hours. The minimum needed to hold the lines was five, and successful offensive operations required at least seven or eight per gun. Russian shell production was estimated at 450,000 a month, compared with 2.5 million for France.[6] In two months of steady retreat on the Warsaw front (sometimes so rapid that the commanders didn't know where they were) there had been losses of 50 per cent in manpower with little hope of replacements. Cartridges were running out, there were no more rifles, and France had none to spare.[7]

"In a year of war the regular Army had vanished," observed Gen. A. A. Brusilov, possibly Russia's best commander. "It was replaced by an army of ignoramuses."[8]

Behind the front the stain of scandal and treason spread. In March Col. S. N. Mayaseyedov was executed as a German agent. He was a close friend of War Minister Sukhomlinov's and, particularly, of Madame Sukhomlinova's. Before the war he had fought a duel with the Octobrist leader Guchkov, who openly called him a spy. When Mayaseyedov missed his shot at fifteen paces Guchkov threw down his pistol saying: "I don't want to save him from his natural death—hanging."[9] Now he was summarily executed.[10] The execution met popular approval. The public was convinced that the Government was riddled with German agents. Madame Sukhomlinova and her husband were popularly believed to be among their number. Even the Czarina joined the clamor about Madame Sukhomlinova. "The fool harms her husband & breaks her neck," she wrote Nicholas. She sympathized with the Minister but told her husband that the "rage of the officers against Sukhomlinov is quite colossal." She blamed his wife and "her bribes" for part of the War Minister's trouble but held him responsible for the fact that "there is no ammunition wh is our curse now."[11] Rumors of Kshesinskaya's being mixed up in bribes for artillery contracts and other irregularities hardly helped the situation.[12]

Prince Serafim Mansyrev told I. V. Kluzhev, an Octobrist member of the Duma who promptly entered the remark in his diary on May 21, 1915, that there was in the country a mood of growing dissatisfaction, a mood which "moves forward on its own, without organization, without plan or system and, therefore, is even more frightening because this may lead not merely to undesirable but to terrifying results."[13]

Or as the vastly rich Alexei Putilov, owner of the Putilov steelworks, observed to Paléologue over a fine dinner, concluded with brandy and Havana cigars: "The days of Tsarism are numbered. It is lost, lost beyond hope. Revolution is now inevitable. . . . A revolution may be a great benefit to a nation if it can reconstruct after having destroyed. . . . But from the bourgeois revolution we shall at once descend to the working-class revolution and soon after to the peasant revolution. And then will begin the most frightful anarchy, interminable anarchy. . . ."[14]

No government, even an autocracy like the Czar's, could move through such times without response. The Czar made changes in his cabinet. First he dropped the unpopular Nikholai A. Maklakov, Interior Minister; then War Minister Sukhomlinov. Alexander Kerensky, who was beginning to win a reputation in the Duma, summed up the public mood: "The fall of Peremyshl—out went Maklakov; the fall of Lvov—out went Sukhomlinov.[15] When Warsaw falls—out goes [Premier] Goremykin."[16]

Goremykin managed to survive Warsaw's fall. Prince N. B. Shcherbatov, an uninspiring right-winger, replaced Maklakov, and Alexei Polivanov, a more lively if not more able man, came in as War Minister. At his first cabinet meeting Polivanov created a sensation by saying (quite reasonably): "I hold it my civic and service duty to declare to the Council of Ministers that the country is in danger."[17] Alexander Krivoshein, the intelligent Agriculture Minister (soon to be fired), chimed in: "Over Russia is hovering some irreparable tragedy."[18]

It was against this background that Nicholas had set out from Tsarskoye Selo on the evening of August 22 to take over command of his armies. Just a month before on July 22 the Czar had asked Polivanov to convey his decision to the Grand Duke. GHQ was being moved from Baranovichi to Mogilev because of the German advance, and it was only on August 8 that Polivanov delivered the Emperor's letter. "I felt my task lightened," Polivanov recalled, "when, after my words that in view of the difficult position of our armies the Czar did not feel he had the right to absent himself from them and had decided to take over the Supreme Command, Nikolai Nikolayevich [who was nearly seven feet tall] made a wide gesture and crossed himself. . . ."[19]

The Czar's closest friends and advisers were appalled by the move. They saw him exposing himself to blame for inevitable disasters while leaving the political front untended and prey to every kind of intrigue.

His Ministers, except for the aging Goremykin who said "the Czar must please himself," opposed the idea, particularly Foreign Minister Sazonov and Agriculture Minister Krivoshein. They sought with no success to change his mind.[20]

Even General Voyeikov, the palace commandant, son-in-law of Count Frederiks, the court chamberlain, a friend of neither the Grand Duke nor the parliamentarians, tried his hand without success, warning of the danger of leaving the home front neglected. Voyeikov's father-in-law also talked to the Czar. Finally eight Ministers formally petitioned, warning him that his action "threatens serious consequences to Russia, to you and to the dynasty." They added a veiled demand that Goremykin resign because the differences between the Premier and themselves could be "disastrous" for the country. The petition was handed to the Czar as he boarded his train for Mogilev to replace the Grand Duke.

Nothing could change Nicholas' mind at this point. He had been subjected to an extraordinary campaign of rhetoric and wheedling from the Czarina since early June. Letter after letter from her, couched in hysterical terms, cited the words of "our Friend." "Never forget that you are and must remain autocratic Emperor," she wrote. And again: "Sweetheart needs pushing always & to be reminded that he is the Emperor & can do whatsoever pleases him—you never profit of this—you must show you have a way & will of yr own & are not lead by N. & his staff." And: "Russia, thank God, is not a constitutional country. . . . Cant you realize that a man who turned simple traitor to a man of Gods cannot be blest, nor his actions be good." (Here she was speaking of the Grand Duke.)[21] She sent Nicholas a small trinket, a stick with a fish holding a bird, which was a present from Rasputin. It had been, she said, originally sent to Rasputin from the Monastery at New Athos. "He used it first & now sends it to you as a blessing—if you can sometimes use it, wld, be nice & to have it in yr compartment near the one Mr. Ph [Dr. Philippe, the French charlatan who preceded Rasputin] touched, is nice too."[22]

Nor was this all. Since mid-June Rasputin had been in Siberia, sent there or persuaded to go because of the growing scandal about him in the newspapers. Now, at the Czarina's orders—conveyed through Goremykin—Rasputin was called back to Petrograd, arriving at 10:30 A.M. July 31.[23] He met twice with the Czar, on July 31 and August 4, supporting the Czarina's insistence that Nicholas take command of the armies.[24] He then reboarded the train for Siberia August 5, seen off at the Petrograd station by Vyrubova and a group of female admirers, including the twenty-six-year-old Princess Shakhovskaya, Baroness Kusova, Madame Malka-Leya-Basya Miller, Ivan Dobrovolsky and his twenty-nine-year-old wife, and Alexandra Von-Pistolkors, Vyrubova's twenty-five-year-old sister.[25] Lest the Czar waver in his intentions, Rasputin bombarded him with telegrams from Siberia.[26]*

Even so the Czarina still did not feel certain the Czar would be able to stick to his resolution and remove the Grand Duke. Rasputin had given the Czar a small comb (much as Philippe had given the Czarina a bell to ward off persons with evil designs). As Nicholas set off to face up to his uncle, the Grand Duke, the Czarina wrote:

"Remember to comb your hair before all difficult talks & decisions, the little comb will bring its help. Don't you feel calm now that you have become 'sure of yourself'—it's not pride or conceit—but sent by God. . . ."[27]

The Czar prayed repeatedly and read and reread the Czarina's letter, then he set out to meet Nikolasha. (Whether he combed his hair with Rasputin's comb he did not record.) To his surprise the meeting went off well. The Grand Duke agreed to leave with his suite within forty-eight hours. "So," the Czar wrote his wife, "begins a new clean page and what will be written on it only the almighty lord knows."[28] The Czar played a game of dominoes before retiring that night and wrote: "Think, my wifey, will you not come to the assistance of your hubby now that he is absent?"[29]—by which he meant would she act as his surrogate while he was at "Czar's Stavka." And, in fact, this role she was already fulfilling and would fulfill until the fatal end, receiving the Ministers and the Premiers as they came and went with such rapidity that Prince Vladimir M. Volkonsky said there should be a sign outside the cabinet room saying: "Piccadilly—Every Saturday a new program."[30]

The Czar settled into the pleasant and comfortable routine of the Czar's Stavka. He quickly moved out of his splendid special train with its broad-windowed saloon cars and gilt Imperial double eagles[31] into the Mogilev governor's mansion, occupying two rooms on the second floor, a sleeping room and a sitting room. When, later, the Czarevich came to stay with him the boy slept on a canvas camp bed next to that of his father.[32] Every afternoon the Czar called for his car, drove out along the Dnieper bluffs, and went for a brisk two- or three-hour walk. Usually young staff members accompanied him; the older ones couldn't keep up with his pace.[33] On Saturdays and Sundays the Czar went to mass. Meals were comparatively simple—three dishes for

---

* Between sending telegrams to the Czar, Rasputin got into a violent brawl on the steamboat taking him from Tyumen to Pokrovskoye. He began drinking with a group of ten soldiers, throwing 25- and 100-ruble bills around. He disrupted the second-class dining room and then the third. When the boat arrived at Pokrovskoye at 8 A.M. Rasputin lay on the floor of his cabin dead drunk. The police agents accompanying him got two strong men to help carry him ashore. (*Krasny Arkhiv*, 1925, Vol. V, pp. 277–79.)

lunch, four for dinner. The Czar ordinarily had two *ryumki* (shot glasses) of vodka with the *zakuski* and drank only port wine at dinner. A bottle was always put beside his place.[34] Mess had cost the officers 3 rubles a day during the Grand Duke's command. Now the price was brought down to 1.50. Once or twice a week movies were shown at the Mogilev theater. Lt. Gen. P. K. Kondzerovsky worried about these programs. He started out presenting newsreels of the war, especially clips showing the Czar at the front or at headquarters. But the Czar asked him to cut down this footage. With some trepidation Kondzerovsky suggested showing a comedy which he liked very much. The Czarina and the three Imperial daughters were visiting the Czar and, as he told Nicholas, "there is a lot of kissing" in the picture. "Only kisses and nothing more?" the Czar inquired. Assured that the film didn't go beyond kisses, the Czar ordered it shown. Both he and his daughters liked it. Then Kondzerovsky got from Pathé a twenty-part serial, called *The Secrets of New York*. He ran two parts per session. This picture was the favorite of the Czarevich to whom Pathé had presented the film projector. He could hardly wait until after dinner when the screening began.[35]

So life ran on at the Czar's Stavka. Once, a few years earlier, in conversation with Premier Stolypin the Czar had pointed out that he shared his birthday, May 6, with the name day of the patriarch Job, the long-suffering. He told Stolypin that he had often thought of the words of Job: "Hardly have I entertained a fear than it comes to pass and all the evils I foresee descend on my head."[36] If Vyrubova is to be believed it was in this spirit that he had assumed the High Command. "Perhaps," she quoted him as telling the Czarina and herself, "a scapegoat is needed to save Russia. I mean to be the victim. May the will of God be done."[37] Nicholas worked hard and conscientiously. He studied the papers his staff prepared for him. His listened to his new chief of staff, Gen. M. V. Alexeyev, report each day the bad news from the fronts. He attended the briefings of the general officers and courteously drank a glass of vodka with them in the mess. He read with care and attention the daily—sometimes three times daily—letters from his wife, often addressed to "my poor much-suffering Job."[38] Sometimes these ran to thousands of hastily but carefully formed words—so many words that Sir Bernard Pares wondered how the Czarina could write so much and how the Czar could find time to read it all. He wrote back to her, warm, endearing letters, for the most part, but far shorter, far more dry then hers, and in a ratio of not more than one of his to three of hers. He carefully responded to each telegram from the Czarina with one in return, always sending his love, his kisses, and frequently reporting on the weather, still a subject of deep interest and concern to him. He was patient when kindly old Goremy-kin ("such a dear," the Empress said of him[39]) came to consult. Most of all he enjoyed the long stays of the Czarevich. The Czar was a father who loved his son intensely and thought that it was very good for him to live in a military atmosphere away from the court and the feminine society of his four sisters, his mother, Vyrubova, and the others. Within the cloistered world of the Stavka, set down in the small white-washed provincial town of Mogilev beside the picturesque Dnieper River, nothing seemed to change. Summer turned to autumn. Autumn to winter. On Sunday the crowds came out to stare at the Czar and his retinue as he went to church. The officers around his big dinner table numbered between twenty and thirty. The talk was pleasant. In the evening after dinner there was a cozy game of dominoes. He ran out of cascara and sent his wife the empty bottle for refilling.[40] Somewhere beyond the orchards and the tethered goats on the outskirts of Mogilev the world went on; men died by the million at the front; the cities grumbled and food grew short; in the villages the peasants plied their tasks, cut the grain with gleaming scythes, beating it on the hard-baked threshing floors, pouring the flinty kernels into bags of hemp, carting them to the granaries. Then they came home to sit around the stove, smoking their rough makhorka, smoking and saying little. Waiting . . .

Ivanov's Tower was long since closed. Now in Petrograd another kind of salon arose to meet the mood of the times. Perhaps the most influential was that of the Baroness Ye. M. Rosen. Here—or so the Czar's last Interior Minister Khvostov was to testify—you could meet almost anyone, especially of the demiworld: journalists and Grand Dukes, fashionable courtesans and great ladies, the Grand Duke Boris Vladimirovich and Boris Rzhevsky, a yellow journalist whose hand touched many dirty affairs, including, it was said, the sale to news-papers of the letters of the Czarina and her daughters to Rasputin, and a go-between in an abortive plot to murder Rasputin.[41] He was an associate of another tainted journalist, Manasevich-Manuilov, also with ties to police and underworld. Sometimes the Minister of Justice, Alexander A. Khvostov, uncle of the Minister of Interior, Alexei N. Khvostov, might turn up (he was a good friend of Countess Rosen's) or an adventuress who had managed to marry one of the Dolgorukys, whose name was the most ancient in Russia. Here any evening might well turn into a drunken orgy. These were people on the prowl, men and women seeking profit and advantage from the disorder of the country and the high stakes of war. What happened at Countess Rosen's salon besides drunkenness and debauchery? Contracts were sold, bribes were paid, and, it was said, spies overheard secrets and passed them on.

A somewhat similar salon had grown up around B. V. Stürmer, who in January 1916, in spite of some qualms on the part of the Czarina about his German name, was to be appointed Premier, thanks to her urging and that of Rasputin, in place of "dear old Goremykin." Stürmer was a political climber with no apparent morals who had established his salon to advance his ambitions and quickly attracted some influential personalities and, most important, Rasputin.[42] In his house were to be met important right-wing politicians like A. A. Rimsky-Korsakov, the aggressive right-wing Duma leader, Nikolai E. Markov 2nd, V. P. Sokolov, a close friend of Rasputin's, Member of the State Council Viktor Didrikhs, Prince Nikolai B. Shcherbatov, S. P. Beletsky, the Deputy Minister of Interior Prince Nikolai D. Golitsyn and his cousin, Fyodor Golitsyn, and Count A. A. Bobrinsky. The Stürmer salon, or circle as some called it, did not indulge in drink and sex. It dealt with politics, political influence, and the policy of the state. The views of the group were conveyed to the Czar (and naturally to the Czarina) at first through Count Frederiks, the court chamberlain, and then more directly through Vyrubova and Rasputin. After Stürmer became Premier the salon was so popular there was hardly room to hold it in his house.[43]

There were other establishments, less respectable. One was the Villa Rode on the outskirts of Petrograd. Here according to Aron Simano-vich, Rasputin's partner in many money affairs, the proprietor built a small wing specially for Rasputin's parties. There were the gypsy dancers and singers whom Rasputin loved so well and here were in-vited "women of society" who, in Simanovich's words, did their best to outdo the chorus girls and chansonettes. Rasputin was a passionate dancer. He loved to dance the traditional Russian dances. Before going to the Villa Rode he would fill his pockets with candy, silk scarves, ribbons, powder puffs, and bottles of perfume—these were presents for his dancing partners "to steal." He then delightedly an-nounced to the assemblage: "The gypsies have robbed me."[44]

There was the inevitable scandal at the Villa Rode. One night in January 1916, a group of young officers appeared suddenly as Raspu-tin was about to take the dance floor. One had a revolver in hand. Rasputin, so Simanovich and others reported, stared them down with his hypnotic glance. "You want to kill me," Rasputin said. "There is no power left which can direct you against me. Go home. I want to stay with my party here and relax."

The officers slunk away like chastised children and the story became the talk of Petrograd.[45]

And Simanovich, who had been a gambling addict until, so he claimed, he was cured by Rasputin, opened a small gambling hall at 14 Fontanka in partnership with some friends, among them Count Tolstoy (not the author) and Baron Roop. It was run by a cavalry officer named Bermont and among those associated with the enterprise were Count Musvits-Shadursky and the Procurator Rozen. Rasputin often dropped in. Simanovich claimed that lotto was the principal game played in the club and that the place was designed as a gathering spot for "likeminded people." In the evenings, he said, there were sometimes programs and concerts. The police had different ideas about the club and closed it down.[46] Their report contended that Simanovich was the real owner of the establishment, that he had a capital of 200,000 rubles, and that his principal business was gambling and usury, catering particularly to young Petrograd spendthrifts, lending his money at exorbitant rates.[47]

The atmosphere in Russia was fetid. The stink of decay was in the air. The Czar got a stuffy nose and wrote his wife he had taken a shot of cocaine to clear it up—it restored his energy, he reported.[48] She wrote back expressing hope "that the cocain helped well."[49] The Empress couldn't sleep because of a stomach-ache, but a hot-water bottle and a dose of opium, she wrote her husband, brought some relief.[50]

Gambling, cocaine, opium, scandal . . . Zinaida Gippius did not want to follow her gloomy thoughts to a logical conclusion—what would the conclusion be? Would it be revolution in the midst of war? All she heard were words, words, words. And they all seemed fatally childish. No one knew where it would end. Life, she thought, cried at the top of its voice for a Russian revolution, a revolution from within. What seemed most likely was an anarchical uprising, not an organized revolution, plotted and carried through by a revolutionary group such as the SRs or the Bolsheviks but "an unorganized revolution" called forth by the fatally stupid actions of the Government. The exiled revolutionaries—Plekhanov and all the others—simply understood nothing about Russia. They saw from the distance, she wrote in her Blue Book, "Nothing. Absolutely nothing." The intelligentsia within Russia were mules. Nothing could move them. As for the revolutionary underground, so far as she could discover, it was dead. She heard nothing of it, saw no propaganda, saw no effects of it in Russian life, at least as of January 1916.[51] Gippius' assessment was supported by that of A. V. Konovalov, a progressive textile manufacturer with large plants in Kostroma and Moscow. Konovalov reported growing unrest among the workers but little organized agitation and no real ideological leadership. He and other progressive Moscow industrialists were eager to put themselves at the head of a quasi-revolutionary movement which would join the interests of the industrialists and workers in support of a constitutional government. Even a conscientious Soviet historian like V. S. Dyakin was compelled more or less to agree with Gippius' assessment although insisting that the role of the Bolsheviks was underevaluated. The truth was that all through 1915 and into 1916 the scale of strikes was insignificant, especially when compared to 1905.[52]

Almost from the beginning of war communications between Lenin, Trotsky, Martov, Dan, Chernov—all the varieties of Russian revolutionaries—and their organizations within Russia had been effectively cut by police arrest and repression. (*Pravda* was suspended at the outbreak of war; the Bolshevik and other Social Democratic Duma members were arrested in November 1914 and exiled to Siberia in February 1915.) It was extremely difficult to communicate between Zurich or Paris and Russia. Mail went through two or three censors and was often intercepted or suppressed. Lenin's letters to his colleagues in Sweden and France often did not reach their destinations—nor did their letters reach him. Revolutionary agitation simply died out, and in Lenin's case, from the beginning of the war, his interest was directed away from Russia rather than toward it. His energies were thrown into the sharp divisions within international socialist ranks. He put himself at the head of the so-called Zimmerwald group of socialists, opposed to war and fanatically antagonistic to their comrades who supported the respective national war efforts. As always, Lenin fought and argued with almost every other revolutionary with whom he was in contact, although occasionally he tried (usually unsuccessfully) to hold himself in check so as not to spoil all of his relations. He wrote more letters to Inessa Armand than to any other correspondent in this period, often writing her every day for periods of several weeks. But even with her his arguments verged on the point of anger. Sometimes Inessa lived in Switzerland (for a long time in a house just across the lane from the one he occupied with Nadezhda Krupskaya) and went on walking trips with Lenin and Krupskaya.

Lenin wrote scores—hundreds—of letters in 1914, 1915, and 1916. But for weeks he never mentioned Russia or Russian events. If he did, it was usually simply to say "the news from Russia is good." Or "there is no news from Russia." For long intervals he saw no Russian paper and got no mail or clandestine correspondence.

Lenin plunged into the Swiss libraries, waiting on the doorstep when they opened at 9 A.M., working until 12, back again at 1 and there until 6 P.M. He worried constantly about money. He wrote bland and ingratiating letters to publishers in Petrograd, trying to get work not only for himself but for Krupskaya. They lived in the cheapest rooms, once taking meals for some weeks in a boardinghouse where they ate at a common table with a prostitute who liked to discuss her professional problems and another lodger who was obviously a criminal. The conversation, Krupskaya noted, was "more human and lively than that heard in the decorous dining rooms of a respectable hotel." But they finally stopped eating there, fearful of scandal. The place where they lived was next to a sausage factory, and the smell was so bad they opened the window only late at night. On leaving the library Lenin would buy two bars of nut chocolate in blue wrappers for fifteen centimes, and they would walk up into the mountains with their books to read awhile.

It was, Krupskaya remarked, "a quiet jog-trot life." By all external signs Lenin could not have been more isolated—and the isolation was not entirely physical. It was of his own making. He was, as never before, absorbed with exile existence, interesting himself more and more in the French left-wing movement, trying *very* unsuccessfully to make a mark on Swiss left-wing thought (he was far too acerbic for the Swiss, who simply refused to listen to him), and attempting at second hand to have some voice in Scandinavian and American labor movements.

"Out there," Krupskaya commented, "the revolutionary struggle was mounting, life was seething, but it was all so far away."[53]

The story of Lenin is different only in detail from that of Trotsky and the others. Trotsky, too, went to Switzerland on the outbreak of war. He, too, plunged into the hectic émigré political life. Then he went to France as a war correspondent for *Kievskaya Mysl,* transferred his activities to *Nashe Slovo* and later to *Golos,* the voice of a conglomerate of left-wing Russians. Essentially Trotsky and his group (like Lenin and his) were talking to themselves. In due course, the chauvinistic French authorities, stimulated by the Russian Embassy, arrested Trotsky and decided to deport him.

And Stalin? He was still in deepest exile in Kureika, on the Arctic Circle. He spent a lot of time fishing and his luck was good. The natives were so impressed they thought he had magical powers. "Osip, thou knowest the word," they said.[54]

XXXI

"For Baby's Sake"

The Grand Duke Nikolai Mikhailovich was one of the more liberal relatives of the Czar (he was a first cousin of the Czar's father, Alexander III). A historian by profession although somewhat of an amateur, he was president of the Imperial Historical Association, and in a modest way he sought to persuade the Czar of the perils and difficulties facing the country. In June of 1916 he made a long journey to his properties in the south where he owned estates comprising six villages and seven colonies of Germans who had been settled there in the time of Alexander II after living for 150 years in Poland. The Germans, originally from Württemberg, were Mennonites opposed to war on religious grounds and not subjected to Russian military service. Nothing much had changed in their villages. Not so with the Russians. The Grand Duke gave the Czar a picture of the village of Grushevka, which had a population of 3,307 when war broke out. Of that total 829 men had been mobilized and 115 had been lost—10 killed, 34 wounded, and 71 missing or prisoners. There had been more than 500 petitions from relatives of men in service, mostly for pensions and aid. To make up for the lost manpower the Grand Duke had obtained 947 Austrian prisoners (mostly Czechs) as well as 36 ordinary prisoners released from jail for farm work.

The question in the Grand Duke's mind was a simple one: Would it be possible to get the crop—it was a very excellent one of wheat—harvested and to market?[1]

This was, to be sure, the heart of the matter. More than 10 million peasants[2] had been taken off the land—most of them the best workers —and sent into the Army, where month by month their bodies piled up in the mountainous casualties at the front. The sown areas of Russia, in consequence, had been cut back by 25 to 30 per cent.[3]

What the Grand Duke's careful report to Nicholas revealed was that the life of a very productive Russian peasant village, in one of the finest grain-producing regions, had been savagely disrupted. Nearly one third of the village manpower had been removed. The women, children, and indifferent war prisoners now working the fields hardly made good the loss.

The Russian gendarmerie, whose reports on the political mood of the country were remarkably accurate, had begun to warn of difficulty in the countryside. All through 1916 these warnings were repeated. "The villages are now going through a most serious moment," one Moscow report said. "For the first time in Russian history the antagonism between the city and the village is clearly seen." The feeling in the countryside, said the police, was sharply opposed not only to the Government but also to "all other [nonvillage] classes—workers, officials, priests and so forth." Another police observer compared the mood of the peasants to that of 1906–7.[4]

At the root of the food crisis was the transport crisis. In 1916 the country had grain reserves as of mid-July of 402.2 million poods despite the heavy military needs. But there was virtually no way of getting the grain from the country to the city. About one third of Russian rolling stock had been commandeered for military use, and nearly half the remainder was being used to bring supplies up from the rear. The heavy equipment losses in the Galicia defeat made matters worse. The volume of grain moved by rail (except for military supplies) dropped to 65 per cent of the prewar level. Many mills were left without grain to turn into flour or fuel to power the mills. Petrograd required 4,000 cars of supplies a day. Deliveries fell to 2,800 a day in the first half of 1916.

Speculation ran riot. Every kind of dealer from large wholesaler to small shopkeeper began to hoard goods to benefit by the dramatic rise in prices. Enormous quantities of sugar, salt, and other commodities were held in Petrograd and Moscow warehouses in the winter of 1916 but not offered for sale. For example, more than 1 million poods of sugar were held in the warehouses of the Vindava-Rybinsk railroad. One Tambov mill was found in September 1916 to be hoarding enough flour to feed the town for a whole year. In 1915 no fewer than 23,000 fines totaling 3 million rubles were levied on merchants for illegal price rises. The financial paper *Birzhevye Vedomosti* reported from Nizhni Novgorod: "In Nizhni Novgorod what is going on is not just a bacchanalia but to speak bluntly—simple guzzling. The sharks are working their gigantic jaws. It is a shameful all-Russian spectacle which carries the brand of the all-Russian merchant class." Again and again officials reported: "The situation is critical," "The situation is alarming."[5] By July 1916 meat prices had risen 332 per cent of prewar, butter to 220 per cent, and flour to 265 per cent. Inflation was rampant. Industrial wages had risen to 142 per cent of prewar but their value in gold rubles had fallen to 69.8 per cent. In the metallurgical industry average monthly wages were 78.6 rubles but their buying power was only 38.7 rubles. Rents in Petrograd were up to 200 to 300 per cent.[6]

How did the people feel? A friend of Prince Andrei Vladimirovich's said that his coachman in Moscow told him that all Russia knew that the generals were traitors—otherwise Russian troops long since would have been in Berlin. Until the end of the war they were going to sit quietly. Then they would settle accounts with the traitors and enemies of the fatherland.[7]

Alexander Dmitriyevich Protopopov was one of the dubious reeds on whom the Czar came to lean in the closing days of Empire. He was a friend of the Mongolian doctor-speculator Zhimsaryan Badmayev's,[8] a protégé of Rasputin, a member of the Duma, and had a certain reputation for political ability. His personality was somewhat more attractive than that of most of the politicians called into the Czar's service in the last years of the reign.[9] Because he was a Duma man, there even seemed a chance that he might bridge the gap between the throne and parliament when in 1916 he was named to the Interior Ministry. This did not work out. Protopopov was an ambitious and sometimes engaging schemer but he did nothing to turn the fatal tide. He left one legacy—a remarkably clear evaluation, after the event, of what went wrong. Testifying in 1917 before the Provisional Government's Extraordinary Investigating Commission, he said:

"In the winter of 1916 there lay under the snowdrifts 60,000 railroad cars filled with fuel, food and forage. The draft had emptied the villages of people and halted agricultural processing industries. The profound shortage of labor was met by the use of prisoners and the contract labor of Persians and Chinese. Their distribution was accidental, without plan and with no particular accounting. . . ."

The general harvest of grain in Russia, he noted, was large enough to more than meet the demands of the troops and the population (because it was no longer possible to export wheat), but distribution was so complicated and so inefficient that it produced local famine, huge rises in the cost of living, and general dissatisfaction.

No one was able to make things work right.

"The Supreme Power ceased to be a source of life and light," he said. "It became the prisoner of stupid influences and stupid forces. It could not get things going. Stupidities were not exposed, mistakes were not brought to view, and the work did not get on. Yet life raced ahead—it demanded answers. But it was impossible to pour new wine into the old skin."

The system, he said, was at odds with itself. The Government made a mistake, the Duma a second, the Government a third, until the catastrophe threatened.

"All levels of the population were dissatisfied," he said. "To many it seemed that only the village was rich but goods did not reach the village, there was nothing there and the village didn't send on its grain. It even, it was said, concealed the grain. But the village without men, husbands, brothers, sons and even young boys, was equally unfortunate. The cities starved, trade was destroyed. The natural way of establishing prices—competition—did not exist. There was little goods; prices rose. . . . Art, literature, academic work was oppressed, workers in industry were turned into soldiers and soldiers into workers. The army was worn out, shortages of everything sent its spirit down and this did not lead to victory. . . .

"No one was happy. The former Czar felt this instinctively."[10]

The Czar did feel it instinctively. He felt it instinctively, and on every side the problems of his country pressed in on him. What was he to do? Hang Guchkov, one of the most perceptive of the new industrial entrepreneurs, as the Czarina kept suggesting? But Guchkov was a leader of the Military Industrial Committee, which was keeping supplies moving to the armies.[11] Shut Guchkov up as Rasputin kept proposing to the Czarina?[12] Or, perhaps, as the Czarina hinted, "a strong railroad accident" would take care of Guchkov.[13] But it was only with the help of the Guchkovs that munitions and arms were being provided to the troops. Should the Czar "smack" the Petrograd Municipal Council (as the Empress recommended) in order to get them to "mind their own business" (taking care of food, fuel, the wounded, etc.) instead of criticizing the Government?[14] Or should he act on the vision of "our Friend" (Rasputin) who one night, Alexandra reported, brought a solution for the food problem. It was a simple one. For three days only trains carrying supplies of flour, butter, and sugar were to move on the railroads. It would, Rasputin calculated, take "forty old soldiers" only an hour or so to load a train and the trains could be directed one after another, principally to Petrograd and Moscow, and "in three days one could bring enough for very many months." Of course, "people will scream and say it's impossible."[15]

The scarcities increased in Moscow and the Czarina warned that even for the rich people "it is hard living."[16] The worry about food and supplies grew as 1916 progressed. Even though "our Friend" tried to assuage the Czar's concern in September with the assurance that "things will arrange themselves," they did not arrange themselves. Through the autumn of 1916 the question of food never left the mind of the Czar nor that of his constant correspondent, the Czarina. It was the single subject most often referred to in letter after letter.[17]

Then there was the eternal question of the Czarevich—his illness—and specifically of preserving his inheritance, the Russian throne. "Life," as the Czarina said, "is a riddle, the future hidden behind a curtain."[18] The essence of the problem, as she told her husband was:

"For Baby's sake we must be firm as otherwise his inheritance will be awful as with his caracter [sic] he wont bow down to others but be his own master, as one must in Russia whilst people are still so uneducated—Mr. Philippe and Gregory said so too—."[19]

Baby, the son and heir, was at the center of the Imperial lives and Imperial concerns. He was now, for the most part, staying with his father at Czar's Stavka.[20] His mother worried every day for him. "We must give a strong country to Baby & dare not be weak for his sake."[21] And over him—his spelling ("is of course queer"[22]), his prayers ("pleas Deary" see that he says them properly[23]), his requests for money ("I have no more money, beg you to send the allowance—I entreat [it's me]"[24]) and family jokes ("Bad Boy wrote today: Papa made smells much and long this morning. Too noughty [sic]"[25]).

There were a wife's worries. Faithfully she reported to Nicholas on her menstrual periods ("Becker came to Tatiana and me today, so kind before time, will be all the better for journey." "Shall come to you and leave Becker behind!"[26] "Becker has just come."[27] "The engineer-mechanic came."[28] When her period coincided with her visits to Czar's Stavka or Nicholas' rare trips back to Tsarskoye Selo, she did not conceal her distress. The physical love of the Imperial couple was strong and vigorous. ("Four months we have not slept together—even more."[29]) In September 1916 Alix was furious at a rumor that Gen. A. N. Grabbe, chief of the Imperial Cossack convoy, was planning to introduce a certain Madame Soldatenko to Nicholas "so as to get you acquainted with her & that she might become yr mistress." Grabbe, moreover, was providing the Czar with what the Czarina called "those exciting books."[30]

Intertwined with these worries were the worries about the war (nothing really important happened from the time the Czar took over in August 1915 all through 1916 and early 1917—the Germans were too heavily engaged in the West to mount major operations in the

East and the operations of the Russians caused heavy casualties but no fundamental change), the worries about Rasputin (in letter after letter after letter the Czarina gave the Czar Rasputin's "advice," complained of attacks upon him, recommended the change of this official or that one consistent with their support or friendship for Rasputin), and always the worry about revolution.

Never was revolution far from the Imperial minds. The war was hardly a year old when "Aunt Olga," the Dowager Queen of Greece, went running to the Czar's uncle, Pavel Alexandrovich, with her fear that revolution had already begun, that the streets would run red with blood and all of the royalty be slaughtered. The Czarina quieted Aunt Olga. But the specter did not vanish.[31] There were recurrent rumors, so the Czarina was told, that Nikolasha, the Grand Duke Nikolai Nikolayevich, would try to take the throne by a coup d'état. As early as 1915 she heard gossip that she, the Empress, was to be shut up in a convent.[32] The rumors increased as months went by.

When all was said and done, as the Empress put it: "I am but a woman fighting for her Master & Child, her two dearest ones on earth —& God will help me being your guardian angel, only dont pull the sticks away upon wh I have found it possible to rest."[33]

The Czar responded thoughtfully, tenderly (and, rarely, a bit irritated at her hysteria), and methodically followed almost every direction he received from her and through her from Rasputin. At times the Empress forwarded an agenda for the Czar to use in his meeting with Ministers ("you may forget something—& so act as your living notebook." "Keep this paper before you."[34]).

On December 31, 1915, the Czarina had written her husband for the last time in that year. For 1916 she wished him victory on the battlefield and "interior calm—to crush these effervescing elements who try to ruin the country and give you endless worry."[35]

At the identical moment the Czar was writing the Czarina his last letter for 1915. He thanked her for her love, her support, and help. Without her he did not know how he could have carried his burdens. He had had trouble getting to sleep the night before but fell to reading a new book, *Girl Millionaire*, the first English novel he had read in a long time. It was, he said, "extraordinarily interesting and quieted the brain." The temperature in the morning, he faithfully reported, was ten degrees centigrade.[36]

XXXII

The Dance Macabre

In the autumn of 1916 there was a particular heaviness in the atmosphere, an especially intense feeling, Zinaida Gippius thought, "of pregnancy." Many persons came to visit her and Dmitri Merezhkovsky. Among them Kerensky, other Duma members and persons connected in one way or another with the SRs with whom the Merezhkovskys had been so close in Paris. The question which concerned them all was revolution. Gippius noted in her diary: "It will come. But will it be the revolution or some monstrosity with an unknown name?"[1] No one any longer doubted that there would be a revolution. What kind and when—those were questions too terrible to think of. The Government was moving ahead in an unbelievable manner, she felt. There was a certain calm despair about everything it did. No one understood what was happening in the war. The Germans overran Romania. There were not enough bullets. Sugar went on the ration. There were, it was said, disorders in Moscow. Merezhkovsky's play *The Romantics* was presented at the Alexandrinsky Theater. What difference did it make? Gippius asked herself. Rasputin changed the Czar's Ministers at his every whim. Between autumn 1915 and autumn 1916 there were five Ministers of the Interior, three Ministers of War, and four Ministers of Agriculture.[2] Now it was Stürmer in the premiership. There were strikes in seventeen factories. The troops seemed to care nothing about suppressing them. People were dying like grass, dropping like dandelion puffs—the young, the old, children—it made no difference.

The stupid and the wise. Everyone, she thought, was stupid—the honest and the thieves together. And everyone, after all, was a thief —or simply insane.[3] Russia was a vast insane asylum. If some evening you were to find yourself in the main hall of a mental institution, you would not understand it. You would not understand anything. Everyone was crazy, only some were confined and some were not.[4]

Among the Imperial family none had longer and more consistently been concerned at the course of events than the Dowager Empress, Mariya Fyodorovna. As far back as 1912 when Rodzyanko was preparing his famous report on Rasputin for the Czar, the Dowager Empress had summoned him to learn what he had discovered. She told Rodzyanko that "unfortunately he [the Emperor] will not believe you and it will give him much pain. His heart is so pure he is not capable of believing such bad things." But later Rodzyanko heard from Prince Yusupov that Mariya Fyodorovna had gone to Nicholas and told him: "Either me or Rasputin," that is, that she would leave unless Rasputin was dismissed. He was not and the Dowager Empress quit St. Petersburg and took up residence in Kiev.[5] She talked frankly with Premier Kokovtsov in those days of her fears for her son, for the dynasty, of her concern about the influence of the Czarina. She had begged Kokovtsov to use any opportunity to convey his warnings to Nicholas. But since leaving the premiership Kokovtsov had not even seen the Emperor. He held nothing but minor posts. All through 1916 he heard more and more talk in government and political circles of the "dark forces" gathering about the throne. But he was helpless to intervene.[6] The industrialist A. I. Putilov said: "We're headed for anarchy. The Russian is not a revolutionary. He is an anarchist. There is a world of difference. The revolutionary means to reconstruct; the anarchist thinks only of destroying."[7]

When Nicholas made himself commander in chief, his mother was in despair. Grand Duke Andrei Vladimirovich visited her—"Aunt Minny"—at her residence on Yelagin Island. He found her shaken. She believed that the removal of Grand Duke Nikolai Nikolayevich would lead directly to the downfall of her son. She blamed Alix for the whole thing. The Dowager Empress had begged her son not to become commander in chief, but he insisted that it was his duty, to save Russia. She argued that he was poorly prepared to lead the Army and that the business of the state demanded his presence in Petrograd. The Czar was not moved. "Where are we going, where are we going?" Aunt Minny asked Andrei. "This is not Nicky, not him. He is gentle and honest and good—it is all her." The Dowager said that Uncle Alex, that is Prince Alexander of Oldenburg, had begged her to keep Nicholas from taking command of the Army. He predicted the most terrible consequences. He fell into such despair, Aunt Minny said, that he rolled on the floor.[8]

Now, for the first time in many months, the Czar paid a visit to Kiev to see his mother. The last time he had gone there the Czarina warned him that "when you see poor Motherdear, you must rather sharply tell her how pained you are, that she listens to slander and does not stop it, as it makes mischief."[9] This time the Czarina gave him no written advice, possibly because he was going directly from Tsarskoye Selo.

The meeting may have been the most important which the Czar held in the months before the final disaster. It concerned the Czarina and Rasputin and all the other "dark forces" gathered around the throne.[10] The full content of these discussions in which Grand Duke Alexander Mikhailovich, Grand Duke Pavel Alexandrovich, and the Grand Duchess Mariya Pavlovna also participated has never been recorded. They lasted two days and, in the words of Pierre Gilliard, the Czarevich's tutor who accompanied the Emperor, the Imperial family did its utmost to convince the Czar of the total gravity of the situation and the need for energetic measures.[11]

"The Czar was greatly influenced by the advice which was given him," Gilliard reported. "He had never seemed to me so worried before. He was usually very self-controlled but on this occasion he showed himself nervous and irritable, and once or twice he spoke roughly to Alexei Nikolayevich [the Czarevich]."[12]

The Czar was back at Mogilev, where General Alexeyev, the chief of staff, was methodically handling the day-by-day conduct of the war, in time to receive another Imperial vistior, the stately and solemn historical Grand Duke Nikolai Mikhailovich. The Grand Duke was so nervous the Czar several times had to provide a light for the Grand Duke's cigarette.[13] He spent a couple of hours with his eminent relative talking on general matters but apparently never mentioned the subject which was in the forefront of his mind—the gathering Imperial crisis. At the end of his interview he handed the Czar a three-page letter in which he warned the Czar that he stood on the brink of a new era of troubles, a time of attempts at his overthrow. He said that only the promptest and firmest action could save the dynasty. The Czar must, the Grand Duke insisted, end the use of his wife as an avenue of influence and a means of imposing decisions. "You have confidence in Alexandra Fyodorovna," he wrote. "That is completely natural. Nonetheless, what she tells you is not the truth. She is only repeating what has been cleverly suggested to her. If you cannot remove these influences from her at least protect yourself from these constant and systematic maneuvers which are being made through the intermediary of the wife whom you love."

The solution, said the Grand Duke, was to establish a responsible government, a ministerial cabinet, and a genuine legislature. He warned against the "occult forces" which constantly intervened in affairs of state and assured the Czar that he spoke not from personal motives but only that Nicholas might "free himself from the chains which had been forged," and "to save your throne and our dear country from the irreparable."[14] The Czar sent the letter unread to his wife, who responded: "I read Nikolai's & am utterly disgusted. Had you stopped him in the middle of his talk & told him that, if he only once more touched that subject or me, you will send him to Siberia—as it becomes next to high treason. He has always hated & spoken badly of me since 22 years . . . at such a time to crawl behind yr Mama & Sisters & not stick up bravely (agreeing or not) for his Emperor's Wife is loathsome & treachery. . . . He & Nikolasha are my greatest enemies in the family, not counting the black women [the Montenegrin princesses Anastasia and Militsa]—& Sergei [Grand Duke Sergei Mikhailovich]."[15]

The ink was not dry on her letter when Nikolasha, the bête noire of the Empress, arrived at Mogilev to try his hand with the Czar. The Czarina had forebodings about her enemy's visit. "I don't like Nikol going to the H.Q.—may be brood [sic] no evil with his people. Don't allow him to go anywhere now, but streight [sic] back to the Caucasus—the revol. party else will hail him again."[16]

Nikolasha spent November 7–8 with the Czar. Perhaps, learning a lesson from his experience with Nikolai Mikhailovich, the Czar did not follow his usual custom—he gave his wife no account whatever of the contents of his conversation.[17] This was probably just as well. Nikolasha didn't mince words, as he later told the Grand Duke Andrei Vladimirovich. His conversation, he said, was sharp. "I wanted to get a rise out of him," the Grand Duke said. "But he just sat silent and shrugged his shoulders. I told him directly: 'I would be more pleased if you swore at me, struck me, kicked me out than at your silence. Can't you see that you are losing your crown? Collect yourself while it's not too late. Give a responsible ministry. As long ago as last June I spoke to you about this. You just procrastinate. For the moment there is still time but soon it will be too late.'"

The Grand Duke accused the Czar of believing he wanted to take away the throne. "Shame on you, Nicky," he said.

"In such a spirit I spoke," said the Grand Duke sadly. "But he sat silent."

When the conversation ended, the Grand Duke felt that it was all over—that there was no hope of saving his nephew.

"It was clear," he told Andrei, "that we were rolling quickly down a slippery incline and that sooner or later he would lose his crown."[18] The Czar's only comment on the talks to the Empress was "all conversations have passed off well."[19]

Within the week—on November 11—the Czar had a letter from another Grand Duke—Georgi Mikhailovich, brother of Nikolai the historian. Georgi wrote after visiting the headquarters of General Brusilov. He reported that "the hatred for Stürmer" in the Army was extreme and said the only remedy was the dismissal of Stürmer and "the formation of a responsible Ministry to protect you against the deceptions of the ministers."

"This measure," he added, "is considered the only one susceptible of avoiding a general catastrophe. The voice of the people is the voice of God and I am sure that the Savior will help you to meet the universal wish and prevent the imminent storm which arises from the interior of Russia."[20]

Yet another Grand Duke joined in the chorus. He was the Grand Duke Mikhail Mikhailovich, resident in England. November 15 he sent the Czar a letter from London reporting that King George V was concerned over the Russian political situation and that intelligence quarters were predicting a revolution. He expressed hope Nicholas would be able to "satisfy the just demands of our people before it is too late."[21]

The members of the Imperial family were not the only ones who sought in these days to turn the Czar from his fatal course. The English ambassador, Sir George Buchanan, spoke with the Czar in late October. He had been urged by two members of the Imperial family to raise the question of Stürmer with the Czar but he felt this was impolitic. Instead, he spoke of the food shortages, the rising discontent, the habit of the Government of trying to solve every situation with force, and, most alarming, the reports of British consuls scattered around the country indicating the peasantry was beginning to lose faith in the Emperor and the aristocracy. The Czar did not seem very pleased with the ambassador's remarks.[22]

And finally, a very Russian, almost mystical representation was made to Nicholas.

Some time shortly after Nicholas was crowned his attention was accidentally drawn to a petty *chinovnik* (bureaucrat) named A. A. Klopov. Nicholas vested in Klopov the right to communicate directly with him, passing on any personal information he had about the mood of the country. Klopov made wide use of this right, particularly after the outbreak of World War I. He had an audience with the Czar at Czar's Stavka in mid-October. In preparation for this he was supposed to meet with the chief of staff, General Alexeyev,[23] who was eager to get Klopov to urge the Czar to get rid of Stürmer. Alexeyev was ill so Prince Lvov acted as an intermediary between Alexeyev and Klopov. Klopov visited the Crimea before meeting with the Czar and probably conferred with some of the Grand Dukes there. He also went to Kiev and had a talk with the Dowager Empress. The content of Klopov's meeting with the Czar is not known, but in late October he submitted to Nicholas a memorandum in which he urged the Czar to agree to the creation of a ministry composed of persons having the confidence of the Duma. The memorandum had been edited and approved by the Grand Duke Nikolai Mikhailovich. Klopov also seems to have sent the Czar a rescript drafted by General Alexeyev for the establishment of a government formed of both official and private political figures united "in a single understanding of the tasks which face Russia and with the capability of working with the Duma majority."[24]

The Duma convened on November 1 and the proceedings shook Russia to its foundations. Pavel Milyukov, leader of the great Kadet party, a center conservative by any reckoning but that of the Czar or his police, delivered the most memorable speech which was to be heard in the brief and unhappy life of Russia's young parliament. He attacked the Government, reciting a series of charges (not all of them true or accurate).[25] After each declaration he paused dramatically, then said: "What is this—stupidity or treason?" By reading a passage in German, culled from the *Neue Freie Presse* of Vienna, Milyukov even managed to introduce the name of the Empress and those of Rasputin and her other associates.[26]

The speech was suppressed by the censorship but circulated in millions of typewritten and duplicated copies, selling for a ruble and more each.[27]

The aim of Milyukov's speech was clear to almost everyone who heard it. He believed the end of the dynasty was at hand and he hoped to place his Kadet party in a position to take power when it fell from the feeble hands of Nicholas. In a letter to his fellow Kadet, Ivan Petrunkevich, in 1919 he said: "I thought that once the moment of revolution was inescapable—and I believed it already was inescapable —I must attempt to take it into my hands."[28]

The Revolution was inescapable. So it seemed to almost everyone. After Milyukov's speech Zinaida Gippius wrote in her diary that the Russians had no inner understanding of time.

"It is too early for revolution (but, of course) and too late for reform (without doubt)"—so she wrote. Long since the country had been alienated from the war by the weariness, the terrible disorder and chaos of the rear. It was threatening.

"Yes, threatening," she wrote. "And if we do nothing—it will be done by 'something.' And the face of that something is dark."

Then she and her husband hurried off to a spa in the Caucasus far from tumescent Petrograd.

There was one more speech to come—then the curtain would go up on the last act. This was the speech of Vladimir Purishkevich, as staunch a reactionary as the Duma boasted, a hater of Jews, an enemy of liberals, a member of the extreme right, a man dedicated to the monarchy, to the divine right of kings, to the Russian autocracy. He had dined with the Czar at Mogilev on November 3 where he was invited to give Nicholas a report on his visit to the Romanian front. He found the Czar's staff in ferment. One after the other, the Grand Dukes and the generals approached him. "Tell him about Stürmer. Point out the pernicious role of Rasputin. Don't spare the colors. The Czar believes you and your word may make an impression on him."

Purishkevich did speak to the Czar—whether as openly as the Czar's couriers wished is not known—but he did compare the cabinet to "caliphs of the hour" and called the Ministers bankrupt and ungifted men.[29] He also called the men surrounding the Czar at headquarters cowards for not speaking up themselves.

Now on November 19 he rose in the Duma. He was, he said, a man of the right. He could not leave the ranks of the right. But there came a moment when it was necessary to speak out—not as a belfry might in some provincial town but like the peal of the Ivan the Great bell in the Kremlin. He spoke, he said, with boundless love for the Crown and firm dedication to his Czar. "All these evils stem from those dark forces, from those influences . . . which are headed by Grishka Rasputin," he said, naming by name Alexander Protopopov, Prince Mikhail M. Andronikov, and other scoundrels who had gathered around the throne. He called on the Ministers to place duty above career, to make their way to Mogilev, throw themselves at the feet of the Czar, and tell him: "It is impossible to go further." "Go on your knees," he said, "and beg leave to open the eyes of the Czar to the terrible reality."[30]

The press was filled with attacks on the Government. Rumors flew that on the Emperor's name day, December 6, a new and responsible government would be formed.* These rumors were false.[31] The Czar had dropped Stürmer November 9 and replaced him with another nonentity, G. F. Trepov, Minister of Communications. But in the face

---

* Grand Duke Pavel, the Czar's uncle, husband of Princess Olga Paley, saw the Czar and Czarina at tea December 3 and urged the Czar to grant a constitution on his name day. The Czar refused. (Princess Paley, Souvenirs de Russie.)

of a hurricane of invective, hysteria, begging, wheedling, meddling, caviling by the Czarina,* nothing was done about Protopopov—in fact, nothing of consequence whatever was done by the Czar.

"Why do people hate me?" ran the Czarina's litany. "Because they know I have a strong will & when am convinced of a thing being right (when besides blessed by Gregory) do not change my mind & that they can't bear. Remember Mr. Phillips words when he gave me the image with the bell. . . . I was to be yr bell, & I wd warn you."[32]

"A country where a man of God helps the Sovereign will never be lost."[33]

"Lovy, do you want me to come for a day to give you courage & firmness? Be the master."[34]

"Be firm, I your wall am behind you & wont give way—I know He leads us right. . . . Only out of love which you bear for me & Baby—take no big steps without warning me and speaking over all quietly."

"Russia loves to feel the whip—it's their nature—tender love & then the iron hand to punish & guide—How I wish I could pour my will into your veins."[35]

The Empress was deaf to all pleas. Her sainted sister, Elizabeth Fyodorovna, widow of the Grand Duke Sergei, came to Tsarskoye Selo December 3. "Remember the fate of Louis XVI and Marie Antoinette," she said. The Empress ordered her sister to leave Petrograd by the first available train.[36]

The Czarina reached a climax in a letter she sent off from Tsarskoye Selo December 14. She had already won her battle. The Czar, as usual, was doing nothing. But she could not be sure and her bugaboo Nikolasha was visiting the Czar again—or so she heard—and she was frightened. "Keep him away, evil genius," she warned adding: "Be Peter the Great, John the Terrible, Emperor Paul—crush them all under you—now don't you laugh noughty [sic] one."[37]

The Empress' victory was, alas, her most terrible defeat. Russia was not only moving down that slippery slope, but it was accelerating with a momentum which could no longer be reversed—not by the Czarina's wild hysteria, not by Rasputin's peasant cunning, not by the scheming of the cheap politicians who made up the Imperial coterie. No one could halt the events under way. Nor could anyone predict their outcome.

* In this period Rasputin met with the Empress almost daily, as did Protopopov. (V. S. Dyakin, *Russkaya Burzhuasiya i Tsarism v gody Pervoi Mirovoi Voiny 1914–17*, p. 246.)

"How terrible it is to have an autocracy without an autocrat," commented Shulgin.[38]

Now, he said, they were dancing on the summits of the nation, an awful dance macabre. It had begun with a *grand rond*, or better speaking, a vicious circle, and now it was moving through the capital from palace to cathedral, from cathedral to dive and back again. The dance was moving from the capital into the depths of Russia and closer, closer, closer to the throne.[39]

XXXIII

Russian Blood

Sitting in the gallery of the white-columned chamber of the Tauride Palace, listening as Purishkevich read his indictment of Rasputin was, among others, Prince Felix Yusupov, the brightest flower of the decadent society which flourished in the feverish salons of wartime Petrograd. The Prince was twenty-nine years old, son of one of the richest and most noble families in Russia. He was a member of the court, part of its inner circle. His wife was the beautiful Princess Irena, daughter of the Grand Duke Alexander Mikhailovich, one of the many Mikhailovichi, brother of Nikolai the historian. Irena was a favorite in the Imperial family, and the Empress herself was fond of her. The Empress was not so fond of the Prince, although for years he had been the best friend of the Grand Duke Dmitri Pavlovich. Dmitri was almost a son to the Czar and the Czarina. He lived with them. He traveled with them. His official residence was the Alexander Palace, but he was in and out of the personal quarters of the Imperial family constantly. In fact, it was said that the Czar and Czarina thought of him as a possible husband for their oldest daughter, Olga. Dmitri was a cousin of the Czar's, but he called Nicholas "Uncle" and Alexandra "Auntie." There was no other member of the vast Romanov family with whom the Imperial couple was on closer terms, terms of warm affection.

The relationship of Prince Felix and Grand Duke Dmitri (three years younger than Felix) was a worry to the Czarina. For several years the young men had been virtually inseparable, and the Czarina was convinced that Felix was a bad influence, so much so that on several occasions the two had been forbidden to see each other. Naturally, these rules and regulations broke down.

One source of the Czarina's concern was the fact that from adolescence Felix' favorite amusement had been to dress up as a woman. His first experiment in transvestism occurred when he was still a schoolboy. In his schoolboy's uniform he was not permitted to visit night clubs or cabarets. Polya, the mistress of his older brother, Nikolai, dressed him in her clothes so that he could go with them to a gypsy cabaret.[1] Polya's clothes fitted Yusupov perfectly and from then on he spent many evenings in drag, sometimes with his brother and Polya, sometimes with others. When he and his brother went to Paris they often repeated the experiment. One night at the Théâtre des Capucines, Yusupov, to his delight, was ogled by King Edward VII. Later Felix got an engagement to sing at a Petersburg cabaret, the Aquarium. He sang six times (in drag) before being recognized by some friends of his mother's who spotted the family jewelry he was wearing.

A suitable scandal ensued but Felix could not be turned from his escapades. After appearing at a fancy dress ball at the Opéra in sequin dress, diamond star in his blond wig, and a sable cape, he let himself be picked up by four Guards officers who took him off to the Bear, a favorite St. Petersburg night club. To escape the amorous attentions of the officers—or so he said—Yusupov broke a bottle of champagne in a mirror, switched off the lights, and fled through the wintry St. Petersburg streets in décolleté and an open sleigh.

There were continuous rows with his family. Years later, Yusupov explained that he was not much attracted to women, although he professed to have had numerous love affairs. He denied in his memoirs that he disliked women. He had seen very few who met his ideal. "Generally speaking," he said, "I have found among men the loyalty and disinterestedness which I think most women lack."[2]

The Prince got to know and admire Anna Pavlova, the dancer, who once told him that "You have God in one eye and the devil in the other."[3]

There had been substantial family objections to the marriage of Felix to the beautiful Irena because of the constantly expanding catalogue of rumor and gossip surrounding him. Finally, however, the couple was married on the eve of the war. The Grand Duke Dmitri was Felix' unsuccessful rival for Irena's hand.

It was this unlikely actor on the center stage of the Russian drama who on November 21, 1916, at 9 A.M. appeared in Purishkevich's flat, dressed in the uniform of a member of the Corps of Pages, olive drab with a high Pershing collar and a white Sam Browne belt.

He was a tall, slender, darkly handsome young man, and Purishkevich, a bald bearded man with pince-nez, was immediately drawn to him. He saw in him a young man of will and character, qualities which he found rare among the Russian artistocracy.[4] The two talked for two hours.

"*Chto zhe delat?*—what shall we do?—"asked Purishkevich, repeating that eternal question which Russians had been asking each other now for a century.

Prince Yusupov smiled, looked Purishkevich straight in the eye, and without blinking said: "Remove Rasputin."

"That's easy to say," Purishkevich responded, "but who will undertake it when there are no resolute people in Russia and the Government which might undertake this itself and do it skillfully supports Rasputin and protects him like the apple of its eye."

"Yes," replied Yusupov. "There is no use counting on the Government. But in Russia such people can be found."

"You think so?" Purishkevich said.

"I am confident," responded Yusupov. "And one of them stands before you."

The two men shook hands and the plot was under way.[5] The truth was that Purishkevich had long since sworn to do away with Rasputin. As early as 1912 when Rodzyanko was investigating the Rasputin scandals Purishkevich had said: "I would give my life to kill this canaille Rasputin."[6] Purishkevich was a devout Orthodox believer. He felt Rasputin was not only destroying the monarchy but also the Russian Orthodox Church.

The motivation of Prince Yusupov was, perhaps, more complex. He had met Rasputin in 1909 through Mariya (Munya) Golovin,[7] a young girl of strongly religious bent, a member of the Imperial circle and a devout follower of Rasputin. She was now serving him in the capacity of a secretary. Most of her days were spent at the Rasputin residence.

According to Yusupov he began to think about assassinating Rasputin some time in 1915 and in the autumn of 1916 deliberately cultivated a friendship with Rasputin through Mlle Golovin.[8] Rasputin seems to have taken to Felix from the start. The young man had made an excuse of having a pain in his chest and Rasputin, according to Felix, hypnotized him. He felt numb. Rasputin's eyes glowed like "two phosphorescent beams of light melting into a great luminous ring." When Felix emerged from hypnosis, Rasputin began to talk about getting him an appointment in the Government, probably a cabinet post, but Felix objected that he was too young and inexperienced.[9] Rasputin then, or so Yusupov insisted, told how he employed some of the "herb medicines" of Badmayev to treat the Czar. They were given in "a tea which causes divine grace to descend on him. His heart is filled with peace, everything looks good and cheerful to him."[10]*

How often Felix met with Rasputin is not certain. He told his friends there had been numerous meetings. Mlle. Golovin testified there were only two, each lasting less than an hour at the end of November or early in December.[11]

Before going to Purishkevich Yusupov had called on Vasily Maklakov, a liberal Duma member who had also spoken against Rasputin. Maklakov was wary of any plot. He doubted that Rasputin was the real problem—rather, just a symptom. Nor did he take Yusupov seriously.[12] The "elimination" of Rasputin was a favorite subject in Petrograd drawing rooms.

It was after Maklakov's refusal that the Prince approached Purishkevich. By the evening of their first encounter the Prince and Purishkevich were actively discussing details with the Grand Duke Dmitri and Captain Sukhotin, a friend of Yusupov's and a member of the Preobrazhensky Regiment.

A plan was quickly agreed upon. Yusupov's beautiful wife, Irena, was in the Crimea visiting her parents. The Prince had already spoken to Rasputin, using Irena as a lure to invite the starets to his residence on the Moika. Rasputin had agreed to come, provided the evening chosen was not one when he had to wait upon the Empress at Tsarskoye Selo.

The conspirators agreed that Rasputin should be lured to the Yusupov Palace and murdered there. Because a police station was located across the street, at No. 61, they decided to use poison rather than a gun which might attract attention. Purishkevich proposed bringing a doctor, S. S. Lazavert, into the plan.

The conspirators decided that Yusupov would go to Rasputin's residence and escort him to the Yusupov home in a car chauffeured by Captain Sukhotin. The monk would be poisoned with a dose of cyanide of potassium provided by Dr. Lazavert. His clothes would be bundled up and burned on a hospital train Purishkevich sponsored.

---

* Rumors that Rasputin employed drugs to strengthen his control over the Imperial couple were common in Petrograd. (Princess Cantacuzene, *Revolutionary Days*, pp. 92, 188.) No real substantiation of the rumors has turned up, but some of the Grand Dukes were convinced the rumors were true. Yusupov quoted Rasputin as urging him to try the herb concoction of Badmayev. "You drink the infusion," Rasputin said, "when your soul is troubled and within the hour it all seems like nonsense and you become so genial and stupid that nothing makes any difference." (V. M. Purishkevich, *Dnevnik*, p. 177.) The words remarkably fit the Czar's frequent moods.

Dmitri's closed car would cart Rasputin's body to a branch of the Neva called the Staraya Nevka. There it would be attached to weights and sunk in the river. A telephone call was then to be made to the Villa Rode, Rasputin's favorite night club, asking if Rasputin had yet arrived. This was designed to throw the police off the track.[13]

The plan was a simple one, and with remarkably little discussion the scenario was arranged. The date depended on Rasputin. When he agreed to come to the Yusupov residence at 1 A.M. December 17 there was little more the conspirators had to do. Characteristically, Yusupov was intensely concerned about the setting for the murder. He brought in some workmen and redecorated a vaulted suite just below street level where he would receive Rasputin. He put down an expensive Persian carpet, placed three large red Chinese porcelain vases in niches hollowed in the walls, set around the room a number of oak chairs and small tables covered with antique embroidery. In the center he placed a Chinese cabinet of inlaid ebony—"a maze," as he described it, "of little mirrors, tiny bronze columns and secret drawers." On the chest was set a beautiful rock crystal and silver crucifix, a sixteenth-century Italian work, and on the big red granite fireplace there were golden bowls, majolica plates, and ivory sculptures.[14] The room was divided in two with a circular arch separating the chambers. The first was a dining room. The second, in the words of Purishkevich, was a "cross between a boudoir and drawing room." The Prince had laid a large white bearskin rug on the floor, placed low pillowed chairs and divans around the walls, and against the wall was a table on which the bottles of wine and cake, suitably flavored by Dr. Lazavert with cyanide, were to stand.[15]

Although the conspirators cautioned themselves to complete secrecy and agreed that all would deny participation in the crime (actually they told themselves that if all went well the fate of Rasputin would never be discovered), in reality they made virtually no attempt to disguise their intentions—in fact, spread them broadside. Purishkevich cornered Maklakov at the Duma and sitting down with him under a bust of Alexander II, tried to persuade him to join the conspiracy. Purishkevich said they needed more hands for the job, but more likely he wanted to broaden the political base of the plot—which now included only right-wing monarchists—by co-opting a leading member of the centrist Kadets. Maklakov again refused to join but promised to undertake the legal defense of the conspirators if they were arrested. To which Purishkevich sighed to himself: "A typical Kadet!"[16] Purishkevich also revealed his plans to Shulgin, whom he encountered in the Catherine Hall of the Tauride Palace. Shulgin was just leaving for Kiev: "Listen, Shulgin," he said—"remember December 16." "Why?"

asked Shulgin. "I'll tell you," he replied. "On the 16th we will kill him." "Whom?" "Grisha." Shulgin, like Maklakov, tried to persuade him the trouble lay deeper than Rasputin. Purishkevich would not listen.[17]

How many others Purishkevich may have spoken with is not known, but at least one Russian newspaperwoman named Becker got the whole story from him with names and even the date. Maklakov had kept Purishkevich's confidence, but when Miss Becker told him what she knew Maklakov decided to consult Kerensky. Kerensky was horrified. He felt the murder of Rasputin would only strengthen the monarchy.[18]

Yusupov was in constant correspondence with his mother, Princess Zinaida Yusupov, who with her husband was at the family estate of Koreiz, near Yalta. Yusupov's wife, Irena Alexandrovna, was with her parents.

Young Yusupov's mother was an open foe of Rasputin and the Czarina. Again and again she wrote her son that the only way to save Russia was to end the country's direction by Rasputin and the unhealthy influence of "Valide," the Yusupovs' code word for the Empress.

All during November and December Yusupov and his mother carried on a semiconspiratorial exchange in which Yusupov dropped deliberately vague hints of his plans, the meaning of which was clear after the event.

With his wife, Irena, the young Prince was open enough so that she was able to follow the drift of his conspiratorial words.

"I see that you are getting ready to do something wild," she wrote. "Please be careful and don't get into some dirty business."

Her principal concern was that Felix had decided to go ahead without her. That, she insisted, was "wild piggishness." She cautioned her husband to be careful, making clear that she understood what Yusupov planned and that they had often discussed Rasputin's removal.[19]

Yusupov's plot was not the first against Rasputin. Once Rasputin had almost been run down by a flying troika in Petersburg, undoubtedly the work of his ecclesiastical enemy, the Monk Illiodor. There had been the attempt of the young officers whom Rasputin stared down and, more serious than these, there had been a plot involving the police themselves only a year previously. The Interior Minister, Alexei Khvostov, who had come to power through Rasputin's influence, ambitiously decided to rid himself of Rasputin and go it alone. He enlisted two lieutenants, Deputy Minister S. P. Beletsky and Mikhail S. Komissarov, the officer in charge of Rasputin's security.

These men had been very close to Rasputin, and Beletsky and Komissarov were suspicious of Khvostov—they feared he wanted them to
get rid of Rasputin, then pin the blame on them. Khvostov had several
ideas for doing away with Rasputin. One was to arrange to have a
woman invite Rasputin to visit her. En route his car could slow down
in a narrow lane. A band of masked men would leap out, throw a
noose around his neck, smother his screams with a handkerchief, and
strangle him. Then his body would be thrown into the Neva (not far
from the point the new conspirators had picked).[20] There were other
versions of this plot—to give Rasputin poison (Khvostov bought some
poison and tried it out on two cats), to shoot him (for this purpose
Khvostov acquired a Browning and began to practice target shooting),[21] or to bribe him with 200,000 rubles to go away. His associates
professed to be shocked by Khvostov's conduct. Beletsky, a man with
buttery face and yellow hands, decided that he could not co-operate in
"turning the government into a Mafia."[22] Nothing came of these plans
(eventually all the men lost their jobs), but Rasputin was alarmed
and for the first time began to take threats to his life more seriously.

He was protected by the two, or possibly three, sets of police—ordinary police for his personal security, a special detachment of
plain-clothes men of the Interior Ministry who were supposed to keep
him constantly under observation, and probably secret agents of the
palace as well. Actually, as their daily reports disclosed, the police not
infrequently lost track of him, particularly late at night when he was
engaged in drunken brawls.[23]

On December 14, the day he last visited Tsarskoye Selo to meet in
Anna Vyrubova's famous "little house" with the Empress, Rasputin
went for a stroll in the Petrograd streets with Munya Golovin. It was a
cold snowy day. The walk was unusual, in the words of the Empress,
because "he never goes out since ages, except to come here." Rasputin
visited the Kazan Cathedral on the Nevsky and St. Isaac's with its
gilded dome, "& not one disagreeable look, people all quiet," the Empress reported to her husband with satisfaction. "Says in 3 or 4 days
things will go better in Roumania & all will go better."[24]

That was Rasputin's last walk.

With all the agitation in the Duma, the newspaper reports, the rumors and gossip flying through Petrograd, Rasputin had displayed
some nervousness. For the last month, according to Vyrubova, he had
feared for his safety and at the end of his last meeting with the Czar
had asked that the Emperor bless him, instead of making the sign of
the cross over Nicholas as was his custom.[25] Members of Rasputin's
circle were now very much on the alert for his safety. His friend Aron
Simanovich, the moneylender, jeweler, usurer, and gambling house

proprietor, was particularly concerned. Through underworld connections he heard rumors of a plot to take Rasputin's life. He got this information from employees of a gambling establishment he owned called the Firemen's Club. Some of his employees also worked at the nearby National Club and they brought him reports of private meetings in the club and talk among noblemen of a plot to kill Rasputin.

Simanovich warned of these rumors, but Rasputin brushed them away, saying: "The nobility is against me but they have no Russian blood. Their blood is mixed. They want me killed because they don't want a Russian muzhik around the Russian throne."[26]

On the sixteenth Rasputin talked to Simanovich about visiting "the youngster" but would not tell Simanovich who the youngster was. They argued and finally Simanovich left him some time during the evening. He claimed he had helped Rasputin to undress and locked his clothes, including his boots, fur hat, and fur coat, in the wardrobe.[27] Protopopov dropped in on Rasputin later that night, just before midnight. He had a bit of gossip for him. He had just come from the railroad station, seeing off Nadezhda Voskoboinikova, one of the Vyrubova circle. She was going to her daughter's side because the daughter's husband had just shot himself.[28] Protopopov stayed ten minutes and Rasputin personally showed him to the door.

Rasputin's two daughters, Mariya (sometimes called Matryona) and Varvara, nineteen and sixteen, were living with their father. So was their eighteen-year-old cousin Anna. The three girls had gone out for the evening, returning home about 11 P.M. As they were going to bed Rasputin told Mariya he was going to visit "the youngster" and warned them not to say anything about the visit to Munya Golovin.[29] Munya herself was at the Rasputin house until 9 or 10 P.M. He had told her that morning that he was going out in the evening but teasingly refused to say where.[30]

The three girls as well as at least two servants knew that when Rasputin referred to "the youngster" he meant Yusupov, so there was no real mystery as to where he would spend the evening. Moreover, about 8 P.M.[31] Anna Vyrubova (whom Alexander Blok, the poet, once called a combination of a fool and a blissful streetwalker) had called on him to deliver, she said, an icon which the Empress was giving him as a present. Rasputin told her that he was going late that evening to the Yusupovs to meet the Prince's wife, Irena. She was ill and he would try to cure her.[32] Vyrubova thought it strange that he would be going so late, but he said Felix wanted to keep the visit secret from his parents. As she left the house Rasputin said to her cryptically: "Whatever else you need from me you have already received." When Vyrubova returned to Tsarskoye Selo, she told the Empress of her conversation. The Empress said there must be some mistake because Princess Irena was still in the Crimea.[33]

When Rasputin went to the door with Protopopov, he may have told the police and plain-clothes men they could go home, that he was not going out for the night. In any event they do not seem to have been around after midnight and they could well have accepted his word, knowing that he had been drunk the night before and that even after visiting the baths across the street at midmorning he came home still half drunk. In any event one of his servants did lock the main door at midnight.[34]

The conspirators assembled at the Yusupov house shortly before midnight. Purishkevich had been nervous all evening. At one point he called up a friend, an actress "N," with whom he gossiped for nearly an hour. For some reason Horace's ode, "Don't ask, Don't pry, Luconius, It is not given to us to know what end God has prepared for you and me," kept running through his mind.[35]

When Purishkevich arrived at the Yusupov home, they descended into the half-cellar where Yusupov had prepared the rooms for receiving Rasputin. The decor reminded Purishkevich of a bonbon shop. There were four bottles of wine on the table—marsala, madeira, port, and a bottle from Kherson—all sweet. Rasputin liked sweet wine and his favorite was madeira. Simanovich claimed he had already drunk at least a dozen bottles of madeira before going to the Yusupovs.[36] Some dark red glasses stood beside the open bottles. All sat down and had a glass of tea and some cake. There were two kinds of cakes, some with rose filling and some with chocolate. Dr. Lazavert put on a pair of rubber gloves, crushed some capsules of cyanide with a knife, and carefully sifted a dose into the center of each of the rose petits fours. He then threw his rubber gloves into the fire which was briskly burning in the fireplace.[37]

Prince Felix surveyed the scene with some satisfaction. The room had lost its grim look. He thought the ancient colored glass lanterns which hung from the ceiling, the heavy red damask portieres, the crackling log fire, gave it a special feeling. It was as though all trace of whatever might happen that night would remain buried within the heavy granite walls.[38]

The conspirators deliberately disarranged the table, leaving tea in glasses half-drunk, napkins tossed aside, bits of cake uneaten. This was to suggest to Rasputin that Princess Irena had been entertaining some women in these quarters and was now just above in the reception room. Then they started up the staircase but the fireplace began to smoke, possibly from Dr. Lazavert's rubber gloves. They set it right and went to the floor above. Yusupov gave Purishkevich some more cyanide capsules which were to be crushed and put into the glasses, just twenty minutes before Rasputin's arrival—to be certain they were fresh and full strength. Then the Prince in a heavy uniform overcoat and Dr. Lazavert in chauffeur's costume left. It was 12:35 A.M. There was the sound of the motorcar departing. Purishkevich took out of his pocket his heavy Savage revolver and laid it on the table. After fifteen minutes had passed Purishkevich and the Grand Duke Dmitri went downstairs, crushed cyanide into two of the glasses, and returned upstairs. A few minutes later they heard a noise outside. It was Yusupov returning with Rasputin.[39]

Felix had arrived at the house at 64 Gorokhova where Rasputin occupied apartment 20 on the ground floor just before 1 A.M. The doorman on duty, Fyodor Korshunov, asked where he was going. He replied: "To Rasputin." The doorman opened the main gate and directed him to the front door but Felix walked straight to the back entrance.[40] Rasputin's housekeeper (a relative),[41] Yekaterina Ivanovna Poterkina, was in the kitchen. After the girls had come home Rasputin had told her to go to bed. He was lying on his bed in his clothes with his boots on, and he said that the youngster was going to pick him up. She knew that this meant the husband of Princess Irena. She had seen him twice before, most recently a week or so ago. She went to the kitchen, and a bit later Rasputin came out asking her to help him with the buttons on the collar of the blue silk blouse he was wearing. At that moment the back door bell rang. Rasputin went to answer it. She heard a voice say: "Nobody's here?" And Rasputin's answer: "No one's here and the children have gone to bed. Come in, youngster." Yekaterina went to her room but saw the other man as he came through the kitchen with Rasputin and recognized him as the same one who had come before. Rasputin led Felix into his bedroom. It was a sparse room, containing only his iron bed, a plain chair, wooden table, and an icon before which was burning an icon lamp. It was to this spartan room Rasputin had brought woman after woman, prostitutes or princesses, bedded them swiftly and brutally, then arising saying vaguely: "*Nu, nu*—now, now, Mother. Everything is in order."[42]

On this evening he made his toilet with care. After lighting a candle he combed his beard. Felix noticed that his silk blouse was embroidered with cornflowers and that he was wearing highly polished boots, seemingly brand-new, and velvet breeches. He smelled of strong cheap soap. Yusupov picked up Rasputin's heavy fur coat, helped him on with it, and they left.[43] Rasputin stopped to tell Katya that he had locked the front door, was leaving by the rear entrance, and to lock it after him. She said: "*Khorosho*. Good." And they went out.[44] The doorman, Korshunov, estimated that about thirty minutes elapsed between Yusupov's entry and his leaving with Rasputin in the car.[45] (It was, incidentally, Purishkevich's car. The engraved Purishkevich arms with the motto *Semper Vem* had been painted over, and other witnesses thought it was a military car.[46])

Purishkevich's sharp ears were the first to distinguish the sound of the returning car. "They've come," he whispered to his companions. Captain Sukhotin quickly set the phonograph going. The record the conspirators had especially gotten for the occasion was "Yankee Doodle Dandy." It was to play over and over that evening until Purishkevich felt he would never get the sound out of his mind. (The record was to make Rasputin think that Princess Irena was still occupied with her friends upstairs.)

The conspirators crept to the staircase and heard Rasputin's voice: "Where to, dear?" as Yusupov showed his guest to the cellar chambers. Hardly breathing, they listened from the stairway—one to a step —first, Purishkevich, then Grand Duke Dmitri, then Sukhotin, then Dr. Lazavert. They kept waiting for the pop of an opening bottle which was to be the signal that all was going well. But they heard nothing but the sound of "Yankee Doodle."[47]

Suddenly the door downstairs opened and Felix came up the stairs. The conspirators retired to his study. "Look," he said, "nothing's happening. That beast is neither eating nor drinking." This was not quite accurate. What had actually occurred, as Felix later explained, was that Rasputin had examined the ebony cabinet with delight. They then sat down and made light conversation. Rasputin asked for some tea. Felix poured it out (nonpoisoned) and Rasputin drank it. Felix offered him some of the chocolate (unpoisoned) cakes. He waved them away but later accepted a cyanide-flavored rose cake. Felix poured out two glasses of wine, again unpoisoned.[48] They sat talking and Yusupov began to lose his nerve.

The Grand Duke Dmitri persuaded Felix to go back downstairs and try again.

This time Yusupov did manage to get Rasputin to drink some poisoned madeira and eat more of the poisoned cakes. Rasputin drank one poisoned glass, then another. Yusupov became more nervous. He thought the poison was not working, although Rasputin complained of being thirsty and asked for tea. Then he asked Felix to play his guitar. The Prince played one sad, sentimental Russian ballad after another. Rasputin sat, his eyes glazed and gloomy. Still the poison didn't seem to take effect. Upstairs "Yankee Doodle Dandy" played on and on.[49]

"What's that noise upstairs?" asked Rasputin, rousing himself.

Yusupov said it was probably the guests leaving. He would go up and see. He appeared upstairs now in a panic. Meantime, Dr.

Lazavert had become ill. He had gone outside for fresh air, fainted, and come to when he fell into a snowdrift.

When Yusupov appeared upstairs again, Purishkevich decided they could no longer wait for the poison to act.[50]

He offered to shoot Rasputin or simply beat his brains out. They set out down the staircase, Purishkevich in the lead with his revolver when Grand Duke Dmitri suddenly halted and they went back. Yusupov asked if he might have the honor of killing Rasputin.

"Please," said Purishkevich. "The question isn't who finishes him off but that he be promptly done away with on this night."

Yusupov rushed to his desk, pulled out a Browning belonging to Dmitri, and ran down the staircase. The others remained in their old positions on the staircase.

Felix found Rasputin sitting where he had left him, breathing slowly and his head drooping. He gave Rasputin a glass of madeira and Rasputin proposed that they visit the gypsies. Felix suggested that it was too late. Rasputin got up and again went to look at the little Chinese cabinet. Felix now drew the revolver from behind his back.

"You'd far better look at the crucifix and say a prayer," he said. As Rasputin stared at the cross, Yusupov raised the gun and shot him.[51]

The men waiting on the staircase heard a revolver shot, then a long-drawn-out scream—Ah-ah-ah—then the sound of a body falling heavily. They leaped down the staircase and found Rasputin half-lying on the white bear rug before the low divan and Yusupov standing over him, the revolver still in hand, perfectly cool, staring at the figure of the starets with undisguised hatred.

The Grand Duke Dmitri, all business, said: "We must quickly take him off the rug and onto the stone floor so that the blood won't soak up and we can get him out of here."

They pulled the body off the rug and were surprised to see no blood. Apparently, they decided, the bleeding was internal.

As he stood over the body, Purishkevich recalled asking himself how this Russian muzhik had been able to make the Czar's will and the Czarina's will his will, how he had factually become the autocrat of all Russia. And the thought came to him of Rasputin's words to Yusupov about the Tibetan herbs of Badmayev and how "with these herbs, dear, he can cure any illness, just with these herbs." Could that have been the secret?

Purishkevich looked at Rasputin's eyes. He was not yet dead, but from his breathing it seemed he must be in the death agony. Purishkevich did not know how long he stood over Rasputin when he heard the Prince's voice: "Now, gentlemen, let's go upstairs. We must finish what we have begun."

Sukhotin donned Rasputin's coat and fur hat and went off with the Grand Duke and Dr. Lazavert to Purishkevich's hospital train. A stove had been kept going in Purishkevich's special car in which to burn Rasputin's effects. They were to leave Purishkevich's automobile there, go by cab to the Grand Duke's residence, pick up his closed sedan, and return to the Moika.

Purishkevich relaxed, smoked a good cigar. Prince Yusupov wandered off into the part of the palace occupied by his parents. Purishkevich was sitting in an armchair, filled with satisfaction, when he suddenly heard a scream: "Purishkevich. Shoot. Shoot. He's alive. He's getting away." Yusupov burst into the room, his face distorted with terror.

Later he explained he had gone back to the room and shaken the corpse. Suddenly one eye opened. Rasputin with an enormous effort staggered to his feet and rushed at the Prince. The Prince tore himself away, Rasputin still holding an epaulette he had ripped from Yusupov's tunic. Rasputin collapsed on the floor, then began moving again.[52]

Purishkevich hesitated a moment. Then he heard the unmistakable heavy steps of a man staggering up the staircase toward the door to the courtyard. He pulled his revolver from his pocket, took off the safety, and ran downstairs.

The door was open and in the courtyard he saw Rasputin staggering through the snow. He could not believe his eyes, but he heard Rasputin muttering: "Felix, Felix. I'll tell it all to the Czarina." Rasputin was staggering along the iron barred fence leading to the street. He had almost reached the gate. Purishkevich leaped after him and fired. Rasputin kept on. Purishkevich fired again. Rasputin struggled on. Purishkevich was a good shot. He practiced regularly at the Semyonov Barracks. How could he miss a man at twenty paces? He fired a third time and hit Rasputin in the back. He fired a fourth bullet aiming for the head. Then he ran up to the body, lying in the snow, and kicked Rasputin in the head with all his strength.

What now to do? Purishkevich was certain the shots had been heard. There seemed little reason for concealment. He remembered seeing two soldiers passing on the street between his first and second shots. He went to the main entrance and called to them.

"I've killed—I've killed Grishka Rasputin, enemy of Russia and the Czar," he said. The men threw themselves on him, embracing and kissing him and shouting: "Thank God. At last it's done!"

Purishkevich asked for their silence.

"Your Excellency," they said. "We are Russian people. Have no doubts of us."

The two soldiers then helped Purishkevich drag the body into the entrance hall of the house.[53]

Purishkevich found Yusupov in the lavatory, vomiting violently. He pulled him away from the basin, assuring him that Rasputin now was really dead. Yusupov kept repeating to himself, "Felix, Felix, Felix, Felix." Purishkevich had the impression something had passed between Rasputin and Yusupov in that moment when Yusupov discovered the monk, apparently returned from the dead.[54] Now, however, Yusupov seemed to come to himself. He rushed to his desk, pulled out a two-pound steel-and-leather billy which he had picked up from Maklakov's desk when visiting him, and rushed at Rasputin's body, beating it again and again. Whether there were signs of life in Rasputin now or whether it was just hysteria is uncertain. But Purishkevich thought he heard a whimper and saw the flicker of an eye. Finally Yusupov was led away.[55]

The question of Rasputin's remarkable vitality has long added to the mystery of his death. The explanation, however, may be fairly simple. When his body was fished out of the Nevka, there was said to have been water in his lungs, suggesting he was still alive when hurled over the bridge. There was no formal autopsy because the Empress objected to this. Five shots in all were fired at Rasputin—one by Yusupov, four by Purishkevich. The conspirators were surprised when they moved Rasputin's body off the bearskin rug to see no blood. Yusupov's bullet may well have missed or simply grazed Rasputin. How much poison he actually ingested is dubious considering the conflicting accounts of Yusupov and his obvious reluctance to offer him the poisoned wine and poisoned cakes. Rasputin may simply have fallen in drunkenness, or possibly as a result of a small amount of the poison in his system.

Later, on being shaken by Yusupov he could easily have begun to come to his senses—especially if he had only been grazed by the bullet, if there was little poison in him, and if he was suffering, principally, from drunkenness. After all, Simanovich claimed Rasputin had already had twelve bottles of madeira before going to Yusupov's. If so the "mystery" of Rasputin's death is largely resolved. Purishkevich missed his first two shots, according to his own testimony. He shot Rasputin in the back with his third, aimed for the head with his fourth. These would match the two principal wounds noted by the police. The conspirators were in such a state of hysteria the wonder is not that Rasputin was shot but that he didn't get away scot free.[56]

What followed was a comedy of sorts. The shots, of course, had been heard by various police and watchmen. They hustled around trying to find out what was going on. Finally, Stepan F. Vlasyuk, a policeman on duty at the corner of Pracheshnaya and Maximilianovsky Pereulok, traced the disturbance to 94 Moika, the Yusupov Palace.

When he came to No. 94 Vlasyuk was told by the doorman that there had been no shots. He stood around, peering into the courtyard, trying to get some clue as to what was happening, when suddenly he was told that Prince Felix wanted to see him. He was led inside, where he met the Prince and a man whom he did not recognize.

The unknown man said: "Are you an Orthodox believer?"

The policeman said: "Of course."

"You are a Russian?"

"Of course."

"You love the Czar and your country?"

"Of course."

"Do you know me?"

"No, I don't."

"And have you heard of Purishkevich?"

"Yes."

"Well, that's who I am. And you've heard of Rasputin and know about him?"

The policeman said he didn't know Rasputin but he'd heard of him.

"Well," said the unknown man, "he's dead and if you love the Czar and the country you must be silent about this and tell no one."

"I understand," the policeman replied.

"Now you can go."

Vlasyuk went back to his post and about twenty minutes later reported to one of his superiors what had happened. The police kept an eye on the palace for the rest of the night. At one point their attention was called to a dog which had been shot in the courtyard. This, they were told, was the reason for the shots. They observed the Grand Duke Dmitri's car leaving and then returning. Purishkevich, Dmitri, Sukhotin, and one of the passing soldiers had gone to dispose of Rasputin's body. It was dumped through a hole in the ice. But in the hurry no weights were put on it, so they put the weights on his fur coat and threw that over the bridge. The conspirators had forgotten to burn his boots. One was left in the car. The other was thrown down from the bridge. It lay on the ice where it would attract the attention of the police and lead to the recovery of Rasputin's body.

In the morning the confusion multiplied. Yusupov called up the Czarina and asked to see her. She refused and he sent her a letter denying he had had anything to do with the murder. He telephoned Munya Golovin and said the same thing. At the same time the conspirators were spreading word of their deed around town. The police at

the instigation of Munya Golovin, Rasputin's daughters, and Simanovich began a cumbersome investigation.

The Czarina took charge of matters in her own way. She brought
Vyrubova into the palace to live with her, fearful "they" would get her
next. She asked the police to prevent Yusupov and the Grand Duke
Dmitri from leaving Petrograd (this was illegal—actions affecting the
upper nobility could only be ordered by the Czar). She hung between
hope and despair as she wrote her husband late on December 17. The
first part of her letter was the usual collection of weather, prayers, politics. She hoped the Czar would finish "the nice English novel" on the
train back to Tsarskoye Selo (he was scheduled to return in a day or
so). She worried about "Baby's 'worm.'" Had it been gotten rid of?

Then she turned to Rasputin. He had disappeared. There was a big
scandal at Yusupov's house last night. "Big meeting," she wrote, "Dmitri, Purishkevich, etc., all drunk. Police heard shots. Purishkevich ran
out screaming to the Police that our Friend was killed."

The police had searched and found nothing. Felix pretended that
Rasputin had not been at his house. "Seems quite a paw," the Empress
wrote. "I still trust in God's mercy that one has only driven Him off
somewhere . . . I cannot & won't believe He has been killed.

"God have mercy."

In the dense forests of Zosima in a quiet monastery, a monk named
Sergei Bulgakov, a holy man who abominated Rasputin's evils and
was dedicated to the throne of Russia, heard the news in the cell
where he had retired to pray.

"Don't they know," he thought, "that the bullet directed at Rasputin
will strike the Czar's family and that with this shot has begun the
Revolution?"[57]

XXXIV

A Quiet Winter

The sun rose in Petrograd a little before 8:30 on January 19, 1917. The fresh winds from the frozen Baltic had dropped since the day before, but it was colder and the mercury stood close to zero. The sky was mostly clear and tinted with that delicate blue which sometimes bathes the winter landscape of the great city on the Neva in pastels of almost unbearable delicacy. Count Kokovtsov, now sixty-four and inactive in politics since his dismissal three years before, rose a bit earlier than usual and, donning his black broadcloth coat with its fine marten collar, once again took the familiar train to Tsarskoye Selo for an audience with the Czar.

Kokovtsov had not seen the Emperor for more than a year, and when he entered the Alexander Palace he found nothing changed— the same old porter in the reception hall, the same books and albums on the tables, the same pictures on the wall, and two old familiars, Count Benkendorf and Dr. Ye. S. Botkin, patiently waiting to be received.

There was an air of peace and continuity about the scene. Kolovtsov could not help thinking of the hundreds of times he had come here in his years of service to the Emperor. He was ushered into the Czar's working cabinet almost immediately and found the Czar standing at a window near the entrance. Instead of moving over to his desk and inviting Kokovtsov to sit down as was his custom, the Czar remained uncomfortably standing where he was.

Kokovtsov noticed that the door to the Czar's toilet was half open—

which he had never before seen—and had the impression that there was someone behind the door throughout his short stay.[1]

It was not the peculiarity of the Czar's conduct which struck Kokovtsov but his appearance. He hardly recognized the Czar, so much had he aged. His face was thin, his cheeks sunken, his eyes almost without color, the whites yellow and the pupils gray and lifeless. They wandered vaguely from object to object.

Kokovtsov could not restrain from voicing his concern. The Czar looked at him vacantly and said that he was quite healthy but possibly hadn't slept well the night before.

The Count thanked the Czar for receiving him—his visit was in connection with becoming trustee of the Alexander Lyceum—and asked whether it was convenient to discuss these affairs now or later. The Czar looked as though he did not understand a word Kokovtsov was saying. A vague smile fluttered over his face, "a strange smile," Kokovtsov recalled. "I would say an almost unconscious one without expression, sort of a sickly smile." The Czar stared at Kokovtsov and after a silence that seemed endless to the former Premier, said that he wasn't ready to talk about the question but would drop Kokovtsov a note. Then his face fell back into the meaningless smile, he gave Kokovtsov his hand and showed him to the door.[2]

Kokovtsov found Benkendorf and Botkin still waiting in the reception room. Botkin was the Czar's personal physician.

"Can't you see the condition the Czar is in?" Kokovtsov asked Botkin, tears flooding his eyes. "He is on the verge of a nervous breakdown."

The pair dismissed Kokovtsov's fears. "He's just tired," they said. But the impression stayed with Kokovtsov to the end of his life that the Czar was now a lost man.[3]

The Czar's days had been anguish. He rushed back to Tsarskoye Selo upon the news of Rasputin's murder and participated with his family and Anna Vyrubova (no one else was present) in a grim ceremony for the starets in the early morning fog and cold of the Imperial Park. The body was buried on a plot of land belonging to Anna Vyrubova. Father Alexander, the Czar's chaplain, read the service. The icon which Anna had brought to Rasputin on the night of his death was placed on his chest in the coffin. It had been signed by the Empress, the four Imperial daughters, and Vyrubova. The Empress laid a spray of white flowers on the coffin and threw the first handful of earth. Then, as the gravediggers began their work, she and Vyrubova, weeping, went back to the palace. The Czar took his usual morning turn in the park.[4]

Rasputin's body rested there until it was dug up and burned on the night of March 8 by a group of revolutionary soldiers. The disinterment took most of the night and was witnessed by several hundred peasants.[5]

In these tense days the Czar was closeted with his wife and children most of the time, carrying on as few official duties as possible. In the evenings he read aloud or engaged in the latest passion of the Imperial family—puzzles. He took his usual long walks, sometimes spending three or four hours in the open. The campaign of the Grand Dukes for a constitutional government and for the end of the Czarina's influence did not halt. The whole family rallied to the support of Grand Duke Dmitri and Prince Yusupov, but the Czar, insisting that "no one has the right to take a man's life, be he Grand Duke or peasant," sent Dmitri off to Persia and Yusupov to Rakitnoye, the Yusupov estate near Kursk.[6]

Petrograd salons and embassies were filled with talk of dynastic plots. Almost every evening in the gloomy depths of the Yacht Club over brandy and port the Grand Dukes played quinze and talked of "saving" Russia by removing the Czarina or both her and the Czar.[7] Who would be set on the throne as regent varied from one evening to the next. Sometimes they spoke of Grand Duke Nikolai Nikolayevich (Nikolasha). Sometimes it was Grand Duke Mikhail, the Czar's brother. And sometimes it was Grand Duke Dmitri, hero of many for his role in Rasputin's death. In the months of December 1916 and January 1917, the diary of Maurice Paléologue, the French ambassador and the liveliest gossip in Petrograd, was filled with talk of plots and coups, of the abdication of the Czar and the exile of his wife to England. There were many who thought Sir George Buchanan, the English ambassador, had a hand in these schemes.[8] Perhaps the most outspoken of the royal dissidents was the Grand Duchess Mariya Pavlovna, widow of the Emperor's uncle Vladimir. She packed her bags and left for Kislovodsk, telling her friends, "I'll not return until all is finished here."[9] Among some of the generals there was similar talk, and in parliamentary circles conspiracy gossip revolved around the president of the Duma, M. V. Rodzyanko.

Grand Duke Alexander Mikhailovich, "Sandro" to the Czar, and his first cousin, made several attempts to penetrate the Czar's isolation and the Czarina's fierce antagonism. He wrote a long letter in four parts, over a period of six weeks, calling on the Czar to act "in this most dangerous of moments," warning that "this situation cannot long last; I repeat again: one cannot lead a country without listening to the voice of the people." He called for dismissal of the incompetent (and some thought deranged) Minister of Interior Protopopov and establishment of a government led by men in whom the nation had confidence.

"In conclusion," said the Grand Duke, "I will say that strange as it seems it is the government which prepares the revolution; the people do not want it but the government employs all possible means to augment the number of the discontented and it succeeds perfectly. We are participating in an unheard of spectacle: the revolution comes from above and not from below."[10]

Alexander saw the Czarina for the last time February 10. She was, as so often, ill and received him in her bedroom off the mauve salon, wearing a white negligee embroidered in lace. The Grand Duke was upset. He had hoped to talk with Alix privately but the Czar sat at her side on the big double bed. One last time the Grand Duke put forward his ideas for change, warning that "perhaps in two months there will be nothing left in this country of ours to remind us we ever had autocrats sitting on the throne of our ancestors."[11]

The Czarina coldly dismissed him. He kissed her hand and went out through the mauve salon where he was surprised to see the Czar's aide, N. P. Linevich, waiting with the Grand Duchess Olga. The Czar had remained with the Czarina and ordered Linevich to stay at hand because "the Grand Dukes were so hostile you could not know what they might do," Vyrubova observed.[12] This feeling may explain why the Imperial family had sent no Christmas presents in December to the Grand Dukes.[13]

The truth was, as V. N. Voyeikov, commandant of the Imperial Palace and a familiar of all of the participants, concluded, the Grand Dukes were only "playing at Revolution." They had no real plans, no genuine conspiracies, no agreed scenarios. As Rodzyanko remarked, they kept asking him, "When will the Revolution be?" With Rodzyanko, too, there was nothing really specific, nothing tangible. After her husband's meeting with the Grand Dukes and Duchesses on December 24 Madame Rodzyanko wrote her close friend, the Princess Zinaida Yusupova: "Holy Russia can not perish from a gang of crazy and low people; too much noble blood has been shed for the glory and honor of Russia for the devil's forces to overturn it all." And ten days later she wrote: "Hatred for her [the Czarina] has reached such a measure that her life is in danger." Agitation, Madame Rodzyanko continued, grew with each day and she felt "the state is threatened with inevitable peril." But, she added, "when the talk comes to her [the Czarina] he [the Czar] pales and says nothing."

After spending the Christmas holidays in the Crimea, Pavel Milyukov, the future Foreign Minister of the Provisional Government, stopped for a few days in Moscow. It was early January and he heard talk of a "palace revolt" on all sides. It seemed to him that the more people seriously concerned themselves with revolution the less they would gossip about it. He remembered being asked one specific question: "Why didn't the Duma take power?" His answer was: "Bring two regiments to the Tauride Palace and we'll take power."[14]

Nor did the military seem more serious than the Grand Dukes. The desire for change was there, but like all the rest the generals waited for someone else to make a move. Gen. A. M. Krymov, one of the Army's best commanders, visited Petrograd in early January. At his request Rodzyanko assembled a group of parliamentarians. The general told them the Army would welcome a coup d'état with joy and that the high command felt a revolution was imminent. "There is no time to lose," he concluded.

General Krymov's words touched off one more of the interminable Petrograd discussions. A. I. Shingarev, a Kadet and middle-of-the-road Duma leader, declared: "A coup d'état is urgent. But who will lead it?" Sergei Shidlovsky, his colleague, responded: "No need for pity on him [the Czar] when he is losing Russia." Another quoted General Brusilov as having said: "If I had to choose between the Emperor and Russia I would choose Russia." M. I. Tereshchenko supported these extreme sentiments. The conversation went on until the small hours of the night. Rodzyanko thought Russia was advancing implacably to the edge of an abyss.[15] But nothing was decided.

The Grand Duke Mikhail Alexandrovich came to see Rodzyanko at about this time. "Do you think there will be a revolution?" he asked. Rodzyanko said revolution was imminent but there was still time to save the throne and the dynasty. "What can we do?" asked the Grand Duke. Rodzyanko urged the Grand Duke once again to speak with his brother.[16]

Nothing, of course, came of this. Rodzyanko had a last chance to try to convince the Czar himself. He was invited to tea February 10. It was the same afternoon the Czar and Czarina had their final angry confrontation with Grand Duke Alexander Mikhailovich. Rodzyanko found the atmosphere cold and hostile. The Czar interrupted Rodzyanko and asked him to cut short his report because the Grand Duke Mikhail was waiting to take tea. Rodzyanko solemnly warned the Czar that this would probably be his final report.

"Why?" asked the Czar.

"Because the Duma will be dissolved and the course the Government is now following will lead to no good. . . . There is still time to change everything with a responsible government but this apparently is not to be. Your Majesty does not share my opinion and all remains as before. I believe that the result of this will be a Revolution and anarchy which no one will be able to control."

The Emperor made no response. He icily showed Rodzyanko to the door.[17] The Czar disliked Rodzyanko intensely and had the habit of filing away his reports unread.

After this last meeting with the Czar, Madame Rodzyanko wrote Zinaida Yusupova on February 12:

"Misha carried away the impression that neither words nor persuasion can anymore have any effect. They are all too confident that force is behind them and that the whole country must be squeezed in their fists. . . .

"Now the danger is that the smallest spark will touch off the fire. Police and troops are everywhere in force, patrols tramp the streets in expectation of Revolution. . . . Bread happily appeared today in large quantities which had a quieting influence. . . .

"It is now clear that A.F. [the Czarina] is not alone guilty but that he as the Russian Czar is even more criminal."[18]

Everything was tried. Even Klopov, the commoner with the right to petition and to meet with the Czar, was brought again into action. He wrote a series of letters to the Czar, five in all, between January 19 and February 13, and on January 29 the Czar laconically noted in his diary that at "6 P.M. received old Klopov." Old Klopov, suitably briefed by the Czar's brother, the Grand Duke Mikhail (who consulted with Rodzyanko and Prince G. Ye. Lvov), tried to convince the Czar that he must name a responsible ministry, summon the Duma into session, proclaim a general amnesty, and appoint Lvov Prime Minister.[19]

The Czar made no more response to Klopov than he did to any of the others. But he was irritated enough at the activities of his Romanov relatives to try to discipline them. He ordered Grand Duke Nikolai Mikhailovich to leave Petrograd for two months on his estates (because Nikolai had been the ringleader in the joint family letter supporting the Grand Duke Dmitri). He sent the Grand Duke Kirill off to Murmansk for naval duty. The Grand Duke Andrei Vladimirovich took the caution of leaving Petrograd for Kislovodsk in late January.

As never before the Czar and the Czarina felt themselves alone against the world. Rasputin was gone but they still prayed to his spirit and found their answer in the confused and often criminal guidance of Rasputin's legacy, the sycophant Interior Minister Protopopov. Protopopov had organized the writing of hundreds of letters and telegrams to the Czarina and the Czar through agents of the police and reactionary organizations such as the Fatherland Union. These letters strengthened the long-held belief, particularly of the Czarina, that the Russian masses truly supported the *batyushka-Czar,* the "little Father," and that the trouble lay with the upper classes, the Imperial family, and the intelligentsia.[20] This conviction was bolstered by the counsel given to the Czar by Nikolai Maklakov, former Interior Minister, who personally believed that "among the lower levels there was a completely patriarchical view toward affairs" and that the Czar had the full support of the simple people.[21]

The Czarina kept a heap of telegrams on her desk and showed them to visitors with pride. One morning an old peasant who worked at Tsarskoye Selo came to the palace and asked a personal audience with the Czar. He told an adjutant that a plot was brewing against the Czar: "They want to kill the *batyushka-Czar* and the *matyushka-Czarina* and send the children to the monastery."

He said the Czar should not be alarmed because "we will come to his rescue. And there are many of us."

The Czar gave the old man a present and sent him on his way. The story became one more strand in the persisting belief of the Czar and his wife that whatever the Grand Dukes might say, whatever Rodzyanko might propose, whatever the Duma might do—the people loved them and would protect them in the end.[22]

There was one man whom the Czar did consult—his dentist, Sergei Sergeyevich Kostritsky. The Czar was fond of Kostritsky and liked to talk with him. Kostritsky traveled a good deal and had just come back from the Caucasus.

"What's new," the Czar now asked him. "What's the mood of the country?"

Kostritsky apologized and then told him of the general concern among the people, the disorders and difficulties. Perhaps, he said, a responsible ministry might help. That was what was on everyone's mind.

The Czar thought a bit and then said: "That would be useful."

Kostritsky was surprised, but the Czar explained that it would be very useful because it would relieve him of many responsibilities. But he did not think it was possible to grant a responsible ministry in wartime. In three or four months, he said, after the victory, then it would be done and the people would accept the reform with thanks.[23]

So January imperceptibly faded into February. The Petrograd weather remained cold but not too cold. Snow covered the ground and there were many bright days. The Czar walked. Sometimes he strolled the palace grounds at night, but usually he spent the evenings with his family. Often there were movies. The last one which Voyeikov remembered seeing in February was *Madame Du Barry*, filled with blood-curdling scenes of the guillotine. It left a heavy feeling in Voyeikov's heart.[24] The last motion picture which the Czar recorded in his diary was something called *Mysterious Hands*. Two days later on February 22, he left Petrograd for military headquarters at Mogilev.[25] He had been assured by Protopopov that all was quiet in Petrograd.[26]

On his way, the Czar read the letter which Alix had tucked under the pillow of his berth before the train departed, a letter in which she said:

"Our dear Friend in the other world also prays for you—He is still so close to us. . . . I think everything will right itself. Only, dearest, be firm, show the power of your fist—that is what the Russians need. You never let a chance pass to show your love and kindness—let them now feel your fist. They themselves ask for this—so many have recently said to me: 'We need the knout.' It is strange but such is the slavic nature—the greatest firmest—harshness even—and warm love. Now that they have begun to 'feel' you and *Kalinin* [her code name for Protopopov] they have begun to quiet down."

When he got to Mogilev, the Czar sent his wife a telegram:

"Arrived safely. Clear, cold, windy. Cough a little. Again feel myself firm but very lonely."

Zinaida Gippius and her husband returned to Petrograd from the spa on Thursday February 2, 1917. She found the capital iron with frost, but the morning sun painted the gardens of the Tauride Palace rose, and even the dead circular cupola of the Duma was bathed in color. For such a Cassandra as herself, she thought, everything was as might be expected. Now that Rasputin was gone, Russia's rulers waited around his grave for a miracle without which there was no hope. Everything was as before. In a sense, she thought, this was a comedy but the laughter caught in her throat, for the shame was Russia's and there was more to come.

The theaters were full. Andrei Bely was back from his mad hegira in Dornach, pale and thin and gray at the temples but somehow more sincere, as Lyubov Blok wrote her husband.[27] Khodasevich was with Bely at Berdyayev's flat in Moscow the night they had news of the killing of Rasputin. He thought Bely close to insanity. The terror never left his pale eyes and his hair stood out as though charged with 100,000 volts of electricity. His talk was all of spies, provocations, "black" forces which had followed him from Switzerland.[28] Twice Bely spoke at the Religious-Philosophical Society. Gippius could not bear the faces of the listeners with their expressions of contented lust. Nor could she stand the pseudopatriotic psalms of the Russophile poet

N. Klyuyev with his fat shiny face. Poor Russia! she exclaimed.[29] Everyone thought there would be trouble when the Duma convened February 14, but nothing happened.

The Merezhkovskys were not the only ones back in Petrograd. The Bloks were there. And so was Mayakovsky, still in the military automobile company but now totally preoccupied with the woman who was to be the love of his life, Lila Brik, wife of Osip Brik, who decided to become Mayakovsky's publisher. Mayakovsky wrote mad verses about love and about Lila Brik. Once he wrote a poem called "Don Juan." Lila was angry. Couldn't he write anything but love poems? Mayakovsky tore it to bits and hurled them to the Petrograd wind. Pasternak came up from Moscow and was welcomed to the Briks' apartment. On the apartment wall hung a paper yellow tunic and a paper representation of a Cloud in Pants. These were Mayakovsky's latest sensations. Mayakovsky wore a yellow tunic and recited the poem "Cloud in Pants" ("I will be irreproachably tender— not a man but a cloud in pants!"). The poets no longer talked of revolution. They simply waited for it, tapping their feet with impatience. One evening Mayakovsky appeared at the Comedians' Inn (formerly the Stray Dog). Lila Brik was with him. They left but Mayakovsky came back in a moment.

"She left her handbag," he explained, picking up a small black pocketbook. At the next table was Larisa Reisner, young, beautiful, soon to become a Bolshevik commissar,[30] and probably in love with Mayakovsky.

"You have found your handbag and now you will carry it all your life," she said.

"I can carry this handbag in my teeth," Mayakovsky replied.[31]

Boris Savinkov, the SR terrorist, and Ilya Ehrenburg, the embryo poet, were still in Paris, both now war correspondents, Savinkov for the war-supporting *Den* and Ehrenburg for the liberal *Birzhevye Vedomosti*. They argued not about the war but about art; not about revolution but about Savinkov's poor novels.

In Moscow, Konstantin Paustovsky, having spent the previous year as a streetcar conductor, was trying to scratch out a living on one of the Moscow newspapers. His editor had an idea: "Go to some God-forsaken place in the provinces and write what Turgenev's Russia is thinking now."

It was early February. Paustovsky made his way to Yefremov in Tula Guberniya. The streets had the sour smell of horse manure, the gravestones in the cemetery were overturned, sheep lived in the peasants' huts, idiot beggars huddled on the church steps, and the woods were filled with bandits. The wind whistled through the bare birch branches and the women wept for their absent men—the soldiers at the front, the living, the wounded, the dead. Paustovsky thought of Blok's words:

> My Russia, my life, must we languish together?
> The Tsar, and Siberia and Yermak and prison . . .

The town was a trading center for grain and for excellent Antonovka apples. On the streets were "white ticket men," exempt from military service. In the hotel the two other guests were Madame Troma, a fortuneteller whose fingers were covered with rings, and a man who introduced himself as "Princess Greza," the author of an advice-to-the-lovelorn column published in cheap provincial magazines.

Paustovsky decided to go deeper into the back country. He went to the village of Bogovo on the bank of the Krasivaya Mecha River and talked to the peasants. The water ran black in the millrace, the first February thaw had come, and there was a smell of woodsmoke and dampness in the air.

The peasants were waiting. Waiting for the end of the war. They did not know when it might halt but they did not think it would simply come to a natural end. Something—they did not know what—had to be done to halt it. And this would happen. And what after that? Well, then there would be justice. That was what they were waiting for. Justice.[32] How they might define justice they did not say. Paustovsky was not the only one to venture into the countryside that winter. A friend of French Ambassador Maurice Paléologue's came back in early February from his estates near Kostroma on the Volga. He said the peasants were tired of the war. They understood nothing except that victory was not possible. They were melancholy rather than aroused. Rasputin's murder had made a deep impression.

"To the muzhiks," Paléologue's friend said, "Rasputin has become a martyr. He was a man of the people; he let the Czar hear the voice of the people. He defended the people against the *pridvornye*, the noblemen. So the *pridvornye* killed him. That's what's being said in all the *izbas*."[33]

Ivan Bunin spent the fall of 1916 and the early winter in the village. He concluded: "The people don't want to fight. They are tired of the war and they don't understand what we are fighting for. The war isn't their business. They grow more furious every day."

Bunin sat in his overcoat on his bed in the darkness of evening. He was waiting, he said, for the peasants to come and burn the house down. They had already run off with the horses.[34]

XXXV

"Only People Changed"

There was one body in Russia which had impeccable evidence of the condition of the country. This was the police. Their agents penetrated everywhere—from the highest circles of the court to the miserable workers' barracks of Petrograd's Vyborg quarter, from the front-line trenches in Galicia to the sugar-beet fields of the Ukraine.

In October 1916 the Okhrana, the security branch of the police, drafted one more of a remarkable series of warnings to the Czarist Government. It was in the form of a carefully written, tightly documented analysis of the condition of Russia after two years of war. The data on which it was based had been collected over a period of nearly a year.

The country, said the Okhrana, stood on the brink of revolution. Not a revolution brought about by revolutionary organizations. The revolutionary underground, the police made clear, had been virtually wiped out. The Bolsheviks were almost nonexistent. The other Social Democrats were little more effective. The SRs still had their strength —but it was in the Duma rather than in party cells.

It was not revolutionaries that the Czar need fear. It was the people.

"Believing that the Government has forgotten about its needs the people like a dark, broad body is embittered not only at the Government but at the principle according to which the Power exercises its direct and normal obligations," said the Okhrana.

The country stood on the verge of events, said the report, "beside which 1905 was child's play."

It was not just the workers of Petrograd whose pay had risen only 50 to 100 per cent while prices had gone up 100 to 500 per cent (and many items of goods or fuel were unavailable at any price). It was the Army. There was an intimate relationship between the workers and the Army, and within the Army the mood was "very, very disturbed not to say 'revolutionary.'" Among the troops, the wildest rumors circulated about conditions in Petrograd and the other large centers (rumors which only too soon could hardly be distinguished from reality) that "a pound of bread costs a ruble" or that "meat is given only to noblemen and landowners" or that "they are opening up a new cemetery for those dying of hunger."

If on just one occasion, warned the police, bread should not appear in the stores, "this will touch off in the capital and other large centers of the Empire the strongest kind of disorders with pogroms and endless street riots."

The mood of businessmen and bankers was gloomy. Many Jewish businessmen were talking of closing up shop because they felt collapse was at hand and that they would be the victim of pogroms.

The state of the Army was especially alarming because, said the police, covert examination of soldiers' mail revealed that the process of "revolutionizing" the troops had been under way steadily since the end of 1915.

"The alarming mood grows stronger each day," said the police. "It penetrates all the principal levels of the population. Never has there been such dissatisfaction."

Despite the weakness of the revolutionary movements, the police warned that when the uprising occurred they would make every effort to put themselves at its head. The strength of the Revolution would be overwhelming because it would have the support of "two-thirds of the former and present soldiers."

What to do? The police made no recommendation but offered a warning:

"The slightest sign of indecisiveness or vacillation in the solution of these complicated and urgent questions threatens the heaviest and most regrettable consequences, the result of which in this grim moment cannot even be calculated."[1]

The words of the Okhrana dissolved in empty air; the paper was filed away to gather dust until exhumed by the archivists of the Revolution ten years later.

By the first week in January the Petrograd Okhrana was reporting that the mood in the capital had taken on an "exceptionally threatening character."

"The wildest rumors circulate in society," the Okhrana said January 5, "about the intention of the Government to take various reactionary steps as well as predictions that hostile elements and groups are preparing for possible revolutionary acts and excesses."

By January 19 the Okhrana was reporting that "the population openly (on the streets, in the streetcars, in the theaters and stores) criticizes in the sharpest tone the Government's program."

It warned that if the Government prorogued the Duma, the whole country might rise. In the Army, the Okhrana said, belief was widespread that the murder of Rasputin was only "the first swallow."

On January 26 the chief of the Petrograd security section, Konstantin Globachev, reported growing talk of a possible "palace coup" among such centrist figures as A. I. Guchkov, Prince Georgi Ye. Lvov, S. M. Tretyakov, A. V. Konovalov, and M. M. Fyodorov. As a result, that evening the Okhrana arrested the workers' group of the Military Industrial Committee. The mood of the workers grew more alarming, and on January 31, February 1, 3, 4, and 5 Globachev reported spreading strikes.

By February 5 the Okhrana was advising: "With every day the food question becomes more acute and it brings down cursing of the most unbridled kind against anyone who has any connection with food supplies."

"Never before," said the police, "has there been so much swearing, argument and scandal. That the population has not yet begun food riots does not mean they will not in the nearest future. . . .

"That any kind of accidental step by the hungry masses will be the first and last step on the way to mindless and merciless excesses of the most terrible kind—anarchistic revolution—there can be no doubt."[2]

Day by day the Okhrana penned the scenario of what was to come—informed, detailed, couched in bureaucratic language which hardly concealed the alarm of the authors. But nothing was done.

In the last ten days of January Petrograd got 21 carloads of grain and flour per day instead of the 120 wagons needed to feed the city. On February 13 Mayor A. P. Balk reported that in the last week the city had received 5,000 poods of flour a day instead of the usual 60,000 poods. The city's bakers got 35,000 poods a day instead of a normal 90,000. Moscow was receiving an average of 39 cars of flour a day in January and only 17 in February. Mikhail V. Chelnokov, chairman of the Union of Cities, reported that "there won't be any bread in February. We have grain for mills that have no fuel, flour where there are no freight cars to haul it and cars where there is no food for the population."[3]

By the end of 1916 thirty-six blast furnaces had been shut down for lack of fuel,[4] and by late February only twenty-eight of sixty-three furnaces in the Donbas and only forty-four of ninety-two in the Urals were operating.[5]

Petrograd was a city of 2,700,000 swollen with an influx of wartime workers, 393,000 now, up 150,000 since July 1914. It was the country's biggest industrial center, its biggest finance center. It counted 70,000 civil servants (*chinovniki*) and a police force of 5,000, which by October 1916 had increased to 6,700.[6]

What of the Army? As of February 1, 1917, there was a garrison of about 420,000 troops in Petrograd and the environs of whom about 200,000 were actually in the capital.[7] Possibly the most important characteristic of the garrison—traditionally the largest in the country —was the change in its social composition since the start of the war.

Key elements were crack regiments like the Preobrazhensky, the Volynsky, the Semyonovsky, and the Pavlovsky, led by officers from the nobility and composed of trained and reliable men deliberately drawn from other parts of the empire. This was no longer the case. The military units in the capital now were *reserve* regiments which bore the famous names but whose composition was radically different. A higher and higher percentage of ordinary soldiers were Petrograd residents, not infrequently factory workers forcibly inducted as a penalty for going on strike. Some were workers forced into the Army after strikes in October 1916. Others were strikers from the Donets Basin coal mines and the Nikolayev shipyard. The nonpeasant elements in the military force had risen from a normal 5 per cent to at least 10 per cent.

There was a change in the peasant composition of the regiments, as well. Many of the Cossacks, that traditional reliant arm of the Russian Czars, now came from the poorest and most downtrodden areas of the Kuban and Don.

So far as officers were concerned, the numbers of nobility in the cadet schools had fallen sharply as a result of huge war casualties. From levels of 40 per cent in the Pavlovsky Infantry School and 90 per cent in the Nikolayevsky Cavalry School the numbers had fallen to 30 and 35 per cent respectively.

Whereas before the war most Petrograd regiments had been quartered in comfortable barracks, many troops now were badly housed in quarters not infrequently located in the heart of working-class districts.[8]

Protopopov, the "fatal man" in Blok's words,[9] was confident of the general reliability of the troops. He thought perhaps 5 per cent might have been affected by antigovernment agitation but that the remainder and especially the training ranks and the officers, except for possibly the highest officers, were conservative and reliable supporters of the regime. "Life demonstrated that I was uninformed," he said later.[10]

But the great trouble, Protopopov formally concluded, was that after the death of Rasputin the Czar and Czarina did not change policy. "Only people changed," he concluded.[11]

Who were the people whom the Czar changed? Blok had an answer. It was nothing but a game of musical chairs within the small palace circle. A circle, in the words of Voyeikov, the Czar's palace commandant (and a leading member of it), composed of manikins,[12] struggling between pride and intrigue—twenty-three persons each of whom had his duties ("I play chess," "I open doors"), each aspiring to the place of the Minister of Court once "dear old Count Frederiks," who was sometimes out of his head, passed on. And as Adm. Konstantin D. Nilov, one of the circle, said: "If the revolution comes we'll all hang on the nearest lampposts."[13] Individuals in this circle traded jobs. But the course of the Empire flowed on unchanged.

With the call-up of autumn 1916, Russia had under mobilization 13 million men—peasants, tillers of the land, mechanics, factory workers, the backbone of the country. Slowly the country was being paralyzed. The arteries feeding the land no longer flowed. The crisis demanded exceptional people, exceptional means.

Neither was at hand.

Early on a wintry evening in January 1917 Lenin and his wife left their little room on the third floor of the old stone building at 14 Spiegelgasse, Zurich, owned by a socialist shoemaker named T. Kammerer, and hurried three blocks down the narrow stone streets to the Volkhaus on Helvetia Platz.

It was an important moment for Lenin. More and more seldom had he appeared in public as the years of exile wore on. His nerves again bothered him. He was no good at meetings and often left before they ended.[14] He felt shy and he envied those like his warm friend Inessa Armand who were able to do a good deal of public speaking.[15] Public life upset him. In fact, although he and Krupskaya tried to go to the theater to while away tedious Zurich evenings, they often left after the first act—a habit that amused their companions.[16] "You are losing your money," they said.

These were not the best of times for Lenin or any of the revolutionaries. Lenin was obsessed with worry about money and the rap-

idly escalating cost of living. Lenin's war chest had been scanty at the
outbreak of war. Even in September 1913 he wrote G. D. Shklovsky
that he "didn't have a groschen." In 1915 he advised the International
Socialist Commission in Bern that "Party funds are very very scanty."
Party work in Russia was suffering as a result. At the time Lenin and
Krupskaya came to Switzerland in the summer of 1914 the Party fund
totaled 150 francs. Lenin counted the characters in each line of *Sotsial-Demokrat* to keep down printing costs and cut the print order to
three hundred copies—one hundred for foreign distribution and two
hundred for Russia (where very few ever arrived).[17] He and Krupskaya filled their letters with financial concerns. At irregular intervals
Lenin's sister or brother-in-law forwarded sums of two hundred or five
hundred rubles, and Lenin earned some money selling articles to
Maxim Gorky's publishing house. Lenin even put up with Gorky's editors cutting out sulphurous passages about his enemy, the German
socialist Kautsky, an almost unheard-of concession and one which
revealed that he was even more prepared to put monetary considerations ahead of Party polemics.[18] He got rid of his spleen by writing
nasty remarks about Gorky ("Oh, the calf!") to Inessa Armand[19] and
began to dream up unrealistic projects for making money. He proposed to set up a publishing house in collaboration with Inessa and
one or two colleagues to issue leaflets and pamphlets in French and
German. He emphasized that the business would have to pay its way
from the beginning and spelled out the proposed operations in detail.[20]
Nothing, of course, came of this enterprise. A few weeks later in
February 1917 he concocted a more elaborate scheme and sent a
prospectus to his brother-in-law, Mark Yelizarov, then working in Petrograd for the Volga Steamship Company. Lenin proposed to publish
a pedagogical dictionary or encyclopedia to be written by Krupskaya,
who had interested herself in such questions in Switzerland. He
wanted to keep the venture in the family, borrowing the necessary
money or going into partnership with a capitalist who would be
willing to take a minority interest. He had no doubt that "an under-
taking would be profitable" and warned his brother-in-law against a
publisher stealing the idea, grabbing the profit, and "enslaving" the
editor. "That happens," he said, underlining the words.[21] In her memoirs Krupskaya poked gentle fun at Lenin's idea, calling it "this fantastic plan of his."[22]

Lenin's concern over funds soon verged on the hysterical. His living
expenses were low. He paid only twenty-eight francs a month for the
little room and kitchen where he and Krupskaya lived. It was lighted
by kerosene lamps and Krupskaya cooked over a spirit stove or the gas
range in the Kammerers' quarters across the street.[23]

At one point he wrote Inessa saying that he was thinking of sending her the Party fund (which was in his possession) to be kept sewn up in a little bag on her person because of the possibility that Switzerland might be drawn into the war. Banks weren't safe.[24]

Lenin wrote his sister Mariya February 1, 1917, thanking her for sending him 808 francs through the Azov-Don bank, adding: "The cost of living makes one despair and I have desperately little capacity for work."

"There are no changes here," he concluded. "We live very quietly. Nadya often feels poorly. The winter has been exceptionally cold."[25]

There was no reason why Lenin should have been in good spirits. He was almost completely cut off from Russia. He had maintained tenuous communications through his sister Anna until her arrest in July 1916, but from then on he heard nothing—or almost nothing—from what remained of the Petrograd Bolshevik organization. M. G. Filiya, a Georgian Bolshevik, recalled Lenin complaining that he gave many instructions to Comrade Fyodor N. Samoilov in Petrograd but had no knowledge of what happened to them. He had sent a number of underground workers into Russia but had heard nothing from them.[26] He saw no Russian newspapers whatever.[27]

Krupskaya wrote plaintively to A. G. Shlyapnikov in Petrograd in late autumn, trying to answer his complaint about the émigrés being out of touch with Russian conditions. "How can it be otherwise when there are no connections with Russia?" she asked. "Only James [Lenin's sister Anna] writes and at that in general lines and more about literary affairs."[28]

Nor did the situation improve. In late December Lenin was writing that "my contacts with Petersburg are exceptionally weak and intolerably slow,"[29] and on Christmas Day he told Inessa that "the picture is 'dark' . . . because the revolutionary movement grows extremely slowly and with difficulty."[30] Two months later on February 5, after getting one of his rare letters from Moscow, he wrote that his correspondent told him ". . . the mood of the masses is a good one, that chauvinism is clearly declining and that *probably* our day will come." As for himself he noted, "things here, as I wrote, are not very good."[31]

The truth was that Lenin's Bolshevik organization had been all but destroyed by the police, by the war, and by his own uncompromising policies. Even before the arrest of the Bolshevik members of the Duma November 1, 1914, communications had broken down between Lenin and his colleagues. Only ninety copies of the first issue of his wartime publication, *Sotsial-Demokrat*, reached Stockholm and only five or six of these got into Russia. Later on twenty copies were smuggled to Petrograd in a pair of shoes.[32] By the end of December 1914,

Lenin's Stockholm agent, Shlyapnikov, had lost communication with Russia completely. In the winter of 1914–15, 157 copies of *Sotsial-Demokrat* and about thirty leaflets were smuggled in, but arrests—411 Bolshevik party members were arrested between the outbreak of war and the end of 1915—wrecked the organization. The Petrograd committee was virtually wiped out and the Moscow organization was heavily infiltrated with police agents. Lenin's only reliable allies were members of his own family, particularly his sisters, Anna and Mariya.[33] There is no record of any significant Bolshevik activity during 1915. Nor for that matter in 1916. Yelena Stasova was released from exile and returned to Petrograd in late September 1916, and the following month Lenin's sister Anna was released from prison but she was too ill to carry on any work. A new Russian Party bureau was created November 16[34] in Petrograd comprising Kasimir Zalutsky, Shlyapnikov, and young Vyacheslav Molotov, who for much of the time had been working almost singlehanded.[35]

But they engaged in no meaningful activities. Work was carried on in what an official Party historian calls "very complicated conditions." He makes clear that the other radical parties had won the sympathies of the workers.[36] The Bolsheviks had hoped to organize a demonstration January 9, 1917, to mark the anniversary of the 1905 uprising. But their print shop was raided by the police, the printers arrested, and no leaflets could be put out.[37] They managed to get out one thousand leaflets calling for a demonstration February 10 to mark the anniversary of the exiling of the Bolshevik Duma deputies, but the workers did not respond.[38]

Shlyapnikov wrote to Lenin on February 11. It was a dismal letter. He had heard only once from Switzerland since the turn of the year. He wondered whether Lenin had received the materials he had sent in December (apparently Lenin had not). Organization work was not bad but "would be much better if we had the people." Nonetheless, the political struggle was sharpening. "You can smell the prerevolutionary hurricane," he said, offering Lenin no evidence in support of this optimistic assessment. He did not even mention the Bolshevik demonstration the day before, February 10, which had been such a fizzle.[39]

As Globachev, chief of the Petrograd Okhrana, accurately observed just before January 9: "A series of liquidations in recent times has significantly weakened the force of the underground and now, according to our agents, on January 9 there will be only individual strikes and attempts to hold meetings and these will have an unorganized character."[40]

The other left-wing parties called for a demonstration February 14 to mark the opening of the Duma but Globachev pointed out that the Bolsheviks were not going to support them. On that day 89,576 workers in fifty-six factories went out on strike but a feeble attempt to send a demonstration to the Tauride Palace was easily thwarted by the police. The next day the number of strikers dropped to 24,840 at twenty factories.[41]

Isolated, Lenin once more turned his attention away from his homeland. More and more rare were his comments on Russian affairs. He filled his letters with exasperation over *Swiss* politics. He struck out at *Swiss* socialists and *Swiss* Social Democrats as savagely as he once had at his Russian opponents. When not trying to play a role in Swiss affairs he cantankerously argued with his fellow émigrés—not about the Russian Revolution but about the international socialist movement. He wrote article after article, one open letter after another, leaflets, pamphlets, studies—and none were published. By late 1916 and early 1917 Lenin's only channel of publication was his own *Sotsial-Demokrat* with its scant circulation or the occasional publication written for money in which his polemics were pruned. Even Inessa Armand took it upon herself to modify an open letter which Lenin wrote to Boris Souvraine (but which was not published in full until 1929).[42]

It was in this atmosphere of alienation, of deep despondency and growing preoccupation with West European affairs, that Lenin set off with Krupskaya on the evening of January 9 for the pseudo-Gothic Volkhaus. The building was headquarters of the Swiss Socialist party and a familiar hall to Lenin. Tonight he had been invited to lecture to a group of young Swiss workers on the lessons of the 1905 Revolution in Russia. As always he had prepared carefully for the talk, assembling a whole portfolio of clippings and working and reworking his remarks.

He spoke in serious, almost scholarly terms, pointing out how the Revolution had erupted spontaneously, through the emotions of simple, uneducated, illiterate men and women who did not realize that they were making a revolution. He told the young Swiss how the movement spread to the countryside and the peasants and how it even began to "shake the 'firmest' and last prop of tsarism," the Army.

The Russian Revolution of 1905, he said, would prove to be the "prologue to the coming European revolution."

"We must not be deceived by the present grave-like stillness in Europe," he said. "Europe is pregnant with revolution."

The moment was not necessarily at hand. But "coming years" would see the victory of socialism in Europe.

"We of the older generation," Lenin concluded, "may not live to see the decisive battles of this coming revolution."

Nowhere in his address did he suggest that Russia once again might be swollen pregnant with revolution. Nowhere did he predict that 1905 was about to repeat itself. Nowhere did he suggest that Russia might lead the way to the "coming proletarian revolution."

His eyes were on Europe. And even there, as his wife said, he wondered rather wistfully whether he[43] might live to see the day of the triumph he[44] had so long dreamed of. It was the speech of a middle-aged man who has put aside the fiery ambitions of youth, the speech of a man who was preparing to hand the torch of his hopes over to the next generation, the speech of an émigré too long in exile, the speech of a man cut off from his homeland yet eternally ill at ease in a distant and alien country.

The next morning Lenin was back again in his accustomed seat in the reading room of the Zurich cantonal library. Each day he made his way here or to the Library for Social Literature on Zeilergraben where he worked over his books, looking to neither right nor left, conversing with no one until noon when he emerged, lunched with Krupskaya, and then, like as not, returned.[45]

By February 22 Lenin was writing Inessa a tired letter about his arguments with the Swiss Social Democrats.[46] He was getting ready to draft an article on Bakunin, and on the same day the faithful Krupskaya wrote to Vyacheslav A. Karpinsky in Geneva saying that for some reason they had had no letters for a long time from their agent in Sweden who kept them informed on Russian affairs and no answers to letters sent two weeks previously.[47]

On February 28 Lenin wrote Inessa a short note, worrying about her silence and failure to reply to his letters. Once again, as so often, he was afraid she had taken offense at some of his sharp remarks. He sounded depressed. Alexander Solzhenitsyn suggests there was a rift in relations this winter between Inessa and Lenin but there is no hint of this in the published correspondence.[48]*

"From Russia," Lenin wrote Inessa, "nothing—not even letters. We are making arrangements via Scandinavia."

---

* Solzhenitsyn's novelistic re-creation of Lenin in Zurich seems off-key and simply does not coincide with historical reality, existing sources, and known facts. The extent of Lenin's correspondence with Inessa in autumn 1916, when Solzhenitsyn postulated a rift between the two and suggested that Inessa was deliberately staying away from Lenin, hardly supports his theory. Lenin sent Inessa at least eight letters between October 6 and November 9, 1916, and from internal evidence received at least three letters from her. It is true that Lenin wanted her to come to Zurich and she did not, but there was nothing unusual in this failure. It had happened often before. The question is carefully examined by Alfred Erich Senn in a paper presented to the convention of the American Association for the Advancement of Slavic Studies, October 1976.

He did not know that in Russia the February Revolution had been under way for five days.

Where were the others? Many of the revolutionaries, like Lenin, were in Switzerland—among them Martov, who, so often Lenin's opponent, was in many respects the Social Democrat whose views were closest to Lenin's, perhaps one reason why they so seldom found agreement. With Martov was his close colleague Axelrod.[49] Like Lenin they were deeply involved in the complexities of émigré polemics. The dean of Russian social democracy, Plekhanov, estranged now from almost all of his colleagues, was suffering through the war years in Paris, writing for a newspaper called *Prizyv*. He was a supporter of the war effort; most of the others opposed it. An old friend, A. P. Aptekman, saw him in 1916: "Lord such a face! Tormented, suffering . . . A martyr, plagued by doubt, by inner division, having lost his way . . . an eagle with broken wings."[50]

Trotsky had unexpectedly been cast up on the shores of America. France, where he had been contributing to the left-wing socialist organ *Nashe Slovo*, suddenly decided to deport him—at the insistence of the Imperial Russian Embassy. *Nashe Slovo* opposed the war, opposed the Czar, favored a new order in Russia. In September 1916 Trotsky was expelled. Switzerland refused him. So did England. Spain was his only alternative. But the Spaniards did not want him either. They took him to Cadiz and proposed to put him on a slow boat to Havana. Finally Trotsky was permitted with his family to sail from Barcelona to New York.

On Sunday January 13 he noted in his diary: "We are nearing New York. At three o'clock in the morning everybody wakes up. We have stopped. It is dark. Cold. Wind. Rain. On land, a wet mountain of buildings. The New World!"

It was the New World, complete, as Trotsky delightedly noted, with electric lights, gas cooking, a bath, a telephone, and even a chute for garbage. He took an apartment "in a workers district" on 164th Street for eighteen dollars a month. But Trotsky hardly left the Old World. Almost immediately he was at work on the Social Democratic paper *Novy Mir*, with offices in St. Marks Place, then as now a run-down neighborhood. Through the window of his newspaper office Trotsky watched an old man fish out a crust of bread from a garbage can.

Bukharin was a collaborator on *Novy Mir*. Alexandra Kollontai was also in the United States, traveling constantly, making speeches.[51] Moisei Volodarsky, later to be assassinated in Petrograd by the SRs, and G. I. Chudnovsky, later to be killed in the Ukraine, were on the *Novy Mir* board along with Trotsky and Bukharin. It was, Trotsky said, "the headquarters for internationalist revolutionary propaganda," and he thought it was gradually making headway against the powerful *Jewish Daily Forward,* then with a circulation of 200,000. Almost overnight Trotsky became a towering figure in the half-world of the Russian revolutionary intelligentsia in New York.[52] He and his wife paid calls Sundays upon the families of other Russian Jewish leftist émigrés. More than one child grew up with the legend of having been "dangled on Trotsky's knee" in a crowded apartment on the Lower East Side.

Deep in Siberia dozens of revolutionaries, Bolsheviks, Mensheviks, SRs, served out their long terms—Dan and Tsereteli among the Mensheviks, both in the Irkutsk area as was Abram Gots of the SRs (Chernov was in Paris and N. A. Natanson in Switzerland) and Yekaterina Breshko-Breshkovskaya. She was in nearby Minusinsk. That winter, as always, she was busy each day writing letters to her friends in America. "Really," she wrote, "my nature is like that of a wild man. Steppes, forest, air, river, sky are the region where I grow young and strong. Without space I feel like a bird in a cage." She was seventy-three years old, but on February 24, 1917, she wrote Miss Julia C. Drury, of Boston: "This furious war, as I hope, will teach the majority of mankind to understand its own interest and to improve life throughout."[53]

Among the Bolsheviks in Siberia were Lev B. Kamenev, Matvei K. Muranov, Yakov Sverdlov, and Stalin.

Stalin had been living in Siberian exile since July 1913 in the little village of Kureika. He did not grow more congenial with the passing of the years and had taken up trapping of hares and fishing.[54] He did maintain a friendship with another exiled Bolshevik from the Caucasus, Suren Spandaryan, an Armenian, who was living in Monastyrskoye. It was technically illegal for Stalin to visit Spandaryan but, as usual, surveillance in Arctic Siberia was minimal. Stalin made no effort at escape and his only Marxist work seems to have been a study of the national question which he sent to Sergei Ya. Alliluyev in Petrograd for forwarding to Lenin in 1913.[55]

Stalin did write Lenin on February 17, 1915, sending "warm warm greetings." He asked after Lenin's health and added: "I live, as before, chew my bread, completing half of my term. It is rather dull but it can't be helped." He expressed hope that Lenin would soon be issuing a newspaper attacking Plekhanov and other Social Democrats, a paper "that will lash them across their mugs."[56]

In October 1916 the Russian Government changed its regulations and began calling up political exiles for military duty. Stalin received notice to report for induction. He made his way first to Monastyrskoye and then to Krasnoyarsk by dog and reindeer sled. In February 1917 he was examined and rejected because of a stiff left arm due to a childhood injury. Then, because his four-year exile was almost completed, he was permitted to settle in Achinsk, a small town on the main line of the Trans-Siberian.[57]

So the actors were scattered to the four winds and three continents. A few, of course, were in Petrograd. There young Molotov still carried on with the Bolshevik party (although without direct contact with Lenin, who, so far as is known, did not even know of his existence).

And there, too, was Alexander Kerensky on the center platform, an active member of the Duma, a participant of almost every hushed conference that took place in the Duma corridors and in the Petrograd drawing rooms.

On February 14, 1917, the day of the opening of the Duma, Kerensky spoke before the members of the Progressive Bloc.

"Have you not realized," said Kerensky, "that . . . the historic task is the immediate overthrow of the medieval regime at all costs?"

The acting president of the Duma asked Kerensky what he meant.

"I was referring," he said, "to what Brutus did in the days of Rome."[58]

XXXVI

"I Think the Revolution Has Begun"

At the end of Kamennoostrov Prospekt where the bridge leads to the island, the park, the palace, and what then were the villas and estates of the wealthy stood one of the countless gray buildings in which the countless gray bureaucracies of the Czarist regime were housed. One tenant chanced to be a section of the Ministry of Agriculture.

On the morning of Tuesday February 21, a day which Nicholas noted in his diary as windy, cold, and snowy,[1] two young typists in this office were overheard talking about the high prices, the difficulty of getting food, the long lines in the streets.

"You know," one said, "it seems to me that the Revolution is beginning. . . ."

The man who overheard the remark, Nikolai Sukhanov, a radical politician who was to go down in history as the diarist of the Revolution, smiled to himself. Just like a couple of chattering women! The Revolution is beginning. Indeed! Later on he was to remember the chattering girls. They, he realized, were the first to notice.[2]

A few days earlier, on the thirteenth, a young American who happened to be in Petrograd wrote his mother-in-law in Moline, Illinois, that life was getting more difficult. He had enjoyed maslenitsa ("pancake week") at the beginning of February. He had eaten blini with melted butter and whipped sour cream, sold by farmers coming in from Finland with their sleighs and jingling bells. But now no pastries could be had in the restaurants; some of the candy stores had closed;

many restaurant orchestras had been dismissed; trains were getting more crowded and scarce. It was hard to find rooms in Petrograd.[3]

The opening of the Duma on February 14 caused less excitement than had been expected by the Government and the Duma members. In part, in the opinion of the brilliant young Kadet deputy, V. V. Shulgin, this was because the "feeling of nearness to Revolution was so terrifying that at the last moment the politicians softened their speeches." Everyone had begun to tread more carefully. Shulgin heard of a meeting of revolutionary workers and soldiers. The workers wanted to demonstrate. The soldiers refused. "After you demonstrate you can go back to your factories but we soldiers can't return—we would be shot."

The fact was, Shulgin concluded later, that "the revolutionaries were not ready but it—the revolution—was ready."

"Alarm and melancholy filled the air," he observed. "During the speeches of Milyukov, the talk of Shulgin, the declaration of Rittikh and the other speeches there was a feeling that all this was unnecessary, too late, of no importance.

"For behind the white columns of the hall grinned Hopelessness and she whispered: 'Why? What for? What difference does it make?' "[4]

On February 17 another of those endless disputes broke out in the Putilov steelworks, the largest and most important military and industrial establishment in Russia with its 26,700 workers. There was nothing unusual about the row. It began in the gun-carriage shop with an argument about the discharge of several workers and wound up with a demand by the shop committee for the return of the workers to their jobs and a 50 per cent increase in pay. Naturally, the Putilov management refused to meet the demands, and on the eighteenth the shop walked out. A couple of days later four other shops joined them, and on the evening of the twenty-first the rest of the factory decided to support their comrades. The next morning the Putilov management declared a lockout.[5]

On the twenty-first—the same day the young typist was overheard saying that "the Revolution is beginning"—Zinaida Gippius noted in her diary: "Today there were disorders. . . ."[6] Maurice Paléologue, the French ambassador, passing a bakeshop, "was struck by the sinister expressions on the faces of the poor folk who were lined up in a queue, most of whom had spent the whole night there."[7]

As the official Bolshevik history comments: "The movement was set off by an intermingling of different causes in which the element of accidentalness was expressed very clearly. No one in essence told himself that he was standing on the threshold of revolution."[8]

On the morning of the twenty-second Vladimir Zenzinov, a member of the Central Committee of the SRs, was working in the cluttered editorial offices of the *Severnye Zapiski*. He was correcting page proofs of the magazine, due for publication at the end of the month. Nothing unusual was going on. Five or six men came into the office and asked to see Alexander Kerensky, an editor of the magazine as well as a close ally of the SRs in the Duma. The workers came from the Putilov factory and they had something important to tell Kerensky which they would not impart to Zenzinov. Fortunately, Zenzinov had Kerensky's home telephone number, 119-60. He rang him up and Kerensky agreed to meet the group at 7 P.M. in the editorial offices. The workers didn't want to go to Kerensky's home; they were afraid the police might interfere.

At 7 P.M. the workers met with the "Citizen Deputy," as they called Kerensky. They told him of the lockout by the Putilov management and said they wanted to share with him the burden of "the profound consequences" which they were convinced would ensue. They spoke with solemnity and simplicity. They told Kerensky that the strike did not have a purely private character, that is, it did not concern simple economic demands nor the high cost of living. The workers, they said, were conscious that this was the beginning of a great political movement and they counted it their duty to warn the deputy. They did not know how the movement would finish but the moment was grave. The quietness and earnestness of the workers gave weight to their words. They spoke with a sense of history.

Zenzinov acknowledged that he had not paid special heed to the visit. He doubted that Kerensky had either. Later he realized that the Putilov workers may have been among the few who already understood the full seriousness of what was happening.[9] Certainly on this day, the day the Czar quietly boarded his train and left Tsarskoye Selo to return to his headquarters at Mogilev, there was no sense of drama. It was true that the lines at the shops had grown longer, the shortages so often predicted from the wartime displacement of economy had finally become acute. In bakery after bakery signs had appeared even before daylight saying: *"Khleba Nyet"*; at the kerosene store signs had gone up: *"Kerosina Nyet"*; candle shops had no candles; flour shops no flour; grocery stores no sugar; butchers no meat.

As Mme. Amélie de Néry, a sharp-eyed French woman, noted, even at temperatures approaching forty below zero, women—workers' wives, wives of the petites bourgeoisies, servants of the great houses, formed up in queues at 3 A.M., waiting for the opening of the butcher shops, the sugar and tea stores, at 9 A.M.

She found that for a small portion of potatoes which cost before the war 15 kopecks the price was now 1 ruble 20 kopecks; butter—if it could be found—cost 1 ruble 20 kopecks a pound. Boots cost 50 to 100 rubles, fashionable women's shoes 60 to 120 rubles, workingwomen's shoes 25 to 35 rubles. Felt boots had trebled in price. Even in fine apartments the temperature was often only a bit above freezing because of the cost of wood.[10]

Day by day the muttering, the shouting when the doors of the shops closed or supplies ran out, grew angrier. More and more often the women shook their fists at the shopkeepers. The police looked on with sympathy. In the long hours they exchanged stories about their hardships.

"How can we live like this?" the women asked.

The police shook their heads. They had no answer.

February 23 was International Women Workers' Day, not a widely observed holiday. Still it had some meaning to women workers. They usually marked the day with meetings and wore their best clothes. Yevgeny Onufuriyev was a worker in the Nevsky quarter and what was rare enough in those days, an underground member of the Bolshevik party. He was reminded of Women's Day when he was awakened on the morning of the twenty-third by his wife.

"Get up, Zhena," she said. "It's time you left for the factory."

His factory, the Anchar plant, was on strike, so he and his friends decided to go over to the big Obukhov factory and see if they wouldn't halt work too. A goodly number came out and Onufuriyev spent the day marching through the streets. Every time they saw a bakery there was a huge line of women. They all shouted together: "*Khle-e-e-ba . . . Khle-e-e-ba . . .* bread . . . bread."

They finally wound up on the Nevsky Prospekt singing:

> "Bravely, comrades, we march
> Our spirit strengthened by battle . . ."[11]

The city authorities, attempting to cope with the situation, had decided to introduce a rationing system. The cards were not yet printed, nor had the size of the ration been decided. But rumors began to fly that it would be a pound a day—insufficient to sustain strength for the Russians, whose diet was based on bread.[12] Possibly in preparation for rationing, authorities forbade the further sale by the Petrograd Consumers Society of flour and bread to workers' co-ops and factory eating places. The stocks of flour and bread of the Consumers Society were seized to add to the general supplies. This action struck heavily in the Vyborg quarter where there were eleven workers' co-ops and eating places serving not less than 30,000 workers and 90,000 to 100,000 members of their families.

The inspector of the Second Vyborg Police Division reported on February 22 that he was getting complaints that people had had no bread for two or three days. Therefore, he concluded, "strong street riots are to be expected."[13]

The afternoon of Thursday February 23 was so bright and warm that Madame de Néry felt spring was just around the corner. The snow had melted from the windows and the balconies, and if there wasn't yet a real thaw the hint was strong enough to give the crowds a special gaiety. She walked down the Morskaya. It seemed as though all the world was on the streets. The softness of the air and the warm sunshine, she thought, could explain that.

She took a streetcar on the Nevsky. At the Kazan Cathedral an enormous throng had gathered. Everyone crowded to the windows.

"What's going on?" Madame de Néry asked.

"It's the workers from the Putilov factory. They've gone on strike and are demanding bread. They've come back from demonstrating at the Duma."

The strikers marched down the street, serious and solemn, with police ranks on either side. Some of the crowd plucked the black plumes from the horses of the mounted officers. The crowd shouted hurrahs. Madame de Néry got off the streetcar and joined the crowd. There was no disorder. It was like a holiday. There was no concern on the faces of the people who kept talking about the strikers: "They're right. The flour has been hidden. Life is too expensive. We can't stand it."

"A revolutionary breeze had already passed over the city," Madame de Néry observed.

Actually, the throngs were made up not only of Putilov workers. Many were women from the textile factories who were celebrating Women's Day. They were joined by strikers of other plants. The demonstrations had started earlier in the day on the Vyborg side and in the Petrograd quarter. The workers then streamed over the bridges and where blocked by the police had crossed the ice of the frozen Neva. The women attacked at least two bakeries where bread was not forthcoming—the big Filippov bakery on Bolshoi Prospekt and another on Kamennoostrov Prospekt. Police didn't interfere. "We value our lives," they said, taking one look at the fierce and determined women.[14]

Some said the Putilov workers would be back at work the next day. Others said no, that the factory had closed down for lack of fuel (this, in fact, was the case). When Madame de Néry got back to the place where she was staying with a friend, she thought the whole thing was almost a dream. Here everything was quiet and normal. No one had heard of any strike or any disorder.[15]

Many in the city were ignorant of anything unusual. The Countess Olga Putyatin was serving as a nurse in the Anglo-Russian Hospital on Nevsky Prospekt at No. 41, the southeast corner of the Fontanka. She saw nothing abnormal except "as always during the past months there stood enormous lines at the bakery and meat stores."[16]

It was, of course, those "enormous lines" which were the visible evidence of what the newspaper Utro Rossii called the "precipice" before which Russia stood.[17] Protopopov, the incompetent Interior Minister, felt the day's demonstrations were entirely spontaneous and without plan or preparation, but he was concerned about the food shortage and called on the city authorities for action.[18]

Gen. Sergei S. Khabalov, commandant of Petrograd, called in Mayor Balk and some of the bakers and ordered that supplies be increased.[19] There was in the city, as of February 23, 500,000 poods of flour. Estimating bakers' needs at 35,000 to 40,000 a day, Khabalov calculated the city had ten or twelve days of flour on hand.[20]

Khabalov ordered that on the city walls by the morning of the twenty-fourth there be posted his proclamation declaring:

"In recent days the distribution of flour to bakers for baking bread in Petrograd has been of the same quantity as previously. There should be no shortage in bread for sale. If in some stores there is not enough bread it is because many people fearing a shortage have bought it to put away as hard tack. There is sufficient rye flour in Petrograd. The delivery of this flour continues without interruption."[21]

There had been no shooting on the twenty-third, although two horses and one rider had been injured by a grenade.[22] Count Louis de Robien, a twenty-nine-year-old attaché at the French Embassy, took a stroll in late afternoon with a friend named Friquet. He found everything calm on the Nevsky except for a few demonstrators. On the Sadovaya the streetcars had halted. He met a friend, who told him there was talk of big demonstrations in the suburbs.

The embassy held a pleasant dinner party that evening. Among the guests were Prince and Princess Gorchakov, Countess Kleinmikhel, Count Tolstoy, former Premier Trepov, one of the Dolgoruky princesses, and the Spanish ambassador, the Marquis of Villasinda. During dinner Alexander Benois, the artist, told Count Robien that it was true, there had been some incidents in the outskirts and that a tram had been overturned.[23]

Ambassador Paléologue spoke with Trepov about the food situation. He did not find Trepov's replies reassuring, but the main subject of conversation was the big party which Princess Leon Radziwill was giving on Sunday—scores of guests, music and dancing.

Paléologue and Trepov stared at each other, then spoke simultaneously:

"What a curious time to arrange a party!"[24]

Zinaida Gippius noted in her diary that the disorders had continued but that "no one knows anything exactly." It was, she said, "like looking into turbid waters—we look and can not see how far away we are from the collapse."[25]

Gippius' words were echoed by V. N. Kayurov, a Bolshevik underground worker leader. He said, "At this moment no one could predict where [this movement] would go."[26]

Protopopov rode down the Nevsky during the evening. There were not many people on the wide avenue which was brilliantly lighted by huge searchlights on the Admiralty spire.[27]

That evening the Czar was disturbed. He had had a telegram from his wife reporting that two of the Imperial children, Olga and the Czarevich, had the measles. It also looked as though Vyrubova was down with the disease. However, things were so quiet at Headquarters and his life was so peaceful that he thought he would again take up dominoes.[28]

Early on Friday the twenty-fourth General Khabalov met with a delegation of bakers, up in arms over his proclamation. They said everyone was blaming them for the shortage, whereas in fact they had no flour. Khabalov finally agreed that they would get at least 35,000 poods a day. They also complained of a shortage of bakers, and Khabalov promised to have the Army release 1,500 as soon as possible. An official named Veis told Khabalov to be careful about releasing flour because reserves were low. He said that he had visited five stores on the Bolshoi Sampsoniyevsky, in the heart of the Vyborg workers' section, and found all had flour on hand. One had five days' supply, another had ten.

Khabalov arranged with the Okhrana, the Czar's security police, to carry out arrests that evening of revolutionaries and suspected revolutionaries.[29] And he decided to strengthen the security forces on the streets, having heard that Cossacks of the First Don Regiment had been very gentle with the crowds, not attacking them, simply letting them slip by.[30]

Friday was another fine day, clear skies and warm sun. Madame de

Néry returned to the Nevsky. The crowds were enormous. She was struck again by their high spirits. Almost all the shops were open. The throng was especially dense near the Kazan Cathedral. Suddenly a young officer commanding a detachment of Cossacks ordered them to charge the crowd. The Cossacks obeyed the order, forming a double file with lances poised. The crowd opened up, let the Cossacks pass through, then re-formed in the rear of the horsemen shouting "Hurrah!" The Cossacks trotted ahead, smiling and nodding to the crowds which cheered them. A worker approached one of the officers: "Your Highness," he said, "remember that we are starving." Some Cossacks told workers: "Push harder and we'll let you through."[31]

Tram movements gradually ground to a halt. Demonstrators boarded the cars and removed the power levers.[32] The police estimated that 197,000 workers were on strike; the Okhrana's estimate was 158,000. The demonstrators thronged the Nevsky and Liteiny prospekts all day long. Amidst the shouting for "*Khleba*" (bread) there began to be occasional shouts of "*Doloi voiny! Doloi tsarskoi monarkhii!* (Down with the war! Down with the Czarist Monarchy!).[33]

From the windows of the Anglo-Russian Hospital at the corner of the Nevsky and the Fontanka the Countess Putyatin watched the crowds and was delighted to see how gingerly the Cossacks treated them. They only charged after shouting or trumpeting at the people.

"I was in the industrial sections of the city toward evening," she wrote in her diary. "At the Pryazhka [canal] and at that end of the Fontanka there are everywhere animated faces and enormous lines but the majority of the people seem to be joking. I saw nothing threatening."[34]

Gippius thought the demonstrators on the Nevsky were "jolly."[35] Count Robien amused himself by watching the Cossacks on their little horses patrolling the Neva quays. They galloped along with a truss of hay tied to their saddles in a net, carrying both lances and carbines. He heard through the Belgian ambassador who had been at Tsarskoye Selo that the Empress was very calm although she spoke of the danger of hungry people. However, she said the Army was loyal and could be relied upon.[36]

Sukhanov decided that his first priority was to collect information on what was happening. He telephoned N. D. Sokolov, an important political figure, sometimes called a Bolshevik but actually more of an independent radical. Sokolov agreed to assemble a group of left-wing representatives in his apartment the following day, Saturday, at 3 P.M., to assess the situation.[37]

The Duma continued to debate the food situation. The Council of Ministers met under Premier Golitsyn. The talk was of provisioning the city. No one mentioned the disorders. When Prince Golitsyn left the meeting, his chauffeur had to take a roundabout route because of the crowds on the Nevsky but Golitsyn didn't notice anything out of the ordinary. The State Censor decided not to permit the morning papers to publish the Duma speeches of Fyodor Rodichev, N. S. Chkheidze, and Kerensky and warned the editors not to leave white blanks where the speeches should have appeared.[38]

The Czar was in a quiet and reflective mood on the evening of the twenty-fourth. With word that three of the children were now down with the measles, he suggested to his wife that Mariya and Anastasia might as well be exposed to get the whole family over it. His brain, he said, was at rest—no Ministers, no disturbing questions, no need to think. "I think that it is useful for me but only for my mind," he wrote his wife. He was worried about supplies for the troops. A blizzard had halted all trains. If food wasn't gotten through in three or four days, there would be real hunger.[39]

Nicholas displayed no sign of concern over the situation in Petrograd. Voyeikov, the "sporting general," as some called him, was worried by reports of the disorders (he was told they were serious but the Government had matters in hand) and that evening tried to persuade the Czar to go back to Tsarskoye Selo. The Czar turned the idea aside. He would stay at Headquarters for three or four days anyway.

XXXVII

The First Shot

What was happening in Petrograd? This was a question which more and more troubled thoughtful citizens. The Kadets (and they were not alone) strongly suspected a Government provocation. They feared that the Government had deliberately created the food crisis in order to provide justification for signing a separate peace with Germany (which had just issued a series of peace feelers). Zinaida Gippius thought this kind of thinking was "blind and stupid."[1] The handful of survivors of the underground Bolshevik organization agreed "with aching hearts," as Kayurov said, that they must go forward with support for the demonstrations but saw little or no hope of any outcome other than the crushing of the movement by the Czar's troops.[2] Up to this point no Bolshevik recognized in what had been happening on the streets of Petrograd any sign of the long-awaited, constantly discussed, and frequently predicted revolution. "No one thought the possibility of revolution was so near," Kayurov admitted.[3]*

* The Bolsheviks in the assessment of their official historian of the twenties, M. N. Pokrovsky, didn't think the country was within "dozens of versts of an armed uprising." (S. P. Melgunov, *Martovskiye Dni 1917 goda*, p. 18.) As Shlyapnikov, Lenin's lieutenant and the most reliable member of the Bolshevik Central Committee, put it: "None of us thought (on Feb. 24) that the movement then underway would be the last and decisive battle with the Czarist regime. We held no such belief." (A. Shlyapnikov, *Semnadsty god*, Vol. I, p. 87.) As Zenzinov, the SR leader, said: "Revolution struck like thunder from a clear sky and caught by surprise not only the Government and existing social organizations. No one predicted that from this movement would emerge the coming revolution." (*Oktyabr- skoye Vooruzhennoye Vosstaniye*, Vol. I, pp. 49–50; V. Zenzinov, *Iz Zhizni Revo-*

Instead of leading, the revolutionaries, like everyone else, had all they could do to keep up with the Russian masses streaming into the broad avenues and prospects of the capital city.

Petrograd from early morning on Saturday the twenty-fifth was a slowly surging sea of people. It seemed that all of the city's 2.5 million citizens had taken to the streets. The crowds flowed out of the Vyborg section, the Narva section, the Petersburg side; they came from Vasilevsky Island, from the Neva district. There were no figures on how many were on strike. Some simply used the figure 306,500—the total working force of the city.[4] One official figure was 304,945. Another was 240,000.[5] Figures didn't matter. No trams ran. No cabs ran. Not an industrial plant operated. Only the most essential services such as gas, electricity, and water were maintained.

Early Saturday morning at General Khabalov's order new proclamations had been plastered on the walls. They warned that if the strikers did not go back to work by Tuesday all those in the classes of 1917, 1918, and 1919 who had been deferred would automatically be called up for army duty.[6]

Nikita Rudkovsky, eleven-year-old son of an Interior Ministry official, went to school as usual Saturday morning. His school, the Larinsky Gymnasium, was on Vasilevsky Island and he had to cross the Tuchkov Bridge in walking from his home on the Petersburg side. His mother hadn't wanted him to go because of the disorders but he had a German quiz he didn't want to miss. At the entrance of the bridge he noticed a small crowd around a grocery store. Suddenly, the crowd broke in, smashing the door and windows, and began to emerge with its loot. Nikita particularly noticed a grinning youngster with a load of chocolate bars. He noticed another thing, a patrol of ten Cossacks clattering by. They paid no heed to the looters, looked straight ahead nonchalantly, and disappeared.[7] Madame de Néry also witnessed some looting. She saw a fourteen-year-old youngster offering mother-of-pearl buttons for sale on the Liteiny, a ruble for six dozen. A friend saw a soldier join in looting a small Jewish shop. She thought the distinction between "yours" and "mine" was beginning to blur. For the most part, she still heard the crowds shouting for bread. She heard no shouting against the Emperor or against the war.[8]

Zenzinov saw a crowd protest when a banner saying: "Down with

lyutsionera, p. 81.) The official history of the Leningrad workers' movement declares: "The activities and instructions of the Bolshevik center lagged behind the mass actions of the proletariat in significant measure. . . . It was not able fully to take over the mass movement which had taken on an extraordinarily wide character." (*Istoriya Rabochikh Leningrada*, p. 521.)

the War" was unfurled, apparently by a Social Democrat group—possibly Bolsheviks. The banner quickly disappeared. However, red flags were becoming commonplace.[9]

The troops still had orders not to fire on the crowds. In fact, Gen. Mikhail A. Belyayev, the War Minister, had given a special caution about firing because of the "bad impression" which pictures of bodies on the Nevsky would make if printed in the newspapers of London and Paris. He recommended that to prevent crowds from crossing the Neva fire be directed onto the ice in front of them to keep the channel open.[10]

From her windows on the Nevsky Countess Putyatin had a front seat for the principal demonstrations. All day on Saturday she and her friends watched the growing friendship between the Cossacks and the crowds. The crowds continued to shout "Hurrah" when the Cossacks appeared. The Cossacks touched their hats and carefully rode around the people.

"In the afternoon," the Countess noted, "the people began to command, halting carriages with officers and forcing them not to ride along the Nevsky but to turn on the Fontanka."

An officer who refused to obey was pulled from his carriage, his sword taken away, bent in two, and thrown into the Fontanka. But the officer was not hurt. The Countess saw a Cossack who had fallen from his horse picked up by the crowd and carefully seated again on his mount.[11]

Zenzinov in midafternoon marched up the Nevsky with a throng toward Znamenskaya Square where under the monument to Alexander III a continuous mass meeting was in progress. Some speakers were workers, some were middle class, and some were students. All kinds of speeches were being made—some for a responsible ministry, some for support of the Duma, and some for war "to a victorious conclusion."[12] Zenzinov noticed several small units of Cossacks stationed around the square but they didn't seem to be interfering. In fact, some observers thought the Cossacks were more interested in listening to the speeches than halting them. Suddenly a Cossack unit moved forward and crossed the jammed square from one corner to another. The crowd simply opened up, let the horsemen through, then closed ranks. The orator at the Alexander III statue went on speaking. Then Zenzinov heard the clatter of hoofs on the stone pavement and a new detachment of horsemen emerged from beside the Nicholas railroad station. These, it turned out, were mounted police, led by a solidly built officer in a tight belt and gray uniform. There was a warning blast of a bugle. And another. Zenzinov heard a shot and Constable Krylov, leader of the mounted police, fell dead. As Zenzinov clearly saw, a

Cossack had raised his gun at the third sounding of the bugle and shot the police officer.[13] Zenzinov turned and ran for his life. So did the crowd. The hour was about 3 P.M.[14] V. N. Katyurov, a worker in the Erickson electrical factory, remembered that when the mounted police began their charge at Znamenskaya that day he and other workers turned to the Cossacks and asked their help against the Pharaohs, as the mounted police were called. When Krylov was shot, the crowd cheered and the Cossacks waved their caps.[15]

Krylov was not the day's only casualty. There were others killed and wounded—three were killed and nine wounded outside the City Duma.[16] But Krylov's death was a turning point. Government forces, the distinguished regiments on which the regime depended to maintain order and to protect the throne, had gone against the police. The Czar's forces had joined with the people.

At about the time that Officer Krylov was losing his life, Nikolai N. Sukhanov, self-appointed historian of the February Days, was beginning to be convinced that he was witnessing the opening of the Russian Revolution. He made his way to the apartment of N. D. Sokolov where at 3 P.M. a select group of political figures was to meet.

On his way Sukhanov dropped in at the offices of Maxim Gorky's magazine, Letopis, on Monetny Place. Nothing was going on there but gossip. No one could see any plan nor reason in the actions by the authorities. At one hour they would cordon off one section of the city, at the next another. Movement was almost entirely free, making clear the lack of power of General Khabalov and General Trepov.

Sukhanov bumped into a group of workers near the Letopis office.

"What we want," one of them said, "is bread, peace with the Germans and equal rights for the Jews."

The meeting at Sokolov's did little to clarify the situation. Kerensky, excitable and talkative, spoke about the confusion in the Duma and the inability of the bourgeois representatives to decide what they wanted. Soon he ran back to the Duma, and somewhat later Zenzinov and Sukhanov made their way to Kerensky's apartment where he agreed to meet them in an hour.[17] It was quiet but Kerensky rang up to report shooting on the Nevsky. His wife, Olga Lvovna, came in from her institute near Kazan Square to say there had been shooting in the square but no one could be certain who had done it or how many casualties there were.

The feeling came strongly to Sukhanov that a climax had been reached. He and Zenzinov waited for Kerensky, who never did appear, then went out into the streets, where dusk was falling. They walked past the Tauride Palace, where the lights burned dimly.

Sukhanov cut across the ice of the empty Neva from the Liteiny to the Troitsky Bridge and went to Maxim Gorky's flat, where he found not only Gorky but two of his editors, V. Bazarov and Alexander Tikhonov, with whom he was soon engaged in violent argument—he wanting to discuss organizing plans for the Revolution, they being interested only in the events of the day. Several Bolsheviks drifted into the apartment. Sukhanov thought them narrow-minded, concentrating on how to organize workers, get out leaflets, and set up illegal presses, whereas he wanted to discuss the broader issues of where Russia was moving.

Finally, toward 11:00, Sukhanov left Gorky's place and went to his flat where he slipped in unnoticed by the porter. He was living illegally in his own apartment and had been for nearly three years, since his official exile from Petrograd.[18]

The Duma, thought Gippius, had occupied a "revolutionary position" in much the same way a tramcar does when it is thrust across the rails. The liberal intelligentsia, so far as she could observe, hadn't the slightest connection with the movement on the streets. They kept whispering: What insanity! We need the Army. We have to go on! Now —everything for the war! But no one was listening.[19]

That evening Paléologue took the Vicomtesse du Halgouet, wife of his secretary, to the Liloty concert at the Mariinsky. The theater was almost empty. Even some orchestra members were absent. They heard the first symphony of a young composer named Saminsky and Saint-Saëns' Fantasia played by Georges Enesco. When they left the Mariinsky, the ambassador noticed that his car was the only one parked in the square. There were troops massed in front of the Litovsky Castle prison and gendarmes guarding the Moika Bridge.[20] Count Robien went to the Mikhail Theater that evening with a colleague, Charlier, and the Countess Kleinmikhel. The play was L'Idée de Françoise. The Mikhail Theater was as empty as the Mariinsky. Charlier didn't think the situation was too serious. Countess Kleinmikhel was less optimistic. She thought there would be defections among the troops.[21] Edward Heald, a young YMCA secretary who had recently arrived in Russia, went with some of his friends that Saturday night to the Mayak (Lighthouse) the Russian equivalent of the Y. Very few young men turned out for the gym class.[22]

Throughout the long Saturday General Khabalov had been closeted with his aides in the Petrograd governor's office. As the situation grew more and more threatening he finally sent to General Alexeyev at Headquarters his account of what had been going on in the past forty-eight hours. He pointed out that the troops had not used their arms against the demonstrators and that on this day, Saturday, efforts of the demonstrators to tie up the Nevsky had been thwarted by the Cossacks; that a number of police had been wounded and Constable Krylov had been killed on the Znamenskaya.

Interior Minister Protopopov telegraphed the Czar's aide Voyeikov that the demonstrations had "an unorganized random character" and that while denouncing the Government the demonstrators cheered the troops. He said the military were taking "energetic measures" to end further disorders and that Moscow was quiet.[23]

Voyeikov told the Czar about Protopopov's telegram and once again (or so he recalled) sought to persuade the Emperor to return to Petrograd but the Czar brushed aside the suggestion.[24]

The Czar had received two telegrams from the Czarina that day. One in the afternoon said that the "city is still quiet" and one in the evening said that "things are still not well in the city."

The Czar's schedule was much as usual—he met with his staff, went for a long automobile ride, got the Petrograd mail at 5 P.M. Gen. Dmitri N. Dubensky thought he looked concerned but his spirits were good. He wore a Caucasian Cossack uniform that Saturday and went to vespers without bothering to put on his overcoat.

The mail brought him a letter from the Czarina, telling him that she was reading *Aunt Helen's Children* to her measles-stricken family and that, the day before, there had been some disorders and the Cossacks had been called out after Filippov's bakery had been attacked.[25] Not until Sunday would he read the letter the Czarina dashed off to him late Saturday explaining that Petrograd had been afflicted by a "hooligan movement, young men and young women who run and shout that they have no bread simply in order to create a disturbance and workers who keep others from working." If the weather were a bit colder, she said, "everyone would just stay at home." Everything would be all right if only the "Duma would behave itself."

Much of her letter, naturally, concerned the children, their temperatures, their spots, and their coughs. But she had a few political observations. She had heard of the incident at Znamenskaya Place. What was needed, she felt, was a real cavalry regiment that would firmly establish order, not these unreliable reserve units made up of Petrograd recruits. Also she thought Khabalov should bring in army field kitchens to bake bread for the populace and she thought there should be a card rationing system and that all factories should be militarized —then there would be no disorders. The strikers simply should be told that if they went on strike they would be sent to the front. There was no need of shooting, only a need to preserve order and control the bridges so the crowds could not move freely. She was afraid the situation would be worse on Sunday.[26]

Before sitting down to dinner the Czar sent a telegram to Khabalov. It said:

> I command you tomorrow to end the disorders in the capital which are not permissible in a time of difficult war with Germany and Austria.
>
> Nikolai[27]

It was about 9 P.M. when Khabalov got the Czar's wire. During the evening an excited meeting took place at the City Duma at which Kerensky, Shingarev, and Matvei I. Skobelev spoke. They made violent protests about the shooting of demonstrators. A resolution demanding freedom of assembly and free speech was approved.[28] While the meeting was in progress police swept through Petrograd arresting revolutionaries and suspected radicals. Among those picked up were Anna Ulyanova-Yelizarova, Lenin's sister, and Yelena Stasova.[29]

"What do I do?" Khabalov asked himself when he received the Czar's telegram. "How do I end it tomorrow? When they said: Give us bread—you give it and that is that. But when on the banner is written 'Down with Autocracy'—how can bread quiet them? The Czar orders: 'You must fire.' I would be killed. Positively killed."

An hour later he called in his lieutenants and told them that instructions had been changed. The Czar had directed that order be restored in the city. Tomorrow, if faced with resisting crowds, the instruction was: Give them three warnings then shoot.[30]

At midnight the Council of Ministers met at Premier Golitsyn's. Before the meeting Rodzyanko had called on the Premier and asked him to resign. Golitsyn shrugged his shoulders and showed Rodzyanko a *papka*, a file in which there was a blank order for the prorogation of the Duma already signed by the Czar. He asked Rodzyanko to arrange a meeting of the Duma leaders with him.

At the council meeting the question turned on the dissolution of the Duma. Golitsyn's colleagues except for Protopopov and two others opposed its dissolution. Protopopov reported on the day's disorders and Khabalov told of the orders he had received from the Czar. Some Ministers wanted the city to be put under a state of siege. Khabalov opposed this. Golitsyn favored more talks with the Duma leaders and warned his colleagues that some might have to be sacrificed. Protopopov, for example. It was 4 A.M. before the meeting broke up. Golitsyn thought Khabalov seemed slow-witted, lacking in energy, and even confused.[31]

The city lay dark and sleeping as the tired Ministers bustled into their heavy coats, sank back in the leather seats of their limousines or the fur-rugged cushions of their sleighs, and wearily made their way homeward. There were troops at the bridges and the intersections, fires burning to keep them warm. But no other sign of life in the city. The dawn of Sunday and a new day was almost at hand.

Not a word was spoken at the Ministers' meeting; nor at the conference of Khabalov and his police aides; nor in Protopopov's sessions; nor in the stormy debate at the City Duma; nor in the gathering of the revolutionaries, radicals, and intellectuals at Sokolov's and at Gorky's of what had been happening Friday evening and during Saturday at many of the factories.

The workers had begun to discuss the idea of naming deputies to a new Workers Soviet, the kind which they had created in 1905. During Saturday many delegates were actually chosen. The Soviet, thus far, was only an aspiration. Yet it was in the minds of hundreds of thousands of Petrograd workers now on the streets.[32]

XXXVIII

Revolutionary Sunday

Sunday the twenty-sixth was another beautiful day—warm, sunny, not quite thawing, with a softness in the air promising that winter's end was near. The morning was so uneventful that General Khabalov telegraphed Stavka that "the city is quiet." So it was. But not for long.

About 4 P.M.[1] Leonid Andreyev, whose apartment was on the same side of the Champs de Mars as the barracks of the Pavlovsky Regiment, saw from his window troops apparently firing at the barracks. He called up his friend, the basso Fyodor Chaliapin, who lived nearby, and told him about it. Neither could make out what might be happening.[2]

The fourth company of the Pavlovsky Regiment had been confined to its barracks that Sunday. Possibly it was being held in reserve. In early afternoon, another unit of the regiment, the training command, opened fire on demonstrators in front of the Kazan Cathedral. Some civilians who worked at the Pavlovsky barracks rushed back and, tears in their eyes, told the troopers what had happened. The troopers, highly disturbed, broke open the armory, took thirty rifles, and came out into the street, moving along the Catherine Canal toward the Nevsky.[3] They hoped to meet their comrades and persuade them to stop firing. As the troop passed along the canal it collided with a unit of mounted police and an exchange of shots took place.[4] At this point someone telephoned General Khabalov reporting firing between two military units not far from the Resurrection Church. Khabalov was told that fifteen hundred men had dashed from the Pavlovsky barracks discharging their guns in the air, and then opening fire on the mounted police. Officers and chaplains of the regiment were sent after the rebellious unit. Colonel Eksten,[5] commander of the Pavlovsky Regiment, making his way back to the barracks to take charge of the turbulent soldiers, was attacked by the crowd and killed. Whether this incident was connected with the other events is not certain.[6] Finally, the rebels returned to the barracks and gave themselves up to the Preobrazhensky Regiment which had been called in to take a hand. Some nineteen of the "worst mutineers" were bustled off to the Peter and Paul Fortress where it was the intent of War Minister Belyayev to have them quickly tried and hanged. This was not to be.[7]

Word of the Pavlovsky mutiny flew from one end of Petrograd to another. By mid-Sunday evening everyone in Petrograd from the Vyborg slums to the Millionnaya Street salons knew that mutiny had appeared in the Czar's forces. As Sukhanov commented: "To the Pavlovsky regiment belongs the honor of having carried out the first revolutionary act of the military against the armed forces of Czarism."[8] It was, he added, a deep "breach in the stronghold of Czarism."

The sunny Sunday had turned into a day of terror. Watching from the windows of the Anglo-Russian Hospital, housed in the palace of the Grand Duke Dmitri, Countess Putyatin had seen the crowded Nevsky suddenly empty—people, soldiers, everyone running for their lives, huddling against the walls of houses, throwing themselves flat on the pavement or behind streetcar poles. Then the rattle of rifle fire in the distance and the snap of bullets against the wall of the corner ward. She saw a line of soldiers dressed in gray (later she heard they were police disguised in military uniforms), deploy across the broad Nevsky Prospekt at the Sadovaya and lay down a continuous volley of rifle fire. The wounded and dead lay "like poor lumps" on the pavement. She counted seven bodies, and later a dozen wounded were brought into the hospital. A young Guards officer carried in his cousin, a cadet, thinking he had only lost consciousness. The cadet had been killed instantly by a bullet.[9]

Khabalov had plastered the city with new posters, forbidding meetings and warning that the troops would use arms to maintain order. In the Znamenskaya Square forty people were killed and many more wounded and ten were killed at the intersection of First Rozhdestvensky and Suvorov streets.[10] Here and there among the crowds appeared persons with weapons, for the most part revolvers, occasionally grenades. "The signs of transition of a people's movement into an armed uprising were present" commented the official Bolshevik chronicler."[11]

The president of the Duma, Rodzyanko, became more and more alarmed. He rose early on Sunday, determined to prod the authorities into positive action. First he went to Agriculture Minister Alexander A. Rittikh, who was supposed to be getting the food situation in hand. He got him out of bed and took him to Defense Minister Belyayev. They talked with General Khabalov by telephone and learned that nothing had been done about the bread supply. To questions from Rodzyanko as to why the troops were firing on the crowds he was told that the soldiers couldn't stand by when the crowds attacked them. Rodzyanko tried unsuccessfully to persuade Belyayev and Khabalov to use fire hoses instead of bullets.

Rodzyanko then sent a telgram to the Czar with a copy to the high commanders of the Army asking that they support his views.

The telegram said:

"Situation serious. Anarchy in the capital. Government paralyzed. Transport of food and fuel in full disorder. Popular discontent growing. Disorderly firing in the streets. Some military units fire on one another. Essential immediately to order persons having the confidence of the country to form new government. Delay impossible. Any delay deadly. I pray to God that in this hour the blame does not fall on the crown."[12]

After regular 5 P.M. tea at Mogilev the Czar told Voyeikov about Rodzyanko's telegram and invited him to read it. Voyeikov asked the Czar how he proposed to respond. The Czar said that since the Duma was being prorogued that evening and since Rodzyanko spoke in the name of the Duma no answer was necessary.[13]*

Protopopov (but not until well after midnight) sent Voyeikov a sanitized version of the day's events, mentioning the Pavlovsky company but only as an exception to the "ardor" of the other troops. He said there was evidence that on Monday the twenty-seventh at least some of the workers planned to go back to their jobs.[14]

The Czarina was by no means sanguine about the situation although she tried to keep up her hopes. She telegraphed the Czar at 11:50 A.M.: "Very concerned about the city."[15] She spelled out her fears in two letters, one written in the morning and the other in midafternoon. In the morning she apologized for mentioning the food situation. "I wrote about that yesterday, I'm an idiot," she said. But she went on to report what her good friend Lily Den had heard from

* According to Count Frederiks the Czar responded to this telegram (or to one from Rodzyanko the following day): "Once again that fat Rodzyanko has written me some kind of rubbish which I am not even going to answer." (*Padeniye Russkoi Revolyutsii*, Vol. V, p. 38.)

questioning the *izvoschiki,* the cab drivers. They reported, according to Lily Den, that students had told them if they didn't go out on strike they would be shot. So, of course, the cab drivers and porters had gone on strike. But it wasn't like 1905, the Empress was certain, because the people adored the Czar. It was just that they wanted bread.

Writing again at 3:30 in the afternoon, she said things had gone poorly but Protopopov thought they would be better on Monday because of the strict measures which had been taken.

"It seems to me," she said, "that it will all be all right. The sun shines so clearly and I felt such peace and quiet at His [Rasputin's] dear grave. He died in order to save us."[16]

There was some concern at Mogilev but mostly among the junior officers. General Dubensky asked in his diary: "Why can't the Czar understand that he must show his will and his power?"[17] It was a question which had been on people's lips since 1896.

The Czar wrote to Alix that he had suffered a sharp pain in the center of his chest for about fifteen minutes while in church that morning. When he stood up, his forehead was covered with perspiration and later his heart began to palpitate. Now, however, he felt better.

"I hope that Khabalov is able quickly to stop these street disorders," he wrote. "Protopopov should give him clear and definite instructions. If only old Golitsyn doesn't lose his head!"

At 9:20 P.M. he sent his wife a telegram saying he would leave for Tsarskoye Selo the day after tomorrow, that is Tuesday.[18]

Then he read a bit and played dominoes.[19]

In Petrograd the Council of Ministers met under Golitsyn's chairmanship at the Mariinsky Palace.[20] Khabalov, appearing even more confused than the evening before, told of the unreliability of the troops.[21] Rittikh reported on his conversations with Duma members in which Vassily Maklakov talked about the possibility of creating a new government. Golitsyn asked General Belyayev to take command of the troops because of Khabalov's incapability. There was discussion about getting in some reliable artillery units,[22] and it was decided to announce a state of siege and to prorogue the Duma, using one of the blank decrees the Czar had signed for this eventuality.[23] When Rodzyanko got back home that evening, he found waiting for him an official decree proroguing the Duma to April "because of the extraordinary situation."[24]

Two other meetings were held in Petrograd that evening. The first was at Gorky's and was a meeting only in a peripheral sense. People streamed in and out of Gorky's flat all day and all night. The apartment had become the information center of the February Days.

Sukhanov got there in the afternoon, went out in midafternoon to have a look at the streets, watched agitators openly haranguing soldiers around the Troitsky Bridge, and took close account of the way the soldiers reacted—some listening attentively some chuckling, none hostile—then went back to Gorky's. Gorky seemed perplexed and baffled. He was horrified by the action of the riflemen who had "cleared" the Nevsky.

Sukhanov sat around Gorky's talking until late at night. When he went home he didn't bother about concealment. He simply rang the porter and went in by the front door.

At Kerensky's apartment the participants included N. D. Sokolov, the leftist Menshevik, Kerensky himself, Matvei I. Skobelev, a right-wing Menshevik, I. Yurenev, a Social Democrat close to the Bolsheviks, P. Alexandrovich, a radical SR, G. Erlikh, a Bundist, Shlyapnikov, a member of the Central Committee of the Bolsheviks, A. V. Peshekhonov, Zenzinov, A. Yermansky, a Menshevik-internationalist (close to the Bolsheviks), Sukhanov(?), and two Trudoviks, M. Ye. Berezin, and S. F. Znamensky, close to Kerensky.[25]

Yurenev, in contrast to all the others present, showed no enthusiasm about the course of events, expressing great skepticism and lack of confidence. "There is not and will be no revolution," he said. "The movement among the troops amounts to nothing. Reaction is increasing. It is clear the workers and the soldiers don't share the same objectives. We must prepare for a long period of reaction."[26]

It was necessary, Yurenev said, to occupy only an "observer's role." "We must wait and see," he insisted. He attacked Kerensky for hysteria and exaggeration. Since Yurenev occupied the extreme left wing, his opinions struck the others like a dash of cold water.

It was clear, Zenzinov said, that Yurenev's position was not a personal one. It was the Party position of the Petersburg Bolshevik organization. Yurenev was against forcing the pace of events, and the only thing he would agree to was that "Kerensky use his social connections and collect money for issuing an information bulletin."[27]

This reserved position, Zenzinov said, was general among the Bolsheviks. It was true, of course, that the Bolsheviks had little or no leadership. "We got no orders," the Bolshevik Kayurov recalled. "The Petersburg Committee was in prison and the Central Committee member Shlyapnikov was in no position to give orders for the next day.[28] When I. D. Chuguran proposed forming "armed commandos," Shlyapnikov opposed the idea. He was afraid this would just antagonize the soldiers.[29]

Late that Sunday night Zinaida Gippius turned to her diary and tried to sum up what had happened:

"The connection between the Duma and the revolutionary movement is very indefinite and invisible. The 'intelligentsia' continue to stand to one side. They are not really even informed. Is there somewhere a Soviet of Workers Deputies, like 1905, working out slogans? . . . But no. It is a headless revolution—the head has been chopped off. It is dead."[30]

Count de Robien and his wife left the French Embassy early in the evening to attend the party of Princess Radziwill at the Fontanka Palace. A car had been sent for them but because of the disturbances the Nevsky was still closed off and they had to go around by other streets.

There was little gaiety when they first arrived. Not even the brilliant lighting, the lackeys in their powdered wigs, and the beautiful setting cheered the guests. All the talk was of the shooting on the Nevsky, the dead, the wounded. The musicians were late. Evidently they had had trouble getting there. They dribbled in in ones and twos. But finally the band struck up and couples, a little nervous, took the floor. The Grand Duke Boris was there. He, too, was nervous.

By midevening, however, everyone seemed to be enjoying themselves. Nonetheless, De Robien and his wife left before midnight. The streets were filled with troops. The Nevsky was barricaded and illuminated only by a single searchlight mounted on the Admiralty spire.

As they drove up to their home a *sotnia* of Cossacks passed along the street, the snow deadening the horses' hoofs but not the clink of arms.[31]

From the windows of Pavel Milyukov's apartment one saw a short lane to the gate of the Volynsky barracks. Early on Monday morning the twenty-seventh, the doorman awakened Mikyukov. He said something was going on in the barracks. Milyukov looked out from his balcony window and saw soldiers waving their caps and milling about. They were shouting to passers-by that they were joining them. Milyukov was not exactly surprised by the scene. After the events of the past few days he was ready for almost anything. Still, he thought, events have reached a new stage.[32]

Milyukov was right.

When the Volynsky soldiers had returned to barracks Sunday evening, they started to talk and argue.

They stayed up most of the night trying to decide what to do. Finally, led by Sgt. T. Ye. Kirpichnikov, they agreed that they would refuse to fire again on the people. About 6 A.M. the unit assembled. Kirpichnikov spoke. As he was speaking Second Lieutenant Kolokolov entered. The men answered his salute as usual. Behind Kolokolov came Commander Lashkevich, who greeted the men, as customary: "Good morning, brothers."

Instead of saluting and responding "At your service!" the men shouted "Hurrah!" Lashkevich repeated his greeting. Again came: "Hurrah!" He turned to Sgt. M. Markov[33] and asked what this meant.

Markov, reaching for his bayonet, shouted: "It's a signal to disobey your orders!"

Rifle butts crashed on the barracks floor. The soldiers shouted: "Get out while you can!" Lashkevich made an attempt to read the Czar's proclamation, proroguing the Duma, then turned and fled with Kolokolov.

Markov and a soldier named Orlov grabbed their rifles, opened the window transom, and when Lashkevich and Kolokolov appeared in the courtyard two shots rang out. Lashkevich fell dead.[34]

Khabalov got word of the mutiny at 6:30 A.M. He went to the scene personally. By this time the Volynsky Regiment had been joined by units of the Preobrazhensky and Litovsky regiments. The troops were drawn up with their weapons outside the barracks. Khabalov hurried away to try to find reliable troops with which to oppose them.[35]

The rebelling troops, joined by growing crowds of demonstrators and led by marching bands, swung down the Liteiny Prospekt, headed for the bridge to the Vyborg side where they planned to "bring out" the Moscow Regiment from its barracks on Sampsoniyevsky Prospekt.

When the crowd reached the Arsenal on the Liteiny, they stormed it, breaking in about 10 A.M. and seizing some 40,000 rifles and 30,000 revolvers, which were promptly distributed.[36]

At this point the mass of troops and demonstrators began to split up. Some troops attacked the gendarme barracks on Kirpochny. Others broke into the Engineer Cadets School.[37] One group went to the House of Detention on Shpalerny Street while others took as their targets the Litovsky Castle, a grim old prison, and the great Kresty Prison on the Vyborg side where so many revolutionaries had been imprisoned over the years.[38]

Soon a heavy column of smoke was rising from the burning District Court Building and the nearby House of Detention. When firemen appeared, the hoses were cut and the crowd prevented them from approaching. Efforts by Khabalov to find troops to save the court buildings failed.[39] The crowds roared through the streets. They wrecked district police offices and stormed the building of the Petrograd Okhrana and the Central Police headquarters.[40] At 2 P.M. the Petrograd telegraph office was put out of commission. Mikhail I.

Kalinin, a Bolshevik underground worker, joined a group of workers and soldiers who seized the Finland Station.[41]

After capturing the station the crowd didn't know what to do. One of the soldiers said: "Where are the leaders? Direct us!"[42]

Kalinin, as he recalled, had little more idea than the others as to what to do next but he was sure of one thing. It was not a moment for delay. The crowd should be led into action. He got up on the station platform and shouted: "If you want to have leaders—they are right next door at the Kresty [Prison]. We've got to begin to liberate the leaders."

A moment later the crowd stormed off, some to the Kresty, some to the military prison to free the prisoners.[43]

For a while the training company of the Moscow Regiment, which had been positioned on the Alexandrovsky Bridge, held back the revolutionary troops which sought to cross to the Vyborg side but soon they were swirling up to the Moscow Regiment barracks on Sampsoniyevsky Prospekt. There they met a company standing outside the barracks without officers. Some officers had been killed, some wounded.[44]

By 4 P.M. Petrograd was in the hands of the revolutionaries except for the commandant's offices at 2 Gorokhovaya Street, the Mariinsky Palace, the Admiralty, the Winter Palace, and the Peter and Paul Fortress.[45]

From the moment at 6 A.M. when the Volynsky Regiment had turned on its officers, the Romanov regime was doomed. No one understood this at that hour. No one understood it as the other military units began to side with the Volynsky troops. Not even when the Arsenal was seized at 10 A.M. and the District Court Building began to burn at 11 A.M. was this clear to the troops, the street crowds, the Czar's authorities, or the observers. By noon of Monday February 27, some 25,000 troops had revolted. This was only a fraction of the forces which the Government had at its nominal command—perhaps a bit more than 5 per cent of the troops and police concentrated in Petrograd and its environs. But it was enough.

It was still not clear to those in the streets that they had triumphed. However, the deterioration of the situation was painfully clear to General Khabalov, commandant of the Petrograd garrison. He was close to nervous and physical collapse. After the rising of the Volynsky Regiment he managed with difficulty to assemble about 1,500 men—two companies of the Kexholm Regiment, two of the Preobrazhensky, a company of the Imperial riflemen—in all six companies, fifteen machine guns, and a squadron and a half of cavalry. He put them under command of Col. A. P. Kutepov of the Preobrazhensky Regiment, a Cavalier of the Order of St. George who had been severely wounded in fighting at the front.[46]

This tiny force was given the task of trying to restore order; to disarm the revolting regiments; to get them back to their barracks; if necessary to compel them by force of arms.

The effort was hopeless. It did not succeed in any of its objectives. Kutepov set out and vanished in the swarm of humanity which had taken over the city streets. Khabalov heard that the unit had gotten to Kirpochny Street, then that it was advancing on Kirpochny toward Spassky. He tried to send some cavalry reinforcements but heard no more. The counterforce was swallowed up in the human sea.

It was the same everywhere. All of Petrograd was in the streets. The people simply drowned any effort to turn them from their course—the overthrow of the hated regime.[47]

Another individual who perceived what was happening was Police Director Alexei T. Vasilyev. He had been up most of the night with Interior Minister Protopopov at a long futile cabinet meeting. He awakened to the news of the Volynsky Regiment at 6:30 A.M. Hour by hour the news grew worse. From his apartment window he could see the scurrying in the streets, the dashing about of military cars, and he heard intermittent rifle fire. Each time the telephone rang it reported a new disaster. The prisons were being broken open, police stations ransacked, policemen caught and torn limb from limb by the crowds. Vasilyev was preparing to go to his office when a courier arrived and warned that he would never make it through the streets. He telephoned police headquarters and ordered his staff to leave the building. Hardly had the order been given than the building was stormed, records tossed into the courtyard and burned.

Moscow police kept calling Vasilyev and asking what was happening. "I replied to Colonel Alexander P. Martynov, chief of the Moscow Okhrana," Vasilyev recalled, "that a serious mutiny had broken out." The disorder was so great that neither the insurgents nor the military authorities thought of occupying the telephone exchange. It continued to work normally.

A bit later Vasilyev abandoned any effort to stay in touch with events. With his wife, a friend, and a passport made out in an assumed name he fled his quarters.

"To tell the truth I did not know where to go," he said. He spent the night in a friend's apartment listening to rifle and machine-gun fire.[48]

Baroness S. Taube-Anichkova saw a crowd dragging a young policeman to the Fontanka Canal. The man had been badly beaten, blood covered his face but even that did not conceal his terror. He pleaded: "Brothers! Brothers! Don't drown me. I swear by God I did nothing wrong. I didn't hurt anyone. Brothers!"

His words seemed to inflame the crowd. They lifted him and threw him over the wall into the canal. The policeman made the sign of the cross and started to swim, hoping that he could save himself. But the crowd gathered up paving stones and hurled them at the struggling figure until it finally disappeared in a widening pool of red-tinted water.[49]

About 2 P.M. Count Kokovtsov and his wife, warmly dressed in their black broadcloth coats and fur collars, she with a marten muff and he with a black caracul hat, left their apartment to see what was happening. They knew that there were disturbances but had no notion of the extent. They took their dog, Zhipik, along for an airing, walking down the Mokhovaya to the Sergeivsky and turning to the right toward Liteiny Prospekt. A blast of rifle fire sent them back in a hurry to the Mokhovaya, where they had to stop and look for Zhipik who had scurried under the nearest gate. As they hunted for the dog Alexander Guchkov emerged from the entrance of the Chief Artillery Administration, accompanied by a young man whom he introduced as M. I. Tereshchenko. Guchkov told Kokovtsov that the Duma had decided to form a new government in which Tereshchenko would be Minister of Finance and asked if Kokovtsov would be kind enough to make himself available for advice.[50]

Vladimir Nabokov, who lived on the Morskaya, walked to work on Monday morning. His job was in the Asian section of the General Staff. He worked until 3 P.M. as usual, then walked home, crossing the Nevsky, which was full of people. That evening, looking from a window which gave a view from the Hotel Astoria on St. Isaac's Square to the Konnogvardeisky Pereulok, Nabokov saw that the Morskaya was completely deserted. An armored car lumbered down the street. There was a sound of rifles and machine guns. An occasional soldier ran fast, hugging the walls of the buildings.[51]

XXXIX

A Year and a Half Too Late

The telephone of V. V. Shulgin, the sardonic monarchist Duma deputy and chronicler of the Revolution, rang at 9 A.M. Monday morning. It was his friend and fellow Duma member Andrei I. Shingarev.

"Is that you, Vasily Vitalyevich?" he said. "This is Shingarev. We must go to the Duma. It's begun."

"What's begun?" Shulgin responded.

"It's begun. We've received the ukase about the prorogation of the Duma. The city is agitated. They are occupying the bridges. We may not get there. They're sending me an automobile. Come immediately and we'll go together."

The two men made their way through the city. The crowds got thicker and thicker. Finally a student climbed on the running board and shouted: "Comrades, make way! These are members of the Duma —Comrade Shingarev!" The crowds cheered and opened a path. At the Troitsky Bridge the student dropped off, saying: "Tell the soldiers you are members of the Duma." The soldiers, too, opened the way and Shingarev remarked: "The Duma still stands between the people and the Government. So far both sides recognize it."

But Shulgin was pessimistic: "I think our role is ending."[1]

Within Tauride Palace the Duma leaders had assembled under the chairmanship of Rodzyanko. Quickly it was clear that the last thing anyone desired was to stand at the head of a revolution.

Some thought the Duma should simply ignore the Czar's ukase closing the session. But when it was pointed out that this would be a step down the revolutionary route, no one was prepared to take it.

In recognition of the Czar's orders it was decided not to meet in Catherine Hall, the traditional home of the Duma, but in the smaller semicircular hall. Still, no one could decide what to do. Outside, in the grandiloquent words of Shulgin, there "stalked One of whom few then thought but whom many felt in their subconscious. . . . In the streets filled with the crowds of thousands stalked Death."

Amid these futile deliberations the chief of the Duma guard burst into the room shouting: "Gentlemen members of the Duma—I beg your protection. I am the chief of the guard, your guard, the protector of the State Duma. Some soldiers have broken in. My assistant has been heavily wounded. They want to kill me. I barely escaped."[2]

Kerensky leaped to his feet: "We must not delay. I am constantly receiving information that the troops are agitated. They are coming to the streets. I now am going to them. It is essential that I know what I can tell them. May I tell them that the Duma is with them, that it takes upon itself responsibility and that it stands at the head of the movement?"

There were a few more words. Shulgin tried to raise the question of whether the advancing mob was for the Duma or against it, supporters of the war or friends of the Germans.

But his words were drowned in the emotion of the moment.

"Kerensky stood there determined," Shugin recollected. "Ready to depart, uttering sharp almost contemptuous words. He grew. He grew in the mud of the Revolution."

Someone whispered to Shulgin: "He is their dictator."

A few moments later the fateful step had been taken. The Duma members unanimously named a "Provisional Committee" of all parties except those of the right. It included: Chkheidze, Social Democrat; Kerensky, Trudovik; I. V. Yefremov, Progressive; V. A. Rzhevsky, Progressive; Milyukov, Kadet; N. V. Nekrasov, Kadet; Sergei Shidlovsky, left Octobrist; N. V. Rodzyanko, Octobrist; Vladimir Lvov, Center; Shulgin, Nationalist Progressive.[3]

The purpose of the committee was "to restore order in the capital and establish contact with public organizations and institutions."

"But," asked Sukhanov later, "did this connect the Duma with the Revolution? Did it provide a shadow of solidarity of the Progressive bloc with the people who were attacking the foundations of Czarism? Did this act mean some kind of solidarity between democracy and the bourgeoisie in the direction of overthrowing autocracy and carrying out the revolution?

"No. The revolutionary act of the bourgeoisie in the person of the

Progressive bloc and the Duma majority was directed at saving the dynasty and the plutocratic dictatorship from the democratic revolution. In those hours hope of saving the Romanov dynasty had far from disappeared."[4]

Outside the palace there was the sound of a distant surf. It grew louder. It was the tramp of thousands of feet, the feet of the people of Petrograd, the workers, the soldiers, the housewives, the hangers-on, the youngsters, the sight-seers. The *narod,* the people. Nearer and nearer it came. Nervousness within the great palace grew. At 1 P.M. the crowd was not yet in sight. Suddenly people began to arrive outside the building. The courtyard began to fill. Someone shouted from the main entrance, "They are arriving." Kerensky had been expecting them for hours. He rushed to the window and saw the soldiers, surrounded by civilians, lining up on the opposite side of the street. He thought the soldiers felt awkward and looked lost without their officers.[5]

Without waiting to put on an overcoat he dashed outside and shouted a greeting:

"Citizen soldiers, on you falls the great honor of guarding the State Duma. I declare you the first revolutionary guard."

But, commented Shulgin, "this 'first revolutionary guard' didn't last long. It was immediately swept away by the crowd."[6]

The gray mass came on and on like the tide of the sea. His Majesty, the Russian people, Shulgin called it, adding: *"Ils viennent jusque dans nos bras."*[7] It flowed into the courtyard and, filling the courtyard, flowed into the building, one room after another, soldiers in their muddy boots, trailing rifles, their overcoats wrinkled and crumpled, some back from the front, men who had not slept for days, bearded, dirt-caked, young blond peasants, hair unruly under their caps, faces red with the wind and the cold. On and on they came, swallowing up the palace, swallowing up the deputies who abandoned pretense of work to greet one company after another, one regiment after another, each new wave of arrivals. Chkheidze, Skobelev, Rodzyanko, Kerensky, met them, each making up some words of welcome, some kind of formless greeting for this protoplastic mass of the Russian people.

What brought them to the Duma? Kerensky recalled that from early morning he had telephoned his friends and asked them to go to the barracks of the troops and urge them to come to the Duma.[8] Kerensky was eager for the troops to come in order to protect the Tauride Palace from an attack by forces loyal to the Czar. He was so eager for the troops to appear that he ran from window to window of the palace, waiting for them to arrive.[9]

But Sergeant Kirpichnikov didn't recall any intention on the part of his comrades to go to the Duma. However, the Tauride Palace lay in the heart of what was called the "military city." It was surrounded by barracks of the Preobrazhensky, the Horse Artillery, the Sappers, the Horse Guards, and others. It was natural for the soldiers to move off in this direction. It could have been sheer accident but no one really accepted that. There were a good many who urged the soldiers to go to the Duma—Kerensky's friends, and V. B. Stankevich and N. D. Sokolov, who later declared that he was responsible for bringing the troops there.

The sharp-eyed French correspondent, Madame de Néry, gave credit to her friend Sonya Morozova, a young woman who played some role in radical circles, an educated woman of simplicity and modesty. On that morning of the twenty-seventh Morozova encountered the Volynsky Regiment shortly after it joined forces with the Preobrazhensky. The soldiers were uncertain what to do next.

Sizing up the situation, Morozova suddenly cried "To the Duma!" Placing herself at the head of the troops, she led them to the palace, shouting to the waiting deputies, "I have brought the Army!"[10]

Whatever the motive or leadership, by midafternoon 30,000 troops had gathered in and around the Tauride.

The storming of Kresty Prison and the House of Detention brought the release of most of the radical leaders of Petrograd, many of whom had been gathered up in police sweeps of the preceding weeks—notably the members of the Workers Section of the Military-Industrial Committee, arrested on January 26. Now in commandeered trucks the central core of a more radical, more revolutionary body made its way through the throngs of workers and soldiers. Led by K. A. Gvozdev, they joined their Duma friends and colleagues Chkheidze, Skobelev, and others and meeting in Room 13 formed a Provisional Executive Committee of the Petrograd Soviet, calling for the Soviet to meet at 7 P.M. There had been scattered elections in Petrograd factories over the last three or four days of delegates for a Soviet along the lines of 1905. Now it was coming into being.[11]

Even before the 7 P.M. meeting the Provisional Committee got to work to try to arrange for provisioning the city and took the first steps toward creating a military organization to protect the Revolution from attack by forces loyal to the Czar.[12] No Bolshevik participated in these preparations. No Bolshevik, so far as is known (and this is supported by all of the memoirs and the Communist histories), was present in the Tauride Palace during these hours.

The leaders in organizing the Soviet, the Bolshevik historians concede, were the Mensheviks, the SRs, the Trudoviks, and all the other left-wing parties. The leading role was played by Gvozdev of the Workers Section of the Military-Industrial Committee and his associate M. I. Broido together with the Menshevik Sokolov, Henryk Erlikh of the Jewish Bund, Chkheidze, and Skobelev.

The Bolsheviks appeared at the Tauride Palace only in the evening of February 27. They "underestimated the question of representation and leadership in the Soviet and its Executive Committee and in the following days the Central Committee sinned particularly in this respect," the Bolshevik official history comments.[13]

The first Bolshevik to arrive at the palace, so far as is known, was Shlyapnikov, probably the most responsible member of the Party then in Petrograd. He arrived around 7 P.M. in company of the memoirist-radical Sukhanov and the writer Alexander Tikhonov. It was an accidental trio. Sukhanov had spent the afternoon dashing about Petrograd gathering "impressions." He wound up at Gorky's flat, from which he had a panorama of the city, watching the trucks filled with armed workers and soldiers roar through the streets, decorated with red banners and cheered by the crowds. Clouds of smoke were rolling up from the burning Court Building and police statons.

It was decided to go to the Tauride Palace. On the way the group— Gorky, Sukhanov, Tikhonov, and several others—encountered Shlyapnikov. They argued about what was going on and finally went back to Gorky's apartment, then started out again. Sukhanov got the impression that Shlyapnikov and his Bolsheviks had no program, had formulated no slogans, and had little knowledge or understanding of what was happening.

Making their way through groups of armed young people, many of them women, motorcars in which soldiers brandished machine guns, trucks filled with ammunition and food supplies, they entered the Tauride Palace. That evening Shlyapnikov was named to the Executive Committee of the Soviet. At its first meeting he made no significant contribution so far as any participant has recorded.[14] Late in the evening, however, one Bolshevik motion was approved. It was made by young Molotov and provided for soldiers as well as workers to join the Soviet.[15]

The Czarina was isolated at Tsarskoye Selo, preoccupied with caring for her children, down with the measles, as was her companion, Madame Vyrubova, too seriously ill to be aware of what was happening. Lily Den, a close friend of Vyrubova's (and of the Czarina's), was also at Tsarskoye Selo. She had come to see Vyrubova and stayed on, partly to help the Czarina, partly because of the dangerous situation in Petrograd.[16]

In an effort to help those who were ill the icon of the Virgin of Znamenskaya Church had been solemnly paraded around the Alexander Palace, carried in a procession of priests and acolytes, chanting Orthodox prayers and swinging incense-laden censors. Alexei Volkov, the Czarina's valet de chambre, who marched in the procession, later insisted he heard a soldier mutter: "You trample on the people and you carry about idols." It was the first breath of the Revolution which Volkov felt at the Imperial household.[17]

By Monday morning the twenty-seventh, the Czarina realized from reports coming in to Tsarskoye Selo that the situation was rapidly moving out of control. At 11:12 A.M. she telegraphed the Czar:

"Revolution yesterday took on terrible scale. I know that more units have joined it. The news is worse than it ever has been."

At 1:03 P.M. she telegraphed:

"Concessions essential. Uprising continues. Many troops have gone to the side of the Revolution."*

At 9:50 P.M. she telegraphed: "Lily has been with us day and night. There hasn't been either a carriage or a motor. The District court is burning."[18]

The Czar's day at Mogilev had begun as usual. He went to General Alexeyev's headquarters for the 11 A.M. report on operations at the front. He spent some time with the general. Presumably they talked about the situation in Petrograd. There was nothing new on the military front to talk about.[19]

The bad news poured in. A little after 1 P.M. another telegram arrived from Rodzyanko warning the Czar that there was not a moment to lose. If the revolutionary movement spread to the Army (it already had!), Rodzyanko said, the Germans would exult, Russia would be crushed and the dynasty along with it. "The hour of your fate and that of Russia is at hand," said Rodzyanko. "Tomorrow may be too late."[20]

Even before Rodzyanko's message the Czar had been advised by General Khabalov of the mutiny of the Volynsky Regiment together with units of the Litovsky and Preobrazhensky. Khabalov urgently asked the Czar for reliable units from the front. Almost simultaneously War Minister Belyayev told General Alexeyev that while the revolt

* Shulgin commented: "This telegram was a year and a half late." (V. V. Shulgin, Dni, p. 180.) The telegrams became the subject of a popular revolutionary joke. Ordinarily the Czar promptly answered every telegram from the Czarina. So far as the record goes he did not answer any of these. The joke, repeated by both Trotsky and Vyrubova, was that the telegrams were returned to the Czarina with the penciled notation: "Address unknown." (S. P. Melgunov, Martovskiye Dni 1917 goda, p. 154.)

had not yet been put down he was "firmly confident of quickly restoring order."[21]

During the afternoon, the Czar may have talked with the Czarina at Tsarskoye Selo. There was a direct telephone connection from Mogilev both to Tsarskoye Selo and to Petrograd.[22]

The Czar noted in his diary that in the afternoon he took his customary constitutional, walking along the highway toward Orsha in the sunny weather.[23]

Despite mounting evidence of crisis the Czar remained firm in his determination not to change his plans. He would leave for Tsarskoye Selo on Tuesday. Nor was he willing to make any political decisions, such as permitting the formation of a new government.[24]

No one in Mogilev, to be sure, had any idea that the situation in Petrograd was already beyond remedy.

The Council of Ministers under Prince Golitsyn assembled in late afternoon in the Mariinsky Palace. General Khabalov was still trying to put bits and pieces of soldiery together. He had obtained a company of soldiers to guard the Mokhovaya approaches to the Mariinsky. He found some troops to occupy the telephone exchange and that was about all. General Belyayev described Khabalov at this point as "hands trembling, indifferent, lacking the ability to lead in this serious moment."[25] Meantime, there had collected in the square in front of the Winter Palace a number of units—some companies of the Preobrazhensky under Prince Arguntinovsky-Dolgoruky, some remnants of the force that had set out in the morning under Colonel Kutepov. Between 5 and 6 P.M. units of the Pavlovsky Regiment, led by a band, marched into the square and joined the other troops.[26] Several thousand troops assembled outside the palace. But they were of uncertain reliability. The council decided to declare a state of siege in Khabalov's name. The proclamation was written out in pencil. The Admiralty press was ordered to strike off one thousand copies—the city's printing press was in the hands of the revolutionaries. Once the proclamations were printed there was no way of posting them. No one had paste or brushes. They were spiked on the iron fences around the Admiralty and by morning the wind had blown them through the streets and into the Alexander Garden.[27]

A bit later in the evening Khabalov went to the Palace Square with Gen. Mikhail I. Zankevich, who was replacing him. The question was where to make a last stand with the handful of troops left. They hoped to hold a hollow square around the Winter Palace, occupying the area between the Moika and the Neva from the Winter Bridge along the Winter Canal. But they did not have enough troops. First the troops were sent to the Admiralty, but Zankevich—over Khaba-lov's objection as he recalled it—decided to occupy the Winter Palace instead. But by this time the Preobrazhensky Regiment had gone back to its barracks. So had the Pavlovskys and some Guards units. They had left only three companies of the Izmailovsky Regiment, one of the Yegersky, one of the Strelkovsky, two batteries, a machine-gun com-pany, and some miscellaneous police units—about two thousand men in all. There was little ammunition.

When they started to enter the palace, the commandant, Gen. Vladimir A. Komarov, urged them not to. However, the troops did go in.[28]

Interior Minister Protopopov, assuming that his ministry would be sacked by the mob, fled his office in early afternoon after filling a heavy briefcase with grisly mementos of his regime—his reports to the Czar, reports to and letters from the Czarina, letters from Vyrubova and Voyeikov, and police photographs of Rasputin's body. He gave the case for safekeeping to his assistant, Pavel Savelyev. Then he put 50,000 rubles which (as he claimed) he was holding for Count Dmitri Tatishchev into a fireproof safe and made his way to Prince Golitsyn's. The two went to the Mariinsky Palace. There the Council of Ministers decided to advise the Czar that most of the troops had gone over to the Revolution; to propose that he name as dictator a very popular general; to enter into discussions with the revolutionary troops; and to give Prince Golitsyn the right to change the composition of the coun-cil and enter discussions with the Duma. It was agreed there was no time to consult the Czar about these decisions.[29] A few moments later Prince Golitsyn turned to Protopopov and suggested that he "offer himself as a sacrifice" and leave the cabinet. Protopopov (who said af-terward that he thought the Czar had already agreed to his retire-ment) did not object. "Now there is nothing left to me but to shoot myself," Protopopov exclaimed.[30] He did not. He spent the night at the office of State Controller Alexander Malinkov[31] and the next day in a tailor's shop.[32]

At Mogilev there was discussion of the situation. The Czar, looking a bit pale and wearing an embroidered shirt, dined with General Alex-eyev and Gen. N. I. Ivanov, who had been invited to join them. Be-fore sitting down to dinner the Czar telegraphed the Czarina that he had ordered troops into Petrograd from Novgorod and he hoped, God willing, that the military disorders would quickly come to an end. He wrote his wife, as always, a tender letter promising to be with her in two days. "This will be my last letter," he said. And, indeed, it was the last. "After the evening news from the city I saw here many frightened faces," he said. "Happily, Alexeyev is confident but suggests that it is essential to name a very energetic individual in order to see that the ministers work for resolution of the questions of food, railroads, coal, etc. It is, of course, quite right."[33]

By this time Prince Golitsyn had sent an almost hysterical telegram reporting the gravity of the situation, the fact that the troops were steadily going over to the side of the workers and mutineers, and asking that he be relieved of duty and replaced by a Premier who would have the confidence of "wide levels of society."[34]

The Czar also knew that Interior Minister Protopopov had left the Government, resigning "on grounds of illness," as the euphemism was.

And Voyeikov had gotten a telephone call from Count Benkendorf at Tsarskoye Selo, saying that the Czarina was extremely concerned for the Imperial children and proposing that she leave and meet the Czar en route. The Minister of War, General Belyayev, had warned her, Benkendorf said, that there was danger of the mob moving on Tsarskoye Selo from Petrograd. The Empress had been unable to get in contact with any other Ministers.

But the Czar would have none of this. He would not even discuss moving the sick children. Instead, he said, he would come to Tsarskoye Selo as rapidly as possible.[35]

And, most importantly, not long before dinner the Czar had decided to send General Ivanov to Petrograd with dictatorial powers and an escort of one battalion of cavaliers of St. George and a company of Nicholas' personal guards.

Ivanov was a veteran military officer of the old school. At dinner the Czar was rather quiet, but Ivanov regaled him with tales of how he'd once quelled a mutiny in Harbin with the aid of two companies without firing a shot and how[36] he single-handedly quelled a rebellious crowd of sailors at Kronshtadt by shouting to one of them, "On your knees!" The stunned sailors sank to their knees and docilely permitted themselves to be led off to the brig.[37]

After dinner the Czar gave Ivanov a scanty sketch of the situation in Petrograd—"disorder among the reserve battalions and strikes at the factories"—and said he had named him commander of the Petrograd military district. Ivanov suggested it was better that he not lead troops into the city until the situation was clear in order to avoid bloodletting. "Yes, of course," said the Czar.[38]

The Council of Ministers was instructed to fulfill all of Ivanov's demands, and a force of eight reliable regiments from the northern and western fronts was to be placed at his disposal.[39]

While Ivanov was concerned about the military situation in Petrograd he felt that the cause of trouble lay deeper—in the food and coal shortages, distribution and political problems. His last words on taking leave of the Czar were: "Your Highness, permit me to remind you regarding the reforms." "Yes, yes," the Czar replied. "General Alexeyev has just reminded me about them."[40]

Did the Czar have reform in mind? Was he even now aware of the nature of the crisis of his Empire?

Some time between 9 P.M. and 10 P.M. his brother, the Grand Duke Mikhail Alexandrovich, called the Czar on the direct wire which connected the War Ministry with Mogilev.

The Grand Duke had gone to the Mariinsky Palace at Golitsyn's request after 8 P.M.[41] Rodzyanko joined the Ministers and an appeal was made to the Grand Duke to become Regent, take command of the troops, and ask Prince G. Ye. Lvov to form a new government. The Grand Duke refused to take control from his brother but agreed to ask the Czar to permit the formation of a new government of popular confidence under Prince Lvov.

With General Belyayev at his side Prince Mikhail asked on the direct wire to be connected with the Czar. The Czar refused to hold a direct conversation with his brother and named General Alexeyev as his deputy. By this time General Alexeyev was ill and hardly able to carry on. Nonetheless, he went to the Hughes wire and talked with the Grand Duke.[42]

Mikhail said he was deeply convinced that the only way to quiet the turbulent situation was to dismiss the cabinet and that Prince Golitsyn concurred in this. It was necessary to name a distinguished man, inspiring public confidence, as Premier and vest in him power to pick a cabinet. Mikhail suggested Prince Lvov as Premier and offered to make the announcement in the Czar's name if the Czar felt this appropriate.

General Alexeyev promised to pass the message on to the Czar who he said was leaving for Tsarskoye Selo the following day. The Grand Duke said he would wait at the War Ministry for a reply and added his personal advice that the Czar should delay his return to Tsarskoye Selo for some days.

After a wait of about half an hour[43] General Alexeyev advised Mikhail that the Czar was leaving for Tsarskoye Selo at 2:30 A.M.,[44] that he would make no changes in the Government before reaching Tsarskoye Selo, that he was sending General Ivanov to Petrograd with a reliable battalion, that tomorrow four reliable infantry and four cavalry regiments would be sent from the northern and western fronts.

The Grand Duke warned Alexeyev that time was running out and that each hour was especially valuable. The general promised the Grand Duke he would again urge the Czar to take the necessary steps "in these decisive moments on which depends the fate and future course of the war and the life of the state."[45]

The Council of Ministers continued to huddle in the Mariinsky Palace, listening to growing turbulence outside. Shortly after 10 P.M. General Khabalov managed to get off a last telegram to General Alexeyev, confessing his inability to fulfill the Czar's orders to restore order. Most of the troops had gone over to the Revolution. He had collected the few remaining soldiers and proposed to make a stand at the Winter Palace with Major General Zankevich.

By now the telegraph operators were warning Mogilev that communications were almost impossible. The operator said he could not handle any telegrams for the Council of Ministers as he had no means of getting through the city on foot and the telephone had ceased working.

A little after midnight General Belyayev sent a final message to Voyeikov at Mogilev. He had telephoned the Mariinsky Palace. The phone was answered by a revolutionary, not a secretary of the Council of Ministers. The revolutionaries had occupied the palace.

All of the Ministers except two, Belyayev said, had escaped safely. He did not know the fate of the missing two.[46]

General Belyayev then telegraphed General Alexeyev at Mogilev:

"The situation in Petrograd has become very serious. The military mutiny continues and loyal units have not succeeded in quenching it. On the contrary many units continue to join the mutineers. Fires have begun and there is no way of fighting them. Essential quickly send reliable fighting units in sufficient quantity to act simultaneously in various parts of city."

Grand Duke Mikhail had stayed on with General Belyayev at the General Staff Building waiting for the shooting in the city streets to die down so that he could return to his palace at Gatchina. About 1 A.M., beginning to despair about getting home, he went over to the Winter Palace with Belyayev, thinking he might spend the night there. He discovered to his surprise and anger that the Winter Palace had been chosen for the last stand of the Government troops.[47]

The Grand Duke asked that the troops be removed from the palace.

"I don't want troops firing on the people from the house of the Romanovs," he said.[48]

Where to go? Khabalov telephoned the Peter and Paul Fortress. The commandant, Baron V. I. Stal, reported that the revolutionaries hadn't taken over but he did not think the troops could reach the fortress because the Troitsky Bridge was occupied. The Prince some time after 2 A.M. left for his home in Gatchina.[49]

Khabalov and Zankevich finally led their force back into the spire-tipped Admiralty Building nearby where there was no ammunition, no food, no water, no forage for the horses. During the night most of the troops melted away.[50]

The Czar's Government had ceased to exist. The greatest empire in the world was a rudderless ship careening through the night. But no one knew this—not the aged Prince Golitsyn, not the Czar preparing to leave on his special train at 2:30, not the generals at the front facing the Germans, not the people on the streets of the city,[51] and certainly not the throngs at the Tauride Palace. As Milyukov observed: "In the capital of Russia there was no Czar, no Duma, no Council of Ministers. The 'disorders had taken on the manifest uniform of Revolution.'"[52]

XL

"Nothing's Left but Russia"

In the Catherine Hall the Soviet had been called to order. Sokolov ran about the hall telling those present whether they had a consultative vote or a real vote. Each delegate was supposed to represent 1,000 workers. About 250 delegates were present for the opening, but no one really knew or cared about this. A Presidium was named. Chkheidze was elected permanent chairman but Skobelev took the chair. There were repeated shouts of: "Order! Order!" The hall was overflowing with soldiers and now they cried for permission to speak. They stood on stools and chairs still clutching their rifles, calling for the floor.

As they began, "the audience," Sukhanov recalled, "listened entranced as though to an absorbing well known fairy tale, holding their breaths, with craning necks and unseeing eyes."

"We're from the Volynsky . . . the Pavlovsky . . . the Litovsky . . . the Kexholm . . . the Saperny . . . the Yegersky . . . the Finlandsky . . . the Grenadersky . . ." the soldiers said.

As each name rang out—the names of Russia's most heroic regiments—a storm of applause broke out. The soldiers said:

"We met . . . We were instructed to say . . . The officers ran away . . . To come to the Soviet of Workers Deputies . . . We were directed to say that we no longer want to serve against the people. . . . We are joining with our brother-workers all together to defend the people's cause. . . . We will lay down our lives for that. . . . Our general meeting sends greetings—Long Live the Revolution!"[1]

This *was* the Revolution.

It was happening before the eyes of the participants. But even here in its heart there was no understanding that these simple men, sweat standing on their foreheads, feet encased in dirty boots, illiterate, none having ever spoken in public, none before this day or yesterday a revolutionary, members of no political party, professing no political faith, unaware of the existence of such words as dialectics, Marxism, socialism, or economics, were *the Revolution*.

"Terrible rifles, hated uniforms, strange words!" thought Sukhanov.

In other chambers of the palace the Duma members were filled with indecision, misgivings, and even fright. Many, many regiments had not yet come over to the movement. Was this irresolution? Was it conscious neutrality? Was it preparation for battle against the internal enemy?

"The situation was still critical," Sukhanov observed. "There was the possibility of bloody battle between the organized regiments and their officers. The Revolution might still be throttled with naked hands."[2]

The soldiers, in truth, were the actual masters of the situation. But, as Milyukov noted, "they were not conscious of this themselves and threw themselves into the Palace, not as victors, but as people fearing punishment for violating discipline, for the murder of their commanders and officers. Even less than we were they confident that the revolution would triumph."[3]

Wildest rumors circulated. The Black Hundreds and policemen out of uniform were leading the crowds in pillage and plunder (not true). Military cadets had been mobilized to put down the people (not true). The police had mounted machine guns on the roofs and were terrorizing the city (doubtful).[4] Loyal troops were marching on the city, both from the front and from nearby provinces (not true). The Peter and Paul Fortress had fallen to the Revolution (not true). The Government had turned the Admiralty into an armed fortress and revolutionary troops were assaulting it. (The bedraggled force assembled by Khabalov and Zankevich wandered off about noon the next morning after the adjutant of the Naval Ministry[5] told them to clear out.) Kronshtadt had joined the Revolution (premature). The 171st Infantry Regiment, loyal to the Czar, had arrived at the Nicholas Station and was giving battle to rebel forces in Znamenskaya Square (not true).[6]

"We're lost," cried A. V. Grinevich, a radical Menshevik. "We're lost."[7] "Now it's the gallows," thought Peshekhonov.[8] Amid the elation whole groups, Peshekhonov recalled, were seized with a paroxysm of "doubt, terror and alarm." Kerensky suddenly feared a "terrible end." Skobelev was seized by panic. So was Stankevich. Chkheidze thought "all is lost" and "only a miracle" would save them. The soldiers' rebellion had terrified Chkheidze, Milyukov recalled.[9] Many feared a military take-over. Gorky shared this view.

He wrote his wife in Moscow that the events seemed "externally grandiose" and even "touching" but that their meaning was neither so profound nor so sublime as appeared. "I am full of scepticism even though the sight of the soldiers coming to the Duma moves me to tears."

"In the revolutionary army—I do not believe," he wrote. Many took part in the Revolution simply because of lack of discipline and organization. Only visionaries, he said, could expect that the Army would stand together with the Soviet.

"There is much more that is absurd than is grandiose," he said. "We can't go back but we are not going forward very far, perhaps only a sparrow's step. And, of course, much blood will be spilled—an unprecedented amount."[10]

All evening long as the endless stream of soldiers bore witness at the Soviet session in the Catherine Hall the Duma Committee struggled with its conscience. Should it take power? Should it not? Rodzyanko held back until the end. He spent the evening in exertions—and futile hope—that he could compel the Czar to act, to accept Prince Golitsyn's proposal, to permit the old cabinet to resign, and to form a new "government of national confidence." But as the evening wore on he began to waver. "I am not a revolutionary," he kept insisting. "I don't want a revolution. I've not made one and I won't make one. I won't go against the Czar's power."

But in the end, like Shulgin with whom he talked, he was won over. Shulgin told him simply: There were two possible conclusions. If the Czar formed a new government they would hand over power to it. If the Imperial Government fell, at least the power would be in their hands, not in those of some "dogs" or "scoundrels."

To Shulgin the monarchy was everything. Without the monarchy there could be no Russia. But for the first time the thought entered his head: "Perhaps in order to save the monarchy we must sacrifice the monarch."[11]

The decision of the Duma Committee to take power into its hands came just in time. Sukhanov, Sokolov, Peshekhonov, Yu. M. Steklov, and Grinevich were hard at work in the Duma chairman's office drafting a proclamation from the Soviet, announcing its creation as a center of revolutionary democracy, appealing for organization and maintenance of order. In a word, the Soviet was about to take power.

At this moment the telephone rang. It was someone from the

Preobrazhensky Regiment wanting to place the whole regiment at the disposal of the Duma. Sukhanov was holding the phone when Milyukov, his face rosy, his eyes puffy, his linen clean but his jacket rumpled, burst into the room. "A decision has been reached," Milyukov said. "We're taking power."

Sukhanov handed the telephone to Milyukov. Milyukov listened a moment.

"Very well," he said, "Colonel Engelhardt will be coming to you immediately in the name of the Provisional Committee of the Duma and will take command of the regiment."[12]

In the morning the walls of Petrograd were plastered with the manifesto of the Duma Committee declaring, "We have found ourselves with the necessity of taking into our hands the reestablishment of governmental and social order."[13]

In the words of Zinaida Gippius, a revolutionary government which contained not a single revolutionary, with the possible exception of Kerensky, had come to pass.[14]

Madame Kshesinskaya was warned on Sunday by Gen. Vladislav F. Galle chief of the Fourth Petrograd Police District, that she had better get out of her house. She did not leave but she put most of her jewels and portable valuables into a small suitcase.

On the evening of the twenty-seventh they were five at dinner—her son, Vova, George A. Pfluger, his tutor, and two dancers, P. N. Vladimirov and Pavel Goncharov, and herself. There had been shooting around the house all day. Suddenly, Kshesinskaya decided it was time to get away. She put on her plainest coat, threw a shawl over her head, and prepared to leave. One man took her bag of jewels, another picked up her fox terrier, Dzhibi, and they made their way to the apartment of Yu. M. Yuryev, a member of the Mariinsky Drama Company. She did not realize that she would never live in her palace again, that it would become, in fact, the headquarters of the Bolshevik party.

Kshesinskaya managed to get most of her more important valuables out of her house.[15]

The indefatigable Countess Kleinmikhel was not fazed by Petrograd's troubles. She held one of her usual dinner parties on the evening of the twenty-seventh—the Prince and Princess Kurakin; the Prince Mingrelsky, both the Barons Pilar, father and son; the last governor of Riga, Zvegintsev; Nilolai Belzac, the vice-president of the Russian Historical Society; Gubastov; and Von Strolnich, later shot by the Bolsheviks.

The party had hardly seated itself at the long dinner table when the servants tumbled into the dining hall shouting: "Run! Run! Armed bandits have broken in the back way. They've wounded two doormen and are coming this way. Run! Run!"

Pilar drew his sword and prepared to defend the party but the Countess grabbed him by the hand and the party ran down the broad front steps, out into the fifteen-degree cold and into the house across the street where Baron Pilar lived. From the windows of Pilar's house they watched the Countess' house lighted as it had not been since the start of the war. Candelabra appeared at each window. Then a motley throng of soldiers and sailors sat down at the table and were served a feast on the Countess' silver plates, drinking dozens of bottles of the best wine from her cellars.

In the mind of the Countess there was no doubt—the Revolution had occurred.[16]

Early in the evening of the twenty-seventh a long ring sounded on the bell of the third-floor apartment at the corner of Shirokaya and Gazovaya streets on the Petrograd side, 27 Shirokaya Ulitsa.

The building was sharply cornered like the prow of a ship and, possibly because its tenant, Mark Timofeyevich Yelizarov, worked for the Volga Steamship Company, his family called their apartment "the Steamboat Flat."

Georgi Lozgachev-Yelizarov, that is Gorushka, as he was called in the family, ran to answer the door. He had just come in from wandering around the streets. He had seen Cossacks bowing to people on the sidewalks; streets full of workers and demonstrators with red flags and all kinds of exciting things. He had hardly gotten off his coat and heavy overshoes when there came the unexpectedly long and steady ring at the door.

As he opened the door a woman dashed past him, laughing and shouting, "I've been liberated by the Revolution."

It was Gorushka's stepmother, Anna Ilyinichina, the sister of Vladimir Ilyich Lenin, who had been arrested in the last sweep of the Czarist secret police on Saturday night, the twenty-fifth. Monday morning her sister, Mariya, had gone to the Okhrana headquarters for an interview with Anna. The clerk laughed and said not to bother —soon everyone would be freed.[17]

Gorushka was hurt that his stepmother had not even noticed him. He stood to one side, biting his lips to hold back his tears. Suddenly Anna looked at him, grabbed him to her, kissed him, and began to tell what had happened:

"You see," she said, "some workers broke into the headquarters. The police didn't even oppose them, just gave them the keys immediately.

They opened our cell and said: 'Comrades, come out. You are free. In Petrograd there is a Revolution.'"

Anna shook her head in wonder.

"God save me," said Lenin's sister, "at last what we have so long awaited!"[18]

Late that night—or early in the morning of Tuesday the twenty-eighth—a young philosophy professor, Pitirim Sorokin, was walking home from the Tauride Palace. The District Court Building was still blazing on the Liteiny.

"Who started that?" a spectator said. "Isn't it necessary to have a court building for the new Russia?"

Sorokin looked at the faces of the crowd, reddened by the flames. They bore expressions of intense satisfaction. They danced and shouted. Vodka bottles were passed around. Here and there Sorokin saw piles of wooden Russian double eagles—the Imperial symbol—torn from Government buildings. The crowd cheered as they were hurled into the fire. The regime was turning into ashes.

"Let them go," one old man said. "When wood is chopped chips fly."[19]

In the backwoods town of Yefremov, Konstantin Paustovsky was reading by the light of a kerosene lamp. It was a snowy, quiet evening. The night watchmen made their rounds, sounding wooden clappers. Nothing had changed in Yefremov since the sixteenth century. A man dashed into the sleepy inn shouting: "There's a Revolution in Petersburg!" Paustovsky and two friends went out into the snowy street. A man came running up, hatless, barefoot, wearing only a long Russian blouse. "Dear Friends," the man shouted. "Have you heard? There's no more Czar. Nothing's left but Russia."[20]

XLI

The Czar on the Run

It was a time of nightmare for Shulgin. He dozed in an armchair in the reception room outside Rodzyanko's office in the Tauride Palace—the Volkonsky Room it was called. The tramp of soldiers' boots still rang in his ears. Outside came occasional bursts of machine-gun fire. He kept awakening. Where was he? What was really happening? Where was Russia headed? What of the Army?

Most of all he thought of Nicholas II. Could Nicholas still govern? Not really. Before there had been Rasputin. Now Nicholas was alone —worse than alone. He stood in the shadow of Rasputin. Cursed muzhik! Shulgin had warned Purishkevich not to kill him. Now Rasputin was dead and it was worse than if he had been alive.

But how to save the throne? Abdication was the only solution, Shulgin decided. The Czar must abdicate. This would save his life and save the throne. That meant a regent—undoubtedly Grand Duke Mikhail Alexandrovich—and a new high command—Grand Duke Nikolai Nikolayevich, Nikolasha. And there would have to be a new government. Shulgin awakened to a new day with these thoughts tumbling through his mind.[1]

Nikolai Sukhanov also slept that night in the palace. He rolled up in his *shuba* (fur coat), used his fur hat for a pillow, and lay down in a corner of the White Chamber of the Duma as the first milky light of dawn appeared in the window. It was past 6 A.M. He slept awhile and then was awakened by a strange sound. The clock said 7:30. Two soldiers in gray coats, their bayonets prying at the canvas from both sides, were slowly pulling down Repin's famous portrait of Nicholas II. In a moment there appeared over the rostrum an empty frame which would yawn in this hall of the Revolution for many months. It did not enter Sukhanov's head to worry about the fate of the painting. He noticed some soldiers watching the proceedings and wondered what they might say.

"Twenty-four hours ago these rank-and-file soldiers," Sukhanov observed, "had been the dumb slaves of the despot who was now hurled down. What had happened inside their heads in these 24 hours?"

Sukhanov listened. They seemed neither surprised nor particularly interested. In fact, they made no intellectual comments whatever. Their remarks were so banal Sukhanov didn't bother to record them.

"No better sign was needed," he said, "of the final decay and inevitable ruin of Czarism."[2]

The Czar, to be certain, had no idea that he had lost his throne. He spent Tuesday the twenty-eighth riding comfortably across the snowy landscapes in his pleasant train. He had finally gotten away from Mogilev at 5 A.M.,[3] a little before Shulgin, Sukhanov, and thousands of others bedded down in and around the Tauride Palace. General Alexeyev's last words to the Czar had been: "*Slava bogu,* don't go. Wait . . ."[4]

He had gotten the same urgent warning from Voyeikov (and possibly Count Frederiks.)[*] But he turned the gloomy words aside. He was certain that once he and Ivanov ("I expect we'll meet tomorrow in Tsarskoye," he told the general[5]) got to Tsarskoye Selo the situation could be dealt with.[6]

The Czar was a bit tired. He hadn't gotten to bed until 3:30 A.M. and he rose at 10 A.M.[7] He had been with General Alexeyev, Voyeikov, Frederiks, and Ivanov until after 3 A.M. He ate a late breakfast and was joined by his suite and two members of the railroad administration. Everything was perfectly normal. As Gen. Dmitri N. Dubensky observed, no one in the entourage believed that a revolution was in progress. All was in order along the railroad. At the stations the Czar's train, as always, was greeted by the local chiefs of gendarmes and the local governors. The train made its way through Smolensk. There was no news from Petrograd. Moscow, according to

---

[*] Gen. A. S. Lukomsky was certain the return to Tsarskoye Selo meant disaster. He urged Voyeikov to try to persuade the Czar not to go. Voyeikov refused. Lukomsky then persuaded General Alexeyev to rise from his sickbed and make one last effort to change the Czar's mind. Alexeyev tried but failed. (A. Lukomsky, *Vospominaniya,* Vol. I, pp. 128–30.)

someone who had been there the day before, was quiet. Dubensky was cheered. That meant the trouble was confined to Petrograd.[8]

From Vyazma at 3 P.M. the Czar sent a telegram to his wife. He told her he had left Mogilev at 5 A.M., that his thoughts were with her and he hoped that she was well and not too disturbed. He was sending "many troops from the front." The weather was "marvellous."[9] At Rzhev the Czar disembarked and went for a little walk while the train took on coal and water.[10]

The Czar's train chuffed into Likhoslavl about 9 P.M. and for the first time they had news from Petrograd—the formation of the Duma Provisional Committee, an announcement that A. A. Bublikov had been named Minister of Communications, in charge of the railroads, and rumors (untrue) that Petrograd Mayor Balk and his deputy Oskar I. Vendorf had been shot and that the Winter Palace had been plundered. There were also reports that the train would not be permitted to proceed farther than Tosno, just outside Petrograd.[11]

En route or possibly at Likhoslavl the Czar received a telegram from his wife, a reassuring one, and he now wired her: "Thanks for the news. Happy that everything is all right with you. Tomorrow morning I hope to be home. I embrace you and the children, God be with you." He wrote a brief note in his diary, recording the weather that day as frosty but sunny.[12]

Among the rumors which spread through the Imperial train during its halt at Likhoslavl was one that the Provisional Government would intercept the Czar at Tosno and take him to Petrograd. Many in the Czar's suite who had opposed the return to Tsarskoye Selo now began to urge the Czar to go, instead, to northern front headquarters of General Ruzsky at Pskov. Ruzsky was regarded as one of Russia's ablest commanders and a stronger supporter of the Czar than General Alexeyev at Mogilev. Before the train went forward there was some discussion of this plan but no decision was made until they reached Malaya Vishera at 2:30 A.M. March 1. Here the special train which always preceded the Czar's had halted. A trainman said the next station toward Petrograd, Lyuban, had been seized by two companies of rebels with arms and machine guns. When the Czar's train pulled up, the commanders of both trains went to the Czar's suite. No one was awake except for Gen. Kirill A. Naryshkin,[13] one of the Czar's aides. He awakened Voyeikov, who went to the Czar and asked what to do. The Czar did not seem disturbed. He told Voyeikov he wanted to go to the nearest point where there was a terminal of the special Hughes direct telegraph wire (used for military communications).[14] The nearest point was Pskov and the train was directed there, backtracking via Bologoye.[15]

At 9 A.M. the train halted at Bologoye.[16] The Czar did not understand it—but he was no longer an Emperor. He was a man on the run.

In Petrograd confusion reigned. The successful revolutionaries did
not realize their success. All day long members of the Government,
high police officials, generals—almost anyone who roving patrols of
workers and soldiers and sailors happened to think might be an
"enemy of the people"—were brought to the Tauride Palace. The first to
be brought in was the chairman of the Czar's Council of Ministers,
Shcheglovitov. A college student "arrested" him in his apartment during the afternoon of the twenty-seventh and escorted him with some
armed soldiers to the Tauride Palace. He was taken to the Catherine
Hall about 3 P.M. where Kerensky confronted him and shouted: "Ivan
Grigoryevich Shcheglovitov—you are under arrest!"

The Minister, a heavy figure, cast down his eyes.

"Ivan Grigoryevich," continued Kerensky, "your life is in danger.
But the State Duma does not shed blood."[17]

At that moment Rodzyanko appeared on the scene, beaming and
smiling:

"Ah, Ivan Grigoryevich," said Rodzyanko. "Do come to my office."

"No," said Kerensky. "Ex-Minister Shcheglovitov has been arrested
in the name of the people."

Kerensky and Rodzyanko stared at each other. Then Shcheglovitov
was led off to the Pavilion of Ministers, the first of the many taken into
protective custody by the Duma.[18]

It was midevening of the next day when A. D. Protopopov, the
hated Minister of Interior, No. 1 criminal of the Czarist state in the
minds of most revolutionaries, straggled into the Tauride Palace. He
had hidden all day in the tailor's shop of Ivan Fyodorovich Pavlov at
12 Yamskaya. Reading in the paper that members of the Government
were turning themselves over to the Duma, he made his way there,
went up to a student standing outside the palace, and said: "I am Protopopov." The student led him in, shouting to the crowd that he had
Protopopov. By the time they reached the Catherine Hall an ugly
crowd was following. Kerensky leaped out of the Volkonsky Room and
confronted the crowd, his eyes blazing, his face pale, his hands
upraised. There was a huge mirror on the wall and in this mirror Shulgin saw behind Kerensky a ring of soldiers with bayonets and in their
middle a feeble figure with a beaten face whom he could hardly recognize.

"Don't touch this man!" cried Kerensky, one hand raised against the
crowd, the other pointing to the miserable Protopopov. "Don't touch
him!"

The crowd froze. Kerensky led the way. Behind him trailed the bedraggled Protopopov and the ring of bayonets. Kerensky led the party through the Catherine Hall, filled with soldiers. There was real danger here. But no one lifted a finger. Again Kerensky shouted: "Don't touch this man!"

Kerensky brought Protopopov safely through the Catherine Hall and the halls beyond it into the Pavilion of Ministers. There he closed the door, motioned to the couch, and said: "Have a seat, Alexander Dmitriyevich!" Protopopov reached in his pocket and handed over to Kerensky the key to his office desk in the Interior Ministry, saying that in the drawer was a key to his fireproof safe where he had deposited fifty thousand rubles.[19]

A bit later Kerensky saved former War Minister Sukhomlinov, who was brought in by a crowd of soldiers.

"Seeing its victim was about to escape the crowd rushed us," Kerensky recalled. "I hastened to shield Sukhomlinov with my body. I yelled that I would not allow them to kill him and dishonor the Revolution. I said they could reach him only over my dead body."

The crowd backed off.[20]

But not all were saved. The sailors at Kronstadt ran riot. Nowhere in the Czar's Empire had there been more repression, more cruel, mindless discipline than in the Russian Navy. Sailors who had participated in the 1905 Revolution still rotted in the Kronstadt dungeons. Capt. I. I. Rengarten was one of the senior officers of the Russian fleet, a close friend and associate of Fleet Adm. Adrian Nepenin. For months before the February Revolution Rengarten and a group of his fellow officers, Flag Capt. Prince Mikhail Cherkassky, Baron Nikolai Tipolt, commander of the mine layer *Pogranichnik*, Vice Adm. Alexander Rusin, chief of the Naval General Staff, and others, had been holding seminars on questions which they felt were linked to the fate of Russia. The group, Nepenin included, regarded themselves as liberals. They openly hoped for the abdication of Nicholas and the rise of a new democratic Russia.

But the Revolution set off a chain reaction in the Navy. First Kronstadt exploded while the Navy remained comparatively calm. The first officer to die was Capt. Mikhail I. Nikolsky, commander of the cruiser *Aurora*, soon to become a symbol of the Revolution. A senior lieutenant on the *Aurora* was badly wounded.

Then the telegraph connecting headquarters with Petrograd was severed. Admiral Nepenin made clear to his staff that in conflict between the Czar and the Duma he would stand beside the Duma. The next word Rengarten had was that Kronstadt was in full anarchy, that Adm. Robert Viren, commander of Kronshtadt, had been killed, and all officers arrested.

The naval bases of Revel and Helsingfors caught the fever. Officers were killed and scores thrown into the brig.

Despite all this, Rengarten noted in his diary March 3: "Now we are at the dawn of a new life for great free Russia!"

"It has been a night without sleep," he wrote, "but what a great joyous and memorable night for the fortunate beginning of the Great Russian revolution!"

Within hours he was asking in bewilderment: "What does it all mean?" The red flag was going up on the Russian warships, officers were compelled to surrender their swords, the men were electing "new commanders." By 5:30 P.M. of the same day Rengarten wrote, "Only a miracle can save us." Masses of sailors and workingmen from the naval yards conducted meetings. Deputations waited on the commanders. Battleship Commander Nebolsin was killed. Adm. Andrei Maximov was elected commander of the battle fleet.

"Yesterday I was arrested," he said, "today I am put in command of the fleet and tomorrow I will be hung!"

At 1:10 P.M. March 4 it was announced that all the officers on the *Krechet* (Rengarten's warship) were arrested. Thirty-five minutes later Admiral Nepenin was killed. A few officers, including Rengarten and Prince Cherkassky, were permitted to remain and, in fact, were named "delegates" for the ship. So it went. Senior Lt. Pyotr G. Von Vitt was killed on his mine layer. So was Capt. Boris N. Rybkin of the *Diana* and Lt. Gen. Veniamin N. Protopopov, commander of Sveaborg port, and Baron Rudolf Shtackelberg. It was, Rengarten finally wrote, a "golgotha," although he still stressed the positive results—it had extinguished differences between officers and men and opened the way (so he thought) to going on with the war.[21]

February surely had not been the "bloodless revolution" of which some observers wrote. Prince Dmitri Leonidovich Vyazemsky, in an officer's uniform, was shot and fatally wounded as he rode beside Guchkov in a car a few hours before Guchkov went off with Shulgin for the last talk with the Czar. It was probably a stray bullet but it was a time when anyone in an officer's uniform might find himself a sudden target.[22] Sixty-three officers were killed in Petrograd on one day, February 28.[23]

The blood and passion at Kronshtadt erupted out of the terrible excesses of the past—and would lead to more excess in the future. Skobelev was sent to Kronshtadt by the Soviet to try to restore order. He reported that considering the past conduct of authorities there it was astonishing there had not been more casualties.[24]

In all February's toll in Petrograd numbered 169 dead of whom 59 were soldiers and 22 workers. There were about 1,000 wounded of whom about 500 were troops and 200 workers.[25]

On March 23—a gray, dark, damp day—was held the most solemn ceremony of the Revolution: the funeral for 184 men, women, and children, dead in the Revolution.[26] All day long the procession of the people moved through Petrograd's streets—a million mourners, a million people paying tribute to the Revolution. Everyone was there. Banners flamed in red for Zemlya i Volya (Land and Freedom), for the People's Republic, for War to Victory over Wilhelm, Workers of the world—Unite, Eternal Memory to those who fell for Freedom. And anarchists, long-bearded, long-haired, Colt revolvers in hand, marched under black banners bearing the slogans: Hail the Social Revolution! Hail Anarchy! Hour after hour the people marched. Sometimes with bands playing the "Varsoviana," sometimes the "Internationale" but more often the "Marseillaise." Groups sang through their tears:

> "You have fallen in the fatal battle
> For the love of the people
> You have given all
> For life, for honor, for liberty."

It was, Madame de Néry thought, the most moving spectacle she would ever see. And it was the most moving when the people walked in simple silence, no bands, no songs, no voices. Just the soft shuffle of hundreds of thousands of feet on Russian pavements.

Night fell before the immense cortege had finally filled the Champs de Mars. There flaming torches lighted the scene as 184 coffins were lowered into the earth without crosses or priests to the rolling sound of 184 cannon. When the last gun sounded, reverberating across the field to the Peter and Paul Fortress on the other side of the Neva and back, the silence was total.[27]

The biggest question with which the men in the Tauride Palace struggled was the question of the Czar. At first men like Rodzyanko had thought of establishing a responsible government, a constitutional monarchy like that of Britain or Italy. But now there was talk that the Czar must go. A regency for the Czar's young son, Alexei, under the Czar's brother, Mikhail Alexandrovich—this was becoming the common aim.

But how to achieve a change? It was plain to the men of the Tauride Palace that the Czar was a long way from making up his mind. If they were unsure of themselves and of the Revolution, the Czar did not even know that a Revolution had occurred.

There was endless milling about. Rodzyanko was eager to go to the Czar. He had a plan worked out for a constitutional monarchy, and by the morning of March 1 when the Czar's train turned back to Bologoye he was preparing to meet the Czar, either there or at Dno, farther along the way.

A naval officer appeared at the Soviet Executive Committee and asked for a special train for Rodzyanko. The Executive Committee, led by Sukhanov, refused on grounds they didn't know what kind of game Rodzyanko was playing. Yet, simultaneously messages were sent to try to hold the Czar's train at Bologoye so the Czar and Rodzyanko could meet. Then Kerensky came raging into the Soviet Executive.

"What have you done? How could you?" Kerensky whispered tragically. "You haven't given a train. . . . Rodzyanko must go in order to get Nicholas to sign his abdication. And you have prevented it. You are playing into the hands of the monarchists, the Romanovs. The responsibility will lie on you!"[28]

Naturally, the Soviet reversed itself and gave permission. But Rodzyanko never did go. Every thirty minutes stationmaster Lomonosov called. Was he ready? The answer came back. Wait a bit. The day went by. Rodzyanko did not go to the Czar. He had changed his mind. The Czar's train left Bologoye. Rodzyanko sent a telegram asking the Czar to wait at Dno. The Czar got the wire when they arrived at Dno about 6 P.M. He asked Voyeikov to find out when Rodzyanko was coming. Petrograd said the special train was standing by but there was no word as to when Rodzyanko was leaving.

The Czar decided there was no use waiting at Dno and went on to Pskov.[29] Even if Rodzyanko started immediately it would be midnight before he arrived.[30]

During the day the Czar had been talking with his suite. He had seen everyone—Frederiks, Nilov, Count Grabbe, Dr. S. P. Fyodorov, Prince Dolgoruky, Georgi M. Likhtenbergsky, and Voyeikov. He had made up his mind to accept a constitutional monarchy with a responsible ministry and he proposed to advise Rodzyanko of his decision when Rodzyanko finally caught up with him.[31]

General Dubensky was ecstatic. He called the night halt at Malaya Vishera "an historic night." The constitutional question had finally been decided. There was a consensus on the train. The Czar would not think of arguing. Nicholas seemed at peace again.

Dubensky had once described the Czar's conduct in terms of a court anecdote. It was said that if soup was served to the Czar and Prince Dolgoruky said, "Your Highness, the soup is not tasty," the Czar would put it aside and eat no more. If someone like Dubensky said the soup was no good, the Czar would go on eating. He gave his full confidence to those he trusted and thus, Dubensky thought, he should make a perfect constitutional monarch.

"Ancient Pskov," Dubensky noted in his diary, would again make a page in Russia's history. Here the Czar would set his dynasty onto a new path in the modern world.[32]

It was not to be. The history which was written at Pskov was not what Dubensky had in mind. Nor the Czar, either, for that matter.

After a pleasant dinner at Pskov—the Czar insisted that they eat first—they got down to business. There was really no disagreement on what must be done. As Ruzsky said, "We must throw ourselves on the mercy of the victors." A full constitution must be granted "otherwise anarchy would grow and Russia would perish."[33]

Ruzsky got in touch by direct wire with Rodzyanko, and a draft of the Czar's proclamation was hammered out. But by the time the final document was completed a major change had occurred. The Czar reserved to himself the appointment of the Ministers of Foreign Affairs, War, and Navy. This last-minute change was apparently inserted under the influence of Voyeikov or Frederiks or both.[34]

At Pskov the Czar finally sent a brief message to the Czarina (but not until after midnight). He hoped everyone was feeling better and that he would soon see them. "God be with you," he added. The message did not reach Alix until nearly 1 P.M. Wednesday March 2.[35]

Before he retired the Czar as usual made a note in his diary. He wrote:

"Last night turned back from M. Vishera because Lyuban and Tosno were occupied by insurrectionists. Went via Valdai, Dno and Pskov where we are stopping for the night. Saw Ruzsky. He, Danilov and Savich dined with me. Gatchina and Luga also appear to be occupied. Shame and infamy! Not to be able to get to Tsarskoye. But my thoughts and feelings are constantly there. That poor Alix should suffer alone the weight of all these events. Help us, O Lord!"[36]

Through the night the exchange of views between Pskov and Petrograd continued. Rodzyanko was backing away from coming, and by morning he made clear to Ruzsky that a constitution was not enough. Now the question came down to the abdication of the Czar in favor of Alexei and a regent, presumably Grand Duke Mikhail.[37]

XLII

The Czar Steps Down

During the night General Ivanov, the designated "dictator of Petrograd," had with little difficulty gotten to Tsarskoye Selo. There he conferred with the Czarina about 2 A.M. The Czar's Guards had gone off to Petrograd, and Tsarskoye Selo was now under protection of troops sent from Petrograd by the revolutionary government. But all was quiet and orderly. The Czarina told Ivanov that, having had no reply from the Czar to her telegrams, she had thought of sending a message by plane but the weather was too bad for the aircraft to take off. She mentioned the long hours she and her daughters had given to the sick and wounded and said she was perplexed at the antagonism of the people. Ivanov told her it had long been growing and that Protopopov was the target of much of it. The Czarina wanted Ivanov to take a letter from her to the Czar but he had no means of doing this. The talk was finally interrupted when someone in a neighboring room called to her. Ivanov heard her speaking for a time in English (which he did not understand) and soon took his leave. He found a telegram from General Alexeyev telling him that conditions were now quiet in Petrograd and that it was hoped after talks between the Czar and the Duma the monarchy could be preserved. Therefore, he was to take no action. A wire from the Czar sent at midnight from Pskov also warned him to take no steps until the Czar himself arrived at Tsarskoye Selo.

Ivanov had thoughtfully attached a second locomotive to the rear of his train in case he had to make a hasty exit. Now he decided to leave town. He went back down the line, winding up at Vyritsa. He waited there a day or so, finally went on to Pskov, and eventually returned to Mogilev. His mission had accomplished nothing.[1]

Events now began to move at a quickened pace.

Dubensky's exhilaration over the history which would be made at Pskov rapidly began to evaporate. When members of the Imperial suite appeared on the station platform on the morning of Thursday March 2, they were surrounded by persons bringing bad news from Petrograd—Count Frederiks' house had been burned, high officials of the Gendarmerie Corps and the police had been killed, the District Court had burned, the prisons emptied, police stations destroyed, members of the Government arrested and confined to the Duma building, armories pillaged, and 200,000 rifles distributed to workers' detachments.[2]

Dubensky was told that Petrograd was in a state of anarchy, in the hands of the "worst elements and the Jews" who were insulting every officer who appeared on the street.[3]

And there was worse news. When Ruzsky saw the Czar at 10:45 A.M.,[4] he told him that Rodzyanko had turned down the Czar's proposal for a constitutional monarchy. The only course now was abdication. Ruzsky was moving in this direction himself. He gave the Czar the general views of General Alexeyev and put before him the telegraph tape of his night-long exchange with Rodzyanko.[5] General Ruzsky was outwardly calm but inwardly in turmoil. The Czar read the telegrams attentively. Then he rose from his chair, went to the window, and a moment of absolute silence followed. He sat down and began speaking quietly about the possibility of abdication. He recalled again his conviction that he was doomed to be a "suffering Job," that he had brought unhappiness to Russia. He had been convinced, he said, as early as yesterday and even before last night that no manifesto would save the situation.

"If it is necessary that I step aside for the good of Russia," he said quietly, "then I am ready."

But he was afraid that the people would not understand. He was not prepared to violate his oath at the coronation.

At that moment the answers to General Alexeyev's circular telegram to the commanders of all the fronts asking their opinion about the Czar's abdication were placed before General Ruzsky and the Czar.[6]

"What do you think, N.V.?" the Czar asked. Ruzsky was shaken. They decided to defer a final decision until after lunch.[7]

When Ruzsky told Voyeikov the Czar was thinking of leaving the throne, Voyeikov immediately went to the Czar. He found him profoundly changed since the talk with Ruzsky. The Czar looked as though he had given up all hope and was submitting himself to his fate, but Voyeikov did not feel he could offer any words of comfort.[8]

The Emperor met his suite for lunch. There was little conversation.

At about this hour the Empress was writing another of her enormously long letters to her husband. This was letter No. 650. Her previous letter, No. 649, which must have been sent off on March 1, never reached the Czar and has vanished. She wrote No. 650 in two versions and gave them to two young aides to try to smuggle through to the Czar in their boots, if necessary. They were written in a small hand on small sheets so as easily to be burned. No. 650 never reached the Czar in either of its versions.

"Everything is shocking," she wrote, "and events have developed with colossal rapidity."

But she had not stopped believing that all would come out all right. She had been relieved to get the Czar's telegram from Pskov. She knew he was being prevented from joining her. She was certain that "they" wanted him to sign "some kind of paper, a constitution or something of that nature." And now the Czar was "caught like a mouse in a trap" without his Army. It was the greatest meanness, unheard-of in history, to detain the ruler. But, she assured him, if he had to make some concessions then he was not obliged "in any case" (she underlined the words) to fulfill anything extorted under duress. She had told the children what was going on, but to Alexei she had told only half. They were still sick but all were getting better.

"Can't give you any advice except to be your dear sweet self," she concluded. "Oh, my holy sufferer!"[9]

At 2:20 lunch was over.[10] Ruzsky went again to the Emperor. This time he took his aides, Generals Danilov and Sergei S. Savich, with him because he had a feeling the Czar was not completely confident in his judgment.[11] He put before the Czar the answers to General Alexeyev's circular telegram. There was no disagreement among the generals—Nikolai Nikolayevich, Brusilov, A. E. Ebert, V. V. Sakharov, Admiral Nepenin, Ruzsky himself—all agreed on abdication. The Czar read Nikolasha's telegram twice.[12]

"But," said the Emperor, "I don't know whether this is what all Russia wants."

Ruzsky let his associates speak. Both supported abdication. A silence followed. All looked at Nicholas. Finally the Czar spoke:

"I have decided. I will give up the throne."

The generals crossed themselves.[13] "I'll go and write the telegram," the Czar said.[14] General Alexeyev had sent a form of abdication.[15] Now the Czar took it with him to his compartment, dated it 3 P.M.

March 2, 1917, and wrote it out in his own hand. He came back and gave it to Ruzsky for transmission to Rodzyanko[16] and Alexeyev. It was now known that Shulgin and Guchkov were on their way to Pskov on a mission for the Duma. It was obvious that they wanted to secure the Czar's abdication.[17] The Czar did not wish to resign under Duma pressure and he was eager to send the abdication before they arrived.

When it was over, the Czar emerged from his car and for a long time walked back and forth between the two Imperial trains, accompanied by Georgi M. Likhtenbergsky. He never missed his walk in the open air. This was the only moment he could spare for it. General Dubensky watched the Czar through the window. Although he was an old man, he could not keep the tears from streaming down his face. As the Czar passed by he looked up, saw the general, smiled, nodded, and waved his hand.

"It was within half an hour of sending his telegram about abdicating the throne," recalled Dubensky. "He was such a fatalist. I can't even imagine it."[18]

There was one more small flutter. When Voyeikov heard that the Czar's telegram had gone off, he rushed to the Czar and tried to stop it. After some confusion the telegram was returned but apparently the copy to Rodzyanko had already gone off.[19]

When Voyeikov got permission to try to stop the Czar's telegram, hopes went up in his suite. Maybe there would be another roll of the dice. But when Naryshkin learned one copy apparently had gone off, all of them—Naryshkin, A. A. Mordvinov, Baron Shtakelberg, and Dubensky—said with one voice: "It's all over."

Dubensky was outraged. It was the fault, he felt, of the "empty, egoistic people" who surrounded the Czar. But the Czar as always was quiet. His only show of feeling came during his walk when he told his companion: "I'll be ashamed to see the foreign military attaches at headquarters and it won't be easy for them to see me."[20]

Dubensky wrote in his diary: "A weak, indecisive but good and clean man he was destroyed by the Empress and her senseless attraction to Grigory. Russia could not forgive this."

About 4 P.M. Dr. S. P. Fyodorov went to the Czar and in talking about the abdication said: "Really, Your Excellency, you suppose that Alexei will stay with you after the abdication?"

"And why not?" the Czar asked with some surprise. "After all he is still a child and naturally should stay with his family while he is not grown. During that time Mikhail Alexandrovich will be regent."

Fyodorov gently said he didn't think things would go this way. It was impossible to imagine Alexei staying with his father.

"Really, do you think that I might carry on some intrigue?" the Czar asked. "I would just live with Alexei and educate him."[21]

The Czar then thought a bit and said, "You know, Sergei Petrovich, that I am a man *terre à terre*. I naturally did not regard Rasputin as a saint but the things that he predicted ordinarily happened. He predicted that if the Czarevich lived to be 17 he would be perfectly healthy. Is that right? Can he become healthy or not?"

The doctor answered that there were no miracles in nature. Science said about the Czarevich's illness that "possibly His Highness will live longer than you and me, Your Highness, but he may die at any moment from the simplest most insignificant circumstance. That is the nature of his illness."[22]

"Then," said the Czar firmly, "I cannot be separated from Alexei. It is beyond my strength."[23]

At this point Count Frederiks entered the room. The Czar was crying.[24]

The Czar decided to renounce the throne on behalf of his son and abdicate in favor of his brother, Mikhail. This was unconstitutional. The Emperor could only abdicate for himself. He had no right to act on the part of his heir.[25]

At five o'clock tea the Czar was outwardly calm as usual. He smiled, spoke quietly, but no one was inclined to draw out the ceremony.[26]

At 9 P.M. Guchkov and Shulgin arrived. The Czar greeted them. He was wearing one of his favorite uniforms—the gray uniform of the Cherkess Cossacks. Guchkov launched into a seemingly endless speech. Ruzsky whispered to Shulgin: "It's all decided. It's been a hard day. There's been a *burya*, a storm."

Finally Guchkov finished and the Czar spoke:

"I have taken the decision to abdicate the throne. Until three o'clock this afternoon I thought of abdicating in favor of my son Alexei. But in this time I changed my decision in favor of my brother Mikhail. I hope you can understand the feeling of a father. . . ."

The Czar went out to his personal car and returned a moment later with his act of abdication. A few changes were made. A word here and there. It was decided to type out a fresh copy, making the changes but keeping the time 3 P.M. The question of a new Premier came up. "Whom do you suggest?" the Czar asked. The delegates named Prince Lvov. "Ah, ha," said the Czar with an air of doubt. "Very well . . . Lvov." There was some small talk. Shulgin asked the Czar what were his plans—would he go at once to Tsarskoye Selo? No, he replied. He wanted to go to headquarters at Mogilev first and then he wanted to see his mother so he would probably go to Kiev.

Only then would he go to Tsarskoye Selo and his family. The time was twenty minutes to midnight. Guchkov and Shulgin shook the Emperor's hand. It seemed to Shulgin that the Czar's handshake was a bit too warm. Then they left to catch the train back to Petrograd.[27]

The Czar returned to his compartment and wrote, as usual, an entry in his diary.

"This morning Ruzsky came and read his long conversation by telegraph with Rodzyanko. In his words the situation in Petrograd is such that now the Ministers of the Duma would be helpless to do anything since against them struggles the Social Democratic party and members of the Workers committee. My abdication is necessary. Ruzsky sent this conversation to headquarters and Alexeyev and all the chief commanders. At 2:30 came the answer from them all. The judgement is that in the name of saving Russia and supporting the Army at the front in calmness it is necessary to decide on this step. I agreed. From the headquarters was sent the project of a manifesto. This evening Guchkov and Shulgin arrived from Petrograd with whom I conversed and gave them the signed and completed manifesto. At 1 A.M. I leave Pskov with heavy heart.

"I am surrounded by treason and cowardice and fraud."

At 2 A.M. March 3 the Czar's special train quietly pulled out of Pskov for the last journey to Mogilev.[28]

Actually two small scenes remained to be played. The next day Grand Duke Mikhail Alexandrovich after a bit of soul searching declined to follow his brother to the throne. He, too, rejected the Crown, and the dynasty came to a formal end. When Mikhail announced his decision to the delegation of the Provisional Government assembled in Prince Putyatin's house, Kerensky stepped forward and said: "Your Supreme Highness, I see that you are an honest man."[29]

That afternoon the Czar's other brother, the Grand Duke Pavel Alexandrovich, was called to Tsarskoye Selo by the Czarina. He had last seen her March 1 when she asked him, "Where is my husband? Is he alive? What must be done to put down the disorders?"

On that occasion he told her of a manifesto which he had prepared with the Grand Dukes Mikhail Alexandrovich and Kirill Vladimirovich calling for establishment of constitutional government in Russia. The Czarina had approved.

Now Grand Duke Pavel appeared again at Tsarskoye Selo. He had in his pocket the latest number of *Izvestiya* with the announcement of the Czar's abdication. He read it to Alexandra Fyodorovna. When he finished reading, she said:

"I don't believe it. It's all lies. The newspaper invented it. I believe in God and the Army. They haven't deserted us yet."

The Grand Duke replied that not only God but the Army had joined the revolutionaries.

"And only then," he said, "the former Czarina was convinced and, it seemed, for the first time understood or attempted to understand all that she, Grishka Rasputin and Protopopov had done to the country and the monarchy."[30]

The Czarevich was not told the news immediately. He spent the day of March 4—he was still recovering from the measles—casting lead bullets and building model houses with Mr. Gibbes, his tutor. The Czarina began to burn her papers—her letters to and from Queen Victoria, her personal diaries, and, presumably, any correspondence with Rasputin.

Not until the day before the Czar returned to Tsarskoye Selo, March 9, was Mr. Gibbes given the delicate task of telling the Czarevich his father had abdicated and would no longer be commander in chief.

"But who's going to be Czar, then?" Alexei asked.

"I don't know," Mr. Gibbes replied. "Perhaps nobody now."[31]

XLIII

The News Spreads

The news traveled slowly in Siberia. In the remote Yenisei region of eastern Siberia, Osip Pyatnitsky* lounged in his wooden hut all day on March 8 without a fire in the stove. He was sick and depressed, and when that evening a peasant and fellow exile, Foma Govorek, burst into the room and told him there was a revolution in Russia, he told him he was in no mood for joking. But Foma finally convinced Pyatnitsky that the wife of one of the exiles had actually attended a meeting in Kansk where the news was announced.[1]

In Irkutsk V. S. Voitinsky, sometime acolyte of Lenin and a Bolshevik deputy of the Second Duma, had long been in exile. He, too, was sick in bed with influenza. A police officer came to his house on March 1 with an order that he was to leave Irkutsk at once. He persuaded the officer to let him stay until he felt better. The next day word arrived of the formation of the Provisional Duma Committee, and on March 2 Irkutsk burst into a mass of red flags. Crowds marched the streets singing revolutionary songs.[2]

The Irkutsk area was a center for revolutionary exiles. The Mensheviks F. I. Dan and I. G. Tsereteli lived there as well as Abram Gots, the SR, and many others less well known.[3]

That evening word of the Revolution reached Tsereteli, who lived in nearby Usolye. He came immediately to Irkutsk and with the other

---

* A leading Bolshevik during the Revolution, later a leader of the Communist International, executed by Stalin in 1939.

revolutionaries formed a Citizens' Committee which took over power. The spirit of the citizenry, Tsereteli recalled, was one of "happy alarm." One thing made a special impression on him—the mood of the Army. Everywhere the soldiers stood at the side of the Revolution and ensured its success but he felt the soldiers were drawn to the Soviet as though it were a kind of idol whereas in reality there was no "intimacy, no nearness, no understanding between us."[4]

"The presence of this element in the first days of the revolution," he later was to write, "aroused alarm for the fate of the revolution—alarm which was not stiffled even in the drunken happiness of the first days."

Tsereteli and the others spent ten days in Irkutsk then left on March 11 on "the Train of the Deputies of the Second Duma" for Petrograd. The locomotive was decorated with red banners and slogans, and the forty political exiles had two cars at their disposal, attached to the regular Trans-Siberian Express. They stopped at every big city for celebration and speeches. A grand welcome had been planned in Petrograd but they were seventeen hours late. The bands and well-wishers had long since dispersed. In the rainy early morning hours of March 20 the exiles were embraced by a few relatives and then scattered out to see what had happened to Petrograd in the long years of absence. Before long most of them turned up at the Tauride Palace.[5]

Yekaterina Breshko-Breskovskyaya got the news on March 4 at Minusinsk. Before evening she was on her way to Achinsk, the nearest railhead, and European Russia. At Moscow she was placed in the Czar's gilt-and-white coach and escorted in triumph to the Moscow Duma, where she declared: "One thought is in my mind. Joy gives place to care. At every station and crossroads there is only one demand. It is the groan of the people for books and teachers." At Petrograd she was welcomed in the Czar's reception room of the Nicholas Station, surrounded by wreaths and flowers, bearing legends: "To our Dear Grandmother" and "To Russia's Martyr Heroine."

She spoke briefly:

"I have come over a long road. I am old and cannot remember everything. As I came out on the platform I saw the people, all around I saw workingmen. I came into this temple of freedom and see military organizations, workmen, Cossacks, sailors.

"Do I not see that you are all children of the same cause? The soldier—isn't he the same as the workingman? You are all children of our great mother, Russia, and why should you suddenly begin to quarrel with one another?"[6]

News of the overthrow of the Czar reached Stalin at Achinsk, and by March 8 he found himself moving westward from Krasnoyarsk along the Trans-Siberian with a group of his Bolshevik colleagues, including Lev B. Kamenev and Matvei K. Muranov. At one Siberian celebration, sharing the platform with Liberals, Populists, and Mensheviks, Kamenev joined in sending a telegram to Grand Duke Mikhail Alexandrovich, congratulating him for renouncing the throne. If Stalin had any objections to this bouquet for a Romanov, he did not record them.[7]

"At first," commented the Bolshevik Duma deputy Fyodor N. Samoilov, "we seemed to have suddenly forgotten our differences of opinion. The path along the railroad was extraordinary and tumultuous, a mass of welcoming demonstrations, meetings and the like."[8]

The bands played the "Marseillaise" (they hadn't yet heard of the "Internationale"); there were gala banquets and talk without end. From Perm the three Bolsheviks telegraphed Lenin in Switzerland: "Fraternal greetings. Leaving today for Petrograd. Kamenev. Muranov. Stalin."[9]

On March 12, the day of their arrival, the Russian Bureau of the Bolshevik Central Committee took up the question of the three prominent returnees—all very senior to the Bolshevik handful in the city. Muranov was admitted immediately to full membership in the bureau. Kamenev received permission to write for *Pravda* but it was stipulated that he must not sign his articles (because of past disagreements within the Party). In Stalin's case when the bureau was told that he had been an "agent" of the Central Committee in 1912 it decided that in view of "his inherent personal characteristics" it would give him only an advisory membership on the committee.[10]

The reference to Stalin's "personal characteristics" reflected the negative opinion of his exiled comrades, formed in the earliest days of his exile in Kureika in 1913 and still unchanged. Thus, from the moment of his arrival in the revolutionary capital the Party members made clear their distaste for Stalin.* Stalin had, however, at least one warm friend—an old comrade from his days in the Caucasus. This was the worker Bolshevik Sergei Alliluyev. Stalin looked him up immediately and was embraced by the whole family—Fyodor, their son, Anna, an

---

* The protocols of the bureau's March meetings were suppressed during Lenin's and Stalin's lifetime and were published only in 1962 as an element of Nikita S. Khrushchev's anti-Stalin campaign. (*Voprosy Istorii KPSS*, 1962, No. 3, p. 43.)

older daughter, and Nadya, the youngest daughter. He told stories about Siberia, imitated the orators who had met the train at station stops proclaiming that "the holy revolution, the long-awaited, dear revolution, has finally arrived." He spent the night with the Alliluyevs and it was agreed that he would room with them in the new flat they were looking for.[11]

Despite Stalin's cool welcome, he and Kamenev quickly overrode the Party bureau and three days later Stalin was named to the bureau Presidium. He and Kamenev took over the editorship of *Pravda* with the issue of March 15.[12]

Pravda had been revived March 5, partly with the help of a subsidy of three thousand rubles provided by the long-suffering Gorky—who just as quickly withdrew his support in disagreement with *Pravda*'s policies.[13]

The first issue had 100,000 circulation.[14]

In Trotsky's words it was in charge of a young college boy (Molotov) and two workingmen (Shlyapnikov and Zalutsky).[15] Molotov launched it on a course as close to Lenin's as he could divine, and in fact, the early Molotov issues did have Lenin's imprint—uncompromising, antagonistic to the Provisional Government and the Duma men, lukewarm if not hostile to the Soviet where the Mensheviks and Socialist Revolutionaries dominated, opposed to the policy of continuing the war to a victorious conclusion.

With the arrival of Kamenev and Stalin *Pravda* veered to moderation. In his first editorial on March 14 Stalin called for land for the peasants, labor legislation for the workers (the eight-hour day), and a "democratic republic for Russia." His revolution was, as Deutscher pointed out, "anti-feudal but not anti-capitalist; it was to be 'bourgeois democratic' not Socialist."[16]

And on March 15 Kamenev wrote in *Pravda* (with Stalin's approval[17]):

"The mere slogan: 'Down with the war' is absolutely impractical. As long as the German Army obeys the orders of the Kaiser, the Russian soldier must stand firmly at his post, answering bullet with bullet and shell with shell."[18]

The next day at the All-Russian Conference of Bolsheviks Stalin declared: "To the extent that the Provisional Government fortifies the march of the Revolution, we must support it. To the extent that it is counter-revolutionary, we cannot support it."[19]

On the agenda of this meeting was Tsereteli's proposal for unity.

"We must agree to this," Stalin declared. "It is necessary to decide upon our propositions on the question of unity. Unity is possible on the platform of Zimmerwald."

Molotov objected.

Stalin rebuked him. "It is not necessary to anticipate and prevent differences of opinion. As members of one party our small differences of opinion will fade away."[20]

The new Party line was introduced with Stalin's customary sharpness. "The comrades who arrived," Shlyapnikov noted, "were critical and negative in their attitude toward our work." And, in fact, the existing *Pravda* directorate was simply pushed aside.[21]

Nor was the Party line welcomed by the Petrograd workers. "The day the transformed *Pravda* appeared," Shlyapnikov later wrote, "was a day of triumph for the Defensists. The whole Tauride Palace . . . buzzed with but one news item—the triumph of the moderate and sensible Bolsheviks over the extremists. In the Executive Committee itself we were greeted with malicious smiles. . . .

"The indignation in the outlying districts was stupendous, and when the proletarians found out that *Pravda* had been taken over by three of its former managing editors recently arrived from Siberia, they demanded the expulsion of the latter from the Party."[22]

Neither *Pravda* nor Stalin nor Kamenev gave more than the faintest lip service to the nominal leader of the Party, Lenin. The truth was that the Russian organization of the Bolsheviks—insofar as it had survived the long years of war and exile—had lost not only physical but philosophical connection with its putative director. Lenin was far away and still in exile. Even now there was no communication with him.[23] The Bolshevik pragmatists were fighting a day-to-day battle for survival. They had lost all the early rounds. The Soviet was in the firm control of the other revolutionaries, the Mensheviks and SRs. The Government was run by moderates. The soldiers were streaming in to the call of the SRs, not the Bolsheviks. In the provinces the Social Democrats everywhere wanted unity, unity of the Bolsheviks and Mensheviks, unity of the whole revolutionary movement. They were tired of secular arguments. The moment called for the triumph of revolutionary ideals and not for arguments about doctrinal differences. And Lenin was still in Switzerland, as always, enmeshed in doctrine.

Early on the afternoon of March 2 Krupskaya was clearing away the lunch dishes from the cluttered kitchen table in the dark flat at 14 Spiegelgasse. Lenin was putting his papers into his battered leather portfolio, preparing to go back to the library where he was gathering materials for another attack on the Swiss Social Democrat Robert Grimm, his latest bête noire. Lenin was upset about a youth Congress that was to be held in Sweden in early May to found a new left-wing party which he feared would be under the influence of Grimm and the German Social Democrat Karl Kautsky, another bitter enemy.[24]

At this moment Mieczyslaw Bronski, a rather good-looking, thirty-five-year-old Polish Social Democrat who had been working closely with Lenin in efforts to bring about closer relations between the émigré revolutionaries and Swiss workers, dashed into the Lenin flat.[25]

"Haven't you heard the news?" he cried. "There's a revolution in Russia."

Lenin and Krupskaya took his announcement with a grain of salt. Lenin had not been following the current newspapers, which had, of course, been publishing reports about the disorders in Petrograd for a week. Bronski told them the Swiss papers had issued extra editions. As soon as Bronski went on his way Lenin and Krupskaya bundled up and went down to the lakeside where new editions of the papers were posted up as rapidly as they came from the presses. Standing there with the wind whipping up whitecaps on Zurich Lake, they hurriedly scanned the headlines in the *Zürcher Post* and the *Neue Zürcher Zeitung*.[26] Then Lenin went to the big newspaper kiosk on Pfauzenplatz where Sergei Y. Bagotsky met him, excitedly turning the pages of the newspapers.[27]

It was true. At least it seemed to be true. Lenin's first comments were reserved and skeptical. In a letter he wrote later that afternoon to his friend Inessa Armand, he began with a down-to-earth discussion of a leaflet which she had prepared. Then he added, "We here in Zurich are in a state of agitation today" because of the reported success of the Revolution.

"If the Germans are not lying, then it's true," he said. "That Russia has for the last few days been *on the eve* of revolution is beyond doubt."

He said, "I am beside myself" that he could not go to—Russia? No —to Scandinavia.[28]

While he told Inessa that for the last few days Russia had "beyond doubt" been on the eve of Revolution, he left behind in the archives not one scrap of paper, not one memo, not one comment (recalled by Krupskaya or anyone else) to indicate that prior to the appearance of Bronski in his flat about 1 P.M. on March 2 he had the faintest notion that the Russian Revolution to which he had devoted his adult life was even on the horizon.

Later on Krupskaya had no recollection of how they spent the rest of the day. Were there excited gatherings with the comrades in Zurich as there had been when the news of the 1905 Revolution reached Switzerland? Perhaps, but there is no trace in the annals of the memoirists. Nor is there the kind of excitement in Krupskaya's narrative and in Lenin's letters which 1905 evoked.

Not until he had gone over the second day's reports in the Swiss and other foreign newspapers did Lenin begin to attune his mind to the idea of revolution in Russia. Yet he was still, as Krupskaya herself admitted, far from understanding what had happened.

"He still gauged it by the scope of the 1905 Revolution," she said, "and said that the most important task of the moment was to combine legal work with illegal."[29]

The scope of Lenin's confusion was revealed in a letter which he wrote that day, March 3, to his loyal ally, Alexandra Kollontai, then in Oslo, Norway. He seemed resigned to the idea that this was not *his* revolution but, of course, he consoled himself it was only the "first stage" of the first revolution and would not be the last, nor would the revolutions be only Russian. He looked forward to a legal party in Russia—if this was permitted—and a continuation of underground work. The goal would be a more revolutionary program than before, legal and illegal work, Republican propaganda, a struggle against imperialism, and, ultimately, an international proletarian revolution and conquest of power by the Soviets.

He spelled out his ideas more fully the same day in another letter to Kollontai and in draft theses over which he and Grigory Zinoviev worked in the course of the day. He was worried, as always, and opposed, as always, to any unity or unification with any other group. He wanted to launch a great organizing campaign among the "backward, the rural, and domestic servants." He placed his revolutionary hopes on the Soviets and wanted to take advantage of whatever freedom of press prevailed to republish his recent writings. He called on Kollontai to "raise up new elements" and "prove to them that peace will be brought only by an armed Soviet of Workers Deputies, if it takes power."[30] In his "theses" he accused the new government of trying to achieve reconciliation with the Romanovs, called for fully democratic elections, the eight-hour day, an immediate cease-fire to be followed by peace and the arming of the workers.

Two days later Lenin spelled out his aims in a telegram to a group of Bolsheviks leaving Scandinavia for Russia.

"Our tactics: no trust in and no support of the new government; Kerensky is especially suspect; arming of the proletariat is the only guarantee: immediate elections to the Petrograd City Council; no rapprochement with other parties. Telegraph this to Petrograd."[31]

Lenin's telegram caused a storm when it reached Petrograd March 13.[32] He issued a clarifying statement which, in effect, made plain that these were his own personal views, not those of the Party. It was equally plain that his views were not widely shared in Petrograd.[33]

Lenin now had finally decided that the Revolution had occurred and he knew he must get to Russia as quickly as possible. But how? Krupskaya said he did not sleep nights for trying to devise a plan. Possibly he could fly to Russia. But that was just fantasy. Or he might borrow the passport of a foreigner. A Swede, perhaps.[34] That would be best. He wrote Vyacheslav A. Karpinsky on March 6 proposing that Karpinsky take out papers for traveling to Russia via France and England. Then Lenin would put on a wig and have his picture taken. He would take Karpinsky's papers and the wigged photo and wearing the wig go to the Bern consulate and get the passport and visas. Karpinsky would disappear for a few weeks (until Lenin got to Sweden). Then he would cable Karpinsky to come out of hiding. The Party would pay Karpinsky's board and lodging while he was hidden away in the mountains.[35] A day or two later Lenin asked Inessa to canvass Russians in Clarens, Switzerland, where she was now living, for a passport which they might lend (not knowing it was to be used by Lenin). He also thought she might find a Swiss who would lend his passport to a Russian.[36] And he even sent his photo (concealed in a book) to Yakov Ganetsky (Furstenberg), the Polish Social Democrat who had made Lenin's arrangements to go to Cracow and now his trusted agent in Stockholm. Lenin asked Ganetsky to find a Swede who looked like him and get his passport. Since Lenin did not speak Swedish, the Swede must be a deaf-mute. Ganetsky thought the idea was hilarious. But he did take the photo to the Swedish Social Democratic newspaper *Politiken*, where it was published a few days later with the caption "Leader of the Russian Revolution."[37] When Lenin told Krupskaya about his plan, she talked him out of it. What would happen, she said, if he fell asleep, began to dream of the Mensheviks, and suddenly started to utter ripe rich Russian oaths?[38] But Lenin's mind continued to range widely. He approved a plan by one of his fellow Bolsheviks, Sofiya Ravich, of marrying a Swiss citizen which would then make her eligible for a passport. He promised to put up one hundred francs of Party money, fifty francs for a lawyer and fifty francs for "a convenient old man" who would be her nominal husband, and suggested that she marry Pavel B. Axelrod, a leading Menshevik who had become a Swiss citizen.[39]

Lenin was disappointed when Inessa did not react favorably to a suggestion that she go to England and try to find out discreetly whether he might be granted transit rights.[40] He put the same question in a more formal way to Ganetsky. Prospects of getting through England seemed gloomy. Lenin was convinced the British would simply intern him and he began to push an idea which had originally been advanced by Martov at a meeting of revolutionaries in Geneva on March 6 to persuade the Germans to permit the revolutionary Russians in Switzerland to transit Germany in return for the release of Germans and Austrians interned in Russia.[41]

Filled with frustration, Lenin consoled himself with writing what he called his "Letters from Afar." There were five in all, and they were intended to guide the Party in Russia through publication in *Pravda* until he got back. Lenin put aside almost all other occupations to concentrate on the letters. He told Karpinsky bluntly on March 8 that he could not deliver a lecture because "I have to write daily for *Pravda*."

Lenin completed his first letter March 7. It was not a well-organized piece of work. He spent a good deal of time discussing the 1905 Revolution (with which, of course, he was more familiar), then developed the thesis that, in effect, the February Revolution was "a plot against Nicholas Romanov" organized by Anglo-French finance capital, Anglo-French imperialism, and "Russian Octobrist-Capital."

The February rising, he insisted, was "a conspiracy of the Anglo-French imperialists" who merely used "Milyukov, Guchkov and Co" to seize power in order to continue the imperialist war. He employed his usual freewheeling invective, calling Kerensky a "balalaika," and A. N. Potresov, Gvozdev, and Chkheidze "traitors to the workers" who were already working to restore the Romanov monarchy.

The only hope for a true revolution, in Lenin's view, was the organization of small peasants and poor people into Soviets and support from the proletariat of other countries. This, he thought, could eventually lead to the establishment of a democratic republic, socialism, peace, bread, and freedom.[42] His second letter, completed March 9, was even more disorganized than the first. It was cast in the form of a rebuttal to a dispatch Lenin had read in the *Times* of London. He continued to warn against a Romanov restoration (and a new Rasputin) and advocated the creation of a "workers' militia or workers' home guard" to replace the Czar's police and to stand guard over the new Provisional Government.

At one point Lenin said of the London *Times* correspondent:

"He is all mixed up, our poor English Guchkovite; he has failed to produce a logical argument, has failed to tell either a whole lie or the whole truth, he has merely given himself away."[43]

The comment could fairly be applied to Lenin's own polemic. Kollontai brought the two letters to Petrograd and turned them over to Stalin and Kamenev March 19. Letter No. 1 appeared in two parts, March 21 and 22, but it was sharply reduced by the *Pravda* editors, about one fifth of its contents being cut, particularly Lenin's strongest polemics—those in which he attacked the leaders of the Revolution, especially the Mensheviks and SRs, his charges of Anglo-French collaboration in the Revolution, his insistence that restoration of the monarchy was contemplated, and his criticism of continuation of the war.[44] The names of Guchkov, Milyukov, Gvozdev, Potresov, and Chkheidze were all cut out.[45]

And that was all. The second letter did not appear. The third, in which Lenin elaborated his idea of a people's militia—the "whole armed population" in which everyone would stand guard once every two weeks and there would be "no police, no army and no bureaucracy"—was not printed. The fourth, in which Lenin said only a workers' and peasants' government could make world peace with other workers and peasants who had overthrown the bourgeois governments of the West, did not appear. The fifth Lenin never finished.

The only circulation Lenin's views achieved was through his personal distribution of the initial two letters among a few Bolsheviks in Switzerland.[46] The Revolution had arrived. The Bolsheviks had returned to Petrograd. *Pravda* was being published. But the views of Lenin were getting no more circulation than they had before Nicholas II left the throne.

Perhaps it was just as well. Not even the most charitable assessment would give "Letters from Afar" a very high rating, even on the turgid scale of Russian revolutionary polemics. "Letters" represented the frantic groping of a narrow, out-of-touch mind to find a connection between sudden dynamic events which he neither expected nor understood and a philosophy which was geared to attack other dialecticians rather than seismic issues such as had been hurled to the forefront by the February events. Lenin had not yet absorbed the reality of the Revolution. He was mired in the conviction that at any moment the Romanovs could return and that the chief perpetrators of February were British and French agents.

The one innovative idea which he presented in "Letters" was the transformation of the total Russian population into an "armed militia" which in some manner would protect the Revolution and take over the entire functioning of the state, replacing Army, police, and bureaucracy. This body would "teach" young people to work, draw women into public life, "ensure public order," see that every child had a bottle of good milk, turn over the palaces and big apartments of the noble and the rich to the poor, and "train the masses for participation in all affairs of state."

But, he hurriedly added, "it would be absurd to think of drawing up any kind of 'plan' for a proletarian militia; when the workers and the entire people set about it practically, on a truly mass scale, they will work it out and organize it a hundred times better than any theoretician."[47]

There was one theme which ran through all of Lenin's unpublished "Letters"—insistence on the primacy of the Soviets. They represented, Lenin insisted, the true revolutionary force in Russia. They must be broadened and *armed,* and, he made clear, this should be the No. 1 objective of the Bolsheviks.

XLIV

To the Finland Station

It was time that Lenin returned to Petrograd. There was more trouble over *Pravda* and the Bolsheviks. M. E. Chernomazov, prewar secretary of *Pravda,* had been arrested as an Okhrana agent (the records were now open). So were Shurkanov (a Bolshevik member of the Third Duma), Ozol, Lucy Serova, and Khakharev.[1] Lenin felt obliged to issue a statement emphasizing that Chernomazov had been removed from the paper on the eve of the war because of suspicions about his activities.[2]

By now arrangements were in full swing for Lenin and a group of revolutionaries to return via Germany. The arrangements were undertaken first by Robert Grimm, the same man with whom Lenin was on such bad terms politically, and then by Friedrich (Fritz) Platten, a left-wing Swiss Social Democrat. Platten conducted the formal negotiations with the German minister in Bern under which the details of the trip were worked out.[3]

The arrangements went smoothly although there were some delays. Once Lenin in a fit of gloom wrote Inessa: "Probably we *won't* manage to get to Russia! Britain *will not let us through*. It can't be done through Germany."[4]

Actually, there was no doubt from the beginning that Germany would let the exiles through. It had been basic German foreign policy from early in the war to encourage Russian revolutionary activity. The delicate arrangements were generally handled by the infamous Parvus

(Helphand) who had once collaborated with Trotsky and who had been on the fringes (and sometimes within the inner circles) of the international revolutionary movement since the early 1900s.

There is no evidence that Parvus had been able to penetrate the Bolshevik apparatus to any material extent up to this point. That is, Lenin had refused to deal with him and there was no indication that the withered Bolshevik apparatus inside Russia benefited in any way from the 2 or 3 millions of marks which Parvus had managed to extract from the German treasury for operations within Russia up to the time of February.

However, Ganetsky, Lenin's trusted agent in Stockholm, was at the same time an employee of Parvus, working in one of Parvus' many corporations. This corporation, in fact, engaged in selling German medical supplies and contraceptives to the Russians through Sweden.[5]

While Grimm and then Platten were dealing formally and openly with the Germans; while Lenin was insisting on every kind of safeguard (he well understood the political perils of accepting favors from the Germans); while efforts were being made to obtain international socialist guarantees of the transit of the revolutionaries through Germany, Parvus was working secretly to smooth the rails for the operation. High German approval had been given almost the moment the Revolution broke out. Of all this Ganetsky was aware. How much Lenin knew through Ganetsky is not clear, but some of Lenin's sly remarks may be revealing. In one letter to Inessa he says: "You will say, perhaps, that the Germans *won't* give a coach. I bet you they *will!*"[6] and in another he tells her, "We have more money for the journey than I thought, enough for 10–12 persons. The comrades in Stockholm have been a *great* help." (The "comrades" is a reference, of course, to Ganetsky).[7]

The fact is that Parvus not only got behind-the-scenes clearance for the trip (which the Germans undoubtedly would have been glad to give in any circumstance) but quite probably was the source of a subvention to Lenin and his comrades to finance the trip, passing on the money through either Ganetsky or another shadowy operative named Alexander Keskula, an Estonian Bolshevik.[8]

There was an enormous flurry of final preparations. First they were going on Wednesday March 22. Only ten persons would make the trip —Lenin, Krupskaya, Inessa, Zinoviev, and six others. Lenin and Krupskaya had to go to Bern to sign the "protocol" of the trip, specifying the rights of the travelers, free transit of Germany, no access to the train by German authorities. Then the date was changed to Monday

March 27. The Mensheviks first planned to go too. Then changed their minds. There was a last-minute firing off of telegrams. Food had to be provided for the journey. Ganetsky was alerted to be ready to meet the travelers once they had transited Germany. There was a final meeting in Bern on the evening of March 26 of the Bolshevik return-ees at which Lenin read the text of his Farewell Letter to Swiss Workers, in which he declared:

"Single-handed, the Russian proletariat cannot bring the socialist revolution to a *victorious* conclusion. But it can give the Russian revo-lution a mighty sweep that would create the most favorable conditions for a socialist revolution and would, in a sense, start it."[9]

Then Lenin, Krupskaya, and the departing Bolsheviks returned to Zurich to board their "sealed" train (actually never sealed). They met at the Zahringer Hof for a farewell lunch—Lenin, Krupskaya, Inessa, the Zinovievs, the G. A. Usiyeviches, the G. I. Safarovs, Sofiya Ravich, A. Abramovich from Chaux-de-Fonds, F. Grebelskaya, M. M. Khari-tonov, Linda Rosenblum, Nikolai Boitsov, Mikha Tskhakaya, E. and M. Marienhoff, Grigory Y. Sokolnikov, and Karl Radek.[10] There they signed a declaration that they understood the conditions of the trip laid down by Platten and the German legation; that they would obey Platten's instructions; that they had heard published reports that the Provisional Government planned to try them all for treason if and when they reached Russia; and that they assumed "full political responsibility" for the trip.[11] There was a demonstration when the group arrived at the Zurich Central Station a little before 3 P.M. Lenin's supporters were there with red banners, and some of his Rus-sian political opponents, supporters of the war, turned up, too, and shouted: "Spies! German spies!"[12] It was a clear sunny day. The sta-tion was almost empty. Not many travelers for Germany from isolated wartime Switzerland. Lenin joked with his friends but Bagotsky felt that his thoughts were a thousand miles away. He kept looking at his watch and asking if it wasn't time for the train to leave. Lunacharsky thought he looked "composed and happy." "When I looked at him standing on the platform of the outward-bound train I felt that inside he was thinking 'At last, at last the thing for which I was created is happening.'"[13]

Finally, the train whistle blew, the guard shouted "All aboard," a little bell rang, and the train pulled out at 3:10 P.M. Soon the train reached the Swiss frontier point of Schaffhausen. The Russian party, strictly shepherded by Platten and forbidden to speak to anyone but him, left the Swiss coaches and boarded the German train.[14] The Swiss waived customs formalities and the strange party passed over into Germany.

Lenin withdrew into himself on the journey, Krupskaya reported. Such talk as there was was trivial. Sokolnikov formed a firm friendship with the only youngster in the group, a four-year-old boy named Robert, son of a woman member of the Bund.[15] (There were thirty-one adult members of the group and Robert.)

The Germans went out of their way to provide good service. The cook served up "good square meals" to which, Krupskaya said, the emigrants were not really accustomed.[16]

Actually, it could hardly have been a more pedestrian, uneventful trip.

There was one minor contretemps. At Frankfurt, Platten, the Swiss guarantor and conductor of the group, got off the train to buy some beer and newspapers. (One of the four doors of the car was not locked.) He asked a couple of German soldiers to help him carry the beer back to the train. Radek greeted the Germans with enthusiasm in violation of the rules and began to "fraternize" with them until the train got under way again.[17]

The train had been given a high traffic priority by the Germans—so high that the German Crown Prince was delayed for two hours to let it pass.[18] There was a several hours' layover in Berlin during which some German Social Democrats boarded the train but were not permitted to communicate with the group.[19] When the train reached the Baltic Sea terminal of Sassnitz on March 30, Lenin cabled Ganetsky that he would arrive at the Swedish port of Trelleborg at 6 P.M.[20] Ganetsky had been shuttling between Malmö and Trelleborg for two days. He persuaded the Swedes to send a radiotelegram to confirm Lenin's arrival. That evening when Lenin and his party debarked Ganetsky discovered that his telegram had produced a council of war among the emigrants. Not knowing who was asking about Lenin's presence, they leaped to the conclusion it was the Swedish police, acting in collusion with the Germans, preparing to arrest Lenin when he set foot on their soil.[21]

But all went swimmingly. In no time at all the party was hustled into a special car which Ganetsky had arranged and set off for Malmö. They dined there and took the night train for Stockholm, talking most of the night, but about 4 A.M. Lenin was persuaded to catch a little sleep.[22] At Stockholm in the morning they were met by whirling motion picture cameras and reporters.[23] Lenin dashed off to buy some new clothes[24]—he didn't want to appear in Russia in the thread-worn suit of his exile—and to pick up some new books, piles of newspapers and magazines. But he also had serious conversations with his agent, Ganetsky, and with Karl Radek, who, it now became apparent, was not going to be permitted to return to Russia (he was an Austrian subject).

Parvus-Helphand had arrived in Stockholm hoping to meet Lenin and to set up an alliance with him, if possible, on behalf of his masters in the German Foreign Office. Lenin shrewdly refused a personal meeting and in an exchange carried on through Ganetsky told Parvus "he was not concerned with diplomacy; his task was social-revolutionary agitation." Parvus responded through Ganetsky that "he may go on agitating; but if he is not interested in statesmanship, then he will become a tool in my hands." If Parvus failed with Lenin personally, this did not mean he failed practically. He spent most of the day with Radek. There is no report of what transpired but as Parvus' biographers, Zeman and Scharau, comment:

"It is unlikely that they spent much time discussing Marxist theories. Helphand was in a position to promise massive support for the Bolsheviks in the forthcoming struggle for political power in Russia; Radek was empowered to accept the offer."

The events of ensuing months, they feel confident, support the conclusion that the two men made a deal.[25]

Before leaving Stockholm Lenin named Ganetsky, Radek, and Vatslav V. Vorovsky as a troika to represent the Party abroad.* One of their chief functions was to be the funneling of German Foreign Office funds into Bolshevik coffers.[26]

Toward the end of the day Lenin's party was under way again by train for Russian Finland. Late Saturday night or early Sunday morning, April 2—Easter Sunday—Shlyapnikov in Petrograd got his first wire from Ganetsky indicating Lenin had successfully transited Germany. He immediately began alerting frontier guards, railroad officials, and Party members about Lenin's impending arrival.[27] Lenin's party made its way onward without real obstacles. They crossed the frontier from Sweden into Finland on Finnish country sleighs on Easter morning, Lenin waving a red scarf tied to an Alpine stock. At Tornio they transferred into rickety Russian third-class coaches. Krupskaya was entranced. Everything was so *Russian!* An elderly Russian soldier cradled the youngster Robert in his arms and fed him *kulich*, Russian Easter cream cheese cake, as the boy chattered away in French. Everyone huddled at the windows drinking in the Finnish countryside—so like the Russian—white birches, scattered pines, snow-covered fields, station platforms crowded with peasants and soldiers. At one station G. A. Usiyevich shouted "Long live

* Vorovsky was assassinated by a white émigré in 1923. Both Ganetsky and Radek were purged by Stalin in 1937.

the world revolution!" The soldiers stared silently and a pale-faced lieutenant, A. S. Savitsky, entered the car. Lenin and Krupskaya talked with him. The lieutenant was a "defensist," in Krupskaya's words—that is, he supported the war. Lenin argued with him. The car filled up with soldiers who listened with open mouths.[28]

Before the train left the Finnish frontier point of Tornio, Lenin sent the last telegram he was ever to dispatch from foreign soil. It was addressed to his two sisters, Mariya and Anna. It read:

Ulyanova
Shirokaya 48/9 Apt 24
Petrograd
Arriving Monday 11 p.m. inform Pravda.

It was sent at 6:12 P.M. April 2 and arrived at Petrograd at 8:08 P.M.[29] Not until the next morning, however, was the message delivered at the steamboat-flat of Mark Yelizarov. The news had been awaited with extraordinary impatience. The whole family knew that Lenin was coming.[30] The Petrograd party was in a fever of preparation. Shlyapnikov got a message similar to that of the Ulyanov sisters on Monday morning. But Monday was a holiday. When Mariya got to the Kshesinskaya mansion, only Nikolai I. Podvoisky was there. They sent the Bolshevik members of the Armored Division guarding the palace scurrying around town to spread the word and round up Bolsheviks for the arrival at Finland Station.[31] The Executive Committee of the Soviet designated Matvei I. Skobelev and Nikolai S. Chkheidze to greet Lenin and his party officially at the Finland Station. (A protocol had begun to be developed for these arrivals.)[32] The Bolshevik Party Bureau decided to go to the Finnish-Russian border point of Beloostrov, a few miles north of Petrograd, and meet the train. The rest would wait at the Finland Station.[33]

When the train drew into Beloostrov at 9 P.M., the platform was crowded with workers from the Sestroretsk arms plant. It was not well lighted and it took A. M. Afanasyev a few minutes to pick out Lenin. He was wearing a topcoat and a new suit—his Stockholm purchase. There was a cry of "Lenin! Lenin!" Lenin quieted the demonstration, spoke a few words, then went into the customs shed. The official group included his sister Mariya, Shlyapnikov, and Lyudmila N. Stal. The railroad buffet was put at the disposal of the party. The workers refused to allow anyone to pay for the sandwiches and beer—which impressed Shlyapnikov. Some women urged Krupskaya to make a speech but she was too excited. Lenin asked the Bolsheviks from Petrograd whether he would be arrested on arrival. They just smiled. As the train pulled out, Afanasyev heard some fashionably dressed people making what he called "wildly malicious" remarks about Lenin and his comrades.[34] In the compartment Lenin almost immediately turned to Kamenev and exploded: "What's this you're writing in *Pravda?* We have seen several issues and really swore at you."[35]

XLV

At Last—Petrograd

The train with its snub-nosed Russian engine and wide cars, decorated with red bunting and Bolshevik party slogans, chuffed off in the night. At 11:10 P.M.[1] it rolled into Petrograd's Finland Station. An honor guard of sailors from "red" Kronshtadt in navy blue uniforms, striped blue shirts, and red pompons lined the platform on both sides. They were backed up by the workers' militia and groups of Red Guards. As the train slowly came to a halt and clouds of steam filled the railroad hall, a brass band struck up the "Marseillaise"—the anthem of the moment—and the guards stood at attention.[2]

The sailors had arrived from Kronshtadt at the last moment. Because of the Easter holiday (April 3 was the Monday after Easter) they had not gotten word of Lenin's impending arrival. They commandeered an icebreaker (the Gulf of Finland was still filled with ice), transferred to a cutter at the Neva, and raced up to the Liteiny Bridge close by the Finland Station, arriving just as the Bolshevik party delegation, two hundred strong, marched into the station from headquarters at the Kshesinskaya mansion.

An armored car was drawn up beside the Imperial reception room at the station.

Lenin and Krupskaya emerged from the fifth car behind the locomotive and a cheer arose.[3] The captain of the honor guard saluted. Lenin, surprised by the gesture, raised his hand and returned the salute.[4]

"What's this about?" Lenin asked.

"It's the greeting of the revolutionary troops and workers," he was told. As Lenin walked down the line of sailors Bonch-Bruyevich whispered to him that the sailors wanted to hear a word from him. Lenin stepped back a pace or two and said (as Bonch-Bruyevich recalled):

"Sailors, comrades I greet you. I don't know as yet whether you all agree with the Provisional Government but I know very well that when they give you sweet speeches and make many promises they are deceiving you, just as they deceive the whole Russian people. The people need peace. The people need bread and the people need land. And they give you war, hunger, no food and the land remains in the hands of the landowners. Sailors, comrades, you must fight for the revolution, fight to the end, for full victory of the proletariat. All hail the world Socialist Revolution!"[5]

The glove was hurled down. Lenin had set the tone of his return to Russia. No compromise. No armistice. War to the end against the new regime. He was forty-six years old. Within a week he would be forty-seven. He was back in his own country—to stay.

Now Lenin and Krupskaya were taken into the Czar's reception room, draped in red banners. Alexandra Kollontai handed him a bouquet of red roses in the name of the Petersburg Bolsheviks. Voitinsky was there. Lenin shook his hand with a twinkle in his eye. "Again with us, Comrade Petrov [Voitinsky's Party name]." "I don't know where you stand," Voitinsky replied.[6] Chkheidze spoke his greetings, expressing hope that Lenin would "close ranks" with the other revolutionary parties, particularly in the task of defending Russia.[7]

Lenin stood listening to him, Kollontai's bouquet in his hands, his round workman's cap on his head. Chkheidze concluded with the words: "We hope you will pursue these goals together with us."

Sukhanov was watching. What would Lenin say to that? Lenin turned toward the group of delegates, sailors, soldiers who had shoved into the room, and spoke, much as he had already in the train hall to the sailors. "The world-wide Socialist revolution has already dawned. . . . Germany is seething. . . . Any day now the whole of European capitalism may crash. . . . The Russian revolution accomplished by you has prepared the way and opened a new epoch. Long live the world-wide Socialist revolution!"[8]

The reception committee listened with open mouths. This was not the kind of speech they had been accustomed to hear from the returning exiles. They didn't seem very enthusiastic, Voitinsky noted.[9] In a moment it was over and Shlyapnikov was leading Lenin outside. The crowd roared. A band was playing. Some were singing revolutionary songs. Inessa Armand shed a tear. She, too, had been on the "sealed train."[*] An effort was made to put Lenin into a closed car but instead Lenin got up on the car and made another speech. Again he lashed out at "shameful imperialist slaughter," "lies and frauds," "capitalist pirates." Sukhanov could only hear occasional phrases. Others heard even less. None of the speeches were recorded for the meticulous hagiography of Lenin which was to grow over the years.[10]

Krupskaya and the others in the party were put into private cars. But Lenin finally mounted the armored car which had stood at the entrance to the Czar's reception room. Searchlights from the nearby Peter and Paul Fortress lighted up the scene from Finland Station along the route down Simbirsk Street, past the Villy Clinic, and across the Sampsoniyevsky Bridge to the Kshesinskaya mansion on the Petrograd side.[11] Crowds surrounded the armored car and several times the procession halted and Lenin again spoke. It was, in the words of Zinaida Gippius, "a pompous welcome"[12] but her husband, Dmitri Merezhkovsky, had been insisting since early March that "our fate will be decided by Lenin."[13]

At the Kshesinskaya mansion Lenin was taken upstairs for a glass of tea.[14] Outside an unending succession of Bolshevik orators harangued the crowd. Lenin sat near an open door to the balcony and listened. Finally a hysterical Bolshevik called for immediate revolution and wildly inflamed the crowd. Lenin was amused but not very pleased. He tried to calm the man and finally himself spoke several times from the balcony, repeating the general theme that he had voiced at Finland Station; against the Government, against the war, for an international revolution.[15]

Sukhanov wandered into the Kshesinskaya mansion some time after midnight. There was little furniture in the once exquisite palace of the Emperor's mistress. Just plain chairs, tables, and desks. Upstairs in the dining room tea was being served. The rooms were filled with happy Bolsheviks. Lenin was again on the balcony but when he came back in he and Sukhanov shook hands.[16] Lenin greeted him with a twinkle in his eyes and recalled their old arguments. A little later Lenin was introduced to the assembled Party workers in Kshesinskaya's ballroom, decorated with white Corinthian columns and golden garlands, and began a long speech—it ran nearly two hours according to Sukhanov. Curiously there is no account of its content in the Bolshevik memoirs, but Shlyapnikov recalled that it generally followed the line of Lenin's "April Theses." As Sukhanov recollected it Lenin said that he had

---

[*] Inessa Armand went to Moscow almost immediately on her return to Russia. She was in Petrograd only once before the October coup. Pavel Podlyashuk, *Tovarishch Inessa*, pp. 205–6.)

feared on arriving in Petrograd he would be taken directly to the Peter and Paul Fortress.

"As we see," he said wryly, "we turned out to be far from that. But let us not lose hope that we may still not escape it."

He attacked the war, the defense policy of the Provisional Government, and the whole idea of government, but he supported the Soviets. That was government enough. His remarks dumbfounded the Bolshevik listeners. They had not read the "Letters from Afar" in which he propounded this idea. They didn't know what to think. As for the countryside—organized seizure of the land by the peasants was his formula. In the cities "armed workers" would stand guard. He attacked all other radicals and socialists and even the name "Social Democracy," which he thought had been "desecrated by treason." He was merciless in his rhetoric against the "traitors, the fools, the lackeys" of the bourgeoisie.[17] He called for a "peace" to be made by Russian regiments fraternizing with German regiments. Let the Soviets seize power and write new laws. Let the landless peasants and poor farm hands take the land as they please. And he called for his party to take the name "Communists" instead of the defiled term "Social Democrats." Voitinsky thought Lenin talked as though he were obsessed by a vision. At the end Lenin asked for questions. No one stood up. Lenin's eyes met Voitinsky's. Voitinsky rose and observed that Lenin's program was not sensible. He was not familiar with actual conditions in Russia. He had not thought out the implications of the war. He had not backed his ideas with facts. He had presented a collection of catch phrases.

Some applause appeared in the audience but Lenin put it down.

"Comrade Petrov," he said, "is mistaken when he says that I am not familiar with conditions in Russia. On the way through Finland to Petrograd I shared a compartment with a soldier from the front. He told me all I need to know about the war and I will not trade his words for the lies of reactionary newspapers that Comrade Petrov considers such wells of wisdom."

Lenin's words drew a thunder of applause.[18]

There was nothing, Sukhanov noted, by way of an analysis of conditions in Russia. Not a word. It was a tour de force, and Sukhanov, not knowing how Lenin's ideas had been evolving, thought he must have made it up on the spur of the moment.

The Party faithful applauded as Lenin sat down. Sukhanov looked at Kamenev, author of Pravda's "moderate" policy. Kamenev shrugged his shoulders and said, "Wait, just wait."[19]

Sukhanov went out into the street. It was beginning to get light. He felt as though he had been beaten around the head by flails.[20] Before they left, Lenin insisted on singing revolutionary songs. He had always loved to sing. Now as the Petrograd dawn began to break he and his revolutionary comrades roared out the "Varskavyanka," the "Marseillaise," and Krylov's "Muzykanty." Lenin wanted to sing the "Internationale" but nobody knew it.[21]

Gora, that is Georgi Lozgachev-Yelizarov, had not been permitted to go with his aunt Mariya, his stepmother Anna, or his stepfather Mark Yelizarov to meet Lenin. The evening was going to be too late and he was too small.

"You know, Gorushka," Anna told him, "Volodya and Nadya are coming to us and will live with us. And tomorrow morning you can meet them for the first time and welcome them without any outsiders being around."

So instead of going to the Finland Station Gora had taken some long strips of paper, colored them with hammers and sickles, and put them up in Mariya's room, which was where "Volodya and Nadya" were going to live. Mariya was moving in with her sister.

The sun had almost risen when Gora was awakened on the morning of Tuesday April 4 by a jumble of voices outside his room. He slipped out of bed, ran into the living room and there, two steps away, he saw a rather small man, thickset, solid, and appearing very wide-shouldered because of his heavy green, rough-textured, semimilitary jacket with stamped leather buttons, like little footballs. He wore green trousers and simple black boots with heavy stitching. He had just been washing himself and stood at the open door of the bathroom, surrounded by his smiling relatives, wiping his face with a towel.

It was, of course, Gora's uncle, Vladimir Ilyich.

"Aha," said Lenin. "There is Gora. At last we get a sight of you."

It suddenly dawned on Gora that "Brother Volodya" and Lenin were one and the same person. Gora was introduced and the whole family sat about listening. Lenin told one funny story after another and even the solemn and serious Mariya could not help laughing.

They were still sitting there when a knock came at the door. A tall good-looking Lett appeared, Robert Matisovich Gabalin, later to become chief of Lenin's personal bodyguard. Now he told Lenin that his car was waiting downstairs.

"Would you like to have a ride?" Lenin asked Gora. Would he! He was eleven years old and had never been in an automobile in his life. He bounced down the stairs with Lenin and they sat together in the car. It was a gray four-seater Renault. Gora sat beside his uncle and they drove off through the nearly empty Petrograd streets in the early morning. In later years Gora remembered almost everything about the ride. Even the straw-woven seat covers. But he could not remember where Lenin went on that first morning that he found himself back in Russia. What did Lenin's eyes see in the thin light of the first hour after dawn? Did he see the Russia that he hoped to build? Not likely. There was no real vision of that in his speech at the Finland Station, his remarks at Kshesinskaya's mansion, nor in his "Letters from Afar" and the April Theses he was now evolving in his mind. But one thing was clear to Lenin: *His* revolution was only beginning.[22]

On the evening of Lenin's return to Petrograd the Czar, as he had been since March 9, was with his wife and family at Tsarskoye Selo. There they lived under arrest. In his first few days the Czar spent hours burning personal papers (but not his diaries or his correspondence with his beloved Alix). Now his time was spent largely in family matters. He had started reading *The Life of Caesar* even before coming back to Tsarskoye Selo. He was starting on the *History of the Byzantine Empire* by Uspensky, which he found "very interesting." Monday the third, as he faithfully recorded, was "a wonderfully sunny day." He and Alexei spent some time chipping away ice from the summer landing. "A crowd of idlers" stood at the iron gates watching them. In the evening he and his wife played *melnitsa*, a two-handed card game similar to bluff. Later on he read aloud to his daughter Tatyana.

The Imperial family had hopes of being permitted to go to England. Politically, in the great empire over which he had ruled until a month before, it was as though the Czar had never existed.[23]*

* The Czar had hoped to go to England with his family and a conditional invitation was issued to him, but the Provisional Government never managed to muster the political courage to permit the exodus, fearing the antagonism of the Soviet, and the invitation was soon quietly withdrawn. (Maurice Paléologue, *An Ambassador's Memoirs*, Vol. III, p. 263; Sir George Buchanan, *My Mission to Russia*, Vol. II, pp. 102–6.) The withdrawal, it has recently been revealed, was on the insistence of the Czar's cousin, King George V. (Anthony Summers and Tom Mangold, *The File on the Tsar*, pp. 246–52.)

XLVI

The Tragedy of Lotarevo

It was the second morning of the Revolution and at dawn Alexander Tikhonov walked down the street from the Kopeika printing plant in Petrograd, his arms full of newspapers. Bonch-Bruyevich had taken over the plant at the point of a machine gun and the presses had just run off the first issue of *Izvestiya*,[1] Tikhonov bumped into Vladimir Mayakovsky on the Nevsky, bareheaded, overcoat unbuttoned. The poet lifted Tikhonov from the sidewalk, kissed him on both cheeks, and shouted to a friend: "Here! Here! Newspapers!"

A moment later there was the sound of shooting toward the Nicholas Station. Mayakovsky ran off.

"Where are you going?" Tikhonov cried.

"They're shooting over there!" Mayakovsky responded.

"But you're not armed."

"I've been running all night to where the shooting is."

"What for?"

"I don't know. Let's run."[2]

As Shklovsky remarked, Mayakovsky entered the Revolution as he would his own home. He went right in and began opening windows.[3]

The Revolution sent the artists and writers careening in every direction. Gorky threw his energies into what Zinaida Gippius called, ironically, the "Committee of Aesthetes." He, the artist Benois, and Chaliapin formed the Commission of Beaux Arts to protect Russia's art treasures against the wild waves of Revolution. It hardly seemed to be the kind of activity to preoccupy Russia's Stormy Petrel, her very symbol of Revolution.

Zinaida Gippius was scornful of Gorky and his friends, riding around in a large requisitioned automobile.[4] Benois had never known what he was, where he was, or why he was. "The role and conduct of Gorky," she observed, "are perfectly fatal." She called him a "kind, soft Hottentot" who passed out beads and top hats. As a political figure, she insisted, he was a zero.[5] Perhaps she was jealous.

The Merezhkovskys had reconstituted their political salon and Andrei Bely was staying with them again. He had been back in Russia six months and had felt from the moment his train crossed the Finnish frontier that Revolution was coming—no, had already come. Russia was gray, gray, gray. Petrograd was filled with gray soldiers in gray uniforms. The Revolution had been carried out before it even started, he mused, and the famous Army Prikaz No. 1, which frightened Russia and frightened him, had been written in the spirit of the country before he even stepped foot on it after five years' absence.[6] Bely was spending his time running back and forth to the Tauride Palace to find out what was happening. Everyone in Petrograd rushed in and out of the Merezhkovskys' flat. Kerensky often dropped in. Gippius could not get out of her mind an image of Kerensky speaking at the Religious-Philosophical Society. In her hand mirror she had seen him in profile and within the same small circle Nicholas II, whose portrait was on the wall behind Kerensky. There was in the two faces, she thought, more than a similarity. Kerensky, she wrote, was, of course, crazy—but pathetically bold, a kind of a Pierrot. Once Kerensky wanted Merezhkovsky to write a pamphlet about the officers who made the Decembrist revolt. Another time he was in a panic about the impending return of Lenin.[7]

Gorky seemed to have a hard time orienting himself. Gippius thought he was completely under the influence of his Bolshevik friends but his letters did not bear this out. He wrote his wife that "Down with war" was an "idiotic" slogan and that the victory of the Germans would be a victory of reaction. He warned against reliance on the Russian soldier "who is just a dark Russian peasant dressed in uniform." It was necessary to support the Provisional Government. He thought misunderstandings between soldiers and workers would grow, particularly over the eight-hour workday. "We sit in the trenches for three days running," the soldiers would respond. Why should others work only eight hours? He had no doubt that counterrevolution would develop quickly and was fearful of the Petrograd garrison "and even more of the muzhiks." All around him, Gorky said, were people bathed in triumph. "They talk in a language which I cannot understand," Gorky said. Nevertheless he started a newspaper, *Novaya Zhizn*, and Mayakovsky wrote for him.

Bunin was staying at the Medved Hotel in Petrograd where he paid twelve rubles a day for a comfortable room with bath. "How seldom have I experienced a life of comfort and how pleasant it is!" he wrote his wife.

Every day there was some hastily organized meeting of artists and writers. Gorky assembled most of literary and artistic Petrograd for a meeting in the Mikhailovsky Theater to launch his Beaux Arts Commission—Chaliapin, Benois, Kuzma Petrov-Vodkin, Nicholas Roerich, Mayakovsky, V. E. Meyerhold, and the composer Sergei Prokofiev. Mayakovsky made a sharp speech, attacking Benois, his World of Art group, and, by implication, the whole Beaux Arts project. A few soldiers, he said loftily, could protect all of Russia's artistic treasures. Mayakovsky was against any artistic left except one composed of himself and his friends David Burlyuk and the artist Mikhail Larionov.[8]

A few days later they all gathered again—for an exhibition of Finnish art. Bunin had a simple, quiet talk with Gorky—the last of Bunin's life as it transpired. Vera Figner, plain and eloquent, spoke. So did Gorky. Later there was a banquet and later still everyone went to the Comedians Shelter. The place was jammed, hot, vulgar. At the banquet Mayakovsky pushed between Bunin and Gorky and started to eat from their plates and drink from their glasses. "Why do you hate me so much?" Mayakovsky asked Bunin.[9]

Night after night Mayakovsky walked the streets of Petrograd. He could not stop walking. Here was the Russian people deciding its fate. Once he was walking at dusk. The Neva bridges were raised. There were lights in the windows but the street lamps were still dark. At the corners were bonfires and groups of soldiers and citizens standing, talking. At one of these bonfires Mayakovsky met Alexander Blok, his fellow poet. Blok still wore his gray soldier's uniform. The two strolled the streets together, talking of Russia, talking of where the great gray current would sweep their land and their people.[10]

The Revolution which the poets had predicted for so many years, the earthquake in Russia's life which they had foreseen, had come. But where the new forces might take them and their country the poets, for the moment, could not foresee. The smashing impact of events had deadened their imaginations. It would be a time before poetic vision once again lighted the way to the terrible future. Only the remarkable Marina Tsvetayeva awaiting the birth of her second child in Moscow had some premonition. She wrote of the revolutionary troops, tramping Moscow's streets, that they bore the color of "ashes and sand" while over the churches blue clouds rode high. Her spirit was suffused with what she called "a lordly, a royal sadness," the depths of which she could not yet understand.[11]

Ehrenburg, finally back in Russia, called on Tsvetayeva in her Moscow apartment. Her five-year-old daughter met him, thin and white, quoting Blok's "What pale dresses! What a strange silence. Embraces full of lilies, eyes empty of thought." Tsvetayeva read him her poem about the Czar: "Many times our children will recall the Byzantine perfidy of your limpid eyes."[12]

Revolution spread slowly over the Russian land. The snows still lay deep when it broke and the news was late in coming to the villages. Not until mid-March even in an advanced guberniya like Tver did word of the Revolution reach the villages, and the peasants were wary of accepting it. "Things can still change and go back to the old," they said, and in Volokolamsk the peasants were warned not to "believe the stupid rumors about the overthrow of the Czar." In the villages of Smolensk Guberniya the news penetrated on tiptoes. Word was whispered from one peasant to another. They were afraid of their neighbors, afraid of their relatives, afraid even of themselves. It was six weeks before the peasants in the Kursk Guberniya heard what had happened. The priest in a volost of Arkhangelsk Guberniya continued to offer prayers to the Czar, and the village policeman went on wearing his epaulets. No one was the wiser. In the Ufa Guberniya the authorities did their best to suppress a rumor that the Czar had fled, given up his throne, and was being chased by soldiers and some kind of workers.

But this was not always the story. Nor was it for long the story.

In the village of Berezovka in Tambov Guberniya the peasants unearthed from the grave the body of State Counselor Luzhenovsky, burned it, and scattered the ashes to the winds.[13] The first rural disorders were reported in the Novgorod region in early March.[14] Within weeks there was trouble nearly everywhere. In Krasnoyarsk proprietors were threatened that their houses would be burned to the ground. "The last moment has arrived," the peasants warned—then made good their threats. Near Kishinev peasants seized two tobacco plantations and drove off the overseers. Near Mtsensk a band appeared at the great estate of Madame Sheremetev, forced its way inside, and pillaged the cellars. Damage was estimated at 7.5 million rubles. Then a crowd of three thousand surged on a nearby distillery. Part of the property was saved when the owners set fire to the alcohol tanks. In a village not far from Moscow a band of hooligans broke into a house.

The peasants seized them and despite the efforts of police simply beat them to death on the village streets.[15]

One thing led to another. In one village the peasants decided to take the landlord's land without payment. They went out to the fields and began quarreling over how to divide it. Someone broke into the landlord's cellar. They got drunk, set fire to the place, and four men were burned to death. A few days later there was another quarrel about dividing the land. Thirteen were killed and four died of wounds. A while later the poor peasants quarreled with the richer over grain reserves. In this fight three were killed and five injured. Three days later a house caught fire. Someone said a peasant had set it. A crowd rushed to the peasant's house and lynched him. Later on they found out the fire had been caused by the carelessness of the peasant's wife. A strong wind was blowing and before the day was over 132 houses had been destroyed.[16]

"The state was falling to pieces like a handful of wet mud," Paustovsky remarked. "The provinces and districts of Russia were no longer ruled by Petrograd and no one knew what they lived on or what was seething inside them."[17]

Paustovsky paid a visit to his mother deep in the countryside. The peasant who drove Paustovsky to Kopan asked when permission would be given for the peasants to take the land "and to drive out all the big Pans and the little pans with our spades, straight to the devil's mother."

The countryside was so dangerous his mother would hardly let Paustovsky out of sight. But she did permit him to visit a little monastery on the Uzh River, ten versts away. The only monks left were a few old helpless men. A bell occasionally sounded in the belfry.

"We really don't know any longer," the monk said, "whether we should ring it or not. So we just ring it gently. A crow sometimes sits on the bell and he doesn't even fly away."

Paustovsky wanted to go again to the monastery but his mother was afraid. There were bandits in the woods. A few weeks later the bandits attacked the monastery, shot the elderly monks, rummaged the buildings for silver, and set fire to the church.[18]

Marc Ferro, after a careful study of resolutions passed by peasants and workers in the early days of the Revolution, concluded that the peasants were far more revolutionary than the workers; far more often called for radical and arbitrary actions than the workers. An analysis of the first one hundred resolutions passed by peasants revealed that the most frequent single demand was for seizure of state lands, crown lands, and large estates and for their distribution to those who worked them. This was followed by demands for establishment of a democratic republic and for a quick just peace.

A peasant comment: "When we take the land from the kulaks [wealthy peasants] it's Anarchy. When they take our sons it's Patriotism."[19]

One thing the peasants quickly made clear—the land was theirs. They had said to the landlords even before liberation: "We are yours but the land is ours." Now they said it again. Or sometimes: The land belongs to God but only those who work it may profit from it. In many areas there was happiness—not violence. The peasants were certain that the new life would be better and that the land would go to them. In fact, the SR leader Chernov was convinced that this was more the rule than the exception and that where landlords were understanding and quick to work out new arrangements violence could be avoided. The villagers of Vorobyevskoye near Klin pointed out that they had only 102 desyatins of land for twenty-eight households and asked that the absentee estates and church and private lands be divided on the principle that land go to those who personally worked it. In other areas the peasants negotiated sharing agreements with landowners who sometimes were to receive a quarter of the proceeds, sometimes as much as one-half, depending on their contribution of tools, animals, and capital investments. In the Saratov region the peasants and landlords agreed to decide on their respective returns when the fall harvest came in.

But Chernov conceded that in most places the landlords regarded themselves as sole owners of their estates, of their cattle, of their farming machinery. They lived under the protection of their own laws. They understood that these laws were to be changed but they recognized only one source of change—the Constituent Assembly—and that had not even been elected. It was a formal, legalistic iron logic. But it was up against the flame of revolution and as Pushkin had warned a hundred years before: "Let not God see the Russian rebellion—the rebellion without mind and without mercy."[20]

The peasants did not know too much about the political process. But as E. Lundberg, traveling in the south of Russia, discovered, they knew what they wanted. One asked him how you went about signing up for a political party. Lundberg answered with a popular joke:

"K.D., S-R, S-D.—spells Anarchist."

They wanted to know which party stood for dividing the land and whether landowners could also sign up. The program of the SDs, the Social Democrats, they felt, was for city folk. But as for the SRs: "That is for us. Because the land is entirely ours, to each his own." They didn't care for the anarchists. "Police—we don't need," they said.

"But courts we do." Nor did they like the idea of agitators coming to tell them what to do. "It's better that we go to them," they said. "We can take a look and they can talk to us."[21]

Among the landed estates in Tambov Guberniya none matched Lotarevo, the model farming establishment of Prince Lenoid Dmitriyevich Vyazemsky, Adjutant General, Member of the State Council, and sometime Minister of Imperial Affairs. It was located in the Usman Uyezd in one of the richest parts of a remarkably rich Russian farming region. Everything about the establishment had been done with care and scientific precision. The stud farm boasted two great lines, one stemming from the American bay Wilbur M., and the other from the pure Orlov champion Zenith, winner of the Russian derby. The farm was stocked with Swiss cattle, a vast poultry establishment, orchards, greenhouses, and surrounded by parks laid out in the English style.

The Ministry of Agriculture brought foreign visitors to inspect Lotarevo and it was known throughout the country as a center for advanced agricultural techniques. New foreign farm machinery, particularly from the United States, was tried out in Lotarevo and adapted to Russian conditions. The estate lay some miles from the nearest railroad at Gryazi. The big peasant village of Korobovka was two versts distant. Most of these peasants worked at Lotarevo and here Prince Vyazemsky had built a church and each summer he brought one of the singers from St. Petersburg's famous Arkhangelsk Choir to teach the local choir new hymns. On a nearby hill in 1903 he had built a hospital for the villagers in memory of his sister, modeling it after the best hospitals in St. Petersburg.

Lotarevo, in a word, represented the best of enlightened Russian management, a conscious and successful attempt to bring to Russia the most productive and scientific agriculture and to raise the cultural and economic level of the backward peasants.

It was true, nonetheless, that the Tambov region had been the scene of violent uprisings in 1905 and of bloody and cruel punitive expeditions in 1906 and 1907. In village after village peasant bodies swung from the gallows and were left to hang, stiff, black, and twisted, for weeks as a warning to the other peasants. One of the officers who led a punitive detachment, or so the villagers firmly believed, was Dmitri Leonidovich Vyazemsky, the Prince's oldest son.

By the time of the February Revolution Prince Leonid was six years dead and Lotarevo was being managed by his son Boris, at thirty-three as shrewd and talented a young man as Russia could boast. He had been one of Premier Stolypin's "bright young men," had specialized in agriculture after graduating from the juridical faculty of St.

Petersburg University with high honors. After Stolypin's assassination and his father's death he had taken over the management of Lotarevo, held many local and government offices, and was chairman of the local Mobilization Committee. He was, in the words of Agriculture Minister Krivoshein, "a young man with a profound future." He and his wife spent the Christmas and New Year's holidays of 1916–17 in Petrograd, staying at Sheremetev Palace (Boris' wife was a Sheremetev) on the Fontanka but by late January he was back at Lotarevo and noting in his diary: "Snowstorm. By evening a *purga*. No roads." It was a normal winter on the Tambov steppe and his diary was a countryman's diary. On March 1, 1917, he recorded: "Misty morning. Thirteen degrees of frost and 'ears' around the sun. Also below the sun a clear, concave rainbow." (He drew a little picture in his diary of the sun's ears.)

It was the next day that his brother Dmitri was killed while riding with Guchkov in Petrograd and on March 3 Boris and his wife left for Petrograd. Not until they were on their way did they hear of the Revolution. They spent a month in Petrograd. (Boris was a member of the Kadet party.) He met with Guchkov, Prince Lvov, Shingarev (the new Agriculture Minister), Milyukov, Nekrasov, and Kerensky and inspected a menagerie which his brother Dmitri had set up and which was now being presented to the Academy of Science.

Back at Lotarevo Boris plunged into the new work of meeting with the Uyezd Executive Committee and peasant representatives. At the start he found the mood "ideal." He spent May Day with the peasants and discussed questions of landownership and requisition.

There were no overt signs of trouble but Boris knew the temper of the peasants well enough to understand that there were passions stirring below the surface. The family wanted Dmitri buried in the church at Korobovka. Boris urged against it, certain there would be trouble because of Dmitri's role in the 1905 reprisals. When the coffin arrived at the railroad station at Gryazi, Boris urged the family to change its plans and return the body to Petrograd. He had just been waited on by the Peasants Committee of Korobovka protesting the burial of Dmitri in the church. But his mother, his sister and sister-in-law insisted, although Boris told his sister, Lidiya, "It's fine for you to be so brave. You will go away. I will remain here and suffer the consequences." He bowed to the family opinion and Dmitri was buried, as planned, although the peasants stood outside the church, their caps on, grumbling and exchanging angry looks.

Spring wore on. The wheat was planted. There was enough labor. The eldest sons had remained with their peasant families. Boris was elected chairman of the Tambov Zemstvo (assembly).

But the undercurrent of trouble more and more came to the surface.[22] A row broke out over farm wages. The peasants threatened a strike. Crowds began to come to the great courtyard of Lotarevo, armed with sticks and clubs. They argued and harangued. There was no shortage of peasant land in the Tambov region. But there was a shortage of pasture, and the good pasture was in the hands of the big estate owners. A scheme was devised to set up an irrigation works to create more pasture, and a detachment of troops was brought in to protect the work. This brought strong resentment from the peasants. They believed Boris was trying to keep them from getting the pastures they needed.

Even so, the harvest went off without incident. The yield, as always, was excellent. Boris spent a whole day inspecting the blooded stock on the farm—the cows, the heifers, the bulls, the mares, and the stallions. The wheat was beginning to go off to the mill and it was haymaking time.

Then, one August morning a young ensign and a soldier scurried into the great house at Lotarevo shouting: "Run for your lives!" A crowd of peasants was following behind. The sound of their angry voices could be heard in the house. The coachman, alerted to trouble, wheeled the troika up to the door. "You must get away now," he said. "In five minutes it will be too late."

But Boris and his wife refused to go. In a moment the angry crowd was upon them. There were shouts about the troops, about Boris' father (whom the peasants feared and disliked),[23] and among the peasants appeared a Bolshevik agitator, a small man from the city, wearing a pince-nez, who told the crowd they were unable to do anything with Boris because in their souls they were still serfs. The elder of Korobovka village then spoke up. "Yes, we've heard all that—the Prince is a swine but these are new times. We want to take his land. Though we respect him we want to finish with him. But as for you" (turning to the agitator) "the time will come when we will hang your brothers."

The argument went on for hours. Boris knew the peasants well. He had talked himself out of difficult situations before. At one point a muzhik said: "Have it as you will, Your Excellency, but we are for Lenin and we will not retreat from him a single step."

Toward evening the couple was taken to the new school which Boris had built recently in Korobovka. Hours later the village *starets* (elder) and some of his comrades appeared and began to argue. By this time all were drunk, having broken into the cellars of Lotarevo.

The principal charge against Boris, the one to which the peasants returned again and again, was that as chairman of the Mobilization

Committee, he had sent many peasant youths to their death at the front. Nothing he could say could budge them from this complaint.

Finally the "court" tired of the discussion, and a verdict was reached—that Boris be compelled to go to the front lines.

During the night some of the muzhiks who knew Boris well attempted to organize a rescue but they could not agree on what to do and nothing was done.

At dawn a military guard appeared to carry out the "verdict." Boris was taken away by the soldiers who were to place him on the train at Gryazi for Moscow where, they decided, he would be sent to the front. The guards were good-natured. They had not been drinking and it was clear they hoped to get their prisoner aboard the train without further trouble. But when they arrived at the Gryazi Station, a train filled with soldiers fleeing the front was standing there. The stationmaster secreted Boris in his office but somehow his presence became known, possibly through the agitator who had appeared at Lotarevo. The crowd of deserters was aroused, smashed down the stationmaster's office door, and almost literally tore the young aristocrat to pieces, some armed with bayonets, others with railroad iron.

Boris' wife finally escaped with the help of friendly neighbors, a friendly soldier, and a few loyal peasants. She brought her husband's body back to Moscow for burial.

Before the year was ended the peasants visited Lotarevo again. First, they demolished the poultry houses and killed the chickens. Next the pigpens. Then the sheep barns, the cow barns, and the milking pens. Then the model stables. Only after that did they turn their attention to the estate house itself. They smashed the tiled stoves that Prince Vyazemsky had brought from Holland. They broke off the door handles. They gutted the building of furniture and furnishings. Not a poker remained, the butler reported later to his mistress in the Crimea. "If a mad dog had run into the house," he told her, "there would have been nothing with which to chase it out."

Lotarevo was gone as if it had existed only in a dream. Why did it happen? Why did Lotarevo happen again and again from one end of Russia to another?

As Georgi I. Vassiltchikov, nephew of Boris, observed:

"Notwithstanding hundreds of years of living in closest proximity or even together and notwithstanding the 'alarm signal' of 1905–6 the peasant revolt of 1917–18 came not less unexpected to most of the Russian landowners than the great peasant revolts of Pugachev, Razin, and Bolotnikov.

"Evidently there is a certain moment in our history when the dialogue between the two, the service ranks and the peasantry, breaks off or more truly said wears out and the people divide into two parts, into 'we' and 'they.'"

True, he acknowledged, there had been propaganda and agitation—by the Bolsheviks and by other revolutionaries. But it fell on hospitable soil—the struggle which had been going on since the time of the Tatars as to whom the land belonged.

In this terrible and merciless struggle, he observed, Prince Boris Leonidovich Vyazemsky fell as one more in a long line of victims—a line that would come to include millions.[24]

XLVII

The Villa Durnovo

On the Vyborg side of the Neva, at the point where the river swings sharply west, to flow past the monuments of Petrograd—the Tauride Palace, the Liteiny and Troitsky bridges, the Peter and Paul Fortress, the Winter Palace, the Admiralty, and all the rest—was located a large park. There stood a villa occupied until his death in 1915 by Pyotr Durnovo, sometime Interior Minister and author of the warning delivered to the Czar in 1914 of the fateful results which war with Germany would bring to Russia.

The villa was one of the most luxurious in Petrograd with its tall white columns reflected in the gray Neva. On the outbreak of the February Revolution it was commandeered by a group of anarchists as their headquarters. The anarchists—never large in numbers—set off a chill of fear when they appeared on the Petrograd streets with their black flags, their black garb, and their ever-present arms. Each carried two or three revolvers and some slung grenades, rifles, and bandoliers of live ammunition over their shoulders.

The anarchists at the Durnovo villa called themselves Anarchist-Communists in contrast to the Anarchist-Syndicalists, a more conservative group. They were close to left-wing elements in the Bolshevik ranks, particularly members of the Bolshevik Military Organization, and had a following among the most revolutionary military organizations, such as the First Machine-Gun Regiment in Petrograd and the turbulent Kronshtadt naval base where the sailors had attempted to set up the "Independent Republic of Kronshtadt."

Petrograd was filled with horror stories about the anarchists and their villa. Everyone *knew* the villa bristled with weapons. God alone knew what went on behind the sinister walls of the isolated mansion, deep in its heavily wooded park—orgies, murders of the bourgeoisie, plots to seize power, schemes to assassinate Government leaders. There was no end to the evil imaginings.

Nor did the anarchists care what people thought of them. Occasionally they made a foray into the city, seized a house, ousted the occupants, installed a colony of their own, and retreated behind the high walls of Durnovo.[1]

Then on June 5 came the act which threw Petrograd into crisis. A band from the villa, seventy in all, armed with rifles, hand grenades, and machine guns, descended on the printing plant of the right-wing paper *Russkaya Volya,* and took possession, declaring that hereafter they would use the printing plant for their own purposes.[2] Troops were called to the plant, disarmed the anarchists, most of them youngsters, and sent them home.[3]

The next day the Minister of Justice gave the anarchists an ultimatum: The Durnovo villa must be evacuated within twenty-four hours. This set off a tempest in a teapot. Until he went to the mysterious villa the Minister did not know that the anarchists were only one of a number of organizations which had taken shelter in its wings. The villa housed, among other things, the headquarters of the Petrograd Bakers Union and the Commissariat of the Workers Militia. Yet it was not all militance. The rambling grounds had become the favorite park of the children of the workers' quarter of Vyborg. The place was filled with baby carriages, children with balls and hoops, and in the evening young people walked down the lanes and sat on the benches, holding hands.[4]

The Durnovo affair quickly roused the whole Vyborg district. Factories went on strike. Crowds gathered to listen to orators denounce the Government for its assault on freedom, and on the other side Viktor M. Chernov, the SR leader, denounced Durnovo as "a citadel from which periodically are carried out armed attacks on every kind of private and public institution."[5]

Within a few hours Petrograd stood on the edge of crisis. The anarchists were calling their friends at Kronshtadt to join in demonstrating against the Government. The Bolsheviks in a hastily convened meeting of their Central Committee, Petersburg Committee, and Military Committee called for a monster demonstration at 2 P.M. Saturday June 10 and the Government was backpedaling in its plans to clean up the wicked Durnovo villa.

The next day, Friday June 9, was spent in hectic preparation. Military units made clear they were going to demonstrate with arms in hand—especially the Kronshtadt sailors. The workers of the Vyborg factories insisted on carrying arms. The potential for trouble was obvious. Were the Bolsheviks and their anarchist allies preparing a coup d'état? Was Lenin about to seize power?

Even today, after the opening of many long-sealed Soviet archives, there is no positive answer to the question. The day before the Durnovo incident Irakli G. Tsereteli was speaking at the All-Russian Congress of Soviets in which the Bolsheviks were a small minority, 105 members in a Congress of 1,090 dominated by the SRs and Mensheviks. "At the present time," Tsereteli said, "there is not a political party which is ready to say: Give us the power. There is no such Party in Russia."

Lenin, speaking from the floor, shouted: "There is. No party has the right to refuse the power and our party does not refuse it. It is ready to assume power at any time."[6]

Lenin went on to talk about the Bolshevik economic program and proposed to arrest fifty or a hundred of the richest Russian millionaires. This drew an acerbic retort from Kerensky, who said that the Bolsheviks "prescribe childish remedies—arrest, kill, destroy. Are you Socialists or policemen of the Old Regime?"[7]

This exchange did not necessarily mean that Lenin was preparing to go into the streets and overthrow the Provisional Government. Only now had he gotten the Bolsheviks pretty well lined up behind him. But the political situation was fluid. The Party was divided between a right wing, represented by Kamenev and Zinoviev, a middle group headed by Lenin (Stalin usually supported Lenin but sometimes stood to his left), and a powerful left wing largely made up of newer Bolsheviks, leaders in the factories, and the Military Committee. Lenin was still plagued by propaganda that he was a German "agent." At one point the Volynsky Regiment had been prepared to arrest him as a traitor, and the Organization of Russian War Cripples publicly demanded that he be jailed.[8]

On his arrival April 3 Lenin had seemed ready to seize power, but when Bolshevik-led workers boiled into the streets on April 10 and 21, demanding "all power to the Soviets," Lenin backed away and his longtime friend and ally Lyudmila Stal urged her comrades not to be "further to the left than Lenin." Nonetheless Bolshevik groups marched in the streets under the slogan "Down with the Provisional Government." Later other demonstrators appeared with banners declaring "Down with Lenin."[9]

Regardless of Lenin's uncertainty as to how close to the brink he should lead his forces, suspicion of his intentions was intense among his political rivals. They had heard his April 3 speeches. They had read his April Theses, echoing the same line—total opposition to the Provisional Government and the war; all power to the Soviets (even though his Bolsheviks were very much in the minority there). Even if Lenin did not seriously think of seizing power in April, other political leaders saw it as a reconnaissance in force. They took the same view of the plans for the June 10 demonstration. And there certainly was ground for suspicion. Martyn I. Latsis, a leader in the Bolshevik Military Committee, and other Military Committee members had agreed that "in case of necessity" they should seize the railroad stations, the banks, the post office, the telegraph office, and the arsenals with the support of the First Machine-Gun Regiment.[10] He was supported by Ivar T. Smilga, a member of the Bolshevik Central Committee, and other influential Party workers.

Sukhanov, the great memoirist of the Revolution, became convinced that Lenin did, indeed, toy with the idea of seizing power in June. Sukhanov was told (he said) by an influential Bolshevik that Lenin's idea was to initiate the armed demonstration, concentrate his forces at the Mariinsky Palace headquarters of the Provisional Government, and then, if circumstances seemed favorable, arrest the Government and take power into his hands. It was not, Sukhanov explained, "a real conspiracy" but "the revolt and the seizure of power ought to be accomplished, given a favorable conjuncture of circumstances."[11] Sukhanov's view had many supporters. Tsereteli came to believe in it implicitly. So did Kerensky. But Trotsky just as firmly denied it.[12] In any event the question, so far as June 10 was concerned, quickly became moot. At 2 A.M. June 10 an emergency meeting of the Bolshevik Central Committee canceled the demonstration after the All-Russian Congress of Soviets in a midnight session voted to bar demonstrations in Petrograd for three days. Five members were present at the Bolshevik Central Committee meeting. V. P. Nogin, Zinoviev, and Kamenev voted to put off the demonstration. Lenin and Sverdlov abstained. Then they rushed down to the *Pravda* plant, pulled out the call for workers to go to the streets, and replaced it with notices of postponement. *Soldatskaya Pravda,* the Bolshevik army paper, was already being run off. They stopped the presses and remade the front page. Latsis, a firebrand who later became one of Felix Dzerzhinsky's chief aides in the Cheka, noted in his diary: "The Central Committee put off the demonstration. It's beaten us to our knees."[13]

It was another setback for the Bolsheviks and a setback for Lenin. It was not easy to turn back the workers' detachments, to persuade Kronshtadt not to descend on Petrograd, to hold back the angry Petrograd regiments. Stalin and Smilga submitted their resignations from the Central Committee—but the committee refused to accept them.[14]

In truth there was no more nervous, politically uncertain capital than Petrograd. The division of authority between the Provisional Government and the Soviet had never worked well. The Soviet had the power but the Government acted in its own name. The Army had grown more and more unreliable. The soldiers simply refused to fight. They did not see any reason for risking their lives. Enough had died. The peasants expressed their view in the villages: "What devil gave us this war—it's not our affair." "Between ourselves we think this—that we have to bring it to an end." "We say to each other: if the Germans demand that we pay—then it's better to pay 10 rubles a head, and in Russia there are so many million heads—than kill people." "It's all the same under whatever Czar we live and under the Germans it can't be worse." "The red cock will be loosed—just as in '05."[15]

Morale and discipline in the Army had steadily deteriorated. The officers blamed this on Order Number One—the first decree of the Petrograd Soviet directed on March 1 to the armed forces. It ordered all military units to elect soldiers' committees directly responsible to the Soviet. The committees were to control all weapons. Soldiers acquired full citizens' rights. Saluting off duty was banned as was the use of the familiar *ty* or thou form by officers in addressing lower ranks. Shulgin thought Order Number One meant the death of the Army. So did Gen. A. I. Spiridovich.[16] This was not quite so. The insistence by the Soviets that all directives to the troops be countersigned by the Soviet was an initial problem but it dissolved as Kerensky emerged as the principal co-ordinator of military operations. To be certain there were constant incidents of humiliation or worse of officers, particularly navy officers. Captain Vechitsky was arrested at Revel, compelled to don a pair of peasant's *lapti* (bark shoes). Another pair of *lapti* was hung around his neck and he was led by a rope through the city streets. Some officers arrested at Kronshtadt were subjected alternatively to buckets of ice-cold water and to coals of fire held to their feet or bodies until they died. Detachments of drunken sailors invaded the dungeons where naval officers were held and to the order of "Show us your arse" compelled them to pull down their trousers.[17]

Louis de Robien, the fashionable and shrewd observer of the French Embassy, thought it was madness to suppose that the Russian Army could mount a new offensive. The soldiers stayed at the front only because the weather was good, they were well fed, had little to do, and the Germans did not disturb them, letting them sun themselves in the open air. "It would be madness not to see that Russia *wants* peace," he observed. Another French attaché came back from the Russian front to report that anarchy was widespread, the troops were filthy, suffering from epidemics, scurvy, and typhus, and more and more often given to murdering their officers.[18] More than 1.3 million deserters were estimated at large in the country.[19]

All of this against a backdrop of the same food shortages, the same disruption of services, the same faults of distribution, as plagued Russia before the Revolution. In the cities conditions grew worse. *Izvestiya* appealed to the peasants: "The Revolution needs bread. Don't forget, brother peasants!" For a few weeks after February things seemed a bit better. Wheat and grain flowed into the city. There was plenty of flour and butter and sugar for Easter cakes. But now queues were lengthening. At daylight the housewives went to the bakeries and the butcher shops. Food was rationed but shops could not meet the demands. Butter disappeared. Milk ran short. Yet travelers from Siberia said that at every station along the Trans-Siberian peasants were selling huge loaves of white bread and pots of cream and milk for a few kopecks. Every day Petrograd needed 80 to 120 carloads of flour. It was not getting them. The trains were running but they arrived late. Often they were commandeered by deserters from the front.[20]

This fed the smoldering fires of frustration, of hatred, of fear, of resentment, among that Russian mass which still called itself "the dark people."

The leadership which was offered to the dark people at this moment came for the most part from a group of men and women who had long been isolated from practical life—they had spent their days in remote Siberian villages or, in the words of Pyotr Ryss, in attics on the side streets of Paris, New York, Brussels, or Geneva. For years they had been occupied with thought, with theory, with plans and fantasies dominated by Russian maximilism, denying a life based on moral principle. They were, Ryss believed, cold and endlessly logical in their own terms. They hated the Government of Russia. They hated the alien cities and villages in which they had been compelled to live. They were accustomed to living within themselves, without discipline, seeing life in the narrow terms of their reading. The theories which they conceived were new to them but often old, already tried in the outer world. And each of these individuals had his *own* theory, his *own* secret for saving humanity. Only give him the opportunity and he would save the world and make people happy.

To the throng of returning exiles from abroad was joined the throng of exiles from prison and Siberia—victims of physical suffering and physical torture. They had spent years studying by flickering lamps and they were merciless in their drive to carry their plans into being—almost insane in this ambition. They hated the system which had distorted their lives. Taken together, these people were, in Ryss's words, the "Jesuits" of socialism, sick spirits alienated from Russian life. Among them, to be sure, were individuals of high nobility and selfless purpose. But mixed with them were poseurs, mountebanks, chatterboxes, egocentrics.

Ryss saw Lenin and his associates as the epigones of this movement, men and women who denied the very idea of a native land and who thought nothing of taking advantage of the courtesy of the enemy seeking to destroy Russia in order to build a new Russia on the extermination of the bourgeoisie.[21]

It was against this background that on June 18 the Russian Army launched a major offensive against Austrian troops on the southwestern front. Kerensky was on hand to witness the take-off after two days of artillery preparation. The Seventh Army kicked off the attack and Russian forces moved ahead making spectacular gains.[22] The start of the attack coincided with a new Government-sponsored demonstration in Petrograd which, as it turned out, was largely dominated by Bolshevik marchers and Bolshevik slogans. But the initial success of the offensive changed the psychology of the nervous Petrograd street crowds and patriotic parades filled the Nevsky Prospekt. For a few days it seemed that the tide might have turned.[23]

But nothing could go smoothly in these days. While the offensive was getting under way on June 18 and while the huge demonstration was filling Petrograd's streets, anarchists from the Durnovo villa carried out a daring raid on Kresty Prison and liberated F. P. Khaustov, a leading Bolshevik member of the Military Organization, and six other prisoners. The operation was carried out by an armed force of fifteen hundred to two thousand men.[24] The Government retaliated with a predawn raid on the Durnovo mansion, arresting sixty persons. In the course of the operation an anarchist named Asnin was killed, probably by the accidental discharge of an anarchist weapon.

Once again the Vyborg section was thrown into turmoil. All day crowds thronged to the Durnovo villa to see the broken windows, the smashed doors, the furniture tossed about, and on display on the doorstep the stiffened, blue, and bloodied corpse of Asnin.[25]

The pot began to bubble. The Government wanted to send some of the idle (and hostile) troops from the Petrograd garrison to beef up the faltering offensive. The garrison troops had no intention of going. They had been promised after February that they would not be sent to the front.

The First Machine-Gun Regiment with its close connections with both the Bolshevik Military Organization and the Anarchist-Communists emerged as the trouble center. The Government demanded that it provide five hundred machine guns for the front and, under a "reorganization plan," send two thirds of its personnel to the front. In little time the First Machine-Gunners were preparing to go into the streets, spurred on by the Durnovo anarchists and many leaders of the Bolshevik Military Organization despite the fact that Lenin himself was strongly opposed to a new test of revolutionary strength. Lenin spoke to a conference of the Bolshevik Military Organization and one of the listeners described his speech as "a cold shower" for the hotheads.[26] One factor weighing heavily on Lenin's mind was the apparent success of the Government's offensive which he felt had turned public sympathy strongly away from the radical left.

For a few days the lid was kept on. Meantime, Lenin vanished from Petrograd. He had, of course, been working in the highest state of tension since his arrival April 3. He was tired and as so often in the past his nerves were frayed.[27] He slept little, returning very late to the steamboat flat of the Yelizarovs and leaving very early. Sometimes he brought his step-nephew Gora to the Kshesinskaya mansion with him, letting the youngster amuse himself while Lenin met with his revolutionary comrades. He liked to go back to the flat for lunch.[28] He liked to play with the youngster. Probably it was a relief from the tensions of his life.

Sometime in the week of June 20–27 Lenin left his sister's flat on Shirokaya Ulitsa. Yelena Stasova, his old associate (and secretary-to-be), recalled that he was concerned over the possibility of some move by the right wing or the Government. She invited him to come and stay with her family. He was suffering from what his sister, Mariya Ilyinichna, called "catarrh of the stomach" but insisted that he needed no special diet or special treatment. Lenin stayed with the Stasovs only a day or two. He left after Stasova got a warning from an officer that it might not be safe for Lenin to stay overnight. He then went to 40 Furshtadtsky Street and stayed in the office of the Central Trade Unions.[29]

For some reason—no one has said why—Lenin saw little or nothing of Krupskaya during these days. She was working day and night in the Vyborg section.[30]

About 5 P.M. on June 29[31] Vladimir D. Bonch-Bruyevich, Lenin's old friend and revolutionary comrade, was relaxing on the porch of his country cottage in the little village of Neivola, not far from Mustamaki, a resort in the Finnish countryside.

He looked up to see the revolutionary poet Demyan Bedny walking up the steps and behind him Lenin, carrying a small suitcase, and Lenin's sister, Mariya Ilyinichna.

"Look at the guests I've brought," Bedny said.

Lenin, it developed, had suddenly decided he had to get out of Petrograd. He had come with his sister to Mustamaki and, by conspiratorial habit, had taken a carriage to Bedny's dacha. Then, after dismissing the coachman, he walked a mile or so to the Bonch-Bruyevich cottage.

Lenin stayed at the cottage, sleeping, sunning himself for hours under the birch trees, swimming in the cold lake (he was such a good swimmer that many of the vacationers wondered who he might be). Bonch-Bruyevich told them he was a sailor from the Baltic Fleet, a relative of his. Lenin read nothing during these days. He walked a bit with Bonch-Bruyevich and sometimes with Mariya Ilyinichna. He talked occasionally with Bonch-Bruyevich. After a few days he began to glance at the papers and to read an English novel or two. And he talked with Bonch-Bruyevich about his work as editor of the magazine, *Zhizn i Znaniye*. He got no messages from Petrograd. He sent none.[32]

On the same evening that Lenin walked up the steps of Bonch-Bruyevich's cottage the fashionable young attaché of the French Embassy, Count de Robien, paid a visit to Tsarskoye Selo—not, of course, to the Czar and the Czarina. They were still under close guard, leading a quiet life. Nicholas worked in his garden, took long walks, sawed wood, and spent some time instructing Alexei in geography and history. He read a good deal—*The Count of Monte Cristo*, something called *La Maison des Hommes Vivants*, Merezhkovsky, and *Arsène Lupin contre Sherlock Holms*. He was pleased and excited at the success of the Russian offensive. De Robien was the guest of the Grand Duke Paul, who was celebrating his birthday. The Grand Duke wore the ribbon of St. George in his buttonhole and had Countess Kleinmikhel on his right and Madame Polovtsev, wife of the Interior Minister, on his left. Other guests were the Grand Duke Boris (who was now free from prison), the Count de Chambrun, Princess Paley, the Grand Duchess Mariya Pavlovna II, very pretty in a white crinoline dress and pearls, Vladimir Paley, Mita Benkendorf, Armand de Saint-Sauveur, and others. The wines, De Robien noted, were remarkable. The service was good but De Robien could not help noting that several servants wore mustaches and that two women were helping. A sign of the times. After dinner the little princesses, Irene and Nathalie Paley, in Pierrot and Pierrette costumes, acted out three short plays.

"The whole thing was delightful," De Robien observed, "how pleasant life could be if only men were sensible."

He drove home with Countess Kleinmikhel in her open barouche. It was the most diaphanous of white nights.[33]

Life went on peacefully for Lenin in the Finnish countryside until six o'clock on the morning of July 4 when Bonch-Bruyevich heard someone knocking on the window of his room. It was Maximilian A. Savelyev. "There's an uprising in Petrograd," he said.

Lenin was awakened. "It's completely untimely," he said. "We've got to go."[34]

XLVIII

Lenin Hunkers Down

The messenger had not exaggerated. Petrograd was about to explode and the spark point had again been provided by the First Machine-Gun Regiment. Sunday July 1 was a beautiful day. In the afternoon the regiment held a "concert" to mark the dispatch of a group of troops to the front and to raise money for agitational literature. Some factory workers and representatives of the Grenadier Regiment were present. Lunacharsky and Trotsky spoke. Trotsky described the mood of the meeting as "exalted" but insisted that no "practical proposal for the immediate future" was made.[1] A resolution was, however, passed that all power should be put in the hands of the Soviets.[2] Unknown to the Bolsheviks—or so they later were to insist—the anarchist leadership called a meeting on Sunday in the "Red Chamber" of the Durnovo villa. The secret meeting, attended by, among others, the anarchists I. Bleikham-Solntsev (a Jewish immigrant who had returned from New York), P. Kolobushkin, D. Nazimov, and A. Fyodorov, decided to call out the masses, around the cadre of the First Machine-Gun Regiment, on July 3. The anarchists were shy of adopting slogans in advance—"Let the streets give us the slogans" was their tactic. But on this occasion there had to be some advance planning. The slogans for the uprising would be: "Down with the Provisional Government" but not "All Power to the Soviets"—that didn't harmonize with their aims. Instead they decided on "For the Soviet"—whatever that might mean. The uprising was set for the next day.

They planned to arrest Kerensky, seize the railroad stations, telephone stations, and newspaper printing plants.[3]

During the night of July 2–3 the four Kadet Ministers of the Provisional Government—A. A. Manilov, V. N. Shakhovsky, A. I. Shingarev, and V. A. Stepanov—decided to leave the Government, adding a ministerial crisis to the general tension. Many workers interpreted the resignations—or the interpretation may have been suggested to them by excited agitators—as a maneuver which had counterrevolutionary implications.[4] Also, it was becoming apparent that the military offensive was not going well. Bleikhman, whose eccentric appearance, curly hair, shirt open at the breast, and vinegar-sharp Jewish-American accent were popular with the soldiers, fired up the First Machine-Gun Regiment.[5] By midmorning of July 3 soldiers and workers once again were pouring into the streets. The Bolshevik Military Organization was probably as eager as the anarchists and the First Machine-Gun Regiment to overthrow the Government. Bolshevik speakers spoke at the rallies, ostensibly urging caution and patience. But as Vladimir I. Nevsky,* the veteran Bolshevik agitator, admitted he spoke "in such a way that only a fool could come to the conclusion that he should not demonstrate."[6]

Confusion about the Bolshevik position was widespread, and many —if not most—Bolsheviks at the factory level or the company level simply went along with the tide—which was into the streets.[7]

By late afternoon of July 3 the workers and soldiers were pouring toward the center of Petrograd. Their first goal was the Kshesinskaya Palace where they flooded into the courtyard and up to the famous balcony from which Lenin so often spoke. Bolshevik orators attempted to cool them off and get the soldiers back to their barracks. Yakov M. Sverdlov, one of the orators, recalled that for the first time he heard derisive shouts and cries of "Down with you!"[8] Finally the Bolsheviks agreed to lead and support the movement. They took the position that to stand to one side, to leave the workers and soldiers without leadership in a situation which might turn into an accidental armed rebellion, was irresponsible.[9]

At 11 P.M. columns of armed soldiers and workers surged toward the Tauride Palace where the Soviet was locked in violent debate. The Machine-Gunners had occupied the Finland Station and posted de-

* Nevsky became a leading Bolshevik historian after the Revolution and director of the Lenin Library, the largest in the Soviet Union. He was arrested in 1935 and executed by Stalin in 1937 after refusing to obey Stalin's orders to remove masses of political literature from the Lenin Library. "I'm not running a baggage room," he said. (Roy A. Medvedev, *Let History Judge*, p, 167.)

tachments at the Neva principal bridges. Soon they occupied the
Nicholas Station and the Peter and Paul Fortress.

Bristling with weapons, three or four machine guns mounted to a
truck, the demonstrators moved down the Nevsky Prospekt. Shooting
broke out as the column passed the Gostiny Dvor. It was never made
clear who fired but there were many casualties. The military units
reached the Tauride Palace at midnight and by 2 A.M. they had been
joined by thirty thousand workers from the Putilov factory. The demonstrators could have seized the Tauride Palace, had they desired.
The total guard force of the Soviet numbered six men.[10]

But the night wore on without decisive action. The demonstrators
argued with the Soviet. The Soviet leaders tried to persuade them to
go away. Everyone grew more and more weary. The Bolsheviks were
on the horns of a dilemma—which way to go? Was it to be a new revolution or one more failed street demonstration with critical consequences for their movement? They argued about it. Kamenev and
Zinoviev feared that failure and a major setback lay ahead. Finally the
Central Committee came down on the side of leading another day's
demonstration—largely because they had no alternative. The Kronshtadt sailors were coming to Petrograd. There was no earthly way of
halting them. Or of getting the workers and soldiers already in the
street back into factories and barracks. The Putilov workers had simply lain down in the courtyard outside the palace and prepared to
catch a cat nap before a new demonstration in the morning. The
Bolsheviks cast the dice—and sent for Lenin.[11]

Lenin caught the 6:45 A.M. train for Petrograd.

He was not in good spirits. Bonch-Bruyevich was fearful Lenin
would be recognized. Everyone on the train was talking about Petrograd. Not all the remarks were complimentary to the Bolsheviks.
Bonch-Bruyevich bought the morning papers and Lenin scanned them
hurriedly. His mood did not improve. "I don't see anything serious
here," he told Bonch-Bruyevich. "It is the normal outburst of the discontented mass of people. The movement must be quickly seized and,
probably, quickly stopped."

Much more serious in Lenin's opinion was a propaganda campaign
against the Bolsheviks which had burst out in almost all of the newspapers.

"This is directly counter-revolutionary," Lenin said. "And it can hurt
us temporarily."

All the way into Petrograd Lenin hunkered down behind his
papers.[12] It was not pleasant reading. *Izvestiya* said the demonstrators
were trying to strangle the Revolution and take all power into their

hands. The Menshevik *Rabochaya Gazeta* called it "a stab in the back."

The SR *Delo Naroda* warned of civil war and the downfall of the Revolution. *Rech* called the demonstration sheer anarchy.[13]

At the Finland Station Bonch-Bruyevich piled Lenin, Mariya Ilyinichna, and Savelyev into a two-seated fly (no streetcars were running), gave the cabbie two rubles, and went home.[14]

Between 10 and 11 A.M. a flotilla of barges, tugboats, and small craft appeared in the Neva—the Kronshtadt sailors ten thousand strong or more.[15] The sailors discharged on the university quays and formed up to march to the Kshesinskaya mansion nearby. Already thousands had gathered there—workers, soldiers from Petrograd regiments. The mood was even more revolutionary than the day before.[16] Sverdlov and Lunacharsky harangued the crowd, which kept shouting for Lenin. Lenin, according to some accounts, didn't want to speak but finally came out on the famous balcony. He talked briefly and unemotionally. He apologized for speaking briefly due to not feeling well, he greeted the sailors in behalf of the Petrograd workers, expressed confidence that the Bolshevik slogan, "All Power to the Soviets," would be carried to victory "despite all the zigzags of history," and appealed to the sailors for "firmness, steadfastness and vigilance."[17] A "very ambiguous" speech, Sukhanov called it.[18] This was not exactly the call to overthrow the Government which the Kronshtadters wanted to hear. The column then swung away from the Kshesinskaya mansion to the Sadovaya, past the Champs de Mars and on to the Nevsky, beginning a slow march to the Tauride. There were at least sixty thousand marchers. The first outburst of shooting—exactly who was firing was never made clear—occurred at the intersection of the Sadovaya and Apriksina, possibly from the Apriksin Palace. Count de Robien saw people being carried away in ambulances, the street littered with caps and sticks and in a corner near the offices of *Novoye Vremya* broken chairs and furniture piled up among parcels from which spilled face powder and ribbons from a looted shop.

There was more shooting on the Liteiny, and in early evening De Robien saw a dozen or more dead horses scattered over the street, and pools of water tinged with blood. There had been many dead and wounded.[19]

The Kronshtadt marchers got to the Tauride Palace by 2 P.M., the Putilov delegation at 3 P.M. All afternoon the columns of workers and soldiers marched through the streets, converging on the Tauride until the palace was once again swamped in humanity.[20]

Voitinsky had been placed in charge of security of the Tauride. It was a hopeless assignment. The palace was simply swallowed up in

armed, angry humanity. But, as he recalled, "there was no real struggle around the Tauride Palace, only a war of nerves with overwhelming forces on the one side and, on the other, a handful of practically
defenseless men who refused to yield."[21]

The Soviet leaders sent out emergency appeals for reliable troops—
from the front, from the provinces, and even from the city. They got
only a handful from the city but front-line troops were dispatched immediately. Meantime, the situation boiled over. Chernov, the SR
leader, went out to address the Kronshtadt forces. He climbed up on a
barrel to speak but the sailors shouted that Chernov was one of those
who shot the people. One worker yelled: "Take power, you son-of-a-
bitch, when it's offered to you." When Chernov sought to leave, the
sailors grabbed him and forced him into an open car to hold him as a
hostage. Word flashed through the Tauride Palace that Chernov had
been captured and might be killed by the sailors. Sukhanov found
F. F. Raskolnikov, the Bolshevik leader of Kronshtadt, and compelled
him to come to the rescue. But Trotsky was already on the scene.
With some difficulty—the sailors seemed no more friendly to Trotsky
than they had been to Chernov—the SR leader was freed by the mob
and permitted to return to the palace.[22] Sukhanov angrily demanded
that Raskolnikov take his sailors away. Raskolnikov mumbled some excuse and later Sukhanov became convinced that Raskolnikov had secret orders from the Bolshevik high command to keep the sailors there
in order to take over the Soviet. Whether or not that was true—and
the total disorganization of the Bolsheviks and obvious reluctance of
Lenin to move in for the kill make the suspicions of Sukhanov and
many other Soviet leaders less plausible than appeared then—within a
short time the Kronshtadt group moved out of the courtyard.[23]

Two things happened. Troops loyal to the Government and Soviet
began to arrive in Petrograd, and rumors swept the city that documents were in the hands of the Government "proving" that Lenin was
a German agent and spy. The two events were closely interconnected
because "neutral" and "loyal" regiments were shown the documents or
told of them and this inflamed their mood and brought them to the
point at which they were willing to move into action against the rebellious forces represented by the Kronshtadt contingent, the Putilov
workers, the First Machine-Gun Regiment, the Bolsheviks, and the
anarchists.

The "evidence" in the hands of Justice Minister P. N. Pereverzev
was weak. It was based on allegations that two German General Staff
officers had named Lenin as one of their agents in Russia. It also contended that Lenin was being supplied with money through a German

espionage organization in Stockholm headed by Parvus. The funds were supposed to come through Lenin's agents Ganetsky and Mechislav Yu. Kozlovsky.[24] Weak as the "evidence" was, it caused a sensation. The Government first forbade the newspapers to print the evidence, largely cables sent by and to Ganetsky. Vladimir L. Burtsev, the exposer of Azef and other Czarist double agents, a longtime enemy of Lenin's, had a hand in preparing the materials. So did G. A. Alexinsky, once a friend and associate of Lenin's. When the Government forbade the newspapers to publish the materials, Alexinsky printed them in a boulevard leaflet, "No Needless Words," which sold like hot cakes on the Nevsky.[25]

The tide turned swiftly in Petrograd, and shortly after midnight with the arrival of the first front-line regiments power flowed back into the hands of the Government and the Soviet. By this time an evening rainstorm had driven many demonstrators home, and when the Izmailovsky regiment arrived at the Tauride Palace about 1 A.M., its band playing the "Marseillaise," it was apparent that a new balance of forces had been struck.[26]

Lenin met with his Central Committee. It was obvious that real danger lay ahead. Unobtrusively *Pravda* was to publish a notice calling off further demonstrations. It was back to the underground again. Lenin and Krupskaya spent what was left of the night of July 4-5 at the flat of M. L. Sulimov, on the Karpovka embankment in the Petrograd district.[27] Early in the morning they walked over to the Vyborg district where they found lodgings with a Bolshevik worker named V. N. Kayurov. As they walked down the street they passed a detachment of the Moskovsky Regiment. It was on its way under orders of the Petrograd commandant, Gen. Alexander A. Polovtsev, to wreck the *Pravda* plant, which Lenin had just left.[28]

The Bolsheviks were in full retreat. They managed to hold a hasty Central Committee meeting during the day of July 6 at the gatehouse of the Renault plant. Lenin flatly opposed a suggestion for a general strike.[29] The Kshesinskaya mansion was occupied by troops. Lenin moved out of the Kayurov flat to that of Sergei Ya. Alliluyev, the old worker friend of Stalin's. The Kayurov flat was regarded as unsafe because, as Krupskaya put it, "his son was an Anarchist and the young people messed around with bombs."

"Aren't they getting ready to shoot us all?" Lenin asked Trotsky. It certainly looked like it.[30] The Provisional Government issued warrants for the arrest of Lenin, Zinoviev, Kamenev, Trotsky, and Lunacharsky Lenin and Zinoviev decided to turn themselves in and Lenin told Mariya Ilyinichna and Krupskaya of his decision—Mariya was opposed to it but Lenin was firm. He embraced Krupskaya and said, "We may not see each other again."[31] That evening Stalin and other members of the Central Committee persuaded Lenin not to give himself up. They argued that the Provisional Government was just looking for a chance to do away with him. Lenin went into hiding.[32]

On the night of July 4 Bonch-Bruyevich had a short talk with Lenin. He had just come back from a brief stroll in the open air. Once again Bonch-Bruyevich was impressed with Lenin's feeling that the demonstrations were not the important thing at the moment. What was important was the counterrevolutionary wave which was about to break, the anti-Bolshevik propaganda, the bringing into Petrograd of front-line troops and Cossacks.

"What do we do?" Bonch-Bruyevich asked.

"An armed uprising," Lenin said. "There is no other way."

"When?"

"It depends on circumstances. But not later than autumn."[33]

Gorky had a word on the July events as well. In his newspaper, *Novaya Zhizn*, he commented:

"The disgusting scenes of the madness which seized Petrograd the day of July 4 will remain in my memory for the rest of my life.

"There, bristling with rifles and machineguns, a truck flashes by like a mad hog; it is tightly packed with motley members of the 'revolutionary army,' among them stands a disheveled youth who shouts hysterically:

"The social revolution, comrades!"

Gorky concluded that the principal stimulus for the drama was provided not by the Leninists, not by the Germans, not by the counter-revolutionaries, but "a more evil and stronger enemy—the oppressive Russian stupidity."[34]

No one seemed to have time for a moment's thought over what had brought Russia to this debacle. The poet Alexander Blok listened to the parade of Czarist officials before the Provisional Government's Extraordinary Commission of Investigation with growing despair. Police officers, asked to explain the introduction of provocateurs like Malinovsky into the Duma, shrugged their shoulders and responded: "Well, there's theory—and there's practice." They had never bothered to ask themselves whether secret examination of private letters was legal. As for the system of arbitrary exile of political prisoners—well, it was essential for the security of the state and besides, other countries did it too. The chief of the Czarist Police Department, Ye. K. Klimovich, insisted that he had done nothing dishonorable although he admitted he may have broken the law. And, in the end, old

Goremykin, one of the Czar's last Premiers, confessed that "it is very hard to tell what is lawful and what is unlawful. There can be different interpretations."

Blok threw up his hands. Russia's ideals, her moral structure, had been shattered. When and how would it be knitted together again?[35]

XLIX

Waiting

Zinaida Gippius and her husband returned to Petrograd from the Caucasus on August 8. Gippius was shocked at what she saw—never had Petrograd looked so disheveled: roving bands of drunken soldiers, unwashed windows, dirty sidewalks, heaps of sunflower shells on the station floor where hundreds of soldiers and peasants squatted day and night waiting for trains. Waiting . . .

She found that she had walked into one of the most confused and tawdry episodes of the Revolution. Within two hours Boris Savinkov, the famous SR revolutionary and her literary protégé, showed up at the apartment. Savinkov, in the latest incarnation of Kerensky's shifting government, had become Deputy Minister of Defense. He painted a gloomy picture to Zinaida. Russia was on the verge of immense territorial losses—Riga and Narva were about to fall to the Germans. In the south Moldavia and Bessarabia were slipping away. The economic situation was catastrophic.[1]

Savinkov was hardly exaggerating. From March to June 1917, 568 factories had closed throwing 104,372 employees out of work. The figures for March to November would total 800 plants and 170,000 workers. Inflation was rampant. Speculation on the Petrograd and Moscow exchanges ran wild.[2] In April 476 million rubles of paper currency had been issued; in May 729 million; in June 869 million; in July 1,070 million; and by November the amount of paper money in circulation would reach 18,917 million rubles. In three years of war nominal pay of workers in Moscow had risen 51.5 per cent but prices of basic foods had gone up 566 per cent and consumer goods 1,109 per cent.[3]

Russia was staying in the war by sheer momentum and habit. Millions of troops still occupied positions in the front lines although desertions were becoming more and more common. The guns were in place although shells were scarce. Most of the old commanders held their posts in nominal charge of armies, divisions, regiments, and companies although many had less and less authority over the men. Most of the troops seemed willing to stay in their places so long as they were not compelled to go on the offense or carry out actions which might imperil their lives. Food still reached most units in fair quantity.

Insofar as there was any military leadership it was provided by Kerensky who spent his time racing from one front to another, haranguing the troops (his oratory was becoming less effective), trying to encourage or brace up the front commanders and somehow substitute words for actions.

The whole thing was, in fact, a charade. The Russian front would have collapsed at any show of strength by the Germans. But the Germans were no fools. They could see Russia disintegrating before their eyes. Why waste men and matériel? The western front was where the action was and to the western front the Germans steadily transferred their best divisions. To the western front they directed the bulk of munitions and on the western front they mounted their terrible 1917 offensives, designed to break the French and British before American support—if it ever came—could be decisive.

Meanwhile, in the East the German lines were as quiet as the Russian. More and more the troops began to fraternize. In some sectors they even played football matches. German teams versus Russian.

No wonder Savinkov said that every minute was precious and the eleventh hour was approaching. He and Kerensky were working with Gen. Lavr G. Kornilov to try to establish "a firm power." Kerensky had been frightened by the July events and he feard that Russia now tottered on the edge of destruction.

Kerensky was trotting along like a three-wheeled cart but he had a new fear—that Savinkov might assassinate him.

In the days that followed the Merezhkovskys lived at the center of the swiftly developing Kornilov affair. Savinkov reported to them almost every day. Kornilov, a rather simple Cossack of peasant origin, had been named commander in chief July 19 by Kerensky. When he came to Petrograd to meet with Kerensky, he swept up to the Winter Palace accompanied by his Tekintsy, a Turkmen bodyguard with high-domed hats, flaring red coats, machine guns at the ready, naked

Turkish scimitars in hand, and *kinzhali*, Caucasian daggers, at their belts.[4] General Alexeyev described Kornilov as a "man with a lion's heart and the brain of a sheep."[5]

Kerensky had installed himself in the Czar's former suite at the Winter Palace. He boasted of sleeping in the Czar's bed.[6] He appeared in public accompanied by two aides, one in naval and one in army dress, and in his speeches used the words "I and my government."[7]

Kerensky took time out at the end of July to move the Czar and his family quietly out of Tsarskoye Selo to Tobolsk in Siberia. The Czar had long hoped to go to England with his family via Murmansk. He did not know that the British Government had, practically speaking, withdrawn its offer of refuge.

The original offer had been made, a bit reluctantly, March 9, but as public opinion built up in England against the Czar and particularly the Czarina, whose difficult character was only too well known to George V and his wife, Queen Mary, King George quietly urged the British Government to withdraw the invitation to the Romanovs. This was done through a series of messages to the British ambassador in Petrograd, Sir George Buchanan, and by mid-April any chance of evacuating the Czar and his family to England had vanished. The news, however, was carefully withheld from the Czar.[8] Failing permission to go abroad, the Czar had continued to hope to go to his beloved Livadia in the Crimea.

Kerensky's attitude toward the Imperial family was equivocal. The original purpose of the Extraordinary Commission to investigate the fall of the Czarist regime, set up in the first days of the Provisional Government, was not merely to establish facts and causes but to lay a basis for indictments and trials. It had been assumed by many that the Czar (if not the Czarina) would be called before the tribunal and later be put on trial. Kerensky circumvented this, taking responsibility for questioning the Czar upon himself. He spent a few hours with Nicholas but conducted nothing like a cross-examination. He also balked a proposal to search the Czar's residence at Tsarskoye Selo for documentary evidence.[9]

Now in July Kerensky made another equivocal move. He kept the Czar in ignorance of his plans until the last moment, only saying that the family should pack "as much warm clothing as possible." The departure was set for the evening of July 31 but the train didn't get away until 6:10 A.M. August 1. Kerensky blamed the delay on the reluctance of railroad men to make up a train for the Czar. Kerensky claimed the move to Tobolsk was for the safety of the Imperial family in case of new outbursts in Petrograd. The Czar busied himself in the days before departure reading *Alexander I* by Merezhkovsky and Conan Doyle's *A Study in Scarlet*. Kerensky carried out the transfer of the Romanovs with great secrecy and did not inform members of the Government that it was taking place. Some suspected Kerensky's move was basically a political gesture to the left.[10]

The curious combination—Savinkov, the onetime plotter of revolutionary assassinations and author of melodramatic novels, Kornilov, the ambitious but ignorant Cossack general, and Kerensky, the silver-tongued Petrograd advocate (now just thirty-six years old)—was enmeshed in a plot in which each hoped to emerge triumphant and with the same prize in hand—the dictatorship of Russia.

The most ambitious was Savinkov. Trotsky had no doubt Savinkov planned to double-cross both Kornilov and Kerensky and make himself master of Russia.[11]

The game rapidly played itself out. There was a spectacle coming in Moscow—a State Conference designed to symbolize the nation's unity. It assembled in the Bolshoi Theater August 12—2,500 delegates representing virtually all strata of Russian political life, except the Bolsheviks (who instigated a general Moscow strike to mark the occasion). Wags said that Kerensky had come to Moscow for his "coronation." Moscow, of course, was the traditional site of the coronation ceremony. But Kornilov and his dashing Moslem Tekintsy were there too, flashing swords as Kornilov prayed at the historic Iversky Chapel in Red Square. To some it looked as though two coronations might be in order.[12] When Kornilov appeared at the Bolshoi Theater meeting, there was an ovation from the right; when Kerensky took the stage, it was from the left.[13]

Savinkov served as go-between. Even with her ringside seat Gippius was never entirely certain who was using whom. Kornilov believed that he was going to become military dictator of Russia. He had the open support of a number of prominent Russian industrialists, headed by A. I. Putilov, owner of the steelworks and a leading Petrograd banker. Others involved in the plot included Guchkov and I. Vyshnegradsky, backers of an organization called the Union for Economic Revival of Russia. According to Kerensky the group had 4 million rubles which it put at Kornilov's disposal.

Kerensky hoped to make use of Kornilov[14] to mobilize some reliable troops which he would then employ to strengthen his hold on Petrograd. That he would use them to make himself dictator was an intention he violently denied to the end of his days. As for Putilov and the other backers of the coup it was the last roll of the dice. Putilov was too shrewd a man to place much hope on any of the conspirators.

The scenario unrolled in late August. On August 27 Kornilov ordered the Savage Cavalry Division to Petrograd, headed by General Krymov. Kerensky through the chance intervention of Vladimir Lvov, former procurator of the Holy Synod, discovered that Kornilov was actually proposing to make himself dictator.

"Warn Kerensky and Savinkov," Kornilov told Lvov (and Lvov told Kerensky), "that I cannot guarantee their personal safety unless they come to Headquarters where I shall personally see that they are well protected.

"The Romanovs will ascend the throne only over my dead body," Kornilov said. "As soon as power is transferred I shall form a cabinet. I no longer trust Kerensky. He does not do anything."

"How about Savinkov?" Lvov asked.

"I don't trust Savinkov either," Kornilov replied. "I really don't know whom he wants to stab in the back, Kerensky or me."

Lvov was a bit puzzled at this. Savinkov had been at Mogilev negotiating with Kornilov only the day before. Lvov asked why Kornilov hadn't arrested Savinkov then but the general had no answer. Instead he said he wouldn't mind making Savinkov Minister of War and Kerensky Minister of Justice in his cabinet.[15] In truth all of the participants in the coup seem to have been thoroughly muddled.

Savinkov in talking with Kornilov on August 20 agreed to Kornilov's dispatch of the troops to Petrograd. He did request, however, that neither the Savage Division nor General Krymov be sent. Kerensky did not think he could rely on the Savage Division, largely Caucasian troops, or on General Krymov.[16]

Everywhere the lines crossed and crisscrossed, the plotters plotting against each other—and "each was trying to use the other for his own aims," Sukhanov remarked.[17]

In the words of Voitinsky:

"Kerensky and Kornilov had hated and distrusted each other for the good reason that each regarded himself alone as the man predestined to save Russia. With two would-be Napoleons, one in Petrograd and the other in Mogilev and both surrounded by unsavory characters, political intrigue filled the air. Counter-revolutionary circles in Mogilev plotted a coup to establish the military dictatorship of Kornilov while Kerensky dreamed of getting rid of the Communists, the Socialists and intractable generals in Mogilev."[18] Chernov called it "a general mix-up in which you can't make out where Kornilov ends and where Filomenko [a Kornilov aide] and Savinkov begin, where Savinkov ends and where begins the Provisional Government as such."[19]

Nonetheless, Kornilov's troops did march on Petrograd. Now Kerensky was confronted with the task of halting the clockwork toys he had set in motion. First, he put the bewildered Lvov under arrest. Then he fired Kornilov and appointed Kornilov's aide, General Lukomsky, in his place. Kornilov refused to be fired and Lukomsky refused to replace him. Kerensky then named Gen. V. N. Klembovsky commander in chief. He, too, refused. Finally on September 1 Kerensky persuaded old General Alexeyev, the Czar's last commander in chief, to bell the cat—to assume Supreme Command and arrest Kornilov. General Krymov came to the Winter Palace, talked with Kerensky, and shot himself presumably because Kornilov's plans for dictatorship, in which Krymov played a leading role, had been given away. By this time the cheap farce—the last to be played out by Kerensky—had virtually reached an end. But its consequences were far from what any of the three—Savinkov, Kerensky, or Kornilov—had imagined. As Gippius put it with her usual precision: "Kerensky is now completely in the hands of the maximalists and the Bolsheviks. The ball is over. They haven't raised their heads yet. They sit. Tomorrow, of course, they'll get on their feet."[20]

After the July debacle, Lenin had gone into deep underground. He and his Party associates were certain that Kerensky would have him killed if he laid hands on him. Lenin stayed first in the attic of a barn belonging to Nikolai A. Yemelyanov, an old Bolshevik worker who lived in Razliv very close to the Finnish border.* He made a bed in the hay and took the air occasionally in the Yemelyanov garden which was protected from the street by heavy lilac bushes. But there was much nervousness about security and soon Yemelyanov rented a place on Razliv Lake, five or six kilometers from the station. Lenin and Zinoviev, who had joined him in hiding, rowed across the lake to a hay barn. The two men took up their profession as "haymakers" living in a rough shed and set up a working space outside it which Lenin called "my green office." The Yemelyanovs rowed across the lake every day with newspapers and food for the "mowers."[21] The biggest hazard was the mosquitoes.[22]

The Party was in retreat—like its leader. The Bolshevik Military Organization, which plunged so heavily into the July events, had suffered a huge setback. Except for Vladimir I. Nevsky, Nikolai I. Podvoisky, and A. I. Semashko, most of its leaders were arrested. The rebellious regiments were broken up and sent out of Petrograd. The Party press was paralyzed for weeks by destruction of *Pravda*'s plant and the Government's suppression of *Pravda, Soldatskaya Pravda*, and

* Yemelyanov and his whole family were arrested by Stalin despite protests by Krupskaya. He was released only after Stalin's death. (Roy A. Medvedev, *Let History Judge*, p. 201.)

other Bolshevik organs July 15. The Party itself was badly shaken and existed in a semilegal state.[23] Lenin and Zinoviev (and some others) were in hiding. Kamenev was arrested July 9 and Kollontai a few days later. Trotsky and Lunacharsky were imprisoned July 22.[24]

It was a period for taking stock, for evaluating the mistakes of July and looking to the future. Lenin had a moment to catch his breath. His communications with Petrograd were looser, more like those he had had in the long periods of exile. He wrote a good deal—between July 3 and August 1 he completed twenty articles, letters, and statements, not all of which were published, and he put his notes in order for the major work *The State and Revolution*, which he had been preparing before the interruption of the July events.[25]

The inevitable differences began to appear between Lenin and the faithful on duty in Petrograd. Most of the disputes seemed to involve Stalin, who began to play a more prominent role because so many other leaders were in hiding or in prison. The problem first arose at a conference of Party leaders July 13–14 and deepened at the Second Petrograd City meeting July 16 when Stalin, despite having in his possession Lenin's evaluation of the July days, referred to Lenin's views only in a general way and gave no answer to a question which was troubling many—should the Bolsheviks begin preparations for an armed uprising?[26] The Party managed by July 23 to get a newspaper going under the name *Worker and Soldier*. Starting with 20,000 circulation it rose to 60,000 by August 10. By the end of July the badly hit military organization had made good its losses and now had 1,800 members.[27] The Party held its Sixth Congress, moving the sessions each day in fear of arrest. Once again differences appeared between Stalin's evaluation of the political situation and Lenin's (as sent to the Congress from his underground hiding place). Delegates representing 240,000 members attended—the Party was now resuming vigorous growth.[28] There was a row over a proposal by Stalin to drop Lenin's famous slogan "All Power to the Soviets." Fifteen delegates spoke in the debate on the question, eight supporting the Lenin slogan, six the Stalin proposal.

As haymaking season wore on, it became more and more difficult to maintain Lenin's disguise and it was decided that he move into Finland. He was photographed in wig and make-up for an identity card in preparation for crossing the border as a locomotive fireman. On August 8 he left his hay barn and, making his way across country where forest and peat fires were burning, arrived at a point near the border. The trip almost ended in disaster. Lenin and his companions arrived late at night at the wrong station. Yemelyanov was arrested and the others almost suffered the same fate.[29] Next day Lenin boarded a locomotive with Engineer Hugo Yalava. When the train got to the border point of Beloostrov, Yalava unhooked his engine and brought it to the water tower. He returned and recoupled the engine to the train just as it was due to pull out, giving the border police no opportunity to inspect Lenin's documents.

For a few days Lenin lived in the village of Yalkala, where he spent his time working on *The State and Revolution,* hunting mushrooms and huckleberries in the forest, swimming in Lake Kafi-Yarvi, rowing a boat, and fishing.[30] It was a quiet and easy life, the kind which had always done much to revive Lenin's spirits. After three or four days he went to Helsingfors, where he stayed at first with the chief of police, who was a Communist. [31] The pace of events was picking up.

From Helsingfors Lenin sought to restore his broken connections with the "Bureau of the Central Committee Abroad"—that is, the organization of Ganetsky and Radek which he had set up in Stockholm. His first letter, written, as he said, "after weeks of interruption," was devoted to trying to put in order the Party defenses against charges of German collaboration raised at the time of the July days. He touched on financial matters only tangentially, asking how the bureau was getting along for money and warning that he couldn't send any. The letter was important only as evidence that from late June to late August Lenin was neither in touch with his Stockholm associates nor receiving any subventions from them. In fact his connections were so poor that although he wrote his letter August 17 he wasn't able to send it off until August 26.[32] So far as is known that was the last of Lenin's communications with his Stockholm colleagues until after the coup that put him in power.

L

The Bolsheviks Begin to Move

The Kornilov plot did not catch the Bolsheviks entirely off guard. Rumors had been swirling about Petrograd, and the Party, concerned against a provocation timed to coincide with the six months' anniversary of the February Revolution, August 26, had warned all factory organizations and troop units to be vigilant and maintain a low profile.

Word of the uprising hit the moribund Soviet like an electric shock. The dual power system of the Soviet on the one hand and Kerensky's government on the other had not changed. Now the Soviet had an opportunity to advance its cause. The Executive Committee met continuously from the morning of August 27 at the Smolny Institute, a school for noblewomen to which it had removed from the Tauride Palace.

The twenty-seventh was a Sunday and Sukhanov, Lunacharsky (just released from prison), and Sukhanov's wife spent a leisurely afternoon, eating at the Vienna Restaurant, wandering about Petrograd's beautiful boulevards, arguing about culture and aesthetics. The sky was clear but there was a breath of autumn in the air. Finally they made their way home across the Troitsky Bridge and Kamennoostrovsky Prospekt. The telephone rang. It was the Soviet Executive Committee with news of the Kornilov rising.[1]

Neither Lunacharsky nor Sukhanov had the slightest fear that Kornilov's men would take Petrograd. In fact, both were exhilarated. It offered a chance for the Soviet to come to life and Sukhanov felt certain the Revolution would now take a new turn. "This was a threat that would clear the unbearably oppressive atmosphere," he thought.[2]

Voitinsky's reaction was the same. He had been acting as commissar on the northern front and had tried futilely to prevent the loss of Riga. With Riga's fall he hurried back to Petrograd, knowing nothing of the Kornilov move until he arrived at Smolny, where he found Chkheidze, Tsereteli, Chernov, and Gots, grim and tired after a sleepless night.

They asked him about Kornilov's forces.

"No regiment and no company of the Northern Front will execute Kornilov's order unless it is confirmed by the Army Committee or by me," he snapped. "No troops will obey [Kornilov] if he orders them to march against the Soviets or the government. Kornilov's troops are phantoms. They will vanish into thin air before the first shot is fired."[3]

A Committee for the People's Struggle Against Counter-Revolution was quickly established by the Soviet and into its composition went Nevsky, chief of the Bolshevik Military Organization, and other members of the Bolshevik military group. The Bolsheviks took leadership in rallying their factory committees and military allies. The Soviet authorized distribution of arms to workers—twenty thousand rifles were put into their hands. The Sestroretsk arms factory handed out guns to new workers' battalions. Flying squadrons dashed about the Petrograd region, alerting detachments and inspecting defense arrangements. The Bolsheviks expanded their Red Guards and by the end of the crisis mustered an armed force of possibly 25,000 men.[4] The Petrograd garrison had been somewhat weakened by transfers carried out at Kornilov's instigation, but the famous regiments—the Volynsky, the Yegersky, the Grenadersky, the Moskovsky, the Izmailovsky, the Preobrazhensky—all the units which won their spurs in February, as well as many others, were flung onto the approaches to Petrograd where Bolshevik agitators raised their fighting morale to a high pitch. Kornilov had sent nearly three thousand officers into Petrograd to act as a "fifth column" and to simulate a Bolshevik uprising which was to be the pretext for his intervention. They had 100,000 rubles put at their disposal by Putilov and friends but it went down the drain. The officer in charge of the Petrograd uprising spent the critical night of August 29 at the Villa Rode resort—once Rasputin's favorite. Others squandered money in bars and houses of prostitution. Many were arrested in their suites at the Astoria Hotel.

In his hiding place in Helsingfors Lenin got news of Kornilov late —not until August 29 or 30—but he reacted instantly. The Party must rally to fight Kornilov but not to support Kerensky. And it must extract every possible concession from Kerensky—specifically to get arms for the workers. An effort should be made to turn the struggle against Kornilov into a truly revolutionary one.

"The development of this war alone can lead *us* to power," Lenin said, "but we must speak of this as little as possible in our propaganda (remembering very well that even tomorrow events may put power into our hands and then we shall not relinquish it)."[5]

That was private advice to his comrades. Publicly he offered a controversial proposal: that all power be placed in the hands of the Soviets with a government of SRs and Mensheviks responsible to them. Then, said Lenin, let there be complete freedom of press and propaganda and may the best side win in the upcoming Constituent Assembly. Lenin himself was uncertain about the wisdom of his proposal. Compromise went against his grain. He wrapped it in qualifications and when it was delayed two days in the mails he almost withdrew the suggestion. His Petrograd comrades didn't like his ideas too much. At first they proposed not to run the article but finally came around to it after a day's consideration.[6] It was published September 6.[7]

Lenin's proposal was not taken up by his rivals. It was the last compromise he was to offer.

From now on, in a rapidly rising crescendo, Lenin was to bombard his colleagues in Petrograd on one topic and one topic alone—the necessity for urgent, immediate, military action to seize power.

As he put it in a letter to a Plenum of the Central Committee scheduled to meet September 3: "The critical situation is inevitably leading the working class—perhaps with catastrophic speed—to a situation in which, due to a change in events beyond its control, it will find itself compelled to wage a determined battle with the counterrevolutionary bourgeoisie and to gain power."[8]

Lenin's conviction was not to change from that moment forward—except to become more urgent, more angry, more demanding, more certain that the hour for seizing power had struck.

To support his confidence he had growing evidence of the revival of the Bolsheviks. On August 20 there had been elections of the Petrograd City Duma. In May the Bolsheviks polled 20 per cent of the vote against 55 per cent for the SRs and Mensheviks. Now the Bolsheviks rolled up 33 per cent. The SR-Menshevik total dropped to 44 and the Kadets fell to 23 per cent from 25. Of the 198 places in the City Duma the Bolsheviks won 67 seats, the SRs 75, Mensheviks 8, the Kadets 42.[9]

The Bolsheviks won a majority in a vote on the night of September 1–2 in the Petrograd Soviet, calling for a government of workers and soldiers—in effect a repudiation of the Kerensky regime. The Bolshevik resolution was approved 279 to 115 with 54 abstaining—to the amazement of both the Bolsheviks and Chkheidze, who was in the chair.[10] An even stronger resolution was approved by the Moscow Soviet September 5 by a vote of 355 to 254. Similar shifts took place in a number of provincial Soviets. But the big and conclusive swing was recorded September 9 in the Petrograd Soviet. All the parties had rounded up their delegates. About 1,000 were present. The Bolshevik resolution was approved 519 votes to 414 with 67 abstaining.[11]

Trotsky remarked: "The new majority applauded like a storm, ecstatically, furiously. It had a right to. The victory had been well paid for. A good part of the road lay behind."[12]

Released from Kresty Prison September 4 on 3,000 rubles bail, Trotsky immediately became chairman of the Petrograd Soviet, the same post he had filled in 1905.

There was one more big election to come—that to the district Dumas in Moscow. It was a shocker. The SRs dropped to 54,000 from the 375,000 votes they polled in June. The Mensheviks almost vanished—16,000 votes against 76,000. The Kadets held their own with 101,000 against 110,000. But the Bolsheviks crashed through with 198,000. In June the SRs registered 58 per cent of the vote. In September the Bolsheviks polled 52 per cent. Significantly the troops voted 90 per cent for the Bolsheviks. In some units 95 per cent.[13]

Why the enormous popular swing? The single overriding issue was the war. Russia was sick of the war. The troops were sick of it. The peasants were sick of it. The workers were sick of it. Almost everyone was sick of it. As Count de Robien noted: "One must have no illusions, all Russians want peace. This wish to have done with it is understandable in this country which is in a state of upheaval and complete anarchy and is on the eve of famine and one really cannot blame them for it."[14]

Only the Bolsheviks stood uncompromisingly for peace, land, and bread—the slogan Lenin had given them in April. There had been no deviation from it. The Provisional Government was dedicated to carrying on the war. The moderate leaders of the Soviet, even the socialist leaders of the Soviet, found themselves tied to the war, tied to the Government's impossible effort to feed the cities, to meet the demands of workers, to curb growing disorder. Behind them loomed the peasant masses more and more rapidly moving to take the land, to seize the manor houses, to burn the barns and granaries, to carry out the Revolution in the countryside regardless of Government, decrees, commissars, authority, or any human force. In the countryside the peasants were still loyal to the SRs, to the tradition that the SRs stood for giving the land back to the people. But in the great capital cities, in the big industrial complexes, in the regional centers like Kiev,

Kharkov, Odessa, Nizhni Novgorod, Yekaterinburg, Krasnodar, and the smaller cities and towns, the country had turned against those whom it blamed for the trouble and toward the one party which consistently spoke for its simplest aspirations.

The meaning of this Lenin spelled out in two blunt letters to his Petrograd colleagues (who did not agree with him) in mid-September. He insisted that the time had come for an armed insurrection in Petrograd and Moscow to take power into the hands of the Bolsheviks. The majority of the people now sided with the Bolsheviks. He warned that Petrograd might soon be surrendered to the Germans, suggested that the British and Germans were talking of separate peace, insisted that the people were fed up with Kerensky and all the other parties and that the Bolsheviks must "assume power *at this very moment*" (his italics). Only the Bolsheviks, he argued, could end the painful vacillation and only the Bolsheviks could save Petrograd from the Germans—through an armistice. An armistice with the Germans now, he said, would mean "to win *the whole world.*"

Every effort must be made immediately to organize the insurrection, to surround the Alexandrinsky Theater, occupy the Peter and Paul Fortress, arrest the General Staff and Government, occupy the telegraph and telephone exchanges, and move against the officer corps.[15]

From now on the day would hardly pass when Lenin would not urge, plead, beg, threaten, and demand from his colleagues that they act, act immediately, act decisively, take power. There was no wavering. The July days were behind him. The June days were of the past. The braggadocio of April was forgotten. Day after day Lenin's words pounded at the skulls of his Party. The tension levels rose and rose. There had been examples before, often enough, when Lenin had whipped himself into a frenzy. But nothing like this. He had total conviction that he was right and that the moment was now. Immediately. This very day. This hour. This minute.

Krupskaya visited her husband twice during these days in Finland. He was totally preoccupied, she recalled, with the problem of the armed seizure of power, with preparations of units of the Finnish Army and Navy for assisting in overthrowing Kerensky, for setting up the apparatus of carrying out the coup d'état.[16] "Ilyich was terribly concerned, sitting there in Finland, that the most favorable moment for the uprising would be lost," Krupskaya said.[17]

Clearly Lenin had entered one of those periods of frenetic activity, a period of exaltation, such as Valentinov had described in Switzerland so many years before. To some his invocations seemed confused, almost hysterical, but his energy was boundless. His arguments shifted from day to day. They partook neither of profound Marxist dialectic nor of the military strategy of Clausewitz. Lenin's attitude seemed more like the aphorism of Napoleon he had once cited: *"On s'engage et puis on voit."* First engage the enemy and then see what happens.[18]

The truth was that Lenin over a long period of years had moved in a classic manic-depressive pattern. He clearly had entered in a down period in late June and early July when he went to rest at Bonch-Bruyevich's cottage in Finland. Now he was going through one of his sharpest upswings. His cry was manic: now or never.

But, as so often, his Party lagged behind. Lenin's letters were discussed at a meeting of his Central Committee September 5. There were sixteen members present. It was the eve of a Democratic Conference of all parties to consider the future course of the Provisional Government. The majority of Central Committee members felt that the period just ahead should be peaceful and that there was a real possibility of compromise with the SRs and Mensheviks, quite possibly along the lines Lenin himself had suggested only a few days earlier. This was the view of the Moscow members as well as that of most of those from Petrograd. Lenin's negative views on the Democratic Conference were sharply criticized. His colleagues particularly didn't care for Lenin's reference to "surrounding the Alexandrinsky Theater." This was where the Democratic Conference was meeting in which the Bolsheviks themselves were taking part. In fact, there was no part of Lenin's reasoning which won enthusiastic response. By a vote of six to four with six members abstaining it was agreed to retain only one copy of Lenin's letters. A suggestion by Stalin that copies be sent to reliable Party organizations for study was put aside. Kamenev was outspoken against Lenin and proposed that the committee declare that his ideas had no practical relevance at present and that resort to the streets was impermissible. Kamenev was voted down but the committee did order members of the Central Committee, directing the work of the Military Committee and the Petersburg Committee, to take steps to see that there be no kind of manifestations by either barracks or factories.[19] Lenin's letters were then buried in the Party archives so deeply that even workers of the Central Committee did not know of their existence.[20]

Not until October 10 did the question of an armed insurrection come up for serious discussion in the higher Party levels. Before that Lenin had fired volleys of rhetoric at his comrades. He had moved from Helsingfors to Vyborg some time between September 15 and 17,[21] where he was only five hours away from Petrograd and could better direct his campaign. He began an independent correspondence with Ivar T. Smilga,* chairman of the regional Bolshevik Committee for the Army, Navy, and Workers of Finland, about deploying troops and naval forces from Finland for his proposed coup d'état. He poured sarcasm on Bolshevik participation in a proposed Pre-Parliament to be held in Petrograd in mid-October and violently opposed holding off insurrectionary plans until the meeting of the All-Russian Soviet scheduled for October 20. Finally in a melodramatic letter of September 29 he warned that world revolution was at hand, mutinies were starting in Germany, France, Italy, and England. In Russia a peasant revolt was beginning, the Bolsheviks had the support of the Soviets of both Moscow and Petrograd, revolts were threatening in Finland and the Ukraine.

Many Party leaders were waiting for the All-Russian Soviet to meet, he said, but to wait "would be utter idiocy or sheer treachery," losing weeks and risking the mobilization of the Cossacks against them.

All that needed to be done was to launch—at this very moment—a surprise attack from Petrograd, Moscow, and the Baltic Fleet. Chances of success were 100 to 1.

To wait, he said, *"is to doom the revolution to failure."*

Therefore, said Lenin, he was tendering his resignation from the Central Committee in order to campaign for his plan among the rank and file and at the Party Congress.[22]

Lenin's suspicions about his Party comrades were, of course, correct. Their sentiment was not for immediate insurrection. They had voted to participate in the Pre-Parliament. They had fixed the day for the All-Russian Congress of Soviets. They saw no particular reason for rushing into the street with guns. They were certain the All-Russian Soviet would simply take into its hands the power of the state—and the Bolsheviks would be in overwhelming majority there. What was the reason for Lenin's urgency? Two weeks more or less and the state would be theirs.

But Lenin was Lenin. After receiving his resignation threat the Central Committee on October 3 voted to summon him to Petrograd for consultation. Two days later the Central Committee began to move toward his views. It agreed that it was not necessary to wait for the meeting of the All-Russian Soviets and that the possibility existed of carrying out an armed uprising before October 20.[23]

Some time in this period Lenin slipped back into Petrograd. To this day Communist researchers have not been able to pinpoint the exact day—a circumstance of considerable importance. It has a direct bearing on the role Lenin played in the preparation of the Bolshevik upris-

---

* Smilga was purged in 1927 and killed by Stalin in 1938.

ing and on the raging argument which he conducted with his associates, he trying to stimulate them to action, they holding back.

There is a good deal of evidence that Lenin came back without sanction from the Party and in violation of the Central Committee's wishes. For many years after 1917 it was said that he had come back before the officially acknowledged date but had stayed in deep underground, dating his communications as though he were still in Finland to throw spies off the track.

When Lenin did return to Petrograd, he went to the home of Margarita Fofanova, who lived with her sister and parents and her sister's children in a large flat, No. 42, in the big apartment house at the corner of Bolshoi Sampsoniyevsky and Serdobolskaya streets.[24] Lenin probably arrived on a Friday. Later Fofanova thought it must have been September 22 or 23. There is strong evidence that this date is too early. He could have come September 29, the day he sent his ultimatum to the Central Committee, although this, too, is uncertain.[25]

Fofanova was an agronomy student, worked in the Vyborg Party section, and came to be a close friend of Krupskaya's.[26] With the passage of years she became convinced that a deliberate attempt was made by higher authorities (presumably Stalin) to confuse the date of Lenin's return. There is much collateral evidence to support the view that the question of the date of return has deep political implications.

The argument between Lenin and the Central Committee over attempting a coup d'état was a violent one. Lenin's "resignation," his threat to carry his fight to the Party membership, and his independent effort to line up military support in Finland are clear evidence of the serious split.

It is reminiscent in many ways of the quarrel between Lenin and the Petrograd Party leadership in March-April 1917, just after the February Revolution. At that time under the leadership of Kamenev and Stalin the Party and *Pravda* took a moderate line, supporting the new Provisional Government and the war. Lenin returned from Switzerland to Petrograd in April breathing smoke and fury. After two or three weeks Lenin's violent line—opposition to the Provisional Government and opposition to the war—won out.

Now again Lenin abroad in Finland had come to a radical conclusion. The Bolsheviks must take power immediately. The leadership in Petrograd—Kamenev, Zinoviev, Stalin, and the rest—took a more moderate view. The Central Committee simply didn't agree with Lenin's analysis. Being on the scene in Petrograd, the Central Committee felt it had better command of the situation than Lenin living in the underground in Finland.

In autumn as in spring it was to take all of Lenin's bulldog tenacity, skill in argument, and passionate conviction to carry the day against his own colleagues.

Against this background it seems not unlikely that Lenin may have slipped back into Petrograd a week or ten days earlier than the official record acknowledges in order to carry on his fight at closer quarters.

The evidence we have is not conclusive. But we do know several things of consequence. Once Lenin died in 1924 and Stalin came into power he deliberately suppressed reminiscences and histories which spoke of an arrival date for Lenin earlier than October 8 or 9. And only after Stalin's death did a few surviving Old Bolsheviks whom Stalin had not executed come forward with strong assertions that Lenin, in defiance of his own Party, came into Petrograd in late September determined to win the day for a quick stroke against the Provisional Government.

The importance of Lenin's daily activity and whereabouts at this period is stressed by Krupskaya in a segment of her memoirs which still lies unpublished in the Central Party Archives. She emphasizes that:

"If you do not *immerse* yourself in that period Ilyich's role in the October coup will not be *totally clear* and the role that was played in the preparation of the coup by years of study of Marxist thought and the open study of preceding revolutions will remain fuzzy. One would also not be able to understand Ilyich as a Revolutionary, as a man and as a Marxist."[27]

What is strongly suggested by all this is that Lenin—and Lenin alone—backed the idea of the October coup; that almost all of his associates opposed him and thought him violently mistaken; that he singlehandedly overcame their opposition and was prepared to go to *any* lengths (including conspiring against his own party) to achieve his goal; and that the historical record has been deliberately suppressed and distorted for sixty years to conceal the dimensions and depth of the conflict.

Regardless of when he arrived, Lenin certainly was in Petrograd by the ninth.[28] On the tenth the Central Committee met for the first time in three months with Lenin present. Twelve members participated in wigs and make-up, false mustaches and beards. Lenin wore a wig of gray hair that fell over his broad brow. It had been made for him in Helsingfors by a wig maker who had worked at the Mariinsky Theater and often made wigs for St. Petersburg noblemen. He couldn't understand why Lenin wanted a gray wig. Usually his clients wanted to look younger.[29] In addition to the wig Lenin wore glasses and had shaved off his beard. Zinoviev wore a beard and had shaved his head.[30]

The meeting took place at 10 P.M. at the apartment of Sukhanov, whose wife, Galina, was a Bolshevik. Her husband was busy at Smolny and had no idea his flat was being used for a high conference by his political rivals.[31] Those present in addition to Lenin were Andrei S. Bubnov, Felix Dzerzhinsky, Grigory Zinoviev, Lev Kamenev, Alexandra Kollontai, A. Lomov, Grigory Y. Sokolnikov, Yakov Sverdlov, Joseph Stalin, Leon Trotsky, and Moisei S. Uritsky. Only Kamenev opposed Lenin's proposal to withdraw from the Pre-Parliament. Then Lenin took the floor. Since the beginning of September, he said, he had observed a certain indifference toward the question of revolt.[32] Much time had been wasted. It was time to turn to the technical side of things. Lenin said it was senseless to wait for the election of the Constituent Assembly in which the Bolsheviks would not have a majority. There was a long discussion (of which no protocol exists). The meeting went on until 3 A.M. and some members had to spend the night at the Sukhanov apartment, but in the end Lenin's proposal—he wrote it out with the stub of a pencil on squared sheets from a child's notebook[33]—won with only two dissenters, Kamenev and Zinoviev. A Politburo to lead preparations for the rising was set up. It comprised Lenin, Bubnov, Zinoviev, Kamenev, Sokolnikov, Stalin, and Trotsky.[34]

At last, at last, Lenin must have sighed as he slipped away from the Sukhanov flat and back to his hideaway in the Vyborg section. He had won. The bold throw for power would now be made. The date had not yet been set. But the coup would come as quickly as preparations could be made. There was one thing the long meeting had not done. It had still taken no practical steps nor approved any general plan of operations. *"On s'engage et pius on voit."*

LI

October Days

Life in Petrograd seemed to move more slowly during the October days of 1917. The Germans seized the islands of Dagö and Ösel in the Baltic Sea off the coast of Estonia, yet alarm over the threat to the capital did not grow. Kerensky was constantly on the go—often at the front. It was as if he did not want to be on the scene to watch his political fate move remorselessly toward disaster. Sir George Buchanan, the British ambassador who had cherished the Kornilov move (and was probably more deeply implicated than he ever put on paper), now expressed concern at the political disarray of the Kerensky Government. He told Foreign Minister Tereshchenko that the Government really existed only on the sufferance of the Soviet and that the Bolsheviks might move at any time.[1]

Trouble gripped the countryside. Train robberies had become frequent in the Caucasus. There was hardly an estate where the owner could feel safe from murder, arson, or pillage.

In Petrograd carriages disappeared from the streets and the few remaining cabmen formed a union and charged five rubles (about six dollars) to go from the French Embassy to the Hôtel de L'Europe. Before the war it cost twenty-five kopecks (thirty cents). There were queues for everything—for cigarettes in the tobacco shop, chocolate in the confectionery stores, flowers in the flower shops. For a few rubles you could hire a soldier to stand in a queue for you. And soldiers sold chocolate bars on the street at eleven rubles a pound. Thousands of deserters wandered through the Petrograd streets. The breakdown of supply and wild inflation turned everyone to the pawnshops and the curiosity markets. Madame Naryshkin was trying to sell a bust of Marie Antoinette to the Louvre. The Count de Robien hoped it could be sold to Paris rather than fall into the hands of "a Transatlantic pork merchant."[2]

Yet it was still possible to get a decent luncheon at Donon's and to dine at Constant's or the Bear. The indomitable Countess Kleinmikhel continued to give dinner parties and Count de Robien enjoyed walking back to the French Embassy in the moonlight with the great golden domes of the Church of the Resurrection sparkling like a scene from *Petrushka*. Zinaida Gippius spent a few days at a cottage in Finland and came back to Petrograd to note in her diary: "Kerensky continues to fall and the Bolsheviks are already the unshakeable masters of the Soviet. Trotsky is chairman. Exactly when will be the slaughter, the cannonade, the uprising, the pogrom in Petersburg— still is not certain. But it will come."[3]

Was the country ready, eager for a new uprising? Sukhanov thought not. He spent a great deal of time in the factories. He felt the mood of the workers was ambiguous. The common strain which united everyone was hatred of what they called "Kerenskyism," fatigue, rage, and a desire for *"peace, bread and land."*[4] But, of course, "peace, bread and land" was Lenin's slogan. Sukhanov believed that regardless of party or person, the people and particularly the soldiers in the trenches and out of them would throw their support to anyone who promised peace. Every soldier in October, in the opinion of the Bolshevik Military Organization leader Podvoisky, was a Bolshevik regardless of whether he had any idea of what Bolshevism meant. That is, he was ready for an end to the war. On the other hand Kamenev didn't think the Petrograd garrison would support an uprising. The French journalist Claude Anet found little militancy in either workshops or barracks and Vladimir I. Nevsky feared the peasants would not support the cities and might halt food supplies.[5]

In late September Petrograd had begun to buzz with rumors of an impending Bolshevik coup. The rumors grew stronger as October advanced. The question was not whether the Bolsheviks would make a move but when. As early as October 8—before Lenin had his showdown with the Central Committee—*Novaya Zhizn* was reporting that everywhere—in the queues, on street corners, on the streets, in streetcars—people were saying there would be a Bolshevik coup and that it was timed to coincide with the meeting of the All-Russian Soviet October 20.[6]

This was natural enough. While the actual decision had not yet been made, Lenin's articles in the Bolshevik press daily called for a rising. He hardly bothered to conceal his language. It was open, impulsive, and eloquent. After the meeting October 10 a message was sent through the party apparatus, as Nikolai V. Krylenko told the Northern Bolshevik Congress, that "the time for words is past." No date was set but the Party apparatus went into action to make plans for troop disposals, seizures, communications, and arrests.[7] The capital became more nervous.

But the Party was never unanimous behind Lenin's urgent decision. Kamenev and Zinoviev had not been convinced that the time was ripe or that there must be resort to arms. They drafted a declaration of opposition asserting that the Party had no right to stake its future, that of the Revolution in Russia and of the Revolution in Europe, "on the card of armed revolt." It was a mistake, they felt, to suppose that the Party in case of failure could draw back again as in July. This would be a decisive battle and on it the cause of Marxist Revolution would stand or fall.

"Against this ruinous policy we raise the voice of warning," they said.[8] The pot bubbled. The SR faction at the Soviet was so convinced that the Bolsheviks were about to move that they discussed the question on October 11, and on October 12 the Petrograd correspondent of the *Russkiye Vedomosti* reported that the Bolshevik coup was expected on October 20, starting as a demonstration demanding that power be placed in the hands of the Soviet. He said that the Government was not alarmed.[9] Almost every day the right-wing newspaper *Rech* published warnings.

The Bolsheviks' position in Petrograd, of course, was very strong. They now had 50,000 Party members and with control of the Petrograd Soviet and eleven of the seventeen regional Soviets they employed these organizations as a legitimate cover for military preparations. They had gotten the Soviet to set up a special Military Revolutionary Committee and they used this as a legal nucleus for arming workers and establishing regional fighting networks. They had not only their Red Guards—10,000 to 12,000 strong—but a rapidly growing Workers Defense contingent. There were about 350,000 troops stationed in Petrograd. Bolshevik influence in most units was strong. It was overwhelming among the 60,000 men of the Baltic Fleet.[10]

In the Soviet Executive Committee meeting of October 15 the Mensheviks tried to cross-examine Trotsky.

Were the Bolsheviks preparing a coup or weren't they? It was Dan who asked the questions and he wanted to know, furthermore, whether they had set a date for their rising and whether they considered the defense of the country the chief task of the moment.[11]

Trotsky retorted: "In whose name has he [Dan] asked this question: in the name of Kerensky, the counter-intelligence, the Secret Police or some other body?"[12]

Lenin had a couple of informal meetings with the Bolshevik chiefs in these days, seeking to quiet the opposition of Kamenev and Zinoviev and solidify support for an immediate uprising. Men in charge of getting units and plans ready, like Nevsky and Podvoisky, wanted more time for preparations. Podvoisky proposed a ten-day postponement. Lenin exploded. The rising could not be delayed. Delay simply played into the hands of the Government.[13] However, Lenin was flexible about how to carry out the coup. He talked of starting it in Moscow or even in a provincial capital like Minsk.[14]

The whole argument about the uprising was gone over again at a special meeting of the Central Committee held in the Petrograd suburb of Lesnoi October 16. Present were eleven members of the Central Committee, eight members of the Petersburg Party Committee, and seven others.

First, Lenin spoke for two hours—his most brilliant speech, Alexander V. Shotman thought.[15]* Then, once again, there was bitter argument.

The reports of the members were not encouraging.

There was no such thing, they said, as a "fighting mood" among the workers of Vasilevsky Island or in red Vyborg, the citadel of Bolshevik strength. It was the same in the Moscow borough, in Narva borough, and, worst of all, the anarchists were beginning to rival the Bolsheviks for influence at the Putilov factory.

Report after report provided the same depressing news. Krylenko called the mood of the troops indifferent. Volodarsky, V. V. Schmidt, Shlyapnikov, N. A. Skrypnik, I. M. Moskvin, G. I. Boky—each one of the regional organizers—were pessimistic.

Shotman summed it up. Speaking of the Military Committee, which had always been the most militant group, he said: "We can not come out but we ought to get ready."

Lenin listened to the dismal assessments as if the words had not been spoken. He could hardly wait for the organizers to finish before he took the floor and demanded that the resolution of October 10 calling for an immediate uprising be carried out.[16]

When V. P. Milyutin argued that the Bolsheviks should not strike

---

* Shotman, one of Lenin's closest associates, was purged by Stalin and shot in 1939. (Roy A. Medvedev, Let History Judge, p. 201.)

the first blow, Lenin simply dismissed the idea. The bourgeoisie were not strong. It was time to go ahead.

Lenin's hard line did not sweep the opposition away. Krylenko and Kamenev felt the time was not ripe. S. I. Skalov and Ya. G. Fenig-shtein were skeptical. Zinoviev came out in open opposition. A. S. Ioffe demanded that the question of timing be reconsidered.

Lenin did not budge.

After much parliamentary maneuvering the committee reaffirmed the idea of an uprising and "expressed confidence" that the Central Committee and the Soviet would pick the most favorable moment for the coup.

The meeting did one more thing. It decided to establish "Revolutionary Center" to be manned by Bubnov, Dzerzhinsky, Sverdlov, Stalin, and M. S. Uritsky.[17]

It was four o'clock in the morning of the seventeenth before Lenin got back to Fofanova's apartment. She was waiting up for him and, in fact, had alerted the Petersburg Committee that something might have happened to him—the hour was so late. Lenin was in low spirits. He said his comrades had been late for the meeting, he had had to walk the streets for two hours waiting for them and had dropped his wig in the mud and it was too dirty to wear. Fofanova agreed to give the wig a good wash in hot water and soap.[18]

Lenin went back into hiding—a discipline he found exhausting. Trotsky noted that Lenin's isolation played on his nerves and caused each hindrance to reflect itself in exaggerated form.[19]

The meeting of the sixteenth did not end the intra-Party struggle. Kamenev and Zinoviev had not given up the fight. The next day, the seventeenth, *Novaya Zhizn*, Gorky's paper, the paper the Bolsheviks considered closest to their very own, a paper with a circulation of tens of thousands among the Petrograd working class, published a leading article warning that the Bolsheviks were preparing an insurrection. If it was only individuals who were preparing an insurrection, that was one thing, V. Bazarov wrote. But if the Party was preparing a rising, that was a crime because it would lead "not only to the crushing of the Party but to the crushing of the working class and the end of the Revolution." He said that among the Bolsheviks there were many who dissented from this decision and that two leading members had circulated through the city a handwritten leaflet against the uprising. "But this is not enough," Bazarov said. "It is their duty to come out before the masses and fight against this adventure in public."[20]

Lenin was already outraged at Kamenev and Zinoviev. As soon as he had returned to his hideaway in the Fofanova flat, he sat down to write a long polemic against the two men for circulation within the

Party answering their arguments and seeking to whip up sentiment for the uprising. Hardly had he finished his article when he received a copy of *Novaya Zhizn* containing the Bazarov article. It was then 8 P.M. Tuesday the seventeenth. He immediately attached a postscript to his article and sent it along directing that it be published as quickly as possible. No longer would he carry forward his preparations for an insurrection privately. His article was to go to the widest circle of readers, regardless of the fact that it spoke openly and in detail about the imminent coup.

"We must agitate also *in favor of* an uprising," he wrote. "Let the anonymous individuals come right out into the light of day and let them bear the punishment they deserve for their shameful vacillations." He spewed venom on the editors of *Novaya Zhizn*. "O contemptible fools," he wrote. "Have they perhaps discovered among the masses an *indifference* to the question of bread, to the prolongation of the war, to land for the peasants?"[21]

But even before Lenin's declaration could appear in *Rabochi Put*, *Novaya Zhizn* on the morning of the eighteenth published a new sensation—a letter signed by Kamenev declaring:

"Not only Zinoviev and I but also a number of practical comrades think that to take the initiative in an armed insurrection at the present moment with the given correlation of social forces, independently of and several days before the Congress of Soviets, is an inadmissible step, ruinous to the proletariat and the revolution."[22]

Nor was this all. Gorky occasionally wrote for his newspaper brief essays with the title "Untimely Thoughts." Now he wrote under the title "I Cannot Be Silent":

"Rumors are more and more persistently being spread that some 'action by the Bolsheviks' will take place on October 20; in other words the disgusting scenes of July 3–5 may be repeated."

Petrograd could expect, Gorky asserted, "trucks tightly packed with people holding rifles and revolvers in hands trembling with fear—and these rifles will fire at the windows of stores, at people, at anything!

"All the dark instincts of the crowd irritated by the disintegration of life and by the lies and filth of politics will flare up and fume, poisoning us with anger, hate and revenge; people will kill one another, unable to suppress their own animal stupidity."

Who needs all this? Gorky asked. "Are there really adventurers who, seeing a decline in the revolutionary energy of the thinking part of the proletariat, hope to stimulate this energy by means of a profuse bloodletting?"

He called on the Bolshevik Central Committee to refute the rumor if it was "not an instrument in the hands of utterly shameless adventurers or crazed fanatics."[23]

Stalin retorted savagely in *Rabochi Put*: "As for the neuresthenics of *Novaya Zhizn* we are at a loss to understand what it is they actually want from us. . . . Their first word is one of reproach directed not to the counter-revolution but to that same revolution about which they talk with enthusiasm over a cup of tea."[24]

Fortunately, perhaps, for the cause of the Bolshevik uprising the Soviet Executive Committee on the seventeenth postponed the meeting of the All-Russian Soviet until October 25. What now unfolded before the fascinated eyes of Petrograd and reverberated at every dinner party, meeting, barracks, and factory hall discussion was an open argument carried out in full public view of the Bolshevik case, for and against a seizure of power. Gone was any vestige of "security." Every issue of the papers brought new statements and counterstatements. Lenin, as might be expected, violently reacted to the Kamenev-Zinoviev open letter.

"I declare outright that I no longer consider either of them comrades and I will fight with all my might both in the Central Committee and at the Congress to secure the expulsion of both of them from the Party," Lenin declared in a letter written to the Party. And in a second letter, close on the heels of his first, Lenin called Zinoviev and Kamenev "strikebreakers." "That is why I demand the expulsion of both the blacklegs, reserving for myself the right (in view of their threat of a split) to publish *everything* when publication becomes possible," he said.[25]

The question flared up in the Petrograd Soviet, still a curious body in which both the Bolsheviks and their enemies were represented. (The Bolsheviks were utilizing the Military Revolutionary Committee of the Soviet as a cover under which they mobilized forces for their proposed coup.) On the eighteenth the Menshevik Martov asked Trotsky point-blank whether a date had been set for the insurrection. Trotsky gave a misleading reply, saying that no move and no date had been set, but that if one was, the workers and soldiers would come out in its support. Kamenev (who was campaigning against the rising) publicly supported Trotsky's position, and the next day the Bolshevik paper, *Rabochi Put*, published a letter by Zinoviev insisting that his views were little different from Lenin's and associating himself with Trotsky's statement in the Soviet. Zinoviev said he was closing ranks and postponing the dispute to a future moment.[26] Stalin appended a note to the Zinoviev letter saying that in view of the declarations of Kamenev and Zinoviev the Party could consider the dispute resolved.

"The sharpness of Lenin's article does not alter the fact that fundamentally we stand united in our views," Stalin wrote.[27]

Nothing was further from the truth than Stalin's bland assertion. Kamenev and Zinoviev had not changed their minds. Stalin was publicly demonstrating sympathy with them for his own reasons—quite possibly he also opposed the early coup. Lenin was furiously demanding their expulsion from the Party. Kamenev had submitted his resignation from the Central Committee. Trotsky was violently denouncing not only Kamenev and Zinoviev but also Stalin for his editorial note.[28] Seldom had a group of plotters for power been more confused and at odds on the eve of their great adventure.

In his distant exile in the quiet Siberian town of Tobolsk, Nicholas II that evening, as was his custom, read aloud to his family. His choice that night was *Dracula*.[29]

October 20 was the date Lenin had set his heart on beginning the coup. Instead the Central Committee met to consider the Kamenev-Zinoviev affair. Lenin, still in hiding, wanted them thrown out. Dzerzhinsky mildly suggested that Kamenev be required to refrain from all political activity. Stalin and Milyutin urged that nothing be done for the moment and that the question be put over to a plenary session. Stalin said it was necessary to preserve the unity of the Party, that exclusion of the two men was not the answer. They should be obliged to submit to the will of the Party but they should remain on the Central Committee.[30] Uritsky supported Stalin and added that the Moscow Committee wanted the question put over. Moreover, he announced, the Moscow Party opposed an armed uprising.[31]

On a vote the resignation of Kamenev from the Central Committee was accepted by five to three with Stalin opposing. By six votes the committee forbade Kamenev and Zinoviev to carry on a campaign against the Central Committee decisions. Stalin opposed this also and submitted his resignation from the editorial board of *Rabochi Put*. The committee refused to accept it.[32]

The committee then turned to practical questions about the uprising. The date was still not yet chosen, but the idea of a rising on the twenty-fifth was beginning to be brought forward. The committee noted (but only with a sense of curiosity) that the morning papers had published an order signed the day before by Kerensky for the arrest of Lenin. Lenin, equipped with wig, spectacles, and a smooth-shaven face, was moving around the city carefully. That evening he again met with some of the chiefs of the Bolshevik Military Organization in the flat of a worker named Pavlov in Lesnoi.[33] And one

night, coat collar turned up and cap pulled down over his forehead,
Lenin appeared at the apartment where his sister Anna, his brother-in-
law Mark Yelizarov, their stepson Gora, and his sister Mariya now
lived at 256 Maly Prospekt on the Petrograd side. Some of Lenin's
comrades joined him and they talked about the coming coup. Gora sat
at the end of a long table, his eyes never leaving Lenin and his mouth
open. He had no idea what the conversation was about but he never
forgot the occasion.[34]

The most publicized, most disorganized, most needless coup in political history was stumbling ahead toward its climax.

Even in the very heart of Bolshevik circles there seemed to be no
rising tension. The sixteen-year-old schoolgirl Nadezhda Alliluyeva
wrote a letter to her girl friend, Alisa Radchenko, on October 19. She
mentioned school lessons, the food shortages in Petrograd, and added:

"People are managing somehow, although we and everybody else
are in an awful frame of mind. Sometimes it makes you cry. It's so dull
and you can't go anywhere. . . . There are rumors going around that
the Bolsheviks are going to do something on October 20, but probably
there's nothing to it."

Nadezhda Alliluyeva's father, Sergei, was a veteran Bolshevik with
years of experience in the Caucasus and Petrograd. He was a close
friend of Stalin's who had been living with the Alliluyevs since his return from Siberia. Later on Stalin would marry this schoolgirl whose
letters reflected so little premonition of great events in the making.[35]

On the Dvinsk front, Baron Alexei Budberg, commander of a corps
and a thoughtful, intelligent officer, watched events march toward their
inevitable conclusion. He was resigned to the fact that the Army no
longer really existed as a military organization. Its discipline was gone
and only a miracle could bring it back—and miracles did not happen
in real life. The slogan "Down with War" was supported by every self-
seeker in uniform and he estimated that this phrase took in 80 per cent
of the troops. More and more units simply refused to go back to the
trenches when their time in a rear area was up.

"It's terrible," he noted in his diary for October 7, "to give an order
without any confidence and often without the slightest hope that it
will be carried out."

In the rear of the Army deserters were attacking and plundering
supply trains bringing food to the front. He thought Russia ought to
go over to a voluntary Army. There was no sense in trying to keep unwilling peasants in the trenches. Let those who wanted go home; those
who wanted to fight could stay. The Army would be perhaps only a

shadow of itself in numbers. But at least that handful could fight. The railroads were staggering under the burden of deserters leaving for their homes. "No power has the strength to halt this hurricane to the east," he wrote.

He had begun to wonder what the difference was between the lies of the Kerensky Government and "those of the villainous ministers and courtiers of the unhappy and blind Nicholas II."

Most of all he was outraged at the "moon people, the political Martians" who did not understand the nature of the Russian peasant. Nikolai Chaikovsky, whom he called the "Grandfather of the Russian Revolution," had once said, "You appeal to their mind but you get an answer from their hide."

The revolutionaries and the Populists had created an image of the "dark" Russian people that bore no resemblance to reality. They had "fantasized, poeticized, beautified and worshiped those who will soon devour them."

The Russian village, he thought, was a nightmare. So was Russia. Everywhere there were beasts, beastly people, beastly deals, beastly greed, beastly harshness.

On October 22 he wrote that the Bolsheviks were gathering strength. There were 200,000 deserters in Petrograd on whom they could rely. Soon they would make a decisive move. The Government of the "blind and light-minded" Kerensky talked of compromise. It did not understand that it had created anarchy, not democracy, and this was the sea in which the Bolsheviks swam.[36]

A young American YMCA worker named Paul Anderson was enjoying his introduction to Russia. He and some of his friends had found lodgings in a mansion that belonged to a manufacturing family named San Galli who were of Swiss origin. It was a beautiful house with a ballroom, great drawing rooms, marble staircases, a fountain, a conservatory, sculpture, and oil paintings. Some of the family including a sixteen-year-old daughter still lived there. The YMCA boys had been invited to stay—although they were not quite clear about this—as a kind of protection against the house being taken over by roving revolutionaries.

Anderson and his friends gave dances on Sunday night in the San Galli ballroom. They invited other young Americans in Petrograd to the parties—a young Harvard graduate named John Reed, who was much interested in the Revolution, Louise Bryant, Reed's girl friend, another American, a liberal named Albert Rhys Williams, and a California newspaper correspondent, Bessy Beatty.

Anderson and his friends had found the Kornilov affair thrilling.

They had seen some of the shooting on the Nevsky because they crossed the wide prospekt every morning going to their office on the Mokhovaya.

Everyone knew that something was going to happen but no one knew what it might be or when. Anderson asked Ed Heald, one of the YMCA men who had been in Russia more than a year, what it was all about.

"There's more and more talk about these Bolsheviks," Heald said. Anderson wasn't much interested. Russian politics seemed too complex to a young American.[37]

To Reed, who had been in Russia since August, nothing could have been more exciting than what he was witnessing in Petrograd. He was a socialist and he had arrived with a list of contacts—mostly Russian radicals who had returned to their homeland from the United States like Volodarsky and V. S. (Bill) Shatov.* Reed dashed from factory meeting to factory meeting. Evenings he and Louise Bryant went to the Cirque Moderne, not far from the Kshesinskaya house, where almost continuous mass meetings were in progress with Bolshevik orators stirring up the Vyborg workers for the coming coup. Alexander Berkman, the American anarchist, spoke at the Cirque, and Reed listened to him. On the ninth Reed and Williams went with Alexandra Kollontai to the Obukhovo arms factory where Lunacharsky was speaking. Reed and Williams both addressed the meeting. When he came away, Reed put down in his notes: "A man with whom I spoke in French at the Obukhovo factory said that they are not going to wait any longer and that soon they will begin to act. And not only the Red Guards but all the people, all the Army."[38]

---

* Shatov, a leader in the American IWW, was one of the most colorful of the American Russian returnees. He served as commissar of the Petrograd fortified region, played a leading role in the Soviet fighting in Siberia and the Far East, directed the construction of the Turk-Sib railroad, and was shot in 1937 in the Stalinist purges. Reed met Russian Americans at almost every turn, among them Semyon Mikhailovich Nakhimson; a factory director named Petrovsky, known as Nelson in the United States; Stepan Semyonovich Dybets, another factory worker; Semyon P. Voskov, a front commander; and many more. Many, if not most, of these men, including Dybets, were killed in the purges.

LII

A Threatening Night

Legend has invested the events of October with heroic stature. They are presented as an epic frieze across which move figures possessing dimensions greater than life. Above them towers the commanding presence of Lenin, the leader, the master strategist, all wise, armed with the guiding truth of Marx, organizing and directing the strategy and tactics of the supreme Revolution. Lenin triumphs against the colossal strength of Russia's capitalist-feudal society, he thwarts false prophets, he confounds enemies within the ranks of his own party and emerges as the tribune of his people, the savior of humanity.

The picture has been painted many times and not only by the eulogists of the Lenin cult. The Bolshevik Revolution, as many insist on calling it, proved to be a watershed in contemporary history. It profoundly changed the lives of the Russian people and the politics of the world and it is natural to expect so germinal an event to be presented on an Olympian stage. Natural—but in the case of Russia's October, totally mistaken.

The October events are encumbered by trivia, petty rivalry, miscalculation, hesitation, ineptitude, posturing, and mistakes. Almost nothing was planned and what did happen was often accidental. The Bolsheviks did not seize power in one bold clandestine move. They blundered into power, divided, fighting against each other, and until the final moments Lenin had only an occasional role in what happened. Kerensky and his Government were not crushed by the steel power of valiant revolutionaries. He and his supporters skedaddled off

the political stage, protesting that they were not really leaving, merely
regrouping strength for the climactic battle—a battle which was never
fought.

Few of the participants understood what they were doing; fewer
witnesses comprehended the significance of what they were seeing.

But if error and confusion was the rule of the day the actual record
is worth the closest study—not as an exercise in revolutionary tactics
but as an illumination of the banality which so often lies at the heart of
great moments in history. Seldom has the contrast between legend and
reality presented a wider gap.

By the evening of Monday October 23 one would have thought that
Kerensky, chief of the Provisional Government which every Petrograd
gossip *knew* was about to be destroyed by a Bolshevik coup, would
have been totally engaged in meeting the crisis which threatened his
existence.

That evening did, indeed, find Kerensky concerned with crisis—but
crisis of a very different order. Kerensky called Gen. Nikolai Nikolayevich Dukhonin, Chief of Staff, at Mogilev by Hughes wire. He wanted
Dukhonin to know that his, Kerensky's, return to the front had been
delayed—but not by rumors of a Bolshevik coup. "That can be taken
care of without me," he said. "Everything is organized." What
Kerensky had on his mind was a serious problem which had arisen
about the War Minister, Gen. Alexander I. Verkhovsky. In fact that
very day the general had gone on leave "for reasons of health" and
would not be returning to his post.[1]

What had happened was that General Verkhovsky had raised in a
secret government meeting the fateful question of Russia's seeking
peace.

Finally he put his full case to a closed meeting of the Government
Council. The situation at the front was beyond repair. The country
could not support an army of 9.5 million. The only way to fight the
Bolsheviks was to cut the ground from under their feet and that meant
peace.

The council's reaction was negative. Most of the members thought
Verkhovsky was talking of a separate Russian peace with Germany.

Kerensky did everything possible to suppress Verkhovsky's views.
The press was forbidden to write about them. But the irrepressible
Burtsev, the exposer of Azef and now a violent opponent of Kerensky,
of the Bolsheviks, and an adherent of Kornilov—a super-patriot in
other words—burst out in his newspaper *Obshcheye Delo* with wild
headlines: "CITIZENS, SAVE RUSSIA." He claimed Verkhovsky pro-

posed a separate peace with Germany, secret from the Allies. "Citizens," he cried. "To your feet! Russia is being betrayed. Save her!"[2] *Zhivoye Slovo* echoed: "General Von der Verkhovsky must immediately be removed."[3]

That was the end of Verkhovsky. Now he had been sent off "on leave," as Kerensky told Dukhonin.[4]

Baron Budberg at the front in Dvinsk wrote in his diary on that same evening of October 23:

"From the point of view of being true to one's word the proposal [for peace] is, of course, insidious but from the point of view of the selfish interests of Russia it may be one hope for salvation; for the masses peace is the trump card and the Bolsheviks want to take it and use it as the only way to power."

Budberg and Verkhovsky were right. But there was no one to heed their counsel.

While Kerensky had been busy suppressing Verkhovsky's remarks about peace, what had he been doing to meet the Bolshevik threat? Literally nothing of any consequence. Interior Minister A. M. Nikitin had warned all provincial authorities to be on guard against an uprising.[5] The self-confident Petrograd commandant, Col. G. B. Polkovnikov, had assured reporters that the Petrograd troops were reliable and on the side of the Government. (Shades of Protopopov and Nicholas II!) Kerensky told Nabokov that "we have more strength than we need." On the "practical side" Polkovnikov ordered that no revolvers be sold without a permit (at a moment when the Red Guards were being handed five thousand rifles by the Sestoretsk factory). He ordered the arrest of Lenin (but not of Trotsky or any of the others). Nor was anything done to follow this up. One city official, out of curiosity, telephoned Mariya Ulyanova and found that Lenin had returned to Petrograd but no one tried to arrest him. Kerensky still had not ordered reinforcements into Petrograd from the front.[6] But several guard posts had been set up on the approaches to the Winter Palace.[7] And the Government had placed 650 cadets of the 1st and 2nd Oranienbaum military schools, a machine-gun unit with six machine guns and seven armored cars, in the palace courtyard.[8] On the twentieth, forty members of a bicycle squad were sent to the palace. By October 22 the defense force at the Winter Palace comprised 37 officers, 696 cadets, 75 soldiers, six field guns, six armored cars, nineteen machine guns, 684 rifles, and forty revolvers.[9]

One more step was taken by Colonel Polkovnikov. Late in the evening of Saturday the twenty-first, eight delegates of the Military Revolutionary Committee had called on him. Their instructions were to "establish control over all orders of the staff" and install three commissars to countersign all orders.[10] Polkovnikov received the delegates politely, listened to their demands, then quietly announced that he would not accept any commissars. When the delegates told him that without the sanction of the Petrograd Soviet his orders would be "poorly received," he said that the garrison was in his hands and would do what was necessary.

"The firmness of Polkovnikov was genuine, there was nothing affected about it," Konstantin A. Mekhonoshin recalled. "Evidently he didn't understand the actual situation in the garrison. There was nothing to do but return to Smolny."

Polkovnikov gave the delegates a car for the ride back, and first thing on the morning of October 22 the delegates instructed the Petrograd garrison to ignore any orders not signed by the Military Revolutionary Committee.

"So," comments the official Soviet historian, "was begun the conflict between the Petrograd Soviet and the Staff of the Command. It was the first open collision of the forces of Revolution and Counter-Revolution. The machine guns and the rifles were still silent and the soldiers of both sides remained in their barracks. But at any moment there might be an ultimatum and the guns would begin to fire."[11]

In fact, in the opinion of Sukhanov, the meeting of the delegates with the commander *was* the Revolution. But neither side had any understanding of what it was doing.

If the Winter Palace had understood the essence of the argument, it could have sent five hundred Cossacks to Smolny then and there to liquidate the Bolsheviks, Sukhanov commented. Had Smolny understood, it would have sent three hundred volunteers to take over the Winter Palace.[12]

On Sunday both sides acted as if they had simply had one more major misunderstanding and began to talk about compromises.[13]

No date had yet been picked for an uprising. On the twenty-first the Military Revolutionary Committee got control of the Petrograd Cartridge Factory. Henceforth ammunition could be issued only on its order.[14] Sunday the twenty-second was tense. There were Soviet meetings and parades all over Petrograd. The Cossacks had planned a solemn religious pilgrimage that day but yielded because of the danger of a collision. Both the Bolsheviks and the Government had worked to smooth this out. Neither side wanted any trouble.

Lenin was still in hiding at Fofanova's apartment, still angry about his "betrayal" by Zinoviev and Kamenev (although both were hard at work with the Bolsheviks in Smolny, preparing the coup as though nothing had happened). But Lenin was so delighted that the Cossack Sunday demonstration had been canceled he dashed off a note to Sverdlov declaring: "Hurrah! If we *attack* with *all our strength,* we shall fully win out in a few days!"[15]

Sir George Buchanan, the British ambassador, invited three of Kerensky's Ministers to lunch that Monday in his sumptuous embassy on the palace embankment. They were Foreign Minister Tereshchenko, Konovalov, and Tretyakov. Buchanan told them he had hardly expected them because of the reports of disturbances. They smiled and said such rumors were premature and that the Government had sufficient strength to handle the situation. Konovolov said the Revolution had passed through three phases and had now arrived at the final phase. Before Buchanan left for England—he was planning to leave soon—he would see a great change.[16]

Monday night was not a pleasant evening—John Reed wrote of the "sour twilight." Reed was everywhere in Petrograd that day—first, at the Mariinsky Palace where the Pre-Parliament was still meeting without the Bolsheviks. As he left the Mariinsky, he reflected that no real voice from the "rough world outside" had penetrated the chamber. The Provisional Government, he thought, "was wrecked—on the same rock of War and Peace that had wrecked the Milyukov Ministry."[17]

A cold wet wind swept Petrograd, and Reed noticed that the City Militia was now mounted and armed with revolvers in new holsters. The city seemed nervous, crowds on the street corners, arguing, streetcars clanging by with people clinging to all sides, deserters selling cigarettes and sunflower seeds.

He went on to Smolny—three long blocks of gray buildings, dominated by a blue and gold cupola—by streetcar. Smolny was the end of the line. The Imperial arms were still emblazoned in stone over the entrance. Within the rooms bore their school designations—Ladies Classroom No. 4, Teachers Office, Third Grade, Fourth Grade.[18]

Smolny was a beehive. The heavy tramp of soldiers' feet filled the corridors. Bobbed-haired girls with armloads of newly printed leaflets ran from office to office, short skirts swirling. There were signs: "Comrades for the sake of your health preserve cleanliness." But the floors were deep in autumn mud chomped from thousands of pairs of boots. The basement dining room provided dinner for two rubles—served from long tables with cauldrons of cabbage soup, hunks of meat, mounds of kasha, and slabs of black bread. Tea in a tin cup was five kopecks.[19]

Reed met a minor Bolshevik carrying a revolver. "The game is on," he said. "Whether we move or not the other side knows it must finish us or be finished."[20]

Despite the frenetic atmosphere at Smolny only one event of consequence occurred on Monday. The Military Revolutionary Committee persuaded the eight thousand troops in the Peter and Paul Fortress to come over to the side of the Bolsheviks—or at least stay neutral. The commandant was arrested and Bolshevik commissars installed. Like so many troops in Petrograd, those at the fortress were passive. "They lacked any tendency whatever toward active armed movements," Boris Sokolov, the Socialist Revolutionary military specialist, said. Trotsky himself conceded that the Petrograd garrison while hostile to the Government "was not capable of fighting on the side of the Bolsheviks." The typical regiments really no longer existed as military units. Their single sentiment was to overthrow Kerensky, disperse, go home, and take over the land.[21]

After midnight most of the electricity in Petrograd was turned off except that supplying the gambling halls, the houses of prostitution, and cabarets, which were filled as never before with freely spending officers and nobility.

Kerensky met with his Ministers at the Winter Palace through the night. Discussions had been going on all day about relations between the Government and the Military Revolutionary Committee. There had been talk of arresting the committee. Now Kerensky decided to order his Minister of Justice to bring a court action against them for illegal activity. It was decided to close down the Bolshevik newspapers *Rabochi Put* and *Rabochi i Soldat* on charges of fomenting revolt and to bring the writers of inflammatory articles to criminal responsibility. The right-wing newspapers *Novaya Rus* and *Zhivoye Slovo* would also be closed.[22]

Still, there was uncertainty. Conversations about the Military Revolutionary Committee went on into the early morning and possibly even during the day of the twenty-fourth.[23]

If this was a coup d'état, it bore no resemblance to any classic example. Instead, it was developing like a Polish minuet, the partners approaching, withdrawing, approaching again, suddenly whirling to the left, now to the right, never quite engaging.

Minute by minute and hour by hour the revolutionaries in public session were advising their opponents exactly what they were doing and proposed to do. Trotsky openly told the Petrograd Soviet that the Military Revolutionary Committee was preparing to take power.

At the same hour Kerensky was in the General Staff Building across the great square from the Winter Palace. Not until this moment had he actually approved any orders for bringing troops into Petrograd. Now he ordered in a rifle regiment from Tsarskoye Selo, another company of cadets, a battery of horse-drawn artillery from nearby Pavlovsk, and the 1st Women's Battalion from Levashovo.[24]

Before the night was over the General Staff offices were strewn with paper—orders to citizens to put all automobiles at the disposal of the staff; a ban on demonstrations; a prohibition to troops to execute orders from sources other than Army Command; an order removing the Petrograd Soviet commissars; and an order for an investigation of all illegal acts with view to possible court-martial.[25]

Nothing came of any of these orders.

Two things were done. Telephone service to Smolny was cut (and soon restored), and at 5:30 A.M. there appeared at the print shop of *Rabochi Put* at 40 Kavalergvardsky Street a detachment of cadets. They confiscated eight thousand copies of *Rabochi Put*, destroyed the stereotypes for the paper, closed and sealed the printing shop.[26] Troops also closed the reactionary newspapers *Novaya Rus* and *Zhivoye Slovo*.

As John Reed walked out of Smolny early in the morning of October 24 he ran into the American IWW, Bill Shatov, just bounding up the steps. "Well," shouted Shatov, "we're off! Kerensky sent the Junkers to close down our papers, *Soldat* and *Rabochi Put*. But our troops went down and smashed the Government seals and now we're sending detachments to seize the bourgeois newspaper offices."[27]

Reed noticed that two machine guns had been mounted at the entrance to Smolny and that there were military detachments in the courtyard.[28]

Until these early morning hours a single company of cadets with a few machine guns and an armored car could have easily captured the Military Revolutionary Committee, most of the Bolshevik leaders, and Smolny itself.[29] It was only in the evening of the twenty-third and the morning of the twenty-fourth that Smolny's defenses got serious attention. Now there were twenty-four machine guns available and a company of the Litovsky Regiment. During Tuesday cords of firewood were piled into the court as a barricade against rifle fire, trucks brought in food and munitions, cannon were emplaced before the columned portico and machine guns on the roof.[30]

LIII

The Coup d'État Begins

At midmorning on Tuesday the twenty-fourth there was still no certainty that the Bolsheviks would move against the Government or the Government against the Bolsheviks. An air of unreality prevailed. The well-to-do industrialist V. A. Auerbakh dropped in to see an old friend, P. I. Palchinsky, chief of Kerensky's Special Defense Council. His offices were in the War Ministry across from St. Isaac's Cathedral. The two friends hadn't seen each other for some time. Auerbakh asked Palchinsky what he thought about the black clouds on the horizon.

Palchinsky laughed. "That's just our regular thunderstorm. It will pass by and everything will be clear. You can sleep quietly."

"Well," said Auerbakh, "that I will. But will you sleep quietly?"

"Look," said Palchinsky. "They are calling me now to the Winter Palace and there I will learn the situation better. Drop by tomorrow."

Palchinsky went downstairs to his waiting limousine. Later in the day Auerbakh met a couple of other friends in the Government. They too recommended that he "sleep quietly." Nevertheless, he sent his wife away from Petrograd to spend a few days in Moscow. Just in case.[1]

The American ambassador, David Francis, a St. Louis politician, wrote a letter to his oldest son Tuesday morning. "It is reported," he said, "that a Bolshevik uprising or 'demonstration' is beginning on the other side of the river. The immediate cause is the suppression of four Bolshevik newspapers [sic] one of them Maxim Gorky's [sic]."

Francis went to the Foreign Office and had a long talk with Foreign Minister Tereshchenko.

"I expect a Bolshevik outbreak tonight," Tereshchenko said.

"If you can suppress it," Francis replied, "I hope it will occur."

"I think we can suppress it," Tereshchenko replied. "I hope it will take place whether we can or not—I am tired of this uncertainty and suspense."[2]

At the front Baron Budberg recorded a strange scene. The trenches were utterly quiet. The German artillery was silent fearing that if they fired their guns the Russian infantry would attack them. At night even the use of flares and rockets by the Germans had ended—apparently, Budberg thought, they had been assured they would not be attacked. Budberg was certain the Germans were awaiting only the success of the Bolsheviks which would give them victory without fighting. There were rumors that a cable had been laid connecting the Germans in front of the XIX Corps with a Bolshevik headquarters somewhere in the rear.

"In Petrograd," he recorded, "there is something in the wind. The new Bolshevik committee is continuously meeting in secret and getting something ready."[3]

There *was*, finally, more than something in the wind. The Bolshevik Central Committee met at 8 A.M.[4] Eleven nembers were present. Lenin was still in hiding. Stalin was at the newspaper office. Zinoviev was absent. Sverdlov was chairman. Kamenev proposed that no member of the committee be permitted to leave Smolny that day without special permission. All members of the Petersburg Committee were to stay in Smolny as well. Members were named for liaison with postal, telegraph, and railroad workers. One member was to keep the Provisional Government under observation. Negotiations with the left SRs were to be carried on. Trotsky proposed that a reserve headquarters be established at the Peter and Paul Fortress. Kamenev wanted a command point on the *Aurora* in case Smolny was destroyed.[5] Sverdlov was designated as liaison on all important questions. Weapons were passed out.[6]

About 9 A.M. a bulletin was sent to all military units: "The Petrograd Soviet is threatened with direct danger." The first leaflets went to the Peter and Paul Fortress, the second batch to the Grenadier Regiment which was directed to prepare a machine-gun command for the protection of Smolny and the Neva bridges. The cruiser *Aurora* was ordered into battle readiness.[7] A proclamation to workers was issued: "The enemies of the people have gone over during the night to the offensive."[8] The Petersburg Bolshevik Committee assembled at Smolny and demanded the immediate overthrow of the Provisional Government and the coming into power of the Soviet.

All of this has the *sound* of a vigorous offensive, of a final decision by Smolny to bring down the Provisional Government. However, in the shifting confusion of the times even this cannot be fully affirmed. There are dozens of tell-tale bits of evidence which suggest Smolny was not really preparing to attack Kerensky, but rather was preparing to defend itself against an attack by Kerensky—an attack which was never to come.[9]

The Government was largely unaware of what Smolny was doing. It had sent small detachments to protect the Telephone Exchange, post office, and telegraph offices. Patrols of cadets went into the streets. They halted cars and directed them to the Winter Palace courtyard. They set up traffic controls and about 3 P.M. an order was given to raise the Neva bridges. Thus, the Troitsky, Liteiny, and Nikolayevsky bridges were opened but the palace bridge was kept in use in order that troops and cadets could be shifted to the Winter Palace. The Bolsheviks did not interfere.[10] The only effect of this was to spread nervousness through the city. Crowds began to appear on the streets. Workers from the Vyborg quarter came to see what was going on. Bolshevik detachments tried to take back some bridges. There were brawls and arguments. Sometimes the Bolsheviks won. Sometimes the Government. No one seemed to want to fight. Some bridges went up and down several times.[11] The Military Revolutionary Committee gave no orders about the bridges but Ilyin-Zhenevsky sent detachments to control the Grenadiersky and the Sampsoniyevsky bridges. A bit later the Tuchkov Bridge across the Maly Neva was taken in hand. About 7 P.M. Bolshevik troops from the Volynsky and Pavlovsky regiments took over the Troitsky and Liteiny bridges, or at least the Petersburg and Vyborg approaches.[12]

What other acts did the Bolsheviks carry out in these preliminary hours of the coup d'état? Very few. They managed to persuade the Pavlovsk cadets and the Pavlovsk cavalry to stay in their barracks. They got the bicycle troops—forty men in all—to leave their posts at the Winter Palace.

Up to 6 P.M. not one shot had been fired. Streetcars rattled serenely through the streets. The stores were open. People strolled the Nevsky. Indeed, until 5 P.M. the Military Revolutionary Committee had not undertaken a single act which was not a response to some move by the Government. Then the pattern was broken. S. S. Pestkovsky together with a friend, Yu. Leshchinsky, was sent to take over the Central Telegraph Office. Neither man was armed. That wasn't thought necessary. The telegraph office was being guarded—for the Government—by units of the Kexholm Regiment, which was favorable to the Bolsheviks. Pestkovsky and Leshchinsky went to the office and talked to the manager, who said he wouldn't interfere. They then spoke to the head of the telegraph workers' union. The union was not very friendly but said it was all right for a commissar to sit in the union hall so long as the troops were removed. The "compromise" was agreed to and the telegraph office was considered to be under Bolshevik control.[13] There was a similar take-over of the Petrograd Telegraph Agency, the official news service, a little later. And, almost accidentally, a small unit of the Izmailovsky Regiment took charge of the Baltic Railroad Station, saying that it had come to maintain order.[14]

Still, the Bolsheviks were spending more time in talk than in action. Early in the evening they asked Kronshtadt to send their sailors into town[15] and ordered the *Aurora* to leave its berth and come up to the bridges.[16]

While this was going on Kerensky, always more partial to oratory than deeds, decided to carry his case to the Pre-Parliament. He told the parliamentarians at the Mariinsky Palace that his Government had worked out a means for turning over the land to the peasants even before the Constituent Assembly gathered in the immediate weeks ahead. Moreover, he was sending a delegation to Paris to discuss with the Allies the "tasks and aims of the war." In other words, Kerensky was now addressing himself for the first time to the basic demands of the people—land and peace. As for the current situation, he said, part of the Petrograd garrison was in a state of insurgency; Lenin was a state criminal and the Government had begun a judicial inquiry into all this.

He pledged his "mind, conscience and honor" to defend Petrograd. He and the Provisional Government were prepared to be killed but they would not betray the life, honor, or independence of the state. It was a theatrical speech in Kerensky's best tradition and it won him an ovation.[17]

But it did not win him what he wanted—a vote of confidence. Instead, after much wrangling, the Pre-Parliament declined to support Kerensky. It voted to condemn the Bolshevik uprising, to blame the Kerensky Government for the conditions which had given rise to it, to call for immediate grants of land and immediate peace, and decided that the task of combating the uprising be turned over to the Committee of Public Safety.

Kerensky told Dan and Gots that after such a resolution the Govern-

ment would fall by morning but he would go ahead and put down the
Bolshevik uprising on his own. Dan replied that Kerensky would only
destroy himself and the Revolution and that he had made it impossible for them to give him any support.[18]

However it seemed from the inside, the external appearance of Petrograd did not suggest that an uprising was in progress. The conservative newspaper *Rech* reported that up to 10 P.M. it was perfectly
plain that "nowhere, not even at one point in the city, had anything
serious happened." *Golos Soldata*, a Menshevik paper, reported that at
10 P.M. Petrograd was perfectly quiet and there were no clashes.[19]

There was one man in Petrograd who could not stand the slow pace
of events, the bowing across the barricades, the indecision in both
Smolny and the Winter Palace. He paced the apartment where he was
confined on the top floor of the big building at the edge of Lesnoi on
the Petrograd outskirts. This man, Lenin, was still in hiding, still
getting most of his information secondhand, still dependent on Fofanova and Party couriers to keep in touch.

Lenin had been left alone most of the day but, Soviet historians insist, he exchanged notes by courier with the Military Revolutionary
Committee.* As the day wore on he became more and more tense,
more and more certain that the time was now. He had felt this for six
weeks. He could not wait longer. It seemed to him the Central Committee was dawdling.[20] And no date and no hour had been set for the
uprising in spite of all his exhortations.

Fofanova had gone off to work. She was busy at her job at the
Devrien Publishing House on Vasilevsky Island until nearly 4 P.M.
when she heard that the Nikolayevsky Bridge over the Neva had been
raised—a sure sign of trouble. She hurried out to verify what she had
heard. The bridge, in fact, had been drawn up, but the Sampsoniyevsky Bridge was in the hands of the Red Guards. Fofanova
dropped in at the Vyborg Party headquarters to see if she could pick
up any further word for Lenin. There were alarming rumors, nothing more. She rushed back to her flat and told Lenin what she had
learned. Lenin listened, then went to his room. Soon he emerged with
a letter in his hand and asked her to deliver it personally to Nadezhda

* The exchange of notes is reported in several Soviet histories and memoirs.
However, no text of any notes from or to Lenin has ever been published. In fact,
there is no hard evidence that any instructions from Lenin were sent to Smolny
during the day. Any reports to him were probably oral. The point is not a small
one. It bears on the question of whether Lenin was directing the uprising. So far
as the day of the twenty-fourth is concerned there is no evidence that he was.

Krupskaya, who was at the Vyborg Party headquarters not far distant. It was now about 6 P.M.[21] and it was necessary, he said, to get on with the uprising this evening. He should be at Smolny this very minute.[22] "I don't understand them," he said of the Central Committee. "What are they afraid of? Just ask them if they have one hundred loyal soldiers or Red Guards with rifles. I don't need anything else!"[23]

Lenin's letter said:

> I am writing these lines on the evening of the 24th. The situation is critical in the extreme. In fact it is now absolutely clear that to delay the uprising would be fatal. . . . We must not wait! We may lose everything! Who must take power? It is not important at present. Let the Revolutionary Military Committee do it or "some other institution.". . .
>
> All districts, all regiments, all forces must be mobilized at once and must immediately send their delegations to the Revolutionary Military Committee and to the Central Committee of the Bolsheviks with the insistent demand that under no circumstances should power be left in the hands of Kerensky & Co—not under any circumstances; the matter must be decided without fail this very evening or this very night.
>
> History will not forgive revolutionaries for procrastination. . . . If we seize power today, we seize it not in opposition to the Soviets but on their behalf. . . . It would be a disaster, or a sheer formality, to await the wavering vote of October 25. The people have the right and are in duty bound to give directions to their representatives, even their best representatives and not to wait for them. . . .
>
> The government is tottering. It must be *given the death blow* at all costs. To delay action is fatal."[24]

In the fourth and fifth editions of Lenin's works this letter is headed: "Letter to Central Committee Members." However, in fact, it bore no such designation and was intended to be distributed to regional Party units for the purpose of bringing pressure to bear on the Central Committee—a fact which is clear from the text. Lenin's note suggests that, in his view, even as late as the evening of the twenty-fourth the Bolsheviks had not actually gone over to carrying out a coup. They were still, he believed, on the defensive against a supposed effort by the Provisional Government to wipe them out.

In other words on the very eve of the coup d'état Lenin was not in charge of the plans for the uprising and had no reason to believe that his colleagues actually intended to go through with the overturn of the Kerensky Government. At this eleventh hour once again he was appealing over the head of the Central Committee to try to compel them to act.[25] The letter is an indication of the almost total lack of liaison between Lenin and the Central Committee and Lenin's deep distrust of the revolutionary resolve of his colleagues. It also places in doubt the extent and reliability of the "messages" which supposedly were exchanged between Lenin and Smolny in these days—messages which have never come to light in the extensive publication of Lenin's works or in Soviet historiography.

After handing over Lenin's letter to Krupskaya at the Vyborg headquarters[26] Fofanova returned to Lenin about 8 P.M. She reported that the palace bridge was still in service because the Government was planning to move the Women's Battalion into the Winter Palace.[27] She brought a note, too, which angered Lenin.[28] He immediately sent her off with another letter demanding Central Committee permission to come to Smolny.[29] Fofanova returned about 9 P.M. with an answer which still did not satisfy Lenin. He sent another note to Krupskaya, saying that if Fofanova was not back by 11 P.M. he would act as he saw fit.[30]

It is difficult to find logical rationale for Lenin's conduct. He was the leader of the Bolshevik party. Why should he have chosen to stay in hiding instead of joining his comrades at Smolny and participating directly with them in the preparations for the uprising? There was an order out for his arrest, but the Government was powerless to carry out such an order in Smolny. By the final days all the Bolshevik leaders were subject to arrest, but nothing was being done to apprehend them.

It is equally difficult to understand why Lenin's associates did not insist that he join them in Smolny. True, the Party leadership had been reluctant for Lenin to leave Helsingfors, and only after his ultimatum about resigning from the Central Committee did they "invite" him to return to Petrograd. Once back in Petrograd he was confined to the Fofanova apartment. It was apparent that Lenin's sense of timing and that of his associates did not coincide—they moving at a deliberate pace, reacting at each point only to his most insistent urgings.

Lenin's liaison with the Central Committee was apparently handled through Stalin, who had indicated that he did not share Lenin's sense of the immediacy of the situation. The possibility exists that Stalin and some of his associates preferred to keep Lenin at a distance because of his feeling that the uprising had to be carried out prior to the All-

Russian Soviet meeting. Or there may have been more sympathy than has been documented for the Kamenev-Zinoviev view that the uprising itself was not needed, that power was certain to fall into the hands of the Bolsheviks without a struggle once the All-Russian Soviet met.

There remains the question of why Lenin himself, in a state of agitation and tension, did not long before the evening of the twenty-fourth take matters into his own hands. He stayed in the apartment all day on the twenty-fourth, boiling with frustration and sending off notes like a schoolboy for permission to come to Smolny. There had been a whiff of this attitude in the whole episode of his staying in the underground in Finland rather than insisting on coming to the center of activity.

However, the habits of half a lifetime must be considered. Lenin since the late 1890s had spent his life except for a short period in 1905–6 far from the center of affairs—in Siberia, in exile abroad, or underground in his own country. It may have seemed more natural to him to be away from the center. And it also may have been more compatible with the state of his nerves. His absence may in a sense have been deliberate—to avoid another attack of depression such as he suffered in late June and early July.

Or it is possible that at the last moment he had actually fallen into another one of his fits of despondency. This is suggested by the fact that after storming back into Petrograd and lashing the Central Committee into reluctant action, after insisting on getting the insurrection going, after excoriating Kamenev and Zinoviev for their doubts, hesitations, and opposition to the coup, Lenin subsided into a state of virtual inactivity.

So far as the record goes—and it is obviously incomplete for this period—Lenin engaged in only a minimum of activity from October 19 to late in the day of October 24. He attended one or possibly two meetings in the period, secondary meetings, not meetings of the Central Committee. He wrote a note or two and worked on some articles. But on October 20, 21, 22, and 23 he seems to have been virtually inactive—and this at a moment when the coup of which he had dreamed, fought, and planned was supposed to be coming to a head.[31]

It is one more strange aspect of the Bolshevik coup that the leader who frantically insisted on it being carried through played no substantive role in the final days of preparation.

In any event the midevening of the twenty-fourth found him still in hiding at the Fofanova apartment.

Soon after Fofanova left, Eino Rahja appeared. He was a Finn who had become close to Lenin during his Finnish underground time and was now acting as a kind of bodyguard. Rahja told Lenin the Government had ordered the bridges raised and that the Vyborg quarter was being cut off from the city center. If Kerensky's tactics succeeded, he might move on the city, quarter by quarter, bringing it all under his control.

Lenin began to pace the room from one corner to another. Suddenly, he told Rahja he must immediately find Stalin. Rahja said that would be difficult. It might take hours. Perhaps Stalin was at the print shop, possibly at Smolny. There was no transportation. Rahja would have to go by foot.

"Well, then," said Lenin, "we'll go to Smolny."

Lenin scrawled a note to Fofanova:

"I've gone where you didn't want me to go. Good-bye. Ilyich."[32]

He and Rahja started out. They were in luck. They caught a streetcar, nearly empty, which took them to the corner of the Botanical Gardens, the end of the line. At the Liteiny Bridge, there was a detachment of Red Guards. They brushed past them and at the middle of the bridge they saw that the other end was held by Government soldiers who were asking for passes. The two men were dressed in old clothes. Lenin had on his wig and wore a cap and a dirty kerchief around his neck. A group of workers was arguing with the soldiers and the two men took advantage of the argument to slip past the guards. They walked down Liteiny Prospekt and soon ran into two cadets who demanded passes. Rahja was armed with two revolvers. He whispered to Lenin to move ahead, he would deal with the Junkers. Lenin faded off into the shadows and after an argument Rahja managed to join him. The cadets had decided they were just a couple of tramps.

At Smolny they were halted at the gates. Rahja had two passes but they were white. The color had been changed to red. Rahja began to shout that they were not admitting a member of the Petrograd Soviet. The diversion succeeded and the two managed to slip through the control and into Smolny where they went up to the second floor. Rahja brought Trotsky and Stalin to Lenin. Quickly, they reported on the situation. As they talked three men came into the room—the Mensheviks Dan and N. I. Liber and Gots, the SR. One of them took a package out of his pocket, unwrapped a sandwich of butter, sausage, and cheese. He raised it to his mouth, lifted his head, saw Lenin, recognized him despite his disguise, gulped, and the three men went back to the Assembly Hall.[33]

Lenin, Stalin, and Rahja then went to a small room where the

Bolshevik leadership had assembled.[34] The uprising for which Lenin had fought so long, so hard, so bitterly, the cause to which he had dedicated his life, was finally, if shakily and even reluctantly, getting under way.

A formal timetable for the rising was never set. It simply went forward propelled by the momentum of events.*

* Small wonder Soviet historians are confused as to when the coup d'état began. They met in formal scholarly session in 1962, forty-five years after the events of October 1917, to try to decide when it started. The meeting broke up in violent disagreement. Academician I. I. Mints insisted it began on the morning of October 24. He was supported by Ye. N. Gorodetsky and V. I. Startsev. Other historians thought it began October 22 or on the afternoon of October 24. The next year a new conference was held to discuss the question. It got no closer to agreement and finally decided that the question "requires further study." (Ye. F. Yerkalov, *Oktyabrskoye Vooruzhennoye Vosstaniye v Petrograd*, pp. 336–37.)

No more evidence is needed to establish the random, accidental, unplanned nature of the famous "revolution."

LIV

The Winter Palace

The Winter Palace stood gloomy in the late October afternoon, its great bulk shielding the city from the granite-bound Neva with a quarter of a mile of ever-repeating ensembles of windows and columns—the palace proper, the old Hermitage of Catherine II, the small Hermitage, and the new Hermitage, gigantic buildings which dominated the city and stood as the symbol of the Russian Empire and the Romanov heritage.

Now, in the waning October days, the vast pile seemed to absorb into the rusty colors of its façade what little light filtered from the gray skies. Along the walls that faced the stone acres of Palace Square was heaped cord after cord of firewood, thousands of cords, the normal housekeeping precaution required to supply the hundreds of fireplaces and furnaces which kept the chill from palace suites during the long Russian winter. There was cordwood along the palace, around the Alexander Column, and beside the remarkable arch of the General Staff.

On the afternoon of October 25 more activity than usual could be observed. Outside the palace, as had been true for days, military men moved about, many wearing the rosettes and visored caps of cadets at the military schools. Beginning at midmorning they had piled cords of wood in the form of a seven-foot barricade to protect the main palace entrance facing the square. At intervals along the wooden barrier they mounted machine guns. Approaches to the sidewalk were blocked by more cordwood. The barricade protected access to the interior courtyard of the palace which lay beyond the main entrance. Within this court stood hundreds of horses belonging to Cossack troops and to the Mikhailovsky artillery school battery which manned three-inch guns at the approach to the palace. At the main entrance stood an armored car. It could not be started because someone, presumably a Bolshevik, had stolen the magneto.

Kerensky had moved the Provisional Government into the Winter Palace in July. The Government occupied the second-floor rooms of the palace with windows looking out on the Admiralty and the Neva. These had formed the Imperial suite of Nicholas II and Alexandra Fyodorovna. Kerensky convened formal meetings in the Malachite Chamber, the most Russian of the palace rooms, adorned with malachite columns, pilasters, fireplaces, tables, and vases—all worked from the green fairy-tale stone of the Urals.

On the third floor in the former suite of Alexander II Kerensky had his personal quarters with a view of the Admiralty spire.

The Government and its officials ordinarily went in and out by the Saltykov entrance and staircase, that is, the staircase opposite the Admiralty Building, not the main entrance on Palace Square or the marble Jordan entrance on the Neva side which the Czars employed in the annual January ceremony of the blessing of the waters.

Most of the enormous building—it had fifteen hundred rooms—was occupied not by the Government but by a hospital for war invalids established by the Empress at the outbreak of war. This filled the rooms on the Neva side and the rooms around the interior courtyard. There were more than five hundred patients in the palace on October 25, together with a large staff of nurses and doctors. The staff came and went by the Jordan entrance from the Neva embankment. Rooms on the third floor with a view of the Palace Square were occupied by the convalescents.

Second-floor rooms overlooking the square had been turned into a dormitory for the Junkers who were guarding the Provisional Government. They used "Their Majesties" entrance on Palace Square. The other entrance on the square, the commandant's entrance, led to service quarters on the lower floors and to the entresol between the lower and middle floor. There was no access to Government suites from this entrance.

Because of danger that the Germans might capture Petrograd, most of the art treasures had been packed for shipment for Moscow, particularly from the three Hermitages. Valuable furniture, sculpture, paintings, and carpets in the suites used for officers and barracks had also been packed but not the furnishings of the Imperial suite. Wooden shipping cases stood in the corridors and anterooms. In some rooms the furniture and walls had been covered with white sheets. In others couches and cots had been installed for secretaries and guards. In the section occupied by the Junkers mattresses had been spread over the floors, and ordinary wooden tables and garden benches brought in to replace the palace treasures.

Just before noon on October 25 automobiles and *izvozchiki* had delivered to the Saltykov entrance, one after another, the Ministers of Kerensky's government: N. M. Kishkin, State Controller S. A. Smirnov, Economic Counsellor S. M. Tretyakov, Naval Minister Adm. D. N. Verderevsky, Interior Minister A. M. Nikitin, Agriculture Minister S. L. Maslov, Justice Minister P. N. Malyantovich, Minister of Communications A. V. Liverovsky, and the rest.[1]

To their surprise they discovered that Kerensky was no longer in the Winter Palace. In fact, he was no longer in Petrograd. The Ministers had last seen him when they filed out of the Malachite Chamber about 2 A.M. that day, tired and worried, after a session at which Kerensky had appeared even more jumpy than usual.[2] After the Ministers left, Kerensky didn't feel safe alone in the Winter Palace.[3] He spent the rest of the night at the General Staff Building, ordering up troops (which never came), arguing with his military advisers, and receiving alarming reports of Bolshevik activity. Kerensky and his deputy Konovalov got back to the Winter Palace about 7 A.M. and lay down for a little rest. When Kerensky awakened, he found that his telephone had been cut off. Looking out the window, he saw that the palace bridge was now guarded by Bolshevik sailors. Kerensky decided he must leave Petrograd, go to the front, rally reliable troops, and return to save the capital.

This was easier said than done. The Bolsheviks had disabled all available cars.

About 10 A.M. Ensign Boris Ippolitovich Knirsha was alone in the motor pool when he was ordered by Colonel Polkovnikov to locate two automobiles in running condition. Kerensky was going to Tosno to meet the troops on route to Petrograd. Polkovnikov thought the British Embassy might provide the cars. Knirsha and Ensign Sobolev went to the British Embassy but got a refusal.[4] They went to Vladimir Nabokov, whom they found still taking his morning bath, and asked whether they could have his car. Somewhat disconcerted Nabokov told them his Benz landau was hardly suitable for a long journey.[5] Then, Knirsha called Prince Sidamon-Eristov, Chief of Militia, who thought he might be able to provide one car. The army quartermaster was no help. Neither was the Italian Embassy.[6] The worried ensigns saw a car flying an American flag standing outside a house. The chauffeur said it belonged to the Americans. (It was in fact a Renault belonging to Assistant Military Attaché E. Francis Rigg.[7]) The car was waiting to pick up Secretary Sheldon Whitehouse. The two ensigns told Whitehouse and his Russian brother-in-law, Baron Ramsey, they wanted the car for Kerensky. According to Knirsha the Americans agreed Kerensky could have the car but wanted to get his personal assurances. The four went to the General Staff Building where Kerensky convinced them he needed the car. Whitehouse pointed to thirty cars parked outside the Winter Palace. Not one, Kerensky said, would run. They bowed to Kerensky's wishes but asked that the American flag be removed from the tonneau. (It wasn't.[8])

Soon Kerensky, accompanied by several aides, emerged and got into an open Pierce-Arrow. Where this machine came from has never been made clear. Perhaps it was provided by Sidamon-Eristov.

Knirsha got into the Renault which was ordered to precede Kerensky. However, the chauffeur of the Renault did not know where they were going. He started his car and made several wide circles of the Palace Square, Kerensky following in the Pierce-Arrow. Hundreds of persons witnessed the curious spectacle. Finally, the Renault chauffeur was waved to go through the General Staff Arch. He got another signal and proceeded down the Morskyaya past the Mariinsky Palace. More hundreds watched the pantomime. Finally, the chauffeur pulled to a stop on the Voznesensky and asked directions. He was ordered to go on the Zabalkansky Prospekt. He moved ahead slowly, and as the cars approached the Catherine Canal the Pierce-Arrow sped ahead at a fast clip. They went out the Pulkovo Highway and reached the palace at Gatchina about noon.[9]

Riding in the open, Kerensky, of course, was seen by thousands. The bailiff of the Pre-Parliament, just gathering in the Mariinsky Palace, told the parliamentarians that Kerensky had been seen crossing the square. What this meant no one could figure out.[10] Nor could anyone guess that this was Kerensky's last public appearance in Petrograd.

From Gatchina Kerensky continued on to Pskov and the headquarters of the northern front. The chauffeur of the Renault ran into a stone on the highway and the car was returned, slightly damaged, to the American Embassy the next day. Had Kerensky delayed his departure an hour more, he might not have made his escape because forces of the Military Revolutionary Committee were beginning to surround the Winter Palace.[11]

A. V. Liverovsky, Minister of Communications, got to the palace about 11:30 A.M. He had paid the *izvozchik* six rubles to bring him from the Ministry and gave ten rubles to the porter who found the *iz-*

vozchik for him. Most of the Ministers had already assembled and all were shocked to be told by Konovalov that Kerensky had left the city and was going by car to meet troops coming to Petrograd to support the Government. Tretyakov told Nabokov that Kerensky had simply abandoned them.[12] The Army Commissar Stankevich told Gen. Mikhail Diterikhs by telephone at Mogilev that it had been impossible to keep Kerensky from leaving.[13] The circumstances of Kerensky's flight suggested panic.

There was no reason for anything other than recriminations on the part of the Ministers. Petrograd, except for the central section embracing the Winter Palace, the General Staff, the Admiralty, the Mariinsky Palace, and the War Ministry on St. Isaac's Square, was in the hands of the Bolsheviks.

The take-over had been improvised almost higgledy-piggledy and virtually no force had been employed. Stimulated by Lenin, the Military Revolutionary Committee had finally begun to act with some energy. It took over the suburban railroad stations and roads connecting with Peterhof in order to prevent more cadets from coming in from Oranienbaum. About 2 A.M. the Nicholas Station and Znamenskaya Square were occupied. A commissar went to the power station and got the workers to cut off electricity to Government-held buildings. Another commissar with a few soldiers from the Kexholm Regiment persuaded the night shift at the post office to accept their authority. A Kexholm commissar called the Central Telephone Exchange and asked that service to the Winter Palace and the General Staff be cut off but the exchange refused. Later a Kexholm detachment took over the exchange after many of the women switchboard operators fled into the street. It had been guarded by three Junkers. The *Aurora* came up to the Nikolayevsky Bridge about 3:30 A.M., accompanied by Trawler No. 15,[14] threw a power line ashore, and the bridge was brought down. About 6 A.M. a sailors' detachment went to the State Bank and sent away a small guard of Junkers. Telephone service to the General Staff and Winter Palace was cut at 7 A.M. However, the interruption was not complete. A number of telephones in both buildings continued in service to the end. During the morning the newspapers *Birzhevye Vedomosti, Russkaya Volya,* and Burtsev's *Obshcheye Delo* were shut down. Burtsev was arrested and taken to the Peter and Paul Fortress.[15]

It was typical of the confusion that the Ministers were not aware of how much of the city was under Bolshevik control. The action had occurred too late for the morning papers which came out with headlines that indicated the coup had not started. *Izvestiya* warned against the Bolsheviks' "mindless adventure." *Novaya Zhizn* advised the Bolsheviks: "Don't fire first!" The Menshevik *Rabochaya Gazeta* said "hope is not yet lost" for a compromise.[16]

But, in fact, with a handful of troops and a few sailors, the Bolsheviks, more by persuasion than by force, had already placed under their control the principal institutions of the city. Bolshevik troops patrolled the streets. They had easily won the "battle of the bridges." More naval vessels and more sailors were arriving from Kronshtadt and the Baltic. The dispatch of Government troops into Petrograd was barred by Bolshevik control of the stations and rail lines entering the city. Meanwhile, most of the famous regiments simply sat in their barracks and did nothing. They were, they said, neutral. They carried out no one's order, either Government or Bolshevik.

The game was over although typically no one realized this. After an hour or two of sleep on a couch with his comrades in Room No. 14 of Smolny, Lenin sat down with a glass of tea to write a manifesto to his fellow Russians announcing: "The Provisional Government has been deposed. State Power has been taken into the hands of the organ of the Petrograd Soviet of workers and soldier deputies—the Military Revolutionary Committee, standing at the head of the Petrograd proletariat and garrison.

"Hail the Revolution of workers, soldiers and peasants!"[17]

Lenin turned to Trotsky with a tired smile:

"Too sudden a transition from the underground and the regime of [Justice Minister] Pereverzev to power . . . *Es schwindelt*. It makes one dizzy."

Lenin raised his hand and made circles around his forehead to convey the dizziness his sudden accession to power had brought.[18]

Had not Lenin issued the proclamation, few citizens of Petrograd would have believed a coup had occurred. Up to this point, so far as any historian has been able to discover, not a shot had been fired. Not one life had been lost. The appearance of the city was close to normal.

De Robien noted that there were not even any of the usual trucks careering around the streets "with their loads of *tovariches* in heroic poses, and in spite of the hallucinations of a few madmen, there had been no fighting." Several diplomats had gone to Smolny on small errands—permits for gasoline, guards for embassies. They had been treated with courtesy.[19] British Ambassador Buchanan said the Bolsheviks met with practically no resistance "as the Government had neglected to organize any force for their own protection." He took a walk along the quays to Palace Square and found things "more or less normal except for the groups of armed soldiers stationed near the bridges."[20]

Crowds in the streets moved freely. The trams continued to circulate even through Palace Square and past the General Staff Arch. Smirnov on his way to the Winter Palace at 11 A.M. had been struck by the business-as-usual atmosphere. Stores were open. Shoppers went in and out. There were no unusual troop concentrations—except for the Junkers around the Winter Palace. And the Junkers showed no sign of alarm. They were sitting at the entrances, telling stories, laughing. Shidlovsky found the streets "extraordinarily quiet." Nowhere were guns going off, troops facing troops. It was just another late October day—October 25, or November 7 by the new calendar.

The peaceful façade was slightly dented at Mariinsky Palace. Under Lenin's pressure the Military Revolutionary Committee decided to take over Mariinsky Palace, where the Pre-Parliament was meeting. A commissar was sent off with a detachment of troops and about 12:30 P.M. they announced they were occupying the building. Nabokov walked out with Milyukov. Both expected to be arrested but they were permitted to leave without interference.[21] However, Education Minister S. N. Prokopovich was arrested a bit later on the embankment near the Winter Canal.[22] Sukhanov showed up at the Mariinsky a few minutes later. He was halted by a group of workers and sailors, one of whom recognized him. They had just chased out the Pre-Parliament, they said. Did he by any chance know where the members of the Government were? They had orders to arrest the Ministers but they hadn't been able to find any of them.[23] Sukhanov said he couldn't help them and was permitted to leave. A bit later the Admiralty was taken over. By this time Kronstadt sailors were landing beside the Nikolayevsky Bridge—2,762 sailors and 943 soldiers. There were 1,061 more sailors in the crews of the vessels.[24]

Within the Winter Palace there was squabbling. The Ministers didn't trust Polkovnikov so they fired him and put the Kadet Minister Kishkin in charge of defense with Gen. Ya. G. Bagratuni as his military chief. Then they had some sandwiches—sausage and cheese on white bread.[25] The decision to put Kishkin in charge didn't help matters very much. The basic problem, as Polkovnikov had at 10:15 that morning telegraphed Dukhonin at Mogilev, was that the Bolsheviks had simply taken over, the Junkers had not opposed them, and the Cossacks were staying in their barracks, creating a situation in which, as Polkovnikov said, the Provisional Government was "in danger of losing power."[26]

In fact, it already had. However, the Ministers didn't realize this and they were encouraged when a detachment of three hundred Cossacks of the 14th Don Regiment showed up at the palace. But Admiral Verderevsky refused to be heartened. As an old military man he thought nothing they were doing made any sense. "I don't understand what this meeting was called for," he said "and why we are sitting here. We haven't any kind of real strength. There's nothing we can undertake and it's senseless to prolong our discussions." But the Ministers insisted that another effort must be made to bring the Cossack regiments to their side. Word came in at 1:35 P.M. of the Bolshevik seizure of the Mariinsky Palace and the closing of the Pre-Parliament. Was there any way to take back the palace? General Bagratuni was doubtful. In fact, he said, there wasn't enough strength even to defend the Winter Palace.[27]

In midafternoon Kishkin, Palchinsky, and Pyotr Rutenberg went over to the General Staff Building to handle the general defense of the Provisional Government. They had two telephone numbers: No. 5-76-62 and No. 2-65-40.[28]

Colonel Ananyev, chief of the Engineer Cadet School, was named to direct the perimeter defense of the Winter Palace. He called the officers of the units into the White Chamber and for the first time, showing them rough sketches of the palace, gave them precise areas for defense.

The Cossacks and the women's detachment were assigned to the rooms on the first floor of the palace on the Millionnaya Street side.[29] The women's detachment was the 2nd Company of the 1st Petrograd Women's Battalion. It was not, as often referred to, the so-called Women's Battalion of Death. Rather, it was a shock company of mixed social composition, the majority coming from working-class families, many from the provinces, and including quite a few Cossack girls.

The company of 137 members had been brought into the Winter Palace about noon October 24, after being told they were to participate in a parade. Many were angered when they learned that, instead, they were to defend the Winter Palace. They had signed up, they said, to fight the foreign foe at the front, not their brother Russians at home.*

Lt. Alexander Sineguba headed a detachment of Engineer School cadets which he led into the Winter Palace in the early afternoon. He found disorder everywhere. The Cossacks were rude and quarrelsome. Many officers and some cadets had been drinking. One grumbled that he had served the Czar for ten years as a colonel, had been thrown out of service by the Revolution, and "now they want us to defend them."

---

* The Women's Battalion became the subject of sensational stories and propaganda after the fall of the Winter Palace. Many people in Petrograd—and around the world—believed they had been raped and slaughtered by the Red Guards. A careful investigation carried out in November 1917, in which the Bolsheviks permitted an independent commission of Mensheviks and Kadets to participate, found no basis for the stories. One woman had committed suicide for personal reasons. (Kh. M. Astrakhan, Istoriya SSR, 1965, No. 5, pp. 93–97.)

Another praised the wonderful wines an old palace steward had brought to the mess hall.

When Ananyev interrupted these discussions to give out staff dispositions, angry arguments erupted. An officer said his cadets "were too tired" and should be put into the reserve. One man after another protested his assignment.

Ananyev warned the officers that they must halt the entry of Bolshevik agitators who were already at work among most of the defense units. Hardly had the defense dispositions been made when an officer of the Konstantinov artillery cadets rushed in. The commandant of the school had ordered the cadets back to their barracks along with the three-inch guns they were manning. The cadets marched out the main palace entrance about 6 P.M. taking their four guns. (They were persuaded to leave two behind.) The cadets were arrested by a detachment of the Pavlovsky Regiment which took their guns and mounted them against the palace.[30] Lieutenant Sineguba went in search of the commissary. He found it guarded by a fat, clean-shaven, important-looking lackey. Inside there was nothing but tobacco smoke, the heavy smell of wine and vodka, and the loud voices of drunken officers. Sineguba fled from the place, muttering under his breath: "Feasting in the time of the plague!"

Things went from bad to worse. Some Cossacks, hostile from the beginning, heard that the artillery men had left. They held a meeting and voted to leave too. Lieutenant Sineguba was ordered to take his cadets and replace the Cossacks on the defenses of the main gate— also to try to persuade the Cossacks to leave their machine guns behind.

Sineguba railed at the Cossacks. They shrugged their shoulders and replied: "When we came here we were told everyone would be here, all the military schools, the artillery and what did we find? Jews and women. Moreover the Government is half full of Jews. And the Russian people are with Lenin."

Sineguba retorted: "Lenin's whole gang are Jews and you saw some Jews here. Well, there are Jews and Jews. And you miserable Cossacks, you beasts and cowards are leaving women and children behind and running off."

The words did not stop the Cossacks. But they did leave their machine guns in a heap in a corner. They made their way out by the Winter Canal entrance to join the Bolshevik agitators who had promised them a free exit.[31]

What was happening within the palace was quite simple. There were hundreds of doors and entrances. Many of them the defenders did not know existed. Just beyond the palace complex on the Millionnaya lay the barracks of the Pavlovsky and Preobrazhensky regiments. The Preobrazhensky Regiment was "neutral." The Pavlovsky favored the Bolsheviks and provided easy access into the palace from the Winter Canal side where none of the entrances were guarded.

Colonel Ananyev tried to get the Junkers to build barricades of cordwood along the Winter Canal and also on the Palace Bridge side. Neither of these orders was carried out.[32]

LV

Before the Storm

As the afternoon wore on nothing seemed to change outside the palace. The Bolsheviks had thrown up picket lines after seizing the Mariinsky Palace so that the approaches to the palace had now been cut off. (They forgot about the War Ministry on St. Isaac's Square and didn't occupy it until about 6 P.M.) The French correspondent Claude Anet arrived on the scene about midafternoon. He was halted by a Bolshevik patrol near the Admiralty but passed through after showing his correspondent's card. The square itself was empty. The palace defenders seemed to be mostly children (many of the cadets were teen-agers). Anet entered the palace and moved from one empty room to another.[1]

Nabokov got a telephoned invitation in midafternoon to join the Ministers at the palace. He took a streetcar to Konnogvardeisky Boulevard and walked to Palace Square. He went up to a soldier, showed his palace pass, and was permitted through with no questions. He found the Ministers chatting idly. Tereshchenko was the most optimistic. If they could hold out forty-eight hours, troops from the front would save them. They had telephoned many prominent citizens asking them to rally at the palace. Nabokov was the only one who showed up. There was really nothing for Nabokov to do. After a word with a journalist, L. M. Klyachko-Lvov, he left and got home without difficulty.[2]

John Reed rose late on the morning of the twenty-fifth. When he went down to the Nevsky, a soldier in front of the State Bank said,

"No more Government." Reed bought a copy of *Rabochi Put* which told him the Soviet had seized power. He went around to the Mariinsky Palace and saw Alexeyev trying to pass the picket lines. "I am General Alexeyev," he was saying. 'As your superior officer and a member of the Council of the Republic I demand to be allowed to pass." He was not passed. Reed, accompanied by Louise Bryant, Albert Rhys Williams, and Alex Gumberg, wandered toward the Winter Palace. Reed's Smolny pass was not honored so they tried their American passports. This got them through. Reed and his friends walked up to the Malachite Chamber but couldn't get in. The Americans strolled around the palace for a while and poked into one of the dormitories where a cadet was drinking from a bottle of white wine.

By the time Reed left the palace the picket lines around the square seemed to have disappeared. He and his friend went to the Hôtel de France for dinner. They were interrupted in the middle of the meal by a pale-faced waiter who said they were going to put out the lights because "there will be much shooting."[3]

Zinaida Gippius and her husband went for a walk down the Sergiyevskaya. The day was gray and quiet. The walls were covered with posters proclaiming "The Government has been overthrown."

"What a beautiful little picture!" Gippius exclaimed. "Between the Revolution and what is now happening is the difference between March and October, between the beaming heavens of spring and to-day's dirty, dark grey slimy clouds."[4]

That was, indeed, the essence of the difference between the two revolutions. In the spring the city had been buoyant, excited, *everyone* went into the streets—workers, soldiers, citizens of all classes. There had been true Russian *sobornost*, togetherness, a feeling that the old had been smashed and an exciting path to the future had been broken through. Hundreds of thousands jammed their way to the Tauride Palace. Not to do anything. Just to *be* there. And on this bleak and gusty October day only a handful of Petrograd citizens knew or cared what was going on. By best estimates there were perhaps 1,500 or 2,000 in the force at the command of the besieged Ministers in the Winter Palace. The Bolsheviks had mustered 6,000 or 7,000 men— 2,500 troops, almost entirely Pavlovsky and Kexholm, 2,500 Kronshtadt sailors, and possibly—just possibly—as many as 2,500 Red Guards.[5] Hardly a popular uprising.

Lenin had been in a frenzy since 11 A.M. because of the delay in taking the Winter Palace. He expected that the palace would be occupied some time before dawn. Why this fell through like so many things that day was not clear. Trotsky blamed the overelaborate plans worked out by Podvoisky and V. A. Antonov-Ovseyenko.[6] That was only part of it. From the moment Lenin arrived at Smolny he fired note after note and order after order to Podvoisky—often just two or three words. "Have you taken the Central Telephone station and telegraph?" "Have you taken the stations and bridges?"[7] But in spite of Lenin's words none of the objectives was taken with dispatch—in part due to lack of forces, in part due to the general slackness. It was only Lenin who was in such a hurry. Podvoisky's plan provided for taking the palace on the morning of the twenty-fifth. But he did not have enough troops. The Soviet was opening and the palace had not yet been seized nor the Ministers arrested. Lenin demanded action. Otherwise he would have the Military Committee shot—instantly![8]

When Lenin issued his declaration that the Provisional Government had been overthrown at 10 A.M., Podvoisky promised he would capture the palace by noon. But this estimate proved no better than the others. He only got around to taking the Mariinsky Palace a little before 1 P.M. He offered a new estimate for the Winter Palace: 3 P.M. This was to be the "conclusive hour."[9]

But the clock was running against Lenin. At 2:35 P.M. at Smolny a meeting of the Petrograd Soviet was called to order. Trotsky spoke. The Revolution had succeeded. Not a drop of blood had been shed. True, the Winter Palace still held out. But its fall could be expected in the next few minutes.[10]

Sukhanov got to Smolny about 3 P.M. When he entered the auditorium, a bald clean-shaven man was speaking. The voice was hoarse and somehow familiar. Suddenly Sukhanov realized—it was Lenin emerging from his four months underground. "Now begins a new era in the history of Russia," Lenin was saying, "and this third Russian revolution must finally lead to the victory of Socialism."[11] There was nothing Lenin could say about the Winter Palace.

At 6:30 P.M., there seeming to be no particular reason against it, the besieged Ministers walked up to the third floor of the Winter Palace and there in Kerensky's private dining room dinner was served—soup, fish, and artichokes. The old palace lackeys in their green service dress waited on them. What they had for dessert was not recorded.[12] Liverovsky was much impressed by the massive silver spoons dated 1843.[13]

At the identical moment the Military Revolutionary Committee at Smolny finally put its plan for seizing the Winter Palace into motion. The details had been worked out (after a tongue-lashing by Lenin) by Antonov-Ovseyenko and, according to his own claim, by a brash young Baltic sailor named Pyotr Malkov.[14] It provided that an ultimatum to surrender be sent to the Winter Palace at 9 P.M. In case of refusal the Peter and Paul Fortress would hoist a red lantern. The cruiser *Aurora* would fire three blank rounds, followed by live fire from the Peter and Paul Fortress. The Bolshevik forces would then storm the palace.[15]

About 6 P.M. Podvoisky telephoned Antonov-Ovseyenko at the Peter and Paul Fortress that Lenin was demanding seizure of the Winter Palace before the Soviet met that evening. Antonov-Ovseyenko sent two bicyclists to the General Staff Building with an ultimatum. The Government and its forces were to surrender within twenty minutes or the guns of the fortress, the *Aurora,* the *Amur,* and other warships would open up. The ultimatum expired at 7:10 P.M. At the moment the ultimatum was being delivered G. I. Chudnovsky, a leader of the Military Revolutionary Committee, was himself within the Winter Palace. He had gone there to talk to the Oranienbaum Junkers who promised him safe conduct and let him come into the palace. When Palchinsky, the palace chief of staff, discovered him, he cried: "Arrest him! Arrest him!" But the Junkers said they had given their word of honor. In the end Chudnovsky was let go to return to the besieging forces. The Junkers decided they would quit the fight and made their way out of the palace. A second committeeman, P. V. Dashkevich, also entered the palace, was arrested, then released, after argument, through the children's entrance on the Neva side. He promptly reported to the Bolsheviks that the entrances on the Neva side were practically unguarded.[16]

The Government Ministers had been in touch with Moscow. There were no signs of revolutionary activities there. This reassured them somewhat. Gvozdev telephoned the Central Committee of the SRs to see if they could help out. Verderevsky talked with Tsentroflot, the naval command. Stankevich had talked with Staff at Mogilev. He was told the Ministers must hold out for twenty-four or forty-eight hours if help was to reach them.[17]

When the Ministers received the Bolshevik ultimatum at about five minutes after seven, it had only five more minutes to run. There was nothing but gloom in Kerensky's state dining room. Nikitin recalled that he telephoned G. I. Shreider, head of the City Duma, for aid but Shreider said there was nothing he could do. Malyantovich noted in his diary: "Around us was emptiness; within us was emptiness." Despite this the Ministers decided not to reply to the ultimatum.[18]

While the Ministers vainly telephoned around town, the General Staff Building across the square was quietly turned over to the Bolsheviks. It seems to have occurred in the same offhand way in which almost everything happened on October 25. The ultimatum had been handed in at the Staff Building. Kishkin, the Government's chief of defense, and General Bagratuni took the document across the square to confer with the Ministers in the Winter Palace. One of the two bicyclists was sent back to the Peter and Paul Fortress with a request for ten minutes more. Within this ten minutes the quartermaster general at Staff, N. N. Poradelov, was to receive an answer from the Government—would they bow to the ultimatum or not?

While this was going on General V. A. Cheremisov, commander of the northern front, called Staff. He wanted to know where the Government was and what was the situation. "The situation is unconditionally lost," Poradelov told him. The general wanted to talk to the palace but the Government was tied up discussing the ultimatum. He waited on the line. Poradelov waited too. He rang back the palace and got no answer. Bolshevik sympathizers of the Pavlovsky Regiment and some Red Guards stood at the door of the Staff Building. Finally Poradelov's nerves broke. At 7:40 P.M. he surrendered to the Bolsheviks. Cheremisov was still waiting on the line for an answer. Someone picked up the telephone: "Staff is occupied by troops of the Military Revolutionary Committee. Work has stopped and we're leaving."

As of 7:40 P.M. the Provisional Government's writ ran only to the confines of the fifteen hundred rooms of the Winter Palace.[19]

This did not end the comedy of errors. The Bolsheviks did nothing about beginning the attack on the Winter Palace. Various excuses are offered in the Bolshevik memoirs. The guns at the Peter and Paul Fortress were in bad condition. They hadn't been cleaned since the February days. They didn't have the right ammunition. They couldn't find a red lantern—all of which was probably true, but Antonov-Ovseyenko and the Peter and Paul Fortress commandant were thrown off by another event. Not long before 8 P.M. a bicyclist arrived and reported that the Winter Palace had surrendered.

At the same time two artillerymen came to inspect the fortress' three-inch guns and advised they could be put in order.

"Now is already too late, comrades," G. I. Blagonavov told them, "the Winter Palace had fallen."

He, Podvoisky, and K. S. Yeremeyev set off to inspect the palace. They sped across the Troitsky Bridge, along the Champs de Mars, and up the Millionnaya to the palace. On both sides of the street stood Pavlovsky troops. A patrol at the bridge across the Winter Canal halted them. When the commissars told them the palace had fallen, the soldiers were skeptical. They had heard nothing of it. Blagonravov and Podvoisky thought troops from the Neva side had probably taken the palace. They drove forward until they actually came under fire from the palace. The chauffeur hastily backed the car to safety and they hurried back to the fortress.[20]

Inside the palace at 9:15, the Ministers took a little break. Tea was served from a bubbling samovar in the crystal glasses and silver glass holders of the palace service.[21]

About 9:30 P.M. the Ministers heard machine-gun fire and then cannon replying in front of the palace.[22] Sailors on the *Aurora* wanted to open fire but got no signal from Peter and Paul. Finally they saw a purplish flare burst out.[23] At 9:40 P.M. the *Aurora* opened fire with blanks and there was a heavier exchange between the cadets at the palace gates and the Bolshevik forces across the square. Armored cars joined in.

The exchange went on intermittently until about 10 P.M. when it came to an end because the three hundred Cossacks of the 14th Don Regiment decided to leave the palace.* They saddled their horses, loaded equipment, and rode out the main entrance and across the wide Palace Square. They went back to their barracks under a pledge of noninterference by the Bolsheviks.[24]

The Ministers, undaunted, dictated over one of the open telephone lines a proclamation addressed "To All, All, All . . ." They gave the text of the Bolshevik ultimatum and added:

"Let the country and the people respond to this insane attempt by the Bolsheviks to raise a rebellion in the rear of the fighting armies."[25]

At 9 P.M. the City Duma convened. The Ministers' message "To All, All, All . . ." reached the Duma and Chairman Shreider told his colleagues: "Within a few seconds the bombardment of the Winter Palace will begin." The Duma decided to send deputations to Smolny, to the Winter Palace, and to the *Aurora* to halt the threatened massacre. No one got through to the palace or the *Aurora*, but Shreider himself went to Smolny and won a promise from the Bolsheviks that he would be permitted to cross their line and enter the palace in an effort to avert bloodshed.

By the time Shreider returned, the Duma had decided to march to the palace in a body and "die together with the Government." They set out in ranks of four. It was a dark night and the street lamps on the Nevsky had been turned off. The three hundred marchers kept strict order and sang the "Marseillaise" as they stepped forward. They could hear intermittent gunfire from the Winter Palace, rifle and machine-gun fire. The column moved slowly along the Nevsky to the

---

* The Postal Telegraph Union sent out a report. "First attack on the Winter Palace beaten off. Palace fired on but only with hand weapons. It is clear that the opponents are weak." (S. P. Melgunov. *Kak Bolvheviki Zakhvatili Vlast*, p. 124.)

Kazan Cathedral Square—only a couple of blocks from the Duma building—where they were halted by a patrol of sailors.[26] The sailors refused to let them through. "I have orders not to let anyone go to the Winter Palace," one grumbled. "But I will send a comrade to telephone Smolny."

The marchers persisted.

"Shoot us if you want to," someone shouted.

"No," the sailor insisted, "I can't let you pass."

"We'll go forward," the crowd said. "What can you do?"

"We'll do something," he repeated. "Go home now and leave us in peace."

Protopovich mounted a box and began to speak. "Let us return to the Duma and discuss the best means of saving the country and the Revolution," he said.[27]

The marchers turned back to the Duma building where they formed a "Committee to Save the Fatherland and the Revolution.[28] In Ryss's bitter words the Duma had taken "all possible measures" to try to save the February Revolution.[29]

LVI

The Storming of the Winter Palace

At the palace the tragicomedy went on. Military strength ebbed away. The women's company slipped out the entrance on Millionnaya Street and was disarmed by the Pavlovsky Regiment. The ensigns from the northern front did the same.[1] The women were taken to the Grenadersky Barracks on the Petrograd side.[2]

More and more Pavlovsky men and Red Guards were filtering into the palace. Now they were coming in groups of fifteen or twenty, mostly through the Millionnaya Street entrances and those on the Winter Canal.

"They came in through various staircases," Palchinsky reported. "I personally led a group of Engineer cadets which disarmed a group of 50 who came in through the Hermitage entrance. They surrendered without opposition. The Pavlovsky troops were down below and all the doors were open."

Palchinsky reported his success to Malyantovich, who commented: "It's happened again. Again they allowed themselves to be disarmed. And again there were a lot of them. How many are already in the Palace? And who, in fact, occupies the Palace? We or the Bolsheviks?"[3]

It was a good question. Lieutenant Sineguba led his Engineer cadets on several sorties through the endless halls of the palace. Again and again they came upon individual agitators or groups of Bolshevik troops. Usually they surrendered without difficulty. Sometimes there was a little argument. Sineguba was spoiling for a fight, but the infiltrators seemed to have no intention of putting up resistance. Suddenly the lights went on over the principal palace entrance silhouetting the barricades and the Junkers at their machine guns. Sineguba hunted down the palace electrician and at revolver point compelled him to turn off the lights. Soon they flared on again. The electrician shrugged his shoulders. His switchboard had been cut off. Somewhere the Bolsheviks had control of the main lines. Finally the lights were shot out by the Junkers.[4]

The mood of the palace defenders improved with the breaking off of fighting at 10 P.M. Many thought this indicated a lack of resolution on the part of the Bolsheviks. Headquarters at Mogilev telephoned that a motorized battalion and other forces were en route to aid. The Ministers were buoyed, too, with the news that the City Duma had decided to send a pilgrimage to rescue the palace. Palchinsky gave the news to Sineguba and told him to spread it through the palace to raise morale. The city fathers and the principal church leaders were marching through Petrograd's streets. Soon the ordeal would be ended. Sineguba dashed off with his news. He told it to a group of cadets gathered in the Temny (dark) Gallery surrounded by paintings of Russia's military heroes. They shouted: "Hurrah! Hurrah for Russia!"[5]

Ambassador Buchanan looked out his embassy windows. The trams were still running over the Troitsky Bridge.[6]

A moment later the deep-throated cannon of the *Aurora* roared from the Neva. The hour was 11 P.M. The final assault was at hand.

Lenin had grown more and more nervous as the evening wore on. For a while he and Trotsky lay down in a room adjoining the meeting hall. Someone, probably Lenin's sister Mariya, had spread a blanket on the floor. The two men tried to get a little rest as they waited. Lenin had sent off his last messages to the Military Revolutionary Committee. He wanted to be certain that the Red Guards played an important role in the seizure of the palace.[7]

Now he and Trotsky talked quietly. He was, Trotsky thought, finally reconciled to the long delay in the uprising. He was interested in the mixed pickets which had been stationed around the Palace Square.

"What a wonderful sight," Lenin said. "A worker with a rifle, side by side with a soldier, standing before a street fire."

Then his worry about the palace surged back.

"What about the Winter Palace?" he exclaimed. "It has not been taken yet. Isn't there danger in that?"

Trotsky started to leap up to telephone someone. Lenin stopped him.

"Lie still," he said. "I'll send someone to find out."[8]*

There were eleven six-inch guns in the Naryshkin Bastion of the Peter and Paul Fortress, six of them facing the Winter Palace. One gun was used every day to fire the noon signal. The others had last been fired March 23 and there was an argument as to whether they were fit for firing. Six three-inch cannon had been mounted on the walls of the Alexeyevsky Ravelin.[9] About 11 P.M. the six-inch guns of the Naryshkin Ravelin finally went into action. Six shells were fired— four blanks and two live. One shot hit the corner window of the reception room of the third-floor suite of Alexander III, sending chips flying in all directions, and embedded itself in the next wall. The second shell fell harmless in Demidov Pereulok near Sennaya Square, several hundred yards from the palace. At the same time gunners opened up with the three-inch cannon of the Alexeyevsky Ravelin and fired between thirty and thirty-five rounds of shrapnel, most of which exploded harmlessly over the Neva. One hit the cornice of the palace. Other cannon mounted under the arc of the General Staff Building joined in the bombardment.

A. V. Liverovsky was called at 10:40 P.M. for direct conversations by telegraph with Headquarters at Mogilev. The telegraph head was in another part of the palace. He left the Malachite Chamber and went down to the lower floor. From the interior courtyard he saw an armored car with two guns facing the palace, but it did not fire until he and the telegraph operator ran across the lighted patch at the main entrance. When he got back to the Malachite Chamber, the Ministers were examining a piece of shrapnel from a shell which had hit near the Alexandrovsky Hall.[10]

Inside the palace confusion mounted. Where before the defenders had disarmed large numbers of Bolsheviks and sent them to the hospital quarters—where they quickly made friends with the wounded— now there were so many Red Guards that they began to disarm the cadets. Sineguba, dashing about the palace on one mission after another, dragged a cadet whom he believed to be a Bolshevik into the Temny Hall. It was so filled with noise and confusion it reminded him (he was given to oratorical flourishes) of Sodom and Gomorrah. In the center of the room he found the palace commandant, Colonel Ananyev, shouting at the chief of staff, Palchinksy, who was shouting at Lieutenant Lokhvinsky, who was shouting back at Palchinksy. Sineguba joined the shouting match and demanded that the suspected Bolshevik be arrested. Then he was sent off to the Hermitage wing to try to halt the hemorrhage of revolutionaries in which the palace was rapidly drowning.[11]

* Other persons describe Lenin as pacing the room like a caged lion, swearing and cursing. (S. P. Melgunov, *Kak Bolsheviki Zakhvatili Vlast,* p. 126.)

The Ministers had not yet given up hope. Pacing the floors of the Malachite Chamber, they were somewhat removed from the turmoil within the palace. Nikitin was still on the telephone, trying to get help from the city. (When one of his friends called the palace back a little later, he heard only "wild noises and the sound of panicky voices."[12]) Palchinsky brought in a shell fragment. Admiral Verderevsky was certain it must have come from one of the Aurora's guns. (It hadn't—it came from one of the cannon firing from the General Staff Arch.[13])

Suddenly two explosions almost burst the Ministers' eardrums. Some sailors had hurled grenades into the Temny Corridor. They had gotten in through one of the doors from the hospital rooms.[14] Two cadets were wounded. Kishkin, a doctor, gave them first aid. Verderevsky lent his handkerchief for a bandage. The hour was ten minutes to midnight.[15] Rutenberg discovered he had no revolver. Liverovsky gave him his small nickel-plated Browning.[16]

By this time the leaders of the Military Revolutionary Committee—Antonov-Ovseyenko, Chudnovsky, and Yeremeyev—had entered the palace, probably from the Admiralty side or the Neva. Chudnovsky immediately went to work to persuade more cadets to leave the palace. Negotiations went well, but when he discovered that there actually was only a handful of cadets still on guard he and Antonov-Ovseyenko ordered the assault on the palace to begin. It was now 1:20 on the morning of the twenty-sixth. The first to notice that the Bolshevik forces were moving in was the telephone operator. Characteristically, she did not realize that a historic moment was at hand. She called the Ministers and said: "A delegation of 300 to 400 is approaching."[17] This crowd—it was more of a crowd than a military attack group—moved into the palace not by the principal entrance on the square where the defenders were concentrated but through the two other entrances which had no barricades in front of them, particularly the left-hand entrance.[18]

Sineguba was just returning from an expedition into the Hermitage corridors where he succeeded in freeing a number of cadets and disarming a larger number of Bolshevik troops. Near the main entrance he encountered a group of Junkers without arms.

"What's the matter?" he asked. "Why are you without arms?"

"We've surrendered the palace," one of them answered gloomily.

"That's nonsense," Sineguba said. He looked out into the square. There was shouting and yelling. He looked up the stairs and saw Ananyev surrounded by a crowd of men. Something had obviously happened. He started up the stairs and a sailor shouted "Halt" and threw his shoulder out to bar Sineguba's path. Sineguba ducked and went up to Colonel Ananyev. Beside Ananyev stood a tall, red-faced life guard of the Pavlovsky Regiment.

The commandant leaned over to Sineguba: "Sanya, I've had to surrender the palace. Listen, don't boil over. It's too late. These are the negotiators. Run quickly to the Government and warn them."

The Junkers were already piling up their weapons. The Oranienbaum cadets had started to leave. Sineguba dashed through the empty halls. He ran through the Temny Corridor. On the floor were rifles, grenades, and mattresses. From their golden frames looked down the great leaders of Russia.

Finally he got to the anteroom outside the Malachite Chamber. A handful of cadets lounged there, the Ministers' life guard. He went into the Malachite Chamber and told Vice-chairman A. V. Konovalov what had happened, then came out and sank exhausted in a chair in the anteroom. Soon a woman came in, saying she was with the press and, representing public opinion, had a right to be present. An official appeared and hurried off with the correspondent. Palchinsky emerged, followed by Tereshchenko.

"No!" Palchinsky was saying. "That is absolutely unacceptable. I categorically state that. We must get back the Junkers."

He turned to Sineguba. "Look, hurry," he said, "bring back the Junkers."

Sineguba looked at him exhausted. "I'll die here," he said, "but I can't run. I just haven't any more strength." He was ashamed of his answer but it was only the truth.

Palchinsky decided to go after the Junkers himself. A young officer in Cherkassian uniform came out and chased after Palchinsky. Minutes passed. What was happening Sineguba could not imagine.

Suddenly Sineguba heard a distant sound. With Antonov-Ovseyenko and Chudnovsky at their head the crowd had poured up the staircase and found themselves in the great White Hall, which was the state dining room of the Romanovs. They fanned out through the corridors until they reached the Temny Corridor. At the end of this corridor they passed through the rotunda and the Arabian Hall. As they came the sound in Sineguba's ears grew louder. It was like the surf of the sea. It was the sound of many voices and many feet.[19] Sineguba looked up and Palchinsky appeared in the door of the small white reception room. By his side was a small man with a sharp face, wearing a sailor's pea jacket and a wide-brimmed artist's hat. It was Antonov-Ovseyenko.

Behind them followed a crowd of men. Sineguba described them as "ugly mugs with beastly, surprisingly stupid faces." Palchinsky went into the Malachite Chamber. Sineguba spoke to the cadets. "Do you

have enough cartridges?" he asked the cadets. "Certainly," they replied.

Antonov-Ovseyenko turned to the crowd: "Hold back, comrades!
Discipline! There are Junkers here!" He spoke in a resonant sharp
voice.

Palchinsky reappeared and motioned Antonov-Ovseyenko to the
Malachite Chamber. The crowd started to press forward.

"Halt!" Palchinsky shouted. "Or the Junkers will open fire."

The cadets gripped their guns firmly, fingers on the triggers. They
were ready to fire. Antonov-Ovseyenko again cautioned his forces and
went into the inner room.[20]

The Ministers—thirteen of them at the end—were gathered at the
table where they had been deliberating. Some stood. As Minister of
Justice Malyantovich recalled it, almost immediately after Palchinsky
and Antonov-Ovseyenko entered, a guard surrounded them.

"This is the Provisional Government," Konovalov said. "What is
your pleasure?"

"I announce that all of you, members of the Provisional Government, are under arrest," said Antonov-Ovseyenko. "I am the representative of the Military Revolutionary Committee Antonov."

The Ministers, Konovalov announced, were submitting in order to
avoid bloodshed.

The hour was 1:50 A.M. October 26.[21]

The door of the Malachite Chamber opened. Sineguba had been
daydreaming how he and the cadets could mow down the crowd of
Bolsheviks. Antonov-Ovseyenko and Palchinsky emerged.

"Quiet, comrades, quiet," Antonov-Ovseyenko said, raising his hand.

There was a moment of silence.

"Comrades," said Antonov-Ovseyenko and his voice took on a wildly
rising note. "Comrades! Hail the proletariat and its Revolutionary Soviet. The power of the capitalists, the power of the bourgeoisie is at
our feet. At the feet of the proletariat. And now Comrades Proletarians you are obliged to show all the firmness of the revolutionary
discipline of proletarian Red Petrograd in order to set an example to
the proletarians of the whole world."[22]

At 2 A.M. Mayor Shreider made one last call from the City Duma to
the Winter Palace. A gruff voice answered saying: "What do you
want? Who's calling?"

"It's the City Administration," Shreider answered. "I want to know
what you are doing."

"I'm the guard," the voice responded, "and we're doing nothing."[23]

It was over. It was over in a kind of massive anticlimax. The
formalities took a few minutes. There were the weapons of the

Ministers—most of them carried revolvers—to collect, the inevitable Russian protocol to be drafted and signed.

A telegram was sent to Smolny: "At 2:04 P.M. Winter Palace was taken. Six men of the Pavlovsky killed." The official protocol was timed at 2:10, listing eighteen persons arrested. Three *papki*, liver-colored file folders, and the portfolio of the Minister of Education were seized.*

John Reed had been at Smolny all evening. He and four other Americans, Louise Bryant, Albert Rhys Williams, Bessy Beatty, and Alex Gumberg, hooked a ride with a truck which took them to the Znamenskaya Square and then down the Nevsky. The truck was filled with leaflets which they hurled out at every corner. Three men stood in the front with rifles ready in case of "provocateurs." When they got to the Morskaya, Americans joined a throng of people moving slowly toward the Winter Palace. They entered the square through the General Staff Arch. Someone shouted: "Watch out, comrades, they will shoot." They ran for the protection of the Alexander Column. The throng hesitated and began to move again. Light streamed out of the palace windows. The Government had surrendered but no one seemed certain that the battle was over. Reed clambered over the wooden barricades and up the main staircase. The rooms were filled with packing boxes of art treasures, glass, porcelain, carpets. The crowds attacked the boxes. Soldiers smashed them in with rifle butts. One man put a bronze clock on his shoulder. Another grabbed an ostrich feather. Reed heard a voice shouting: "Comrades! Don't touch anything. This is the property of the people." At first no one paid heed. Gradually, Party members began to take loot out of the hands of the soldiers and workers. Officers tried to clear the halls: "All out! All out!" they shouted. Sentries at the landings and entrances searched the liberating throng. Heaps of pictures, rugs, bedspreads, damask, vases, statuettes, blankets, and art objects were recovered—but by no means all, of course. As Rhys Williams commented, "prowlers and vandals" made off with many valuables.[24]

Reed watched as the Ministers filed out—Kishkin, his face pale, Tereshchenko staring coldly at Reed. They were taken to the Peter

---

* Liverovsky's diary recorded the last minutes (*Istorichesky Arkhiv*, 1960, No. 6, p. 47):

1:20 A.M. Telephone operator reports approach to Winter Palace of delegation of 300–400.
1:50 A.M. Arrest—prepare protocol.
2:10 A.M. Leave under guard.
3:40 A.M. Arrive at Fortress.
5:05 A.M. I am in cell No. 54.

and Paul Fortress. At one point they had to flatten out with their guards on the bridge to avoid being shot down.

Reed and his companions went back to the Malachite Chamber. The green baise table was just as it had been left. Blank paper. Doodles. Reed picked a sheet of paper on which Konovalov had started to dash off a proclamation, then blacked it out with scratches and circles.

Finally, the Americans were seized by an angry group of soldiers, certain they must be provocateurs. The idea of provocateurs filled everyone's mind. They stumbled out of the palace after 3 A.M. The Nevsky lights were on again. The cannon had disappeared but soldiers huddled around bonfires. Reed went back to Smolny.

All evening long the All-Russian Soviet had been meeting. Lenin waited in the wings but never made an appearance. The meeting had gotten under way after endless delays at the very moment the Military Revolutionary Committee finally unlimbered the Winter Palace assault. There were about 650 delegates in the hall, many of them morose, indifferent men in gray overcoats. Three hundred ninety were Bolsheviks, 159 SRs, and 80 Mensheviks. Sukhanov could not recall a more disorderly meeting since the Revolution began. A presidium consisting mostly of Bolsheviks and headed by Lenin was approved. Martov called for an end to hostilities. Blood was flowing on the Petrograd streets. The Soviet could not stand by indifferently. Lunacharsky replied for the Bolsheviks. They had nothing against the idea. Martov's proposal was made item No. 1 on the agenda. Then the debate fell apart. It was announced that the City Duma chairman had offered to undertake negotiations with the Winter Palace and that the Military Revolutionary Committee had sent its representative to cooperate in finding a solution.

Martov argued for approval of his resolution and Trotsky attacked him. "No compromise is possible," Trotsky shouted. "To those who tell us to do this we must say: you are miserable bankrupts, your role is played out. Go where you ought to be: into the dustbin of history."

It was after 1 A.M. A recess was ordered. Everyone was angry, spiteful, weary. When Sukhanov returned to the chamber, Kamenev, the chairman, was speaking. "We have just received the following telephone message. The Winter Palace has been taken by the troops of the Military Revolutionary Committee. The whole Provisional Government was arrested there except Kerensky who has fled."[25] The hour was 3:10 A.M. Everyone had already heard the news but Kamenev made it official.[26]

Reed got back to Smolny just in time to hear the end of Kamenev's statement. A big peasant, a left SR, rose.

"We insist on the immediate release of the Socialist Ministers," he shouted. "Do you know that four comrades who risked their lives and freedom fighting against the tyranny of the Czar have been flung into Peter and Paul prison?"[27]

This touched off another wrangle. Then Lunacharsky read a proclamation which Lenin had written, proclaiming Soviet power, a quick democratic peace for all people, land for the peasants, and workers' direction of production. About 4 A.M. Lenin slipped out the back door of Smolny and went to Bonch-Bruyevich's apartment. He rested a bit but before going to bed he started to write a decree on land.[28]

The meeting of the Soviet went on and on. It finally ended at 5:15 A.M. The Petrograd skies were still dark as the delegates straggled out of brilliantly lighted Smolny. Troops stood at every hand. Machine guns guarded the doorway. Armored cars filled the courtyard.[29]

There was, Reed wrote, only a faint unearthly pallor stealing over the silent streets and dimming the watch fires, "the shadow of a terrible dawn grey-rising over Russia."[30] It was the first day of the Government of the Soviet of Workers, Peasants, and Soldiers' Deputies, and its leader had not yet made a public appearance.

What, after all, did it mean? That was the thought that filled John Reed's mind as he made his way back to his hotel in the grim hours before dawn. Would Russia rise up and follow Red Petrograd? What of Moscow? And what about the world? What would a Soviet Government be like? Would, indeed, the workers of the world in Marx's classic phrase of the *Communist Manifesto* now rise and strike off their chains?

LVII

The Day After

When the young American YMCA worker, Paul Anderson, awakened on the morning of Thursday October 26, he was puzzled. His house, 62 Ligovsky Prospekt, stood on a busy traffic-filled street. Legovsky intersected Nevsky Prospekt at Znamenskaya Square where the Nicholas railroad station stood. Ordinarily Anderson heard the rumble of trucks and the rattle of streetcars through the thick walls of the great San Galli mansion where he lived with two other young Americans.

But this morning all was quiet and the quietness puzzled Anderson. When he emerged on the street, he saw hardly any traffic. Something must have happened. There had been rumors of an uprising for several days—ever since the Kornilov affair, in fact. He decided to go to the Astoria Hotel and see if his friend, John Reed, could cast any light on the situation. Anderson hurried down the Nevsky. There were no droshkies. He walked the whole distance, a good two miles. At the Astoria he found Reed, Louise Bryant, and Rhys Williams. It was after noon. They were tired and excited. They had not gotten to bed until dawn.

"What happened?" Anderson asked.

"Well," said Reed, "we had the Revolution last night. We were at the Winter Palace."

Reed told how they had climbed over the barricades and entered the palace with the crowd. "There were no guards," he said. "Nobody stopped us at all. We went right into the palace."

Reed described the shooting, the firing by the *Aurora* and the Peter and Paul Fortress. Anderson was amazed. He had been home all evening and hadn't heard a thing.

"Come on," Reed said. "We're going over to Smolny. Wouldn't you like to join us?"

Anderson wanted to go very much. But he was afraid they wouldn't let him in.

"You fellows are journalists and red-card Socialists," he said. "How can I get in?"

"Oh, that's no problem," Reed said airily. "You can be our *dometchnik*, our interpreter."

That sounded fine to Anderson. He and the others caught the No. 17 streetcar, paid their three kopecks to the conductor, and were off.[1]

Tamara Karsavina did not get to bed until dawn on the twenty-sixth. She danced at the Mariinsky Wednesday evening. Although the city was filled with rumors, the performance had not been canceled. She took the precaution of leaving early for the theater from her flat on the Millionnaya. Many members of the company were absent but the curtain went up at 8 P.M. promptly. There was only a handful in the audience. Throughout the evening the sound of cannon could be faintly heard from the stage and more plainly from the dressing rooms.

After the ballet Karsavina and some friends had been invited to supper with Edward Cunard, whose flat on the Millionnaya was hardly a hundred yards from the Palace Square. There were pickets on the street but they managed to talk their way through and sat down to supper to the sound of machine-gun and rifle fire.

After supper Cunard brought out some cards and the company played a game called Cheating. They played and played, waiting for the streets to quiet. The candles burned down. Finally the gray light of dawn came through the curtains. The gentlemen esscorted the ladies to their homes. A new world had been born while the cards whisked around the table on the Millionnaya, but what kind it might be Karsavina had no idea.[2]

Count de Robien had spent the evening in the company of the actors of the Michel Theater at the Pension Choisy. It was a pleasant evening, and when he left at eleven he discovered that there was fighting going on around the Winter Palace but the troops would not permit him to approach. At home he found Armand de Saint-Sauveur, who had gone to the Narodny Dom to hear Chaliapin sing. He had come home by streetcar with no trouble.

De Robien busied himself during the morning of the twenty-sixth learning about the revolutionary events of the night and after lunch dropped by Countess Kleinmikhel's house, where he encountered Madame de Scavenius. Together they went to the palace embankment. The palace façade had been riddled with bullets, making thousands of white pockmarks on the dull red exterior. Some windows were broken and under the main entrance the windows were shattered.

De Robien found the city perfectly quiet. He was not unpleased to learn that the former Ministers including Tereshchenko, whom he personally disliked, had been locked up in the Peter and Paul Fortress. In general, he had not cared for the Provisional Government, which he called glorified riffraff.

"Kerensky in Alexandra's bed!" he exclaimed. "Lenin at least, like Christ of old, brings something new and talks a different language to that of the governments of today. . . . They are perhaps dreamers, but I prefer their dreams to the gross realism of the 'get-out-and-let-me-in people' of the first Revolution."[3]

Zinaida Gippius had only one comment for her diary: "The Petersburgers are now in the hands of and at the disposition of the 200,000 band of the garrison, headed by a handful of swindlers."[4]

It was late afternoon before the Americans got to Smolny. The building was ringed by guards and the courtyard jammed with guns and troops, but they had no trouble in getting through. Reed had his Smolny pass. He simply pointed to Anderson and said, "Dometchnik," and the guards let him through. Inside the building thousands of people milled about. The Americans walked through the corridors. Doors bore signs like: Left SR faction, Bundist faction. They walked into some of the rooms and talked with those they met. One office, Anderson recalled, had Lenin's name on it but they did not enter there.

A meal was being served downstairs so the Americans descended and got in line. Each received a bowl and wooden spoon. A great pot filled with boiled beef stood on a long table. They took a piece of meat, poured some cabbage soup in the bowl, and picked up a hunk of bread. It was the former dining room of the girls' school. Dinner cost three rubles.[5]

"If there were any famous people there," Anderson recalled, "we weren't aware of it."

About 8:30 the Americans went upstairs to the auditorium and took their places at a table in the very front. There were some other journalists there, Alex Gumberg and Raymond Robins of the American Red Cross.

The hall slowly filled up with deputies—serious people, workers, peasants, intelligentsia, many soldiers who carried their rifles and bristling bandoliers of cartridges. Red Guards with their red arm bands stood about the room.[6]

The Bolsheviks had been busy all day. Never in the history of mankind, Trotsky thought, had so many orders been issued, by word of mouth, by penciled note, by typewriter, by telegraph—thousands and thousands of them.[7]

Lenin and the others had got only two or three hours of sleep. Lenin, it transpired, finished his decree on land before going to sleep. It was, as he openly conceded, a direct steal from the left SR land program. In fact, he had worked it out from a copy of the leftist SR newspaper, *Peasant Izvestiya*, during the days he was in hiding at Fofanova's and had showed it to her. "We'll use it as the basis for our law concerning land," he said with glee, "and see if the Left SR's dare to reject it."[8]

Bonch-Bruyevich had expected Lenin to sleep late but he appeared early, fully clothed, full of energy, fresh, and happy.

"Congratulations on the first day of the Socialist Revolution," he said to Bonch-Bruyevich as he sat down for a glass of tea with Krupskaya, who had also spent the night with Bonch-Bruyevich. Taking out of his pocket his decree on land, he began to talk about how it could be most widely publicized.

Then Lenin and Bonch-Bruyevich set out on foot. They walked a bit and caught a streetcar for Smolny.[9]

Lenin could hardly wait for evening and the meeting of the All-Russian Soviet. But it was a day of furious activity—efforts, not too successful, to mobilize military forces against the expected counteroffensive by Kerensky and efforts, not much more successful, to find some formula for collaboration with the other left-wing groups.

A government had to be formed but what to call it. "Anything but ministers," Lenin said. "That's such a vile hackneyed word."

"We might call them commissars," Trotsky suggested. "Perhaps, Supreme Commissars? No 'supreme' does not sound well. What about 'people's commissars'?"

"'People's commissars'? Well, that might do, I think," Lenin said. "And the Government as a whole?"

"A Soviet, of course . . . the Soviet of People's Commissars, eh?"

"The Soviet of People's Commissars?" Lenin repeated. "That's splendid; smells terribly of Revolution."[10]

But who were to be those "Commissars"? Would they be all Bolsheviks? Or would the rest of the left join in? The left—that is, the Mensheviks, most of the SRs, and the other left factions—had walked

out of the Soviet the night before. Still the Bolshevik Central Committee with the possible exception of Lenin rather thought it would be
better to share power with the extreme left. But the left SRs headed
by Mariya Spiridonova wanted to mediate between the Bolsheviks
and those who walked out. Krupskaya recalled Lenin arguing with
Spiridonova two hours before the opening of the second meeting of
the Soviet, trying to convince her and her comrades to join the Government. They were together in a small room in Smolny. Spiridonova sat
on a small dark red settee and Lenin stood beside her arguing in "a
sort of gentle earnest manner."[11]

No agreement was reached and it was decided to go ahead with an
all-Bolshevik government. At first Lenin did not want to head the Government and proposed Trotsky. Trotsky violently objected. Lenin was
the leader, there could be no other choice. "Why not?" Lenin said.
"You were at the head of the Petrograd Soviet that seized power."[12]
On Trotsky's motion the proposal was tabled. Lenin became Chairman, Trotsky Foreign Commissar.

Outside Smolny the Military Revolutionary Committee was hard at
work. It had shut down a number of the principal newspapers during
the night. Now it busied itself closing more. Sailors were sent to
Rech and *Sovremennoye Slovo*. They confiscated all copies of the newspapers and burned them in the streets. Raiding parties hurried down
the Nevsky, the Liteiny, and Kamennoostrovsky Prospekt attacking
newspaper kiosks and dumping all but the Bolshevik papers into the
streets. Nothing like this had been seen in Czarist days. Czarist authorities often closed newspapers but they would reappear the next
day (or even the same day) with a slightly changed name and a new
"responsible" proprietor, usually an unemployed or retired man who
allowed the use of his name and, if necessary, went to jail for a few
days in return for an honorarium of a few hundred rubles.[13]

The second session of the Soviet had been set to meet at 1 P.M. but
it was 8:40 before the chairman, Kamenev, finally rang his little bell
and called the meeting to order. Kamenev, to strong applause, announced that the death penalty had been abolished at the front and in
Russia, generally; that all political prisoners (except the new ones the
Bolsheviks were busily sending into the jails) had been released; that
orders for the arrest of Kerensky and Kornilov (who had just walked
out of Bykhov jail) had been issued and for confiscation of food stocks
in private hands.[14]

Anderson was all eyes. The Presidium had taken its place on the
platform, among them Lenin, whom he was seeing for the first (and
last) time. If Stalin was present he made no impression on Anderson.
He had never heard of him. Nor was Stalin's name mentioned by any

other witness. If, as Sukhanov once said, Stalin in the early days of the Revolution was a "grey blur, looming up now and then, dimly and not leaving any trace," he was even more of a blur in these founding moments of Soviet power. He left no mark whatsoever.[15]*

Now Kamenev called on Lenin to present the report on peace. There was an ovation as Lenin, a short stocky figure with big eyes, a snub nose (Reed in his notes called it "snubby"), bald head, clean-shaven chin, trousers too long for him and clothes rather shabby, gripped the podium and waited for the applause to quiet. He then began to read a long declaration proposing to all warring governments immediate negotiations for peace without annexations or indemnities, suggesting a three-month armistice, denouncing all secret treaties and secret diplomacy, and calling on the workers of the advanced capitalist countries of Britain, France, and Germany to join in bringing a prompt end to the bloody war.[16]

Sukhanov got to Smolny toward the end of Lenin's speech. For the first time he entered the Soviet as a spectator, not a participant. He had no trouble finding an empty seat in the back rows. There was an outburst when Lenin finished, a unanimous vote of approval,[17] and then the singing of the "Internationale" and the Funeral March:

> You fell in the fatal fight
> For the liberty of the people, for the honor of the people . . .

Reed saw Kollontai wipe away a tear.[18]

The whole Presidium, headed by Lenin, stood and sang "with exalted faces and blazing eyes," in Sukhanov's words. The delegates whom he had thought tired and disinterested now sparkled with excitement.

"They were beginning to be persuaded of the imminence of peace, land and bread," Sukhanov recalled. "But I didn't believe in the victory, the success, the 'rightfulness' or the historic mission of a Bolshevik regime. Sitting in the back seats, I watched this celebration with a heavy heart. How I longed to join in and merge with this mass and its leaders in a single feeling. But I couldn't."

Next Lenin read his decree on land. Its essence was the abolition of private property in land. All estates, private, Imperial, and Church holdings, were placed at the disposal of rural agrarian committees and Soviets pending action by the Constituent Assembly. Property interest in land was abolished in perpetuity but the land of ordinary peasants and Cossacks would not be confiscated. The right to the use of the land

*Nor was Stalin mentioned in John Reed's classic *Ten Days that Shook the World.*

belonged to all citizens provided they worked it themselves. Hired labor was forbidden. Land resources were subject to periodic reallocation.

Lenin had difficulty in reading the decree—probably because he had scribbled it in such haste in the morning. When he finished he added:

"Voices can be heard here saying that the decree was drawn up by the SRs. Very well. Isn't it all the same who composed it?"[19]

Anderson was not impressed with Lenin's delivery. "It was a professional *doklad*, a professional report," he said. "He held a paper in his hand and read it off. No oratory. But the debate that followed was moving. Soldiers, members of the intelligentsia, peasants rose and spoke their thoughts."

It was, he thought, a real Soviet. He was particularly impressed by a peasant who was wearing a homemade sheepskin jacket, the wool inside, and a ragged fur cap with floppy ears which he carefully removed and placed beside him on the rostrum before beginning to speak.

"Tovarishchi," the peasant said. "We have won the Revolution."[20]

The crowd roared. The peasant went on, bowing to the four corners of the room and running a hand through his long disheveled hair.

"I wish you well, comrades and citizens," he said. "There are some Kadets walking around outside. You arrested our Socialist peasants—why not arrest them, too?"[21]

A soldier took the rostrum. He had a tangled beard and fiery eyes:

"You sit here and talk about giving the land to the peasants and you commit an act of tyrants and usurpers against the peasants' chosen representatives! I tell you" (he raised his fist) "if one hair of their heads is harmed, you'll have a revolt on your hands!"[22]

The soldier was referring to the Revolutionary Ministers whom the Bolsheviks had thrown into Peter and Paul Fortress. The crowd stirred uneasily. There were obviously guilty consciences in the Smolny auditorium. Trotsky rose and rather lamely said orders had been given to release the Ministers and that if they were still in prison it was because everyone had been too busy to let them out.

But, he warned, and it was a warning which his listeners would have been well advised to heed closely, the Ministers would be held under house arrest and their conduct carefully investigated.[23]

The meeting went on. The land decree was approved. B. V. Avilov, once a Bolshevik, now one of Gorky's associates on *Novaya Zhizn*, young, intelligent-looking, wearing a frock coat, spoke some words of warning. The coup d'état had succeeded not because of the strength of the left but because of the inability of the Provisional Government to give the people peace and bread. Could the new government solve these questions? He was not certain. Grain was scarce. The peasants probably would not co-operate too well. Peace would be even more difficult. The Allies would not help. There was no counting on revolutionary movements in Germany, France, and England. No one party could solve all these difficulties. He called for a coalition.[24]

The Soviet approved the all-Bolshevik Government. Then it heard another warning—this one from the All-Russian Railwaymen's Union, the most powerful trade union in Russia, a citadel of revolutionary strength, the key factor in the 1905 rising, the organization which had tipped the balance against the Czar, against Kornilov, and against Kerensky, an organization in which the Bolsheviks had virtually no influence and which they had studiously excluded from the Soviet.

Now the railroad men demanded recognition and a place in the high councils. The union condemned the seizure of power by one party; government should be responsible to the whole revolutionary democracy; until and unless such a government was created the union would control all railroad lines; it would not permit counterrevolutionary troops to reach Petrograd but movements would be sanctioned only by the union.[25]

At 5:15 A.M. the Soviet came to an end. Sukhanov walked home with Lunacharsky, who was staying with him for the night in a flat near the Tauride Gardens. Lunacharsky was in ecstasy. He tried to persuade Sukhanov to become Foreign Minister in the new Bolshevik Government ignoring the fact Trotsky had already agreed to be Foreign Commissar. Sukhanov's head was reeling.[26]

Anderson left before the proceedings concluded. He walked a good part of the way back to the San Galli mansion. It stood dark and silent like the streets of Petrograd. He rang the bell and the butler appeared, still in his formal dress and white gloves.

"*Gde vy byli?*" he asked. "Where have you been?"

"I've been to the Revolution," Anderson replied.

In the morning Madame San Galli and her daughter Sonya came down to the breakfast table.

"We missed you last night," they said to Anderson.

"I went to the Soviet," Anderson explained.

"Oh, the Soviet," they laughed. "It will be gone in two weeks."[27]

LVIII

Permanent Crisis

Life turned into a reddish blur. Lenin and his comrades worked eighteen, twenty, twenty-four hours a day. The crises came so swiftly and so imposed one on the other that it was difficult to say at a given moment whether the most urgent task was Kerensky's attack from Gatchina, the violent resistance of the embattled Junkers in the Moscow Kremlin, who (for a time) threatened to overwhelm the poorly led Bolshevik forces, or the political threat in Petrograd itself.

Krupskaya almost lost track of her husband. She saw him occasionally late at night. She continued to work in the Vyborg headquarters, then shifted to the Education Commissariat. A flat was furnished for Lenin and Krupskaya on the second floor of Smolny. There were two pleasant rooms, a kitchen, a warm bathroom, a private elevator, a corridor to the back courtyard in case Lenin had suddenly to flee. There were two iron beds, formerly used by the schoolmistresses, a table, a few chairs, a small mirror, and the trunks of the Ulyanovs which were brought over from Yelizarov's apartment.[1]

But Lenin had not a moment for relaxation. What was apparent to all was that while the Bolsheviks had seized power in Petrograd, had taken over the Winter Palace, had arrested the Provisional Government, and driven out Kerensky, their writ ran only a short distance and even in Petrograd it seemed that most citizens agreed with Madame San Galli that a fortnight would see the Bolsheviks gone.

When Alexandra Kollontai and A. A. Ioffe, the future diplomat, appeared at the City Duma on the morning of Friday the twenty-seventh, they were greeted, as the Bolshevik representatives, with cries of: "Murderers! Rapists! Out! To prison! To the gallows!"

They took their places, smiled a bit nervously, sat awhile, and left never to return.[2]

The City Duma overnight became the rallying point for those numerous forces opposed to the Bolsheviks: the other socialist parties, the Mensheviks, the SRs, the Internationalists; the bourgeois parties, chiefly the Kadets; Vikzhel, the all-powerful railroad workers' union; other anti-Bolshevik unions, including telegraphers, postal workers, some of the printing trades. They rallied around the Committee to Save the Fatherland and the Revolution. Debate went on night and day in the Duma Hall on the Nevsky. Speech after speech. Rumors fed the excitement. Kerensky's forces were marching on Petrograd. The Bolshevik party was splitting up. Lenin's enemies were coming out on top.[3]

Suddenly the quiet, the ease, the calm, of the Bolshevik coup d'état was sundered by blows that came from every side. Kerensky had—with a good deal of difficulty—gotten General Krasnov to move on Petrograd with a small force of Cossacks (no one at Smolny knew how small). He was advancing on Gatchina and the outskirts of Petrograd. Could he be halted? Who in the Bolshevik Military Revolutionary Committee could be certain?

Lenin flung himself into a frenzy of activity. His first step was an attempt to seize control of all channels of information. Petrograd up to October 26 had enjoyed an extraordinarily free press. It represented every view from extreme reactionary to opinion far to the left of the Bolsheviks. The capital boasted newspapers as responsible as *The Times* of London and gutter boulevard sheets whose filth could not be matched in Europe.

As his first act in the new Soviet of People's Commissars Lenin presented a decree abolishing freedom of the press (freedom of the press had always been a basic Bolshevik demand) in Russia—a freedom stifled to this day.[4] The decree called the bourgeois press a powerful weapon directed against the Soviet power, no less dangerous than bombs and machine guns. It must be quashed. Any newspaper judged antagonistic to Soviet power or charged with publishing untruthful reports about the Soviet would be suppressed and its editors tried for criminal responsibility.[5]

This violated a stand Lenin had taken publicly as recently as September 15 when in a long discussion in *Rabochi Put* he had called for what he described as a "much more democratic" and "incomparably more complete" freedom of press than then existed. He proposed that all kinds of opinion should flourish. The state would take over all printing presses and newsprint and allot their resources equitably.

Part would go to a state press serving the whole country; part to a press representing each of the large political parties; part to a smaller press representing the small parties; and finally groups of ordinary citizens who collected a given number of signatures would be entitled to have their press too.

This, he asserted, "would provide real freedom of the press for all and not just for the rich. It would be state aid to the people's enlightenment and not to their stultification and deception."[6]

Lenin's first postrevolutionary act cut across his brave words of September. No one understood then, not even his closest colleagues, that this would only be the initial manifestation of a Lenin-in-power who would halt at no step to retain, consolidate, and strengthen that power. If long since he had been prepared to utilize any means to his ends, from now on the sole criterion of every move was not to be: Is it principled? Is it Marxist? Has it been promised? From now on the fight to hold power would totally dominate Lenin. No measure would seem too extreme to serve his purpose. As Krupskaya commented, his one great fear was that the Revolution would show too much leniency. He had become convinced, she said, that the Paris Commune of 1870 had collapsed because it showed too much humanity toward its enemies. This would not be his mistake. If the Bolshevik regime fell, it would not be because Lenin had permitted a feeling of compassion to temper revolutionary ferocity.

With his first act Lenin set the tone of what was to follow.[7]

To be sure in the emerging first hours of Soviet power Lenin found he had sailed into most dangerous waters. From the morning of the twenty-sixth onward he had no real assurance that power might not slip from his hands at any time. The warnings of his comrades against the coup d'état echoed in his ears from that moment. They had said the country was not yet ready. The city was not ready. The Army and the workers were not ready. The Party was not ready.

And on October 27 and increasingly on the twenty-eighth and subsequent days it looked more and more as though the Party had been right and Lenin had been wrong—wrong and stubborn-headed, incredibly overoptimistic, and blind to political reality.

By 3 P.M. of the twenty-seventh the Kerensky-Krasnov forces had taken Gatchina without a fight. They now held the perfect jumping-off point for a direct assault on Petrograd,[8] and by midday Lenin himself had moved into the Petrograd military district headquarters and assumed direction of defense. Nothing that the Military Revolutionary Committee had done satisfied him. He challenged each decision, particularly their failure to call on Kronshtadt, Vyborg, and Helsingfors for support.

He himself got onto the Hughes wire.

"Can you move the greatest possible number of destroyers and other warships to Petrograd at once?" he asked A. L. Sheinman, chairman of the Helsingfors Soviet.

"Let me call the chairman of Tsentrobalt because this is purely a naval matter," Sheinman replied, referring to the commander of the Baltic Fleet. "What's new in Petrograd?"

"There is a report that Kerensky's troops have moved up and have taken Gatchina and since a part of the Petrograd troops are tired it is imperative that we have the strongest reinforcements as soon as possible," Lenin responded.

"Anything else?" Sheinman asked.

"Instead of 'anything else,'" Lenin said, "I expected you to say you were ready to set out and fight."

I. Mikhailov, chairman of the military department, came on the line and asked: "How many men do you need?"

Lenin replied: "As many as possible but only loyal men who are ready to fight." Mikhailov promised to send five thousand within twenty-four hours. Lenin asked him if they had heard of the new government and how the news had been received.

"We heard about the government only from the papers," Mikhailov said. "People over here are enthusiastic about power passing into the hands of the Soviets."

N. F. Izmailov, the Tsentrobalt representative, promised to send to Petrograd the battleship *Republic* and two destroyers. They should arrive within eighteen hours. Lenin said he wanted to put the battleship in the Ship Canal as close to the shore as possible, but Izmailov, with an air of superiority, told him the battleship was not to be anchored near the shore but in the roads close to the cruiser *Aurora* "because its guns have a range of 25 versts" (about 16.5 miles).

"In short," Izmailov added, "let the sailors and their command handle this."

Lenin asked for all available stocks of rifles and ammunition. Izmailov promised to send what they had.

"Good-by, good luck," Lenin said.

"Good-by," Izmailov said. "Was that you speaking? Will you tell me your name?"

"Lenin," was the reply.

"Good-by," Izmailov said. "We're setting everything in motion."[9]

When Lenin told Sheinman that "part of the Petrograd troops are tired," this was, of course, a euphemism. The truth was that today, after the Bolshevik seizure of power just as before and during the coup, most of the Petrograd garrison was continuing to declare itself "neutral." The troops were on a sit-down strike. They had no intention of fighting anyone or for anyone and especially they had no intention of fighting their fellow Russian soldiers. To a considerable extent this was the attitude, as well, of the Petrograd workers, which, of course, affected the fighting capabilities of the Red Guard.

The plain truth was that outside of a few—very few—units, like the Kexholm Regiment (which was, in theory at least, not Russian but Finnish)—Lenin had almost no reliable fighting men. His only certain resources were the naval detachments from Kronshtadt and the Baltic Fleet. He had virtually no artillery, which was why he was hysterically eager to get ships of the Baltic Fleet into Petrograd to use as floating artillery.

The next day the news was worse—or so it seemed to Lenin and his worried associates at Smolny. Krasnov's III Cossack Corps swept into Tsarskoye Selo. There were rumors of fresh anti-Bolshevik troops moving on Petrograd from the front. In Moscow anti-Bolshevik Junkers and other opponents centered in the Kremlin had fought the new Soviet power to a standstill. Lenin had thought Moscow a stronger Bolshevik citadel than Petrograd and had at one time proposed to launch his coup d'état from Moscow. Now it was obvious that his judgment of Bolshevik strength in Moscow had been wrong. The outcome of the Moscow battle was very much in doubt and Lenin had no forces to send in as reinforcements and even if he had, the railroad union, Vikzhel, would not permit their movement. Vikzhel was "neutral" and adamant against spreading the flames of civil war.

Uncertain whether he could halt Kerensky and Krasnov, Lenin called for twenty thousand workers to throw up trenches on the approaches to the capital (there is no evidence that any such number turned out). He was consumed with worry that the workers would not stand by the Bolshevik regime and amidst his concerns himself went to the Putilov works to give a rallying speech.[10] There was sound basis for Lenin's concern. District and factory Bolshevik leaders were reporting signs of "fatigue" among the workers and "total indifference." The workers opposed civil war, opposed shedding blood, and they wanted differences resolved by "peaceful means." Trotsky admitted that within a day or two of the coup it was obvious that the revolutionary mood of the workers had been exaggerated. The truth was, of course, that the Bolshevik field workers had stressed again and again the lack of revolutionary fire among the factory proletariat. Lenin strongly overrode this opinion. Antonov-Ovseyenko reported that the Petrograd garrison had collapsed. It could not be depended upon for anything. An old friend found Lenin pale and his face twitching with nervousness. Raskolnikov said that Lenin's nervousness sharply increased after the fall of Gatchina. "The situation of the Revolution is in deadly danger," Lenin told him. His associates were near panic. Lozovsky asked John Reed what "a mere crowd" could do against trained soldiers and Petrovsky feared a whole army corps might appear against them on the morrow. "But they will not take us alive," he insisted. The new regime's orders were ignored. Petrograd had been placed in a state of siege but crowds surged along the Nevsky, indifferent to the Government's edict. When a band of fifty Red Guards tried to interfere, they were disarmed by the crowds, most of them workers.[11]

The news got worse. At 2 A.M. on the twenty-eighth Krasnov's cavalry moved out of Gatchina. Kerensky—at Krasnov's orders—stayed behind. The Cossacks advanced cautiously. There was no fighting. Kerensky was on tenterhooks. Krasnov was no more eager than anyone else for real combat. He hesitated on the outskirts of Tsarskoye Selo until Stankevich, the Provisional Government's Army Commissar, arrived from Petrograd full of optimism about overthrowing the Bolsheviks and putting Kerensky back in power.[12] This emboldened Krasnov. Toward evening Voitinsky, another Provisional Government Army Commissar who by a fluke had managed to escape from Pskov, found Krasnov speaking from an army truck on the outskirts of Tsarskoye Selo. A handful of mounted Cossacks stood around him. In the field beside the road had assembled ten thousand soldiers of the Tsarskoye Selo garrison.

"Enough foolishness, lads," Krasnov was saying. "The people of Russia will not yield to the garrison of a single city. Lay down your arms and return in peace to your barracks. Do not compel me to use force."

There was some shuffling. The Cossacks set up a gun.

One of the soldiers shouted: "Don't fire, you devils! We don't want trouble."

"I don't want trouble either," Krasnov replied. "Put the guns and shells back on the truck."

Voitinsky went up to Krasnov and asked what forces he had. He took a little notebook from his pocket and read: "October 27, 6 A.M. three *sotni*, six artillery pieces. October 27, 6 P.M. six sotni, 16 artillery pieces, six machine guns with crew." A sotnya was a regiment of cavalry—between one hundred and two hundred men. Krasnov's units, however, averaged about seventy men per sotnya.

By evening Krasnov had occupied Tsarskoye Selo, and by morning of the twenty-ninth his muster had risen to twelve sotni, a four-car armored train, a tank, and one infantry company.[13]

The force which threatened to take Petrograd and which had driven Lenin and his associates to panic numbered a little more than twelve hundred men.

But the panic was real and it became more real. On Saturday night in Moscow the Bolsheviks lost the Kremlin, the post office, the telephone and telegraph offices, and many local headquarters.[14] In the early morning hours of Sunday the twenty-ninth in Petrograd a patrol of Red Guards arrested two men near the Kshesinskaya mansion and took them to the Peter and Paul Fortress. One proved to be a member of the Central Committee of the SRs, named A. S. Bruderer, and he had in his pocket instructions from the Committee to Save the Fatherland and the Revolution naming special commissars for the cadet schools and ordering them to a state of military readiness for taking the offensive. Alarmed by the arrests (to which the Bolsheviks paid little heed), the committee sent its forces into action prematurely. Headquarters were set up in the Engineers Castle. Five cadet schools joined in an attack on the Bolsheviks.

At 8:50 on the morning of the twenty-ninth a squad of cadets, disguised as Red Guards, appeared at the Central Telephone Station, overpowered a detail of the Kexholm Regiment, and took over the station, cutting communications at Smolny, the Peter and Paul Fortress, and other important offices. Other cadet details seized the Astoria Hotel and the State Bank. Cadet street patrols began to halt traffic.[15] Their ultimate objective was an attack on Smolny and the Peter and Paul Fortress.

That morning, Albert Rhys Williams, the American correspondent and Bolshevik sympathizer, heard there was trouble at the telephone station. He went up to the stone building on the Morskaya and slipped inside, where he found the cadets fortifying the place under the direction, he later insisted, of a French officer. When Williams showed his American passport, he was greeted as a friend. He looked on as the cadets piled up barricades, stacked boxes, and halted automobiles on the street outside. Suddenly there was a cheer and some cadets brought in a prize—Antonov-Ovseyenko, the Soviet military chief who had been sent to oust the cadets. The cadets were jubilant. How could they help winning now they had captured the enemy commander?

But the battle intensified. Machine guns chattered away on both sides. An officer pasted huge red crosses on a car, invited Williams to come along, and the automobile pushed out of the entranceway and up to the Red Guard lines. After a little parley the car was permitted through to pick up Red Cross supplies. Instead, it hurried to the Engineers Castle to call for reinforcements. Then back again the car went, loaded with hand grenades and provided with newly forged credentials of the Bolshevik Military Revolutionary Committee. Again it passed the Red Guard lines and entered the telephone headquarters. What Williams thought he was doing in this caper he never made clear.

The daring maneuver did not save the day. The Bolsheviks brought up an armored car and broke through the barricades. Soon Red Guards were storming up the staircase. Now the cadets turned to Williams and begged him to go to the captured Antonov-Ovseyenko. Williams was to offer Antonov-Ovseyenko freedom in exchange for their lives.

"So," Antonov said to Williams, "I am not to be a corpse, but a commander." He put on his broad-brimmed artist's hat and joined the Junkers.

"Tovarishch Antonov," the cadets begged. "Give us your word as a Bolshevik, a true Bolshevik."

"My word," he said. "I give it. If they kill you they must first kill me."

A moment later the Red Guards stormed into the room wild with rage. They were about to slaughter the cadets with a burst of machine-gun fire.

"Wipe out the butchers!" they shouted. "Kill the White devils."[16]

Antonov-Ovseyenko halted them.

"They have given up their arms," he said. "I have given them their lives."

"You may give them their lives. We don't. We give them the bayonet," a big peasant shouted.

Antonov-Ovseyenko pulled out a huge revolver: "The first man who lays hands on a prisoner—I will kill him on the spot."

The crowd recoiled growling and angry. Antonov-Ovseyenko turned to Williams. "Speak to them, comrade," he said, playing for time. Williams stepped to the front and began a long harangue in English. No one understood a word he said but as time passed passions simmered down. Antonov was able to get the cadets out of the telephone exchange. They were marched to the Peter and Paul Fortress. Near the Winter Palace crowds broke through the lines and mauled some of them but the Red Guards managed to save them. However, this was not to be the case throughout Petrograd. Or in the prisons. Not a few cadets were torn limb from limb. Special orders were given to the prisons to try to protect them.[17]* Often the orders were not carried out.

* There was hundreds if not thousands of brutal murders by Red Guards, sailors, soldiers, and Bolshevik sympathizers in the days, weeks, and months to follow. One of the earliest and least excusable was that of Gen. N. N. Dukhonin, the Stavka commander who was discharged by Lenin for refusal to enter into armistice talks with the Germans. When his successor, Naval Ensign N. V. Krylenko, arrived at Mogilev to take over as commander in chief, a mob of sailors who accompanied Krylenko murdered Dukhonin in Krylenko's presence, running a bayonet through his back. Krylenko found it "not possible" to identify the murderers. (M. A. Bonch-Bruyevich, *Vsye Vlast Sovetam*, pp. 218–20.)

Exactly how many were killed and wounded in the Sunday uprising will never be known. Sukhanov estimated each side lost about two hundred killed and wounded.[18] *Izvestiya* reported the next day that twenty-four persons—eleven workers and thirteen soldiers—were killed and seventeen wounded. *Novaya Zhizn* put the over-all total at about two hundred killed and wounded.[19]

It was a trivial engagement, crudely prepared, carried out in confusion, filled with accident and coincidence. But this was the pattern of events in these revolutionary days.

Arthur T. Dailey, an American working for the Petrograd branch of the National City Bank of New York, saw a Russian general shot down in the street outside the bank's offices on the English Embankment. As the body lay on the sidewalk young girls came by, dipped the toes of their boots in the blood, and walked on, laughing. On another day a company of soldiers was marching past. Two of them fell into violent argument. One raised his rifle and shot the other through the head. The company marched on leaving the body lying where it fell.[20]

This pattern of trivial almost accidental engagements held true at the "front"—the Kerensky-Krasnov front—as well.

Now Krasnov was advancing on Pulkovo, site of Russia's astronomical observatory and the heights which commanded the southern approaches to Petrograd. Lenin had put together a ragtag force—some Red Guards, some sailors, some troops. The Bolsheviks had three or four armored cars, they had dug some shallow trenches and had mounted a number of machine guns. The terrain was not suitable for maneuver by Krasnov's cavalry. They had to dismount and act as infantry.[21] Krasnov contended that his twelve hundred men were up against fifty thousand Bolshevik troops—granted they were badly handled—but he did not dare press forward in his engagement. His forces would simply be smothered. He ordered a pullback to Gatchina.[22]

The balance, little by little, was tipping toward the Bolsheviks. Not because of their strength but because of the opposition's weakness and disorganization. This is easier seen in retrospect than it was at the time.

In the course of Sunday, with the outcome of the battle with the cadets still in doubt, a Bolshevik Central Committee meeting (not attended by Lenin and Trotsky, who presumably were trying to put down the Petrograd revolt) voted to accept the ultimatum of the big railroad union, Vikzhel, and enter conversations to broaden the base of the Government by including members of other socialist parties.

The Bolsheviks agreed to include the parties on a basis proportionate to their representation in the All-Russian Soviet, and to admit as well representatives of the railroad unions, postal-telegraph workers, and similar organizations. The vote to enter the talks was five to one with three members abstaining. Kamenev and Sokolnikov were named to represent the Bolsheviks.[23]

The Bolshevik coup was four days old. Already Lenin's comrades were moving on a conciliatory course which Lenin had sworn he would never take. He had forced the coup almost singlehanded. He had insisted that it be a Bolshevik coup with no one else (except a few left SRs) participating. Now with Soviet power less than ninety-six hours old his associates were ready to form a coalition regime. Whatever Lenin thought at this moment (and his thoughts and views were not marked down by any of his associates), it is hard to believe he could have shared their willingness to yield to the tough-talking railroad men or to bargain with his socialist rivals of so many years. His subsequent conduct supports this view.

The talks began at the Vikzhel headquarters late Sunday, a few hours after the Bolshevik acceptance. From the beginning Vikzhel was insistent that there be agreement between all parties. The Bolsheviks regarded Vikzhel as openly hostile; the other socialist parties suspected Vikzhel was a Communist tool.[24] The truth was Vikzhel was playing as neutral a role as was possible in a confused and overheated situation.

From the beginning many delegates—including those of the City Duma—insisted that no Bolsheviks should sit in the new Government and particularly that neither Lenin nor Trotsky should participate. When An—sky, speaking for the Duma, proposed that Lenin and Trotsky be excluded, the Bolshevik delegate D. B. Ryazanov exploded.

On Monday morning the thirtieth, after the quelling of the Junkers uprising, the Bolshevik Military Revolutionary Committee issued a decree ordering all participants in the revolt tried before special "military revolutionary courts."

At the Vikzhel meeting three veteran revolutionary opponents of the Bolsheviks—Martov, Dan, and V. N. Filippovsky—accused the Bolsheviks of employing "red terror" to cling to power. It was the first time this charge was uttered. The Vikshel participants finally instructed the Bolshevik Lozovsky and the Menshevik internationalist Martov to draft a resolution declaring that employment of political terror including the use of exceptional courts was "impermissible."[25]

The delegates were still arguing at 3 A.M. when the doorman reported that a delegation of Putilov workers was outside, demanding to be admitted. After some argument the workers pushed their way in.

"For a week there's been bloodletting between both revolutionary camps," the Putilov leader shouted. "Civil war has begun. That's enough. You've already had two sessions. We aren't going to permit any more civil war. The hell with Lenin and Chernov! Let's hang them both! We're telling you: bring an end to this disorder—or we'll take care of you!"

Several delegates, including the Bolshevik Ryazanov and the Duma delegate An—sky, tried to answer the angry workers by explaining the nature of their disagreements. They got nowhere.

"The devil take you," the workers shouted, "whichever of you may be right. We'll hang you all from the same tree and let the country be at peace. Come on, lads, there's nothing for us to do here."

They marched out into the dark raw night.[26]

The angry discussions among the political parties went on, but finally an agreement was hammered out late on the evening of the thirty-first. There was to be a new Soviet with one hundred workers' representatives, seventy-five peasants, one hundred delegates from the Petrograd and Moscow Dumas, fifty representing Tsentroflot, fifteen representing Vikzhel, and twenty representing other trade unions.

Agreement was reached on a new government to be headed by Chernov. Neither Lenin nor Trotsky was included. Five Bolsheviks were named in a cabinet of eighteen.[27] Whether the Bolshevik delegates who agreed to these proposals really thought that they would win the approval of the Party (and particularly of Lenin and Trotsky) is not entirely clear. The Bolshevik delegates were Kamenev, Sokolnikov, and Ryazanov. Later they would be charged with violating their instructions, with endangering the Party and the cause of the Revolution.[28] In truth, in agreeing to compromises to broaden the base of the Government and to eliminate the controversial figures of Lenin and Trotsky, the delegates were much closer to the mainstream of Party and revolutionary opinion than their critics.

The stand of the Putilov delegates supported the conciliatory line, and on the very night when the final Vikzhel agreement was being hammered out delegations from the Litovsky and other regiments appeared at the Bolshevik Military Revolutionary Committee and raised the question of talks with the Kerensky troops with a view to ending the fighting which pitted Russian soldier against Russian soldier. The Bolsheviks were strongly opposed to this, but the Litovsky Regiment insisted it was going to send its delegates both to Kerensky and to the Committee to Save the Fatherland and the Revolution. Stalin and Zinoviev tried to argue them out of it. The best the Bolsheviks could do was to set up a commission headed by Zinoviev and Uritsky to work with the regiment in drafting proposals for their talks with Kerensky's Cossacks.[29]

The same attitude appeared at Gatchina, where late on October 31 and early November 1 the Cossacks and Lenin's military representative Ensign P. Ye. Dybenko, entered into conversations. The Cossacks had never loved Kerensky, and Dybenko had little difficulty in convincing them that they should turn over Kerensky to the Bolsheviks. In return he would give them safe conduct to the Don, letting them take their horses and their arms. According to General Krasnov, Dybenko, from the beginning, suggested an exchange. The Cossacks would give him Kerensky and he would give them Lenin. The Cossacks were delighted with the proposal and came running to General Krasnov, ready to hang Kerensky in the Gatchina Palace courtyard.[30]

Kerensky managed to make his escape from Gatchina, dressed as a sailor, to the violent anger of the Cossacks.[31] Nonetheless they sat down with Dybenko to work out the agreement.

Voitinsky, who had gone to Luga to try to get some reinforcements, returned to Gatchina as the talks were getting under way. He found ten Cossack representatives on one side of a long table facing a row of sailors. Dybenko stood out amongst them. He was a huge handsome man with broad shoulders and a tanned face, black beard, and bright arrogant eyes.

Dybenko had agreed to terms for the safe conduct of the Cossacks back to the Don. Now the Cossacks were demanding the release of officers and military cadets held by the Bolsheviks. Dybenko refused. Then he relented. "I would not mind turning those blackguards over to them," he said to his companion, Tushin. "Why should we feed them?"

So it was agreed that all officers and military cadets arrested after October 23 in Petrograd would be released.

"Now," said the chairman of the Cossacks, "about Lenin and Trotsky. They must go."

"None of your business!" Dybenko shouted.

"Make it fair," the Cossacks said. "You told us Kerensky must not be in the Government until he cleared himself of having conspired with Kornilov. We agreed. Well, weren't Lenin and Trotsky charged with being German spies? Until they clear themselves, they must not be in the Government."

Wild argument raged. Finally Tushin said: "Let them have their way. I rather like their guts."

So solemnly was written into the agreement: "Lenin and Trotsky will withdraw from the government and abstain from any public activity until they have cleared themselves of the charge of having worked for the enemy."

To the amazement of Voitinsky, Dybenko calmly signed the agreement. The Cossacks assembled. They were permitted to keep their arms and horses and, in very little time, had made their way back to the Don, there to become the central force in the civil war which would break out against Soviet power. Krasnov and Voitinsky were arrested and taken to Moscow.[32]

Dybenko's agreement was repudiated by Lenin and his associates. Dybenko, they said, had exceeded his authority. He was authorized only to negotiate about the Cossacks, not about political matters. But there was only a light censure of him.

As for the agreement of Kamenev, Sokolnikov, and Ryazanov in the Vikzhel talks for a government without Lenin and Trotsky—this, too, was overturned by Lenin in a series of meetings of the Central Committee in which he and others excoriated Kamenev for exceeding his instructions. As Lenin remarked: "The negotiations were only to serve as a diplomatic cover for military operations."[33]

In other words, so far as Lenin was concerned, the idea of compromise, of joining forces with the other parties of the left, of diluting the Bolshevik regime, was pure hypocrisy.

Now, with the tide running his way against Kerensky, with the Junkers shattered in Petrograd and the battle in Moscow beginning to turn, he had no more need of "diplomatic cover."

As Voitinsky noted on being imprisoned in the Peter and Paul Fortress:

"A dictatorship began to emerge from the chaos. Printing plants were taken over by the government. Political clubs were closed. All meetings except for those called by the government parties were prohibited. Jails emptied by the March revolution were packed again."[34]

Lenin went before the Petrograd Soviet on November 4 to appeal for support. A number of delegates from front-line units were there.

"We are accused," he said, "of resorting to terrorism but we have not resorted and I hope will not resort to the terrorism of the French revolutionaries who guillotined unarmed men. I hope we shall not resort to it because we have strength on our side."[35]

The truth was, as Lenin knew, that the terror was already well under way.

LIX

Full Steam Ahead Through the Swamp

No one irritated Zinaida Gippius as did Gorky. She could forgive Blok and Bely for their support of the Bolsheviks. They were, after all, "lost children." In fact, Blok had even described himself to her as a "lost child." To argue with them was useless. Bely was irresponsible and timid and now he had gone back to Moscow, romping with the Bolsheviks, as Gippius put it.[1] But Gorky was something else. Gippius' spirits had steadily sunk since the Bolshevik take-over. She was not surprised at the failure of Kerensky and Krasnov at Gatchina. Nothing Kerensky had done since July had been done right. Nor was her mood improved by word that Boris Savinkov had gone to Gatchina. Inevitably he would join Kerensky and Krasnov. Inevitably they would fail. What lay ahead? "Civil war without end and without limit"—this was her fear.[2] Meantime there was the question of the prisoners in Peter and Paul Fortress, the Kerensky Ministers, Tereshchenko, Konovalov, Tretyakov, and the others. Conditions were terrifying. No one had any control over the guards. The lives of all prisoners balanced on sword's edge. The only hope was intervention by Lenin or Trotsky and the only person to whom Gippius could turn was Gorky, who was already being called in Petrograd salons, "The Negro in a silk hat," the servant, in other words, of his Bolshevik masters.[3]

Gippius and a friend spoke to Gorky. She described him as "dark and black and grim" and his voice sounded like the barking of a dog.

"I am . . . organically . . . unable . . . to speak with those—scoundrels . . . Lenin and Trotsky," he said when asked to intervene.

He had, however, just written an article for *Novaya Zhizn* on the subject. Gippius was outraged.

"The devil with your articles!" she cried. "None of your articles are going to set you apart from those Bolshevik scoundrels, as you call them. You must get out of this company. Aside from all the shadows which fall over you from your closeness to the Bolsheviks—what about yourself? What does your own conscience tell you?"

Gorky got up and barked deeply:

"And if I leave . . . with whom will I be?"

"You will be with Russia," Gippius snapped.[4]

Gippius' indignation was not well placed. The article to which Gorky referred was no small thing. It was a raging indictment of the Bolsheviks and his comrade of so many years, Lenin.

"Lenin, Trotsky and their companions have already become poisoned with the filthy venom of power and this is evidenced by their shameful attitude toward freedom of speech, the individual and the sum total of those rights for the triumph of which democracy struggled," Gorky wrote in *Novaya Zhizn* of November 7.

"Lenin and his associates," he declared, "consider it possible to commit all kinds of crimes, such as the slaughter outside St. Petersburg [the battle of Pulkovo], the destruction of Moscow [the Kremlin had been badly damaged by Bolshevik cannon], the abolition of free speech and senseless arrests—all the abominations which Plehve and Stolypin once perpetrated."

Gorky summoned the proletariat to repudiate Lenin.

"The workers," he said, "must not allow adventurers and madmen to heap shameful, senseless and bloody crimes on the head of the proletariat, for which not Lenin but the proletariat itself will pay." He called Lenin "not an omnipotent magician but a cold-blooded trickster who spares neither the honor nor the life of the proletariat."[5]

This was only the beginning. Three days later he charged that Lenin was introducing a socialist order "By Nechayev's method—'full steam ahead through the swamp.'"

The experiment was doomed to failure, but this did not, Gorky said, bother Lenin, whom he called "a 'leader' and a Russian nobleman not without certain psychological traits of this extinct class."

"The inevitable tragedy does not disturb Lenin, the slave of dogma, or his cronies—his slaves," he said. "Life in all its complexity is unknown to Lenin. He does not know the popular masses, he has not lived with them. . . . The working class is for Lenin what ore is for a metalworker. . . . He works like a chemist in a laboratory."

Gorky's views were strong but he was by no means alone. When Lenin presented his resolution suspending freedom of the press to the

Central Committee, Kamenev, A. I. Rykov, Milyutin, Zinoviev, and Nogin resigned. And Rykov, Milyutin, I. A. Teodorovich, Ryazanov, Shlyapnikov, and N. I. Derbyshev quit the Soviet of People's Commissars. Lunacharsky and Lozovsky supported them. Lunacharsky was so outraged he wrote a violent letter which was published by *Novaya Zhizn:* "What next? Where are we going? I can't support this. It is more than I can stand. I am helpless to halt this terror. That is why I am resigning from the Soviet of People's Commissars." His resignation was refused and Lunacharsky continued in the Government.[6] Zinoviev, typically, withdrew his resignation the next day. But Lozovsky stuck to his guns. He condemned Lenin's "regime of the bayonet and the saber" and refused to join with the Bolshevik faction which had stated "that for one of ours we shall kill five opponents."[7] Lenin had Lozovsky expelled from the Party but he was permitted to return in December 1919.*

The issue had been joined. What kind of a revolution were the Bolsheviks going to make?

Gorky for his part had taken his stand. The Lenin Revolution was not the one for which he had labored for twenty years. He soon became the center of a whirlwind. *Pravda* and the other Bolshevik organs centered their attack on him. He was called a betrayer. *Pravda* published a letter from three noncommissioned officers, asking whether Gorky was naïve or just a liar. "Who is defaming the Russian revolution more—Comrades Lenin and Trotsky or you, Comrade Gorky?"

Gorky stuck to his guns.

"I think that to gag with a fist the mouth of *Rech* and other bourgeois newspapers only because they are hostile to democracy is a disgrace to democracy," he insisted. "To frighten by terror and violence those who do not wish to participate in Mr. Trotsky's frenzied dance on the ruins of Russia is disgraceful and criminal."[8]

Pravda retorted that Gorky was beginning to speak the language of the enemies of the working class. Gorky replied:

"I cannot regard as 'inevitable' such facts as the plundering of national wealth in the Winter Palace, the Gatchina Palace and others.

"I am especially suspicious, especially distrustful, of a Russian when he gets power into his hands. Not long ago a slave, he becomes the most unbridled despot as soon as he has the chance to become his neighbor's master."[9]

Gorky wrote his wife in Moscow on December 2 that while he was not ill his nerves had been shattered. "I can't sleep and my mood is so

* Lozovsky, who became the principal Soviet Government spokesman in World War II, was purged and shot by Stalin in the so-called Jewish Anti-Fascist Committee case in 1952. (Roy A. Medvedev, *Let History Judge*, p. 484.)

heavy that it is simply a catastrophe. I try not to show it to those close
to me but—how can I not show it?

"Things are very bad with Russia. Very bad."[10]

Gorky's bleak forebodings were not shared by Mayakovsky. He
went to Smolny on October 25 and saw Lenin there. "To take part or
not to take part," Mayakovsky wrote in his autobiography. "For me
(and for other Moscow-Futurists) there was no such question. It was
my Revolution. I went to Smolny. Worked. Did everything that came
along. Meetings began to be held."

A friend who saw him at Smolny said Mayakovsky was moved to
the point of tears by the spectacle of the workers and peasants in the
hall.[11] He hailed the Bolshevik coup with a not-very-good poem which
he called "Our March." (*Happiness sing! Sing! In our veins Spring
overflows. Heart! Beat for battle! Our breast is a copper kettledrum.*)
There was no hint in these words of the power of "Left March!" (*Who
there marches right? Left! Left! Left!*), which he would write within a
year.[12]

Mayakovsky was finally released from further liability for military
service. He wrote his mother that he was going to have his "teeth and
nose" fixed. Then he was going to Moscow.[13] The fact was he was having trouble making ends meet in Petrograd. He caught a train for
Moscow and joined his old friends David Burlyuk and Vasily Kamensky. Kamensky had persuaded Filippov, the Moscow baker (his
shops had been the center of struggle during the February Days and
even earlier during the 1905 revolt in Moscow), to subsidize a small
café for poets.[14] It was located in an old laundry on a small pereulok
called Nastasyinsky just off the Tverskaya.[15]

Mayakovsky came to Burlyuk and Kamensky. "How, brothers," he
said, "do you take me in?" They agreed and the receipts of the Poets
Café henceforth were divided three ways between Burlyuk, Kamensky, and Mayakovsky.[16]

The walls of the café were decorated by Burlyuk in what he called
cannibal orange and covered with drawings by Mayakovsky and others
whose eccentricities were calculated to arouse the public. On one wall
Mayakovsky scrawled a quotation from an early poem—"I like watching children die." This was designed to shock. Every night Mayakovsky in his yellow tunic recited his verses. David Burlyuk would
take the platform, his face heavy with powder, lorgnette in hand, and
declaim: "I like pregnant men. . . ." That, too, was calculated to
shock. A man named Vladimir Goldshmidt dyed two locks of his hair
gold, demonstrated his strength by splintering boards and throwing
drunks out of the café, and one day put up a nude statue of himself in

Teatralnaya Square, opposite the Bolshoi Theater, where it remained for quite a while before some brawlers smashed it down.

The café did not fill up until after the theaters. Then drifted in profiteers, former officers, prostitutes, sailors who had no other place to go, burly men in overcoats with revolvers stuck in their belts, some with ammunition belts over their shoulders, anarchists, a mysterious man named Guido who wore a colored silk shirt, jewels around his neck, rings on his fingers, and two revolvers in his belt, members of a "commune" that seemed to be made up of the "poet-singer" Aristrakh Klimov and a number of young girls.

One night the café was filled with anarchists. They brought along a café singer who took the stage and began to sing:

> Soldiers, soldiers, down the street are marching!
> Soldiers, soldiers, songs are singing!

Mayakovsky went into a rage. He banged the table so hard many thought a gun had exploded. "Get off the platform," he shouted. "Get that scoundrel away."

Yakov Blyumkin, the left SR who later was to murder the German ambassador, Baron Wilhelm von Mirbach, shouted back at Mayakovsky:

"Do you think, Mayakovsky, that sailors understand your poems?"

The anarchists swarmed toward Mayakovsky. Then a patrol of Red Guards sitting in the back surged forward, rifles in hand. An anarchist fired his revolver into the ceiling, the crowd quieted, and Mayakovsky began to shout out his poem "Revolution": "Citizens! Today is being destroyed the thousand-year-old Past! Today we are looking at the world anew! Today to the last button of our coats life is being made anew!"[17]

As Mayakovsky wrote to the Briks: "The café for the time being is a pleasant gay establishment. We send the public to the devil. At midnight we divide the till. That's all . . . A lot of fun. Imagine, for instance, how Vysotsky, Marants and Shatklov (and the banks are closed) listen, straining all their attention to Dodya's 'He terribly loved flies with fat abdomens.'"[18]

What was happening in the world outside the doors of the former laundry on Nastasyinsky Pereulok? It could not easily be guessed from the poems, from the rows, from the scandals. Mayakovsky did not know. He wrote the Briks: "All women love me. All men respect me. All women are sticky and boring. All men—scoundrels. . . . Do write! How's Lila's little knee?"[19]

Paustovsky was in Moscow, too, working on one of the few remaining non-Bolshevik papers. One evening he walked in the park. There was an early thaw. Melting snow dropped from the trees and the smell of rotten leaves was in the air.

"Words thundered over the country," he remembered. "Insistent summons to struggle, impatient, exultant, accusing, threatening . . .

"It was no time for nature. But the woods went on rustling just as vaguely, the ice on the rivers turned blue and watery. The same gloomy shaggy hoarfrost covered the linden trees on the Moscow boulevards in the mornings. . . .

"Everyone was caught up and deafened by the storm raging in his own consciousness. A man did not even glance at nature."[20]

Perhaps it was so for Lenin, too. Problem piled upon problem. Lenin moved relentlessly toward force and more force. Exasperated by the foot-dragging of officials of the State Bank who refused to cooperate, he turned to drastic measures. The director of the bank, I. P. Shipov, was arrested and brought to Smolny, where he was confined to a room where N. P. Gorbunov, secretary of the Soviet of People's Commissars, and V. P. Menzhinsky, Commissar of Finance, slept. Gorbunov let Shipov have his bed and slept in a chair. But the arrest of Shipov changed nothing. Finally Lenin called in Gorbunov and sent him and N. Osinsky, (V. V. Obelensky), State Bank Commissar, to the bank with a decree ordering the bank to give them 10 million rubles. "Don't come back without the money," Lenin said.

The pair went to the bank. Red Guards surrounded the building. Junior clerks and bank couriers supported the Soviet officials, and under the muzzles of the bank's own guards 10 million rubles was stuffed into old bags. Gorbunov and Osinsky put the bags over their shoulders, walked out to their automobile, and took the sacks to Smolny. Lenin was not in his office so Gorbunov dropped the bags on the floor and sat down with a cocked revolver to guard them. Soon Lenin returned. He was greatly pleased. The sacks were put in an old wardrobe in an adjoining office, chairs were put around in a semicircle, and a sentry stood duty over the first Soviet treasury.[21]

A bit later Lenin declared the leaders of the Kadet party "enemies of the people," liable to arrest and trial by revolutionary tribunal,[22] and swept them up (Countess S. V. Panina, Vladimir D. Nabokov, N. N. Aninov, A. I. Shingarev, F. F. Kokoshkin, and Prince Pavel Dolgorukov) in a quick series of arrests—all outside the law since the Kadet leaders had been elected to the Constituent Assembly which guaranteed parliamentary immunity from arrest.[23] Lenin cared nothing for this. Almost alone among his associates he had from the beginning insisted that the Constituent Assembly, that long-awaited, crowning jewel in Russian democratic life, be suppressed for the simple reason that the Bolsheviks would be unable to control it.[24]

True, Lenin had been compelled, because of the country's enormous faith in the Assembly, to declare to the Second Congress of Soviets on the evening of October 26 that the Bolsheviks would accept the verdict of the popular masses if they lost the elections.

But this had not kept him from lobbying privately to delay the elections, to postpone them, to wiggle out of the dilemma in some way. When the vote revealed that in a total of 707 the Bolsheviks would have only 175 members against 370 Socialist Revolutionaries, 40 left SRs, 17 Kadets, and 16 Mensheviks, his attitude toward the Constituent Assembly hardened.[25]

He told an old friend that he didn't yet want to say anything publicly but he added: "The 'Constituent' is already an old fairytale which there is no reason to carry on further. We have actually already passed this stage. But—well, we shall see. We promised—and so we'll see. In any case no 'Constituent' is going to knock us out of our position. No!"[26]

Lenin had already gotten rid of the Petrograd City Duma, that stubborn center of resistance to the Bolsheviks, by the device the Czar so often used. He simply ordered it prorogued and set new elections which the Bolsheviks were sure to win for November 26.[27] He employed, for the most part, the Military Revolutionary Committee to carry out repressive measures. This soon seemed neither efficient enough nor forceful enough.

On December 7 he took a historic step. He approved the creation of what was called the All-Russian Extraordinary Commission for Struggle against Counter-Revolution and Sabotage. The Russian initials for "Extraordinary Commission" were Ch. K. (pronounced Cheka) and became the most notorious term in the Russian language, just as it and its initialed successors, the GPU, the OGPU, the NKVD, the MVD, the KGB, and all the other Soviet instruments of police terror would become notorious throughout the world.[28]

A few days earlier Bonch-Bruyevich had submitted to Lenin evidence of a whole series of counterrevolutionary acts. Lenin wrinkled his brow, got up, and nervously began to pace up and down his office.

"Where are we going to find our Fouquier-Tinville?" he asked. Antoine Fouquier-Tinville was the tribune of the French Revolution who had, in the inexorable course of events, finally lost his own head to the guillotine to which he had sent so many others. Now Lenin found his Fouquier in Felix Edmundovich Dzerzhinsky, the thin-faced, saturnine, fiery-eyed single-minded Polish Communist who was named the first chairman and became, in fact, the creator of the Cheka.[29]

On the very next night Lenin sent a note to the Petrograd Party Committee: "Please send not less than 100 persons, *absolutely* reliable Party members, to room No. 75, second floor—the Committee to Combat Looting. (For performance of *commissar* duties)

"The matter is arch-important. The Party is responsible. Approach the districts and factories."[30]

Night after night the Cheka commandos swept out over Petrograd. On the night before Christmas Yelizaveta Drabkina was sitting with some of her young Communist friends in a former gambling house near the Ligovsky Prospekt which they had requisitioned as a center. A friend named Lenya Petrovsky appeared. They had been summoned to the Cheka for all-night duty. Before morning they were whisked by truck to the very end of Kamennoostrovsky Prospekt, where they stormed into the mansion of Count and Countess Vorontsov. Both were arrested and Drabkina was saved by a friend from a shot fired by the Count in a vain attempt to thwart the Cheka raiding party.[31]

The Vorontsovs were participants in one of the countless antiBolshevik plots. So it was alleged and so, no doubt, Lenin believed. There were so many real plots it was hard to separate rumor from fact and fantasy from reality. Night after night parties of soldiers were sent to try to halt the looting of liquor supplies that was turning Petrograd into a nightmare. The huge vaults of the Winter Palace contained thousands of barrels and tens of thousands of bottles. So did countless warehouses and residences of the rich and the royal. Bonch-Bruyevich and the other Bolsheviks became convinced the bourgeoisie were deliberately seeking to undermine the Revolution by besotting the soldiers and Red Guards with drink. Regiment after regiment was sent to protect the liquor supplies only to fall victim to temptation. All through December liquor stocks were confiscated, burned, or poured down the sewers that the Revolution might survive.

Food began to run out. The Czarist bureaucrats in one ministry after another refused to carry out orders or co-operate with the new regime. Lenin had thought any clerk could learn banking overnight. Now he was discovering how naïve he had been. On the same day he set up the Cheka he sent a telegram to his representative in Stockholm, V. V. Vorovsky: "Urgently find and send here three highly skilled accountants to work on reform of the banks. Knowledge of Russian is not essential. Fix their remuneration yourself in accordance with local conditions."[32]

Talks with the Germans had shakily gotten under way. An armistice was in effect until January 14 and Lenin had sent Trotsky to Brest-Litovsk to negotiate for the Soviet side. Lenin told Trotsky: "To delay negotiations there must be some one to do the delaying." Delay, Lenin felt, could only play into his hands because it was difficult to imagine falling into a position more weak or difficult.[33]

Breaking his public reticence, Lenin now spoke bluntly for the use of terror.

"The good of the revolution, the good of the working class is the highest law," he wrote in *Pravda*. "The 'good of the revolution' now demands a grim fight against saboteurs, organizers of military cadet insurrections, and newspapers run by bankers."

He quoted Plekhanov on the use of terror to protect the Revolution and added: "the enemies of socialism may be deprived for a time not only of inviolability of the person and not only of freedom of the press but of universal suffrage as well."

Kerensky and others, he charged, had used "terror against the workers, soldiers and peasants." Now:

"The Soviet government is taking strong measures against the landowners, marauders and their underlings—in the interests of the workers, soldiers and peasants.[34]

In other words—henceforth no quarter was to be given.

LX

The Twelve

Finally, on the day before Christmas Lenin decided to get out of Petrograd. Once again he was worn out—the same old story, frayed nerves, headaches, sleepless nights. Krupskaya had been trying for days to persuade him to take a holiday. Alexandra Kollontai joined in the plot to get Lenin to take a vacation. Her commissariat had just the place for him—a warm rest house called Khalila at Ysikirkka in Karelia. It was clean and bright and there was even hunting in the lovely forests around it.

At first Lenin objected, but gradually he came around to the idea. Perhaps nostalgia for the old days on the Volga and the merry Christmas times with his mother, his father, his brothers and sisters may have played a part in this. In any event Kollontai made the arrangements, and on the morning of the twenty-fourth Lenin appeared at the Finland Station, wearing his fall overcoat and a broad-brimmed hat. Krupskaya and Mariya Ilyinichna were with him. So was Eino Rahja, his faithful Finnish bodyguard, now acting as commissar of Finnish Railroads.

Kollontai found Lenin slumped in the corner seat of a compartment in a second-class car. Lenin thought that if he traveled second class he was less likely to attract attention and the security risk would be smaller. Kollontai brought three fur coats with her—one for Lenin, one for Krupskaya, and one for Mariya Ilyinichna. She had taken them out of the stocks of her Social Security Commissariat. (Red Guards in the first days of the Revolution had visited the houses and flats of the rich, confiscating fur coats and warm clothing for the benefit of soldiers and the poor.) The coats still bore their inventory marks.

Lenin accepted the coats. Then he suddenly remembered he had no Finnish money. He sent Kollontai off to get one hundred Finnish marks. She had hardly any money with her and brought Lenin back something less than he had asked for.[1]

Finally the train pulled out. Despite Lenin's "security" precautions his departure had attracted considerable attention from spectators in the station.[2] Soon Lenin was engaged in a conversation with a Finnish woman with Rahja acting as interpreter. Lenin wanted to know what her life was like. The woman said that before the Revolution she had had to pay the forest police for every twig of kindling she picked up in the forest. Now the soldiers helped her to gather wood. "Now," she said, "we no longer fear the man with the gun."[3]

The spotless Finnish cleanliness, the white curtains at the windows, the new-swept floors, reminded Lenin of his past stays in Finland, particularly the weeks he spent there waiting for events to move forward to the October Revolution. But somehow it wasn't the same. It wasn't much of a success as a holiday, Krupskaya recalled. Lenin couldn't seem to get into the mood. He dropped his voice when speaking, just as in the old conspiratorial days. He and Krupskaya went for long walks as they used to do in Switzerland but, as she said, "there was no real zest in them."

He tried to write but that went no better. He wrote three articles— one on consumer communes, another on competition, and a third on the old order and the certainty of victory of the new. But he was not satisfied with them. They went into his files and were not published until five years after his death when he was beginning to be turned into an icon and every scrap of paper to which he set his hand was treated as gospel.

Whether they had a *yolka* (Christmas tree) on the twenty-fifth, whether they tried to sing the old songs that had made the holiday at Simbirsk so warm and wonderful, Krupskaya did not record.* The

---

* The significance of Christmas, Orthodox Christian Christmas, in Lenin's life is not to be underestimated. Not only did he preserve his feeling for Christmas but it seemed to grow to the very end. The last formal function of Lenin's life was a Christmas party with a tree, arranged at his specific desire, at Gorki, the estate outside Moscow where he was confined after a succession of strokes rendered him semiparalyzed. The Christmas tree was set up at Gorki on his instruction on January 7, 1924, that is, December 25 by the Orthodox calendar, and neighborhood children were invited in. Lenin sat in a chair, smiling and enjoying himself, although unable to speak. Two weeks later, January 21, Lenin died. (L. A. Fotiyeva, *V. I. Lenin-Rukovoditel i Tovarishch*, p. 86.) It is characteristic of tendentious Soviet "scholarship" that the current official biography of Lenin, issued under the general

only good memory she recorded was of a glorious sleigh ride over the white Finnish snows on a winter road through the pine trees as they set out on the morning of the twenty-eighth to return to Petrograd.[4]

Lenin was hardly refreshed by his Finnish Christmas and he came back to the same troubles which he had left. The pressure of his critics had not relaxed. Day after day Gorky attacked. No threats swerved him from his course.

"The reformers from Smolny do not care about Russia," Gorky thundered, "they are cold-bloodedly sacrificing her to their dream of world or European revolution."

"As long as I am able," Gorky said, "I shall tell the Russian proletariat again and again:

"You are being led to ruin, you are being used as material for an inhuman experiment, and in the eyes of your leaders you are still not human beings."

A day later he wrote: "There is no poison more foul than power over people."

And the next day he simply described a street scene. A group of people was standing at the Fontanka. On the bridge was a dense crowd.

Gorky listened to the people talk.

"They're drowning thieves."

"Did they catch many?"

"Three, they say."

"They beat one, a youngster."

"Killed him?"

"What else did you expect?"

"They've got to beat them to death, otherwise they'll make your life a misery. . . ."

"Hey, he's howling!"

The crowd, Gorky said, became silent, straining to better hear the screams of the dying.

Nowhere, Gorky commented, was man beaten so often and with such zeal and joy as in Russia.

"It looks," he said, "as if these people brought up on torture have now been given the right to torture one another freely."[5]

New Year's Eve brought Lenin some jubilation. At Krupskaya's urging—she was still trying to lift him out of his depression—they went to the Mikhailovskoye Cadet School (the former Artillery Cadet

editorship of Pyotr P. Pospelov of the Institute of Marxism-Leninism, states that Lenin's children's party was held on New Year's Eve rather than on January 7, Orthodox Christmas. (V. I. Lenin, *Biografia*, p. 654.)

School) to attend a send-off the Vyborg district had arranged for some Red Guards who were going to the front for propaganda work. It was not easy getting there. Snow was piled deep in the streets. There were no more janitors. They had been "abolished" in one of the free and easy gestures of the early Revolution and now the chauffeur could hardly get the car containing Lenin and Krupskaya out of the Smolnaya Square. Snow was heaped shoulder-high. Finally they arrived at the Mikhailovskoye School about half an hour before midnight.

Lenin gave a little talk and then was hoisted up by the workers in his chair and hauled around the room.[6] It was a bright flicker in a dark period. The next day, New Year's Day, Lenin went to the Mikhailovsky Menage to address the first detachment of socialist troops who were going to the front. His spirits had fallen again. He made a dull, wooden speech. The applause was hesitant. It was the first time Albert Rhys Williams had heard Lenin fail with a crowd. The depression had not lifted.[7]

Lenin left the dark hall and got into his car to return to Smolny. As the car crossed the Simeonovsky Bridge across the Fontanka three shots were fired at it,[8] crashing through the windshield and body. Lenin's life was saved by Fritz Platten, the Swiss Social Democrat, who pushed Lenin's head down and was himself wounded in the hand.*

The perpetrators of the assassination attempt were never identified but the incident touched off a wave of terror and arrests.[9] Six days later the Kadet leaders Shingarev and Kokoshkin were murdered in their beds at the Mariinsky Hospital where they had been taken from the Peter and Paul Fortress because of the condition of their health. The murders were committed by sailors who broke into the hospital. Lenin gave orders that every effort be made to apprehend the murderers but the conviction remained that the responsibility for the crime lay, in fact, with Lenin and with the Bolshevik leaders who had whipped up the emotions of their followers to a murderous pitch.[10] This at least was to be the verdict of Lenin's political opponents, both left and right.[11]

Nor was the feeling mitigated by Lenin's handling of the Constituent Assembly. The Bolsheviks met the approach of the Assembly as though it were a plot to achieve their overthrow—which, to be certain, was the aim of some of its members. Lenin brought in fresh troops, particularly Lettish regiments. He put ashore fighting naval

* Fritz Platten was the man who was the guarantor of the "sealed" train across Germany. Lenin had invited him to the Soviet Union and credited him with saving his life. Stalin, however, purged Platten. He died in a concentration camp at Kargopol. (Roy A. Medvedev, *Let History Judge*, p. 201.)

detachments from the cruiser *Aurora* and the battleship *Republic* and assigned them to the Tauride Palace, where the Constituent Assembly was to meet. Commissars were named to protect security in the region of Smolny, the Tauride Palace, and the Peter and Paul Fortress. A special decree specified that any act by an individual or institution to take upon itself the function of state power would be regarded as counterrevolutionary. This was directed to the Constituent Assembly. If it declared itself to be what it was elected to be, that is, the supreme parliamentary power in the country, it was liable to arrest as a counterrevolutionary body.[12]

The Constituent Assembly convened on January 5, a day of special significance for Lenin. Lenin had been haunted by the bloody fate of the Paris Commune. Again and again he had asked his comrades whether they thought the Soviet would last as long as the Paris Commune. Just before he left for his Christmas holiday he had said again: "Ten more days and we shall have lived seventy days—as long as the Paris Commune."[13] Actually the Paris Commune endured seventy-one days, from March 18, 1871, to May 28, 1871. Now on this January 5 the Soviet regime equaled the record of the Paris Commune. Nothing —nothing—must be permitted to prevent it from outdistancing the Paris record.

Bonch-Bruyevich outdid himself in security arrangements. He spent the morning of the fifth dashing back and forth between the Tauride Palace and Smolny. There was an outbreak of firing at the intersection of the Nevsky and the Liteiny. Exactly who was responsible for the clash never became clear but a hundred people were killed and wounded.[14] Bonch-Bruyevich accompanied Lenin from Smolny to the Tauride Palace. Krupskaya, Mariya Ilyinichna, and Bonch-Bruyevich's wife rode with them. Bonch-Bruyevich had the car pick them up at an almost unused entrance to Smolny. The machine swung through back streets to an equally obscure entrance to the Tauride Palace, where the party was conducted to a guarded room set aside for Lenin's use. Krupskaya thought this cloak-and-dagger business irritated Lenin. He was even more irritated when he was about to enter the hall for the Constituent Assembly meeting at 4 P.M. He had left his Browning revolver in his overcoat pocket. He went to get it but the gun was gone. He rebuked Dybenko roundly. Dybenko was in charge of security at the hall.[15] It was the second rebuke of the day. On his way to the Tauride in a sleigh Uritsky had been held up by two thieves in an alley who robbed him of his fur coat. Lenin ordered Bonch-Bruyevich to get Uritsky's coat back. No trace of either coat or thieves could be found.[16]

The Constituent Assembly began on a sour note. Lenin had taken his place on the platform. Sverdlov, as head of the Bolshevik faction, had been instructed by Lenin to open the meeting. Sverdlov was a bit late, and S. P. Shvetsov, a Socialist Revolutionary and the senior delegate, made his way to the speaker's podium. It was the Russian (and European custom) that parliamentary sessions be opened by the senior member.

Shvetsov had just begun to call the meeting to order when Sverdlov, broad-shouldered, leather-coated, a lock of hair over his forehead, rushed up, roughly shoved Shvetsov away from the podium, grabbed the little bell, rang it for order, and opened the meeting (to catcalls[17]) with a demand that the Assembly as its first act approve a declaration drafted by Lenin decreeing that Russia was a Republic of Soviets of Workers, Soldiers, and Peasants' Deputies; approving all laws passed by the Second Soviet Congress; endorsing all acts of the Soviet of People's Commissars (including the decree that "any attempt on the part of any person or institution whatever to assume one or another function of state power will be regarded as a counterrevolutionary act"; and, finally, announcing its own dissolution with the statement:

"The Constituent Assembly considers its tasks completed with the establishment of the fundamental basis for a socialist remodelling of society."[18]

In other words if the Constituent Assembly were pleased to rubberstamp the Bolshevik coup of October 25, approve all its acts, and declare itself dead—it would be permitted to meet peacefully for the length of time required to complete these formalities.

Lenin did not speak. He sat uncomfortably in an armchair on the platform. Bonch-Bruyevich had never seen him so pale and nervous. His eyes were wide and sparkled with what Bonch-Bruyevich called "steel flames," ranging over the Assembly like those of a raging beast.[19] Later on he relaxed a bit, smiled ironically, joked, and jotted down notes. Krupskaya thought that he felt out of it all.[20] Finally, Lenin got up, walked to the back of the platform, and sprawled on the red-carpeted steps. He remained there awhile, his head nodding, his eyes closed, then returned to his box where he was promptly bearded by John Reed and Albert Rhys Williams. They couldn't get him to talk about the Constituent Assembly but when they got onto the subject of the Russian language he brightened up. He told the young Americans they must break the backbone of the language by learning all the nouns; then the verbs; then the adverbs and adjectives. Only at the end should they tackle the grammar.[21]

Viktor Chernov was elected chairman over the left SR Spiridonova, 244 to 151, and the Bolshevik proposal that the Constituent Assembly approve the Bolshevik regime and then quit was voted down 247 to

146. Lenin had had enough. He ordered his Bolshevik colleagues and their left SR allies to leave the Assembly. Later on he jotted down his impressions in a never-to-be-finished article. He spoke of "a tiresome, painful, dreary day in the elegant rooms of the Tauride Palace whose very appearance differs from that of Smolny as elegant but lifeless bourgeois parliamentarism differs from the proletarian, simple Soviet apparatus which, though in many ways, still disorderly and unfinished, is alive and vital."[22]

The Assembly went on. The great speakers of Russia's democracy took the rostrum, one after another—Chernov, Tsereteli (Bolshevik sailors in a casual act of hooliganism pointed their rifles at him as he spoke, others snapped their pistols in his face),[23] M. I. Skobelev, the Menshevik, and the others—as the audience in the galleries dwindled.

One of those who stayed to the end was Yelizaveta Drabkina. She and four friends had gotten spectators' tickets at Smolny. The talk went on and on, one living corpse after another, as she said. Midnight passed. One A.M., 2 A.M., 3 A.M., 4 A.M. Finally a tall blue-eyed sailor appeared behind Chernov on the platform. He came forward and said: "I invite all those present to leave the hall. The guard is tired."

"Who are you?" Chernov asked.

"I'm the chief of the guard for the Tauride Palace," he replied. He was Anton Zheleznyakov and he had orders from Dybenko to bring the session to an end.

"The members of the Constituent Assembly are also tired," Chernov said. "But exhaustion cannot interrupt our work which all Russia is watching."[24]

Chernov went on reading. The Assembly approved a decree declaring Russia a federal republic. It voted the transfer of land to the peasants and for a democratic peace program. "Dovolno, enough," the sailors shouted.[25]

Slowly the lights in the hall began to go off, one by one, first the side lights and then the central chandeliers. The sailor guards were plunging the hall into darkness.[26] Finally at 4:40 A.M. Chernov declared the session adjourned. It was to meet later that day, January 6, at noon.[27]

Yelizaveta Drabkina* and her friends came down to the palace entrance. Outside they found the Tauride Gardens filled with jolly sailors, delighted that their long vigil had come to an end. Yelizaveta's father, S. I. Gusev, Lenin's long-time Petrograd agent, appeared at the big double door. He took out of his brief case a huge brass key marked with the crown and wreath of Prince Potemkin-Tavridsky. He

---

* Yelizaveta Drabkina was arrested in the 1937 purge and survived seventeen years of prison camp life to be released in 1954.

fitted the key in the door and locked the Tauride Palace doors as Yelizaveta and her friends watched.

Did we go home and go to sleep? Yelizaveta asked many years later. By no means. It wasn't possible. The youngsters went out to help gather wood for the freezing city.[28]

When the delegates to the Constituent Assembly appeared at the Tauride Palace for the noon session, the doors were still locked and sailors armed with rifles, machine guns, and two fieldpieces prevented them from entering. The Soviet of People's Commissars had issued a decree proroguing the Assembly.[29] Newspapers that published accounts of the meeting were seized from the kiosks and burned.[30] The experiment in democracy for which Russia had waited three generations was at an end. The lights which Lenin's sailors darkened in the Tauride Palace would not go on again—for how many years no one yet knows.

But the Soviet regime had been saved—whatever the cost—and Lenin five days later would go before the Third All-Russia Congress of Soviets, a Bolshevik-packed body which he had hastily summoned to try to drive away the bad taste of the Constituent Assembly, and declare that the Soviet regime had now eclipsed the record of the Paris Commune by five days.

"If we compare the preceding dictatorship of the proletariat," said Lenin, "with the present one we shall see at once what a gigantic stride the international working-class movement has made, and in what an immeasurably more favorable position Soviet power in Russia finds itself, notwithstanding the incredibly complicated conditions of war and economic ruin."[31]

Suppression of the Constituent Assembly did not clear Lenin's skies. There remained the terrible question of making peace with Germany. On this Lenin fought, dodged, procrastinated, argued. Trotsky negotiated at Brest-Litovsk, finally proposing a policy of no-war-no-peace, whatever that might mean. The Germans held all the trumps. They revved up their military machine and began to advance. Lenin's support within the Central Committee evaporated. His comrades, outraged by German demands for annexations and dismemberment of Russia, voted for "revolutionary war." On January 8 at a meeting of Party leaders Lenin's peace resolution got only 15 votes against 32 for Bukharin's thesis of revolutionary war against Germany. Trotsky's idea of stopping the fighting but signing no peace got 16 votes. At a Central Committee meeting three days later Lenin ran into so much opposition he modified his position, and Trotsky's no-war-no-peace formula was approved by a vote of 9 to 7. At a meeting of the Petrograd Committee January 15 there was a large majority against Lenin.[32] Lenin's opponents included many of the outstanding members of the Party—Bukharin, Bubnov, Kollontai, Radek, S. V. Kosior, S. M. Yaroslavsky, G. L. Pyatakov, Uritsky, V. Kuibyshev, and Béla Kun. In the ranks of the opposition, a staunch advocate of revolutionary war, appeared Inessa Armand—the first time Lenin's dear friend had taken a public position radically opposed to his.[33]

For all this Lenin won out in the end. Terms for peace were agreed on February 23 (new style).* Once again Lenin had threatened to resign. Once again he had maneuvered and maneuvered until he managed to find a majority in the Central Committee, helped by the ever more Draconian terms advanced by the Germans. Now Lenin must give away not only Poland, the Ukraine, and the Baltic provinces but part of Belorussia and the cities of Kars, Batum, and Ardahan (to Turkey). The Russians must make peace with the Ukrainian Nationalist Rada regime, pay Germany a 6 billion mark indemnity, withdraw all troops from Finland and the Ukraine, and demobilize the Army.[34]

Peace was signed with the Germans March 3. The Soviet regime once more was preserved—but at what a price! Lenin privately assured his comrades he would violate every provision of the treaty which he could get away with. But there was no turning from the fact that he had signed away half the empire's western domain. He had split his party more badly than ever before. The Germans still stood at the gates to Petrograd. What might happen now, whether the life of the Soviet would really run much longer than that of the Paris Commune, no one could say.

Krupskaya remembered the winter of 1917–18 as one of the most difficult she had known. As never before Lenin was worried and distraught. The year had started badly and it did not improve. Sometimes in the early evening she and Lenin went for walks along the Neva near Smolny. One evening they walked along the embankment at dusk. The western sky flamed with a crimson sunset that reminded Krupskaya of the evening she walked back along the Neva with some comrades after her first meeting with Lenin at a blini party at maslenitsa in 1894. Here they were, Lenin and she, walking along the same embankment twenty-four years later as Lenin kept turning over in his mind the reasons why the formula of no-peace-no-war would not work. He had staked so much on a revolution in Germany. Daily he scanned the horizon for clues that it might be forthcoming. Now, he told her, "You never know!" like an inveterate gambler going back to the roulette table for one more turn of the wheel. But when they ar-

* The Soviet regime introduced the Western calendar to Russia in February 1918. The calendar ran January 29, 30, 31, then February 14 (instead of February 1 in the old Russian style).

rived at Smolny there was no news of revolution. Only the deadly reports of the German Army moving forward all along the Russian front,
drawing nearer and nearer to Petrograd.[35]

Hardly had peace been signed than Lenin gave the order: move to
Moscow. The danger of trying to maintain the Soviet Government in
Petrograd under the guns of the Germans was too great. At any move-
ment they might lash forward and stamp out the Revolution.

On March 11, the day Lenin took the train for Moscow, the Soviet
ruled a land not much bigger than that controlled by the early duchy
of Moscow five hundred years before. The whole northern and western portion had been lost down to the approaches of Petrograd and
Moscow. The South was gone. In the Don and the Cossack country
the White counterrevolutionary forces were gathering. To the east in
Siberia a weak Bolshevik hold on the larger cities was soon to be
shaken off, and in the deep forests and countryside the peasants had
hardly heard that Lenin and his men had taken power.

That day Lenin wrote an editorial for *Izvestiya*. He took as his
theme Nekrasov's famous poem "Who Can Be Happy and Free in
Russia":

> Thou art so wretched,
> Poor and sorrowful,
> Thou are so abundant
> Thou art mighty
> Thou are impotent,
> Mother Russia![36]

We must, said Lenin, measure fully, to the very depths, the abyss of
defeat, dismemberment, enslavement, and humiliation into which we
have been thrown. Only then could Russia rise anew, mighty, abun-
dant—and *socialist!*[37]

The words were grim. The times were grim. Lenin had exceeded
the record of the Paris Commune by fifty-one days. How many more
days lay ahead neither he nor his comrades could guess.

On that same day Gorky wrote in *Novaya Zhizn:*

"To kill is simpler and easier than to convince—but was it not acts
of violence committed against the people which brought about the destruction of the power of the monarchy?

"Just because you divide among yourselves the material wealth of
Russia, she will become neither richer nor happier, nor will you be
better, more human."[38]

Moscow. The ancient Russian capital in March. Grim. Cold. Buildings run down. Thousands of shabby people gathered at the great

street markets, Smolenskaya and Sukharevskaya. Hungry, worn out with war, revolution, suffering. Never so many people without work. There was no coal or wood to heat the buildings. The food stores were empty. If this was the new day of the Revolution, it was a hollow-cheeked, red-eyed tubercular Revolution, wearing a ragged uniform, carrying a battered gun with an icy doorstep to sleep in at night and nothing but worry over what the bitter morrow would bring. Lenin moved into a two-room suite in the National Hotel (rechristened the First House of Soviets), looking out onto what was then Okhotny Ryad, the farmers' market. Beyond these low buildings he could see the Kremlin where suites for the Government were hastily being prepared. Steel-eyed spade-bearded Felix Dzerzhinsky looked for quarters in which to house his new Cheka. He found them in a handsome building on Lubyanka Square occupied by the Rossiya Insurance Building, No. 22. It was one of the biggest buildings in Moscow, many rooms, many entrances, and spacious cellars. The cellars, time would demonstrate, were particularly useful. Executions by the hundreds could be carried out there with no one on the outside the wiser. The thick walls muffled the sound of machine-gun and revolver fire. No need to back up a truck and keep its motor running to conceal the crackle of gunfire.

In the cafés harlots sang and poets made fools of themselves to the golden clink of black market rubles. Not all the poets spent their nights in smoke-filled, liquor stinking halls, shouting obscenities to shock the demimonde. Blok had been in Moscow all winter and the Revolution had penetrated his being. From January onward he was in its thrall. He saw it in the dark snow-choked streets, in the coarse faces of the peasant soldiers, in the rifle shots in the night, in the crunch of rifle butt on plate glass, in women's screams, and the whine of rich old men trying to save their gold watches and sable coats from hawk-faced thieves.

Revolution! This was it. The death of the old and the birth of the new. Blok fell into a passion. His notebook overflowed. Ideas poured into it like lava from a volcano. In a week he had written a declaration of faith in the Revolution—*Intelligentsia and the Revolution*. All around he heard the voices—Russia is being destroyed . . . Russia no longer exists . . . May Russia rest in peace. But this was not so. Russia was a storm, a *burya,* and out of this Siberian hurricane democracy was being born. Peace and the brotherhood of man—that was the banner of the Revolution. No need to worry about the destruction of the Kremlin, the burning of palaces, the loss of pictures and books. If the Kremlin was wiped from the face of the earth, it was no longer a

Kremlin, no more than the Czar stepping down from his throne was any longer a Czar.

What did people think—that the Revolution was an idyll? That creation did not destroy? It was, he thought, shameless to stand around, complaining and wringing one's hands, when over Russia was flying a revolutionary cyclone. He had, he said, put his whole body, his whole heart, his whole consciousness, at the service of the Revolution.[39]

He had not yet completed this declaration of revolutionary faith— which brought down on him the anathema of the non-Bolshevik intelligentsia like Gippius—that he was outlining a play based on the life of Jesus Christ, a play he was never to write. Instead, the next day he plunged into *Dvenadtsat* (The Twelve). The Revolution was to get its epiphany. Blok felt shaken to his depths. He worked all day on the poem. The next day he finished his essay on revolution, then lay in darkness on his bed. He heard a distant roar in his ears—he thought an earthquake was beginning. He wrote in his diary: "What is the secret of Russia?" It was, he decided, the fact that in Europe the subject of art was death; in Russia it was life. He fell into despondency and wandered for hours through the dirty, slushy streets of Moscow. A thaw came on and the wind rose. For a few days his poem did not advance. His room was cold and damp. Yesenin telephoned to tell him that Blok and Bely had been attacked by the Merezhkovskys as "traitors." Suddenly, the ice jam broke. *The Twelve* went forward in a fury of creation. Again around him Blok heard a frightful noise. It came, he understood, from within himself. Gogol had suffered the same thing. "Today," Blok wrote, "I am—a genius." The poem was finished.

On March 3—the day the ravaging peace with Germany was signed —*The Twelve* was published in the newspaper *Znamya Truda* and the Russian world was changed:

> Cherny vecher.
> Bely sneg.
> Veter, veter!
> Na nogakh ne stoit chelovek.
> Veter, Veter—
> Na vsem bozhem svete!

> Black night.
> White snow.
> Wind, wind!
> A man can't stand.
> Wind, wind—
> All over God's world![40]

Twelve Red Guards appear out of the night, the cold, the snow. A soldier sleeps with Katya, a prostitute; Katya is killed by an angry shot from Petrukha's gun; Petrukha fills with remorse; there is a glimpse of Katya's dismal history; a glimpse of a *burzhui*, a bourgeois, standing on a street corner, his nose hidden in his collar, looking like a mangy dog.

The Twelve march on through the stormy night, the *purga* filling the downtrodden streets, their clothes in tatters, their destination and duties unknown.

> So they march with solemn tread—
> Behind—the hungry dog.
> Ahead—with bloody flag
> Unseen by the blizzard,
> Untouched by bullets,
> With gentle steps above the storm
> In a white crown of roses.
> Ahead—goes Jesus Christ.[41]

Blok's poem did not create a sensation. It *was* an explosion, an explosion which echoed through the tawdry streets of Moscow, the grimy factories of Petrograd, the bustling bureaucracy of the Kremlin. The Revolution had found its voice, its symbol, its icon. One cold night a reading of *The Twelve* was arranged. (Blok himself never recited *The Twelve*.) The gathering listened with awe. Then Ivan Bunin spoke:

"What a cheap, unconvincing trick; he takes a winter evening in Petersburg, so terrible just now, where people are perishing of cold and hunger, where even in daytime you cannot go out in the streets for fear of being attacked and stripped to the skin, and he says: look what the drunken savage soldier-mob is doing—but in the end that saturnalia is justified by the complete destruction of old Russia; and at their head, he says, goes Christ Himself. They are His twelve apostles, their essence is the same as His:

"Comrades, take aim and don't be scared,

"Let's blast away at Holy Russia."[42]

Bunin hated Blok, hated the Revolution, hated *The Twelve*. He knew as did everyone who heard *The Twelve* not only the power, the overwhelming power of Blok's images, but the power, the overwhelming power of the terrible Revolution which Blok celebrated.

The Bolsheviks were nervous about *The Twelve*. Lenin never mentioned it. Kamenev once said that Lunacharsky was writing an article about the poem. But Lunacharsky never did perhaps because, as Kamenev said, "it celebrates what we, old socialists, fear most of all."

What they feared (and of this Gorky reminded Lenin again and again) was the primitive force of the Russian people, The Twelve, ignorant, lice-ridden, casual murderers and consorts of whores moving through the streets of the Russian capitals, trudging along the dusty roads of the deep provinces, elemental, fierce, the "dark people," the *narod*, the remorseless force of the Russian *burya*, sweeping over taiga and city slum, over the black chernozem and government office buildings, storming, storming, storming, as it had from the time of Pugachev and the terrible rebellions of Catherine's day, burning, killing, raping, destroying. It was a specter to haunt the Revolution, to haunt its leaders, to haunt the world. This was Russia's Revolution and it had nothing in common with intellectuals like Lenin and his Bolsheviks who were now trying to harness the whirlwind.

"Have you ever happened to walk the city streets on a dark night," Blok asked his friend S. M. Aliansky, "in a snowstorm or driving rain when a frenzied wind tears and pulls at everything all around, when you can hardly keep on your feet and think only about not being knocked down, swept away.

"Suddenly, in the nearest pereulok there flashes a bright or brightly lighted spot . . . maybe it's a big flapping flag. . . . On one stormy winter night I had a vision of such a bright spot. It grew bigger and bigger. Around this both The Twelve and Christ came to my mind."[43]

For better, for worse, the Russian Revolution had come to the world. Lenin stood at its head. Or did he? Lenin could never be certain. Perhaps Blok was right. Perhaps it *was* the figure of Christ that borne by the wind of the *burya* led the dark people toward their inevitable fate.

LXI

The House of Special Designation

On Monday March 11, 1918, the day Lenin and his Government abandoned Petrograd for Moscow, the former Czar worked quietly and quite happily for many hours in the courtyard of the not unpleasant governor's house at Tobolsk, the old Siberian town to which he and his family had been transferred by Kerensky the preceding August. The Czar's name had long vanished from the newspapers; he was not mentioned in political speeches, either by the Bolsheviks or by their opponents; he and his family had their problems—what family does not—but his spirit was good, and if he fretted from time to time over his treatment by the guards, over close confinement to the house and courtyard, over the problems of going to religious services and other matters of daily life, no one would have called him despondent, despairing, or downtrodden. It is fair to say that he was, in his way, as happy in his imprisonment as was Lenin in his years in Nicholas' prisons and in Siberian exile. Possibly happier. Nicholas still kept a monotonously cheerful record of his days, and on March 11 (he was still using the old-style calendar and headed the entry February 26) he noted that it was the birthday of his late beloved father, Alexander III. The weather was cold and snow fell in the courtyard. Nonetheless, he and his daughters worked heartily at their self-imposed task of sawing and chopping wood. The commandant of what was euphemistically called "the House of Freedom"* had brought in a whole sleigh load of logs a couple of days previously in order that

* The House was located on Svoboda (Freedom) Street.

Nicholas might enjoy his favorite exercise. He and his family had established generally good relations with their guards, and on this day three young riflemen from Orlov helped Nicholas and the girls carry wood into the barn.

The Czar spent many evenings reading to his family. He had now almost finished *Anna Karenina* and was soon to start on a volume of Lermontov's verses. The Imperial Princesses loved amateur theatricals and so did their companions, particularly the English schoolteacher, a Mr. Gibbes. On March 3, the day the Brest-Litovsk treaty was signed —news of the event was not to reach Tobolsk for nearly two weeks— the Grand Duchess Mariya Nikolayevna and Mr. Gibbes presented a play called *The Crystal Gazer*, by Leopold Montague, and then Olga, Mariya, and Nicholas himself did Chekhov's *The Bear*. On March 10 Mariya, Anastasia, and young Alexei presented something entitled *Packing Up*, which was a great favorite. They had done it as recently as February 4, and in the finale a draft whisked up Mr. Gibbes's dressing gown which Anastasia was wearing, exposing her husky thighs and behind clad in the Czar's woollies. The Czar and Czarina shrieked with laughter.[1]

Of course, it was not all so idyllic. On the anniversary of his abdication from the throne, March 15, Nicholas uttered a cri de coeur: "How much longer will our unhappy motherland be torn up and tortured by foreign and internal enemies? It seems sometimes that there isn't strength to suffer more and that I don't even know what to hope for or what to wish. Only God knows! It will be as He wishes!"[2]

Tobolsk was a curious quiet corner. It had a population of 27,000 and lay 260 versts from the railhead. It had hardly been touched by the Revolution. In fact, Bolshevik power was not really established in the old Siberian city. As Pierre Gilliard, the thoughtful tutor of Alexei, observed in his diary on March 17 there was—five long months after October—still no actual representative of the Bolshevik Government in Tobolsk. The chief of the guards, Colonel Yevgeny Kobylinsky, strongly sympathized with the imprisoned family. "Never was the situation more favorable for escape," Gilliard noted. "It would be easy to trick the insolent but careless vigilance of our guards." All that was needed was some organization and a few bold spirits.

Some months earlier in mid-December an attempt had been made by the Czarina to get in touch with the English Royal family in hope that a rescue effort might be made. It was impossible for the Czarina to communicate directly since all her communications went through the hands of guards and commissars. However, Mr. Gibbes wrote a letter to Miss Margaret Jackson, who had been Alix' teacher in Hesse-Darmstadt thirty years before.

Miss Jackson was living in retirement in a home for governesses in Regent's Park, London. Gibbes, of course, had never met her. He nonetheless wrote a careful letter describing conditions in Tobolsk, the location of the house in which the Imperial family was kept, briefly described the disposition of guards, noted when and where they attended church, and enclosed a crude floor plan of the House of Freedom.

As a key to Miss Jackson that the communication was intended for the Royal family he incorporated the lines:

"I hear that David is back from France, how are his father and mother? And the cousins are they also at the Front?"

David was the Prince of Wales. His father and mother were King George V and Queen Mary.

The letter went forward from Tobolsk December 15, 1917, to the British Embassy at Petrograd and was duly forwarded in the diplomatic bag to London. The Czarina was certain Miss Jackson would take the letter to the Queen. But there is no indication that the communication reached the British Royal family. If it did the British did not act upon it.[3]

The hope for a rescue seemed doomed. The Czar would not think of his family being separated nor of leaving Russia, and the Czarina told Gilliard: "I wouldn't leave Russia on any consideration, for it seems to me that to go abroad would be to break our last link with the past which would then be dead forever."

Moreover, the situation of the family was already in the process of change. Within a week a detachment of one hundred Red Guards arrived from Omsk with instructions to tighten security around the former Czar and his family, and, in fact, as of March 1, on orders from Moscow the family had been put on military rations and instructed that expenses must be limited to 600 rubles each per month—4,200 a month for the Imperial household. This meant that ten servants had to be dismissed.[4]

As Bolshevik troubles mounted, violence became more and more common. So did nervousness increase among top Bolsheviks about the Imperial family. The former Grand Duke Mikhail, whose friendliness to the Revolution was well known, had been permitted to live in virtual freedom at his palace in Gatchina. Now, just after the signing of the Brest-Litovsk treaty, Mikhail and his English secretary, Nicholas Johnson, were arrested and brought to Smolny. Mikhail was interrogated by Uritsky, head of the Petrograd Cheka. The Grand Duke offered to sign any declaration that might be desired, affirming his complete and total withdrawal from political life and acceptance of the Bolshevik regime.[5]

But Uritsky was not satisfied. As he told Count V. P. Zubov, curator of the Gatchina Palace, who was arrested at the same time, "he [Mikhail] can sign anything that's necessary and with complete good faith and then he can act otherwise. That's why his declaration has no value to me."

Zubov and Uritsky discussed the case of Nicholas. Uritsky said that he was not entirely confident that the Government had been right not to shoot the Czar out of hand. There might come a time, he said, when this would be necessary. But he left Zubov with the impression that he was by no means confident that the Soviet Government would survive that long.[6]

The arrest of Grand Duke Mikhail, Uritsky's talk with Zubov, and the tightening of the regime at Tobolsk reflected discussions by Lenin and his associates which cannot be fully documented. However, Lenin's order exiling Mikhail and Johnson has been published.[7] The two were taken to Perm in the Urals and permitted, for a time, to live in comparative freedom in a hotel although, of course, under constant surveillance.[8]

Actually, a crisis over the Imperial family was developing—not in Siberia but in the Crimea where there had already been savage outbreaks of Red terror. On January 16, 17, and 18, 1918, possibly as many as one thousand officers had been killed on the transports *Rumyniya* and *Tryvor*, the bodies simply being shoved into the sea.[9] While no evidence has turned up that specific instructions for the extermination of the officers came from Petrograd, enough general orders for the shooting of enemies of the Revolution had been issued so that there could be no surprise if local authorities took their pistols in hand. As Martyn Latsis, Dzerzhinsky's aide in the Cheka, was to explain a few months later:

"We are not carrying out war against individuals. We are exterminating the bourgeoisie as a class. We aren't looking for evidence or witnesses to reveal deeds or words against the Soviet power. The first question which we ask is—to what class does he belong, what are his origins, upbringing, education, or profession. These questions define the fate of the accused. This is the essence of Red Terror."*[10]

In the Crimea had gathered the Dowager Empress Mariya Fyodorovna, mother of Nicholas, and her daughter, the Grand Duchess Olga Alexandrovna, the Grand Duke Nikolai Nikolayevich (Nikolasha) and his wife, Anastasia, the Grand Duke Pyotr Nilolayevich,

---

* *Pravda*, Oct. 18, 1918, commented that under this definition the first one to be shot would be Lenin.

the Grand Duke Alexander Mikhailovich, his wife, the Grand Duchess Xenia, his six sons, his daughter Irena, and her husband Prince Yusupov. The family had been compelled to live together in the thick-walled villa of Grand Duke Pyotr called Dulber, at the insistence of the representatives of the Sevastopol Soviet, Batuk and Zabolotny, a black-haired, six-foor-four-inch sailor. The Grand Dukes protested. They did not get on well and detested living together. But Batuk and Zabolotny knew what they were about. They fortified Dulber against attack (Grand Duke Alexander helped them place the machine guns), and in the showdown it was the thick walls of Dulber and the determination of Batuk and Zabolotny to defend their prisoners which saved the lives of these Romanovs.[11] In early April as the Germans entered the Crimea and approached the coast commandos of the Yalta Soviet attempted to seize Dulber and execute the Romanovs. Zabolotny defended his Imperial captives and with the arrival of the Germans the threat ended. All eventually were safely evacuated from the Crimea by the British.

Whether orders were sent by Moscow to the Yalta Soviet in the first days of April to execute the Romanovs has not been established. But a pattern and an attitude was beginning to take shape and it cast an ominous shadow ahead.[12] Red terror was now not just a flamboyant phrase. It was a fact and the time was soon to come, as A. D. Naglovsky recalled, when during a meeting of the Soviet of People's Commissars Lenin passed a note to Dzerzhinsky: "How many hardened counterrevolutionaries have we in prison?" Dzerzhinsky passed the slip back with the notation: "Around 1,500." Lenin read it, frowned, marked an "X" beside Dzerzhinsky's answer, and returned the slip. The discussion (about railroad affairs) went on. Dzerzhinsky quietly rose and left the room. Only the next day did it emerge that he had given an order for the 1,500 to be shot. But as Lenin's secretary Fotiyeva* explained to Naglovsky, this was not Lenin's intention. He hadn't wanted the 1,500 shot. It was simply his ordinary custom to make a check mark to indicate he had read a reply. Dzerzhinsky misinterpreted the "X."[13]

Steadily the times grew more tense. The peace with Germany had not kept German troops from pushing steadily eastward and southward in the Ukraine. The White generals in the Don and the Kuban drilled their troops and made their alliances. Lenin's erstwhile left Socialist Revolutionary allies plotted his overthrow. The anarchists stirred up trouble. The armed forces were a shambles and Trotsky had not yet created the Red Army. The Japanese were landing in Siberia. The temper of the times was reflected in Lenin's telegrams, letters,

---

* Lidiya Fotiyeva died in 1975 at the age of ninety-four. She survived persecution and imprisonment under Stalin.

and orders: "Our difficulties are extremely grave," "no trust can be put in assurances," "The situation in Pskov guberniya is desperate," "the catastrophic food situation," "in the Ukraine there had been a coup d'état," "In view of the hopelessness of the situation as certified by the supreme military authorities, the fleet must be destroyed forthwith," "Obviously we shall perish and ruin the whole revolution if we do not conquer famine in the next few months."[14]

It was against this background and signs of increasing French and British hostility to the Bolsheviks and support for their opponents that the somnolent and largely beneficent regime at Tobolsk began to change. General B. A. Tatishchev, Prince Vasily Dolgoruky, and Countess Hendrikov, members of the Imperial entourage, were ordered into the House of Freedom, henceforth to be treated like the Imperial family as prisoners. A ceremonial *kinzhal* (dagger), worn by the Czar with his Cossack uniform, was taken away. The Czar and Alexei were forbidden to wear shoulder straps indicating officer's rank on their uniforms. ("This swinishness I will not forget!" Nicholas angrily wrote in his diary.) And on April 22 for the first time since the Bolshevik regime was established there arrived at Tobolsk an emissary bearing credentials signed by the new regime, specifically by Sverdlov, chairman of the Central Executive Committee of the Soviet, an office equivalent to the Soviet President. The representative was Vasily Vasilyevich Yakovlev.[15] Yakovlev lost no time in visiting the House of Freedom. Warned that he was coming, the Imperial children burned their letters and Mariya and Anastasia burned their diaries (all of the Romanovs seemed to have been brought up from childhood to keep diaries).[16]

Chairman Sverdlov had been concerned with the situation of the Czar and his family at least since January when a delegation of the Tsarskoye Selo Regiment guarding the Czar at Tobolsk complained about the Czar's security.

The delegates gave Sverdlov clippings from the Tobolsk papers saying that "Dark forces have said that here they will light the flames of Civil War." The stories talked of counterrevolutionary moves among the military cadets, correspondence of Nicholas with the former Court Chamberlain Count Benkendorf, and quoted Nicholas as saying that his relations with the guard detail "are completely correct."

There was also a clipping from the Menshevik paper, *Tobolsk Rabochi*, saying of the town that "happily we are not Bolsheviks." Sverdlov had assured the soldier delegates that they had the Government's full confidence and ordered them to guard the Romanovs carefully *until they could be brought to trial.*

The question of the Czar's trial was actually discussed in the Council of People's Commissars at a session in February just before the Brest-Litovsk treaty was signed. It was raised by a delegation from the Peasant Congress which demanded that the Czar and his family be returned from Tobolsk and stand trial. I. N. Steinberg, a left Socialist Revolutionary then serving as Minister of Justice, opposed the proceeding as being too dangerous. Lenin also doubted that the moment was opportune but Steinberg was instructed to prepare documents for an ultimate trial.[17]

After the Bolsheviks moved to Moscow in March new evidence came to Sverdlov from Yekaterinburg, Tyumen, and Omsk about "monarchist plots," including a story that someone intended to spirit the Romanovs out of Russia to England via the River Ob and the Barents Sea or possibly via the Far East.

In Tobolsk the Bolsheviks were so weak that they had to operate half underground whereas, in Sverdlov's opinion, the monarchists could maneuver almost openly. He sent Red Guard units to take up positions to block possible Czarist escape routes and to establish Bolshevik authority more firmly in Tyumen.

Not long after the Soviet regime left Petrograd F. I. Goloshchekin, the Urals regional commissar, came to Moscow, advised Sverdlov of the unsatisfactory situation in Tobolsk, and asked that Nicholas be sent to Yekaterinburg where he could be put "under the reliable guard" of Urals workers detachments. Thus, the plans of the monarchists would be foiled. Sverdlov agreed in principle with the plan and placed on Goloshchekin personal responsibility for holding Nicholas in security *until he could be brought to trial.* Apparently Sverdlov spelled this out in a letter written April 9.

There was fear, Sverdlov acknowledged, that anarchists and provocateurs might seize the Czar and kill him out of hand.

The mission of the new emissary, Yakovlev, was in line with previous discussions by Sverdlov in which Lenin certainly participated. Yakovlev, a member of the Central Committee of the left SRs, had instructions to remove the Imperial family and its entourage from Tobolsk and take them to Yekaterinburg. Simultaneous with his arrival in Tobolsk, however, a second (and hostile) detachment arrived from Yekaterinburg. These were Red Guard units, headed by Brysatsky and Zaslavsky.[18]

But a complication arose. Alexei was seriously ill with one of his periodic hemophilic attacks. Yakovlev called Moscow on the telegraph wire and was instructed to take the Czar away immediately with whoever wished to accompany him. He would return later for Alexei and the others. He promised that the family would be reunited within three weeks.[19] He would not say where he was taking them, but the

Czar and Colonel Kobylinsky, chief of the guard, assumed that the destination must be Moscow: Only Moscow would fit the time frame. The Czar leaped to the conclusion that he was to be taken to Moscow to countersign the Brest-Litovsk treaty because the Germans had no faith in the Bolshevik regime.[20] The Czarina, ever clutching at straws, insisted: "They're going to try to force his hand by making him anxious about his family. The Czar is necessary to them; they feel that he alone represents Russia."[21] After tormenting struggle she decided to accompany the Czar and leave behind her beloved, suffering, bedridden son.

At 3:30 A.M. on April 26 in the raw Siberian night a convoy of *koshevy*, springless, seatless Siberian carriages, drew up before the House of Freedom. These were two-horse vehicles except for one troika. Gilliard and some others found straw in the courtyard and put it in the vehicles. They got a mattress for the carriage in which the Czarina rode with her daughter Mariya. The Czar rode with Yakovlev. Botkin, the Imperial physician, Dolgoruky, and three servants, Terenty I. Chemodurov, Ivan Sednev, and Anna Demidova, accompanied them. At 8:40 April 30 on the morning of a day which Nicholas described as "wonderful and warm" the Imperial prisoners arrived at Yekaterinburg.[22]

Whether Yakovlev originally intended to take them to Yekaterinburg is a matter of controversy. In fact, the Yakovlev episode is shrouded in mystery and confusion out of which have arisen many myths. From the beginning Yakovlev demonstrated unusual concern and unusual respect for his prisoners. He was under obvious stress to get them away as quickly as possible. He immediately got into conflict with the Red Guards detachment which had simultaneously arrived from Yekaterinburg. He "lacked confidence in them," according to one Soviet account, and "behaved very strangely."[23] However, he communicated frequently with Moscow and had his instructions verified by Sverdlov.[24]

In any event he set out with his prisoners by land over the difficult spring roads, deep in mud, making 130 versts on the first day of leaving Tobolsk. The second day at 9:30 P.M. he arrived with his party at the Tyumen railhead. Here there were two routes to Moscow, one via Yekaterinburg, the other via Omsk. By this time Yakovlev had concluded (for whatever reasons) that he would not take his prisoners to Yekaterinburg. He started for Omsk instead. Yekaterinburg learned of this and issued orders to all Siberian railroad authorities to halt him. Yakovlev—advised of the order—stopped the Czar's train at Lyubinskaya and hurried on himself by special coach and locomotive to Omsk.[25]

From Omsk, Yakovlev spoke with Chairman Sverdlov by direct wire and urged that the Romanovs be taken to Ufa, where their security could be guaranteed.[26] Sverdlov rejected the Ufa proposal but did give Yakovlev permission to bring his prisoners to Omsk.[27]

At the same time the Urals detachment got on the wire and telegraphed back to Sverdlov the text of the letter Sverdlov had written April 9 authorizing the transfer of the Romanovs to Yekaterinburg, where they would be given into custody of the Urals Regional Soviet. The Urals representatives told Sverdlov they had halted Yakovlev's train and proposed to arrest Yakovlev and bring him with the Romanovs to Yekaterinburg.

Yakovlev, they said, was a "traitor." They refused to accept Yakovlev's contention that he had "other orders" and insisted that if Nicholas was not brought to Yekaterinburg "the conflict may take a very sharp form because we don't think it is necessary to run Nicholas around the Siberian roads and he ought to be in Yekaterinburg under strong guard."

Sverdlov was caught in the middle. According to his Soviet biographers, he demanded a guarantee that if Nicholas was taken over by the Urals group, he would be brought to and kept in Yekaterinburg safe and sound.

The Urals group said that provided these instructions were conveyed through the Regional Soviet they would give their guarantee. It is apparent from the Sverdlov exchange that he had doubts of the reliability of the Urals Bolsheviks and would have preferred that the Czar be taken to a more safe place.

But rather than provoke an armed clash between the Urals detachment and Yakovlev's (smaller) forces with the probable result that the Czar would not survive the conflict, Sverdlov bowed to the Urals' demands. He had, after all, absolutely no power to compel the enforcement of his orders by the competing Bolshevik groups in Siberia.[28]

On May 9 Sverdlov told the Soviet Executive Committee that Nicholas had been removed to Yekaterinburg, where his security would be guaranteed, and that the former Czar would now realize that he was an *arestant*, "a prisoner of Soviet power."[29]

He also advised the Central Executive Committee that Bishop Germogen and Prince Dolgoruky had been arrested after their correspondence had implicated them in plotting to free the Czar.[30]

Why should Moscow have wanted to move the Czar out of Tobolsk? There were many reasons—the fragile hold the Bolsheviks had on Tobolsk, the growing disorder in Siberia and the country generally, soon to escalate with the rising of the Czechoslovak prisoner-of-war detachments against the Soviet regime, and a desire to have the Czar easily available in the event it was finally decided to try him formally for the crimes of the Romanov regime and—inevitably—execute him. The idea for such a trial had been in the minds of Lenin and his associates all along—probably since long before the October coup d'état. It is almost ritual for a new revolutionary regime to place on trial the ruler who has been overthrown, provided he has not already been killed in the first bloody hours. Trotsky, for one, had been a strong advocate of a public trial and had suggested that he would make a very effective public prosecutor.[31] Lenin had not spoken publicly on the question but it is reasonable to suppose that in the gloomy spring of 1918 when revolutionary power was hanging by a thread the fate of the Romanovs would cross his mind. After all if the Revolution was to go down, it must certainly bring down "bloody Nicholas" with it.

There was a gnawing fear in Moscow that somehow Nicholas might slip through their fingers. There had been a number of poorly thought-out, badly managed attempts by a handful of monarchists to try to establish connection with the Czar and make plans for his rescue. At least some details of these efforts were known to the Bolsheviks—it was impossible for a former Czarist officer from Petrograd to turn up in Tobolsk or nearby Siberian towns without his presence arousing suspicion, and the conspirators could hardly have been more naïve in their operations. The Czarina had managed to maintain a remarkably active correspondence with Madame Vyrubova, who was the inspirer of some of these undertakings (despite the fact that she herself had only with difficulty gotten released from the Peter and Paul Fortress).[32]

Despite the lack of realism in these efforts the Bolsheviks inevitably exaggerated the possibility of a successful escape if for no other reason than the fact that they had so little control of the Siberian reaches.

Whatever the genesis of the move from Tobolsk, the Czar's arrival in Yekaterinburg was sudden and unexpected. The prisoners were taken to a roomy, solid, and ugly merchant's house in the center of Yekaterinburg which belonged to a well-to-do engineer named Ipatyev.[33] Nicholas and Alexandra arrived there on the morning of April 30. The Ipatyevs had been removed from the house—with no prior notice—only at 3 P.M. the day before. The guards were an accidental group of Red Army men, units hastily withdrawn from prisons and other places.[34] Despite this, Nicholas found the house "good and clean" with four large rooms put at their service and a small garden. But it was ugly. A wooden fence had been thrown up, cutting off a view of the street; there were guards on the same floor with the Imperial party (in fact, they had to pass a guard and the guard room in going to the bathroom and toilet)[35]; there were guards around the house, inside the fence, and in the little garden.[36] The Ipatyev house stood (and still stands) on a dusty unpaved (now paved) street in the heart of town. There were and are lindens shading the street, a view (cut off by the fence) up a hill toward an old church and from the back over neighboring courtyards. Built as it was at the intersection of two streets the house fell away toward the back. At the rear the bared windows of the extensive ground floor were above the street whereas in the front of the house the first floor was a semibasement.[37]

Life in the gloomy Ipatyev house was more like prison than anything Nicholas had endured. The dusty provincial house was called by the Yekaterinburg Soviet a "House of Special Designation." "Special" was a favorite word of the Revolution and a house of "Special Designation" seemed to suit the pallisaded building of faded Empire style.

Prince Dolgoruky had been separated from the Czar's entourage on arrival. Soon word reached the Czar that his old friend was being held in prison.

It was not until May 23 that Alexei and the other children finally joined their parents at the House of Special Designation. They had left Tobolsk on Monday May 20, on the same steamer *Rus* which had brought them there. They arrived at Tyumen on the twenty-second, boarded a special train, and arrived at Yekaterinburg late in the evening, the train halting some distance from the station. At 9 A.M. on the twenty-third several carriages drove up. Alexei's sailor escort Nagorny carried him from the railroad car, followed by the Grand Duchesses, carrying their bags and belongings, Tatyana last, struggling with her heavy brown valise and her little black and ginger Japanese dog, called Gemmy or Jamie.[38] Nagorny tried to help her but was shoved aside by a sentry. A few moments later the carriages drove off with the children. It was the last time the tutor Gilliard was to see his pupils. The Imperial party was broken up. General Tatishchev, Countess Hendrikov, and Mademoiselle Shneider were taken off to prison. The servants, the Czar's valet Volkov, the footman Alexei Tropp, and all the others except for the chef, I. M. Kharitonov, and the fifteen-year-old kitchen boy, Leonid Sednev, son of one of the footmen, went straight to prison. Kharitonov and Leonid were taken to the House of Special Designation. Baroness de Buxhoeveden, Mr. Gibbes, and Gilliard were simply turned loose and ordered to leave Urals territory without delay.[39] A bit later footman Tropp and Nagorny were permitted to join the Czar at the Ipatyev house but soon Nagorny and the elder Sednev were taken off for questioning and never returned.

At the House of Special Designation the joy at reunion of the family overshadowed the harshness of what the Czar now sometimes called a "prison regime." On the first night the girls had no beds and had to sleep on the floor but the next day beds were provided from the heavy baggage they brought from Tobolsk. But, as the Czar wrote, the weather, the wet snow, and the freezing temperatures fairly reflected their mood. Alexei had banged his knee and was in pain. A guard fired his gun into the house—he claimed he thought someone was signaling from a window, but the Czar concluded he was just fiddling with his weapon in the time-honored manner of sentries.

The weather improved and so did the Czar's spirits. Alix successfully cut his hair, Alexei's pain began to diminish, the family walked and relaxed in the sunshine in the courtyard, and in the evening the Czar read aloud from the works of the Russian satirist Saltykov-Shchedrin, which he had found in the house and which he greatly enjoyed (never having read him before),* and played trik-trak or bezique. On June 5 the Czar put his watch forward two hours—double daylight savings time had been introduced. The family was now well but the Czar himself suffered a couple of days from piles.

On Saturday June 8 the Czar did not make an entry in his diary. The omission might seem trivial but there was no precedent for this in the Czar's methodical life. He was meticulous in his entries. For him to skip a day without even a line on the weather was almost as traumatic as a heart attack. His entry the next day, June 9 (Sunday May 27 in the Czar's diary—he never gave up the old calendar), offered no clue to the omission. He wrote that he had left his sickbed. It was a sunny day. The family took its daily stroll in two parties, Alix, Alexei, Olga, and Mariya before lunch, the Czar, Tatyana, and Anastasia before tea. The grass was a stunning green and its smell filled his nostrils. He read from the twelfth volume of Saltykov-Shchedrin in the evening.

It was warm again the next day. On Monday June 10 the Czar observed that a number of the boxes and trunks containing things which had been sent from Tobolsk had been broken into in the barn where they were kept. The Czar was indignant. "Disgusting!" he exclaimed. Moreover, the attitude of the guard and officers had changed in the past week. The guards tried not to talk with their prisoners. They were not at ease. Some kind of danger seemed to be in the air. "I can't understand it!" he observed. But the following day the Czar was calm as usual, recording Tatyana's twenty-first birthday and expressing pleasure at a night breeze which had swept out the humid air from their quarters.

* Another fan of Saltykov-Shchedrin was Stalin.

But he made no entry for June 12 (May 30 old style) and from now on his diary's consistency vanished. In the month of June (old style) he would write in his diary only on ten of the thirty days.

Why did the Czar suddenly stop writing regularly? Melgunov suggested that the monotony of life in the Ipatyev house, the absence of impressions from outside, caused the Czar to reduce his entries. This hardly seems tenable. No matter how dull his life the Czar had *always* made a daily notation in his diary. Was, in fact, his diary censored by the Soviet authorities before being made public? Almost certainly not. A number of the Czar's June entries refer to events or impressions of days when he did not write. No discontinuity is apparent. Moreover, the originals of the diaries were seen by a number of foreigners in the early revolutionary days. The suppression of parts of the diary by the Bolsheviks would only be likely if the Czar reported events embarrassing to them, such as mistreatment, torture, or the like. The existing entries, their calm and normal nature, negate that possibility. Did the Czar get some clue as to what lay ahead or record it? Was he growing more and more despondent? Could he possibly have had rising expectations of a change in status—even his rescue—and did this inhibit him from his usual daily notations? There simply is no way to be certain. But there is some reason to suspect that he detected a rising personal danger.

LXII

"The Terrorists Will Consider Us Old Women"

Lenin's position in these days was weakening catastrophically. From early winter and particularly from the time of the signing of the Brest-Litovsk treaty he and the other Bolsheviks had begun to regard the Urals and the lands beyond the Volga as a refuge, a citadel to which they might retire if the pressures on Petrograd and Moscow grew insupportable. A large portion of the Russian gold reserve, 651.5 million rubles,[1] had been sent to the Urals for safekeeping.[2] Some two hundred hostages from the Baltic had been dispatched to Yekaterinburg. An official evacuation commission had been set up in April to make plans for the Government's transfer to the Urals if necessary.[3] Lenin had said during debate over the Brest treaty that he was prepared to give up Petrograd and Moscow and retire to the East if necessary to save the Revolution. It was no accident that the Imperial family had been concentrated in the Urals—at Yekaterinburg, Perm, and Alapayevsk. The Urals with their great mining and industrial establishments, Lenin felt, were a stronghold of Bolshevik and revolutionary sentiment, second only to Petrograd. Here behind the low- wall of the Urals, protected by the Russian distance, the Revolution could hold out against any enemy until that fateful happy long-awaited day when the Revolution broke out in Germany and the European comrades came to the rescue of their hard-pressed Bolshevik fellows.

But a quirk of fate demolished Lenin's Urals fortress.[4] There were in Russia between forty thousand and fifty thousand Czechoslovak prisoners of war,[5] forced soldiery of the Austrian Army, who had freely surrendered to the Russians, unwilling to fight for the Austrian throne. The Czech soldiers, armed and officered, were on their way out of Russia via the Trans-Siberian and Vladivostok, headed for the western front, under arrangements made by the Czech government-in-exile. They were strung out across Russia from the Volga eastward, through the Urals and Siberia. Progress was painfully slow. Some units spent two months in freight cars covering a distance which should have taken no more than two days.[6] Disputes flared. The Bolsheviks tried to propagandize the Czechs to stay in Russia and fight for the Revolution. One thing led to another. On May 14 a row broke out at Chelyabinsk in the Urals between Czech soldiers and Hungarians, also prisoners of war. The local Soviet arrested several Czech soldiers, and on May 17 the Czechs marched into town, released the prisoners, and disarmed the Red Guards. Within a week the Czechs had moved to the offensive and were taking over one Siberian town after another: Maryanovka near Omsk May 15; Mariinsk farther east on the Trans-Siberian the same day; then Chelyabinsk and Novo-Nikolayevsk (now Novosibirsk) May 26; Penza and Syzran (on the Volga) May 28 and 29; Tomsk May 31; Omsk June 7; Samara, the central Volga capital, June 8.[7]

Lenin was as close to panic as he was ever to be. The Bolshevik position in Siberia crumbled by the hour. The Trans-Siberian had been cut. The Volga River route had been cut. All this at a moment when Lenin was straining every resource in an effort to seize grain from the peasants and move it into the starving cities. Lenin telegraphed Zinoviev in Petrograd. "The greatest peril," he said, menaced food supplies. Every effort, every extraordinary measure, was needed to meet the threat.[8] The circle was closing. The Urals peasants were restive. Revolt spread from village to village. The Bolsheviks responded with bloody repressions. Even before the Czech rising the Urals had been troubled.[9] After the uprising the Bolsheviks were overthrown in the towns of Semipalatinsk, Biisk, Omsk, and Krasnoyarsk even before the Czechs put in an appearance.[10]

It was, as Krupskaya recalled, "a very difficult time." Lenin got little sleep. He wrote very little.[11] As he said in a message to Petrograd: "Time is short: after painful May will come still more painful June and July and perhaps part of August."[12] The times were bad and they grew worse. Lenin's revolution was threatened from within and from without, and he was compelled to watch growing signs that it was being rejected by the workers and peasants in whose name he had made it.

Mikhail Alexandrovich Romanov, the Czar's brother, and his English secretary, Mr. Johnson, were living quietly in the Korolevskiye

Nomera, the King's Rooms, on Sibirskaya Street in Perm. The Grand
Duke's morganatic wife, Countess Brasova, visited him in May with
no apparent difficulty.[13] He and Johnson walked freely about the
town, visited the market, and talked with passers-by. It was true that
a squad of plain-clothes Cheka agents was quartered in the hotel and
followed the Grand Duke about. But it appeared to be nominal surveillance. The Grand Duke carried on a certain amount of correspondence. He had written his brother, the former Czar. As late as the
end of May and the beginning of June a traveler had no problem in
visiting him.

On the evening of June 12, shortly before dark, that is at some time
after 8 P.M., two men, one named Kobelev, an old resident[14] of the
hotel, and the other named Kurumnikov, owner of a store selling precious Urals stones, were playing cards when they heard a dispute in
the corridor. They opened the door of their room and saw the Grand
Duke surrounded by half a dozen men armed with revolvers who
were insisting that he come with them. The Grand Duke demanded to
see an official order from the Soviet. The men refused. Mikhail attempted to use the telephone but was prevented by one of the armed
men. Finally, after a whispered conversation the Grand Duke took his
hat from his room and left with the escort. After some hesitation Johnson accompanied them.[15]

The next day the Perm newspaper announced that "a band of White
Guardists" with forged papers had spirited the Grand Duke and Johnson away. A search failed to disclose their whereabouts.

The men had been taken to a deserted tract six versts from town
and murdered by a Cheka detail headed by the chairman of the local
Party committee, a left Communist named A. F. Myasnikov. Later
Myasnikov was to boast that he permitted Mikhail Romanov to "escape" just as the Germans permitted the murdered Communists Rosa
Luxemburg and Karl Liebknecht to "escape."[16] The Grand Duke and
Johnson were simply taken to the tract of land belonging to the Mo-
tovilikha factory and shot. Mikhail's body was destroyed in the factory
smelter. That of Johnson was buried in the woods.[17] Investigation has
never positively established that Moscow or Yekaterinburg (which
had jurisdiction over Perm) gave positive orders for the killing of the
Grand Duke, but Myasnikov's action was promptly reported to Lenin
and Sverdlov by Yekaterinburg in a telegram which implied that it
was taken in fulfillment of a directive by Moscow. And Moscow,
aware of the fact that Mikhail and Johnson had been murdered, for
months spread the story that the pair had "mysteriously escaped." The
Grand Duke was long thought to be "in hiding," and as late as autumn
1918, he was still being mentioned as the possible head of a moderate

constitutional monarchy, precisely the role which the Bolsheviks feared he might fill. This fear had been expressed several times in early June by the Perm newspapers, just before the murder.[18]

Yekaterinburg was not Tobolsk. It was not some sleepy bear's corner of Russia. It was the capital of the Urals, the principal center of Russia's heavy industrial region, the largest city in the Urals with 75,000 population, and an important Bolshevik center. There was a constant traffic in and out of the city. Not only had the Bolsheviks transferred activities here from Moscow and Petrograd but refugees had come to the city, including agents of various right-wing organizations. The Academy of the General Staff had been moved to Yekaterinburg from Petrograd. The city bustled with officers, attached to the academy or passing through for one purpose or another. Some supported the Revolution, many did not.

Everyone knew that the Czar and his family were confined in the Ipatyev house. The Municipal Gardens with their afternoon and evening concerts was nearby. So was the Church of the Ascension and the Club, somewhat diminished in brilliance, where the local Urals millionaires, officers, and bureaucrats traditionally gathered to play cards, overeat, and overdrink. Nearby were the leading hotels, the former Palais Royal and the Amerikanskaya.[19] There was a constant procession of sight-seers, and some who were not sight-seers, past the Ipatyev house. Unlike Tobolsk news flowed swiftly in and out of Yekaterinburg. Word of the Czech uprising, the success of the Czechs, their advances in Siberia and the Urals, spread rapidly. News of the disappearance of the Grand Duke Mikhail was reported the next day in the Yekaterinburg papers. The isolation of the Romanovs was by no means complete. Priests visited the house to celebrate mass. Dr. Vladimir Derevenko was permitted to come to treat the Czarevich and the Czarina. The former Czar sometimes talked at length with Alexander Avdeyev, commandant of the house, and Dr. Botkin spoke with Avdeyev every day. For the most part relations with the house guards were not too bad. The Grand Duchesses were lively, attractive girls. They enjoyed talking and for all the rules they talked freely and easily with the sentries who, after all, loved small talk and gossip with pretty girls.

Nor were these the only routes of communication. Arrangements had been made under which sisters of the Novotikhvinsky Monastery regularly brought milk, eggs, butter, cream, meat, sausage, radishes, cucumbers, different kinds of pastry, and nuts for the use of the Imperial prisoners. They even brought tobacco for the Czar when Commandant Avdeyev personally requested it for "the Emperor." The supplies were delivered regularly by Sisters Antonina and Mariya.[20] Correspondence, it is true, dried up. Only a handful of letters sent by members of the family from Yekaterinburg have survived, in contrast to the almost uninhibited correspondence, for example, which the Czarina was able to carry on from Tobolsk.[21]

Among those moving through Yekaterinburg was the Serbian Princess Yelena Petrovna, wife of the Grand Duke Ioann Konstantinovich who had been exiled to Alapayevsk, a mine and steel town of nine thousand population about sixty versts from Yekaterinburg. She spent three weeks in Yekaterinburg in May and several days later in June. She even went to the Ipatyev house and tried to gain admission. Of course, it was refused. Soon thereafter a Serbian officer named Maximović arrived and sought an interview with Nicholas. He claimed he wanted to discuss historical questions "concerning the war."[22] Actually Maximović had brought thirty thousand rubles to help the Czar's financing. He was refused admission. In June a whole Serbian delegation, including the chief of the Serbian Military Mission Mičić, arrived in Yekaterinburg. There were English and French consuls stationed in the city. The English consul had a view of the Ipatyev house and used to report to his consular colleagues daily that "the goods is still in the station."[23]

There can be no doubt that no news of major importance could long be prevented from reaching the Czar. He certainly knew by late May, if not before, of the Czech uprising and would have understood its significance: The Czechs might seize control of the Urals and Yekaterinburg. There is no mention of this in his diary but he would have been cautious to avoid any expression in view of the growing tension within the house. The possibility that he received communications from the outside, smuggled in one way or another into Ipatyev house, cannot be excluded.

On June 13–14 the routine of the House of Special Designation was broken. June 13 (May 31 old style) was Ascension Day. The Imperial family had expected a priest to conduct services. They waited all morning but no one came. Finally, they were told all the priests were too busy at the churches. Nor was the family permitted to take its usual walk in the garden. Late in the day Commandant Avdeyev arrived and had a long talk with Dr. Botkin, telling him the Regional Soviet was concerned over a possible outbreak by the anarchists and that possibly the family would have to leave hurriedly—in all probability for Moscow. He asked them to get ready for departure but warned that they must pack quietly so as not to attract the attention of the officers of the guard.

The family quickly assembled the minimum of travel requirements and awaited instructions. Avdeyev returned about 11 P.M. and said departure would be delayed several days. The family left the bags packed and went to bed after midnight. The next day, Saturday, was a fine warm day. The Czar and his family went for a walk as usual in two shifts. After the evening meal Avdeyev appeared, reporting that the anarchists had been taken in hand and departure had been put off. The Czar was disappointed. Later that evening he played his usual game of bezique.[24]

Was it coincidence that the alarm was raised at Ipatyev house on the night of June 13–14—at the very moment when at Perm the Czar's brother, the man in whose favor he had abdicated, was being lured from his hotel and murdered by Soviet agents? Yekaterinburg controlled Perm and both were controlled by Moscow. Moscow's orders to Perm were usually transmitted via Yekaterinburg. When the Czar learned of his brother's disappearance, did he connect the two events of June 13?[25] There is no notation about Mikhail in the Czar's diary, but from this time forward his lapses become more frequent and the entries lose their air of almost immutable calm. They become thin, erratic, nervous. They convey a feeling of the unknown, of events half-perceived, half-hidden in the background. Some small mystery is posed in almost every entry. On Sunday June 16 once again no priest appeared to conduct services. For some reason the family had been promised that the missing servants, the footman, Sednev, and Nagorny, the Czarevich's companion, would return that day. But they never did.[26]

The Czar finished reading the life of Czar Paul I by Shilder that day. He found it "very interesting." Paul was, of course, one of the many Czars whose career was ended by murder—in his case with the sanction and probable participation of his son, Alexander I.[27]

June was a month of rising tension in Moscow. Martial law had been declared May 29 because of discovery by the Cheka of a widespread conspiratorial organization headed by Boris Savinkov, Zinaida Gippius' old friend and onetime collaborator with Kerensky. A military uprising broke out in Tambov June 17. In Petrograd workmen in the Obukhov factory conducted a sit-in strike under the influence of the SRs, and the torpedo-boat squadron rebelled. There were angry strikes in Tula and Sormovo, put down with the use of weapons. Strikers at the Bublino plant outside Moscow were arrested by Cheka agents. Outbreaks occurred in the workshops of the Alexander railroad and on the Nicholas line connecting Moscow and Petrograd.[28] Trotsky was on the run, trying to whip up a military force to cope with the disaster which overhung the Revolution. He was in and out of Moscow half a dozen times. On one of his fleeting visits he talked with Lenin about the trial of the Czar for "the crimes of the Romanovs." There was a suggestion that it might be held in Yekaterinburg, "capital of the red Urals." Lenin seemed to favor the idea but wondered if "there might not be enough time."[29] The question was left open.

The disappearance and quickly suspected murder of the Grand Duke Mikhail and the advance of the Czechs into the Urals touched off rumors published both in Moscow and abroad that the Czar had been murdered. One monarchist after another tried to get the German ambassador, Count Mirbach, to intervene in behalf of the Czar or at least the Czarina and the "German Princesses." Mirbach steadfastly rejected these demands, insisting that there was no other power than the Bolsheviks with whom the Germans could deal and that, as he told Prince Dmitri Obolensky, a steel magnate and Germanophile: *"Aidez vous-mêmes et Dieu vous aidera.* I would rephrase it thus: aid yourself and Germany will help you." Nonetheless, a quiet German inquiry was now made about the Czar's situation.[30]

Lenin himself grew concerned about the Romanovs' security although probably for other reasons. In any event on June 22, as the Czar recorded in some amazement, a commission of six men arrived to carry out a thorough investigation of the regime at Ipatyev house. The Czar personally and Dr. Botkin on his behalf had for two weeks been arguing with the commandant about the windows in their quarters. The weather was hot, the house was sweltering, and there was no air except for the *fortochka,* the small Russian winter ventilation pane. They were not allowed to open any regular windows. Now the Czar leaped to the conclusion that the government commission had been sent to inquire into the window question. A mind-boggling exercise in bureaucracy! The members went through all the rooms, met the members of the family, and observed the conditions of their life. They were not the first to look into the window question, the Czar pointed out. A number of others had come, silently examined the windows, and departed.

The next day, the twenty-third, the Czar jubilantly reported that since morning one window had been opened. Not only were they breathing fresh air but by evening it was even cold in the quarters. He also corrected his earlier impression. The commission was not, as he first thought, made up of members of the Regional Soviet but had come from Moscow.[31] In fact it was headed by Ye. P. Berzin, later to become Dzerzhinsky's secretary.* He was acting as commander of the

* Berzin was purged and shot by Stalin in 1938. (Roy A. Medvedev, *Let History Judge,* p. 216.)

North Urals Siberian Front. He had been directed to carry out the inspection by Bonch-Bruyevich, director of the Soviet of People's Commissars, at the order of Lenin or Sverdlov. On June 27 Berzin formally reported to Sovnarkom, the Soviet of People's Commissars, that on June 21 (the Czar calls it June 22) he had carried out an examination of how Nicholas and his family were being confined, had checked the guards and security detachments, all members had verified the fact that Nicholas and his family were alive, and, therefore, "all reports about his murder and so on were provocations."[32]

The report at least gave Lenin up-to-date information about the Czar's conditions of confinement, information which could be used to counter rumors and reports of his assassination or execution.

But the times had not grown more quiet and Lenin's tendency to terror was accelerated. On June 20 Volodarsky, a leading Petrograd Bolshevik, editor of *Krasnaya Gazeta* and a Russian émigré who had returned from the United States to join the Revolution, was shot to death by an SR terrorist named Sergeyev. Immediately the call for reprisals and mass terror arose. This was not enough for Lenin. He wrote Zinoviev, his lieutenant for Petrograd, June 26 in violent terms:

> Only today we have heard at the CC that in Petrograd the workers wanted to reply to the murder of Volodarsky by mass terror and that you . . . restrained them.
> I protest most emphatically!
> We are discrediting ourselves; we threaten mass terror . . . yet when it comes to action we *obstruct* the revolutionary initiative of the masses, a *quite* correct one.
> This is im-pos-sible;
> The terrorists will consider us old women. This is wartime above all. We must encourage the energy and mass character of the terror against the counter-revolutionaries, and particularly in Petrograd, the example of which is *decisive*.
> Greetings![33]

It was now clear, had it ever been obscure, that when Lenin spoke of terror, he meant terror. He was not talking about terror to frighten with words. He was demanding genuine, awful terror—the swift, mass, remorseless killing of his fellow Russians, be they guilty or simply unfortunate enough to come from a particular class or chance to be swept up in a Cheka roundup. Only thus did he believe he could save the Revolution from collapse. Intimidation by mass murder.

And, as the *Uralsky Krai*, the Yekaterinburg newspaper, warned:

"Romanov and his relatives will not escape the Court of the People when the hour sounds."[34]

When would the hour of the Romanovs sound? On the fourth of July, Alexander Beloborodov, chairman of the Urals Soviet, and several other officials appeared at Ipatyev house.[*] He announced that Avdeyev had been replaced as commandant by a dark-complexioned man named Yakov Yurovsky.[†] Yurovsky had appeared once before at Ipatyev house on May 26, accompanied by Dr. Derevenko, who had come to treat Alexei. The Czar mistook him for a doctor.[35] Actually, Yurovsky was chief of the local Cheka. The change in regime was attributed to Avdeyev's slackness in permitting the Romanov trunks to be broken in on.[36] Yurovsky and his aide, Prokopy Nikulin, spent most of the day making an inventory of valuables in the possession of the family. They took the greater part of the jewelry, mostly rings and bracelets, and sealed them in a box after permitting the family to check the accuracy of the inventory against the property sealed in the box. Yurovsky also reported to the Czar that much of the food sent from the monastery had been appropriated by Avdeyev's guards for their own use. Within a couple of days a new and more firm regime had been installed in the House of Special Designation.

July 4 was a critical day.[37] On the same day that the new regime went into effect at Ipatyev house a strict new order was established over the other Imperial prisoners held at Alapayevsk. Here had been assembled the Grand Duchess Yelizaveta Fyodorovna, sister of the Czarina and widow of the Grand Duke Sergei, attended by two nuns of the order of Marfo-Mariinskaya, the Grand Duke Sergei Mikhailovich, the three sons of the Grand Duke Konstantin Konstantinovich— Igor, Ioann, and Konstantin—the Prince Vladimir Pavlovich Paley, son of Grand Duke Pavel Alexandrovich, and their servants. They had been living under a very light regime in a school building on the outskirts of town. They had been permitted to work in the big garden, walk in the fields, go to and from church, and buy provisions in the market. Now the servants were sent off, except for one nun for the Grand Duchess Yelizaveta, and a servant for Grand Duke Sergei. Just as at the Ipatyev house the property of the Imperial relatives was examined. Their jewelry and valuables were taken away. So were extra clothing, extra pairs of shoes, and linen. No longer were they permit-

---

[*] Beloborodov, who went on to become a hero of the Soviet Civil War, was purged and shot by Stalin in 1937. (Alexander Solzhenitsyn, *The Gulag Archipelago*, Vols. I–II, p. 333.)

[†] Yurovsky was purged and shot by Stalin as a Trotskyite. (Stefan T. Possony, *Lenin: The Compulsive Revolutionary*, p. 287.)

ted to stroll in the fields or go to church.[38] A "prison regime" was established about which Grand Duke Sergei complained by telegraph to Beloborodov in Yekaterinburg.[39] He also sent a message to his brother, Nikolai in Vologda, which read: "Salyue m. Kopre e le Per Lustre." It was a childish code but it deceived the telegraph operators. It said that he was in prison and his correspondence was subject to examination.[40]

One more event had occurred behind the scenes, probably unknown to the Czar and his family. Bishop Germogen, who in Tobolsk had shown sympathy for them, had been arrested and brought to Yekaterinburg on suspicion of plotting to rescue the Imperial family. His fellow religionists had raised 100,000 rubles bond and gotten the Yekaterinburg authorities to agree to let Germogen return to Tobolsk. He was en route back to Tobolsk when Czech forces broke through and seized the city. The armed convoy of Yekaterinburg Red Guards escorting Germogen got as far as the Tura River near Pokrovskoye, Rasputin's birthplace. There they threw Germogen into the river and drowned him.[41]

LXIII

"No News from Outside"

July is a warm month in the Urals. The winds flow over the low mountains from the interior deserts to the south and the temperature mounts into the nineties or even higher. There is little rain and the sun stands high in cloudless skies. July 13, a Saturday, was a warm day in Yekaterinburg yet not too warm to be unpleasant. Nicholas, writing less often in his diary, recorded that Alexei had had his first bath since leaving Tobolsk in May. His knee was much better but he could not yet completely straighten it.

The Czar added one more sentence: "No news from outside." These were the last words he was to record. What news had he been expecting? The expression was not one which he had used before. Never had he spoken of any absence of news—either from within or from without. It was for him a curious observation. Two days before he had permitted himself one of his rare bursts of anger. That morning three workmen had suddenly appeared in his room, installed a heavy grating over his window, and strengthened its outer frame. He described what had happened and said of the new commandant, Yurovsky: "This type pleases me less and less!"*

Yurovsky seemed to be fearful—or pretended to be fearful—that the Czar might escape from the House of Special Designation.[1]

The Czar had a special reason for being upset over the new iron grating. Or so he must have thought. Two weeks earlier, a few days

---

* "Type" in Russian has a special meaning. It describes a low fellow, perhaps a scoundrel.

before Yurovsky appeared on the scene, Nicholas and his family had passed what the Czar called "an alarming night." Apparently they had spent most of the night, fully dressed, in expectation of a rescue attempt. They had received two letters, one after the other, the Czar noted, which warned them to be prepared to be spirited away by "some dedicated people." But time passed, nothing happened, and "the expectation and uncertainty was very torturing." For a week thereafter the Czar wrote not a line in his diary.[2]

P. M. Bykov, chairman of the Yekaterinburg Soviet, later insisted that as the Czechs neared Yekaterinburg the Czar received letters from officers who planned to free him.

"The hour of liberation is nearing and the days of the usurpers are numbered," he quoted one letter as saying. "The Slav army is getting closer and closer to Yekaterinburg. It is only a few versts from the city. The moment has come. It is time to act."

Another letter said: "The long awaited hour has come."[3]

No news from the outside . . . Perhaps, it was this "long awaited hour" for which the Czar hoped.

The next day was Sunday July 14, the anniversary of the storming of the Bastille in the French Revolution. Father Storozhev and Deacon Buimirov were called to conduct mass at Ipatyev house. Both had served mass to the Imperial family on previous occasions. The Czar, his graying beard neatly trimmed, wore his uniform, but whether he had his St. George's medal on his breast Father Storozhev was never able to remember. Storozhev thought the Czar and his daughters seemed depressed although the Czarina in a flowing gown of pale lilac was in good spirits. The girls wore dark skirts and white blouses, and their hair—cut off when they had the measles—had grown down to their shoulders. Alexei wore a sailor suit and sat in a wheel chair. The Cheka Commandant Yurovsky sat in a far corner watching the proceedings. Father Storozhev had been warned not to hold any personal conversation.

The service was conducted without incident. When the prayer Be at Peace with His Holiness was chanted, Father Storozhev heard the Imperial family behind him sink to their knees. At the end of the service the Father passed close to the Grand Duchesses. One of them murmured: "Thank you."

As the priest and deacon walked home the deacon mentioned that for the first time in the services at Ipatyev house none of the Romanovs had joined in the singing.[4]

Monday July 15: cleaning day. Four women were summoned from the trade union hall to wash the floors of Ipatyev house. They arrived about midday and found the family and Dr. Botkin gathered in the dining room. The washerwomen, Mariya Starodumova recalled, were not permitted to speak with the family, but the Grand Duchesses helped them move the furniture and clean up the quarters, talking among themselves in jolly fashion. Alexei was still in his wheel chair. Yurovsky sat beside him and asked about his health.

The next day the family walked in the garden as usual. They came inside about 4 P.M. Two guards saw them return—Mikhail Letemin and Anatoly Yakimov. The Czarina did not go out that day nor apparently did the Czarevich. "I didn't notice anything special that time," Letemin observed.[5]

No news from the outside . . . At the Bolshoi Theater in Moscow there convened July 4 the Fifth All-Russian Soviet Congress. Of the 1,035 delegates 678 were Communists and 269 left Socialist Revolutionaries. Bruce Lockhart, the British agent, sat in the box from which he had often heard Chaliapin sing *Boris Gudunov*. Now he looked out on a sea of Russian revolutionaries, the Bolsheviks mostly soldiers in uniform and the left SRs in peasant blouses with unruly blond hair and brawny shoulders. The Bolsheviks were on the defensive. Sverdlov apologized for the German occupation. He defended the "Poverty Committees," the armed worker detachments Lenin had sent into the villages to seize grain for the cities. And he defended the reinstatement of death sentences and terror.

Then arose the electric figure of Mariya Spiridonova, thirty-two years old, the assassin of Luzhinovsky in Tambov in 1906, victim of a Cossack rape, sentenced to life in solitary imprisonment under the Czar. She was simply dressed, dark hair brushed straight back, wearing pince-nez. Her words came like bullets—aimed at the heart of the Bolsheviks.

"I accuse you," she told Lenin, "of betraying the peasants, of making use of them for your own ends.

"In Lenin's philosophy," she coolly told her peasant followers, "you are only dung—only manure. When the peasants, the Bolshevik peasants, the left SR peasants and the non-party peasants are alike humiliated, oppressed and crushed—crushed as peasants—in my hand you will find the same pistol, the same bomb, which once forced me to defend . . ."

Her words, Lockhart recorded, were lost in a storm of violence—applause by her supporters, indecencies shouted by the Bolsheviks.

Lockhart returned to the Bolshoi at 4 P.M. July 6. It was a hot, sultry day. Many seats on the platform were vacant. Trotsky was absent. So was Lenin. So was Radek. By 5 P.M. most of the Bolshevik Executive Committee members had disappeared. Spiridonova sat calm and composed. At 6 P.M. Sidney Reilly, another British agent, slipped into Lockhart's box. The theater had been surrounded by troops. There was fighting in the city. At that moment the building rocked under a grenade explosion.[6] No one seemed to understand what was happening.

At 2:30 P.M. Yakov Blyumkin and Nikolai Andreyev, left SRs, entered the German Embassy with forged Cheka credentials. They won admission to German Ambassador Mirbach's presence. After a few words Blyumkin drew his Browning and shot Mirbach and two of his aides. Andreyev threw a grenade which exploded with a tremendous roar, the men jumped from the window and fled, Blyumkin breaking his leg in the process.

SR troops at the Pokrovsky Barracks moved out into the city and captured the telegraph office from where they sent messages all over the country announcing they had overthrown the Bolshevik Government. Felix Dzerzhinsky, the Cheka chief, hurried to the barracks where the SRs disarmed him and declared him under arrest. Latsis, Dzerzhinsky's chief lieutenant, was captured when the SRs seized the Lubyanka, as was P. G. Smidovich, chairman of the Moscow Soviet.[7]

Lenin telephoned Trotsky at the War Commissariat.

"Do you know what's happened?" Lenin asked.

"No, what is it?"

"The left SRs threw a bomb at Mirbach," Lenin exclaimed.

Trotsky went to Lenin's office. While they talked word came in that Mirbach had died. It was decided that Lenin, Sverdlov, and Foreign Commissar G. V. Chicherin would go personally to the German Embassy and express condolences.[8]

"How does one express 'condolences'?" Lenin asked nervously. "I've already talked to Radek. I want to say 'Mitleid.' But apparently one has to say 'Beileid.'"[9]

That day Savinkov, with the aid of a force largely composed of SR officers, seized the city of Yaroslavl. The Left SR Boris Donskoi assassinated the German commander in the Ukraine, Gen. Hermann von Eichhorn, in Kiev, and Gen. M. A. Muravyev, the Soviet commander in Kazan and an SR, "declared war on Germany" and moved on Simbirsk with some troops loyal to himself. The Simbirsk Soviet, however, refused to follow his lead and he was killed in a shoot-out with loyal Soviet forces who were trying to arrest him.[10]*

Trotsky moved quickly to meet the threat. Two Lettish regiments surrounded the Bolshoi Theater. The SRs were driven from their barracks. Blyumkin escaped but Andreyev was captured and shot at

---

* Muravyev managed to arrest Mikhail Tukhachevsky, commander of the First Soviet Army and later commander in chief of the Red Army, purged and shot by Stalin in 1937.

Kursk railroad station.* A detachment led by the Hungarian revolutionary Béla Kun recaptured the telegraph office.[11] Spiridonova and the other SRs at the Bolshoi were arrested. Spiridonova, who was hoping to announce the SR rising to the Fifth Congress of Soviets, was instead hustled into confinement in the Kremlin.† Twenty SR hostages were shot. The Socialist Revolutionary coup to overthrow the Bolsheviks had failed. Subsequently before an investigating commission Spiridonova declared:

"I organized the matter of killing Mirbach from beginning to end. Learning about the assassination I went with a report about it to the Congress of Soviets, in order to explain the act and in order to assume responsibility before all the workers and before the International."[12]

Lenin's mood had never been more grim. At 1 A.M. on the seventh he telegraphed Stalin, who was requisitioning food at Tsaritsyn (later Stalingrad, now Volgograd), of the SR rising:

"We are liquidating it mercilessly this very night and we shall tell the people the whole truth; we are a hair's breadth from war. We have hundreds of Left SRs as hostages. Everywhere it is essential to crush mercilessly these pitiful and hysterical adventurers who have become tools in the hands of the counter-revolutionaries. All who are against war will be for us."[13]

After the SRs had been arrested and their headquarters seized Lenin drove with Krupskaya to inspect the scene. On the way their car was halted near the Nicholas Station by armed Bolsheviks who fired from behind a corner. Lenin and Krupskaya then proceeded to the former Morozov mansion, SR headquarters. The only thing that interested Lenin was the heap of torn-up SR documents. He decided to go for a ride in Sokolniki Park. Here a Young Kommunist patrol halted them, sneered at their documents, and took them to the nearest police station. Released, they went back to Sokolniki Park, where they were stopped by another patrol.[14] Lenin could hardly complain. He had given orders: "All cars are to be detained and held for a triple check."[15]

As Krupskaya remarked: "The situation was extremely difficult throughout July."[16]

In Petrograd, Count V. N. Kokovtsov, the Czar's elderly onetime Prime Minister, was being held for investigation. He had been taken

---

* Blyumkin escaped, was pardoned in 1919, but was purged and shot by Stalin as a Trotskyite in 1929. (Robert Conquest, *The Great Terror*, p. 29.)

† Spriridonova spent most of the remainder of her life in prison and exile. She was still alive in 1941 in the isolator at Orel. With the approach of the Germans she was taken out with other prisoners, it is said, and shot. (*Politicheskii Dnevnik 1964–1970*, Amsterdam, 1972, p. 726.)

to the former office of the city commandant, now headquarters of the Cheka. Here he found himself in the company of a pliad of notables—among them Generals Raikh and Goldgaur, the wealthy grain dealer Mukhin, Prince Yu. I. Trubetskoi, former Petrograd Governor-General Palchinsky, and former War Minister Verkhovsky. Kokovtsov was interrogated by the deputy head of the Cheka, Gleb I. Boky.*

Kokovtsov's case dragged on until July 9 when he was suddenly called in at 11 A.M. by Uritsky, head of the Petrograd Cheka. Uritsky had returned that morning from Moscow. He and Kokovtsov had a long conversation, much of it about the Czar. Uritsky wanted to know whether Kokovtsov felt that the Czar was sane. Kokovtsov told Uritsky that up to the time he left office in 1914 the Czar was "perfectly healthy" but that when he saw him for the last time on January 19, 1917, the Czar had radically changed and his condition had aroused in him "profound spiritual suffering and alarm." The Czar, he felt, was a sick man.

Uritsky wanted to know whether the Czar was aware of "the evil which the Emperor had caused to Russia."

Kokovtsov took issue with this concept. He told Uritsky the Czar believed in Russia, believed in the Russian man, and was dedicated to Russia. Kokovtsov was confident that there was no sacrifice the Czar would not have made for his country if he knew the country needed it. But Kokovtsov conceded the Czar was not always well advised. Nor did he choose people well. The greatest sins, Kokovtsov insisted, were committed not by the Czar but by the people around him. He told Uritsky that there had never been a time when the Czar did not permit him to present his views, no matter how strong, and heard them with no sign of dissatisfaction. Kokovtsov always spoke openly. But how the Czar acted on these views—that was another question.

Uritsky finally brought the discussion to a close. It had been decided by the Soviet Government, he said, to bring the Czar before a people's court. Kokovtsov would, of course, be called as a witness in the case.[17]

At the end of June or in early July, F. I. Goloshchekin, the military commissar of the Urals, returned to Moscow.† He stayed with his old friend Chairman Sverdlov in his Kremlin apartment. Soon, the Urals Soviet Chairman Alexander Beloborodov sent Goloshchekin a ciphered telegram reporting that his Cheka chief, Yurovsky, had now been installed in the Ipatyev house with the Czar.[18]

* Boky was arrested in 1937 by Stalin and died in 1941. (Alexander Solzhenitsyn, The Gulag Archipelago, Vols. I–II, p. 622.)

† Goloshchekin, purged by Stalin, died in a concentration camp in 1941. (Roy A. Medvedev, Let History Judge, p. 247.)

It is difficult to imagine that Goloshchekin did not discuss the Czar's case in the Kremlin and, in fact, Bykov, who would have known (he was chairman of the Yekaterinburg Soviet), insisted that Goloshchekin was sent to Moscow to consult the Kremlin about the Czar. Yekaterinburg was unanimous in desiring the Czar's execution but wanted Moscow's sanction. Goloshchekin found the Kremlin inclined to favor an open trial, and, in fact, it had been intended to raise the question of the Czar's fate at the Fifth All-Russian Soviet Congress. But because of the SR rising this was not done. Instead, Goloshchekin was sent back to the Urals with instructions to prepare for a trial in late July. Uritsky's conversation with Kokovtsov on July 9 reflected these discussions. The question was still in balance—execution without trial or execution with trial—but Moscow was inclining toward a trial.[19]

Moscow was maintaining the closest liaison with Yekaterinburg. Not only was Goloshchekin present in the Kremlin, in fact living with Chairman Sverdlov, but Lenin as early as July 7 had ordered arrangements made so that the Urals Soviet boss Beloborodov in Yekaterinburg could be connected with the Kremlin by direct wire.[20] Moreover, it should be noted that Goloshchekin was a trusted associate of Lenin. He had been a member of the Central Committee since 1912.[21] Lenin surely met with Goloshchekin. He had received him before he went to the Urals in 1917 and on other return trips.[22]

Goloshchekin got back to Yekaterinburg July 12. A meeting of the Regional Soviet was immediately called. Moscow's idea for a trial was threatened by the rapid approach of the Czechs. The front commander was asked how long he thought he could hold them off. He reported that they were advancing on two sides and the city might not be held more than three days.[23]

On July 14 the Yekaterinburg *Izvestiya*, organ of the Urals Soviet, reported: "Last night the Chairman of the Soviet [Beloborodov] had a long conversation by direct wire with Moscow with the Chairman of the Sovnarkom Lenin. The conversation concerned a military review and the security of the former Czar Nikolai Romanov."[24]

Did Lenin at long last sanction the execution of the Czar and his family? Was he told that Yekaterinburg could no longer guarantee their security and that there was no safe method of evacuating them? There is no written evidence. Three versions have been offered: that Lenin said, "Do as you wish"; that he said, "Act in accordance with the orders of the Soviet"; or that Sverdlov had already given a written order, "Act at your discretion."[25] Trotsky wrote (many years later) that he was told in late July by Sverdlov that the Czar and all the family had been shot. "Who made the decision?" Trotsky asked. "We decided it here. Ilyich believed we shouldn't leave the Whites a live

banner to rally around, especially under the present difficult circumstances . . . ," Sverdlov replied.[26] Trotsky agreed with the decision.
Krupskaya wrote simply: "On July 16 we had him [the Czar] and
his family shot."[27]

Whether the sanction was brought by Goloshchekin, whether it was
given by Lenin on the evening of the thirteenth, whether it was conditional or absolute, made little objective difference. Everyone by now
knew what the outcome would be. The Urals Soviet met at 10 P.M. in
Yekaterinburg July 14. All members were present.

It took the following action and stamped the edict "Top Secret":

"On the proposal of the Military Commissar [Goloshchekin] and
also the Chairman of the Military Revolutionary Committee [Mebiyis]
the meeting unanimously agreed to liquidate the former Czar Nikolai
Romanov and his family and also those in their service.

"It was further decided that the decision would be carried out not
later than July 18, 1918, and responsibility for this was given to Comrade Yurovsky, Ya. —member of the Cheka."[28]

On the morning of the sixteenth Yurovsky sought out the young
kitchen boy, fifteen-year-old Leonid Sednev, and had him taken over
to the neighboring Popov house where the guard lived. About 7 P.M.
Yurovsky called in Pavel Medvedev, chief of the guard, and told him
to collect the revolvers of the sentries. There were twelve of them, all
Russian Nagants. Yurovsky laid them out on his desk and told Medvedev that the family was to be shot at midnight and to warn the
guards so that they would not be disturbed by the noise.

The family went to bed as usual. Some time after midnight
Yurovsky appeared at their quarters.[29] He awakened them and told
them an alarming situation had arisen and that the Ipatyev house
might be attacked at any moment. The family must come down to the
lower floor for safety. The Romanovs rose, hurriedly washed and
dressed, and went down the staircase to the ground floor, then
through the back rooms of the house to a room adjoining the semisub-
merged side door that led out to Voznesensky Pereulok. Yurovsky and
his assistant, Prokopy Nikulin, went ahead, carrying kerosene lamps
which cast a swaying shadow over the procession. The Czar followed,
carrying Alexei, whose leg was bound with a heavy bandage. Next
came Alexandra and the Grand Duchesses, Anastasia carrying in her
arms her sister Tatyana's little Japanese dog.[30] Then came Dr. Botkin,
the housemaid Anna Demidova, carrying two pillows, the footman
Tropp, and the cook, Kharitonov. The guards chief Medvedev followed behind. Yurovsky announced that they would wait in the
semibasement room until automobiles were brought around. Three
chairs were brought in at the Czar's request. The Czar sat down in the

middle of the room. Alexei was at his right hand, the Czarina on his left. There were pillows on the chairs of the Czarevich and Alexandra. To one side near the wall with windows stood Anastasia. The other girls stood behind their mother.

There were a few moments of quiet. Then came a noise in the neighboring room—the executioners were assembling. Outside car motors started up. The hour was 3:15 A.M. (by daylight time). Yurovsky entered the room followed by his commando of eleven Chekists.[31] He stepped forward and said: "Nikolai Alexandrovich, by the decision of the Urals district committee we are going to shoot you and your family."[32]

"What?" said the Czar, starting up and turning to his family.[33]

For an answer Yurovsky opened fire, as did the eleven agents, each having selected a target before entering the room. The Czar fell immediately. Several of the girls screamed. Their screams were choked by shots from the Nagants.[34] Alexei was still alive. Yurovsky finished him off with two shots of his revolver. Anna Demidova tried to protect herself with her pillows but bayonets ended her life. It was over in two or three minutes.

Later that night the bodies were loaded into a truck, taken to a lonely mine called the Four Brothers. There they were chopped up, burned, drenched with acid, and thrown down an abandoned mine shaft.

By 9 P.M. on July 17 Gorbunov, secretary of the Sovnarkom in Moscow, had received from Beloborodov a ciphered telegram saying:

"Inform Sverdlov that all the family have met the same fate as the head. Officially family died during evacuation."

Was this the first word the Kremlin had of the extermination of the Romanovs? Possibly. But Beloborodov's telegram seems to imply that Moscow had already been informed as to the fate of the head of the Romanov family.[35]

The next day, the eighteenth, the Central Executive Committee of the Soviet was meeting at the Metropole Hotel, then called the Second House of Soviets. Before the meeting the Bolshevik faction gathered in Sverdlov's corner suite, No. 237.[36] Sverdlov read a telegram he had received from the Yekaterinburg Soviet. It said that because of the danger that they hadn't sufficient forces to defend Yekaterinburg the former Czar Nicholas might be liberated by the White Guards who would turn him into "a banner of counter-revolution." Not having a possibility of evacuating the Czar, the Executive Committee had decided to shoot him and his family. Yekaterinburg asked for Soviet approval of this "needed step." Yu. Flaxerman, an old Bolshevik present at the meeting, recalled that the request did not arouse any great happiness, but "the deed was done and there was no point in discussing it." Sverdlov proposed that the faction give approval and this was done unanimously.[37]

That evening the Soviet of People's Commissars met at 8:30 with Lenin in the chair. N. A. Semashko, the Commissar of Health, was presenting a proposal when Sverdlov entered the room. When Semashko concluded his presentation, Sverdlov asked for permission to speak out of order. Lenin gave him the floor. He reported that Nicholas had been shot at the instruction of the Urals Regional Soviet because of "fear that he would escape." The Urals Soviet asked approval of the Presidium of the Central Executive Committee and this had been given. There was no discussion. Lenin simply said: "Let's return to the proposal and take it up point-by-point."[38]

The next day newsboys ran screaming through the streets of Moscow shouting: "Death of the Czar!" *Izvestiya* announced the execution and said Alexandra and the daughters "had been taken to a safe place." Documents about a White Guard plot to rescue the former Czar were being sent to Moscow. The Executive Committee now had in its possession a number of important documents—Nicholas' diary, diaries of his wife and daughters, correspondence with Rasputin. All this material was to be published at the earliest possible moment.[39]

The Romanov tragedy was ended. All that remained was the tidying up. On the seventeenth the Romanovs at Alapayevsk were murdered by a commando of the Urals Soviet and it was announced they had been "attacked by an unknown band of marauders."[40] Lenin wanted their blood but he did not want public responsibility for killing children, uncles, aunts, servants, and other persons who hardly fitted even his most generous definition of "terror." There was a final back and forth with Yekaterinburg. Yekaterinburg was told it might publish the news of the Czar's execution and it was announced by Goloshchekin at a meeting on July 21 and the news (identical with Moscow's false announcement) appeared in the Yekaterinburg papers July 23.[41] Already Yekaterinburg was being evacuated. On July 22 the Ipatyev house, most—but not all—of the blood scrubbed from the floor and otherwise in badly disordered condition, was turned back to its owners. In the evening of the twenty-fifth the Czech troops and their Russian allies entered the city, a guard was placed at the house, and on August 2 an investigation was begun to try to discover what had happened. It has now gone on for nearly sixty years and many details are still unknown. But one thing was certain from the beginning—Lenin's remorseless course had carried him far from the clean, simple, and noble morality of the family in which he grew up and which had produced his martyred brother, Alexander, and his dedicated sisters.

The young Lenin, formed by the stern and puritanical views of his school inspector father and his saintly mother, had now come full circle. Lenin had committed the final act for which his brother had been willing openly to give his life. But Lenin in sanctioning the murder of Nicholas was only willing to admit ex post facto approval.

In his great act of vengeance he refused public responsibility. Rather, he falsified the record, and in the process the Czar's epithet, "Bloody Nicholas," was transferred to his successor, who became known as "Bloody Lenin."

Lenin lacked the clarifying and terrible simplicity of the high priest of Russian revolutionary terror, Nechayev, upon whom some critics insisted Lenin secretly modeled himself. Lenin had praised Nechayev for presenting formulas "so simple and clean that they could be understood by every person then living in Russia."

For instance, said Lenin, Nechayev was asked once by a fellow revolutionary the question: If all of the Romanovs are gathered together in church, which of them should be assassinated? Nechayev answered: "The whole House of Romanov."

This, said Lenin, "is simplicity to the point of genius."

In deed Lenin followed Nechayev. In word he was silent.

Lenin, in the reasoned opinion of the Russian philosopher Berdyayev, who had made the calvary from belief in Karl Marx to belief in Jesus Christ, "was not a vicious man."

"There was," Berdyayev believed, "a great deal that was good in him [Lenin]. He was not mercenary and absolutely devoted to an idea; he was not even a particularly ambitious man or a great lover of power; he thought little about himself; but the sole obsession of a single idea led to a dreadful narrowing of thought and to a moral transformation which permitted entirely immoral methods of carrying on the conflict."[42]

Lenin, Berdyayev believed, was a man of fate. Without Lenin, it seems entirely clear, the vast insurgence of the Russian people would not have taken the turn it did. And without the raw turbulence and cruelty of the people Lenin's course would not have taken a turn so brutal and inhuman.

Just before the Romanov murders Gorky in one of his last "Untimely Thoughts" (his paper was finally closed down July 16—a coincidence?) declared:

"Everything that I said about the Bolsheviks' savage crudeness, about their cruelty which approaches sadism, about their lack of culture, about their ignorance of the psychology of the Russian people, about the fact that they are performing a disgusting experiment on the people and are destroying the working class—all this, and much more that I said about 'Bolshevism' retains its full force."[43]

Or, as the saintly old anarchist Prince P. A. Kropotkin was to declare in a famous letter to Lenin in 1920:

"Really can't there be found around you someone to remind you that such measures [a new terror had just been proclaimed] inevitably return us to the worst times of the Middle Ages and the religious wars —unworthy of people seeking to create a future society on Communist foundations? Is there really no one amongst you who understands what a hostage is? That it means that a man is thrust into prison not because he is guilty of any kind of crime but simply in order to threaten your opponents with his death. 'Kill one of ours and we will kill so many of yours.' Don't your comrades really understand that this indifference is nothing but torture for those imprisoned and their relatives?"[44]

It was, alas, too late—and still too early—for Lenin to hear Kropotkin's humanitarian voice.

LXIV

Where Is My Home?

There was no heat in the flats of Moscow in the winter of 1919–20. The Revolution sat on the city like an unearthly presence. In the snow-choked streets hawk-faced patrols with peaked Budenny caps, dull red stars, and bayoneted rifles tramped endlessly, the wind whipping the skirts of their long gray coats. The people in the flats waited hungry and cold and worried where to get a bit of wood or a heel of bread. Sometimes they wondered where Russia would end. What had Lenin's Revolution wrought? The country seemed lost in a wasteland of spent passion and desiccated dreams. The old order was dead but the new was a stillborn monster. Hope had died and there was no law but the bullet.

It seemed to the poet Balmont that a white mist filled the air, blurring the outlines of buildings and dissolving the figures of passers-by. It was as hard to see the city as it was the future. He was too cold to stay in bed, too cold to stay in his flat. There was no warm place in Moscow but he often went to the poet Marina Tsvetayeva. Her flat was as cold as his; still, as they huddled in their coats over a glass of tea, the words flew back and forth and soon the dark streets of the Arbat vanished, the frost melted, and they found themselves in the bright world of imagination, of beauty, of golden images, laughter, and dreams.°

° Balmont, a revolutionary who broke with the Bolsheviks, left Russia in 1922 and died impoverished and insane in France in 1943. Tsvetayeva left Russia in

On this winter day Balmont had already had tea with Tsvetayeva. Both Tsvetayeva and he had twelve-year-old daughters. Now Balmont brought Marina's Alya to meet his Mirochka and left them together, eating a dish of warm kasha in his flat while he set out to rejoin Marina at the Café of Poets. Balmont walked down the Bronnaya, a narrow street, both sides lined with dirty old buildings at dusk, the sunset painting the horizon crimson like the glow of a distant fire. The street was empty and as he looked at the darkening sky he saw the pale arc of a young moon.

Balmont's thoughts were distant. It was a harsh moment for poets— especially for poets like himself and Tsvetayeva whose sympathy for revolution had soured. It was a harsh moment for Russia. Nowhere could he see a gleam of light.

Suddenly out of the dusk appeared before him a woman dressed as a peasant, wearing a peasant's winter *valenki* (felt boots), a long dark kaftan, almost like a monk's robe, and a warm white shawl over her head. Balmont could not tell whether she was beautiful or not but he knew he could not take his eyes from her face and that she was young.

The woman spoke and Balmont halted.

"Dyadenka, uncle," she said, "where is my home?"

She spoke in the soft voice of a child who turns to an adult in absolute confidence that her question will be answered.

A strange feeling overcame Balmont and he started to go ahead but the woman came abreast and touched his right hand:

"Dyadenka, where is my home?"

"I don't know," Balmont said, his heart filling with despair.

"You *do* know," she said, her voice like a trusting girl's. "You know, dyadenka, that it's right nearby. Show me where my house is."

The woman's face seemed strange and her question was strange but it did not seem strange to Balmont. They walked past a row of houses. No one appeared. Again the woman asked: "Where is my house? Where is my house?"

"I can't help you," Balmont said with falling heart. "I just don't know."

"Oh," said the woman, "you should be ashamed, dyadenka."

Balmont felt a blush sweep over his face.

"It's not," she said, "where you are going."

Balmont's head whirled and his heart beat fast. Some monstrous desire arose in him—was it monstrous or holy? He could not be certain. All he knew was that he wanted to take this woman into a snow-

---

1922, returned in 1939, and committed suicide in 1941, living in neglect, poverty, and oppression in her homeland. He tells this story in his sketch, *Gdye Moi Dom,* published in 1924 in Prague after he had gone into exile from Russia.

filled courtyard, sit with her under the portico, and embrace her passionately. To oblivion.

At that moment a man emerged from a gate. It was too dark to see his face. The woman ran to the man, spoke to him quickly, and in a moment they had vanished into the darkness of the courtyard, he with his arm over her shoulder.

For a moment Balmont halted, waiting for what he did not know. All was quiet. Then he went on to the café where Marina Tsvetayeva sat. She glanced at Balmont's shaken face and cried:

"Brother! What's happened?"

He told her of his brief encounter. A solemn look came over Marina's face and it seemed to Balmont that her eyes saw something deep within herself. She took Balmont's hand in hers.

"You should have brought her with you," she said. "You should have. She was—Russia."

Source Notes and Acknowledgments

All studies of the Russian Revolutions inevitably begin with that classic work of Russian scholarship and jurisprudence the seven-volume steno-graphic report of the Extraordinary Investigating Commission of the 1917 Provisional Government, called *Padeniye Tsarskogo Rezhima*, the Fall of the Czarist Regime.

The commission was set up two days after the Czar's abdication and con-cluded its inquiry just in time—October 11, 1917. A few days later the Pro-visional Government was overthrown by the Bolsheviks. The commission had begun its inquiry March 18, 1917, with the questioning of Minister of Justice A. H. Khvostov. It conducted eighty-eight examinations of witnesses of which eighty-seven are published in its stenographic report (the record of one session, a second examination of Finance Minister V. N. Kokovtsov, was lost).

Almost every individual of consequence in the Romanov regime was heard. Some were responsive, some were not. Even when they were not, as in the case of Anna Vyrubova, the close friend of the Czarina, the testimony was marvelously revealing of the ambience of the court circle, its psychol-ogy, the narrowness of its perspectives, the intrigue, the scandal, the para-noia, the ignorance.

All the politicians and the policemen appeared. The police were defensive but as they told their stories and offered their excuses the raw underbelly of the Czarist system was wantonly exposed.

It is a commentary on the high standards of Soviet scholarship in the early revolutionary period that the seven volumes of *Padeniye* were pub-lished in the years 1924–27. The editing was meticulous and careful. No effort was made to distort, slant, or suppress the commission's findings.

Padeniye stands as a monument to a vanished era. Its detail and richness can never be equaled.

But this is only one of a number of magnificent collections of revolutionary source materials. Enormous efforts were made after the 1905 Revolution to probe and study the continuing social upheaval. Everyone wanted to know *why* and *how* and *who*. A stream of documents, studies, and revelations was presented in such publications as *Byloye* and *Golos Minuvshego*. The report by Lubov Ya. Gurevich in *Byloye* on the events of 1905 is a classic on which all subsequent accounts have had to draw.

The two Revolutions of 1917 freed from the Government's archives a mountain of materials—secret reports of the police on the deterioration of social and political life, the memoranda of high officials to the Czar, warning him of the onrushing peril, the letters of the Romanov Grand Dukes, the Czar's uncles, brothers, and cousins, seeking to persuade him to change course, the diaries of public men in which they recorded their fear-haunted observations over the years—those, for example, of Count A. A. Bobrinsky, A. A. Polovtsev, War Minister A. N. Kuropatkin, and the Grand Dukes Konstantin Konstantinovich and Andrei Vladimirovich.

And, of course, along with these materials came the most significant evidence of all—the private diaries and letters of Nicholas II and Alexandra Fyodorovna.

The published Romanov materials include segments of the personal diary of the Czar covering the important period from December 16, 1916, to his final entry, June 30, 1918, a few days before his death, the letters and telegrams exchanged between himself and his wife in the period 1914–17.

Several other Romanov documents have been made public: portions of the Czar's diary beginning in 1890 and ending in 1906; a portion of his diary for July 1–31, 1914; letters exchanged between himself and Kaiser Wilhelm of Germany; some letters exchanged between himself and his mother, Mariya Fyodorovna, at the time of the 1905 Revolution and in the years 1907–10; his correspondence with Premier Stolypin; and a few other random letters.

But there are many Romanov materials which have never been published by Soviet archivists for reasons by no means clear. Access to these materials is not permitted to foreign scholars and is only irregularly granted to Soviet researchers. However, a few recent Soviet historical works do cite unpublished letters, telegrams, and diaries of Nicholas.

The publishing record of the Romanov materials has been curious from the beginning. Both Nicholas and Alexandra were meticulous correspondents and record keepers. Almost all the Romanovs, even the children, kept diaries. When Alexandra finally realized that the February Revolution had succeeded, she spent several days in early March 1917 destroying correspondence, including all of her letters to and from Queen Victoria of England (her letters to Victoria had been returned to her on Victoria's death). She destroyed her diary and correspondence from or about Rasputin, including letters from Vyrubova. The Czar spent his first days in detention at

Tsarskoye Selo destroying correspondence and records, as he noted in his diary.

The children destroyed some but not all of their letters and diaries before they left exile at Tobolsk for exile in Yekaterinburg. Alexei's diary was not destroyed and was found by the investigators of the Romanov murders but it has not been published except for a few entries.

Neither the Czar nor the Czarina destroyed the letters they had exchanged. The Czarina's letters to the Czar, for example, were found at Yekaterinburg in a black box and returned to Moscow, where they were put in the State Archives. The same was true of the Czar's diaries and correspondence found at Yekaterinburg. In fact, it was announced in July 1918, coincident with the Czar's execution, that quantities of materials, including information about Rasputin's activities, had been seized and would be made public. Some segments of the Czar's diaries were, in fact, published by the Bolshevik newspapers, but publication was quickly suspended when it proved to be creating sympathy for Nicholas.

In the early days of the Revolution access to these and other State Archives was relatively simple. A number of foreign correspondents, among them Isaac Don Levine, were able to win entry to the archives and purchase materials from the archivists who were glad to earn a little money copying off the letters of the Czar and the Czarina. These copies found their way to the West, and portions of the Czar's diary and the Czarina's letters were first published in book form in Berlin by the Slovo publishing house and later in Paris and London.

Levine obtained a substantial quantity of the Czarina's letters to the Czar in 1919. These were published in the Chicago *Daily News* and formed the basis for the Berlin Slovo edition of the Czarina's letters and later editions published in Paris and London.

At this time, as Levine recalls, he saw both the Czar's diary and the diary of the Czarina in the State Archives, the Czar's diary in large thin bound volumes and the Czarina's diary, or at least the last volume of it, a small volume. He found the Czar's diary so uninteresting that he did not bother to try to obtain a copy. Some extracts from the Czarina's diary were published in the Chicago *Daily News*.

Later on Levine negotiated with the Russians for the Czar's letters, and excerpts from them were published in the Hearst newspapers.

According to some accounts, notably that of Gen. M. K. Diterikhs, one of the investigators of the Yekaterinburg tragedy, Kerensky took possession of the Czar's letters and the Czarina's letters in the spring of 1917 at the time of the Provisional Government's inquiry into the Romanov regime. This contradicts other reports that the correspondence was seized at Yekaterinburg.

Irritated by these publications, Soviet authorities announced that they would publish their own edition of the correspondence of the Czar and the Czarina. The complete file, they said, from the late 1880s to the Czar's last letter of March 7, 1917, was in the State Archives. The Soviet archivists criticized inaccuracies and inadequacies in Slovo's Berlin edition which contained the Czarina's letters beginning with No. 232 (she always carefully numbered her letters to the Czar) and ending with letter No. 630, December 15, 1916.

They promptly published in *Krasny Arkhiv*, No. 4 for 1923, letters 631–53, the last of the Czarina's correspondence.

Then they began what was intended to be publication of the full correspondence of Nicholas and Alexandra. In 1925 Volume III of a projected five-volume edition of their correspondence was published. Volume III contained correspondence of 1914–15; Volumes IV and V contained 1916 and 1917. Volumes I and II were supposed to contain correspondence from the end of the 1890s to 1914, but they were never issued.

No explanation for this failure to publish has ever been made. Careful examination of the published letters shows no indication of tampering. They have been published fully and with scholarly concordance. There is, however, one serious defect in the Soviet publication. The Czar and the Czarina wrote in English. No English edition was published. Instead, the Soviet edition contains translations of the correspondence into Russian, inevitably losing much of the intimate flavor of the originals, which were often ungrammatical and full of misspellings. The Imperial couple sometimes used simple code to disguise individuals they mentioned (Kalinin for Protopopov, the "old man" for Count Fredriks, the "black ones" for the Montenegrin princesses, Anastasia and Militsa).

The Imperial letters were edited by the Soviet archivist A. A. Sergyev, with meticulous scholarship.

As he noted: "Nicholas and Alexandra Romanov wrote each other always in English except for a few dozen telegrams sent in the Russian language."

He recorded that Alexandra made an error in numbering her letters. After letter No. 545 (July 17, 1916) she numbered the next one on July 18 No. 555, an error which Nicholas pointed out to her in one of his last letters. The only letter in the whole series which the editors could not locate was No. 649, sent between February 26, 1917, and March 2, undoubtedly lost somewhere en route.

Pokrovsky, the general editor of the series, lamented the fact that because of the Czar's swift return to Tsarskoye Selo after the murder of Rasputin there are no letters between December 17, 1916, and February 22, 1917, one of the most critical periods of the regime.

Sergyev was able to decipher almost all the simple code words with which the Czar and Czarina sought to cloak the identity of some of those of whom they wrote. But he was unable to identify *krasnaya shapka* (red hat) and *tsvetushchi* (the blooming one), cover names appearing in some of the Czarina's last letters.

At the time Volumes III, IV, and V of the Czar's correspondence were published the editors apologized that they had been unable to locate copies of telegrams sent by the Czarina to the Czar in 1917. There is evidence that at least some of these (which may have originally been in Blok's possession) have been found but they have not been published.

According to Sir Bernard Pares, who edited the collection of the Czarina's letters for 1914–16 published in England, the Czarina's earlier letters also reached England but were not published. He also believed that a "mass of letters" exchanged by the Czarina and Vyrubova survived. If so they have not seen the light of day.

A pathetic collection of letters dispatched by the Imperial family from imprisonment has recently been published by the Holy Trinity Monastery of Jordanville, New York, under the editorship of Ye. E. Alferev. It contains 227 letters, 6 from the Czar, 82 from the Czarina (including a number to Vyrubova), and the remainder from the children, many of them greeting cards. There are no letters from Yekaterinburg although it is known that some did reach the children in Tobolsk from their mother and their sister, the Grand Duchess Mariya Nikolayevna, before the children departed to join the others in Yekaterinburg. There is no indication that any letters emerged from the Ipatyev house in Yekaterinburg during the final weeks.

It is doubtful that access to thus far unavailable materials in Soviet hands would radically change the impressions conveyed by the mass already published. However, important insights would be forthcoming if free access could be had to many secondary materials still closely held in Soviet archives. This can be deduced from the work of contemporary Soviet historians who like V. S. Dyakin, for instance, have had access to unpublished diaries and telegrams of Nicholas; to the important archive of A. A. Klopov, a curious kind of Russian ombudsman who had unique access to Nicholas and to many other top figures in the last years of the Romanov regime; and to other unpublished diaries and letters. Because of this kind of access, recent Soviet historical works by such writers as Dyakin, Ye. N. Burdzhalov, V. Ya. Laverychev, Yu. Z. Polevoi, Ye. D. Chermensky, and the excellent two-volume study of the 1917 Revolutions called *Oktyabrskoye Vooruzhennoye Vosstaniye*, published under the editorship of A. L. Fraiman and others, provide valuable insights despite inevitable bows to the Party line. There is much in contemporary Soviet historiography which deepens our comprehension of the revolutionary events. The publication since 1953 of a mass of Party protocols, reports, and correspondence brings into clearer perspective the role of Lenin's Bolsheviks, particularly their extreme weakness and estrangement from both the 1905 and February 1917 Revolutions.

The same cannot be said, alas, for Soviet scholarship concerning the icon figure of V. I. Lenin. The extraordinary achievement of assembling Lenin's writings, letters, notebooks, telegrams (even his doodles) in the collected works (the recent fifth edition is far and away the best) and in the so-called *Leninsky Sbornik*, an irregular repository of minor Leniniana, cannot be minimized. No student of the last years of the Romanov dynasty and the three revolutions can do without these collections.

All of this renders the lacuna, deliberate suppression, and distortion more painful. Such simple questions as the ethnic origin of Lenin's grandfather, Dr. Blank (was he a German or a Jew?); the financial standing of the Ulyanov family before and after the death of Lenin's father; the source of the money which for so long supported Lenin, his brother, and his sisters in their years of revolutionary activities (probably funds carefully doled out by Lenin's mother); the details of Lenin's marriage to Krupskaya (certainly celebrated in conventional Russian Orthodox style); Lenin's reaction to the execution of his brother Alexander for the failed attempt on the life of Alexander III; the full story of Lenin's romantic involvement with Inessa Armand (in recent years quantities of Lenin's letters to *her* have been published but only two or three business letters of hers to him although presumably huge numbers survive in the archives, unless Krupskaya destroyed them); the story of Lenin's relationship with Maxim Gorky after the Revolution when Gorky was devoting every effort to save writers, artists, and even nobility from the Red Terror; the details of Lenin's actions with respect to the execution of the Romanovs (certainly preserved by the pettifogging bureaucrats who have conserved every scrap of paper on which Lenin wrote his name); the full scope of his relationship with Helphand (Parvus); how much German money was sent into Bolshevik hands and how.

There is also the carefully glossed over but critical question of the extent to which Lenin was in disagreement with his fellow Bolsheviks about the timing and tactics of the October coup d'état. Exactly when, for example, did Lenin sneak back into Petrograd from Finland in the autumn of 1917 and why did he remain in hiding, only in intermittent and difficult touch with his Bolshevik colleagues at their Smolny headquarters? Where are his notes and plans for the uprising, the scribbled orders that went back and forth between Lenin in his hiding place and Smolny? In fact, were there such communications?

This merely touches lightly on the kind of issues which cannot be resolved through the official collections of Lenin materials. That substantial numbers of Lenin documents have not yet been made public is certain. This can be deduced, for example, by the recent publication of a series of Lenin letters on the question of the disputed Schmidt inheritance funds. These are the funds of the young radical Moscow entrepreneur who died at the time of the 1905 Revolution and wished his money to go to the Social Democratic revolutionaries. By remarkably tricky maneuvers Lenin got hold of the money. The Mensheviks said it was theirs, or at least that it should be divided. An ugly wrangle went on for years. Only in 1975 did Soviet authorities finally publish in *Leninsky Sbornik*, No. 38, Lenin's correspondence on the subject and they did so only after a group of Lenin's letters had turned up in Swiss archives and been made public in Zurich and Germany.

In general the best materials on the Revolutions published under Soviet auspices emerged during the early years before the death of Lenin. After his death the suppressive and revisionist hand of Stalin became more and more evident. Historians like Pokrovsky who had done a scholarly job in editing memoirs and archival materials in the 1920s were attacked and purged. As the 1930s advanced many early reminiscences were suppressed and their authors executed. The role of men like Trotsky, Zinoviev, Kamenev, Bukharin, and Lenin were falsified (or eliminated) and the portrait of Stalin as a prime mover in 1917 grew larger and larger.

Among the best of the Lenin memoirs are, of course, those of his family, particularly those of his wife, Nadezhda Krupskaya. There are also memoirs of his sisters, Anna and Mariya, and his brother Dmitri as well as those of Anna's adopted son, Georgi Lozgachev-Yelizarov, Anna's husband, and a few snippets from the Veretennikov cousins.

Additional family materials are still locked in the archives. The Soviet historical journal *Voprosy Istorii* has commented that there are "many, many" unpublished letters of Lenin's mother. Stalin rigorously repressed most of Lenin's relatives. Krupskaya herself was threatened. Even Georgi Lozgachev-Yelizarov was exiled to Central Asia. It is possible that a substantial Ulyanov family archive still exists although it is also possible these materials were destroyed by Stalin or at his orders. There is also known to be a substantial unpublished Krupskaya archive.

Some of the best and most revealing Lenin memorabilia were written outside the Soviet Union—several by Trotsky (although he was never really close to Lenin in prerevolutionary days), by Nikolai Valentinov (N. V. Volsky), a sensitive observer who was Lenin's acolyte in the 1904–5 period, and by Angelica Balabanoff, the remarkable selfless Russian revolutionary who was deeply offended by the vulgarity of Lenin's pragmatism, the cruelty of his tactics and of his strategy.

A whole bibliographic study could be written on the publishing history of such secondary participants in the Revolutions as Bonch-Bruyevich, Gusev, Antonov-Ovseyenko, Lunacharsky, and Lepeshinsky. For their honest, direct recollections of events one must go back to the first publications in the early journals. Here their memories appear uncolored except by their own emotions and political biases. Through the years they will be reprinted again and again, each time with different editing, different suppressions, different distortions designed to fit the aberrations of the current and ever-shifting Party line.

In the period since Stalin's death there has been some improvement. Some new collections have retrieved the original accurate accounts but not all. And, now and then, a new untarnished reminiscence will be published, extracted from long-suppressed archives. How many more accounts lie still locked in the vast filing cabinets of the Party and the vaults of the Institute of Marxism-Leninism probably not even the most knowledgeable Soviet researchers know.

In dealing with Russia's cultural revolution, the explosion in arts, letters, and music which presaged and prefigured the political upheavals, another situation prevails. Here there is magnificent material. It has been published all through the years (except the worst Stalin years).

The problem is one of selection. Every one of the brilliant figures in Russian intellectual life kept a personal record, published his or her observations and correspondence. The task of reconstructing Russia's "Silver Age," of reconstituting the incredible tensions and imagination which marked Russian poetry and painting in the years leading up to World War I, the long premonitory shadows cast ahead of the Revolutions-to-come, is one of sorting through a treasure chamber. Here the writings of Zinaida Gippius-

Merezhkovsky, her magnificent *Sinyaya Kniga*, Bryusov, Bely, Blok, Khoda-sevich, Mayakovsky, Burlyuk, and the many, many others provide a narra-tive of enormous richness. No one has done a better job of re-creating these times than Konstantin Mocholsky in his many studies of the lives of those gifted individualists.

Perhaps nowhere has the flavor of the era which came to an end in Feb-ruary 1917 been more vividly conveyed than in that illustrated weekly jour-nal which was pored over by almost every middle- and upper-class Russian family in the years from the 1880s onward—*Niva*, published by A. F. Marks, something like *Harper's Weekly* or the *Illustrated London News*, a mixture of often second-rate serialized fiction and art and illustrated fea-tures on the great events of the times. *Niva's* portrait of Russia in the three decades before 1917 is far more vivid than that of the daily newspapers in-cluding *Pravitelstvenny Vestnik* (the government journal) and all the rest.

The best narrative of the February 1917 Revolution is that written by the poet Alexander Blok, at the commission of the Provisional Government and published in the great collection edited by the Menshevik Gessen, in Berlin, called *Arkhiv Russkii Revolyutsii*. The ARR was published monthly for about four years and included many basic historical studies and reminis-cences, essential to understanding the complex political-social events of 1917–18. Blok's study of the February Revolution was based on full access to the materials of *Padeniye*. He was the official editor and chronicler of the Investigating Commission. He saw some telegrams and messages of the Czar and Czarina which have never since come to light—probably having been lost in his personal files.

All, or almost all, of the great February participants wrote their memoirs —Kerensky, Chernov, Chkheidze, Tsereteli, and the rest. So did the impor-tant diplomats—Maurice Paléologue, the sophisticated French ambassador, David Francis, the bumbling American, and Sir George Buchanan, the well-informed but closemouthed British ambassador. The political memoirs are uneven, inconsistent, and often concentrate on sectarian and doctrinal ques-tions. The authors are self-serving, self-justifying. Kerensky wrote his four times, changing his version each time, never to the neglect of his personal image. The best and most perceptive memoir is that of V. V. Shulgin, whose *Dni* gives us sharply etched portraits of all the political figures and some cryptic images of the great events, particularly the abdication of the Czar. One of the best eyewitness accounts is that of the French newspaper-woman Mme Amélie de Néry.

The Rasputin story has been told by all of its participants, except Grand Duke Dmitri. None of the accounts is entirely satisfactory and a great deal of nonsense has been written about Rasputin from the days before his assas-sination. Sir Bernard Pares, who knew all of the participants, is excellent in putting the facts into some perspective. The secret reports of the Okhrana published after the Revolution are good on the hard facts. A small study of the Tibetan adventurer Badmayev gives insight into the atmosphere in and around the court in which Rasputin operated. A good deal of archival material on Rasputin and his circle probably remains unpublished in the Soviet files.

Almost all accounts of the October Revolution draw heavily on John Reed's "classic" *Ten Days that Shook the World* and on Sukhanov's brilliant seven-volume memoir. Each is invaluable but neither is entirely satisfactory. Reed's account is spotty and flawed by errors of fact. Sukhanov's is marvelously gossipy but wanders off into endless political speculation and controversies obscure at the time and long since forgotten. This is why Joel Carmichael's abridgment of Sukhanov is much better reading than the original. Blok's diary, notebook, and letters give detail and flavor of the era in Petrograd and Moscow but, alas, his wife is said to have destroyed any firsthand accounts he wrote of February and October.

Going beyond these accounts, there is a wealth of detail in seldom-consulted memoirs including a diary of Communications Minister Liverovsky, who was in Winter Palace during the fateful night of October 25–26, recently published in Moscow. Another recently published memoir by an insider is that of Count Zubov. There is also a remarkable story by Ensign Sineguba, who assisted in the defense of the Winter Palace, and an excellent eyewitness account by Vladimir Nabokov, the Kadet leader and father of the famous novelist, as well as many others, including those of the young French diplomat Count de Robien, the French correspondent Claude Anet, and the newly published memoirs of Yelizaveta Drabkina. The best reconstruction of the events leading up to the revolutions is to be found in the works of S. P. Melgunov, a participant in the events who devoted thirty years of life in Paris to writing a series of comprehensive fact-packed volumes on the February events, the October Revolution, and the Romanov tragedy.

On the Romanov murders the account of the investigator Sokolov will always be the best, supplemented with such revealing Soviet documents as the account of P. M. Bykov, chief of the Yekaterinburg Soviet. Sokolov's original investigative file appears to have been lost together with some Romanov relics, including bones found at the execution site. A copy of most of his materials, however, is on deposit at the Houghton Library at Harvard University. Very little has been published on the Romanov tragedy by the Soviets in recent years, but a few significant details regarding Lenin and his deputy, Sverdlov, can now be pieced together from disparate Soviet materials. These are sufficient to remove any doubt that Lenin and Moscow knew precisely what was going on in Yekaterinburg. If Lenin did not give actual orders for the executions, he did grant general authority for them.

Much detail in this narrative was drawn from personal archives and personal reminiscences. Some of the more important are those of Princess Lidiya Vassiltchikova; V. L. and El. Dm. Vyazemsky; the observations of G. I. Vassiltchikov; the personal reminiscences of Paul Anderson, one of the young American members of the YMCA group in Petrograd during the revolutionary days; and the archives of several of his associates. The advice and guidance of Alexandre Tarsaidze was helpful on several critical points, and the work would not have been possible without the constant assistance of the Slavonic Division of the New York Public Library, its resources and remarkable staff. I have also had the co-operation of several Soviet specialists and historians who have helped to untangle some knotty questions. In this connection I must acknowledge with particular gratitude their assistance in providing me from the Institute of Marxism-Leninism in Moscow copies of some of the original manuscript materials of Nadezhda Krupskaya, bearing on the question of the date of Lenin's return to Petrograd on the eve of the October Revolution.

My thanks for special assistance to Georgi Lozgachev-Yelizarov; E. E. Schmidt, of the Danish Press Museum, Aarhus, Denmark; Thomas P. Whitney; Theodore Shabad; Arthur T. Dailey; Professor John A. Hangin, of the University of Indiana; the late Countess Bezobrazov; Princess Vera Konstantinova; Bart McDowell; Prince Andrew Konstantinovich Bagration; and Nikita D. Roodkowsky, of Natick, Massachusetts. And particularly to my editors, Sam Vaughn, Betty Heller, and Nancy Kojima.

Notes and Sources

Sources

RUSSIAN BOOKS

Adamchevsky, Ya., and Potsekha, Yusef. *Lenin v Krakove*. Krakov, 1974.
Akatov, V. S. *O Pozitivnykh Osnovakh Noveshego Spiritualisma*. Moscow, 1909.
Alferev, Ya. F., ed. *Pisma Tsarskoi Semyi iz Zatocheniya*. Jordanville, N.Y., 1974.
Alliluyeva, A. S. *Vospominaniya*. Moscow, 1946.
Almazov, Boris. *Rasputin i Rossiya*. Prague, 1922.
Ananich, B. V. *Rossiya i Mezhdunarodnii Kapital 1897–1914*. Leningrad, 1969.
Andreyev, A. A. *O Vladimirye Ilyiche Lenine*. Moscow, 1970.
Andreyev, Leonid. *Povesti i Rasskasy*. Vol. II. Moscow, 1971.
Andrikanis, Yevgeni Nikolayevich. *Khozyain "Chertova Gnezda."* Moscow, 1975.
Anfimov, A. M. *Krupnoye Pomeshchichye Khozyaistvo Evropeiskoi Rossii*. Moscow, 1969.
———. *Rossiikaya Derevya v gody Pervoi Mirovoi Voiny*. Moscow, 1962.
Anichkova, S. (Baronessa Taube). *Zagadka Lenina, iz Vospominanii Redakortora*. Prague, n.d.
Anin, D. *Revolyutsiya 1917 goda Glazami Yeyo Rukovoditelei*. Rome, 1971.
Antonova, L. V. *Kogda i Kak Postroyen Ermitazh*. Leningrad, 1965.
Aristov, V. *Prochitano Ilyichem*. Kazan, 1970.
Armand, Inessa Fyodorovna. *Stati, Rechi, Pisma*. Moscow, 1975.
Aronson, Grigory. *Rossiya v Epokhu Revolyutsii*. New York, 1966.
Artybashev, M. *Sanin*. Nice, 1909.
Askoldov, S. A., et al. *Iz Glubiny. Sbornik Statei o Russkoi Revolyutsii*. Paris, 1967.
Astrakhan, Kh. M. *Bolsheviki i ich Politicheskie Protivniki v 1917 goda*. Leningrad, 1973.
Avrekh, A. Ya. *Stolypin i Tretya Duma*. Moscow, 1968.
Avtorkhanov, A. *Proiskhozhdeniye Partokratii*. 2 vols. Frankfurt/Main, 1973.

Avvakumov, S. I., et al. *Oktyabrskoye Vooruzhennoye Vosstaniye v Petrograde. Sbornik Statei*. Moscow-Leningrad, 1957.

Baborenko, A. *I. A. Bunin. Materialy dlya Biografii*. Moscow, 1967.

Badayev, A. Ye. *Bolsheviki v Gosudarstvennoi Dume*. Moscow-Leningrad, 1930.

Bakh, A. N. *Zapiski Narodovoltsa*. Leningrad, 1931.

Bakh, S. *Tsar Golod. Popularnye Ekonomicheskiye Ocherki*. Berlin, n.d.

Balmont, K. D. *Gdye Moi Dom. Ocherki 1920–1923*. Prague, 1924.

Baranovskaya, V., *Soldaty-Pavlovtsy*. Leningrad, 1968.

Bazanov, V. G., et al. *A. V. Lunacharsky. Neizdannye materialy.* (*Literaturnoye Nasledstvo*, Vol. LXXXII.) Moscow, 1970.

Beisembayev, S. B., and Aidarov, Kh. G. *Oni Vstrechalis c Leninym.* (*Vospominaniya.*) Alma Ata, 1968.

Bely, Andrei. *Mezhdu Dvukh Revolyutsii*. Leningrad, 1934.

———. *Nachalo Veka*. Moscow-Leningrad, 1933.

———. *Vospominaniya ob Aleksandre Bloke*. London, 1964.

———. *Zapiski Chudaka*. 2 vols. Moscow-Berlin, 1922.

———; Ivanov-Razumnik; and Steinberg, A. Z. *Pamyati Aleksandra Bloka*. Petersburg, 1922.

Belyayevsky, V. A. *Golgofa. Ocherki iz Moikh Vospominanii 1883–1964*. São Paulo, 1965.

Benua, Aleksandr. *Zhizn Khudozhnika*. 2 vols. New York, 1955.

Berdyayev, N. A., et al. *Vekhi.* (*Sbornik Statei o Russkoi Intelligentsii*.) Moscow, 1909.

Berezhnoi, A. F. *Tsarskaya Tsenzura i Borba Bolshevikov Za Svobodu Petchati (1895–1914)*. Leningrad, 1967.

Bezveselny, S. F., and Grinberg, D. Ye. *O Lenine. Vospominaniya Zarubezhnykh Sovremennikov*. Moscow, 1962.

Blok, A. A., and Bely, Andrei. *Perepiska*. Moscow, 1940.

Blok, Aleksandr. *Posledniye Dni Imperatorskoi Vlasti*. Petersburg, 1921.

———. *Sobraniye Sochinenii*. 8 vols. Moscow, 1960.

———. *Sochineniya*. 2 vols. Moscow, 1955.

———. *Zapisnye Knizhki*. Moscow, 1965.

Bogdanovich, P. N. *Vtorzheniye v Vostochnuyu Prussiyu v Avguste 1914 goda*. Buenos Aires, 1964.

Bok, M. P. *Vospominaniya o Moyem Otse P. A. Stolypine*. New York, 1953.

Bonch-Bruyevich, M. D. *Vsye Vlast Sovetem*. Moscow, 1964.

Bonch-Bruyevich, V. V. *I. Lenin v Petrograde i v Moskve*. Moscow, 1956.

———. *Vospominaniya o Lenine*. Moscow, 1969.

Bondarevskaya, T. P. *Peterbyrgskii Komitet RSDRP v Revolyutsii 1905–07 gg.* Leningrad, 1975.

———, et al. *Ocherki Istorii Leningradskoi Organizatsii KPSS*. Part I, 1883–Oktyabr 1917 gg. Leningrad, 1962.

Brusilov, A. A. *Moi Vospominaniya*. Moscow-Leningrad, 1929.

Bryusov, Valery, *Iz Moei Zhizni*. Moscow, 1926.

———. *Kon Bled*. Leningrad, 1964.

Bulatsky, G. V., and Plavnik, A. A. *Lunacharsky—Revolyutsioner—Publitsist (1905–1907 gg)*. Minsk, 1971.

Bulgakov, Sergei. *Avtobiograficheskiye Zametki*. Paris, 1946.

Burdzhalov, Ye. N. *Vtoraya Russkaya Revolyutsiya. Moskva, Front, Periferiya*. Moscow, 1971.

Burenin, N. Ye. *Pamyatnye gody. Vospominaniya*. Leningrad, 1967.

Burtsev, V. L. *V Borbe s Bolshevikami i Nemtsami.* Paris, 1919.

———. *Prestupleniya i Nekazaniye Bolshevikov.* Paris, 1938.

Byalik, B. *Sudba Maxima Gorkogo.* Moscow, 1968.

Bystrykh, F. P., ed. *Ocherki Istorii Kommunisticheskikh Organizatsii Urala.* Sverdlovsh, 1971.

Chermensky, E. D. *Istoriya SSSR Period Imperializma.* Moscow, 1973.

Chernov, V. M. (Viktor). *Pered Burei. Vospominaniya.* New York, 1953.

Chernov, Viktor. *Rozhdeniye Revolyutsionnoi Rossii.* Paris, 1934.

———. *Rozhdeniye Revolyutsionnoi Rossii (Fevralskaya Revolyutsiya).* Prague, 1934.

Chicherin, Boris Nikolayevich. *Vospominaniya Zemstvo i Moskovskaya Duma.* Moscow, 1934.

Chikin, S. Ya. *D. I. Ulyanov.* Moscow, 1974.

Dan, F. *K istorii poslednikh dnei Vremennogo Pravitelstva. Letopis Revolyutsii.* Kniga I. Berlin, 1923.

Danilov, Yu. N. *Velikii Knyaz Nikolai Nikolayevich.* Paris, 1930.

Denisov, Y. E., ed. *V gody Podpolya.* Moscow, 1964.

Detushev, I. F., et al. *Velikiye Nezabyvayemye Dni. Sbornik Vospominanii Ychastnikov Revolyutsii 1905–07 godov.* Moscow, 1970.

Diterikhs, M. K. *Ubiistvo Tsarskoi Semi i chelenov doma Romanovykh na Urale.* Vladivostok, 1922.

Dnevnik, B. Velikogo Knyazya Andreya Vladimirovicha. Leningrad, 1925.

Dolgorukov, Kn. Pavel Dmitr. *Velikaya Razrukha.* Madrid, 1964.

Dostoyevsky, Fyodor. *Sobraniye Sochinenii.* Vol. IX. (*Bratya Karamozovy.*) Moscow, 1958.

Drabkina, Yelizaveta. *Chernye Sukhari.* Moscow, 1963.

———. *A. I. Ulyanova-Yelizarova.* Moscow, 1970.

Dubensky, Gen. D. N. *Ostrechenye Nikolai II.* Edited by P. Ye. Shchegolev. Leningrad, 1927.

Dubinskaya, A. *Byl o Legendarnom Komissarye.* (*Aleksandr Vermishev.*) Moscow, 1963.

Dubinsky-Mukhadze, I. M. *Kamo.* Moscow, 1974.

Dyakin, V. S. *Russkaya Burzhuaziya i Tsarizm v gody Pervoi Mirovoi Voiny 1914–17.* Leningrad, 1967.

Dzeniskevich, A. R., et al. *Istoriya Rabochikh Leningrada, 1703–1965* 2 vols. Leningrad, 1972.

Eder-Yezhova, Mariye. *Shestdesyat Let v Ryadakh Leninskoi Partii.* Tallin, 1972.

Fabritsky, S. S. *Iz Proshlago. Vospominaniya Fligel-adyutanta Gosudarya Imperatora Nikolaya II.* Berlin, 1926.

Figner, Vera (N.). *V. Borbe.* Leningrad, 1966.

———. *Posle Shlisselburga.* Leningrad, 1925.

Fomin, N. D., ed. *Za Vlast Sovetov. Vospominaniya Uchastnikov Oktyabrskoi Revolyutsii v Simbirskoi Gubernii.* Saratov, 1967.

Fotiyeva, L. A. *Iz Zhizni V. I. Lenina.* Moscow, 1967.

Fraiman, A. L., chief ed. *Oktyabryskoye Vooruzhennoye Vosstaniye.* 2 vols. Leningrad, 1967.

Garibdzhanyan, G. V. *V. I. Lenin i Bolsheviki Zakavkazya.* Erevan, 1971.

Gershuni, Grigory. *Iz Nedavnego Proshlago.* Paris, 1908.

Gilyarovsky, Vladimir A. *Izbrannoye.* 3 vols. Moscow, 1960.

———. *Moskva i Moskvichi.* Moscow, 1955.

Gippius-Merezhkovskaya, Z. (Zinaida). *Dmitrii Merezhkovsky.* Paris, 1951.

————. *Sinyaya Kniga, Petersburgsky Dvevnik 1914–1918.* Belgrade, 1929.

————. *Zhivyya Litsa.* Prague, 1925.

Golikov, G. N., ed. *Vladimir Ilyich Lenin. Biograficheskaya Khronika.* Moscow, 1974.

————, et al. *Vospominaniya o Vladimir Ilyiche Lenine.* 5 vols. Moscow, 1969.

Gorky, A. M. (Maxim). *Arkhiv A. M. Gorkogo. Pisma k Ye. P. Peshkovoi 1906–1932.* Moscow, 1966.

————. *Publitsisticheskaye Statii.* Leningrad, 1931.

————. *Sobraniye Sochinenii.* Vols. IV, XII. Moscow-Leningrad, 1947.

————. *V Epokhu Revolyutsii 1905–1907 godov. Materialy, Vospominaniya, Issledovaniya.* Moscow, 1957.

————. *Zhizn Klima Samgina.* Moscow, 1955.

————; Molotov, V.; Voroshilov, K., et al. *Istoriya Grazhdanskoi Voiny v SSSR.* 5 vols. Moscow, 1936.

Gorodetsky, Sergei. *Valery Bryusov.* Moscow, 1929.

Gorodetsky, Ye., and Shuranov, Yu. P. *Sverdlov.* Moscow, 1961.

————. *Sverdlov.* Moscow, 1971.

Gorokhov, I.; Zamyatin, L.; and Zemskov, I. *G. V. Chicherin.* Moscow, 1973.

Grigorenko, V. V., ed. *V. Mayakovsky v Vospominaniyakh Sovremennikov.* Moscow, 1963.

Grinko, V. A., et al. *Borba Partii Bolshevikov Protiv Trotskizma (1903–Fevral 1917 g).* Moscow, 1968.

Gurko, V. I. *Tsar i Tsaritsa.* Paris, 1927.

Ignatyev, V. K., ed. *Partiya Bolshevikov v gody Mirovoi Imperialisticheskoi Voiny. (1914 god—Fevral 1917 goda).* Moscow, 1963.

Ilyin, A., and Ilyin, V. A. *Rozhdeniye Partii 1883–1904.* Moscow, 1962.

Imenburg, B. S., and Chernyakh, A. Ya. *Zhizn Aleksandra Ulyanova.* Moscow, 1966.

Imperator Nikolai II. *Dnevnik.* Berlin, 1922.

Ioffe, A. M. *Izdatelskaya Deyatelnost Bolshevikov v 1905–1907 gg.* Moscow, 1971.

Iroshinikov, M. P. *Predsedatel Soveta Narodnykh Komissarov Vl. Ulyanov (Lenin). Ocherki Gosudarstvennoi Deyatelnosti v 1917–1918 gg.* Leningrad, 1974.

Isaakyan, G. A. *"Pravda" (1912–Oktyabr 1917 g.) i Sotsial-Demokrat (1908–1917 gg.) o Zakavkaze.* Erevan, 1968.

Ivanov-Razumnik (R. V.). *Istoriya Russkoi Obshchestevnnoi Mysli.* 2 vols. St. Petersburg, 1908.

————. *Istoriya Russkoi Obshchestevnnoi Mysli. Devyatisotiye gody.* Vol. VII. Petrograd, 1918.

————. *Tyurmy i Ssylki.* New York, 1953.

Ivansky, A. I. *Molodye Gody V. I. Lenina. Po Vospominanyam Sovremennikov i Dokumentam.* Moscow, 1960.

————. *Zhizh Kak Fakel. Istoriya Geroicheskoi Borby I Tragicheskoi Gibeli Aleksandra Ulyanova Rasskazannaya Yeyo Sovremennikami.* Moscow, 1966.

Kaganova, R. Yu. *Lenin vo Frantsii.* Moscow, 1972.

Kadesnikov, N. S. *Kratki Ocherk Russkoi Istorii XX Veka.* New York, 1967.

Kalinin, A. F., and Mandel, S. Z. *Lenin i Petersburgsky Universitet.* Leningrad, 1969.

Kalinin, M. I. *Za eti gody.* Kniga III. Moscow-Leningrad, 1929.

Kalinychev, F. I., comp. *Gosudarstvennaya Duma v Rossii v Dokumentakh i Materialakh.* Moscow, 1957.

Kanivets, Vladimir, *Ulyanovy. Istorichesky Roman*. Moscow, 1972.

Katanyan, V. A. *Mayakovsky. Literaturnaya Khronika*. Moscow, 1961.

Khigerovich, Rafail I. *Mladshii Brat. Dokumentalnaya Povest o Dmitrii Ilyiche Ulyanove*. Moscow, 1969.

Khodasevich, Vladislav F. *Nekropol*. Brussels, 1939.

Kleinmikhel, Grafinya M. *Iz Pontonuvshego Mira*. Berlin, n.d.

Knyaz Oleg. Petrograd, 1915.

Knyaz, Yu. *Imperator Nikolai II*. Nice, 1910.

Knyazev, S. P., ed. *Ocherkii Istorii Leningradskoi Organizatsii KPSS*. Leningrad, 1962.

Kobylin, Viktor S. *Imperator Nikolai II i General-adyutant M. V. Alexeyev*. New York, 1970.

Kokovtsov, Graf Vladimir N. *Iz Moego Proshlego. Vospominaniya 1903–1919*. 2 vols. Paris, 1933.

Kollontai, Aleksandra M. *Izbrannye Stati i Rechi*. Moscow, 1972.

Kondakov, A. I. *Direktor Narodnykh Uchilishch I. N. Ulyanov*. Moscow-Leningrad, 1948.

Kondzerovsky, Pyotr K. *V. Stavke Verkovnogo 1914–1917*. Paris, 1967.

Kovnator, R. *Olga Ulyanova*. Moscow, 1971.

KPSS v Rezolyutsiyakh is Resheniyakh Seyezdov, Konferentsi i Plenumov TsK. Moscow, 1970–73.

Krastyn, Ya. P. *Istoriya Latyshkikh Strelkov*. Riga, 1971.

Kropotkin, Pyotr A. *Zapiski Revolyutsionera*. Moscow-Leningrad, 1933.

Krulova, Agrippina Ilyinichna. *Nezabyvayemoye*. Leningrad, 1963.

Krupskaya, N. K. *Oktyabrskiye Dni*. Moscow, 1967.

———. *Vospominaniya o Lenine*. Moscow, 1957.

Kudryavtsev, Anatoly S.; Muravyena, L. L.; and Sivolap-Kaftanova, I. I. *Lenin v Berne i Tsyurikhe*. Moscow, 1972.

Kukin, D. M., ed. *Partiya Bolshevikov v Fevralskoi Revolyutsii 1917 goda*. Moscow, 1917.

Kutsentov, Dmitri G. *Deyateli Petersburgshogo "Soyuza Borby Za Osvobozhdeniye Rabochego Klassa."* Moscow, 1962.

Laverychev, V. Ya. *Po tu Storonu Barrikad. Iz Istorii Borby Moskovskoi Burzhuzii c Revolyutsii*. Moscow, 1967.

———. *Tsarizm i Rabochi Vopros v Rossii 1861–1917*. Moscow, 1975.

Lavrin, V. A. *Bolshevistskaya Partiya v Nachale Pervoi Mirovoi Imperialisticheskoi Voiny*. Moscow, 1972.

Lavrov, P. A., and Yakovlev, B. V. *Lenin i "Izvestiya."* Moscow, 1975.

Lebidova, S. M., and Salita, E. G. *Yelena Dmitriyevna Stasova (Biograficheskii Ocherk)*. Leningrad, 1969.

Lenin, N. *K Derevenskoi Bednot*. Geneva, 1903.

Lenin, N. (V. Ulyanov). *Izbranniye Stati i Rechi*. Moscow, 1924.

Lenin, V. I. *Pisma V. I. Lenina k Rodnykh*. 3 vols. Moscow, 1969.

———. *Polnoye Sobraniye Sochinenii*. 5th ed. Moscow, 1967–72.

———, and Gorky, A. M. *Pisma, Vospominaniya, Dokumenty*. Moscow, 1969.

———, and Lunacharsky, A. V. *Perepiska, Doklody, Dokumenty. Literaturnoye Nasledstvo*, Vol. LXXX. Moscow, 1971.

Lepeshinskaya, Olga B. *Vstrechi c Ilyichem*. Moscow, 1968.

Lepeshinsky, P. (Panteliemon N.). *Kak Voznikla Leninskaya Partiya*. Moscow, 1933.

———. *Na Povorote*. Petersburg, 1922.

———. *Vladimir Ilyich v Turmei i izganii*. Moscow, 1934.

Loginov, V. T. *Lenin i Pravda 1912–1914 godov*. Moscow, 1962.

Lozgachev-Yelizarov, Georgi Yakovlevich. *Nezabyvayemoye*. 4th ed. Kiev, 1963.

———. *Nezabyvayemoye*. 5th ed. Saratov, 1966.

Lukomsky, Aleksandr S. *Vospominaniya*. Berlin, 1922.

Lunacharsky, Anatoly V. *Vospominaniya i Vpechatleniya*. Moscow, 1968.

Lundberg, E. *Zapiski Pisatelya*. Berlin, 1922.

Lyubimov, I. N. *Revolyutsiya 1917 goda. Khronika Sobytii*. Vol VI. Moscow-Leningrad, 1930.

Maklakov, Vasily A. *Iz Vospominanii*. New York, 1954.

———. *Pervaya Gosudarstvennaya Duma. Vospominaniya Sovremennika*. Paris, 1930.

———. *Vtoraya Gosudarstvennaya Duma*. Paris, n.d.

Malakhov, A. *Velikaya Russkaya Revolyutsiya i Rol v Nei Kommunistov*. London, 1921.

Malkov, P. (Pavel D.). *Zapiski Komendanta Moskovskogo Kremlya*. Moscow, 1962.

Marks (Marx), Karl. *Kapital*. St. Petersburg, 1872.

Mayakovskaya, L. V., and Koloskova, A. I., eds. *Vladimir Mayakovsky v Vospominaniyakh Rodnykh i Druzei*. Moscow, 1968.

Mayakovsky, Vladimir V. *Sobraniye Sochinenii*. 8 vols. Moscow, 1968.

Meier, I. L. *Kak Pogibla Tsarskaya Semya*. Munich, 1957.

Melgunov, S. (Sergei P.). *Kak Bolsheviki Zakhvatili Vlast*. Paris, 1953.

———. *Krasny Terror v Rossii 1918–1923*. Berlin, 1924.

———. *Martovskiye Dni 1917 goda*. Paris, 1961.

———. *Nikolai II. Materialy dlya Kharakteristiki Lichnost i Tsarstvovaniya*. Moscow, 1917.

———. *Rossiiskaya Kontr-Revolyutsiya. Metody i Vyvody Gen. Golovina*. Paris, 1938.

———. *Sudba Imperatora Nikolaya II Posle Ostrecheniya*. Paris, 1951.

———. *Vospominaniya i Dneviki. Vypusk I*. Paris, 1964.

Milyukov, Pavel N. *Vospominaniya (1859–1917)*. 2 vols. New York, 1955.

Mochulsky, K. *Andrei Bely*, Paris, 1955.

———. *Valery Bryusov*. Paris, 1962.

———. *Vladimir Solovyev*. Paris, 1951.

More, N. M., and Savitsky, R. M. *Vospominaniya o Vladimire Ilyiche Lenine*. 2 vols. Moscow, 1956.

Morozov, Nikolai A. *Povesti Moyei Zhizni*. 4 vols. Moscow-Petrograd, 1918.

Moskalev, Mikhail A. *V. I. Lenin v Sibiri*. Moscow, 1957.

Mstislavsky, Sergei D. *Pyat Dnei. (Nachalo i Konets Fevralskoi Revolyutsii)*. Moscow, 1922.

Naumov, A. I. *Larisa Reisner*. Moscow, 1969.

Nazhivin, Ivan F. *Zapiski o Revolyutsii*. Vienna, 1921.

Nevsky, Vladimir I., ed. *Nikolai II i Velikiye Knyazya, Rodstvenniye Pisma k poslednemy Tsaryu*. Leningrad-Moscow, 1925.

———. *Rabocheye Dvizheniye v lanvarskii Dni 1905 goda*. Moscow, 1930.

Nikiforov, Pyotr M. *V gody Bolshevitskogo Podpolya*. Moscow, 1952.

Nikitin, V. *Rokovye Gody*. Paris, 1937.

Nogin, V. *Na Polyuse Kholoda*. Moscow-Petrograd, 1923.

Novikov, V. I. *V. I. Lenin i Pskovskiye Iskovtsy*. Leningrad, 1968.

Novorussky, M. (Mikhail) V. *Zapiski Shlisselburzhtsa 1887–1905*. Petersburg, 1920.

Olkhovsky, E. P. *Leninskaya "Iskra" v Peterburge.* Leningrad, 1975.

Olminsky, M. *Iz Epokhi Zvezdy i Pravdy 1911–1914 gg.* Moscow-Leningrad, 1929.

Oniani, V. *Bolshevistskaya Partiya i Intelligentsiya v Pervoi Russkoi Revolyutsii.* Tbilisi, 1970.

Onufriyev, Ye. P. *Za Nevskoi Zastavoi.* Moscow, 1968.

Pamyati Yego Imp. Vysochestva. V. Knyazh K. K. (K. R.). New York, 1956.

Pavlov, Nikolai A. *Yevo Velichestvo Gusudar Nikolai II.* Paris, 1927.

Perepiska V. I. Lenina i Redaktsii Gazety Iskra s Sotsial-Demokraticheskimi Organizatsiyami v Rossii, 1900–1903 gg. 3 vols. Moscow, 1969.

Perepiska V. I. Lenina i Rukhovodymykhim Uchrezhdenii RSDRP c Partiinymi Organizatsiyami, 1903–1905 gg. 3 vols. Moscow, 1973.

Perepiska Vilgelma II s Nikolayem II, 1894–1914 gg. Moscow-Petrograd, n.d.

1 Marta 1887 Delo P. Shevyreva, A. *Ulyanova i drugikh* (Stenographic report of Special Session of Senate on the affair of March 1.) Moscow-Leningrad, 1927.

Petersburzhets (Takhtarev, Konstantin M.). *Ocherk Petersburgskogo Rabochogo Dvizheniya 90-kh Godov.* London, 1902.

Petrogradsky Voyenno-Revolyutsionny Komitet. Dokumenty i Materialy. 3 vols. Moscow, 1966.

Petrov, I. M. (Toivo Vyakhya). *Krasnye Finny. Vospominaniya.* Petrozavodsk, 1970.

Petrovsky, Grigory I. *Nash Mudry Vozhd.* Moscow, 1970.

Pilyavsky, V. I. *Zimni Dvorets.* Leningrad, 1960.

Pisma Imperatritsy Aleksandry Fyodorovny k Imperatory Nikolayu II. 2 vols. Berlin, 1922.

Pisma P. B. Akselroda i Yu. D. Martova. Berlin, 1924.

Pitkin, L. M., ed. *Lenin v Peterburg.* Leningrad, 1957.

Plekhanov, Georgi V. *Gody na Rodine. Polnoye Sobraniye Statei i Rechi 1917–1918* 2 vols. Paris, 1921.

———. *Literaturnoye Naslediye.* Vol. I. Moscow, 1934.

Podlyashuk, Pavel. *Tovarishch Inessa. Dokumentalnaya Povest.* 2nd ed. Moscow, 1965.

———. *Tovarishch Inessa. Dokumentalnaya Povest.* 3rd ed., Revised. Moscow, 1973.

Pogossky, V. *V Mestnoye Samoupravleniye na Demokraticheskikh nachalakh.* Moscow, 1917.

Pokrovsky, M. N., ed. *Perepiska Nikolaya i Alexandry Romanovykh, 1914–1915.* Vols. III, IV, V. Moscow-Leningrad, 1925–27.

Polevoi, Yu. Z. *Zarozhdeniye Marksizma v Rossii. 1883–1894.* Moscow, 1959.

Politicheskii Dnevnik 1964–1970. Amsterdam, 1972.

Popov, I. V. *Vospominaniya.* Moscow, 1971.

Pospelov, Pyotr N. (chief ed.). *Istoriya Kommunisticheskoi Partii Sovetskogo Soyuza.* 6 vols. Moscow, 1964–72.

———, chief ed. *Vladimir Ilyich Lenin. Biografiya.* Moscow, 1963.

Potresov, A. N., and Nikolaevsky, B. I. *Sotsial-Demokraticheskoye Dvizheniye v Rossii. Materialy.* Moscow-Leningrad, 1928.

Pronin, Vasily M. *Posledniye Dni Tsarskoi Stavki.* Belgrade, 1929.

Protokoly Tsentralnoyo Komiteta RSDRP (b), Avgust 1917–Fevral 1918. Moscow, 1958.

Prugavin, Aleksandr S. *V. Kazematakh.* St. Petersburg, 1909.

Purishkevich, Vladimir Mitrofanovich. *Dnevnik.* Riga, 1924.

————. *Ubiistvo Rasputina.* Buenos Aires, 1944.
Pyatnitsky, Osip. *Izbrannye Vospominaniya i Stati.* Moscow, 1969.
Rakitin, Anton. *V. A. Antonov Ovsenko.* Leningrad, 1975.
Raskolnikov, Fyodor F. *Kronshtadt i Piter v 1917 gody.* Moscow-Leningrad, 1925.
Rerberg, F. P. *Istoricheskiye Tainy, Velikikh Pobed i Neobyasnimykh Porazhenii.* Madrid, 1967.
"Revolyutsiya 1917 Goda." *Khronika Sobytii,* Vol. VI.
Revolyutsionnoye Dvizheniye v Rossi v Avguste 1917 g. Razgrom Kornilovskogo Myatezha. Dokumenty i Materialy. Moscow, 1959.
Ropshin, V. (Boris Savinkov). *Kon Bledny.* Nice, 1913.
Rudnev, V. (Vladimir M.). *Pravda o Tsarskoi Semye i Temnykh Silakh.* Berlin, 1920.
Ryabtsev, I. G., chief ed. *Bolsheviki v Borbe Protiv Melkoburzhuaznykh Partii v Rossii.* Moscow, 1969.
Ryss, Pyotr. *Russkii Opyt. Istoriko-Psikhologicheskii Ocherk Russkoi Revolyutsii.* Paris, 1921.
Sazonov, Ivan S., and Kylyshev, Yu. S., eds. *Petrograd v Dni Velikogo Oktyabrya.* Leningrad, 1967.
Semanov, S. N. *Krovavoye Voskresenye.* Leningrad, 1965.
Semashko, Nikolai A. *Prozhitoye i Perezhitoye.* Moscow, 1960.
Semennikov, V. P., ed. *Za Kulisami Tsarisma. Arkhiv Tibetskogo Vracha Badmayeva.* Leningrad, 1925.
Semin, N. *Zdes uchilsya V. I. Lenin.* Moscow, 1969.
Shaginyan, Mariyetta. *Chetyre Uroka u Lenina.* Moscow, 1970.
Shaumyan, L. *Kamo.* Moscow, 1959.
Shaurov, V. *1905 God. Vospominaniya Uchastnika Revolyutsii 1905–1907 godov.* Moscow, 1965.
Shchegoloyev, P. Ye., ed. *Otrecheniye Nikolai II. Vospominaniya Ochevidtsev, Dokumentov.* Leningrad, 1927.
————, ed. *Padeniye Tsarskogo Rezhima, Stenograficheskye Otchety Doprosev i Pokazanii, Dannikh v 1917 g. V Chrezvychainoi Sledstvennoi Komissii Vremennogo. Pravitelstva.* 7 vols. Leningrad-Moscow, 1924–27.
Shelavin, K. *1905 God v Peterburge.* Leningrad-Moscow, 1925.
Shibayeva, N. *Partiya Bolshevikov v Period Reaktsii (1907–1910 gg.).* Moscow, 1965.
Shidlovsky, S. I. *Vospominany.* 2 vols. Berlin, 1923.
Shlikhter, A. *Ilyich, Kakim Ya Yego Znal.* Moscow, 1970.
Shlyapnikov, A. *Semnadtsty god.* 5 vols. Moscow-Petrograd, 1923.
Shneider, Ilya. *Zapiski Starogo Moskvicha.* Moscow, 1970.
Shulgin, V. V. *Dni.* Belgrade, 1925.
Shulgin, Vitaly. *O Sostoyanii Zhenshchein v Rossii do Petra Velikogo.* Kiev, 1850.
Sidelnikov, S. M. *Agrarnaya Reforma Stolypina.* Moscow, 1973.
Simanovich, Aron. *Rasputin i Yevrei.* Riga, n.d.
Skitalets. *Les Razgoralsya.* Stuttgart, 1906.
Skrypnik, Mariya. *Vospominaniya ob Ilyiche.* Moscow, 1965.
Smolnikov, I. G. *A. Lopatin.* Leningrad, 1968.
Sokolov, N. *Ubiistvo Tsarskoi Semyi.* Berlin, 1925.
Solomon, G. A. *Lenin i Yego Semya.* Paris, 1931.
————. *Sredi Krasnikh Vozhdei.* 2 vols. Paris, 1930.
Solzhenitsyn, A. *Lenin v Tsyurikhe.* Paris, 1975.
Sorokin, A. M. *V Preddverii Oktyabrya.* Moscow, 1973.

Spasovsky, M. M. *V. V. Rozanov v Posledniye gody Svoei Zhizni.* New York, 1968.

Spiridovich, General A. I. *Velikaya Voina i Fevralskaya Revolyutsiya 1914–1917 gg.* 3 vols. New York, 1960.

Staponenko, L. S. *Rabochi Klass Rossii v 1917 godu.* Moscow, 1970.

Startsev, A. *Russkiye Bloknoty Dzhona Rida.* Moscow, 1968.

Startsev, V. I. *Ocherki po istorii Petrogradskoi Krasnoi gvardi i Rabochei Militsii (Mart 1917–Aprel 1918g).* Leningrad, 1965.

Stepanyak-Kravchinsky, S. M. *V Londonskoi Emigratsii.* Moscow, 1968.

Stishov, M. I., ed., et al. *Iz Istorii Velikoi Oktyabrskoi Sotsialisticheskoi Revolyutsii. Sbornik Statei.* Moscow, 1957.

Struve, Pyotr. *Rasmyshleniya o Russkoi Revolyutsii.* Sofia, 1931.

Sukharev, G. I. *Za Vlast Sovetov. Vospominaniya Uchastnikov Revolyutsionnikh Sobytii 1917 goda v Saratovskoi Gubernii.* Saratov, 1957.

Sukhanov, Nik. *Zapiski o Revolyutsii.* 7 vols. Berlin, 1922.

Sukhomlinov, Vladimir Aleksandrovich. *Vospominaniya. S Predsloviyem V. Nevskoyo.* Moscow-Leningrad, 1926.

Sultanova, Ye. A., ed. *Ob Ilyiche: Vospominaniya Pitersev.* Leningrad, 1970.

Surguchev, Ilya. *Detstvo Imperatora Nikolaya.* Paris, 1953.

Sutyrin, Vladimir. *Aleksandr Ulyanov (1866–1887).* Moscow, 1971.

———. *Aleksandr Ulyanov (1866–1887).* 2nd ed. Moscow, 1975.

Suvorov, K. I., chief ed. *Iz Istorii Stanovleniya i Razvitya Partii Bolshevikov v Dooktyabrskii Period.* Moscow, 1968.

Sverdlov, Ya. M. *Izbranniye Proizvedeniya.* 3 vols. Moscow, 1957.

———. *Izbranniye Proizvedeniya. Stati, Rechi, Pisma.* Moscow, 1976.

Taganov, A. *Bessmenny Chasovoi. (Tovarishch Kamo).* Moscow, 1960.

Tagantsev, N. S. *Perezhitoye.* Moscow, 1919.

Taneyeva, A. (Vyrubova). *Stranitsy iz moei zhizni.* Berlin, 1923.

Tarsaidze, Aleksandr. *Chetyre Mifa.* New York, 1969.

Tatarukhin, A., ed. *Lenin v Moskve.* Moscow, 1957.

Tokaryev, Yu. S. *Petrogradskii Sovet Rabochikh I Soldatskikh Deputatov v Marte-Aprile 1917 g.* Leningrad, 1976.

Tretii Syezd RSDRP. Moscow: 1955.

Tsarskii Listok. Doklady Ministra Vnutrennikh del Nikolaya II za 1897 god. Paris, 1909.

Tsereteli, I. G. *Vospominaniya o Fevralskoi Revolyutsii.* 2 vols. Paris, 1963.

Ugarov, I., and Velichhina V. *Na Barrikadakh Moskvu.* Moscow, 1975.

Ulyanov, V. *Lyubyashonii Tebya. Pisma V. I. Lenina Materi.* Moscow, 1967.

Ulyanova-Yelizarova, A. I. *A. I. Ulyanov i Delo 1 Marta 1887. Sbornik.* Moscow, 1927.

Urazov, Arkadi Ivanovich, ed. *My Videli i Slyshali Lenina.* Simferopol, 1969.

Ushakov, A. V. *Revolyutsionnoyi Dvizheniye Demokratichskoi Intelligentsii v Rossii 1895–1904.* Moscow, 1976.

Valentinov, V. (Nikolai Vladislavich Volsky). *Maloznakomy Lenin.* Paris, 1972.

———. *Vstrechi s Leninym.* New York, 1953.

Varustin, L., and Frolov, M. *Poezd No. 4001.* Leningrad, 1968.

Vasilyev, I. *O Yevreiskikh Predkakh Lenina.* Buenos Aires, 1964.

Velikaya Oktyabrskaya Sotsialisticheskaya Revolyutsiya, Khronika Sobytii. 4 vols. Moscow, 1957.

Veresov, A. *Krepost "Oreshek."* Leningrad, 1967.

Veretennikov, N. *Volodya Ulyanov, Vospominaniya s Detskikh i Yunosheskikh Godov V. I. Lenin v Kokushkino.* Moscow, 1966.

Verkhos, V. *Krasnaya Gvardiya v Oktyabroi Revolyutsii.* Moscow, 1975.

Vinberg, F. *Krestny Put.* Munich, 1922.

Vinogradov, V. V., ed. *Literaturnoye Nasledstvo.* Vol. LXVIII (Chekhov). Moscow, 1960.

Vinogradskaya, P. S. *Pamyatnye Vstrechi.* Moscow, 1972.

Vitte (Witte), Graf S. Yu. *Vospominaniya. Tsartvovaniye Nikolai II.* 2 vols. Berlin, 1922.

Voitinaky, Vl. *Gody Pobed i Porazhenii.* 1905-ii god. Berlin, 1923.

Voitsekhovsky, S. L. *Trest. Vospominaniya i Dokumenty.* London, Ontario, 1974.

Volin, B. M. *Iz Vospominanii.* Moscow, 1972.

———. *V. I. Lenin v Povolzhye.* Moscow, 1955.

Volin, Ya. R., ed. *Istoriografiya Petersburgshogo "Soyuza Borby Za Osvobozhdeinye Rabochyego Klassa."* Perm, 1974.

Volk, S. S. *Narodnaya Volya, 1879–1882.* Moscow, 1966.

Volkonskaya, Kn. S. A. *Gore Pobezhdennym. Vae Victis. Vospominaniya.* Paris, n.d.

Volper, I. N. *Psevdonimy V. I. Lenina.* Leningrad, 1968.

Vorobtsova, Yu. I. *Internatsionalnaya Deyatelnost Bolshevistskoi Partii v Period Podgotovki Oktyabrya (Fevral–Oktyabr 1917).* Leningrad, 1975.

Voyeikov, V. N. *S Tsarem i Bez Tsarya.* Helsingfors, 1936.

Voznesenky, A. *Sovetskaya Yustitsiya.* Moscow, 1937.

Vyazhemskikh, Kn. V. L. Kn. El. Dm. *Lotarevskaya Kniga Sudbe.* N.p., n.d.

Yakushina, A. P. *Zagraninchnye Organizatsii RSDRP (1905–1917 gg.).* Moscow, 1967.

Yarotsky, Boris. *Ulyanov Mladshii.* Simferopol, 1970.

Yelizarov, P. P. *Mark Yelizarov i Semya Ulyanovykh.* Moscow, 1967.

Yemelyanov, N. P. G. Z. *Yeliseyev Publitsist.* Leningrad, 1971

Yenikeyev, Z. A. *Deyatelnost Kazanskikh Bolshevikov po Revolyutsionnomy Vospitaniyu Studencheskoi Molodezhi (1905–Fevral 1917 gg.).* Kazan, 1973.

Yerman, L. K. *Intelligentsiya v Pervoi Russkoi Revolyutsii.* Moscow, 1966.

Yerokhin, A. S. *Shushensky Arsenal.* Moscow, 1971

Yerykalov, Ye. F., ed. *Geroi Oktyaburya.* 2 vols. Leningrad, 1967.

———. *Oktyabrskoye Vooruzhennoye Vosstaniye v Petrograde.* Leningrad, 1966.

Yubilei Nikolaya Poslednago, 1894–1904 gg. (*Partiya Sotsialistov-Revolyutsionerov*) Pamphlet. Paris(?), 1904(?).

Yusupov, Kn. F. F. *Konets Rasputina. Vospominaniya.* Paris, 1927.

Zarnitsky, S. B., and Trofimova, L. I. *Sovetskoi Strany Diplomat.* (*Leonid Borisovich Krasin*). Moscow, 1968.

Zavarzin, P. P. *Zhandarmy i Revolyutsionery. Vospominaniya.* Paris, 1930.

Zazayevsky, Ye., and Lyubarsky, A. *Lenin Emigratsiyna i Rossiya.* Moscow, 1975.

Zelinsky, Korneli. *Na Rubezhe Dvukh Epokh.* Moscow, 1959.

Zenzinov, Vladimir. *Iz Zhizni Revolyutsionera.* Paris, 1919.

———. *Perezhitoye.* New York, 1953.

Zhikov, G. S. *Peterburskye Marksisty i Gruppa "Osvobozhdeniye Truda."* Leningrad, 1975.

Zhilyar, P. *Imperator Nikolai II i Yego Semya.* Vienna, 1921.

Zubov, Gr. V. P. *Stradnye Gody Rossii (Vospominaniya o Revolyutsii 1917–1925).* Munich, 1968.

Akhalkin, Yu. A. "Meeting on a Train; an Episode in Lenin's Life." *Prometei,* 1967, No. 4.

An—sky, S. "After the Coup of Oct. 25, 1917." *Arkhiv Russkoi Revolyutsii* (Berlin), 1923, Vol. VIII.

Armand, I. A. "Recollections about Vladimir Ilyich Lenin." *Voprosy Istorii KPSS,* 1966, No. 1.

Armand, Inna Alexandrovna. "Letters of Inessa Armand." *Novy Mir,* 1970, No. 6.

Astrakhan, Kh. M. "The Women's Battalion that Defended the Winter Palace." *Istoriya SSSR,* 1965, No. 5.

Auerbakh, V. A. "Revolutionary Society, Based on Personal Recollections." *Arkhiv Russkoi Revolyutsii* (Berlin), 1924, Vol. XIV.

Avdeyev, N. "Around Gatchina." *Krasny Arkhiv* 1925, Vol. II (9).

Bazylev, L. "The Mystery of Sept. 1, 1911." *Voprosy Istorii,* No. 7, 1975.

Blok, Aleksandr. "The Last Days of the Old Regime." *Arkhiv Russkoi Revolyutsii* (Berlin), 1922, Vol. IV.

Bobrinsky, A. A. "Recollections." *Krasny Arkhiv,* 1928, No. 26.

Bonch-Bruyevich, V. D. "Lenin's Views About Fictional Literature." *Tritsat Dnei,* 1934, No. 1.

Bondarevskaya, T. P., and Kuznetsova, D. S. "Eino Abramovich Rahja." *Voprosy Istorii KPSS,* No. 6, 1975.

Budberg, Baron Aleksei. "Diary of 1917–1918." *Arkhiv Russkoi Revolyutsii* (Berlin), 1923, Vol. XII.

Bykov, P. M. "The Last Days of the Last Czar." *Arkhiv Russkoi Revolyutsii* (Berlin), 1926, Vol. XVII.

Conversation between A. F. Kerensky and N. N. Dukhonin during the night from October 23 to 24, 1917. *Arkhiv Russkoi Revolyutsii* (Berlin), 1922, No. 7.

Correspondence between N. A. Romanov and P. A. Stolypin. *Krasny Arkhiv,* 1924, Vol. V.

Correspondendence between Nicholas Romanov and Alexandra Fyodorovna, Dec. 4, 1916 to Mar. 7, 1917. *Krasny Arkhiv,* 1923, Vol. IV.

Correspondence of N. Lenin and N. K. Krupskaya with M. Litvinov. *Proletarskaya Revolyutsiya,* 1925, No. 2.

Correspondence of N. Lenin and N. K. Krupskaya with S. I. Gusev. *Proletarskaya Revolyutsiya,* 1925, No. 2.

Derenkovsky, G. M. "The Armed Uprising of December 1905 in Moscow." *Voprosy Istorii,* 1975, No. 12.

Flaxerman, Yu. "Pages from the Past." *Novy Mir,* 1968, No. 11.

Fofanova, M. V. "Lenin in the Pre-October Days." *Istorichesky Arkhiv,* 1956, No. 4; 1958, No. 2.

Ganetsky, Ya. S. "With Lenin." *Voprosy Istorii KPSS,* 1970, No. 3.

Gapon, Georgi. "Letters of January and February 1906." *Krasny Arkhiv,* 1925, Vol. II (9).

Gelis, I. "General Ivanov's Drive Against Petrograd." *Krasny Arkhiv,* 1926, Vol. VI (17).

———. "The Romanovs and the Allies in the First Days of the Revolution." *Krasny Arkhiv,* 1926, Vol. III (16).

Golubstov, V. "About a Scientific Edition of the Literary Works of N. K. Krupskaya." *Novy Mir,* 1965, No. 10.

Gorky, M. "On Lenin." *Russky Sovremennik*, 1924, No. 1

Gorodetsky, Sergei. "Valery Bryusov." *Krasnya Niva*, 1925, No. 41.

Govorukhin, O. M. "Recollections." *Oktyabr*, 1927, Nos. 3 and 4.

———. "The Attempt Against the Life of Alexander III." *Golos Minyuvshego*, 1926, No. 2.

Gurevich, L. "The People's Movement of Jan. 9, 1905, in St. Petersburg." *Byloye*, 1906, No. 1.

Iliodor, Byusher. "Holy Devil." *Golos Minyuvshego*, 1917, No. 3.

Ivanov, V. I. "The Last Day and First Day." *Prometei*, 1967, No. 4.

Ivansky, Anatoly. "Three Days in April." *Novy Mir*, 1977, No. 4.

Izgoyev, A. "Five Years in Soviet Russia." *Arkhiv Russkoi Revolyutsii* (Berlin), 1923, Vol. X.

Kiselev, A. "The Visit of Bolshevik Delegates to Lenin in Austria in July 1914 and the Organization of Revolutionary Actions During the War." *Byloye*, n.s., 1933, No. 46.

Knersha, Boris. "Around Gatchina." *Krasny Arkhiv*, 1924, No. 9.

Kokovtsov, V. N. "Reports to Nicholas II on Jan. 5, 11, 16, and 19, 1905." *Krasny Arkhiv*, 1925, Vols. IV–V (11–12).

Koronen, M. M. "V. I. Lenin and the Finnish Revolutionaries." *Voprosy Istorii*, 1967, No. 8.

Korovin, V. V. "The Boris Savinkov Case." *Istoriya SSSR*, 1967, No. 6.

Krulova, S. "Leninist Features." *Znamya*, May, 1966.

Krupskaya, N. K. Correspondence, 1912. *Istorichesky Arkhiv*, 1959, No. 1.

———. Correspondence with A. S. Shlyapnikov. *Voprosy Istorii KPSS*, 1965, No. 9.

———. "Pages from Party History." *Prometei*, 1967, No. 4.

Kuropatkin, A. N. Diary. *Krasny Arkhiv*, 1924, Vol. VII; 1925, Vol. I (8); 1922, Vol. II.

Letters from Grand Duke Alexander Mikhailovich to Nicholas II from Dec. 24, 1916 to Feb. 4, 1917. *Arkhiv Russkoi Revolyutsii* (Berlin), 1922, No. 5.

Letter from Leo Tolstoy to Nicholas II of Jan. 16, 1902. *Byloye*, July 1917, No. 1 (23).

Liberovsky, A. V. Diary. *Istorichesky Arkhiv*, 1960, No. 6.

Letter from Leo Tolstoy to Nicholas II of Jan. 16, 1902. *Byloye*, July 1917, Government in the Eyes of A. A. Blok." *Voprosy Istorii*, 1977, No. 2.

Lukashevich, Josef. "Recollections About the Affair of March 1, 1887." *Byloye*, 1917, Nos. 1–2.

Lyvbimov, D. N. "Gapon and January 9." *Voprosy Istorii*, 1965, Nos. 8 and 9.

Maisky, B. Yu. "The Stolypinshchina and the End of Stolypin." *Voprosy Istorii*, 1966, Nos. 1 and 2.

Mirolyubov, N. "Report of the Kazan Judicial Chamber." *Gryaduschchaya Rossiya*, February 1920.

"The Murder of Rasputin; Official Inquiry." *Byloye*, July 1917, No. 1 (23).

Nabokov, Vlad. "The Provisional Government." *Arkhiv Russkoi Revolyutsii* (Berlin), 1921, No. 1.

Naglovsky, A. D. "Lenin." *Novy Zhurnal*, 1967, No. 88.

Nemirovich-Danchenko, Vlad. V. "Correspondence." *Niva*, May 11–June 8, 1896, Nos. 19–23.

Nevsky, V. "From the History of the Social-Democratic Movement in St. Petersburg in 1905." *Byloye*, May 1907.

Nevsky, V. I. "January Days in St. Petersburg." *Krasnaya Letopis*, 1922, No. 1.

Nicholas Romanov's diary, Dec. 16, 1916–June 30, 1918. *Krasny Arkhiv*, 1927, Vol. I (20), Vol. II (21), Vol. III (22); 1928, Vol. II (27).

Niva. St. Petersburg–Petrograd, 1896–1917.

Novorussky, Mikhail. "Notes of a Shlisselburg Inmate." *Byloye*, 1906, No. 4.

Oldenburg, S. F. "Emperor Nicholas II." *Russkaya Letopis* (Paris), 1925, Vol. VII.

Orekhekova, Ye. D. "The Make-up of the Petrograd Military Revolutionary Committee." *Istoriya SSSR*, 1971, No. 2.

Ospipova, T. V. "The All-Russian Council of Landowners 1917." *Istoriya SSSR*, 1976, No. 3.

Pankratova, M. Ya. "New Lenin Documents." *Voprosy Istorii KPSS*, April 1975, No. 4.

Pokrovsky, M. "The Beginning of the Proletarian Revolution in Russia." *Krasny Arkhiv*, 1925, Vols. IV–V (11–12).

———. "The Political Situation in Russia on the Eve of the February Revolution as Reported by the Police." *Krasny Arkhiv*, 1926. Vol. VI (17).

———. "The Romanov Family Correspondence." *Krasny Arkhiv*, 1923, Vol. I.

Polovtsev, A. A. Diary. *Krasny Arkhiv*, Vols. III–IV.

Pravitelstvenny Vestnik. St. Petersburg, February–May 1887.

Protocols of the St. Petersburg Committee of the Russian Social Democratic Workers Party. *Proletarskaya Revolyutsiya*, 1925, No. 1 (36).

Protocols of the St. Petersburg Party Committee, 1917. *Voprosy Istorii*, 1962, Nos. 3, 5.

Protopopov, A. D. Dairy. *Krasny Arkhiv*, 1925, Vol. III (10).

———. "Testimony in the Extraordinary Investigation Commission of the Provisional Government." *Krasny Arkhiv*, 1925, Vol. II (9).

Rahja, E. "Comrade V. I. Lenin in 1917." *Voprosy Istorii*, 1967, No. 10.

———. "Lenin's Last Time in Hiding." *Krasnaya Letopis*, 1934, No. 1.

Rakhmetov, V. "April 1917 in Petrograd. *Krasny Arkhiv*, 1929, Vol. XXXIII.

Rengarten, I. I. Diary. *Krasny Arkhiv*, 1929, Vol. XXV (26), Vol. XXIII.

Rodzyanko, M. V. "The Last Report [to the Czar] on Feb. 14, 1917." *Arkhiv Russkoi Revolyutsii* (Berlin), 1922, No. 6.

———. "Russia's economic situation before the Revolution. Notes, February 1917." *Krasny Arkhiv*, 1925, Vol. III (10).

Romanov, Konstantin. Diary. *Krasny Arkhiv*, 1931, Nos. 44, 45.

Romanov, V. Kn., Andrei V. Diary for 1916–1917. *Krasny Arkhiv*, 1928, Vol. I (26).

Rutenberg, Pyotr. "The End of Gapon." *Byloye*, 1909, No. 11/12.

Sadikov, P. "History of the Last Days of the Czarist Regime." *Krasny Arkhiv*, 1926, Vol. I (14).

Savinkov, Boris Viktorovich. "Memoirs." *Byloye*, 1917, No. 1 (23), No. 2 (24), No. 3 (25).

Savitskaya, R. "Pages from the Memoirs about V. I. Lenin." *Novy Mir*, 1964, No. 12.

Selivachev, V. I. "1917 Diary." *Krasny Arkhiv*, 1925, Vol. II (9).

Sergeyev, A. A. "In Lieu of a Bibliography: The Publication Abroad of the Letters of the Former Empress Alexandra." *Krasny Arkhiv*, 1923, Vol. III.

———. "Nicholas Romanov from Feb. 28 to Mar. 4, 1917." *Krasny Arkhiv*, 1925, Vol. I (8).

Shlyapnikov, A. "The February Revolution." *Voprosy Istorii KPSS*, 1965, No. 9.

Shub, D. "The Merchant of Revolution, Parvus and the German-Bolshevik Conspiracy." *Novy Zhurnal*, 1967, No. 87.

Sidorov, K. "The Struggle Against the Strike Movement on the Eve of the World War." *Krasny Arkhiv*, 1929, Vol. XXXIV.

Silvin, M. A. "Memoirs." *Proletarskaya Revolyutsiya*, 1924, No. 7.

Sinegub, Aleksandr. "The Defense of the Winter Palace." *Arkhiv Russkoi Revolyutsii* (Berlin), 1922, No. 4.

Solovyev, M. E. "Unaccomplished Escape." *Voprosy Istorii*, 1973, No. 10.

Sovokin, A. M. "Creating the Revolutionary Circle Around Petrograd on the Eve of the October Uprising." *Voprosy Istorii*, 1967, No. 11.

Starkov, V. V. "V. I. Lenin." *Krasnaya Nov*, 1925, No. 8.

Stasova, Yelena Dmitriyevna. "Lenin." *Pravda*, Oct. 15, 1963.

Stolyarov, A. "Diary Excerpts and Recollections of 1917," *Prometei*, 1968, No. 6.

Tamarov, I. "Nicholas II in 1905." *Krasny Arkhiv*, 1925, Vols. IV–V (11–12).

Tarle, Ye. "Emperors Wilhelm II and Nicholas II in 1904–1907. Unpublished Correspondence." *Byloye*, July 1917, No. 1 (23).

Tarsaidze, A. "The Disappearance of the Czarist Relics." *Rossiya*, Apr. 22, 23, 24, 29, 30, May 2, 3, 1958.

Ulyanov, Dmitri. "Lenin's Childhood Years." *Krasnaya Nov*, Nov. 1938, No. 3.

Ulyanova, Aleksandra Ilyinichna. "Letters." *Voprosy Istorii KPSS*, 1966, No. 5.

Ulyanova, M. I. "Aleksandr Ilyich Ulyanov." *Pravda*, Feb. 18, 1963.

———. Letters. *Istorichesky Arkhiv*, 1958, No. 1.

Ulyanova-Yelizarova, A. I. "About Lenin." *Proletarskaya Revolyutsiya*, 1927, Nos. 2–3.

Valentinov, V. "Lenin's Early Years (Lenin's brother A. Ulyanov)." *Novy Zhurnal*, 1954, No. 40.

Veresov, A. "The Last Three Days (on the Centennial of the Birth of A. I. Ulyanov)." *Neva*, 1966. No. 4.

Veselina, M. S. "The Gathering of Lenin's Documentary Heritage." *Voprosy Istorii*, 1974, No. 4.

Vilshai, V. L. "I. F. Armand." *Voprosy Istorii KPSS*, Nov. 1976, No. 11.

Vodovozov, V. "My Acquaintance with Lenin." *Goloso Minuvshom Chuzhoi Storone*, 1925, Vol. XII.

———. "Deliberation at Tsarskoye Selo." *Byloye*, Oct. 1917, No. 4 (26).

Volin, E. "Lenin in Kokushkino and Alakayevka." *Istorichesky Zhurnal*, 1945, Vol. IV.

Wilhelm II. Letters About the Russo-Japanese War and the 1905 Revolution. *Krasny Arkhiv*, 1925, Vol. II (9).

Yakhontov A. N. "Painful Days." *Arkhiv Russkoi Revolyutsii*, Vol. XVIII.

Yakovenko, E. I. "The Second March 1." *Katorga i Ssylka*, 1927, Vol. XXXII.

Yakovlev, V. "The Years of Iskra; Lenin's Autobiographical Comments. (1900–1903)." *Novy Mir*, 1963, No. 7.

———. "On the Eve of the Party's Founding; Lenin's Autobiographical Comments (1893–1900)." *Novy Mir*, 1965, No. 6.

———. "The Beginning of the Road; Lenin's Autobiographical Comments (1886–1893). *Novy Mir*, 1965, No. 4.

Yermolov, A. S. "Notes of Jan. 17 and Jan. 31, 1905." *Krasny Arkhiv*, 1925, Vol. I (3).

Yusupov, Kn. F. F. Letters from Count Sumarokov-Elston to Princess Z. N. Yusupova. *Krasny Arkhiv*, 1926, Vol. I (14).

Zenzinov, V. "The February Days." *Novy Zhurnal*, 1953, Nos. 34, 35.

Alexander, Grand Duke of Russia. *Once a Grand Duke*. New York, 1932.

Allilyueva, Svetlana. *Only One Year*. New York, 1969.

————. *Twenty Letters to a Friend*. New York, 1967.

Almedingen, E. M. *Tomorrow Will Come*. New York, 1968.

Anet, Claude. *La Révolution Russe*. Paris, 1915.

Anweiler, Oskar. *The Soviets: The Russian Workers, Peasants, and Soldiers Councils, 1905–1921*. New York, 1974.

Avilov, Lydia. *Chekhov in My Life*. London, 1950.

Baedeker, Karl. *Russia with Teheran, Port Arthur, and Peking*. New York, 1914.

Balabanoff, Angelica. *Impressions of Lenin*. Ann Arbor, Mich., 1964.

Baron, Samuel. *Plekhanov*. Stanford, 1963.

Basily, Nicholas de. *Memoirs*. Stanford, 1973.

Bassow, Whitman. "La Pravda de 1912 à 1914." Thèse de Doctorat d'Université, Faculté des Lettres, Université de Paris, 1953.

Baynac, Jacques; Engelstein, Laura; Girault, René; Keenan, E. L.; and Yassour, Avraham. *Sur 1905*. Paris, 1974.

Bedford, C. Harold. *The Seeker: D. S. Merezhkovsky*. Lawrence, Kans., 1975.

Bejalski, Risto. "Report from Moscow." Borba, June 28, 29, 30, 1964. Belgrade, U. S. Foreign Broadcast Reports, July 7, 1964.

Bely, Andrei. *St. Petersburg*. New York, 1959.

Berdyayev, Nikolai. *The Origins of Russian Communism*. Ann Arbor, Mich., 1960.

————. *The Russian Idea*. New York, 1948.

————. *The Russian Revolution*. Ann Arbor, Mich., 1961.

Brancovan, C. E. "Lenin's Ancestry." *The Times Literary Supplement*, July 21, 1971.

Breshkovsky, Catherine. *The Little Grandmother of the Russian Revolution: Reminiscences and Letters*. Boston, 1919.

Bryant, Louise. *Mirrors of Moscow*. New York, 1923.

————. *Six Red Months in Russia*. New York, 1918.

Buchanan, Meriel. *Dissolution of an Empire*. London, 1937.

Buchanan, Sir George. *My Mission to Russia*. Boston, 1923.

Bulygin, Captain Paul. *The Murder of the Romanovs*. New York, 1935.

Bunin, Ivan. *Memories and Portraits*. London, 1951.

Burliuk, David. *Color and Rhyme*, No. 31, 1956.

Cantacuzene, Princess. *Revolutionary Days*. New York, 1919.

Care, Norman S. M. "The Russians as Philosophers." *The New Republic*, Sept. 25, 1965.

Carmichael, Joel. "German Money and Bolshevik Honour." *Encounter*, June 1974.

Chamberlain, William Henry. *The Russian Revolution*. 2 Vols. New York, 1935.

Chernyshevsky, N. G. *What Is to Be Done?* New York, 1961.

Colton, Ethan T., Sr. *Memoirs*. New York, 1969.

Conquest, Robert. *The Great Terror*. New York, 1968.

————. *The Great Terror: Stalin's Purge of the Thirties*. Rev. ed. New York, 1973.

Curtiss, John Shelton, ed. *Essays in Russian and Soviet History*. New York, 1963.

Dan, Theodore. *The Origins of Bolshevism*. New York; 1964.

Daniels, Robert V. *Red October: The Bolshevik Revolution of 1917*. New York, 1967.

Davis, Donald, and Trani, Eugene P. "An American in Russia: Russell M. Story and the Bolshevik Revolution, 1917–1919." *The Historian*, Vol. XXXVI, No. 4 (Aug. 1974).

———. "The American YMCA and the Russian Revolution." *Slavic Review*, Sept. 1974.

Denikin, Anton I. *The Career of a Tsarist Officer, Memoirs, 1872–1916*. Minneapolis, 1975.

De Robien, Louis. *The Diary of a Diplomat in Russia, 1917–1918*. London, 1969.

Deutscher, Isaac. *Stalin*. 2nd ed. New York, 1967.

Dreier, Katherine. *Burliuk*. New York, 1944.

Dukes, Sir Paul. *Red Dusk and the Morrow*. London, 1922.

Ehrenburg, Ilya. *People and Life, 1891–1921*. New York, 1962.

Elsworth, J. D. *Andrey Bely*. Letchworth, England, 1972.

Elwood, Ralph Carter. "Lenin and *Pravda*, 1912–1914." *Slavic Review*, June 1972.

Ferro, Marc. *The Russian Revolution of February 1917*. New York, 1972.

———. *La Révolution de 1917*. 2 vols. Paris 1967, 1976.

Fischer, George. *Russian Liberalism*. Cambridge, Mass., 1958.

Fischer, Louis. *The Life of Lenin*. New York, 1964.

Fitzpatrick, Sheila. *The Commissariat of Enlightenment: Soviet Organization of Education and the Arts under Lunacharsky*. London, 1970.

Footman, David. *Red Prelude: The Life of the Russian Terrorist Zhelyabov*. New Haven, 1945.

Francis, David R. *Russia from the American Embassy, April, 1916–November, 1918*. New York, 1921.

Franklin, Bruce. *The Essential Stalin: Major Theoretical Writings 1905–1952*. New York, 1972.

Fülöp-Miller, René. *Rasputin: The Holy Devil*. Garden City, N.Y.: 1928.

Furtell, Michael. *Northern Underground*. New York, 1963.

Galitzine, Princess Nicholas. *Spirit to Survive: The Memoirs of Princess Nicholas Galitzine*. London, 1976.

Germanis, Uldis. "Some Observations on the Yaroslav Revolt in July, 1918." *Journal of Baltic Studies*, Vol. IV, No. 3 (Fall 1975).

Getzler, Israel. *Martov*. London, 1967.

Geva, Tamara. *Split Seconds*. New York, 1972.

Gilliard, Pierre. *Thirteen Years at the Russian Court*. London, 1921.

Gorky, Maxim. *Untimely Thoughts*. London, 1970.

Goul, Roman. *Azef*. New York, 1962.

Gourfinkel, Nina. *Gorky*. London, 1960.

Gray, Camilla. *The Russian Experiment in Art, 1863–1922*. London, 1962.

Grigoriev, S. L. *The Diaghilev Ballet, 1909–1929*. London, 1960.

Harcave, Sidney. *The Russian Revolution of 1905*. New York, 1970.

Heald, Edward T. *Witness to Revolution*. Kent State University Press, 1972.

Hedlin, Myron. "Zinoviev's Revolutionary Tactics in 1917." *Slavic Review*, Mar. 1975.

Herzen, Alexander. *From the Other Shore*. Cleveland, 1963.

Hingley, Ronald. *Chekhov*. London, 1950.

Hough, Richard. *The Potemkin Mutiny*. New York, 1961.

Hyde, H. Montgomery. *Stalin*. New York, 1972.

Iswolsky, Alexandre (Aleksandr Izvolsky). *Mémoires 1906–1910*. Paris, 1923.

Karlinsky, Simon. *Marina Cvetaeva: Her Life and Art.* Berkeley and Los Angeles, 1966.

Karsavina, Tamara. *Theatre Street.* New York, 1961.

Kennan, George. *Russia Leaves the War.* Princeton, 1956.

Kerensky, Alexander. *Russia and History's Turning Point.* New York, 1965.

Kerzhentsev, P. *Life of Lenin.* Moscow, 1937.

Kochubei, Princess Varvara Alexandrovna. *Gone Forever. Memoirs.* Privately Printed, n.d.

————. *Some More of Gone Forever.* Privately Printed, n.d.

Kohn, Richard. *La Révolution Russe.* Paris, 1963.

Krupskaya, N. K. *Reminiscences of Lenin.* Moscow, 1959.

Kschessinska, Mathilde. *Dancing in Petersburg.* New York, 1961.

Kuprin, Alexandre. *Yama, the Pit.* New York, 1960.

Landau-Aldanov, M. A. *Lenine.* Paris, 1919.

Lenin, V. I. *Collected Works.* In English. 4th ed. Moscow, 1963–70.

Lensen, George Alexander. *War and Revolution: Excerpts from the Letters and Diaries of the Countess Olga Poutiatine.* Tallahassee, Fla., 1971.

Lerner, Warren. *Karl Radek: The Last Internationalist.* Stanford, 1969.

Letters of the Tsaritsa to the Tsar, 1914–1916. With an Introduction by Sir Bernard Pares. London, 1923.

Lettres de Nicolas II et de Sa Mère. Translated by Paul L. Leon. Paris, 1928.

Lettres des Grand-Ducs à Nicolas II. Paris, 1926.

Levin, Dan. *Stormy Petrel: The Life and Work of Maxim Gorky.* New York, 1965.

Levine, Isaac Don. *The Russian Revolution.* New York, 1917.

Liebman, Marcel. *The Russian Revolution.* New York, 1970.

Lockhart, R. H. Bruce. *British Agent.* New York, 1933.

Loukomsky, A. (Gen. Aleksandr Sergeyevich Lukomsky). *Memoirs of the Russian Revolution.* London, 1922.

Lukacs, George. *Lenin: A Study on the Unity of His Thought.* London, 1970.

Lunacharsky, Anatoly Vasilyevich. *Revolutionary Silhouettes.* New York, 1968.

Lyashchenko, Peter I. *History of the National Economy of Russia to the 1917 Revolution.* New York, 1949.

Lyons, Marvin. *Nicholas II: The Last Tsar.* New York, 1974.

Malkov, P. *Reminiscences of a Kremlin Commandant.* Moscow, n.d.

Marcu, Valeriu. *Lenin.* New York, 1929.

Markovitch, Marylie (Mme Amélie de Néry). *La Révolution Russe Vue par une Française.* Paris, 1917.

Marsden, Victor E. "A New Passion Play: Russian Grand Duke's Production." *The Times* (London), Feb. 20, 1914.

Marshall, Herbert. *Mayakovsky.* London, 1965.

Matlaw, Ralph E., ed. *Belinsky, Chernyshevsky, and Dobrolyubov: Selected Criticism.* New York, 1962.

Maynard, Sir John. *Russia in Flux.* New York, 1948.

Meck, Galina von. *As I Remember Them.* London, 1973.

Medvedev, Roy A. *Let History Judge.* New York, 1971.

Melgounov, Sergey Petrovich (S. P. Melgunov). *Red Terror.* London 1926.

Metternich, Tatiana. *Tatiana, Five Passports in a Shifting Europe.* London, 1976.

Meyer, Alfred G. *Leninism.* Cambridge, Mass., 1957.

Miliukov, Paul. *Russia and Its Crises.* New York, 1964.

Monro, H. H. *The Short Stories of Saki.* New York, 1930.

Nabokov, Vladimir D. *The Provisional Government, 1917.* New Haven, 1975.

Nemirovitch-Dantchenko, Vladimir. *My Life in the Russian Theater.* New York, 1968.

New York *Times,* 1917–18.

Nicky-Sunny Letters, Correspondence of the Tsar and the Tsaritsa, 1914–1917. Hattiesburg, Miss., 1970.

Paléologue, Maurice. *An Ambassador's Memoirs.* 3 vols. New York, 1925.

Paley, Princess. *Souvenirs de Russie.* Paris, 1923.

Pares, Sir Bernard. *A History of Russia.* New York, 1947.

———. *My Russian Memoirs.* London, 1931.

———. *The Fall of the Russian Monarchy.* New York, 1961.

Paustovsky, Konstantin. *The Story of a Life.* New York, 1964.

Payne, Robert. *The Life and Death of Lenin.* New York, 1964.

Pearlsteen, Edward W. *Revolution in Russia! As reported by the New York Tribune and the New York Herald, 1894–1921.* New York, 1967.

Pethybridge, Roger, ed. *Witnesses to the Russian Revolution.* London, 1964.

Pinchuk, Ben-Cion. *The Octobrists in the Third Duma, 1907–1912.* Seattle, 1974.

Pipes, Richard. *Social Democracy and the St. Petersburg Labor Movement 1885–1897.* Cambridge, Mass., 1963.

———. *The Russian Intelligentsia.* New York, 1961.

Poggioli, Renato. *The Poets of Russia, 1890–1930.* Cambridge, Mass., 1960.

Pokrovsky, M. N. *Brief History of Russia.* London, 1933.

Possony, Stefan T. *Lenin: The Compulsive Revolutionary.* Chicago, 1964.

Rabinowitch, Alexander. *Prelude to Revolution: The Petrograd Bolsheviks and the July 1917 Uprising.* Bloomington, Ind., 1968.

———. *The Bolsheviks Come to Power.* New York, 1976.

Rasputin, Maria. *My Father.* London, 1934.

Reed, John. *Ten Days that Shook the World.* New York, 1919.

———. *Ten Days that Shook the World.* Edited by Bertram D. Wolfe. New York, 1960.

Reeve, F. D. *Aleksandr Blok Between Image and Idea.* New York, 1962.

Reitzel, Raymond J. *All in a Lifetime.* Privately printed, 1973.

Riha, Thomas. *Readings in Russian Civilization.* 3 vols. Chicago, 1964.

Rodzianko, M. V. *Mémoires: Le Regne de Raspoutine.* Paris, 1928.

Rosdolsky, Roman. "The February Regime." *The Times Literary Supplement,* Oct. 20, 1966.

Rosenberg, William G. *Liberals in the Russian Revolution.* Princeton, N.J., 1974.

Rosenstone, Robert A. *Romantic Revolutionary: A Biography of John Reed.* New York, 1975.

Sablinsky, Walter. *The Road to Bloody Sunday.* Princeton, N.J., 1976.

Salisbury, Harrison E. "Lenin's Ancestry." *The Times Literary Supplement,* June 18, July 30, 1971.

Samuel, Maurice. *Blood Accusation: The Strange History of the Beiliss Case.* New York, 1966.

Sazonov, Serge. *Fateful Years, 1909–1916.* London, 1927.

Schapiro, Leonard. *The Communist Party of the Soviet Union.* New York, 1960.

Schwartz, Solomon. *The Russian Revolution of 1905.* Chicago, 1907.

Seaton-Watson, Hugh. *The Decline of Imperial Russia.* London, 1952.

Senn, Alfred Erich. "The Myth of German Money During the First World War." *Soviet Studies,* Jan. 1970, Vol. XXVIII, No. 1.

————. *The Russian Revolution in Switzerland, 1914–1917*. Madison, Wis., 1971.

Serge, Victor. *Memoirs of a Revolutionary, 1901–1941*. London, 1963.

————. *Year One of the Russian Revolution*. London, 1972.

Seroff, Victor. *The Real Isadora*. New York, 1972.

Shklovsky, Viktor. *Mayakovsky and His Circle*. New York, 1972.

Shub, David. *Lenin*. New York, 1948.

Simmons, Ernest J. *Leo Tolstoy*. 2 vols. New York, 1960.

————, ed. *Continuity and Change in Russian and Soviet Thought*. Cambridge, Mass., 1955.

Slonim, Marc. *From Chekhov to the Revolution: Russian Literature 1900–1917*. New York, 1962.

————. *Modern Russian Literature from Chekhov to the Present*. New York, 1953.

Smith, Edward Ellis. *The Young Stalin*. New York, 1967.

Sokoloff, Boris. *The White Nights*. New York, 1956.

Solzhenitsyn, Aleksandr. *The Gulag Archipelago, 1918–1956*. Vols. I–II, III–IV. New York, 1974, 1975.

Sorokin, P. *Leaves from a Russian Diary*. New York, 1924.

Souvarine, Boris. *Stalin*. New York, 1939.

Stavrou, Theofanis George, ed. *Russia Under the Last Tsar*. Minneapolis, 1969.

Subbotin, Z. *Lenin's Study and Flat in the Kremlin*. Moscow, n.d.

Sukhanov, N. N. *The Russian Revolution, 1917*. Edited, abridged, and translated by Joel Carmichael. New York, 1955.

Summers, Anthony, and Mangold, Tom. *The File on the Tsar*. London, 1976.

Szebfeld, Ignacy. "Elizaveta Drabkina." *Radio Liberty Papers*, May 13, 1974.

Tarasov-Rodionov, Aleksei. *February 1917*. New York, 1931.

Tarsaidze, Alexandre. *Katia, Wife Before God*. New York, 1970.

Tchernoff, Olga (Olga E. Chernova-Kolbasina). *New Horizons*. London, 1936.

Trewin, J. C. *The House of Special Purpose*. New York, 1975.

Trotsky, Leon. *The History of the Russian Revolution*. 3 vols. London, 1932.

————. *Lenin*. New York, 1962.

————. *My Life*. New York, 1960.

————. *1905*. New York, 1971.

————. *On Lenin: Notes Towards a Biography*. London, 1971.

————. *Stalin*. New York, 1941.

————. *Trotsky's Diary in Exile, 1935*. New York, 1953.

————. *The Young Lenin*. New York, 1972.

Tschebotarieff-Bill, Valentine. "The Morozovs." *Russian Review*, Apr. 1955, No. 2.

Tucker, Robert C. *Stalin as Revolutionary, 1879–1929*. New York, 1973.

Ulam, Adam B. *Stalin*. New York, 1973.

Valentinov, Nikolai (N. V. Volsky). *The Early Years of Lenin*. Ann Arbor, Mich., 1969.

————. *Encounters with Lenin*. London, 1968.

Venturi, Franco. *Roots of Revolution: A History of the Populist and Socialist Movements in 19th Century Russia*. New York, 1966.

Viroubova, Anna. *Souvenirs de Ma Vie*. Paris, 1927.

Volkov, Alexis. *Souvenirs d'Alexis Volkov, Valet de Chambre de La Tsarine Alexandra Feodorovna, 1910–1918*. Paris, 1928.

Von Lahe, T. H. "Sergei Witte on the Industrialization of Imperial Russia." *Journal of Modern History*, Vol. XXVI.

Walder, David. *The Short Victorious War: The Russo-Japanese Conflict, 1904–5.* New York, 1974.

Wallace, Sir Donald MacKenzie. *Russia on the Eve of War and Revolution.* New York, 1961.

Walsh, Warren B. *Readings in Russian History.* Vol. III. Syracuse, N.Y., 1963.

Wasilieff, A. T. *Police Russe et Révolution.* Paris, 1936.

Weidle, Wladimir. *Russia: Absent and Present.* New York, 1961.

Williams, Albert Rhys. *Lenin: The Man and His Work (With the Impressions of Col. Raymond Robins and Arthur Ransome).* New York, 1919.

———. *Through the Russian Revolution.* New York, 1921.

Wilson, Colin. *Rasputin and the Fall of the Romanovs.* New York, 1964.

Wolfe, Bertram D. *The Bridge and the Abyss.* New York, 1967.

———. *An Ideology in Power: Reflections on the Russian Revolution.* New York, 1969.

———. "Lenin and Inessa Armand." *Encounter,* Feb. 1964.

———. *Three Who Made a Revolution.* Boston, 1955.

Woroszylski, Wiktor. *The Life of Mayakovsky.* New York, 1970.

Woytinsky, W. S. (V. S. Voytinsky) *Stormy Passage: A Personal History Through Two Russian Revolutions to Democracy and Freedom, 1905–1960.* New York, 1961.

Wyziemeld, Marcin. "Lenin and Inessa Armand." *Slavic Review,* Mar. 1963, Vol. XXII, No. 1.

———. "Lenin's Ancestry." *The Times Literary Supplement,* May 21, 1971.

Yarmolinsky, Avram. *Road to Revolution: A Century of Russian Radicalism.* New York, 1962.

Yershov, Peter. *Letters of Gorky and Andreev, 1899–1912.* London, 1958.

Youssoupoff, Prince Felix. *Lost Splendor.* New York, 1953.

Zeman, Z. A. B. *Germany and the Revolution in Russia, 1915–1918.* London, 1958.

———, and Scharlau, W. B. *The Merchant of Revolution: The Life of Alexander Israel Helphand (Parvus), 1867–1924.* London, 1965.

Notes

I. A Quiet Execution PAGES 1–4

1. Some accounts say there was a convoy of three small cutters, one for the prisoners, one for guards, one for the prison staff. (See A. Veresov, in *Neva*, 1966, No. 4, p. 161.)

2. A. S. Prugavin, *V Kazematakh*, p. 137.

3. E. I. Yakovenko, *Katorga i Ssylka*, 1927, Vol. III, p. 29.

4. Ibid.

5. Two of the seven prisoners taken to Shlisselburg were not executed. They were Mikhail Novorussky and Iosif Lukashevich, who were brought to the fortress on the same steamer which conveyed the five men who had been condemned to death. Novorussky and Lukashevich had been sentenced to life imprisonment. When he was freed in 1906, Novorussky published his memoirs, and over the years new and revised editions kept appearing. The 1933 edition contained this passage: "Three days were spent in preparing the gallows which was erected outside the prison court and brought there in semi-prepared state. Here, in the courtyard, at the entrance to the old building, it was put up without sawing and without hammering and in the night of May 8 when we slept they soundlessly led out five of our comrades with Ulyanov at the head and soundlessly took their lives. . . ." (Mikhail Novorussky, *Zapiski Shlisselburzhtsa*, p. 362.) The first version which Novorussky published contained a brief tribute to Ulyanov (whom Novorussky had met only a half dozen times) but not a word about the execution of Ulyanov and the others. This account appeared in *Byloye*, 1906, No. 4 (p. 65), eleven years before the Revolution. The name of Ulyanov then had only limited significance. In the first post-Revolution version, published in Petrograd in 1920, Novorussky tells of learning of the executions from a friendly jailer several years after the event. The melodramatic references to the prisoners being "soundlessly" led out and "soundlessly" executed are not included. His story seems to have grown with the telling. Actually the fortress walls were so thick that no spe-

cial precautions were needed to keep the executions secret from the other prisoners.

II. But for How Long? PAGES 5–13

1. Yu. Z. Polevoi. *Zarozhdeniye Marksizma v Rossii*, pp. 79–80.
2. Ibid., pp. 79, 80, 82, 88, 104.
3. A. V. Ushakov, *Revolyutsionnoye Dvizheniye Demokraticheskoi Intelligentsii v Rossii 1894–1904*, pp. 18–19.
4. Polevoi, *Zarozhdeniye*, p. 279.
5. "I was surprised how well Sasha spoke. So confidently, so forcefully. I didn't think he could speak so well," his mother said. She was so upset, however, that she had to leave the courtroom before he finished. (*A. I. Ulyanov i Delo 1 Marta 1887*, p. 122.
6. The Czar invited nine agents and two policemen to his country residence at Gatchina where he thanked them. They were given pensions of 250 rubles a year but by 1909 they were petitioning for more, saying they could not live on this small sum. (A. Azotzy, in *Krasny Arkhiv*, 1925, No. 9, pp. 297–99.)
7. B. S. Imenburg and A. Ya. Chernyakh. *Zhizn Aleksandra Ulyanova*, pp. 142–45.

III. Volga Mat' PAGES 14–16

1. Address: V. I. Lenin, *Biograficheskaya Khronika*, Vol. I, p. 2.
2. Anna I. Ulyanova-Yelizarova, *Vospominaniya o Aleksandr Ulyanov*, pp. 41–43.
3. I. F. Popov, in *Novy Mir*, 1963, No. 4, p. 160.
4. Vladimir Kanivets, *Ulyanovy. Istoricheskii Roman*, p. 34.
5. M. I. Ulyanova, *Voprosy Istorii KPSS*, 1964, No. 4, pp. 39–41.
6. Kanivets, *Ulyanovy*, p. 38.
7. Leon Trotsky, *The Young Lenin*, p. 7.
8. P. P. Semenov, *Rossiya*, Vol. VI, pp. 391–92. More than eighty years later I visited Simbirsk, now called Ulyanovsk. It was still a sleepy backwater town, drowsing on the Volga bluffs. Russian tourists waxed indignant at the unpaved streets, run-down droshkies, unkempt parks, and paintless houses. They thought it a disgrace to Lenin's memory. Simbirsk seemed to have gone to sleep at the turn of the century. In recent years, particularly in connection with Lenin's Centennial in 1970, it was spruced up a bit.
9. The possibility that Dr. Alexander Dmitriyevich Blank, Mariya Ulyanova's father, was a Jew has been raised by several biographers, notably David Shub. Shub cites the fact that Blank originally came from Odessa, that a number of Jews named Blank lived in Odessa, and that rumors long circulated that he was, in fact, a Jew, possibly a converted Jew. Nikolai Valentinov (who knew Lenin) and Boris Nicolayevsky, a painstaking researcher in Leninana, both doubted the theory of Jewishness. There is no really hard evidence available, but it must be noted that whereas Soviet historians and haleographers have meticulously searched out the origins and family data of the Ulyanov line, there is little material available on the origin of Blank or his background. Interestingly, even Trotsky admitted he did not know Blank's nationality. (Trotsky, *Young Lenin*, p. 19.) The principal facts of his career, however, seem fairly clear. He completed the St. Petersburg Medical Surgical Academy in 1824, served his internship in a Petersburg hospital, did epidemic duty in Olonets Guberniya, served as a medical inspector in Perm, directed a factory hospital in the Zlatovst mining area of the Urals, and served as a police surgeon in St. Petersburg for seven years. His salary was apparently 561.80 rubles

a year. (Kanivets, *Ulyanovy*, p. 36.) He retired in 1849 to the estate which he purchased in Kokushkino, acquiring a number of serfs in the process. He was a state counselor of the Fifth Class, a member of the nobility, and a man of some means. (R. A. Kovnator, *Olga Ulynova*, p. 104.) So far as Christmas is concerned there is no doubt from many reminiscences that Mariya Ulyanova was brought up to observe it in the traditional German way and that Christmas was an important holiday in the Blank family. Of course, Dr. Blank's wife, Mariya Ulyanova's mother, was a German and a Lutheran. Shub reported that he was told by S. M. Ginsburg, a historian who worked for some years in the early Soviet period in the archives of the Holy Synod in Petrograd, that he had discovered a medical assistant in Odessa named Alexander Blank who had been converted to Catholicism. Ginsburg recalled that Moscow suddenly sent for this file and he suspected that it must relate to Lenin's grandfather. The affair has little but historical-polemical value since Blank died when Lenin was only four years old and any sign of Jewish culture or influence in Lenin's life or that of the Ulyanov family is absent. However, the "Jewish" grandfather story has long been used by anti-Semitic, anti-Soviet propagandists. (D. Shub–N. Valentinov exchange, *Novy Zhurnal*, Nos. 61, 63, 1960; also letter signed "Istorik," Dec. 2, 1960, *Novy Zhurnal*, No. 63; H. E. Salisbury–C. E. Brancovan exchange, *Times Literary Supplement*, July 2 and 30, 1971; I. Vasilyev, *O Yevreiskikh Predkakh Lenina*, Buenos Aires, 1964.) The poet Alexander Blok, who listened to Lenin's testimony before the Extraordinary Investigating Commission after the February Revolution, interestingly, asked himself the question as to whether Lenin "didn't have Jewish blood" but then answered his question in the negative. (Alexander Blok, *Zapisniye Knizhki*, p. 325.)

10. Anna Ulyanova described her father as a "genuine and profoundly devout man who educated his children in this spirit." She called his religious feeling spiritually clean and devoid of narrow sectarianism. (Anna I. Ulyanova-Yelizarova, in *Vospominaniya o V. I. Lenine*, Vol I, p. 23)

11. Ulyanova-Yelizarova, *Aleksandr Ulyanov*, p. 34, in Ivansky, *Zhizh Kak Fakel*, p. 40; A. I. Kondakov, *Direktor Narodnykh Uchilishch I. N. Ulyanov*, p. 21.

12. Anna I. Ulyanova-Yelizarova, *A. I. Ulyanov i Delo 1 Marta 1887*, p. 43.

13. Kovnator, *Olga Ulyanova*, pp. 30–31.

14. Ibid., pp. 35.

15. P. P. Yelizarov, *Mark Yelizarov i Semya Ulyanovykh*, pp. 24, 38.

16. A. I. Ivansky, *Molodye Gody V. I. Lenina*, p. 58.

17. *Novy Mir*, 1963, No. 4, p. 158.

18. Ulyanova-Yelizarova, *Aleksandr Ulyanov*, in Ivansky, *Zhizh Kak Fakel*, p. 55; Dmitri Ulyanov, in Ivansky, *Lenina*, p. 77.

19. Kondakov, *I. N. Ulyanov*, p. 11.

20. *Novy Mir*, 1963, No. 4, p. 158.

21. Kanivets, *Ulyanovy*, p. 10.

22. Ulyanova-Yelizarova, *Aleksandr Ulyanov*, in Ivansky, *Zhizh Kak Fakel*, pp. 13–14; *Ivansky Lenina*, p. 121.

23. Kovnator, *Olga Ulyanova*, pp. 31–32.

24. Ibid., p. 15.

25. Dmitri Ulyanov, in *Krasnaya Nov*, 1938, No. 5, pp. 142–43.

26. Kovnator, *Olga Ulyanova*, pp. 12–13.

27. Ulyanova-Yelizarova, *Aleksandr Ulyanov*, pp. 31–34, in Ivansky, *Zhizh Kak Fakel*, p. 34.

28. The house was purchased in the name of Mariya Ivanovna, rather than that of her husband. Whether this was merely a legal convenience or whether Mariya

Ivanovna put up the money to buy the house is not known. Mariya Ivanovna's father was well-to-do and the funds may have come from him or his estate. (Lenin, *Biograficheskaya Khronika*, Vol. I, p. 6.) Mariya received a fifth of her father's estate as a wedding dowry (Trotsky, *Young Lenin*, p. 2), but there is no record of what this amounted to.

29. Ivansky, *Lenina*, p. 57.
30. Ulyanov, ibid, p. 72.
31. Kovnator, *Olga Ulyanova*, pp. 8–9
32. Ulyanov, in Ivansky, *Lenina*, pp. 72–74.
33. Trotsky, *Young Lenin*, p. 14.
34. Ulyanova-Yelizarova, A. I. *Ulyanov*, p. 43, quoted in Ivansky, *Lenina*, p. 78.
35. N. Veretennikov, *Volodya Ulyanov, Vospominaniya s Detskhikai Yunesheskikh Godakh V. I. Lenin v Kokushkino*, pp. 9–20, quoted in Ivansky, *Lenina*, pp. 78–88.
36. Kondakov, *I. N. Ulyanov*, p. 15.
37. Nikolai Valentinov, *Maloznakomy Lenin*, pp. 106–8.
38. Ulyanova-Yelizarova, *Detskiye i shkoliye gody Ilyicha*, pp. 8–10, quoted in Ivansky, *Lenina*, p. 60.
39. Ivansky, *Lenina*, pp. 130–38.

IV. *"The Best and Most Thoughtful"* PAGES 25–33

1. Alexander Kerensky, *Russia and History's Turning Point*, pp. 4–5.
2. V. M. Chernov, *Pered Burei*, pp. 17–28.
3. There is much ostentatious and tendentious Soviet scholarship trying to establish deeper roots of Alexander's political orientation. He is even presented as an "early Marxist." This is nonsense as the memoirs of the Ulyanov family, their friends and contemporaries in the radical movement make clear. He worked with enormous concentration on his studies, winning a gold medal, until his final year when his interest in sociopolitical conditions was suddenly stimulated in part by the world around him, in part undoubtedly by his fellow students in an eating club of students from the Volga area to which he belonged. Possibly he was giving some thought to social problems in his last summer at home, the summer of 1886, but this seems not likely. His sister, Anna, who knew him best, did not believe so and there are no anecdotes in the memoirs. He seems to have devoted himself to his studies. In free moments he played endless games of chess with his brother Vladimir, silent concentrated games in which both brothers seemed hardly conscious of their surroundings, so devoted to their play they exchanged no words.
4. B. S. Imenburg and A. Ya. Chernyakh, *Zhizn Aleksandra Ulyanova*, p. 124.
5. Ibid., pp. 133–34.
6. Nikolai Berdyayev, *The Origins of Russian Communism*, pp. 25–35.
7. A. I. Ivansky, *Zhizh Kak Fakel*, p. 498.
8. A. I. Ivansky, *Molodye Gody V. I. Lenina*, pp. 223–39.
9. A. Kalinin and S. Mandel, *Lenin i Petersburgskii Universitet*, p. 69, quoting S. F. Oldenburg, in *Krasnaya Letopis*, Vol. 24, No. 2.
10. When Vladimir's younger sister, Olga, heard the news of Alexander's execution, she threw herself on the ground, weeping wildly and crying: "I hate the Czar. I will kill him." If Vladimir shared her emotion, he kept his feelings under control. (R. A. Kovnator, *Olga Ulyanova*, p. 41.)
11. Anna Yelizarova-Ulyanova, in *Proletarskaya Revolyutsiya*, Feb.–Mar. 1927, Nos. 2–3 (61–62), p. 284.
12. In later years Vladimir would often inveigh with unrestrained anger against

the ostracism displayed by the "liberal" society of Simbirsk against the Ulyanovs and particularly toward his mother after the news broke of his brother's arrest and execution. He was bitter at the fact that Mariya Alexandrovna could find no one to accompany her when she went to St. Petersburg to try to save her son's life. Regardless of the conduct of others, it is clear that Kerensky did not turn his back on the Ulyanov family and, indeed, did his best to help them.

13. Ivansky, *Lenina*, p. 248. The advertisement for the sale of the house appeared in the Simbirsk *Vedomosti* May 30, 1887. It said: "Because of moving away will sell house with garden, grand piano and furniture. Moskovskaya Ulitsa, Ulyanov house." The grand piano was not sold but most of the furnishings went, including Ilya Nikolayevich's maps, which were bought by G. Ya. Kokurochnikov, a third-grade teacher and inspector in the Smibirsk schools, for twelve rubles. (Kovnator, *Olga Ulyanova*, p. 45.)

V. Up Against the Wall PAGES 34–38

1. Mariya Alexandrovna's father died in 1873. (Vladimir Kanivets, *Ulyanovy. Istoricheskii Roman*, pp. 192–93.) She was one of five daughters—a brother died in childhood. All five visited Kokushkino during Dr. Blank's lifetime but later Kokushkino came to be shared largely by the Ulyanovs and the Veretennikovs. Madame Veretennikova was Mariya Alexandrovna's sister, Anna. The estate stayed in the family until about 1898 when it was apparently sold, presumably for quite a substantial sum, but Soviet historians have never made public any information about this, probably seeking to minimize the middle-class wealth of the Ulyanovs. There are references to negotiations for its sale in Lenin's letters, but those letters commenting in detail on these matters (and letters from his mother and sister Mariya concerning the same subject) have not been published. The last reference to Kokushkino in Lenin's correspondence occurs in a letter to his mother, March 8, 1898. (V. I. Lenin, *Collected Works*, Vol. XXXVII, pp. 118, 120, 150, 166. See also Nikolai Valentinov, *The Early Years of Lenin*, pp. 58–59.) Valentinov, an indefatigable investigator of the Ulyanov family finances, was never able satisfactorily to establish the financial arrangements involved in the disposal of Kokushkino. An editor's note in Vol. XXXVII of Lenin's collected works suggests that the death of Mariya Alexandrovna's sister, L. A. Ponomareva (apparently in 1897), compelled Mariya Alexandrovna and her sister, Madame Veretennikova, to share the debts of the Kokushkino estate. If this was correct, they presumably would also have shared the proceeds of the estate's sale. (Lenin, *Collected Works*, Vol. XXXVII, p. 636.)

2. Nikolai Valentinov, *Vstrechi s Leninym*, pp. 161–64; M. M. Essen, in *Novy Mir*, 1963, No. 4, pp. 161–64.

3. Essen, pp. 164–65.

4. It was true that Marx started to learn Russian for the specific purpose of reading Chernyshevsky.

5. Essen, p. 165.

6. Avram Yarmolinsky, *Road to Revolution*, p. 114.

7. Vladimir Ulyanov, possibly taking his cue from Chernyshevsky, was a vigorous proponent of physical exercise. When confined to prison, he kept himself fit by doing fifteen minutes of nip-ups and knee bends every morning and strongly urged all his comrades to do the same.

8. Essen, p. 164.

9. Pavel Milyukov, *Vospominaniya* (*1859–1917*), Vol. I, pp. 162–63.

10. Kn. Pavel Dmitriyevich Dolgorukov, *Velikaya Razrukha*, pp. 429–30; Anton I. Denikin, *The Career of a Tsarist Officer*, p. 176. The Dolgoruky family is usually

considered the oldest and most distinguished in Russia. It descended from Prince Michael of Chernigov who died in 1246. His seventh direct descendant, Prince Ivan, in the fourteenth century changed his name from Prince Obolensky, and began to call himself Prince Ivan Dolgoruky. His son was called Dolgorukov. Thus, there are two branches of the family, the Dolgorukys and the Dolgorukovs. Generally, the Dolgorukys were considered more wealthy than the Dolgorukovs. (Alexandre Tarsaidze, *Katia, Wife Before God*, p. 86.)

11. Theodore Dan, *The Origins of Bolshevism*, p. 189.
12. V. Vodovozov, in *Na Chuzhoi Storone*, 1925, Vol. XII.
13. N. G. Chernyshevsky, *What Is to Be Done?*, p. 241.
14. Ralph E. Matlaw, *Belinsky, Chernyshevsky, and Dobrolyubov*, pp. 133ff.
15. Yu. Z. Polevoi, *Zarozhdeniye Marksizma v Rossiya*, p. 360.
16. Anna I. Ulyanova-Yelizarova, in *Vospominaniya o V. I. Lenine*, Vol. I, pp. 9–13.
17. Nadezhda Krupskaya, *Vospominaniya o Lenine*, p. 37; *Novy Mir*, 1963, No. 4, p. 169.
18. Angelica Balabanoff, *Impressions of Lenin*, pp. 3–4.

VI. What Is to Be Done? PAGES 42–46

1. Yu. Z. Polevoi, *Zarozhdeniye Marksizma v Rossii*, p. 277.
2. F. A. Brokgauz and I. A. Efron, *Entsyklopedicheskii Slovar*, Vol. XXVI, p. 910.
3. Polevoi, *Zarozhdeniye Marksizma*, p. 350.
4. Ibid., pp. 62–69.
5. The censor's comment was: "Although the author is by conviction a complete socialist and his book carries a definite socialist character . . . taking into consideration that the exposition can hardly be called popular and that, on the other hand, the method of argumentation is couched in strict mathematical and scientific form the committee does not find it appropriate to submit this work to court proceedings and has decided to permit the book's publication." (A. Ilyn and V. Ilyn, *Rozhdeniye Partii*, p. 21.)
6. Polevoi, *Zarozhdeniye Marksizma*, p. 367.
7. Ibid., p. 366.
8. Leon Trotsky, *The Young Lenin*, p. 133.
9. B. Volin, in *Istorichesky Zhurnal*, 1945, Vol. IV, p. 10.
10. Nikolai Valentinov, *Maloznakomy Lenin*, p. 30.
11. Volin, in *Istorichesky Zhurnal*, 1945, Vol. IV, p. 12.
12. Valentinov, *Maloznakomy Lenin*, p. 30.
13. Vladimir Kanivets in a supposedly factual historical novel about the Ulyanov family gives Ilya's salary as 73.50 rubles a month, not a likely figure in the light of the 100-ruble monthly pension. (Kanivets, *Ulyanovy. Istoricheskii Roman*, p. 244.)
14. Louis Fischer, *The Life of Lenin*, p. 88.
15. Trotsky, *Young Lenin*, pp. 123, 133.
16. Valentinov, *Maloznakomy Lenin*, pp. 34ff. The major difficulty in establishing the facts about the Ulyanov finances is the suppression of basic archival materials by the Soviet Government. The extent of the suppressions cannot be measured precisely, but Lenin and his family ordinarily exchanged at least one letter a week, more if the occasion warranted. They wrote with extreme regularity, as is evident from repeated references and allusions in the correspondence. However, the published correspondence shows only fifteen letters from Lenin to his relatives in 1901, ten in 1902, three in 1903, and six in 1904.
17. R. A. Kovnator, *Olga Ulyanova*, p. 81.

18. Current Moscow dicta contends that Vladimir brought Marxism and Social Democratic theory to Samara and turned the Narodniki group into Social Democrats. (Polevoi, *Zarozhdeniye Marksizma*, pp. 408–15). A number of Samara citizens are cited in support of this. However, M. A. Silvin, a more knowledgeable and reliable witness, a genuine Marxist and the first contact whom Vladimir met in St. Petersburg, quotes him as saying then that "there was no Marxism in Samara whatever." (*Proletarskaya Revolyutsiya*, 1924, No. 7, pp. 66–73.)

19. Hearing that his younger brother Dmitri had been arrested, Vladimir, then himself in exile, wrote him February 7, 1898: "Most important. Do not forget daily obligatory gymnastics, setting yourself to do each exercise tens of times without stopping. This is very important." He recommended at least 50 bends to the floor, hands touching each time. V. Kanun, in *Novy Mir*, 1963, No. 6, p. 173.

20. Anna I. Ulyanova-Yelizarova, in *Vospominaniya o V. I. Lenine*, p. 68.

21. V. V. Starkov, in *Krasnaya Nov*, 1925, No. 8.

22. A. Kalinin and S. Mandel, *Lenin i Petersburgskii Universitet*, p. 84.

23. Nadezhda Krupskaya, *Vospominaniya o Lenine*, p. 37; *Novy Mir*, 1963, No. 4, p. 159.

24. Silvin, in *Proletarskaya Revolyutsiya*, 1924, No. 7, pp. 66–73.

25. Ibid., p. 74.

26. Kalinin, and Mandel, *Lenin i Petersburgskii Universitet*, pp. 96–97.

27. P. Kerzhentsev, *Life of Lenin*, quoting L. Blumenthal, p. 17. "It was not his brusqueness that was unpleasant. There was something more than ordinary brusqueness, a kind of mockery, partly deliberate, partly irresistibly organic, breaking through from the inmost depths of his being, in Lenin's way of dealing with those on whom he looked as his adversaries." (Pyotr B. Struve, in *Slavonic Review*, 1934, No. 36, pp. 590–95.)

28. I. N. Volper, *Psevdonimy V. I. Lenina*, pp. 144–46.

VII. Life for the Czar PAGES 50–58

1. Maxim Gorky, *Zhizh Klim Samgin, Sobraniye Sochinenii*, Vol. XII, pp. 450–55.

2. Von Derviz, a wealthy industrialist, went bankrupt three years later in the panic of August 1899. (Hugh Seaton-Watson, *Decline of Imperial Russia*, p. 129.)

3. Where later on June 21, 1897, Nemirovich-Danchenko and Konstantin Stanislavsky were to start their famous eighteen-hour conversation which led to the founding of the Moscow Art Theater and where, as Chekhov fondly recalled, tough-fisted Moscow merchants used to gather and drink tea so hot and in such quantity that sweat poured from their foreheads.

4. Ilya Shneidr, *Zapiski Starogo Moskvicha*, p. 5.

5. S. P. Melgunov, *Nikolai II*, quoting Pierre d'Alheim, pp. 105–6.

6. Gorky, *Zhizh Klim Samgin*, p. 461.

7. *Prometei*, 1969, No. 7, pp. 446–48.

8. The official police figure was 1,360 dead, 644 wounded. Police investigators concluded the deaths began even before the mugs began to be distributed. The distribution had been planned for 10 A.M. but was started at 6 A.M. because of the crush. Police officers on the spot asked for reinforcements several times during the night. Only 100 were sent. (*Krasny Arkhiv*, 1936, Vol. LXXVI, pp. 31–48.)

9. Melgunov, *Nikolai II*, p. 113; Graf S. Yu. Vitte, *Vospominaniya Tsartvovaniye Nikolai II*, Vol. I, p. 65.

10. Melgunov, *Nikolai II*, p. 144.

11. *Niva*, May 11–June 8, 1896, Nos. 19–23, correspondence of Vladimir V.

Nemirovich-Danchenko. The details of Khodyinka came largely from these superlative reports.

VIII. *The Seeds Are Planted* PAGES 59–69

1. I. N. Volper, *Psevdonimy V. I. Lenina*, p. 32.
2. M. Moskalev, *V. I. Lenin v Sibiri*, pp. 17–31.
3. M. A. Silvin, in *Proletarskaya Revolyutsiya*, 1924, No. 7, pp. 74–76.
4. Richard Pipes, *Social Democracy and the St. Petersburg Labor Movement*, pp. 106–7.
5. Nadezhda Krupskaya, in *Vospominaniya o V. I. Lenine*, Vol. I, p. 50.
6. Israel Getzler, *Martov*, p. 36.
7. Bertram D. Wolfe, *An Ideology in Power*, p. 63ff.
8. V. I. Gurko, *Tsar i Tsaritsa*, p. 22.
9. S. P. Melgunov, *Nikolai II*, p. 51.
10. Leon Trotsky, *History of the Russian Revolution*, Vol. I., pp. 74–75.
11. Melgunov, *Nikolai, II*, p. 41.
12. Sir Bernard Pares, *The Fall of the Russian Monarchy*, pp. 31–34.
13. Maurice Paléologue, *An Ambassador's Memoirs*, Vol. I, p. 324.
14. Alexandre Iswolsky, *Mémoires 1906–1910*, p. 266.
15. Pares, *Russian Monarchy*, pp. 56–57.
16. Imperator Nikolai II, *Dnevnik*, p. 23.
17. Anna Viroubova, *Souvenirs de Ma Vie*, p. 20.
18. Izwolsky, *Mémoires*, p. 280.
19. Melgunov, *Nikolai II*, p. 60.
20. Nadezhda Krupskaya, *Reminiscences of Lenin*, p. 32. Oskar Alexandrovich Engberg was a rather illiterate Finnish worker of vague revolutionary inclinations. Lenin and Krupskaya became fond of him. Lenin looked him up when he was in Finland in 1906, and Engberg paid a visit to Krupskaya in Moscow in 1935. He died in Helsinki in 1955. (M. M. Koronen. "V. I. Lenin and Finnish Revolutionaries." *Voprosy Istorii*, 1967, No. 8.)
21. Moskalev, *Lenin v Sibiri*, pp. 96–97.
22. V. I. Lenin, *Collected Works*, Vol. XXXVIII, letters of May 10, 1898, June 7, 1898; P. P. Yelizarov, *Mark Yelizarov i Semya Ulanovykh*, pp. 24, 42.
23. Nikolai Valentinov, *Maloznakomy Lenin*, p. 54.
24. Lenin, *Collected Works*, Vol. XXXVII, pp. 376–79.
25. V. Kanun, in *Novy Mir*, 1963, No. 6, p. 180.
26. Krupskaya, *Reminiscences*, p. 40.
27. Silvin, in *Proletarskaya Revolyutsiya*, 1924, No. 7, p. 78.
28. Valentinov, *Maloznakomy Lenin*, pp. 39–40.
29. Moskalev, *Lenin v Sibiri*, p. 157.
30. Leon Trotsky, *My Life*, p. 50.

IX. *On the Eve* PAGES 70–73

1. V. Ya. Laverychev, *Po tu Storonu Barrikad*, p. 23.
2. Graf S. Yu. Vitte, *Vospominaniya. Tsartvovaniye Nikolai II*, Vol. I, pp. 467–73.
3. T. H. Von Lahe, in *Journal of Modern History*, Vol. XXVI, pp. 61–74.
4. Hugh Seaton-Watson, *The Decline of Imperial Russia*, p. 201.
5. *Krasny Arkhiv*, 1923, Vol. II, p. 81, Kuropatkin diary.
6. Ibid., pp. 34–38.

7. Imperator Nikolai II, *Dnevnik*, p. 125.

8. It is entirely possible that the Buryat-Mongol doctor, Zhamsaryn Badmayev, played some role in the Czar's decision to send the Kalmyks off to Tibet. Badmayev had tried to persuade Alexander III to link China to Russia by a railroad through Mongolia. He proposed this as the first step in joining Russia, Mongolia, Tibet, and China. On January 1, 1904, Badmayev wrote the Czar: "Who masters Tibet can master Kokonor and the province of Szechwan; who masters Kokonor masters the Buddhist world, not excluding Russian Buddhists, and who masters Sinkiang masters China and may have influence on the one side over Turkestan and the other over Manchuria." (V. P. Semennikov, *Za Kulisami Tsarisma. Arkhiv Tibetskogo Vracha Badmayeva*, pp. 6, 110.) Badmayev's language is remarkably reminiscent of the geopolitical theories of Sir Halford J. Mackinder, who declared in 1918 that "who rules the Heartland commands the World Island; who rules the World Island commands the world." Mackinder's "Heartland" and Badmayev's Tibet-Kokonor-Sinkiang are virtually identical. Badmayev was a durable character. He survived to collaborate intimately with Rasputin and play a minor but measurable role in the dynasty's last days. (See Semennikov, *Za Kulisami*; also Imperator Nikolai II, *Dnevnik*, p. 115.)

9. *Krasny Arkhiv*, 1923, Vol. III, A. A. Polovtsev diary, dated February 17, 1901.

10. Ibid., Vol. II, p. 67, Kuropatkin diary.

11. Ibid., pp. 31–32.

12. Ibid., p. 44.

13. Ibid., p. 83.

14. Laverychev, *Po tu Storonu Barrikad*, pp. 24–26.

15. Leon Trotsky, *My Life*, p. 128.

16. S. M. Lebidova and E. G. Salita, *Yelena Dmitriyevna Stasova*, pp. 15–26.

17. Ibid., pp. 62–63.

18. Ernest J. Simmons, *Leo Tolstoy*, Vol. II, p. 307.

19. *Literaturnoye Nasledsto*, 1960, Vol. LXVIII, p. 459.

20. *Krasny Arkhiv*, 1923, Vol. III, p. 82, Polovtsev diary.

21. R. V. Ivanov-Razumnik, *Tyurmy i Ssylki*, pp. 19–32.

X. The Stage Is Set PAGES 81–86

1. Pavel Milyukov, *Vospominaniya* (*1859–1917*), Vol. I, p. 193.

2. Milyukov refused the editorship of *Osvobozhdeniye* but prepared the principal programmatic statement carried in its first issue. Pyotr Struve was its editor. The publication was financed by a 100,000-ruble contribution from the wealthy landowner, Yevgeny Zhukovsky. (George Fischer, *Russian Liberalism*, p. 125.)

3. Paul Miliukov, *Russia and Its Crises*, pp. 16–17.

4. Mariya Vetrova, a young revolutionary student confined in the Peter and Paul Fortress, was raped in her cell by a gendarme officer. She immolated herself by pouring the kerosene from her lamp onto her dress and setting it afire. (Maurice Paléologue, *An Ambassador's Memoirs*, Vol. I, p. 203.)

5. I. N. Volper, *Psevdonimy V. I. Lenin*, pp. 82–83.

6. Leon Trotsky, *My Life*, pp. 95–142.

7. Some scholars have long suspected that Djugashvili became an informer for the Okhrana about this time. Evidence has not been found to support this theory but such connections on the part of young revolutionaries were far from rare. Alexander Solzhenitsyn in *The Gulag Archipelago* comments on these rumors and suggests that the destruction of some Okhrana records immediately after the Revo-

lution may be connected with Stalin's past. Also see Edward Ellis Smith, *The Young Stalin*, pp. 99–100.

8. Isaac Deutscher, *Stalin: A Political Biography*, pp. 16–59.
9. Miliukov, *Russia and Its Crises*, pp. 163–64.
10. Ibid., p. 149.
11. Ibid., p. 137.
12. *Krasny Arkhiv*, 1923, Vol. II, pp. 60–80, Kuropatkin diary.
13. Nicholas had instructed War Minister Kuropatkin to tell the Ulyanovs "to stir up the Tibetans against the English" and to keep their mission secret from Foreign Minister Lamsdorf. (Ibid., p. 101.)
14. Imperator Nikolai II, *Dnevnik*, pp. 124–30.

XI. "A Small Victorious War" PAGES 90–97

1. *Niva*, 1904, No. 7, p. 136.
2. Ibid.
3. Ibid., p. 135.
4. Ibid., No. 6, p. 113.
5. Later he put out an antiwar pamphlet, "Bethink Yourselves," published in London. (Ernest J. Simmons, *Leo Tolstoy*, Vol. II, p. 357.)
6. Imperator Nikolai II, *Dnevnik*, p. 133.
7. In fact, there are only three brief references to the war in his writings of 1904. (Bertram Wolfe, *Three Who Made a Revolution*, p. 278.)
8. V. I. Lenin, *Collected Works*, Vol VII, p. 526, "Letter to the Comrades," written November 29, 1904.
9. Nikolai Valentinov, *Encounters with Lenin*, p. 149.
10. Lenin had a similar breakdown after the traumatic London Congress of 1903. (Leon Trotsky, *My Life*, p. 161; Nadezhda Krupskaya, *Reminiscences of Lenin*, p. 95.)
11. P. N. Lepeshinsky, *Na Povorote*, p. 198.
12. Krupskaya, *Reminiscences*, pp. 105–6.
13. Valentinov, *Encounters*, p. 115.
14. Trotsky, *My Life*, p. 165.
15. The total record of Stalin's activity in 1904 is so slender that one biographer has suggested that it was in this year that he became a secret agent for the Russian Gendarme Administration. There is, however, no proof for this, merely speculation, based on an unusually blank record. (Edward Ellis Smith, *The Young Stalin*, pp. 123–30.)
16. Imperator Nikolai II, *Dnevnik*, pp. 130–31; *Niva*, 1904, No. 6, pp. 113–14; *Niva*, 1904, No. 7, p. 136; Valentinov, *Encounters*, pp. 111–51.
17. Graf S. Yu. Vitte, *Vospominaniya. Tsartvovaniye Nikolai II*, Vol. I, p. 262.
18. *Krasny Arkhiv*, 1923, Vol. II, p. 86, Kuropatkin diary.
19. *Perepiska Vilgelma II s Nikolayem II 1894–1914 gg*, pp. 55ff.
20. *Krasny Arkhiv*, 1923, Vol. II, pp. 103–11, Kuropatkin diary.
21. Grand Duke Alexander, *Once a Grand Duke*, p. 214.
22. S. P. Melgunov, *Nikolai II*, p. 67.
23. *Krasny Arkhiv*, 1923, Vol. II, pp. 103–11, Kuropatkin diary.
24. Ibid., p. 109.
25. Melgunov, *Nikolai II*, p. 70.
26. *Krasny Arkhiv*, 1923, Vol. II, p. 111, Kuropatkin diary; Vitte, *Vospominaniya*, Vol. I, pp. 265–66.
27. The Czar attended a mass for Makarov on the day he received news of the

loss of the Petropavlovsk. General Rydzevsky met the Czar after the service. "What weather!" the Czar exclaimed, looking out at the new-fallen snow. "It would be great to go hunting. Let's see—what day is today—Friday? Should we go hunting tomorrow?" A few moments later Rydzevsky saw the Czar out in the garden shooting crows with a small rifle. (Melgunov, *Nikolai II*, p. 71.)

28. Imperator Nikolai II, *Dnevnik*, p. 149.

XII. *Not a Good Summer* PAGES 98–106

1. Vladimir Nemirovich-Danchenko, *My Life in the Russian Theater*, p. 233.
2. Konstantin Pavstovsky, *The Story of a Life*, p. 272.
3. Alexandre Kuprin, *Yama the Pit*.
4. Vl. Gilyarovsky, *Moskva i Moskvichi*, pp. 3–90; V. A. Gilyarovsky, *Izbrannoye*, Vol. I, pp. 447–60.
5. Marc Slonim, *From Chekhov to Revolution*, p. 129.
6. B. Byalik, *Sudba Maxima Gorkogo*, p. 161.
7. *Krasny Arkhiv*, 1923, Vol. II, p. 73, Kuropatkin diary.
8. Graf S. Yu. Vitte, *Vospominaniya. Tsartvovaniye Nikolai II*, Vol. I, pp. 189–91.
9. On February 6, 1906, the Czar received a report on the terrible pogrom at Gomel in which the burgomaster, a member of the anti-Semitic Union of Russian Patriots, had stood by without interference while Jews were being killed. He noted in the margin of the report: "What have I to do with this?" (*Krasny Arkhiv*, 1925, Vol. XII, p. 439.) Thirty-six Jews were killed at Gomel. The Czar gave Police Agent Rachkovsky 75,000 rubles June 20, 1906, which was used to buy a press on which to print anti-Semitic posters. (S. P. Melgunov, *Nikolai II*, pp. 14, 73.)
10. War Minister Kuropatkin, after talking with Plehve, April 14, 1903—that is, a week after the Kishinev pogrom—noted in his diary: "I heard from him as I had from the Czar that it was necessary to teach the Jews a lesson, that they were putting on airs and placing themselves at the forefront of the revolutionary movement." (*Krasny Arkhiv*, 1923, Vol. II, p. 43.)
11. Maurice Paléologue, *An Ambassador's Memoirs*, Vol. I, p. 168. After the 1917 Revolution, Goujon (or Gougeon as the name is sometimes spelled) took refuge with his Russian wife in the Crimea. He was murdered there in the autumn of 1918, apparently by right-wing White Russians. (Unpublished memoirs, Princess Lidiya Vassiltchikov.) Goujon, or a relative, also owned the Moscow steel plant now known as Serp i Molot. (Yu. Flaxerman, in *Novy Mir*, 1968, No. 11, pp. 239–40.)
12. In February 1917, being informed of the Revolution, Zubatov got up from the family dinner table, walked into the next room, and shot and killed himself. (Walter Sablinsky, *The Road to Bloody Sunday*, p. 57.)
13. V. Ya. Laverychev, *Po tu Storonu Barrikad*, p. 24.
14. *Krasny Arkhiv*, 1923, Vol. II, pp. 81–82, Kuropatkin diary; Vitte, *Vospominaniya*, Vol. I, p. 194–98.
15. S. N. Semanov, *Krovavoye Voskresenye*, p. 20.
16. L. Gurevich, in *Byloye*, Jan. 1906, No. 1, pp. 195–97.
17. I. F. Detushev, *Velikiye Nezabyvayemye Dni*, pp. 11–12.
18. Boris Viktorovich Savinkov, in *Byloye*, July 1917, pp. 149–95.
19. Vitte, *Vospominaniya*, Vol. I, pp. 198–99.
20. Plehve was the second successive Minister of Interior to be assassinated by an SR terrorist. His predecessor, Dmitri Sergeyevich Sipyagin, was shot and killed April 2, 1902, as he was about to enter the Mariinsky Palace in St. Petersburg by

a man dressed in an officer's uniform who stopped him to deliver "a packet from the Grand Duke Sergei Alexandrovich in Moscow." The man, who described himself as an anarchist and former student named Stepan Balmashev, then shot Sipyagin. Balmashev, in reality, was a member of the Fighting Organization of the SRs. Sipyagin kept a diary in which he expressed many frank opinions. After Sipyagin's death the diary was turned over to Nicholas to read. He never returned it to Sipyagin's widow. According to Count Sheremetov the Czar personally destroyed it. (Vitte, *Vospominaniya*, pp. 182–83; V. M. Chernov, *Pered Burei*, pp. 164–67.) Count V. N. Kokovtsov, Minister of Finance, had a slightly different version of the Plehve affair. He said the report on Witte was not found in Plehve's portfolio as Witte believed but among the papers on Plehve's desk. It consisted of two unattributed items, excerpted by the censorship from private unnamed correspondents. One said that Witte was in the closest contact with revolutionary circles within Russia and abroad; the other expressed surprise that the Government had not detected so dangerous an enemy within its own ranks. The report was initialed as having been seen by the Czar. (V. N. Kokovstov, *Iz Moego Proshlego*, Vol. I, p. 48.)

21. Imperator Nikolai II, *Dnevnik*, p. 170.

XIII. *The Night Before*   PAGES 108–13

1. S. I. Semanov, *Krovavoye Voskresenye*, pp. 7, 40.
2. Ibid., p. 20.
3. L. Gurevich, in *Byloye*, 1906, No. 1, pp. 203–4.
4. There has been much confusion about the place of this meeting. Maxim Gorky recalled it as being at the newspaper, *Syn Otechestva* (Son of the Fatherland). His memory misled him. (Gorky, *V Epokhu Revolyutsii 1905–1907*, p. 26.)
5. Graf S. Yu. Vitte, *Vospominaniya. Tsartvovaniye Nikolai II*, Vol I, p. 308.
6. V. N. Kokovtsov, *Iz Moego Proshlego*, Vol. I, pp. 52–53.
7. Semanov, *Krovavoye Voskresenye*, pp. 46–47. A remarkable firsthand account of this evening and of the events of January 9 is given in a memoir by D. N. Lyubimov, chief of the chancellory of the Czar's Ministry of Internal Affairs. Lyubimov was present during many of the official deliberations before and after January 9 and saw much of the action on the streets. He wrote his memoirs in emigration and they were brought back to the Soviet by his son, L. D. Lyubimov, who returned to Russia in 1948. Excerpts from the Lyubimov document have been published in Soviet journals. The passages dealing with 1905 appeared in *Voprosy Istorii*, 1965, Nos. 8 and 9, edited and somewhat shortened by A. L. Sidorov. An excellent general analysis of 1905 is provided by Solomon M. Schwartz, *The Russian Revolution of 1905* (Chicago, 1967).
8. V. Nevsky, *Rabocheye Dvizheniye v Ianvarskii Dni 1950 goda*, p. 100.
9. Semanov, citing S. Balk, *Krasnaya Letopis*, 1925, No. 1 (12), p. 39.
10. Gorky, *V Epokhu Revolyutsii*, pp. 28–30.
11. L. Gurevich, in *Byloye*, 1906, No. 1, pp. 195–210.
12. Semanov, *Krovavoye Voskresenye*, p. 72.
13. Imperator Nikolai II, *Dnevnik*, p. 194.
14. Sir Bernard Pares, *The Fall of the Russian Monarchy*, p. 40.
15. Hugh Seaton-Watson, *The Decline of Imperial Russia*, pp. 156–57.
16. Pares, *Russian Monarchy*, p. 84.
17. Warren B. Walsh, *Readings in Russian History*, Vol. III, pp. 535–37.
18. Victor Serge, *Year One of the Revolution*, p. 46.
19. *Krasny Arkhiv*, 1923, Vol. II, pp. vii–ix; M. Turgan-Baranovsky, *Geschichte der Russischen Fabrik*, p. 425, cited in Seaton-Watson, *Imperial Russia*, p. 123.

20. One sign of his liberalism was the release of three surviving Narodovoltsy, including Vera Figner, after twenty years in Shlisselburg prison. (Schwartz, *Russian Revolution*, p. 33.)

21. George Fischer, *Russian Liberalism*, pp. 175-96.

22. E. D. Chermensky, in *Istoriya SSSR*, 1965, No. 5, p. 56.

23. V. Ya. Laverychev, *Po tu Storonu Barrikad*, pp. 26-27.

24. Sidney Harcave, *The Russian Revolution of 1905*, p. 58.

25. George Vassiltchikov, personal conversation.

26. Pavel Milyukov, *Vospominaniya* (*1859-1917*), Vol. I, pp. 270-71.

27. Vitte, *Vospominaniya*, pp. 294-301. The Czar told Witte before issuing his decree December 12, 1904: "I will never in any case agree to a representative form of government because I regard it as harmful to the belief of God's people in me." (Ibid., p. 300. See also Imperator Nikolai II, *Dnevnik*, pp. 186-87.)

28. Imperator Nikolai II, *Dnevnik*, p. 193.

XIV. Bloody Sunday PAGES 117-18

1. L. Gurevich, in *Byloye*, 1906, No. 1, p. 198.

2. The Gapon Society records were seized by the police after January 9 and the exact membership is not known. One estimate places it at 8,000, a very impressive total if accurate. (S. I. Semanov, *Krovavoye Voskresenye*, p. 40.)

3. As is so often the case the actual facts were quickly lost from sight. Only Sergunin had actually been fired—because of injuries he had been unable to meet the demands of his job. Fyodorov was threatened with being fired but the threat was not carried out. Ukolev was requested to sign a declaration that he would not get drunk again. The facts didn't matter; what mattered was that the plant workers *believed* four comrades had been unjustly dismissed. (V. I. Nevsky, *Rabocheye Dvizheniye v Ianvarskii Dni 1905 goda*, p. 67.)

4. I. F. Detushev, *Velikiye Nezabyvayemye Dni*, (quoting D. Ya. Odintsov), pp. 16-17; Nevsky, *Rabocheye Dvizheniye*, pp. 67ff.

5. V. I. Nevsky, in *Krasnaya Letopis*, 1922, No. 1, pp. 13-19.

6. *Krasny Arkhiv*, 1925, Vol. XI, p. 3, V. N. Kokovtsov to Nikolai II, dated Jan. 3, 1905.

7. Nevsky, *Rabocheye Dvizheniye*, p. 75.

8. Ibid., p. 72; Nevsky, in *Krasnaya Letopis*, 1922, No. 1, p. 21.

9. *Proletarskaya Revolyutsiya*, 1925, No. 2, pp. 17-24.

10. "Perepiska N. Lenina i N. K. Krupskoy s M. Litvinovym," *Proletarskaya Revolyutsiya*, 1925, No. 2, p. 78.

11. Gusev to Lenin, dated Jan. 20, 1905, in *Proletarskaya Revolyutsiya*, 1925, No. 2, pp. 17-74.

12. *Proletarskaya Revolyutsiya*, 1925, No. 36, pp. 110-13.

13. *Tretii Syezd RSDRP*, pp. 565-66.

14. Nevsky, *Rabocheye Dvizheniye*, p. 73. This is the evidence of Nevsky in *Byloye*, May 1907. A collection of SD leaflets issued in St. Petersburg in 1905, published by the Leningrad Section of the 1st Parti, the Bolshevik history unit, reprints texts of two leaflets supposedly distributed January 5 and 7, 1905. (Yu. V. Shaurov, *1905 God*, pp. 12-15.)

15. Nevsky, in *Krasnaya Letopis*, 1922, No. 1, p. 24.

16. Nevsky, *Rabocheye Dvizheniye*, p. 82.

17. *Tretii Syezd RSDRP*, p. 547-61.

18. Yelizaveta Drabkina, *Chernye Sukhari*, pp. 26-27.

19. "Perepiska N. Lenina i N. K. Krupskoy s S. I. Gusevym," *Proletarskaya Revolyutsiya*, 1925, No. 2, pp. 17-74.

20. Nevsky, in *Krasnaya Letopis*, 1921, No. 1, p. 29. Contrast Krupskaya's honest concern with a contemporary Soviet history which contends that the Bolshevik influence in Petersburg factories was stronger than any other and that the Bolsheviks had seven circles and 50 members at the Putilov plant compared with one Menshevik circle with 15 members (M. M. Gitelman, B. Glebov, and A. Veyansky, *Istoriya Putilovskogo Zavoda*, p. 466). Actually Gusev estimated his total worker membership January 1, 1905, at 300 to 400, probabably double the real figure (S. I. Gusev, *Leningradskogo Pravda*, No. 13, cited by S. N. Semanov, *Krovavoye Voskresenye*, p. 68). Incidentally, Gusev, one of Lenin's oldest lieutenants, was *posthumously* decreed to be an "enemy of the people" by Stalin in 1936 (Roy A. Medvedev, *Let History Judge*). The Bolshevik activist and historian V. I. Nevsky estimated in 1930 (before history began to be so critically distorted at Stalin's order) that the maximum Bolshevik membership in St. Petersburg could not have exceeded 500 and that between them the Bolsheviks and Mensheviks did not muster more than 1,000 adherents (Nevsky, *Rabocheye Dvizheniye*, p. 84). Julius Martov estimated Menshevik membership as 1,200 to 1,500 and Bolshevik membership at "some hundreds" (Shaurov, *1905 God*, pp. iii–iv). Six months later, in July 1905, a conservative estimate of the Bolshevik membership in St. Petersburg was 1,000 members of whom only 50 were workers of the Narva quarter. In the Putilov plant, in spite of Lenin's frantic urging, there was still no Bolshevik organization. Most Bolsheviks were still not workers but members of the intelligentsia—students, writers, professional people, etc. (A. D. Naglovsky, *Novy Zhurnal*, 1967, No. 88.)

21. Drabkina, *Chernye Sukhari*, p. 27.

22. Gurevich, in *Byloye*, 1906, No. 1, p. 201.

23. Detushev, *Velikiy Nezabyvayemye Dni*, pp. 16–22.

24. Gurevich, in *Byloye*, 1906, No. 1, pp. 203–4.

25. Ibid., p. 206.

26. Semanov, *Krovavoye Voskresenye*, p. 76.

27. Gurevich, in *Byloye*, 1906, No. 1, p. 213.

28. Semanov, *Krovavoye Voskresenye*, p. 85.

29. Nevsky, *Rabocheye Dvizheniye*, p. 109.

30. *Byloye*, 1909, No. 11/12, p. 29.

31. Gurevich, *Byloye*, 1906, No. 1, pp. 210–15.

32. Nevsky, *Rabocheye Dvizheniye*, p. 109. The military report on activity January 9, 1905, stated that forty persons were killed and wounded at the Narva Gates. (*Voprosy Istorii*, 1975, No. 1, p. 112.)

33. Semanov, *Krovavoye Voskresenye*, p. 112.

34. Gurevich, in *Byloye*, 1906, No. 1, p. 216.

35. Semanov, *Krovavoye Voskresenye*, p. 78.

36. *Krasny Arkhiv*, 1925, Vol. XII, p. 466.

37. B. Byalik, *Sudba Maxima Gorkogo*, p. 174.

38. Graf S. Yu. Vitte, *Vospominaniya. Tsartvovaniye Nikolai II*, Vol. I, p. 308.

39. Alexander Kerensky, *Russia and History's Turning Point*, pp. 48–49.

40. V. N. Kokovtsov, *Iz Moego Proshlego*, Vol. 1, pp. 53–54.

41. Semanov, *Krovavoye Voskresenye*, p. 92.

42. Sidney Harcave, *The Russian Revolution of 1905*, p. 92. D. N. Lyubimov reported in his memoirs that the order to fire was given by Capt. N. N. Mansurov. (*Voprosy Istorii*, 1965, No. 9, p. 115.)

43. *Voprosy Istorii*, 1975, No. 1, p. 113.

44. *Short Stories of Saki*, (New York: Modern Library, 1958), pp. 682–84.

45. S. M. Lebidova and E. G. Salita, *Yelena Dmitriyevna Stasova*, p. 126. The

lack of Bolshevik participation in the events of the day is candidly revealed in the report of the Petersburg Committee to the 3rd Congress of the Party in April 1905. The report said: "The mood of the workers after noon was so strong that agitation was perfectly useless. From 10 in the morning to 5 I walked on the Nevsky with our agitators, looking for crowds which needed rousing words. Such crowds we did not find. Words were irrelevant. Coachmen were carrying away bodies. Crowds were following them, crying: 'Down with the Czar' . . . In the evening the mood toward organization sharply changed. Our agitators were listened to with enthusiasm." The author of the report was not identified but may have been Stasova. (*Tretii Syezd RSDRP*, pp. 564–66.)

46. Z. Gippius-Merezhkovskaya, *Dmitrii Merezhkovsky*, p. 131.
47. Gurevich, in *Byloye*, 1906, No. 1, pp. 16–22.
48. Andrei Bely, *Nachalo Veka*, p. 418.
49. Ibid., pp. 416–21.
50. Maxim Gorky, *Epokhu Revolyutsii 1905–1907*, pp. 32–34.
51. Z. Gippius-Merezhkovskaya, *Dmitrii Merezhkovsky*, p. 132.
52. Tamara Karsavina, *Theatre Street*, p. 153.
53. Maxim Gorky, *Sobraniye Sochinenii*, Vol. IV, pp. 249–56; Semanov, *Krovavoye Voskresenye*, pp. 95–96.
54. Dan Levin, *Stormy Petrel*, p. 121.
55. Isidora Duncan, *My Life*, p. 161.
56. Andrei Bely, *Vospominaniya ob Aleksandre Bloke*, p. 170.
57. A. Vanag, in *Krasny Arkhiv*, 1923, Vol. XI, pp. 26–27.

XV. The Czar Sleeps PAGES 129–31

1. *Krasny Arkhiv*, 1928, Vol. XXVI, p. 132, Bobrinsky diary.
2. Ibid., p. 131.
3. Dan Levin, *Stormy Petrel*, p. 109.
4. Morozov had inherited control of an enormously profitable complex of textile, machine-tool, and manufacturing enterprises from his father, Timofei, who had succeeded his own father, Savva, a serf who bought his freedom and that of his family for 17,000 rubles in 1820. The Morozov textile factories alone were throwing off a profit of 2,000,000 rubles a year by the mid-1880s. Morozov contributed 2,000 rubles a month toward publication of *Iskra*, according to Gorky, from an annual income of about 100,000 rubles. According to rumor he put up 10,000 rubles to bail Gorky out of jail following the January 9 incidents. He also gave heavily to the Red Cross, to the support of political exiles, and to various special Social Democratic causes. His mother, Mariya Fyodorovna, became increasingly incensed at Savva's support of revolutionary enterprises and in April 1905 succeeded in ousting him from direction of the family business. He went first to Switzerland, then to Cannes, where he took out a large insurance policy in favor of Gorky's wife to provide more funds for the Bolsheviks. He was in a highly nervous state and had spoken with Gorky of his fear of insanity, which he said ran in the Morozov family. He entered a small sanatorium at Vichy and on May 13, 1905, traced the outline of his heart on his chest with a chemical pencil and put a bullet through it. (Levin, *Stormy Petrel*, p. 117; Valentine Tschebotarieff Bill, *Russian Review*, April 1955, No. 2, p. 109; Maxim Gorky, *V Epokhu Revolyutsii 1905–1907*, pp. 34–35.)
5. Gorky, *V Epokhu Revolyutsii*, pp. 33–34.
6. L. K. Yerman, *Intelligentsiya v Pervoi Russkoi Revolyutsii*, pp. 57–58.
7. Ernest J. Simmons, *Leo Tolstoy*, Vol. II, p. 362.
8. *Byloye*, July 1912, pp. 16–21.

9. *Krasny Arkhiv*, 1925, Vol. XI, pp. 3–6.

10. V. N. Kokovtsov, *Iz Moego Proshlego*, Vol. I, p. 56.

11. Solomon Schwartz, *The Russian Revolution of 1905*, p. 79.

12. A. S. Yermolov, in *Krasny Arkhiv*, 1925, Vol. VIII, p. 59.

13. Schwartz, *Russian Revolution*, p. 81.

14. Kokovtsov, *Iz Moego Proshlego*, Vol. I, p. 57.

15. Graf S. Yu. Vitte, *Vospominaniya. Tsartvovaniye Nikolai II*, Vol. I, p. 313.

16. L. Gurevich, in *Byloye*, Jan. 1906, No. 1, p. 223.

17. Yermolov, in *Krasny Arkhiv*, 1925, Vol. VIII, pp. 50–58.

18. Ibid., pp. 58–59.

19. For example, May 8, 1905, General Trepov passed on to the Czar an eloquent plea for rural reforms drafted by I. Ya. Gofshtetter, who employed the curious argument that the struggle of the intelligentsia was sharpening "the blind hatred" against them on the part of the common people. "By this path," Gofshtetter reasoned, "the internal chaos of Russia leads to bloody revolution, to a blind *Pugachevshchina*, to the annihilation of the cultured classes, to harsh executions by the brutal crowd—in a word, to inescapable death and destruction." Only his program, he warned, could save "the dynasty from destruction, Russia from bloody revolt, the intelligentsia from total annihilation, and the Russian nation from final political dissolution." His logic may not have tracked but his forecast was uncannily accurate. (*Krasny Arkhiv*, 1925, Vol. XII, pp. 452–54.)

20. Grand Duke Alexander, *Once a Grand Duke*, pp. 143, 173.

21. The uncles resembled Nicholas' father, Alexander III, a bull of a man who could bend a horseshoe between his hands.

22. Alexander, *Grand Duke*, p. 178.

23. Vitte, *Vospominaniya*, Vol. I, p. 342.

24. Alexander, *Grand Duke*, pp. 139–40.

25. Roman Goul, *Azef*, p. 149.

26. Imperator Nikolai II, *Dnevnik*, pp. 197–98.

27. Anna Viroubova, *Souvenirs de Ma Vie*, p. 15.

28. Prince Felix Youssoupoff, *Lost Splendor*, p. 118.

29. *Krasny Arkhiv*, 1930, Vol. XLIII, p. 108. Konstantin Romanov diary.

30. Sidney Harcave, *The Russian Revolution of 1905*, pp. 130–131.

31. *Perepiska Vilgelma II s Nikolayem II 1894–1914; Krasny Arkhiv*, 1925, Vol. IX, pp. 64–65.

32. *Krasny Arkhiv*, 1931, Vol. XLIV, pp. 126–32, Konstantin Romanov diary.

XVI. Lenin PAGE 138

1. V. I. Lenin, *Biograficheskaya Khronika*, Vol. 1, p. 546.

2. The Russian colony in Geneva, largely revolutionaries and students, was the largest in Europe. By 1911 it numbered 5,000 to 6,000. (A. P. Yakushina, *Zagranichnye Organizatsii RSDRP 1905–1917*, pp. 3–4.)

3. The canteen was run by Panteleimon Nikolayevich Lepeshinsky and his wife, Olga. Panteleimon had literary pretensions and after the Revolution served in the Commissariat of Education. His wife, known to every Russian émigré in Geneva for her tasty pirogi and her succulent borsch, became one of Stalin's most eminent pseudoscientists. She invented a soda-water bath which was much publicized as a cure for the aging process. Stalin himself was said to have taken her baths with great success. On her eightieth birthday in September 1951 there was a celebration at the Academy of Sciences. She did not die until 1963, surviving Stalin by ten years, possibly because of the soda baths. (Nikolai Valentinov, *Encounters with Lenin*, p. 85.)

4. O. Lepeshinskaya, *Vstrechi c Ilyichem*, p. 42.

5. Ibid., p. 43.

6. N. M. More and R. M. Savitsky, *Vospominaniya Vladimir Ilyich Lenin*, Vol. I, pp. 286–87.

7. Nadezhda Krupskaya, *Reminiscences of Lenin*, p. 519.

8. P. N. Lepeshinsky, *Na Povorote*, pp. 211ff.

9. Nadezhda Krupskaya, *Reminiscences*, pp. 110–11.

10. Bertram Wolfe, *Three Who Made a Revolution*, p. 288.

11. Leon Trotsky, *My Life*, pp. 167–68.

12. P. N. Lepeshinsky, *Na Povorote*, pp. 211ff.

13. Gusev to Lenin, correspondence, Jan. 5 or 6, 1905, *Proletarskaya Revolyutsiya*, 1925, No. 2, pp. 17–74.

14. Gusev, writing Lenin from St. Petersburg January 5 or 6, 1905, reported the first issue of *Vpered* just received. Two weeks later he was writing: "When can we see *Vpered?* Except for the first issue (of which we have a single example) we have seen nothing." (Ibid.)

15. V. I. Lenin, *Collected Works*, Vol. VIII, pp. 21–23.

16. A. V. Lunacharsky, *Revolutionary Silhouettes*, pp. 44–45. In contrast Lunacharsky thought that Trotsky, despite his youth, showed himself "the best prepared" of the revolutionary leaders in the 1905 period (pp. 60–61).

17. Ibid., pp. 45–56.

18. Nadezhda Krupskaya, *Reminiscences*, p. 86.

19. Ibid., p. 95.

20. Ibid., p. 100

21. Ibid., p. 105.

22. Wolfe, *Three Who Made a Revolution*, p. 123.

23. A. Naglovsky, in *Novy Zhurnal*, 1967, No. 88.

24. Lenin, *Biograficheskaya Khronika*, Vol. I, p. 579.

25. Leninski Sbornik, 1926, Vol. V, p. 149.

26. Ibid., p. 151.

27. *Proletarskaya Revolyutsiya*, 1905, No. 2, pp. 17–74.

28. *Vpered i Proletarii*, 1924, No. 1, p. 2.

29. Lenin i Lunacharsky, *Literaturnoye Nasledstvo*, Vol. LXXX, p. 609. Lenin had been very worried at Lunacharsky's failure to arrive in Geneva. Apparently he feared Lunacharsky might fall into the hands of his rival revolutionaries. Finally he went to Paris and rapped on the door of Lunacharsky's room at the Golden Lion Hotel at the crack of dawn, apologizing that his train had arrived so early but adding (as Lunacharsky recollected): "If you think that I've come to you too early, I, on the other hand think that I've come too late because you are just losing time here." (*Lunacharskii-Revolyutsioner-Publitsist*, G. V. Bulatsky and A. A. Plavnik, p. 27; *Lunacharskii Vospominaniya i Vpechatlenniya*, p. 84.)

30. Lunacharsky, *Revolutionary Silhouettes*, pp. 44, 48.

31. Ibid., p. 38.

32. Trotsky, *My Life*, pp. 161–62.

33. Trotsky, *Lenin*, p. 16.

34. Ibid., p 60.

35. Valentinov, *Encounters*, p. 41.

36. Andrei Bely, *Mezhdu Dvukh Revolyutsii*, pp. 256–57.

37. Valentinov, *Encounters*, pp. 54–55.

38. Ibid., p. 122.

39. Ibid., p. 182

40. Ibid.
41. Ibid., pp. 242–43.
42. Trotsky, *Lenin*, p. 127.
43. A. D. Naglovsky, in *Novy Zhurnal*, 1967, No. 88, p. 177.
44. V. I. Lenin, *Collected Works*, Vol. XII, pp. 423–26.
45. W. S. Woytinsky, *Stormy Passage*, pp. 119–20.
46. Date: Lenin, *Biograficheskaya Khronika*, Vol. I, p. 561.
47. Angelica Balabanoff, *Impressions of Lenin*, p. 7.
48. V. V. Starkov, in *Krasnaya Nov*, 1925, No. 8, p. 111.
49. Valentinov, *Encounters*, pp. 122–33.
50. M. A. Silvin, *Proletarskaya Revolyutsiya*, 1924, No. 7, p. 76.
51. Wolfe, *Three Who Made a Revolution*, p. 253, quoting Trotsky in his Report of the Siberian Delegation and Our Political Tasks.
52. P. N. Lepeshinsky, *Vladimir Ilyich v Tyurme i Izgami*, p. 27.
53. Krupskaya, *Reminiscences*, pp. 110–19; Lenin, *Collected Works*, Vol. XVIII, pp. 158–66; Wolfe, *Three Who Made a Revolution*, p. 332.
54. Krupskaya, *Reminiscences*, p. 116.
55. Michael Furtrell, *Northern Underground*, pp. 66–68.
56. Viktor Chernov, *Pered Burei*, pp. 234–35.
57. Pyotr Rutenberg, in *Byloye*, 1909, No. 11/12, p. 119; *Krasny Arkhiv*, 1923, Vol. II, pp. 294–96; Graf S. Yu. Vitte, *Vospominaniya. Tsartvovaniye Nikolai II*, Vol. II, pp. 166–69; Krupskaya, *Reminiscences*, p. 116; Walter Sablinsky, *The Road to Bloody Sunday*, pp. 316–22.

XVII. The Dress Rehearsal PAGES 150–53

1. Anna Viroubova, *Souvenirs de Ma Vie*, p. 18.
2. Ibid., p. 19.
3. Imperator Nikolai II, *Dnevnik*, pp. 215–18.
4. *Lettres de Nicolas II et de Sa Mère*, pp. 54–55.
5. Ibid., Nikolai II to Mariya Fyodorovna, Sept. 29, 1905; Graf S. Yu. Vitte, *Vospominaniya. Tsartvovaniye Nikolai II*, Vol. I, p. 422.
6. Viroubova, *Souvenirs*, pp. 18–19.
7. Sir Bernard Pares, *The Fall of the Russian Monarchy*, p. 127.
8. V. I. Lenin, *Collected Works*, Vol. XXXIV, p. 336.
9. A. D. Naglovsky, in *Novy Zhurnal*, 1967, No. 88.
10. Bertram Wolfe, *Three Who Made a Revolution*, p. 287; Nadezhda Krupskaya, *Reminiscences of Lenin*, pp. 114–15.
11. N. E. Burenin, *Pamyatnye Gody. Vospominaniya*, pp. 78ff.
12. *Leninsky Sbornik*, Vol. V, 1926, pp. 464–66.
13. Ibid., p. 522.
14. V. I. Lenin, *Collected Works*, Vol. XXXIV, pp. 360–61.
15. To a complaint from P. A. Krasnikov, a Petersburg Bolshevik, about this practice Lenin wrote: "'They're printing Trotsky's leaflets.' There's nothing bad about that if the leaflets are reasonable and proof-read. I'm advising the St. Petersburg Committee to print his leaflets after they've been edited, let's say, by you" (*Leninsky Sbornik*, 1926, Vol. V, p. 497).
16. Leon Trotsky, *My Life*, p. 175.
17. Leon Trotsky, *1905*, p. 86; I. F. Detushev, *Velikiye Nezabyvayemye Dni*, pp. 124–28.
18. Sidney Harcave, *The Russian Revolution of 1905*, p. 176.
19. Pares, *The Fall of the Russian Monarchy*, pp. 81–82.

20. Andrei Bely, *Mezhdu Dvukh Revolyutsii*, pp. 36-37.

21. Harcave, *Russian Revolution*, pp. 182-83; Trotsky, *1905*, pp. 86-87.

22. Imperator Nikolai II, *Dnevnik*, p. 221.

23. Trotsky, *1905*, pp. 88-94.

24. Solomon Schwartz, *The Russian Revolution of 1905*, pp. 172ff.

25. Trotsky, *My Life*, p. 178.

26. Trotsky, *1905*, p. 105.

27. S. P. Melgunov, *Nikolai II*, p. 21.

28. Wolfe, *Three Who Made a Revolution*, p. 321.

29. Andrei Bely, *St. Petersburg*, p. 57.

30. *Krasny Arkhiv*, 1925, Vol. XI, p. 40.

31. *Lettres de Nicolas II*, pp. 82-83.

32. W. S. Woytinsky, *Stormy Passage*, pp. 30ff.

33. Witte reported that Count Benkendorf, Marshal of the Court, was concerned that the five royal children and particularly the hemophilic Czarevich Alexei would present a serious complication if the family had to be taken out of Peterhof by sea (Vitte, *Vospominaniya*, Vol. II, p. 31).

34. Alexander Kerensky, *Russia and History's Turning Point*, p. 53.

35. *Krasny Arkhiv*, 1923, Vol. II, pp. 54-56; Vitte, *Vospominaniya*, Vol. II, pp. 7ff.

36. Vitte, *Vospominaniya*, Vol. II, p. 35.

37. Ibid., pp. 33-36; Imperator Nikolai II, *Dnevnik*, pp. 222-23.

38. Grand Duke Alexander, *Once a Grand Duke*, p. 168.

39. Imperator Nikolai II, *Dnevnik*, p. 222.

40. Viroubova, *Souvenirs*, p. 22.

41. *Krasny Arkhiv*, 1923, Vol. IV, p. 86, Polovtsev diary.

42. For months the Czar had been complaining about "meetings." Commenting on a meeting the Moscow Pedagogical Society held March 28, 1905, at which a collection was taken up for "propaganda among workers," he said: "It is necessary to end this kind of mischief." Of a meeting called by the Moscow Duma May 24, 1905, on the question of ending the Russo-Japanese War he commented: "I hope this session won't be permitted. They have gossiped enough." Of another Moscow meeting in early July he noted: "Where are my loyal servants?" (*Krasny Arkhiv*, 1925, Vol. XII, pp. 433-34).

43. *Lettres de Nicolas II*, pp. 75-82.

44. *Krasny Arkhiv*, 1928, Vol. XXVI, p. 199.

XVIII. The First Scene PAGES 160-62

1. Pavel Milyukov, *Vospominaniya* (*1859-1917*), Vol. I, pp. 310-11.

2. It was Professor Ye. V. Tarle, the famous Russian historian. He was wounded by a saber blow, but rumors that he had been killed were widespread. (See Diary of A. A. Polovtsev, Oct. 19, 1905, *Krasny Arkhiv*, Vol. IV, pp. 78-79.)

3. There were all kinds of demonstrations on the St. Petersburg streets that day. V. S. Voitinsky, a Bolshevik of about ten days' standing, encountered monarchists carrying the tricolor flag who were supporting the Czar's Manifesto and who behaved in perfectly friendly manner toward those demonstrating against it. (Woytinsky, *Stormy Passage*, p. 43.) Crowds gathered at the Winter Palace to cheer the Manifesto while students with red flags jeered. (*Krasny Arkhiv*, 1923, Vol. IV, p. 18, Polovtsev diary.)

4. V. Shaurov, *1905 God. Vospominaniya Uchastnika revolyutsii*, pp. 42-47.

5. Leon Trotsky, *1905*, pp. 116-17.

6. Leon Trotsky, *My Life*, p. 179.

7. W. S. Woytinsky, *Stormy Passage*, p. 44. Trotsky recalled that the demonstration was abandoned when word (false) was received that the Czar had granted an amnesty. (Trotsky, *1905*, p. 125.)

8. Now the Moscow City Soviet on Gorky Street.

9. I. F. Detushev, *Velikiye Nezabyvayemye Dni*, pp. 215–16.

10. *Krasny Arkhiv*, 1925, Vol. XII, pp. 442–43; Bolshaya Sovetskaya Entsiklopediya, 1st ed., Vol. V, pp. 79–81.

11. The police estimated the crowd at 100,000 (Sidney Harcave, *The Russian Revolution of 1905*, p. 200).

12. Dan Levin, *Stormy Petrel*, p. 119.

13. Milyukov, *Vospominaniya*, Vol. I, p. 313.

14. Ilya Ehrenburg, *People and Life*, p. 36; P. A. Arsky, in *Velikiye Nezabyvayemye Dni*, pp. 165–70.

15. The building is now the reception office of the Presidium of the Supreme Soviet. Vozdvizhenka Street has been renamed Kalinin Street in honor of Mikhail Kalinin, who was Chairman of the Presidium and long occupied this office.

16. Maxim Gorky, *V Epokhu Revolyutsii 1905–1907*, p. 39.

17. Levin, *Stormy Petrel*, p. 119.

18. *Krasny Arkhiv*, 1924, Vol. VII, pp. 55–69.

19. *Perepiska Vilgelma II s Nikolayem II 1894–1914*, pp. 129–30, dated Jan. 29, 1906.

20. The police were deeply involved in the pogroms. Prince Urusov, Deputy Interior Minister, told the first Duma that he had been informed by a police official, M. S. Komissarov, that he could arrange any kind of a pogrom, "involving 10 people, if you like or 10,000 if you like." The pogroms were usually whipped up by tendentious newspaper articles (sometimes, special newspapers or pamphlets were issued) alleging terrible Jewish atrocities or "blood rituals." Or that the Jews and revolutionaries were planning or had attacked icons and the Czar's portraits. Mobs were assembled from the countryside and city outskirts, a special mass was said in the cathedral, followed by a patriotic procession with flags, bands, and police. An incident was created—and then the mob turned loose. (Trotsky, *1905*, pp. 133–35.) An estimated 4,000 persons were killed and 10,000 wounded in October and November 1905, in pogroms and punitive expeditions. A theater in Tomsk was deliberately set afire by pogromists and 1,000 persons burned to death. (S. P. Melgunov, *Nikolai II*, p. 22.) The Czar's attitude toward the perpetrators of pogroms as reportedly expressed to an Odessa supporter, Konovnitsyn, was that regardless of the "pedantic strictness" of the courts he stood ready on all occasions to commute or pardon offenders convicted by the courts. (Ibid., p. 34.)

21. *Lettres de Nicolas II et de Sa Mère*, pp. 84–86.

22. Ibid., p. 96.

23. Ibid., p. 135.

24. Sir Bernard Pares, *The Fall of the Russian Monarchy*, p. 91.

25. *Krasny Arkhiv*, 1925, Vol. XII, p .439.

26. S. P. Melgunov, *Nikolai II*, p. 23.

XIX. The Last Stages   PAGES 168–69

1. Bertram, Wolfe, *Three Who Made a Revolution*, pp. 317–18.

2. N. E. Burenin, *Pamyatnye Gody*, pp. 83–84.

3. Nadezhda Krupskaya, *Reminiscences of Lenin*, pp. 134–37.

4. Z. Gippius-Merezhkovskaya, *Dmitrii Merezhkovsky*, pp. 141–42.

5. Minsky managed to hang on somehow. He firmly believed he could build a bridge from Marxism to religion. When the debacle came it was he who was arrested while Lenin and his associates escaped into the underground. (Ibid., p. 145.)

6. Leon Trotsky, *1905*, pp. 176–77.

7. Andrei Bely, *Mezhdu Dvukh Revolyutsii*, pp. 77–78. Andrei Bely used Savinkov as the model for the terrorist who played a leading role in his novel *St. Petersburg*.

8. Ibid., pp. 34–35.

9. Trotsky, *1905*, pp. 232–33.

10. Krupskaya, *Reminiscences*, pp. 140–41.

11. Joseph Stalin, speech to Kremlin students, Jan. 28, 1928, in *Vospominaniya o V. I. Lenine*, Vol. II, pp. 128–29.

12. *Lettres de Nicolas II et de Sa Mère*, p. 109. As so often Witte's role seemed equivocal. No one had fought harder than he for the October 17 Manifesto and Constitutional Government yet as he once told Sir Bernard Pares: "I have a Constitution in my head but in my heart . . ." He broke off the sentence and spat on the floor. (Sir Bernard Pares, *The Fall of the Russian Monarchy*, p. 86.)

13. A curious light is cast on the Czar's meetings with the Guards regiments and their commanders by a note in the diary of A. A. Polovtsev, chairman of the Imperial Russian Historical Society. He was informed on excellent authority that the commanders of these regiments warned the Petersburg commandant that sentiment among their troops was so strong that there was danger of a military counterrevolution. Grand Duke Nikolai Nikolayevich (Nikolasha) promised the commanders he himself would lead such a movement if it was necessary but, for the present, ordered them to keep their troops in line. Nikolasha then told Witte about the situation and shortly thereafter the Government's vigorous campaign of arrests and suppression began. (*Krasny Arkhiv*, 1923, Vol. IV, p. 110.)

14. Imperator Nikolai II, *Dnevnik*, pp. 227–30.

15. Trotsky, *1905*, p. 238.

16. Trotsky estimated the active fighting units in Presnya at "about 200, not more," armed with eighty guns and revolvers (ibid., p. 244). He put the total armed revolutionary force in Moscow at about 1,600, including 500 Social Democrats, 250–300 SRs, 500 railroad workers, and 400 printers (ibid., p. 246). A Bolshevik estimate of December 4, 1905, put the revolutionary forces at 900–1,000; that is, 300 Bolsheviks, 300 Srs, 100 Mensheviks, and 300 others (M. Liadou, *Iz Zhizni partii v 1903–1907 godak. Vospominaniya*, pp. 131, 133).

17. Now the Trekhgornaya Manufactura, one of the principal Soviet textile establishments.

18. Lenin had hoped to disrupt operations of the Moscow-Petersburg line but his lieutenants were unable to raise the forces needed. (G. M. Derenkovsky, in *Voprosy Istorii*, 1975, No. 12.)

19. *Lettres de Nicolas II*, p. 106.

20. Yelizaveta Drabkina, *Chernye Sukhari*, pp. 32–34.

21. Trotsky, *1905*, pp. 196, 245.

22. Trotsky estimated casualties at 1,000 killed, 1,000 wounded, and "several hundred" soldiers killed and wounded (Ibid., p. 248).

23. I. F. Detushev, *Velikiye Nezabyvayemye Dni*, pp. 224–36; Bertram Wolfe, *Three Who Made a Revolution*, p. 311.

24. Imperator Nikolai II, *Dnevnik*, p. 228.

25. S. P. Melgunov, *Nikolai II*, p. 30.

26. Krupskaya, *Reminiscences*, p. 143.

27. Schmidt's name was spelled in Russian "Shmit." Lenin consistently transliterated it "Shmidt." (*Leninsky Sbornik*, Vol. XXXVIII, p. 66.)

28. Nikolai Valentinov, *Maloznakomy Lenin*, p. 110.

29. *Leninsky Sbornik*, Vol. XXXVIII, p. 36.

30. Nikolai Burenin was first proposed as the bridegroom for Yelizaveta Schmidt. He was told the "matter is too important to let any sentiment stand in the way." But he managed to wiggle out of the assignment. (N. Ye. Burenin, *Pamyatnye Gody*, pp. 262–63.)

31. Ibid., p. 265.

32. Detushev, *Velikiye Nezabyvayemye Dni*, pp. 301–11. Later endless arguments concerning the sum turned over to the Bolsheviks from the inheritance of Schmidt developed. Martov estimated the sum at 730,000 French francs. Ye. M. Yaroslavsky placed the total at 776,000 gold francs. (Valentinov, *Maloznakomy Lenin*, p. 120.) Valentinov put the sum at 190,000 gold rubles, the equivalent of 510,000 gold francs. The sum of the Schmidt inheritance is given by contemporary Soviet scholars as 251,966.70 rubles, exclusive of personal property. (*Leninsky Sbornik*, Vol. XXXVIII, p. 36.)

33. Leon Trotsky, *My Life*, p. 186.

34. Nadezhda Krupskaya, *Vospominaniya o Lenine*, p. 130

XX. *From the Tower*   PAGES 177–82

1. Sergei Gorodetsky, *Valery Bryusov*, pp. 20–21.

2. Briefly the husband of the greatest contemporary Russian poet, Anna Akhmatova, who died in 1969. Gumilev was shot soon after the Revolution for alleged participation in a rather childish anti-Soviet plot.

3. K. Mochulsky, *Andrei Bely*, p. 277.

4. Andrei Bely, *Nachalo Veka*, pp. 313–28.

5. Andrei Bely, *Vospominaniya ob Aleksandre Bloke*, p. 113.

6. Mochulsky, *Bely*, p. 85.

7. R. V. Ivanov-Razumnik, *Istoriya Russkoi Obshchestevnnoi Mysli*, Vol. II, p. 431.

8. Bely, *Aleksandre Bloke*, p. 88.

9. Andrei Bely, *Mezhdu Dvukh Revolyutsii*, p. 50.

10. Gorodetsky, *Bryusov*, p. 202, citing *Krasnaya Niva*, 1925, No. 41.

11. K. Mochulsky, *Blok*, p. 145.

12. Bely, *Mezhdu Dvukh Revolyutsii*, p. 50.

13. Mochulsky, *Blok*, p. 143.

14. Mochulsky, *Valery Bryusov*, pp. 112–13.

15. Pavel Milyukov, *Vospominaniya* (*1859–1917*), Vol. I, p. 280.

16. Bely, *Nachalo Veka*, p. 460.

17. Ibid., p. 460.

18. Milyukov, *Vospominaniya*, Vol. I, pp. 278–79.

19. Bely, *Nachalo Veka*, p. 460.

20. Ivanov-Razumnik, *Istoriya*, Vol. II, p. 431.

21. Mochulsky, *Bely*, pp. 82–83.

22. Ibid., p. 37.

23. Ibid., p. 40.

24. Ibid., p. 25.

25. Bely, *Aleksandre Bloke*, p. 112.

26. Bely, *Nachalo Veka*, pp. 173, 418.

27. Z. Gippius-Merezhkovskaya, *Dmitrii Merezhkovsky*, pp. 144–45.

28. Bely, *Nachalo Veka*, p. 422.

29. Semyonov had been a devoted monarchist, an idealist. He could believe no evil of the Czar. In this belief he marched with Gapon's followers to the Winter Palace and fell under fire from the troops. The experience so shocked him that for a long time he dreamed of assassinating a member of the Imperial family. (Bely, *Aleksandre Bloke*, p. 171.)

30. Ibid., p. 51.

31. Mochulsky, *Bely*, p. 50.

32. V. F. Khodasevich, *Nekropol*, pp. 7–10.

33. Marc Slonim, *From Chekhov to the Revolution*, p. 8.

34. Mochulsky, *Bryusov*, p. 42.

35. Bely, *Aleksandre Bloke*, p. 153.

36. Alexander Blok, *Sobraniye Sochinenii*, Vol. VII, p. 82.

37. V. F. Khodasevich, *Konetz Renata*, pp. 10–22, 44; Bely, *Nachalo Veka*, pp. 270–87; Mochulsky, *Bryusov*, pp. 54–57.

38. Valery Bryusov, *Iz Moei Zhizni*, p. 82.

39. Ilya Ehrenburg, *People and Life*, Vol. I, p. 41.

40. Mochulsky, *Bryusov*, pp. 17, 21, 22, 155ff.

41. Ehrenburg, *People and Life*, Vol. I, p. 41.

42. S. P. Melgunov, *Nikolai II*, p. 30.

43. Bely, *Aleksandre Bloke*, p. 192.

44. Mochulsky, *Bely*, p. 92.

45. Bely, *Aleksandre Bloke*, pp. 101, 108, 110.

XXI. The Arts Explode   PAGES 187–92

1. *Lettres de Nicolas II et de Sa Mère*, p. 207.

2. He made several trips to Tibet and finally in the 1920s came to New York to found a museum and a cult. Vice-president Henry Wallace was attracted to his circle for a time during the New Deal.

3. K. Mochulsky, *Valery Bryusov*, p. 78.

4. Andrei Bely, *Mezhdu Dvukh Revolyutsii*, p. 226.

5. Ibid.

6. The Shchukin and Morozov collections were exhibited at the Museum of Modern Western Art in Moscow until World War II when the museum was closed, ostensibly as a wartime measure but actually because of Stalin's hatred for modern art. The works were placed in the reserve collections of the Pushkin Museum in Moscow and the Hermitage in Leningrad and barred from public exhibition. Only after 1959 were the collections finally taken out of the vaults and placed on exhibition in the Hermitage and Pushkin galleries.

7. Ryabushinsky's remarkable collection, including many fine early Rouaults and early Kuznetsovs, Saryans, Larionovs, and Goncharovas, was destroyed by fire in 1911. For *Zolotoye Runo* he commissioned paintings of Balmont by V. A. Serov, Bely by L. S. Bakst, Ivanov by K. A. Sumov, and Bryusov by Vrubel. At that time Vrubel was living in a psychiatric hospital in Petrovsky Park and Bryusov was terrified at his appearance. Vrubel's face and eyes reminded him of a shark. (Mochulsky, *Bryusov*, p. 125; Sergei Gorodetsky, *Valery Bryusov*.)

8. Much of this detail is drawn from Camilla Gray's classic *The Russian Experiment in Art 1863–1922* (London, 1962), which is a unique study of this fascinating era. Mrs. Gray tragically died in 1971 at the untimely age of thirty-five.

9. Ernest J. Simmons, *Leo Tolstoy*, pp. 414–15.

10. Andreyev's story was based on the execution of a group of young people, be-

trayed by the police spy, Azef, as they were preparing an attempt on Minister of Justice I. G. Shcheglovitov. They were executed in the fortress at Lisy Nos, outside St. Petersburg, February 17, 1908. (Leonid Andreyev, *Povesti i Rasskazy*, Vol. II, p. 415.)

11. S. P. Melgunov, *Nikolai II*, p. 29.

12. *Lettres de Nicolas*, p. 194, dated Oct. 11, 1906, from the Czar to his mother.

13. Melgunov, *Nikolai II*, p. 19.

14. B. Savinkov, in *Byloye*, July 1917, p. 158.

15. *Krasny Arkhiv*, 1924, Vol. V, p. 102, correspondence between N. A. Romanov and P. A. Stolypin.

16. *Lettres de Nicolas II*, p. 169, dated Aug. 16, 1906.

17. Ibid., p. 274, dated Aug. 30, 1906.

18. Melgunov, *Nikolai II*, p. 25.

19. *Krasny Arkhiv*, 1924, Vol. IV, p. 120.

20. Imperator Nikolai II, *Dnevnik*, p. 246. Actually this was the undress uniform of the infantry battalion of the Imperial family. The Czar enjoyed wearing the uniform especially when drinking with battalion members. (Melgunov, *Nikolai II*, p. 80.)

21. Valery Bryusov, *Kon Bled*, pp. 283–84.

XXII. "What a Bad Joke Is Man!"   PAGES 195–99

1. Warren B. Walsh, *Readings in Russian History*, Vol. III, pp. 536–37.

2. Alexander Blok, *Sochineniya*, Vol I, p. 398.

3. *Krasny Arkhiv*, 1929, Vol. XXXIV, p. 96.

4. Andrei Bely, *Mezhdu Dvukh Revolyutsii*, pp. 197–98; Andrei Bely, *Nachalo Veka*, p. 374.

5. Bely, *Nachalo Veka*, p. 374.

6. V. V. Rozanov was ultimately expelled from Merezhkovsky's Religious-Philosophical Society because of his viciously anti-Semitic writings in the black reactionary weekly *Zemshchina* at the time of the notorious Beilis affair. Beilis was a Jew falsely accused in a typical police conspiracy of ritual murder. Rozanov *defended* Beilis from the "Jewish" standpoint, insisting on the right of Jews to conduct blood rituals! (Z. Gippius-Merezhkovskaya, *Dmitrii Merezhkovsky*, pp. 207ff.) Rozanov wrote for the reactionary *Novoye Vremya* at the same time as he wrote liberal articles for *Russkoye Slovo*. He once said: "My works are blended with neither water nor blood but semen." (Marc Slonim, *Modern Russian Literature from Chekhov to the Present*, p. 110.)

7. Bely, *Mezhdu Dvukh Revolyutsii*, pp. 196–97.

8. Ibid., pp. 197–98.

9. K. Mochulsky, *Andrei Bely*, p. 170. This image Bely incorporated in his famous mystical symbolist novel, *Petersburg*, written in 1913.

10. Z. Gippius-Merezhkovskaya, *Dmitrii Merezhkovsky*, p. 208.

11. Ibid.

12. Mochulsky, *Bely*, p. 110.

13. Now the restaurant of the Hotel Sovetskaya which has been built around it. For a long time it was Moscow's Aero Club. The decor today is almost exactly what it was before World War I.

14. Grand Duke Alexander, *Once a Grand Duke*, p. 254.

15. Ibid., p. 256.

16. On November 11, 1910, three days after Tolstoy's death, Nicholas wrote

his mother: "As you've heard Tolstoy has died and about that death much has been said and written—too much. Happily he was buried very quickly so that comparatively few people were able to get to Yasnaya Polyana and everything there was all right and quiet. But everyone expected demonstrations and disorder and now they are surprised that it did not happen." (*Krasny Arkhiv*, 1932, Vol. L–LI, p. 193.)

17. Ibid., 1926, Vol. XXVI, pp. 137–44, Bobrinsky diary.

18. After the February Revolution Kshesinskaya's palace was requisitioned by the Bolshevik party for its headquarters.

19. *Krasny Arkhiv*, 1926, Vol. XXVI, pp. 142–43, Bobrinsky diary. In her memoirs Madame Kshesinskaya makes no mention of these rumors. But she does deny that before and after the February Revolution she received bribes for artillery orders. These rumors were so widespread that they reached the ears of the Czarina, who noted in her diary June 24, 1915: "Kshesinskaya is mixed up again—she behaved like Mme. Sukhomlinova it seems with bribes and the artillery orders—one hears it from many sides." And on January 9, 1916: "There are very unclear, unclean stories about her and bribes, etc., which all speak about and the artillery is mixed up into it." (Mathilde Kschessinska, *Dancing in Petersburg*, p. 97.)

20. V. S. Akatov, *O Positivnykh Osnovakh Noveishego Spiritualizma*.

21. Andrei Bely, *Vospominaniya ob Aleksandre Bloke*, pp. 105–6.

22. Mochulsky, *Bely*, pp. 121, 135–37.

23. Bely, *Mezhdu Dvukh Revolyutsii*, pp. 355–62.

24. Mochulsky, *Bely*, pp. 165–66.

25. Bely, *Mezhdu Dvukh Revolyutsii*, p. 354.

XXIII. The Starets PAGES 203–6

1. A. Taneyeva (Vyrubova), *Stranitsi iz Moei Zhizni*, pp. 80–81.

2. V. I. Gurko, *Tsar i Tsaritsa*, pp. 52–53.

3. Fyodor Dostoyevsky, *Sobraniye Sochinenii*, Vol. IX, p. 38.

4. Sir Bernard Pares, *The Fall of the Russian Monarchy*, p. 131.

5. *Padeniye Tsarkogo Rezhima*, Vol. VIII, p. 403.

6. *Krasny Arkhiv*, 1923, Vol. III, Polovtsev diary, dated Sept. 1, 1902.

7. Anna Viroubova, *Souvenirs de Ma Vie*, p.106. Philippe Nizier-Vachot, son of a butcher, was born April 25, 1849, at Leisieux in Savoy and died at Arbesle after a short illness August 2, 1905, only a year or so after he had been expelled from Russia. French records disclosed that he had been convicted three times for illegal practice of medicine. He was introduced to the Czar and Czarina September 20, 1901, during their visit to France, the intermediary being the Grand Duchesses Militsa and Anastasia. Rumors circulated at the Russian court that the Empress suffered not a false pregnancy but a miscarriage in September 1902. (Maurice Paléologue, *An Ambassador's Memoirs*, Vol. I, pp. 203–10.) When Philippe was sent back to France, the Czar wrote the French President, Émile Loubet, recommending Philippe for a scientific post. (S. P. Melgunov, *Nikolai II*, p. 61; Grand Duke Alexander, *Once a Grand Duke*, pp. 181–82.)

8. V. P. Semennikov, *Za Kulisami Tsarizma*, pp. iv–v.

9. Charges of adherence to the *khlysti* were brought against Rasputin by the Tobolsk consistory at the order of Bishop Anthony but the case was never brought to trial because Rasputin simply vanished for a while. (Pares, *Russian Monarchy*, p. 134.) A detailed report on the matter was made to Nicholas II by Rodzyanko (at the Czar's request) in 1912. The Czar, however, suppressed the report, possibly without reading it. (V. N. Kokovtsov, *Iz Moego Proshlego*, Vol. II, pp. 48–49.)

See also Semennikov, *Za Kulisami Tsarizma*, pp. lv–lvii.) These investigations as well as those of A. I. Guchkov did not support the theory that Rasputin was a formal adherent of the *khlysti* sect. Nor did a similar inquiry by Bonch-Bruyevich, who had several long conversations with Rasputin through the intermediary of Baroness V. I. Uexküll. (Gurko, *Tsar i Tsaritsa*, pp. 103–5.)

10. Pares, *Russian Monarchy*, p. 130.

11. Aron Simanovich, *Rasputin i Yevrei*, pp. 22–26.

12. Ibid., pp. 12–14.

13. Pares, *Russian Monarchy*, p. 136.

14. Imperator Nikolai II, *Dnevnik*, p. 229.

15. Ibid., p. 224.

16. Ibid., p. 247.

17. Semennikov, *Za Kulisami Tsarizma*, p. 141.

18. Simanovich, *Rasputin*, p. 9.

19. Z. Gippius-Merezhkovskaya, *Dmitrii Merezhkovsky*, pp. 199–203.

20. Kokovtsov, *Iz Moego Proshlego*, Vol. II, p. 38.

21. Some idea of Badmayev's nostrums can be gathered from a letter he sent to Tsarskoye Selo October 6, 1912, on hearing of a new illness of the Czarevich. He sent three envelopes containing various powders. One was called *dabsen-tan*, to be given every four hours in bouillon, porridge, or milk; a second was a stomatic to be taken one hour after eating; and the third was *gabyr-nirnga*, which was to reduce temperature. (Semennikov, *Za Kulisami Tsarizma*, p. 17.) *Dabsen-tan* appears to be a Mongol phrase which describes a decoction containing various kinds of salt. *Gabyr-nirnga* is a Tibetan phrase describing a compound consisting of camphor and twenty-five other ingredients. (Personal communication, Prof. John C. Hangin, Department of Uralic and Altaic Studies, Indiana University.)

22. Byusher Iliodor, in *Golos Minyushego*, 1917, No. 3, pp. 7, 25–26.

23. Kokovtsov, *Iz Moego Proshlego*, Vol. II, p. 42.

24. Iliodor, in *Golos Minyushego*, 1917, No. 3, p. 31.

25. Semennikov, *Za Kulisami Tsarizma*, p. 10.

26. Kokovtsov, *Iz Moego Proshlego*, Vol. II, pp. 20, 44; Semennikov, *Za Kulisami Tsarizma*, p. vi.

27. Kokovtsev, *Iz Moego Proshlego*, Vol. II, p. 20.

28. Ibid., p. 342.

29. Gilliard, *Thirteen Years*, pp. 141–43.

30. Gurko, *Tsar i Tsaritsa*, p. 90.

31. Konstantin Paustovsky, *The Story of a Life*, pp. 215–16.

32. *Krasny Arkhiv*, 1929, Vol. XXXV, Nicholas to Mariya Fyodorovna, pp. 209–10; Pares, *Russian Monarchy*, p. 125.

33. Kokovtsov, *Iz Moego Proshlego*, Vol. I, pp. 474–88. According to another version the Czar arrived at the hospital late at night after Stolypin had lost consciousness. Nicholas wrote his mother that Stolypin's wife had "not permitted" him to see her husband. There is preserved in the archives an unpublished letter in which Madame Stolypin expresses her deep dedication to the Czar. (L. Bazylev, in *Voprosy Istorii*, 1975, No. 7, p. 122.)

34. Ibid., pp. 120–22.

35. A recent Soviet re-examination of the Stolypin affair fails to come to any firm conclusion in what it calls the "Riddle of Sept. 1, 1911." The study is notable in that it draws almost entirely on prerevolutionary inquiries and studies published abroad largely by White Russian sources. There is virtually no material from Russian archives which may mean that the police purged their files of incriminating materials long before the Revolution. (L. Bazylev, ibid., pp. 115ff.) There is

is some evidence that the police tried to persuade Bogrov to declare that he had really intended to kill the Czar, not Stolypin. Kokovtsev told the examining commissioner for the Provisional Government's Extraordinary Investigating Commission in 1917 that he was warned at 2 A.M. September 2 by General Trepov that a pogrom was expected in the streets of Kiev that morning and that he did not have security forces to prevent it. Kokovtsov took responsibility for diverting two regiments of troops from maneuvers to handle the emergency. (B. Yu. Maisky, in *Voprosy Istorii,* 1966, Nos. 1 and 2.)

36. *Perepiska Nikolaya i Aleksandry Romanovykh* (1914–15), foreword by M. N. Pokrovsky, Vol. III, p. vi.
37. Prince Felix Youssoupoff, *Lost Splendor,* p. 146.
38. *Dnevnik B. Velikogo Knyazya Andreya Vladimirovicha,* p. 64.
39. *Padeniye Tsarskago Rezhima,* Vol. III, pp. 39–45.
40. Ibid., pp. 230–32.
41. Paustovsky, *Story of a Life,* p. 217.
42. *Padeniye Tsarskogo Rezhima,* Vol. VI, p. 53.
43. V. V. Shulgin, *Dni,* pp. 105–7.
44. Kokovtsov, *Iz Moego Proshlego,* Vol. I, pp. 493–94.
45. Ibid., p. 498.
46. Ibid., Vol. II, p. 20.
47. Semennikov, *Za Kulisami Tsarizma,* Vol. VII, pp. 138–39.
48. Kokovtsov, *Iz Moego Proshlego,* Vol. II, pp. 27–35.
49. *Padeniye Tsarkogo Rezhima,* Vol. VI, pp. 252–55.

XXIV. On the Brink PAGES 216–21

1. Maurice Paléologue, *An Ambassador's Memoirs,* Vol. I, p. 260.
2. Andrei Bely, *Mezhdu Dvukh Revolyutsii,* p. 160.
3. Z. Gippius-Merezhkovskaya, *Dmitrii Merezhkovsky,* pp. 155–56.
4. Ilya Ehrenburg, *People and Life,* p. 101.
5. S. L. Grigoriev, *The Diaghilev Ballet 1909–1929,* pp. 30–37.
6. Ehrenburg, *People and Life,* p. 147.
7. Ibid., p. 127.
8. Bely, *Mezhdu Dvukh Revolyutsii,* p. 161.
9. Ehrenburg, *People and Life,* p. 146.
10. Gippius-Merezhkovskaya, *Merezhkovsky,* p. 169.
11. V. Ropshin, *Kon Bledny.*
12. Gippius-Merezhkovskaya, *Merezhkovsky,* p. 194.
13. Ibid., p. 185.
14. Bely, *Mezhdu Dvukh Revolyutsii,* p. 188.
15. Nadezhda Krupskaya, *Reminiscences of Lenin,* p. 176.
16. V. I. Lenin, *Collected Works,* Vol. XXXVII, p. 373.
17. Krupskaya, *Reminiscences,* p. 179.
18. Ibid., pp. 172–82.
19. Ibid., p. 183.
20. Ibid., p. 190.
21. Ibid., pp. 215–26.
22. Ibid., p. 216.
23. David Shub, *Lenin,* p. 61.
24. Stefan T. Possony, *Lenin: The Compulsive Revolutionary,* p. 102.
25. Kamo, a rather simple-minded but cunning and daring adventurer, fought for the Bolsheviks in the Civil War. He died at 3 A.M. July 15, 1922, in Tiflis, a few hours after being hit by an automobile as he was cycling home. (I. Dubinsky-

Mukhadze, *Kamo,* p. 219.) There have been suspicions that this was suicide. (Possony, *Lenin.*) Very little was published about Kamo after his death and it is only in recent years that a series of biographies including one by Lev Shaumyan have appeared. Each emphasizes Kamo's closeness to Lenin, Maxim Litvinov, Sergo Ordzhonikidze, and other enemies of Stalin. (Lev Stepanovich Shaumyan, *Kamo.*)

26. Krupskaya, *Reminiscences,* p. 206.
27. Shub, *Lenin,* p. 62. Trotsky opposed the expropriations and this, he said, led to the "sharpest conflict with Lenin in my whole life." See Leon Trotsky, *My Life,* p. 222.
28. Possony, *Lenin,* pp. 114-16.
29. Louis Fischer, *The Life of Lenin,* pp. 71-72.
30. Possony, *Lenin,* p. 117.
31. Lenin obligated himself to turn over to the trustees 75,000 francs immediately and 400,000 francs more in installments over a two-year period. The agreement broke down before the transfers were complete. Lenin is believed to have turned over not less than 100,000 francs but, in any case, not more than 200,000. (Nikolai Valentinov, *Maloznakomy Lenin,* p. 125.) Some of the funds deposited in German banks by the trustees were apparently frozen by the German Government after the outbreak of World War I. Lenin wrote letter after letter to Clara Zetkin trying to get the funds released and even began a study of civil law in preparation for going to court to force her to turn over the inheritance. (*Voprosy Istorii KPSS,* 1975, No. 4, p. 8.)

Twenty-two letters of Lenin's, mostly dealing with maneuvers to get the Schmidt money back, were retained in Swiss national archives and in 1967 were published in Switzerland. This action stimulated the Moscow keepers of Lenin's archive. In 1975 in Volume XXXVIII of *Leninsky Sbornik* they suddenly "discovered" forty-four Lenin letters hitherto unpublished and presented them along with the twenty-two Swiss letters, providing a comprehensive view of the row over the Schmidt inheritance. It is still not possible to determine exactly how much money the Bolsheviks got from the legacy. However, 275,966.70 rubles represented Schmidt's principal capital. This was divided equally between his two sisters Yekaterina and Yelizaveta (who engaged in the marriage of convenience with Ignatyev at Lenin's order). Yelizaveta turned over her half share of 128,983 rubles plus 34,558.65 francs, representing proceeds of a sale of Schmidt's real property to the Bolsheviks. Yekaterina's share was subject to a separate wrangle. Her husband, N. A. Andrikanis, opposed giving the money to the Bolsheviks. A Party arbitration court was set up in 1907-8 and under its ruling of June 7, 1908, is said to have conveyed 85,000 rubles of her inheritance to the Bolsheviks, retaining 43,983 to compensate her for various expenses including court costs and pensions for Schmidt factory workers. These financial details, still not published in any basic Lenin historical documents, are drawn from Yekaterina Schmidt's personal archive quoted in a new biography of Nikolai Schmidt published by Yekaterina's son, Yevgeny Nikolayevich Andrikanis. (Yevgeny Andrikanis, *Khozyain "Chertova Gnezda,"* pp. 229-31.) As late as 1910 Lenin was complaining that only part of the money had been paid. Lenin's stubborn and tortured fight over the Schmidt money, now revealed in all its unloveliness by the forced publication of long-suppressed documents, is one of the less savory episodes of his career. (*Leninsky Sbornik,* Vol. XXXVIII, pp. 36-170.) In the end Lenin enlisted a Paris lawyer, Georges Ducos de la Haille, with the idea of bringing a civil action to recover the money from the German trustees. He was still vainly pursuing this cause in the months before the outbreak of World War I, finally winding up in a row with

Ducos over legal fees. Inessa Armand translated some of his letters into French. (*Leninsky Sbornik*, Vol. XXXVIII, pp. 36–170; V. Sedych, "Three Meetings," *Znamya*, 1977, No. 4, pp. 163–65.)

32. Shub, *Lenin*, p. 64.

33. Ibid. When Taratuta was brought before a Party investigating commission on charges of "political unreliability and inadmissible conduct," Lenin strongly defended him. A. Bogdanov called Taratuta a "dishonorable man." Ignatyev (who married Yelizaveta Schmidt) and N. A. Natanson, who became a leading SR, supported the charges of misconduct by Taratuta. (*Leninsky Sbornik*, Vol. XXXVIII, pp. 35–36.)

34. Angelica Balabanoff, *Impressions of Lenin*, pp. 28–29.

35. W. S. Woytinsky, *Stormy Passage*, pp. 121–22.

36. Valentinov, *Maloznakomy Lenin*, p. 190.

37. Lenin, *Collected Works*, Vol. XXXVII, p. 396.

38. Krupskaya, *Reminiscences*, p. 191.

39. Israel Getzler, *Martov*, p. 119.

40. Ehrenburg, *People and Life*, p. 67.

41. Lenin, *Collected Works*, Vol. XXXVII, p. 402; Krupskaya, *Reminiscences*, p. 192.

42. Valentinov calculated Lenin's income in these years as being in excess of 4,000 francs, his income from Party sources being 300–500 francs a month, and the remainder coming from the "Ulyanov family fund." (*Maloznakomy Lenin*, pp. 127–30.) Certainly Lidiya Alexandrovna Fotiyeva, Lenin's faithful secretary, is mistaken in her assertion that Lenin and all of the Ulyanov family earned their living by literary work and that only in extreme cases did they draw any Party funds. This merely reflects the Party propaganda line, continued over many years, which attempts to present Lenin's finances as considerably more modest than they actually were. (L. A. Fotiyeva, *V. I. Lenin-Rukovoditel i tovarishch*, p. 78.)

43. Krupskaya, *Reminiscences*, p. 193.

44. Anatoly V. Lunacharsky, *Revolutionary Silhouettes*, p. 48.

45. Letter from Lenin to Anna Ulyanova, dated July 1, 1908, in Lenin, *Collected Works*, Vol. XXXIV, p. 395.

46. Ibid., Vol. XXXVII, p. 431.

47. Krupskaya, *Reminiscences*, p. 208.

48. Lenin, *Collected Works*, Vol. XXXIV, p. 421.

49. Bertram Wolfe, *Three Who Made a Revolution*, p. 558.

50. Anna Yelizarova-Ulyanova, in *Proletarskaya Revolyutsiya*, No. 4, pp. 128–29. Krupskaya recalled this remark as: "I do not know whether I'll live to see the next rise of the tide" (*Reminiscences*, p. 233). David Shub quotes Lenin as saying to Anna: "I do not know whether I will live to see a revival of the Party" (*Lenin*, p. 69).

51. Lenin, *Collected Works*, Vol. XXXIV, p. 411.

52. Letters of Mariya Ulyanova, dated Aug. 31, 1910 and Sept. 3, 1910, in *Istorichesky Arkhiv*, 1958, No. 1, pp. 14–15.

53. Letter from Lenin to Gorky, dated Nov. 22, 1910, in Lenin, *Collected Works*, Vol. XXXIV, p. 435.

54. Letter from Lenin to Gorky, dated Jan. 2, 1911, ibid., p. 437.

XXV. Three Hundred Years PAGES 226–27

1. Nadezhda Krupskaya, *Reminiscences of Lenin*, pp. 204–5.

2. V. I. Lenin, *Collected Works*, Vol. XVII, p. 305.

3. S. I. Gopner, who was there, mistakenly says Lenin spoke in French. See V. I. Lenin, *Vospominaniya*, Vol. II, p. 297.

4. Yelena Stasova gives the date of the meeting as 1909 but this is almost certainly mistaken. (See Yelena Stasova, *Pravda*, Jan. 5, 1964.)

5. Pavel Podlyashuk, *Tovarishch Inessa*, 2d rev. ed., pp. 7–83.

6. Ibid., p. 86.

7. Bertram Wolfe, in *Encounter*, Feb., 1964, p. 90.

8. *Bolshevik*, 1939, No. 13.

9. From 1890 onward Lenin only addressed two other persons outside his family with the "ty" form. These were Martov and Krzhizhnovsky and in both cases he used the familiar form only for a short time. (Nikolai Valentinov, *Maloznakomy Lenin*, p. 189.)

10. Podlyashuk, *Tovarishch Inessa*, 2d rev. ed. See also I. F. Armand, *Stati, Rechi, Pisma*. The first substantial collection of Inessa's letters to be published (not including any to Lenin) appeared in the magazine *Novy Mir*, No. 6, 1970. Twenty-eight letters were published, including sixteen to her husband, A. E. Armand, and nine to her lover, V. E. Armand. There was one letter to her children and two to political associates. The letters were edited by Inessa's oldest daughter, Inna, and were severely pruned, obviously to omit personal and emotional references. The 1975 edition of Armand's articles, speeches, and letters includes forty-seven letters. It omits two early letters to her husband included in the *Novy Mir* collection and includes fourteen previously unpublished letters, including eleven to her daughter Inna. It includes four letters to Krupskaya, three of which had been published in 1955, and five other letters dealing with Party matters which had appeared over the years in various publications. The book collection eliminates personal material even more severely than the *Novy Mir* collection but does present, apparently in full, an eloquent letter to her daughter Inna on the subject of love, marriage, women's liberation, and sex, designed as an answer to Tolstoy's ideas presented in the *Kreutzer Sonata*.

11. V. L. Vilshai, in *Voprosy Istorii KPSS*, 1976, No. 11.

12. V. I. Lenin, *Biograficheskaya Khronika*, Vol. III, pp. 569–610.

13. Lenin, *Collected Works*, Vol. XXXV, pp. 180–85.

14. Ibid., Vol. XXXVII, pp. 610–13. Trotsky regarded Lenin as chaste and pure where women were concerned. "Passion was the basis of his nature," Trotsky wrote, "but it was supplemented by—I find it difficult to think of another word— chastity. The natural merger of these two elements, passion and chastity, precludes any idea of immorality or impropriety. Vladimir had no need of any moral shackles in order to rise above others; his inborn revulsion from vulgarity and triviality sufficed." (Leon Trotsky, *The Young Lenin*, p. 202.) Since Trotsky certainly was acquainted with the facts of the relationship of Lenin and Inessa, his view suggests he believed it was intellectual and emotional but not sexual.

15. Krupskaya, *Reminiscences*, p. 194.

16. Lenin, *Collected Works*, Vol. XXXVII, p. 447.

17. Letter from Lenin to his sister, Anna, dated Mar. 24, 1912, in *Collected Works*, Vol. XXXVII, p. 474.

18. Nadezhda Krupskaya, *Vospominaniya o Lenine*, p. 173.

19. Mathilde Kschessinska, *Dancing in St. Petersburg*, p. 143.

20. Sir Bernard Pares, *My Russian Memoirs*, p. 262. Since 1905 the Czar's public appearances had been held to a minimum by security precautions, so much so that he complained he was a "prisoner of Tsarskoye Selo." The first and only occasion on which Nicholas is known to have appeared informally in public occurred one

day in the autumn of 1894 when he went, unaccompanied, for a stroll one afternoon after 3:00 along the Nevsky Prospekt. He had passed the Milyutin Row, a block of shops, when the St. Petersburg prefect, General Von Val, came past in his carriage en route to the Winter Palace. General Von Val halted his carriage, rushed up to Nicholas, and said: "This is not possible, Your Highness." Nicholas protested but Von Val insisted. "It is not possible, Your Highness," he repeated. "I pray you to return to your palace." A crowd collected, recognized the Czar, and shouted "Hurrah!" But Nicholas sadly permitted himself to be escorted back to the Anichkov Palace where he was reprimanded by his mother, the Dowager Empress. (U. Gardenin, *Ubilie Nikolakaya Postlednyavo*, SR Pamphlet, 1905, pp. 7–8.)

21. Peter Yershov, *Letters of Gorky and Andreev*, p. 109; letter dated Aug. 12, 1911.

22. V. N. Kokovtsov, *Iz Moego Proshlego*, Vol. II, pp. 150–62.

23. *Perepiska Vilgelma II c Nikolayem II 1894–1914*, pp. 146–65.

24. *Niva*, 1913, No. 23, pp. 417–59; *Niva*, 1913, No. 25, p. 494.

XXVI. Last Warnings PAGES 235–41

1. Mathilde Kschessinska, *Dancing in Petersburg*, p. 146.

2. The Countess' salon was famous. It was frequented by all the leading St. Petersburg political and diplomatic personages, particularly the French ambassador, Maurice Paléologue. In his early Petersburg days Rasputin was made much of by the Countess and her good friend, the Countess Ignatyeva. (Aron Simanovich, *Rasputin i Yevrei*, p. 101.)

3. Grafinya M. Kleinmikhel, *Iz Potonuvshego Mira*, pp. 191–95; Nicholas de Basily, *Memoirs*, pp. 26–27.

4. Princess Lidiya Vassiltchikova, "Reminiscences of a Russian Refugee." Unpublished manuscript.

5. *Niva*, 1914, No. 1, pp. 19–20.

6. *The Times* (London), Feb. 20, 1914.

7. V. N. Kokovtsov, *Iz Moego Proshlego*, Vol. II, p. 355. Alexander Izvolsky, Russian ambassador to Paris and later Foreign Minister, called Kokovtsov capable of prestigious work and distinguished by a universally recognized probity. (*Mémoires de Alexandre Iswolsky*, p. 129.)

8. Kokovtsov, *Iz Moego Proshlego*, Vol. II, pp. 387–89.

9. V. N., Voyeikov, *S Tsarem i Bez Tsarya*, pp. 37–47.

10. *Byloye*, 1922, No. 19, pp. 101–76.

11. Serge Sazonov, *Fateful Years 1909–1916*, pp. 126–27.

XXVII. Impotence Before Fate PAGES 242–43

1. V. T. Loginov, *Lenin i Pravda 1912–1914*, pp. 32–35.

2. V. I. Lenin, *Collected Works*, Vol. XXXVII, p. 478.

3. Ya. S. Ganetsky, "With Lenin," *Voprosy Istorii KPSS*, 1970, No. 3, pp. 96–101, written in 1927, previously unpublished. Ralph Carter Elwood has presented an excellent exposé of the myth of Lenin's role in establishing *Pravda* in the *Slavic Review*, June 1972, pp. 355–80. A detailed account of the establishment of the paper by M. Olminsky emphasizes that it was founded as a "workers' paper" in response to working class interest in St. Petersburg and that its principal backers were the eight Bolshevik members of the Duma. Lenin's name is hardly mentioned but there is a cryptic sentence saying: "The closest foreign friends of *Pravda* were occupied in May and June with other affairs and in

the first two months sent few articles." (M. Olminsky, *Iz Epokhi Zvezdy i Pravdy*, pp. 40–45.)

4. Letter from Lenin to his mother, dated July 1, 1912, in Lenin, *Collected Works*, Vol. XXXVII, p. 479.

5. Ibid., pp. 482, 519.

6. Ibid., p. 502 letter dated July 26, 1913.

7. Ibid., p. 509 letter from Nadezhda and Lenin to Lenin's mother.

8. Ibid., p. 507 letter dated Dec. 16, 1913.

9. M. V. Rodzyanko, in *Padeniye Tsarkogo Rezhima*, Vol. VII, p. 168. Rodzyanko seems to have known some time previously of Malinovsky's connection with the Okhrana or so N. S. Chkheidze testified before the Provisional Government's inquiry into the fall of the Czarist regime. (*Padeniye Tsarskogo Rezhima*, Vol. III, pp. 500–1.) See also B. F. Livchak, in *Voprosy Istorii*, 1977, No. 2.)

10. A. E. Badayev, *Bolsheviki v Gosudarstvennoi Dume*, pp. 273–89.

11. Nadezhda Krupskaya, *Reminiscences of Lenin*, pp. 275–76.

12. Nevertheless, Krupskaya, careful as always, wrote to the Moscow Party Bureau May 14 that Malinovsky's conduct was so "odd" that it opened the door to any kind of surmise. She ordered the bureau to "change all the addresses which might be known to Malinovsky." (*Istoricheskii Arkhiv*, 1959, No. 1, p. 21.)

13. V. F. Dzhunkovsky, in *Padeniye Tsarskogo Rezhima*, Vol. V, pp. 69ff.

14. Krupskaya, *Reminiscences*, p. 276.

15. Louis Fischer, *Life of Lenin*, p. 83.

16. Badayev, *Bolsheviki*, pp. 228–29. Lenin did not appear before the full Extraordinary Commission. He gave his testimony to an examiner, N. A. Kolokolov, and thus his statement does not appear in the commission's report. A substantial extract from Lenin's statement was published by Badayev. Roughly the same extracts are to be found in the *Collected Works*, Vol. XXXII, p. 354 and footnotes. The sensitivity of the Malinovsky subject after sixty years is betrayed by the continuing failure of Soviet historiographers to present the text of the Lenin interrogatory. Alexander Blok, who was present at the questioning, described Lenin as testifying "with great confidence." Lenin said "many interesting things but *acknowledged nothing*." (Blok's italics.) (Alexander Blok, *Zapisnye Knizhki*, p. 325.)

17. Dzhuvkovsky, in *Padeniye Tsarskogo Rezhima*, Vol. V, pp. 69ff.

18. *Byloye*, 1933, No. 46, pp. 126–30.

19. Lenin, *Collected Works*, Vol. XLIII, p. 392.

20. Ibid., Vol. XXXV, p. 153.

21. Ibid., p. 154.

22. Roy A. Medvedev, *Let History Judge*, pp. 5–6.

23. Letter to L. Besser, dated Mar. 22, 1914, Ya. M. Sverdlov, in *Izbranniye Provizvedeniya*, Vol. I, pp. 268–69.

24. Svetlana Allilyueva, *Only One Year*, pp. 381–83.

25. Lenin, *Collected Works*, Vol. XLIII, pp. 469, 498.

26. Leon Trotsky, *My Life*, p. 227.

27. Catherine Breshkovsky, *The Little Grandmother of the Russian Revolution: Reminiscences and Letters*, pp. 180–81.

XXVIII. "We Are Kalutsky . . ."   PAGES 250–51

1. Maurice Paléologue, *An Ambassador's Memoirs*, Vol. I, pp. 11–28. Paléologue may have exaggerated a bit about the length of his talk with the Czar. Nicholas recorded in his diary that he was back by 11 P.M. He was considerably more meticulous than Paléologue. (*Krasny Arkhiv*, 1934, Vol. LXIV, p. 135.)

2. Alexandre Tarsaidze, *Chetyre Mifa*, p. 11.

3. *Krasny Arkhiv*, 1923, Vol. IV, p. 8.

4. Pierre Gilliard, *Thirteen Years at the Russian Court*, p. 99.

5. Mathilde Kschessinska, *Dancing in Petersburg*, pp. 148–49.

6. In his diary Nicholas wrote: "I said a few words." (*Krasny Arkhiv*, 1934, Vol. LXIV, p. 136.)

7. Sir Bernard Pares, *Fall of the Russian Monarchy*, p. 188.

8. M. V. Rodzyanko, *Mémoires: Le Regne de Raspoutine*, p. 132.

9. *Krasny Arkhiv*, 1929, Vol. XXXIV, p. 96.

10. Viktor Chernov, *Rozhdeniye Revolyutsionnoi Rossi*, p. 84.

11. Nadezhda Krupskaya, *Reminiscences of Lenin*, pp. 276–77.

12. Chernov, *Rozhdeniye Revolyutsiannoi Rossi*, p. 75.

13. Pavel Milyukov, *Vospominaniya* (*1859–1917*), Vol. II, p. 183.

14. Nikolai Berdyayev, *The Origins of Russian Communism*, p. 136.

15. Oliver H. Radkey, in Ernest J. Simmons, *Continuity and Change in Russian and Soviet Thought*, p. 69.

16. Chernov, *Rozhdeniye Revolyutsionnoi Rossi*, pp. 59–60, 82–86.

17. Berdyayev, *Russian Communism*, pp. 133–34.

18. Rasputin's daughter, Mariya, said that Guseva was nothing but a "wretched prostitute." (Mariya Rasputin, *My Father*, p. 21.)

19. A. Taneyeva (Vyrubova), *Stranitsy iz Moei Zhizni*, p. 49.

20. Gilliard, *Thirteen Years*, p. 100.

21. Taneyeva (Vyrubova), *Stranitsy iz Moei Zhizni*, p. 49. A recent Soviet history strongly suggests that the Czar was maneuvered into World War I by clever British and French diplomacy. The version draws heavily on émigré and White Russian sources, particularly the memoirs of Kadet leaders, citing P. N. Milyukov, F. F. Kokoshkin, P. L. Bark, I. Gessen, as well as Foreign Minister S. D. Sazonov. Most improbably, Countess Kleinmikhel is relied upon for an account of a last-minute intervention by Count Frederiks and the Czarina, who sought to convince the Czar to revoke his order for general Russian mobilization. The meeting, Kleinmikhel asserted, was arranged after Court Pourtales, the German ambassador, begged Frederiks with tears in his eyes to make one last attempt to avert war. Frederiks and the Czarina urged the Czar to withdraw the order but Foreign Minister Sazonov warned Nicholas that he would be signing his death sentence because Russia would never forgive such a cowardly act. Nicholas, who had been hesitating, then determined to stand by his mobilization. The account contends that Nicholas was powerfully influenced against the war by Rasputin's telegrams including one saying: "Don't declare war, Nikolasha will win. If you announce war they again will shout: Down! It will go bad for you and Alexei." (E. D. Chermensky, *Istoriya SSSR Period Imperializma*, pp. 355–57; Grafinya M. Kleinmikhel, *Iz Potonuvshego Mira*, pp. 214–15.)

22. V. V. Shulgin, *Dni*, p. 60.

23. Wiktor Woroszylski, *The Life of Mayakovsky*, pp. 130–32.

24. Vladimir Mayakovsky, "Ya Sam," *Sobraniya Sochinenii*, Vol. I, p. 22. Later Mayakovsky was drafted and Gorky got him assigned to a motor company as a draftsman. (Viktor Shklovsky, *Mayakovsky and His Circle*, p. 88.)

25. Z. Gippius-Merezhkovskaya, *Dmitrii Merezhkovsky*, p. 216.

26. Dan Levin, *Stormy Petrel*, p. 183.

27. A. Baborenko, and I. A. Bunin, *Materialy dlya Biografii*, pp. 200, 201, 290.

28. Valentin Katayev, *The Grass of Oblivion*, p. 38.

29. Zinaida Gippius, *Sinyaya Kniga*, p. 21.

30. K. Mochulsky, *Valery Bryusov*, pp. 163–64.

31. K. Mochulsky, *Andrei Bely*, pp. 190–92.

32. Gippius-Merezhkovskaya, *Merezhkovsky*, p. 213.

33. The Czar was persuaded to change the name of the capital because St. Petersburg—Sankt-Peterburg—was in fact a German name. Petrograd was the Slav equivalent. The French ambassador, Paléologue, shared Gippius' distaste for "Petrograd." He called the Czar's ukase "not only a mistake but an historical contradiction" since St. Petersburg was not and never had been intended by Peter the Great to be a Slav city. (Paléologue, *Memoirs*, Vol. I, p. 108.)

34. Gippius, *Sinyaya Kniga*, pp. 7-13.

35. Tamara Karsavina, *Theatre Street*, p. 252.

36. Konstantin Paustovsky, *The Story of a Life*, pp. 264-67; Gippius, *Sinyaya Kniga*, pp. 13-14.

37. Paustovsky, *Story of a Life*, p. 266.

38. *Dnevnik B. Velikogo Knyazya Andreya Vladimirovicha*, pp. 35-36.

39. Lt. Gen. P. K. Kondzerovosky, *V Stavke Verkhovnovo*, p. 24; Paléologue, *Memoirs*, Vol. I., p. 304.

40. *Padeniye Tsarkogo Rezhima*, Vol. VII, pp. 126-27.

XXIX. "A Healthy War"   PAGES 259-62

1. *Knyaz Oleg*, pp. 169-70.

2. *Dnevnik B. Velikogo Knyazya Andreya Vladimirovicha*, pp. 101-5.

3. Wiktor Woroszylski, *The Life of Mayakovsky*, pp. 133-35.

4. Viktor Shklovsky, *Mayakovsky and His Circle*, pp. 86-87; Tamara Karsavina, *Theatre Street*, pp. 254-55.

5. Shklovsky, *Mayakovsky*, p. 66; Woroszylski, *Mayakovsky*, pp. 138-39.

6. Shklovsky, *Mayakovsky*, p. 87.

7. *Letters of the Tsaritsa to the Tsar, 1914-1916*, p. 9.

8. Sir Bernard Pares, *The Fall of the Russian Monarchy*, p. 237.

9. Maurice Paléologue, *An Ambassador's Memoirs*, Vol. I, p. 222.

10. V. V. Shulgin, *Dni*, p. 76.

11. Nikolai Valentinov, *Maloznakomy Lenin*, pp. 144-45.

12. Nadezhda Krupskaya, *Reminiscences of Lenin*, pp. 277-89.

13. V. I. Lenin, *Collected Works*, Vol. XXXV, pp. 177-78.

14. Ibid., pp. 161-71.

15. Letter of A. I. Ulyanov to M. I. Ulyanov, dated Sept. 25, 1924, in *Perepiska Semii Ulyanovikh*, p. 341. To the astonishment of Valentinov, who well knew the strictness of Lenin's views on Marx, Lenin permitted the encyclopedia to edit his article radically, cutting out many important quotations of Marx and toning down Lenin's language in order to win the approval of the censor. In Lenin's struggle between Marxist principles and need for money, his monetary cause came first. Valentinov took this as further evidence of the decay of Lenin's moral qualities. (Nikolai Valentinov, *Maloznakomy Lenin*, pp. 147-48.)

16. Paléologue, *Memoirs*, Vol. I, p. 122.

17. Ibid., p. 183.

18. Sir George Buchanan, *My Mission to Russia*, pp. 221-22.

19. This was not the first instance of concordance of views between Witte and Rasputin. This had been noted by Rasputin's financial ally, Simanovich, and also by Kokovtsov, who was told that Rasputin had campaigned to get Witte back as Premier in 1911. (V. N. Kokovstov, *Iz Moego Proshlego*, Vol. II, pp. 22-23; S. R. Beletsky, in *Padeniye Tsarskogo Rezhima*, Vol. IV, p. 147.) Izvolsky heard that Witte had approached Rasputin before the war, hoping to regain the Czar's

favor through Rasputin's influence. (Alexandre Iswolsky, *Mémoires 1906–1910*, p. 173.)

20. Surgeon Fyodorov, who treated Vyrubova, told Gen. A. I. Spirodovich that in the course of his examination he found Vyrubova to be a virgin which he thought should put to rest gossip she was Rasputin's mistress or the Empress' lesbian partner (A. I. Spiridovich, *Velikaya Voina i Fevralskaya Revolyutsiya*, Vol. I, p. 86.)

21. A. Taneyeva (Vyrubova), *Stranitsy iz Moei Zhizni*, pp. 56–57.

22. *Krasny Arkhiv*, 1924, Vol. V, pp. 272–73.

23. Sir Bernard Pares, *Russian Monarchy*, p. 224.

24. Paléologue, *Memoirs*, Vol. I, pp. 229–30; R. H. Bruce Lockhart, *British Agent*, p. 126.

25. *Padeniye Tsarskogo Rezhima*, Vol. V, pp. 101–6, Dzhunkovsky testimony.

26. Ibid., Vol. IV, pp. 150–51, Beletsky testimony.

27. *Letters of the Tsaritsa to the Tsar*, pp. 105–6.

28. *Padeniye Tsarskogo Rezhima*, Vol. V, p. 103, Dzhunkovsky testimony.

29. M. P. Bok, *Vospominaniya o Moyem Otse P. A. Stolypine*, p. 331.

30. M. V. Rodzyanko, *Mémoires: Le Regne de Raspoutine*, p. 27.

31. Ibid., p. 28.

32. *Letters of the Tsaritsa to the Tsar*, pp. xxxii–xxxv.

XXX. The Little Comb PAGES 266–69

1. Sir Bernard Pares, *The Fall of the Russian Monarchy*, p. 250.

2. *Arkhiv Russkoi Revolyutsii*, Vol. XVIII, p. 65.

3. *Dnevnik B. Velikogo Knyazya Andreya Vladimirovicha*, p. 49.

4. Ibid., p. 31.

5. V. S. Dyakin, *Russkaya Burzhuasiya i Tsarism v gody Pervoi Mirovoi Voiny 1914–1917*, pp. 132–33.

6. *Dnevnik Andreya Vladimirovicha*, p. 42.

7. Ibid., p. 59. Actually Russian military production had increased substantially —rifle production rose from 525,000 a year to a rate of 1,600,000 by January 1917; artillery from 2,106 guns in 1915 to 5,135 in 1916. But demand increased even more. (E. D. Chermensky, *Istoriya SSSR Period Imperializma*, p. 371.)

8. A. A. Brusilov, *Moi Vospominaniya*, p. 138.

9. Maurice Paléologue, *An Ambassador's Memoirs*, Vol. I, p. 300.

10. A careful postrevolutionary study disclosed conclusively that whatever his past had been Mayaseyedov did not engage in spying for the Germans and was not guilty of the charges brought against him. (Dyakin, *Russkaya Burzhuasiya*, p. 78.)

11. *Letters of the Tsaritsa to the Tsar, 1914–1916*, pp. 34, 89.

12. Ibid., p. 221. Rodzyanko, the Duma leader, reported that Grand Duke Nikolai told him in 1915 while still commander in chief that Kshesinskaya played an active role in artillery contracts. (M. V. Rodzyanko, *Mémoires: Le Regne de Raspoutine*, p. 161.)

13. Dyakin, *Russkaya Burzhuasiya*, p. 74.

14. Paléologue, *Memoirs*, Vol. I, pp. 349–50.

15. The Czar managed to muffle the Sukhomlinov dismissal and bring down wrath upon himself by sending the Minister a personal letter of dismissal in which he spoke of how "difficult it is to make this decision" and "how many years we have worked together and never had a misunderstanding." The Czar thanked the Minister "warmly for all your work and for the strength which you have put to the

service of building up our national army." (Sukhomlinov, *Vospominaniya*, p. 260.) The Czarina indignantly wrote the Csar that Sukhomlinov should be reprimanded for "showing your private letter to him, right & left & others have copies of it." (*Letters of the Tsaritsa to the Tsar*, p. 108.)

16. Dyakin, *Russkaya Burzhuasiya*, p. 81, quoting Kluzhev's diary entry for June 13, 1915.

17. Pares, *Russian Monarchy*, p. 225, quoting A. N. Yakhontov, *Tyazhelye Dni*, pp. 10ff.

18. Yakhontov, ibid., p. 21.

19. Yu. N. Danilov, *Velikii Knyaz Nikolai Nikolayevich*, pp. 263-65.

20. Ibid., pp. 265-67. Sazonov walked out of a cabinet meeting with Goremykin on September 2, 1915, in hysterics shouting: "I do not want to say goodbye or shake the hand of this madman. *Il est fou, c'est vieillard.*" (A. N. Yakhontov, in *Arkhiv Russkoi Revolyutsii*, Vol. XVIII, p. 128.)

21. *Letters of the Tsaritsa to the Tsar*, pp. 100, 109, 110.

22. Ibid., p. 94.

23. *Krasny Arkhiv*, 1923, Vol. V, p. 277.

24. Dyakin, *Russkaya Burzhuasiya*, p. 113, quoting unpublished diaries of Nicholas.

25. *Krasny Arkhiv*, 1924, Vol. V, p. 278.

26. Dyakin, *Russkaya Burzhuasiya*, p. 113, based on unpublished telegrams in Soviet archives.

27. *Letters of the Tsaritsa to the Tsar*, p. 117.

28. *Perepiska Nikolaya i Aleksandry Romanovykh*, Vol. III, pp. 266-68.

29. Ibid., p. 267.

30. *Padeniye Tsarskogo Rezhima*, Vol. VI, p. 138.

31. Paléologue, *Memoirs*, Vol. I, p. 302.

32. Pierre Gilliard, *Thirteen Years at the Russian Court*, p. 150; Lt. Gen. P. K. Kondzerovsky, *V Stavke Verkhovnovo 1914-1917*, p. 75.

33. Kondzerovsky, *V Stavke Verkhovnovo*, pp. 78-79.

34. Ibid., pp. 77-79.

35. Ibid., pp. 90-95; J. C. Trewin, *The House of Special Purpose*, p. 42.

36. V. I. Gurko, *Tsar i Tsaritsa*, p. 48; Paléologue, *Memoirs*, Vol. I, p. 98. The Czarina shared this feeling on occasion. Once she told Sophia Fersen that she felt she was a "pechvogel," a bird of ill omen. (*Memoirs of Princess Varvara Aleksandrovna Kochubei*, privately printed, p. 78.)

37. Paléologue, *Memoirs*, Vol. II, p. 65.

38. *Letters of the Tsaritsa to the Tsar*, p. 190.

39. Ibid., p. 127.

40. *Perepiska Nikolaya i Alexandry Romanovykh*, Vol. III, p. 230.

41. *Padeniye Tsarskogo Rezhima*, Vol. VII, p. 405.

42. Ibid., Vol. IV, p. 381, Beletsky testimony.

43. Ibid., pp. 381-89. I. F. Manasevich-Manuilov, hardly a reliable witness, claimed Stürmer promised Rasputin to fulfill his every wish in return for Rasputin's support of his candidacy for the premiership. (*Padeniye Tsarskogo Rezhima*, Vol. II, pp. 46-47.)

44. Aron Simanovich, *Rasputin i Yevrei*, p. 32.

45. Ibid., pp. 31-32; Pares, *Russian Monarchy*, p. 300.

46. Simanovich, *Rasputin*, pp. 97-100.

47. S. P. Beletsky, in *Padeniye Tsarskogo Rezhima*, Vol. IV, pp. 350-51.

48. *Perepiska Nikolaya i Alexandry Romanovykh*, Vol. III, p. 453.

49. *Letters of the Tsaritsa to the Tsar*, p. 224.

50. Ibid., p. 265.
51. Zinaida Gippius, *Sinyaya Kniga*, pp. 22-46.
52. Dyakin, *Russkaya Burzhuasiya*, pp. 196-97.
53. Nadezhda Krupskaya, *Reminiscences of Lenin*, pp. 312-35.
54. A. S. Alliluyeva, *Vospominaniya*, pp. 189-90.

XXXI. "For Baby's Sake" PAGES 278-82

1. *Lettres des Grand-Ducs à Nicholas II*, pp. 119-22.
2. The Russian armed forces totaled 1,423,000 men on July 18, 1914. Within two weeks 3,915,000 men had been mobilized to bring its total to 5,338,000. During the whole course of the war (1914-1917) 14,375,000 men were drafted bringing the total to 15,798,000 (V. A. Lavrin, *Bolshevistskaya Partiya v Nachale Pervoi Mirovoi Imperialisticheskoi Voiny*, pp. 191, 222).
3. Pyotr Ryss, *Russkii Opyt*, p. 29.
4. Viktor Chernov, *Rozhdeniye Revolyutsionnoi Rossii*, pp. 82-83.
5. V. S. Dyakin, *Russkaya Burzhuasiya i Tsarism v gody Pervoi Mirovoi Voiny 1914-1917*, pp. 207-11.
6. Sir Bernard Pares, *The Fall of the Russian Monarchy*, pp. 331-32, citing Strumlin, *Wages in Russian Industry*, p. 90.
7. *Dnevnik B. Velikogo Knyazya Andreya Vladimirovicha*, p. 100.
8. Rodzyanko, in *Padeniye Tsarskogo Rezhima*, Vol. VII, pp. 140-41.
9. Rodzyanko thought Protopopov was insane. Once they were playing cards when Protopopov started talking so wildly that both Rodzyanko and Shingarev, another Duma leader, told him to go home and take a bromide. Protopopov refused to go, saying: "I am saving Russia. I have been called." Rodzyanko told him: "Go home. You need treatment." Rodzyanko told the Czar he thought Protopopov had lost his mind. The Czar shook his head and said nothing. (Ibid., pp. 145-46.)
10. Ibid., Vol. IV, pp. 21-23, Protopopov testimony.
11. *Letters from the Czarina to Czar Nicholas II*, p. 135.
12. Ibid., p. 130.
13. Ibid., p. 156.
14. Ibid., p. 125.
15. Ibid., p. 195.
16. Ibid., p. 214.
17. Ibid., pp. 408, 420, 426, 431, 432, 439, 441, etc.
18. Ibid., p. 217.
19. Ibid., p. 305.
20. Pierre Gilliard, the Czarevich's faithful tutor, came to the conclusion in the summer of 1916 that the boy was not benefiting by life at the Czar's Stavka. His studies were interrupted and he had become nervous and fretful. He recommended that the youngster be returned to Tsarskoye Selo. However, both the Czar and the Czarina insisted that the Czarevich stay with the Czar. The Czarina felt that it was good preparation for his eventual duties as Czar. (Gilliard, *Thirteen Years at the Russian Court*, pp. 166-68.)
21. *Letters from the Czarina to Czar Nicholas II*, p. 453.
22. Ibid., p. 249.
23. Ibid., p. 183.
24. Ibid., p. 359.
25. Ibid., p. 191.
26. Ibid., pp. 366, 368.

27. Ibid., p. 346.
28. Ibid., p. 267.
29. Ibid., p. 394.
30. Ibid., pp. 391–392
31. Ibid., p. 143.
32. Ibid., pp. 254, 164, 206.
33. Ibid., p. 441.
34. Ibid., p. 417.
35. Ibid., p. 246.
36. *Perepiska Nikolaya i Alexandry Romanovykh,* Vol. III, p. 512.

XXXII. The Dance Macabre   PAGES 284–87

1. Z. Gippius-Merezhkovskaya, *Dmitrii Merezhkovsky,* pp. 217–19.
2. M. V. Rodzyanko, *Mémoires: Le Regne de Raspoutine,* p. 277.
3. Zinaida Gippius, *Sinyaya Kniga,* pp. 51–54.
4. Ibid., p. 57.
5. Rodzyanko, *Mémoires,* pp. 56–57.
6. V. N. Kokovtsov, *Iz Moego Proshlego,* Vol. II, pp. 389, 396–97.
7. Maurice Paléologue, *An Ambassador's Memoirs,* Vol. III, pp. 15, 34.
8. *Dnevnik B. Velikogo Knyazya Andreya Vladimirovicha,* pp. 76–77.
9. *Letters from the Czarina to Czar Nicholas II,* p. 170.
10. V. S. Dyakin, *Russkaya Burzhuasiya i Tsarism v gody Pervoi Mirovoi Voiny 1914–1917,* p. 244.
11. The Grand Duchess Mariya Pavlovna was the aunt of Nicholas II, the widow of his uncle, the Grand Duke Vladimir Alexandrovich. Some idea of her views can be gained from a conversation which she and her three sons had with Rodzyanko shortly after the Kiev meeting. She telephoned Rodzyanko late at night, asking him to join her at 1 A.M. to discuss *"une affaire importante."* Rodzyanko, fearing gossip, put off the meeting until morning. The Grand Duchess inveighed on the state of the country, the incapability of the Government, the problem of Protopopov and of the Empress. She said the Czarina's interference in affairs of state was leading the country into peril and that all of the Imperial family was menaced. It was necessary "to change, to eliminate, to destroy." "How to eliminate?" Rodzyanko asked. "I don't know," the Grand Duchess replied. "Something must be invented. You understand yourself. The Duma must find a means. It is necessary that she disappear." "Whom do you mean?" asked Rodzyanko. "The Empress," she replied. (Rodzyanko, *Mémoires,* pp. 285–86.) The Grand Duke Alexander Mikhailovich seems to have left no record of this talk. He does refer to making five visits to the Czar's Stavka to try to persuade the Czar to act against Rasputin and the Czarina's influence. His efforts met no success. "I believe in no one but my wife," the Grand Duke quoted the Czar as saying (Grand Duke Alexander, *Once a Grand Duke,* p. 275).
12. Pierre Gilliard, *Thirteen Years at the Russian Court,* p. 178. Nicholas wrote his wife: "Mama was very good and kind. In the evening we played *putzl* and had long talks" (A. I. Spirodovich, *Velikaya Voina: Fevralskaya Revolyutsiya,* Vol. II, p. 271).
13. Spirodovich, *Velikaya Voina,* Vol. II, pp. 171–72.
14. *Lettres des Grands-Ducs à Nicholas II,* pp. 257–60.
15. *Letters from the Czarina to Czar Nicholas II,* p. 433. There is a contradiction in reports about Grand Duke Nikolai Mikhailovich's interview with the Czar at the Czar's Stavka. The correspondence of the Czar and Czarina clearly states that

the Czar did not read the Grand Duke's letter and the Grand Duke did not inform the Czar of its contents. However, V. V. Shulgin, the Duma member whose memoir *Dni* is one of the most accurate, best informed, and best written of the period, quotes a conversation in which he and Prince N. N. Lvov were told by the Grand Duke about the letter just after its delivery. The Grand Duke said that he had consulted the Dowager Empress in Kiev before drafting it and decided to deliver the letter personally to the Czar. He went to the Czar on November 1 and asked the Czar's permission to read the letter. The Czar listened to the end and then said: "It's strange. I've just returned from Kiev. Never, it seems to me have I been received as on this occasion. . . ." The Grand Duke told the Czar that this was possibly because he had gone alone with the Czarevich and without the Czarina. To Lvov's question as to whether his letter had produced an impression on the Czar, the Grand Duke said he didn't know but that, all the same, he had done what had to be done. (Shulgin, *Dni*, pp. 117–19.)

16. *Letters from the Czarina to Czar Nicholas II*, pp. 424–25.

17. *Perepiska Nikolaya i Alexandry Romanovykh*, Vol. V. pp. 136, 141.

18. *Krasny Arkhiv*, 1928, Vol. XXVI, p. 197.

19. *The Nicky-Sunny Letters*, p. 296.

20. *Lettres des Grands Ducs à Nicholas II*, pp. 219–21.

21. Alexander, *Grand Duke*, p. 185.

22. Sir George Buchanan, *My Mission to Russia*, Vol. II, pp. 25–27.

23. General Alexeyev had engaged in discussion with some political and military figures about ending the Emperor's role in politics and possibly the abdication of the Czar, but the talks came to no firm conclusion, possibly because of Alexeyev's illness. The date of the proposed coup was to be January 1917. (Spiridovich, *Velikaya Voina*, Vol. II, p. 178.)

24. Dyakin, *Russkaya Burzhuasiya*, p. 245. The text of Klopov's correspondence with the Czar has never been published but presumably exists in the restricted archives of the Soviet Government. Protopopov described to the Provisional Government's Extraordinary Investigating Commission a letter from Klopov probably sent to the Czar in December 1916, recommending establishment of a responsible ministry. Alexander Blok, who was present while Protopopov was being questioned, noted that Klopov was also in correspondence with Grand Duke Nikolai Nikolayevich. (*Padeniye Tsarskogo Rezhima*, Vol. V., pp. 270–71; Alexander Blok, *Zapisnye Khnizhki*, p. 368.)

25. Milyukov long afterward admitted he did not have the "facts" to support his charges of treason (Milyukov, *Vospominaniya* (*1859–1917*), Vol. II, pp. 170–71). Burtsev called it "an historic speech but it was all fashioned on lies" (S. Melgunov, *Po Putyakh k Dvortsomomy Perevoroty*, p. 72).

26. Milyukov, Vospominaniya, Vol. II, p. 277.

27. Ibid.

28. Dyakin, *Russkaya Burzhuasiya*, p. 243, quoting unpublished letter of Milyukov dated Oct. 2, 1919, in Soviet archives.

29. V. M. Purishkevich, *Dnevnik*, pp. 7–8.

30. Ibid., p. 6a.

31. Dyakin, *Russkaya Burzhuasiya*, p. 252.

32. *Letters from the Czarina to Czar Nicholas II*, p. 442.

33. Ibid., p. 444.

34. Ibid., p. 449.

35. Ibid., p. 453.

36. Spiridovich, *Velikaya Voina*, Vol. II, p. 186.

37. *Letters from the Czarina to Czar Nicholas II*, p. 455. Nicholas replied on

December 16: "Tender thanks for the severe written scolding. I read it with a smile because you speak as to a child. . . . Your poor little weak-willed hubby." (*Krasny Arkhiv*, 1923, Vol. IV, p. 189.)
38. Shulgin, *Dni*, p. 101.
39. Ibid., p. 115.

XXXIII. Russian Blood   PAGES 293–300

1. Prince Felix Youssoupoff, *Lost Splendor*, pp. 78–80.
2. Ibid., pp. 82–84.
3. Ibid., pp. 134–51.
4. V. M. Purishkevich, *Dnevnik*, pp. 11–13.
5. Ibid., pp. 11–13.
6. M. V. Rodzyanko, *Mémoires: Le Regne de Raspoutine*, p. 38.
7. Prince Yusupov in his memoirs calls her "Mlle G." He describes going to the Golovin mansion on the Winter Canal. Madame Golovin and her daughter were waiting in the drawing room. Rasputin entered, put his arms around each woman in turn, and kissed her resoundingly. (Youssoupoff, *Lost Splendor*, pp. 139–40.) The police inquiry identified the young woman accurately as Mariya Yevgenyevna Golovina. Her nickname was Munya. (*Byloye*, July 1917, p. 69.)
8. Youssoupoff, *Lost Splendor*, pp. 139, 206–7.
9. When Felix told his co-conspirators about Rasputin's offer they laughed and the Grand Duke Dmitri exclaimed: "*C'est ravissant, mais c'est vraiment ravissant!*" (Purishkevich, *Dnevnik*, p. 33).
10. Youssoupoff, *Lost Splendor*, pp. 218–20.
11. *Byloye*, July 1917, p. 69.
12. Youssoupoff, *Lost Splendor*, p. 225; Sir Bernard Pares, *The Fall of the Russian Monarchy*, p. 401.
13. Youssoupoff, *Lost Splendor*, pp. 225–26; Pares, *Russian Monarchy*, pp. 402–3; Purishkevich, *Dnevnik*, pp. 19–24.
14. Youssoupoff, *Lost Splendor*, pp 230–32.
15. Purishkevich, *Dnevnik*, p. 64.
16. Ibid., pp. 29–30.
17. V. V. Shulgin, *Dni*, pp. 119–21.
18. Pares, *Russian Monarchy*, p. 404.
19. *Krasny Arkhiv*, 1926, Vol. XIV, pp. 231–40.
20. Beletsky, in *Padeniye Tsarskogo Rezhima*, Vol. IV, pp. 363–65.
21. Protopopov, ibid., p. 69.
22. Ibid.
23. *Krasny Arkhiv*, 1924, Vol. V, pp. 270ff.
24. *Letters from the Czarina to Czar Nicholas II*, p. 457.
25. A. Taneyeva (Vyrubova), *Stranitsy iz Moei Zhizni*, p. 120.
26. Aron Simanovich, *Rasputin i Yevrei*, pp. 154–58.
27. Ibid., pp. 160–61.
28. *Padeniye Tsarskogo Rezhima*, Vol. IV, p. 31.
29. In her book, *My Father*, published in London in 1934, Mariya Rasputin (Telivyev) says she and her sister hid her father's boots to keep him from going out. In her testimony to Gendarme Major General Popov in Petrograd, December 18, 1916, she made no mention of this. Nor did she claim to have heard her father leave the house after exclaiming: "It's the children again—they've hidden my boots" (p. 12).
30. *Byloye*, July 1917, pp. 68–70, Official Police Protocols.

31. *Padeniye Tsarskogo Rezhima,* Vol. IV, p. 503.

32. Ibid.

33. A. Taneyeva (Vyrubova), *Stranitsy iz Moei Zhizni,* p. 72. None of those in the Rasputin house questioned by the police seems to have noted Vyrubova's visit. Two of the witnesses reported that a blonde woman about twenty-five years old of medium height visited him about 10 P.M. and stayed an hour. This could not have been Vyrubova as both witnesses said they had never seen the woman before. (*Byloye,* July 1917, pp. 72–73.) One said she was called "Sister Mariya but she was not a nurse." Since Rasputin had just been at Tsarskoye Selo and seen the Czarina on the fourteenth it seems curious she would send Vyrubova into town two days later to deliver an icon. However, the story about the icon may have been used by Vyrubova as an excuse for one of her almost daily meetings with Rasputin. There are many minor but not material discrepancies in the stories of Rasputin's last hours.

34. *Byloye,* July 1917, pp. 72–73.

35. Purishkevich, *Dnevnik,* pp. 59–60.

36. Simanovich, *Rasputin,* Vol. I, p. 61.

37. Purishkevich, *Dnevnik,* pp. 64–65.

38. Youssoupoff, *Lost Splendor,* pp. 231–32.

39. Purishkevich, *Dnevnik,* pp. 46–47.

40. *Byloye,* July 1917, pp. 74–75.

41. Simanovich, *Rasputin,* p. 27.

42. Ibid., p. 26.

43. Youssoupoff, *Lost Splendor,* p. 223.

44. *Byloye,* July 1917, pp. 75–76.

45. Ibid., p. 74.

46. Purishkevich, *Dnevnik,* p. 59; *Letters from the Czarina to Czar Nicholas II,* p. 461.

47. Purishkevich, *Dnevnik,* pp. 68–70.

48. Youssoupoff, *Lost Splendor,* pp. 235–36.

49. Ibid., pp. 237–39.

50. Yusupov's and Purishkevich's accounts differ. Yusupov recalled running upstairs only once; Purishkevich said he came up three times.

51. Youssoupoff, *Lost Splendor,* pp. 239–40.

52. Ibid., pp. 242–43.

53. Purishkevich, *Dnevnik,* pp. 78–82.

54. Later Yusupov told Purishkevich Rasputin opened his eyes, dragged himself to his feet exclaiming: "Felix, Felix, Felix . . ." (Purishkevich, *Dnevnik,* pp. 82–83).

55. Ibid., pp. 81–84.

56. Beletsky, in *Padeniye Tsarskogo Rezhima,* Vol. IV, pp. 502–3; Pares, *Russian Monarchy,* p. 409; A. I. Spiridovich, *Velikaya Voina i Fevralskaya Revolyutsiya,* Vol. II, pp. 217–18; Viroubova, *Souvenirs de Ma Vie,* p. 95.

57. Prot. Sergei Bulgakov, *Avtobiograficheskiye Zametki,* pp. 87–88.

XXXIV. A Quiet Winter PAGES 309–10

1. A wooden staircase had been built through the wall from the Empress' study to a platform behind the toilet. Here, concealed by a curtain, the Czarina could lie on a couch and listen to the Czar's conversations. (Sir Bernard Pares, *The Fall of the Russian Monarchy,* p. 414.)

2. The Czar, usually meticulous in recording his visitors, failed to mention

Kokovtsov in his diary entry for January 29. (*Krasny Arkhiv*, 1927, Vol. XX, p. 129.)

3. V. N. Kokovtsov, *Iz Moego Proshlego*, Vol. II, pp. 401–4. On July 10, 1918, when Kokovtsov was under examination by the Bolshevik Cheka, he was asked by Uritsky whether he regarded the Czar as psychologically healthy and whether he did not think that since the time of the sword blow on the head which he received in Japan during his visit in 1891 he had not been a sick man. (Ibid., p. 404.) It is true that Nicholas suffered severe headaches from that time forward.

4. A. Taneyeva (Vyrubova), *Stranitsy iz Moei Zhizni*, pp. 73–74; Nikolai Romanov, Diary, in *Krasny Arkhiv*, 1927, Vol. XX, p. 126; A. I. Spiridovich, *Velikaya Voina i Fevralskaya Revolyutsiya*, Vol. II, pp. 218–19.

5. Maurice Paléologue, *An Ambassador's Memoirs*, Vol. III, pp. 266–67.

6. Grand Duke Alexander, *Once a Grand Duke*, p. 279; A. Taneyeva (Vyrubova), *Stranitsy iz Moei Zhizni*, p. 74; Spiridovich, *Velikaya Voina*, Vol. II, p. 220. Sixteen members of the Imperial family in a joint letter to the Czar begged that Dmitri be permitted to go to the family estate of Yusovo or Ilyinsk instead of Persia. (*Krasny Arkhiv*, 1928, Vol. XXVI, pp. 190–92.)

7. Ibid., p. 190.

8. Princess Cantacuzene, *Revolutionary Days*, p. 114.

9. V. N. Voyeikov, *S Tsarem i Bez Tsarya*, p. 193.

10. *Lettres des Grands-Ducs à Nicholas II*, pp. 206–17.

11. Grand Duke Alexander, *Once a Grand Duke*, pp. 283–84.

12. Taneyeva, *Stranitsy iz Moei Zhizni*, pp. 93–94.

13. Ibid., p. 98.

14. Pavel Milyukov, *Vospominaniya* (*1859–1917*), Vol. II, p. 281.

15. M. V. Rodzyanko, *Mémoires: Le Regne de Raspoutine*, pp. 283–84.

16. Ibid., pp. 287–89.

17. Ibid., pp. 299–300.

18. *Krasny Arkhiv*, 1925, Vol. XII, pp. 237–46.

19. V. S. Dyakin, *Russkaya Burzhuasiya i Tsarism v gody Pervoi Mirovoi Voiny 1914–1917*, p. 265; *Krasny Arkhiv*, 1927, Vol. XX, p. 131. One factor which held back the Czar from taking decisive action was his stubborn if ill-founded belief that spring would bring a victorious Russian offensive which would enhance his prestige and resolve his political problems. He expressed these views to the Irkutsk governor-general, A. I. Pilts, January 22. (E. D. Chermensky, *Istoriya SSSR Period Imperializma*, p. 403.) Nicholas' hopes for success of the spring offensive may also have caused him to turn his back on all suggestions of a separate peace. (Dyakin, *Russkaya Burzhuasiya*, pp. 287–88).

20. *Padeniye Tsarskogo Rezhima*, Vol. IV, pp. 484–85.

21. Ibid., Vol. III, p. 271.

22. Spiridovich, *Velikaya Voina*, Vol. II, p. 232.

23. Ibid., Vol. III, pp. 23–24. Kostritsky was one of the very few individuals permitted to visit the Czar and his family in Tobolsk. He spent the third week of October 1917 in Tobolsk treating the Czar, the Czarina, and members of the family. (*Krasny Arkhiv*, 1928, Vol. XXVII, pp. 82–83.)

24. Voyeikov, *S Tsarem i Bez Tsarya*, p. 191.

25. *Krasny Arkhiv*, 1927, Vol. XX, p. 135.

26. Voyeikov, *S Tsarem*, pp. 192–93.

27. J. D. Elsworth, *Andrey Bely*, pp. 91–92.

28. V. F. Khodasevich, *Nekropol*, p. 8.

29. Zinaida Gippius, *Sinyaya Kniga*, pp. 65–71.

30. Viktor Shklovsky, *Mayakovsky and His Circle*, p. 214.

31. Wiktor Worozylsky, *The Life of Mayakovsky*, pp. 159–72; Shklovsky, *Mayakovsky*, pp. 93–98.

32. Konstantin Paustovsky, *The Story of a Life*, pp. 260–69.

33. Paléologue, *Memoirs*, Vol. III, pp. 188–89. Milyukov had predicted the peasant reaction to Rasputin's murder precisely. He said the peasant would say of his brother's murder: "Look, finally a muzhik gets to the Czar's ear and speaks the truth to the Czar—and the noblemen murder him." (Milyukov, *Vospominaniya*, Vol. II, p. 281.)

34. A. Baborenko and I. A. Bunin, *Materialy dlya Biografii*, pp. 210–11.

XXXV. "Only People Changed" PAGES 319–23

1. *Krasny Arkhiv*, 1926, Vol. XVII, pp. 3–55.

2. Alexander Blok, in *Arkhiv Russkoi Revolyutsii*, Vol. VI, pp. 13–21.

3. V. S. Dyakin, *Russkaya Burzhuasiya i Tsarism v gody Pervoi Mirovoi Voiny 1914–1917*, pp. 312–13.

4. I. G. Ryabtsev, *Bolsheviki v Borbe Protiv Melkoburzhuaznykh Partii v Rossii*, p. 33.

5. *Krasny Arkhiv*, 1927, Vol. XXI, p. 67.

6. *Oktyabrskoye Vooruzhennoye Vosstaniye*, Vol. I, p. 14. The stated force was 6,700, but the actual numbers may have been slightly larger. Police pay had not kept pace with the rise in the cost of living and there had been a police strike on this account in Moscow. (Protopopov, in *Padeniye Tsarkogo Rezhima*, Vol. IV, p. 79.)

7. *Oktyabrskoye Vooruzhennoye Vosstaniye*, Vol. I, p. 21.

8. Ibid., pp. 21–24. It has frequently been reported that the question of the reliability of these forces gave the Czar some disquiet and that he ordered General Gurko, acting chief of staff, to send four cavalry regiments to the capital from the front and that, instead, Gurko moved in three units of sailors. (Protopopov, in *Padeniye Tsarskogo Rezhima*, Vol. IV, p. 93.) This account, spread by Vyrubova and Protopopov, has been convincingly demolished by S. P. Melgunov (*Martovskiye Dni 1917 goda*, pp. 165–66). Melgunov demonstrates that actually Stavka asked whether two cavalry regiments might not be sent *from* Petrograd to the front, rather than the other way around. About the same time a plan was drawn up by General Khabalov, the military commandant, and Mayor Balk to divide the city into sixteen defense districts in case of civil disorders but this did not essentially change anything. Petrograd was separated from the northern front command three weeks before the overturn but this does not seem to have had material effect on the ability of the authorities to cope with an internal uprising. (Protopopov, in *Padeniye Tsarskogo Rezhima*, Vol. IV, p. 46.) General Ruzsky, commander of the northern front, attributed the change which took Petrograd out of his jurisdiction to a violent argument with Protopopov in which Ruzsky was trying to get action on proposals to improve the Petrograd food situation. (*Krasny Arkhiv*, 1928, Vol. XXVI, pp. 202–3.)

9. *Arkhiv Russkoi Revolyutsii*, Vol. IV, p. 12.

10. Protopopov, in *Padeniye Tsarskogo Rezhima*, Vol. IV, pp. 82–84.

11. Ibid., p. 26.

12. Voyeikov, ibid., Vol. III, p. 76.

13. Dubensky, ibid., Vol. VI, p. 394; Blok, in *Arkhiv Russkoi Revolyutsii*, Vol. IV, p. 7.

14. V. I. Lenin, *Collected Works*, Vol. XLII, pp. 602, 609.

15. Ibid., pp. 597, 614.

16. V. Valentinov, *Maloznakomy Lenin*, quotes Krupskaya, p. 168.

17. *Voprosy Istorii KPSS*, 1975, No. 4, p. 8, commenting on *Leninsky Sbornik*, Vol. XXXVIII, pp. 113, 170.

18. Lenin, *Collected Works*, Vol. XLIII, pp. 586, 590.

19. Ibid., Vol. XXXV, p. 259.

20. Ibid., Vol. XLIII, pp. 590–93.

21. Ibid., Vol. XXXVII, pp. 537–38.

22. Nadezhda Krupskaya, *Reminiscences of Lenin*, p. 333.

23. A. S. Kudryavtsev, *Lenin v Berne i Tsyurikhe*, pp. 133–38.

24. Lenin, *Collected Works*, Vol. LXIII, p. 603.

25. Ibid., Vol. XXXVII, pp. 535–36. The evidence seems conclusive that up to this point Lenin was receiving none of the German funds which later were to be funneled to the Bolsheviks by Alexander Helphand, the famous Parvus. Z. A. B. Zeman and W. B. Scharlau, who have made the most extensive investigation of these funds and their use, agree on this point. (Z. A. B. Zeman and W. B. Scharlau, *The Merchant of Revolution*, p. 181.) This view is supported by Alfred Erich Senn, who has made probably the most careful inquiry into the relevant German and Swiss materials. (See Alfred Erich Senn, "The Myth of German Money During the First World War," *Soviet Studies*, Jan. 1976, Vol. XXVII, No. 1, pp. 83–90.) There is also no sign of any infusion of funds into the vestigial Bolshevik organization within Russia. However, Valentinov feels that Lenin and Krupskaya were not always completely honest in their professions of poverty. (Valentinov, *Maloznakomy Lenin*, pp. 163–81.)

26. V. Shavneva, *Partyiya Bolshevikov v gody Mirovoi Imperialicheskoi Voiny*, p. 306.

27. Lenin, *Collected Works*, Vol. XXXVII, p. 530.

28. *Voprosy Istorii KPSS*, 1965, No. 9, p. 79.

29. Lenin, *Collected Works*, Vol. XXXV, p. 262.

30. Ibid., p. 266.

31. Ibid., pp. 288–89.

32. V. A. Lavrin, *Bolshevistskaya Partiya v Nachale Pervoi Mirovoi Imperialisticheskoi Voiny*, pp. 93–95.

33. Ibid., pp. 252, 267, 273, 275, 283.

34. *Oktyabrskoye Vooruzhennoye Vosstaniye*, Vol. I, p. 42.

35. S. M. Lebidova and E. G. Salita, *Yelena Dmitriyevna Stasova*, pp. 223–24.

36. *Oktyabrskoye Vooruzhennoye Vosstaniye*, Vol. I, p. 43.

37. Shavneva, *Partiya Bolshevikov*, p. 155.

38. Ibid., pp. 216, 254.

39. *Voprosy Istorii KPSS*, 1965, No. 9, p. 81.

40. Blok, in *Arkhiv Russkoi Revolyutsii*, Vol. IV, p. 14.

41. Ibid., p. 25.

42. Lenin, *Collected Works*, Vol. XXIII, pp. 399–400.

43. Krupskaya, *Reminiscences*, p. 335.

44. Lenin, *Collected Works*, Vol. XXIII, pp. 236–53.

45. Kudryavtsev, *Lenin v Berne*, pp. 168–69.

46. Lenin, *Collected Works*, Vol. XLIII, p. 614.

47. *Leninsky Sbornik*, Vol. XI, p. 254.

48. A. Solzhenitsyn, *Lenin v Tsurikhe*, pp. 167ff.

49. Israel Getzler, *Martov*, pp. 144–45.

50. Samuel Baron, *Plekhanov*, pp. 335–36.

51. Kollontai wrote Lenin about Trotsky's collaboration on *Novy Mir*. This inspired Lenin to a typical outburst. He gathered that Trotsky had taken control of

the paper from Bukharin. "What a swine this Trotsky is!" Lenin exclaimed (*Collected Works*, Vol. XXXV, p. 285).

52. Leon Trotsky, *My Life*, pp. 250–76.
53. Catherine Breshkovsky, *The Little Grandmother of the Russian Revolution*, pp. 298–308.
54. Leon Trotsky, *Stalin*, p. 172.
55. Ibid., p. 174.
56. Ibid., pp. 175–76.
57. Robert C. Tucker, *Stalin as Revolutionary 1879–1929*, pp. 160–61.
58. Alexander Kerensky, *Russia and History's Turning Point*, p. 52.

XXXVI. "*I Think the Revolution Has Begun*" PAGES 332–39

1. *Krasny Arkhiv*, 1928, Vol XX, p. 135.
2. Nikolai Sukhanov, *Zapiski o Revolyutsii*, Vol. I, p. 16.
3. Edward T. Heald, *Witness to Revolution*, p. 45.
4. V. V. Shulgin, *Dni*, p. 139.
5. *Ocherkii istorii Leningradskoi Organizatsii KPSS*, Part I, pp. 438–40; *Istoriya Rabochikh Leningrada*, pp. 507–511.
6. Z. Gippius-Merezhkovskaya, *Dmitrii Merezhkovsky*, p. 220.
7. Sir Maurice Paléologue, *An Ambassador's Memoirs*, Vol. III, p. 213.
8. *Oktyabryskoye Vooruzhennoye Vosstaniye*, Vol. I, p. 49.
9. Vladimir Zenzinov, in *Novy Zhurnal*, 1953, Nos. 34–35; Vladimir Zenzinov, *Iz Zhizni Revolyutsionera*, pp. 81–82.
10. Marylie Markovitch, *La Révolution Russe*, pp. 3–4.
11. Ye. P. Onufuriyev, *Za Nevskoi Zastavoi*, pp. 126–28.
12. Khabalov, in *Padeniye Tsarskogo Rezhima*, Vol. I, p. 184.
13. *Istoriya Rabochikh Leningrada*, pp. 512–13.
14. *Oktyabryskoye Vooruzhennoye Vosstaniye*, Vol. I, pp. 51–52.
15. Markovitch, *Révolution Russe*, pp. 43–47.
16. George Alexander Lensen, *War and Revolution*, p. 23.
17. V. S. Dyakin. *Russkaya Burzhuasiya i Tsarism v gody Pervoi Mirovoi Voiny 1914–1917*, p. 317.
18. *Krasny Arkhiv*, 1925, Vol. X, pp. 176–77, Protopopov diary.
19. *Padeniye Tsarskogo Rezhima*, Vol. I, p. 184.
20. Ibid., p. 186.
21. Alexander Blok, in *Arkhiv Russkoi Revolyutsii*, 1922, Vol. IV, p. 26.
22. *Krasny Arkhiv*, 1925, Vol. X, p. 177.
23. Louis de Robien, *The Diary of a Diplomat in Russia 1917–1918*, pp. 7–8.
24. Paléologue, *Memoirs*, Vol. III, p. 214.
25. Zinaida Gippius, *Sinyaya Kniga*, pp. 71–72.
26. S. P. Melgunov, *Martovskiye Dni 1917 goda*, p. 19.
27. *Padeniye Tsarskogo Rezhima*, Vol. IV, p. 96.
28. *Krasny Arkhiv*, 1923, Vol. IV, pp. 203–4.
29. The arrests were actually carried out the night of February 25–26.
30. Khabalov, in *Padeniye Tsarskogo Rezhima*, Vol. I, pp. 187–88.
31. *Oktyabrskoye Vooruzhennoye Vosstaniye*, Vol. I, p. 53.
32. Zenzinov, *Iz Zhizni Revolyutsionera*, p. 82.
33. *Oktyabrskoye Vooruzhennoye Vosstaniye*, Vol. I, p. 55.
34. Lensen, *War and Revolution*, pp. 44–45.
35. Gippius, *Sinyaya Kniga*, p. 15.
36. De Robien, *Diary of a Diplomat*, pp. 8–9.

37. Blok, in *Arkhiv Russkoi Revolyutsii*, Vol IV, pp. 26-27.
38. *Krasny Arkhiv*, 1923, Vol. IV, pages 206-8.
39. V. N. Voyeikov, *S Tsarem i Bez Tsarya*, pp. 196-97.

XXXVII. The First Shot   PAGES 341-48

1. Zinaida Gippius, *Sinyaya Kniga*, pp. 51-52.
2. S. P. Melgunov, *Martovskiye Dni 1917 goda*, p. 18.
3. Ibid., p. 19.
4. *Istoriya Rabochikh Leningrada*, p. 518.
5. *Oktyabrskoye Vooruzhennoye Vosstaniye*, Vol. I, p. 56.
6. Alexander Blok, in *Arkhiv Russkoi Revolyutsii*, Vol. IV, p. 27.
7. Nikita D. Roodkowsky, a personal reminiscence.
8. Marylie Markovitch, *La Révolution Russe*, pp. 19-21.
9. Vladimir Zenzinov, *Iz Zhizni Revolyutsionera*, p. 83.
10. Marc Ferro, *The Russian Revolution of February 1917*, p. 37.
11. George Alexander Lensen, *War and Revolution*, pp. 45-46.
12. *Oktyabrskoye Vooruzhennoye Vosstaniye*, Vol. I, p. 58.
13. According to another version Krylov was cut down by M. G. Filatov of the 6th Sotnya of the 1st Cossack Regiment after Krylov struck another Cossack in the face. (V. Baranovskaya, *Soldaty-Pavlovtsy*, p. 22.)
14. Zenzinov, *Iz Zhizni Revolyutsionera*, p. 83; D. Anin, *Revolyutsiya 1917 Goda Glazami Yeyo Rukovoditelei*, pp. 159-60.
15. *Oktyabrskoye Vooruzhennoye Vosstaniye*, Vol. I, p. 58.
16. Ibid.
17. There is a conflict about Zenzinov's presence. Zenzinov places himself at the Znamenskaya Square at about 3 P.M. Sukhanov remembers him at the Sokolov meeting.
18. Nikolai Sukhanov, *Zapiski o Revolyutsii*, Vol. I, pp. 36-51.
19. Gippius, *Sinyaya Kniga*, pp. 75-76.
20. Maurice Paléologue, *An Ambassador's Memoirs*, Vol. III, pp. 215-16.
21. Louis de Robien, *The Diary of a Diplomat in Russia 1917-1918*, p. 10.
22. Edward T. Heald, *Witness to Revolution*, p. 51.
23. Blok, in *Arkhiv Russkoi Revolyutsii*, Vol. IV, p. 28.
24. V. N. Voyeikov, *S Tsarem i Bez Tsarya*, p. 197.
25. *Krasny Arkhiv*, 1923, Vol. IV, p. 206.
26. Ibid., pp. 208-10.
27. Blok, in *Arkhiv Russkoi Revolyutsii*, Vol. IV, p. 29.
28. Zenzinov, *Iz Zhizni Revolyutsionera*, p. 85; Anin, *Revolyutsiya 1917*, pp. 155-56.
29. *Oktyabrskoye Vooruzhennoye Vosstaniye*, Vol. I, p. 59; S. M. Lebidova and E. G. Salita, *Yelena Dmitriyevna Stasova*, p. 229.
30. Khabalov, in *Padeniye Tsarskogo Rezhima*, Vol. I, pp. 191-93.
31. Blok, in *Arkhiv Russkoi Revolyutsii*, Vol. IV, pp. 29-30.
32. *Oktyabrskoye Vooruzhennoye Vosstaniye*, Vol. I, p. 56; Sukhanov, *Zapiski o Revolyutsii*, Vol. I, p. 35.

XXXVIII. Revolutionary Sunday   PAGE 349

1. Khabalov gave the hour as 4 P.M. (*Padeniye Tsarskogo Rezhima*, Vol. I, pp. 195-96). Protopopov gave it as 6 P.M. (V. S. Dyakin, *Russkaya Burzhuasiya i Tsarism v gody Pervoi Mirovoi Voiny 1914-1917*, p. 324).
2. Nikolai Sukhanov, *Zapiski o Revolyutsii*, Vol. I, pp. 58-59.

3. *Oktyabrskoye Vooruzhennoye Vosstaniye*, Vol. I, p. 62.
4. Ibid., p. 62.
5. *Krasny Arkhiv*, 1923, Vol. XXI, p. 7.
6. Khabalov reported that Eksten was attacked by demonstrators. When he tried to draw his revolver, he was struck a blow by a sword which severed three fingers. A second sword blow severed his head from his body. (*Padeniye Tsarskogo Rezhima*, Vol. I, p. 202.)
7. Vladimir Zenzinov, *Iz Zhizni Revolyutsionera*, p. 86.
8. Sukhanov, *Zapiski o Revolyutsii*, Vol. I, p. 58.
9. George Alexander Lensen, *War and Revolution*, pp. 46-48.
10. *Oktyabrskoye Vooruzhennoye Vosstaniye*, Vol. I, p. 60.
11. Ibid., p. 62.
12. Alexander Blok, in *Arkhiv Russkoi Revolyutsii*, Vol. IV, p. 31.
13. V. N. Voyeikov, *S Tsarem i Bez Tsarya*, pp. 198-99.
14. Blok, in *Arkhiv Russkoi Revolyutsii*, Vol. IV, p. 33.
15. Ibid.
16. *Krasny Arkhiv*, 1923, Vol. IV, pp. 210-13.
17. Blok, in *Arkhiv Russkoi Revolyutsii*, Vol. IV, p. 33.
18. *Krasny Arkhiv*, 1923, Vol. IV, pp. 212-13.
19. Ibid., 1927, Vol. XX, p. 136.
20. *Padeniye Tsarskogo Rezhima*, Vol. IV, p. 99.
21. Ibid., Vol. I, pp. 195-96.
22. Ibid., Vol. IV, p. 199.
23. Dyakin, *Revolyutsiya 1917*, pp. 324-25.
24. Blok, in *Arkhiv Russkoi Revolyutsii*, Vol. IV, p. 33.
25. Sukhanov, *Zapiski o Revolyutsii*, Vol. I, pp. 53-61. There are several discrepancies between Sukhanov's and Zenzinov's account of this evening. Zenzinov seems to place Sukhanov at the Kerensky apartment instead of Gorky's. Sukhanov places Skobelev at the Duma but Zenzinov has him at Kerensky's. In view of the hectic times occasional discrepancies seem natural. (Ibid., pp. 53-78; Vladimir Zenzinov, in *Novy Zhurnal*, 1953, No. 34, pp. 53-54.) The Okhrana had planned to raid this meeting but nothing came of the plan. See *Arkhiv Russkoi Revolyutsii*, Vol. IV, p. 3.
26. Marc Ferro, *The Russian Revolution of February 1917*, p. 41.
27. Petrograd police records indicate that the Petersburg Bolshevik Committee decided on February 25 to set up as quickly as possible an "Information Bureau" and an Information Bulletin. (*Oktyabrskoye Vooruzhennoye Vosstaniye*, Vol. I, p. 56.)
28. Ferro, *Russian Revolution*, pp. 38-39.
29. Ibid., p. 40.
30. Zinaida Gippius, *Sinyaya Kniga*, pp. 77-79.
31. Louis de Robien, *The Diary of a Diplomat in Russia, 1917-1918*, p. 11.
32. Pavel Milyukov, *Vospominaniya*, Vol. II, pp. 291-92; Milyukov, in *Padeniye Tsarskogo Rezhima*, Vol. VI, p. 352.
33. *Istoriya Rabochikh Leningrada*, p. 528.
34. *Oktyabrskoye Vooruzhennoye Vosstaniye*, Vol. I, p. 64; Ferro, *Russian Revolution*, pp. 42-43. Another version had it that Lashkevich committed suicide. (Khabalov, in *Padeniye Tsarskogo Rezhima*, Vol. I, p. 198.)
35. Ibid., pp. 198-99.
36. *Istoriya Rabochikh Leningrada*, p. 529.
37. Blok, in *Arkhiv Russkoi Revolyutsii*, Vol. IV, p. 34.

38. *Istoriya Rabochikh Leningrada*, p. 530.
39. Khabalov, in *Padeniye Tsarskogo Rezhima*, Vol. I, p. 199.
40. *Istoriya Rabochikh Leningrada*, p. 532.
41. Kalinin later was to become the venerable, goateed "President of the Soviet Union."
42. The Vyborg Bolsheviks hoped to turn the Finland Station into the center of the revolutionary movement. They issued an appeal: "Let the Finland station be the center where the Revolutionary staff assembles." However, the station did not become the revolutionary center because, as one Communist historian observed, "of the impetuous development of events and weak connections with other districts." (*Istoriya Rabochikh Leningrada*, p. 527.)
43. M. I. Kalinin, *Za eti gody*, Vol. III, p. 432; *Oktyabrskoye Vooruzhennoye Vosstaniye*, Vol. I, p. 67; *Ocherki Istorii Leningradskoi Organizatisii KPSS*, p. 446.
44. Blok, in *Arkhiv Russkoi Revolyutsii*, Vol. IV, p. 34.
45. *Oktyabrskoye Vooruzhennoye Vosstaniye*, Vol. I, p. 66.
46. *Istoriya Rabochikh Leningrada*, p. 532; Sir Bernard Pares, *The Fall of the Russian Monarchy*, p. 444; Khabalov, in *Padeniye Tsarskogo Rezhima*, Vol. I, p. 198. Kutepov, a leader in the postrevolutionary White Russian anti-Bolshevik movement, was kidnaped from Paris by the Soviet secret police January 26, 1930, and spirited back to Russia where he was shot. (S. L. Voitsekhovsky, *Trest. Vospominaniya i Dokumenty*, p. 30.)
47. Khabalov, in *Padeniye Tsarskogo Rezhima*, Vol. I, pp. 198–99.
48. Pares, *Russian Monarchy*, pp. 445–48, quoting A. T. Wasilieff, *Police Russe et Révolution*, pp. 166–70.
49. S. Anichkova, *Zagadka Lenina iz Vospominanii Redaktora*, pp. 10–11.
50. V. N. Kokovtsov, *Iz Moego Proshlego*, Vol. II, p. 405.
51. *Arkhiv Russkoi Revolyutsii*, Vol. I, pp. 12–13.

XXXIX. A Year and a Half Too Late PAGES 359–63

1. V. V. Shulgin, *Dni*, pp. 149–56.
2. Cadet L. A. Obolensky had a different version of this. He said he and some armed soldiers and workers had arrived at the Tauride Palace. At first they gathered outside the iron fence, then entered the courtyard. Some Socialist deputies came out and tried to quiet them but soon the crowd grew restive. A shot rang out, a member of the Tauride guard fell wounded, and the crowd stormed into the building. (E. D. Chermensky, *Istoriya SSSR Period Imperializma*, quoting the unpublished memoirs of Obolensky in Soviet archives, p. 413.)
3. Shulgin, *Dni*, pp. 150–62.
4. Nikolai Sukhanov, *Zapiski o Revolyutsii*, Vol. I, pp. 80–90.
5. Alexander Kerensky, *Russia and History's Turning Point*, p. 196.
6. Shulgin, *Dni*, p. 161.
7. Ibid., pp. 163, 166.
8. Kerensky, *Russia*, p. 194.
9. S. P. Melgunov, *Martovskiye Dni 1917 goda*, p. 29.
10. Ibid.; Marylie Markovitch, *La Révolution Russe*, pp. 26–27.
11. Oscar Anweiler, *The Soviets*, p. 104.
12. Sukhanov, *Zapiski o Revolyutsii*, Vol. I, pp. 86–88.
13. *Oktyabrskoye Vooruzhennoye Vosstaniye*, Vol. I, p. 74.
14. Sukhanov, *Zapiski o Revolyutsii*, Vol. I, pp. 92–98. Sukhanov noted that no resolution to take over the power of government was placed before the Soviet. Ad-

vocates of an immediate dictatorship by the Soviet might well have been the Bolshevik Shlyapnikov or the left SR Alexandrovich. But neither said a word. "As it happened," Sukhanov observed, "both these groups were weak, not prepared, had no initiative and were unable to orient themselves in the situation." (Ibid., p. 127.) Early in the evening Shlyapnikov had approved the text of a Bolshevik manifesto which was published the next morning in issue No. 1 of *Izvestiya* of the Petrograd Soviet of Workers' Deputies. It called for: creation of a provisional revolutionary government guarded by a revolutionary people's army with temporary powers; confiscation of the land and giving it to the peasants; an eight-hour day; and election of a constituent assembly on a basis of popular suffrage. There was no word in the Bolshevik declaration about the Soviet. Nor was there any call for an end to the war. (*Oktyabrskoye Vooruzhennoye Vosstaniye*, Vol. I, pp. 68-70.) The manifesto was apparently drafted earlier in the day, possibly before the formal call for the Soviet meeting went out at 3 P.M. In many Communist archives it is erroneously dated "Feb. 26" but its text makes clear that it must have been prepared during the day of the twenty-seventh. The authors of the document were Vyacheslav Molotov, M. I. Khakharev, and V. Kayurov. It was typewritten by Shlyapnikov and turned over for publication *after* Shlyapnikov became aware of the impending meeting of the Soviet. (Marc Ferro, *The Russian Revolution of February 1917*, pp. 46-47.)

A very careful effort by the Soviet historian Yu. S. Tokaryev to demonstrate that the Bolsheviks played a leading role in creation of the Soviet proves only the reverse. He cites evidence from the Czarist Okhrana that the Petersburg committee had plans to set up an Information Bureau which proposed to take the lead with factory committees in setting up a Soviet. But, by this time, of course, the Soviet was already coming into being. He admits that "the extreme barrenness of source materials" makes it difficult to show what role the Bolsheviks played. He is right about the "barrenness." It is this which demonstrates that the Bolsheviks, in fact, played no role in the creation of the Soviet. (Yu. S. Tokaryev, *Petrogradskii Sovet Rabochikh i Soldatskikh Deputatov v Marte-Aprile 1917 g.*, pp. 18-20.)

15. Ferro, *Russian Revolution*, p. 51.

16. A. Taneyeva, (Vyrubova), *Stranitsy iz Moei Zhizni*, pp. 96-98.

17. Alexis Volkov, *Souvenirs d'Alexis Volkov*, pp. 86-87.

18. Alexander Blok, in *Arkhiv Russkoi Revolyutsii*, Vol. IV, p. 38.

19. V. M. Pronin, *Posledniye Dni Tsarskoi Stavki*, pp. 14-15.

20. *Krasny Arkhiv*, 1927, Vol. XXI, pp. 6-7.

21. Ibid., p. 7.

22. A. S. Lukomsky, *Vospominaniya*, Vol. I, p. 128. Gen. A. S. Lukomsky's chronology of events on February 27 is so mistaken as to both time and person that his evidence is not reliable. He reports that after receiving Rodzyanko's telegram the Czar spent an hour on the telephone and that "all were confident" that he spoke with the Czarina in Tsarskoye Selo. Nicholas de Basily, the Czar's diplomatic-legal adviser at Mogilev, states flatly that the Czar had a telephone conversation with his wife that evening. (Nicholas de Basily, *Memoirs*, p. 110.) Princess Cantacuzene, reflecting Petrograd gossip, said there were several calls. (Princess Cantacuzene, *Revolutionary Days*, pp. 133, 136, 137.) N. A. Sokolov, the investigator of the murder of the Czar and his family, states that the Czar spoke with the Czarina for about an hour in the evening of the twenty-seventh. He cited no source but Sir Bernard Pares thought he might have gotten the information from Pierre Gilliard, the tutor of the Czarevich. (N. Sokolov, *Ubistvo Tsarskoi Semii*, p. 6; Pares, *The Fall of the Russian Monarchy*, p. 464.) If the Czar spoke on the telephone with his wife, this would explain his failure to ac-

knowledge her telegrams and, perhaps, his insistence on returning to Tsarskoye before making any major decisions.

23. *Krasny Arkhiv*, 1927, Vol. XX, p. 136.

24. V. N. Voyeikov, *S Tsarem i Bez Tsarya*, p. 199.

25. Blok, in *Arkhiv Russkoi Revolyutsii*, Vol. IV, p. 34.

26. The situation in Palace Square gave rise to many misconceptions. Count de Chambrun wrote his fiancé in France that he had watched the Pavlovsky Regiment march into the square, band playing. It entered the palace and soon thereafter the Imperial flag came slowly down. (Ferro, *Russian Revolution*, p. 43.) If the flag came down, it was because dusk had fallen. The palace was not occupied by revolutionaries that night.

27. Blok, in *Arkhiv Russkoi Revolyutsii*, Vol. IV, pp. 35–36, 38.

28. Ibid., p. 38.

29. When the Czar was finally informed about the council's actions about midnight, he disapproved them. (*Krasny Arkhiv*, 1927, Vol. XXI, p. 13.)

30. Blok, in *Arkhiv Russkoi Revolyutsii*, Vol. IV, p. 36.

31. *Krasny Arkhiv*, 1925, Vol. X, p. 179, Protopopov diary.

32. Protopopov, in *Padeniye Tsarskogo Rezhima*, Vol. IV, pp. 101–2.

33. *Krasny Arkhiv*, 1922, Vol. IV, p. 213.

34. Golitsyn, in *Padeniye Tsarskogo Rezhima*, Vol. II, p. 267. Golitsyn recalled sending the message between 6 and 7 P.M. but it may not have arrived in Mogilev before late evening. (Ferro, *Russian Revolution*, p. 67.) Ladyzhensky recalled giving the telegram to the chancellery at 6 P.M. (Blok, in *Arkhiv Russkoi Revolyutsii*, Vol. IV, p. 36.) Almost all the eyewitness accounts err by placing action earlier than it occurred—often by hours, sometimes by days.

35. Voyeikov, *S Tsarem i Bez Tsarya*, pp. 200–1. The communications between Voyeikov and Benkendorf apparently occurred before dinner since at 8:15 P.M. after his conversation Voyeikov sent a ciphered message to Protopopov (not knowing he had been compelled to resign), saying the Czar was leaving Mogilev at 2:30 A.M. for Tsarskoye Selo via Orsha, Likhoslavl, and Tosno. (Blok, in *Arkhiv Russkoi Revolyutsii*, Vol. IV, p. 40.)

36. Blok, in *Arkhiv Russkoi Revolyutsii*, Vol. IV, p. 38–39.

37. Ivanov, in *Padeniye Tsarskogo Rezhima*, Vol. V, p. 320.

38. Blok, in *Arkhiv Russkoi Revolyutsii*, Vol. IV, p. 39.

39. Ivanov, in *Padeniye Tsarskogo Rezhima*, Vol. V, pp. 317–20; V. S. Dyakin, *Russkaya Burzhuasiya i Tsarism v gody Pervoi Mirovoi Voiny 1914–1917*, p. 332.

40. Ivanov, in *Padeniye Tsarskogo Rezhima*, Vol. V, p. 318.

41. Blok, in *Arkhiv Russkoi Revolyutsii*, Vol. IV, p. 36.

42. Belyayev, in *Padeniye Tsarskogo Rezhima*, Vol. II, p. 242; Dyakin, *Russkaya Burzhuasiya*, pp. 329–30.

43. Possibly as much as an hour. (Blok, in *Arkhiv Russkoi Revolyutsii*, Vol. IV, p. 36.)

44. The Czar and his suite boarded the train about midnight but it did not leave until nearly 5 A.M. because arrangements were not completed for the movement. (Ibid., p. 38.)

45. *Krasny Arkhiv*, 1927, Vol. XXI, pp. 11–12.

46. Ibid., pp. 15–16. The missing men were the Minister of Communications and the Minister of Foreign Affairs. Actually, as Belyayev learned in a later call from an official named Putilov, they were hiding in another room of the palace and wanted Belyayev to rescue them. He, of course, had no troops to send to help. (Blok, in *Arkhiv Russkoi Revolyutsii*, Vol. IV, p. 37.)

47. *Krasny Arkhiv*, 1927, Vol. XXI, pp. 9, 11–12.
48. A. I. Spiridovich, *Velikaya Voina i Fevralskaya Revolyutsiya 1914–1917 gg.*, Vol. III, p. 143.
49. *Krasny Arkhiv*, 1927, Vol. XXI, p. 242.
50. Khabalov, in *Padeniye Tsarskogo Rezhima*, Vol. I, pp. 199–204.
51. Dyakin, *Russkaya Burzhuasiya*, p. 33.
52. Pavel Milyukov, *Vospominaniya*, Vol. II, p. 290.

XL. "Nothing's Left but Russia" PAGES 371–76

1. Nikolai Sukhanov, *Zapiski o Revolyutsii*, Vol. I, pp. 126–31.
2. Ibid., p. 131.
3. Pavel Milyukov, *Vospominaniya*, Vol. II, p. 295.
4. This rumor was believed by almost everyone in Petrograd. Postrevolutionary inquiry by both Communist and non-Communist historians indicates few, if any, machine guns were in the hands of the police, and in all probability none were mounted on rooftops as almost everyone in the city believed. (*Oktyabrskoye Vooruzhennoye Vosstanniye*, Vol. I, p. 66, citing evidence of Provisional Government: Extraordinary Investigating Committee, in A. D. Sidorov, *Materialy o Sverzhenii Tsarizma v fonde Chrezvychainoi Sledstvennoi Kommissii Vremennogo Pravitelstva*, pp. 139–49.)
5. Alexander Blok, in *Arkhiv Russkoi Revolyutsii*, Vol. IV, p. 42.
6. Sukhanov, *Zapiski o Revolyutsii*, Vol. I, pp. 57, 58, 66.
7. Ibid., p. 139.
8. Marc Ferro, *The Russian Revolution of February 1917*, p. 49.
9. S. P. Melgunov, *Martovskiye Dni 1917 goda*, pp. 20–21.
10. *Arkhiva A. M. Gorkogo*, Vol. IX, p. 194.
11. V. V. Shulgin, *Dni*, pp. 178–79, 181.
12. Sukhanov, *Zapiski o Revolyutsii*, Vol. I, pp. 142–44. Col. B. A. Engelhardt was an Octobrist Duma deputy who was named to head the Military Commission of the Duma. The Soviet had already named a Military Commission headed by S. D. Mstislavsky (Maslovsky). (*Oktyabrskoye Vooruzhennoye Vosstaniye*, Vol. I, p. 73.) For the time being Mstislavsky agreed to subordinate himself to Engelhardt. (Sukhanov, *Zapiski o Revolyutsii*, Vol. I, p. 144.) Shidlovsky had a different version of this episode. His nephew, Nelidov, was an officer of the Preobrazhensky. Nelidov telephoned Shidlovsky telling him that the regiment wished to place itself at the disposal of the Duma. Shidlovsky gave this word to Rodzyanko and this decided Rodzyanko on his course. (S. I. Shidlovsky, *Vospominany*, Vol. II, pp. 67–68.)
13. V. S. Dyakin, *Russkaya Burzhuasiya i Tsarism*, p. 331.
14. Zinaida Gippius, *Sinyaya Kniga*, p. 96.
15. She kept most of her jewelry in a safe-deposit vault at Fabergé. Later she moved it to a bank. In the end she was compelled to leave the bulk of her jewels behind when she escaped from Russia. (Mathilde Kschessinska, *Dancing in Petersburg*, pp. 163–73.) Tamara Karsavina in her memoir mistakenly places Kshesinskaya in the Crimea when the Revolution broke out. (*Theatre Street*, p. 260.)
16. Grafinya M. Kleinmikhel, *Iz Potonuvshavo Mira*, pp. 264–70.
17. *Oktyabrskoye Vooruzhennoye Vosstaniye*, Vol. I, p. 66.
18. G. Lozgachev-Yelizarov, *Nezabyvayemoye*, pp. 96–97, 124–26; P. P. Yelizarov, *Mark Yelizarov i Semya Ulyanovykh*, p. 117.

19. P. Sorokin, *Leaves from a Russian Diary*, pp. 12–13.
20. Konstantin Paustovsky, *The Story of a Life*, p. 474.

XLI. *The Czar on the Run* PAGES 377–82

1. V. V. Shulgin, *Dni*, pp. 181–84.
2. Nikolai Sukhanov, *Zapiski o Revolyutsii*, Vol. I, pp. 158–59.
3. *Krasny Arkhiv*, 1925, Vol. VIII, p. 245.
4. V. M. Pronin, *Posledniye Dni Tsarskoi Stavki*, p. 18.
5. Ivanov, in *Padeniye Tsarskogo Rezhima*, Vol. V, pp. 315–19.
6. V. N. Voyeikov, *S Tsarem i Bez Tsarya*, pp. 201–2.
7. *Krasny Arkhiv*, 1927, Vol. XX, p. 136.
8. Dubensky, in *Padeniye Tsarskogo Rezhima*, Vol. VI, p. 402.
9. *Krasny Arkhiv*, 1923, Vol. IV, p. 214.
10. Ibid., 1925, Vol. VIII, p. 245.
11. Dubensky, in *Padeniye Tsarskogo Rezhima* Vol. VI, p. 402.
12. *Krasny Arkhiv*, 1927, Vol. XX, p. 136.
13. Dubensky, in *Padeniye Tsarskogo Rezhima*, Vol. VI, pp. 402–3.
14. The Hughes apparatus was a system of keyboard telegraph transmission invented by David E. Hughes of New York, first put into use in the 1860s. It was much admired by the Russians, and as late as World War II an improved Hughes system was relied upon by Stalin as his principal means of communication with his generals. (*Bolshaya Sovetskaya Entsyklopediya*, 1st ed., Vol. LXV, pp. 164–65.)
15. Voyeikov, *S Tsarem i Bez Tsarya*, p. 204; *Padeniye Tsarkogo Rezhima*, Vol. III, p. 74. The conventional version of this event is that the Czar was unable to get back to Tsarskoye Selo because the new Minister of Communications, Bublikov, alerted the railroad men and they played cat-and-mouse with the Czar, placing such obstacles in his path that he was compelled to go off to Pskov. Melgunov has examined the evidence carefully and has concluded that it was actually a decision of the Czar and his suite which sent the train to Pskov. Most accounts contend that the seizure of the railroad station at Tosno was what blocked the Czar from returning to his palace. In fact, Tosno was not blocked nor was Lyuban (as reported by the trainman). All that happened was that a reserve unit had created a disturbance in the Lyuban station restaurant. Voyeikov's accounts are very confused. He mentions Tosno but never refers to Lyuban which was where the trouble was reported to be. (S. P. Melgunov, *Martovskiye Dni*, pp. 54, 170–71; Voyeikov, *S Tsarem i Bez Tsarya*, pp. 204–5; Voyeikov, Vol. II, p. 74, and Dubensky, Vol. VI, pp. 402–3, in *Padeniye Tsarskogo Rezhima*.)
16. S. P. Melgunov, *Martovskiye Dni 1917 goda*, p. 54.
17. Shulgin, *Dni*, pp. 170–71.
18. Sukhanov, *Zapiski o Revolyutsii*, Vol. I, pp. 110–11.
19. Shulgin, *Dni*, pp. 190–92; Protopopov, in *Padeniye Tsarskogo Rezhima*, Vol. IV, pp. 101–2; *Krasny Arkhiv*, 1925, Vol. X, pp. 180–81, Protopopov diary.
20. Marc Ferro, *The Russian Revolution of February 1917*, p. 52.
21. *Krasny Arkhiv*, 1929, Vol. XXXII, p. 88–115.
22. Princess Lidiya Vassiltchikova, unpublished memoirs.
23. Marylie Markovitch, *La Révolution Russe*, p. 58.
24. Sukhanov, *Zapiski o Revolyutsii*, Vol. I, p. 179. Two hundred officers were slain in the Kronshtadt massacre according to Zinaida Gippius. (*Sinyaya Kniga*, p. 106).

25. *Oktyabrskoye Vooruzhennoye Vosstaniye*, Vol. I, p. 66.
26. Gippius, *Sinyaya Kniga*, p. 130.
27. Markovitch, *Révolution Russe*, pp. 128–33.
28. Sukhanov, *Zapiski o Revolyutsii*, Vol. I, pp. 245–46.
29. Voyeikov, *S Tsarem i Bez Tsarya*, pp. 205–6.
30. Voyeikov in *Padeniye Tsarskogo Rezhima*, Vol. III, p. 76.
31. Voyeikov, *S Tsarem i Bez Tsarya*, p. 206.
32. Dubensky, in *Padeniye Tsarskogo Rezhima*, Vol. III, p. 396–404.
33. Blok, in *Arkhiv Russkoii Revolyutsii*, Vol. IV, p. 48.
34. Some hours later the Czar rewrote his proposal, making it clearly a grant of Constitutional Government and withdrawing the right to name any Ministers. (*Krasny Arkhiv*, 1928, Vol. XXVI, p. 204.)
35. *Krasny Arkhiv*, 1923, Vol. IV, p. 214.
36. Ibid., 1927, Vol. XX, p. 136.
37. Blok, in *Arkhiv Russkoi Revolyutsii*, Vol. IV, pp. 46–48; Voyeikov, *S Tsarem i Bez Tsarya*, pp. 206–12.

XLII. The Czar Steps Down PAGES 386–90

1. *Padeniye Tsarskogo Rezhima*, Vol. V, pp. 314–26; Alexander Blok, in *Arkhiv Russkoi Revolyutsii*, Vol. IV, pp. 45–50.
2. V. N. Voyeikov, *S Tsarem i Bez Tsarya*, pp. 209–10.
3. Dubensky, in *Padeniye Tsarskogo Rezhima*, Vol. VI, p. 408.
4. *Krasny Arkhiv*, 1924, Vol. VIII, p. 245.
5. The conversation went on from about 4 A.M. to 7 A.M. (Ibid., 1928, Vol. XXVI, p. 204.)
6. General Lukomsky believes Alexeyev sent the circular telegram at General Ruzsky's request. All other sources suggest it was sent at Alexeyev's initiative. (A. S. Lukomky, *Vospominaniya*, Vol. I, p. 136.)
7. S. P. Melgunov, *Martovskiye Dni 1917 goda*, p. 182.
8. Voyeikov, *S Tsarem i Bez Tsarya*, p. 211.
9. *Krasny Arkhiv*, 1923, Vol. IV, pp. 215–16.
10. Ibid., 1925, Vol. VIII, p. 245.
11. Ibid., 1928, Vol. XXVI, p. 206.
12. Ibid.
13. Melgunov, *Martovskiye Dni*, pp. 182–84.
14. *Krasny Arkhiv*, 1928, Vol. XXVI, p. 206.
15. General Lukomsky says the form was composed by himself and the chief of headquarters diplomatic section, Basily. He says it was sent to Pskov after the Czar's decision at 3 P.M. and that Rodzyanko was then informed by Alexeyev of the Czar's action. (Lukomsky, *Vospominaniya*, Vol. I, p. 138.)
16. *Padeniye Tsarskogo Rezhima*, Vol. VI, p. 409; *Krasny Arkhiv*, 1928, Vol. XXVI, p. 206, diary of Grand Duke Andrei Vladimirovich.
17. Dubensky, in *Padeniye Tsarskogo Rezhima*, Vol. VI, p. 409.
18. Ibid., p. 393.
19. Ibid., p. 409; Voyeikov, *S Tsarem i Bez Tsarya*, pp. 212–21.
20. Dubensky, in *Padeniye Tsarskogo Rezhima*, p. 409.
21. Ibid., p. 394.
22. A. I. Spiridovich, *Velikaya Voina i Fevralskaya Revolyutsiya 1914–1917 gg.*, Vol. III, pp. 297–98, relating personal conversation with Fyodorov.
23. Melgunov, *Martovskiye Dni*, pp. 187–88.
24. *Padeniye Tsarskogo Rezhima*, Vol. VI, p. 394.

25. *Krasny Arkhiv*, 1925, Vol. VIII, p. 245. Ruzsky and Shulgin discussed this question but decided there was nothing they could do about it. (*Krasny Arkhiv*, 1928, Vol. XXVI, p. 207.)
26. Melgunov, *Martovskiye Dni*, p. 189.
27. V. V. Shulgin, *Dni*, pp. 267-79.
28. *Krasny Arkhiv*, 1925, Vol. VIII, p. 245.
29. Ibid., 1928, Vol. XXVI, p. 290.
30. *Nikolai II i Velikiye Knyazya*, pp. 144-45.
31. J. C. Trewin, *The House of Special Purpose*, pp. 52-55.

XLIII. The News Spreads PAGES 393-400

1. Osip Pyatnitsky, *Izbrannye Vospominaniya i Stati*, p. 222.
2. W. S. Woytinsky, *Stormy Passage*, pp. 243-44.
3. I. G. Tsereteli, *Vospominaniya o Fevralskoi Revolyutsii*, pp. 3-4.
4. Ibid., Vol. I, p. 20.
5. Woytinsky, *Stormy Passage*, p. 253; Tsereteli, *Vospominaniya*, Vol. I, pp. 33-34.
6. Catherine Breshkovsky, *The Little Grandmother of the Russian Revolution*, pp. 309-14.
7. Leon Trotsky, *Stalin*, p. 181.
8. Ibid.
9. V. I. Lenin, *Collected Works*, Vol. XLIII, p. 625. The telegram was probably sent on March 10 but Lenin did not report receiving it until March 22.
10. *Voprosy Istorii KPSS*, 1962, No. 3, pp. 143-46. Actually Stalin had been an "agent" of the Central Committee in 1910. In 1912 he was co-opted to membership in the CC.
11. A. S. Alliluyeva, *Vospominaniya*, pp. 165-69.
12. *Voprosy Istorii KPSS*, 1962, No. 3, p. 148.
13. Grigory Aronson, *Rossiya v Epokhu Revolyutsii*, p. 42.
14. *Oktyabrskoye Vooruzhennoye Vosstaniye*, Vol. I, p. 111.
15. Trotsky, *Stalin*, p. 186.
16. Isaac Deutscher, *Stalin*, p. 133.
17. Trotsky, *Stalin*, p. 187.
18. David Shub, *Lenin*, p. 103.
19. Ibid.
20. *Voprosy Istorii KPSS*, 1966, No. 6, p. 140.
21. Trotsky, *Stalin*, p. 187.
22. A. Shlyapnikov, *Semnadtsty god*, Vol. II, p. 180.
23. A Shlyapnikov, in *Leninsky Sbornik*, Vol. II, pp. 448-49.
24. V. I. Lenin, *Collected Works*, Vol. XXXV, pp. 290-92.
25. *Bolshaya Sovetskaya Entsyklopedia*, 1st ed., Vol. VII, p. 631.
26. Nadezhda Krupskaya, *Reminiscences of Lenin*, pp. 335-36.
27. A. S. Kudryavtsev, *Lenin v Berne i Tsurikhe*, p. 226.
28. Lenin, *Collected Works*, Vol. XXXV, p. 294.
29. Krupskaya, *Reminiscences*, p. 336.
30. Lenin, *Collected Works*, Vol. XXXV, pp. 297-99.
31. Ibid., p. 292.
32. Ibid., Vol. XXIII, p. 406.
33. Ibid., p. 293. The telegram was read at the Petrograd Party Bureau March 13 and provoked much antagonism, particularly to Lenin's last two points. (*Oktyabrskoye Vooruzhennoye Vosstaniye*, Vol. I, p. 155.) The Central Committee

considered these points "insufficiently clear" and telegraphed Lenin, asking for clarification; meantime, the telegram was set aside. (*Vosprosy Istorii KPSS*, 1962, No. 3, p. 140.)

34. Krupskaya, *Reminiscences*, p. 337.

35. Lenin, *Collected Works*, Vol. XXXV, p. 300.

36. Ibid., Vol. XLIII, pp. 616–17.

37. Ya. Ganetsky, in *Vospominaniya o V. I. Lenine*, Vol. I, pp. 557–58.

38. Krupskaya, *Reminiscences*, p. 337.

39. Lenin, *Collected Works*, Vol. XLIII, p. 622.

40. Ibid., p. 616.

41. Ibid., Vol. XXXVI, p. 420.

42. Ibid., Vol. XXIII, pp. 297–308.

43. Ibid., pp. 309–19.

44. Ibid., pp. 406–7.

45. *Oktyabrskoye Vooruzhennoye Vosstaniye*, Vol. I, P. 109.

46. Lenin, *Collected Works*, Vol. XXIII, p. 407.

47. Ibid., pp. 328–29.

XLIV. To the Finland Station PAGES 404–6

1. Grigory Aronson, *Rossiya v Epokhu Revolyutsii*, p. 42.

2. V. I. Lenin, *Collected Works*, Vol. XXIII, pp. 363–64.

3. Ibid., pp. 416–17.

4. Ibid., p. 307.

5. Z. A. B. Zeman and W. B. Scharlau, *The Merchant of Revolution*, pp. 162–63. Careful examination of the German, French, and Swiss evidence, including records of Parvus' Swiss bank accounts, leads Alfred Erich Senn to the conclusion that most of the German and Austrian funds went to nationality groups, Ukrainian, Baltic, and Caucasian. A little money trickled into Lenin's hands via the Ukrainians in 1915, but he stopped taking it when he learned the source probably through the revelations and polemics of Grigory Alexinsky, a onetime Bolshevik who had now become a strong supporter of the war. Alexinsky played a leading role in 1917 in spreading charges that Lenin was financed with German funds. (Alfred Erich Senn, in *Soviet Studies*, Vol. XXVIII, No. 1 (Jan. 1970), pp. 83–90; Alfred Erich Senn, *The Russian Revolution in Switzerland*, pp. 54–55.)

6. Lenin, *Collected Works*, Vol. XLIII, p. 618.

7. Ibid., p. 624.

8. Parvus overplayed his hand early in the negotiations, proposing not only to arrange for Lenin and Zinoviev to transit Germany but to pay their expenses as well. Lenin immediately turned the proposal down, writing Ganetsky: "I thank you with all my heart for the trouble you are taking and for your help. I cannot, of course, make use of the services of people who are connected with the publisher of *Die Glocke*," that is, Parvus. (Ibid., Vol. XXV, p. 308.) It seems likely, despite this, that Parvus' friends did help finance the Bolsheviks' trip.

9. Ibid., Vol. XXIII, pp. 372, 418.

10. Nadezhda Krupskaya, *Reminiscences*, p. 344; *Leninsky Sbornik*, 1924, Vol. II, pp. 405–16.

11. Lenin, *Collected Works*, Vol. XXIII, p. 417.

12. David Shub, *Lenin*, p. 106.

13. Lenin i Lunacharsky, *Literaturnoye Nasledstvo*, Vol. LXXX, p. 644.

14. A. S. Kudryavtsev, *Lenin v Berne i Tsyurikhe*, pp. 247–50.

15. Krupskaya gives the total as thirty-one (Krupskaya, *Reminiscences*, p. 344). Of the thirty-two, nineteen were Bolsheviks (*Oktyabrskoye Vooruzhennoye Vosstaniye*, Vol. I, p. 179).

16. Krupskaya, *Reminiscences*, p. 345.

17. Richard Kohn, *La Révolution Russe*, pp. 251–52, quoting Platten and Radek.

18. Stefan T. Possony, *Lenin: The Compulsive Revolutionary*, p. 212.

19. Krupskaya, *Reminiscences*, pp. 345–46.

20. Lenin, *Collected Works*, Vol. XLV, p. 628.

21. Ya. Ganetsky, in *Vospominaniya o V. I. Lenine*, Vol. I, pp. 561–62.

22. Ibid., Vol. II, pp. 376–77.

23. Ibid., Vol. I, p. 563.

24. M. G. Tskhakaya, ibid., Vol. II, p. 380.

25. Zeman and Scharlau, *Merchant of Revolution*, pp. 216–17.

26. The German Foreign Office on March 21 had obtained from the Treasury a new sum of 5 million marks to be spent for "political purposes" in Russia. How much of this was channeled to the Bolsheviks after Lenin's return to Petrograd has not been established despite careful efforts by Zeman, Scharlau, and others. (Ibid., p. 219.)

27. A. Shlyapnikov, in *Leninsky Sbornik*, Vol. II, p. 400.

28. Krupskaya, *Reminiscences*, p. 346; Anatoly Ivansky, *Novy Mir*, 1977, No. 4, pp. 210–11.

29. Lenin, *Collected Works*, Vol. XXXVII, p. 540.

30. Georgi Lozgachev-Yelizarov, *Nezabyvayemoye*, 4th ed., p. 136.

31. *Oktyabrskoye Vooruzhennoye Vosstaniye*, Vol. I, p. 179.

32. Plekhanov had arrived a day or two earlier from Paris, and on April 7 Boris Savinkov, the famous SR terrorist and friend of Zinaida Gippius, was expected. (Zinaida Gippius, *Sinyaya Kniga*, p. 132.)

33. Shlyapnikov, in *Leninsky Sbornik*, Vol. II, p. 452.

34. Krupskaya, *Reminiscences*, p. 346; A. M. Afanasyev, in *Vospominaniya o V. I. Lenine*, Vol. II, pp. 382–83; Shlyapnikov, ibid., p. 452.

35. Fyodor F. Raskolnikov, *Kronshtadt i Piter v 1917 godu*, p. 54.

XLV. At Last—Petrograd   PAGES 411–14

1. *Oktyabrskoye Vooruzhennoye Vosstaniye*, Vol. I, p. 180.

2. A. Shlyapnikov, in *Leninsky Sbornik*, Vol. II, p. 452.

3. V. D. Bonch-Bruyevich, *Vospominaniya o Lenine*, pp. 71–72.

4. Nadezhda Krupskaya, *Reminiscences*, p. 347.

5. Bonch-Bruyevich, *Vospominaniya*, pp. 72–73.

6. W. S. Woytinsky, *Stormy Passage*, p. 265.

7. Shlyapnikov, in *Leninsky Sbornik*, Vol. II, p. 452.

8. Nikolai Sukhanov, *Zapiski o Revolyutsii*, Vol. I, pp. 273–74.

9. Woytinsky, *Stormy Passage*, p. 265.

10. Sukhanov, *Zapiski o Revolyutsii*, Vol. I, p. 274.

11. S. M. Lebidova and E. G. Salita, *Yelena Dimitriyevna Stasova*, p. 239.

12. Zinaida Gippius, *Sinyaya Kniga*, p. 134.

13. Z. Gippius-Merezhkovskaya, *Dmitrii Merezhkovsky*, p. 222.

14. Krupskaya, *Reminiscences*, p. 348.

15. Bonch-Bruyevich, *Vospominaniya*, pp. 74–75.

16. Madame de Néry listened to Lenin speaking on the balcony one evening. She called him "un revolutionaire élégant" with diamond cuff links and a new pointed beard. (Marylie Markovitch, *La Révolution Russe*, p. 14.)

17. Woytinsky, *Stormy Passage*, p. 265.

18. Ibid., p. 266.

19. Lenin's "April Theses" formally incorporating these views were published in *Pravda* April 7. The next day *Pravda* published an editorial note declaring them "unacceptable" because they were based on the concept that the bourgeois revolution had been completed and that it was now time to proceed to the socialist revolution. Lenin had little support in the Central Committee or the Petersburg Committee for his extreme views. In fact his only backing came from three leading Bolshevik women, two of whom had accompanied him on the "sealed train"— Alexandra Kollontai, Inessa Armand, and Nadezhda Krupskaya. (A. Avtorkhanov, *Proiskhozhdeniye Partokratti*, Vol. I, pp. 278–79.) Shlyapnikov, Lenin's faithful Petrograd lieutenant, observed: "The position of Vladimir Ilyich was to the left of our left." (*Leninsky Sbornik*, Vol. II, p. 454.)

20. Sukhanov, *Zapiski o Revolyutsii*, pp. 283–85.

21. Lebidova and Salita, *Stasova*, p. 241.

22. Georgii Lozgachev-Yelizarov, *Nezabyvayemoye*, 4th ed., pp. 136–39. According to some accounts Lenin visited his mother's grave at Volkov cemetery on that first ride. Other sources say he made the trip later in the day. (*Novy Mir*, 1977, No. 4, p. 223.)

23. *Krasny Arkhiv*, 1927, Vol. XX, pp. 136–43.

XLVI. The Tragedy of Lotarevo PAGES 417–25

1. Zinaida Gippius, *Sinyaya Kniga*, p. 109.

2. N. Serebrov (Tikhonov), in *V. Mayakovsky, v Vospominaniyakh Sovremennikov*, pp. 140–41.

3. Viktor Shklovsky, *Mayakovsky and His Circle*, p. 97.

4. Z. Gippius-Merezhkovskaya, *Dmitrii Merezhkovsky*, p. 222.

5. Gippius, *Sinyaya Kniga*, pp. 106–7.

6. Andrei Bely, *Zapiski Chudaka*, Vol. II, pp. 215–18.

7. Gippius, *Sinyaya Kniga*, pp. 91, 118, 119, 130.

8. Wiktor Woroszylski, *The Life of Mayakovsky*, pp. 175–79.

9. A. Baborenko and I. A. Bunin, *Materialy dlya Biografii*, pp. 209–10; Woroszylski, *Mayakovsky*, pp. 179–80.

10. Shklovsky, *Mayakovsky*, pp. 103–4.

11. Simon Karlinsky, *Marina Cvetaeva: Her Life and Art*, p. 141.

12. Ilya Ehrenburg, *People and Life 1891–1921*, pp. 252–53.

13. Viktor Chernov, *Rozhdeniye Revolyutsionnoi Rossii*, pp. 216–17.

14. Gippius, *Sinyaya Kniga*, p. 109.

15. Marylie Markovitch, *La Révolution Russe*, pp. 197–206.

16. Roger Pethybridge, *Witnesses to the Russian Revolution*, pp. 174–75, quoting F. Golder, *Documents of Russian History* (1927).

17. Konstantin Paustovsky, *The Story of a Life*, p. 484.

18. Ibid., pp. 492–94.

19. Marc Ferro, *The Russian Revolution of February 1917*, pp. 122–125, 158.

20. Chernov, *Rozhdeniye Revolyutsionnoi Rossii*, pp. 316–28.

21. E. Lundberg, *Zapiski Pisatelya*, p. 73.

22. Between March and June there were 196 agrarian outbreaks in the Tambov Guberniya. Analagous outbreaks occurred in other rural areas but Tambov was a center of most violent unrest. (T. V. Ospipova, in *Istoriya SSSR*, 1976, No. 3, p. 119.)

23. The peasants did not regard the Prince as a liberal despite the fact that the Czar had temporarily banished him from St. Petersburg in 1901 for interfering with the Cossacks' beating up demonstrators at Kazan Cathedral.

24. Princess Lidiya Vassiltchikova, unpublished memoirs; Kn. V. L. i Kn. E. Dm. Vyazemskikh. *Lotarevskaya Kniga Sudbe;* personal observations of G. I. Vassiltchikov.

XLVII. The Villa Durnovo PAGES 428-37

1. Nikolai Sukhanov, *Zapiski o Revolyutsii*, Vol. I, p. 386.
2. *Oktyabrskoye Vooruzhennoye Vosstaniye*, Vol. I, pp. 288-89.
3. Wiktor Woytinsky, *Stormy Passage*, p. 290.
4. *Oktyabrskoye Vooruzhennoye Vosstaniye*, Vol. I, p. 269.
5. Ibid., p. 289.
6. Ibid., p. 286.
7. Marc Ferro, *The Russian Revolution of February 1917*, pp. 308-9.
8. *Oktyabrskoye Vooruzhennoye Vosstaniye*, Vol. I, pp. 205-6.
9. Ibid., pp. 224-25.
10. Leon Trotsky, *The History of the Russian Revolution*, Vol. I, p. 451.
11. Sukhanov, *Zapiski o Revolyutsii*, Vol. I, pp. 404-5.
12. Trotsky, *Russian Revolution*, Vol. I, pp. 484-86.
13. *Oktyabrskoye Vooruzhennoye Vosstaniye*, Vol. I, pp. 294-95.
14. Ibid., p. 288. Years later in emigration Kerensky told Gippius he would have arrested Lenin and Trotsky in June but "he didn't know their address." (Zinaida Gippius, *Sinyaya Kniga*, p. 226.)
15. N. Maximov, *V Gody Voiny*, Letopis Revolyutsii, Vol. I, pp. 243-46.
16. A. I. Spiridovich, *Velikaya Voina i Fevralskaya Revolyutsiya 1914-1917 gg.*, Vol. III, p. 210.
17. Marylie Markovitch, *La Révolution Russe*, pp. 253-61.
18. Louis de Robien, *The Diary of a Diplomat in Russia, 1917-1918*, pp. 72, 74.
19. Maurice Paléologue, *An Ambassador's Memoirs*, Vol. III, p. 322.
20. Markovitch, *Révolution Russe*, pp. 243-47.
21. Pyotr Ryss, *Russkii Opyt*, pp. 82-88.
22. Alexander Kerensky, *Russia and History's Turning Point*, pp. 284-86.
23. Woytinsky, *Stormy Passage*, pp. 294-97.
24. Alexander Rabinowitch, *Prelude to Revolution*, p. 107. On the same day more than 460 ordinary criminals escaped from two other Petrograd prisons due to the carelessness or connivance of the authorities. (*Oktyabrskoye Vooruzhennoye Vosstaniye*, Vol. I, p. 309.)
25. Ibid., pp. 308-9.
26. Rabinowitch, *Prelude to Revolution*, p. 121.
27. As early as June 26 he wrote Radek that he had been ill for several days and still was not in good health. (V. I. Lenin, *Collected Works*, Vol. XLIII, p. 628.)
28. Georgii Lozgachev-Yelizarov, *Nezabyvayemoye*, 5th ed., p. 141.
29. S. M. Lebidova and E. G. Salita, *Yelena Dmitriyevna Stasova*, pp. 245-46.
30. Nadezhda Krupskaya, *Reminiscences of Lenin*, p. 364.
31. The date is given as June 29 by *Oktyabrskoye Vooruzhennoye Vosstaniye*, Vol. I, p. 321; and by Trotsky, in his *History of the Russian Revolution*, Vol. II, p. 28; and by Lenin himself, in his *Collected Works*, Vol. XXV, p. 208. Bonch-Bruyevich gives it as June 27.
32. V. D. Bonch-Bruyevich, *Vospominaniya o Lenine*, pp. 96-106.
33. De Robien, *Diary of a Diplomat*, pp. 81-82.
34. Bonch-Bruyevich, *Vospominaniya*, pp. 96-106.

XLVIII. *Lenin Hunkers Down*

1. Leon Trotsky, *A History of the Russian Revolution,* Vol. II, p. 24.
2. *Oktyabrskoye Vooruzhennoye Vosstaniye,* Vol. I, p. 323.
3. Ibid., pp. 323–24.
4. Ibid., pp. 325–26.
5. Trotsky, *Russian Revolution,* Vol. II, p. 25.
6. V. I. Nevsky, in *Katorga i Ssylka,* 1932, Nos. 96–97, p. 30.
7. Alexander Rabinowitch, *Prelude to Revolution,* pp. 150–51.
8. *Istoriya SSSR,* 1957, No. 2, p. 126.
9. *Oktyabrskoye Vooruzhennoye Vosstaniye,* Vol. I, p. 338.
10. Ibid., p. 343.
11. Nikolai Sukhanov, *Zapiski o Revolyutsii,* Vol. I, pp. 434–38; Trotsky, *Russian Revolution,* Vol. II, pp. 40–42.
12. V. D. Bonch-Bruyevich, *Vospominaniya o Lenine,* pp. 105–7.
13. *Oktyabrskoye Vooruzhennoye Vosstaniye,* Vol. I, pp. 349–50.
14. Bonch-Bruyevich, *Vospominaniya,* p. 107. Bonch-Bruyevich instructed the cabbie to take Lenin home and then to the Tauride Palace. Lenin probably went home but he appeared very soon at the Bolshevik headquarters at the Kshesinskaya Palace.
15. Sukhanov estimated the numbers at 20,000. (Sukhanov, *Zapiski o Revolyutsii,* Vol. I, p. 441.)
16. *Oktyabrskoye Vooruzhennoye Vosstaniye,* Vol. I, p. 349.
17. V. I. Lenin, *Collected Works,* Vol. XXV, pp. 209–10.
18. Sukhanov, *Zapiski o Revolyutsii,* Vol. I, p. 441. This proved to be Lenin's last public speech until after the coup d'état in which he seized power October 26.
19. Louis de Robien, *The Diary of a Diplomat in Russia, 1917–1918,* pp. 84–85.
20. *Oktyabrskoye Vooruzhennoye Vosstaniye,* Vol. I, pp. 352–55.
21. W. S. Woytinsky, *Stormy Passage,* p. 302.
22. Sukhanov, *Zapiski o Revolyutsii,* Vol. I, pp. 445–47; Trotsky, *Russian Revolution,* Vol. II, p. 52.
23. Sukhanov, *Zapiski o Revolyutsii,* Vol. II, pp. 447–49.
24. Lenin, of course, was not a German spy nor a German agent, and no genuine evidence in support of such allegations has ever turned up despite intensive search by his enemies. But he was quite prepared to accept support from almost any source, and the Bolsheviks had been and were in receipt of German funds—exactly how much is still a matter of controversy. Parvus and Ganetsky were, in fact, the agents for their disbursement. One of Lenin's first letters on his return to Petrograd was directed April 12 to Ganetsky and Radek and complained: "Up to now we have received nothing, absolutely nothing from you—no letters, no packets, no money. . . . Write as often as you can and be very regular and careful in your contacts." (Lenin, *Collected Works,* Vol. XXXVI, pp. 444–45.) On April 21 Lenin wrote Ganetsky confirming the receipt of funds (2,000) from Kozlovsky and indicating that a courier system was being set up. (Ibid., Vol. XLIII, pp. 629–30.) Count Louis de Robien, no friend of the Bolsheviks, said of the Government charges at the time: "It seems to me that this accusation must be false, at any rate as regards Lenin who is a sincere and dedicated man. But this accusation will enable the men who make it to pose as patriots and incorruptibles and thereby regain some popularity." (De Robien, *Diary of a Diplomat,* p. 88.)
25. Sir Bernard Pares, *My Russian Memoirs,* pp. 464–65.
26. Sukhanov, *Zapiski o Revolyutsii,* Vol. I, p. 445.

27. S. P. Knyazev, *Ocherkii Istorii Leningradskoi Organizatsii KPSS*, Vol. I, p. 316.

28. *Oktyabrskoye Vooruzhennoye Vosstaniye*, Vol. I, p. 360.

29. Knyazev, *Ocherkii*, Vol. I, p. 516.

30. Trotsky, *Russian Revolution*, Vol. II, p. 104.

31. Some time between July 5 and 7 Lenin hastily penned a note to Kamenev saying. "Entre nous: if they do me in, I ask you to publish my notebook: 'Marxism on the State' (it got left behind in Stockholm). It's bound in a blue cover. . . . The condition: all this is absolutely entre nous!" (Lenin, *Collected Works*, Vol. XXXVI, p. 454.)

32. Nadezhda Krupskaya, *Reminiscences of Lenin*, pp. 365-71.

33. Bonch-Bruyevich, *Vospominaniya*, pp. 108-9.

34. Maxim Gorky, *Untimely Thoughts*, p. 75.

35. Alexander Blok, *Zapisnye Knizhki 1901-1920*, pp. 336-76.

XLIX. Waiting PAGES 446-52

1. Zinaida Gippius, *Sinyaya Kniga*, p. 150; Z. Gippius-Merezhkovskaya, *Dmitrii Merezhkovsky*, p. 224.

2. *Oktyabrskoye Vooruzhennoye Vosstaniye*, Vol. II, p. 38.

3. A. M. Sovokin, *V Preddverii Oktyabrya*, pp. 13-16.

4. Leon Trotsky, *A History of the Russian Revolution*, Vol. II, p. 142.

5. Ibid., p. 154.

6. Ibid., p. 147.

7. W. S. Woytinsky, *Stormy Passage*, p. 333.

8. Anthony Summers and Tom Mangold, *The File on the Czar*, pp. 250-51.

9. Alexander Blok, *Sobraniye Sochinenii*, Vol. VII, pp. 289-90; S. Vizavadsky, in *Arkhiv Russkoi Revolyutsii*, Vol. XI, pp. 49-50.

10. S. P. Melgunov, *Sudba Imperatora Nikolaya II*, p. 191.

11. Trotsky, *Russian Revolution*, Vol. II, p. 204.

12. Ibid., p. 160.

13. Ibid., p. 172.

14. Kerensky, *Russia*, p. 362.

15. V. V. Lvov, in *Posledniye Novosti*, Dec. 17, 1930, quoted ibid., pp. 278-79.

16. P. N. Finisov, an aide to Kornilov, in *Posledniye Novosti*, Mar. 6, 1937, quoted ibid., p. 377.

17. N. Sukhanov, *Zapiski o Revolyutsii*, Vol. I, p. 503.

18. Woytinsky, *Stormy Passage*, p. 348.

19. Trotsky, *Russian Revolution*, Vol. II, p. 326.

20. Gippius, *Sinyaya Kniga*, p. 182.

21. P. N. Pospelov, *Vladimir Ilyich Lenin. Biografiya*, pp. 334-35.

22. Emelyanov, in *Vospominaniya o V. I. Lenine*, Vol. II, p. 409.

23. Alexander Rabinowitch, *Prelude to Revolution*, pp. 219-22.

24. Nadezhda Krupskaya, *Reminiscences of Lenin*, p. 369.

25. *Oktyabrskoye Vooruzhennoye Vosstaniye*, Vol. I, p. 382.

26. Ibid., pp. 382-83.

27. Ibid., pp. 384-86. The Bolshevik press in late June had numbered some twelve dailies. *Pravda* with 90,000-95,000 copies plus 15,000 distributed at the front was the largest, followed by *Soldatskaya Pravda* with 63,000. (Marc Ferro, *The Russian Revolution of February 1917*, p. 232.) The size and strength of the Bolshevik press has caused some to speculate that German funds went into these enterprises.

28. *Oktyabrskoye Vooruzhennoye Vosstaniye*, Vol. II, p. 92.
29. *Vospominaniya o V. I. Lenine*, Vol. II, p. 426.
30. Pospelov, *Lenin. Biografiya*, pp. 341–42.
31. *Vospominaniya o V. I. Lenine*, Vol. II, p. 436.
32. V. I. Lenin, *Collected Works*, Vol. XXXV, pp. 318–24.

L. The Bolsheviks Begin to Move   PAGES 454–61

1. N. N. Sukhanov, *The Russian Revolution, 1917*, pp. 499–501.
2. Ibid., p. 500.
3. W. S. Woytinsky, *Stormy Passage*, pp. 347–49.
4. The usual estimate of Red Guards in Communist literature is 40,000. Recent studies indicate the number could not have been more than 25,000. The number of organized Red Guards at the time of the October coup was significantly less than 40,000. Some estimates place the August total as low as 13,000–15,000. (*Oktyabrskoye Vooruzhennoye Vosstaniye*, Vol. II, p. 159.)
5. V. I. Lenin, *Collected Works*, Vol. XXV, pp. 288–89.
6. *Oktyabrskoye Vooruzhennoye Vosstaniye*, Vol. II, p. 188.
7. Lenin, *Collected Works*, Vol. XXV, pp. 305–10.
8. Ibid., pp. 311–17.
9. *Oktyabrskoye Vooruzhennoye Vosstaniye*, Vol. II, p. 126.
10. Leon Trotsky, *A History of the Russian Revolution*, Vol. II, p. 304.
11. *Oktyabrskoye Vooruzhennoye Vosstaniye*, Vol. II, p. 192.
12. Trotsky, *Russian Revolution*, Vol. II, p. 306.
13. Ibid., p. 287.
14. Louis de Robien, *The Diary of a Diplomat in Russia, 1917–1918*, p. 128.
15. Lenin, *Collected Works*, Vol. XXVI, pp. 19–27.
16. Nadezhda Krupskaya, *Reminiscences of Lenin*, pp. 372–73.
17. Nadezhda Krupskaya, *Oktyabrskiye Dni*, p. 4.
18. Melgunov, the anti-Bolshevik but conscientious historian, suggested that the frenzy and disorientation of Lenin's arguments might be a symptom of syphilis which some anti-Bolsheviks affected to believe might have been the cause of Lenin's final fatal illness of 1922–24. There seem no medical grounds for this suspicion. (S. P. Melgunov, *Kak Bolsheviki Zakhvatili Vlast*, p. 22.)
19. *Oktyabrskoye Vooruzhennoye Vosstaniye*, Vol. II, pp. 206–7.
20. Many Party histories and personal memoirs mistakenly speak of circulating these letters of Lenin. Actually the reference is to letters written in late September and October. (Ibid., p. 225.)
21. Ibid., p. 207.
22. Lenin, *Collected Works*, Vol. XXVI, pp. 69–84.
23. *Oktyabrskoye Vooruzhennoye Vosstaniye*, Vol. II, pp. 225–8.
24. Krupskaya, *Reminiscences*, pp. 373, 386.
25. *Voprosy Istorii KPSS*, 1974, No. 1, pp. 114–15. Fofanova insisted to the end of her days (she died in 1976) that Lenin arrived from Finland about September 22, 1917. She first presented her views in an article in *Istoricbesky Arkhiv*, 1956, No. 4. Her conclusions were challenged, particularly by Isaak I. Mints, of the Institute of Marxism-Leninism. Mints supported his argument with evidence that a Finn who helped to conceal Lenin made a note on his calendar for October 7: "Old Man arrived." The Finn's wife's diary also said Lenin arrived October 7. Moreover, it was known that Lenin met Stalin October 8. Fofanova buttressed her case with the following evidence: a letter from Lenin's secretary Stasova of July 29, 1957, saying that Lenin came to Petrograd before permission of the Central Committee was given October 3; a book published on Lenin's fiftieth

birthday referring to his "self-willed" action in coming to Petrograd, the word "self-willed" twice underlined in red pencil by Lenin himself; Alexander V. Shotman's reminiscence published in 1934 saying that Lenin came in late September, held meetings in Kalinin's apartment and elsewhere, a recollection supported by Eino Rahja; Rahja's recollection that he came to Stalin after Lenin's arrival and said Lenin wanted to see him. Stalin said: "But I can't go to Finland." Rahja told him Lenin was already in Petrograd. Stalin burst out in rage that Rahja had brought Lenin there, demanding: "What right did you have?"; the original manuscript of Krupskaya's memoirs which, Fofanova insisted, placed the date in September but was changed by the editor. She asked that the original manuscript be checked to verify her recollection of the change. (*Istorichesky Arkhiv*, 1958, No. 2, pp. 166ff.) Fofanova reiterated her case in a strongly worded speech at a conference of historians in Leningrad in 1962. She contended that the October 7 date was arbitrarily and incorrectly "fixed" by a Central Committee resolution. She contended that in earlier years she had been told not to mention the September date and later on was just brushed aside. She suggested there must be a reason for official insistence on the later date. (Risto Bejalski, *Report from Moscow,* June 28, 29, 30, 1964.)

Actually, there exists strong evidence that Fofanova, Shotman, and Rahja may be mistaken as to the September date. Certainly they are mistaken about September 22. Lenin's letter to the Finnish Communist Smilga, dated September 27, contains unequivocal internal evidence of being written from Vyborg. If Lenin returned to Petrograd as early as September 29, the question arises as to why he did not participate in the Central Committee meetings of October 1, 3, and 5. And there is evidence in Lenin's writings of October 7 and 8 that he is not familiar with events in Petrograd, suggesting that he was still in Vyborg.

But questions do remain. Lenin had asked the Finnish Communist military leader Smilga to meet with him in Vyborg. Smilga spent October 2–3 in Vyborg but did not see Lenin. Certainly the meeting would have occurred had Lenin been there. Does this mean he had gone on to Petrograd by October 2–3? (A. M. Sovokin, *Voprosy Istorii,* 1967, No. 11, p. 52.)

There exists a brief reminiscence of Lenin published by Rahja in 1925 in which he says Lenin asked him to come to Vyborg and bring him back to Petrograd. After making arrangements with Hugo Yalava, the locomotive engineer who had earlier transported Lenin to Finland, Rahja went to Vyborg and met Lenin in the apartment of the Finnish journalist E. V. Kisanova. (In a 1933 version Rahja said the message from Lenin came through Nadezhda Krupskaya "in September." This version was published in a collection called *Lenin v pervye mesyatsy Sovetskoi vlastov,* Moscow, 1933.) Rahja said he found Lenin in a very disturbed state because of delays in communication with Petrograd. Lenin told Rahja he had determined to return to Russia despite the dangers. "The Revolution should be carried out in the course of the nearest weeks," Rahja quoted Lenin as saying, "and if we are not prepared for this we will suffer a defeat not to be compared with that of the July days because the bourgeoisie are trying to strangle the Revolution with all their strength and they will do it with such harshness as has not been known in the history of the world." This recollection, written January 23, 1924, the day after Lenin's death, was published in a collection of memoirs by Finnish Communists by the Leningrad Finnish-language publishing house Kirya, in an edition of 3,000 copies in 1925 and was not translated into Russian until 1967. It is notable that Rahja gives no indication he was called to Vyborg because of any decision of the Central Committee.

He presents the decision as being that of Lenin alone. Unfortunately Rahja gave no dates, or if he did they have been eliminated in the belated republication of the memoir in *Voprosy Istorii*, 1967, No. 10, pp. 170–71.

As early as September 6, 1918, Zinoviev in a speech to the Petrograd Soviet said Lenin had "arbitrarily" or "willfully" returned to Petrograd, presumably meaning without Central Committee sanction. This version was frequently published in the early 1920s when Lenin was alive and could easily have corrected it. Some Soviet scholars say they believe an unpublished letter by Zinoviev supporting the early date exists in the archive.

Fofanova's assertion that Krupskaya changed the date of Lenin's arrival in her memoirs does not seem to be borne out, although the issue is still not completely clear.

In the first edition of Krupskaya's memoirs published in 1931 she gave the date of the return as October 7. But in the third edition she changed the date to October 9. In the manuscript version of her article "Na Poroge Oktyabra" (On the Eve of October), published in *Pravda*, No. 212, November 21, 1932, the handwritten text and typescript of which were provided the author by the Institute of Marxism-Leninism in Moscow, she uses the date October 9. The outline for her memoir uses the date October 7 and she used this date again in a speech November 11, 1934. In that speech she observed that "now some of the comrades have begun to grumble 'he came without permission' but at that time there wasn't any grumbling." She didn't identify the grumblers. Apparently she never used the "end of September" date and Rahja in an unpublished memoir (dictated February 7, 1935, and still in Party archives) said he had argued with Krupskaya over the date, she insisting it was "October 8" while he insisted it was the "end of September."

No evidence has been reported by Soviet specialists as to why Krupskaya shifted her choice from October 7 to October 9. There are many corrections and changes in the manuscript and typescript of Krupskaya's November 21, 1932, version but none in the dates. Possibly, changes were made in the 1931 manuscript as Fofanova contended, but the 1931 manuscript text has not been made available by the Institute of Marxism-Leninism. In fact, the institute says it doesn't possess the manuscript. A facsimile of Krupskaya's rather muddled notes for the text clearly specifies "7 Oktyabr."

The problem of Krupskaya's memoirs is complicated by other factors. She herself repeatedly warned that she had a bad memory for dates and names. Although she did her best to verify facts, she wrote largely from memory. This, as R. Savitskaya, a researcher of the Institute of Marxism-Leninism, has pointed out, is a problem in almost all memoir material about Lenin. (R. Savitskaya, *Novy Mir*, 1964, No. 12, p. 198.) In Krupskaya's case it is compounded by what the editors of *Novy Mir* as long ago as 1965 called numerous "excisions" and "inexplicable variant readings." The magazine cited a dozen of these and called for a new and complete edition of Krupskaya's works, declaring there lay in the archives a mass of unpublished correspondence and memoir materials. Some of the published Krupskaya reminiscences, *Novy Mir* said, have been so severely edited as to lose completely Krupskaya's literary style and thought. (V. Golubtsov, *Novy Mir*, 1965, No. 10, pp. 276–78.)

Fofanova, in a taped interview with Bart McDowell, a writer for the *National Geographic*, in November 1974, said Lenin arrived at her apartment September 23, 1917. Her mind was sharp and lucid and she recalled the events of the period with clarity and precision. She also made clear her own antagonism to Stalin and recalled Lenin warning her in 1922 against working for Stalin in the Workers-Peasant Inspectorate.

Why so much attention to this point and what is the significance of the controversy? The suspicion persists that in some manner Stalin was involved. The discrepancies in dates seem to have attracted no special attention in Lenin's lifetime and indeed were incorporated into the fourteenth volume of the first edition of his collected works, which was published in 1921. This said he returned to Petrograd at the end of September. The latest official history of the Communist Party which appeared volume by volume from 1964 through 1972 did not attempt to take sides in the controversy, simply reporting that those who had something to do with organizing Lenin's movement from Finland to Petrograd (Rahja, Shotman, and Fofanova) supported a date "at the end of September," whereas some other sources including Krupskaya supported the date of October 7. "This date entered literature at the beginning of the 1930s," the editors added. It is obvious that only after Lenin's death did the question become sensitive. Possibly Stalin was antagonized from the start at Lenin's return. It hardly seems likely that Rahja could have invented Stalin's anger over the news of Lenin's return. The fact that the date was "frozen" as October 9 for the last twenty years of Stalin's life is telling. Possibly, the conflict between Lenin and the Central Committee over the revolutionary coup was sharper than the existing record shows—as is hinted in Krupskaya's unpublished comments. And, of course, all parties may have wanted to conceal the fact that Lenin, the great advocate of Party discipline, so flagrantly violated it in an effort to get his own way. But this seems far too trivial a reason for such strenuous efforts to establish a firm Party line and for the evident emotion among the parties to the dispute. Whatever the net weight of the various considerations, there can be no question that the issue of the dates has great importance in real fact. The best published summaries of the arguments are to be found in *Voprosy Istorii KPSS*, 1963, No. 12, A. A. Panfilova and others, and *Voprosy Istorii KPSS*, 1974, No. 1, S. P. Kirukhin and others.

A senior Soviet historian who is preparing a major study on this question (but who did not wish to be quoted in advance of publication of his work) feels (he told the author) that the weight of available evidence supports no date earlier than October 7. He believes Lenin actually returned either late on the evening of October 9 or after midnight in the early hours of October 10. He does not believe Lenin would have returned in advance of the Central Committee's resolution of October 3, giving him permission to come to Petrograd, and sets aside the evidence of Fofanova, Rahja, and Shotman as containing internal contradictions. His conclusion is strongly weighted by his study of Lenin's letters, particularly their internal evidence indicating his presence in Finland and his lack of knowledge of events in Petrograd and of decisions of the Central Committee. He points to a lack of evidence as to what Lenin may have been doing between October 8 and October 10 as suggesting this may have been the period of his moving to Petrograd. He is inclined toward a later date because he does not believe Lenin would have waited in Petrograd two days from October 8 to October 10 to meet with the Central Committee. However, he concedes that this reconstruction is only a hypothesis. In fact, of course, if Lenin had been underground in Petrograd during that period, unknown to the Central Committee, he would necessarily have been somewhat uninformed and presumably would have masked his correspondence to indicate that he was still in Vyborg.

26. *Vospominaniya o Lenine*, Vol. II, pp. 443–44.

27. Tsentral Partii Arkhivi, Institut Marksizm-Leninizm, f.12, op.2, d.56, l.14.

28. *Oktyabrskoye Vooruzhennoye Vosstaniye*, Vol. II, p. 231.

29. *Vospominaniya o Lenine,* Vol. II, p. 440.

30. N. N. Sukhanov, *The Russian Revolution, 1917,* p. 556.

31. Yu. Flaxerman, *Novy Mir,* 1968, No. 11, p. 213–14.

32. *Petrogradsky Voyenno-Revolyutsionny Komitet,* Vol. I, p. 36. (Protocol of Session.)

33. Trotsky, *Russian Revolution,* Vol. III, p. 106.

34. *Oktyabrskoye Vooruzhennoye Vosstaniye,* Vol. II, pp. 232–33. Trotsky recalled that it was agreed to carry out the uprising "if possible" not later than October 15. Stalin insisted Trotsky's memory betrayed him. (Trotsky, *Russian Revolution,* Vol. III, p. 156.) Contemporary Soviet historians tend to skip over this question, contending that such an early uprising could not have been properly prepared. It seems probable, however, that Lenin hoped for this early date.

LI. *October Days* PAGES 464–68

1. Sir George Buchanan, *My Mission to Russia,* Vol. II, p. 187.

2. Louis de Robien, *The Diary of a Diplomat in Russia, 1917–1918,* pp. 122–27. There were two statuettes, one an exact copy, and they could not be told apart. Madame Naryshkin sold both, one in 1917, one in 1924. She hoped to use the proceeds to live on and to pay the costs of going into emigration but inflation ate up the first sale and she was swindled in the second. (Princess Nicholas Galitzine, *Spirit to Survive,* pp. 67, 112.)

3. Zinaida Gippius, *Sinyaya Kniga,* p. 199.

4. Nikolai Sukhanov, *The Russian Revolution,* p. 558.

5. S. P. Melgunov, *Kak Bolsheviki Zakhvatili Vlast,* pp. 21–24.

6. *Oktyabrskoye Vooruzhennoye Vosstaniye,* Vol. II, pp. 251–52.

7. Sukhanov, *Russian Revolution,* p. 559.

8. Melgunov, *Kak Bolsheviki,* p. 21.

9. Ibid., p. 48.

10. *Oktyabrskoye Vooruzhennoye Vosstaniye,* Vol. II, pp. 251–57. This is the figure used by all early Soviet historians. However, V. I. Startsev employs a substantially higher figure—35,700. He concludes that the early statistics did not cover all regions and units. (V. I. Startsev, *Ocherki po Istorii Petrogradskoi Krasnoi Gvardii i Rabotchei Militsii* (*Mart 1917–Aprel 1918 g.,* p. 200.)

11. Ibid., p. 254.

12. Sukhanov, *Russian Revolution,* p. 562.

13. N. I. Podvoisky, in *Kommunist,* 1957, No. 1, p. 34.

14. *Oktyabrskoye Vooruzhennoye Vosstaniye,* Vol. II, p. 254.

15. E. F. Yerykalov, *Oktyabrskoye Vooruzhennoye Vosstaniye v Petrograde,* p. 53.

16. *Petrogradsky Voyenno-Revolyutsionny Komitet* (Protocols), Vol. I, pp. 41–50.

17. In Stalin's day much was heard of the "Revolutionary Center." Stalin was its guiding spirit and, through it, guided the Revolution at Lenin's side. With Stalin's death the "Revolutionary Center" vanished into the mists of Soviet historiography, and the Military Revolutionary Committee, which, in fact, directed the insurrection, was restored to its rightful place in the story of the events. Contemporary Soviet histories hardly find a place to mention Stalin in the narrative of the overturn. This may be a slight overcompensation but study of the records of the Military Revolutionary Committee make clear that it was, in fact, in direct charge of all the practical activities of the uprising and Stalin played no role in it.

18. Fofanova to Burt McDowell, personal communication, Nov. 1974.

19. Leon Trotsky, *A History of the Russian Revolution,* Vol. III, p. 158.

20. Sukhanov, *Russian Revolution*, p. 568; *Oktyabrskoye Vooruzhennoye Vosstaniye*, Vol. II, p. 266.
21. V. I. Lenin, *Collected Works*, Vol. XXVI, pp. 214–15.
22. Trotsky, *Russian Revolution*, Vol. III, p. 161.
23. Maxim Gorky, *Untimely Thoughts*, pp. 83–84.
24. Isaac Deutscher, *Stalin*, pp. 170–71.
25. Lenin, *Collected Works*, Vol. XXVI, pp. 217–18, 227.
26. Trotsky, *Russian Revolution*, Vol. III, p. 161.
27. Ibid., p. 163; *Oktyabrskoye Vooruzhennoye Vosstaniye*, Vol. II, p. 267.
28. Trotsky, *Russian Revolution*, Vol. II, pp. 163–67.
29. *Krasny Arkhiv*, 1927, Vol. XXII, p. 82.
30. *Petrogradsky Voyenno-Revolyutsionny Komitet* (Protocols), Vol. I, p. 54.
31. Ibid., p. 53.
32. *Oktyabrskoye Vooruzhennoye Vosstaniye*, Vol. II, pp. 271–72; Trotsky, *Russian Revolution*, Vol. III, p. 164.
33. *Oktyabrskoye Vooruzhennoye Vosstaniye*, Vol. II, p. 273.
34. Georgi Lozgachev-Yelizerov, *Nezabyvayemoye*, 5th ed., p. 52–53. Bolshevik historians seem to have been unable to verify this visit although both Mariya Ulyanova and Krupskaya read and approved Yelizarov's version in 1924.
35. Svetlana Alliluyeva, *Twenty Letters to a Friend*, pp. 90–91.
36. Baron Alexei Budberg, in *Arkhiv Russkoi Revolyutsii*, Vol. XII, pp. 197–225.
37. Paul Anderson, personal reminiscence.
38. A. Startsev, *Russkiye Bloknoty Dzhona Rida*, pp. 34–57.

LII. A Threatening Night PAGES 475–80

1. *Arkhiv Russkoi Revolyutsii*, Vol. VII, p. 281. The conversation is mistakenly dated "Night of 21 to 22 October 1917" instead of 23–24 October when it actually occurred.
2. V. L. Burtsev, *V Borbe s Bolshevikami i Nemtsami*, p. 78.
3. E. F. Yerykalov, *Oktyabrskoye Vooruzhennoye Vosstaniye v Petrograde*, p. 279.
4. When the Bolshevik coup occurred, rumors swept Petrograd that Verkhovsky was leading it. (Zinaida Gippius, *Sinyaya Kniga*, p. 213.)
5. S. P. Melgunov, *Kak Bolsheviki Zakhvatili Vlast*, p. 49.
6. Ibid., pp. 50–55.
7. *Oktyabrskoye Vooruzhennoye Vosstaniye*, Vol. II, p. 264.
8. Melgunov, *Kak Bolsheviki*, p. 268.
9. *Oktyabrskoye Vooruzhennoye Vosstaniye*, Vol. II, pp. 272–76.
10. Melgunov, *Kak Bolsheviki*, p. 69.
11. *Oktyabrskoye Vooruzhennoye Vosstaniye*, Vol. II, p. 276–77.
12. Nikolai Sukhanov, *The Russian Revolution*, pp. 588–89.
13. Melgunov, *Kak Bolsheviki*, p. 68.
14. V. I. Starets, in *Prometei*, 1967, No. 4, p. 101.
15. V. I. Lenin, *Collected Works*, Vol. XLI, pp. 450–51.
16. Sir George Buchanan, *My Mission to Russia*, Vol. II, 203–4.
17. John Reed, *Ten Days that Shook the World* (1960 ed.), pp. 84–85.
18. Leon Trotsky, *A History of the Russian Revolution*, Vol. III, p. 200.
19. Reed, *Ten Days*, pp. 40–41, 87, 88.
20. Ibid., p. 89.
21. Trotsky, *Russian Revolution*, Vol. III, pp. 182–83.
22. Melgunov, *Kak Bolsheviki*, pp. 74–75.

23. *Oktyabrskoye Vooruzhennoye Vosstaniye*, Vol. II, pp. 285–86. The record of these conversations is confused. Kamenev reported on them at a Bolshevik Central Committee meeting on the morning of October 24. Stalin told the Bolshevik faction at the All-Russian Soviet that there had been "an attempt at conversations between 5 and 6 A.M. on the 24th." Kerensky told the Pre-Parliament on the morning of the 24th that he had been told at 3 A.M. that the Revolutionary Committee had accepted the General Staff's conditions.

24. Ibid., p. 292. At 5:30 A.M. Sunday the twenty-second, General Bagratuni arranged by telephone with V. S. Voitinsky, commissar of the northern front, for speedy dispatch of reliable troops to Petrograd as soon as Kerensky gave the order. No order was ever given. (Ibid., p. 282.)

25. Sukhanov, *Russian Revolution*, pp. 600–1.

26. *Oktyabrskoye Vooruzhennoye Vosstaniye*, Vol. II, p. 292; Melgunov, *Kak Bolsheviki*, p. 75.

27. Reed, *Ten Days*, p. 90.

28. Ibid., p. 89.

29. Sukhanov, *Russian Revolution*, p. 602.

30. *Oktyabrskoye Vooruzhennoye Vosstaniye*, Vol. II, p. 302; Trotsky, *Russian Revolution*, Vol. III, pp. 206–7.

LIII. The Coup d'État Begins PAGES 482–85

1. V. A. Auerbakh, in *Arkhiv Russkoi Revolyutsii*, Vol. XIV, pp. 23–24.

2. David Francis, *Russia from the American Embassy*, pp. 177–78.

3. *Arkhiv Russkoi Revolyutsii*, Vol. XII, pp. 227–28.

4. *Oktyabrskoye Vooruzhennoye Vosstaniye*, Vol. II, p. 293.

5. *Petrogradsky Voyenno-Revolyutsionny Komitet*, Vol. I, p. 80.

6. Leon Trotsky, *A History of the Russian Revolution*, Vol. III, pp. 207–11.

7. Ye. F. Yerykalov, *Oktyabrskoye Vooruzhennoye Vosstaniye v Petrograde*, p. 336.

8. *Oktyabrskoye Vooruzhennoye Vosstaniye*, Vol. II, pp. 292–96.

9. Ibid., p. 297. Robert V. Daniels in *Red October* points out that there is virtually no evidence to support the claim that the Petersburg City Committee did in fact meet on the morning of the twenty-fourth and issue this demand. He also collates evidence suggesting that the Bolshevik moves were actually defensive rather than offensive. (Robert V. Daniels, *Red October*, pp. 128–36.)

10. Ibid., pp. 303–4.

11. Nikolai Sukhanov, *The Russian Revolution*, pp. 604–5.

12. *Oktyabrskoye Vooruzhennoye Vosstaniye*, Vol. II, pp. 304–5.

13. Ibid., pp. 307–8.

14. Ibid., pp. 314–15. Some reports said the Baltic Station was not taken over until 1 A.M. of the twenty-fifth.

15. Ibid., pp. 315–16.

16. Yerykalov, *Oktyabrskoye Vooruzhennoye Vosstaniye v Petrograde*, p. 206.

17. S. P. Melgunov, *Kak Bolsheviki Zakhvatili Vlast*, pp. 79–80. The text of Lenin's hastily scrawled proclamation has been preserved. It reveals an interesting change. Lenin first wrote that the Military Revolutionary Committee was convening a meeting of the Petrograd Soviet at 12 noon to take "immediate measures to establish a Soviet Government." Then he scratched this sentence out, leaving the "power," such as it was, in the hands of the Revolutionary Committee. The change is not a small one. It clearly reflects Lenin's desire to keep the closest possible control of events, especially since at 10 A.M. October 25 it was

by no means clear in whose hands real power was actually invested. This point never seems to have been commented on in the mass of Soviet studies of the October days. (V. I. Lenin, *Collected Works*, Vol. XXVI, pp. 236-37; Marc Ferro, *La Révolution de 1917*, Vol. I, pp. 412-13.)

18. F. Dan, *Letopis Revolyutsii*, Book 1, pp. 163-75.

19. Yerykalov, *Oktyabrskoye Vooruzhennoye Vosstaniye*, pp. 340-41.

20. *Oktyabrskoye Vooruzhennoye Vosstaniye*, Vol. II, p. 312.

21. *Oktyabrskoye Vooruzhennoye Vosstaniye*, Vol. II, p. 312.

22. Fofanova, in *Vospominaniya o V. I. Lenine*, Vol. II, pp. 445-46.

23. Fofanova, in Ye. A. Sultanova, *Ob Ilyiche*, p. 348.

24. V. I. Lenin, *Collected Works*, Vol. XXVI, pp. 234-35.

25. There is substantial controversy over this letter of Lenin's and its significance. The respected Soviet historian Ye. N. Gorodetsky first noted the mistaken attribution given to the letter at a historians' conference in 1962. It was his view that the letter was directed only to the Petersburg Committee and regional committees. Other Soviet historians insist that a copy was also sent to the Central Committee at Smolny. Whether or not the copy went to Smolny, Lenin's intent is clear from his wording—to light a fire under the Central Committee. While Fofanova recalls delivering the letter to Krupskaya at Vyborg Party headquarters, Rahja thinks that he delivered it. In his memoirs he recalls giving it to Zhenya Yegorova at the Vyborg headquarters and says she typed it up for distribution to the regional organizations. He mistakenly dates the action to October 23 rather than 24. (*Vospominaniya o V. I. Lenine*, Vol. II, pp. 430-31.) In an earlier version Rahja gives the date correctly as October 24. He says that he reported to Lenin that the factories and barracks were in ferment. "Lenin wrote a letter to the regional committees in which he recommended that they begin decisive battle. I took this letter to the Vyborg regional committee where it was copied and sent to the soldiers and workers." (Originally published by Finnish-language publishing house Kirya in Petrograd, January 1924, republished in *Voprosy Istorii*, 1967, No. 10.) *Oktyabrskoye Vooruzhennoye Vosstaniye*, Vol. II, p. 312, mistakenly says Krupskaya took the letter to Smolny. Ye. F. Yerykalov, another careful scholar of the revolutionary events, finds it hard to believe Lenin did not send the Central Committee a copy of so important a document and insists that other important Lenin communications were forwarded to the Central Committee through the Vyborg district headquarters. (Yerykalov, *Oktyabrskoye Vooruzhennoye Vosstaniye v Petrograde*, pp. 351-52.)

26. Krupskaya, *Reminiscences of Lenin*, p. 386.

27. Krupskaya, in *Vospominaniya o V. I. Lenine*, Vol. II, p. 446.

28. *Oktyabrskoye Vooruzhennoye Vosstaniye*, Vol. II, p. 312.

29. Krupskaya, *Reminiscences*, p. 386.

30. *Vospominaniya o V. I. Lenine*, pp. 445, 446; *Oktyabrskoye Vooruzhennoye Vosstaniye*, Vol. II, p. 312. Neither the second nor third note to Nadezhda nor the notes to Lenin have ever been published. Krupskaya's memoirs mention only two notes from Lenin. (Krupskaya, *Reminiscences*, p. 386.)

31. V. I. Lenin, *Biograficheskaya Khronika*, Vol. IV, pp. 394-99.

32. During the evening the Central Committee did finally decide to send for Lenin. T. A. Slovatinsky was directed to find Krupskaya and deliver the message through her that Lenin was wanted at Smolny. It was late evening before he found Krupskaya. (Ibid., p. 399.) Krupskaya was upset. Zhenya Yegorova, Vyborg organizational secretary, asked young Yelizaveta Drabkina to go with Krupskaya— where or why Yelizaveta did not know. She was just told that if anyone stopped

them to say that Grandma was sick and they were going for a doctor. When they got to a big apartment building on the Bolshaya Samsoniyevskaya, Krupskaya told her to wait while she went in. Soon she emerged more upset than ever and they hurried back to Vyborg headquarters. (Yelizaveta Drabkina, *Chernye Sukhari,* pp. 74-75.) Then Krupskaya and Yegorova got a ride on a truck to Smolny where Lenin had already arrived. (Krupskaya, *Reminiscences,* p. 397.) Drabkina, daughter of S. I. Gusev, Lenin's St. Petersburg lieutenant of 1905 and a secretary of the Military Revolutionary Committee, took an active part in the coup d'état and became an important Soviet functionary.

33. Trotsky first described this scene in a reminiscence published in 1924, shortly after Lenin's death. He did not mention Stalin's presence. When Rahja's memoir was published in 1933, Trotsky had vanished from the anecdote but Stalin had appeared! (Leon Trotsky, *Lenin,* p. 101 [first published in Moscow in 1924]; *Vospominaniya o V. I. Lenine,* Vol. II, pp. 432-33, reprinting Rahja's memoir first published in 1933.) There is now a third version by M. P. Yefremov, a member of the Military Revolutionary Committee. He remembers going up the staircase at Smolny with Lenin that night. Lenin went to the third floor and waited there "some time" for Yakov M. Sverdlov. (*Voprosy Istorii,* 1967, No. 5, p. 106.) This version neatly gets rid of both the present unmentionables—Trotsky and Stalin!

34. *Vospominaniya o V. I. Lenine,* Vol. II, pp. 431-35.

LIV. The Winter Palace PAGES 492-97

1. V. I. Ivanov, in *Prometei,* 1967, No. 4, pp. 118-23.

2. Two Ministers, Kartashev and Galperin, were arrested on the Millionaya after leaving the palace by pickets of the Pavlovsky Regiment and taken to Smolny where they were later released, and the troops reprimanded for "premature" action. (S. P. Melgunov, *Kak Bolsheviki Zakhvatili Vlast,* p. 95.)

3. V. P. Zubov, *Stradnye Gody Rossii* (*Vospominaniya o Revolyutsii 1917-1925*), p. 16.

4. Count Zubov, who got the story from Knirsha, was told that Kerensky believed his only hope of getting out of Petrograd was in a car provided by a foreign embassy. Zubov saw Kerensky's car arrive at Gatchina and recollected that it flew an English flag. (Ibid., pp. 16-17.) A. V. Liverovsky, Kerensky's Minister of Communications, in a note entered in his diary on October 25, that very day, said he was told by Konovalov that Kerensky left "in an automobile of the English embassy." (*Istorichesky Arkhiv,* 1960, No. 6, p. 41.)

5. Vladimir Nabokov, in *Arkhiv Russkoi Revolyutsii,* Vol. I, p. 84.

6. Melgunov, *Kak Bolsheviki,* pp. 100-1.

7. George F. Kennan, *Russia Leaves the War,* pp. 72-73.

8. David Francis, *Russia from the American Embassy,* pp. 179-80.

9. B. I. Knirsha, in *Krasny Arkhiv,* 1925, Vol. IX, pp. 179-81.

10. Nabokov, in *Arkhiv Russkoi Revolyutsii,* Vol. I, p. 85.

11. *Oktyabrskoye Vooruzhennoye Vosstaniye,* Vol. II, pp. 326-27.

12. *Arkhiv Russkoi Revolyutsii,* Vol. I, p. 87.

13. Melgunov, *Kak Bolsheviki,* p. 102.

14. Ye. F. Yerykalov, *Oktyabrskoye Vooruzhennoye Vosstaniye v Petrograde,* p. 206.

15. *Oktyabrskoye Vooruzhennoye Vosstaniye,* Vol. II, pp. 319-25; *Byloye,* Vol. II, No. 47, p. 5.

16. *Oktyabrskoye Vooruzhennoye Vosstaniye,* Vol. II, p. 322.

17. Ibid., pp. 328-29.

18. Leon Trotsky, *On Lenin, Notes Towards a Biography*, pp. 91–92.
19. Louis de Robien, *The Diary of a Diplomat in Russia, 1917–1918*, p. 131.
20. Sir George Buchanan, *My Mission to Russia*, p. 206.
21. Nabokov, in *Arkhiv Russkoi Revolyutsii*, Vol. I, p. 86.
22. *Oktyabrskoye Vooruzhennoye Vosstaniye*, Vol. II, p. 331.
23. Nikolai Sukhanov, *The Russian Revolution*, pp. 624–25.
24. *Oktyabrskoye Vooruzhennoye Vosstaniye*, Vol. II, p. 331.
25. *Istorichesky Arkhiv*, 1960, No. 6, p. 42, Liverovsky diary.
26. Yerykalov, *Oktyabrskoye Voruzhennoye Vosstaniye v Petrograde*, pp. 110–11.
27. *Oktyabrskoye Vooruzhennoye Vosstaniye*, Vol. II, p. 339.
28. *Istorichesky Arkhiv*, 1960, No. 6, p. 44, Liverovsky diary.
29. *Oktyabrskoye Vooruzhennoye Vosstaniye*, Vol. II, p. 340.
30. Ibid., p. 341.
31. Alexander Sineguba, in *Arkhiv Russkoi Revolyutsii*, Vol. IV, pp. 162–64.
32. *Oktyabrskoye Vooruzhennoye Vosstaniye*, Vol. II, p. 340.

LV. Before the Storm   PAGES 502–6

1. *Oktyabrskoye Vooruzhennoye Vosstaniye*, Vol. II, p. 112.
2. *Arkhiv Russkoi Revolyutsii*, Vol. I, pp. 86–87.
3. John Reed, *Ten Days that Shook the World* (1960 ed.), pp. 110–19.
4. Zinaida Gippius, *Sinyaya Kniga*, pp. 212–13.
5. *Prometei*, 1967, No. 4, p. 127.
6. Leon Trotsky, *A History of the Russian Revolution*, Vol. III, pp. 243–44.
7. N. I. Podvoisky, in *Vospominaniya o V. I. Lenine*, Vol. II, pp. 449–50.
8. Ibid., p. 450.
9. Trotsky, *Russian Revolution*, Vol. III, p. 245.
10. Ibid., p. 235.
11. Nikolai Sukhanov, *The Russian Revolution*, p. 629.
12. *Oktyabrskoye Vooruzhennoye Vosstaniye*, Vol. II, p. 341.
13. *Istorichesky Arkhiv*, 1960, No. 6, p. 45, Liverovsky diary.
14. In later years Malkov became Kremlin commandant. His account is detailed but not trustworthy. No one else seems to have recalled Malkov playing any particular role in these events. According to another version, the specifics of the attack on the Winter Palace were worked out in ten or fifteen minutes early on the morning of the twenty-fifth by Lenin himself. (S. Melgunov, *Kak Bolsheviki Zakhvatili Vlast*, p. 107.) Actually the most careful search by Soviet historians has failed to turn up *any* plan for the coup. Operations *seem* to have been in charge of a troika of the Military Revolutionary Committee, N. I. Podvoisky, V. A. Antonov-Ovseyenko, and G. I. Chudnovsky. The existing memoirs suggest that these three were huddled over some kind of plans in a very small room, No. 10, at Smolny on the evening of October 24 when Lenin walked in the door. They were so preoccupied they did not notice him at once. They had a map of Petrograd before them. No plan for the uprising has ever turned up in the voluminous published records of the Military Revolutionary Committee nor anything but a handful of orders. (Yerykalov, *Oktyabrskoye Vooruzhennoye Vosstaniye v Petrograde*, pp. 356–57.)
15. P. Malkov, *Reminiscences of a Kremlin Commandant*, pp. 42–44.
16. *Oktyabrskoye Vooruzhennoye Vosstaniye*, Vol. II, pp. 344–45.
17. *Istorichesky Arkhiv*, 1960, No. 6, pp. 44–45, Liverovsky diary.
18. *Prometei*, 1967, No. 4, p. 129.
19. *Oktyabrskoye Vooruzhennoye Vosstaniye*, Vol. II, pp. 342–44.

20. Ibid., pp. 346–47, and Ye. A. Yerykalov, *Oktyabrskoye Vooruzhennoye Vosstaniye v Petrograde*, p. 440. The shouts of the Bolsheviks entering the General Staff frightened the nearby Pavlovsky troops who thought the Junkers were attacking. Many of them fled to the Champs de Mars. (Melgunov, *Kak Bolsheviki*, p. 124.)

21. *Istorichesky Arkhiv*, 1960, No. 6, p. 46, Liverovsky diary.

22. Ibid.

23. *Oktyabrskoye Vooruzhennoye Vosstaniye*, Vol. II, p. 350.

24. Ibid.

25. Ibid., p. 348.

26. Vladimir Zenzinov, *Iz Zhizn Revolyutsionera*, pp. 94–95.

27. Reed, *Ten Days*, pp. 135–36.

28. Melgunov, *Kak Bolsheviki*, p. 129.

29. Pyotr Ryss, *Russkii Opyt*, p. 148.

LVI. The Storming of the Winter Palace PAGES 509–15

1. *Prometei*, 1967, No. 4, p. 133.

2. *Istoriya SSR*, 1965, No. 5, p. 95.

3. *Prometei*, 1967, No. 4, p. 132. The continued infiltration of the palace, the successful efforts by delegates of the Pavlovsky Regiment and the Military Revolutionary Committee to persuade groups of defenders to abandon its defense, the emphasis which was placed on agitation, propaganda, and persuasion, strongly suggest that the slow pace of the attack on the palace was more than a technical question and that, in fact, the Military Revolutionary Committee hoped by peaceful means to bring about the surrender of the Provisional Government without armed attack. The fact that some of the leading members of the Committee were sent into the palace supports this view.

4. Alexander Sineguba, in *Arkhiv Russkoi Revolyutsii*, Vol. IV, pp. 167–79.

5. Ibid., p. 173.

6. Sir George Buchanan, *My Mission to Russia*, Vol. II, p. 20.

7. *Oktyabrskoye Vooruzhennoye Vosstaniye*, Vol. II, p. 349.

8. Leon Trotsky, *My Life*, pp. 327–28.

9. *Oktyabrskoye Vooruzhennoye Vosstaniye*, Vol. II, p. 346.

10. Ibid., pp. 355–56.

11. *Arkhiv Russkoi Revolyutsii*, Vol. IV, p. 177.

12. S. P. Melgunov, *Kak Bolsheviki Zakhvatili Vlast*, p. 131.

13. Leon Trotsky, *A History of the Russian Revolution*, Vol. III, p. 161; *Oktyabrskoye Vooruzhennoye Vosstaniye*, Vol. II, p. 356.

14. *Oktyabrskoye Vooruzhennoye Vosstaniye*, Vol. II, p. 356.

15. *Istorichesky Arkhiv*, 1960, No. 6, p. 47, Liverovsky diary.

16. Ibid.

17. Ibid.

18. *Oktyabrskoye Vooruzhennoye Vosstaniye*, Vol. II, p. 357.

19. Ibid., pp. 357–58.

20. Sineguba, in *Arkhiv Russkoi Revolyutsii*, Vol. IV, pp. 182–84.

21. *Oktyabrskoye Vooruzhennoye Vosstaniye*, Vol. II, p. 358.

22. *Arkhiv Russkoi Revolyutsii*, Vol. IV, p. 185.

23. Ye. F. Yerykalov, *Oktyabrskoye Vooruzhennoye Vosstaniye v Petrograde*, p. 456, quoting *Stenograficheski Otchetye Dumy*, Vol. I, p. 88.

24. Albert Rhys Williams, *Through the Russian Revolution*, pp. 112–13. Actually there was rather substantial looting at the palace, largely of small, easily con-

cealed objects. Not all of this occurred on the night the palace fell. The palace was left open for several days and thousands of curiosity seekers swarmed through it, making off with silver, clocks, mirrors, vases of precious and semiprecious stones, and the like. Reed estimated the losses at $50,000, undoubtedly an undervaluation. An SR paper estimated them at 500,000,000 rubles, an obvious overvaluation. Several decrees and notices were issued by the authorities in an attempt to regain the lost objects. (John Reed, *Ten Days that Shook the World* [1960 ed.], pp. 153–54.)

25. Nikolai Sukhanov, *The Russian Revolution*, pp. 635–45.
26. *Oktyabrskoye Vooruzhennoye Vosstaniye*, Vol. II, p. 360.
27. Reed, *Ten Days*, p. 146.
28. V. D. Bonch-Bruyevich, *Vospominaniya o Lenine*, pp. 123–24; V. I. Lenin, *Biograficheskaya Khronika*, Vol. V, pp. 2–3.
29. *Oktyabrskoye Vooruzhennoye Vosstaniye*, Vol. II, p. 362.
30. Reed, *Ten Days*, p. 150.

LVII. The Day After PAGES 518–23

1. Paul Anderson, personal reminiscence, 1975.
2. Tamara Karsavina, *Theatre Street*, pp. 263–65.
3. Louis de Robien, *The Diary of a Diplomat in Russia, 1917–1918*, pp. 133–34.
4. Zinaida Gippius, *Sinyaya Kniga*, p. 215.
5. Yelizaveta Drabkina, *Chernye Sukhari*, p. 85.
6. Anderson, personal reminiscence.
7. Leon Trotsky, *A History of the Russian Revolution*, Vol. III, p. 316.
8. Nadezhda Krupskaya, *Reminiscences of Lenin*, pp. 390–91.
9. V. D. Bonch-Bruyevich, *Vospominaniya o Lenine*, pp. 125–26.
10. Leon Trotsky, *My Life*, pp. 337–38.
11. Krupskaya, *Reminiscences*, p. 394.
12. Trotsky, *My Life*, p. 339.
13. Nikolai Sukhanov, *The Russian Revolution*, pp. 649–50.
14. Ibid., p. 656; John Reed, *Ten Days that Shook the World* (1960 ed.), p. 171. The Military Revolutionary Committee had abolished the death penalty on the morning of October 25. Lenin was not present and he was enraged when he was told of the action. "Nonsense," he said. "How can one make a revolution without firing squads? Do you think you will be able to deal with all your enemies by laying down your arms? What other means of repression do you have? It is a mistake. An inadmissible weakness, a pacifist illusion." Finally he was persuaded to let the action stand. Someone said: "It would be better simply to have recourse to a firing squad when it becomes obvious there is no other way." Lenin accepted that. (Leon Trotsky, *On Lenin, Notes Towards a Biography*, p. 115.)
15. Sukhanov, *The Russian Revolution*, p. 230.
16. John Reed's classic account reports that Lenin opened his remarks by saying: "We shall now proceed to construct the Socialist order." (Reed, *Ten Days*, p. 172.) There is substantial evidence that Lenin made no such remark and that Reed simply got his notes confused. There is no stenographic report of the session because the official stenographers withdrew along with the protesting Mensheviks and SRs. (Trotsky, *Russian Revolution*, Vol. III, p. 318.) However, the accounts of others present do not report Lenin making such a dramatic statement. Nor does Reed include such a quotation in his own notes taken that night at Smolny. In speaking to the Petrograd Soviet the day before, October 25, Lenin had used the

phrase: "In Russia we now must occupy ourselves with constructing the prole-tarian socialist state." Reed was not present at that meeting but his notebook con-tains a phrase: "7 November (25 Oct) Lenin said: "Now soc. state." And another note: "Lenin 7 November at the Session of Soviets when the battle was going on in the streets: "We proceed now to con. soc. stat." Apparently in writing *Ten Days that Shook the World* nearly a year later he confused his notes. (A. Startsev, *Russkiye Bloknoty Dzhona Rida*, pp. 88–89.)

Albert Rhys Williams, who was with Reed in Smolny that night, quotes Lenin as saying: "Comrades, we shall now take up the formation of the Socialist State." He almost certainly got the quotation from Reed. (Albert Rhys Williams, *Lenin*, p. 47.) The same is true, for example, of Yu. Flaxerman, who quotes the Reed phrase in a memoir about Lenin published in *Novy Mir*, 1968, No. 11, p. 208.

17. Sukhanov, *Russian Revolution*, pp. 658–59.
18. Reed, *Ten Days*, p. 178.
19. Sukhanov, *The Russian Revolution*, pp. 658–62.
20. Anderson, personal reminiscence.
21. Reed, *Ten Days*, p. 182.
22. Ibid., p. 181.
23. Ibid.; Trotsky, *Russian Revolution*, Vol. III, pp. 327–28.
24. Reed, *Ten Days*, pp. 188–89; Trotsky, *Russian Revolution*, Vol. III, pp. 330–31.
25. Trotsky, *Russian Revolution*, Vol. III, p. 335.
26. Sukhanov, *Russian Revolution*, p. 666.
27. Anderson, personal reminiscence.

LVIII. Permanent Crisis PAGES 526-28

1. V. D. Bonch-Bruyevich, *Vospominaniya o Lenine*, pp. 135–37; Nadezhda Krupskaya, *Reminiscences of Lenin*, pp. 379, 411–14. There is no evidence as to what happened to Lenin's relationship with Inessa Armand in this period. She went to Moscow almost immediately after arriving in Russia in March and made one brief trip to Petrograd in April. She was heavily engaged in Party activities in Moscow but from November 1917 through January 1918 "worked in the Cen-tral Committee of the Party, peasant section," in Petrograd. She then returned to Moscow where, of course, Lenin and his Government moved in March 1918. In April 1918 Inessa became chairman of the Moscow Guberniya Economic Coun-cil. She held this job until February 1919. (*Istorichesky Arkhiv*, 1959, No. 5, p. 250.) No letters of Lenin to Inessa during her Moscow period have been pub-lished. Perhaps none were written but Lenin had been corresponding with her at the rate of a letter or more a day for weeks before their departure together from Switzerland. Inessa had personal difficulties in Moscow; one of her boys was ill with tuberculosis. It seems unlikely that the intimate relationship of Switzerland perished in the hurly-burly of Russia, especially since it is known that they re-tained their deep affection until Inessa's death in 1920 of cholera. Presumably, once again the written record has been suppressed by the Soviet historical censor-ship. (Pavel Podlyashuk, *Tovarishch Inessa*, p. 189.)

2. S. An—sky, in *Arkhiv Russkoi Revolyutsii*, Vol. VIII, p. 43.
3. *Oktyabrskoye Vooruzhennoye Vosstaniye*, Vol. II, pp. 370–73; An—sky, in *Arkhiv Russkoi Revolyutsii*, Vol. VIII, pp. 43–44.
4. Bonch-Bruyevich, *Vospominaniya o Lenine*, p. 129.
5. *Oktyabrskoye Vooruzhennoye Vosstaniye*, Vol. II, p. 374.
6. V. I. Lenin, *Collected Works*, Vol. XXV, pp. 378–79.

7. By October 28 Lenin had shut down more than ten Petrograd newspapers. (Ye. F. Yerykalov, *Oktyabrskoye Vooruzhennoye Vosstaniye v Petrograde*, p. 410.) Among them were *Den, Rech, Sovremennoye Slovo, Petrogradsky Listok, Petrogradskaya Gazeta, Birzhevye Vedomosti, Novoye Vremya, Novaya Rus, Zhivoye Slovo*, and *Kopeika*. In the next few days the Bolsheviks closed *Narodnoye Slovo, Mira, Khleba i Svobody, Vechernyaya Pochta, Utro, Trudovoye Slovo, Russkiye Novosti, Dni, Volnost, Russkaya Volya*, and *Groza*. (M. I. Stishov, *Iz Istorii Velikoi Oktyabrskoi Sotsialisticheskoi Revolyutsii*, pp. 28–31.) The printing trade unions vigorously protested, but the Bolsheviks brushed aside the complaints, contending the printers were all Mensheviks. (Ibid., p. 29.)

8. *Oktyabrskoye Vooruzhennoye Vosstaniye*, Vol. II, p. 377.

9. Lenin, *Collected Works*, Vol. XXVI, pp. 266–68.

10. Krupskaya, *Reminiscences*, p. 400; *Oktyabrskoye Vooruzhennoye Vosstaniye*, Vol. II, p. 381.

11. S. P. Melgunov, *Kak Bolsheviki Zakhvatili Vlast*, pp. 181–83.

12. Ibid., p. 162.

13. W. S. Woytinsky, *Stormy Passage*, pp. 381–82.

14. I. N. Nebimov, in *Revolyutsiya 1917 Goda Khronika Sobyii*, Vol. VI, p. 15.

15. *Oktyabrskoye Vooruzhennoye Vosstaniye*, Vol. II, pp. 383–84.

16. The designation "white" as the opposition to the "reds" arose in Finland during the 1905 Revolution. The "Red" Guards in Helsingfors wore red armbands. Their opponents wore white armbands. Thus, the term "white" gradually came into general usage for the opponents of the Bolsheviks. (*Bolshaya Sovetskaya Entsiklopediya*, 1st ed., Vol. V, p. 275.)

17. Albert Rhys Williams, *Through the Russian Revolution*, pp. 123–49.

18. Melgunov, *Kak Bolsheviki*, p. 200.

19. *Oktyabrskoye Vooruzhennoye Vosstaniye*, Vol. II, p. 390.

20. Arthur T. Dailey, personal archive.

21. Krasnov, in *Arkhiv Russkoi Revolyutsii*, Vol. I, pp. 165–72.

22. Woytinsky, *Stormy Passage*, pp. 384–85.

23. I. N. Lyubimov, *Revolyutsiya 1917 goda*, p. 21.

24. An—sky, in *Arkhiv Russkoi Revolyutsii*, Vol. VIII, p. 44.

25. Lyubimov, *Revolyutsiya 1917 goda*, p. 30.

26. An—sky, in *Arkhiv Russkoi Revolyutsii*, Vol. VIII, pp. 48–49.

27. Ibid., pp. 408–9; Lyubimov, *Revolyutsiya 1917 goda*, p. 39.

28. *Oktyabrskoye Vooruzhennoye Vosstaniye*, Vol. II, p. 409.

29. Lyubimov, *Revolyutsiya 1917 goda*, p. 38.

30. I. Krasnov, in *Arkhiv Russkoi Revolyutsii*, Vol. I, pp. 172–73.

31. Kerensky was to live in emigration for more than fifty years until his death in New York. Never after Gatchina was he to play a meaningful role in Russian politics. He stayed underground in Russia until June 1918 when he sailed from Murmansk on a British destroyer, arriving in England June 20–21, 1918. (Alexander Kerensky, *Russia and History's Turning Point*, pp. 445–85.)

32. Woytinsky, *Stormy Passage*, pp. 387–89.

33. V. I. Lenin, *Collected Works*, Vol. XXVI, p. 275.

34. Woytinsky, *Stormy Passage*, p. 392.

35. Lenin, *Collected Works*, Vol. XXVI, p. 294.

LIX. Full Steam Ahead Through the Swamp PAGE 539

1. Zinaida Gippius, *Sinyaya Kniga*, pp. 211–12.

2. Ibid., p. 221.

3. Dan Levin, *Stormy Petrel: The Life and Work of Maxim Gorky*, p. 194.
4. Gippius, *Sinyaya Kniga*, pp. 232–33.
5. Maxim Gorky, *Untimely Thoughts*, pp. 85–87.
6. *Lenin i Lunacharsky, Literaturnoye Nasledstve*, Vol. LXXX, p. 46.
7. Leon Trotsky, in *Goda 1917*, Vol. II, p. 358.
8. Gorky, *Untimely Thoughts*, pp. 92–93.
9. Ibid., pp. 93–95.
10. *Arkhiv A. M. Gorkogo*, Vol. IX, pp. 204–6.
11. V. Katanyan, *Mayakovsky. Literaturnaya Khronika*, pp. 90–91.
12. V. V. Mayakovsky, *Sobraniye Sochinenii*, Vol. I, pp. 235–36, 255–56.
13. Ibid., p. 428.
14. Filippov had a beautiful wife, enjoyed literary company, and fancied himself something of a poet as well. He issued anonymously a collection of his poems in an imposing volume published on heavy paper, entitled *My Gift*. (S. D. Spassky, in V. V. Grigorenko, *V. Mayakovsky v Vospominamyakh Sovremennikov*, p. 162.)
15. Ibid., pp. 161–63.
16. D. and M. Burlyuk, in *Color and Rhyme*, 1956, No. 31.
17. Mayakovsky, *Sobraniye Sochinenii*, Vol. I, pp. 220–24.
18. Wiktor Woroszylski, *The Life of Mayakovsky*, pp. 200–12; V. F. Mulkin, O. V. Grozshaya, P. Autokolsky, and S. D. Spassky, in Grigorenko, *V. Mayakovsky*, pp. 145–82; Ilya Ehrenburg, *People and Life*, pp. 166–270.
19. Woroszylski, *Mayakovsky*, p. 212.
20. Konstantin Paustovsky, *The Story of a Life*, pp. 511–12.
21. *Vospominaniya o V. I. Lenine*, Vol. III, pp. 58–59. When Lenin decided to nationalize the banks in December 1917, Bonch-Bruyevich went to Smolny Commandant Malkov and had him prepare a good-sized room with twenty-eight cots, tables and chairs, also a guard and facilities for feeding twenty-eight persons (there were twenty-eight banks in Petrograd). Then commandos were sent to each bank, the director was arrested, brought back to Smolny, and Bolshevik Commissars sent to run each bank. In many cases after short confinement the bank director agreed to go back and run his institution under Bolshevik direction. (David Shub, *Lenin*, p. 144.)
22. V. I. Lenin, *Collected Works*, Vol. XXVI, p. 351.
23. V. M. Purishkevich, one of the Rasputin conspirators, and a number of others who were, in fact, actively engaged in a plot to overthrow the Bolsheviks had been arrested in early November. (*Oktyabrskoye Vooruzhennoye Vosstaniye*, Vol. II, p. 426.)
24. Pavel Dmitri Dolgorukov, *Velikaya Razrukha*, pp. 57–62.
25. Leonard Schapiro, *The Communist Party of the Soviet Union*, pp. 180–81.
26. G. A. Solomon, *Sredi Krasnikh Vozhdei*, Vol. I, pp. 16–17.
27. *Oktyabrskoye Vooruzhennoye Vosstaniye*, Vol. II, p. 427.
28. Ibid., pp. 418–19.
29. V. D. Bonch-Bruyevich, *Vospominaniya o Lenine*, pp. 152–53.
30. Lenin, *Collected Works*, Vol. XLIV, p. 48.
31. Yelizaveta Drabkina, *Chernye Sukhari*, pp. 86–92.
32. Lenin, *Collected Works*, Vol. XLIV, p. 50.
33. *Vospominaniya o V. I. Lenine*, Vol. III; Nadezhda Krupskaya, *Reminiscences of Lenin*, pp. 500–1; Leon Trotsky, *My Life*, pp. 362–63.
34. Lenin, *Collected Works*, Vol. XLII, pp. 48–49.

LX. The Twelve

1. The day after he came back to Petrograd Lenin returned the three fur coats with a letter of thanks to Kollontai. He apologized for not being able to give her back Finnish money but enclosed eighty-three rubles, which he calculated was about equal to the money she had lent him. *Vospominaniya o V. I. Lenine,* Vol. III, p. 141.)
2. Alexandra Kollontai, ibid., Vol. I, pp. 139–41.
3. V. I. Lenin, *Biograficheskaya Khronika,* Vol. V, p. 156.
4. Nadezhda Krupskaya, *Reminiscences of Lenin,* pp. 425–26; Lenin, *Biograficheskaya Khronika,* Vol. V, pp. 156–57.
5. Maxim Gorky, *Untimely Thoughts,* pp. 107–18.
6. Krupskaya, *Reminiscences,* pp. 424–25.
7. Albert Rhys Williams, *Lenin,* pp. 70–71.
8. Ibid., p. 73.
9. *Oktyabrskoye Vooruzhennoye Vosstaniye,* Vol. II, p. 429.
10. Ibid., p. 430.
11. Gorky was contemptuous of this so-called assassination attempt. He said, somewhat later: "Probably everyone remembers that after a certain joker or bored idler punctured with a penknife the body of the automobile used by Lenin, Pravda, regarding the damage to the car's body as an attempt on the life of Vladimir Ilyich sternly declared: 'For each of our heads we shall take a hundred bourgeois heads.'" Gorky thought the Bolsheviks had deliberately exaggerated the event to stir up their supporters. (Gorky, *Untimely Thoughts,* pp. 150–51.) According to Bonch-Bruyevich, three men charged with carrying out the attempt on Lenin were arrested but were freed at Lenin's order when they volunteered to go to the Pskov front and fight the advancing Germans. (V. D. Bonch-Bruyevich, in *Novy Mir,* 1930, No. 1.)
12. *Oktyabrskoye Vooruzhennoye Vosstaniye,* Vol. II, pp. 498–99.
13. Albert Rhys Williams, *Through the Russian Revolution,* p. 177.
14. David Shub, *Lenin,* p. 149; V. D. Bonch-Bruyevich, *Vospominaniya o Lenine,* pp. 164–65. The enemies of the Bolsheviks charged that the incident was a deliberate provocation.
15. Krupskaya, *Reminiscences,* pp. 433–34.
16. Bonch-Bruyevich, *Vospominaniya,* p. 166.
17. S. Mstislavsky, *Pyat Dnei,* p. 83.
18. Krupskaya, *Reminiscences,* pp. 434–35.
19. Bonch-Bruyevich, *Vospominaniya,* p. 167.
20. Krupskaya, *Reminiscences,* p. 437.
21. Williams, *Lenin,* pp. 79–80.
22. Krupskaya, *Reminiscences,* pp. 437–38.
23. Shub, *Lenin,* p. 150.
24. Yelizaveta Drabkina, *Chernye Sukhari,* pp. 99–100.
25. Mstislavsky, *Pyat Dnei,* p. 92.
26. Drabkina, *Chernye Sukhari,* p. 100.
27. V. M. Chernov, *Pered Burei,* p. 366.
28. Drabkina, *Chernye Sukhari,* p. 101.
29. *Oktyabrskoye Vooruzhennoye Vosstaniye,* Vol. II, pp. 502–3.
30. Shub, *Lenin,* p. 151.
31. V. I. Lenin, *Collected Works,* Vol. XXVI, p. 455.
32. A. Avtorkhanov, *Proiskhozhdeniye Partakratii,* Vol. I, pp. 432–42.
33. Louis Fischer, *The Life of Lenin,* p. 191.

34. When the Central Committee—the day before—was exploring the possibility of getting aid from the Allies in order to carry on "revolutionary war" Lenin sent in a note saying: "Please include my vote in favor of getting potatoes and arms from the bandits of Anglo-French imperialism." (Lenin, *Collected Works*, Vol. XLIV, p. 67.)

35. Krupskaya, *Reminiscences*, pp. 448–49.

36. Ibid., p. 450; Lenin, *Collected Works*, Vol. XXVII, p. 159.

37. Lenin, *Collected Works*, Vol. XXVII, pp. 160–61.

38. Gorky, *Untimely Thoughts*, p. 152.

39. Alexander Blok, *Sochineniya*, Vol. II, pp. 218–19.

40. Ibid., p. 523.

41. Ibid., p. 534.

42. Ivan Bunin, *Memories and Portraits*, p. 163.

43. F. D. Reeve, *Aleksandr Blok Between Image and Idea*, p. 248.

LXI. The House of Special Designation   PAGES 562–69

1. J. C. Trewin, *The House of Special Purpose*, pp. 82–83.

2. *Krasny Arkhiv*, 1928, Vol. XXVII, pp. 118–22, Romanov diary.

3. Trewin, *House of Special Purpose*, pp. 88–91, quoting letters of Charles Sydney Gibbes.

4. Pierre Gilliard, *Thirteen Years at the Russian Court*, pp. 254–56.

5. V. P. Zubov, *Stradyne Gody Rossii*, pp. 55, 66.

6. Ibid., pp. 70–71.

7. P. Malkov, *Reminiscences of a Kremlin Commandant*, p. 117. This is one of the few decrees about the Romanovs in Lenin's name which has been published. The existence of others still concealed in the secret archives is certain.

8. Zubov, *Stradnye Gody Rossii*, pp. 78–79.

9. Sergei P. Melgunov, *Red Terror*, p. 82; Yu. I. Danilov, *Veliki Knyaz Nikolai Nikolayevich*, p. 332.

10. Latsis, *Yezhenedelnik Chrez Komiss Kazan*, Nov. 1, 1918, No. 1, quoted in S. P. Melgunov, *Krasny Terror v Rossii*, p. 36.

11. Zabolotny was later shot by the Germans despite efforts by Grand Duke Alexander to protect him.

12. Grand Duke Alexander, *Once a Grand Duke*, pp. 296–313; Danilov, *Nikolai Nikolayevich*, pp. 330–35.

13. A. D. Naglovsky, in *Novy Zhurnal*, 1967, No. 88, p. 183.

14. V. I. Lenin, *Collected Works*, Vol. XLIV, pp. 75–95.

15. N. Sokolov, *Ubiistvo Tsarskoi Semyi*, p. 39.

16. *Krasny Arkhiv*, 1928, Vol. XXVI, p. 124.

17. I. N. Steinberg, *In the Workshop of the Revolution*, pp. 143–44.

18. Ye. Gorodetsky, and Yu. Shuranov, *Sverdlov* (1971 ed.), pp. 309ff.

19. *Krasny Arkhiv*, 1928, Vol. XXVI, p. 125.

20. Sokolov, *Ubiistvo Tsarskoi Semyi*, p. 45. This rumor in various forms circulated in Moscow. Even the English ambassador, Buchanan, believed that the Czar could have saved his life had he been willing to sign the Brest treaty. In that case, Buchanan reasoned, the Germans would have rescued him. (Sir George Buchanan, *My Mission to Russia*, Vol. II, p. 85.)

21. Gilliard, *Thirteen Years*, p. 260.

22. Now Sverdlovsk. Renamed after his death in 1919 for Yakov Sverdlov, who spent some time as a Bolshevik underground worker in the Urals, principally in Perm and Yekaterinburg.

23. Ya. M. Sverdlov, *Izbranniye Proizvedeniya*, pp. 309ff.

24. P. M. Bykov, in *Arkhiv Russkoi Revolyutsii*, Vol. XVII, pp. 309–10.

25. S. P. Melgunov, *Sudba Imperatora Nikolaya II Posle Ostrecheniya*, p. 290.

26. Sverdlov, *Izbranniye Proizvedeniya*, p. 312.

27. Bykov, in *Arkhiv Russkoi Revolyutsii*, Vol. XVII, p. 310.

28. There seems no evidence to support the suggestion of some Romanov romanticists that Yakovlev was actually trying to spirit the Imperial family out to Siberia and escape from the Bolshevik regime. Such allegations were made against him by the Urals Bolsheviks, but the fact is that when Yakovlev went back to Moscow he soon was given command of the Second Army, active against the Czechoslovak troops and the White Volunteer army on the Volga and in the Urals. He would not have been placed in this responsible post had there been any suspicion that he harbored Romanov sympathies. He was eventually removed from command in connection with the "anarchistic" mood of his troops, and his further fate is uncertain. Sokolov, the brilliant investigator of the Romanov tragedy, believes that Yakovlev left the Bolsheviks, offered his services to the Czech General Shenik, and was later executed. Melgunov, an equally careful researcher, feels the evidence for this conclusion is shaky, noting that for ten years or more Soviet historians made no mention of any treason in connection with Yakovlev's name. The point is interesting only for the light it might throw on Yakovlev's character and whether, in fact, he was a secret sympathizer of the Czar. (Sokolov, *Ubiistvo Tsarskoi Semyi*, pp. 53–54; Melgunov, *Sudba Imperatora Nikolaya II*, pp. 292–94.)

29. Gorodetsky and Shuranov, *Sverdlov*, pp. 253–54.

30. Ibid., p. 312.

31. Leon Trotsky, *Trotsky's Diary in Exile*, pp. 80–81.

32. Vyrubova even approached Gorky, asking him to intercede with Lenin on behalf of the Imperial family. Whether Gorky undertook the petition is not known. He was still on extremely bad terms with Lenin during the spring and early summer of 1918. (Anna Vyroubova, *Souvenirs de Ma Vie*, p. 196.) Her principal agent in Siberia was Boris Solovyev, who had married Matryona (Mariya), the daughter of Rasputin.

33. Alexandre Tarsaidze, personal conversation.

34. Sokolov, *Ubiistvo Tsarskoi Semyi*, p. 52.

35. In a day or two the guards and guardroom were removed to the lower floor.

36. *Krasny Arkhiv*, 1928, Vol. XXVI, p. 126.

37. The Ipatyev house still stands, unchanged externally, from the time of the Czar's incarceration. For many years it was a museum open to the public but at least since World War II has been closed to outsiders and is used to house local Soviet offices. It was last seen by Americans in 1959 at the time of then Vice-president Nixon's visit to the Soviet Union. Sverdlovsk is normally closed to foreigners.

38. Trewin, *House of Special Purpose*, p. 129.

39. Gilliard, *Thirteen Years*, pp. 270–71.

LXII. *"The Terrorists Will Consider Us Old Women"*   PAGE 575

1. William Henry Chamberlain, *The Russian Revolution*, Vol. II, p. 16.

2. In fact, it never got to the Urals. It got no further than Kazan where it fell into the hands of the White Guards. (S. P. Melgunov, *Sudba Imperatora Nikolaya II Posle Ostrecheniya*, p. 350.)

3. Ibid.

4. Leon Trotsky, *On Lenin*, pp. 102–3.

5. Louis Fischer, *The Life of Lenin*, p. 290.

6. Chamberlain, *Russian Revolution*, Vol. II, p. 4.

7. Ibid., pp. 7–8. The Bolsheviks contended the British and French instigated the uprising. Actually it seems to have been spontaneous in origin but the Allies were swift to support it and take advantage of it.

8. V. I. Lenin, *Collected Works*, Vol. XXXV, p. 334.

9. Melgunov, *Sudba Imperatora Nikolaya II*, p. 350.

10. Chamberlain, *Russian Revolution*, Vol. II, p. 8.

11. Nadezhda Krupskaya, *Reminiscences of Lenin*, p. 470.

12. Lenin, *Collected Works*, Vol. XXVII, p. 390.

13. Ya. F. Alferev, *Pisma Tsarskoi Semyi iz Zatocheniya*, p. 395.

14. Melgunov, *Sudba Imperatora Nikolaya II*, p. 392.

15. Ibid., pp. 392, 394.

16. Ibid., p. 389.

17. The Bolsheviks were extremely sensitive about Johnson's death, fearing British reprisals.

18. Melgunov, *Sudba Imperatora Nikolaya II*, pp. 350–51, 388–96; Sokolov, *Ubiistvo Tsarskoi Semyi*, pp. 265–66; Alferev, *Pisma Tsarskoi Semyi*, pp. 393–94.

19. Karl Baedecker, *Russia with Teheran, Port Arthur, and Peking* (1914), p. 260.

20. Melgunov, *Sudba Imperatora Nikolaya II*, p. 376.

21. A. Taneyeva (Vyrubova), *Stranitsy iz Moei Zhizni*, pp. 147–53; Alferev, *Pisma Tsarskoi Semyi*, pp. 112–76. Apparently a great many letters were directed to the Czar. How many he was permitted to receive is not clear. (P. M. Bykov, in *Arkhiv Russkoi Revolyutsii*, Vol. XVII, p. 312.)

22. Bykov, in *Arkhiv Russkoi Revolyutsii*, Vol. XVII, p. 312.

23. Melgunov, *Sudba Imperatora Nikolaya II*, pp. 362, 376; *Krasny Arkhiv*, 1928, Vol. XXVI, pp. 130–35.

24. *Krasny Arkhiv*, 1928, Vol. XXVI, pp. 134–35. Perhaps because of excitement and confusion in the evening of June 13 the Czar did not make his diary entry until the evening of the fourteenth. He dated it June 13 but covered the events of 13–14—another deviation from his habit.

25. P. M. Bykov, chairman of the Yekaterinburg Soviet, claimed there was constant pressure on the Soviet from extreme left-wing SR members to execute the Czar. This pressure apparently increased in June with the left SRs denouncing the Soviet for its dilatoriness. (*Arkhiv Russkoi Revolyutsii*, Vol. XVII, p. 313.) But Bykov offers no support for Avdeyev's remarks about an "anarchist plot." However, many Bolshevik sources insist there actually was some kind of plot to kill the Czar as Avdeyev claimed. (Melgunov, *Sudba Imperatora Nikolaya II*, p. 375.) Bykov's memoir was first published in 1921 in an edition of 1,000 copies which was almost immediately suppressed. In 1925 he published a revised and expanded version. (Ibid., p. 399.)

26. The pair had been taken from Ipatyev house May 27 and lodged in the local prison with the other members of the Imperial party and staff. Gilliard, by chance, was passing Ipatyev house that day. He saw two carriages out in front with a large detachment of Red Guards. Sednev was placed in the first, Nagorny in the second. Nagorny saw Gilliard, who was accompanied by Dr. Derevenko and Mr. Gibbes, stared at them without a smile of recognition, took his seat, and was driven off with Sednev in the direction of the prison. (Pierre Gilliard, *Thirteen Years at the Russian Court*, p. 272.)

27. *Krasny Arkhiv*, 1928, Vol. XXVI, p. 135.

28. Chamberlain, *Russian Revolution*, Vol. II, pp. 48–49.

29. Leon Trotsky, *Trotsky's Diary in Exile*, p. 80.

30. Melgunov, *Sudba Imperatora Nikolaya II*, pp. 228-31.

31. The question of the windows of the Ipatyev house was to bulk large in Soviet historiography. Bykov, the Yekaterinburg Soviet chairman, contended that an elaborate system of signaling through open windows had formed part of a Czarist plot to free the Romanovs. From the moment Nicholas arrived in Yekaterinburg there had been concern about his windows, particularly the corner window of the room occupied by Nicholas and Alexandra in the front of the house at the intersection of Voznesensky Prospekt and Voznesensky Pereulok. Examination of the Soviet allegations, the Czar's diary references, and the stories of surviving servants and guards offers no support for the theory that a signaling system had been agreed upon. (Ibid., pp. 266-67.)

32. Ibid., pp. 377-78; *Krasny Arkhiv*, 1928, Vol. XXVI, p. 135.

33. Lenin, *Collected Works*, Vol. XXXV, p. 336.

34. Melgunov, *Sudba Imperatora Nikolaya II*, p. 365.

35. *Krasny Arkhiv*, 1928, Vol. XXVI, pp. 132, 136.

36. Worker guards had stolen a number of pieces of jewelry and had been caught selling them in the black market.

37. An Anglo-French expeditionary force landed at Murmansk July 1, and preparations for landing at Archangel were under way.

38. Sokolov, *Ubiistvo Tsarskoi Semyi*, pp. 256-58.

39. Ibid., p. 258.

40. Melgunov, *Sudba Imperatora Nikolaya II*, p. 386.

41. Ibid., p. 370.

LXIII. *"No News from Outside"* PAGES 585-90

1. There were disorders in Yekaterinburg July 13, the so-called "revolt of evacuated invalids," wounded officers and soldiers evacuated to Yekaterinburg. It was put down ruthlessly by the local Soviet. Simultaneously a group of officers which had been talking about a rescue of the Czar and his family slipped out of town to join the advancing Czechs. (S. P. Melgunov, *Sudba Imperatora Nikolaya II Posle Ostrecheniya*, p. 370.)

2. *Krasny Arkhiv*, 1928, Vol. XXVI, pp. 136-37.

3. P. M. Bukov, in *Arkhiv Russkoi Revolyutsii*, Vol. XVII, p. 313.

4. Sokolov, *Ubiistvo Tsarskoi Semyi*, pp. 142-48.

5. Ibid., p. 148.

6. R. H. Bruce Lockhart, *British Agent*, pp. 292-98.

7. Ibid., pp. 298-300; William Henry Chamberlain, *The Russian Revolution*, Vol. II, pp. 53-55; Yelizaveta Drabkina, *Chernye Sukhari*, pp. 191-92; Ya. P. Krastyn, *Istoriya Latyshkikh Strelkov*, p. 254.

8. I. Gorokhov, L. Zamyatin, and I. Zemskov, *G. V. Chicherin*, pp. 91-93.

9. Leon Trotsky, *On Lenin*, pp. 130-31.

10. M. D. Bonch-Bruyevich, *Vsye Vlast Sovetem*, p. 203.

11. Krastyn, *Istoriya Latyshkikh Strelkov*, p. 257.

12. Chamberlain, *Russian Revolution*, Vol. II, p. 54.

13. V. I. Lenin, *Collected Works*, Vol. XXVII, p. 533.

14. Nadezhda Krupskaya, *Reminiscences of Lenin*, pp. 476-77; V. I. Lenin, *Biograficheskaya Khronika*, Vol. V, p. 617.

15. Lenin, *Collected Works*, Vol. XXXV, p. 340.

16. Krupskaya, *Reminiscences*, p. 477.

17. V. N. Kokovtsov, *Iz Moego Proshlego. Vospominaniya 1903-1919*, Vol. II, pp. 449-61.

18. Sokolov, *Ubiistvo Tsarskoi Semyi*, p. 245.

19. Melgunov, *Sudba Imperatora Nikolaya II*, p. 400. Lenin was described as being opposed to executing the whole family. He felt taking the lives of the children would have a bad effect on public opinion. Some members of the Soviet wanted to use the Imperial family as a bargaining chip in negotiations with the Germans. (Ibid., p. 401.)

20. Lenin, *Biograficheskaya Khronika*, Vol. V, p. 616.

21. Roy A. Medvedev, *Let History Judge*, p. 249.

22. Lenin, *Biograficheskaya Khronika*, Vol. V, pp. 64, 288.

23. Ya. M. Sverdlov, *Izbranniye Proizvedeniya*, p. 312.

24. Melgunov, *Sudba Imperatora Nikolaya II*, p. 402.

25. Ibid.

26. Leon Trotsky, *Trotsky's Diary in Exile*, p. 81.

27. Krupskaya, *Reminiscences*, p. 478. V. L. Panyushkin, a Communist Party member since 1907, was named in April 1918 extraordinary military commissar for the struggle with counterrevolutionaries in the Tula Guberniya. He spent much time in the Kremlin. In the Central Party archives he left a notation of his observations at that time in which he said that he was completely confident that Lenin and Sverdlov "constantly consulted each other and decided many questions together." He said not only he but many of his comrades felt certain that the two men "always agreed between themselves" and decided all questions on a friendly basis. Other data in the archives support this view. (M. P. Iroshnikov, *Predsedatel Soveta Narodnykh Komissarov Vl. Ulyanov*, p. 57.)

28. Ya. F. Alferev, *Pisma Tsarskoi Semyi iz Zatocheniya*, pp. 398-99.

29. *Pisma* gives the hour "soon after midnight"; Melgunov puts it at 2 A.M. (Ibid., p. 401; *Sudba Imperatora Nikolaya II*, p. 382.) Apparently *Pisma* is using standard time, Melgunov double daylight.

30. V. Kobylin, *Imperatora Nikolai II i General-adyutant M. V. Alexeyev*, p. 418.

31. Alferev, *Pisma Tsarskoi Semyi*, p. 402.

32. Melgunov, *Sudba Imperatora Nikolaya II*, p. 383.

33. Bykov quoted him as saying: "You mean you're not taking us somewhere?" (*Arkhiv Russkoi Revolyutsii*, Vol. XVII, p. 314.)

34. Melgunov, *Sudba Imperatora Nikolaya II*, p. 382.

35. A curious coincidence has turned up in the record of Lenin's life painstakingly being published, volume by volume, under the auspices of the Institute of Marxism-Leninism in Moscow. In Volume V in the record of Lenin's actions on July 16 there is the notation that some time before 4 P.M. he sent off to the Danish newspaper *National Tidende* a reply in English to an inquiry about rumors that the Czar had been shot. The next day, the seventeenth, at twelve noon he received a letter from Yekaterinburg and wrote on the envelope "Received. Lenin." Neither the text of Lenin's reply to the Copenhagen newspaper nor his communication from Yekaterinburg has ever been made public. Yekaterinburg could not so swiftly have informed him of the execution of the Romanovs. But it could have informed him that it was acting on his previously received instructions. (Lenin, *Biograficheskaya Khronika*, Vol. V, pp. 640, 642.) A search of the remaining archives of the *National Tidende* (no longer published) now held in the Danish Press Museum and Archive at Aarhus has failed to turn up Lenin's telegram. The *National Tidende* reported the execution of the Czar in two telegrams from Berlin in the issue of July 21. Some additional details were carried July 22 in a report by the Wolff Bureau from Berlin. The Lenin telegram was never published, possibly having been outdated by events. (Communication from E. E. Schmidt, Danish Press Museum and Archives, Aarhus, Denmark, September 1975.)

36. Drabkina, *Chernye Sukhari*, p. 160.

37. Yu. Flaxerman, in *Novy Mir*, 1968, No. 11, p. 229.

38. Lenin, *Biograficheskaya, Khronika*, Vol. V, p. 648; Melgunov, *Sudba Imperatora Nikolaya II*, p. 407. In June and early July repeated reports of the Czar's death were published both inside and outside Russia. Rumors of the killing of the Czar and his family circulated widely in Vologda where the diplomatic corps had moved in early June. (Louis de Robien, *The Diary of a Diplomat in Russia, 1917–1918*, pp. 267–68.) Similar rumors appeared in the New York *Times* June 26, July 1, and July 4. Most of these rumors came from Sweden and one was attributed to the *National Tidende* of Copenhagen. Another allegedly had been published in Russia by *Novaya Zhizn*. The July 4 report quoted *The Times* (London) and said that while the Czar's death could not be confirmed "rumors of the escape of Prince Michael are better founded." On July 12 the New York *Times* quoted a Stockholm report that Alexei had been frightened to death by a bomb which had been thrown at his father. July 15 the New York *Times* reported that Grand Duke Mikhail had appeared at Kiev. The actual news of the Czar's execution was front-page news in the New York *Times* July 21, 1918, and simply quoted the official Soviet report as transmitted by wireless.

39. The Soviet press began serial publication of the Czar's diary but quickly broke it off. It simply aroused sympathy for the Czar. Only bits and pieces of the promised materials were ever made public. (Lockhart, *British Agent*, p. 301.)

40. Except for Chemodurov, Volkov, young Sednev, and Dr. Derevenko, all those who came with the Romanovs from Tobolsk were also executed—Nagorny, Sednev, and Prince Dologoruky. Tatishchev, Hendrikov, and Shnieder were shot August 22 at Perm. The valet Volkov made his escape under fire as the execution was about to occur. The Grand Duchess Yelizaveta, the four Grand Dukes Sergei Mikhailovich, Igor, Ioann, and Konstantin Kontantinovich, and Prince Paley together with two servants were shot at Alapaevsk on the night of July 17. There was one more Romanov tragedy to come. The Grand Dukes Pavel Alexandrovich, Dmitri Konstantinovich, Nikolai Mikhailovich, and Georgi Mikhailovich were shot January 27, 1919, in the courtyard of the Peter and Paul Fortress in Petrograd as "hostages" in retaliation for the murders of Rosa Luxemburg and Karl Liebknicht in Germany. Gorky tried to save their lives. He went from Petrograd to Moscow, obtained an order from Lenin sparing the lives of the Grand Dukes, but on his way back to Petrograd to present it to Zinoviev learned that the executions had already been carried out. (Melgunov, *Sudba Imperatora Nikolaya II*, pp. 386–87; Alferev, *Pisma Tsarskoi Semyi*, p. 421.)

41. Melgunov, *Sudba Imperatora Nikolaya II*, pp. 398–99.

42. Nikolai Berdyayev, *The Origins of Russian Communism*, p. 118.

43. Maxim Gorky, *Untimely Thoughts*, p. 216.

44. S. P. Melgunov, *Krasny Terror v Rossii*, p. 15.

Index

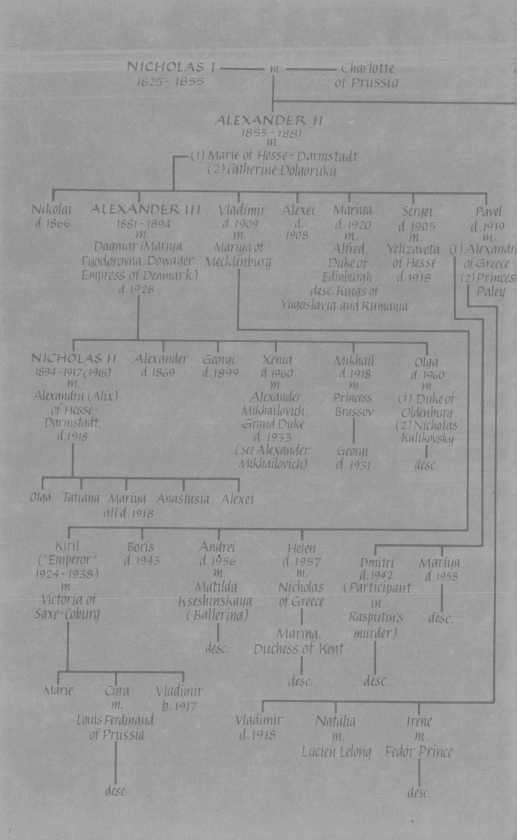

NICHOLAS I ——— m. ——— Charlotte
1825 – 1855   of Prussia

ALEXANDER II
1855 – 1881
m.
(1) Marie of Hesse – Darmstadt
(2) Catherine Dolgoruky

Nikolai	ALEXANDER III	Vladimir	Alexei	Mariya	Sergei	Pavel
d. 1866	1881 – 1894	d. 1909	d.	d. 1920	d. 1905	d. 1919
	m.	m.	1908	m.	m.	m.
	Dagmar (Mariya	Mariya of		Alfred,	Yelizaveta	(1) Alexandr
	Fyodorovna, Dowager	Mecklenburg		Duke of	of Hesse	of Greece
	Empress of Denmark.)			Edinburgh	d. 1918	(2) Princess
	d. 1928			desc. Kings of		Paley
				Yugoslavia and Rumania		

NICHOLAS II	Alexander	Georgi	Xenia	Mikhail	Olga
1894 – 1917 (1918)	d. 1869	d. 1899	d. 1960	d. 1918	d. 1960
m.			m.	m.	m.
Alexandra (Alix)			Alexander	Princess	(1) Duke of
of Hesse-			Mikhailovich,	Brassov	Oldenburg
Darmstadt,			Grand Duke		(2) Nicholas
d. 1918			d. 1933		Kulikovsky
			(see Alexander	Georgi	
			Mikhailovich)	d. 1931	desc.

Olga Tatiana Mariya Anastasia Alexei
all d. 1918

Kiril	Boris	Andrei	Helen	Dmitri	Mariya
("Emperor"	d. 1943	d. 1956	d. 1957	d. 1942	d. 1958
1924 – 1938)		m.	m.	(Participant	
m.		Matilda	Nicholas	in	
Victoria of		Kseshinskaya	of Greece	Rasputin's	desc.
Saxe-Coburg		(Ballerina)		murder)	
			Marina,		
			Duchess of Kent		
		desc.		desc.	

Marie	Cyra	Vladimir	Vladimir	Natalia	Irene
	m.	b. 1917	d. 1918	m.	m.
	Louis Ferdinand			Lucien Lelong	Fedor Prince
	of Prussia				
	desc.				desc.